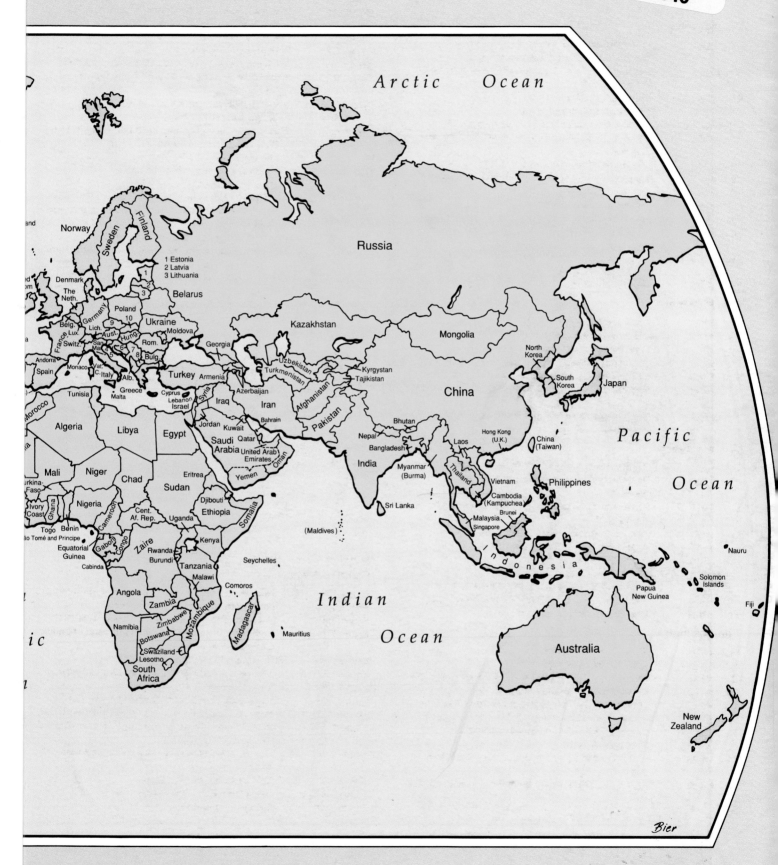

HUMAN GEOGRAPHY

Human Geography

Landscapes of Human Activities

FIFTH EDITION

JEROME FELLMANN
University of Illinois, Urbana-Champaign

·

ARTHUR GETIS
San Diego State University

·

JUDITH GETIS

·

WCB
McGraw-Hill

Boston, Massachusetts   Burr Ridge, Illinios   Dubuque, Iowa
Madison, Wisconsin   New York, New York   San Francisco, California   St. Louis, Missouri

WCB/McGraw-Hill

A Division of The **McGraw·Hill** *Companies*

Book Team

Managing Editor *Ed Bartell*
Acquisitions Editor *Scott Spoolman*
Production Editor *Ann Fuerste*
Proofreading Coordinator *Carrie Barker*
Designer *Chris Reese*
Art Editor *Miriam Hoffman*
Photo Editor *Rose Deluhery*
Permissions Coordinator *Gail I. Wheatley*
Production Manager *Beth Kundert*
Marketing Manager *Amy Halloran*
Copywriter *Jennifer Smith*
Proofreader *Ann Morgan*

Basal Text *10/12 Veljovic Book*
Display Type *Herculenium*
Typesetting System *Macintosh™ QuarkXPress™*
Paper Stock *Mirror matte*

Executive Vice President and General Manager *Bob McLaughlin*
Vice President, Business Manager *Russ Domeyer*
Vice President of Production and New Media Development *Victoria Putman*
National Sales Manager *Phil Rudder*
National Telesales Director *John Finn*

The credits section for this book begins on page 525 and is considered an extension of the copyright page.

Cover image © *1996 PhotoDisc, Inc.—Volume 5, World Commerce and Travel*

Proofread by Patsy Adams

Library of Congress Catalog Card Number: 96–85762

ISBN: 0–697–29038–7

Printed in the United States of America

10 9 8 7 6 5 4 3 2

CONTENTS

Preface   xi

INTRODUCTION: 1

SOME BACKGROUND BASICS   1

GETTING STARTED   2

Evolution of the Discipline   2

Geography and Human Geography   3
Human Geography   4
The Structure of This Book   7

BACKGROUND BASICS   8

Basic Geographic Concepts   8
Location, Direction, and Distance   9
  Location   9
  Direction   10
  Distance   11
Size and Scale   11
Physical and Cultural Attributes   12
The Changing Attributes of Place   13
Interaction among Places   14
The Structured Content of Place   15
  Density   15
  Dispersion   15
  Pattern   16
Place Similarity and Regions   16
  The Characteristics of Regions   17
  Types of Regions   17

Maps   18
Map Scale   19
The Globe Grid   20
How Maps Show Data   21
Mental Maps   23

Systems, Maps, and Models   27

SUMMARY   27
KEY WORDS   28
FOR REVIEW   28
SELECTED REFERENCES   28

THEMES AND FUNDAMENTALS OF HUMAN GEOGRAPHY   31 1

ROOTS AND MEANING OF CULTURE   33 2

Components of Culture   35
Interaction of People and Environment   36
Environments as Controls   37
Human Impacts   38
Roots of Culture   40
Seeds of Change   43
Agricultural Origins and Diffusions   44
Neolithic Innovations   46
Culture Hearths   47
The Structure of Culture   51
Culture Change   52
Innovation   54
Diffusion   55

Contact between Regions   57
Cultural Modification and Adoption   60
  SUMMARY   60
  KEY WORDS   61
  FOR REVIEW   61
  SELECTED REFERENCES   61

SPATIAL INTERACTION AND SPATIAL BEHAVIOR   63 3

Bases for Interaction   64
A Summarizing Model   65
  Complementarity   65
  Transferability   65
  Intervening Opportunity   66
Measuring Interaction   66
  Distance Decay   67
  The Gravity Concept   68
  Interaction Potential   68
  Movement Biases   69
Human Spatial Behavior   70
Individual Activity Space   70
The Tyranny of Time   72
Distance and Human Interaction   72
Spatial Interaction and the Accumulation of Information   73
  Information Flows   76
Information and Perception   77
  Perception of Environment   77
  Perception of Natural Hazards   79

Migration 82

Principal Migration Patterns 83
Types of Migration 83
Controls on Migration 85

SUMMARY 91

KEY WORDS 92

FOR REVIEW 92

SELECTED REFERENCES 92

PATTERNS OF
DIVERSITY
AND UNITY 131 11

Islam 166
Hinduism 168
Buddhism 170
East Asian Ethnic Religions 172

SUMMARY 174

KEY WORDS 174

FOR REVIEW 175

SELECTED REFERENCES 175

POPULATION: 4

WORLD PATTERNS,
REGIONAL TRENDS 95

Population Growth 96
Some Population Definitions 98
Birth Rates 98
Fertility Rates 99
Death Rates 102
Population Pyramids 104
Natural Increase 107
Doubling Times 108
The Demographic Transition 109
The Western Experience 110
A World Divided 113
The Demographic Equation 113
Population Relocation 114
Immigration Impacts 114
World Population Distribution 116
Population Density 119
Overpopulation 120
Urbanization 122
Population Data and Projections 122
Population Data 123
Population Projections 124
Population Controls 125
Population Prospects 126

SUMMARY 127

KEY WORDS 128

FOR REVIEW 128

SELECTED REFERENCES 128

LANGUAGE AND
RELIGION: 5

MOSAICS OF
CULTURE 133

THE GEOGRAPHY OF
LANGUAGE 135

Classification of Languages 135
World Pattern of Languages 136
Language Spread 137
Language Change 142
The Story of English 143
Standard and Variant Languages 144
Standard Language 144
Dialects 145
Dialects in America 147
Pidgins and Creoles 149
Lingua Franca 149
Official Languages 149
Language, Territoriality, and
Identity 152
Language on the Landscape:
Toponymy 154

PATTERNS OF RELIGION 156

Religion and Culture 156
Classification of Religion 156
Patterns, Numbers, and Flows 158
The World Pattern 158
The Principal Religions 159
Judaism 159
Christianity 160
Regions and Landscapes of
Christianity 163

ETHNIC
GEOGRAPHY: 6

THREADS OF
DIVERSITY 177

Ethnic Diversity and Separatism 179
Immigration Streams 181
Acculturation and Assimilation 184
Areal Expressions of Ethnicity 186
Charter Cultures 186
Ethnic Clusters 188
Black Dispersions 189
Hispanic Concentrations 191
Asian Contrasts 194
French Uniformity 195
Urban Ethnic Diversity and
Segregation 196
External Controls 198
Internal Controls 198
Shifting Ethnic Concentrations 199
Typologies and Spatial Results 200
Native Born Dispersals 202
Cultural Transfer 202
The Ethnic Landscape 204
Land Survey 205
Settlement Patterns 206
Ethnic Regionalism 207

SUMMARY 209

KEY WORDS 209

FOR REVIEW 210

SELECTED REFERENCES 210

FOLK AND POPULAR CULTURE:

DIVERSITY AND UNIFORMITY 213

FOLK CULTURAL DIVERSITY AND REGIONALISM 215

North American Hearths 216
Folk Building Traditions 218
The Northern Hearths 220
The Lower St. Lawrence Valley 220
Southern New England 222
The Hudson Valley 223
The Middle Atlantic Hearths 224
The Delaware Valley 224
Chesapeake Bay 224
The Southern Hearths 225
The Southern Tidewater 225
The Mississippi Delta 225
Interior and Western Hearths 226
Architectural Diffusions 226
Folk Fencing in North America 227
Nonmaterial Folk Culture 228
Folk Food and Drink Preferences 229
Folk and Customary Foods 229
Drink 231
Folk Music 232
Folk Medicines and Cures 234
The Oral Folk Tradition 235
Folk Cultural Regions of Eastern United States 235
The Passing of Folk Cultural Regionalism 237

PATTERNS OF POPULAR CULTURE 238

National Uniformities 239
The Shopping Mall 240
Outside the Mall 242
Diffusion Tracks 243
Regional Emphasis 244
Vernacular Regions 247
SUMMARY 248
KEY WORDS 249
FOR REVIEW 249
SELECTED REFERENCES 249

DYNAMIC PATTERNS OF THE SPACE ECONOMY 253

LIVELIHOOD AND ECONOMY:

PRIMARY ACTIVITIES 255

The Classification of Economic Activity and Economies 256
Categories of Activity 257
Types of Economic Systems 258
Primary Activities: Agriculture 260
Subsistence Agriculture 261
Extension Subsistence Agriculture 261
Intensive Subsistence Systems 264
Costs of Territorial Extension 266
The Green Revolution 266
Commercial Agriculture 267
Production Controls 268
A Model of Agricultural Location 270
Intensive Commercial Agriculture 271
Extensive Commercial Agriculture 272
Special Crops 275
Agriculture in Planned Economies 276
Primary Activities: Resource Exploitation 278
Resource Terminology 278
Fishing 279
Forestry 282
Mining and Quarrying 283
Metallic Minerals 284
Nonmetallic Minerals 286
Mineral Fuels 287
Trade in Primary Products 289
SUMMARY 290
KEY WORDS 291
FOR REVIEW 291
SELECTED REFERENCES 292

LIVELIHOOD AND ECONOMY:

FROM BLUE COLLAR TO GOLD COLLAR 293

Components of the Space Economy 294
Concepts and Controls 295
Secondary Activities: Manufacturing 296
Locational Decisions in Manufacturing 296
Principles of Location 297
Raw Materials 297
Power Supply 298
Labor 298
Market 299
Transportation 299
Transportation and Location 302
Industrial Location Theories 304
Least-Cost Theory 304
Locational Interdependence Theory 305
Profit-Maximization Approaches 306
Other Locational Considerations and Controls 307
Agglomeration Economies 307
Comparative Advantage 307
Transnational Corporations 309
Imposed Considerations 310
Industrial Location in Planned Economies 310
Major Manufacturing Regions of the World 310
Eastern Anglo America 312
Other Anglo American Concentrations 314
Western and Central Europe 315
Eastern Europe 316
Eastern Asia 318
Japan 318
China 319
The "Dragons" 321
High-Tech Patterns 323
Tertiary and Beyond 325
SUMMARY 327
KEY WORDS 327
FOR REVIEW 328
SELECTED REFERENCES 328

PATTERNS OF
DEVELOPMENT
AND CHANGE 331

Development as a Cultural Variable 333
Dividing the Continuum: Definitions of Development 333
Explanations of Underdevelopment 335
The Core-Periphery Argument 336
Economic Measures of Development 336
The Diffusion of Technology 338
The Complex of Development 340
Gross National Product and PPP Per Capita 340
Energy Consumption Per Capita 342
Percentage of the Workforce Engaged in Agriculture 344
Landlessness 344
Poverty, Calories, and Nutrition 348
Composite Assessment of Economic Development 349
A Model for Economic Development 350
Noneconomic Measures of Development 352
Education 352
Public Services 354
Health 354
Aggregate Measures of Development and Well-Being 358
The Role of Women 360
SUMMARY 366
KEY WORDS 366
FOR REVIEW 366
SELECTED REFERENCES 367

LANDSCAPES OF
FUNCTIONAL
ORGANIZATION
369

URBAN SYSTEMS
AND URBAN
STRUCTURES 371

The Urbanizing Century 373
Merging Metropolises 373
Settlement Roots 377
The Nature of Cities 379
Some Definitions 380
The Location of Urban Settlements 380
The Functions of Cities 381
The Economic Base 381
Base Ratios 382
Systems of Urban Settlements 383
The Urban Hierarchy 383
Rank-Size and Primacy 384
Urban Influence Zones 385
Central Places 385
Inside the City 388
The Competitive Bidding for Land 388
Land Values and Population Density 390
Models of Urban Land Use Structure 392
Social Areas of Cities 393
Social Status 393
Family Status 394
Ethnicity 394
Institutional Controls 396
Suburbanization in the United States 396
Central City Change 398
World Urban Diversity 400
The Anglo American City 400
The West European City 403
The East European City 404
Cities in the Developing World 406
The Asian City and African City 408
The Latin American City 410
SUMMARY 411
KEY WORDS 412
FOR REVIEW 412
SELECTED REFERENCES 412

THE POLITICAL
ORDERING
OF SPACE 415

National Political Systems 417
States, Nations, and Nation-States 417
The Evolution of the Modern State 419
Geographic Characteristics of States 419
Size 420
Shape 420
Location 424
Cores and Capitals 425
Boundaries: The Limits of the State 425
Classification of Boundaries 426
Boundary Disputes 428
State Cohesiveness 429
Nationalism 429
Unifying Institutions 430
Organization and Administration 431
Transportation and Communication 431
Nationalism and Centrifugal Forces 433
The Projection of Power 434
Geopolitical Assessments 435
International Political Systems 436
The United Nations and Its Agencies 437
Maritime Boundaries 438
An International Law of the Sea 438
Regional Alliances 439
Economic Alliances 440
Military and Political Alliances 443
Local and Regional Political Organization 443
The Geography of Representation: The Districting Problem 444
The Fragmentation of Political Power 445
Unified Government 449
Predevelopment Annexation 450
SUMMARY 450
KEY WORDS 451
FOR REVIEW 451
SELECTED REFERENCES 452

HUMAN ACTIONS AND ENVIRONMENTAL IMPACTS 453

HUMAN IMPACTS ON NATURAL SYSTEMS:

GEOGRAPHIC OUTLOOKS ON GLOBAL CONCERNS 455

Physical Environments and Cultural Impacts 456

Climates, Biomes, and Change 457
Global Warming 460
Acid Rain 464
The Trouble with Ozone 465

Land Use and Land Cover 467
Tropical Deforestation 468
Desertification 470
Soil Erosion 472

Water Supply and Water Quality 475
Patterns of Availability 476
Water Use and Abuse 476

Garbage Heaps and Toxic Wastes 478
Solid Wastes and Rubbish 480
   Landfill Disposal 481
   Incineration 481
   Ocean Dumping 483
Toxic Wastes 483
   Radioactive Wastes 483
Exporting Waste 484

Prospects and Perspectives 486
SUMMARY 487
KEY WORDS 487
FOR REVIEW 487
SELECTED REFERENCES 488

APPENDICES
A: MAP PROJECTIONS 491
B: 1996 WORLD POPULATION DATA 501
C: NORTH AMERICAN REFERENCE MAP 507

GLOSSARY 509
CREDITS 525
INDEX 529

PREFACE

his fifth edition of *Human Geography* preserves the pattern set by its predecessors. Designed for students enrolled in a one-semester or one-quarter course, it seeks to introduce them to the scope and excitement of human geography while making clear the relevance of its content to their daily lives and roles as citizens of an increasingly interrelated world community. To that end, the current edition builds on the extensive revisions that marked the earlier ones, making selective, significant changes in text but not in basic subject matter or topical sequence.

Some of the alterations represent expansions or contractions of text coverage in response to user advice or requests. Others reflect data, research results, and interpretations newly available since the last edition. Finally, of course, rapidly changing world political, social, and economic events have made obsolete many of the patterns and interactions that were considered fundamental and controlling in the recent past. In consequence, corresponding alterations in text descriptions and maps have been required and made.

All textbook authors strive to be current in their data and relevant in their interpretations. The rapidity of late 20th-century changes in economic, political, social, and population structures and relationships makes those goals elusive and unrealistic. The time lapse between world events and the publication date of a book means inevitably that events will outpace analysis. The further delay between the time of book publication and actual class assignment means that at best, some of the text's content will be out of date and at worst, some may be glaringly wrong at the time of student use. Not since the post-World War II period of rapid decolonization and political and economic realignments has the partnership between geography textbook authors and classroom instructors been more essential and mutually supportive than it is now. We have done our best in the text of this fifth edition to reflect world events and patterns evident and in place at the time of its final editing. We—and most importantly, the students—rely on the instructor to provide the currency of information and the interpretation of new patterns of human geographic substance essential to correct a text overtaken by events.

These concerns with current events do not diminish the importance we place on the basic content and enduring values we attempt to incorporate in the book. We recognize, for example, that for many of its readers their course in human geography may be their first or only work in geography and this their first or only textbook in the discipline. For those students particularly, we take seriously the obligation not only to convey the richness and breadth of human geography but also to give insight into the nature and intellectual challenges of the field of geography itself.

Chapter 1 addresses that goal of disciplinary overview, introducing geography as an enduring and meaningful orientation of intellect and action and identifying the place of human geography within the larger field of study. It reviews the scope, methods, and "background basics" of geography, including the unifying questions, themes, and concepts that structure all geographic inquiry and the tools—especially maps—that all geographers employ. It is supplemented by Appendix A that gives a more detailed treatment of map projections than is appropriate in a general introductory chapter. We realize, of course, that not all instructors will find either this chapter or the projections appendix necessary to the course as they teach it. Both are designed to be helpful, with content supportive of, not essential to, the later chapters of the text.

The arrangement of those chapters reflects our own sense of logic and teaching experiences and follows the ordering of material in earlier editions of *Human Geography*. The chapters are unevenly divided among five parts, each with a brief orienting introduction. We begin by examining the basis of culture, culture change, and cultural regionalism. We then proceed to a review of concepts and models of spatial interaction and spatial behavior, and complete Part I with a consideration of population structures, patterns, and change. Parts II through IV (Chapters 5 through 12) build on the fundamentals of the early chapters to examine the landscapes of culture and organization resulting from human occupance of the earth and from spatial similarities and differences that occupation has engendered. These include cultural patterns of linguistic, religious, ethnic, folk, and popular geographic differentiation of peoples and societies and those of economic, urban, and political organization of space.

Chapter 13—Part V—draws together in sharper focus selected aspects of the human–environmental interface, of the human impact on the natural landscape. It documents in some detail the relationships between human geographic patterns and processes and matters of current national and world environmental concern. Its purpose is to make clear to students the relevance of the earlier-studied human geographic concepts and landscapes to their lives and roles as citizens in a complex, changing world.

Among those concepts, of course, is the centrality of gender issues. Socially created distinctions between male and female role assignments and rewards are cultural spatial variables that underlie all facets of human geographic inquiry. Because they are so pervasive and significant, we felt it unwise to relegate their consideration to a single separate chapter. To do so would artificially and arbitrarily isolate women and women's concerns from all the topics of human geography for which recognition of gender differences and concerns is relevant. Rather, we felt it much better and more meaningful to incorporate significant gender/female issues within the chapters where those issues apply—either within the running text of the chapter or, very often, highlighted in boxed discussions. Such broader incorporation, we feel, is more appropriate and pointed than segregating women and their interests to an isolated chapter and ignoring them in the remainder of the text.

By means of chapter clusters and sequence, we have tried to convey to students the logic and integration we recognize in the broad field of human geography. Our sense of organization and continuity, of course, is not necessarily that of instructors using this text. Recognizing that, we have designed each chapter to be reasonably self-contained, able to be assigned and discussed in any sequence or combination that satisfies the arrangement preferred by the instructor or found to be of greatest interest to students. It is our firm opinion that the format of any course should reflect the joint contributions of instructor and textbook and not be dictated by the structure of the text alone.

Instructor contributions are gratefully acknowledged by the content changes incorporated in this current edition. They are found throughout the text, perhaps most prominently in the amplification of discussions of migration (Chapter 3), international population policy (Chapter 4), religious landscapes (Chapter 5), ethnicity, race, and the increase in multiethnic societies (Chapter 6), mining on public lands (Chapter 8), transnational corporations (Chapter 9), economic measures of development, development theory, and the role of women in development (Chapter 10), and ethnicity and ethnic change in American cities (Chapter 11). New data and changing world conditions and human geographic patterns—for example, the political restructuring of Eastern Europe and the former USSR—are reflected in text alterations and new maps and photographs. We have continued our practice of using map and photograph captions as teaching opportunities, conveying additional information and explanation as integral parts of the text. The attention

aroused by the graphic is therefore used as an additional tool of instruction, not as a diversion.

As in earlier editions of *Human Geography,* chapter introductions take the form of vignettes designed to capture students' interest, arouse their curiosity in the sketch itself, and sustain their attention for the subject matter that follows. Many of the boxed inserts that are part of each chapter are new to this edition, though they perform the same function as before—expanding on ideas included within the text proper or introducing related examples of applications of chapter concepts and conclusions, often in gender-related contexts. The boxes are not just for "reader relief" but are designed to amplify and instruct. Instructors report that they are valuable as the basis for more extended classroom discussions or for additional lecture topics.

We have included in each chapter at least one special-purpose box labeled "For Your Consideration." These begin with a discussion of a topic of current national or international interest or debate and conclude with a set of questions designed to induce thought, discussion, and even class argumentation as students debate the subject and view it against the background of human geographic insights they have mastered. The Cairo Conference, the urban homeless, the Official English debate, racial gerrymandering, and foreign aid are among the topics receiving that special treatment.

We also continue our practice of identifying new terms and special usages of common words and phrases by boldface or italic type. These are included in *Key Words,* a list at the end of each chapter. Boldfaced and italicized words and phrases are defined in an inclusive glossary at the end of the text. As a further student aid, many glossary definitions identify by cross-reference other, related terms that students can review to build up a more inclusive understanding of the item in question.

In addition to its key words list, each chapter also includes a repeated series of pedagogical aids. *Summary* reiterates the main points and arguments of the chapter and provides a bridge linking it to the chapter that follows. *For Review* contains questions that again direct student attention to important concepts developed within the chapter; these questions may serve as study guides for the individual reader or, if the instructor chooses, as the basis for written assignments. *Selected References* suggests a number of book and journal articles that expand on topics presented within the chapter and provide the basis for further study or class paper preparation. Of course, new materials constantly appear, but the suggested titles can serve as a starting point for specific student interests and needs.

Appendix B at the end of the book is a modified version of the Population Reference Bureau's *1996 World Population Data Sheet* containing economic and demographic data and projections for countries, regions, and continents. Although inevitably dated and subject to change, these statistics will provide for some years a wealth of useful comparative data for student projects, regional and topical analyses, and study of world patterns. Finally, Appendix C is a single-page "Anglo American Reference Map," providing name identification of all U.S. states and Canadian provinces and showing the location of principal cities.

To assist the instructor, an *Instructor's Manual* highlights the main ideas of each chapter, offers topics for class discussions, and provides 50 suggested text questions for each chapter. The publisher also makes available a set of slides reproducing maps and drawings in the text; a set of acetate transparencies of key text illustrations, including an expanded collection of North American vernacular house types; computerized testing materials (MicroTest III) for instructors; and a *Study Guide* for students. In addition, instructors may order the text packaged with the *Nystrom Student Atlas* at a significant savings. Also available for packaging is the *Student Atlas of World Politics*. And Brown & Benchmark offers CourseKits™ in which students may purchase the text and the *Annual Editions® Geography* reader at a reduced price.

It is with great pleasure that we repeat our previously acknowledged debts of gratitude to those who have given generously of their time and knowledge in response to our requests. Our departmental colleagues—at the University of Illinois, Urbana–Champaign and at both San Diego State University and the University of California, Santa Barbara— all willingly gave us guidance and help when asked. Among them, particular thanks are owed to Professors John A. Jakle and Colin E. Thorn for permitting us to reproduce some of the many excellent photographs from their personal collections; to John Jakle for advice and information on North American vernacular housing (though any retained errors of fact and interpretation are the authors', not his); to Geoffrey J. D. Hewings who read passages and gave counsel on economic geographic topics; and to Luc Anselin,

Thomas J. Bassett, and John Thompson for help on, respectively, matters European, African, and Latin American. The maps and diagrams have all again been prepared by Mr. James A. Bier, emeritus member of the Department of Geography of the University of Illinois at Urbana–Champaign. We take pride and pleasure once more in acknowledging his indispensable contribution to this work and expressing appreciation for many years of his unstinting assistance and warm friendship.

We wish to recognize with gratitude the advice, suggestions, corrections, and general assistance in matters of content and emphasis provided by the following reviewers of the manuscript for this edition: Sarah Bednarz, *Texas A & M University;* Michael Marchioni, *East Tennessee State University;* Daniel Montello, *University of California, Santa Barbara;* Thomas Orf, *Prestonsburg Community College;* Madhusudana Rao, *Bridgewater State College;* and Gerard Rushton, *University of Iowa.*

We appreciate their invaluable help, as we do that of the many other previous reviewers recognized in earlier editions of this book.

We continue to be indebted to W. D. Brooks and C. E. Roberts, Jr., of Indiana State University for the modified van der Grinten projection used for many of the maps in the book. We gratefully thank these and unnamed others for their help and contributions; none, of course, is responsible for final decisions on content or for errors of fact or interpretation the reader may detect.

A final note of thanks is reserved for the publisher's "book team" members separately named on the copyright page. It is a privilege to emphasize here their professional competence, unflagging interest, and always courteous helpfulness.

C H A P T E R

INTRODUCTION:

SOME BACKGROUND BASICS

GETTING STARTED   2

Evolution of the Discipline   2
Geography and Human Geography   3
Human Geography   4
The Structure of This Book   7

BACKGROUND BASICS   8

Basic Geographic Concepts   8
Location, Direction, and Distance   9
   Location   9
   Direction   10
   Distance   11
Size and Scale   11
Physical and Cultural Attributes   12
The Changing Attributes of Place   13
Interaction Among Places   14
The Structured Content of Place   15
   Density   15
   Dispersion   15
   Pattern   16
Place Similarity and Regions   16
   The Characteristics of Regions   17
   Types of Regions   17
Maps   18
Map Scale   19
The Globe Grid   20
How Maps Show Data   21
Mental Maps   23
Systems, Maps, and Models   27

   SUMMARY   27
   KEY WORDS   28
   FOR REVIEW   28
   SELECTED REFERENCES   28

*Amish farmers have created an intricate
cultural landscape replacing the original
natural landscape of Lancaster
County, Pennsylvania.*

The fundamental question asked by geographers is "Does it make a difference where things are located?" If for any one thing or group of things the answer is "You bet it does," the geographer's interest is aroused and geographic investigation is appropriate. For example, it matters a great deal that languages of a certain kind are spoken in certain places. But knowledge of the location of a specific language group is not of itself particularly significant. Geographic study of a language requires that we try to answer questions about why and how the language shows different characteristics in different locations and how the present distribution of its speakers came about. In the course of our study, we would logically discuss such concepts as migration, acculturation, the diffusion of innovation, the effect of physical barriers on communication, and the relationship of language to other aspects of culture. As geographers, we are interested in how things are interrelated in different regions and give evidence of the existence of "spatial systems."

Geography is often referred to as the *spatial* science, that is, the discipline concerned with the use of earth space. In fact, *geography* literally means "description of the earth," but that task is really the responsibility of nearly all the sciences. Geography might better be defined as the study of spatial variation, of how—and why—things differ from place to place on the surface of the earth. It is, further, the study of how observable spatial patterns evolved through time. If things were everywhere the same, if there were no spatial variation, the kind of human curiosity that we call "geographic" simply would not exist. Without the certain conviction that in some interesting and important way landscapes, peoples, and opportunities differ from place to place, there would be no discipline of geography.

But we do not have to deal in such abstract terms. You consciously or subconsciously display geographic awareness in your daily life. You are where you are, doing what you are doing, because of locational choices you faced and spatial decisions you made. You cannot be here reading this book and simultaneously be somewhere else—working, perhaps, or at the gym. And should you now want to go to work or take an exercise break, the time involved in going from here to there (wherever "there" is) is time not available for other activities in other locations. Of course, the act of going implies knowing where you are now, where "there" is in relation to "here," and the paths or routes you can take to cover the distance.

These are simple examples of the observation that "space matters" in a very personal way. You cannot avoid the implications of geography in your everyday affairs. Your understanding of your hometown, your neighborhood, or your college campus is essentially a geographic understanding. It is based on your awareness of where things are, of their spatial relationships, and of the varying content of the different areas and places you frequent. You carry out your routine activities in particular places and move on your daily rounds within defined geographic areas, following logical paths of connection between different locations.

Just as geography matters in your personal life, so it matters on the larger stage as well. Decisions made by corporations about the locations of manufacturing plants or warehouses in relation to transportation routes and markets are spatially rooted. So, too, are those made by shopping center developers and locators of parks and grade schools. At an even grander scale, judgements about the projection of national power or the claim and recognition of "spheres of influence and interest" among rival countries are related to the implications of distance and area.

Geography, therefore, is about space and the content of space. We think of and respond to places from the standpoint not only of where they are but, rather more importantly, of what they contain or what we think they contain. Reference to a place or an area usually calls up images about its physical nature or what people do there and often suggests, without conscious thought, how those physical things and activities are related. "Colorado," "mountains," and "skiing" might be a simple example. The content of area, that is, has both physical and cultural aspects, and geography is always concerned with understanding both (Figure 1.1).

Evolution of the Discipline

Geography's combination of interests was apparent even in the work of the early Greek geographers, who first gave structure to the discipline. Geography's name was reputedly coined by the Greek scientist Eratosthenes over 2200 years ago from the words *geo,* "the earth" and *graphein,* "to write." From the beginning, that writing focused both on the physical structure of the earth and on the nature and activities of the people who inhabited the different lands of the known world. To Strabo (*ca.* 64 B.C.–A.D. 20) the task of geography was to "describe the several parts of the inhabited world . . . to write the assessment of the countries of the world [and] to treat the differences between countries."

FIGURE 1.1 Ski development at Whistler Mountain, British Columbia: the interaction of physical environment and human activity. Climate and terrain have made specialized human use possible. Human development has placed a cultural landscape on the natural environment, thereby altering it.

Greek (and, later, Roman) geographers measured the earth, devised the global grid of latitudes and longitudes, and drew upon that grid surprisingly sophisticated maps (Figure 1.2). Employing nearly modern concepts, they discussed patterns and processes of climates, vegetation, and landforms and described areal variations in the natural landscape. Against that physical backdrop, they focused their attention on what humans did in home and distant areas—how they lived; what their distinctive similarities and differences were in language, religion, and custom; and how they used, altered, and perhaps destroyed the lands they inhabited.

These are enduring and universal interests. The ancient Chinese, for example, were as involved in geography as an explanatory viewpoint as were Westerners, though there was no exchange between them. Further, as Christian Europe entered its Dark and Middle Ages between A.D. 800 and 1400 and lost its knowledge of Greek and Roman geographical work, Muslim scholars—who retained that knowledge—undertook to describe and analyze their known world in its physical, cultural, and regional variation (see "Roger's Book").

Modern geography had its origins in the surge of scholarly inquiry that, beginning in the 17th century, gave rise to many of the traditional academic disciplines we know today. In its European rebirth, geography from the outset was recognized—as it always had been—as a broadly based integrative study. Patterns and processes of the physical landscape were early interests, as was concern with humans as part of the earth's variation from place to place. The rapid development of geology, botany, zoology, and other natural sciences by the end of the 18th century strengthened regional geographic investigation and increased scholarly and popular awareness of the intricate interconnections of things in space and between places. By that same time, accurate determination of latitude and longitude and scientific mapping of the earth made assignment of place information more reliable and comprehensive. During the 19th century, national censuses, trade statistics, and ethnographic studies gave firmer foundation to human geographic investigation.

By the end of the 19th century, geography had become a distinctive and respected discipline in universities throughout Europe and in other regions of the world where European academic examples were followed. The proliferation of professional geographers and geography programs resulted in the development of a whole series of increasingly specialized disciplinary subdivisions.

Geography and Human Geography

Geography's specialized subfields are not divisive but are interrelated. Geography in all its subdivisions is characterized by three dominating interests. The first is in the areal variation of physical and human phenomena on the surface of the earth. Geography examines relationships between human societies and the natural environments that they occupy and modify. The second is a focus on the spa-

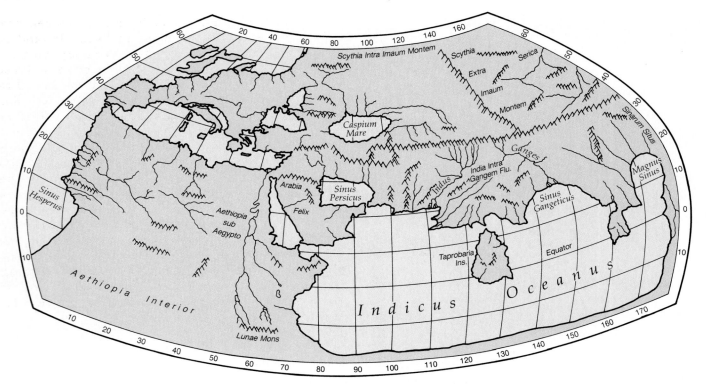

FIGURE 1.2 **World map of the 2nd century A.D. Roman geographer-astronomer Ptolemy.** Ptolemy (Claudius Ptolemaeus) adopted a previously developed map grid of latitude and longitude based on the division of the circle into 360°, permitting a precise mathematical location for every recorded place. Unfortunately, errors of assumption and measurement rendered both the map and its accompanying six-volume gazetteer inaccurate. Many variants of Ptolemy's map were published in the 15th and 16th centuries. The version shown here summarizes the extent and content of the original.

tial systems[1] that link physical phenomena and human activities in one area of the earth with other areas. Together, these interests lead to a third enduring theme, that of regional analysis: geography studies human–environmental—or ecological—relationships, and the systems of spatial interaction are studied in specific areal settings. This areal orientation pursued by some geographers is called *regional geography.*

Other geographers choose to identify particular classes of things, rather than segments of the earth's surface, for specialized study. These *systematic geographers* may focus their attention on one or a few related aspects of the physical environment or of human populations and societies. In each case, the topic selected for study is examined in its interrelationships with other spatial systems and areal patterns. *Physical geography* directs its attention to the natural environmental side of the human–environment

structure. Its concerns are with landforms and their distribution, with atmospheric conditions and climatic patterns, with soils or vegetation associations, and the like. The other systematic branch of geography—and the subject of this book—is *human geography.*

Human Geography

Human geography deals with the world as it is and with the world as it might be made to be. Its emphasis is on people: where they are, what they are like, how they interact over space, and what kinds of landscapes of human use they erect upon the natural landscapes they occupy. It encompasses all those interests and topics of geography that are not directly concerned with the physical environment or, like cartography, are technical in orientation. Its content provides integration for all of the social sciences, for it gives to those sciences the necessary spatial and systems viewpoint that they otherwise lack. At the same time, human geography draws upon other social sciences in the analyses identified with its subfields, such as *behavioral, political, social,* or *economic geography* (Figure 1.3).

---

[1] A "system" is simply a group of elements organized in a way that every element is to some degree directly or indirectly interdependent with every other element. For geographers, the systems of interest are those that distinguish or characterize different regions or areas of the earth.

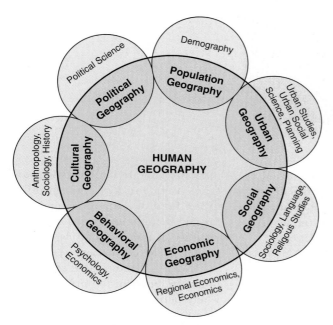

FIGURE 1.3 Some of the subdivisions of human geography and the allied fields to which they are related. Geography, "the mother of sciences," initiated in antiquity the lines of inquiry that later led to the development of these and other separate disciplines. That geography retains its ties to them and shares their insights and data reinforces its role as an essential integrator of all data, concepts, and models that have integrative regional and spatial implications.

Human geography admirably serves the objectives of a liberal education. It helps us to understand the world we occupy and to appreciate the circumstances affecting peoples and countries other than our own. It clarifies the contrasts in societies and cultures and in the human landscapes they have created in different regions of the earth. Its models and explanations of how things are interrelated in earth space give us a clearer understanding of the economic, social, and political systems within which we live and operate. Its analyses of those spatial systems make us more aware of the realities and the prospects of our own society in an increasingly troubled and competitive world. Our study of human geography, therefore, can help make us better-informed citizens, more able to understand the important issues facing our communities and our countries and better prepared to contribute to their solutions. Importantly, it can also help open the way to wonderfully rewarding and diversified careers as professional geographers (see "Working in Geography").

ROGER'S BOOK

The Arab geographer Idrisi, or Edrisi (c. A.D. 1099–1154), a descendant of the Prophet Mohammed, was directed by Roger II, the Christian King of Sicily in whose court he served, to collect all known geographical information and assemble it in a truly accurate representation of the world. An academy of geographers and scholars was gathered to assist Idrisi in the project. Books and maps of classical and Islamic origins were consulted, mariners and travelers interviewed, and scientific expeditions dispatched to foreign lands to observe and record. Data collection took 15 years before the final world map was fabricated on a silver disc some 200 centimeters (80 inches) in diameter and

weighing over 135 kilograms (300 pounds). Lost to looters in 1160, the map is survived by "Roger's Book," containing the information amassed by Idrisi's academy and including a world map, 71 part maps, and 70 sectional itinerary maps.

Idrisi's "inhabited earth" is divided into the seven "climates" of Greek geographers, beginning at the equator and stretching northward to the limit at which, it was supposed, the earth was too cold to be inhabited. Each climate was then subdivided by perpendicular lines into 11 equal parts beginning with the west coast of Africa on the west and ending with the east coast of Asia. Each of the resulting 77 square compartments was then discussed in sequence in "Roger's Book."

Though Idrisi worked in one of the most prestigious courts of Europe, there is little evidence that his work had any impact on European geographic thought. He was strongly influenced by Ptolemy's work and misconceptions and shared the then common Muslim fear of the unknown western ocean. Yet Idrisi's clear understanding of such scientific truths as the roundness of the earth, his grasp of the scholarly writings of his Greek and Muslim predecessors, and the faithful recording of information on little-known portions of Europe, the Near East, and North Africa set his work far above the mediocre standards of contemporary Christian geography.

FOR YOUR CONSIDERATION

WORKING IN GEOGRAPHY

Recognizing geography's role in a rounded liberal education leads logically to a further interest: Can it, as well, be a pathway to employment for those who wish to specialize in the discipline? The answer is "yes," in a number of various types of jobs. One broad cluster is concerned with supporting the field itself, through teaching and research. Teaching opportunities exist at all levels, from elementary to university post-graduate. Teachers with some training in geography are increasingly in demand at the elementary and high school level in the United States, reflecting geography's inclusion as a core subject in the federally adopted *Goals 2000: Educate America Act* (Public Law 103–227) and the national determination to create a geographically literate society. At the college level, specialized teaching and research in all branches of geography have long been established, and geographically trained scholars are prominently associated with urban, community, and environmental studies, regional science, locational economics, and other interdisciplinary programs.

Because of the breadth and diversity of this field, training in geography involves the acquisition of skills and approaches applicable to a wide variety of jobs outside the academic world. Modern geography is both a physical and social science and fosters a wealth of technical skills. The employment possibilities it presents are as many and varied as are the agencies and enterprises dealing with the natural environment and human activities and with the acquisition and analysis of spatial data.

About a quarter of all professional geographers work in government, either at the state or local level or in a variety of federal agencies and international organizations. Although many positions do not carry a geography title, physical geographers serve as water and natural resource analysts, weather and climate experts, soil scientists, and the like. An area of recent high demand is for environmental managers and technicians. Geographers who have specialized in environmental studies find jobs in both public and private agencies. Their work may include assessing the environmental impact of proposed development projects on such things as air and water quality and endangered species; and also includes preparing the environmental impact statements required before construction can begin.

Human geographers work in many different roles in the public sector. Jobs include data acquisition and analysis in health care, transportation, population studies, economic development, and international economics. Many geography graduates find positions as planners in local and state governmental agencies concerned with housing and community development, park and recreation planning, and urban and regional planning. They map and analyze land use plans and transportation systems, monitor urban land development, make informed recommendations about the location of public facilities, and engage in basic social science research.

Many of these same specializations are found in the private sector, where perhaps another quarter of geographers work. Geographic training is ideal for such tasks as business planning and market analysis; factory, store, and shopping center site selection; community and economic development programs for banks, public utilities, and railroads; and similar applications. Publishers of maps, atlases, news and travel magazines, and the like, employ geographers as writers, editors, and mapmakers.

The combination of traditional, broad-based liberal arts perspective with the technical skills required in geographic research and analysis gives geography graduates a competitive edge in the current labor market. These field-based skills include familiarity with geographic information systems (GIS), cartography and computer mapping, remote sensing and photogrammetry, and competence in data analysis and problem solving. In particular, students with expertise in GIS, who are knowledgeable about data sources, hardware, and software, are finding they have ready access to employment opportunities.

The Structure of This Book

By way of getting started, it is useful for you to know how the organization and topics of this text have been structured to help you reach the kinds of understandings we seek.

We begin by exploring the roots and meaning of culture (Chapter 2), establishing the observed ground rules of spatial interaction and spatial behavior (Chapter 3), and examining the areal variations in patterns of population distribution and change (Chapter 4). These set the stage for following separate discussions of spatial patterns of language and religion, ethnic distinctions, and folk and popular culture. These are the principal expressions of unity and diversity and of areal differentiation among the peoples and societies of the earth. Understanding their spatial patterns and interrelations goes far toward providing the world view that is our objective.

Beginning with Chapter 8, our focus shifts more to the economic and organizational landscapes humans have created. In turn, we look at economic geography and economic development, urban systems and structures, and patterns of the political ordering of space. Finally, in Chapter 13, dealing with human impacts, we return to the underlying concern of all geographic study: the relationship between human geographic patterns and processes and both the present conditions and the future prospects of the physical and cultural environments we occupy, create, or modify.

To help clarify the connections between the various topics of human geography, the chapters of this book are grouped by common theme and separately introduced. For students new to geography as a subject and for those who want a reminder of its unifying objectives and shared techniques of study, the remainder of this first chapter will serve as introduction and review.

Basic Geographic Concepts

The topics included in human geography are diverse, but that very diversity emphasizes the reality that all geographers—whatever their particular topical or regional specialities—are united by the similar questions they ask and the common set of concepts they employ to consider their answers. Of either a physical or cultural phenomenon they will inquire: What is it? Where is it? How did it come to be what and where it is? Where is it in relation to other things that affect it or are affected by it? How is it part of a functioning whole? How does its location affect people's lives and the content of the area in which it is found?

These questions are spatial in focus and systems analytical in approach and are derived from enduring central themes in geography. In answering them, geographers draw upon a common store of concepts, terms, and methods of study that together form the basic structure and vocabulary of geography. Collectively, they reflect the fundamental truths addressed by geography: that things are rationally organized on the earth's surface and that recognizing spatial patterns is an essential starting point for understanding how people live on and shape the earth's surface. That understanding is not just the task and interest of the professional geographer; it should be, as well, part of the mental framework of all informed persons. As the publication *Geography for Life* summarizes,

THE NATIONAL STANDARDS

 eography is a core subject in the nationally adopted *Goals 2000: Educate America Act.* Its inclusion reflects a national conviction that a grasp of the skills and understandings of geography are essential in an American educational system "tailored to the needs of productive and responsible citizenship in the global economy." The National Geography Standards 1994 were developed to help achieve that goal. They specify the essential subject matter, skills, and perspectives that students who have gone through the U.S. public school system should acquire and use. Although not all of the standards are relevant to our study of human geography, together they help frame the kinds of understanding we will seek in the following pages and suggest the purpose and benefit of further study of geography.

The 18 standards from *Geography for Life* tell us:

The geographically informed person knows and understands:

The World in Spatial Terms

1. *How to use maps and other geographic tools and technologies to acquire, process, and report information from a spatial perspective.*
2. *How to use mental maps to organize information about people, places, and environments in a spatial context.*
3. *How to analyze the spatial organization of people, places, and environments on Earth's surface.*

Places and Regions

4. *The physical and human characteristics of places.*
5. *That people create regions to interpret Earth's complexity.*
6. *How culture and experience influence people's perceptions of places and regions.*

Physical Systems

7. *The physical processes that shape the patterns of Earth's surface.*
8. *The characteristics and spatial distribution of ecosystems on Earth's surface.*

Human Systems

9. *The characteristics, distribution, and migration of human populations on Earth's surface.*
10. *The characteristics, distribution, and complexity of Earth's cultural mosaics.*
11. *The patterns and networks of economic interdependence on Earth's surface.*
12. *The processes, patterns, and functions of human settlement.*
13. *How the forces of cooperation and conflict among people influence the division and control of Earth's surface.*

Environment and Society

14. *How human actions modify the physical environment.*
15. *How physical systems affect human systems.*
16. *The changes that occur in the meaning, use, distribution, and importance of resources.*

Uses of Geography

17. *How to apply geography to interpret the past.*
18. *How to apply geography to interpret the present and plan for the future.*

Source: *Geography for Life: National Geography Standards 1994.* Washington, D.C.: National Geographic Research and Exploration, 1994.

"There is now a widespread acceptance . . . that being literate in geography is essential . . . to earn a decent living, enjoy the richness of life, and participate responsibly in local, national, and international affairs." (See "The National Standards".)

Geographers use the word *spatial* as an essential modifier in framing their questions and forming their concepts. Geography, they say, is a *spatial* science. It is concerned with *spatial behavior* of people, with the *spatial relationships* that are observed between places on the earth's surface, and with the *spatial processes* that create or maintain those behaviors and relationships. The word *spatial* comes, of course, from *space,* and to geographers it always carries the idea of the way things are distributed, the way movements occur, and the way processes operate over the whole or a part of the surface of the earth. The geographer's space, then, is earth space, the surface area occupied or available to be occupied by humans. Spatial phenomena have locations on that surface, and spatial interactions occur between places, things, and people within the earth area available to them. The need to understand those relationships, interactions, and processes helps frame the questions that geographers ask.

Those questions have their starting point in basic observations about the location and nature of places and about how places are similar to or different from one another. Such observations, though simply stated, are profoundly important to our comprehension of the world we occupy.

- **Places have location, direction, and distance with respect to other places.**
- **A place may be large or small; scale is important.**
- **A place has both physical structure and cultural content.**
- **The characteristics of places develop and change over time.**
- **Places interact with other places.**
- **The content of places is rationally structured.**
- **Places may be generalized into regions of similarities and differences.**

These are basic notions understandable to everyone. They also are the means by which geographers express fundamental observations about the earth spaces they examine and put those observations into a common framework of reference. Each of the concepts is worth further explanation, for they are not quite as simple as they at first seem.

Location, Direction, and Distance

Location, direction, and *distance* are everyday ways of assessing the space around us and identifying our position in relation to other things and places of interest. They are also essential in understanding the processes of spatial interaction that figure so importantly in the study of human geography.

Location

The location of places and things is the starting point of all geographic study as well as of all our personal movements and spatial actions in everyday life. We think of and refer to location in at least two different senses, *absolute* and *relative.*

Absolute location is the identification of place by some precise and accepted system of coordinates; it therefore is sometimes called *mathematical location.* We have several such accepted systems of pinpointing positions. One of them is the global grid of latitude and longitude (discussed later on page 20). With it the absolute location of any point on the earth can be accurately described by reference to its degrees, minutes, and seconds of *latitude* and *longitude* (Figure 1.4).

Other coordinate systems are also in use. Survey systems such as the township, range, and section description of property in much of the United States give mathematical locations on a regional level, while street address precisely defines a building according to the reference system of an individual town. Absolute location is unique to each described place, is independent of any other characteristic or observation about that place, and has obvious value in the legal description of places, in measuring the distance separating places, or in finding directions between places on the earth's surface.

When geographers—or real estate agents—remark that "location matters," however, their reference is usually not to absolute but to **relative location**—the position of a

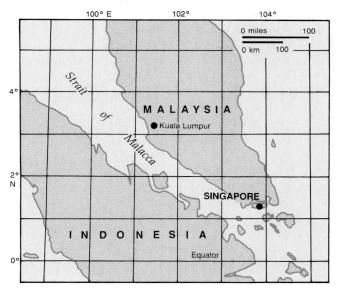

FIGURE 1.4 **The latitude and longitude of Singapore** is 1° 20′ N, 103° 57′ E (read as 1 degree, 20 minutes north; 103 degrees, 57 minutes east). The circumference of the earth measures 360 degrees; each degree contains 60 minutes and each minute has 60 seconds of latitude or longitude. What are the coordinates of Kuala Lumpur?

place in relation to that of other places or activities. Relative location expresses spatial interconnection and interdependence. On an immediate and personal level, we think of the location of the school library not in terms of its street address or room number but where it is relative to our classrooms, or the cafeteria, or some other reference point. On the larger scene, relative location tells us that people, things, and places exist not in a spatial vacuum but in a world of physical and cultural characteristics that differ from place to place (Figure 1.5).

New York City, for example, may in absolute terms be described as located at (approximately) latitude 40° 43′ N and longitude 73° 58′ W. We have a better understanding of the *meaning* of its location, however, when reference is made to its spatial relationships: to the continental interior through the Hudson-Mohawk lowland corridor or to its position on the eastern seaboard of the United States. Within the city, we gain understanding of the locational significance of Central Park or the Lower East Side not solely by reference to the street addresses or city blocks they occupy but by their spatial and functional relationships to the total land use, activity, and population patterns of New York City.

In view of these different ways of looking at location, geographers make a distinction between the *site* and the *situation* of a place. **Site** refers to the physical and cultural characteristics and attributes of the place itself. It is more than mathematical location, for it tells us something about

the internal features of that place. The site of Philadelphia, for example, is an area bordering and west of the Delaware River north of its intersection with the Schuylkill River in southeast Pennsylvania (Figure 1.6). **Situation,** on the other hand, refers to the external relations of a locale. It is an expression of relative location with particular reference to items of significance to the place in question. The situation of Chicago might be described as at the deepest penetration of the Great Lakes system into the interior of the United States, astride the Great Lakes–Mississippi waterways, and near the western margin of the manufacturing belt, the northern boundary of the corn belt, and the southeastern reaches of a major dairy region. Reference to railroads, coal deposits, and ore fields would amplify its situational characteristics (Figure 1.7).

Direction

Direction is a second universal spatial concept. Like location, it has more than one meaning and can be expressed in absolute or relative terms. **Absolute direction** is based on the cardinal points of north, south, east, and west. These appear uniformly and independently in all cultures, derived from the obvious "givens" of nature: the rising and setting of the sun for east and west, the sky location of the noontime sun and of certain fixed stars for north and south.

We also commonly use **relative** or *relational* **directions.** In the United States we go "out West," "back East," or "down South"; we worry about conflict in the "Near East" or economic competition from the "Far Eastern countries." These directional references are culturally based and locationally variable, despite their reference to cardinal compass points. The Near and the Far East locate

FIGURE 1.5 **The reality of relative location** on the globe may be strikingly different from the impressions we form from flat maps. The position of Russia with respect to North America when viewed from a polar perspective emphasizes that relative location properly viewed is important to our understanding of spatial relationships and interactions between the two world areas.

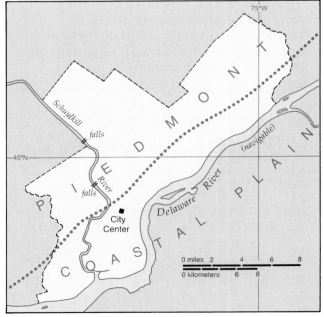

FIGURE 1.6 **The site of Philadelphia.**

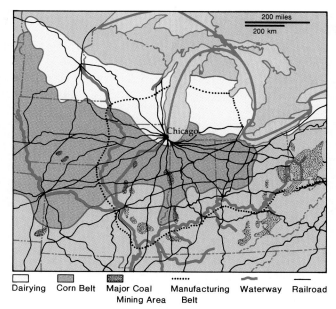

FIGURE 1.7 **The situation of Chicago** helps suggest the reasons for its functional diversity.

Legend: Dairying | Corn Belt | Major Coal Mining Area | Manufacturing Belt | Waterway | Railroad

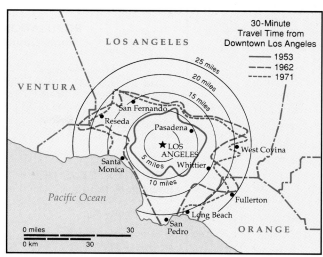

FIGURE 1.8 **Lines of equal travel time** (*isochrones*) mark off different linear distances from a given starting point, depending on the condition of the route and terrain and changes in the roads and traffic flows over time. On this map, the areas within 30 minutes' travel time from downtown Los Angeles are recorded for the period 1953 to 1971.

parts of Asia from the European perspective; they are retained in the Americas by custom and usage, even though one would normally travel westward across the Pacific, for example, to reach the "Far East" from California, British Columbia, or Chile. For many Americans, "back East" and "out West" are reflections of the migration paths of earlier generations for whom home was in the eastern part of the country, to which they might look back. "Up North" and "down South" reflect our accepted custom of putting north at the top and south at the bottom of our maps.

Distance

Distance joins location and direction as a commonly understood term that has dual meanings for geographers. Like its two companion spatial concepts, distance may be viewed in both an absolute and a relative sense.

Absolute distance refers to the spatial separation between two points on the earth's surface measured by some accepted standard unit such as miles or kilometers for widely separated locales, feet or meters for more closely spaced points. **Relative distance** transforms those linear measurements into other units more meaningful for the space relationship at question.

To know that two competing malls are about equidistant in miles from your residence is perhaps less important in planning your shopping trip than is knowing that because of street conditions or traffic congestion one is 5 minutes and the other 15 minutes away (Figure 1.8). Most people, in fact, think of time distance rather than linear distance in their daily activities; downtown is 20 minutes by bus, the library is a 5-minute walk. In some instances, money rather than time may be the

distance transformation. An urban destination might be estimated to be a $5 cab ride away, information that may affect either the decision to make the trip at all or the choice of travel mode to get there.

A *psychological* transformation of linear distance is also frequent. The solitary late-night walk back to the car through an unfamiliar or dangerous neighborhood seems far longer than a daytime stroll of the same distance through familiar and friendly territory. A first-time trip to a new destination frequently seems much longer than the return trip over the same path. Distance relationships, their measurement, and their meaning for human spatial interaction are fundamental to our understanding of human geography. They are a subject of Chapter 3, and reference to them recurs throughout this book.

Size and Scale

When we say that a place may be large or small, we speak both of the nature of the place itself and of the generalizations that can be made about it. In either instance, geographers are concerned with **scale,** though we may use that term in different ways. We can, for example, study a problem—say, population or agriculture—at the local scale, the regional scale, or on a global scale. Here the reference is purely to the size of unit studied. More technically, scale tells us the relationship between the size of an area on a map and the actual size of the mapped area on the surface of the earth. In this sense, scale is a feature of every map and essential to recognizing the areal meaning of what is shown on that map.

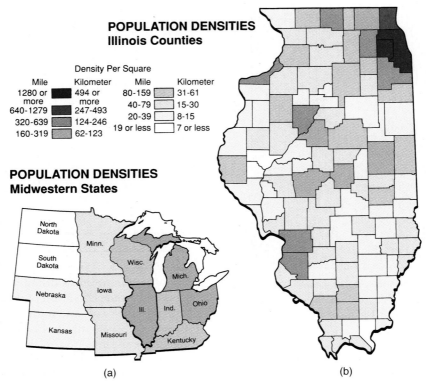

POPULATION DENSITIES
Illinois Counties

Density Per Square

Mile	Kilometer	Mile	Kilometer
1280 or more	494 or more	80-159	31-61
640-1279	247-493	40-79	15-30
320-639	124-246	20-39	8-15
160-319	62-123	19 or less	7 or less

POPULATION DENSITIES
Midwestern States

(a)   (b)

FIGURE 1.9 **Population density and map scale.** "Truth" depends on one's scale of inquiry. Map (*a*) reveals that the maximum population density of Midwestern states is no more than 123 people per square kilometer (319 per sq. mi.). From map (*b*), however, we see that population densities in two Illinois counties exceed 494 people per square kilometer (1280 per sq. mi.). Were we to reduce our scale of inquiry even further, examining individual city blocks in Chicago, we would find densities as high as 2000 people per square kilometer (5200 per sq. mi.). Scale matters!

In both senses of the word, *scale* implies the degree of generalization represented (Figure 1.9). Geographic inquiry may be broad or narrow; it occurs at many different size scales. Climate may be an object of study, but research and generalization focused on climates of the world will differ in degree and kind from study of the microclimates of a city. Awareness of scale is of great importance because in geographic work, concepts, relationships, and understandings that are found to have meaning at one scale may not be applicable when the same problem is examined at another scale. For example, the study of world agricultural patterns may refer to global climatic regimes, cultural food preferences, levels of economic development, and patterns of world trade. These large-scale relationships are of little concern in the study of crop patterns within single counties of the United States, where topography, soil and drainage conditions, farm size, ownership, and capitalization, or even personal management preferences may be of greater explanatory significance.

Physical and Cultural Attributes

All places have physical and cultural traits that distinguish them from other places. Their attributes give them character, potential, and meaning. Geographers are concerned with identifying and analyzing the details of those attributes and, particularly, with recognizing the interrelationship between the physical and cultural components of area—the human–environmental interface.

Physical characteristics refer to such natural aspects of a locale as its climate and soil, the presence or absence of water supplies and mineral resources, its terrain features, and the like. These **natural landscape** attributes provide the setting within which human action occurs. They help shape—but do not dictate—how people live. The resource base, for example, is physically determined, though how resources are perceived and utilized is culturally conditioned.

People modify the environmental conditions of a given place simply by occupying it. The existence of the U.S. Environmental Protection Agency (and its counterparts elsewhere) is a reminder that humans are the active and frequently harmful agents in the continuing spatial interplay between the cultural and physical worlds (Figure 1.10). Virtually every human activity leaves its imprint on an area's soils, water, vegetation, animal life, and other resources and on the atmosphere common to all earth space. The impact of humans has been so universal and so long exerted that essentially no "natural landscape" any longer exists. The visible expression of that human activity is the **cultural landscape.** It, too, exists at different scales and dif-

FIGURE 1.10 Sites (and sights) such as this devastation of ruptured barrels and petrochemical contamination near Texas City, Texas, are all-too-frequent reminders of the adverse environmental impacts of humans and their waste products. Many of those impacts are more subtle, hidden in the form of soil erosion, water pollution, increased stream sedimentation, plant and animal extinctions, deforestation, and the like.

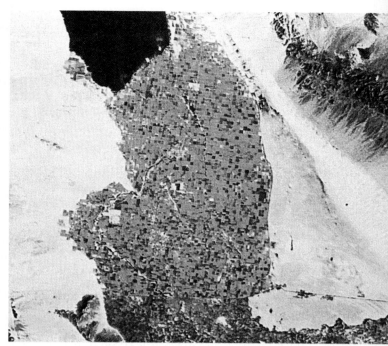

FIGURE 1.11 This Landsat image reveals contrasting cultural landscapes along the Mexico-California border. Move your eyes from the Salton Sea (the dark patch at the top of the image) southward to the agricultural land extending to the edge of the picture. Notice how the regularity of the fields and the bright colors (representing growing vegetation) give way to a marked break, where irregularly shaped fields and less prosperous agriculture are evident. Above the break is the Imperial Valley of California; below the border is Mexico.

ferent levels of visibility. Differences in agricultural practices and land use between Mexico and Southern California are evident in Figure 1.11, while the signs, structures, and people of, for instance, Los Angeles's Chinatown, leave a smaller, more confined imprint within the larger cultural landscape of the metropolitan area itself.

Although the focus of this book is on the human characteristics of places, geographers are ever aware that the physical content of an area is also important in understanding the activity patterns of people and the interconnections between people and the environments they occupy and modify. Those interconnections and modifications are not static or permanent, however, but are subject to continual change.

The Changing Attributes of Place

The physical environment surrounding us seems eternal and unchanging but, of course, it is not. In the framework of geologic time, change is both continuous and pronounced. Islands form and disappear; mountains rise and are worn low to swampy plains; vast continental glaciers form, move, and melt away, and sea levels fall and rise in response. Geologic time is long, but the forces that give shape to the land are timeless and relentless.

Even within the short period of time since the most recent retreat of continental glaciers—some 10,000 or 11,000 years ago—the environments occupied by humans have been subject to change. Glacial retreat itself marked a period of climatic alteration, extending the area habitable by humans to include vast reaches of northern Eurasia and North America formerly covered by thousands of feet of ice. With moderating climatic conditions came associated changes in vegetation and fauna. On the global scale, these were natural environmental changes; humans were as yet too few in number and too limited in technology to alter materially the course of physical events. On the regional scale, however, even early human societies exerted an impact on the environments they occupied. Fire was used to clear forest undergrowth, to maintain or extend grassland for grazing animals and to drive them in the hunt, and, later, to clear openings for rudimentary agriculture.

With the dawn of civilizations and the invention and spread of agricultural technologies, humans accelerated their management and alteration of the now no longer "natural" environment. Even the classical Greeks noted how the landscape they occupied differed—for the worse—from its former condition. With growing numbers of people and particularly with industrialization and the spread of European exploitative technologies throughout the world, the pace of change in the content of area accelerated. The built landscape—the product of human effort—increasingly replaced the natural landscape. Each new settlement or city, each agricultural assault on forests, each new mine, dam, or factory changed the content of regions and altered the temporarily established spatial interconnections between humans and the environment.

Characteristics of places today, therefore, are the result of constantly changing past conditions. They are, as well, the forerunners of differing human–environmental balances yet to be struck. Geographers are concerned with places at given moments of time. But to understand fully the nature and development of places, geographers must view them as the present result of past operation of distinctive physical and cultural processes (Figure 1.12).

You will recall that one of the questions geographers ask of a place or thing is: How did it come to be what and where it is? This is an inquiry about process and about becoming. The forces and events shaping the physical and explaining the cultural environment of places today are an important focus of geography. They are, particularly in their human context, the subjects of most of the separate chapters of this book. To understand them is to appreciate more fully the changing human spatial order of our world.

Interaction among Places

The concepts of relative location and distance that we earlier introduced lead directly to a fundamental spatial reality: Places interact with other places in structured and comprehensible ways. In describing the processes and patterns of that **spatial interaction,** geographers add *accessibility* and *connectivity* to the ideas of location and distance.

A basic law of geography tells us that in a spatial sense, everything is related to everything else but that relationships are stronger when things are near one another. Our observation, therefore, is that interaction between places diminishes in intensity and frequency as distance between them increases—a statement of the idea of *distance decay,* which we explore in Chapter 3.

Consideration of distance implies assessment of **accessibility.** How easy or difficult is it to overcome the "friction of distance"? That is, how easy or difficult is it to surmount the barrier of the time and space separation of places? Distance isolated North America from Europe until the development of ships (and aircraft) reduced the effective distance between the continents. All parts of the ancient and medieval city were accessible by walking; they were "pedestrian cities," a status lost as cities expanded in area and population with industrialization. Accessibility between city districts could only be maintained by the development of public transit systems whose fixed lines of travel increased ease of movement between connected points and reduced it between areas not on the transit lines themselves.

FIGURE 1.12 The process of change in a cultural landscape. Before the advent of the freeway, this portion of suburban Long Island, New York, was largely devoted to agriculture (left). The construction of the freeway and cloverleaf interchange ramps altered nearby land use patterns (right) to replace farming with housing developments and new commercial and light industrial activities.

INTRODUCTION: SOME BACKGROUND BASICS

Accessibility therefore suggests the idea of **connectivity,** a broader concept implying all the tangible and intangible ways in which places are connected: by physical telephone lines, street and road systems, pipelines and sewers; by unrestrained walking across open countryside; by radio and TV broadcasts beamed outward uniformly from a central source. Where routes are fixed and flow is channelized, *networks*—the patterns of routes connecting sets of places—determine the efficiency of movement and the connectedness of points.

There is, inevitably, interchange between connected places. **Spatial diffusion** is the process of dispersion of an idea or an item from a center of origin to more distant points with which it is directly or indirectly connected. The rate and extent of that diffusion are affected by the distance separating the originating center of, say, a new idea or technology from other places where it is eventually adopted. Diffusion rates are also affected by population densities, means of communication, obvious advantages of the innovation, and importance or prestige of the originating *node.* These ideas of diffusion are further explored in Chapter 2.

Geographers study the dynamics of spatial relationships. Movement, connection, and interaction are part of the social and economic processes that give character to places and regions (Figure 1.13). Geography's interest in those relationships recognizes that spatial interaction is not just an awkward necessity but a fundamental organizing principle of human life on earth.

The Structured Content of Place

A starting point for geographic inquiry is how things are distributed in area—for example, the placement of churches or supermarkets within a town. That interest distinguishes geography from other sciences, physical or social, and underlies many of the questions geographers ask: Where is a thing located? How is that location related to other items? How did the location we observe come to exist? Such questions carry the conviction that the contents of an area are comprehensibly arranged or structured. The arrangement of things on the earth's surface is called **spatial distribution** and may be analyzed by the elements common to all spatial distributions: *density, dispersion,* and *pattern.*

Density

The measure of the number or quantity of anything within a defined unit of area is its **density.** It is therefore not simply a count of items but of items in relation to the space in which they are found. When the relationship is absolute, as in population per square kilometer, for example, or dwelling units per acre, we are defining *arithmetic density* (see Figure 1.9). Sometimes it is more meaningful to relate item numbers to a specific kind of area. *Physiological density,* for example, is a measure of the number of persons per unit area of arable land. Density defined in population terms is discussed in Chapter 4.

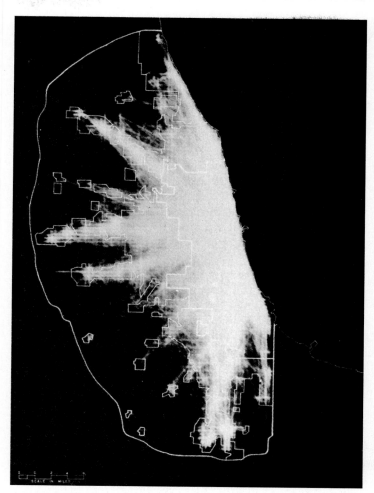

FIGURE 1.13 The routes of the 5 million automobile trips made each day in Chicago during the late 1950s are recorded on this light-display map. The boundaries of the region of interaction that they created are clearly marked. Those boundaries (and the dynamic region they defined) were subject to change as residential neighborhoods expanded or developed, as population relocations occurred, and as the road pattern was altered over time.

A density figure is a statement of fact but not necessarily one useful in itself. Densities are normally employed comparatively, relative to one another. High or low density implies a comparison with a known standard, with an average, or with a different area. Ohio, with (1994) 105 persons per square kilometer (271 per sq. mi.) might be thought to have a high density compared to neighboring Michigan at 64 per square kilometer (167 per sq. mi.), and a low one in relation to New Jersey at 411 (1065 per sq. mi.).

Dispersion

Dispersion (or its opposite, **concentration**) is a statement of the amount of *spread* of a phenomenon over an area. It tells us not how many or how much but how far things are spread out. If they are close together spatially, they are considered *clustered* or *agglomerated*. If they are spread out, they are *dispersed* or *scattered* (Figure 1.14).

If the entire population of a metropolitan county were all located within a confined central city, we might say the population was clustered. If, however, that same population redistributed itself, with many city residents moving to the suburbs and occupying a larger portion of the county's territory, it would become more dispersed. In both cases, the *density* of population (numbers in relation to area of the county) would be the same, but the distribution would have changed. Since dispersion deals with separation of things one from another, a distribution that might be described as *clustered* (closely spaced) at one scale of reference might equally well be considered *dispersed* (widely spread) at another scale.

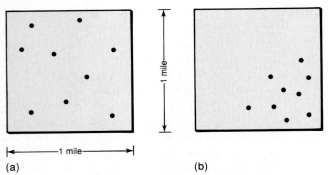

(a)   (b)

FIGURE 1.14   Density and dispersion each tell us something different about how items are distributed in an area. *Density* is simply the number of items or observations within a defined area; it remains the same no matter how the items are distributed. The density of houses per square mile, for example, is the same in both (*a*) and (*b*). *Dispersion* is a statement about nearness or separation. The houses in (*a*) are more *dispersed* than those shown *clustered* in (*b*).

Pattern

The geometric arrangement of things in space is called **pattern.** Like dispersion, pattern refers to distribution, but that reference emphasizes design rather than spacing (Figure 1.15). The distribution of towns along a railroad or houses along a street may be seen as *linear.* A *centralized* pattern may involve items concentrated around a single node. A *random* pattern may be the best description of an unstructured irregular distribution.

The rectangular system of land survey adopted in much of the United States under the Ordinance of 1785 creates a checkerboard rural pattern of "sections" and "quarter-sections" of farmland (see Figure 6.25). As a result, in most American cities, streets display a *grid* or *rectilinear* pattern. The same is true of cities in Canada, Australia, New Zealand, and South Africa, which adopted similar geometric survey systems. The *hexagonal* pattern of service areas of farm towns is a mainstay of central place theory discussed in Chapter 11. These references to

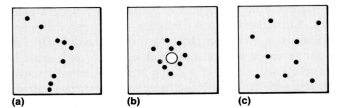

(a)   (b)   (c)

FIGURE 1.15   *Pattern* describes spatial arrangement and design. The *linear* pattern of towns in (*a*) perhaps traces the route of a road or railroad or the course of a river. The central city in (*b*) with its nearby suburbs represents a *centralized* pattern, while the dots in (*c*) are *randomly* distributed.

the geometry of distribution patterns help us visualize and describe the structured arrangement of things in space. They help us make informed comparisons between areas and use the patterns we discern to ask further questions about the interrelationship of things.

Place Similarity and Regions

The distinctive characteristics of places in content and structure immediately suggest two geographically important ideas. The first is that no two places on the surface of the earth can be *exactly* the same. Not only do they have different absolute locations, but—as in the features of the human face—the precise mix of physical and cultural characteristics of a place is never exactly duplicated.

Since geography is a spatial science, the inevitable uniqueness of place would seem to impose impossible problems of generalizing spatial information. That this is not the case results from the second important idea: The physical and cultural content of an area and the dynamic interconnections of people and places show patterns of spatial similarity. Often the similarities are striking enough for us to conclude that spatial regularities exist. They permit us to recognize and define **regions**—earth areas that display significant elements of internal uniformity and external difference from surrounding territories. Places are, therefore, both unlike and like other places, creating patterns of areal differences and of coherent spatial similarity.

The problem of the historian and the geographer is similar: each must generalize about items of study that are essentially unique. The historian creates arbitrary but meaningful and useful historical periods for reference and study. The "Roaring Twenties" and the "Victorian Era" are shorthand summary names for specific time spans, internally quite complex and varied but significantly distinct from what went before or followed after. The region is the geographer's equivalent of the historian's epoch. It is a device of areal generalization, an attempt to separate the otherwise overwhelming diversity and complexity of the earth's surface into recognizable component parts. In both the time and the space need for generalization, attention is focused on key unifying elements or similarities of the

INTRODUCTION: SOME BACKGROUND BASICS

era or area selected for study. In both the historical and geographical cases, the names assigned to those times and places serve to identify the time span or region and to convey a complex set of interrelated attributes.

All of us have a general idea of the meaning of region, and all of us refer to regions in everyday speech and action. We visit "the old neighborhood" or "go downtown"; we plan to vacation or retire in the "Sunbelt"; or we speculate about the effects of weather conditions in the "corn belt" on next year's food prices. In each instance we have mental images of the areas mentioned, and in each we have engaged in an informal place classification to pass along quite complex spatial, organizational, or content ideas. We have applied the **regional concept** to bring order to the immense diversity of the earth's surface.

What we do informally as individuals, geography attempts to do formally as a discipline—define and explain regions (Figure 1.16). The purpose is clear: to make the infinitely varying world around us understandable through spatial summaries. That world is only rarely subdivided into neat, unmistakable "packages" of uniformity. Neither the environment nor human areal actions present us with a compartmentalized order, any more than the sweep of human history has predetermined "eras" or all plant specimens come labeled in nature with species names. We all must classify to understand, and the geographer classifies in regional terms.

Regions are spatial expressions of ideas or summaries useful to the analysis of the problem at hand. Although as many possible regions exist as there are physical, cultural, or organizational attributes of area, the geographer studies selected areal variables that contribute to the understanding of a specific topic or areal problem. All other variables are disregarded as irrelevant. Regional boundaries are assumed to be marked where the region's internal unifying characteristics change so materially that different regional summaries are required.

The Characteristics of Regions

The regional concept tells us that all regions share certain common characteristics related to earth space.

- **Regions have *location,*** often expressed in the regional name selected, such as the Middle West, the Near East, North Africa, and the like. This form of regional name underscores the importance of *relative location.*
- **Regions have *spatial extent.*** They define territories across which uniform sets of physical, cultural, or organizational features are found.
- **Regions have *boundaries*** based on the areal spread of the features selected for study. Since regions are the recognition of the features defining them, their boundaries are drawn where those features no longer occur or dominate (Figure 1.17). Regional boundaries are rarely as sharply defined as those suggested by Figure 1.17 or by the regional maps in this and other geography texts. More frequently, broad zones of transition from one distinctive core area to another exist, as the dominance of the defining regional features gradually diminishes outward from the core to the regional periphery. Linear boundaries are arbitrary divisions made necessary by the scale of world regional maps and by the summary character of most regional discussions.
- **Regions are *hierarchically arranged.*** Although regions vary in scale, type, and degree of generalization, none stands alone as the ultimate key to areal understanding. Each defines a part of spatial reality (Figure 1.18) and at the same time exists as a part of a larger, equally valid regional unit.

Types of Regions

Regions may be either *formal, functional,* or *perceptual.* **Formal** or **uniform regions** are areas of essential uniformity in one or a limited combination of physical or

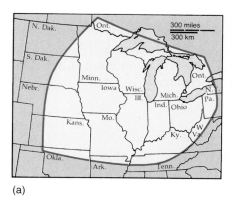
(a)

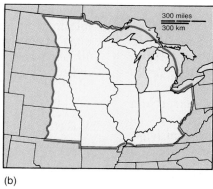
(b)

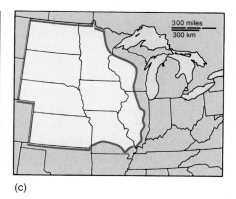
(c)

FIGURE 1.16 The Middle West as seen by different professional geographers. Agreement on the need to recognize spatial order and to define regional units does not imply unanimity in the selection of boundary criteria. All the sources concur in the significance of the Middle West as a regional entity in the spatial structure of the United States and agree on its core area. These sources differ, however, in their assessment of its limiting characteristics.

Sources: (a) John H. Garland, ed., *The North American Midwest* (New York: John Wiley & Sons, 1955); (b) John R. Borchert and Jane McGuigan, *Geography of The New World* (Chicago: Rand McNally, 1961); and (c) Otis P. Starkey and J. Lewis Robinson, *The Anglo-American Realm* (New York: McGraw-Hill, 1969).

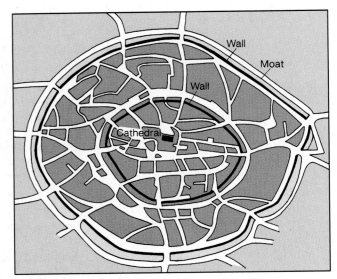

FIGURE 1.17 **Aachen, Germany, in 1649.** The acceptance of regional extent implies the recognition of regional boundaries. At some defined point, *urban* is replaced by *nonurban,* the Midwest ends and the Plains begin, or the rain forest ceases and the savanna emerges. Regional boundaries are, of course, seldom as precisely and visibly marked as were the limits of the walled medieval city. Its sprawling modern counterpart may be more difficult to define, but the boundary significance of the concept of *urban* remains.

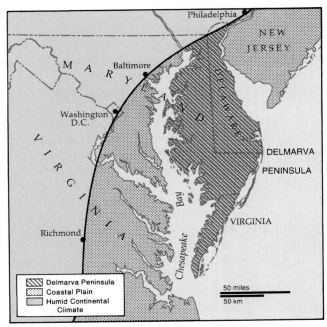

FIGURE 1.18 **A hierarchy of regions.** One possible nesting of regions within a regional hierarchy defined by differing criteria. On a formal regional scale of size progression, the Delmarva Peninsula of the eastern United States may be seen as part of the Atlantic Coastal Plain, which is in turn a portion of the eastern North American humid continental climatic region. Each regional unit has internal coherence. The recognition of its constituent parts aids in understanding the larger composite areal unit.

cultural features. Your home state is a precisely bounded formal political region within which uniformity of law and administration is found. Later in this book we will encounter formal (homogeneous) cultural regions in which standardized characteristics of language, religion, ethnicity, or economy exist. The foldout maps of landform regions and country units show other formal regional patterns. Whatever the basis of its definition, the formal region is the largest area over which a valid generalization of attribute uniformity may be made. Whatever is stated about one part of it holds true for its remainder.

The **functional** or **nodal region,** in contrast, is a spatial system defined by the interactions and connections that give it a dynamic, organizational basis (Figure 1.19). Its boundaries remain constant only as long as the interchanges establishing it remain unaltered.

Perceptual regions are less rigorously structured than the formal and functional regions geographers devise. They reflect feelings and images rather than objective data and because of that may be more meaningful in the lives and actions of those who recognize them than are the more abstract regions of geographers.

Ordinary people have a clear idea of spatial variation and employ the regional concept to distinguish between territorial entities. People individually and collectively agree on where they live. The *vernacular regions* they recognize have reality in their minds and are reflected in regionally based names employed in businesses, by sports teams, or in advertising slogans. The frequency of references to "Dixie" in the southeastern United States represents that kind of regional consensus and awareness. Such vernacular regions reflect the way people view space, assign their loyalties, and interpret their world. At a different scale, such urban ethnic enclaves (see Chapter 6) as "Little Italy" or "Chinatown" have comparable regional identity in the minds of their inhabitants. Less clearly perceived by outsiders but unmistakable to their inhabitants are the "turfs" of urban clubs or gangs. Their boundaries are sharp, and the perceived distinctions between them are paramount in the daily lives and activities of their occupants.

Maps

Maps are tools to identify regions and to analyze their content. The spatial distributions, patterns, and relations of interest to geographers usually cannot easily be observed or interpreted in the landscape itself. Many, such as landform or agricultural regions or major cities, are so extensive spatially that they cannot be seen or studied in their totality from one or a few vantage points. Many, such as regions of language usage or religious belief, are spatial phenomena but are not tangible or visible. Many

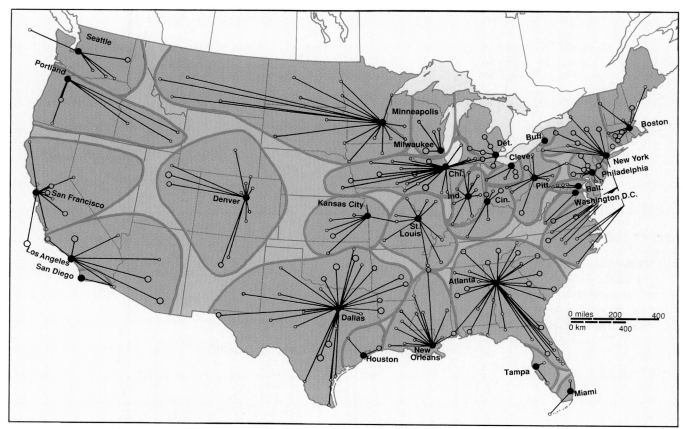

FIGURE 1.19 The *functional regions* shown on this map are based on linkages between large banks of major central cities and the "correspondent" banks they serve in smaller towns. The regions suggest one form of *connectivity* between principal cities and locales beyond their own immediate metropolitan area.

interactions, flows, and exchanges imparting the dynamic quality to spatial interaction may not be directly observable at all. And even if all things of geographic interest could be seen and measured through field examination, the infinite variety of tangible and intangible content of area would make it nearly impossible to isolate for study and interpretation the few matters of regional interest selected for special investigation.

Therefore, the map has become the essential and distinctive tool of geographers. Only through the map can spatial distributions and interactions of whatever nature be reduced to an observable scale, isolated for individual study, and combined or recombined to reveal relationships not directly measurable in the landscape itself. But maps can serve their purpose only if their users have a clear idea of their strengths, limitations, and diversity and of the conventions observed in their preparation and interpretation.

Map Scale

We have already seen that scale (page 11) is a vital element of every map. Because it is a much reduced version of the reality it summarizes, a map generalizes the data it displays. *Scale*—the relationship between size or length of a feature on the map and the same item on the earth's surface—determines the amount of that generalization. The smaller the scale of the map, the larger is the area it covers and the more generalized are the data it portrays. The larger the scale, the smaller is the depicted area and the more accurately can its content be represented (Figure 1.20). It may seem backward, but large-scale maps show small areas, and small-scale maps show large areas.

Map scale is selected according to the amount of generalization of data that is acceptable and the size of area that must be depicted. The user must consider map scale in evaluating the reliability of the spatial data that are presented. Regional boundary lines drawn on the world maps in this and other books or atlases would cover many kilometers or miles on the earth's surface. They obviously distort the reality they are meant to define, and on small-scale maps major distortion is inevitable. In fact, a general rule of thumb is that the larger the earth area depicted on a map, the greater is the distortion built into the map.

This is so because a map has to depict the curved surface of the three-dimensional earth on a two-dimensional sheet of paper. The term **projection** designates the method chosen to represent the earth's curved surface as a flat map. Since absolutely accurate representation is

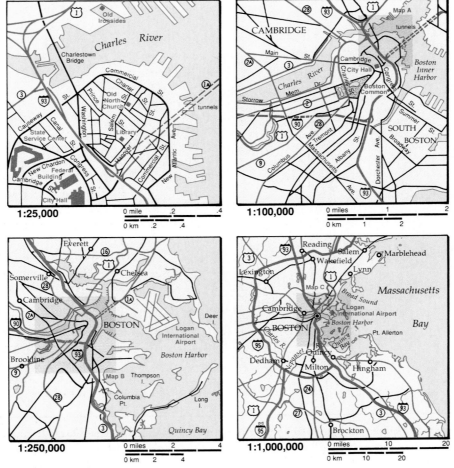

FIGURE 1.20 **The effect of scale on area and detail.** The larger the scale, the greater the number and kinds of features that can be included. Scale may be reported to the map user in one (or more) of three ways. A *verbal* scale is given in words ("1 centimeter to 1 kilometer" or "1 inch to 1 mile"). A *representative fraction* (such as that placed at the left and below each of the four maps shown here) is a statement of how many linear units on the earth's surface are represented by one unit on the map. A *graphic* scale (such as that placed at the right and below each of these maps) is a line or bar marked off in map units but labeled in ground units.

impossible, all projections inevitably distort. Specific projections may be selected, however, to minimize the distortion of at least one of the four main map properties—area, shape, distance, and direction.[2]

The Globe Grid

Maps are geographers' primary tools of spatial analysis. All spatial analysis starts with locations, and all locations are related to the global grid of latitude and longitude. Since these lines of reference are drawn on the spherical earth, their projection onto a map distorts their grid relationships. The extent of variance between the globe grid and a map grid helps tell us the kind and degree of distortion the map will contain.

The key reference points in the *grid system* are the North and South poles and the equator, which are given in nature, and the *prime meridian,* which is agreed on by cartographers. Because a circle contains 360 degrees, the distance between the poles is 180 degrees and between the equator and each pole, 90 degrees (Figure 1.21). *Latitude* measures distance north and south of the equator (0°), and *parallels* of latitude run due east-west. *Longitude* is the angular distance east or west of the prime meridian and is depicted by north-south lines called *meridians,* which converge at the poles. The properties of the globe grid the mapmaker tries to retain and the map user should look for are as follows:

1. **All meridians are of equal length; each is one-half the length of the equator.**
2. **All meridians converge at the poles and are true north-south lines.**

---

[2] A more complete discussion of map projections, including examples of their different types and purposes, may be found in Appendix A, beginning on page 491.

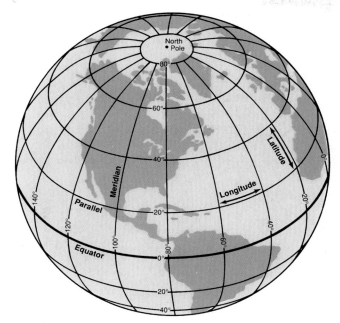

FIGURE 1.21 **The grid system of parallels of latitude and meridians of longitude.** Since the meridians converge at the poles, parallels become increasingly shorter away from the equator. On the globe, the 60th parallel is only one-half as long as the equator, and a degree of longitude along it measures only about 55½ kilometers (about 34½ miles) compared to about 111 kilometers (about 69 miles) at the equator (0°).

3. **All lines of latitude (parallels) are parallel to the equator and to each other.**
4. **Parallels decrease in length as one nears the poles.**
5. **Meridians and parallels intersect at right angles.**
6. **The scale on the surface of the globe is everywhere the same in every direction.**

Only the globe grid itself retains all of these characteristics. To project it onto a surface that can be laid flat is to distort some or all of these properties and consequently to distort the reality the map attempts to portray.

How Maps Show Data

The properties of the globe grid and of various projections are the concern of the cartographer. The geographer is more interested in the depiction of spatial data and in the analysis of the patterns and interrelationships those data present. Out of the myriad items comprising the content of an area, the geographer must, first, select those that are of concern to the problem at hand and, second, decide on how best to display them for study or demonstration.

A *thematic map* is the general term applied to a map of any scale that presents a specific spatial distribution or a single category of data. The way the information is shown on such a map may vary according to the type of information to be conveyed and the level of generalization

that is desired. A *statistical map* records the actual numbers or occurrences of the mapped item per established unit area or location (Figure 1.22). The actual count of each state's colleges and universities shown on an outline map of the United States or the number of traffic accidents at each street intersection within a city are examples of statistical maps. A *cartogram* uses such statistical data to transform territorial space so that the largest areal unit on the map is the one showing the greatest statistical value (Figure 1.23).

A *dot map* gives a different view of data by representing quantities or occurrences by a dot placed on the map in the approximate location of the occurrence or, perhaps, uniformly distributed within the unit area of occurrence (Figure 1.24). The numerical value of a single dot is determined by the compiler and recorded in the map legend. The dot map serves not only to record data but to suggest their spatial pattern, distribution, and dispersion. A *choropleth map* presents average value of the data studied per unit area—dwelling unit rents or assessed values by city block, for example, or (in the United States) population densities by individual townships within counties. Each unit area on the map is then shaded or colored to suggest the magnitude of the event or item found within its borders (Figure 1.25).

4	9	13	11	9	4
8	13	15	17	12	10
6	19	18	12	7	3
9	15	12	10	8	3
8	9	10	8	5	2
5	6	7	6	1	1

FIGURE 1.22 **The starting point of quantitative thematic maps is the location and magnitude of things or events. Here observations are assigned to their areas of occurrence. The spatial arrangement of events is recorded, but their pattern of occurrence is difficult to see.**

McCarty/Lindberg, *A Preface to Economic Geography,* © 1966, p. 31. Redrawn by permission of Prentice-Hall, Inc., Upper Saddle River, NJ.

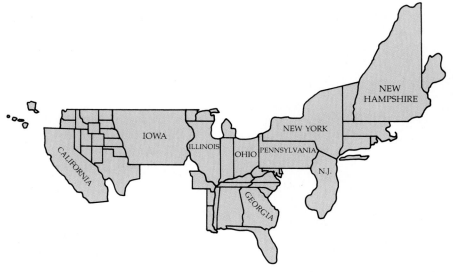

FIGURE 1.23 A cartogram with states drawn in proportion to news coverage of the 1984 presidential nomination contests.

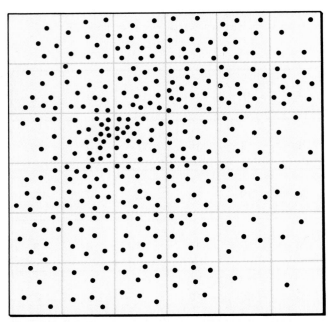

FIGURE 1.24 **A dot map example.** In this dot map the data of Figure 1.22 are represented by dots placed randomly within the areal statistical units.

McCarty/Lindberg, *A Preface to Economic Geography,* © 1966, p. 33. Redrawn by permission of Prentice-Hall, Inc., Upper Saddle River, NJ.

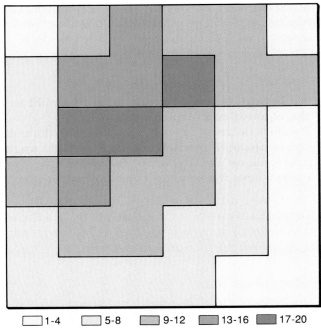

1-4   5-8   9-12   13-16   17-20

FIGURE 1.25 **A choropleth map example.** This choropleth map is derived from Figure 1.22. Data are assigned to class intervals, and colors are used to distinguish magnitudes of occurrences. The selection of data intervals and choice of colors can alter the message and impact of the map.

McCarty/Lindberg, *A Preface to Economic Geography,* © 1966, p. 35. Redrawn by permission of Prentice-Hall, Inc., Upper Saddle River, NJ.

An *isoline map* features lines (*isolines*) that connect points registering equal values of the item mapped (*iso* means "equal"). The *isotherms* shown on the daily weather map connect points recording the same temperature at the same moment of time or the same average temperature during the day. Identical elevations above sea level may be shown by a form of isoline called a *contour* line. Were you to walk along a mapped contour line, you would never go up or downhill but remain always on the level, eventually returning to your starting point (Figure 1.26). U.S. Geological Survey topographic maps show a great deal more than topography and contour lines, as Figures 1.26 and 1.27 document.

On many maps, isolines are drawn to connect points showing identical calculated values, such as percentage of total possible sunlight received at a location. On others, the calculation refers not to a point but to an areal statistic—for example, persons per square kilometer or average percentage of cropland in corn—and the isoline connects average values for unit areas. For emphasis, the area enclosed by isolines may be shaded to indicate approximate uniform occurrence of the thing mapped, and the isoline itself may be treated as the boundary of a uniform region (Figure 1.28).

Mental Maps

Maps that shape our understanding of distributions and locations or influence our understanding of the world around us are not always drawn on paper. We carry with us *mental maps* that in some ways are more accurate in reflecting our view of spatial reality than the formal maps created by geographers or cartographers. **Mental maps**

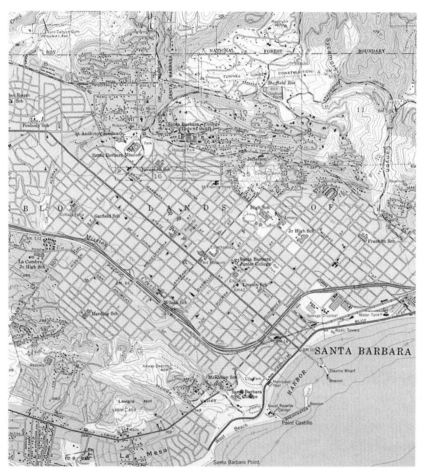

FIGURE 1.26   A portion of the Santa Barbara, California, topographic quadrangle of the U.S. Geological Survey 1:24,000 series. Where contour lines are closely spaced in the upper-right quadrant, they indicate a rapid change in elevation—that is, a steep slope. Widely spaced contours tell us the slope (elevation change) is gradual. The practiced user of topographic maps can visualize terrain with the same ease as if viewing a three-dimensional model. Color and symbols on topographic maps also tell us much about the landscape. Here, the pink tint indicates built-up areas, in which only landmark buildings are shown. The light purple tint is used to indicate extensions of urban areas. The scale of the original map no longer applies to this photographic reduction.

BOUNDARIES

National ....
State or territorial ....
County or equivalent ....
Civil township or equivalent ....
Incorporated-city or equivalent ....
Park, reservation, or monument ....
Small park ....

LAND SURVEY SYSTEMS

U.S. Public Land Survey System:
  Township or range line ....
    Location doubtful ....
  Section line ....
    Location doubtful ....
  Found section corner; found closing corner ....
  Witness corner; meander corner ....

Other land surveys:
  Township or range line ....
    Section line ....
  Land grant or mining claim; monument ....
  Fence line ....

ROADS AND RELATED FEATURES

Primary highway ....
Secondary highway ....
Light duty road ....
Unimproved road ....
Trail ....
Dual highway ....
Dual highway with median strip ....
Road under construction ....
Underpass; overpass ....
Bridge ....
Drawbridge ....
Tunnel ....

BUILDINGS AND RELATED FEATURES

Dwelling or place of employment: small; large ...
School; church ....
Barn, warehouse, etc.: small; large ....
House omission tint ....
Racetrack ....
Airport ....
Landing strip ....
Well (other than water); windmill ....
Water tank: small; large ....
Other tank: small; large ....
Covered reservoir ....
Gaging station ....
Landmark object ....
Campground; picnic area ....
Cemetery: small; large ....

RAILROADS AND RELATED FEATURES

Standard gauge single track; station ....
Standard gauge multiple track ....
Abandoned ....
Under construction ....
Narrow gauge single track ....
Narrow gauge multiple track ....
Railroad in street ....
Juxtaposition ....
Roundhouse and turntable ....

TRANSMISSION LINES AND PIPELINES

Power transmission line: pole; tower ....
Telephone or telegraph line ....
Aboveground oil or gas pipeline ....
Underground oil or gas pipeline ....

CONTOURS

Topographic:
  Intermediate ....
  Index ....
  Supplementary ....
  Depression ....
  Cut; fill ....

Bathymetric:
  Intermediate ....
  Index ....
  Primary ....
  Index Primary ....
  Supplementary ....

MINES AND CAVES

Quarry or open pit mine ....
Gravel, sand, clay, or borrow pit ....
Mine tunnel or cave entrance ....
Prospect; mine shaft ....
Mine dump ....
Tailings ....

SURFACE FEATURES

Levee ....
Sand or mud area, dunes, or shifting sand ......
Intricate surface area ....
Gravel beach or glacial moraine ....
Tailings pond ....

VEGETATION

Woods ....
Scrub ....
Orchard ....
Vineyard ....
Mangrove ....

COASTAL FEATURES

Foreshore flat ....
Rock or coral reef ....
Rock bare or awash ....
Group of rocks bare or awash ....
Exposed wreck ....
Depth curve; sounding ....
Breakwater, pier, jetty, or wharf ....
Seawall ....

BATHYMETRIC FEATURES

Area exposed at mean low tide; sounding datum .
Channel ....
Offshore oil or gas: well; platform ....
Sunken rock ....

RIVERS, LAKES, AND CANALS

Intermittent stream ....
Intermittent river ....
Disappearing stream ....
Perennial stream ....
Perennial river ....
Small falls; small rapids ....
Large falls; large rapids ....
Masonry dam ....
Dam with lock ....
Dam carrying road ....
Intermittent lake or pond ....
Dry lake ....
Narrow wash ....
Wide wash ....
Canal, flume, or aqueduct with lock ....
Elevated aqueduct, flume, or conduit ....
Aqueduct tunnel ....
Water well; spring or seep ....

GLACIERS AND PERMANENT SNOWFIELDS

Contours and limits ....
Form lines ....

SUBMERGED AREAS AND BOGS

Marsh or swamp ....
Submerged marsh or swamp ....
Wooded marsh or swamp ....
Submerged wooded marsh or swamp ....
Rice field ....
Land subject to inundation ....

FIGURE 1.27 Standard U.S. Geological Survey topographic map symbols.

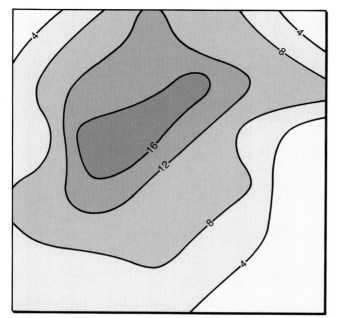

FIGURE 1.28 An isoline generalization of areal data.
The basic assumptions of such a map are that (1) events occur
at the central point of the statistical unit they represent and
(2) events occur continuously across the map in smooth
gradients. The isolines are drawn by estimating values
between actual numerical amounts. The shadings applied to
areas between the isolines on this map are those of Figure
1.25 class intervals.

McCarty/Lindberg, *A Preface to Economic Geography*, © 1966, p. 35. Redrawn by
permission of Prentice-Hall, Inc., Upper Saddle River, NJ.

are images about an area or an environment developed by
an individual on the basis of information or impressions
received, interpreted, and stored. We use this information—this mental map—in organizing our daily activities:
selecting our destinations and the sequence in which they
will be visited, deciding on our routes of travel, recognizing where we are in relation to where we wish to be.

Such maps are every bit as real to their creators (and
we all have them) as are the street maps or highway maps
commercially available and they are a great deal more immediate in their impact on our spatial decisions. We may
choose routes or avoid neighborhoods not on objective
grounds but on emotional or perceptual ones. Whole sections of a community may be voids on our mental maps,
as unknown as the interiors of Africa and South America
were to Western Europeans two centuries ago. Our areas
of awareness generally increase with the increasing mobility that comes with age (Figure 1.29), affluence, and education and may be enlarged or restricted for different
social groups within the city (Figure 1.30).

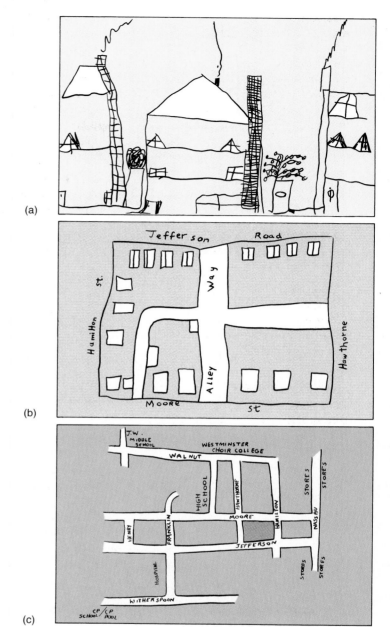

FIGURE 1.29 Three children, aged 6, 10, and 13, who
lived in the same house, were asked to draw maps of their
neighborhood. They received no further instructions. Notice
how perspectives broaden and neighborhoods expand with
age. (*a*) For the 6-year-old, the "neighborhood" consists of the
houses on either side of her own. (*b*) The square block on
which she lives is the neighborhood for the 10-year-old.
(*c*) The wider horizons of the 13-year-old are reflected in her
drawing. The square block the 10-year-old drew is shaded in
this sketch.

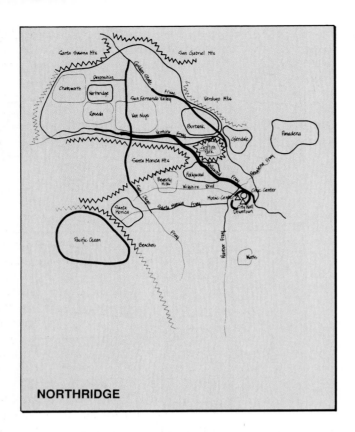

NORTHRIDGE

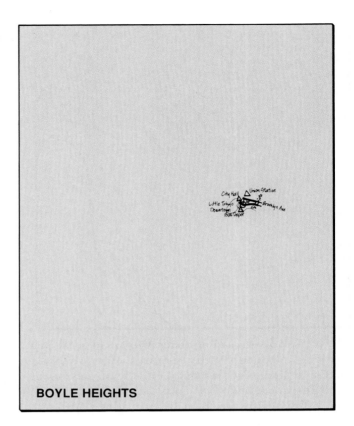

BOYLE HEIGHTS

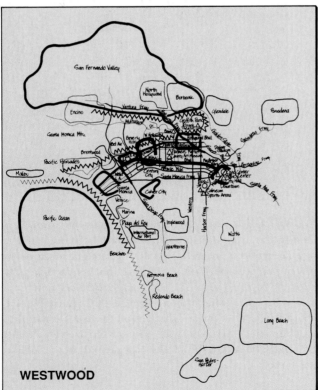

WESTWOOD

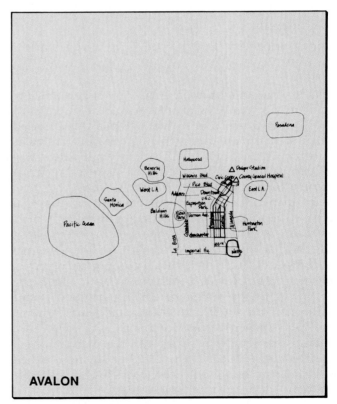

AVALON

FIGURE 1.30 **Four mental maps of Los Angeles.** The upper-middle-income residents of Northridge and Westwood have expansive views of the metropolis, reflecting their mobility and area of travel. Residents of Boyle Heights and Avalon, both minority districts, have a much more restricted and incomplete mental image of the city. Their limited mental maps reflect and reinforce their spatial isolation within the metropolitan area.

Systems, Maps, and Models

The content of area is interrelated and constitutes a **spatial system** that, in common with all systems, functions as a unit because its component parts are interdependent. Only rarely do individual elements of area operate in isolation, and to treat them as if they do is to lose touch with spatial reality. The systems of geographic concern are those in which the functionally important variables are spatial: location, distance, direction, density, and the other basic concepts we have reviewed. The systems that they define are not the same as regions, though spatial systems may be the basis for regional identification.

Systems have components, and the analysis of the role of components helps reveal the operation of the system as a whole. To conduct that analysis, individual system elements must be isolated for separate identification and, perhaps, manipulated to see their function within the structure of the system or subsystem. Maps and models are the devices geographers use to achieve that isolation and separate study.

Maps, as we have seen, are effective to the degree that they can segregate at an appropriate level of generalization those system elements selected for examination. By compressing, simplifying, and abstracting reality, maps record in manageable dimension the real-world conditions of interest. A **model** is a simplified abstraction of reality, structured to clarify causal relationships. Maps are a kind of model. They represent reality in an idealized form so that certain aspects of its properties may be more clearly seen. They are a special form of model—their abstractions are rendered visually and at a reduced scale so they may be displayed, for example, on the pages of this book.

The complexities of spatial systems analysis—and the opportunities for quantitative analysis of systems made possible by computers and sophisticated statistical techniques—have led geographers to use other kinds of models in their work. Model building is the technique social scientists use to simplify complex situations, to eliminate (as does the map) unimportant details, and to isolate for special study and analysis the role of one or more interacting elements in a total system.

An interaction model discussed in Chapter 3, for instance, suggests that the amount of exchange expected between two places depends on the distance separating them and on their population size. The model indicates that the larger the places and the closer their distance, the greater is the amount of interaction. Such a model helps us to isolate the important components of the spatial system, to manipulate them separately, and to reach conclusions concerning their relative importance. When a model satisfactorily predicts the volume of intercity interaction in the majority of cases, the lack of agreement between what is observed and what is expected in a particular case leads to an examination of the circumstances contributing to the disparity. The quality of connecting roads, political barriers, or other variables may affect the specific places examined, and these causative elements may be isolated for further study.

Indeed, the steady pursuit of more refined and definitive analysis of human geographic questions—the "further study" that continues to add to our understanding of how people occupy and utilize the earth, interact with each other, and organize and alter earth space—has led to the remarkably diversified yet coherent field of modern human geography. With the content of this introductory chapter as background to the nature, traditions, and tools of geography, we are ready to begin its exploration.

Summary

Geography is about earth space and its physical and cultural content. Throughout its long history, geography has remained consistent in its focus on human–environmental interactions, the interrelatedness of places, and the likenesses and differences in physical and cultural content of area that exist from place to place. The collective interests of geographers are summarized by the spatial and systems analytical questions they ask. The responses to those questions are interpreted through basic concepts of location, distance, direction, content evolution, spatial interaction, and regional organization.

Geographers employ maps and models to abstract the complex reality of space and to isolate its components for separate study. Maps are imperfect renderings of the three-dimensional earth and its parts upon a two-dimensional surface. In that rendering, some or all of the characteristics of the globe grid are distorted, but convenience and data manageability are gained. Spatial information may be depicted visually in a number of ways, each designed to simplify and to clarify the infinite complexity of spatial content. Geographers also use verbal and mathematical models for the same purpose, to abstract and analyze.

In their pursuit of the study of the earth's surface as the occupied and altered space within which humans operate, geographers may concentrate on the integration of physical and cultural phenomena in a specific earth area (regional geography). They may, instead, emphasize systematic geography through study of the earth's physical systems of spatial and human concern or, as here, devote primary attention to people. This is a text in *human geography*. Its focus is on human interactions both with the physical environments people occupy and alter and with the cultural environments they have created. We are concerned with the ways people perceive the landscapes and regions they occupy, act within and between them, make choices about them, and organize them according to the varying cultural, political, and economic interests of human societies. This is a text clearly within the social sciences, but like all geography, its background is the physical earth as the home of humans. As a human geography, its concern is with how that home has been altered by societies and cultures. Culture is the starting point, and in the next chapter we begin with an inquiry about the roots and nature of culture.

KEY WORDS

absolute direction   10
absolute distance   11
absolute location   9
accessibility   14
concentration   15
connectivity   15
cultural landscape   12
density   15
dispersion   15
formal region   17
functional region   18

mental map   23
model   27
natural landscape   12
nodal region   18
pattern   16
perceptual region   18
projection   19
region   16
regional concept   17
relative direction   10

relative distance   11
relative location   9
scale   11, 19
site   10
situation   10
spatial diffusion   15
spatial distribution   15
spatial interaction   14
spatial system   27
uniform region   17

FOR REVIEW

1. In what two meanings and for what different purposes do we refer to *location?*

2. Describe the *site* and the *situation* of the town where you live, work, or go to school.

3. What kinds of distance transformations are suggested by the term *relative distance?* How is the concept of *psychological distance* related to relative distance?

4. What are the common elements of *spatial distribution?* What different aspects of the spatial arrangement of things do they address?

5. What are the common characteristics of *regions?* How are *formal* and *functional* regions different in concept and definition? What is a *perceptual region?*

6. List at least four properties of the globe grid. Why are globe grid properties apt to be distorted on maps?

7. What does *prime meridian* mean? What happens to the length of a degree of longitude as one approaches the poles?

8. What different ways of displaying statistical data on maps can you name and describe?

SELECTED REFERENCES

Abler, Ronald F., Melvin G. Marcus, and Judy M. Olson, eds. *Geography's Inner Worlds: Pervasive Themes in Contemporary American Geography.* New Brunswick, NJ: Rutgers University Press, 1992.

Demko, George J., with Jerome Agel and Eugene Boe. *Why in the World: Adventures in Geography.* New York: Anchor Books/Doubleday, 1992.

Dent, Borden D. *Cartography: Thematic Map Design.* 3d ed. Dubuque, IA: Wm. C. Brown, 1993.

Dickinson, Robert E., and Osbert J. R. Howarth. *The Making of Geography.* Oxford: Clarendon Press, 1933.

Fenneman, Nevin M. "The Circumference of Geography." *Annals of the Association of American Geographers* 9 (1919): 3–11.

Gaile, Gary L., and Cort J. Willmott, eds. *Geography in America.* Columbus, OH: Merrill, 1989.

Gersmehl, Phil. *The Language of Maps.* NCGE *Pathways in Geography P-1.* Indiana, PA: National Council for Geographic Education, 1991.

Goodall, Brian. *The Facts on File Dictionary of Human Geography.* New York: Facts on File Publications, 1987.

Gould, Peter, and Rodney White. *Mental Maps.* 2d ed. Boston: Allen & Unwin, 1986.

Gritzner, Charles F., Jr. "The Scope of Cultural Geography." *Journal of Geography* 65 (1966): 4–11.

Holt-Jensen, Arild. *Geography: Its History & Concepts.* 2d ed. Totowa, NJ: Barnes and Noble, 1988.

Johnston, Ronald J., Derek Gregory, and David M. Smith. *The Dictionary of Human Geography.* 3d ed. Oxford: Blackwell Publishers, 1994.

Johnston, Ronald J., J. Hauer, and G. A. Koekveld, eds. *Regional Geography: Current Developments and Future Prospects.* New York: Routledge, 1990.

Lanegran, David A., and Risa Palm. *An Invitation to Geography.* 2d ed. New York: McGraw-Hill, 1978.

Larkin, Robert P., and Gary L. Peters. *Dictionary of Concepts in Human Geography.* Westport, CN: Greenwood Press, 1983.

Ley, David. "Cultural/Humanistic Geography." *Progress in Human Geography* 5 (1981): 249–257; 7 (1983): 267–275.

Livingstone, David N. *The Geographical Tradition.* Cambridge, MA: Blackwell Publishers, 1992.

Lobeck, Armin K. *Things Maps Don't Tell Us: An Adventure into Map Interpretation.* Chicago, IL: University of Chicago Press, 1993.

Marshall, Bruce, ed. *The Real World: Understanding the Modern World through the New Geography.* Boston: Houghton Mifflin, 1991.

Martin, Geoffrey J., and Preston E. James. *All Possible Worlds: A History of Geographical Ideas.* 3d ed. New York: John Wiley & Sons, 1993.

Massey, Doreen. "Introduction: Geography Matters," in Doreen Massey and John Allen, eds., *Geography Matters! A Reader.* Pp. 1–11. New York: Cambridge University Press, 1984.

McDonald, James R. "The Region: Its Conception, Design and Limitations." *Annals of the Association of American Geographers* 56 (1966): 516–528.

Monmonier, Mark. *Mapping It Out: Expository Cartography for the Humanities and Social Sciences.* Chicago: University of Chicago Press, 1993.

Morrill, Richard L. "The Nature, Unity and Value of Geography." *Professional Geographer* 35 (1983): 1–9.

Muehrcke, Phillip C., and Juliana O. Muehrcke. *Map Use: Reading, Analysis, and Interpretation.* 3d ed. Madison, WI: J. P. Publications, 1992.

Pattison, William D. "The Four Traditions of Geography." *Journal of Geography* 63 (1964): 211–216.

Robinson, J. Lewis. "A New Look at the Four Traditions of Geography." *Journal of Geography* 75 (1976): 520–530.

Rogers, Ali, Heather Viles, and Andrew Goudie. *The Student's Companion to Geography.* Cambridge, MA: Blackwell Publishers, 1992.

Rowntree, Lester. "Cultural/Humanistic Geography." *Progress in Human Geography* 10 (1986): 580–586.

Sobel, Dava. *Longitude. The True Story of a Lone Genius Who Solved the Greatest Scientific Problem of His Time.* New York: Walker & Company, 1995.

Thomson, J(ames) Oliver. *History of Ancient Geography.* New York: Biblo and Tannen, 1965.

Tuan, Yi-fu. "Humanistic Geography." *Annals of the Association of American Geographers* 66 (1976): 266–276.

Wheeler, James O. "Notes on the Rise of the Area Studies Tradition in U.S. Geography, 1910–1929." *Professional Geographer* 38 (1986): 53–61.

White, Gilbert F. "Geographers in a Perilously Changing World." *Annals of the Association of American Geographers* 75 (1985): 10–15.

Whittlesey, Derwent. "The Regional Concept and the Regional Method." Chapter 2 in *American Geography: Inventory and Prospect,* edited by Preston E. James and Clarence F. Jones. Syracuse, NY: Syracuse University Press, 1954.

Wood, Denis. *The Power of Maps.* New York: Guilford Press, 1992.

Wood, T. F. "Thinking in Geography." *Geography* 72 (1987): 289–299.

THEMES AND FUNDAMENTALS OF HUMAN GEOGRAPHY

Rush hour in Jaipur, Rajasthan, India. People in spatial interaction are the starting point of human geography.

Human geography studies the ways in which people and societies are regionally different in their distinguishing characteristics. Additionally, it examines the ways that different societies perceive, use, and alter the landscapes they occupy. These interests would seem to imply an unmanageable range and variety of topics. The implication is misleading, however, for the diversified subject matter of human geography can be accommodated within two general themes connected by one continuing and unifying thread of concern.

One theme considers the traits of *culture* that characterize different social groups and comprise the individual pieces of the human geographic mosaic. These are matters of learned behaviors, attitudes, and group beliefs that are fundamental and identifying features of specific social groups and larger societies. They are cultural identifiers that are transmitted within the group by tradition, example, and instruction. A second theme has to do with the *systems* of production, livelihood, spatial organization, and administration—and the institutions appropriate to those systems—that a society erects in response to opportunity, technology, resources, conflict, or the need to adapt and change. This second theme recognizes what French geographers early in this century called *genre de vie*—the way of life—of a population that might be adopted or pursued no matter what the other intangible cultural traits of that social group might be. Interwoven with and unifying these primary themes is the continuing background concern of geographers: humans and environments in interaction.

We shall pursue each of these themes in separate sections of this book and address the unifying interest in human impact on the earth surface both as an integral part of each chapter and as the topic of our concluding chapter. Throughout, we shall keep returning to a small number of basic observations that underlie all of human geographic study: (1) People and the societies they form are differentiated by a limited set of identifying cultural characteristics and organizational structures; (2) Without regard to those cultural and organization differences, human spatial behavior has common and recurring motivations and patterns; (3) Cultural variations and spatial actions are rooted in the distribution, numbers, and movements of people.

These observations are the concerns of the following three chapters, which together make up this first part of our study of human geography. We begin by setting the stage in Chapter 2 with a review of the meaning, components, and structure of *culture* and of the processes of cultural change, diffusion, and divergence. Those processes underlie an observable world mosaic of culture regions and realms. Despite regional distinctiveness, however, common characteristics of *spatial behavior* affect and unify all peoples and social systems. These are the topics of Chapter 3 and might be called the "ground rules" of spatial interaction. They are physical and behavioral constants whose recognition is a necessary first step in understanding the world, regional, and local patterns of people and social systems that are so central to human geography.

To conclude the first section of our study, Chapter 4 focuses on *population:* people in their numbers, movements, distributions, and growth trends. Part of our understanding of those matters, in both their world and regional expressions, is based on the examination of cultural origins and diffusions and the principles of spatial interaction conducted in Chapters 2 and 3.

The first phase of our exploration of human geography, then, expresses a unifying concern with the cultural processes and spatial interactions of an unevenly distributed and expanding world population.

ROOTS AND MEANING OF CULTURE

Components of Culture   35

**Interaction of People and
    Environment   36**

Environments as Controls   37

Human Impacts   38

Roots of Culture   40

Seeds of Change   43

Agricultural Origins and Diffusions   44

Neolithic Innovations   46

Culture Hearths   47

The Structure of Culture   51

Culture Change   52

Innovation   54

Diffusion   55

Contact between Regions   57

Cultural Modification and Adoption   60

SUMMARY   60

KEY WORDS   61

FOR REVIEW   61

SELECTED REFERENCES   61

*Dogon dancers of Mali, West Africa. Cultural
differences still remain in a world of increasing
human geographic similarity.*

They buried him there in the cave where they were working, less than 6 kilometers (4 miles) from the edge of the ice sheet. Outside stretched the tundra, summer feeding grounds for the mammoths whose ivory they had come so far to collect. Inside, near where they dug his grave, were stacked the tusks they had gathered and were cutting and shaping. They prepared the body carefully and dusted it with red ochre, then buried it in an elaborate grave with tundra flowers and offerings of food, a bracelet on its arm, a pendant about its throat, and 40 to 50 polished rods of ivory by its side. It rested there, in modern Wales, undisturbed for some 18,000 years until discovered early in the 19th century. The 25-year-old hunter had died far from the group's home some 650 kilometers (400 miles) away, near present-day Paris, France. He had been part of a routine annual summer expedition overland from the forested south across the as-yet-unflooded English Channel to the mammoths' grazing grounds at the edge of the glacier.

As always, they were well prepared for the trip. Their boots were carefully made. Their sewn skin leggings and tunics served well for travel and work; heavier fur parkas warded off the evening chill. They carried emergency food, fire-making equipment, and braided cord that they could fashion into nets, fishing lines, ropes, or thread. They traveled by reference to sun and stars, recognizing landmarks from past journeys and occasionally consulting a crude map etched on bone.

Although the hunters returned bearing the sad news of their companion's death, they also brought the ivory to be carved and traded among the scattered peoples of Europe from the Atlantic Ocean to the Ural Mountains.

As shown by their tools and equipment, their behaviors and beliefs, these Stone Age travelers displayed highly developed and distinctive characteristics, primitive only from the vantage point of our own different technologies and customs. They represented the culmination of a long history of development of skills, of invention of tools, and of creation of life-styles that set them apart from peoples elsewhere in Europe, Asia, and Africa who were the inheritors of still different cultural heritages.

To writers in newspapers and the popular press, "culture" means the arts (literature, painting, music, and the like). To a social scientist, **culture** is the specialized behavioral patterns, understandings, adaptations, and social systems that summarize a group of people's learned way of life. In this broader sense, culture is an ever-present part of the regional differences that are the essence of human geography. The visible and invisible evidences of culture—buildings and farming patterns, language, political organization, and ways of earning a living, for example—are all parts of the spatial diversity human geographers study. Cultural differences over time may present contrasts as great as those between the Stone Age ivory hunters and modern urban Americans. Cultural differences in area result in human landscapes with variations as subtle as the differing "feel" of urban Paris, Moscow, or New York or as obvious as the sharp contrasts of rural Zimbabwe and the Prairie Provinces of Canada (Figure 2.1).

(a)

(b)

FIGURE 2.1   Visible cultural contrasts are clearly evident between (*a*) a subsistence maize plot in Zimbabwe and (*b*) the broad regularity of extensively farmed fields of the Canadian prairies.

Since such tangible and intangible cultural differences exist and have existed in various forms for thousands of years, human geography addresses the question, Why? Why, since humankind constitutes a single species, are cultures so varied? What and where were the origins of the different culture regions we now observe? How, from whatever limited areas individual culture traits developed, were they diffused over a wider portion of the globe? How did people who had roughly similar origins come to display significant areal differences in technology, social structure, ideology, and the other myriad expressions of human geographic diversity? In what ways and why are there distinctive cultural variations even in presumed "melting pot" societies such as the United States and Canada or in the outwardly homogeneous long-established countries of Europe? Part of the answer to these questions is to be found in the way separate human groups developed techniques to solve regionally varied problems of securing food, clothing, and shelter and, in the process, created areally distinctive customs and ways of life.

Components of Culture

Culture is transmitted within a society to succeeding generations by imitation, instruction, and example. In short, it is learned, not biological. It has nothing to do with instinct or with genes (see "The Question of Race," p. 180). As members of a social group, individuals acquire integrated sets of behavioral patterns, environmental and social perceptions, and knowledge of existing technologies. Of necessity, each of us learns the culture in which we are born and reared. But we need not—indeed, cannot—learn its totality. Age, sex, status, or occupation may dictate the aspects of the cultural whole in which an individual becomes fully indoctrinated.

A culture, that is, despite overall generalized and identifying characteristics and even an outward appearance of uniformity, displays a social structure—a framework of roles and interrelationships of individuals and established groups. Each individual learns and adheres to the rules and conventions not only of the culture as a whole, but also of those specific to the subgroup to which he or she belongs. And that subgroup may have its own recognized social structure (Figure 2.2).

Culture is a complexly interlocked web of behaviors and attitudes. Realistically, its full and diverse content cannot be appreciated, and in fact may be wholly misunderstood, if we concentrate our attention only on limited, obvious traits. Distinctive eating utensils, the use of gestures, or the ritual of religious ceremony may summarize and characterize a culture for the casual observer. These are, however, individually insignificant parts of a much more complex structure that can be appreciated only when the whole is experienced.

Out of the richness and intricacy of human life we seek to isolate for special study those more fundamental cultural variables that give structure and spatial order to societies. We begin with *culture traits,* the smallest distinctive

(a)

(b)

FIGURE 2.2 (*a*) Both the traditional rice farmer of rural Japan and (*b*) the harried commuter of Tokyo are part of a common Japanese culture. They occupy vastly different positions in its social structure.

items of culture. **Culture traits** are units of learned behavior ranging from the language spoken to the tools used or the games played. A trait may be an object (a fishhook, for example), a technique (weaving and knotting of a fishnet), a belief (in the spirits resident in water bodies), or an attitude (a conviction that fish is superior to other animal protein). Such traits are the most elementary expression of culture, the building blocks of the complex behavioral patterns of distinctive groups of peoples.

Individual cultural traits that are functionally interrelated comprise a **culture complex.** The existence of such complexes is universal. Keeping cattle was a *culture trait* of the Masai of Kenya and Tanzania. Related traits included the measurement of personal wealth by the number of cattle owned, a diet containing milk and the blood of cattle, and disdain for labor unrelated to herding. The assemblage of these and other related traits yielded a culture complex descriptive of one aspect of Masai society (Figure 2.3). In exactly analogous ways, religious complexes, business behavior complexes, sports complexes, and others can easily be recognized in American or any other society.

Culture traits and complexes have areal extent. When they are plotted on maps, the regional character of the components of culture is revealed. Although human geographers are interested in the spatial distribution of these individual elements of culture, their usual concern is with the **culture region,** a portion of the earth's surface occupied by populations sharing recognizable and distinctive cultural characteristics. Examples include the political organizations societies devise, the religions they espouse, the form of economy they pursue, and even the type of clothing they wear, eating utensils they use, or kind of housing they occupy. There are as many such culture regions as there are culture traits and complexes recognized for population groups. Their recognition will be particularly important in discussions of ethnic, folk, and popular cultures in later chapters of this book.

Finally, a set of culture regions showing related culture complexes and landscapes may be grouped to form a **culture realm.** The term recognizes a large segment of the earth's surface having an assumed fundamental uniformity in its cultural characteristics and showing a significant difference in them from adjacent realms. Culture realms are, in a sense, culture regions at the broadest scale of recognition. In fact, the scale is so broad and the diversity within the recognized realms so great that the very concept of realm may mislead more than it informs. One of many possible divisions of human cultures into realms is offered in Figure 2.4. The spatial pattern and characteristics of these generalized realms will help us place the discussions and examples of human geography of later chapters in their regional context.

FIGURE 2.3   The formerly migratory Masai of Kenya are now largely sedentary, partially urbanized, and frequently owners of fenced farms. Cattle formed the traditional basis of Masai culture and were the evidence of wealth and social status. They provided, as well, the milk and blood important in the Masai diet. Here, a herdsman catches blood released from a small neck incision he has just made.

Interaction of People and Environment

Culture develops in a physical environment that, in its way, contributes to differences among people. In primitive societies, the acquisition of food, shelter, and clothing, all parts of culture, depends on the utilization of the natural resources at hand. The interrelations of people to the environment of a given area, their perceptions and utilization of it, and their impact on it are interwoven themes of **cultural ecology**—the study of the relationship between a culture group and the natural environment it occupies.

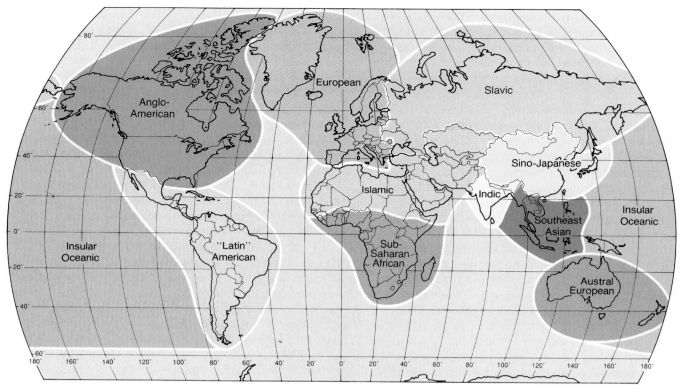

FIGURE 2.4 **Culture realms of the modern world.** This is just one of many possible subdivisions of the world into multifactor cultural regions.

Environments as Controls

Geographers have long dismissed as intellectually limiting and demonstrably invalid the ideas of **environmental determinism,** the belief that the physical environment exclusively shapes humans, their actions, and their thoughts. Environmental factors alone cannot account for the cultural variations that occur around the world. Levels of technology, systems of organization, and ideas about what is true and right have no obvious relationship to environmental circumstances.

The environment does place certain limitations on the human use of territory. Such limitations, however, must be seen not as absolute, enduring restrictions but as relative to technologies, cost considerations, national aspirations, and linkages with the larger world. Human choices in the use of landscapes are affected by group perception of the feasibility and desirability of their settlement and exploitation. These are not circumstances inherent in the land. Mines, factories, and cities were (and are being) created in the formerly nearly unpopulated tundra and forests of Siberia as a reflection of Russian developmental programs, not in response to recent environmental improvement. **Possibilism** is the viewpoint that people, not environments, are the dynamic forces of cultural development. The needs, traditions, and level of technology of a culture affect how that culture assesses the possibilities of an area and shape what choices the culture makes regarding them. Each society uses natural resources in accordance with its circumstances.

Changes in a group's technical abilities or objectives bring about changes in its perceptions of the usefulness of the land. Simply put, the impact of the environment appears inversely related to the level of development of a culture, while perception of environmental opportunities increases directly with growth in economic and cultural development.

Map evidence suggests the nature of some environmental limitations on use of area. The vast majority of the world's population is differentially concentrated on less than one-half of the earth's land surface, as Figure 4.21 suggests. Areas with relatively mild climates that offer a supply of fresh water, fertile soil, and abundant mineral resources are densely settled, reflecting in part the different potentials of the land under earlier technologies to support population. Even today, the polar regions, high and rugged mountains, deserts, and some hot and humid lowland areas contain very few people. If resources for feeding, clothing, or housing ourselves within an area are lacking, or if we do not recognize them there, there is no inducement for people to occupy the territory.

Environments that do contain such resources provide the framework within which a culture operates. Coal, oil, and natural gas have been in their present locations throughout human history, but they were of no use to preindustrial cultures and did not impart any recognized advantage to their sites of occurrence. Not until the Industrial Revolution did these deposits gain importance and come to influence the location of such great industrial complexes as the Midlands in England, the Ruhr in Germany, and the steelmaking districts formerly so important in parts of northeastern United States. American Indians made one use of the environment around Pittsburgh, while 19th-century industrialists made quite another.

Human Impacts

People are also able to modify their environment, and this is the other half of the human–environment relationship of geographic concern. Geography, including cultural geography, examines the reactions of people to the physical environment and also their impact on that environment. We modify our environment through the material objects we place on the landscape: cities, farms, roads, and so on (Figure 2.5). The form these take is the product of the kind of culture group in which we live. The **cultural landscape,** the earth's surface as modified by human action, is the tangible physical record of a given culture. House types, transportation networks, parks and cemeteries, and the size and distribution of settlements are among the indicators of the use that humans have made of the land.

Human actions, both deliberate and inadvertent, modifying or even destroying the environment are perhaps as old as humankind itself. People have used, altered, and replaced the vegetation in wide areas of the tropics and midlatitudes. They have hunted to extinction vast herds and whole species of animals. They have, through overuse and abuse of the earth and its resources, rendered sterile and unpopulated formerly productive and attractive regions.

Fire has been called the first great tool of humans, and the impact of its early and continuing use is found on nearly every continent. Poleward of the great rain forests of equatorial South America, Africa, and South Asia lies the *tropical savanna* of extensive grassy vegetation separating scattered trees and forest groves (Figure 2.6). The trees appear to be the remnants of naturally occurring tropical dry forests, thorn forests, and scrub now largely obliterated by the use, over many millennia, of fire to remove the unwanted and unproductive trees and to clear off old grasses for more nutritious new growth. The grasses supported the immense herds of grazing animals that were the basis of hunting societies. After independence, the government of Kenya in East Africa sought to protect its national game preserves by prohibiting the periodic use of fire. It quickly found that the immense herds of gazelles, zebras, antelope, and other grazers (and the lions and other predators that fed on them) that tourists came to see were being replaced by less-appealing browsing species—rhinos, hippos, and elephants. With fire prohibited, the forests began to reclaim their natural habitat and the grassland fauna was replaced.

The same form of vegetation replacement occurred in midlatitudes. The grasslands of North America were greatly extended by Native Americans who burned the forest margin to extend grazing areas and to drive animals in the hunt. The control of fire in modern times has resulted in the advance of the forest once again in formerly grassy areas ("parks") of Colorado, northern Arizona, and other parts of the United States West.

FIGURE 2.5 The physical and cultural landscapes in juxtaposition. Advanced societies are capable of so altering the circumstances of nature that the cultural landscapes they create become the controlling environment. The city of Cape Town, South Africa, is a "built environment" largely unrelated to its physical surroundings.

FIGURE 2.6 The parklike landscape of grasses and trees characteristic of the tropical savanna is seen in this view from Kenya, Africa.

THEMES AND FUNDAMENTALS OF HUMAN GEOGRAPHY

Examples abound. The *Pleistocene overkill*—the Stone Age loss of whole species of large animals on all inhabited continents—is often ascribed to the unrestricted hunting to extinction carried on by societies familiar with fire to drive animals and hafted (handled) weapons to slaughter them. With the use of these, according to one estimate, about 40% of African large-animal genera passed to extinction. In North America, most of the original large-animal species had disappeared by 10,000 years ago under pressure from the hunters migrating to and spreading across the continent. Although some have suggested that climatic changes were at least partially responsible, human action seems the more likely explanation for the abrupt faunal losses. No uncertainty exists in the record of faunal destruction by the Maoris of New Zealand or of Polynesians who had exterminated some 80% to 90% of South Pacific bird species—as many as 2000 in all—by the time Captain Cook arrived in the 18th century.

Not only destruction of animals but of the life-supporting environment itself has been a frequent consequence of human misuse of area (see "Chaco Canyon Desolation"). North Africa, the "granary of Rome" during the empire, became wasted and sterile in part because of mismanagement. Roman roads standing high above the surrounding barren wastes give testimony to the erosive power of wind and water when natural vegetation is unwisely removed and farming techniques are inappropriate. Easter Island in the South Pacific was covered lushly with palms and other trees when Polynesians settled there about A.D. 400. By the beginning of

CHACO CANYON DESOLATION

It is not certain when they first came, but by A.D. 1000 the Anasazi people were building a flourishing civilization in present-day Arizona and New Mexico. In the Chaco Canyon alone, they erected as many as 75 towns, all centered around pueblos, huge stone-and-adobe apartment buildings as tall as five stories and with as many as 800 rooms. These were the largest and tallest buildings of North America prior to the construction of iron-framed "cloudscrapers" in major cities at the end of the 19th century. An elaborate network of roads and irrigation canals connected and supported the pueblos. About A.D. 1200, the settlements were abruptly abandoned. The Anasazi, advanced in their skills of agriculture and communal dwelling, were forced to move by the ecological disaster their pressures had brought to a fragile environment.

They needed forests for fuel and for the hundreds of thousands of logs used as beams and bulwarks in their dwellings. The pinyon-juniper woodland of the canyon was quickly depleted. For larger timbers needed for construction, the Anasazi first harvested stands of ponderosa pine found some 40 kilometers (25 miles) away. As early as A.D. 1030 these, too, were exhausted, and the community switched to spruce and Douglas fir from mountaintops surrounding the canyon. When they were gone by 1200, the Anasazi fate was sealed—not only by the loss of forest but by the irreversible ecological changes deforestation and agriculture had occasioned. With forest loss came erosion that destroyed the topsoil. The surface water channels that had been built for irrigation were deepened by accelerated erosion, converting them into enlarging arroyos useless for agriculture.

The material roots of their culture destroyed, the Anasazi turned upon themselves; warfare convulsed the region. Smaller groups sought refuge elsewhere, recreating on reduced scale their pueblo way of life but now in nearly inaccessible, highly defensible mesa and cliff locations. The destruction they had wrought destroyed the Anasazi in turn.

the 18th century, Easter Island had become the barren wasteland it remains today. Deforestation increased soil erosion, removed the supply of timbers needed for the vital dugout fishing canoes, and made it impossible to move the massive stone statues that were significant in the islanders' religion (Figure 2.7). With the loss of livelihood resources and the collapse of religion, warfare broke out and the population was decimated. A similar tragic sequence is occurring on Madagascar in the Indian Ocean today. Despite current romantic notions, not all primitive societies lived in harmony with their environment.

The more technologically advanced and complex the culture, the more apparent is its impact on the natural landscape. In sprawling urban-industrial societies, the cultural landscape has come to outweigh the natural physical environment in its impact on people's daily lives. It interposes itself between "nature" and humans, and residents of the cities of such societies—living and working in climate-controlled buildings, driving to enclosed shopping malls—can go through life with very little contact with or concern about the physical environment.

Roots of Culture

Earlier humans found the physical environment more immediate and controlling than we do today. Some 11,000 years ago, the massive glaciers—moving ice sheets of great depth—that had covered much of the land and water of the Northern Hemisphere (Figure 2.8) began to retreat. Animal, plant, and human populations that had been spatially confined by both the ice margin and the harsh climates of middle-latitude regions, began to spread, colonizing newly opened territories. The name *Paleolithic* (Old Stone Age) is used to describe the period near the end of glaciation during which small and scattered groups like the ivory hunters at this chapter's start began to develop regional variations in their ways of life and livelihood.

All were **hunter-gatherers,** preagricultural people dependent on the year-round availability of plant and animal foodstuffs they could secure with the limited variety of rudimentary stone tools and weapons at their disposal. Even during the height of the Ice Age, the unglaciated sections of western, central, and northeastern Europe (the continent with the best-documented evidence of Paleolithic culture) were covered with tundra vegetation, the mosses, lichens, and low shrubs typical of areas too cold to support forests. Southeastern Europe and southern Russia had forest, tundra, and grasslands, and the

FIGURE 2.7   Now treeless, Easter Island once was lushly forested. The statues (some weighing up to 85 tons) dotting the island were rolled to their locations and lifted into place with logs.

FIGURE 2.8   **Maximum extent of glaciation.** In their fullest development, glaciers of the most recent Ice Age covered large parts of Eurasia and North America. Even areas not covered by ice were affected as ocean levels dropped and rose and climate and vegetation regions changed with glacial advance and retreat.

THEMES AND FUNDAMENTALS OF HUMAN GEOGRAPHY

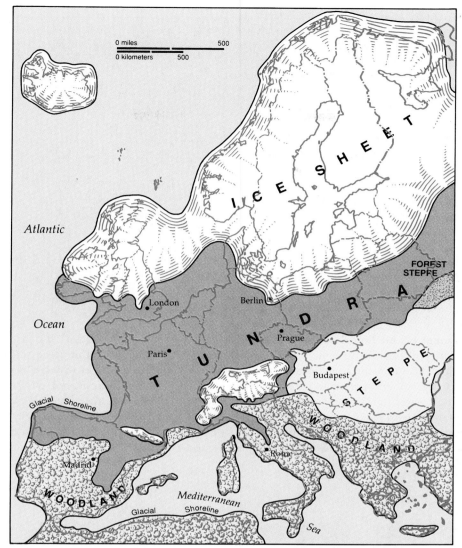

FIGURE 2.9   **Late Paleolithic environments of Europe.** During the late Paleolithic period new food-gathering, shelter, and clothing strategies were developed to cope with harsh and changing environments, so different from those in Europe today.

Mediterranean areas had forest cover (Figure 2.9). Gigantic herds of herbivores—reindeer, bison, mammoth, and horses—browsed, bred, and migrated throughout the tundra and the grasslands. An abundant animal life filled the forests.

Human migration northward into present-day Sweden, Finland, and Russia demanded a much more elaborate set of tools and provision for shelter and clothing than had previously been required. It necessitated the crossing of a number of ecological barriers and the occupation of previously avoided difficult environments. By the end of the Paleolithic period, humans had spread to all the continents but Antarctica, carrying with them their common hunting-gathering culture and social organization. The settlement of the lands bordering the Pacific Ocean is suggested in Figure 2.10.

While spreading, the total population also increased. But hunting and foraging bands require considerable territory to support a relatively small number of individuals. There were contacts between groups and, apparently, even planned gatherings for trade, socializing, and selecting spouses from outside the home group. Nevertheless, the bands tended to live in isolation. Estimates place the Paleolithic population of the entire island of Great Britain, which was on the northern margin of habitation, at only some 400–500 persons living in widely separated families of 20–40 people. Total world population at about 9000 B.C. probably ranged from 5 to 10 million. Variations in the types of tools characteristic of different population groups steadily increased as people migrated and encountered new environmental problems (Figure 2.11).

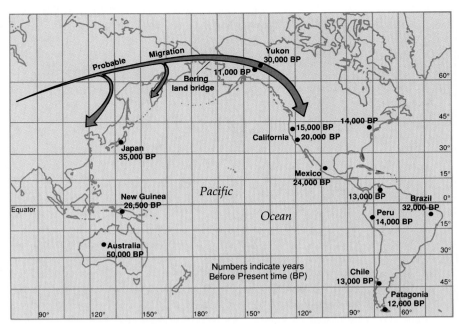

FIGURE 2.10   **Settlement of the Americas and the Pacific basin.** Genetic studies suggest humans spread around the globe from their Old World origins beginning some 100,000 years ago. Their time of arrival in the Western Hemisphere, however, is uncertain. Geological evidence indicates that the Bering Strait land bridge—over which it is speculated migrants from northern China and northeastern Siberia passed in three different migration waves—disappeared about 14,000 years ago when glacier melt released sufficient water to raise sea levels several hundred feet worldwide. Recent genetic and linguistic research suggests that the first Asian arrivals in America came no later than 22,000 years ago and more likely 29,000 years ago. Disputed radiocarbon dates from northeastern Brazil indicate cave dwellers were there as early as 32,000 and perhaps even 45,000 years ago. A Pennsylvania rock shelter is thought to have been occupied some 14,000 years ago.

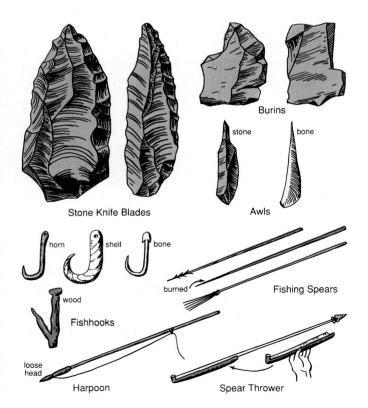

FIGURE 2.11   **Representative tools of the Paleolithic period in Europe.** The basis of many Stone Age tools was the stone blade, formed by new techniques of flaking stone that permitted efficient manufacture of special-purpose implements. Among these was the *burin,* a chisel-edged blade for working wood, bone, and antlers. The wooden or bone spear-thrower (called the *atlal* after its Aztec name) permitted more reliable harvesting of large game. Development of bone and antler fishhooks and harpoons made possible a sedentary life based on fishing. Clothing and tents could be fashioned with bone awls, needles, and fasteners.

Improved tool technology greatly extended the range of possibilities in the use of locally available materials. The result was more efficient and extensive exploitation of the physical environment than earlier had been possible. At the same time, regional contrasts in plant and animal life and in environmental conditions accelerated the differentiation of culture between isolated groups who under earlier, less varied conditions had shared common characteristics.

Within many environments, even harsh ones, the hunting and foraging process was not particularly demanding of either time or energy. Recent studies of South African San people (Bushmen), for example, indicate that such bands survive well on the equivalent of a 2½-day workweek. Time was available for developing skills in working flint and bone for tools, in developing regionally distinctive art and sculpture, and in making decorative beads and shells for personal adornment and trade. By the end of the Ice Age (about 11,000 years ago), language, religion, long-distance trade, permanent settlements, and social stratification within groups appear to have been well developed in many European culture areas.

What was learned and created was transmitted within the cultural group. The increasing variety of adaptive strategies and technologies and the diversity of noneconomic creations in art, religion, language, and custom meant an inevitable cultural variation of humankind. That diversification began to replace the rough cultural uniformity among hunting and gathering people that had been based on their similar livelihood patterns, informal leadership structures, small-band kinship groups, and the like (Figure 2.12).

Seeds of Change

The retreat of the last glaciers marked the end of the Paleolithic era and the beginning of successive periods of cultural evolution leading from primitive hunting and gathering economies at the outset through the development of agriculture and animal husbandry to, ultimately, the urbanization and industrialization of modern societies and economies. Since not all cultures passed through all stages at the same time, or even at all, **cultural divergence** between human groups became evident.

Glacial recession brought new ecological conditions to which people had to adapt. The weather became warmer, and forests began to appear on the open plains and tundras of Europe and northern China. In the Middle East, where much plant and animal domestication would later occur, savanna (grassland) vegetation replaced more arid landscapes. Populations grew and, through hunting depleted the large herds of grazing animals already retiring northward with the retreating glacial front.

Further population growth demanded new food bases and production techniques, for the **carrying capacity**—the number of persons supportable within a given area by the technologies at their disposal—of the earth for

FIGURE 2.12 Hunter-gatherers practiced the most enduring life-style in human history, trading it for the more arduous life of farmers under the necessity to provide larger quantities of less diversified foodstuffs for a growing population. For hunter-gatherers (unlike their settled farmer rivals and successors), age and sex differences, not caste or economic status, were and are the primary basis for the division of labor and of interpersonal relations. Here a San (Bushman) hunter of Botswana, Africa, stalks his prey. Men also help collect the gathered food that constitutes 80% of the San diet.

hunter-gatherers is low. The *Mesolithic* (Middle Stone Age) period, from about 11,000 to 5000 B.C. in Europe, marked the transition from the collection of food to its production. These stages of the "Stone Age"—occurring during different time spans in different world areas—mark distinctive changes in tools, tasks, and social complexities of the cultures that experience the transition from "Old" to "Middle" to "New."

Agricultural Origins and Diffusions

The population of hunter-gatherers rose slowly at the end of the glacial period. As rapid climatic fluctuation adversely affected their established plant and animal food sources, people independently in more than one world area experimented with the *domestication* of plants and animals. There is no agreement on whether the domestication of animals preceded or followed that of plants. The sequence may well have been different in different areas. What appears certain is that animal domestication—the successful breeding of species that are dependent on human beings—began during the Mesolithic, not as a conscious economic effort by humans but as outgrowths of the keeping of small or young wild animals as pets and the attraction of scavenger animals to the refuse of human settlements. The assignment of religious significance to certain animals and the docility of others to herding by hunters all strengthened the human–animal connections that ultimately led to full domestication.

Radiocarbon dates suggest the domestication of pigs in southeastern Turkey and of goats in the Near East as early as 8000 to 8400 B.C., of sheep in Turkey by about 7500 B.C., and of cattle and pigs in both Greece and the Near East about 7000 B.C. North Africa, India, and southeastern Asia were other Old World domestication sources, as were—less successfully—Meso-America and the Andean Uplands. Although there is evidence that the concept of animal domestication diffused from limited source regions, once its advantages were learned, numerous additional domestications were accomplished elsewhere. The widespread natural occurrence of species able to be domesticated made that certain. Cattle of different varieties, for example, were domesticated in India, north-central Eurasia, Southeast Asia, and Africa. Pigs and various domestic fowl are other examples.

The domestication of plants, like that of animals, appears to have occurred independently in more than one world region over a time span of between 10,000 and perhaps as long as 20,000 years ago. A strong case can be made that most widespread Eurasian food crops were first cultivated in the Near East beginning some 10,000 years ago and dispersed rapidly from there across the midlatitudes of the Old World. However, clear evidence also exists that African peoples were raising crops of wheat, barley, dates, lentils, and chickpeas on the floodplains of the Nile River as early as 18,500 years ago. In other world regions, farming began more recently.

Familiarity with plants of desirable characteristics is universal among hunter-gatherers. In those societies, females were assigned the primary food-gathering role and thus developed the greatest familiarity with nutritive plants. Their fundamental role in initiating crop production to replace less reliable food gathering seems certain. Indeed, women's major contributions as innovators of technology—in food preparation and clothing production, for example—or as inventors of such useful and important items as baskets and other containers, baby slings, yokes for carrying burdens, and the like are unquestioned.

Agriculture itself, however, seems most likely to have been not an "invention" but the logical extension to food species of plant selection and nurturing habits developed for nonfood varieties. Plant poisons applied to hunting arrows or spread on lakes or streams to stun fish made food gathering easier and more certain. Plant dyes and pigments were universally collected or prepared for personal adornment or article decoration. Medicinal and mood-altering plants and derivatives were known, gathered, protected, and cultivated by all primitive cultures. Indeed, persuasive evidence exists to suggest that early gathering and cultivation of grains was not for grinding and baking as bread but for brewing as beer, a beverage that became so important in some cultures for religious and nutritional reasons that it may well have been a first and continuing reason for sedentary agricultural activities.

Nevertheless, full-scale domestication of food plants, like that of animals, can be traced to a limited number of origin areas from which its techniques spread (Figure 2.13). Although there were several source regions, certain uniformities united them. In each, domestication focused on plant species selected apparently for their capability of providing large quantities of storable calories or protein. In each, there was a population already well fed and able to devote time to the selection, propagation, and improvement of plants available from a diversified vegetation. Some speculate, however, that grain domestication in the Near East may have been a forced inventive response, starting some 12,000 years ago, to food shortages reflecting abrupt increases in summertime temperatures and aridity in the Jordan Valley. That environmental stress—reducing summer food supplies and destroying habitats of wild game—favored selection and cultivation of short-season annual grains and legumes, whose seeds could be stored and planted during cooler, wetter winter growing seasons.

In the tropics and humid subtropics, selected plants were apt to be those that reproduced vegetatively—from roots, tubers, or cuttings. Outside of those regions, wild plants reproducing from seeds were more common and the objects of domestication. Although there was some duplication, each of the origin areas developed crop complexes characteristic of itself alone, as Figure 2.13 summarizes. From each, there was dispersion of crop plants to other areas, slowly at first under primitive systems of population movement and communication, and then more rapidly and extensively with the onset of European exploration and colonization after A.D. 1500 (Figure 2.14).

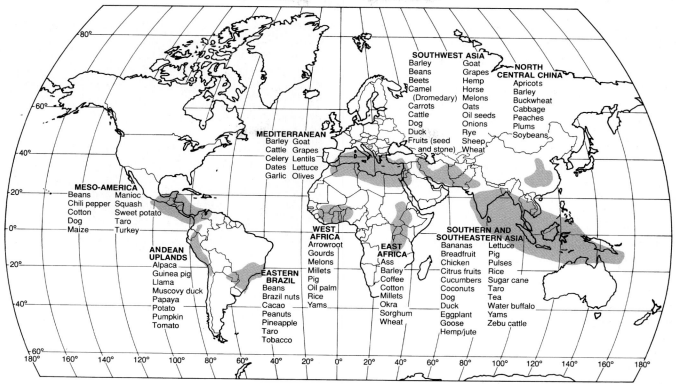

SOUTHWEST ASIA
Barley — Goat
Beans — Grapes
Beets — Hemp
Camel — Horse
(Dromedary) — Melons
Carrots — Oats
Cattle — Oil seeds
Dog — Onions
Duck — Rye
Fruits (seed — Sheep
and stone) — Wheat

NORTH CENTRAL CHINA
Apricots
Barley
Buckwheat
Cabbage
Peaches
Plums
Soybeans

MEDITERRANEAN
Barley — Goat
Cattle — Grapes
Celery — Lentils
Dates — Lettuce
Garlic — Olives

MESO-AMERICA
Beans — Manioc
Chili pepper — Squash
Cotton — Sweet potato
Dog — Taro
Maize — Turkey

ANDEAN UPLANDS
Alpaca
Guinea pig
Llama
Muscovy duck
Papaya
Potato
Pumpkin
Tomato

EASTERN BRAZIL
Beans
Brazil nuts
Cacao
Peanuts
Pineapple
Taro
Tobacco

WEST AFRICA
Arrowroot
Gourds
Melons
Millets
Pig
Oil palm
Rice
Yams

EAST AFRICA
Ass
Barley
Coffee
Cotton
Millets
Okra
Sorghum
Wheat

SOUTHERN AND SOUTHEASTERN ASIA
Bananas — Lettuce
Breadfruit — Pig
Chicken — Pulses
Citrus fruits — Rice
Cucumbers — Sugar cane
Coconuts — Taro
Dog — Tea
Duck — Water buffalo
Eggplant — Yams
Goose — Zebu cattle
Hemp/jute

FIGURE 2.13 **Chief centers of plant and animal domestication.** The southern and southeastern Asian center was characterized by the domestication of plants such as taro, which are propagated by the division and replanting of existing plants (vegetative reproduction). Reproduction by the planting of seeds (e.g., maize and wheat) was more characteristic of Meso-America and the Near East. The African and Andean areas developed crops reproduced by both methods. The lists of crops and livestock associated with the separate origin areas are selective, not exhaustive.

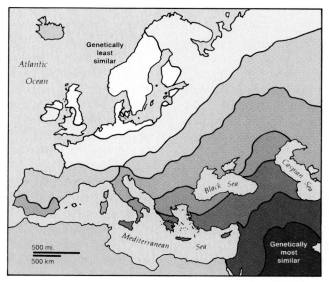

FIGURE 2.14 **The migration of first farmers** out of the Middle East into Europe starting about 10,000 years ago is presumably traced by blood and gene markers. If the gene evidence interpretation is valid, the migrants spread at a rate of about one kilometer (five-eighths of a mile) per year, gradually replacing the indigenous European hunter-gatherers throughout that continent.

While adapting wild plant stock to agricultural purposes, the human cultivators, too, adapted. They assumed sedentary residence to protect the planted areas from animal, insect, and human predators. They developed labor specializations and created more formalized and expansive religious structures in which fertility and harvest rites became important elements. The regional contrasts between hunter-gatherer and sedentary agricultural societies increased. Where the two groups came in contact, farmers were the victors and hunter-gatherers the losers in competition for territorial control.

The contest continued into modern times. During the past 200 years, European expansion totally dominated the hunting and gathering cultures it encountered in large parts of the world such as North America and Australia. Even today, in the forests of Zaire in central Africa, Bantu farmers put continuing pressure on hunting and gathering Pygmies; and in southern Africa, Hottentot herders and Bantu farmers constantly advance on the territories of the San (Bushmen) hunter-gatherer bands. The contrast and conflict between the hunter-gatherers and agriculturalists provide dramatic evidence of cultural divergence.

Neolithic Innovations

The domestication of plants and animals began during the Mesolithic period, but in its refined form it marked the onset of the *Neolithic* (New Stone Age). Like other Stone Age levels, the Neolithic was more a stage of cultural development than a specific span of time. The term implies the creation of an advanced set of tools and technologies to deal with the conditions and needs encountered by an expanding, sedentary population whose economy was based on the agricultural management of the environment (Figure 2.15).

Not all peoples in all areas of the earth made the same cultural transition at the same time. In the Near East, from which most of our knowledge of this late prehistoric period comes, the Neolithic lasted from approximately 8000 to 3500 B.C. There, as elsewhere, it brought complex and revolutionary changes in human life. Culture began to alter at an accelerating pace, and change itself became a way of life. In an interconnected adaptive web, technological and social innovations came with a speed and genius surpassing all previous periods.

Humans learned the arts of spinning and weaving plant and animal fibers. They learned to use the potter's wheel and to fire clay and make utensils. They developed techniques of brick making, mortaring, and construction, and they discovered the skills of mining, smelting, and casting metals. On the foundation of such technical advancements, a more complex exploitative culture appeared, a stratified society to replace the rough equality of adults in hunting and gathering economies. Special local advantages in resources or products promoted the development of long-distance trading connections, which the invention of the sailboat helped to maintain.

(a)

(b)

FIGURE 2.15   The Mediterranean scratch plow, the earliest form of this basic agricultural tool, was essentially an enlarged digging stick dragged by an ass, an ox, or—as here near Cairo, Egypt—by a pair of oxen. The scratch plow represented a significant technological breakthrough in human use of tools and animal power in food production. Its earliest evidence is found in Egyptian tomb drawings and in art preserved from the ancient Middle East but was elsewhere either independently invented or introduced by those familiar with its use. See also Figure 2.18*a*.

By the end of the Neolithic period, certain spatially restricted groups, having created a food-producing rather than a foraging society, undertook the purposeful restructuring of their environment. They began to modify plant and animal species; to manage soil, terrain, water, and mineral resources; and to utilize animal energy to supplement that of humans. They used metal to make refined tools and superior weapons—first pure copper and later the alloy of tin and copper that produced the harder, more durable bronze. Humans had moved from adopting and shaping to the art of creating.

As people gathered together in larger communities, new and more formalized rules of conduct and control emerged, especially important where the use of land was involved. We see the beginnings of governments to enforce laws and specify punishments for wrongdoers. The protection of private property, so much greater in amount and variety than that carried by the nomad, demanded more complex legal codes, as did the enforcement of the rules of societies increasingly stratified by social privileges and economic status.

Religions became more formalized. For the hunter, religion could be individualistic, and his worship was concerned with personal health and safety. The collective concerns of farmers were based on the calendar: the cycle of rainfall, the seasons of planting and harvesting, the rise and fall of waters to irrigate the crops. Religions responsive to those concerns developed rituals appropriate to seasons of planting, irrigation, harvesting, and thanksgiving. An established priesthood was required, one that stood not only as intermediary between people and the forces of nature but also as authenticator of the timing and structure of the needed rituals.

In daily life, occupations became increasingly specialized. Metalworkers, potters, sailors, priests, merchants, scribes, and in some areas, warriors complemented the work of farmers and hunters.

Culture Hearths

The social and technical revolutions that began in and characterized the Neolithic period were initially spatially confined. The new technologies, the new ways of life, and the new social structures diffused from those points of origin and were selectively adopted by people who were not a party to their creation. The term **culture hearth** is used to describe such centers of innovation and invention from which key culture traits and elements moved to exert an influence on surrounding regions.

The hearth may be viewed as the "cradle" of a culture group whose developed systems of livelihood and life created distinctive cultural landscapes. All hearth areas developed the trappings of *civilizations*. The definition of that term is not precise, but indicators of its achievement are commonly assumed to be: writing, metallurgy, long-distance trade connections, astronomy and mathematics, social stratification and labor specialization, formalized governmental systems, and a structured urban culture.

Several major culture hearths emerged in the Neolithic period. Prominent centers of early creativity were found in Egypt, Crete, Mesopotamia, the Indus Valley of the Indian subcontinent, northern China, southeastern Asia, several locations in sub-Saharan Africa, in the Americas, and elsewhere (Figure 2.16). They arose in widely separated areas of the world, at different times, and under differing ecological circumstances. Each displayed its own unique mix of culture traits and amalgams, some aspects of which are summarized in Table 2.1.

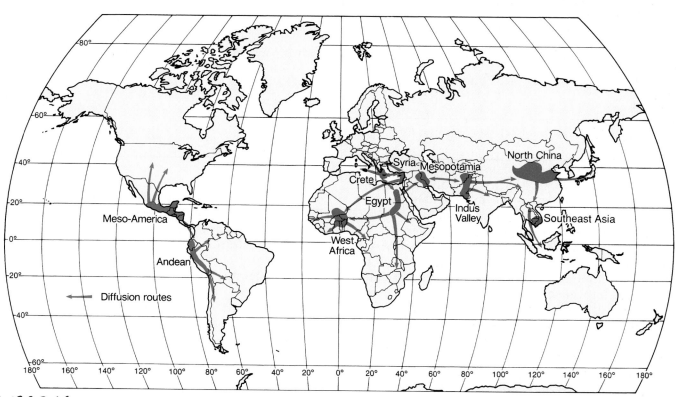

FIGURE 2.16   **Early culture hearths of the Old World and the Americas.** Generalized hearth characteristics are summarized in Table 2.1.

TABLE 2.1 Emerging Culture Hearths: Periods and Features of Development

HEARTH REGION	BEFORE 10,000 B.C.	10,000–8000 B.C.	8000–6000 B.C.	6000–4000 B.C.	4000–2000 B.C.	2000 B.C.–A.D. 1	A.D. 1–1000
Near East	Earliest domestication of dog Early hunter-gatherer villages	Domestication of sheep and goats First permanent communities Long-distance trade	First farming villages Wheat, barley, legumes Sophisticated houses Metalworking Pottery, textiles	First irrigation Early records on clay tablets Potter's wheel	First cities Earliest writing Wheeled vehicles First legal codes Bronze Age Plow	First alphabet Glass Iron smelting Birth of Christ	Birth of Mohammed (A.D. 570) Arab/Muslim expansion
Nile Valley	Evidence of cultivation of wheat, barley, lentils, dates		Pottery Fishing villages	Domestication of cattle Metalworking Farming villages	Cattle herding Farming Cloth Sailing ships Cities Writing Long-distance trade		
Indus Valley					Village farming Rise of cities Long-distance trade	End of Indus Valley cities (1600 B.C.)	
East Asia			Cultivation of rice; root crops, beans, millet Pottery	Settled villages Wide range of crops, domestic animals Plow Irrigation	Metalworking (bronze) First Chinese city	Chinese walled cities Buddha (563–483 B.C.) Confucius (551–479 B.C.) Ideographic script Iron working (China)	First Southeast Asian cities

Adapted with permission from John E. Pfeiffer, *The Emergence of Society: A Prehistory of the Establishment.* Copyright © 1977 McGraw-Hill Publishing Company, New York, NY.

All were urban centered, the indisputable mark of civilization first encountered in Mesopotamia 5500–6000 years ago, but the urbanization of each was differently arrived at and expressed (Figure 2.17). In some hearth areas, such as Mesopotamia and Egypt, the transition from settled agricultural village to urban form was gradual and prolonged. In Minoan Crete, urban life was less explicitly developed than in the Indus Valley, where early trade contacts with the Near East suggest the importance of exchange in fostering urban growth (see "Cities Brought Low"). Trade seems particularly important in the development of West African culture hearths, such as Ghana and Kanem. Coming later (from the 8th to the 10th centuries) than the Nile or Mesopotamian centers, their numerous stone-built towns seem to have been supported both by an extensive agriculture whose origins were probably as early as those of the Middle East and, particularly, by long-distance trade across the Sahara. The Shang kingdom on the middle course of the Huang He (Yellow River) on the North China Plain had walled cities containing wattle-and-daub buildings but no monumental architecture.

Each culture hearth showed a rigorous organization of agriculture resulting in local productivity sufficient to enable a significant number of people to engage in non-farm activities. Therefore, each hearth region saw the creation of a stratified society that included artisans, warriors, merchants, scholars, priests, and administrators. Each also developed or adopted astronomy, mathematics, and the all-essential calendar. Each, while advancing in cultural diversity and complexity, exported technologies, skills, and learned behaviors far beyond its own boundaries.

Writing appeared first in Mesopotamia and Egypt at least 5000 years ago, as cuneiform in the former and as hieroglyphics in the latter. The separate forms of writing have suggested to some that they arose independently in

HEARTH REGION	BEFORE 10,000 B.C.	10,000–8000 B.C.	8000–6000 B.C.	6000–4000 B.C.	4000–2000 B.C.	2000 B.C.–A.D. 1	A.D. 1–1000
Europe	Cave art Ivory, stone figurines	Long-distance trade	First farming in Greece and Aegean	Megalithic tombs	Olive, grape domestication First European cities Copper working	Minoan civilization on Crete Mycenaean culture in Greece "Golden Age" of Greece and Rome	Fall of Roman Empire Dark Ages
West Africa				Pottery	Yam cultivation Farming	Village clusters	Ceramic art First cities Well-developed agriculture Iron smelting Long-distance trade Empire of Ghana
Andean America		Roots, tubers (potato) as food crops	Beans, pepper, other plant domestications		Pottery	Metalworking Ceramics Textiles	City formation City-state conquests
Meso-America			Maize domestication (Mexico)	Beans, squash, chili peppers	First farming villages	Olmec culture Early cities Early Mayan culture Astronomy Writing Raised field agriculture	Apex of Mayan culture

separate hearths. Others maintain that the idea of writing originated in Mesopotamia and diffused outward to Egypt, to the Indus Valley, to Crete, and perhaps even to China, though independent development of Chinese ideographic writing is usually assumed. The systems of record keeping developed in New World hearths were not related to those of the Old, but once created they spread widely in areas under the influence of Andean and Meso-American hearths. Skill in working iron, so important in Near Eastern kingdoms, was an export of sub-Saharan African hearths.

The anthropologist Julian Steward (1902–1972) proposed the concept of **multilinear evolution** to explain the common characteristics of widely separated cultures developed under similar ecological circumstances. He suggested that each major environmental zone—arid, high altitude, midlatitude steppe, tropical forest, and so on—tends to induce common adaptive traits in the cultures of those who exploit it. Those traits were, at base, founded on the development of agriculture and the emergence of similar cultural and administrative structures in the several culture hearths. But *similar* does not imply *identical*. Steward simply suggested that since comparable sequences of developmental events cannot always or even often be explained on the basis of borrowing or exporting of ideas and techniques (because of time and space differences in cultures sharing them), they must be regarded as evidence of parallel creations based on similar ecologies. From similar origins, but through separate adaptations and innovations, distinctive cultures emerged.

Nonetheless, the common characteristics deriving from multilinear evolution and the diffusion of specific culture traits and complexes contained the roots of **cultural convergence.** That term describes the sharing of technologies, organizational structures, and even cultural traits and artifacts that is so evident among widely

FIGURE 2.17   Urbanization was invariably a characteristic of culture hearths of both the Old and the New Worlds. Pictured is the Pyramid of the Moon and Avenue of the Dead at Teotihuacán, a city that, at its height between A.D. 300 and 700, spread over nearly 18 square kilometers (7 square miles). Located some 50 kilometers (30 miles) northeast of Mexico City in the Valley of Mexico, the planned city of Teotihuacán featured broad, straight avenues and an enormous pyramid complex. The Avenue of the Dead, bordered with low stone-faced buildings, was some 3 kilometers (nearly 2 miles) in length.

CITIES BROUGHT LOW

Sustainable development requires a long-term accommodation between human actions and environmental circumstances. When that accommodation is broken either through poor management of resources by an exploiting culture or through natural environmental alteration unrelated to human actions—such as the catastrophic drought between A.D. 800 and 1000 thought to have caused the collapse of Mayan culture in Meso-America—a society's use and development of a region are no longer "sustainable" in the form and patterns previously established. Just as the activities of humans may alter or destroy their environment, that is, so may spontaneous changes in the environment bring low the works of organized society. Recent research suggests that one of the world's great early cultures, that of the Indus Valley of Pakistan, was destroyed not by fire or sword but by drowning in a sea of mud.

The great cities of the civilization, among them Harappa and Mohenjo-Daro, underwent an abrupt downfall about 2000 B.C. Excavations showing deep accumulations of mud, the erosional collapse of city walls, and recurring attempts to rebuild city structures document a losing battle against rising water backed up behind a dam created by earthquakes, rock shifts, and mudslides. The Indus was converted from a free-flowing stream to a huge, swampy lake, trapping mud formerly carried to the sea. As the lake rose, it destroyed forests and ruined agriculture. Although people erected dikes and brick walls to shield the cities, their food bases and very life were choked. The dam was cut through by the river and replugged at least five times, each flood recurrence taking its toll of urban life. The degeneration of pottery and other evidences of cultural decline record the losing struggle with an altering environment.

separated societies in a modern world united by instantaneous communication and efficient transportation.

The Structure of Culture

Understanding a culture fully is, perhaps, impossible for one who is not part of it. For analytical purposes, however, the traits and complexes of culture—its building blocks and expressions—may be grouped and examined as subsets of the whole. The anthropologist Leslie White (1900–1975) suggested that for analytical purposes, a culture could be viewed as a three-part structure composed of subsystems that he termed *ideological, technological,* and *sociological.* In a similar classification, the biologist Julian Huxley (1887–1975) identified three components of culture: *mentifacts, artifacts,* and *sociofacts.* Together, according to these interpretations, the subsystems—identified by their separate components—comprise the system of culture as a whole. But they are integrated; each reacts on the others and is affected by them in turn.

The **ideological subsystem** consists of ideas, beliefs, and knowledge of a culture and of the ways in which these things are expressed in speech or other forms of communication. Mythologies and theologies, legend, literature, philosophy, and folk wisdom make up this category. Passed on from generation to generation, these abstract belief systems, or **mentifacts,** tell us what we ought to believe, what we should value, and how we ought to act. Beliefs form the basis of the socialization process (see "The Gauda's Son"). Often we know—or think we know—what the beliefs of a group are from their oral or written statements. Sometimes, however, we must depend on the actions or objectives of a group to tell us what its true ideas and values are. "Actions speak louder than words" or "Do as I say, not as I do" are commonplace recognitions of the fact that actions, values, and words do not always coincide. Two basic strands of the ideological subsystem—language and religion—are the subject of Chapter 5.

The **technological subsystem** is composed of the material objects, together with the techniques of their use, by means of which people are able to live. The objects are the tools and other instruments that enable us to feed, clothe, house, defend, transport, and amuse ourselves. We must have food, we must be protected from the elements, and we must be able to defend ourselves. Huxley termed the material objects we use to fill these basic needs **artifacts** (Figure 2.18). In Chapter 10 we will examine the relationship between technological subsystems and regional patterns of economic development.

The **sociological subsystem** of a culture is the sum of those expected and accepted patterns of interpersonal relations that find their outlet in economic, political, military, religious, kinship, and other associations. These **sociofacts**

THE GAUDA'S SON

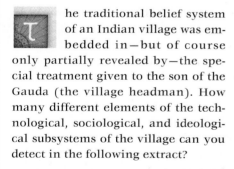

he traditional belief system of an Indian village was embedded in—but of course only partially revealed by—the special treatment given to the son of the Gauda (the village headman). How many different elements of the technological, sociological, and ideological subsystems of the village can you detect in the following extract?

The Gauda's son is eighteen months old. Every morning, a boy employed by the Gauda carries the Gauda's son through the streets of Gopalpur. The Gauda's son is clean; his clothing is elegant. When he is carried along the street, the old women stop their ceaseless grinding and pounding of grain and gather around. If the child wants something to play with, he is given it. If he cries, there is consternation.

If he plays with another boy, watchful adults make sure that the other boy does nothing to annoy the Gauda's son.

Shielded by servants, protected and comforted by virtually everyone in the village, the Gauda's son soon learns that tears and rage will produce anything he wants. At the same time, he begins to learn that the same superiority which gives him license to direct others and to demand their services places him in a state of danger. The green mangoes eaten by all of the other children in the village will give him a fever; coarse and chewy substances are likely to give him a stomachache. While other children clothe themselves in mud and dirt, he finds himself constantly being washed. As a Brahmin [a religious leader], he is taught to avoid all forms of pollution and to carry out complicated daily rituals of bathing,

eating, sleeping, and all other normal processes of life.

In time, the Gauda's son will enter school. He will sit motionless for hours, memorizing long passages from Sanskrit holy books and long poems in English and Urdu. He will learn to perform the rituals that are the duty of every Brahmin. He will bathe daily in the cold water of the private family well, reciting prayers and following a strict procedure. The gods in his house are major deities who must be worshipped every day, at length and with great care.

Excerpt from *Gopalpur: A South Indian Village* by Alan R. Beals, copyright © 1962 by Holt, Rinehart and Winston, Inc. Renewed 1990 by Alan R. Beals, reprinted by permission of the publisher.

(a)

(b)

FIGURE 2.18 (*a*) This Balinese farmer working with draft animals uses tools typical of the lower technological levels of subsistence economies. (*b*) Cultures with advanced technological subsystems use complex machinery to harness inanimate energy for productive use.

define the social organization of a culture. They regulate how the individual functions, relative to the group—whether it be family, church, or state. There are no "givens" as far as the patterns of interaction in any of these associations are concerned, except that most cultures possess a variety of formal and informal ways of structuring behavior. Differing patterns of behavior are learned and are transmitted from one generation to the next (Figure 2.19).

Classifications are of necessity arbitrary, and these classifications of the subsystems and components of culture are no exception. The three-part categorization of culture, while helping us appreciate its structure and complexity, can simultaneously obscure the many-sided nature of individual elements of culture. A dwelling, for example, is an artifact providing shelter for its occupants. It is, simultaneously, a sociofact reflecting the nature of the family or kinship group it is designed to house, and a mentifact summarizing a culture group's convictions about appropriate design, orientation, and building materials of dwelling units. In the same vein, clothing serves as an artifact of bodily protection appropriate to climatic conditions, available materials and techniques, or the activity in which the wearer is engaged. But garments also may be sociofacts, identifying an individual's role in the social structure of the community or culture, and mentifacts, evoking larger community value systems (Figure 2.20).

Nothing in a culture stands totally alone. Changes in the ideas that a society holds may affect the sociological and technological systems just as changes in technology force adjustments in the social system. The abrupt alteration of the ideological structure of Russia following the 1917 communist revolution from a monarchical, agrarian, capitalistic system to an industrialized, communistic society involved sudden, interrelated alteration of all facets of that country's culture system. The equally abrupt disintegration of Russian communism in the early 1990s was similarly disruptive of all its established economic, social, and administrative structures. The interlocking nature of all aspects of a culture is termed **cultural integration.**

Culture Change

The recurring theme of cultural geography is change. No culture is, or has been, characterized by a permanently fixed set of material objects, systems of organization, or even ideologies. Admittedly, all of these may be long enduring within a society at equilibrium with its resource base and totally isolated from need or influence for change. But such isolation and stagnation have always been rare. On the whole, while cultures are essentially conservative, they are simultaneously constantly changing. They are always in a state of flux. Some changes are major and pervasive. The transition from hunter-gatherer to sedentary farmer, as we have seen, affected markedly every facet of the cultures experiencing that change. Profound, too, has been the impact of the Industrial Revolution and its associated urbanization on all societies it has touched.

THEMES AND FUNDAMENTALS OF HUMAN GEOGRAPHY

FIGURE 2.19 All societies prepare their children for membership in the culture group. In each of these settings, certain values, beliefs, skills, and proper ways of acting are being transmitted to the youngsters.

(a)   (b)   (c)

FIGURE 2.20   (*a*) When clothing serves primarily to cover, protect, or assist in activities, it is an *artifact*. (*b*) Some garments are *sociofacts,* identifying a role or position within the social structure: the distinctive "uniforms" of a soldier, a cleric, or a beribboned ambassador immediately proclaim their respective roles in a culture's social organizations. (*c*) The mandatory chadors of Iranian females are *mentifacts,* indicative not specifically of the role of the wearer but of the values of the culture the wearer represents.

Not all change is so pervasive as that following the introduction of agriculture or the Industrial Revolution. Many changes are so slight individually as to go almost unnoticed at their inception, though cumulatively they may substantially alter the affected culture. Think of how the culture of the United States differs today from what you know it to have been in 1940—not in essentials, perhaps, but in the innumerable electrical, electronic, and transportational devices that have been introduced and in the social, behavioral, and recreational changes they have wrought. Such cumulative changes occur because the cultural traits of any group are not independent; they are clustered in a coherent and integrated pattern. Change in an apparently minor and limited fashion will have wide repercussions as associated traits arrive at accommodation with the adopted adjustment. Change, both major and minor, within cultures is induced by *innovation* and *diffusion.*

Innovation

Innovation implies changes to a culture that result from ideas created within the social group itself and adopted by the culture. The novelty may be an invented improvement in material technology, like the bow and arrow or the jet engine. It may involve the development of nonmaterial forms of social structure and interaction: feudalism, for example, or Christianity.

Primitive and traditional societies characteristically are not innovative. For societies at equilibrium with their environment and with no unmet needs, change has no adaptive value and no reason to occur. Indeed, all societies have an innate resistance to change. Complaints about youthful fads or the glorification of times past are familiar cases in point. However, when a social group is inappropriately unresponsive—mentally, psychologically, or economically—to changing circumstances and to innovation, it is said to exhibit **cultural lag.**

Innovation—invention—frequently under stress, has characterized the history of humankind. As we have seen, growing populations at the end of the Ice Age necessitated an expanded food base. In response, domestication of plants and animals appears to have occurred independently in more than one world area. Indeed, a most striking fact about early agriculture is the universality of its development or adoption within a very short span of human history. In 10,000 B.C., the world population of no more than 10 million was exclusively hunter-gatherers. By A.D. 1500, only 1% of the world's 350 million people still

THEMES AND FUNDAMENTALS OF HUMAN GEOGRAPHY

followed that way of life. The revolution in food production affected every facet of the threefold subsystems of culture of every society accepting it. All innovation has a radiating impact on the web of culture; the more basic the innovation, the more pervasive its consequences.

In most modern societies, innovative change has become common, expected, and inevitable. The rate of invention, at least as measured by the number of patents granted, has steadily increased, and the period between idea conception and product availability has been decreasing. A general axiom is that the more ideas available and the more minds able to exploit and combine them, the greater the rate of innovation. The spatial implication is that larger urban centers of advanced technologies tend to be centers of innovation. This is not just because of their size but because of the number of ideas interchanged. Indeed, ideas not only stimulate new thoughts and viewpoints but also create circumstances in which the society must develop new solutions to maintain its forward momentum (Figure 2.21).

Diffusion

Diffusion is the process by which an idea or innovation is transmitted from one individual or group to another across space. Diffusion may assume a variety of forms, each different in its impact on social groups. Basically, however, two processes are involved: (1) People move, for any of a number of reasons, to a new area and take their culture with them. For example, immigrants to the American colonies brought along crops and farming techniques, building styles, or concepts of government alien to their new home. (2) Information about an innovation (e.g., hy-

brid corn or compact discs) may spread throughout a society, perhaps aided by local or mass media advertising; or new adopters of an ideology or way of life—for example, a new religious creed—may be inspired or recruited by immigrant or native converts. The former is known as **relocation diffusion,** the latter as **expansion diffusion** (Figure 2.22).

Expansion diffusion involves the spread of an item or idea from one place to others. In the process the thing diffused also remains—and is frequently intensified—in the origin area. Islam, for example, expanded from its Arabian Peninsula origin locale across much of Asia and North Africa. At the same time it strengthened its hold over its

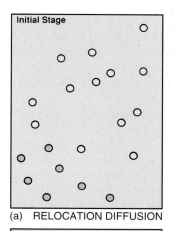
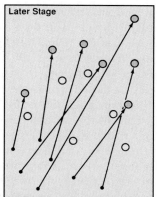

(a) RELOCATION DIFFUSION

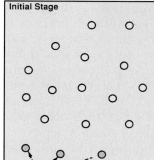
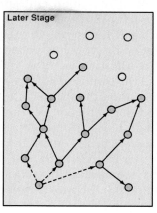

(b) EXPANSION DIFFUSION

FIGURE 2.22 **Patterns of diffusion.** (*a*) In *relocation diffusion,* innovations or ideas are transported to new areas by carriers who permanently leave the home locale. The "Pennsylvania Dutch" barn (Figure 6.23) was brought to Pennsylvania by German immigrants and spread to other groups and areas southward through Appalachia and westward into Ohio, Indiana, Illinois, and Missouri. Not all farmers or farm districts in the path of advancement adopted the new barn design. (*b*) In *expansion diffusion,* a phenomenon spreads from one place to neighboring locations, but in the process remains and is often intensified in the place of origin (see Figure 5.29).

Redrawn by permission from *Spatial Diffusion,* Peter R. Gould, p. 4, Association of American Geographers, 1969.

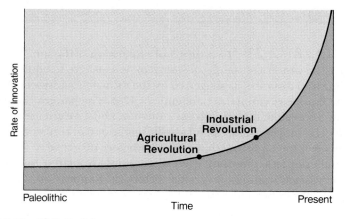

FIGURE 2.21 **The rate of innovation through human history.** Hunter-gatherers, living in easy equilibrium with their environment and their resource base, had little need for innovation and no necessity for cultural change. Increased population pressures led to the development of agriculture and the diffusion of the ideas and techniques of domestication, urbanization, and trade. With the Industrial Revolution, dramatic increases in innovation began to alter cultures throughout the world.

Near Eastern birthplace by displacing pagan, Christian, and Jewish populations. When expansion diffusion affects nearly uniformly all individuals and areas outward from the source region, it is termed **contagious diffusion.** The term implies the importance of direct contact between those who developed or have adopted the innovation and those who newly encounter it, and is reminiscent of the course of infectious diseases (Figures 2.23*a* and 5.23).

In some instances, however, geographic distance is less important in the transfer of ideas than is communication between major centers or important people. News of new clothing styles, for example, quickly spreads internationally between major cities and only later filters down irregularly to smaller towns and rural areas. The process of transferring ideas first between larger places or prominent people and only later to smaller or less important points or people is known as **hierarchical diffusion** (Figure 2.23*b*). The Christian faith in Europe, for example, spread from Rome as the principal center to provincial capitals and thence to smaller Roman settlements in largely pagan occupied territories.

In relocation diffusion, the innovation or idea is physically carried to new areas by migrating individuals or populations that possess it (Figure 2.22*a*). Mentifacts or artifacts are therefore introduced into new locales by new settlers who become part of populations not themselves associated or in contact with the origin area of the innovation. The spread of religions by settlers or conquerors is a clear example of relocation diffusion, as was the diffusion of agriculture to Europe from the Middle East (Figure 2.14). Christian Europeans brought their faiths to areas of colonization or economic penetration throughout the world. At the world scale, massive and pervasive relocation diffusion resulted from the European colonization and economic penetration that began in the 16th century. More localized relocation diffusion continues today as Asian refugees or foreign "guest workers" bring their cultural traits to their new areas of settlement in Europe or North America.

Innovations in the technological or ideological subsystems may be relatively readily diffused to, and accepted by, cultures which have basic similarities and compatibilities. Continental Europe and North America, for example, could easily and quickly adopt the innovations of the Industrial Revolution diffused from England with which they shared a common economic and technological background. Industrialization was not quickly accepted in Asian and African societies of totally different cultural conditioning. On the ideological level, too, successful diffusion depends on acceptability of the innovations. The Shah's attempt at rapid westernization of traditional Iranian, Islamic culture after World War II evoked a traditionalist backlash and revolution that deposed the Shah and reestablished clerical control of the state.

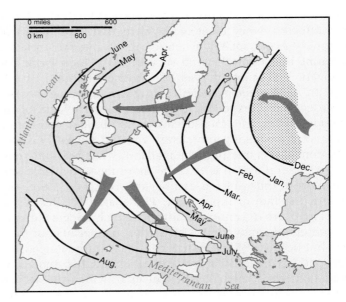

(a)

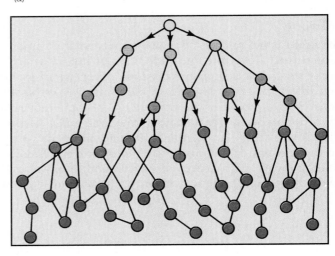

FIGURE 2.23 Two forms of expansion diffusion.

(*a*) The process of *contagious diffusion* is sensitive to both time and distance, as suggested by the diffusion pathways of the European influenza pandemic of 1781. The pattern there was a wavelike radiation from a Russian nodal origin area. (*b*) The process of *hierarchical diffusion* is one of transfer between the large and the important before dispersal to the smaller or less important. New discoveries are shared among scientists at leading universities before they appear in textbooks or become general knowledge through the public press. Prosperous and locally important farmers in any region are the first to adopt new agricultural techniques that only later are understood and taken up by their less adventurous neighbors.

(*a*) Based on Gerald F. Pyle and K. David Patterson, *Ecology of Disease* 2, no. 3, (1984): p. 179.

(*b*) Based on *Spatial Diffusion*, Peter R. Gould, p. 6, Association of American Geographers, 1969.

It is not always possible, of course, to determine the precise point of origin or the routes of diffusion of innovations now widely adopted (see "Documenting Diffusion"). Nor is it always certain whether the existence of a cultural trait in two different areas is the result of diffusion or of **independent** (or *parallel*) **invention.** Cultural similarities do not necessarily prove that diffusion has occurred. The pyramids of Egypt and of the Central American Maya civilization most likely were separately conceived and are not necessarily evidence, as some have proposed, of pre-Columbian voyages from the Mediterranean to the Americas. A monument-building culture, after all, has only a limited number of shapes from which to choose.

Historical examples of independent, parallel invention are numerous: logarithms by Napier (1614) and Burgi (1620); the calculus by Newton (1672) and Leibnitz (1675); the telephone by Elisha Gray and Alexander Graham Bell (1876) are commonly cited. It appears beyond doubt that agriculture was independently developed not only in both the New World and the Old but also in more than one culture hearth in each of the hemispheres.

Contact between Regions

All cultures are amalgams of innumerable innovations spread spatially from their points of origin and integrated into the structure of the receiving societies. It has been estimated that no more than 10% of the cultural items of any society are traceable to innovations created by its members and that the other 90% come to the society through diffusion (see "A Homemade Culture"). Since, as we have seen, the pace of innovation is affected strongly by the mixing of ideas among alert, responsive people and is increased by exposure to a variety of cultures, the most active and innovative historical hearths of culture were those at crossroad locations and those deeply involved in distant trade and colonization. Ancient Mesopotamia and classical Greece and Rome had such locations and involvements, as did the West African culture hearth after the 5th century and, much later, England during the Industrial Revolution and the spread of its empire.

Recent changes in technology permit us to travel farther than ever before, with greater safety and speed, and to communicate without physical contact more easily and completely than was previously possible. This intensification of contact has resulted in an acceleration of innovation and in the rapid spread of goods and ideas. Several millennia ago, innovations such as smelting of metals took hundreds of years to diffuse. Today, worldwide diffusion—through Internet interest groups, for example—may be almost instantaneous.

Obstacles do exist, of course. **Diffusion barriers** are any conditions that hinder either the flow of information or the movement of people and thus retard or prevent the acceptance of an innovation. Because of the *friction of distance,* generally the farther two areas are from each other,

the less likely is interaction to occur. The concept of *distance decay* tells us that, all else being equal, the amount of interaction decreases as the distance between two areas increases. Distance as a factor in spatial interaction is further explored in Chapter 3. For now it is sufficient to note that distance may be an *absorbing barrier,* halting the spread of an innovation.

Interregional contact can also be hindered by the physical environment and by a lack of receptivity by a contacted culture. Oceans and rugged terrain can and have acted as physical *interrupting barriers,* delaying or deflecting the path of diffusion. Cultural obstacles that are equally impenetrable may also exist. For example, for at least 1500 years most California Indians were in contact with cultures utilizing both maize and pottery, yet they failed to accept either innovation. Should such reluctant adopters intervene between hearths and receptive cultures, the spread of an innovation can be slowed. It can also be delayed when cultural contact is overtly impeded by governments that interfere with radio reception, control the flow of foreign literature, and discourage contact between their citizens and foreign nationals.

More commonly, barriers are at least partially *permeable;* they permit passage (acceptance) of at least some innovations encountering them. The more similar two cultural areas are to each other, the greater is the likelihood of the adoption of an innovation, for diffusion is a selective process. The receiver culture may adopt some goods or ideas from the donor society and reject others. The decision to adopt is governed by the receiving group's own culture. Political restrictions, religious taboos, and other social customs are cultural barriers to diffusion. The French Canadians, although close geographically to many centers of diffusion, such as Toronto, New York, and Boston, strive to be only minimally influenced by such centers. Both their language and culture complex govern their selective acceptance of Anglo influences, and restrictive French-only language regulations are enforced to preserve the integrity of French culture. Traditional groups, perhaps controlled by firm religious conviction, may very largely reject culture traits and technologies of the larger society in whose midst they live (Figure 7.2).

Adopting cultures do not usually accept intact items originating outside the receiving society. Diffused ideas and artifacts commonly undergo some alteration of meaning or form that makes them acceptable to a borrowing group. The process of the fusion of the old and new is called **syncretism** and is a major feature of culture change. It can be seen in alterations to religious ritual and dogma made by convert societies seeking acceptable conformity between old and new beliefs; the mixture of Catholic rites and voodooism in Haiti is an example. On a more familiar level, syncretism is reflected in subtle or blatant alterations of imported cuisines to make them conform to the demands of America's palate and its fast-food franchises (Figure 2.24).

he places of origin of many ideas, items, and technologies important in contemporary cultures are only dimly known or supposed, and their routes of diffusion are at best speculative. Gunpowder, printing, and spaghetti are presumed to be the products of Chinese inventiveness; the lateen sail has been traced to the Near Eastern culture world. The moldboard plow is ascribed to 6th-century Slavs of northeastern Europe. The sequence and routes of the diffusion of these innovations has not been documented.

In other cases, such documentation exists, and the process of diffusion is open to analysis. For example, hybrid corn was originally adopted by imaginative farmers of northern Illinois and eastern Iowa in the mid-1930s. By the late 1930s and early 1940s, the new seeds were being planted as far east as Ohio and north to Minnesota, Wisconsin, and northern Michigan. By the late 1940s, all commercial corn-growing districts of the United States and southern Canada were cultivating hybrid corn varieties.

Clearly marked as well is the diffusion path of the custom of smoking tobacco, a practice that originated among Amerindians. Sir Walter Raleigh's Virginia colonists, returning home in 1586, introduced smoking in English court circles, and the habit very quickly spread among the general populace. England became the source region of the new custom for northern Europe. Smoking was introduced to Holland by English medical students in 1590. Dutch and English together spread the habit by sea to the Baltic and Scandinavian areas and overland through Germany to Russia, where by 1634, laws were being passed to curb the practice of smoking. The innovation continued its eastward diffusion, and within a hundred years tobacco had spread across Siberia and was, in the 1740s, reintroduced to the American continent at Alaska as both a habit and an item of trade carried by Russian fur traders. A second route of diffusion for tobacco smoking can be traced from Spain, where the custom was introduced in 1558, and from which it spread more slowly through the Mediterranean area into Africa, the Near East, and Southeast Asia.

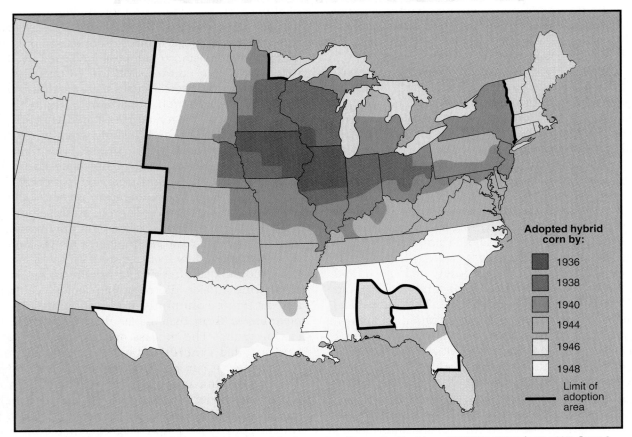

Adopted hybrid corn by:

- 1936
- 1938
- 1940
- 1944
- 1946
- 1948
- Limit of adoption area

Source: Redrawn from data in Zvi Griliches, "Hybrid Corn and the Economics of Innovation" in *Science,* 132(3422): 277 (July 29, 1960), figure 3.

eflecting on an average morning in the life of a "100% American," Ralph Linton noted:

Our solid American citizen awakens in a bed built on a pattern which originated in the Near East but which was modified in Northern Europe before it was transmitted to America. He throws back covers made from cotton, domesticated in India, or linen, domesticated in the Near East, or wool from sheep, also domesticated in the Near East, or silk, the use of which was discovered in China. All of these materials have been spun and woven by processes invented in the Near East. . . . He takes off his pajamas, a garment invented in India, and washes with soap invented by the ancient Gauls. . . .

Returning to the bedroom, . . . he puts on garments whose form originally derived from the skin clothing of the nomads of the Asiatic steppes [and] puts on shoes made from skins tanned by a process invented in ancient Egypt and cut to a pattern derived from the classical civilizations of the Mediterranean. . . . Before going out for breakfast he glances through the window, made of glass invented in Egypt, and if it is raining puts on overshoes made of rubber discovered by the Central American Indians and takes an umbrella invented in southeastern Asia. . . .

[At breakfast] a whole new series of borrowed elements confronts him. His plate is made of a form of pottery invented in China. His knife is of steel, an alloy first made in southern India, his fork a medieval Italian invention, and his spoon a derivative of a Roman original. He begins breakfast with an orange, from the eastern Mediterranean, a cantaloupe from Persia, or perhaps a piece of African watermelon. With this he has coffee, an Abyssinian plant. . . . [He] may have the egg of a species of bird domesticated in Indo-China, or thin strips of flesh of an animal domesticated in Eastern Asia which have been salted and smoked by a process developed in northern Europe.

When our friend has finished eating . . . he reads the news of the day, imprinted in characters invented by the ancient Semites upon a material invented in China by a process invented in Germany. As he absorbs the accounts of foreign troubles he will, if he is a good conservative citizen, thank a Hebrew deity in an Indo-European language that he is 100 percent American.

Ralph Linton, *The Study of Man: An Introduction,* ©1936, pp. 326–327. Reprinted by permission of Prentice-Hall, Inc., Upper Saddle River, NJ.

FIGURE 2.24 Foreign foods modified for American tastes and American palates accustomed to dishes from all cultures together represent *syncretism* in action.

FIGURE 2.25 Baseball, an import from America, is one of the most popular sports in Japan, attracting millions of spectators annually.

Cultural Modification and Adoption

A culture group may undergo major modifications in its own identifying traits by adopting some or all of the characteristics of another, dominant culture group. Such is the case in *acculturation*—discussed at greater length in Chapter 6 (pp. 184)—as immigrant populations take on the values, attitudes, customs, and speech of the receiving society. A different form of contact and subsequent cultural alteration may occur in a conquered or colonized region where the subordinate or subject population is either forced to adopt the culture of the new ruling group, introduced through relocation diffusion, or does so voluntarily, overwhelmed by the superiority in numbers or the technical level of the conqueror. Tribal Europeans in areas of Roman conquest, native populations in the wake of Slavic occupation of Siberia, and Native Americans stripped of their lands following European settlement of North America experienced this kind of cultural modification or adoption.

In many instances, close contact between two different groups may involve adjustments of the original cultural patterns of both. For example, changes in Japanese political organization and philosophy were imposed by occupying Americans after World War II, and the Japanese voluntarily adopted some more frivolous aspects of American life (Figure 2.25). In turn, American society was enriched by the selective importation of Japanese cuisine, architecture, and philosophy, demonstrating the two-way nature of cultural diffusion.

Summary

The web of culture is composed of many strands. Together, culture traits and complexes in their spatial patterns create human landscapes, define culture regions, and distinguish culture groups. Those landscapes, regions, and group characteristics change through time as human societies interact with their environment, develop for themselves new solutions to collective needs, or are altered through innovations adopted from outside the group itself. The cultural uniformity of a preagricultural world composed solely of hunter-gatherers was lost as domestication of plants and animals in many world areas led to the emergence of culture hearths of wide-ranging innovation and to a cultural divergence between farmers and gatherers. Innovations spread outward from their origin points, carried by migrants through relocation diffusion or adopted by others through a variety of expansion diffusion processes. Although diffusion barriers exist, most successful or advantageous innovations find adopters, and both cultural modification and cultural convergence of different societies result. The details of the technological, sociological, and ideological subsystems of culture define the differences that still exist between world areas.

The ivory hunters who opened our chapter showed how varied and complex the culture of even a primitive group can be. Their artifacts of clothing, fire making, hunting, and fishing displayed diversity and ingenuity. They were part of a structured kinship system and en-gaged in organized production and trade. Their artistic efforts and ritual burial customs speak of a sophisticated set of abstract beliefs and philosophies. Their culture complex did not develop in isolation; it reflected at least in part their contacts with other groups, even those far distant from their Paris Basin homeland. As culture groups have done always and everywhere, the hunters carried on their own pursuits and interacted with others in spatial settings. They exhibited and benefited from structured *spatial behavior,* the topic to which we next turn our attention.

KEY WORDS

artifact 51	culture hearth 47	independent invention 57
carrying capacity 43	culture realm 36	innovation 54
contagious diffusion 56	culture region 36	mentifact 51
cultural convergence 49	culture trait 36	multilinear evolution 49
cultural divergence 43	diffusion 55	possibilism 37
cultural ecology 36	diffusion barrier 57	relocation diffusion 55
cultural integration 52	environmental determinism 37	sociofact 51
cultural lag 54	expansion diffusion 55	sociological subsystem 51
cultural landscape 38	hierarchical diffusion 56	syncretism 57
culture 34	hunter-gatherers 40	technological subsystem 51
culture complex 36	ideological subsystem 51	

FOR REVIEW

1. What is included in the concept of *culture?* How is culture transmitted? What personal characteristics affect the aspects of culture that any single individual acquires or fully masters?

2. What do we mean by *domestication?* When and where did the domestication of plants and animals occur? What impact on culture and population numbers did plant domestication have?

3. What is a *culture hearth?* What new traits of culture characterized the early hearths? Identify and locate some of the major culture hearths that emerged at the close of the Neolithic period.

4. What do we mean by *innovation?* By *diffusion?* What different patterns of diffusion can you describe? Discuss the role played by innovation and diffusion in altering the cultural structure in which you are a participant from that experienced by your great-grandparents.

5. Differentiate between *culture traits* and *culture complexes.* Between *environmental determinism* and *possibilism.*

6. What are the components or subsystems of the three-part system of culture? What cultural characteristics are included in each of the subsystems?

SELECTED REFERENCES

Brown, Lawrence A. *Innovation Diffusion: A New Perspective.* London and New York: Methuen, 1981.

Bryan, Alan L., ed. *New Evidence for the Pleistocene Peopling of the Americas.* Orono: University of Maine, Center for the Study of Early Man, 1986.

Coe, Michael, Dean Snow, and Elizabeth Benson. *Atlas of Ancient America.* New York: Facts on File Incorporated, 1986.

Cowan, C. Wesley, and Patty Jo Watson, eds. *The Origins of Agriculture: An International Perspective.* Washington, D.C.: Smithsonian Institution Press, 1992.

Crosby, Alfred W. *Ecological Imperialism: The Biological Expansion of Europe 900–1900.* Cambridge: Cambridge University Press, 1986.

Deane, Phyllis. *The First Industrial Revolution.* 2d ed. New York: Cambridge University Press, 1979.

Denevan, William M. "The Pristine Myth: The Landscape of the Americas in 1492." *Annals of the Association of American Geographers* 82, no. 3 (1992):369–385.

Frankfort, Henri. *The Birth of Civilization in the Near East.* Garden City, NY: Doubleday, 1956.

Gebauer, Anne B., and T. Douglas Price, eds. *Transitions to Agriculture in Prehistory.* Monographs in World Archeology No. 4. Madison, WI: Prehistory Press, 1992.

Gould, Peter. *Spatial Diffusion.* Association of American Geographers, Commission on College Geography. *Resource Paper* No. 4. Washington, D.C.: Association of American Geographers, 1969.

Haggett, Peter. "Geographical Aspects of the Emergence of Infectious Diseases." *Geografiska Annaler* 76B, no. 2 (1994):91–104.

Henderson, John S. *The World of the Ancient Maya.* Ithaca, NY: Cornell University Press, 1981.

Isaac, Erich. *Geography of Domestication.* Englewood Cliffs, NJ: Prentice-Hall, 1970.

Keatinge, Richard W., ed. *Peruvian Prehistory.* New York: Cambridge University Press, 1987.

Kroeber, Alfred L., and Clyde Kluckhohn. "Culture: A Critical Review of Concepts and Definitions." Harvard University. *Papers of the Peabody Museum of American Archaeology and Ethnology* 47, no. 2 (1952).

MacNeish, Richard S. *The Origins of Agriculture and Settled Life.* Norman: University of Oklahoma Press, 1991.

Morrill, Richard, Gary L. Gaile, and Grant Ian Thrall. *Spatial Diffusion.* Scientific Geography Series, Vol. 10. Newbury Park, CA: SAGE Publications, 1988.

Morris, Craig, and Adriana von Hagen. *The Inka Empire and its Andean Origins.* New York: Abbeville Press, 1993.

"The Peopling of the Earth." *National Geographic* (October 1988):434–503.

Pfeiffer, John E. *The Emergence of Society: A Prehistory of the Establishment.* New York: McGraw-Hill, 1977.

Platt, Robert S. "Determinism in Geography." *Annals of the Association of American Geographers* 38 (1948):126–132.

Redman, Charles L. *The Rise of Civilization: From Early Farmers to Urban Society in the Ancient Near East.* San Francisco: W. H. Freeman, 1978.

Rodrique, Christine M. "Can Religion Account for Early Animal Domestications . . . ?" *Professional Geographer* 44, no. 4 (1992):417–430.

Rogers, Alisdair, ed. *Peoples and Cultures.* The Illustrated Encyclopedia of World Geography. New York: Oxford University Press, 1992.

Rogers, Everett M. *Diffusion of Innovations.* 3d ed. New York: Free Press, 1983.

Runnels, Curtis N. "Environmental Degradation in Ancient Greece." *Scientific American* (March 1995):96–99.

Sauer, Carl. *Agricultural Origins and Dispersals.* New York: American Geographical Society, 1952.

Sebastian, Lynne. *The Chaco Anasazi: Sociopolitical Evolution in the Prehistoric Southwest.* New York: Cambridge University Press, 1992.

Sjoberg, Gideon. "The Origin and Evolution of Cities." *Scientific American* 213 (1965):54–63.

Steward, Julian H. *Theory of Culture Change.* Urbana: University of Illinois Press, 1955.

Thomas, William L., Jr., ed. *Man's Role in Changing the Face of the Earth.* Chicago: University of Chicago Press, 1956.

Wagner, Philip L., and Marvin W. Mikesell. *Readings in Cultural Geography.* Chicago: University of Chicago Press, 1962.

White, Leslie A. *The Science of Culture: A Study of Man and Civilization.* New York: Farrar, Straus and Giroux, 1969.

White, Randall. *Dark Caves, Bright Visions: Life in Ice Age Europe.* New York: American Museum of Natural History in Association with W. W. Norton & Company, 1986.

Wilbanks, Thomas J. " 'Sustainable Development' in Geographic Perspective." *Annals of the Association of American Geographers* 84, no. 4 (1994):541–556.

Zohary, Daniel, and Mari Hopf. *Domestication of Plants in the Old World.* 2d ed. Oxford, England: Clarendon Press, 1993.

SPATIAL INTERACTION AND SPATIAL BEHAVIOR

Bases for Interaction   64
A Summarizing Model   65
  Complementarity   65
  Transferability   65
  Intervening Opportunity   66
Measuring Interaction   66
  Distance Decay   67
  The Gravity Concept   68
  Interaction Potential   68
  Movement Biases   69
Human Spatial Behavior   70
Individual Activity Space   70
The Tyranny of Time   72
Distance and Human Interaction   72
Spatial Interaction and the Accumulation
  of Information   73
  Information Flows   76
Information and Perception   77
  Perception of Environment   77
  Perception of Natural Hazards   79
Migration   82
Principal Migration Patterns   83
Types of Migration   83
Controls on Migration   85

  SUMMARY   91
  KEY WORDS   92
  FOR REVIEW   92
  SELECTED REFERENCES   92

People and goods in economic and social interaction along the autobahn in Germany .

Early in January of 1849 we first thought of migrating to California. It was a period of National hard times . . . and we longed to go to the new El Dorado and "pick up" gold enough with which to return and pay off our debts.

Our discontent and restlessness were enhanced by the fact that my health was not good. . . . The physician advised an entire change of climate thus to avoid the intense cold of Iowa, and recommended a sea voyage, but finally approved of our contemplated trip across the plains in a "prairie schooner."

Full of the energy and enthusiasm of youth, the prospects of so hazardous an undertaking had no terror for us, indeed, as we had been married but a few months, it appealed to us as a romantic wedding tour.[1]

So begins Catherine Haun's account of their 9-month journey from Iowa to California, just two of the quarter-million people who traveled across the continent on the Overland Trail in one of the world's great migrations. The migrants faced months of grueling struggle over badly marked routes that crossed swollen rivers, deserts, and mountains. The weather was often foul, with hailstorms, drenching rains, and burning summer temperatures. Graves along the route were a silent testimony to the lives claimed by buffalo stampedes, Indian skirmishes, cholera epidemics, and other disasters.

What inducements were so great as to make emigrants leave behind all that was familiar and risk their lives on an uncertain venture? Catherine Haun alludes to economic hard times gripping the country and to their hope for riches to be found in California. Like other migrants, the Hauns were attracted by the climate in the West, which was said to be always sunny and free of disease. Finally, like most who undertook the perilous journey West, the Hauns were young, moved by restlessness, a sense of adventure, and a perception of greater opportunities in a new land. They, like their predecessors back to the beginnings of humankind, were acting in space and across space on the basis of acquired information and anticipation of opportunity—prepared to pay the price, in time, money, and hardship costs, of overcoming distance.

A fundamental question in human geography is, What considerations influence how individual human beings use space and act within it? Related queries include: Are there discernible controls on human spatial behavior? How does distance affect human interaction? How do our perceptions of places influence our spatial activities? How do we overcome the consequences of distance in the exchange of commodities and information? How are movement and migration decisions (like that of the Hauns) reached? These are questions addressing geography's concern with understanding spatial interaction.

Spatial interaction means the movement of peoples, ideas, and commodities within and between areas. The Hauns were engaging in spatial interaction (Figure 3.1). International trade, the movement of semitrailers on the expressways, radio broadcasts, and business or personal telephone calls are more familiar examples. Such movements and exchanges are designed to achieve effective integration between different points of human activity. Movement of whatever nature satisfies some felt need or desire. It represents the attempt to smooth out the spatially differing availability of required resources, commodities, information, or opportunities. Whatever the particular purpose of a movement, there is inevitably some manner of trade-off balancing the benefit of the interaction with the costs that are incurred in overcoming spatial separation. Because commodity movements represent simple demonstrations of the principles underlying all spatial interactions, let us turn to them first.

Bases for Interaction

Neither the world's resources nor the products of people's efforts are uniformly distributed. Commodity flows are responses to these differences; they are links between points of supply and locales of demand. Such response may not be immediate or even direct. Matters of awareness of supplies

FIGURE 3.1   Cross-country movement was slow, arduous, and dangerous early in the 19th century, and the price of long-distance spatial interaction was far higher in time and risks than a comparable journey today.

1. From Catherine Haun, "A Woman's Trip Across the Plains in 1849," in Lillian Schlissel, *Women's Diaries of the Westward Journey* (New York: Schocken Books, 1982).

or markets, the presence or absence of transportation connections, costs of movement, ability to pay for things wanted and needed—all and more are factors in the structure of trade. Underlying even these, however, is a set of controlling principles governing spatial interaction.

A Summarizing Model

The conviction that spatial interaction reflects areal differences led the geographer Edward Ullman (1912–1976) to speculate on the essential conditions affecting such interactions and to propose an explanatory model. He observed that spatial interaction is effectively controlled by three flow-determining factors that he called *complementarity, transferability,* and *intervening opportunity.* Although Ullman's model deals with commodity flows, it has—as we shall see—applicability to informational transfers and patterns of human movements as well.

Complementarity

For two places to interact, one place must have a supply of an item for which there is an effective demand in the other, as evidenced by desire for the item, purchasing power to acquire it, and means to transport it. The word describing this circumstance is **complementarity.** *Effective* supply and demand are important considerations; mere differences from place to place in commodity surplus or deficit are not enough to initiate exchange. Greenland and the Amazon basin are notably unalike in their natural resources and economies, but their amount of interaction is minimal. Supply and market must come together, as they do in the flow of seasonal fruits and vegetables from California's Imperial Valley to the urban markets of the American Midwest and East or in the movement of manganese from Ukraine to the steel mills of Western Europe. The massive movement of crude and refined petroleum between spatially separated effective supplies and markets clearly demonstrates complementarity in international trade (Figure 3.2). More generalized patterns of complementarity underlie the exchanges of the raw materials and agricultural goods of less developed countries for the industrial commodities of the developed states.

Transferability

Even when complementarity exists, spatial interaction occurs only when conditions of **transferability**—acceptable costs of an exchange—are met. Spatial movement responds not just to availability and demand but to considerations of time and cost. Transferability is an expression of the mobility of a commodity, and is a function of three interrelated conditions: (1) the characteristics and value of the product; (2) the distance, measured in time and money penalties,

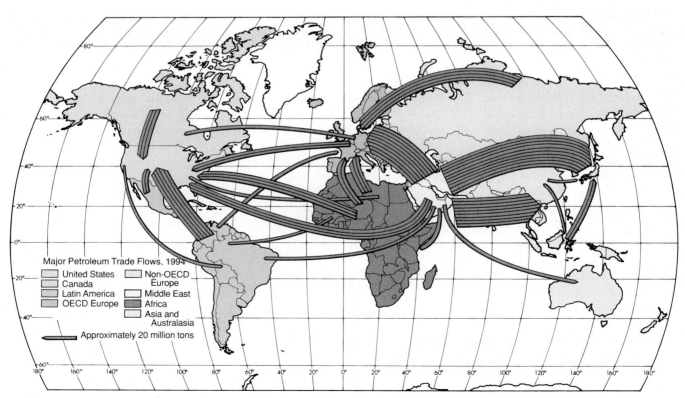

FIGURE 3.2 **Interregional trade in oil, 1994.** Complementarity is so basic in initiating interaction that even relatively low-value bulk commodities such as coal, fertilizer, and grain move in trade over long distances. For many years, despite fluctuating prices, petroleum has been the most important commodity in international trade. The line widths are proportional to average daily movements.

over which it must be moved, and (3) the ability of the commodity to bear the costs of movement. If the time and money costs of traversing a distance are too great, exchange does not occur. That is, mobility is not just a physical matter but an economic one as well. If a given commodity is not affordable upon delivery to an otherwise willing buyer, it will not move in trade, and the potential buyer must seek a substitute or go without.

Transferability is not a constant condition. It differs between places, over time, and in relation to what is being transferred and how it is to be moved. The opening of a logging road will connect a sawmill with stands of timber formerly inaccessible (nontransferable). An increasing scarcity of high-quality ores will enhance the transferability of lower-quality mine outputs by increasing their value. Low-cost bulk commodities not economically moved by air may be fully transferable by rail or water. Poorly developed and costly transportation may inhibit exchanges even at short distance between otherwise willing traders (see "Roads as Barriers in Medieval Europe"). In short, transferability expresses the changing relationships between the costs of transportation and the value of the product to be shipped.

Intervening Opportunity

Complementarity can be effective only in the absence of more attractive alternative sources of supply or demand closer at hand or cheaper. **Intervening opportunities** serve to reduce supply-demand interactions that otherwise might develop between distant complementary areas. A supply of Saharan sand is not enough to assure its flow to sand-deficient Manhattan Island because supplies of sand are more easily and cheaply available within the New York metropolitan region. For reasons of cost and convenience, a purchaser is unlikely to buy identical commodities at a distance when a suitable nearby supply is available. When it is, the intervening opportunity serves to demonstrate complementarity at a shorter distance.

Similarly, markets and destinations are sought, if possible, close at hand. Growing metropolitan demand in California reduces the importance of midwestern markets for western fruit growers. The intervening opportunities offered by Chicago or Philadelphia reduce the number of job seekers from Iowa searching for employment in New York City. More people from New England take winter vacations in Florida, which is relatively near and accessible, than in Southern California, which is not. That is, opportunities that are discerned closer at hand reduce the pull of opportunities offered by a distant destination (Figure 3.3). Patterns of spatial interaction are dynamic, reflecting the changeable structure of apparent opportunity.

Measuring Interaction

Complementarity, transferability, and intervening opportunity—the controlling conditions of commodity movement—help us understand all forms of spatial interaction, including

ROADS AS BARRIERS IN MEDIEVAL EUROPE

Europe at the start of the 12th century was poised for rapid change and growth, sparked by population increase, spread of settlement, and the revival of commerce. That revival and the promise it held for economic specialization and spatial interaction were, however, hampered by the terrible condition of the continent's road network, as the following passage makes clear.

As much use as possible was made of navigable waterways for the movement of bulky and heavy goods, but most were transported overland on the backs of pack animals. Wherever possible the Roman roads were still followed, but these had never been built north of the Danube and east of the Rhine, and elsewhere bridges had in many places collapsed and the roads had fallen into disrepair.

Furthermore, the cities on which the Roman roads had focussed were not necessarily those which the early medieval traveller wished to visit.

Most roads were merely tracks. Bridges were very few, and rivers were generally forded. Many roads, especially in central and eastern Europe, were not clearly defined, consisting of multiple paths through the forest and waste. The Alps aroused considerable fears, and the roads across their passes were avoided whenever possible. Crossing the passes was strenuous and dangerous, but the most hazardous part of the journey was usually the approach to the high mountains. Here, where the roads ran alternately through defiles and wide valleys, they could be more easily blocked and the traveller harassed by robbers and burdened with tolls.

It is convenient to divide Medieval trade into, first, local or short-distance trade and, second, long-distance commerce. The former consisted essentially of the products of agriculture and forestry, which were transported to the nearest monastery, market, or town. In terms of volume the local trade was much the greater. Long-distance commerce consisted in general of luxury goods. Their price, when they reached their destination, included not only the production cost, but also the value added by transport by sea-going ship, by river boat and pack animal, together with the cost of tolls and doubtless a high insurance against all risks which the merchants ran.

Source: Norman J. G. Pounds, *An Historical Geography of Europe, 450 B.C.–A.D. 1330* (New York: Cambridge University Press, 1973).

THEMES AND FUNDAMENTALS OF HUMAN GEOGRAPHY

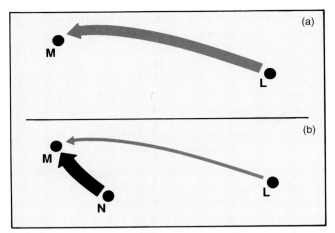

FIGURE 3.3   (a) The volume of expected flow of a good between centers L and M, based solely on their complementarity and distance apart, may be (b) materially reduced if an alternate supplier is introduced as an intervening opportunity nearer to the market.

the placing of long-distance phone calls, the residential locational decisions of commuters, and the once-in-a-lifetime transcontinental adventure of the Hauns. Interaction of whatever nature between places is not, of course, meaningfully described by the movement of a single commodity, by the habits of an individual commuter, or the once-only decision of a migrant. The discovery of an Inuit (Eskimo) ivory carving in a Miami gift shop does not establish significant interaction between the Arctic coast and a Florida resort.

The study of unique events is suggestive but not particularly informative. We seek general principles that govern the frequency and intensity of interaction both to validate the three preconditions of spatial exchange and to establish the probability that any given potential interaction will actually occur. Our interest is similar to that of the physical scientist investigating, for example, the response of a gas to variations in temperature and pressure. The concern there is with *all* of the gas molecules and the probability of their collective reactions; the responses of any particular molecule are of little interest. Similarly, we are concerned here with the probability of aggregate, not individual, behavior.

Distance Decay

In all manner of ways, our lives and activities are influenced by the **friction of distance.** That phrase reminds us that distance has a retarding effect on human interaction because there are increasing penalties in time and cost associated with longer-distance, more expensive interchanges. We visit nearby friends more often than distant relatives; we go more frequently to the neighborhood convenience store cluster than to the farther regional shopping center. Telephone calls or mail deliveries between nearby towns are greater in volume than those to more distant locations.

Our common experience, clearly supported by maps and statistics tracing all kinds of flows, is that most interactions occur over short distances. That is, interchange decreases as distance increases, a reflection of the fact that transferability costs increase with distance. More generally stated, **distance decay** describes the decline of an activity or function with increasing distance from its point of origin. As the examples in Figure 3.4 demonstrate, near destinations have a disproportionate pull over more distant points in commodity movements. However, it is also evident that the rate of distance decay varies with the type of activity.

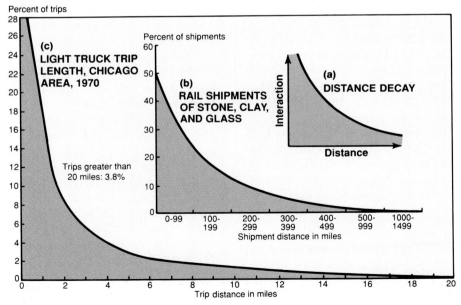

FIGURE 3.4   **The shape of distance decay.** The geographer W. Tobler summarized the concept of distance decay in proposing his "first law of geography: everything is related to everything else, but near things are more related than distant things." Distance decay curves vary with the type of flow: (a) is a generalized statement of distance decay, (b) summarizes U.S. data for 1963, and (c) suggests the primary use of light trucks as short-haul pickup and delivery vehicles.

Study of all manner of spatial interconnections has led to the very general conclusion that interaction between places is inversely related to the square of the distance separating them. That is, volume of flow between two points 80 kilometers (50 miles) apart would probably be only one-quarter of that between centers at 40 kilometers (25 miles) apart. Such a rigid *inverse-square* relationship is well documented in the physical sciences. For social, cultural, and economic relations, however, it is at best a useful approximation. In human interaction, linear distance is only one aspect of transferability; cost and time are often more meaningful measures of separation.

When the friction of distance is reduced by lowered costs or increased ease of flow, the slope of the distance decay curve is flattened and more total area is effectively united than when those costs are high. When telephone calls are charged by uniform area rates rather than strictly by distance, more calls are placed to the outer margins of the rate area than expected. Expressways extend commuting travel ranges to central cities and expand the total area conveniently accessible for weekend recreation. Figure 3.4 shows that shipping distances for high-cost truck transport are, on the average, shorter than for lower-cost rail hauls.

The Gravity Concept

Interaction decisions are not based on distance or distance–cost considerations alone. The large regional shopping center attracts customers from a wide radius because of the variety of shops and goods its very size promises. We go to distant big cities "to seek our fortune" rather than to the nearer small town. We are, that is, attracted by the expectation of opportunity that we associate with larger rather than smaller places. That expectation is summarized by another model of spatial interaction, the **gravity model,** also drawn from the physical sciences.

In the 1850s, Henry C. Carey (1793–1879), in his *Principles of Social Science,* observed that the law of "molecular gravitation" is an essential condition in human existence and that the attractive force existing between areas is akin to the force of gravity. According to Carey, the physical laws of gravity and motion developed by Sir Isaac Newton (1642–1727) have applicability to the aggregate actions of humans.

Newton's *law of universal gravitation* states that any two objects attract each other with a force that is proportional to the product of their masses and inversely proportional to the square of the distance between them. Thus, the force of attraction, F, between two masses, M_i and M_j, separated by distance, d, is

$$F = g \; \frac{M_i M_j}{d_{ij}^2},$$

where g is the "gravitational constant."

Carey's interests were in the interaction between urban centers and in the observation that a large city is more likely to attract an individual than is a small hamlet. His first interest could be quickly satisfied by simple analogy. The expected interaction (I) between two places, i and

j, can be calculated by converting physical mass in the gravity model to population size (P), so that

$$I_{ij} = \frac{P_i P_j}{D_{ij}^2}$$

Exchanges between any set of two cities, A and B, can therefore be quickly estimated:

$$I_{AB} = \frac{\text{population of } A \times \text{population of } B}{(\text{distance between } A \text{ and } B)^2}$$

In social—rather than physical—science applications of the gravity model, distance may be calculated by travel time or travel cost modifications rather than by straight line separation. Whatever the unit of measure, however, the model assures us that although spatial interaction always tends to decrease with increasing distance between places, at a given distance it tends to expand with increases in their size.

Carey's second observation—that large cities have greater drawing power for individuals than small ones—was subsequently addressed by the *law of retail gravitation,* proposed by William J. Reilly (1899–1970) in 1931. Using the population and distance inputs of the gravity model, Reilly concluded that the *breaking point* (BP) or boundary marking the outer edge of either of the cities' trade area could be located by the expression

$$BP = \frac{d_{ij}}{1 + \sqrt{\dfrac{P_2}{P_1}}}$$

where

BP = distance from city 1 to the breaking point (or boundary)
d_{ij} = distance between city 1 and city 2
P_1 = population of city 1
P_2 = population of city 2

Any farm or small town resident located between the two cities would be inclined to shop in one or the other of them according to that resident's position relative to the calculated breaking point. Since the breaking point between cities of unequal size will lie farther from the larger of the two, its spatially greater drawing power is assured (Figure 3.5).

Later studies in location theory, city systems, trade area analysis, and other social topics all suggest that the gravity model can be used to account for a wide variety of flow patterns in human geography, including population migration, commodity flows, journeys to work or to shop, telephone call volumes, and the like. Each such flow pattern suggests that size as well as distance influences spatial interaction. Carey's observation made nearly 150 years ago initiated a type of analysis that has continuing relevance. In modified form it is used today for a variety of practical studies that help us better understand the "friction of distance."

Interaction Potential

Spatial interaction models of distance decay and gravitational pull deal with only two places at a time. The world of reality is rather more complex. All cities, not just city pairs,

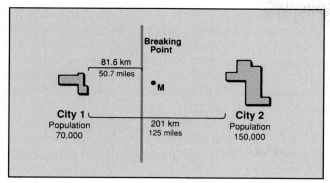

FIGURE 3.5   The *law of retail gravitation* provides a quick determination of the trade boundary (or breaking point) between two cities. In the diagram, cities 1 and 2 are 201 kilometers (125 miles) apart. Reilly's law tells us that the breaking point between them lies 81.6 kilometers (50.7 miles) distant from city 1. A potential customer located at *M*, midway (100.5 km or 62.5 mi) between the cities, would lie well within the trade zone of city 2. A series of such calculations would define the "trade area" of any single city.

within a regional system of cities have the possibility of interacting with each other. Indeed, the more specialized the goods produced in each separate center—that is, the greater their collective complementarity—the more likely is it that such multiple interactions will occur.

A **potential model,** also based on Newtonian physics, provides an estimate of the interaction opportunities available to a center in such a multicentered network. It tells us the relative position of each point in relation to all other places within a region. It does so by summing the size and distance relationships between all points of potential interaction within an area. The concept of potential is applicable whenever the measurement of the intensity of spatial interaction is of concern—as it is in studies of marketing, land values, broadcasting, commuting patterns, and the like.

Movement Biases

Distance decay and the gravity and potential models help us understand the bases for interaction in an idealized area without natural or cultural barriers to movement or restrictions on routes followed, and in which only rational interaction decisions are made. Even under those idealized conditions, the pattern of spatial interaction that develops for whatever reason inevitably affects the conditions under which future interactions will occur. An initial structure of centers and connecting flows will tend to freeze into the landscape a mutually reinforcing continuation of that same pattern. The predictable flows of shoppers to existing shopping centers make those centers attractive to other merchants. New store openings increase customer flow; increased flow strengthens the developed pattern of spatial interaction. And increased road traffic calls for the highway improvement that encourages additional traffic volume.

Such an aggregate regularity of flow is called a **movement bias.** We have already noted a *distance bias* favoring short movements over long. There is also *direction bias,* in which of all possible directions of movement, actual flows are restricted to only one or a few. Direction bias is simply a statement that from a given origin, flows are not random (Figure 3.6); rather, certain places have a greater attraction than do others. The movement patterns from an isolated farmstead are likely oriented to a favored shopping town. On a larger scale, in North America or Siberia long-distance freight movements are directionally biased in favor of east-west flows. Direction bias reflects not just the orientation but also the intensity of flow. Movements from a single point—from Novosibirsk in Siberia, for example, or from Winnipeg, Canada, or Kansas City in the United States—may occur in all directions; they are in reality more intense along the east-west axis.

Such directional biases are in part a reflection of *network bias,* a shorthand way of saying that the presence or absence of connecting channels strongly affects the likelihood that spatial interaction will occur. A set of routes and the set

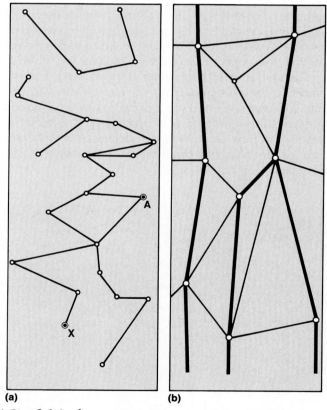

(a)   (b)

FIGURE 3.6   **Direction bias.** (*a*) When direction bias is absent, movements tend to be almost random, occurring in all possible directions, but less likely between points, such as A and X, not directly connected. (*b*) Direction bias indicating predominantly north-south movements. Direction bias implies greatest intensity of movement within a restricted number of directions.

of places that they connect are collectively called a **network.** Flows cannot occur between all points if not all points are linked. In Figure 3.6a, the interchange between A and X, though not necessarily impossible, is unlikely because the routeway between them is indirect and circuitous. In information flows, a worker on the assembly line is less likely to know of company production plans than is a secretary in the executive offices; these two workers are tied into quite different information networks.

A recognition of movement biases helps to refine the coarser generalizations of spatial interaction based on complementarity, transferability, and intervening opportunity. Other modifying statements have been developed, but each further refinement moves us away from aggregate behavior toward less predictable individual movements and responses. The spatial interaction questions we ask and the degree of refinement of the answers we require determine the modifications we must introduce into the models we employ.

Human Spatial Behavior

Humans are not commodities and individually do not necessarily respond predictably to the impersonal dictates of spatial interaction constraints. Yet, to survive, people must be mobile and collectively do react to distance, time, and cost considerations of movement in space and to the implications of complementarity, transferability, and intervening opportunity. Indeed, an exciting line of geographic inquiry involves how individuals make spatial behavioral decisions and how those separate decisions may be summarized by models and generalizations to explain collective actions.

Two aspects of human spatial behavior concern us. The first is the daily or temporary use of space—the journeys to stores or to work or to school. The second is the longer-term commitment related to decisions to travel, to migrate, or to settle away from the home territory. Both aspects imply a time dimension. Humans' spatial actions are not instantaneous. They operate over time, frequently imparting a rhythm to individual and group activity patterns and imposing choices among time-consuming behaviors. Elements of both aspects of human spatial behavior are also embodied in how individuals perceive space and act within it and how they respond to information affecting their space-behavioral decisions.

Individual Activity Space

One of the realities of life is that groups and countries draw boundaries around themselves and divide space into territories that are, if necessary, defended. Some see the concept of **territoriality**—the emotional attachment to and the defense of home ground—as a root explanation of much of human action and response. It is true that some individual and collective activity appears to be governed by territorial defense responses: the conflict between street groups in claiming and protecting their "turf" (and their fear for their lives when venturing beyond it) and the sometimes violent rejection by ethnic urban neighborhoods of an advancing black, Hispanic, or other population group. On a more individualized basis, each of us claims as **personal space** the zone of privacy and separation from others our culture or our physical circumstances require or permit. North Americans demand greater face-to-face separation in conversations than do Latin Americans. Personal space on a crowded beach or in a department store is acceptably more limited than it is in our homes or when we are studying in a library (Figure 3.7).

(a)

(b)

FIGURE 3.7   Our demanded *personal space* is not necessarily uniform in shape or constant in size. We tolerate strangers closer to our sides than directly in front of us; we accept more crowding in an elevator than in a store. We tend to distance ourselves from others in a library, but accept the press of the crowd on a popular beach—as do these vacationers (a) along the Costa Blanca in Spain.

For most of us, our personal sense of territoriality is a tempered one. We regard our homes and property as defensible private domains but open them to innocent visitors, known and unknown, or to those on private or official business. Nor do we confine our activities so exclusively within controlled home territories as street-gang members do within theirs. Rather, we have a more or less extended home range, an **activity space** or area within which we move freely on our rounds of regular activity, sharing that space with others who are also about their daily affairs. Figure 3.8 suggests probable activity spaces for a suburban family of five for a day. Note that the activity space is different and for the mapped day rather limited for each individual, even though two members of the family use automobiles. If one week's activity were shown, more paths would be added to the map.

The types of trips that individuals make and thus the extent of their activity space depend on at least three interrelated variables: their stage in the life cycle; the means of mobility at their command; and the demands or opportunities implicit in their daily activities. The first variable, *stage in the life cycle,* refers to membership in specific age groups. School-age children usually travel short distances to lower schools and longer distances to upper-level schools. After-school activities tend to be limited to walking or bicycle trips to nearby locations. Greater mobility is characteristic of high school students. Adults responsible for household duties make shopping trips and trips related to child care as well as journeys

away from home for social, cultural, or recreational purposes. Wage-earning adults usually travel farther from home than other family members. Elderly people may, through infirmity or interests, have less extensive activity spaces.

The second variable that affects the extent of activity space is *mobility,* or the ability to travel. An informal consideration of the cost and effort required to overcome the friction of distance is implicit. Where incomes are high, automobiles are available, and the cost of fuel is reckoned minor in the family budget, mobility may be great and individual activity space large. In societies or neighborhoods where cars are not a standard means of conveyance, the daily nonemergency activity space may be limited to walking, bicycling, or taking infrequent trips on public transportation. Wealthy suburbanites are far more mobile than are residents of inner-city slums, a circumstance that affects ability to seek or retain work and to have access to medical care, educational facilities, and social services.

A third factor limiting activity space is the individual assessment of the existence of possible activities or *opportunities.* In primitive societies, where the needs of daily life are satisfied at home, the impetus for journeys away from home is minimal. Without stores, schools, factories, or even roads, expectations and opportunities are limited. Not only are activities spatially restricted, but **awareness space**—knowledge of opportunity locations beyond normal activity space—is minimal, distorted, or absent. In low-income neighborhoods of modern cities in any country, poverty

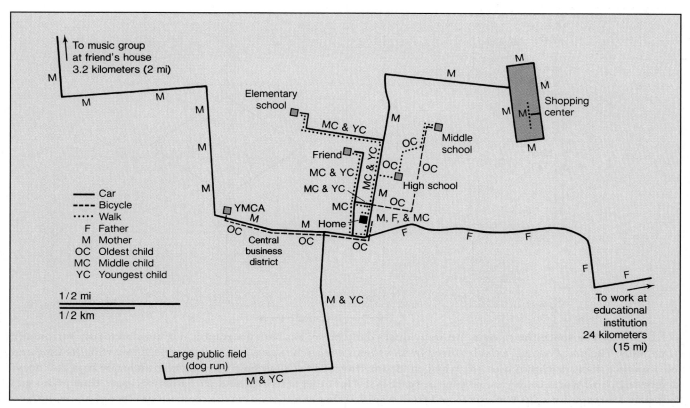

FIGURE 3.8   Activity space for each member of one of the author's family of five for a typical weekday. Routes of regular movement and areas recurrently visited help to foster a sense of territoriality and to color one's perceptions of space.

and isolation restrict access to information about opportunities and therefore reinforce other limitations on activity space (Figure 1.30).

The Tyranny of Time

The daily activities of humans—eating, sleeping, traveling between home and destination (and back), working or attending classes—all consume time as well as involve space. An individual's spatial reach is restricted because one cannot be in two different places at the same moment or engage simultaneously in activities that are spatially separate. Further, since there is a finite amount of time within a day and each of us is biologically bound to a daily rhythm of day and night, sleeping and eating, time tyrannically limits the spatial choices we can make and the activity space we can command.

Our daily space-time constraints—our *time-geography*—may be represented by a **space-time prism,** the volume of space and length of time within which our activities must be confined. Its size and shape are determined by our mobility; its boundaries define what we can or cannot accomplish spatially or temporally (Figure 3.9). If our circumstances demand that we walk to work or school (3.9*b*), the sides of our prism are steep and the space available for our activities is narrow. We cannot use time spent in transit for other activities, and the area reasonably accessible to the pedestrian is limited. The space-time prism for the driver (3.9*c*) has flattened sides and the individual's spatial range is wide. The dimensions of the prism determine what spatially defined activities are possible, for no activity can exceed the bounds of the prism (see "Space, Time, and Women"). Since most activities have their own time constraints, the choices of things you can do and the places you can do them are strictly limited. Defined class hours, travel time from residence to campus, and dining hall location and opening and closing hours, for example, may be the constraints on your *space-time path* (Figure 3.10). If you also need part-time work, your choice of jobs is restricted by their respective locations and work hours, for the job, too, must fit within your daily space-time prism.

Distance and Human Interaction

People make many more short-distance trips than long ones, a statement in human behavioral terms of the concept of *distance decay.* If we drew a boundary line around our activity space, it would be evident that trips to the boundary are taken much less often than short-distance trips around the home. The tendency is for the frequency of trips to fall off very rapidly beyond an individual's **critical distance**—the distance beyond which cost, effort, and means strongly influence our willingness to travel. Figure 3.11 illustrates the point with regard to journeys from the homesite.

Regular movements defining our individual activity space are undertaken for different purposes and are differently influenced by time and distance considerations. The kind of activities individuals engage in can be classified according to type of trip: journeys to work, to school, to shop,

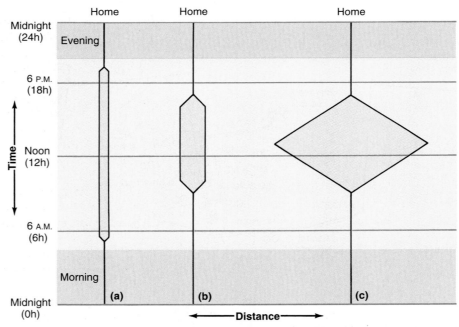

FIGURE 3.9   **The space-time prism.** An individual's daily prism has both geographical limits and totally surrounding space-time walls. The *time* (vertical axis) involved in movement affects the space that is accessible, along with the time and space available for other than travel purposes. (*a*) When collecting firewood for household use may take an entire day, as it does in some deforested Third World countries, no time or space is left for other activities, and the gatherer's space-time prism may be represented by a straight line. (*b*) Walking to and from work or school and spending the required number of hours there leave little time to broaden one's area of activity. (*c*) The automobile permits an extension of the geographical boundaries of the driver's space-time prism; the range of activity possibilities and locations is expanded for the highly mobile.

THEMES AND FUNDAMENTALS OF HUMAN GEOGRAPHY

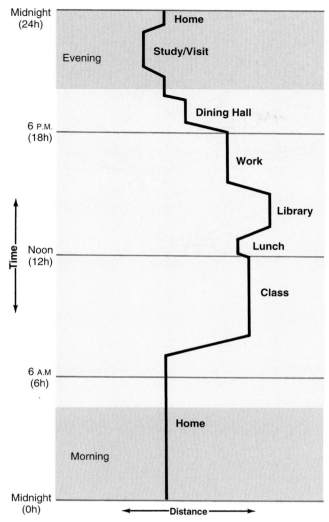

FIGURE 3.10 School-day space-time path for a hypothetical college student.

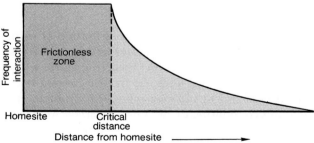

FIGURE 3.11 **Critical distance.** This general diagram indicates how most people observe distance. For each activity, there is a distance beyond which the intensity of contact declines. This is called the *critical distance* if distance alone is being considered, or the *critical isochrone* (from Greek *isos,* "equal," and *chronos,* "time") if time is the measuring rod. The distance up to the critical distance, is identified as a *frictionless zone,* in which time or distance considerations do not effectively figure in the trip decision.

for recreation, and so on. People in nearly all parts of the world make these same types of journeys, though the spatially variable requirements of culture, economy, and personal circumstance dictate their frequency, duration, and significance to an individual (Figure 3.12). A small child, for example, will make many trips up and down the block but is inhibited by parental admonitions from crossing the street. Different but equally effective distance constraints control adult behavior.

The journey to work plays a decisive role in defining the activity space of most adults. Formerly restricted by walking distance or by the routes and schedules of mass transit systems, the critical distances of work trips have steadily increased in Western European and North American cities as the private automobile figures more importantly in the movement of workers (Figure 3.13). Daily or weekly shopping may be within the critical distance of an individual, and little thought may be given to the cost or the effort involved. That same individual, however, may relegate shopping for special goods to infrequent trips and carefully consider their cost and effort. The majority of our social contacts tend to be at short distance within our own neighborhoods or with friends who live relatively close at hand; longer social trips to visit relatives are less frequent. In all such trips, however, the distance decay function is clearly at work (Figure 3.14).

Spatial Interaction and the Accumulation of Information

Critical distances, even for the same activity, are different for each person. The variables of life-cycle stage, mobility, and opportunity, together with an individual's interests and demands, help define how often and how far a person will travel. On the basis of these variables, we can make inferences about the amount of information a person is likely to acquire about his or her activity space and the area beyond. The accumulation of information about the opportunities and rewards of spatial interaction helps increase and justify movement decisions.

For information flows, however, space has a different meaning than it does for the movement of commodities. Communication, for example, does not necessarily imply the time-consuming physical relocations of freight transportation (though in the case of letters and print media it usually does). Indeed, in modern telecommunications, the process of information flow may be instantaneous regardless of distance. The result is space-time convergence to the point of the obliteration of space. A Bell System report tells us that in 1920, putting through a transcontinental telephone call took 14 minutes and eight operators. By 1940, the call completion time was reduced to less than 1½ minutes. In the 1960s, direct distance dialing allowed a transcontinental connection in less than 30 seconds, and electronic switching has now reduced the completion time to that involved in dialing a number and answering a phone.

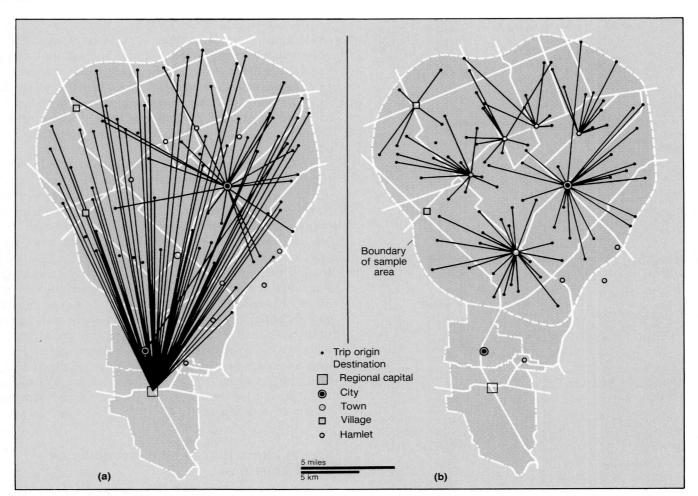

FIGURE 3.12 **Travel patterns for purchases of clothing and yard goods** of (*a*) rural cash-economy Canadians and (*b*) Canadians of the Old Order Mennonite sect. These strikingly different travel behaviors demonstrate the great differences that may exist in the action spaces of different culture groups occupying the same territory in midwestern Canada. They suggest that "modern" rural Canadians, owning cars and wishing to take advantage of the variety of goods offered in the more distant regional capital, are willing to travel longer distances than are people of a traditionalist culture who have different mobility and whose different demands in clothing and other consumer goods are satisfied in nearby small settlements.

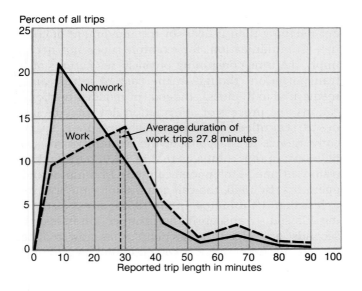

FIGURE 3.13 **The frequency distribution of work and nonwork trip lengths in minutes in Toronto.** Work trips are usually longer than other recurring journeys. In the United States, the average work trip in 1990 covered 17.1 kilometers (10.6 miles) and took about 19.7 minutes; for suburbanites commuting to the central business district, the journey to work took between 30 and 45 minutes. In western Canada, average work trip length in Calgary and Edmonton, Alberta, was 11 kilometers (6.8 miles) and took 18 minutes. For North American metropolitan areas, at least, 20 to 30 minutes seemed to be the upper limit of commuting time before people began to consider time and distance to work seriously in their choice of homesite. Most nonwork trips are relatively short.

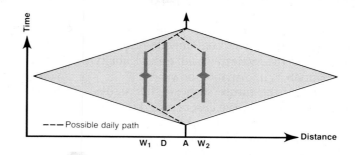

From a time-geographic perspective it is apparent that many of the limitations women face in their choices of employment or other activities outside the home reflect the restrictions that women's time budgets and travel paths place on their individual daily activity mixes.

Consider the case* of the unmarried working woman with one or more children of preschool age. The location and operating hours of available child-care facilities may have more of an influence on her choice of job than do her labor skills or the relative merits of alternative employment opportunities. From the diagram we see that the woman cannot leave her home base, A, before a given hour because the only available full-day child-care service, D, is not open earlier. She must return at the specified child pick-up time and arrive home to prepare food at a reasonable (for the child) dinnertime. Her travel mode and speed determine the outer limits of her daily space-time prism.

Both of two solid job offers, W_1 and W_2, have the same working hours and fall within her space-time prism. The preferred, better paying job is W_2, but she cannot accept it because drop-off time at the child-care center would make her late for work, and work hours would make her miss the center's closing time. On the other hand, although W_1 is acceptable from a child-care standpoint, it leaves no time (or store options) for shopping or errands except during the lunch hour (indicated by the small subprism). Job choice and shopping opportunities are thus determined not by the woman's labor skills or awareness of store price comparisons but by her time-geographic constraints. Other women in other job-skill, parenthood, locational, or mobility circumstances experience different but comparable space-path restrictions.

Mobility is a key to activity mix, time-budget, and space-path configurations. Again, research indicates that women are frequently disadvantaged. Because of their multiple work, child-care, and home maintenance tasks, women on average make more—though shorter—trips than men, leaving less time for alternate activities. Although the automobile reduces those time demands, women have less access to cars than do males, in part because in many cities they are less likely to have a driver's license and because they typically cede use of a single family car to husbands. The lower income level of many single women with or without children limits their ability to own cars and leads them to use public transit disproportionately to their numbers—to the detriment of both their money and time-space budgets. They are, it has been observed, "transportation deprived and transit dependent."

*Suggested by Risa Palm and Allan Pred, *A Time-Geographic Perspective on Problems of Inequality for Women.* Institute of Urban and Regional Development, Working Paper no. 236. University of California, Berkeley, 1974.

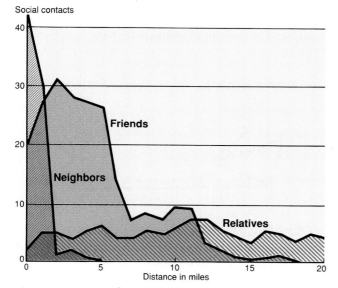

FIGURE 3.14 **Social interaction as a function of distance.** Visits with neighbors on the same street are frequent; they are less common with neighbors around the corner and diminish quickly to the vanishing point after a residential relocation. Friends exert a greater spatial pull, though the distance decay factor is clearly evident. Visits with relatives offer the greatest incentive for longer-distance (though relatively infrequent) journeys.

Internet and communication satellites have made worldwide personal and mass communication immediate and data transfers for economic integration instantaneous. The same technologies that have led to communication space-time convergence have tended toward a space-cost convergence (Figure 3.15). Domestic mail, which once charged a distance-based postage, is now carried nationwide or across town for the same price. In the modern world, transferability is no longer a consideration in information flows.

A speculative view of the future suggests that as distance ceases to be a determinant of the cost or speed of communication, the spatial structure of economic and social decision making may be fundamentally altered. Determinations about where people live and work, the role of cities and other existing command centers, flows of domestic and international trade, constraints on human mobility, and even the concepts and impacts of national boundaries may fundamentally change with new and unanticipated consequences for patterns of spatial interaction.

Information Flows

Spatially significant information flows are of two types: individual (person-to-person) exchanges and mass (source-to-area) communication. A further subdivision into formal and informal interchange recognizes, in the former, the need for an interposed channel (radio, press, postal service, or telephone, for example) to convey messages. Informal communication requires no such institutionalized message carrier.

Short-range informal individual communication is as old as humankind itself. Contacts and exchanges between individuals and within small groups tend to increase as the complexity of social organization increases, as the size and importance of the population center grows, and as the range of interests and associations of the communicating person expands. Each individual develops a **personal communication field,** the informational counterpart of that person's activity space. Its size and shape are defined by the individual's contacts in work, recreation, shopping, school, or other regular activities. Those activities, as we have seen, are functions of the age, sex, education, employment, income, and so on of each person. An idealized personal communication field is suggested in Figure 3.16.

Each interpersonal exchange constitutes a link in the individual's personal communication field. Each person, in turn, is a node in the communication field of those with whom he or she makes or maintains contact. The total number of such separate informal networks equals the total count of people alive. Despite the number of those networks, all people, in theory, are interconnected by multiple shared nodes (Figure 3.17). Experimentation has demonstrated that through such interconnections, no person in the United States is more than five links removed from any other person, no matter where located or how unlikely the association.

Mass communication is the formal, structured transmission of information in essentially a one-way flow between single points of origin and broad areas of reception. There are few transmitters and many receivers. The mass media are by nature "space filling." From single origin points they address their messages by print, radio, or television to potential receivers within a defined area. The number and location of disseminating points, therefore, are related to their spatial coverage characteristics, to the minimum size of area and population necessary for their support, and to the capability of the potential audiences to receive their message. The coverage area is determined both by the nature of the medium and by the corporate intent of the agency.

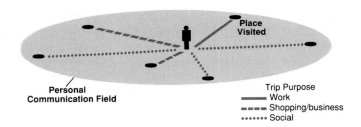

FIGURE 3.16   **A personal communication field** is determined by individual spatial patterns of communication related to work, shopping, business trips, social visits, and so on.

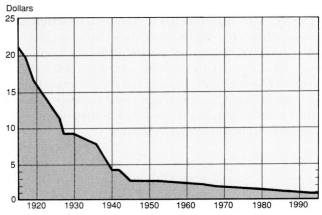

FIGURE 3.15   **Space-cost convergence in telephone tolls** between New York and San Francisco, 1915–1995. The rates shown are a smooth-curve summary of frequently adjusted charges for station-to-station daytime 3-minute calls.

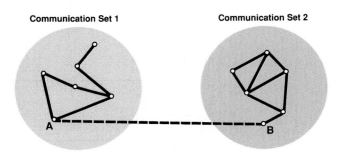

FIGURE 3.17   Separate population sets are interconnected by the links between individuals. If link *A–B* exists, everyone in the two sets is linked.

THEMES AND FUNDAMENTALS OF HUMAN GEOGRAPHY

There are no inherent spatial restrictions on the dissemination of printed materials. In the United States, much book and national magazine publishing has localized in New York City, as have the services supplying news and features for sale to the print media located there and elsewhere in the country. Paris, Buenos Aires, Moscow, London—indeed, the major metropolises and/or capital cities of other countries—show the same spatial concentration. Regional journals emanate from regional capitals, and major metropolitan newspapers, though serving primarily their home market, are distributed over (or produce special editions for distribution within) tributary areas whose size and shape depend on the intensity of competition from other metropolises. A spatial information hierarchy has thus emerged.

Hierarchies are also reflected in the market-size requirements for different levels of media offerings. National and international organizations are required to expedite information flows (and, perhaps, to control their content), but market demand is heavily weighted in favor of regional and local coverage. In the electronic media, the result has been national networks with local affiliates acting as the gatekeepers of network offerings, and adding to them locally originating programs and news content. A similar market subdivision is represented by the regional editions of national newspapers and magazines. At a different scale, the spatial distribution of newspapers in Kansas (Figure 3.18) shows their hierarchical pattern.

The technological ability to fill space with messages from different mass media is useless if receiving audiences do not exist. In illiterate societies, publications cannot inform or influence. Unless the appropriate receivers are widely available, television and radio broadcasts are a waste of resources. Perhaps no invention in history has done more to weld isolated individuals and groups of purely person-to-person communicators into national societies exposed to centralized information flows than has the low-cost transistor radio. Its battery-powered transportability converts the remotest village and the most isolated individual into a receiving node of entertainment, information, and political messages. The direct satellite broadcast of television programs to community antennae or communal sets brings that mass medium to remote areas of Arctic Canada, India, Indonesia, and other world areas able to invest in the technology but as yet unserved by ground stations.

Information and Perception

Human spatial interaction, as we have seen, is conditioned by a number of factors. Complementarity, transferability, and intervening opportunities help pattern the movement of commodities and peoples. Flows between points and over area are influenced by distance decay and partially explained by gravity and potential models. Individuals in their daily affairs operate in activity spaces that are partly determined by stage in life cycle, mobility, and a variety of socioeconomic characteristics. In every instance of spatial interaction, however, decisions are based on information about opportunity or feasibility of movement, exchange, or want satisfaction.

More precisely, actions and decisions are based on **place perception**—the awareness we have, as individuals, of home and distant places and the beliefs we hold about them. Place perception involves our feelings and understandings, reasoned or irrational, about the natural and cultural characteristics of an area and about its opportunity structure. Whether our view accords with that of others or truly reflects the "real" world seen in abstract descriptive terms is not the major concern. Our perceptions are the important thing, for the decisions people make about the use of their lives or about their actions in space are based not necessarily on reality but on their assumptions and impressions of reality.

Perception of Environment

Psychologists and geographers are interested in determining how we arrive at our perceptions of place and environment both within and beyond our normal activity space. The images we form firsthand of our home territory have been in

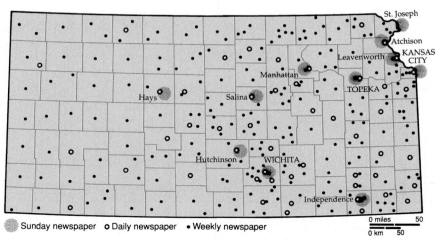

FIGURE 3.18   The hierarchy of newspaper coverage in Kansas in the 1970s. The counties in sparsely populated western Kansas had only weekly papers. The more populous eastern part of the state had daily and Sunday papers, with wide-area distribution.

part reviewed in the discussion of mental maps in Chapter 1. The perceptions we have of more distant places are less directly derived (Figure 3.19). In technologically advanced societies, television and radio, magazines and newspapers, books and lectures, travel brochures and hearsay all combine to help us develop a mental picture of unfamiliar places and of the interaction opportunities they may contain. Again, however, the most effectively transmitted information seems to come from word-of-mouth reports. These may be in the form of letters or visits from relatives, friends, and associates who supply information that helps us develop lines of attachment to relatively unknown areas.

There are, of course, barriers to the flow of information, including that of distance decay. Our knowledge of close places is greater than our knowledge of distant points; our contacts with nearby persons theoretically yield more information than we receive from afar. Yet in crowded areas with maximum interaction potential, people commonly set psychological barriers around themselves so that only a limited number of those possible interactions and information exchanges actually occur. We raise barriers against information overload and to preserve a sense of privacy that permits the filtering out of information that does not directly affect us. There are obvious barriers to long-distance information flows as well, such as time and money costs, mountains, oceans, rivers, and differing religions, languages, ideologies, and political systems.

Barriers to information flow give rise to what we earlier (page 69) called *direction bias*. In the present usage, this implies a tendency to have greater knowledge of places in some directions than in others. Not having friends or relatives in one part of a country may represent a barrier to individuals, so that interest in and knowledge of the area beyond the "unknown" region are low. In the United States, both northerners and southerners tend to be less well informed about each other's areas than about the western part of the country. Traditional communication lines in the United States follow an east-west rather than a north-south direction, the result of early migration patterns, business connections, and the pattern of the development of major cities. In Russia, directional bias favors a north-south information flow within the European part of the country and less familiarity with areas far to the east. Within Siberia, however, east-west flows dominate.

When information about a place is sketchy, blurred pictures develop. These influence the impression—the perception—we have of places and cannot be discounted. Many important decisions are made on the basis of incomplete information or biased reports, such as decisions to visit or not, to migrate or not, to hate or not, even to make war or not. Awareness of places is usually accompanied by opinions about them, but there is no necessary relationship between the depth of knowledge and the perceptions held. In general, the more familiar we are with a locale, the more sound the factual basis of our mental image of it will be. But individuals form firm impressions of places totally unknown to them personally, and these may color interaction decisions.

One way to determine how individuals envisage home or distant places is to ask them what they think of different locales. For instance, they may be asked to rate places ac-

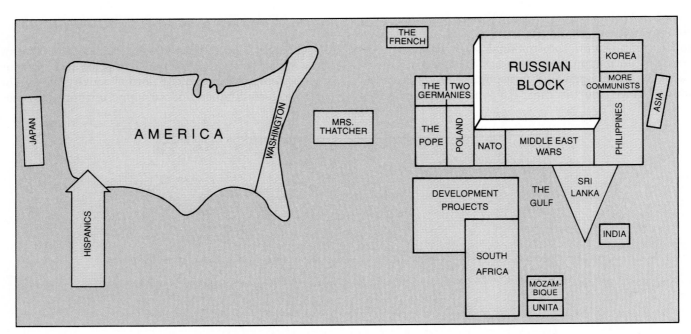

FIGURE 3.19   A view of the world as fashioned from newscasts heard by a Peace Corps volunteer working in the Central African Republic. The map is based on several months of listening to the Africa Service of the Voice of America (VOA) during 1987. Both areas and topics shown were those in the news and selected for emphasis by the broadcasters, whose choices helped form the mental maps and awareness patterns of their listeners. The "Russian Block" took on a three-dimensional reality not intended by the VOA.

cording to desirability—perhaps residential desirability—or to make a list of the 10 best and the 10 worst cities in their country of residence. Certain regularities appear in such inquiries. Figure 3.20 presents some residential desirability data elicited from college students in three provinces of Canada. These and comparable mental maps derived from studies conducted by researchers in many countries suggest that near places are preferred to far places unless much information is available about the far places. Places of similar culture are favored, as are places with high standards of living. Individuals tend to be indifferent to unfamiliar places and areas and to dislike those that have competing interests (such as distasteful political and military activities or conflicting economic concerns) or a physical environment perceived to be unpleasant.

On the other hand, places perceived to have superior climates or landscape amenities are rated highly in mental map studies and favored in tourism and migration deci-sions. The southern and southwestern coast of England is attractive to citizens of generally wet and cloudy Britain, and holiday tours to Spain, the south of France, and the Mediterranean islands are heavily booked by the English. A U.S. Census Bureau study indicates that "climate" is, after work and family proximity, the most often reported reason for interstate moves by adult individuals of all ages. International studies reveal a similar migration motivation based not only on climate but also on concepts of natural beauty and amenities.

Perception of Natural Hazards

Less certain is the negative impact on spatial interaction or relocation decisions of assessments of *natural hazards,* processes or events in the physical environment that are not caused by humans but that have consequences harmful to them. Distinction is made between chronic, low-level hazards

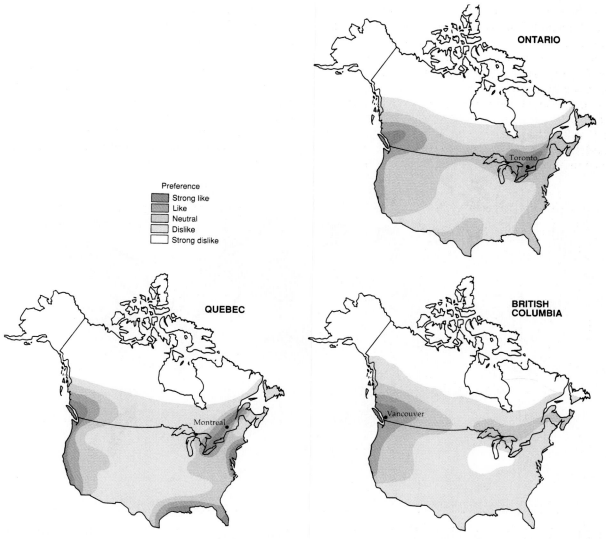

FIGURE 3.20 **Residential preferences of Canadians.** Each of these maps shows the residential preference of a sampled group of Canadians from the provinces of British Columbia, Ontario, and Quebec, respectively. Note that each group of respondents prefers its own area, but all like the Canadian and U.S. west coasts.

(health-affecting mineral content of drinking water, for example) and high-consequence/low-probability events such as hurricanes, earthquakes, landslides, and the like. Remedial low-level hazards do not appear to create negative space perceptions, though highly publicized chronic natural conditions, such as suspected cancer-related radon emissions (Figure 3.21) may be an exception. Space perception studies do reveal, however, a small but measurable adverse assessment of locales deemed "dangerous," no matter what the statistical probability of the hazard occurring.

Mental images of home areas do not generally include as an overriding concern an acknowledgment of potential natural dangers. The cyclone that struck the delta area of Bangladesh on November 12, 1970, left dead at least 500,000 people, yet after the disaster the movement of people into the area swelled the population above precyclone levels—a resettlement repeated after other cyclones in 1985 and 1991. The July 28, 1976, earthquake in the Tangshan area of China devastated a major urban-industrial complex, with casualties estimated to lie between 700,000 and 1 million. Rebuilding began almost immediately, as it usually does following earth-

quake damage (Figure 3.22). The human response to even such major and exceptional natural hazards is duplicated by a general tendency to discount dangers from more common hazard occurrences. Johnstown, Pennsylvania, has suffered recurrent floods, and yet its residents rebuild; violent storms strike the Gulf and East coasts of the United States, and people remain or return. Californians may be concerned about Kansas tornadoes if contemplating a move there but be unconcerned about earthquake dangers at home.

Why do people choose to settle in areas of high-consequence hazards in spite of the potential threat to their lives and property? Why do hundreds of thousands of people live along the San Andreas fault in California, build houses in Pacific coastal areas known to experience severe erosion during storms, return to flood-prone river valleys in Europe or Asia, or avalanche-threatened Andean valleys? What is it that makes the risk worth taking? Ignorance of natural hazard danger is not necessarily a consideration. People in seismically active regions of the United States and Europe, at least, do believe that damaging earthquakes are a possibility in their districts but, research indicates, are reluctant to do

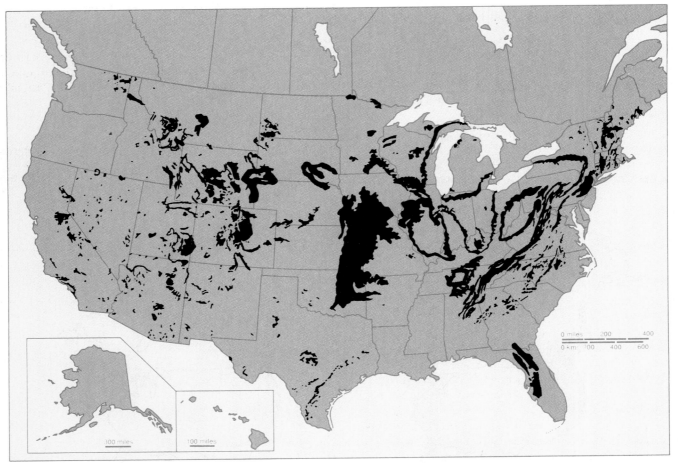

FIGURE 3.21   **Areas with potentially high radon levels.** The radon "scare" began in 1984 with the discovery that a Pennsylvania family was being exposed in its home to the equivalent of 455,000 chest X rays per year. With the estimate that as many as 20% of the nation's annual lung-cancer deaths may be attributable to radon, homeowners and seekers were made aware of a presumed new but localized environmental hazard.

THEMES AND FUNDAMENTALS OF HUMAN GEOGRAPHY

FIGURE 3.22 Destruction from the San Francisco earthquake and fire. The first shock struck San Francisco early on the morning of April 18, 1906, damaging the city's water system. Fire broke out and raged for three days. It was finally stopped by dynamiting buildings in its path. When it was over, some 500 people were dead or missing, and 25,000 buildings had been destroyed. Locally, the event is usually referred to as the Great Fire of 1906, suggesting a denial of the natural hazard in favor of assigning blame to correctable human error. Post-destruction reconstruction began at once. Rebuilding following earthquake damage is the rule, though the immediate return of population to northern Italian areas after a major quake in 1976 was followed by an abrupt exodus after a subsequent, much weaker shock.

anything about the risk. Similar awareness and reticence accompanies other low-incidence/high-consequence natural dangers. Less than one-tenth of 1% of respondents to a federal survey in the mid-1970s gave "natural disaster" as the reason for their interstate residential move.

There are many reasons why natural hazard risk does not deter settlement or adversely affect space-behavioral decisions. Of importance, of course, is the persistent belief that the likelihood of an earthquake or a flood or other natural calamity is sufficiently remote so that it is not reasonable or pressing to modify behavior because of it. People are influenced by their innate optimism and the predictive uncertainty about timing or severity of a calamitous event and by their past experiences in high-hazard areas. If they have not suffered much damage in the past, they may be optimistic about the future. If, on the other hand, past damage has been great, they may think that the probability of repetition in the future is low (Table 3.1).

Perception of place as attractive or desirable may be quite divorced from any understanding of its hazard potential. Attachment to locale or region may be an expression of emotion and economic or cultural attraction, not just a rational assessment of risk. The culture hearths of antiquity

TABLE 3.1	Common Responses to the Uncertainty of Natural Hazards
ELIMINATE THE HAZARD	
Deny or Denigrate Its Existence	*Deny or Denigrate Its Recurrence*
"We have no floods here, only high water."	"Lightning never strikes twice in the same place."
"It can't happen here."	"It's a freak of nature."
ELIMINATE THE UNCERTAINTY	
Make It Determinate and Knowable	*Transfer Uncertainty to a Higher Power*
"Seven years of great plenty . . . After them seven years of famine."	"It's in the hands of God."
"Floods come every five years."	"The government is taking care of it."

Burton and Kates, "The Perception of Natural Hazards in Resource Management," 3 *Natural Resources Journal* 435 (1964). Used by permission of the University of New Mexico School of Law, Albuquerque, NM.

discussed in Chapter 2 and shown on Figure 2.16 were for the most part sited in flood-prone river valleys; their enduring attraction was undiminished by that potential danger. The home area, whatever disadvantages an outside observer may discern, exerts a force not easily dismissed or ignored.

Indeed, high-hazard areas are often sought out because they possess desirable topography or scenic views, as do, for instance, coastal areas subject to storm damage. Once people have purchased property in a known hazard area, they may be unable to sell it for a reasonable price even if they so desire. They think that they have no choice but to remain and protect their investment. The cultural hazard—loss of livelihood and investment—appears more serious than whatever natural hazards there may be.

Carried further, it has been observed that spatial adjustment to perceived natural hazards is a luxury not affordable to impoverished people in general or to the urban and rural poor of Third World countries in particular. Forced by population growth and economic necessity to exert ever-greater pressures on fragile environments or to occupy at higher densities hazardous hillside and flood-plain slums, their margin of safety in the face of both chronic and low-probability hazards is minimal to nonexistent (Figure 3.23).

FIGURE 3.23   Many of the poor of Rio de Janeiro, Brazil, occupy steep hillside locations above the reach of sewer, water, and power lines that hold the more affluent at lower elevations. Frequent heavy rains cause mudflows from the saturated hillsides that wipe away the shacks and shelters that insecurely cling to them, and deposit the homes and hopes of the poor in richer neighborhoods below.

Migration

When continental glaciers began their retreat some 11,000 years ago, the activity space and awareness space of Stone Age humans were limited. As a result of pressures of numbers, need for food, changes in climate, and other inducements, those spaces were collectively enlarged to encompass the world. **Migration**—the permanent relocation of residential place and activity space—has been one of the enduring themes of human history. It has contributed to the evolution of separate cultures, to the diffusion of those cultures and their components by interchange and communication, and to the frequently complex mix of peoples and cultures found in different areas of the world.

Massive movements of people within countries, across national borders, and between continents have emerged as a pressing concern of the late 20th century. They affect national economic structures, determine population density and distribution patterns, alter traditional ethnic, linguistic, and religious mixtures, and inflame national debates and international tensions. Because migration patterns and conflicts touch so many aspects of social and economic relations and have become so important a part of current human geographic realities, their specific impact becomes an important part of several of our topical concerns. Portions of the story of migration have been touched on already in Chapter 2; other elements of it are part of later discussions of population (Chapter 4), ethnicity (Chapter 6), economic development (Chapter 10), urbanization (Chapter 11), and international political relations (Chapter 12). Because migration is, above all, the result of individual and family decisions, our interest here is with migration as an unmistakable, recurring, and near-universal expression of human spatial behavior. Reviewing that behavioral basis of migration now will give us common ground for understanding its impacts in other contexts later.

Migration embodies all the principles of spatial interaction and space relations we have already reviewed. Complementarity, transferability, and intervening opportunities and barriers all play a role. Space information and perception are important, as are the sociocultural and economic characteristics of the migrants and the distance relationships between their original and prospective locations of settlement. In less abstract terms, mass and individual migration decisions may express real-life responses to poverty, rapid population growth, environmental deterioration, or international and civil conflict or war. In its current troubling dimensions, migration may be as much a strategy for survival as an unforced but reasoned response to economic and social opportunity.

Although all spatial movement incorporates the same theoretical interaction principles, not all long-distance interaction involves migration. That term is reserved for movements presumed to be permanent relocations, though seasonal and short-term moves are often imprecisely considered "migratory" (Figure 3.24). Naturally, the length of

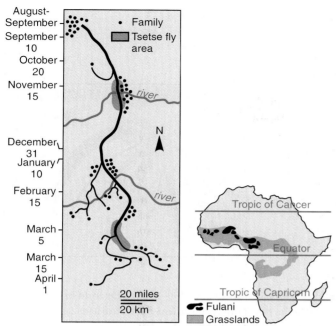

FIGURE 3.24 **Fulani movement paths.** Nomadic people have regular routes of "migration" that involve near-continuous movement in response to the needs of their herds or flocks. Their moves are always temporary and involve a circuit, not a one-way flow. The groups of Fulani families herd their cattle within the savanna of West Africa. On their southward trek during the dry season, the groups separate; when returning north during the wet season, they reunite. Migration circuits may be changed annually in response to the availability of pasture and the location of areas free of the tsetse fly, the transmitter of "sleeping sickness."

the move and its degree of disruption of established activity space patterns raise distinctions important in the study of migration. A change of residence from the central city to the suburbs certainly changes both residence and activity space of schoolchildren and of adults in many of their non-working activities. But the working adults may still retain the city—indeed, the same place of employment there—as an action space. On the other hand, immigration from Europe to the United States and the massive farm-to-city movements of rural Americans late in the 19th and early in the 20th centuries meant a total change of all aspects of behavioral patterns.

Principal Migration Patterns

Migration flows may be discussed at different scales, from massive intercontinental torrents to individual decisions to move to a new house or apartment within the same metropolitan area. At each level, the factors influencing the spatial interaction are different, with differing impacts on population patterns and cultural landscapes.

At the broadest scale, *intercontinental* movements range from the earliest peopling of the habitable world to the most recent flight of Asian refugees to countries of Europe or the Western Hemisphere. The population structure

of the United States, Canada, Australia and New Zealand, Argentina, Brazil, and other South American countries—as Chapter 4 suggests—is a reflection and result of massive intercontinental flows of immigrants that began as a trickle during the 16th and 17th centuries and reached a flood during the 19th and early 20th (Figure 4.20). World War II and its immediate aftermath involved more than 25 million permanent population relocations, all of them international but not all intercontinental.

Intracontinental and *interregional* migrations involve movements between countries and within countries, most commonly in response to individual and group assessments of improved economic conditions or changes in life cycle, but often reflecting flight from disastrous environmental, economic, or political conditions. The millions of actual and potential refugees from adverse circumstances in their homelands following the dissolution of Eastern European communist states and economic systems exemplify that kind of flight. Between 1980 and 1995, Europe received some 17 million migrants, often refugees, who joined the 15 million labor migrants ("guest workers") already in West European countries in the early 1980s (Figure 3.25).

North America has its counterparts in the hundreds of thousands of immigrants coming (many illegally) to the United States each year from Mexico, Central America, and the Caribbean region. The Hauns, whose westward trek opened this chapter, were part of a massive 19th-century regional shift of Americans that continues today (Figure 3.26). The former USSR experienced a similar, though eastward, flow of people in this century. Some 100 million people—nearly 2% of world population—lived in a country other than the country of their birth in the mid-1990s, and migration had become a world social, economic, and political issue of first priority.

In the 20th century, nearly all countries have experienced a great movement of peoples from agricultural areas to the cities, continuing a pattern of *rural-to-urban* migration that first became prominent during the 18th- and 19th-century Industrial Revolution in advanced economies, and now is even more massive than international migrant flows. While the rate of urban growth is decreasing in the more developed countries, urbanization in the developing world continues apace, as will be discussed more fully in Chapter 11.

Types of Migration

Migrations may be forced or voluntary or, in many instances, reluctant relocations imposed on the migrants by circumstances.

In *forced migrations,* the relocation decision is made solely by people other than the migrants themselves (Figure 3.27). Perhaps 10 to 12 million Africans were forcibly transferred as slaves to the Western Hemisphere from the late 16th to early 19th centuries. Half or more were destined for the Caribbean and most of the remainder for Central and South America, though nearly a million arrived in the United States. Australia owed its earliest European settlement to convicts

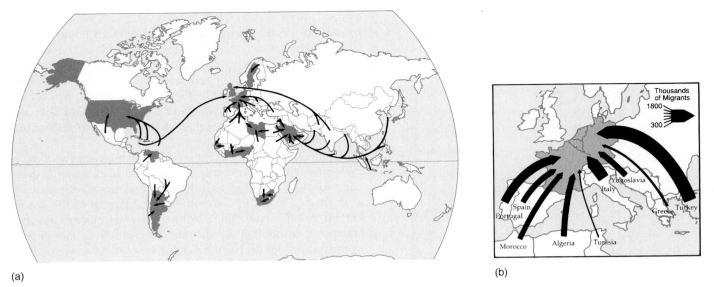

(a)

(b)

FIGURE 3.25   International labor flows. (*a*) Major international labor migration flows 1960–1980. The industries of Western Europe, oil and construction work in Arabia, mining in South Africa, urban and agricultural opportunities in the United States, and similar economic attractions elsewhere sparked international labor movements from widely scattered source regions. Economic stagnation and domestic unemployment in many economies in the later 1980s and 1990s changed both the incidence of perceived opportunity for labor migrants and the willingness of formerly receptive countries to accept them. (*b*) European "guest worker" flows. For prosperous, but labor-short Western Europe (West Germany, France, Belgium, Netherlands, and Switzerland), major source regions for labor immigrants in the early 1980s were southern and southeastern Europe, Turkey, and North Africa.

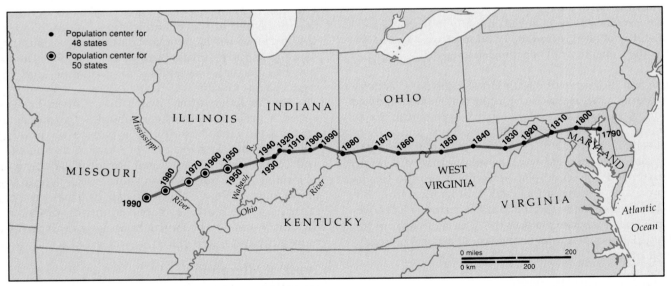

FIGURE 3.26   Westward shift of population, 1790–1990. Two hundred years of western migration and population growth are recorded by the changing U.S. center of population. (The "center of population" is that point at which a rigid map of the United States would balance, reflecting the identical weights of all residents in their location on the census date.) The westward movement was rapid for the first 100 years of census history and slowed between 1890 and 1950. Some of the post-1950 acceleration reflects population growth in the "Sunbelt." However, the two different locations for the population center in 1950 and the symbol change indicate the geographical pull on the center of population exerted by the admission of Alaska and Hawaii to statehood.

THEMES AND FUNDAMENTALS OF HUMAN GEOGRAPHY

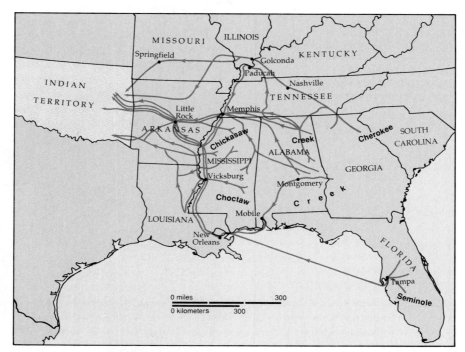

FIGURE 3.27   **Forced migrations: The Five Civilized Tribes.** Between 1825 and 1840, some 100,000 southeastern Amerindians were removed from their homelands and transferred by the Army across the Mississippi River to "Indian Territory" in present-day Oklahoma. By far the largest number were members of the Five Civilized Tribes of the South: Cherokees, Choctaws, Chickasaws, Creeks, and Seminoles. Settled, Christianized, literate small-farmers, their forced eviction and arduous journey—particularly along what the Cherokees named their "Trail of Tears" in the harsh winter of 1837–1838—resulted in much suffering and death.

transported after the 1780s to the British penal colony established in southeastern Australia (New South Wales). More recent involuntary migrants include millions of Soviet citizens forcibly relocated from countryside to cities and from the western areas to labor camps in Siberia and the Russian Far East beginning in the late 1920s. Nigeria expelled 2 million foreign workers in 1983 and another 700,000 in 1985 to reduce unemployment among its own citizens. Germany and other European countries restricted immigration and encouraged repatriation of foreign nationals within their borders beginning in 1990. Other examples abound.

Less than fully voluntary migration—*reluctant relocation*—of some 6 million Indonesians has taken place under an aggressive governmental campaign begun in 1969 to move people from densely settled Jawa (Java, roughly 580 per km² or 1500 people per sq. mi.) to other islands and territories of the country in what has been called the "biggest colonization program in history." International refugees from war and political turmoil or repression annually numbered some 20 million or more in the mid-1990s, according to the United Nations and the World Refugee Survey. In the past, refugees sought asylum mainly in Europe and other developed areas. More recently, the flight of people is primarily from developing countries to other developing regions, and many countries with the largest refugee populations are among the world's poorest. About 80% of

the officially recorded refugees have found asylum in Southeast Asia, southern and eastern Africa, the Near East and South Asia, and South and Central America (Table 3.2). Sub-Saharan Africa alone housed some 6 million refugees in 1995 (Figure 3.28). Worldwide, an additional 26 million people are "internally displaced." In a search for security or sustenance, they have left their home areas but not crossed an international boundary.

The great majority of migratory movements, however, are *voluntary* (volitional), representing individual response to the factors influencing all spatial interaction decisions. At root, migrations take place because the migrants believe that their opportunities and life circumstances will be better at their destination than they are at their present location (see "Why People Migrate").

Controls on Migration

Economic considerations crystallize most migration decisions, though nomads fleeing the famine and spreading deserts of the Sahel obviously are impelled by different economic imperatives than is the executive considering a job transfer to Montreal or the resident of Appalachia seeking factory employment in the city. Among the aging, affluent populations of highly developed countries, retirement amenities figure importantly in perceptions of residential attractiveness of areas. Educational opportunities, changes in

TABLE 3.2	Top 10 Origin and Destination Countries of Refugees, 1995 Estimates	
	REFUGEE NUMBERS (ROUNDED TO NEAREST 50,000)	
Origin Countries		
Afghanistan	3,400,000	
Palestine	2,800,000	
Rwanda	1,700,000	
Former Yugoslavia	1,400,000	
Liberia	750,000	
Somalia	450,000	
Sudan	400,000	
Angola	350,000	
Eritrea	350,000	
Viet Nam	300,000	
Receiving Countries		
Iran	2,000,000	
Pakistan	1,500,000	
Zaire	1,400,000	
Jordan	1,100,000	
Gaza Strip	600,000	
Sudan	600,000	
Tanzania	600,000	
Guinea	550,000	
West Bank	500,000	
Germany	400,000	

Source: U.S. Committee for Refugees, 1995.

FIGURE 3.28   Rwandan refugees near the border of Rwanda and Tanzania. Approximately 1 million Rwandans fled into neighboring Zaire, Tanzania, Uganda, and Burundi in 1994 to escape civil war in their home country. Fleeing war, repression, and famine, millions of people in developing nations have become reluctant migrants from their homelands.

life cycle, and environmental attractions or repulsions are but a few other possible migration motivations.

Migration theorists attribute international economic migrations to a series of often overlapping mechanisms. Differentials in wages and job opportunities between home and destination countries are perhaps the major driving force in such individual migration decisions. Those differentials are in part rooted in a built-in demand for workers at the bottom of the labor hierarchy in more prosperous developed countries whose own workers disdain low-income, menial jobs. Migrants are available to fill those jobs, some argue, because advanced economies make industrial investment in developing or colonial economies to take advantage of lower labor costs there. New factories inevitably disturb existing peasant economies, employ primarily short-term female workers, and leave a residue of unemployed males available and prone to migrate in search of opportunity. If successful, international economic migrants, male or female, help diversify sources of family income through their remittances from abroad, a form of household security that in itself helps motivate some international economic migration.

Negative home conditions that impel the decision to migrate are called **push factors.** They might include loss of job, lack of professional opportunity, overcrowding or slum clearance, or a variety of other influences including poverty, war, and famine. The presumed positive attractions of the migration destination are known as **pull factors.** They include all the attractive attributes perceived to exist at the new location—safety and food, perhaps, or job opportunities, better climate, lower taxes, more room, and so forth. Very often migration is a result of both perceived push and pull factors. It is *perception* of the areal pattern of opportunities and want satisfaction that is important here, whether or not perceptions are supported by objective reality. In China, for example, a "floating" population of more than 100 million surplus workers has flooded into cities from the countryside, seeking urban employment that exists primarily in their anticipation.

Some 2 billion of the world's 5.7 billion people live in poverty, the vast majority of them in the developing countries of Asia, Africa, and Latin America. Poor people in poor countries are major components of the growing tide of human movement within and between countries for reasons summarized in the following account.

Poor people may move from village to town, from town to city or from one country to another. But all respond to the same basic forces—the push of poverty and the pull of opportunity.

Poverty in developing countries is greatest in the rural areas—home to around 750 million of the world's poorest people. Of these, around 20 to 30 million move each year to the towns and cities. And an increasing proportion of these migrants are "environmental refugees," whose land is so eroded or exhausted that it can no longer support them.

People in towns and cities have greater opportunities. They often earn twice as much as those in rural areas—and may live 10 years longer. They have on average twice as much access to health services and safe water—and four times the access to safe sanitation services.

Developing countries have made enormous progress over the past three decades, but they still have less than one-twentieth of the per capita income of the industrial countries. And around 40% of the labor force is unemployed or under-employed—compared with an average unemployment rate of between 6% and 7% in the North.

People in developing countries are also much more likely to be disrupted by natural disasters, civil strife and war. During the past four decades, there were more than 200 armed conflicts on the developing countries' soil, claiming more human lives than World War II.

Migration from one country to another is usually difficult—and sometimes dangerous. But for many of the world's poorest people, it is the most rational move. About 75 million people from developing countries are on the move each year as refugees, displaced persons, transient workers, or legal or illegal migrants.

From *Human Development Report 1992,* by the United Nations Development Programme. Copyright © 1992 by the United Nations Development Programme. Reprinted by permission of Oxford University Press, Inc.

The concept of place utility helps us to understand the decision-making process that potential voluntary migrants undergo. **Place utility** is the measure of an individual's satisfaction with a given residential location. The decision to migrate is a reflection of the appraisal—the perception—by the prospective migrant of the current homesite as opposed to other sites of which something is known or hoped for. In the evaluation of comparative place utility, the decision maker considers not only perceived value of the present location, but also expected place utility of potential destinations.

Those evaluations are matched with the individual's *aspiration level,* that is, the level of accomplishment or ambition that the person sees for herself or himself. Aspirations tend to be adjusted to what one considers attainable. If one finds present circumstances satisfactory, then **spatial search** behavior—the process by which locational alternatives are evaluated—is not initiated. If, on the other hand, dissatisfaction with the home location is felt, then a utility is assigned to each of the possible migration locations. The utility is based on past or expected future rewards at various sites. Because new places are unfamiliar to the searcher, the information received about them acts as a substitute for the personal experience of the homesite. The decision maker can do no more than sample information about place alternatives and, of course, there may be sampling errors.

One goal of the potential migrant is to avoid physically dangerous or economically unprofitable outcomes in the final migration decision. Place utility evaluation, therefore, requires assessments not only of hoped-for pull factors of new sites but also of the potentially negative economic and social reception the migrant might experience at those sites. An example of that observation can be seen in the case of the large numbers of young Mexicans and Central Americans who have migrated both legally and illegally to the United States. Faced with poverty and overpopulation at home, they regard the place utility in Mexico as minimal. With a willingness to work, they learn from friends and relatives of job opportunities north of the border and, hoping for success or even wealth, quickly place high utility on relocation to the United States. Many know that dangerous risks are involved in entering the country illegally, but even legal immigrants face legal restrictions or rejections that are advocated or designed to reduce the pull attractions of the United States (See "Backlash").

Another migrant goal is to reduce uncertainty. That objective may be achieved either through a series of transitional relocation stages or when the migrant follows the example of known predecessors. **Step migration** involves the place transition from, for example, rural to central city residence through a series of less extreme locational changes—from farm to small town to suburb and, finally, to the major central city itself. **Chain migration** assures that the mover is part of an established migrant flow from a common origin to a prepared destination. An advance group of migrants, having established itself in a new home area, is followed by second and subsequent migrations originating in the same

FOR YOUR CONSIDERATION

BACKLASH

Migrants can enter a country legally—with a passport, visa, work permit, or other authorization—or illegally. Some aliens initially enter a country legally but on a temporary basis (as a student or tourist, for example), but then remain after their departure date. Others may arrive claiming the right of political asylum but actually seeking economic opportunity. The easily accessible politically open states of Western Europe and North America have been particularly subject to such incursions, and in all measures of resistance and prohibition have been discussed or enacted in recent years.

The United States has seen a rising tide of emotion against the estimated 4 to 5 million people who reside illegally in the country, a sentiment that has been reflected in a number of actions. Greater efforts, for example, are being made to deter illegal crossings along the Mexican border by both increasing the number of Border Patrol agents and by building steel fences near El Paso, Texas, Nogales, Arizona, and San Ysidro, California. Four states—Florida, Texas, Arizona, and California—have sued the federal government to win reimbursement for the costs of illegal immigration. The governor of California proposed an amendment to the Constitution to deny citizenship to children born on American soil if their parents are not legal residents of the United States. Finally, and most dramatically, in November 1994, California voters approved by a overwhelming margin a proposition that would deny certain public services to illegal aliens.

Proposition 187, as it is known, prohibits state and local government agencies from providing publicly funded education, nonemergency health care, welfare benefits, and social services to any person they cannot verify as either a U.S. citizen or a person legally admitted to the country. The measure also requires state and local agencies to report suspected illegal immigrants to the Immigration and Naturalization Service and to certain state officials. Both provisions were struck down by U.S. District Court in late 1995.

Proponents of Proposition 187 argued that California can no longer support the burden of high levels of immigration, especially if the immigrants cannot enter the more skilled professions. They contended that welfare, medical, and educational benefits are magnets that draw illegal aliens into the state. These unauthorized immigrants are estimated to cost California taxpayers more than $3.5 billion per year and result in overcrowded schools and public health clinics, and the reduction of services to legal residents. Why should the latter pay for benefits for people who are breaking the law?, 187-supporters asked.

Those opposed to 187 contended that projected savings are illusory because the proposition collides with federal laws that guarantee access to public education for all children in the United States. It also violates federal Medicaid laws, so California will be in danger of losing all regular Medicaid funding. Forcing an estimated 300,000 children out of school and onto the streets will increase the risk of juvenile crime. Forbidding doctors from giving immunizations or basic medical care to anyone suspected of being an illegal immigrant will encourage the spread of communicable diseases throughout the state, putting everyone at risk. Educators, doctors, and other public service officials would be turned into immigration officers, a task for which they are ill-suited. Finally, opponents argued that the proposition will not stop the flow of illegal aliens because it does nothing to increase enforcement at the border or to punish employers who hire undocumented workers.

Questions:

1. *What do you think are the magnets that draw immigrants across the border: jobs or benefits? Is the denial of services likely to reduce the perceived place utility of the United States and thus reduce illegal immigration?*

2. *Do you believe the federal government has an obligation to help states bear the costs of education, medical care, and incarceration for unauthorized immigrants? Why or why not?*

3. *Should the United States require citizens to have a national identification card? Why or why not?*

4. *If you had been able to vote on Proposition 187, how would you have voted? Why?*

5. *Is it good policy not to educate or give basic medical care to any persons, even those not legally in the country?*

home district and frequently united by kinship or friendship ties. Public and private services for legal migrants and informal service networks for undocumented or illegal migrants become established and contribute to the continuation or expansion of the chain migration flow. Ethnic and foreign-born enclaves in major cities and rural areas in a number of countries are the immediate result, as we shall see more fully in Chapter 6.

Sometimes the chain migration is specific to occupational groups. For example, nearly all newspaper vendors in New Delhi, in the north of India, come from one small district in Tamil Nadu, in the south of India. Most construction workers in New Delhi come either from Orissa, in the east of India, or Rajasthan, in the northwest. The diamond trade of Bombay, India, is dominated by a network of about 250 related families who come from a small town several hundred miles to the north.

A corollary of all out-migration flows is **counter** (or **return**) **migration**—the likelihood that as many as 25% of all migrants will return to their place of origin. For the United States, return migration—defined as moving back to one's state of birth—makes up about 20% of all domestic moves. That figure varies dramatically between states. More than a third of in-migrants to West Virginia, for example, were returnees—as were over 25% of those moving to Pennsylvania, Alabama, Iowa, and a few other states. Such widely different states as New Hampshire, Maryland, California, Florida, Wyoming, and Alaska were among the several that found returnees were fewer than 10% of their in-migrants. Interviews suggest that states deemed attractive draw new migrants in large numbers, while those with high proportions of returnees in the migrant stream are not perceived as desirable destinations by other than former residents.

Once established, origin and destination pairs of places tend to persist. Areas that dominate a locale's in- and out-migration patterns make up the **migration fields** of the place in question. As we would expect, areas near the point of origin comprise the largest part of the migration field, though larger cities more distantly located may also be prominent as the ultimate destination of hierarchical step migration. Some migration fields reveal a distinctly *channelized* pattern of flow. The channels link areas that are in some way tied to one another by past migrations, by economic trade considerations, or some other affinity. The flow along them is greater than otherwise would be the case (Figure 3.29) but does not necessarily involve individuals with personal or family ties. The former streams of southern blacks and whites to northern cities, of Scandinavians to Minnesota and Wisconsin, and of U.S. retirees to Florida and Arizona or their European counterparts to Iberia or the Mediterranean coast are all examples of **channelized migration.**

Voluntary migration is responsive to other controls that influence all forms of spatial interaction. Push-pull factors may be equated with *complementarity;* costs (emotional and financial) of a residence relocation are expressions of *transferability.* Other things being equal, large cities exert a stronger migrant pull than do small towns, a reflection of the impact of the *gravity model.* The *distance decay* effect has often been noted in migration studies (Figure 3.30). Movers seek to minimize the *friction of distance.* In selecting between two potential destinations of equal merit, a migrant tends to choose the nearer as involving less effort and expense. And since information about distant areas is less complete and satisfying than awareness of nearer localities, short moves are favored over long ones. Research indicates that determined migrants with specific destinations in mind are unlikely to be deterred by distance considerations. However, groups for whom push factors are more determining than specific destination pulls are likely to limit their migration distance in response to encountered apparent opportunities. For them, *intervening opportunity* affects locational decisions.

Observations such as these were summarized in the 1870s and 1880s as a series of "laws of migration" by E. G. Ravenstein (1834–1913). Among those that remain relevant are the following:

1. Most migrants go only a short distance.
2. Longer-distance migration favors big-city destinations.
3. Most migration proceeds step-by-step.
4. Most migration is rural to urban.
5. Each migration flow produces a counterflow.
6. Most migrants are adults; families are less likely to make international moves.
7. Most international migrants are young males.

The latter two "laws" introduce the role of personal attributes (and attitudes) of migrants: their age, sex, education, and economic status. Migrants do not represent a cross section of the populace from which they come. Selectivity of movers is evident, and the selection shows some regional differences. In most societies, young adults are the most mobile (Figure 3.31). In the United States during the 1980s, mobility peaked among those in their twenties, especially the later twenties, and tended to decline thereafter. Among West African cross-border migrants, a World Bank study reveals, the age group 15–39 predominated.

Ravenstein's conclusion that young adult males are dominant in economically-pushed international movement is less valid today than when first proposed. In reality, women and girls now comprise between 40–60% of all international migrants worldwide. It is true that legal and illegal migrants to the United States from Mexico and Central America are primarily young men, as were first-generation "guest workers" in European cities. But population projections for West European countries suggest that women will shortly make up the largest part of their foreign-born population, and in one-third of the countries of sub-Saharan Africa, including Burkina Faso, Swaziland, and Togo, the female share of foreign-born populations was as large as the male. Further, among rural-to-urban migrants in Latin America since the 1960s, women have been in the majority.

Female migrants are motivated primarily by economic pushes and pulls. Surveys of women migrants in Southeast Asia and Latin America indicate that 50%–70% moved in

FIGURE 3.29 Channelized migration flows.

(*a*) Place-specific flows from the rural South to midwestern cities of medium size. Distance is not necessarily the main determinant of flow direction. Perhaps through family and friendship links, the rural southern areas are tied to particular midwestern destinations. (*b*) International migration streams into Senegal are less place specific, as these immigration paths of resident immigrants suggest. Distance from home country is a prime consideration, but some flows ignore proximity and follow predecessor migrants to more distant areas.

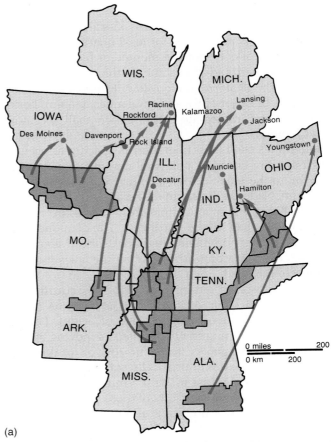

(a)

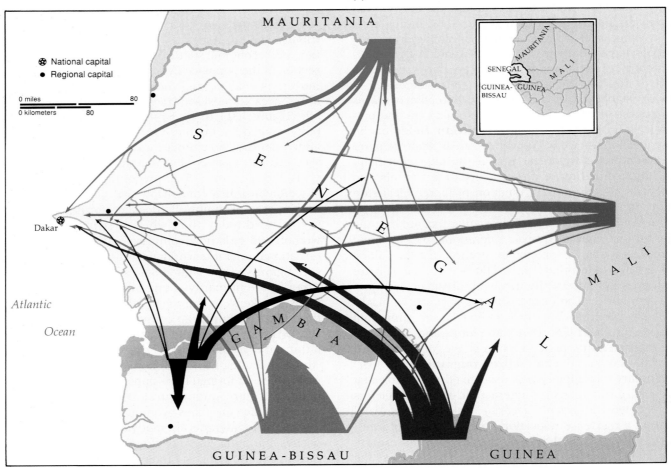

(b)

THEMES AND FUNDAMENTALS OF HUMAN GEOGRAPHY

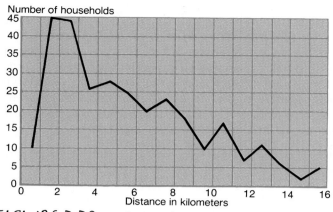

FIGURE 3.30   Distance between old and new residences in the Asby area of Sweden. Notice how the number of movers decreased with increasing distance.

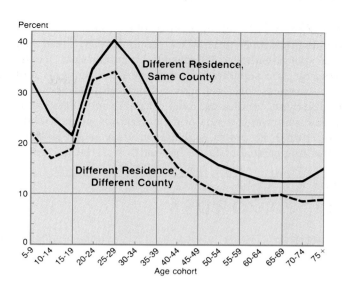

FIGURE 3.31   Percentage of 1994 population over 5 years of age with a different residence than in 1993. Young adults figure most prominently in both short- and long-distance moves in the United States, an age-related pattern of mobility that has remained constant over time. The 1990 census revealed that among people between the ages of 15 and 24, more than 7 in 10 had recently moved. Among those 75 and older, the mobility rate was about 1 in 20.

search of employment and commonly first moved while in their teens. The proportion of young, single women is particularly high in rural-to-urban migration flows, reflecting their limited opportunities in increasingly overcrowded agricultural areas. To the push-and-pull factors normally association with migration decisions, there are sometimes added family pressures that encourage young women with few employment opportunities to migrate as part of a household's survival strategy. In Latin America, the Philippines, and parts of Asia, emigration of young girls from large, landless families is more common than from smaller families or those with land rights. Their remittances of foreign earnings help maintain their parents and siblings at home.

For modern Americans in interregional moves, the decisions to migrate are more ordinary but individually just as compelling. They appear to involve (1) changes in life cycle (e.g., getting married, having children, getting a divorce); (2) changes in the career cycle (getting a first job or a promotion, receiving a career transfer, seeking work in a new location, retiring); (3) changes of residence associated with individual personality. Work-related relocations are most important in U.S. interstate migrations. Some people, of course, simply seem to move often for no discernible reason, whereas others, *stayers,* settle into a community permanently. For other developed countries, a different set of summary migration factors may be present.

Summary

Spatial interaction is the dynamic evidence of the areal differentiation of the earth's surface and of the interdependence between geographic locations. The term refers to the movement of goods, information, people, ideas—indeed, of every facet of economy and society—between one place and another. It includes the daily spatial activities of individuals and the collective patterns of their short- and long-distance behavior in space. The principles and constraints that unite,

define, and control spatial behavior in this sense constitute an essential organizing focus for the study of human geographic patterns of the earth.

We have seen that whatever the type of spatial behavior or flow, a limited number of recurring mechanisms of guidance and control are encountered. Three underlying bases for spatial interaction are: *complementarity,* which encourages flows between areas by balancing supply with demand or satisfying need with opportunity; *transferability,* which affects movement decisions by introducing cost, effort, and time considerations; and *intervening opportunities,* which suggests that costs of overcoming distance may be reduced by finding closer alternate points where needs can be satisfied. The flows of commodities, ideas, or people governed by these interaction factors are interdependent and additive. Flows of commodities establish and reinforce traffic patterns, for example, and also channelize the movement of information and people.

Those flows and interactions may further be understood by the application of uniform models to all forms of spatial interaction from interregional commodity exchanges to an individual's daily pattern of movement. Distance decay tells us of the inevitable decline of interaction with increasing distance. The gravity model suggests that major centers of activity can exert interaction pulls that partly compensate for distance decay. Recognition of movement biases explains why spatial interaction in the objective world may deviate from that proposed by abstract models.

Humans in their individual and collective short- and long-distance movements are responsive to these impersonal spatial controls. Their spatial behaviors are also influenced by their separate circumstances. Each has an activity and awareness space reflective of individual socioeconomic and life-cycle conditions. Each differs in mobility. Each has unique wants and needs and perceptions of their satisfaction. Human response to distance decay is expressed in a controlling critical distance beyond which the frequency of interaction quickly declines. That decline is partly conditioned by unfamiliarity with distant points outside normal activity space. Perceptions of home and distant territory therefore color interaction flows and space evaluations. In turn, those perceptions, well or poorly based, underlie travel and migration decisions, part of the continuing spatial diffusion and interaction of people. It is to people and their patterns of distribution and regional growth and change that we turn our attention in the following chapter.

KEY WORDS

activity space 71
awareness space 71
chain migration 87
channelized migration 89
complementarity 65
counter migration 89
critical distance 72
distance decay 67
friction of distance 67

gravity model 68
intervening opportunity 66
migration 82
migration field 89
movement bias 69
network 70
personal communication field 76
personal space 70
place perception 77

place utility 87
potential model 69
pull factor 86
push factor 86
space-time prism 72
spatial interaction 64
spatial search 87
step migration 87
territoriality 70
transferability 65

FOR REVIEW

1. What is *spatial interaction?* What are the three fundamental conditions governing all forms of spatial interaction? What is the distinctive impact or importance of each of the conditions?

2. What variations in *distance decay* curves might you expect if you were to plot shipments of ready-mixed concrete, potato chips, and computer parts? What do these respective curves tell us about transferability?

3. What is *activity space?* What factors affect the areal extent of an individual's activity space?

4. On a piece of paper, and following the model of Figure 3.10, plot your *space-time path* for your movements on a typical class day. What alterations in your established movement habits might be necessary (or become possible) if (*a*) instead of walking, you rode a bike, (*b*) instead of biking, you drove a car, (*c*) instead of driving, you had to use the bus or go by bike or on foot?

5. What does the thought that transportation and communication are *space adjusting* imply? In what ways has technology affected the "space adjustment" in commodity flows? In information flows?

6. Recall the places you have visited in the past week. In your movements, were the rules of *distance decay* and *critical distance* operative? What variables affect *your* critical distances?

7. What considerations appear to influence the decision to migrate? How do perceptions of *place utility* induce or inhibit migration?

8. What is a *migration field?* Some migration fields show a *channelized* flow of people. Select a particular channelized migration flow (such as the movement of Scandinavians to Michigan, Wisconsin, and Minnesota, or people from the Great Plains to California, or southern blacks to the North) and speculate why a channelized flow developed.

SELECTED REFERENCES

Andrew, Caroline, and Beth Moore Milroy. *Life Spaces: Gender, Household, Employment.* Vancouver: University of British Columbia Press, 1988.

Barkan, Elliott Robert. *Asian and Pacific Islander Migration to the United States: A Model of New Global Patterns.* Westport, CT: Greenwood Press, 1993.

Brown, Lawrence A. *Innovation Diffusion: A New Perspective.* New York: Methuen, 1981.

Brunn, Stanley, and Thomas Leinbach. *Collapsing Space and Time: Geographic Aspects of Communication and Information.* Winchester, MA: Unwin Hyman, 1991.

Burton, Ian, Robert W. Kates, and Gilbert F. White. *The Environment as Hazard.* 2d ed. New York: Guilford Publications, 1993.

Castles, Stephen, and Mark J. Miller. *The Age of Migration: International Population Movements in the Modern World.* New York: Guilford Publications, 1993.

Clark, W. A. V. *Human Migration*. Vol. 7, *Scientific Geography Series*. Newbury Park, CA: Sage, 1986.

Clarke, John I., Peter Curson, S. L. Kayastha, and Prithvish Nag, eds. *Population and Disaster*. Oxford, England: Basil Blackwell, 1989.

Constantinou, Stavros T., and Nicholas D. Diamantides. "Modeling International Migration: Determinants of Emigration from Greece to the United States, 1820–1980." *Annals of the Association of American Geographers* 75 (1985):352–369.

Demko, George J., and William B. Wood. "International Refugees: A Geographical Perspective." *Journal of Geography* 86 (1987):225–228.

Fligstein, Neil. *Going North: Migration of Whites and Blacks from the South, 1900–1950*. New York: Academic Press, 1981.

Gober, Patricia. "Americans on the Move." *Population Bulletin* 48, no. 3. Washington, D.C.: Population Reference Bureau, 1993.

Golledge, Reginald G., and Robert J. Stimson. *Analytical Behavioral Geography*. London: Croom Helm, 1987.

Hägerstrand, Torsten. *Innovation Diffusion as a Spatial Process*. Chicago: The University of Chicago Press, 1967.

Hall, Peter, and Paschal Preston. *The Carrier Wave: New Information Technology and the Geography of Innovation, 1846–2003*. Winchester, MA: Unwin Hyman, 1988.

Hanson, Susan, and Geraldine Pratt. "Geographic Perspectives on the Occupational Segregation of Women." *National Geographic Research* 6, no. 4 (1990):376–399.

Hay, Alan. "The Geographical Explanation of Commodity Flow." *Progress in Human Geography* 3 (1979):1–12.

Jakle, John A., Stanley Brunn, and Curtis C. Roseman. *Human Spatial Behavior: A Social Geography*. North Scituate, MA: Duxbury Press, 1976. Reprint. Prospect Heights, IL: Waveland Press, 1985.

Kane, Hal. *The Hour of Departure: Forces That Create Refugees and Migrants*. Worldwatch Paper 125. Washington, D.C.: Worldwatch Institute, 1995.

Kellerman, Aharon. *Telecommunications and Geography*. New York: John Wiley & Sons, 1993.

King, Russel, ed. *The New Geography of European Migrations*. New York: John Wiley & Sons, 1994.

Lee, Everett S. "A Theory of Migration." *Demography* 3 (1966):47–57.

Lenntorp, Bo. *Paths in Space-Time Environments*. Lund Studies in Geography. *Series B. Human Geography*, no. 44, Lund, Sweden: Lund University, 1976.

Lewis, G. J. *Human Migration: A Geographical Perspective*. London: Croom Helm, 1982.

Lindsay, Beverly, ed. *African Migration and National Development*. University Park: Pennsylvania State University Press, 1985.

Long, Larry H. *Migration and Residential Mobility in the United States*. New York: Russell Sage Foundation, 1988.

Lowe, John C., and S. Moryadas. *The Geography of Movement*. Boston: Houghton Mifflin, 1975.

Massey, Douglas S., et al. "International Migration Theory: The North American Case." *Population and Development Review* 20, no. 4 (1994):699–751.

Massey, Douglas S., et al. "Theories of International Migration: A Review and Appraisal." *Population and Development Review* 19, no. 3 (1993):431–466.

Michelson, William. *From Sun to Sun: Daily Obligations and Community Structure in the Lives of Employed Women and Their Families*. Totowa, NJ: Rowman & Allanheld, 1985.

Morrill, Richard L., Gary L. Gaile, and Grant Ian Thrall. *Spatial Diffusion*. Vol. 10, *Scientific Geography Series*. Newbury Park, CA: Sage, 1988.

Murdie, Robert A. "Cultural Differences in Consumer Travel." *Economic Geography* 41 (1965):211–233.

Newland, Kathleen. *International Migration: The Search for Work*. Worldwatch Paper 33. Washington, D.C.: Worldwatch Institute, 1979.

Newland, Kathleen. *Refugees: The New International Politics of Displacement*. Worldwatch Paper 43. Washington, D.C.: Worldwatch Institute, 1981.

Palm, Risa. *Natural Hazards*. Baltimore, MD: Johns Hopkins University Press, 1990.

Palm, Risa. "Women in Nonmetropolitan Areas: A Time-Budget Survey." *Environment and Planning A* 13 (1981):373–378.

Plane, David A. "Age-Composition Change and the Geographical Dynamics of Interregional Migration in the U.S." *Annals of the Association of American Geographers* 82, no. 1 (1992):64–85.

Ravenstein, E. G. "The Laws of Migration." *Journal of the Royal Statistical Society* 48 (1885):167–227; 52 (1889):241–301.

Rogge, John R., ed. *Refugees: A Third World Dilemma*. Totowa, NJ: Rowman & Littlefield, 1987.

Roseman, Curtis C. "Channelization of Migration Flows from the Rural South to the Industrial Midwest." *Proceedings of the Association of American Geographers* 3 (1971):140–146.

Russell, Sharon Stanton, and Michael Teitelbaum. *International Migration and International Trade*. World Bank Discussion Papers, no. 160. Washington, D.C.: The World Bank, 1992.

Segal, Aaron. *An Atlas of International Migration*. Providence, NJ: K. G. Saur, 1993.

Simon, Rita James, and Caroline B. Brettell, eds. *International Migration: The Female Experience*. Totowa, NJ: Rowman & Allenheld, 1986.

Stouffer, Samuel. "Intervening Opportunities: A Theory Relating Mobility and Distance." *American Sociological Review* 5 (1940):845–867.

Stutz, Frederick P. "Distance and Network Effects on Urban Social Travel Fields." *Economic Geography* 49 (1973):134–144.

Stutz, Frederick P. *Social Aspects of Interaction and Transportation.* Association of American Geographers, Commission on College Geography. *Resource Paper* No. 76-2. Washington, D.C.: Association of American Geographers, 1976.

Svart, Larry M. "Environmental Preference Migration: A Review." *Geographical Review* 66 (1976):314–330.

Szalai, Alexander, ed. *The Use of Time: Daily Activities of Urban and Suburban Populations in Twelve Countries.* The Hague: Mouton, 1972.

Tinkler, Keith. "Reilly's 'Law' Revisited." *The Operational Geographer* 10, no. 1 (1992):12–16.

Tocalis, Thomas R. "Changing Theoretical Foundations of the Gravity Concept of Human Interaction." In *The Nature of Change in Geographical Ideas,* edited by Brian J. L. Berry, pp. 66–124. Perspectives in Geography 3. DeKalb: Northern Illinois University Press, 1978.

Ullman, Edward L. "The Role of Transportation and the Basis for Interaction." In *Man's Role in Changing the Face of the Earth,* edited by William E. Thomas, Jr., pp. 862–880. Chicago: University of Chicago Press, 1956.

United Nations. High Commissioner for Refugees. *The State of the World's Refugees: The Search for Solutions.* New York: Oxford University Press, 1995.

White, Paul, and Robert Woods. *The Geographical Impact of Migration.* London: Longman, 1980.

Wood, William B. "Forced Migration: Local Conflicts and International Dilemmas." *Annals of the Association of American Geographers* 84, no. 4 (1994):607–634.

Zachariah, K. C., and Julien Condé. *Migration in West Africa: Demographic Aspects.* New York: Oxford University Press for the World Bank, 1981.

POPULATION:

WORLD PATTERNS, REGIONAL TRENDS

Population Growth   96
Some Population Definitions   98
Birth Rates   98
Fertility Rates   99
Death Rates   102
Population Pyramids   104
Natural Increase   107
Doubling Times   108
The Demographic Transition   109
The Western Experience   110
A World Divided   113
The Demographic Equation   113
Population Relocation   114
Immigration Impacts   114
World Population Distribution   116
Population Density   119
Overpopulation   120
Urbanization   122
Population Data and Projections   122
Population Data   123
Population Projections   124
Population Controls   125
Population Prospects   126

SUMMARY   127
KEY WORDS   128
FOR REVIEW   128
SELECTED REFERENCES   128

This 1990 New York Earth Day gathering emphasizes the world's increasing population numbers and densities.

Zero, possibly even negative [population] growth was the 1972 slogan proposed by the prime minister of Singapore, an island country in Southeast Asia. His nation's population, which stood at 1 million at the end of World War II (1945), had doubled by the mid-1960s. To avoid the overpopulation he foresaw, the government decreed "Boy or girl, two is enough" and refused maternity leaves and access to health insurance for third or subsequent births. Abortion and sterilization were legalized, and children born fourth or later in a family were to be discriminated against in school admissions policy. In response, birth rates by the mid-1980s fell to below the level necessary to replace the population, and abortions were terminating more than one-third of all pregnancies.

"At least two. Better three. Four if you can afford it" was the national slogan proposed by that same prime minister in 1986, reflecting fears that the stringencies of the earlier campaign had gone too far. From concern that overpopulation would doom the country to perpetual Third World poverty, Prime Minister Lee Kuan Yew was moved to worry that population limitation would deprive it of the growth potential and national strength implicit in a youthful, educated workforce adequate to replace and support the present aging population. His 1990 national budget provided for sizable long-term tax rebates for second children born to mothers under 28. Not certain that financial inducements alone would suffice to increase population, the Singapore government annually renews its offer to take 100,000 Hong Kong Chinese who might choose to leave when China takes over their territory in 1997.

The policy reversal in Singapore reflects an inflexible population reality: The structure of the present determines the content of the future. The size, characteristics, growth trends, and migrations of today's populations help shape the well-being of peoples yet unborn but whose numbers and distributions are now being determined. The numbers, age, and sex distribution of people; patterns and trends in their fertility and mortality; their density of settlement and rate of growth all affect and are affected by the social, political, and economic organization of a society. Through them, we begin to understand how the people in a given area live, how they may interact with one another, how they use the land, what pressure on resources exists, and what the future may bring.

Population geography provides the background tools and understandings of those interests. It focuses on the number, composition, and distribution of human be-ings in relation to variations in the conditions of earth space. It differs from **demography,** the statistical study of human population, in its concern with *spatial* analysis—the relationship of numbers to area. Regional circumstances of resource base, type of economic development, level of living, food supply, and conditions of health and well-being are basic to geography's population concerns. They are, as well, fundamental expressions of the human–environmental relationships that are the substance of all human geographic inquiry.

Population Growth

Sometime during the summer of 1995, a human birth raised the earth's population to 5.7 billion people. In 1965 there were about 3.3 billion. That is, over the 30 years between those two dates, the world's population grew on average by about 80 million people annually, or some 220,000 per day. That growth has increased in recent years, fluctuating between 85 and 95 million people added annually, or between 240,000 and 260,000 per day. It is generally agreed that we will see a year 2000 population of about 6.3 billion (the 20th century began with fewer than 2 billion) inhabitants. Demographers assume that world population will stabilize at about 11.6 billion after the year 2150, with over 95% of the growth occurring in countries now considered "developing." (Figure 4.1). We will return to these projections, and the difficulties inherent in making them, later in this chapter.

Just what is implied by numbers in the millions and billions? With what can we equate the 1995 population of Gabon in Africa (about 1.2 million) or of China (about 1.2 billion)? Unless we have some grasp of their scale and meaning, our understanding of the data and data manipulations of the population geographer can at best be superficial. It is difficult to appreciate a number as vast as 1 million or 1 billion, and the great distinction between them. Some examples offered by the Population Reference Bureau may help in visualizing their immensity and implications.

- A 2.5-centimeter (1-inch) stack of U.S. paper currency contains 233 bills. If you had a *million* dollars in thousand-dollar bills, the stack would be 11 centimeters (4.3 inches) high. If you had a *billion* dollars in thousand-dollar bills, your pile of money would reach 109 meters (357 feet)—about the length of a football field.
- You had lived a *million* seconds when you were 11.6 days old. You won't be a *billion* seconds old until you are 31.7 years of age.
- The supersonic airplane the Concorde could theoretically circle the globe in only 18.5 hours at its cruising speed of 2150 kilometers (1340 miles) per hour. It would take 31 days for a passenger to journey a *million* miles on the Concorde, while a trip of a *billion* miles would last 85 years.

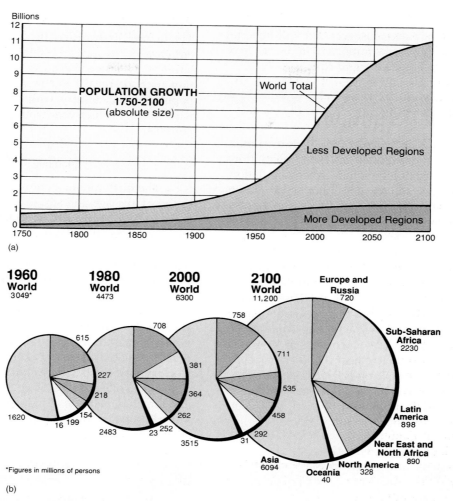

FIGURE 4.1 **World population numbers and projections.** (*a*) After two centuries of slow growth, world population began explosive expansion after World War II. United Nations projections are for a global population of about 6.3 billion in A.D. 2000 and for 9.8 billion in 2050. The total may rise to over 11 billion by the end of the 21st century. (*b*) The greatest numerical growth during the 1990s will occur in Asia, and sub-Saharan Africa will show the highest percentage increase, but the relative population rankings of major world regions will remain the same throughout this century. "Europe and Russia" includes the Eastern European and Caucasian states that were republics of the former Soviet Union and all of Russia, including Siberia.

The implications of the present numbers and the potential increases in population are of vital current social, political, and ecological concern. Population numbers were much smaller some 11,000 years ago when continental glaciers began their retreat, people spread to formerly unoccupied portions of the globe, and human experimentation with food sources initiated the Agricultural Revolution. The 5 or 10 million people who then constituted all of humanity obviously had considerable potential to expand their numbers. In retrospect, we see that the natural resource base of the earth had a population-supporting capacity far in excess of the pressures exerted on it by early hunting and gathering groups.

Some observers maintain that despite present numbers or even those we can reasonably anticipate for the future, the adaptive and exploitive ingenuity of humans is in no danger of being taxed. Others, however, compare the earth to a self-contained spaceship and declare with chilling conviction that a finite vessel cannot bear an ever-increasing number of

passengers. They point to recurring problems of malnutrition and starvation (though these are realistically more a matter of failures of distribution than of inability to produce enough foodstuffs worldwide). They cite dangerous conditions of air and water pollution, the loss of forest and farmland, the nearing exhaustion of many minerals and fossil fuels, and other evidences of strains on world resources as foretelling the discernible outer limits of population growth.

Why are we suddenly confronted with what seems to many an insoluble problem—the apparently unending tendency of humankind to increase in numbers? On a worldwide basis, populations grow only one way: The number of births in a given period exceeds the number of deaths. Ignoring for the moment regional population changes resulting from migration, we can conclude that the observed and projected dramatic increases in population must result from the failure of natural controls to limit the number of births or to increase the number of deaths, or from the success of human ingenuity in circumventing such controls when they exist. The implications of these observations will become clearer after we define some terms important in the study of world population and explore their significance.

Some Population Definitions

Demographers employ a wide range of measures of population composition and trends, though all their calculations start with a count of events: of individuals in the population, of births, deaths, marriages, and so on. To those basic counts demographers bring refinements that make the figures more meaningful and useful in population analysis. Among them are *rates* and *cohort measures.*

Rates simply record the frequency of occurrence of an event during a given time frame for a designated population—for example, the marriage rate as the number of marriages performed per 1000 population in the United States last year. **Cohort** measures refer data to a population group unified by a specified common characteristic—the age cohort of 1–5 years, perhaps, or the college class of 1999 (Figure 4.2). Basic 1996 counts and rates useful in the analysis of world population and population trends have been reprinted with the permission of the Population Reference Bureau as Appendix B to this book. Examination of them will document the discussion that follows.

Birth Rates

The **crude birth rate** (CBR), often referred to simply as the *birth rate,* is the annual number of live births per 1000 population. It is "crude" because it relates births to total population without regard to the age or sex composition of that population. A country with a population of 2 million and with 40,000 births a year would have a crude birth rate of 20 per 1000.

$$\frac{40,000}{2,000,000} = 20 \text{ per } 1000$$

The birth rate of a country is, of course, strongly influenced by the age and sex structure of its population, by the customs and family size expectations of its inhabitants, and by its adopted population policies. Since these conditions vary widely, recorded national birth rates vary—in 1996, from a high of 55 per 1000 in Gaza to the low of 9 per 1000 in 7 European countries. Although birth rates greater than 30 per 1000 are considered *high,* some 30% of the world's people live in countries with rates that are that high or higher (Figure 4.3). In these countries the population is prominently agricultural and rural, and a high proportion of the female population is young. They are found chiefly in Africa, western and southern Asia, and Latin America.

Birth rates of less than 20 per 1000 are reckoned *low* and are characteristic of industrialized, urbanized countries. Most European countries including Russia, Anglo America,

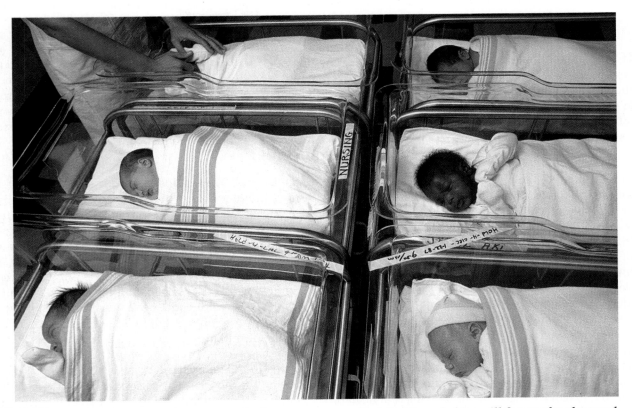

FIGURE 4.2   Whatever their differences may be by race, sex, or ethnicity, these babies will forever be clustered demographically into a single *birth cohort.*

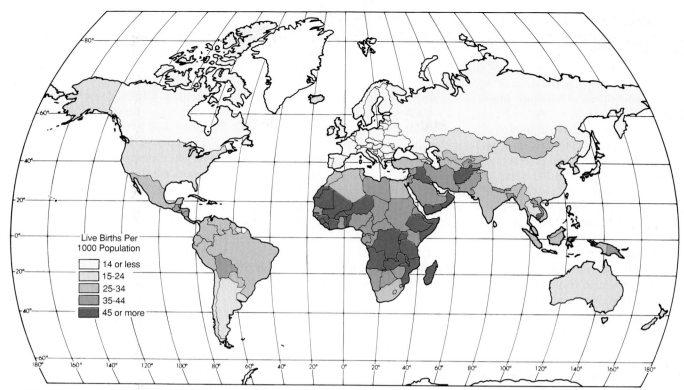

FIGURE 4.3   **Crude birth rates.** The map suggests a degree of precision that is misleading in the absence of reliable, universal registration of births. The pattern shown serves, however, as a generally useful summary of comparative reproduction patterns if class divisions are not taken too literally. Reported or estimated population data vary annually, so this and other population maps may not agree in all details with the figures recorded in Appendix B.

Japan, Australia, and New Zealand have low rates as, importantly, do an increasing number of developing states such as China (see "China's Way—and Others") that have adopted stringent family-planning programs. *Transitional* birth rates (between 20 and 30 per 1000) characterize some, mainly smaller, "developing" countries.

As the recent population histories of Singapore and China indicate, birth rates are subject to change. The decline to present low birth rates of European countries and of some of the areas that they colonized is usually ascribed to industrialization, urbanization, and in recent years, maturing populations. While restrictive family planning policies in China rapidly reduced the birth rate from over 33 per 1000 in 1970 to 18 per 1000 in 1986, industrializing Japan experienced a 15-point decline in the decade 1948–1958 with little governmental intervention. Indeed, the stage of economic development appears closely related to variations in birth rates among countries, although rigorous testing of this relationship proves it to be imperfect (Figure 4.3). As a group, the more developed states of the world showed a crude birth rate of 12 per 1000 in 1996; less developed countries (excluding China) registered 31 per 1000.

Religious and political beliefs can also affect birth rates. The convictions of many Roman Catholics and Muslims that their religion forbids the use of artificial birth control techniques often lead to high birth rates among believers. However, dominantly Catholic Italy shows Europe's lowest birth rate, and Islam itself does not prohibit contraception. Similarly, some European governments—concerned about birth rates too low to sustain present population levels—subsidize births in an attempt to raise those rates. Regional variations in projected percentage contributions to world population growth are summarized in Figure 4.4.

Fertility Rates

Crude birth rates may display such regional variability because of differences in age and sex composition or disparities in births among the reproductive-age, rather than total, population. **Total fertility rate** (TFR) is a more accurate statement than the birth rate in showing the amount of reproduction in the population (Figure 4.5). This rate tells us the average number of children that would be born to each woman if, during her childbearing years, she bore children at the current year's rate for women that age. The fertility rate minimizes the effects of fluctuation in the population structure and is thus a more reliable figure for regional comparative and predictive purposes than the crude birth rate.

A total fertility rate of 2.1 is necessary just to replace present population. On a worldwide basis, the TFR for 1996 was 3.0. The more developed countries recorded a 1.6 rate, while less developed states (excluding China) had a collective TFR of 4.0, down from 5.0 in the mid-1980s. Indeed, the

A n ever larger population is "a good thing," Chairman Mao announced in 1965 when China's birth rate was 37 per 1000 and population totalled 540 million. At Mao's death in 1976, numbers reached 852 million. During the 1970s, when it became evident that population growth was consuming more than half of the annual increase in the country's gross domestic product, China introduced a well-publicized campaign advocating the "two-child family" and providing services, including abortions, supporting that program. In response, China's growth rate dropped to 15.7 per 1000.

"One couple, one child" became the slogan of a new and more vigorous population control drive launched in 1979, backed by both incentives and penalties to assure its success in China's tightly controlled society. Late marriages were encouraged; free contraceptives, cash awards, abortions, and sterilizations were provided to families limited to a single child. Penalties, including steep fines, were levied for second births. At the campaign's height in 1983, the government ordered the ster-

ilization of either husband or wife for couples with more than one child. Tragically, infanticide—particularly the exposure or murder of female babies—was a reported means both of conforming to a one-child limit and of increasing the chances that the one child would be male. By 1986, China's growth rate had fallen to 1%, far below the 2.4% then registered among the rest of the world's less developed countries. (The comparable mid-1990s figures were 1.1% and 2.2%).

Concerned with their own growing numbers, many developing countries have introduced less-extreme programs of family planning stressing access to contraception and sterilization. International agencies have encouraged these programs, buoyed by such presumed success as the 21% fall in fertility rates in Bangladesh from 1970 to 1990 as the proportion of married women of reproductive age using contraceptives rose from 3% to 40% under intensive family planning encouragement and frequent adviser visits. The costs per birth averted, however, were reckoned at an unsupportable $180 in 1987, about 120% of the country's per capita gross domestic product.

Research suggests, however, that fertility falls because women decide they want smaller families, not because they have unmet needs for contraceptive advice and devices. Nineteenth-century northern Europeans without the aid of science, it is observed, had lower fertility rates than their counterparts today in middle-income countries. With some convincing evidence, improved women's education has been proposed as a surer way to reduce fertility than either encouraged contraception or China's coercive efforts. Studies from individual countries indicate that one year of female schooling can reduce the fertility rate by between 5% and 10%. Yet the fertility rate of uneducated Thai women is only two-thirds that of Ugandan women with secondary education. Obviously, the demand for babies is not solely a function of ignorance.

Instead, that demand seems closely tied to the use value placed on children by poor families in some parts of the developing world. Where those families share in such communal resources as firewood, animal fodder, grazing land, fish, and the like, the more of those collective resources that can be converted to private family property and use, the better off is the family. Indeed, the more communal resources that are available for "capture," the greater are the incentives for a household to have more children to appropriate them. Some population economists conclude that only when population numbers increase to the point of total conversion of communal resources to private property—and children have to be supported and educated rather than employed—will poor families in developing countries want fewer children. If so, coercion, contraception, and education may be less effective as checks on fertility than the economic consequence of population increase itself.

行计划生育 是我国的一项基本国策
FAMILY PLANNING—A BASIS NATIONAL POLICY OF CHINA

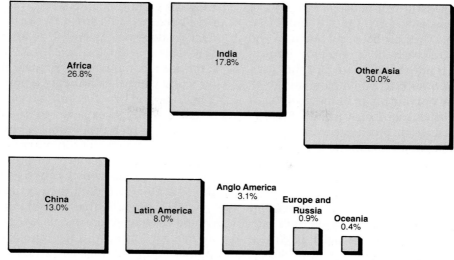

FIGURE 4.4 **Projected percentage contributions to world population growth, by region, 1995–2010.** Birth rate changes affecting differently sized regional populations are altering the world pattern of population increase. Africa, containing 12.5% of world population in the mid-1990s, will probably account for 27% of total world increase between 1995 and 2010. Between 1965 and 1975, China's contribution to world growth was 2.5 times that of Africa; between 1995 and 2010, Africa's numerical growth will be over twice that of China. China added 65 million more people to world population than did India between 1970 and 1980. Between 1995 and 2010, India will add at least 68 million more people than China and will be overtaking China as the world's most populous country by A.D. 2045. Between 1990 and 2025, the UN projects, no less than 95% of global population growth will be in the developing countries of Africa, Asia, and Latin America.

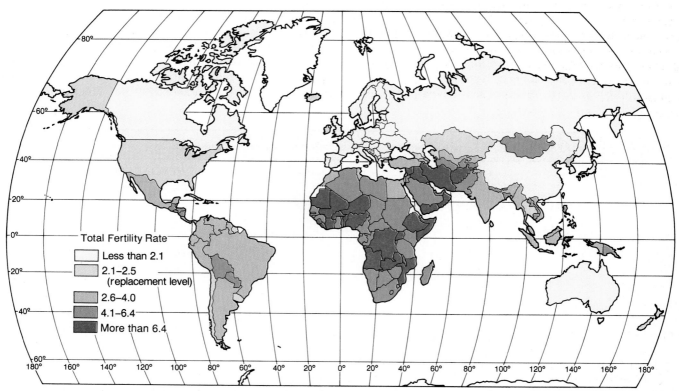

FIGURE 4.5 **Total fertility rate (TFR)** indicates the average number of children that would be born to each woman if, during her childbearing years, she bore children at the same rate as women of those ages actually did in a given year. Since the TFR is age-adjusted, two countries with identical birth rates may have quite different fertility rates and therefore different prospects for growth. Depending on mortality conditions, a TFR of 2.1 to 2.5 children per woman is considered the "replacement level," at which a population will eventually stop growing.

fertility rates for many less developed countries have dropped dramatically since the early 1960s (Table 4.1). China's drop from a TFR of 5.9 births per woman in the early 1960s to below 2.0 in the early 1990s was most impressive and demographically significant because of China's status as the world's foremost state in population. Although fertility rates are still 6 or over per woman in much of Africa and in many smaller Asian countries (see Appendix B), their worldwide impressive declines in recent years make it at least possible for total population to stabilize at the projected 11.6 billion level by A.D. 2150.

Death Rates

The **crude death rate** (CDR), also called the **mortality rate,** is calculated in the same way as the crude birth rate: the annual number of events per 1000 population. In the past, a valid generalization was that the death rate, like the birth rate, varied with national levels of development. Characteristically, highest rates (over 20 per 1000) were found in the less developed countries of Africa, Asia, and Latin America; lowest rates (less than 10) were associated with developed states of Europe and Anglo America. That correlation became decreasingly valid as dramatic Third World reductions in crude death rates occurred in the years following World War II. Infant mortality rates and life expectancies improved as antibiotics, vaccination, and pesticides to treat diseases and control disease carriers were made available in almost all parts of the world and as increased attention was paid to funding improvements in urban and rural sanitary facilities and safe water supplies.

Distinctions between more developed and less developed countries in mortality, indeed, have been so reduced that by the mid-1990s death rates for less developed countries as a group actually were lower than those for the more developed states (Figure 4.6). Notably and tragically, that reduction does not extend to maternal mortality rates (see "The Risks of Motherhood"). Like crude birth rates, death rates are meaningful for comparative purposes only when we study identically structured populations. Countries with a high proportion of elderly people, such as Denmark and Sweden, would be expected to have higher death rates than those with a high proportion of young people, such as Iceland, assuming equality in other national conditions affecting health and longevity. The pronounced youthfulness of populations in developing countries is an important factor in the recently reduced mortality rates of those areas.

To overcome that lack of comparability, death rates can be calculated for specific age groups. The *infant mortality rate,* for example, is the ratio of deaths of infants aged 1 year or under per 1000 live births:

$$\frac{\text{deaths age 1 year or less}}{1000 \text{ live births}}$$

Infant mortality rates are significant because it is at these ages that the greatest declines in mortality have occurred, largely as a result of the increased availability of health services. The drop in infant mortality accounts for a large part of the decline in the general death rate in the last few decades, for mortality during the first year of life is usually greater than in any other year.

Two centuries ago, it was not uncommon for 200–300 infants per 1000 to die in their first year. Even today, despite significant declines in those rates over the last 60 years in many individual countries (Figure 4.7), striking world regional and national variations remain. For all of Africa, infant mortality rates exceed 90 per 1000, and individual

TABLE 4.1	Total Fertility Rate Change in Selected Less Developed Countries and Regions		
REGION OR COUNTRY	EARLY 1960S[A]	MID-1990S[B]	PERCENT CHANGE
East Asia	5.3	1.8	−66.0
China	5.9	1.9	−67.8
South Asia	6.1	3.8	−37.7
Afghanistan	7.0	6.9	−1.4
Bangladesh	6.7	4.3	−35.8
India	5.8	3.4	−41.4
Nepal	5.9	5.8	−1.7
Thailand	6.4	2.2	−65.6
Africa	6.7	5.8	−13.4
Egypt	7.1	3.9	−45.1
Kenya	8.2	5.7	−30.5
Nigeria	6.9	6.3	−8.7
Latin America	5.9	3.1	−47.5
Brazil	6.2	2.9	−53.2
Guatemala	6.8	5.4	−20.6
Mexico	6.7	3.1	−53.7

Sources: [A]Thomas W. Merrick, with PRB staff, "World Population in Transition," *Population Bulletin* 41, no. 2 (Washington, D.C.: Population Reference Bureau, 1986), and [B]*World Population Data Sheet,* Population Reference Bureau.

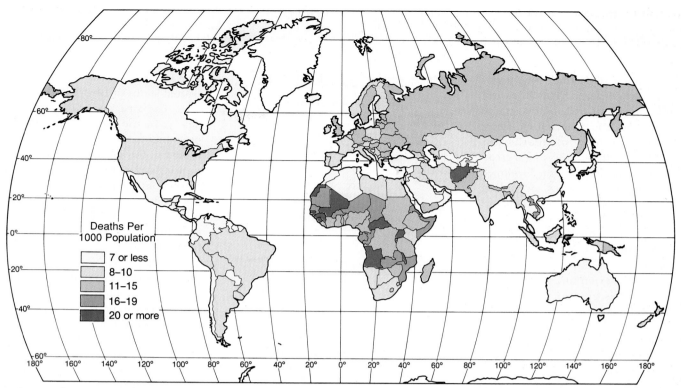

FIGURE 4.6 **Crude death rates** show less worldwide variability than do the birth rates displayed in Figure 4.3, the result of widespread availability of at least minimal health protection measures and a generally youthful population in the developing countries, where death rates are frequently lower than in "old age" Europe.

African states (for example, Guinea-Bissau and Sierra Leone) showed rates above 140 in the mid-1990s. Nor are rates uniform within single countries. The former Soviet Union reported a national infant mortality rate of 23 (1991), but it registered above 110 in parts of its Central Asian region. In contrast, infant mortality rates in Anglo America and Western Europe are more uniformly in the 6–8 range.

Modern medicine and sanitation have increased life expectancy and altered age-old relationships between birth and death rates. In the early 1950s, only 5 countries, all in northern Europe, had life expectancies at birth of over 70 years. By the mid-1990s, some 40 countries outside of Europe and North America—though none in Africa—were on that list. The availability and employment of modern methods of health and sanitation have varied regionally, and the least developed countries have least benefited from them. In such underdeveloped and impoverished areas as much of

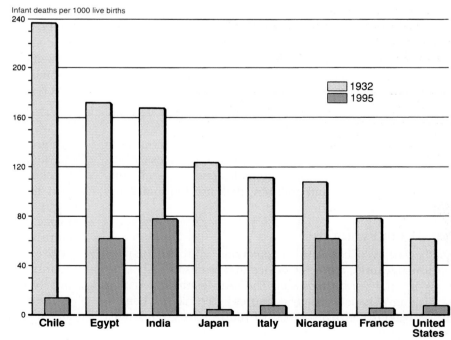

FIGURE 4.7 **Infant mortality rates for selected countries.** Dramatic declines in the rate have occurred in all countries, a result of international programs of health care delivery aimed at infants and children in developing states. Nevertheless, the decreases have been proportionately greatest in the urbanized, industrialized countries, where sanitation, safe water, and quality health care are more widely available.

he worldwide leveling of crude death rates does not apply to pregnancy-related deaths. In fact, the maternal mortality ratio—the number of deaths per 100,000 live births—is the single greatest health disparity between developed and developing countries. According to the World Health Organization, over half a million women die each year from causes related to pregnancy or its management; 99% of them live in less-developed states where, as a group, the maternal mortality ratio is some 40 times greater than in the more developed countries. Complications of pregnancy, childbirth, and unsafe abortions are the leading slayers of women of reproductive age throughout the developing world, though the incidence of maternal mortality is by no means uniform, as the charts indicate.

Excluding China, less developed countries as a group in the early 1990s had a maternal mortality rate of 410. While 60% of all maternal deaths occurred in Asia where the majority of the world's women live, sub-Saharan African women were at greatest statistical risk. There, maternal death rates

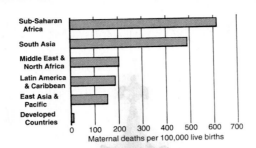

(a) **Regional Ratios of Maternal Deaths, 1990s**

Maternal deaths per 100,000 live births

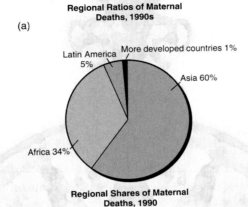

(b) **Regional Shares of Maternal Deaths, 1990**

ranged as high as over 2000 in Mali as a whole and were at least that high in less-accessible parts of several other states. In contrast, the rate in developed countries as a group is 10, and in some—Norway and Ireland, for example—it is as low as 2

or 3 (it was 5 in Canada and 8 in the United States in 1990–92).

The vast majority of maternal deaths in the developing world are preventable. Most result from causes rooted in the social, cultural, and economic barriers confronting females in their home environment throughout their lifetimes: malnutrition, anemia, lack of access to timely basic maternal health care, physical immaturity due to stunted growth, unavailability of adequate prenatal care or trained medical assistance at birth. Part of the problem is that women are considered expendable in societies where their status is low, although the correlation between women's status (Figure 10.28) and maternal mortality is not exact. In those cultures, little attention is given to women's health or their nutrition, and pregnancy, although a major cause of death, is simply considered a normal condition warranting no special consideration or management.

Sources: Graph data from UNICEF, WHO, and Population Reference Bureau.

sub-Saharan Africa, the chief causes of death are those no longer of concern in more developed lands: diseases such as malaria, intestinal infections, typhoid, cholera, and especially among infants and children, malnutrition and dehydration from diarrhea.

Population Pyramids

Another means of comparing populations is through the **population pyramid,** a graphic device that represents a population's age and sex composition. The term *pyramid* describes the diagram's shape for many countries in the 1800s, when the display was created: a broad base of younger age groups and a progressive narrowing toward the apex as older populations were thinned by death. Now many different shapes are encountered, each reflecting a different population history (Figure 4.8). By grouping several generations of people, the pyramids highlight the impact of "baby booms," population-reducing wars, birth rate reductions, and external migrations.

A rapidly growing country such as Kenya has most people in the lowest age cohorts; the percentage in older

age groups declines successively, yielding a pyramid with markedly sloping sides. Typically, female life expectancy is reduced in older cohorts of less developed countries, so that for Kenya the proportion of females in older age groups is lower than in, for example, Sweden. Female life expectancy and mortality rates may also be affected by cultural rather than economic developmental causes (see "100 Million Women Are Missing"). In Sweden, a wealthy country with a very slow rate of growth, the population is nearly equally divided among the age groups, giving a "pyramid" with almost vertical sides. Among older cohorts, as Austria shows, there may be an imbalance between men and women because of the greater life expectancy of the latter. The impacts of war, as Russia's pyramid vividly shows, are evident in that country's depleted age cohorts and male-female disparities. The sharp contrasts between the composite pyramids of sub-Saharan Africa and Western Europe summarize the differing population concerns of the developing and developed regions of the world (Figure 4.9).

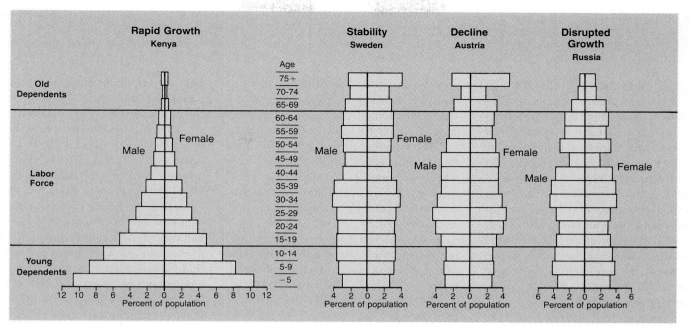

FIGURE 4.8 **Four patterns of population structure.** These diagrams show that population "pyramids" assume many shapes. The age distribution of national populations reflects the past, records the present, and foretells the future. In countries like Kenya, social costs related to the young are important and economic expansion is vital to provide employment for new entrants in the labor force. Austria's negative growth means a future with fewer workers to support a growing demand for social services for the elderly. The 1992 pyramid for Russia reports the sharp decline in births during World War II as a "pinching" of the 45–49 cohort and shows the heavy male mortality of both World Wars in the large deficits of men above age 65.

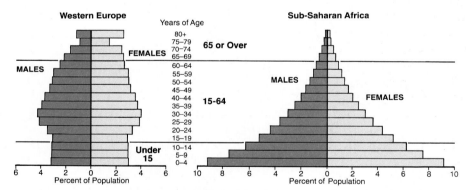

FIGURE 4.9 **Summary population pyramids, 1995.** The economically less developed countries of sub-Saharan Africa show a much younger age profile than do more developed Western European countries. In the mid-1990s, nearly 50% of their population was below age 15; in many developed regions, only about one-fifth was in that youthful cohort. In contrast, the proportion of population above 65 in Western Europe is five times that of sub-Saharan countries.

Source: Lori S. Ashford, "New Perspectives on Population: Lessons from Cairo," *Population Bulletin* 50, no. 1 (1995), Figure 3.

The population pyramid provides a quickly visualized demographic picture of immediate practical and predictive value. For example, the percentage of a country's population in each age group strongly influences demand for goods and services within that national economy. A country with a high proportion of young has a high demand for educational facilities and certain types of health delivery services. Additionally, of course, a large portion of the population is too young to be employed (Figures 4.9 and 4.10). On the other hand, a population with a high percentage of elderly people also requires medical goods and services specific to that age group (Figure 4.11), and these people must be supported by a smaller proportion of workers. The **dependency ratio** is a simple measure of the number of dependents, old or young, that each 100 people in the productive years (usually, 15–64) must support. Population pyramids give quick visual evidence of that ratio.

Worldwide, some 100 million females are missing, victims of nothing more than their sex. In China, India, Pakistan, New Guinea, and many other developing countries a traditional preference for boys has meant neglect and death for girls, millions of whom are killed at birth, deprived of adequate food, or denied the medical attention afforded to favored sons. Increasingly in China and India ultrasound and amniocentesis tests are employed to determine the sex of a fetus so that it can be aborted if it's a female.

The evidence for the missing women starts with one fact: About 105 males are conceived and born for every 100 females. Normally, girls are hardier and more resistant to disease than boys, and in populations where the sexes are treated equally in matters of nutrition and health care, there are about 105 to 106 females for every 100 males. However, the 1990 census of China found just 93.8 females for every 100 males and the 1991 census of India found just 92.9 females for every 100 males. In both cases, the ratios were more unfavorable than they had been in censuses taken just a decade earlier.

Ratio deviations are most striking for second and subsequent births. In China, South Korea, Taiwan, and Hong Kong, for example, the most recent figures for first child sex ratios are near normal, but rise to 121 boys per 100 girls for a second Chinese child to 185 for a third Korean. On that evidence, the problem of missing females is getting worse. Conservative calculations suggest there are nearly 50 million females missing in China alone, about 4% of the national population and more than are unaccounted for in any other country.

The problem is seen elsewhere. In much of South and West Asia and North Africa there are only some 94 females for every 100 males, a shortfall of about 12% of normal (Western) expectations. But not all poor countries show the same disparities. In sub-Saharan Africa, where poverty and disease are perhaps more prevalent than on any other continent, there are 102 females for every 100 males, and in Latin America and the Caribbean there are equal numbers of males and females. Cultural norms and practices, not poverty or underdevelopment, seem to determine the fate and swell the numbers of the world's 100 million missing women.

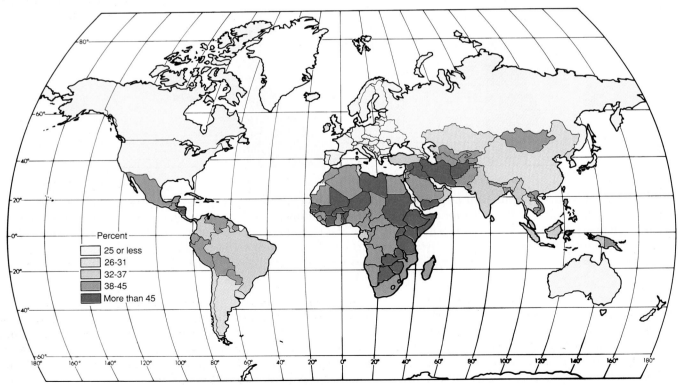

FIGURE 4.10 **Percentage of population under 15 years of age.** A high proportion of a country's population under 15 increases the dependency ratio of that state and promises future population growth as the youthful cohorts enter childbearing years.

FIGURE 4.11 As these Dutch senior citizens exemplify, Europe is an aging continent with an ever-growing proportion of the elderly dependent on the financial support of a reduced working-age population. Rapidly growing developing countries, in contrast, face increasing costs for the needs of the very young.

They also foretell future problems resulting from present population policies or practices. The strict family-size rules and widespread preferences for sons in China, for example, skews the pyramid in favor of males. At current trends, about 1 million excess males will enter an imbalanced marriage market in China beginning about 2010. Millions of bachelors, unconnected to society by wives and children, may pose threats to social order and, perhaps, national stability not foreseen or planned when family control programs were put in place, but clearly suggested when made evident by population pyramid distortions.

Natural Increase

Knowledge of their sex and age distributions also enables demographers to forecast countries' future population levels, though the reliability of projections decreases with increasing length of forecast (Figure 4.12). Thus, a country with a high proportion of young people will experience a high rate of natural increase unless there is a very high mortality rate among infants and juveniles or fertility and birth rates change materially. The **rate of natural increase** of a population is derived by subtracting the crude death rate from the crude birth rate. *Natural* means that increases or decreases due to migration are not included. If a country had a birth rate of 22 per 1000 and a death rate of 12 per 1000 for a given year, the rate of natural increase would be 10 per 1000. This rate is usually expressed as a percentage, that is, as a rate per 100 rather than per 1000. In the example given, the annual increase would be 1%.

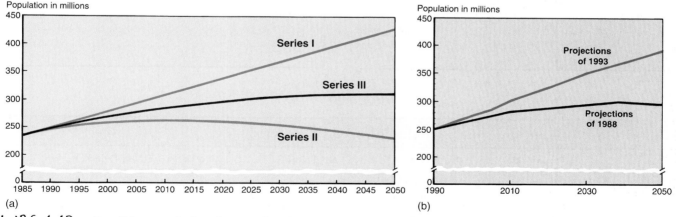

(a) (b)

FIGURE 4.12 **Possible population futures for the United States.** As these population projections to 2050 illustrate, expected future numbers vary greatly because the birth and death rates and immigration flow assumptions they are based on are different. (*a*) Depending on the assumptions, 1985 Census Bureau projections of U.S. population in 2050 ranged from 231 million (low series) to 429 million (high series). (*b*) The Bureau's new 1988 middle series projection was again revised in late 1993, reflecting actual population counts and new assumptions about fertility, immigration, and racial and ethnic differentials in births and deaths. Those counts and assumption revisions increased the earlier A.D. 2050 projection by 31%.

Source: U.S. Bureau of the Census.

Doubling Times

The rate of increase can be related to the time it takes for a population to double, that is, the **doubling time.** Table 4.2 shows that it would take 70 years for a population with a rate of increase of 1% (approximately the rate of growth of New Zealand or South Korea in the mid-1990s) to double. A 2% rate of increase—recorded in the early 1990s by the developing world as a whole—means that the population will double in only 35 years. (Population doubling time can be closely determined by dividing the growth rate into the number "69." Thus, 69 ÷ 2 = 35 years.) How could adding only 20 people per 1000 cause a population to grow so quickly? The principle is the same as that used to compound interest in a bank. Table 4.3 shows the number yielded by a 2% rate of increase at the end of successive 5-year periods.

For the world as a whole, the rates of increase have risen over the span of human history. Therefore, the doubling time has decreased. Note in Table 4.4 how the population of the world has doubled in successively shorter periods of time. It will reach 9.5 billion during the first half of the 21st century if the present rate of growth continues (Figure 4.1). In countries with high rates of increase (Figure 4.13),

the doubling time is less than the 46 years projected for the world as a whole (at growth rates recorded in 1996). Should world fertility rates decline (as they have in recent years), population doubling time will correspondingly increase as it has since 1990 (Figure 4.14).

Here, then, lies the answer to the question posed earlier. Even small annual additions accumulate to large total increments because we are dealing with geometric or exponential (1, 2, 4, 8) rather than arithmetic (1, 2, 3, 4) growth. The ever-increasing base population has reached such a size that each additional doubling results in an astronomical increase in the total. A simple mental exercise suggests the inevitable consequences of such doubling, or **J-curve,** growth. Take a very large sheet of the thinnest paper you can find and fold it in half. Fold it in half again. After seven or eight folds the sheet will have become as thick as a book—too thick for further folding by hand. If you could make 20 folds, the stack would be nearly as high as a football field is long. From then on, the results of further doubling are astounding. At 40 folds, the stack would be well on the way to the moon and at 70 it would reach twice as far as the distance to the nearest star. After 100

TABLE 4.2	Doubling Time in Years at Different Rates of Increase	
ANNUAL PERCENTAGE INCREASE		DOUBLING TIME (YEARS)
0.5		140
1.0		70
2.0		35
3.0		24
4.0		17
5.0		14
10.0		7

TABLE 4.3	Population Growth Yielded by a 2% Rate of Increase
YEAR	POPULATION
0	1000
5	1104
10	1219
15	1345
20	1485
25	1640
30	1810
35	2000

TABLE 4.4	Population Growth and Approximate Doubling Times since A.D. 1	
YEAR	ESTIMATED POPULATION	DOUBLING TIME (YEARS)
1	250 million	
1650	500 million	1650
1804	1 billion	154
1927	2 billion	123
1974	4 billion	47
World population may reach 2021	8 billion	47[a]

[a]The leveling of doubling time reflects assumptions of decreasing and stabilizing fertility rates. No current projections contemplate a further doubling to 16 billion people.

Source: United Nations.

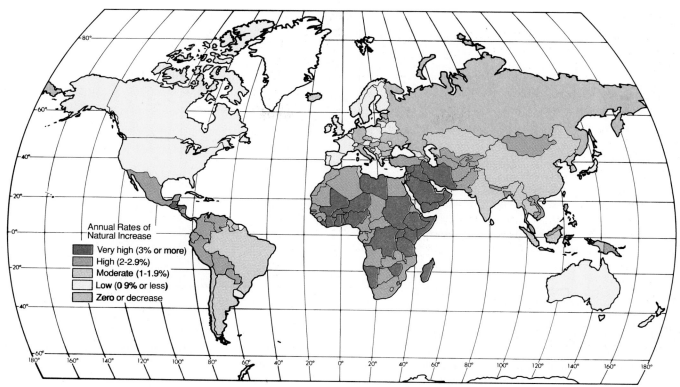

FIGURE 4.13 **Annual rates of natural increase.** The world's 1995 rate of natural increase (1.5%) would mean a doubling of population in 45 years. Many individual continents and countries, of course, deviate widely from the global average rate of growth and have vastly different doubling times. Africa as a whole has the highest rates of increase, followed by western Asia and Central and South America. Europe and North America are prominent among the low-growth areas, with such countries as Italy actually experiencing single year negative growth and showing doubling times measured in millennia.

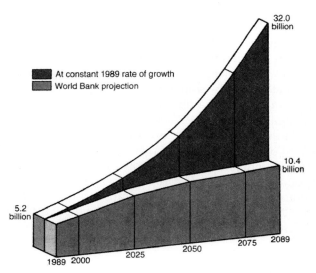

FIGURE 4.14 The "doubling time" calculation illustrates the long-range effect of growth rates on populations. It should never be used to suggest a prediction of future population size, for population growth reflects not just birth rates, but death rates, age structure, and migration. Demographers generally assume that high present growth rates will gradually be reduced. Therefore, if population does double, it will take longer to do so than is suggested by a "doubling time" based on the current rate.

folds, our paper would be more than ten billion light years across and span the known universe. Rounding the bend on the J-curve, which world population has done (Figure 4.15), poses problems and has implications for human occupance of the earth of a vastly greater order of magnitude than ever faced before.

The Demographic Transition

The theoretical consequence of exponential population growth cannot be realized. Some form of braking mechanism must necessarily operate to control totally unregulated population growth. If voluntary population limitation is not undertaken, involuntary controls of an unpleasant nature may be set in motion.

One attempt to summarize an observed voluntary relationship between population growth and economic development is the **demographic transition** model. It traces the changing levels of human fertility and mortality presumably associated with industrialization and urbanization. Over time, the model assumes, high birth and death rates will gradually be replaced by low rates (Figure 4.16). The *first stage* of that replacement process—and of the demographic transition model—is characterized by high birth and high but fluctuating death rates.

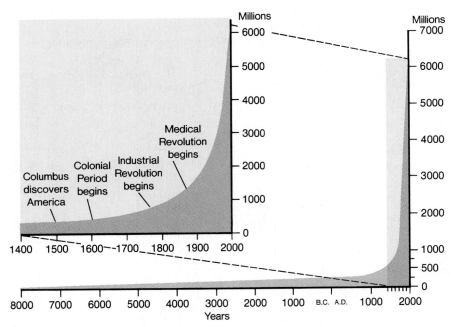

FIGURE 4.15 **World population growth 8000 B.C. to A.D. 2000.** Notice that the bend in the J-curve begins in about the mid-1700s when industrialization started to provide new means to support the population growth made possible by revolutionary changes in agriculture and food supply. Improvements in medical science and nutrition served to reduce death rates near the opening of the 20th century in the industrializing countries.

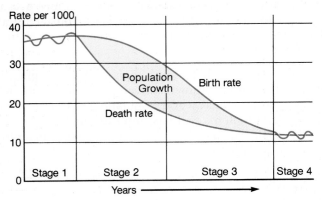

FIGURE 4.16 **Stages in the demographic transition.** During the first stage, birth and death rates are both high, and population grows slowly. When the death rate drops and the birth rate remains high, there is a rapid increase in numbers. During the third stage, birth rates decline and population growth is less rapid. The fourth stage is marked by low birth and death rates and, consequently, by a low rate of natural increase or even by decrease if death rates should exceed those of births. Indeed, the negative growth rates of, particularly, Eastern European countries and Russia have suggested to some that a fifth state of population decline is—at least regionally—a logical extension of the transition model.

As long as births only slightly exceed deaths, even when the rates of both are high, the population will grow only slowly. This was the case for most of human history until about A.D. 1750. Demographers think that it took from approximately A.D. 1 to A.D. 1650 for the population to increase from 250 million to 500 million, a doubling time of more than a millennium and a half. Growth was not steady, of course. There were periods of regional expansion that were usually offset by sometimes catastrophic decline. Wars, famine, and other disasters took heavy tolls. For example, the bubonic plague (the Black Death), which swept across Europe in the 14th century, is estimated to have killed over one-third of the population of that continent. The first stage of the demographic transition model is no longer found in any country. In the middle 1990s, the highest death rates—found in a few African and Asian countries—were in the low 20s per 1000; but the birth rates in some of those same countries were even higher, near or above 50 per 1000.

The Western Experience

The demographic transition model was developed to explain the population history of Western Europe. That area entered a *second stage* with the industrialization that began about 1750. Its effects—declining death rates accompanied by continuing high birth rates—have been dispersed worldwide even without universal conversion to an industrial economy. Rapidly rising populations during the second demographic stage result from dramatic increases in life expectancy. That, in turn, reflects falling death rates due to advances in medical and sanitation practices, improved foodstuff storage and distribution, a rising per capita income, and the urbanization that provides the environment in which sanitary, medical, and food distributional improvements are concentrated (Figure 4.17). Birth rates do not fall as soon as death rates; ingrained cultural patterns change more slowly than technologies. In many agrarian societies, large families are considered advantageous. Children contribute to the family by starting to work at an early age and by supporting their parents in old age.

Many countries in Latin America and parts of southern and southeastern Asia display the characteristics of this second stage in the population model. Syria, with a birth rate of 44 and a death rate of 6, and Guatemala, with respective rates of 36 and 7 (1996 estimates), are typical. The annual rates of increase of such countries are near or above 30 per 1000, and their populations will double in about 20 to 25 years. Such rates, of course, do not mean that the full impact of the Industrial Revolution has been worldwide; they do mean that the underdeveloped societies have been beneficiaries of the life preservation techniques associated with it.

The *third stage* follows when birth rates decline as people begin to control family size. The advantages that having many children bring in an agrarian society are not so evident in urbanized, industrialized cultures. In fact, such cultures may view children as economic liabilities rather than assets. When the birth rate falls and the death rate remains low, the population size begins to level off.

FIGURE 4.17 Vienna, Austria, in the 1870s. A modernizing Europe experienced improved living conditions and declining death rates during the 19th century.

Chile, Sri Lanka, and Thailand are among the many countries now displaying the low death rates and transitional birth rates of the third stage.

The demographic transition ends with a *fourth* and final stage. Essentially all European countries, Canada, Australia, and Japan are among the 40 or so states that have entered this phase. Because it is characterized by very low birth and death rates, it yields at best only very slight percentage increases in population. Population doubling times may be as long as a thousand years or more if those present low birth rates continue. In a few countries of Central and Eastern Europe death rates have begun to equal or exceed birth rates, and populations are declining (see "Europe's Population Dilemma"), an extension of the fourth stage into a fifth so far confined to the developed world in general, not just to Europe. Japan's current slight natural increase, for example, will become a decrease in A.D. 2006, and Taiwan forecasts zero or negative population growth by 2035.

The demographic transition model describes the experience of northwest European countries as they went from rural-agrarian societies to urban-industrial ones. It may not fully reflect the prospects of contemporary developing countries. In Europe, church and municipal records, some dating from the 16th century, show that people tended to marry late or not at all. In England before the Industrial Revolution as many as half of all women in the 15–50 age cohort were unmarried. Infant mortality was high, life expectancy low. With the coming of industrialization in the 18th and 19th centuries, immediate factory wages instead of long apprenticeship programs permitted earlier marriage and more children. Since improvements in sanitation and health came only slowly, death rates remained high. Around 1800, 25% of Swedish infants died before their first birthday. Population growth rates remained below 1% per year in France throughout the 19th century.

Beginning about 1860, first death rates and then birth rates began their significant, though gradual, decline. This "mortality revolution" came first, as an *epidemiologic transition* echoed the demographic transition with which it is associated. Many formerly fatal epidemic diseases became endemic, that is, essentially continual within a population. As people developed partial immunities, mortalities associated with them declined. Improvements in animal husbandry, crop rotation and other agricultural practices, and new foodstuffs (the potato was an early example) from overseas colonies raised the level of health of the European population in general.

At the same time, sewage systems and sanitary water supplies became common in larger cities, and general levels of hygiene improved everywhere (Figure 4.18). Deaths due to infectious, parasitic, and respiratory diseases and to malnutrition declined, while those related to chronic illnesses associated with a maturing and aging population increased. Western Europe passed from a first-stage "Age of Pestilence and Famine" to an ultimate "Age of Degenerative and Human-Origin Diseases." However, recent increases in

Although international dismay may be expressed over rising world populations, some European states are facing an opposite domestic concern. Europe's population is older than that of any other continent, and for many of its countries, population is stagnating or declining. The fertility rates (TFRs) of 37 of the continent's 40 states in 1996 were below the **replacement level**—the level of fertility at which populations replace themselves—of 2.1. None of the larger countries are at present replacing their population through natural increase. With 1996 fertility rates of 1.2 to 1.3 Germany, Italy, Slovenia, and Spain stand at the bottom of the international reproduction scale. Not surprisingly, Western Europe also has the oldest population in the world, with a small proportion of young and a large share of middle-aged and retired persons in its population pyramid. Indeed, almost all of Europe has the same problem of declining population growth, reduced work-age cohorts, and an aging citizenry. The continent's population could begin to decline in the 1990s, barring a dramatic increase in birth rates or massive Asian and African in-migration. By the early 21st century, Europe will have more older than younger people and its population "pyramid" will be inverted.

Spatially, Europe's remaining fertility is peripheral. Catholic Ireland in the west has a fertility rate at or a little above the replacement level, as do Lutheran Iceland in the far west and Sweden in the north. In the southeast, Muslim Albania shows high reproduction rates and is far above the replacement fertility point. The former communist states of Eastern Europe, which before 1989 generally had pro-natal policies and relatively high birth rates by Western European standards, have experienced sharp decreases in their reproduction rates since their liberation. Between 1989 and mid-1993, birth rates in eastern Germany dropped by more than 60%. In the same period, the birth rate fell more than 20% in Poland, around 25% in Bulgaria, over 30% in Estonia and Romania, and 35% in Russia. By 1991, deaths exceeded births in most areas of Eastern Europe, bringing its population trends in line with the West's. "In demographic terms," France's prime minister remarked, "Europe is vanishing."

The national social and economic consequences of population stability or reduction are not always perceived by those who advocate **zero population growth,** a condition achieved when births plus immigration equal deaths plus emigration. An exact equation of births and deaths means an increasing proportion of older citizens, fewer young people, and a rise in the median age of the population. Actual population decline, now the common European condition, exaggerates those consequences. Already, schools are closing and universities cut back in the face of permanently reduced demand. Governments will have to provide pensions and social services for the one-quarter of their citizens older than 60 and pay for them by taxes on a diminishing workforce. Germany in 1991 had 4 pensioners for every 10 workers; by 2030, the numbers will be equal. Unless European birth rates rise dramatically, or the massive immigration of the early 1990s continues, the continent's "old-age dependency ratio" will double by 2040. Once a population starts to age it is difficult to reverse the trend.

FIGURE 4.18 Pure piped water replacing individual or neighborhood wells, and sewers and waste treatment plants instead of privies, became increasingly common in urban Europe and North America during the 19th century. Their modern successors, such as the Windsor, Ontario, treatment plant shown here, helped complete the *epidemiologic transition* in developed countries.

drug- and antibiotic-resistant diseases, pesticide resistance of disease-carrying insects, and such new scourges of both the less developed and more developed countries as AIDS (acquired immune deficiency syndrome) cast doubt on the finality of that "ultimate" stage.

Malaria and tuberculosis have staged comebacks in resistant forms, and the World Health Organization estimates that there will be worldwide perhaps a million deaths a year from AIDS, with the greatest impact in Africa. Even these old and new scourges are unlikely to have serious long-term demographic consequences. The United Nations, for example, has estimated that in a hypothetical worst case—that is if all of Africa were affected by AIDS on the same scale as its worst known affected areas—Africa's population growth rate would still be about 1.8% at the end of the century. On a global scale, reproduction rates seem certain to outpace disease mortality rates.

In Europe, the striking reduction in death rates was echoed by similar declines in birth rates as societies began to alter their traditional concepts of ideal family size. In cities, child labor laws and mandatory schooling meant that children became a burden, not a contribution, to family economies. As "poor-relief" legislation and other forms of public welfare substituted for family support structures, the insurance value of children declined. Family consumption patterns altered as the Industrial Revolution made more widely available goods that served consumption desires, not just basic living needs. Children hindered rather than aided the achievement of the age's promise of social mobility and life-style improvement. Perhaps most important, and by some measures preceding and independent of the implications of the Industrial Revolution, were changes in the status of women and in their spreading conviction that control over childbearing was within their power and to their benefit.

A World Divided

The demographic transition model described the presumed inevitable course of population events from the high birth and death rates of premodern (underdeveloped) societies to the low and stable rates of advanced (developed) countries. The model failed to anticipate, however, that by the 1990s many developing societies would seemingly be locked in the second stage of the model, unable to realize the economic gains and social changes necessary to progress to the third stage of falling birth rates. The population history of Europe was apparently not inevitably or fully applicable to all developing countries of the middle and late 20th century.

The introduction of Western technologies of medicine and public health including antibiotics, insecticides, sanitation, immunization, infant and child health care, and eradication of smallpox, quickly and dramatically lowered the death rates in developing countries. Such imported technologies and treatments accomplished in a few years what it took Europe 50 or 100 years to experience. Sri Lanka, for example, sprayed extensively with DDT to combat malaria; life expectancy jumped from 44 years in 1946 to 60 only 8 years later. With similar public health programs, India also experienced a steady reduction in its death rate after 1947. Simultaneously, with international sponsorship, food aid cut the death toll of developing states during drought and other disasters. The dramatic decline in mortality, which emerged only gradually throughout the European world but occurred so rapidly in contemporary developing countries, has been the most fundamental demographic change in human history.

Corresponding reductions in birth rates have been harder to achieve and depend less on supplied technology and assistance than they do on social acceptance of the idea of fewer children and smaller families (Figure 4.19). The consequence is a world polarized demographically. Roughly one-quarter of the world's countries—voluntarily or through national plan—have limited their rates of natural increase to about 0.8% annually. The other three-quarters are growing, on average, at triple that rate. In both instances, the established pattern tends to become self-reinforcing. Low growth permits the expansion of personal income and accumulation of capital that enhance the quality and security of life and make large families less attractive or essential.

When the population doubles each generation, as it must at the fertility rates of the highest-growth portion of the divided world, a different reinforcing mechanism operates. Population growth consumes in social services and assistance the investment capital that might promote economic expansion. Increasing populations place ever greater demands on limited soil, forest, water, grassland, and cropland resources. Those pressures may, through human-induced deforestation and desertification, for example, consume the environmental base itself. Productivity declines and population-supporting capacities are so diminished as to make difficult or impossible the economic progress upon which the demographic transition depends, an apparent equation of increasing international concern (see "The Cairo Plan").

The Demographic Equation

Births and deaths among a region's population—natural increases or decreases—tell only part of the story of population change. Migration involves the long-distance movement of people from one residential location to another. When that relocation occurs across political boundaries, it affects the population structure of both the origin and destination jurisdictions. The **demographic equation** summarizes the contribution made to regional population change over time by the combination of *natural change* (difference between births and deaths) and *net migration* (difference between in-migration and out-migration). On a global scale, of course, all population change is accounted for by natural change. The impact of migration on the demographic equation increases as the population size of the areal unit studied decreases.

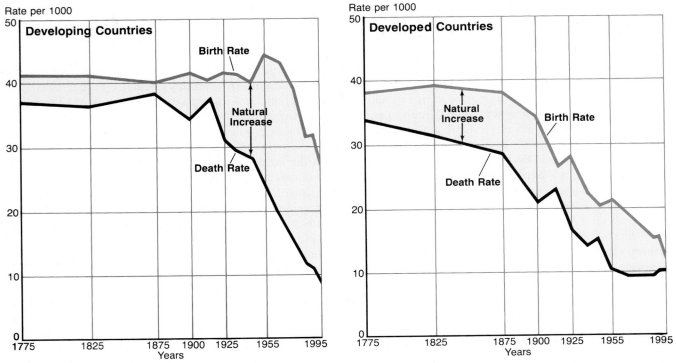

FIGURE 4.19   **World birth and death rates.** The "population explosion" after World War II (1939–1945) reflected the effects of drastically reduced death rates in developing countries without simultaneous and compensating reductions in births. By 1995, however, three interrelated trends had appeared in many developing world countries: (1) fertility had overall dropped further and faster than had been predicted 20 years earlier, (2) contraceptive acceptance and use had increased markedly, and (3) age at marriage was rising. In consequence, the demographic transition had been compressed from a century to a generation in some developing states. In others, fertility decline began to slacken in the mid-1970s reflecting the average number of children—four or more—still desired in many societies.

Population Relocation

In the past, emigration proved an important device for relieving the pressures of rapid population growth in at least some European countries (Figure 4.20). For example, in one 90-year span, 45% of the natural increase in the population of the British Isles emigrated, and between 1846 and 1935 some 60 million Europeans of all nationalities left that continent. Despite recent massive movements of economic and political refugees across Asian, African, and Latin American boundaries, emigration today provides no comparable relief valve for developing countries (Table 4.5). Total population numbers are too great to be much affected by migrations of even millions of people. In only a few countries—Afghanistan, Cuba, El Salvador, and Haiti, for example—have as many as 10% of the population emigrated in recent decades. A more detailed treatment of the processes and patterns of international and intranational migrations as expressions of spatial interaction is presented in Chapter 3.

Immigration Impacts

Where cross-border movements are massive enough, migration may have a pronounced impact on the demographic equation and result in significant changes in the population structures of both the origin and destination regions. Past European and African migrations, for example, not only altered but substantially created the population structures of new, sparsely inhabited lands of colonization in the Western Hemisphere and Australasia. In some decades of the late 18th and early 19th centuries 30% to more than 40% of population increase in the United States was accounted for by immigration. Similarly, eastward-moving Slavs colonized underpopulated Siberia and overwhelmed native peoples.

Migrants are rarely a representative cross section of the population group they leave, and they add an unbalanced age and sex component to the group they join. A recurrent research observation is that emigrant groups are heavily skewed in favor of young singles. Whether males or females dominate the outflow seems to vary with circumstances. Although males traditionally far exceeded females in international flow, in recent years females have accounted for between 40% and 60% of all transborder migrants.

At the least, then, the receiving country will have its population structure altered by an outside increase in its younger age and, probably, unmarried cohorts. The results are both immediate, in a modified population pyramid, and potential, in future impact on reproduction rates and excess of births over deaths. The origin area will have lost a portion of its young, active members of childbearing years.

THE CAIRO PLAN

After a sometimes rancorous nine-day meeting in Cairo in September 1994, the United Nations International Conference on Population and Development endorsed a strategy for stabilizing the world's population at 7.27 billion by no later than 2015. The 20-year "program of action" accepted by over 150 signatory countries seeks to avoid the environmental consequences of population growth that could put world totals at 11 to 12 billion or more by 2050. Its proposals were therefore linked to discussions and decisions of the UN Conference on Environment and Development held in Rio de Janeiro in June 1992.

The Cairo plan abandons several decades of policies that promoted "population control" (a phrase no longer employed) based on frequently coercive targets and quotas and, instead, embraces for the first time policies giving women greater control over their lives, greater economic equality and opportunity, and a greater voice in reproduction decisions. It recognizes that limiting population growth depends on programs that increase the educational and economic prospects and political rights of women, leading women to want fewer children and making them partners in economic development. In that recognition the Conference builds on extensive evidence that increased educational access and economic opportunity for women are invariably linked to falling birth rates and smaller families. Earlier population conferences—1974 in Bucharest and 1984 in Mexico City—did not fully address these issues of equality, opportunity, education, and political rights; their adopted goals failed to achieve hoped-for changes in births in large part because women in many traditional societies had no power to enforce contraception and feared their other alternative, sterilization.

The earlier conferences carefully avoided or specifically excluded abortion as an acceptable family planning method. It was the more open discussion of abortion in Cairo that elicited much of the spirited debate that registered religious objections by the Vatican and many Muslim and Latin American states to the inclusion of legal abortion as part of health care, and to language suggesting approval of sexual relations outside of marriage. Even though the final text of the conference declaration did not promote any universal right to abortion and excluded it as a means of family planning, some 20 of the 150 delegations still registered reservations to its wording on both sex and abortion. At conference close, however, the Vatican endorsed the declaration's underlying principles, including the family as "the basic unit of society," the need to stimulate economic growth, and to promote "gender equality, equity, and the empowerment of women."

Islamic and Christian reservations on abortion were matched by even broader complaints that demands for action on population growth are apt to be tied to aid for poorer countries, selectively limiting their opportunities for economic development and progress. The argument runs that the burden of limiting population continues to fall on the poor while the richer industrialized states are, in reality, the greater danger to world environment and development because of their disproportionate demands on natural resources and the production of pollution.

The Cairo plan assumes a three-fold increase in the world amount spent on population stabilization, from about $5 billion in 1994 to about $17 billion by 2000. Some $5.7 billion is to come from donor countries while countries with existing successful programs combining family planning, education, and economic opportunities for women are to share their expertise. Both the World Bank and the U.S. Agency for International Development (A.I.D.) propose launching integrated health, education, and loan programs for women, and the U.S. Congress approved $585 million for population aid in fiscal 1995, double the 1992 figure, but far short of the annual $1.9 billion U.S. contribution needed to meet Cairo's A.D. 2000 goal.

Questions:

1. *Do you think it is appropriate or useful for international bodies to promote policies affecting such purely personal or national concerns as reproduction and family planning? Why or why not?*

2. *Do you think that current international concerns over population growth, development, and the environment are sufficiently valid and pressing to risk the loss of long-enduring cultural norms and religious practices in many of the world's traditional societies? Why or why not?*

3. *Do you think that the financial obligations implied for developed, donor countries by the Cairo Plan are justified in light of the many other international needs and domestic concerns faced by their governments? Why or why not?*

4. *Many environmentalists see the world as a finite system unable to support ever-increasing populations; to exceed its limits would cause frightful environmental damage and global misery. Many economists counter that free markets will keep supplies of needed commodities in line with growing demand and that science will as necessary supply technological fixes in the form of substitutes or expansion of production. In light of such diametrically opposed views of population growth consequences, is it appropriate or wise to base international programs solely on one of them? Why?*

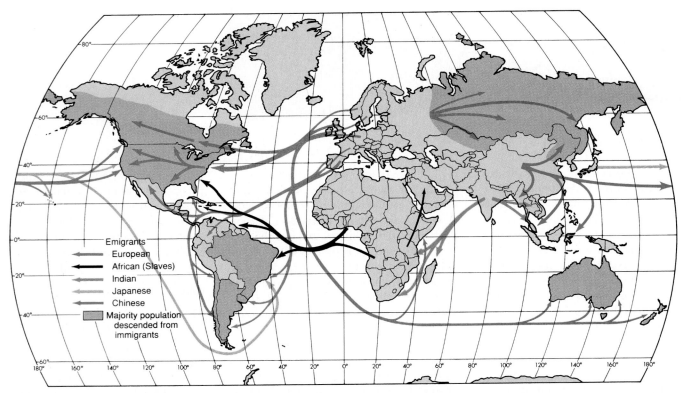

FIGURE 4.20   **Principal migrations of recent centuries.** The arrows suggest the major free and forced international population movements since about 1700. The shaded areas on the map are regions whose present population is more than 50% descended from the immigrants of recent centuries.

TABLE 4.5   Percentage of Natural Population Increase that Permanently Emigrated

PERIOD	EUROPE	ASIA[A]	AFRICA	LATIN AMERICA[A]
1851–1880	11.7	0.4	[B]	0.3
1881–1910	19.5	0.3	[B]	0.9
1911–1940	14.4	0.1	[B]	1.8
1940–1960	2.7[C]	0.1	[B]	1.0
1960–1970	5.2	0.2	0.1	1.0
1970–1980	4.0	0.5	0.3	2.5

[A]The periods from 1850 to 1960 report emigration only to the United States.

[B]Less than 0.1 percent

[C]Emigration only to the United States.

Source: World Bank, *World Development Report 1984*, p. 69. Note: Numbers are calculated from data on gross immigration in Australia, Canada, New Zealand, and the United States.

It perhaps will have suffered distortion in its young adult sex ratios, and it certainly will have recorded a statistical aging of its population. The receiving society will likely experience increases in births associated with the youthful newcomers and, in general, have its average age reduced. As we shall see in Chapter 6, a more profound effect of immigration on receiving societies may be a partial or substantial modification of their existing ethnic mix as newcomers from different racial, religious, and national backgrounds alter the established cultural structure.

World Population Distribution

The millions and billions of people of our discussion are not uniformly distributed over the earth. The most striking feature of the world population distribution map (Figure 4.21) is the very unevenness of the pattern. Some land areas are nearly uninhabited, others are sparsely settled, and still others contain dense agglomerations of people. More than half of the world's people are found—unevenly concentrated, to

THEMES AND FUNDAMENTALS OF HUMAN GEOGRAPHY

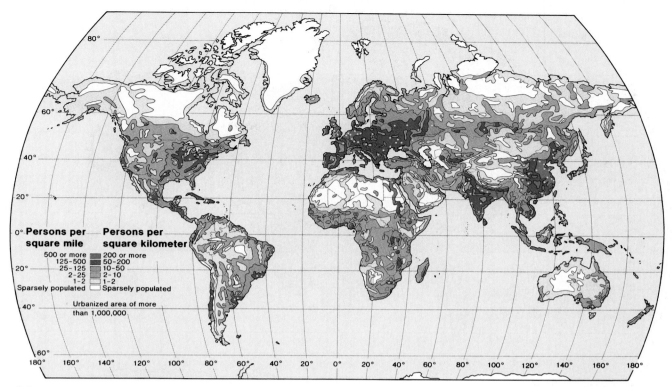

FIGURE 4.21　World population density.

be sure—in rural areas. More than 40% are urbanites, however, and a constantly growing proportion are residents of very large cities of 1 million or more.

Earth regions of apparently very similar physical makeup show quite different population numbers and densities, perhaps the result of differently timed settlement or of settlement by different cultural groups. Had North America been settled by Chinese instead of Europeans, for example, it is likely that its western sections would be far more densely settled than they now are. Northern and Western Europe, inhabited thousands of years before North America, contain more people than the United States on 70% less land.

We can draw certain generalizing conclusions from the uneven but far from irrational distribution of population shown in Figure 4.21. First, almost 90% of all people live north of the equator and two-thirds of the total dwell in the midlatitudes between 20° and 60° North (Figure 4.22). Second, a large majority of the world's inhabitants occupy only a small part of its land surface. Over half the people live on about 5% of the land, two-thirds on 10%, and almost nine-tenths on less than 20%. Third, people congregate in lowland areas; their numbers decrease sharply with increases in elevation. Temperature, length of growing season, slope and erosion problems, even oxygen reductions at very high altitudes, all appear to limit the habitability of higher elevations. One estimate is that between 50% and 60% of all people live below 200 meters (650 feet), a zone containing less that 30% of total land area. Nearly 80% reside below 500 meters (1650 feet).

Fourth, although low-lying areas are preferred settlement locations, not all such areas are equally favored. Continental margins have attracted densest settlement. About two-thirds of world population is concentrated within 500 kilometers (300 miles) of the ocean, much of it on alluvial lowlands and river valleys. Latitude, aridity, and elevation, however, limit the attractiveness of many seafront locations. Low temperatures and infertile soils of the extensive Arctic coastal lowlands of the Northern Hemisphere have restricted settlement there. Mountainous or desert coasts are sparsely occupied at any latitude, and some tropical lowlands and river valleys that are marshy, forested, and disease infested are unevenly settled.

Within the sections of the world generally conducive to settlement, four areas contain great clusters of population: East Asia, South Asia, Europe, and northeastern United States/southeastern Canada. The *East Asia* zone, which includes Japan, China, Taiwan, and South Korea, is areally the largest cluster. The four countries forming it contain 25% of all people on earth; China alone accounts for one in five of the world's inhabitants. The *South Asia* cluster is composed primarily of countries associated with the Indian subcontinent—Bangladesh, India, Pakistan, and the island state of Sri Lanka—though some might add to it the Southeast Asian countries of Cambodia, Myanmar, and Thailand. The four core countries alone account for another one-fifth, 21%, of the world's inhabitants. The South and the East Asian concentrations are thus home to nearly one-half of the world's people.

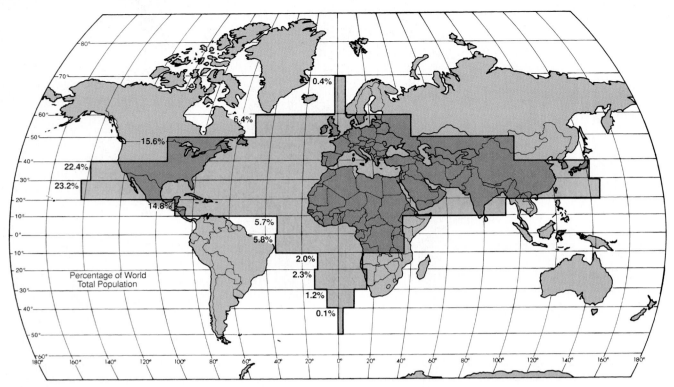

FIGURE 4.22 **The population dominance of the Northern Hemisphere** is strikingly evident from this bar chart. Only one out of nine people lives south of the equator—not because the Southern Hemisphere is underpopulated, but because it is mainly water.

Europe—southern, western, and eastern through Ukraine and much of European Russia—is the third extensive world population concentration, with another 13% of its inhabitants. Much smaller in extent and total numbers is the cluster in *northeastern United States and adjacent Canada.* Other such smaller but pronounced concentrations are found around the globe: on the island of Jawa (Java) in Indonesia, along the Nile River in Egypt, and in discontinuous pockets in Africa and Latin America.

The term **ecumene** is applied to permanently inhabited areas of the earth's surface. The ancient Greeks used the word, derived from their verb "to inhabit," to describe their known world between what they believed to be the unpopulated searing southern equatorial lands and the permanently frozen northern polar reaches of the earth. Clearly, natural conditions are less restrictive than Greek geographers believed. Both ancient and modern technologies have rendered habitable areas that natural conditions make forbidding. Irrigation, terracing, diking, and draining are among the methods devised to extend the ecumene locally (Figure 4.23).

At the world scale, the ancient observation of habitability appears remarkably astute. The **nonecumene,** or *anecumene,* the uninhabited or very sparsely occupied zone, does include the permanent ice caps of the Far North and

Antarctica and large segments of the tundra and coniferous forest of northern Asia and North America. But the nonecumene is not continuous, as the ancients supposed. It is discontinuously encountered in all portions of the globe and includes parts of the tropical rain forests of equatorial zones, midlatitude deserts of both the Northern and Southern Hemispheres, and high mountain areas.

Even parts of these unoccupied or sparsely occupied districts have localized dense settlement nodes or zones based on irrigation agriculture, mining and industrial activities, and the like. Perhaps the most anomalous case of settlement in the nonecumene world is that of the dense population in the Andes Mountains of South America and the plateau of Mexico. Here Native Americans found temperate conditions away from the dry coast regions and the hot, wet Amazon basin. The fertile high basins have served a large population for more than a thousand years.

Even with these locally important exceptions, the nonecumene portion of the earth is extensive. Some 35–40% of all the world's land surface is inhospitable and without significant settlement. This is, admittedly, a smaller proportion of the earth than would have qualified as uninhabitable in ancient times or even during the last century. Since the end of the Ice Age some 11,000 years ago, humans have steadily expanded their areas of settlement.

FIGURE 4.23   Terracing of hillsides is one device to extend a naturally limited productive area. The technique is effectively used here at the Malegcong rice terraces on densely settled Luzon Island of the Philippines.

Population Density

Margins of habitation could only be extended, of course, as humans learned to support themselves from the resources of new settlement areas. The numbers that could be sustained in old or new habitation zones were and are related to the resource potential of those areas and the cultural levels and technologies possessed by the occupying populations. The term **population density** expresses the relationship between number of inhabitants and the area they occupy.

Density figures are useful, if sometimes misleading, representations of regional variations of human distribution. The **crude density** or **arithmetic density** of population is the most common and least satisfying expression of that variation. It is the calculation of the number of people per unit area of land, usually within the boundaries of a political entity. It is an easily reckoned figure. All that is required is information on total population and total area, both commonly available for national or other political units. The figure can, however, be misleading and may obscure more of reality than it reveals. The calculation is an average, and a country may contain extensive regions that are only sparsely populated or largely undevelopable (Figure 4.24) along with intensively settled and developed districts. A national average density figure reveals nothing about either class of territory. In general, the larger the political unit for which crude or arithmetic population density is calculated, the less useful is the figure.

Various modifications may be made to refine density as a meaningful abstraction of distribution. Its descriptive precision is improved if the area in question can be subdivided into comparable regions or units. Thus it is more revealing to know that in the early 1990s New Jersey had a density of 405 and Wyoming of 2 persons per square kilometer (1050 and 5 per sq. mi.) of land area than to know only that the figure for the conterminous United States (48 states) was 34 per square kilometer (88 per sq. mi.). If large, sparsely populated Alaska is added, the U.S. density figure drops below 29 per square kilometer (74 per sq. mi.). The calculation may also be modified to provide density distinctions between classes of population—rural versus urban, for example. Rural densities in the United States rarely exceed 115 per square kilometer (300 per sq. mi.), while portions of major cities can have tens of thousands of people in equivalent space.

Another revealing refinement of crude density relates population not simply to total national territory but to that area of a country that is or may be cultivated, that is, to *arable* land. When total population is divided by arable land area alone, the resulting figure is the **physiological density** which is, in a sense, an expression of population pressure exerted on agricultural land. Table 4.6 makes evident that countries differ in physiological density and that the contrasts between crude and physiological densities of countries point up actual settlement pressures that are not revealed by arithmetic densities alone. But the calculation of physio-

FIGURE 4.24   Tundra vegetation and landscape, Ruby Range, Northwest Territories, Canada. Extensive areas of northern North America and Eurasia are part of the one-third or more of the world's land area considered as *nonecumene,* sparsely populated portions of total national territory that affect calculations of arithmetic density.

TABLE 4.6   Comparative Densities for Selected Countries

COUNTRY	CRUDE DENSITY (MI^2)	(KM^2)	PHYSIOLOGICAL DENSITY[A] (MI^2)	(KM^2)
Argentina	32	12	246	95
Australia	6	2	98	38
Bangladesh	2320	896	3255	1257
Canada	8	3	163	63
China	331	128	3222	1244
Egypt	153	59	5912	2283
India	794	307	1393	538
Iran	97	37	1072	414
Japan	860	332	6918	2671
Nigeria	279	108	811	313
United Kingdom	636	246	2163	835
United States	74	29	355	137

[A]Includes arable land and land in permanent crops.

Sources: UN Food and Agriculture Organization (FAO), *Production Yearbook;* United States Department of Agriculture, *World Agriculture: Trends and Indicators;* and *World Population Data Sheet,* Population Reference Bureau.

logical density depends on uncertain definitions of arable and cultivated land, assumes that all arable land is equally productive and comparably used, and includes only one part of a country's resource base.

Overpopulation

It is an easy and common step from concepts of population density to assumptions about overpopulation or overcrowding. It is wise to remember that **overpopulation** is a value judgement reflecting an observation or conviction that an environment or territory is unable to support its present population. (A related but opposite concept of *underpopulation* refers to the circumstance of too few people to develop the resources of a country or region sufficiently to improve the level of living of its inhabitants.)

Overpopulation is not the necessary and inevitable consequence of high density of population. Tiny Monaco, a principality in southern Europe about half the size of New York's Central Park, has a crude density of nearly 20,000 people per square kilometer (50,000 people per sq. mi.). Mongolia, a sizable state of 1,565,000 square kilometers (604,000 sq. mi.) between China and Siberian Russia, has 1.5

persons per square kilometer (4 per sq. mi.); Iran, only slightly larger, has 37 per square kilometer (96 per sq. mi.). Macao, an island possession of Portugal off the coast of China, has more than 26,000 persons per square kilometer (67,000 per sq. mi.); the Falkland Islands off the Atlantic coast of Argentina count at most 1 person for every 6.5 square kilometers (2.5 sq. mi.) of territory. No conclusions about conditions of life, levels of income, adequacy of food, or prospects for prosperity can be drawn from these density comparisons.

Overcrowding is a reflection not of numbers per unit area but of the **carrying capacity** of land—the number of people an area can support on a sustained basis given the prevailing technology. A region devoted to efficient, energy-intensive commercial agriculture that makes heavy use of irrigation, fertilizers, and biocides can support more people at a higher level of living than one engaged in the slash-and-burn agriculture described in Chapter 8. An industrial society that takes advantage of resources such as coal and iron ore and has access to imported food will not feel population pressure at the same density levels as a country with rudimentary technology.

Since carrying capacity is related to the level of economic development, maps such as Figure 4.21, displaying present patterns of population distribution and density, do not suggest a correlation with conditions of life. Many industrialized, urbanized countries have lower densities and higher levels of living than do less-developed ones. Densities in the United States, where there is a great deal of unused and unsettled land, are considerably lower than those in Bangladesh, where essentially all land is arable and which, with nearly 900 people per square kilometer (2300 per sq. mi.), is the most densely populated nonisland state in the world. At the same time, many African countries have low population densities and low levels of living, whereas Japan combines both high densities and wealth.

Overpopulation can be equated with levels of living or conditions of life that reflect a continuing imbalance between numbers of people and carrying capacity of the land. One measure of that imbalance might be the unavailability of food supplies sufficient in caloric content to meet individual daily energy requirements or so balanced as to satisfy normal nutritional needs. Unfortunately, dietary insufficiencies—with long-term adverse implications for life expectancy, physical vigor, and mental development—are most likely to be encountered in the developing countries, where much of the population is in the younger age cohorts (Figure 4.10).

If those developing countries simultaneously have rapidly increasing population numbers dependent on domestically produced foodstuffs, the prospects must be for continuing undernourishment and overpopulation. Much of sub-Saharan Africa finds itself in this circumstance. Africa's per capita food production decreased 25% between 1960 and 1990, and a further 30% drop is predicted over the following quarter century as the population-food gap widens (Figure 4.25). Egypt already must import more than half the food it

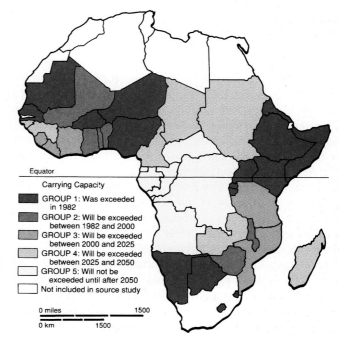

Carrying Capacity

■ GROUP 1: Was exceeded in 1982
▨ GROUP 2: Will be exceeded between 1982 and 2000
▨ GROUP 3: Will be exceeded between 2000 and 2025
▨ GROUP 4: Will be exceeded between 2025 and 2050
□ GROUP 5: Will not be exceeded until after 2050
□ Not included in source study

0 miles 1500
0 km 1500

FIGURE 4.25 **Carrying capacity and potentials in sub-Saharan Africa.** The map assumes that (1) all cultivated land is used for growing food; (2) food imports are insignificant; (3) agriculture is conducted by low-technology methods.

consumes. Africa is not alone. The international Food and Agriculture Organization (FAO) projects that by A.D. 2000, no less than 65 separate countries with some 30% of the population of the developing world will be unable to feed their inhabitants from their own national territories at the low level of agricultural technology and inputs apt to be employed. Even rapidly industrializing China, an exporter of grain until 1994, has become a net grain importer; if its massive and growing population continues its new dependence on imported basic foodstuffs, world grain surpluses and food aid flows will be seriously affected.

In the contemporary world, insufficiency of domestic agricultural production to meet national caloric requirements cannot be considered a measure of overcrowding or poverty. Only a few countries are agriculturally self-sufficient. Japan, a leader among the advanced states, is the world's biggest food importer and supplies from its own production only 40% of the calories its population consumes. Its physiological density is high, as Table 4.6 indicates, but it obviously does not rely on an arable land resource for its present development. Largely lacking in either agricultural or industrial resources, it nonetheless ranks well on all indicators of national well-being and prosperity. For countries such as Japan, a sudden cessation of the international trade that permits the exchange of industrial products for imported food and raw materials would be disastrous. Domestic food production could not maintain the dietary levels now enjoyed by their populations and they, more starkly than many underdeveloped countries, would be "overpopulated."

Urbanization

Pressures on the land resource of countries are increased not just by their growing populations but by the reduction of arable land caused by such growth. More and more of world population increase must be accommodated not in rural areas but in cities that hold the promise of jobs and access to health, welfare, and other public services. As a result, the *urbanization* (transformation from rural to urban status) of population in developing countries is increasing dramatically. Since the 1950s, cities have grown faster than rural areas in nearly all developing states. Although Latin America, for example, has experienced substantial overall population increase, the size of its rural population is actually declining. Asian and African countries that were mostly rural in the mid-1990s will experience most of their future growth in cities. As recently as 1950 only two African cities (Johannesburg and Cairo) had reached the 1 million size; by 2025, it is estimated that the continent will have 36 cities of 4 million or more inhabitants and an average size of 9 million.

Largely because of population increases, the number and size of cities everywhere are growing. In 1950, less than 30% of the world's population lived in urban areas; by 1995 over 43% of a much larger total population were urban dwellers (Figures 4.26 and 11.2). Developing countries have spurred that change. By the mid-1990s, over one-third of their inhabitants were urban, and collectively the less developed areas contained nearly two-thirds of the world's city population. On UN projections, some 97% of all world population increase between 1990 and 2025 will be in urban areas.

The sheer growth of those cities in people and territory has increased pressures on arable land and adjusted upward both arithmetic and physiological densities. Urbanization consumes millions of hectares of cropland each year. In Egypt, for example, urban expansion and development between 1965 and 1985 took out of production as much fertile soil as the Aswan dam made newly available through irrigation with the water it impounds. By themselves, some of these cities, which are surrounded by concentrations of people living in uncontrolled settlements, slums, and shantytowns (Figure 11.40), are among the most densely populated areas in the world. They face massive problems in trying to provide housing, jobs, education, and adequate health and social services for their residents. These and other matters of urban geography are the topics of Chapter 11.

Population Data and Projections

Population geographers, demographers, planners, governmental officials, and a host of others rely on detailed population data to make their assessments of present national and world population patterns and to estimate future conditions.

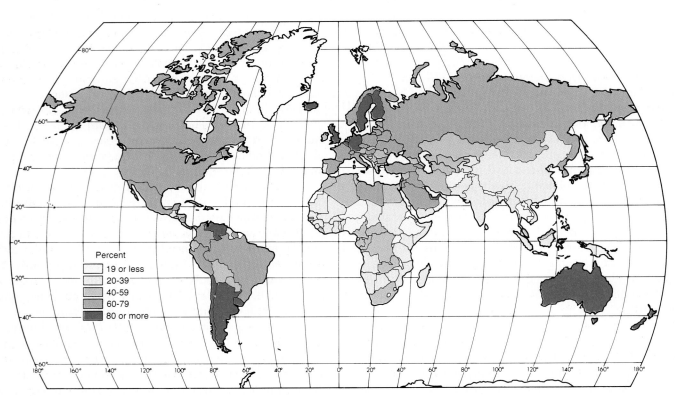

FIGURE 4.26 **Percentage of national population classified as urban.** Urbanization has been particularly rapid in the developing continents. In 1950, only 17% of Asians and 15% of Africans were urban; by the middle 1990s, over 30% of both Asians and Africans were city dwellers.

Percent
- 19 or less
- 20-39
- 40-59
- 60-79
- 80 or more

FIGURE 4.27   Taking the census in rural China in 1982. The sign identifies the "Third National Census. Mobile Registration Station." A new Fourth Population Census, requiring 7 million census workers to conduct, was undertaken on July 1, 1990.

Birth rates and death rates, rates of fertility and of natural increase, age and sex composition of the population, and other items are all necessary ingredients for their work.

Population Data

The data that students of population employ come primarily from the United Nations Statistical Office, the World Bank, the Population Reference Bureau, and ultimately, from national censuses and sample surveys. Unfortunately, the data as reported may on occasion be more misleading than informative. For much of the developing world, a national census is a massive undertaking. Isolation and poor transportation, insufficiency of funds and trained census personnel, high rates of illiteracy limiting the type of questions that can be asked, and populations suspicious of all things governmental serve to restrict the frequency, coverage, and accuracy of population reports.

However derived, detailed data are published by the major reporting agencies for all national units even when those figures are poorly based on fact or are essentially fictitious. For years, data on the total population, birth and death rates, and other vital statistics for Somalia were regularly reported and annually revised. The fact was, however, that Somalia had never had a census and had no system whatsoever for recording births. Seemingly precise data were regularly reported, as well, for Ethiopia. When that country had its first-ever census in 1985, at least one data source had to drop its estimate of the country's birth rate by 15% and increase its figure for Ethiopia's total population by more than 20%. And a disputed 1992 census of Nigeria officially reported a population of 88.5 million, still the largest in Africa but far below the generally accepted and widely cited estimates of between 110 and 120 million Nigerians.

Fortunately, census coverage on a world basis is improving. Almost every country has now had at least one census of its population, and most have been subjected to periodic sample surveys (Figure 4.27). However, only about 10% of the developing world's population live in countries with anything approaching complete systems for registering births and deaths. Estimates are that 40% or less of live births in Indonesia, Pakistan, India, or the Philippines are officially recorded. Apparently, deaths are even less completely reported than births throughout Asia. And whatever the deficiencies of Asian states, African statistics are still less complete and reliable. It is, of course, on just these basic birth and death data that projections about population growth and composition are founded.

Even the age structure reported for national populations, so essential in many areas of population analysis, must be viewed with suspicion. In many societies, birthdays are not noted, nor are years recorded by the Western calendar. Non-Western ways of counting age also confuse the record. The Chinese, for example, consider a person to be 1 year old at birth and increase that age by 1 year each [Chinese] New Year's Day. Bias and error arise from the common tendency of people after middle age to report their ages in round numbers ending in *0*. Also evident is a bias toward claiming an age ending in the number 5 or as an even number of years. Inaccuracy and noncomparability of reckoning added to incompleteness of survey and response conspire to cloud national comparisons in which age or the implications of age are important ingredients.

Population Projections

For all their inadequacies and imprecisions, current data reported for country units form the basis of **population projections,** estimates of future population size, age, and sex composition based on current data. Projections are not forecasts, and demographers are not the social science equivalent of meteorologists. Weather forecasters work with a myriad of accurate observations applied against a known, tested model of the atmosphere. The demographer, in contrast, works with sparse, imprecise, and missing data applied to human actions that will be unpredictably responsive to stimuli not yet evident.

Population projections, therefore, are based on assumptions for the future applied to current data that are, themselves, frequently suspect. Since projections are not predictions, they can never be wrong. They are simply the inevitable result of calculations about fertility, mortality, and migration applied to each age cohort of a population now living, and the making of birth rate, survival, and migration assumptions about cohorts yet unborn. Of course, the perfectly valid *projections* of future population size and structure resulting from those calculations may be dead wrong as *predictions.*

Since those projections are invariably treated as scientific expectations by a public that ignores their underlying qualifying assumptions, agencies such as the UN that estimate the population of, say, Africa in the year 2025, do so by not one but by three or more projections: high, medium, and low, for example (see "World Population Projections"). For areas as large as Africa, a medium projection is assumed to benefit from compensating errors and statistically predictable behaviors of very large populations. For individual African countries and smaller populations, the medium projection may be much less satisfying. The usual tendency in projections is to assume that something like current conditions will be applicable in the future. Obviously, the more distant the future, the less likely is that assumption to remain true. The resulting observation should be that the further into the future one wishes to project the population structure of small areas, the greater is the implicit and inevitable error (see Figure 4.12).

WORLD POPULATION PROJECTIONS

hile the need for population projections is obvious, demographers face difficult decisions regarding the assumptions they use in preparing them. Assumptions must be made about the future course of birth and death rates and, in some cases, about migration.

Demographers must consider many factors when projecting a country's population. What is the present level of the birth rate, of literacy, and of education? Does the government have a policy to influence population growth? What is the status of women?

Along with these questions must be weighed the likelihood of socioeconomic change, for it is generally assumed that as a country "develops," a preference for smaller families will cause fertility to fall to the replacement level of about two children per woman. But when can one expect this to happen in less developed countries? And for the majority of more developed countries with fertility currently below replacement level, can one assume that fertility will rise to avert eventual disappearance of the population and, if so, when?

Predicting the pace of fertility decline is most important, as illustrated by one set of United Nations long-range projections for Africa. As with many projections, these were issued in a "series" to show the effects of different assumptions. The "low" projection for Africa assumed that replacement level fertility will be reached in 2030, which would put the continent's population at 1.4 billion in 2100. If attainment of replacement level fertility is delayed to 2065, the population would reach 4.4 billion in 2100. That difference of 3 billion should serve as a warning that using population projections requires caution and consideration of *all* the possibilities.

Unfortunately, demographers usually cast their projections in an environmental vacuum, ignoring the realities of soils, vegetation, water supplies, and climate that ultimately determine feasible or possible levels of population support. Inevitably, different analysts present different assessments of the absolute carrying capacity of the earth. At a perhaps unrealistically low level, the World Hunger Project calculates that the world's ecosystem could, with present agricultural technologies and with equal distribution of food supplies, support on a sustained basis no more than 5.5 billion people, even if all lived on a vegetarian diet and all cropland was used for food, not industrial crops. Many agricultural economists, in contrast—citing present trends and prospective increases in crop yields, fertilizer efficiencies, and intensification of production methods—are confident that the earth can readily feed 10 billion or more on a sustained basis. Nearly all observers, however, agree that physical environmental realities make unrealistic purely demographically-based projections of a world population three or four times its present size.

Population Controls

All population projections include an assumption that at some point in time population growth will cease and plateau at the replacement level. Without that assumption, future numbers become unthinkably large. For the world at unchecked present growth rates, there would be 1 trillion people three centuries from now, 4 trillion four centuries in the future, and so on. Although there is reasonable debate about whether the world is now overpopulated and about what either its optimum or maximum sustainable population should be, totals in the trillions are beyond any reasonable expectation.

Population pressures do not come from the amount of space humans occupy. It has been calculated, for example, that the entire human race could easily be accommodated within the boundaries of the state of Delaware. The problems stem from the food, energy, and other resources necessary to support the population and from the impact on the environment of the increasing demands and the technologies required to meet them. Rates of growth currently prevailing in many countries make it nearly impossible for them to achieve the kind of social and economic development they would like.

Clearly, at some point population will have to stop increasing as fast as it has been. That is, either the self-induced limitations on expansion implicit in the demographic transition will be adopted or an equilibrium between population and resources will be established in more dramatic fashion. Recognition of this eventuality is not new. "[The evils of] pestilence, and famine, and wars, and earthquakes have to be regarded as a remedy for nations, as the means of pruning the luxuriance of the human race," was the opinion of the theologian Tertullian during the 2d century A.D.

Thomas Robert **Malthus** (1766–1834), an English economist and demographer, put the problem succinctly in a treatise published in 1798: All biological populations have a potential for increase that exceeds the actual rate of increase, and the resources for the support of increase are limited. In later publications, Malthus amplified his thesis by noting the following:

1. Population is inevitably limited by the means of subsistence.
2. Populations invariably increase with increase in the means of subsistence unless prevented by powerful checks.
3. The checks that inhibit the reproductive capacity of populations and keep it in balance with means of subsistence are either "private" (moral restraint, celibacy, and chastity) or "destructive" (war, poverty, pestilence, and famine).

The deadly consequences of Malthus's dictum that unchecked population increases geometrically while food production can increase only arithmetically have been reported throughout human history, as they are today. Starvation, the ultimate expression of resource depletion, is no stranger to the past or present. By conservative estimate, some 70 people worldwide will starve to death during the 2 minutes it takes you to read this page; half will be children under 5. They will, of course, be more than replaced numerically by new births during the same 2 minutes. Losses are always recouped. All battlefield casualties, perhaps 50 million, in all of humankind's wars over the last 300 years equal less than a 7-month replacement period at present rates of natural increase.

Yet, inevitably—following the logic of Malthus, the apparent evidence of history, and our observations of animal populations—equilibrium must be achieved between numbers and support resources. When overpopulation of any species occurs, a population dieback is inevitable. The madly ascending leg of the J-curve is bent to the horizontal, and the J-curve is converted to an S-curve. It has happened before in human history, as Figure 4.28 summarizes. The top of the **S-curve** represents a population size consistent with and supportable by the exploitable resource base. When the population is equivalent to the carrying capacity of the occupied area, it is said to have reached a **homeostatic plateau.**

In animals, overcrowding and environmental stress apparently release an automatic physiological suppressant of fertility. Although famine and chronic malnutrition may reduce fertility in humans, population limitation usually must be either forced or self-imposed. The demographic transition to low birth rates matching reduced death rates is cited as evidence that Malthus's first assumption was wrong: Human populations do not inevitably grow geometrically. Fertility behavior is conditioned by social determinants, not solely by biological or resource imperatives.

Although Malthus's ideas were discarded as deficient by the end of the 19th century in light of the European population experience, the concerns he expressed were revived during the 1950s. Observations of population growth in underdeveloped countries and the strain that growth placed on their resources inspired the viewpoint that improvements in living standards could be achieved only by raising investment per worker. Rapid population growth was seen

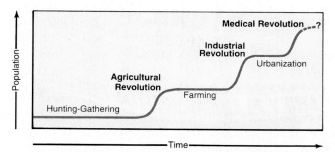

FIGURE 4.28 The steadily higher *homeostatic plateaus* (states of equilibrium) achieved by humans are evidence of their ability to increase the carrying capacity of the land through technological advance. Each new plateau represents the conversion of the J-curve into an S-curve.

as a serious diversion of scarce resources away from capital investment and into unending social welfare programs. Raising living standards required that existing national efforts to lower mortality rates be balanced by governmental programs to reduce birth rates. **Neo-Malthusianism,** as this viewpoint became known, has been the underpinning of national and international programs of population limitation primarily through birth control and family planning (Figure 4.29).

Neo-Malthusianism has had a mixed reception. Asian countries, led by China and India, have in general—though with differing successes—adopted family planning programs and policies. In some instances, success has been declared complete. Singapore established its Population and Family Planning Board in 1965, when its fertility rate was 4.9 lifetime births per woman. By 1986, that rate had declined to 1.7, well below the 2.1 replacement level for developed countries, and the board was abolished as no longer necessary. Caribbean and South American countries, except the poorest and most agrarian, have also experienced declining fertility rates, though often these reductions have been achieved despite pronatalist views of governments influenced by the Roman Catholic church. Africa and the Middle East have generally been less responsive to the neo-Malthusian arguments because of ingrained cultural convictions among people, if not in all governmental circles, that large families—6 or 7 children—are desirable. Although total fertility rates have begun to decline in several sub-Saharan African states, they still remain nearly everywhere far above replacement levels. Islamic fundamentalism opposed to birth restrictions also is a cultural factor in the Near East and North Africa.

Other barriers to fertility control exist. When first proposed by Western states, neo-Malthusian arguments that family planning was necessary for development were rejected by many less developed countries. Reflecting both nationalistic and Marxist concepts, they maintained that remnant colonial social, economic, and class structures rather than population increase hindered development. Some government leaders think that there is a correlation between population size and power and pursue pronatalist policies, as did Mao's China during the 1950s and early 1960s. And a number of American economists called *cornucopians* expressed the view, beginning in the 1980s, that population growth is a stimulus, not a deterrent, to development and that human minds and skills are the world's ultimate resource base. Since the time of Malthus, they observe, world population has grown from 900 million to 5.7 billion without the predicted dire consequences—proof that Malthus failed to recognize the importance of technology in raising the carrying capacity of the earth. Still higher population numbers, they suggest, are sustainable, perhaps even with improved standards of living for all.

A third view, modifying cornucopian optimism, admits that products of human ingenuity such as the Green Revolution (see page 266) increase in food production have managed to keep pace with rapid population increases since 1970. But its advocates argue that scientific and technical ingenuity to enhance food production does not automatically appear; both complacency and inadequate research support have hindered continuing progress in recent years. And even if further advances are made, they observe, not all countries or regions have the social and political will or capacity to take advantage of them. Those that do not, third view advocates warn, will fail to keep pace with the needs of their populace and will sink into varying degrees of poverty and environmental decay, creating national and regional—though not necessarily global—crises.

Yet global crisis is exactly what is being predicted by some as the logical outcome of China's combination of expanding population and booming prosperity. Projecting from recent Chinese population trends, cropland and water scarcity, and increasing grain, dairy, and meat consumption, some worry that within 35 years China's demand for grain will so far exceed its own production capacity and place such massive demands on world grain supplies that global shortages and rocketing food costs will result. Ominously growing food scarcity, they fear, not military aggression may be the real threat to future world economic and political stability.

Population Prospects

Regardless of population philosophies, theories, or cultural norms, the fact remains that in many parts of the world developing countries are showing significantly declining population growth rates. But reducing fertility levels even to the replacement level of 2.1 births per woman does not mean an immediate end to population growth. Because of the age

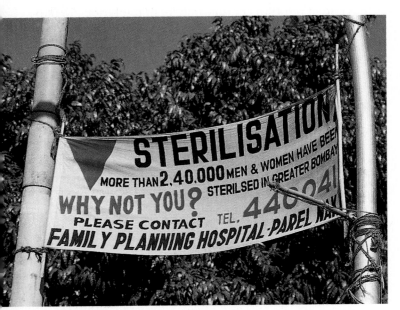

FIGURE 4.29 A Bombay, India, sign promoting the government's continuing program to reduce the country's high fertility rate. Sterilization accounts for 70% of all contraception in India.

composition of many societies, numbers of births will continue to grow even as fertility rates per woman decline. The reason is to be found in **demographic** (or **population**) **momentum.**

When a high proportion of the population is young, the product of past high fertility rates, larger and larger numbers enter the childbearing age each year. One-third of the people now on earth are under 15 (Figure 4.10). For Africa as a whole, the figure in the mid-1990s was 45%, and in many individual African states almost half the population is in that age bracket (Figure 4.9), as it is in some Asian countries. The consequences of the fertility of these young people are yet to be realized. They will continue to be felt until the now youthful groups mature and work their way through the population pyramid. Inevitably, while this is happening, even the most stringent national policies limiting growth cannot stop it entirely. A country with a large present population base will experience large numerical increases despite declining birth rates. Indeed, the higher fertility was to begin with and the sharper its drop to low levels, the greater will be the role of momentum.

Eventually, of course, young populations grow older, and even the youthful developing countries are beginning to face the consequences of that reality. The problems of a rapidly aging population that already confront the industrialized economies are now being realized in the developing world as well. The growth rate of people aged 55 and over is three times as high in developing countries as in developed ones; in most, the rate is highest for those 75 and over. More than 1.2 million people worldwide reach the age of 55 each month; of that number, 80% live in developing countries that generally lack, health, income, and social service support systems adequate to the needs of their older citizens. To the social and economic implications of their present population momentum, therefore, developing countries must add the aging consequences of past patterns and rates of growth (Figure 4.30).

FIGURE 4.30 These senior citizens at exercise in Havana, Cuba, are part of the rapidly aging population of many developing countries. Worldwide, the over-60 cohort will number some 1.5 billion by 2030, some 16% of total population. But by 2020, a third of Singapore citizens will be 55 or older, and China will have as large a share of its population over 60—about one in four—as will Europe. Some developing countries will soon be aging faster than the developed West but without the old-age assistance and welfare programs advanced countries have put in place.

Summary

Birth, death, fertility, and growth rates are important in understanding the numbers, composition, distribution, and spatial trends of population. Recent "explosive" increases in human numbers and the prospects of continuing population expansion may be traced to sharp reductions in death rates, increases in longevity, and the impact of demographic momentum on a youthful population largely concentrated in the developing world. Control of population numbers historically was accomplished through a demographic transition first experienced in European societies that adjusted their fertility rates downward as death rates fell and life expectancies increased. The introduction of advanced technologies of preventive and curative medicine, pesticides, and famine relief have reduced mortality rates in developing countries without always a compensating reduction in birth rates.

Although population control programs have been differentially introduced and promoted, the 5.7 billion human beings present in the mid-1990s will likely nearly double in number by the year 2100. That growth will largely reflect increases unavoidable because of the size and youth of populations in developing countries. Eventually, a new balance between population numbers and carrying capacity of the world will be reached, as it has always been following past periods of rapid population increase.

People are unevenly distributed over the earth. The ecumene, or permanently inhabited portion of the globe, is discontinuous and marked by pronounced differences in population concentrations and numbers. East Asia, South Asia, Europe, and northeastern United States/southeastern Canada represent the world's greatest population clusters, though smaller areas of great density are found in other regions and continents. Since growth rates are highest and population doubling times generally shorter in world regions outside these four present main concentrations, new patterns of population concentration and dominance are taking form.

A respected geographer once commented that "population is the point of reference from which all other elements [of geography] are observed." Certainly, population geography is the essential starting point of the human component of the human–environment concerns of geography.

But human populations are not merely collections of numerical units; nor are they to be understood solely through statistical analysis. Societies are distinguished not just by the abstract data of their numbers, rates, and trends. They have, as we saw in Chapter 2, unifying and differentiating structures of culture in constant flux and change. In their infinite diversity they have created landscapes of activity and cultural traits of basic human geographic interest. Two of those distinctive cultural landscapes, those of language and religion, are the topics of the following chapter.

KEY WORDS

arithmetic density   119
carrying capacity   121
cohort   98
crude birth rate   98
crude death rate   102
crude density   119
demographic equation   113
demographic (population)
   momentum   127
demographic transition   109
demography   96

dependency ratio   105
doubling time   108
ecumene   118
homeostatic plateau   125
J-curve   108
Malthus   125
mortality rate   102
natural increase   107
neo-Malthusianism   126
nonecumene   118
overpopulation   120

physiological density   119
population density   119
population geography   96
population projection   124
population pyramid   104
rate   98
rate of natural increase   107
replacement level   112
S-curve   125
total fertility rate   99
zero population growth   112

FOR REVIEW

1. How do the *crude birth rate* and the *fertility rate* differ? Which measure is the more accurate statement of the amount of reproduction occurring in a population?

2. How is the *crude death rate* calculated? What factors account for the worldwide decline in death rates since 1945?

3. How is a *population pyramid* constructed? What shape of "pyramid" reflects the structure of a rapidly growing country? Of a population with a slow rate of growth? What can we tell about future population numbers from those shapes?

4. What variations do we discern in the spatial pattern of the *rate of natural increase* and, consequently, of population growth? What rate of natural increase would double population in 35 years?

5. How are population numbers projected from present conditions? Are projections the same as predictions? If not, in what ways do they differ?

6. Describe the stages in the *demographic transition*. Where has the final stage of the transition been achieved? Why do some analysts doubt the applicability of the demographic transition to all parts of the world?

7. Contrast *crude population density* and *physiological density*. For what differing purposes might each be useful? How is *carrying capacity* related to the concept of density?

8. What was Malthus's underlying assumption concerning the relationship between population growth and food supply? In what ways do the arguments of *neo-Malthusians* differ from the original doctrine? What governmental policies are implicit in *neo-Malthusianism*?

9. Why is *demographic momentum* a matter of interest in population projections? In which world areas are the implications of demographic momentum most serious in calculating population growth, stability, or decline?

SELECTED REFERENCES

Ashford, Lori S. "New Perspectives on Population: Lessons from Cairo." *Population Bulletin* 50, no. 1. Washington, D.C.: Population Reference Bureau, 1995.

Beaujot, Roderic. *Population Change in Canada: The Challenges of Policy Adaptation*. Markham, Ontario: McClelland & Stewart, 1991.

Bongaarts, John. "Can the Growing Human Population Feed Itself?" *Scientific American* 270, no. 3 (1994):36–42.

Bongaarts, John. "Population Policy Options in the Developing World." *Science* 263 (Feb. 11, 1994):771–776.

Brown, Lester R., and Hal Kane. *Full House: Reassessing the Earth's Population Carrying Capacity*. New York: W. W. Norton, 1994.

Caldwell, John C., I. O. Orbulove, and Pat Caldwell. "Fertility Decline in Africa: A New Type of Transition?" *Population and Development Review* 19, no. 2 (1992):211–242.

Castles, Stephen, and Mark J. Miller. *The Age of Migration: International Population Movements in the Modern World.* New York: Guilford Press, 1993.

Daugherty, Helen Ginn, and Kenneth C. W. Kammeyer. *An Introduction to Population.* 2d ed. New York: Guilford Publications, 1995.

De Vita, Carol J. "The United States at Mid-Decade." *Population Bulletin* 50, no. 4. Washington, D.C.: Population Reference Bureau, 1996.

Dyson, Tim. "Population Growth and Food Production: Recent Global and Regional Trends." *Population and Development Review* 20, no. 2 (1994):397–411.

Gould, Peter. *The Slow Plague: A Geography of the AIDS Pandemic.* Cambridge, MA: Blackwell, 1993.

Grigg, David B. "Migration and Overpopulation." Chapter 5 in *The Geographical Impact of Migration,* edited by Paul White and Robert Woods. London and New York: Longman, 1980.

Grigg, David B. "Modern Population Growth in Historical Perspective." *Geography* 67 (1982):97–108.

Hall, Ray, and Paul White, eds. *Europe's Population: Towards the Next Century.* Bristol, PA: UCL Press/Taylor & Francis, 1995.

Haub, Carl. "Population Change in the Former Soviet Republics." *Population Bulletin* 49, no. 4. Washington, D.C.: Population Reference Bureau, 1994.

Haub, Carl. "Understanding Population Projections." *Population Bulletin* 42, no. 4. Washington, D.C.: Population Reference Bureau, 1987.

Hirschman, Charles, and Philip Guest. "The Emerging Demographic Transitions of Southeast Asia." *Population and Development Review* 16, no. 1 (March 1990):121–152.

Hornby, William F., and Melvyn Jones. *An Introduction to Population Geography.* Cambridge, England: Cambridge University Press, 1993.

Hsu, Mei-Ling. "Population of China: Large is not Beautiful." *Focus* (American Geographical Society) 42, no. 1 (1992):13–16.

Johnson, Stanley. *World Population—Turning the Tide.* London: Graham & Trotman/Martinus Nijhoff, 1994.

Jones, Huw R. *Population Geography.* 2d ed. New York: Guilford, 1991.

Keyfitz, Nathan, and Wilhelm Flinger. *World Population Growth and Aging: Demographic Trends in the Late 20th Century.* Chicago: University of Chicago Press, 1991.

King, Russell, ed. *Mass Migrations in Europe: The Legacy and the Future.* London and New York: Belhaven Press and John Wiley & Sons, 1995.

Lutz, Wolfgang. "The Future of World Population." *Population Bulletin* 49, no. 1. Washington, D.C.: Population Reference Bureau, 1994.

Mattson, Mark T. *Atlas of the 1990 Census.* New York: Macmillan Reference, USA: 1992.

McFalls, Joseph A., Jr. "Population: A Lively Introduction." *Population Bulletin* 46, no. 2. Washington, D.C.: Population Reference Bureau, 1991.

McIntosh, C. Alison, and Jason L. Finkle. "The Cairo Conference on Population and Development: A New Paradigm?" *Population and Development Review* 21, no. 2 (1995):223–260.

Mosley, W. Henry, and Peter Cowley. "The Challenge of World Health." *Population Bulletin* 46, no. 4. Washington, D.C.: Population Reference Bureau, 1991.

Omran, Abdel R. "The Epidemiologic Transition: A Theory of the Epidemiology of Population Change." *Milbank Memorial Fund Quarterly* 49 (1971):509–538.

Omran, Abdel R., and Farzaneh Roudi. "The Middle East Population Puzzle." *Population Bulletin* 48, no. 1. Washington, D.C.: Population Reference Bureau, 1993.

Parnwell, Mike. *Population Movements and the Third World.* London and New York: Routledge, 1993.

Peters, Gary L., and Robert P. Larkin. *Population Geography: Problems, Concepts, and Prospects.* Dubuque, IA: Kendall/Hunt Publishing Company, 1993.

Phillips, David R. "Epidemiological Transition: Implications for Health and Health Care Provision." *Geografiska Annaler* 76B (1994):71–88.

Population Reference Bureau. *World Population: Fundamentals of Growth.* 2d ed. Washington, D.C.: Population Reference Bureau, 1990.

Robey, Bryant, Shea O. Rutstein, and Leo Morris. "The Fertility Decline in Developing Countries." *Scientific American* 269 (December 1993):30–37.

Simon, Julian. *The Ultimate Resource.* Princeton, NJ: Princeton University Press, 1981.

Smil, Vaclav. "How Many People Can the Earth Feed?" *Population and Development Review* 20, no. 2 (1994):255–292.

Tien, H. Yuan. *China's Strategic Demographic Initiative.* New York: Praeger, 1991.

United Nations Population Fund. *The State of World Population.* New York: United Nations. Annual.

van de Kaa, Dirk J. "Europe's Second Demographic Transition." *Population Bulletin* 42, no. 1. Washington, D.C.: Population Reference Bureau, 1987.

Weeks, John R. "The Demography of Islamic Nations." *Population Bulletin* 43, no. 4. Washington, D.C.: Population Reference Bureau, 1988.

Yi, Zeng, et al. "Causes and Implications of the Recent Increase in the Reported Sex Ratio at Birth in China." *Population and Development Review* 19, no. 2 (June 1993):283–302.

PATTERNS OF
DIVERSITY AND
UNITY

 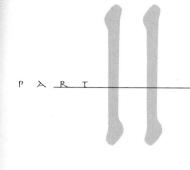

Dressed for confirmation at a Chicago Ukrainian church, these girls show the close association of ethnicity and religion in the American mosiac.

The concerns of Part I of our study were the cultural processes and spatial interactions of an unevenly distributed world population. The understandings we sought were those that stressed the common characteristics, collective processes, behavioral constants, and unifying traits that form the background to human occupation of the earth and the development of distinctive cultural landscapes upon it.

Our attention now turns to the distinguishing features of the culture groups creating those landscapes. Our concern now is not with common features but with cultural differences and with the spatial cultural mosaic that those differences create. The topics of interest are the principal expressions of unity and diversity among and between different social groups. We ask: In what pronounced ways are populations distinctive? How, if at all, are those elements of distinctiveness interrelated and part of the composite cultures of recognizably different social groups? What notable world and regional spatial patterns of cultural differentiation can we recognize? How do cultural traits and composites change over time and through contact with other, differently constituted groups? And, finally, in what ways and to what extent are cultural contrasts evident in the landscapes built or modified by different social groups?

Although human populations are distinguished one from another in innumerable detailed ways, major points of contrast are relatively few in number and commonly recognized as characteristic traits of distinctive social groups. Languages spoken, religions practiced or espoused, and the composite distinguishing features of ethnic or folk cultural communities are among those major elements of contrast; they will claim our attention in the next three chapters.

Language and religion are prominent threads in the tapestry of culture, serving both to identify and classify individuals within complex societies and to distinguish populations and regions of different tongues and faiths. *Language* is the means of transmission of culture and the medium through which its beliefs and standards are expressed. *Religion* has had a pervasive impact on different culture groups, coloring their perceptions of themselves and their environments and of other groups of different faiths with whom they come in contact. As fundamental components and spatial expressions of culture, language and religion command our attention in Chapter 5.

They are also contributors to the complex of cultural characteristics that distinguish *ethnic* groups, populations set off from other groups by feelings of distinctiveness commonly fostered by some combination of religion, language, race, custom, or nationality. Ethnic groups—either as local indigenous minorities within differently structured majority populations or as self-conscious immigrant groups in pluralistic societies—represent another form of cultural differentiation of sufficient worldwide importance to require our attention in Chapter 6. In Chapter 7, we pursue two separate but related themes of cultural geography. The first is that a distinctive and pervasive element of cultural diversity is rooted in f*olk culture*—the material and nonmaterial aspects of daily life preserved and transmitted by groups insulated from outside influences through spatial isolation or cultural barriers. The second theme is that the diversity formerly evident in many culturally complex societies is being eroded and levelled by the unification implicit in the spread of *popular cultures* that, at the same time, provide a broadening of the opportunities and choices available to individuals.

Our concerns in chapters 5–7, then, are the learned behaviors, attitudes, and beliefs that have significant spatial expression and serve in the intricate mosaic of culture as fundamental identifying traits of distinctive social groups.

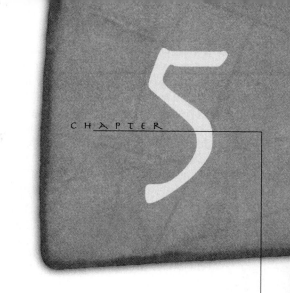

CHAPTER 5

LANGUAGE AND RELIGION:

MOSAICS OF CULTURE

THE GEOGRAPHY OF LANGUAGE 135

Classification of Languages 135

World Pattern of Languages 136

Language Spread 137

Language Change 142

The Story of English 143

Standard and Variant Languages 144

Standard Language 144

Dialects 145

Dialects in America 147

Pidgins and Creoles 149

Lingua Franca 149

Official Languages 149

Language, Territoriality, and Identity 152

Language on the Landscape: Toponymy 154

PATTERNS OF RELIGION 156

Religion and Culture 156

Classification of Religion 156

Patterns, Numbers, and Flows 158

The World Pattern 158

The Principal Religions 159

Judaism 159

Christianity 160

Regions and Landscapes of Christianity 163

Islam 166

Hinduism 168

Buddhism 170

East Asian Ethnic Religions 172

SUMMARY 174

KEY WORDS 174

FOR REVIEW 174

SELECTED REFERENCES 174

Tibetan lamas—Vajrayana Buddhist monks—in exile at a monastery in Sikkim.

When God saw [humans become arrogant], he thought of something to bring confusion to their heads: he gave the people a very heavy sleep. They slept for a very, very long time. They slept for so long that they forgot the language they had used to speak. When they eventually woke up from their sleep, each man went his own way, speaking his own tongue. None of them could understand the language of the other any more. That is how people dispersed all over the world. Each man would walk his way and speak his own language and another would go his way and speak in his own language. . . .

God has forbidden me to speak Arabic. I asked God, "Why don't I speak Arabic?" and He said, "If you speak Arabic, you will turn into a bad man." I said, "There is something good in Arabic!" And He said, "No, there is nothing good in it! . . ."

Here, I slaughter a bull and I call [the Muslim] to share my meat. I say, "Let us share our meat." But he refuses the meat I slaughter because he says it is not slaughtered in a Muslim way. If he cannot accept the way I slaughter my meat, how can we be relatives? Why does he despise our food? So, let us eat our meat alone. . . . Why, they insult us, they combine contempt for our black skin with pride in their religion. As for us, we have our own ancestors and our own spirits; the spirits of the Rek, the spirits of the Twic, we have not combined our spirits with their spirits. The spirit of the black man is different. Our spirit has not combined with theirs.[1]

Language and religion are basic components of cultures, the learned ways of life of different human communities. They help identify who and what we are and clearly place us within larger communities of people with similar characteristics. At the same time, as the words of Chief Makuei suggest, they separate and divide peoples of different tongues and faiths. In the terminology introduced in Chapter 2, language and religion are *mentifacts*, components of the *ideological subsystem* of culture that help shape the belief system of a society and transmit it to succeeding generations. Both within and between cultures, language and religion are fundamental strands in the complex web of culture, serving to shape and to distinguish people and groups.

They are ever-changing strands, for languages and religions in their present-day structure and spatial patterns are simply the temporary latest phase in a continuing progression of culture change. Languages evolve in place, responding to the dynamics of human thought, experience, and expression and to the exchanges and borrowings ever more common in a closely integrated world. They disperse in space, carried by streams of migrants, colonizers, and conquerors. They may be rigorously defended and preserved as essential elements of cultural identity, or abandoned in the search for acceptance into a new society. To trace their diffusions, adoptions, and disappearances is to understand part of the evolving course of historical cultural geography. Religions, too, are dynamic, sweeping across national, linguistic, and cultural boundaries by conversion, conviction, and conquest. Their broad spatial patterns—distinctive culture regions in their own right—are also fundamental in defining the culture realms outlined in Figure 2.4, while at a different scale religious differences may contribute to the cultural diversity and richness within the countries of the world (Figure 5.1).

FIGURE 5.1   Advertised evidence of religious diversity in the United States.

[1]The words of Chief Makuei Bilkuei of the Dinka, a Nilotic people of the southern Sudan. His comments are directed at the attempts to unite into a single people the Arabic Muslims of the north of the Republic of the Sudan with his and other black, Luo-speaking animist and Christian people of the country's southern areas. Recorded by Francis Mading Deng, *Africans of Two Worlds: The Dinka in Afro-Arab Sudan.* Copyright © 1978 Yale University Press, New Haven, CT. Reprinted by permission of the author.

Forever changing and evolving, language in spoken or written form makes possible the cooperative efforts, the group understandings, and shared behavior patterns that distinguish culture groups. Language is the most important medium by which culture is transmitted. It is what enables parents to teach their children what the world they live in is like and what they must do to become functioning members of society. Some argue that the language of a society structures the perceptions of its speakers. By the words that it contains and the concepts that it can formulate, language is said to determine the attitudes, the understandings, and the responses of the society to which it belongs.

If that conclusion be true, one aspect of cultural heterogeneity may be easily understood. The nearly 6 billion people on earth speak many thousands of different languages. Knowing that as many as 1500 languages and language variants are spoken in sub-Saharan Africa gives us a clearer appreciation of the political and social divisions in that continent. Europe alone has more than 100 languages and dialects, and language differences were a partial basis for drawing boundaries in the political restructuring of Europe after World War I. Language, then, is a hallmark of cultural diversity, a frequently fiercely defended symbol of cultural identity helping to distinguish the world's diverse social groups.

Classification of Languages

On a clear, dark night the unaided eye can distinguish between 4000 and 6000 stars, a number comparable to some estimates of the probable total number of the world's languages. In reality, no precise figure is possible, for even today in Africa, Latin America, New Guinea, and elsewhere, linguists are still in the process of identifying and classifying the tongues spoken by isolated peoples. Even when they are well known, languages cannot always be easily or unmistakably recognized as distinctly separate entities.

In the broadest sense, language is any systematic method of communicating ideas, attitudes, or intent through the use of mutually understood signs, sounds, or gestures. For our geographic purposes, we may define **language** as an organized system of spoken words by which people communicate with each other with mutual comprehension. But such a definition fails to recognize the gradations among and between languages or to grasp the varying degrees of mutual comprehension between two or more of them. The language commonly called "Chinese," for example, is more properly seen as a group of related languages—Mandarin, Cantonese, Hakka, and others—that are as different from each other as are such comparably related European languages as Spanish, Italian, French, and Romanian. "Chinese" has uniformity only in the fact that all of the varied Chinese languages

are written alike. No matter how it is pronounced, the same symbol for "house" or for "rice," for example, is recognized by all literate speakers of any Chinese language variant (Figure 5.2). Again, the language known as "Arabic" represents a number of related but distinct tongues, so that Arabic spoken in Morocco differs from Palestinian Arabic roughly as Portuguese differs from Italian.

Languages differ greatly in their relative importance, if "importance" can be taken to mean the number of people using them. More than half of the world's inhabitants are speakers of just eight of its thousands of tongues. That restricted language dominance reflects the reality that the world's linguistic diversity is rapidly shrinking. In prehistory, humans probably spoke between 10,000 and 15,000 tongues. Of the at most 6000 still remaining, between 20% and 50% are no longer being learned by children and are effectively dead. One estimate anticipates that no more than 600 of the world's languages will still be in existence in A.D. 2100. Table 5.1 lists those languages currently spoken by 40 million or more people, a list that includes four-fifths of the world's population. At the other end of the scale are a number of rapidly declining languages whose speakers number in the hundreds or, at most, the few thousands.

The diversity of languages is simplified when we recognize among them related *families*. A **language family** is a group of languages descended from a single, earlier tongue. By varying estimates, from at least 30 to perhaps 100 such families of languages are found worldwide. The families, in turn, may be subdivided into subfamilies, branches, or groups of more closely related tongues. Some 2000 years ago, Latin was the common language spoken throughout the Roman Empire. The fall of the empire in the 5th century A.D. broke the unity of Europe, and regional variants of Latin began to develop in isolation. In the course of the next several centuries, these Latin derivatives, changing and developing as all languages do, emerged as the individual *Romance* languages—Italian, Spanish, French, Portuguese, and Romanian—of modern Europe and of the world colonized by their speakers. Catalan, Sardinian, Provençal, and a few other spatially restricted tongues are also part of the Romance language group.

HOUSE　　　　　RICE　　　　　TREE

FIGURE 5.2　　All literate Chinese, no matter which of the many languages of China they speak, recognize the same ideographs for house, rice, and tree.

TABLE 5.1	Languages Spoken by More than 40 Million People, 1996
LANGUAGE	**MILLIONS OF SPEAKERS**
Mandarin (China)	971
English	481
Hindi[a] (India, Pakistan)	440
Spanish	393
Russian	268
Arabic	225
Bengali (Bangladesh, India)	201
Portuguese	185
Malay-Indonesian	157
French	126
Japanese	125
German	118
Urdu[a] (Pakistan, India)	103
Punjabi (India, Pakistan)	95
Telugu (India)	75
Korean (Korea, China, Japan)	74
Marathi (India)	71
Tamil (India, Sri Lanka)	70
Cantonese (China)	69
Wu (China)	67
Javanese	64
Vietnamese	64
Italian	62
Turkish	60
Tagalog (Philippines)	54
Min (China)	51
Thai	51
Swahili (East Africa)	50
Ukrainian	48
Kannada (India)	45
Polish	43
Gujarati (India, Pakistan)	42

[a]Hindi and Urdu are basically the same language: Hindustani. Written in the Devangari script, it is called *Hindi,* the official language of India; in the Arabic script it is called *Urdu,* the official language of Pakistan.

Family relationship between languages can be recognized through similarities in their vocabulary and grammar. By tracing regularities of sound changes in different languages back through time, linguists are able to reconstruct earlier forms of words and, eventually, determine a word's original form before it underwent alteration and divergence. Such a reconstructed earlier form is said to belong to a **protolanguage.** In the case of the Romance languages, of course, the well-known ancestral language was Latin, which needs no such reconstruction. Its root relationship to the Romance languages is suggested by modern variants of *panis,* the Latin word for "bread": *pane* (Italian), *pain* (French), *pan* (Spanish), *pão* (Portuguese), *pîine* (Romanian). In other lan-

guage families, similar word relationships are less confidently traced to their protolanguage roots. For example, the *Germanic* languages, including English, German, Dutch, and the Scandinavia tongues, are related descendants of a less well-known proto-Germanic language spoken by peoples who lived in southern Scandinavia and along the North Sea and Baltic coasts from the Netherlands to western Poland. The classification of languages by origin and historical relationship is called a *genetic classification.*

Further tracing of language roots tells us that the Romance and the Germanic languages are individual branches of an even more extensive family of related languages derived from *proto-Indo-European* or simply *Indo-European.* Of the principal recognized language clusters of the world, the Indo-European family is the largest, embracing most of the languages of Europe and a large part of Asia, and the introduced—not the native—languages of the Americas (Figure 5.3). All told, languages in the Indo-European family are spoken by about half the world's peoples.

By recognizing similar words in most Indo-European tongues, linguists deduce that the Indo-European people— originally hunters and fishers but later becoming pastoralists and learning to grow crops—developed somewhere in eastern Europe or the Ukrainian steppes about 6000 years ago (though some conclude that central Turkey was the more likely site of origin). About 2500 B.C. their society apparently fragmented; they left the homeland, carrying segments of the parent culture in different directions. Some migrated into Greece, others settled in Italy, still others crossed central and western Europe, ultimately reaching the British Isles. Another group headed into the Russian forestlands, and still another branch crossed Iran and Afghanistan, eventually to reach India. Wherever this remarkable people settled, they appear to have dominated local populations and imposed their language on them. For example, the word for sheep is *avis* in Lithuanian, *ovis* in Latin, *avis* in Sanskrit (the language of ancient India), and *hawi* in the tongue used in Homer's Troy. Modern English retains its version in *ewe.* All, linguists infer, derive from an ancestral word *owis* in Indo-European. Similar relationships and histories can be traced for other protolanguages.

World Pattern of Languages

The present world distribution of major language families (Figure 5.4) records not only the migrations and conquests of our linguistic ancestors but also the continuing dynamic pattern of human movements, settlements, and colonizations of more recent centuries. Indo-European languages have been carried far beyond their Eurasian homelands from the 16th century onward by western European colonizers in the Americas, Africa, Asia, and Australasia. In the process of linguistic imposition and adoption, innumerable indigenous languages and language groups in areas of colo-

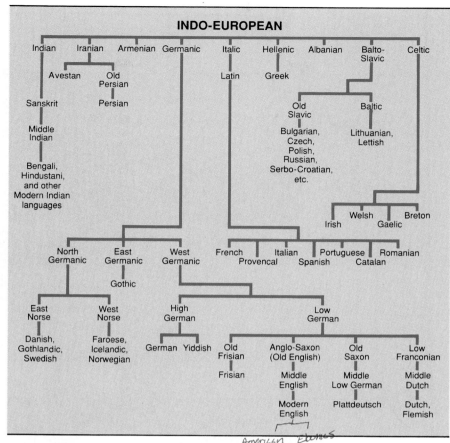

INDO-EUROPEAN

Indian — Iranian — Armenian — Germanic — Italic — Hellenic — Albanian — Balto-Slavic — Celtic

Avestan — Old Persian

Sanskrit · Persian

Middle Indian

Bengali, Hindustani, and other Modern Indian languages

Latin · Greek

Old Slavic · Baltic

Bulgarian, Czech, Polish, Russian, Serbo-Croatian, etc. · Lithuanian, Lettish

Welsh · Breton
Irish · Gaelic

North Germanic — East Germanic — West Germanic — French — Italian — Portuguese — Romanian
Provencal — Spanish — Catalan

Gothic

East Norse — West Norse — High German — Low German

Danish, Gothlandic, Swedish · Faroese, Icelandic, Norwegian · German — Yiddish · Old Frisian — Anglo-Saxon (Old English) — Old Saxon — Low Franconian

Frisian · Middle English · Middle Low German · Middle Dutch

Modern English · Plattdeutsch · Dutch, Flemish

Americzn Etomes

FIGURE 5.3   The Indo-European linguistic family tree.

nization have been modified or totally lost. Most of the estimated 1000 to 2000 *Amerindian* tongues of the Western Hemisphere disappeared in the face of European conquest and settlement (Figure 5.5).

The Slavic expansion eastward across Siberia beginning in the 16th century obliterated most of the *Paleo-Asiatic* languages there. Similar loss occurred in Eskimo and Aleut language areas. Large linguistically distinctive areas comprise the northern reaches of both Asia and America (Figure 5.4). Their sparse populations are losing the mapped languages as the indigenous people adopt the tongues of the majority cultures of which they have been forcibly made a part. In the Southern Hemisphere, the several hundred original *Australian* languages also loom large spatially on the map but have at most 50,000 speakers, exclusively Australian aborigines. Numerically and effectively, English dominates that continent.

Examples of linguistic conquest by non-Europeans also abound. In Southeast Asia, formerly extensive areas identified with different members of the *Austro-Asiatic* language family have been reduced through conquest and absorption by *Sino-Tibetan* (Chinese, Thai, Burmese, and Lao, principally) expansion. Arabic—originally a minor

Afro-Asiatic language of the Arabian Peninsula—was dispersed through much of North Africa and southwestern Asia, where it largely replaced a host of other locally variant tongues and became the official or the dominant language of more than 20 countries and over 225 million people. The more than 300 Bantu languages found south of the "Bantu line" in sub-Saharan Africa are variants of a proto-Bantu carried by an expanding, culturally advanced population that displaced more primitive predecessors (Figure 5.6).

Language Spread

Language spread as a geographical event represents the increase or relocation through time in the area over which a language is spoken. The Bantu of Africa or the English-speaking settlers of North America displaced preexisting populations and replaced as well the languages previously spoken in the areas of penetration. Therefore, we find one explanation of the spread of language families to new areas of occurrence in massive population relocations, such as those accompanying the colonization of the Americas or of Australia. That is, languages may spread because their speakers occupy new territories.

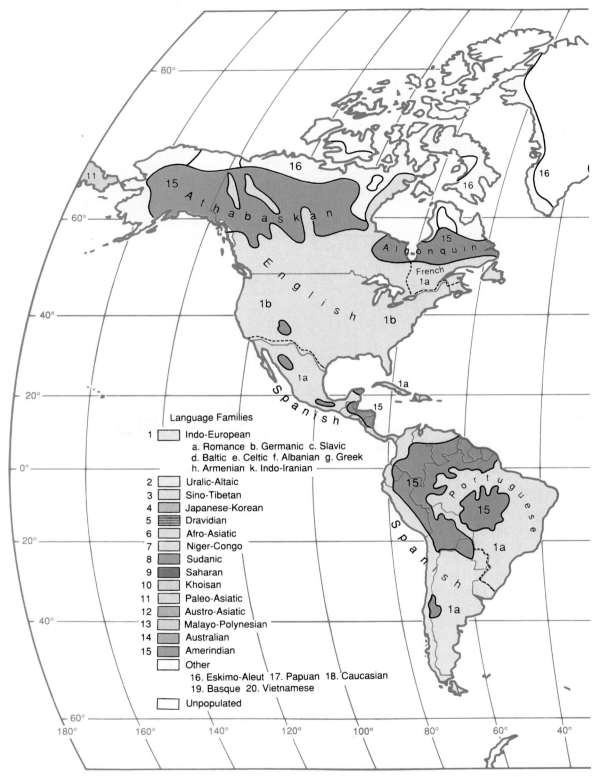

FIGURE 5.4 **World language families.** Language families are groups of individual tongues that had a common but remote ancestor. By suggesting that the area assigned to a language or language family uses that tongue exclusively, the map pattern conceals important linguistic detail. Many countries and regions have local languages spoken in territories too small to be recorded at this scale. The map also fails to report that the population in many regions is fluent in more than one language or that a second language serves as the necessary vehicle of commerce, education, or government. Nor is important information given about the number of speakers of different languages; the fact that there are more speakers of English in India or Africa than in Australia is not even hinted at by a map at this scale.

PATTERNS OF DIVERSITY AND UNITY

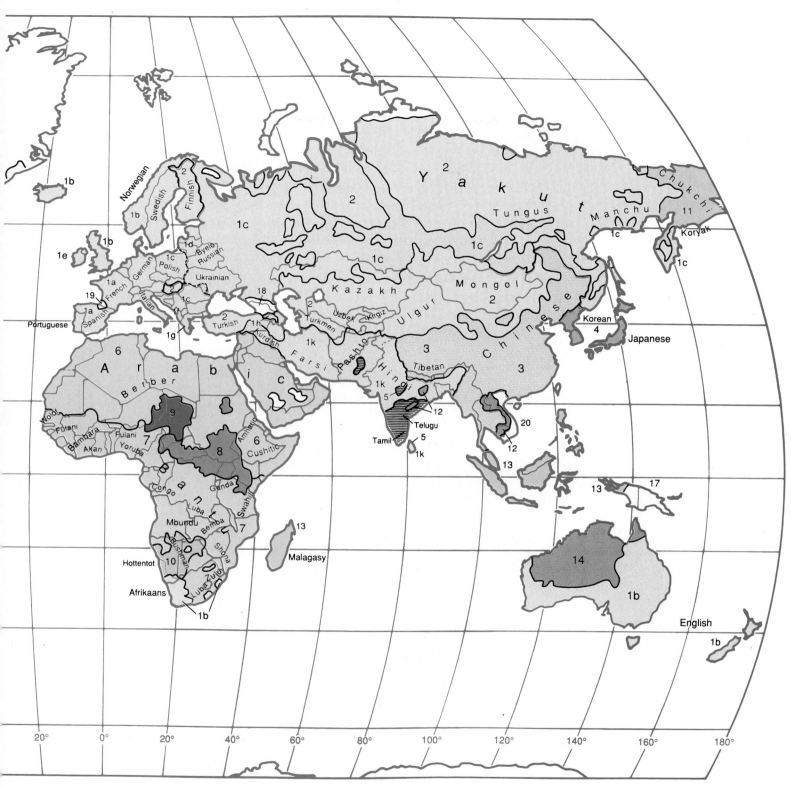

FIGURE 5.4 Continued

FIGURE 5.5 **Amerindian language families of North America.** As many as 300 different North American and more than 70 Meso-American tongues were spoken at the time of first European contact. The map summarizes the traditional view that these were grouped into 9 or 10 language families in North America, as many as 5 in Meso-America, and another 10 or so in South America. More recent research, however, suggests close genetic relationships between Native American tongues, clustering them into just 3 families: Eskimo-Aleut in the extreme north and Greenland; Na-Dené in Canada and the U.S. Southwest, and Amerind elsewhere in the hemisphere. Because each family has closer affinities with Asian language groups than with one another, it is suggested that each corresponds to a separate wave of Asian migration to the Americas: the first giving rise to the Amerind family, the second to the Na-Dené, and the last to the Eskimo-Aleut. Many Amerindian tongues have become extinct; others are still known only to very small groups of mostly elderly speakers.

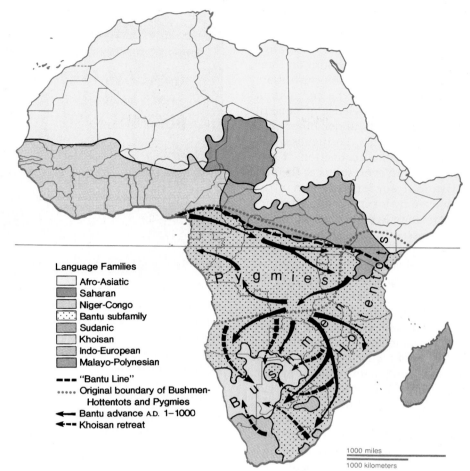

FIGURE 5.6 **Bantu advance, Khoisan retreat in Africa.** Linguistic evidence suggests that proto-*Bantu* speakers originated in the region of the Cameroon-Nigeria border, spread eastward across the southern Sudan, then turned southward to Central Africa. From there they dispersed slowly eastward, westward, and against slight resistance, southward. The earlier *Khoisan*-speaking occupants of sub-Saharan Africa were no match against the advancing metal-using Bantu agriculturalists. Pygmies, adopting a Bantu tongue, retreated deep into the forests; Bushmen and Hottentots retained their distinctive Khoisan "click" language but were forced out of forests and grasslands into the dry steppes and deserts of the southwest.

Latin, however, replaced earlier Celtic languages in western Europe not by force of numbers—Roman legionnaires, administrators, and settlers never represented a majority population—but by the gradual abandonment of their former languages by native populations brought under the influence and control of the Roman Empire. Adoption rather than eviction of language was the rule followed in perhaps the majority of historical and contemporary instances of language spread. Knowledge and use of the language of a dominating culture may be seen as a necessity when that language is the medium of commerce, law, civilization, and personal prestige. It was on that basis, not through numerical superiority, that Indo-European tongues were dispersed throughout Europe and to distant India, Iran, and Armenia. Likewise, Arabic became widespread in western Asia and North Africa not through massive population relocations but through conquest, religious conversion, and

superiority of culture. That is, languages may spread because they acquire new speakers.

Either form of language spread—dispersion of speakers or acquisition of speakers—represents one of the *spatial diffusion* processes introduced in Chapter 2. Massive population relocation in which culture is transported to and made dominant in a new territory is a specialized example of *relocation diffusion*. When the advantages of a new language are discerned and it is adopted by native speakers of another tongue, a form of *expansion diffusion* has occurred along with partial or total *acculturation* of the adopting population. Usually, those who are in or aspire to positions of importance are the first to adopt the new language of control and prestige. Later, through schooling, daily contact, and business or social necessity, other, lower social strata of society may gradually be absorbed into the expanding pool of language adopters.

Such *hierarchical diffusion* of an official or prestigious language has occurred in many societies. In India during the 19th century, the English established an administrative and judicial system that put a very high premium on their language as the sole medium of education, administration, trade, and commerce. Proficiency in it was the hallmark of the cultured and educated person (as knowledge of Sanskrit and Persian had been in earlier periods under other conquerors of India). English, French, Dutch, Portuguese, and other languages introduced during the acquisition of empires retain a position of prestige and even status as the official language in multilingual societies, even after independence has been achieved by former colonial territories. In Uganda and other former British possessions in Africa, a stranger may be addressed in English by one who wishes to display his or her education and social status—though standard Swahili, a second language for many different culture groups, may be chosen if certainty of communication is more important than pride.

As a diffusion process, language spread may be impeded by barriers or promoted by their absence. Cultural barriers may retard or prevent language adoption. Speakers of Greek resisted centuries of Turkish rule of their homeland, and the language remained a focus of cultural identity under foreign domination. Breton, Catalan, Gaelic, and other localized languages of Europe remain symbols of ethnic separateness from surrounding dominant national cultures and controls.

Physical barriers to language spread have also left their mark (Figure 5.4). Migrants or invaders follow paths of least topographic resistance and disperse most widely where access is easiest. Once past the barrier of the Pamirs and the Hindu Kush mountains, Indo-European tongues spread rapidly through the Indus and Ganges river lowlands of the Indian subcontinent but made no headway in the mountainous northern and eastern border zones. The Pyrenees Mountains serve as a linguistic barrier separating France and Spain. They also house the Basques, who speak the only language—*Euskara,* in their tongue—in southwestern Europe that survives from pre-Indo-European times (Figure 5.7). Similarly, the Caucasus Mountains between the Black and Caspian seas separate the Slavic speakers to the north and the areas of *Ural-Altaic* languages to the south. At the same time, in their rugged topography they contain an extraordinary mixture of languages, many unique to single valleys or villages and lumped together spatially, if not genetically, into a separate *Caucasian* language family.

Language Change

Migration, segregation, and isolation give rise to separate, mutually unintelligible languages because the society speaking the parent protolanguage no longer remains unitary. Comparable changes occur normally and naturally within a single language in word meaning, pronunciation, vocabulary, and *syntax* (the way words are put together in phrases and sentences). Because they are gradual, minor, and made

FIGURE 5.7 In their mountainous homeland, the Basques have maintained a linguistic uniqueness despite more than 2000 years of encirclement by dominant lowland speakers of Latin or Romance languages. This sign of friendly farewell gives its message in both Spanish and the Basque language, Euskara.

part of group use and understanding, such changes tend to go unremarked. Yet, cumulatively, they can result in language change so great that in the course of centuries an essentially new language has been created. The English of 17th-century Shakespearean writings or the King James Bible (1611) sounds stilted to our ears. Few of us can easily read Chaucer's 14th-century *Canterbury Tales,* and 8th-century *Beowulf* is practically unintelligible.

Change may be gradual and cumulative, with each generation deviating in small degree from the speech patterns and vocabulary of its parents, or it may be massive and abrupt. English gained about 10,000 new words from the Norman conquerors of the 11th century. In some 70 years (1558–1625) of literary and linguistic creativity during the reigns of Elizabeth I and James I, an estimated 12,000 words—based on borrowings from Latin, Greek, and other languages—were introduced.

Discovery and colonization of new lands and continents in the 16th and 17th centuries greatly and necessarily expanded English as new foods, vegetation, animals, and artifacts were encountered and adopted along with their existing aboriginal American, Australian, Indian, or African names. The Indian languages of the Americas alone brought more than 200 relatively common daily words to English, 80 or more from the North American native tongues and the rest from Caribbean, Central, and South American. An additional two thousand or more specialized or localized words were also added. *Moose, raccoon, skunk, maize, squash, succotash, igloo, toboggan, hurricane, blizzard, hickory, pecan,* and a host of other names were taken directly into English; others were adopted second hand from Spanish variants of South

American native words: *cigar, potato, tobacco, hammock.* More recently, and within a short span of years, new scientific and technological developments have enriched and expanded the vocabularies not only of English but of all languages spoken by modern societies by adding many words of Greek and Latin derivation.

The Story of English

English itself is a product of change, an offspring of proto-Germanic (Figure 5.3) descending through the dialects brought to England in the 5th and 6th centuries by conquering Danish and North German Frisians, Jutes, Angles, and Saxons. Earlier Celtic-speaking inhabitants found refuge in the north and west of Britain and in the rugged uplands of what are now Scotland and Wales. Each of the transplanted tongues established its own area of dominance, but the West Saxon dialect of southern England emerged in the 9th and 10th centuries as Standard Old English (Figure 5.8) on the strength of its literary richness.

It lost its supremacy after the Norman Conquest of 1066, as the center of learning and culture shifted northeastward from Winchester to London, and French rather than English became the language of the nobility and the government. When the tie between France and England was severed after the loss of Normandy (1204), French fell into disfavor and English again became the dominant tongue, although now as the French-enriched Middle English used by Geoffrey Chaucer and mandated as the official language of the law courts by the Statute of Pleading (1362). During the 15th and 16th centuries, English as spoken in London emerged as the basic form of Early Modern English.

During the 18th century, attempts to standardize and codify the rules of English were unsuccessful. But the *Dictionary* of Samuel Johnson (published 1755)—based on cultured language of contemporary London and the examples of major authors—helped establish norms of proper form and usage. A worldwide diffusion of the language resulted as English colonists carried it as settlers to the Western Hemisphere and Australasia; through merchants, conquest, or territorial claim, it established footholds in Africa and Asia. In that spatial diffusion, English was further enriched by its contacts with other languages. By becoming the accepted language of commerce and science, it contributed in turn to the common vocabularies of other tongues (see "Language Exchange").

Within some 400 years, English has developed from a localized language of 7 million islanders off the European coast to a truly international language with some 400 million native speakers, perhaps the same number who use it as a second language, and another 300–400 million who have reasonable competence in English as a foreign language. English serves as an official language of more than 40 countries (Figure 5.9), far exceeding in that role French (27), Arabic (21), or Spanish (20), the other leading international languages. No other language in history has assumed so important a role on the world scene.

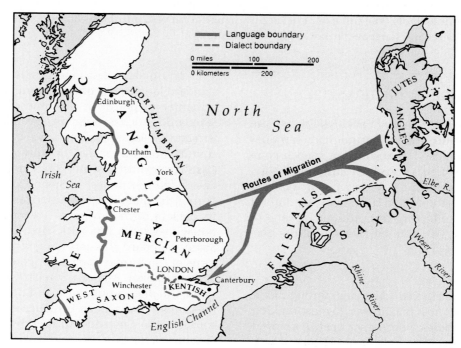

FIGURE 5.8 **Old English dialect regions.** In structure and vocabulary, Old English brought by the Frisians, Angles, Saxons, and Jutes was purely Germanic, with many similarities to modern German. It owed practically nothing to the Celtic it displaced, though it had borrowings from Latin. Much of Old English vocabulary was lost after the Norman conquest. English today has twice as many words derived from Latin and French as from the Germanic.

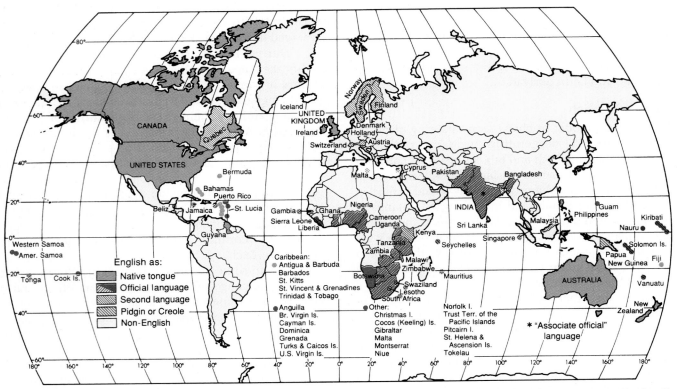

FIGURE 5.9 **International English.** In worldwide diffusion and acceptance, English has no past or present rivals. Along with French, it is one of the two working languages of the United Nations, and some two-thirds of all scientific papers are published in it. English is the sole or joint official language of more nations and territories, some too small to be shown here, than any other tongue. It also serves as the effective unofficial language of administration in other multilingual countries with different formal official languages. "English as a second language" is indicated for countries with near-universal or mandatory English instruction in public schools. The full extent of English penetration of Continental Europe, where 83% of secondary school students study it as a second language, is not evident on this map.

Standard and Variant Languages

People who speak a common language such as English are members of a **speech community,** but membership does not necessarily imply linguistic uniformity. A speech community usually possesses both a **standard language**—comprising the accepted community norms of syntax, vocabulary, and pronunciation—and a number of more or less distinctive *dialects,* reflecting the ordinary speech of areal, social, professional, or other subdivisions of the general population.

Standard Language

A dialect may become the standard language through identity with the speech of the most prestigious, highest-ranking, and most powerful members of the larger speech community. A rich literary tradition may help establish its primacy, and its adoption as the accepted written and spoken norm in administration, economic life, and education will solidify its position, minimizing linguistic variation and working toward the elimination of deviant, nonstandard forms.

The dialect that emerges as the basis of a country's standard language is often the one identified with its capital or center of power at the time of national development. Standard French is based on the dialect of the Paris region, a variant that assumed dominance in the latter half of the 12th century and was made the only official language in 1539. Castilian Spanish became the standard after 1492 with the Castile-led reconquest of Spain from the Moors and the export of the dialect to the Americas during the 16th century. Its present form, however, is a modified version associated not with Castile but with Madrid, the modern capital of Spain. Standard Russian is identified with the speech patterns of the former capital, St. Petersburg, and Moscow, the current capital. Modern Standard Chinese is based on the Mandarin dialect of Beijing. In England, *British Received Pronunciation*—the speech of educated people of London and southeastern England and used by the British Broadcasting System—is the accepted standard.

Other forces than the political may affect language standardization. In its spoken form, Standard German is based on norms established and accepted in the theater, the universities, public speeches, and radio and television. The nglish has a happily eclectic vocabulary. Its foundations are Anglo-Saxon (*was, that, eat, cow*) reinforced by Norse (*sky, get, bath, husband, skill*); its superstructure is Norman-French (*soldier, Parliament, prayer, beef*). The Norman aristocracy used their words for the food, but the Saxon serfs kept theirs for the animals. Its decor comes from Renaissance and Enlightenment Europe: 16th-century France yielded *etiquette, naive, reprimand,* and *police.*

Italy provided *umbrella, duet, bandit,* and *dilettante;* Holland gave *cruise, yacht, trigger, landscape,* and *decoy.* Its elaborations come from Latin and Greek: *misanthrope, medi-tate,* and *parenthesis* all first appeared during the 1560s. In this century, English adopted *penicillin* from Latin, *polystyrene* from Greek, and *sociology* and *television* from both. And English's ornaments come from all round the world: *slogan* and *spree* from Gaelic, *hammock* and *hurricane* from Caribbean languages, *caviar* and *kiosk* from Turkish, *dinghy* and *dungarees* from Hindi, *caravan* and *candy* from Persian, *mattress* and *masquerade* from Arabic.

Redressing the balance of trade, English is sharply stepping up its linguistic exports. Not just the necessary *imotokali* (motor car) and *izingilazi* (glasses) to Zulu; or *motokaa* and *shillingi* (shilling) to Swahili; but also *der Best-seller, der Kommunikations Manager, das Teeshirt* and *der Babysitter* to German; and, to Italian, *la pop art, il popcorn* and *la spray.* In some Spanish-speaking countries you might wear *un sueter* to *el beisbol,* or witness *un nocaut* at *el boxeo.* And in Russia, *biznesmen* prepare a *press rilis* on the *lep-top kompyuter* and print it by *lazerny printer.* Indeed, a sort of global English word list can be drawn up: *airport, passport, hotel, telephone; bar, soda, cigarette; sport, golf, tennis; stop, OK,* and increasingly, *weekend, jeans, know-how, sex appeal* and *no problem.*

Excerpted by permission from *The Economist,* London, December 20, 1986.

Classical or Literary Arabic of the Koran became the established norm from the Indian Ocean to the Atlantic Ocean. Standard Italian was derived from the Florentine dialect of the 13th and 14th centuries, which became widespread as the language of literature and economy.

In many societies, the official or unofficial standard language is not the dialect of home or daily life, and populations in effect have two languages. One is the regional dialect they employ with friends, at home, and in local community contacts; the other is the standard language used in more formal situations. In some cases, the contrast is great; regional variants of Arabic may be mutually unintelligible. Most Italians encounter Standard Italian for the first time in primary school. In India, the several totally distinct official regional languages are used in writing and taught in school but have no direct relationship to local speech; citizens must be bilingual to communicate with government officials who know only the regional language but not the local dialect.

Dialects

Just as no two individuals talk exactly the same, all but the smallest and most closely knit speech communities display recognizable speech variants called **dialects.** Vocabulary, pronunciation, rhythm, and the speed at which the language is spoken may set groups of speakers apart from one another and, to a trained observer, clearly mark the origin of the speaker. In George Bernard Shaw's play *Pygmalion,* on which the musical *My Fair Lady* was based, Henry Higgins—a professor of phonetics—is able to identify the London neighborhood of origin of a flower girl by listening to her vocabulary and accent. In many instances such variants are totally acceptable modifications of the standard language; in others, they mark the speaker as a social, cultural, or regional "outsider" or "inferior." Professor Higgins makes a lady out of the poor flower girl simply by teaching her upper-class pronunciation.

Shaw's play tells us dialects may coexist in space. Cockney and cultured English share the streets of London; black English and Standard American are heard in the same school yards throughout the United States. In many societies, **social dialects** denote social class and educational level. Speakers of higher socioeconomic status or educational achievement are most likely to follow the norms of their standard language; less-educated or lower-status persons are more likely to use the **vernacular**—nonstandard language or dialect native to the locale.

Different dialects may be part of the speech patterns of the same person. Professionals discussing, for example, medical, legal, financial, or scientific matters with their peers employ vocabularies and formal modes of address and sentence structure that are quickly changed to informal colloquial speech when the conversation shifts to sports, vacations, or personal anecdotes. Even sex may be the basis for linguistic differences added to other determinants of social dialects (see "Male and Female Language").

More commonly, we think of dialects in spatial terms. Speech is a geographic variable; each locale is apt to have its own, perhaps slight, language differences from neighboring places. Such differences in pronunciation, vocabulary, word meanings, and other language characteristics tend to accumulate with distance from a given starting point. When they

Sex differentiation in language seems to be universal, appearing in some more or less prominent form among all language families. Most of the observed differences have to do with vocabulary choice and with grammatical devices peculiar to individual cultures, though *sociolinguistics*—the study of the relationship between language and society—explores a number of ways in which males and females everywhere obviously or subtly use language differently.

They may, for example, pronounce the same words differently or produce some sounds—either consonants or vowels or both—with consistent sex-related differences, as do (or did) the Gros Ventre Amerindians of Montana, the Koasati of southwestern Louisiana, and the Yana speakers in California. Similar consistent sound changes have been noted elsewhere—among, for example, the Cham in Vietnam, Bengali speakers of India, and in the Chukchi language of Siberia. Grammatical differences also occur. Speakers of Kurukh, a Dravidian language of northern India, construct verbs differently depending on who is speaking and who is listening. Male to male, male to female, female to female, and female to male conversations all involve possible variants in verb forms in both singular and plural persons and in different tenses. Vocabularies themselves may differ. Among the Caribs of the Caribbean, the Zulu of Africa, and elsewhere, men have words that women through custom or taboo are not permitted to use, and "the women have words and phrases which the men never use, *or they would be laughed to scorn,*" one informant reports.

Evidence from both English and such unrelated languages as Koasati indicate that, apparently as a rule, female speakers use forms considered to be "better" or "more correct" than males of the same social class. They tend to be more "conservative" and less "innovative" in the words and phrases they employ. Presumably these and other linguistic sex varieties arise because language is a *social* phenomenon closely related to social attitudes. The greater and more inflexible the difference in the social roles of men and women in a particular culture, the greater and more rigid the linguistic differences between the sexes.

---

are mapped, they help define the **linguistic geography**—the study of the character and spatial pattern of dialects and languages—of a generalized speech community.

Every dialect feature has a territorial extent. The outer limit of its occurrence is a boundary line called an *isogloss* (the term *isophone* is used if the areal variant is marked by difference in sound rather than word choice), as shown in Figure 5.10. Each isogloss is a distinct entity, but taken together isoglosses give clear map evidence of dialect regions that in their turn may reflect topographic barriers and corridors, long-established political borders, or past migration flows and diffusions of word choice and pronunciation.

Geographic or **regional dialects** may be recognized at different scales. On the world scene, for example, British, American, Indian, and Australian English are all acknowledged distinctive dialects of the same language. Regionally, in Britain alone, one can recognize Southern British English, Northern British English, and Scottish English, each containing several more localized variants. Italy contains the Gallo-Italian and Venetan dialect groups of the north, the Tuscan dialects of the center, and a collection of southern Italian dialects. Japanese has three recognized dialect groups.

Indeed, all long-established speech communities show their own structure of geographic dialects whose number and diversity tend to increase in areas longest settled and most fragmented and isolated. For example, the local speech of Newfoundland—isolated off the Atlantic coast of mainland Canada—retains much of the 17th-century flavor of the four West Counties of England from which the overwhelm-

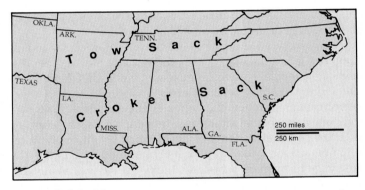

FIGURE 5.10 **Dialect boundaries.** Descriptive words or terms for common items are frequently employed indicators of dialect difference. The limit of their areas of use is marked by an **isogloss,** such as that shown here for a term describing a coarse sack. Usually such boundary lines appear in clusters or *bundles;* together, they help define the frontier of the dialect under study (see Figure 5.13).

ing majority of its settlers came. Yet the isolation and lack of cultural mixing of the islanders have not led to a general Newfoundland "dialect"; settlement was coastal and in the form of isolated villages in each of the many bays and indentations. There developed from that isolation and the passage of time nearly as many dialects as there are bay settlements, with each dialect separately differing from Standard English in accent, vocabulary, sounds, and syntax. Isolation has led to comparable linguistic variation among the

47,000 inhabitants of the 18 Faeroe Islands between Iceland and Scotland; their Faeroese tongue has 10 dialects.

Dialects in America

Mainland North America had a more diversified colonization than did Newfoundland, and its more mobile settlers mixed and carried linguistic influences away from the coast into the continental interior. Nonetheless, as early as the 18th century, three distinctive dialect regions had emerged along the Atlantic coast of the United States (Figure 5.11) and are evident in the linguistic geography of North America to the present day.

With the extension of settlement after the Revolutionary War, each of the dialect regions expanded inland. Speakers of the Northern dialect moved along the Erie Canal and the Great Lakes. Midland speakers from Pennsylvania travelled down the Ohio River, and the related Upland Southern dialect moved through the mountain gaps into Kentucky and Tennessee. The Coastal Southern dialect was less mobile, held to the east by plantation prosperity and the long resistance to displacement exerted by the Cherokees and the other Civilized Tribes (Figure 5.12).

Once across the Appalachian barrier, the diffusion paths of the Northern dialect were fragmented and blocked by the time they reached the Upper Mississippi. Upland Southern speakers spread out rapidly: northward into the old Northwest Territory, west into Arkansas and Missouri, and south into the Gulf Coast states. But the Civil War and its aftermath halted further major westward movements of the Southern dialects. The Midland dialect, so apparently restricted along the eastern seaboard became, almost by default, the basic form for much of the interior and West of the United States. It was altered and enriched there by contact with the Northern and Southern dialects, by additions from Native American languages, by contact with Spanish culture in the Southwest, and by contributions from the great non-English immigrations of

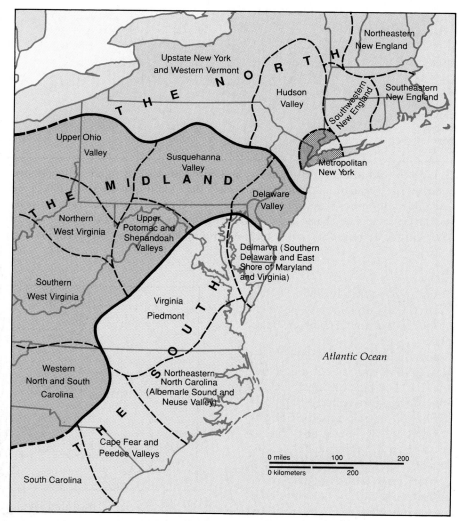

FIGURE 5.11 **Dialect areas of the eastern United States.** The Northern dialect and its subdivisions are found in New England and adjacent Canada (the international boundary has little effect on dialect borders in Anglo America), extending southward to a secondary dialect area centered on New York City. Midland speech is found along the Atlantic Coast only from central New Jersey southward to central Delaware, but spreads much more extensively across the interior of the United States and Canada. The Southern dialect dominates the East Coast from Chesapeake Bay south.

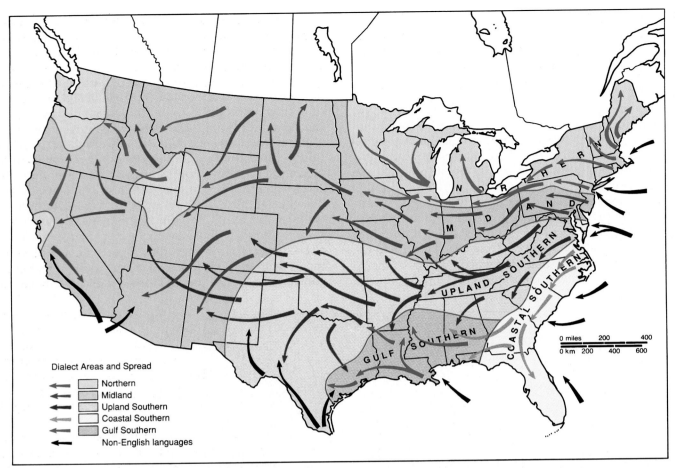

FIGURE 5.12   **Speech regions and dialect diffusion in the United States.** This generalized map is most accurate for the eastern seaboard and the easternmost diffusion pathways where most detailed linguistic study has been concentrated. West of the Mississippi River the Midland dialect becomes dominant, though altered through modifications reflecting intermingling of peoples and speech patterns. Northern speech characteristics are still clearly evident in the San Francisco Bay area, brought there in the middle of the last century by migrants coming by sea around Cape Horn. Northerners were also prominent among the travelers of the Oregon Trail.

the late 19th and early 20th centuries. Naturally, dialect subregions are found in the West, but their boundary lines—so clear in the eastern interior (Figure 5.13)—become less distinct from the Plains states to the Pacific.

Far from becoming more uniform linguistically, all evidence suggests increasing regional and social dialectical divergences in the United States. The black English vernacular of urban America is becoming more differentiated not only from the standard English of the mass media but also from the white regional dialects of the same areas. The social and spatial segregation of black inner-city residents encourages their development of a distinctive pronunciation, grammar, vocabulary, and idiom pool. Some linguists maintain that regional dialect differences within the white community are also increasing despite the assumed unifying influences of national television and press. In areas with strong infusions of Hispanic, Asian, and other immigrant groups, language mixing tends locally to accelerate language change and to create or perpetuate pockets of linguistically unassimilated peoples.

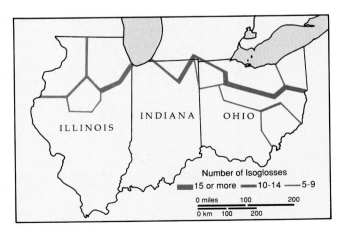

FIGURE 5.13   **Bundled isoglosses in the Midwest** help define the boundary between Northern and Midland dialect regions in the interior United States. Migration patterns strongly influence dialect differentiation. The predominantly east-west orientation of isoglosses reflects the westward stream of migration across the continental interior.

Pidgins and Creoles

Language is rarely a total barrier in communication between peoples, even those whose native tongues are mutually incomprehensible. Bilingualism or multilingualism may permit skilled linguists to communicate in a jointly understood third language, but long-term contact between less able populations may require the creation of new language—a pidgin—learned by both parties.

A **pidgin** is an amalgamation of languages, usually a simplified form of one, such as English or French, with borrowings from another, perhaps non-European local language. In its original form, a pidgin is not the mother tongue of any of its speakers; it is a second language for everyone who uses it, a language generally restricted to such specific functions as commerce, administration, or work supervision. For example, such is the variety of languages spoken among the some 270 ethnic groups of Zaire that a special tongue called Lingala, a hybrid of Congolese dialects and French, has been created to permit, among other things, issuance of orders to army recruits drawn from all parts of the country.

Pidgins are characterized by a highly simplified grammatical structure and a sharply reduced vocabulary, adequate to express basic ideas but not complex concepts. If a pidgin becomes the first language of a group of speakers—who may have lost their former native tongue through disuse—a **creole** has evolved. In their development, creoles invariably acquire a more complex grammatical structure and enhanced vocabulary.

Creole languages have proved useful integrative tools in linguistically diverse areas; several have become symbols of nationhood. Swahili, a pidgin formed from a number of Bantu dialects, originated in the coastal areas of East Africa and spread by trade during the period of English and German colonial rules. When Kenya and Tanzania gained independence, they made Swahili the national language of administration and education. Other examples of creolization are Afrikaans (a pidginized form of 17th-century Dutch used in the Republic of South Africa); Haitian Creole (the language of Haiti, derived from the pidginized French used in the slave trade); and Bazaar Malay (a pidginized form of the Malay language, a version of which is the official national language of Indonesia).

Lingua Franca

A **lingua franca** is an established language used habitually for communication by people whose native tongues are mutually incomprehensible. For them it is a *second language,* one learned in addition to the native tongue. Lingua franca, literally "Frankish tongue," was named from the dialect of France adopted as their common tongue by the Crusaders assaulting the Muslims of the Holy Land. Later, it endured as a language of trade and travel in the eastern Mediterranean, useful as a single tongue shared in a linguistically diverse region.

Between 300 B.C. and A.D. 500, the Mediterranean world was unified by Common Greek. Later, Latin became a lingua franca, the language of empire and, until replaced by the vernacular European tongues, of the Church, government, scholarship, and the law. Outside the European sphere, Aramaic served the role from the 5th century B.C. to the 4th century A.D. in the Near East and Egypt; Arabic followed Muslim conquest as the unifying language of that international religion after the 7th century. Mandarin Chinese and Hindi in India both formerly and today have a lingua franca role in their linguistically diverse countries. The immense linguistic diversity of Africa has made regional lingua francas there necessary and inevitable (Figure 5.14).

Official Languages

Governments may designate a single tongue as a country's **official language,** the required language of instruction in the schools and universities, government and business, the courts, and other official and semiofficial public and private activities. In societies in which two or more languages are in common use (**multilingualism**), such an official language may serve as the approved national lingua franca, guaranteeing communication among all citizens of differing native tongues. In many immigrant societies, such as the United States, only one of the many spoken languages may have implicit or official government sanction (see "An Official U.S. Language?")

Nearly every country in linguistically complex sub-Saharan Africa has selected a European language—usually that of their former colonial governors—as an official language (Figure 5.15), only rarely designating a native language or creole as an alternate official tongue. Indeed, less than 10% of the population of sub-Saharan Africa live in countries with any indigenous African tongue given official status. Nigeria has some 350 clearly different languages and is dominated by 3 of them: Hausa, Yoruba, and Ibo. For no Nigerian is English a native tongue, yet throughout the country English is the sole language of instruction and the sole official language. Effectively, all Nigerians must learn a foreign language before they can enter the mainstream of national life. Most Pacific Ocean countries, including the Philippines (with between 80 and 110 Malayo-Polynesian languages) and Papua New Guinea (with over 750 distinct Papuan tongues), have a European language as at least one of their official tongues.

In some countries, multilingualism has official recognition through designation of more than a single state language. Belgium and Canada, for example, have two official languages (*bilingualism*), reflecting rough equality in numbers or influence of separate linguistic populations comprising a single country. In a few multilingual countries, more than two official languages have been designated. Bolivia has three official tongues and Switzerland has four. South Africa's constitution designates 11 official languages, and India gives official status to 15 languages at the regional, though not at the national, level.

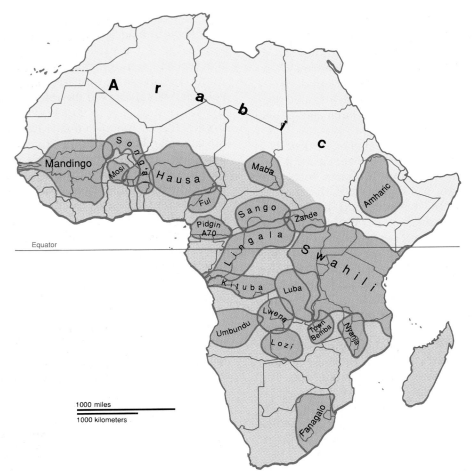

FIGURE 5.14 **Lingua francas of Africa.** The importance and areal extent of competing lingua francas in sub-Saharan Africa change over time, reflecting the spread of populations and the relative economic or political stature of speakers of different languages. In many areas, an individual may employ different lingua francas, depending on activity: dealing with officials, trading in the marketplace, conversing with strangers. Among the elite in all areas, the preferred lingua franca is apt to be a European language. Throughout northern Africa, Arabic is the usual lingua franca for all purposes.

English
French
Portuguese
Spanish

FIGURE 5.15 **Europe in Africa through official languages.** Both the linguistic complexity of sub-Saharan Africa and the colonial histories of its present political units are implicit in the designation of a European language as the sole or joint "official" language of the different countries. In some countries, the former colonial language is widely used but not recognized as official. In Kenya, for example, English is common but the designated official language is Swahili.

Multilingualism may reflect significant cultural and spatial divisions within a country. In Canada, the Official Languages Act of 1969 accorded French and English equal status as official languages of the Parliament and of government throughout the nation. French speakers are concentrated in the Province of Quebec, however, and constitute a culturally distinct population sharply divergent from the English-speaking majority of other parts of Canada (Figure 5.16). Within sections of Canada, even greater linguistic diversity is recognized; the legislature of the Northwest Territories, for example, has 8 official languages—6 native plus English and French.

Few countries remain purely *monolingual,* with only a single language of communication for all purposes among all citizens, though some are officially so. Past and recent movements of peoples as colonists, refugees, or migrants have assured that most of the world's countries contain linguistically mixed populations. Maintenance of native languages among such populations is not assured, of course. Where numbers are small or pressures for integration into an economically and socially dominant culture are strong, immigrant and aboriginal (native) linguistic minorities tend to adopt the majority or official language for all purposes. On the other hand, isolation and relatively large numbers of speakers may serve to preserve native tongues. In Canada, for example, aboriginal languages with large populations of speakers—Cree, Ojibwe, and Inuktitut—are well maintained in their areas of concentration (respectively, northern Quebec, the northern prairies, and the Northwest Territories). In contrast, much smaller language groups in southern and coastal British Columbia have a much lower ratio of retention among native speakers.

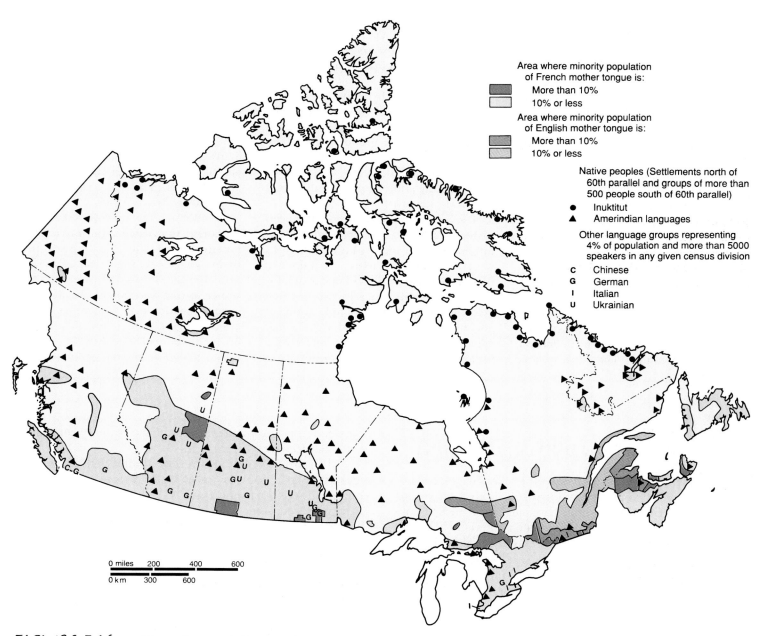

FIGURE 5.16 **Bilingualism and diversity in Canada.** The map shows areas of Canada which have a minimum of 5000 inhabitants and include a minority population identified with an official language.

FOR YOUR CONSIDERATION

AN OFFICIAL U.S. LANGUAGE?

In Lowell, Massachusetts, public school courses are offered in Spanish, Khmer, Lao, Portuguese, and Vietnamese, and all messages from schools to parents are translated into 5 languages. Polyglot New York City gives bilingual programs in Spanish, Chinese, Haitian Creole, Russian, Korean, Vietnamese, French, Greek, Arabic, and Bengali. In most states, it is possible to get a high-school-equivalency diploma without knowing English, because tests are offered in French and Spanish. In 39 states, driving tests are available in foreign languages; California provides 39 varieties, New York 23, and Michigan 20, including Arabic and Finnish. And the 1965 federal Voting Rights Act requires multilingual ballots in 375 electoral jurisdictions.

These, and innumerable other evidences of governmentally sanctioned linguistic diversity, may come as a surprise to those many Americans who assume that English is the official language of the United States. It isn't; nowhere does the Constitution provide for an official language, and no federal law specifies one. The country was built by a great diversity of cultural and linguistic immigrants who nonetheless shared an eagerness to enter mainstream American life. In the 1990s, more than 15% of all U.S. residents speak a language other than English in the home. In California public schools, 1 out of 3 students uses a non-English tongue within the family. In Washington, D.C. schools, students speak 127 languages and dialects, a linguistic diversity duplicated in other major city school systems.

Nationwide bilingual teaching began as an offshoot of the civil rights movement in the 1960s, was encouraged by a Supreme Court opinion authored by Justice William O. Douglas, and has been actively promoted by the U.S. Department of Education under the Bilingual Education Act of 1974 as an obligation of local school boards. Its purpose has been to teach subject matter to minority-language children in the language in which they think, while introducing them to English, with the hope of achieving English proficiency in two or three years. Opponents of the implications of governmentally encouraged multilingual education, bilingual ballots, and ethnic separatism argue that a common language is the unifying glue of the United States and all countries; without that glue, they fear, the process of "Americanization" and *acculturation*—the adoption by immigrants of the values, attitudes, ways of behavior, and speech of the receiving society—will be undermined. Convinced that early immersion and quick proficiency in English is the only sure way for minority newcomers to gain necessary access to jobs, higher education, and full integration into the economic and social life of the country, proponents of "English only" use in public education, voting, and state and local governmental agencies, successfully passed Official English constitutional amendments in 22 states during the late 1980s and early 1990s.

Although the amendments were supported by sizeable majorities of the voting population, resistance to them—and to their political and cultural implications—was in every instance strong and persistent. Ethnic groups, particularly Hispanics, who are the largest of the linguistic groups affected, charged that they were evidence of blatant Anglo-centric racism,

Language, Territoriality, and Identity

The designation of more than one official language does not always satisfy the ambitions of linguistically distinct groups for recognition and autonomy. Language is an inseparable part of group identity and a defining characteristic of ethnic and cultural distinction. The view that cultural heritage is rooted in language is well established and found throughout the world, as is the feeling that losing linguistic identity is the worst and final evidence of discrimination and subjugation. Language has often been the focus of separatist movements, especially of spatially distinct linguistic groups outside the economic heartlands of the strongly centralized countries to which they are attached.

In Europe, highly centralized France, Spain, Britain—and Yugoslavia and the Soviet Union before their dismemberment—experienced such language "revolts" and acknowledged, sometimes belatedly, the local concerns they express. Until 1970, when the ban on teaching regional tongues was dropped, the spoken regional languages and dialects of France were ignored and denied recognition by the state. Since the late 1970s, Spain not only has relaxed its earlier total rejection of Basque and Catalan as regional languages and given state support to instruction in them, but also has recognized Catalan as a co-official language in its

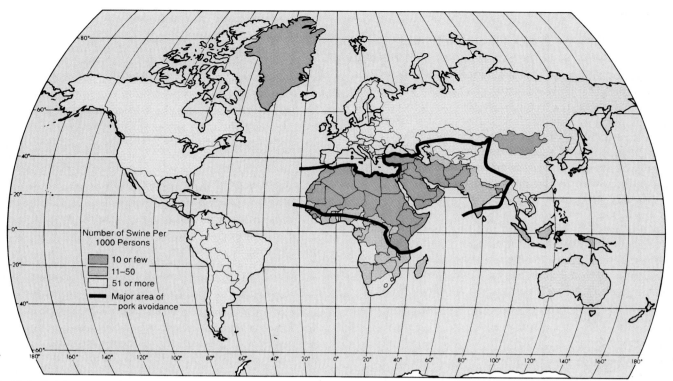

FIGURE 5.18   **Pattern of swine production.** Religious prohibition against the consumption of pork, particularly among those of the Jewish and Muslim faiths, finds spatial expression in the incidence of swine production. Because production figures are national summaries, the map does not faithfully report small-area distributions of either religious affiliation or animal raising.

classifying religions as they were in studying languages. A distinction between **monotheism,** belief in a single deity, and **polytheism,** belief in many gods, is frequent but not particularly spatially relevant. Simple territorial categories have been offered recognizing origin areas of religions: Western versus Eastern, for example, or African, Far Eastern, or Indian. With proper detail such distinctions may inform us where particular religions had their roots but do not reveal their courses of development, paths of diffusion, or current distributions.

Our geographic interest in classification of religions is different from that of, say, theologians or historians. We are not so concerned with the beliefs themselves or with their birthplaces (though both help us understand their cultural implications and areal arrangements). We are more interested in religions' patterns and processes of diffusion once they have developed, with the spatial distributions they have achieved, and with the impact of the practices and beliefs of different religious systems on the landscape. To satisfy at least some of those interests, geographers have found it useful to categorize religions as *universalizing, ethnic,* or *tribal (traditional).*

Christianity, Islam, and Buddhism are the major world **universalizing religions,** faiths that claim applicability to all humans and that seek to transmit their beliefs through missionary work and conversion. Membership in universal-

izing religions is open to anyone who chooses to make some sort of symbolic commitment, such as baptism in Christianity. No one is excluded because of nationality, ethnicity, or previous religious belief.

Ethnic religions have strong territorial and cultural group identification. One becomes a member of an ethnic religion by birth or by adoption of a complex life-style and cultural identity, not by simple declaration of faith. These religions do not usually proselytize, and their members form distinctive closed communities identified with a particular ethnic group or political unit. An ethnic religion—for example, Judaism, Indian Hinduism, or Japanese Shinto—is an integral element of a specific culture; to be part of the religion is to be immersed in the totality of the culture.

Tribal or **traditional religions** are special forms of ethnic religions distinguished by their small size, their unique identity with localized culture groups not yet fully absorbed into modern society, and their close ties to nature. **Animism** is the name given to their belief that life exists in all objects, from rocks and trees to lakes and mountains, or that such inanimate objects are the abode of the dead, of spirits, and of gods. **Shamanism** is a form of tribal religion that involves community acceptance of a *shaman,* a religious leader, healer, and worker of magic who, through special powers, can intercede with and interpret the spirit world.

Patterns, Numbers, and Flows

The nature of the different classes of religions is reflected in their distributions over the world (Figure 5.19) and in their number of adherents. Universalizing religions tend to be expansionary, carrying their message to new peoples and areas. Ethnic religions, unless their adherents are dispersed, tend to be regionally confined or to expand only slowly and over long periods. Tribal religions tend to contract spatially as their adherents are incorporated increasingly into modern society and converted by proselytizing faiths.

As we expect in human geography, the map records only the latest stage of a constantly changing cultural reality. While established religious institutions tend to be conservative and resistant to change, religion as a culture trait is dynamic. Personal and collective beliefs may alter in response to developing individual and societal needs and challenges. Religions may be imposed by conquest, adopted by conversion, or defended and preserved in the face of surrounding hostility or indifference.

The World Pattern

Figure 5.19 (at this scale) cannot present a full picture of religious affiliation or regionalization. Few societies are homogeneous, and most modern ones contain a variety of different faiths or, at least, variants of the dominant professed religion. Frequently, members of a particular religion show areal concentration within a country. Thus, in urban Northern Ireland, Protestants and Catholics reside in separate areas whose boundaries are clearly understood and respected. The "Green Line" in Beirut, Lebanon marked a guarded border between the Christian East and the Muslim West sides of the city, while within the country as a whole, regional concentrations of adherents of different faiths and sects are clearly recognized (Figure 5.20). Religious diversity within countries may reflect the degree of toleration a majority culture affords minority religions. In dominantly (90%) Muslim Indonesia, Christian Bataks, Hindu Balinese, and Muslim Javanese live in easy coexistence. By contrast, the fundamentalist Islamic regime in Iran has persecuted and executed those of the Baha'i faith.

Data on religious affiliation are not precise. Most nations do not have religious censuses, and different religious groups differently and inconsistently report their membership. When communism was supreme in the Soviet Union and Eastern bloc countries, official atheism dissuaded many from openly professing or practicing any religion; in nominally Christian Europe and North America, many who claim to be believers are not active church members and others renounce religion altogether. More than half of the world's

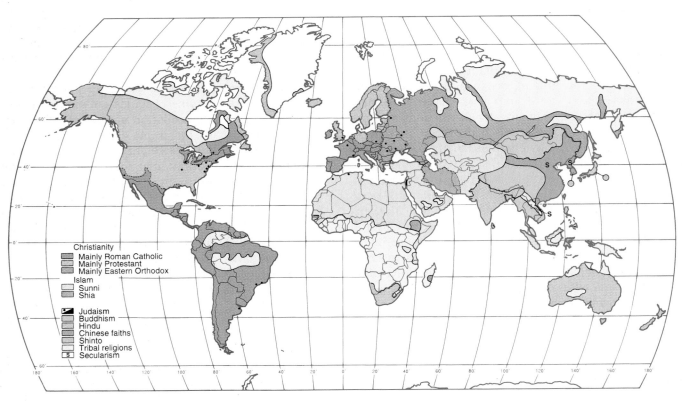

FIGURE 5.19   Principal world religions.

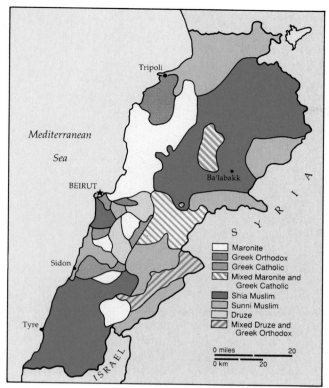

FIGURE 5.20 **Religious regions of Lebanon.**
Religious territoriality and rivalry have contributed to the
prolonged period of conflict and animosity in this
troubled country.

population probably adhere to one of the major universalizing religions: Christianity, Islam, or Buddhism. Of these three, Figure 5.19 indicates Christianity and Islam are most widespread; Buddhism is largely an Asian religion. Hinduism, the largest ethnic faith, is essentially confined to the Indian subcontinent, showing the spatial restriction characteristic of most ethnic and traditional religions even when found outside their homeland area. Small Hindu emigrant communities in Africa, southeast Asia, England, and the United States, for example, tend to remain isolated even in densely crowded urban areas. Although it is not localized, Judaism is also included among the ethnic religions because of its identification with a particular people and cultural tradition.

Extensive areas of the world are peopled by those who practice tribal or traditional religions, often in concert with the universalizing religions to which they have been outwardly converted. Tribal religions are found principally among peoples who have not yet been fully absorbed into modern cultures and economies or who are on the margins of more populous and advanced societies. Although the areas assigned to tribal religions in Figure 5.19 are large, the number of adherents is small and declining.

One cannot assume that all people within a mapped religious region are adherents of the designated faith or that membership in a religious community means active participation in its belief system. **Secularism,** an indifference to or rejection of religion and religious belief, is an increasing part of many modern societies, particularly of the industrialized nations and those now or formerly under communist regimes. In England, for example, the state Church of England claims only 20% of the British population as communicants, and less than 2% of the population attends its Sunday services. Two-thirds of the French describe themselves as Catholic, but less than 10% regularly go to church. Even in devoutly Roman Catholic South American states, low church attendance witnesses the rise of at least informal secularism. In Colombia, only 18% of people attend Sunday services; in Chile, the figure is 12%, in Mexico 11%, and Bolivia 5%.

The Principal Religions

Each of the major religions has its own unique mix of cultural values and expressions, each has had its own pattern of innovation and spatial diffusion (Figure 5.21), and each has had its own impact on the cultural landscape. Together they contribute importantly to the worldwide pattern of human diversity.

Judaism

We begin our review of world faiths with **Judaism,** whose belief in a single God laid the foundation for both Christianity and Islam. Unlike its universalizing offspring, Judaism is closely identified with a single ethnic group and with a complex and restrictive set of beliefs and laws. It emerged some 3000 to 4000 years ago in the Near East, one of the ancient culture hearth regions (Figure 2.16). Early Near Eastern civilizations, including those of Sumeria, Babylonia, and Assyria, developed writing, codified laws, and formalized polytheistic religions featuring rituals of sacrifice and celebrations of the cycle of seasons.

Judaism was different. The Israelites' conviction that they were a chosen people, bound with God through a covenant of mutual loyalty and guided by complex formal rules of behavior, set them apart from other peoples of the Near East. Theirs became a distinctively *ethnic* religion, the determining factors of which are descent from Israel (the patriarch Jacob), the Torah (law and scripture), and the traditions of the culture and the faith. Early military success gave the Jews a sense of territorial and political identity to supplement their religious self-awareness. Later conquest by nonbelievers led to their dispersion (*diaspora*) to much of the Mediterranean world and farther east into Asia by A.D. 500 (Figure 5.22).

Alternately tolerated and persecuted in Christian Europe, occasionally expelled from countries, and usually, as outsiders of different faith and custom, isolated in special residential quarters (ghettos), Jews retained their faith and their sense of community. Between the 13th and 16th centuries, many Jews seeking refuge from intolerable persecution in western and central Europe settled in Poland and

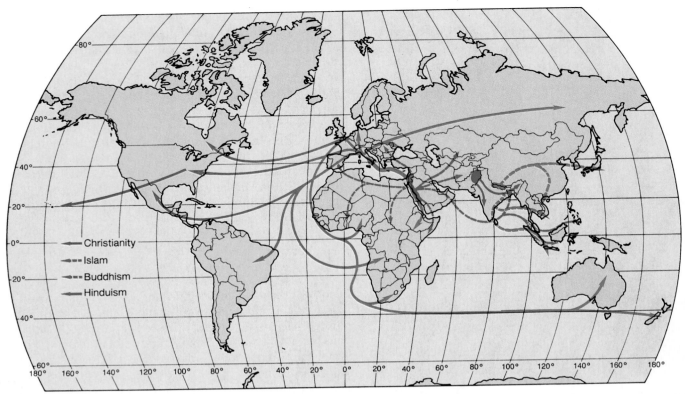

FIGURE 5.21   **Innovation areas and diffusion routes of major world religions.** The monotheistic (single deity) faiths of Judaism, Christianity, and Islam arose in southwestern Asia, the first two in Palestine in the eastern Mediterranean region and the last in western Arabia near the Red Sea. Hinduism and Buddhism originated within a confined hearth region in the northern part of the Indian subcontinent. Their rates, extent, and directions of diffusion are suggested here and detailed on later maps.

Russia (Figure 5.22). It was from eastern Europe that many of the Jewish immigrants to the United States came during the later 19th and early 20th centuries, though German-speaking areas of central Europe were also important source regions. The mass destruction of Jews in Europe before and during World War II—the Holocaust—drastically reduced their representation among the continent's total population.

The establishment of the state of Israel in 1948 was a fulfillment of the goal of *Zionism,* the belief in the need to create an autonomous Jewish state in Palestine. It demonstrated a determination that Jews not lose their identity by absorption into alien cultures and societies. The new state represented a reversal of the preceding 2000-year history of dispersal and relocation diffusion. Israel became largely a country of immigrants, an ancient homeland again identified with a distinctive people and an ethnic religion.

Judaism's imprint on the cultural landscape has been subtle and unobtrusive. The Jewish community reserves space for the practice of communal burial; the spread of the cultivated citron in the Mediterranean area during Roman times has been traced to Jewish ritual needs; and the religious use of grape wine assured the cultivation of the vine in their areas of settlement. The synagogue as place of worship has tended to be less elaborate than its Christian counterpart. The essential for religious service is a community of at least 10 adult males, not a specific structure.

Christianity

Christianity had its origin in the life and teachings of Jesus, a Jewish preacher of the 1st century of the modern era, whom his followers believed was the Messiah promised by God. The new covenant he preached was not a rejection of traditional Judaism but a promise of salvation to all humankind rather than to just a chosen people.

Christianity's mission was conversion. As a universal religion of salvation and hope, it spread quickly among the underclasses of both the eastern and western parts of the Roman Empire, carried to major cities and ports along the excellent system of Roman roads and sea lanes (Figure 5.23). *Expansion diffusion* followed the establishment of missions and colonies of converts in locations distant from the hearth region. Important among them were the urban areas that became administrative seats of the new religion. For the Western church, Rome was the principal center for dispersal, through *hierarchical diffusion,* to provincial capitals and smaller Roman settlements of Europe. From those nodes and from monasteries established in pagan rural areas, *contagious diffusion* disseminated Christianity throughout the continent. The acceptance of Christianity as the state religion of the empire by the Emperor Constantine in A.D. 313 was also an expression of *hierarchical diffusion* of great importance in establishing the faith throughout the full

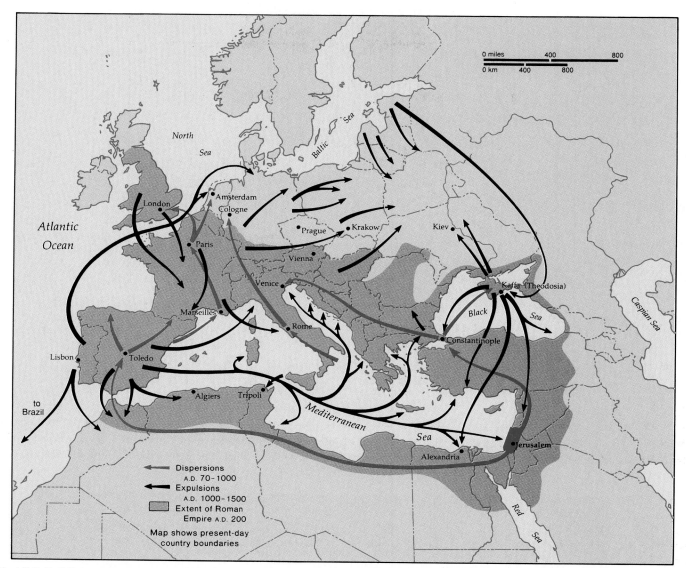

FIGURE 5.22   Jewish dispersions, A.D. 70–1500. A revolt against Roman rule in A.D. 66 was followed by the destruction of the Jewish Temple four years later and an imperial decision to Romanize the city of Jerusalem. Judaism spread from the hearth region by *relocation diffusion,* carried by its adherents dispersing from their homeland to Europe, Africa, and eventually in great numbers to the Western Hemisphere. Although Jews established themselves and their religion in new lands, they did not lose their sense of cultural identity and did not seek to attract converts to their faith.

extent of the Roman world. Finally, and much later, *relocation diffusion* brought the faith to the New World with European settlers (Figure 5.19).

The dissolution of the Roman Empire into a western and an eastern half after the fall of Rome also divided Christianity. The Western Church, based in Rome, was one of the very few stabilizing and civilizing forces uniting western Europe during the Dark Ages. Its bishops became the civil as well as ecclesiastical authorities over vast areas devoid of other effective government. Parish churches were the focus of rural and urban life, and the cathedrals replaced Roman monuments and temples as the symbols of the social order (Figure 5.24). Everywhere, the Roman Catholic church and its ecclesiastical hierarchy were dominant.

Secular imperial control endured in the eastern empire, whose capital was Constantinople. Thriving under its protection, the Eastern church expanded into the Balkans, eastern Europe, Russia, and the Near East. The fall of the eastern empire to the Turks in the 15th century opened eastern Europe temporarily to Islam, though the Eastern Orthodox Church (the direct descendant of the Byzantine state church) remains, in its various ethnic branches, a major component of Christianity.

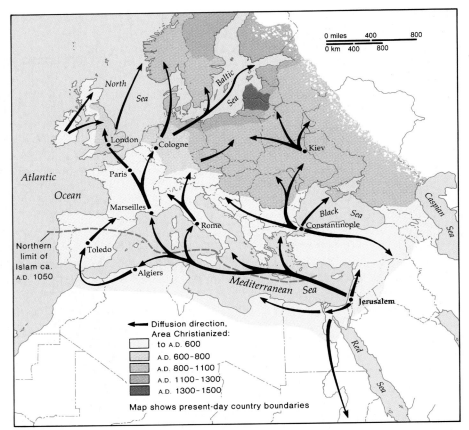

FIGURE 5.23   **Diffusion paths of Christianity, A.D. 100–1500.** Routes and dates are for Christianity as a composite faith. No distinction is made between the Western church and the various subdivisions of the Eastern Orthodox denominations.

FIGURE 5.24   The building of Notre Dame Cathedral of Paris, France, begun in 1163, took more than 100 years to complete. The first of the French Gothic churches, it was part of the great period of cathedral construction in Western Europe during the late 12th and the 13th centuries. Between 1170 and 1270, some 80 cathedrals were constructed in France alone. The cathedrals were located in the center of major cities; their plazas were the sites of markets, public meetings, morality plays, and religious ceremonies. They were the focus of public and private life and the symbol not only of the faith but of the pride and prosperity of the towns and regions that erected them.

PATTERNS OF DIVERSITY AND UNITY

The Protestant Reformation of the 15th and 16th centuries split the church in the west, leaving Roman Catholicism supreme in southern Europe but installing a variety of Protestant denominations and national churches in western and northern Europe. The split was reflected in the subsequent worldwide dispersion of Christianity. Catholic Spain and Portugal colonized Latin America, taking both their languages and the Roman church to that area (Figure 5.21), as they did to colonial outposts in the Philippines, India, and Africa. Catholic France colonized Quebec in North America. Protestants, many of them fleeing Catholic or repressive Protestant state churches, were primary early settlers of Anglo America, Australia, New Zealand, Oceania, and South Africa.

In Africa and Asia, both Protestant and Catholic missions attempted to convert nonbelievers. Both achieved success in sub-Saharan Africa, though traditional religions are shown in Figure 5.19 as dominant through much of that area. Neither was particularly successful in China, Japan, or India, where strong ethnic religious cultural systems were barriers largely impermeable to the diffusion of the Christian faith. Although accounting for nearly one-third of the world's population and territorially the most extensive belief system, Christianity is no longer numerically important in or near its original hearth. Nor is it any longer dominated by Northern Hemisphere adherents. In 1900, two-thirds of all Christians lived in Europe and North America; by 2000, two-thirds of a projected 2 billion total will live elsewhere—in South America, Africa, and Asia.

Regions and Landscapes of Christianity

All of the principal world religions have experienced theological, doctrinal, or political divisions; frequently these have spatial expression. In Christianity, the early split between the Western and Eastern churches was initially unrelated to dogma but nonetheless resulted in a territorial separation still evident on the world map. The later subdivision of the Western church into Roman Catholic and Protestant branches gave a more intricate spatial patterning in western Europe that can only be generally suggested at the scale of Figure 5.19. Still more intermixed are the areal segregations and concentrations that have resulted from the denominational subdivisions of Protestantism.

In Anglo America, the beliefs and practices of various immigrant groups and the innovations of domestic congregations have created a particularly varied spatial patterning (Figure 5.25a and b), though intermingling rather than rigid territorial division is characteristic of the North American, particularly United States, scene (Figure 5.1). While 85% of Canadian Christians belong to one of three denominations (Roman Catholic, Anglican, or United Church of Canada), it takes at least 20 denominations to account for 85% of Americans. Nevertheless, for the United States, one observer has suggested a pattern of "religious regions" of the country (Figure 5.26a) that, he believes, reflects a larger cultural regionalization of the United States. The extent of the underlying areal concentration and domination of at least two U.S. Protestant denominations is demonstrated in Figure 5.26b.

Strongly French-, Irish-, and Portuguese-Catholic New England, the Hispanic-Catholic Southwest, and the French-Catholic vicinity of New Orleans (evident on both Figure 5.25a and 5.26a) are commonly recognized regional subdivisions of the United States. Each has a cultural identity that includes, but is not limited to, its dominant religion. The western area of Mormon (more properly, Church of Jesus Christ of Latter-day Saints, or LDS) cultural and religious dominance is prominent and purely American. The Baptist presence in the South and that of the Lutherans in the Upper Midwest help determine the boundaries of other distinctive composite regions. The zone of cultural mixing across the center of the country from the Middle Atlantic states to the western LDS region—so evident in the linguistic geography of the United States (Figure 5.12)—is again apparent on both maps. No single church or denomination dominates, a characteristic as well of the Far Western zone.

Indeed, in no large section of the United States is there a denominational dominance to equal the overwhelming (88 + %) Roman Catholic presence in Quebec suggested, on Figure 5.25b, by the absence of any "second rank" religious affiliation. The "leading" position of the United Church of Canada in the Canadian West and of the Anglican Church in the Atlantic region of Newfoundland is much less commanding. Much of interior Canada shows a degree of cultural mixing and religious diversity only hinted at by Figure 5.25b, where only the largest church memberships are noted.

The mark of Christianity on the cultural landscape has been prominent and enduring. In pre-Reformation Catholic Europe, the parish church formed the center of life for small neighborhoods of every town, and the village church was the centerpiece of every rural community. In York, England, with a population of 11,000 in the 14th century, there were 45 parish churches, 1 for each 250 inhabitants. In addition, the central cathedral served simultaneously as a glorification of God, a symbol of piety, and the focus of religious and secular life (Figure 5.24). The Spanish Laws of the Indies (1573) perpetuated that landscape dominance in the New World, decreeing that all Spanish American settlements should have a church or cathedral on a central plaza (Figure 5.27a).

Protestantism placed less importance on the church as a monument and symbol, although in many communities—in colonial New England, for example—the churches of the principal denominations were at the village center (Figure 5.27b). They were often adjoined by a cemetery; Christians—in common with Muslims and Jews—practice burial in areas reserved for the dead. In Christian countries in particular, the cemetery—whether connected to the church, separate from it, or unrelated to a specific denomination—has traditionally been a significant land use within urban areas. Frequently, the separate cemetery, originally on the outskirts of the community, becomes with urban expansion a more central land use and often one that distorts or blocks the growth of the city.

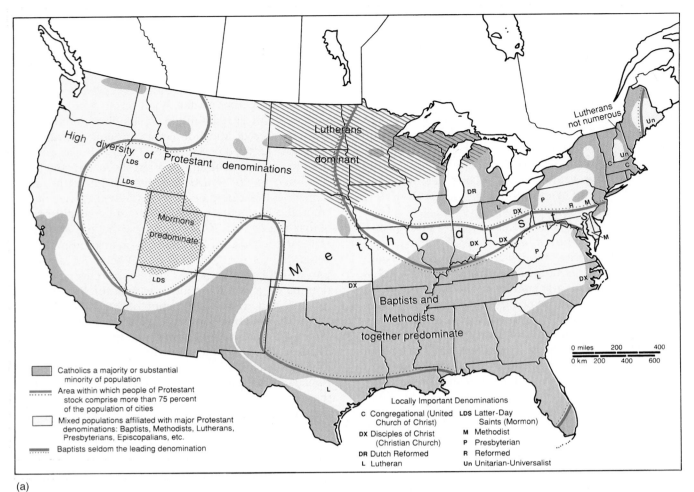

(a)

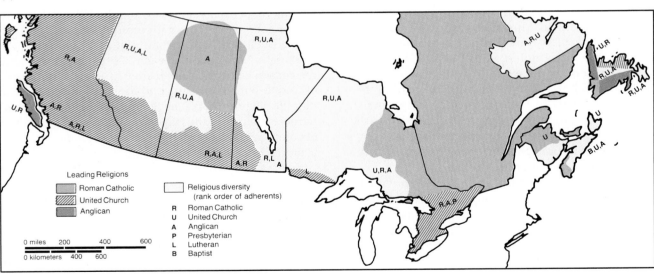

(b)

FIGURE 5.25 *(a)* **Religious affiliation in the conterminous United States.** *(b)* **Religious affiliation in Canada.** The richness of Canadian religious diversity is obscured by the numerical dominance of a small number of leading Christian denominations.

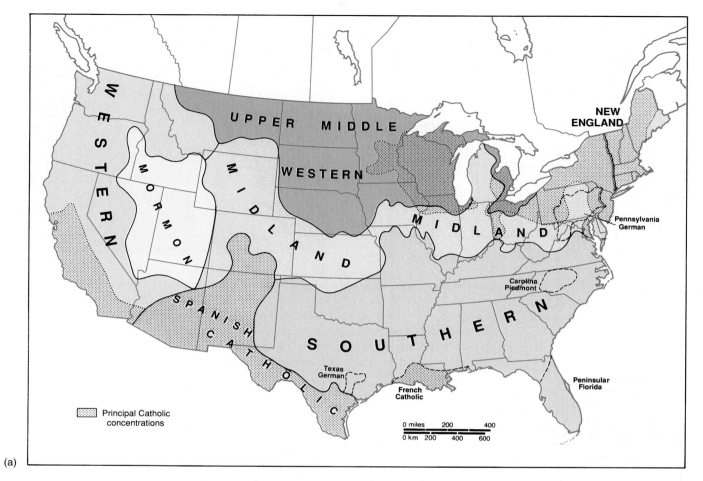

(a)

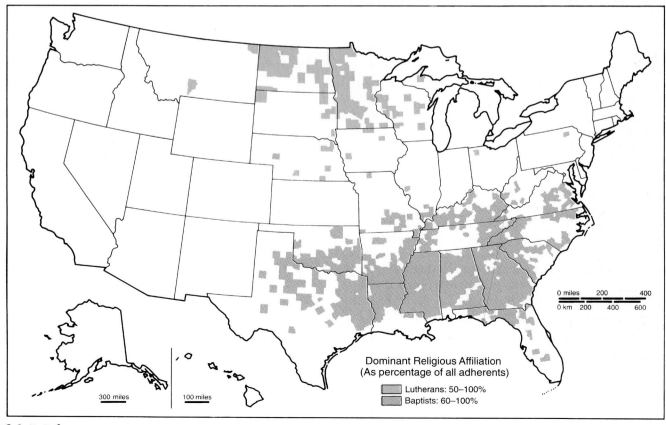

(b)

FIGURE 5.26   (a) **Major religious regions of the United States.** (b) **Regional concentration of Baptists and Lutherans.**

(a) After Wilbur Zelinsky.

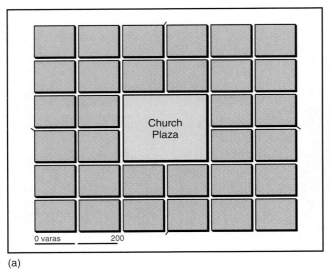

(a)

(b)

FIGURE 5.27   In Christian societies the church assumes a prominent central position in the cultural landscape. (*a*) By royal decree, Spanish planned settlements in the New World were to focus on the cathedral and plaza centered within a gridiron street system. On average, 1 vara equals about 84 centimeters (33 inches). (*b*) Individually less imposing than the central cathedral of Catholic areas, the several Protestant churches common in small and large Anglo American towns collectively constitute an important land use, frequently seeking or claiming space in the center of the community. The distinctive New England spired church became a model for Protestant edifices elsewhere in the United States and a symbol of religion in national life.

Islam

Islam—the word means "submission" (to the will of God)—springs from same Judaic roots as Christianity and embodies many of the same beliefs: There is only one God, who may be revealed to humans through prophets; Adam was the first human; Abraham was one of his descendents. Mohammed is revered as the prophet of *Allah* (God), succeeding and completing the work of earlier prophets of Judaism and Christianity, including Moses, David, and Jesus. The Koran, the word of Allah revealed to Mohammed, contains not only rules of worship and details of doctrine but also instructions on the conduct of human affairs. For fundamentalists, it thus becomes the unquestioned guide to matters both religious and secular. Observance of the "five pillars" (Figure 5.28) and surrender to the will of Allah unite the faithful into a brotherhood that has no concern with race, color, or caste.

That law of brotherhood served to unify an Arab world sorely divided by tribes, social ranks, and multiple local deities. Mohammed was a resident of Mecca but fled in A.D. 622 to Medina, where the Prophet proclaimed a constitution and announced the universal mission of the Islamic community. That flight—*Hegira*—marks the starting point of the Islamic (lunar) calendar. By the time of Mohammed's death in 11 A.H. (anno—the year of—Hegira, or A.D. 632), all of Arabia had joined Islam. The new religion swept quickly by *expansion diffusion* outward from that source region over most of Central Asia and, at the expense of Hinduism, into northern India (Figure 5.29).

The advance westward was particularly rapid and inclusive in North Africa. In western Europe, 700 years of Muslim rule in much of Spain were ended by Christian reconquest in 1492. In eastern Europe, conversions made under an expansionary Ottoman Empire are reflected in Muslim components in Bosnia and Kosovo regions of former Yugoslavia, in Bulgaria, and in the 70% Muslim population of Albania. Later, by *relocation diffusion,* Islam was dispersed into Indonesia, southern Africa, and the Western Hemisphere. Muslims now form the majority population in 39 countries.

Asia has the largest absolute number and Africa the highest proportion of Muslims among its population—more than 42%. Islam, with an estimated 1.25 billion adherents worldwide, is the fastest-growing major religion at the present time and a prominent element in recent and current political affairs. Sectarian hatreds fueled the 1980–1988 war between Iran and Iraq; Afghan *mujahedeen*—"holy warriors"—found inspiration in their faith to resist Soviet occupation of their country, and Chechens drew strength from their faith in resisting the Russian 1995 assault on their Caucasian homeland. Islamic fundamentalism led to the 1979 overthrow of Iran's shah, Muslim separatism is a recurring theme in Philippine affairs, and militant groups seek establishment of religiously rather than secularly based governments in several Muslim states.

The mosque—place of worship, community club house, meeting hall, and school—is the focal point of Islamic communal life and the primary imprint of the religion on the cultural landscape. Its principal purpose is to accommodate the Friday communal service mandatory for all male Muslims. It is the congregation rather than the structure that is important. Small or poor communities are as well served by a bare whitewashed room as are larger cities by architecturally splendid mosques with domes and minarets. The

FIGURE 5.28   Worshipers gathered during *hajj,* the annual pilgrimage to Mecca. The black structure is the Ka'bab, the symbol of God's oneness and of the unity of God and humans. Many rules concerning daily life are given in the Koran, the holy book of the Muslims. All Muslims are expected to observe the five pillars of the faith: (1) repeated saying of the basic creed; (2) prayers five times daily, facing Mecca; (3) a month of daytime fasting (Ramadan); (4) almsgiving; and (5) if possible, a pilgrimage to Mecca.

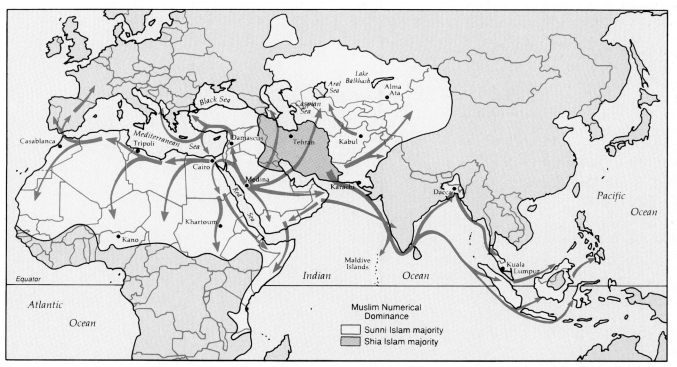

FIGURE 5.29   **Spread and extent of Islam.** Islam predominates in over 35 countries along a band across northern Africa to former Soviet Central Asia, northwestern China, and the northern part of the Indian subcontinent. Still farther east, Indonesia has the largest Muslim population of any country. Islam's greatest development is in Asia, where it is second only to Hinduism, and in Africa, where some observers suggest it may be the leading faith. Current Islamic expansion is particularly rapid in the Southern Hemisphere.

earliest mosques were modeled on or converted from Christian churches. With time, however, Muslim architects united Roman, Byzantine, and Indian design elements to produce the distinctive mosque architecture found throughout the world of Islam. With its perfectly proportioned, frequently gilded or tiled domes, its graceful, soaring towers and minarets (from which the faithful are called to prayer), and its delicately wrought parapets and cupolas, the carefully tended mosque is frequently the most elaborate and imposing structure of the town (Figure 5.30).

Hinduism

Hinduism is the world's oldest major religion. Though it has no datable founding event or initial prophet, some evidence traces its origin back 4000 or more years. Hinduism is not just a religion but an intricate web of religious, philosophical, social, economic, and artistic elements comprising a distinctive Indian civilization. Its estimated 760 million adherents are largely confined to India, where it claims 80% of the population.

Hinduism derives its name from its cradle area in the valley of the Indus River. From that district of present-day Pakistan, it spread by *contagious diffusion* eastward down the Ganges River and southward throughout the subcontinent and adjacent regions by amalgamating, absorbing, and eventually supplanting earlier native religions and customs. Its practice eventually spread throughout southeastern Asia, into Indonesia, Malaysia, Cambodia, Thailand, Laos, and Vietnam as well as into neighboring Myanmar (Burma) and Sri Lanka. The largest Hindu temple complex is in Cambodia, not India, and Bali remains a Hindu pocket in dominantly Islamic Indonesia.

No common creed, single doctrine, or central ecclesiastical organization defines the Hindu. A Hindu is one born into a caste, a member of a complex social and economic—as well as religious—community. Hinduism accepts and incorporates all forms of belief; adherents may believe in one god or many or none. It emphasizes the divinity of the soul and is based on the concepts of reincarnation and passage from one state of existence to another in an unending cycle of birth and death in which all living things are caught. One's position in this life is determined by one's *karma,* or deeds and conduct in previous lives. Upon that conduct depends the condition and the being—plant, animal, or human—into which a soul, after a stay in heaven or hell, is reborn. All creatures are ranked, with humans at the top of the ladder.

FIGURE 5.30   The common architectural features of the mosque make it an unmistakable landscape evidence of the presence of Islam in any local culture. The Badashi Mosque in Lahore, Pakistan would not be out of place architecturally in Muslim Malaysia or Indonesia.

But humans themselves are ranked, and the social caste into which an individual is born is an indication of that person's spiritual status. The goal of existence is to move up the hierarchy, eventually to be liberated from the cycle of rebirth and redeath and to achieve salvation and eternal peace through union with the *Brahman,* the universal soul.

The **caste** (meaning "birth") structure of society is an expression of the eternal transmigration of souls. For the Hindu, the primary aim of this life is to conform to prescribed social and ritual duties and to the rules of conduct for the assigned caste and profession. Those requirements comprise that individual's *dharma*—law and duties. To violate them upsets the balance of society and nature and yields undesirable consequences. To observe them improves the chance of promotion at the next rebirth. Traditionally, each craft or profession is the property of a particular caste: brahmins (scholar-priests), kshatriyas (warrior-landowners), vaishyas (businessmen, farmers, herdsmen), sudras (servants and laborers). Harijans, *untouchables* for whom the most menial and distasteful tasks were reserved and backwoods tribes—together accounting for around one-fifth of India's population—stand outside the caste system. The castes are subdivided into thousands of *jati* groups defined by geography and occupation. Caste rules define who you can mingle with, where you can live, what you may wear, eat, and drink, and how you can earn your livelihood.

The practice of Hinduism is rich with rites and ceremonies, festivals and feasts, processions and ritual gatherings of literally millions of celebrants. It involves careful observance of food and marriage rules and the performance of duties within the framework of the caste system. Pilgrimages to holy rivers and sacred places are thought to secure deliverance from sin or pollution and to preserve religious worth (Figure 5.31). In what is perhaps the largest periodic gathering of humans in the world, millions of Hindus of all castes, classes, and sects gather about once in 12 years for ritual washing away of sins in the Ganges River near Allahabad. Worship in the temples and shrines that are found in every village and the leaving of offerings to secure merit from the gods are required (see "Religion in Nanpur"). The doctrine of *ahimsa*—also fundamental in Buddhism—instructs Hindus to refrain from harming any living being.

Temples and shrines are everywhere; their construction brings merit to their owners—the villages or individuals who paid for them. Temples must be erected on a site that is beautiful and auspicious, in the neighborhood of water since the gods will not come to other locations. Within them, innumerable icons of gods in various forms are enshrined, the

FIGURE 5.31 Pilgrims at dawn worship in the Ganges River at Varanasi (Banares), India, one of the seven most sacred Hindu cities and the reputed earthly capital of Siva, Hindu god of destruction and regeneration. Hindus believe that to die in Varanasi means release from the cycle of rebirth and permits entrance into heaven.

objects of veneration, gifts, and daily care. All temples have a circular spire as a reminder that the sky is the real dwelling place of the god who temporarily resides within the temple (Figure 5.32). The temples, shrines, daily rituals and worship, numerous specially garbed or marked holy men and ascetics, and the ever-present sacred animals mark the cultural landscape of Hindu societies—a landscape infused with religious symbols and sights that are part of a total cultural experience.

Buddhism

Numerous reform movements have derived from Hinduism over the centuries, some of which have endured to the present day as major religions on a regional or world scale. *Jainism,* begun in the 6th century B.C. as a revolt against the authority of the early Hindu doctrines, rejects caste distinctions and modifies concepts of karma and transmigration of souls; it counts perhaps 4 million adherents.

Sikhism developed in the Punjab area of northwestern India in the late 15th century A.D., rejecting the formalism of both Hinduism and Islam and proclaiming a gospel of universal toleration. The great majority of some 20 million Sikhs still live in India, mostly in the Punjab, though others have settled in Malaysia, Singapore, East Africa, the United Kingdom, and North America.

The largest and most influential of the dissident movements has been **Buddhism,** a universalizing faith founded in the 6th century B.C. in northern India by Siddhartha Gautama, the Buddha (*Enlightened One*). The Buddha's teachings were more a moral philosophy that offered an explanation for evil and human suffering than a formal religion. He viewed the road to enlightenment and salvation to lie in understanding the "four noble truths": Existence involves suffering; suffering is the result of desire; pain ceases when desire is destroyed; the destruction of desire comes through knowledge of correct behavior and correct thoughts. In Bud-

FIGURE 5.32   The Hindu temple complex at Khajraho in central India. The creation of temples and the images they house has been a principal outlet of Indian artistry for more than 2000 years. At the village level, the structure may be simple, containing only the windowless central cell housing the divine image, a surmounting spire, and the temple porch or stoop to protect the doorway of the cell. The great temples, of immense size, are ornate extensions of the same basic design.

PATTERNS OF DIVERSITY AND UNITY

he villagers of Nanpur are Hindus. They are religious. They believe in God and his many incarnations. For them He is everywhere, in a man, in a tree, in a stone. According to . . . the village Brahmin, God is light and energy, like the electric current. To him there is no difference between the gods of the Hindus, Muslims and Christians. Only the names are different.

Every village has a local deity. In Nanpur it is a piece of stone . . . called Mahlia Buddha. He sits under the ancient *varuna* tree protecting the village. Kanhai Barik, the village barber, is the attendant to the deity. Kanhai, before starting his daily work, washes the deity, decorates it with vermilion and flowers and offers food given by the villagers. Clay animals are pre-sented. It is believed that the deity rides them during the night and goes from place to place guarding the village. . . . In the old days Mahlia Buddha had a special power to cure smallpox and cholera. Now, although modern medicines have brought the epidemics under control, the power of the deity has not diminished. People believe in him and worship him for everything, even for modern medicines to be effective.

Religious festivals provide entertainment. There is one almost every month. The most enjoyable is the Spring festival of Holi when people throw colored powder and water on each other as an expression of love. As the cuckoo sings, hidden among the mango blossoms, the villagers carry Gopinath (Krishna) in a palanquin [a chair with carrying poles] around the village accompanied by musicians. . . .

The women in Nanpur worship Satyapir, a Hindu-Muslim god, to bless them with sons. "Satyka" is the Hindu part meaning "truth," and "pir" in Islam means "prophet." It was a deliberate attempt to bring the two communities together through religion. There is a large Muslim settlement three kilometers from Nanpur, and in a village on the other side of the river a single Muslim family lives surrounded by Brahmins. In spite of Hindu-Muslim tensions in other parts of India, the atmosphere around the village has remained peaceful.

Source: Reprinted from the *UNESCO Courier,* June 1983, Prafulla Mohanti.

dhism, which retains the Hindu concept of *karma,* the ultimate objectives of existence are the achievement of *nirvana,* a condition of perfect enlightenment, and cessation of successive rebirths. The Buddha instructed his followers to carry his message as missionaries of a doctrine open to all castes, for no distinction among people was recognized. In that message all could aspire to ultimate enlightenment, a promise of salvation that raised the Buddha in popular imagination from teacher to savior and Buddhism from philosophy to universalizing religion.

Contact or *contagious diffusion* spread the belief system throughout India, where it was made the state religion in the 3rd century B.C. It was carried elsewhere into Asia by missionaries, monks, and merchants. While expanding abroad, Buddhism began to decline at home as early as the 4th century A.D., slowly but irreversibly reabsorbed into a revived Hinduism. By the 8th century, its dominance in northern India was broken by conversions to Islam; by the 15th century, it had essentially disappeared from all of the subcontinent.

Present-day spatial patterns of Buddhist adherence reflect the schools of thought, or *vehicles,* that were dominant during different periods of dispersion of the basic belief system (Figure 5.33). Earliest, most conservative, and closest to the origins of Buddhism was *Theravada* (Vehicle of the Elders) Buddhism, which was implanted in Sri Lanka and Southeast Asia beginning in the 3rd century B.C. Its emphasis is on personal salvation through the four noble truths; it mandates a portion of life to be spent as a monk or nun.

Mahayana (Greater Vehicle) was the dominant tradition when Buddhism was accepted into East Asia—China, Korea, and Japan—in the 4th century A.D. and later. Itself subdivided and diversified, Mahayana Buddhism considers the Buddha divine and, along with other deities, a savior for all who are truly devout. It emphasizes meditation (contemplative Zen Buddhism is a variant form), does not require service in monasteries, and tends to be more polytheistic and ritualistic than does Theravada Buddhism.

Vajrayana (the Diamond Vehicle) was dominant when the conversion of Tibet and neighboring northern areas began, first in the 7th century and again during the 10th and 11th centuries as a revived Lamaist tradition. That tradition originally stressed self-discipline and conversion through meditation and the study of philosophy, but it later became more formally monastic and ritualistic, elevating the Dalai Lama as the reincarnated Buddha, who became both spiritual and temporal ruler. Before Chinese conquest and the flight of the Dalai Lama in 1959, as many as one out of four or five Tibetan males was a monk whose celibacy helped keep population numbers stable. Tibetan Buddhism was further dispersed, beginning in the 14th century, to Mongolia, northern China, and parts of southern Russia.

In all of its many variants, Buddhism imprints its presence vividly on the cultural landscape. Buddha images in stylized human form began to appear in the first century A.D. and are common in painting and sculpture throughout the Buddhist world. Equally widespread are the three main

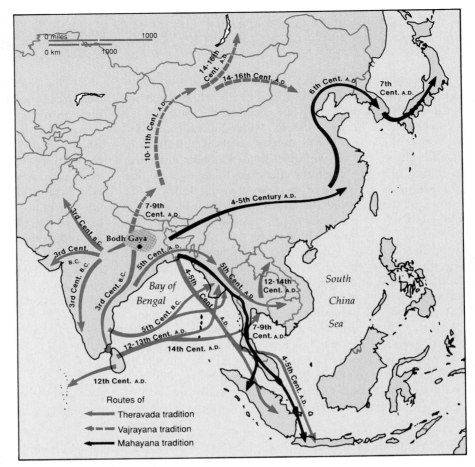

FIGURE 5.33   Diffusion paths, times, and "vehicles" of Buddhism.

types of buildings and monuments: the *stupa*, a commemorative shrine; the temple or pagoda enshrining an image or relic of the Buddha; and the monastery, some of them the size of small cities (Figure 5.34). Common, too, is the *bodhi* (or *bo*) tree, a fig tree of great size and longevity. Buddha is said to have received enlightenment seated under one of them at Bodh Gaya, India, and specimens have been planted and tended as an act of reverence and symbol of the faith throughout Buddhist Asia.

Buddhism has suffered greatly in Asian lands that came under communist control: Inner and Outer Mongolia, Tibet, North Korea, China, and parts of Southeast Asia. Communist governments abolished the traditional rights and privileges of the monasteries. In those states, monks were no longer prominent in numbers or presence; Buddhist religious buildings were taken over by governments and converted into museums or other secular uses, abandoned, or destroyed. In consequence, the number of adherents of Buddhism can now be only roughly and uncertainly estimated.

East Asian Ethnic Religions

When Buddhism reached China from the south some 1500 to 2000 years ago and was carried to Japan from Korea in the 7th century, it encountered and later amalgamated with already well established ethical belief systems. The Far Eastern ethnic religions are **syncretisms,** combinations of different forms of belief and practice. In China the union was with Confucianism and Taoism, themselves becoming intermingled by the time of Buddhism's arrival. In Japan it was with Shinto, a polytheistic animism and shamanism.

Chinese belief systems address not so much the hereafter as the achievement of the best possible way of life in the present existence. They are more ethical or philosophical than religious in the pure sense. Confucius (K'ung Fu-tzu), a compiler of traditional wisdom who lived about the same time as Gautama Buddha, emphasized the importance of proper conduct—between ruler and subjects and between family members. The family was extolled as the nucleus of the state, and filial piety was the loftiest of virtues. There are no churches or clergy in **Confucianism,** though its founder believed in a heaven seen in naturalistic terms, and the Chinese custom of ancestor worship as a mark of gratitude and respect was encouraged. After his death the custom was expanded to include worship of Confucius himself in temples erected for that purpose. That worship became the official state religion in the 2nd century B.C., and for some 2000 years—until the start of the 20th century A.D.—Confucianism, with its emphasis on ethics and morality rooted in Chinese traditional wisdom, formed the basis of the belief system of China.

FIGURE 5.34   The golden stupas of the Swedagon pagoda, Yangon, Myanmar (Rangoon, Burma).

It was joined by, or blended with, **Taoism,** an ideology that according to legend was first taught by Lao-tsu in the 6th century B.C. Its central theme is *Tao,* the Way, a philosophy teaching that eternal happiness lies in total identification with nature and deploring passion, unnecessary invention, unneeded knowledge, and government interference in the simple life of individuals. Beginning in the 1st century A.D., this philosophical naturalism was coupled with a religious Taoism involving deities, spirits, magic, temples, and priests. Buddhism, stripped by Chinese pragmatism of much of its Indian otherworldliness and defining a *nirvana* achievable in this life, was easily accepted as a companion to these traditional Chinese belief systems. Along with Confucianism and Taoism, Buddhism became one of the honored Three Teachings, and to the average person there was no distinction in meaning or importance between a Confucian temple, Taoist shrine, or Buddhist stupa.

Buddhism also joined and influenced Japanese Shinto, the traditional religion of Japan that developed out of nature and ancestor worship. **Shinto**—the Way of the Gods—is basically a structure of customs and rituals rather than an ethical or moral system. It observes a complex set of deities, including deified emperors, family spirits, and the divinities residing in rivers, trees, certain animals, mountains and, particularly, the sun and moon. Buddhism, at first resisted, was later amalgamated with traditional Shinto. Buddhist deities were seen as Japanese gods in a different form, and Buddhist priests assumed control of most Shinto shrines. In more modern times, Shinto divested itself of many Buddhist influences and became, under the reign of the Emperor

Meiji (1868–1912), the official state religion, emphasizing loyalty to the emperor. The centers of worship are the numerous shrines and temples in which the gods are believed to dwell and which are approached through ceremonial *torii,* or gateway arches (Figure 5.35).

FIGURE 5.35   A Shinto shrine, Nikko Park, Honshu Island, Japan.

Summary

Language and religion are basic threads in the web of culture. They serve to identify and categorize individuals within a single society and to separate peoples and nations of different tongues and faiths. By their pronunciation and choice of words we quickly recognize districts of origin and educational levels of speakers of our own language and easily identify those who originally had different native tongues. In some societies, religion may serve as a similar identifier of individuals and groups who observe distinctive modes or rhythms of life dictated by their separate faiths. Both language and religion are mentifacts, parts of the ideological subsystem of culture; both are transmitters of culture as well as its identifiers. Both have distinctive spatial patterns—reflecting past and present processes of spatial interaction and diffusion—that are basic to the recognition of world culture realms.

Languages may be grouped genetically—by origin and historical development—but the world distribution of language families depends as much on the movement of peoples and histories of conquest and colonization as it does on patterns of linguistic evolution. Linguistic geography studies spatial variations in languages, variations that may be minimized by encouragement of standard and official languages or overcome by pidgins, creoles, and lingua francas. Toponymy, the study of place names, helps document that history of movement.

Religion is a less pronounced identifier or conveyer of culture than is language. While language characterizes all peoples, religion varies in its impact and influence on culture groups. Some societies are dominated in all aspects by their controlling religious belief: Hindu India, for example, or Islamic Iran. Where religious beliefs are strongly held, they can unite a society of adherents and divide nations and peoples holding divergent faiths. Although religions do not lend themselves to easy classification, their patterns of distribution are as distinct and revealing as are those of languages. They, too, reflect past and present patterns of migration, conquest, and diffusion, part of the larger picture of dynamic cultural geography.

While each is a separate and distinct thread of culture, language and religion are not totally unrelated. Religion can influence the spread of languages to new peoples and areas, as Arabic, the language of the Koran, was spread by conquering armies of Muslims. Religion may conserve as well as disperse language. Yiddish remains the language of religion in Hasidic Jewish communities; church services in German or Swedish, and school instruction in them, characterize some Lutheran congregations in Anglo America. Until the 1960s, Latin was the language of liturgy in the Roman church, and Sanskrit remains the language of the Vedas, sacred in Hinduism. Sacred texts may demand the introduction of an alphabet to nonliterate societies: the Roman alphabet follows Christian missionaries, Arabic script accompanies Islam. The Cyrillic alphabet of eastern Europe was developed by missionaries. The tie between language and religion is not inevitable. The French imposed their language but not their religion on Algeria; Spanish Catholicism but not the Spanish language became dominant in the Philippines.

Language and religion are important and evident components of spatial cultural variation. They are, however, only part of the total complex of cultural identities that set off different social groups. Prominent among those identities is that of *ethnicity,* a conviction of members of a social group that they have distinctive characteristics in common that significantly distinguish and isolate them from the larger population among which they reside. Our attention turns in the next chapter to the concept and patterns of ethnicity, a distinctive piece in the mosaic of human culture.

KEY WORDS

animism 157
Buddhism 170
caste 169
Christianity 160
Confucianism 172
creole 149
dialect 145
ethnic religion 157
geographic (regional) dialect 146
Hinduism 168
Islam 166
isogloss 146
Judaism 159

language 135
language family 135
lingua franca 149
linguistic geography 146
monotheism 157
multilingualism 149
official language 149
pidgin 149
polytheism 157
protolanguage 136
religion 156
secularism 159

shamanism 157
Shinto 173
social dialect 145
speech community 144
standard language 144
syncretism 172
Taoism 173
toponym 154
toponymy 154
tribal (traditional) religion 157
universalizing religion 157
vernacular 145

FOR REVIEW

1. Why might one consider language the dominant differentiating element of culture separating societies?

2. In what way may religion affect other cultural traits of a society? In what cultures or societies does religion appear to be a growing influence? What might be the broader social or economic consequences of that growth?

3. In what way does the concept of *protolanguage* help us in linguistic classification? What is meant by language family? Is *genetic* classification of language an unfailing guide to spatial patterns of languages? Why or why not?

4. What spatial diffusion processes may be seen in the prehistoric and historic spread of languages? What have been the consequences of language spread on world linguistic diversity?

5. In what ways do *isoglosses* and the study of *linguistic geography* help us understand other human geographic patterns?

6. Cite examples that indicate the significance of religion as a cultural dominant in the internal and foreign relations of countries.

7. How does the classification of religions as *universalizing, ethnic,* or *tribal* help us to understand their patterns of distribution and spatial diffusion?

SELECTED REFERENCES

Beer, William R., and James E. Jackob. *Language Policy and National Unity.* Totowa, NJ.: Rowman & Allanheld, 1985.

Beinart, Haim. *Atlas of Medieval Jewish History.* New York: Simon & Schuster, 1992.

Bryson, Bill. *The Mother Tongue: English and How it Got That Way.* New York: Wm. Morrow, 1990.

Burnaby, Barbara, and Roderic Beaujot. *The Use of Aboriginal Languages in Canada.* Ottawa: Minister of Supply and Services Canada, 1987.

Caldarola, Carlo, ed. *Religions and Societies: Asia and the Middle East.* Berlin and New York: Mouton Publishers, 1982.

Cartright, Don. "Language Policy and Internal Geopolitics: The Canadian Situation." In *Language in Geographic Context,* edited by Colin H. Williams, pp. 238–266. Clevedon, England and Philadelphia: Multilingual Matters Ltd., 1988.

Carver, Craig. *American Regional Dialects: A Word Geography.* Ann Arbor: University of Michigan Press, 1987.

Chadwick, Henry, and G. R. Evans, eds. *Atlas of the Christian Church.* New York: Facts on File Publications, 1987.

Chambers, J. K., ed. *The Languages of Canada.* Montreal: Didier, 1979.

Cooper, Robert L., ed. *Language Spread: Studies in Diffusion and Social Change.* Bloomington: Indiana University Press, 1982.

Crystal, David, ed. *The Cambridge Encyclopedia of the English Language.* Cambridge, England: Cambridge University Press, 1995.

Dutt, Ashok K., and Satish Davgun. "Patterns of Religious Diversity." In *India: Cultural Patterns and Processes,* edited by Allen G. Noble and Ashok K. Dutt, pp. 221–246. Boulder, CO: Westview Press, 1982.

Earhart, H. Byron. *Japanese Religion: Unity and Diversity.* 3d ed. Belmont, CA: Dickenson, 1982.

Edwards, Viv. *Language in a Black Community.* San Diego, CA: College-Hill Press, 1986.

Esposito, John L., ed. *The Oxford Encyclopedia of the Modern Islamic World.* New York: Oxford University Press, 1995.

al-Faruqi, Isma'il R., and Lois L. al-Faruqi. *The Cultural Atlas of Islam.* New York: Macmillan, 1986.

al-Faruqi, Isma'il R., and David E. Sopher, eds. *Historical Atlas of the Religions of the World.* New York: Macmillan, 1974.

Fishman, Joshua A., Charles A. Ferguson, and Jyotirindra Das Gupta, eds. *Language Problems of Developing Nations.* New York: John Wiley & Sons, 1968.

Gamkrelidze, Thomas V., and V. V. Ivanov. "The Early History of Indo-European Languages." *Scientific American* 262 (March 1990):110–116.

Gaustad, Edwin S. *Historical Atlas of Religion in America.* New York: Harper and Row, 1976.

Greenberg, Joseph H., and Merritt Ruhlen. "Linguistic Origins of Native Americans." *Scientific American* 267, no. 5 (November 1992):94–99.

Hall, Robert A., Jr. *Pidgin and Creole Languages.* Ithaca, NY: Cornell University Press, 1966.

Halvorson, Peter L., and William M. Newman. *Atlas of Religious Change in America, 1952–1990.* Atlanta, GA: Glenmary Research Center, 1994.

Heatwole, Charles A. "Sectarian Ideology and Church Architecture." *Geographical Review* 79 (1989):63–78.

Heine, Bernd. *Status and Use of African Lingua Francas.* Munich and New York: Weltforum Verlag and Humanities Press, Inc., 1970.

Hemmasi, Mohammed. "Spatial Diffusion of Islam: A Teaching Strategy." *Journal of Geography* 91, no. 6 (1992):263–272.

Hill, Samuel S. "Religion and Region in America." *Annals, American Academy of Political and Social Science* 480 (July 1985):132–141.

Isaac, Erich. "Religion, Landscape, and Space." *Landscape* 9, no. 2 (Winter 1959–60):14–18.

Jackson, Richard H. "Religion and Landscape in the Mormon Cultural Region." In *Dimensions of Human Geography: Essays on Some Familiar and Neglected Themes,* edited by Karl W. Butzer, pp. 100–127. Chicago: University of Chicago, Department of Geography, *Research Paper 186,* 1978.

Journal of Cultural Geography (Popular Culture Association and The American Cultural Association) 7, no. 1 (Fall/Winter 1986). Special issue devoted to geography and religion.

Kaplan, David H. "Population and Politics in a Plural Society: The Changing Geography of Canada's Linguistic Groups." *Annals of the Association of American Geographers* 84, no. 1 (March 1994):46–67.

Karp, Ivan, and Charles S. Bird, eds. *Explorations in African Systems of Thought.* Washington, D.C.: Smithsonian Institution Press, 1987.

Katzner, Kenneth. *The Languages of the World.* Rev. ed. London: Routledge & Kegan Paul, 1986.

Key, Mary Ritchie. *Male/Female Language.* Metuchen, NJ: The Scarecrow Press, Inc., 1975.

King, Noel Q. *African Cosmos: An Introduction to Religion in Africa.* Belmont, CA: Wadsworth, 1986.

Kurath, Hans. *A Word Geography of the Eastern United States.* Ann Arbor: University of Michigan Press, 1949.

Lind, Ivan. "Geography and Place Names." In *Readings in Cultural Geography,* edited by Philip L. Wagner and Marvin Mikesell, pp. 118–128. Chicago: University of Chicago Press, 1962.

Marty, Martin E. *Pilgrims in Their Own Land: 500 Years of Religion in America.* Boston: Little, Brown, 1984.

McCrum, Robert, William Cran, and Robert MacNeil. *The Story of English.* New York: Elizabeth Sifton Books/Viking, 1986.

Moseley, Christopher, and R. E. Asher, eds. *Atlas of the World's Languages.* London, England and New York: Routledge, 1994.

Newman, William M., and Peter L. Halvorson. *Patterns in Pluralism: A Portrait of American Religion.* Washington, D.C.: Glenmary Research Center, 1980.

Nielsen, Niels C., Jr., et al. *Religions of the World.* New York: St. Martin's Press, 1983.

Park, Chris. *Sacred Worlds: An Introduction to Geography and Religion.* New York: Routledge, 1994.

Renfrew, Colin. "World Linguistic Diversity." *Scientific American* 270, no. 1 (January 1994):116–123.

Scott, Jamie, and Paul Simpson-Housley, eds. *Sacred Places and Profane Spaces: Essays in the Geographics of Judaism, Christianity, and Islam.* New York: Greenwood Press, 1991.

Shortridge, James R. "Patterns of Religion in the United States." *Geographical Review* 66 (1976):420–434.

Simoons, Frederick J. *Eat Not This Flesh: Food Avoidances in the Old World.* Madison: University of Wisconsin Press, 1961.

Simoons, Frederick J. "Fish as Forbidden Food: The Case of India." *Ecology of Food and Nutrition* 3 (1974):185–201.

Sopher, David E. "Geography and Religions." *Progress in Human Geography* 5 (1981):510–524.

Sopher, David E. *The Geography of Religions.* Englewood Cliffs, NJ: Prentice-Hall, 1967.

Stewart, George R. *Names on the Globe.* New York: Oxford University Press, 1975.

Stewart, George R. *Names on the Land.* 4th ed. San Francisco: Lexikos, 1982.

Thompson, Laurence G. *Chinese Religion: An Introduction.* 3d ed. Belmont, CA: Dickenson, 1979.

Topping, Gary. "Religion in the West." *Journal of American Culture* 3 (Summer 1980):330–350.

Trudgill, Peter. *On Dialect: Social and Geographical Perspectives.* Oxford, England: Basil Blackwell, 1983.

Weatherford, Jack. *Native Roots: How the Indians Enriched America.* New York: Ballantine Books, 1991.

Williamson, Juanita V., and Virginia M. Burke, eds. *A Various Language: Perspectives on American Dialects.* New York: Holt, Rinehart and Winston, Inc., 1971.

Wolff, Philippe. *Western Languages:* A.D. 100–1500. New York: World University Library/McGraw-Hill Book Company, 1971.

Zelinsky, Wilbur. "Some Problems in the Distribution of Generic Terms in the Place-Names of the Northeastern United States." *Annals of the Association of American Geographers* 45 (1955):319–349.

Zelinsky, Wilbur. "An Approach to the Religious Geography of the United States: Patterns of Church Membership in 1952." *Annals of the Association of American Geographers* 51 (1961):139–193.

ETHNIC GEOGRAPHY:

THREADS OF DIVERSITY

CHAPTER 6

Ethnic Diversity and Separatism 179
Immigration Streams 181
Acculturation and Assimilation 184
Areal Expressions of Ethnicity 186
Charter Cultures 186
Ethnic Clusters 188
Black Dispersions 189
Hispanic Concentrations 191
Asian Contrasts 194
French Uniformity 195
**Urban Ethnic Diversity and
    Segregation 196**
External Controls 198
Internal Controls 198
Shifting Ethnic Concentrations 199
Typologies and Spatial Results 200
Native Born Dispersals 202
Cultural Transfer 202
The Ethnic Landscape 204
Land Survey 205
Settlement Patterns 206
Ethnic Regionalism 207

    SUMMARY 209
    KEY WORDS 209
    FOR REVIEW 210
    SELECTED REFERENCES 210

*These dancers in a San Francisco Cinco de
Mayo festival parade celebrate their
Hispanic heritage.*

We must not forget that these men and women who file through the narrow gates at Ellis Island, hopeful, confused, with bundles of misconceptions as heavy as the great sacks upon their backs—we must not forget that these simple, rough-handed people are the ancestors of our descendants, the fathers and mothers of our children.

So it has been from the beginning. For a century a swelling human stream has poured across the ocean, fleeing from poverty in Europe to a chance in America. Englishman, Welshman, Scotchman, Irishman; German, Swede, Norwegian, Dane; Jew, Italian, Bohemian, Serb; Syrian, Hungarian, Pole, Greek—one race after another has knocked at our doors, been given admittance, has married us and begot our children. We could not have told by looking at them whether they were to be good or bad progenitors, for racially the cabin is not above the steerage, and dirt, like poverty and ignorance, is but skin-deep. A few hours, and the stain of travel has left the immigrant's cheek; a few years, and he loses the odor of alien soils; a generation or two, and these outlanders are irrevocably our race, our nation, our stock.[1]

The United States is a cultural composite—as increasingly are most of the countries of the world. North America's peoples include aborigine and immigrant, native born and new arrival. Had this chapter's introductory passage been written in the 1990s rather than 80 years earlier, the list of foreign origins would have been lengthened to include many Latin American, African, and Asian countries as well as the European sources formerly most common.

The majority of the world's societies, even those outwardly seemingly most homogeneous, house distinctive **ethnic groups,** populations that feel themselves bound together by a common origin and set off from other groups by ties of culture, race, religion, language, or nationality. Ethnic diversity is a near-universal part of human geographic patterns; the current nearly 200 or so independent countries are home to at least 5000 ethnic groups. European states house increasing numbers of African and Asian immigrants and guest workers from outside their borders (Figure 6.1) and have effectively become multiethnic societies. Refugees and jobseekers are found in alien lands throughout both hemispheres. Cross-border movements and resettlements in Southeast Asia and Africa are well-reported current events. European colonialism created pluralistic societies in tropical lands through introduction of both ruling elites and, frequently, nonindigenous laboring groups. Polyethnic Russia, Afghanistan, China, India, and most African countries have native—rather than immigrant—populations more characterized by racial and cultural diversity than by uniformity. Tricultural Belgium has a nearly split personality in matters political and social. The idea of an ethnically pure nation-state is no longer realistic.

Like linguistic and religious differences within societies, such population interminglings are masked by the "culture realms" shown in Figure 2.4 but are, at a larger scale, important threads in the cultural-geographic web of our complex world. The multiple movements, diffusions, migrations, and mixing of peoples of different origins making up that world are the subject of **ethnic geography.** Its concerns are those of spatial distributions and interactions of ethnic groups however defined, and of the cultural characteristics and influences underlying them.

Ethnicity is always based on a firm understanding by members of a group that they are in some fundamental ways different from others who do not share their distinguishing characteristics or cultural heritage. Ethnicity is, at root, a spatial concept. Ethnic groups are associated with clearly recognized territories—either larger homeland districts or smaller rural or urban enclaves—in which they are primary or exclusive occupants and upon which they have placed distinctive cultural marks. Since territory and ethnicity are inseparable concepts, ethnicity becomes an important concern in the cultural patterning of space and clearly an item of human geographic interest. Further, since ethnicity is often identified with language or religious practices

FIGURE 6.1 "Guest workers"—frequently called by their German name, *Gastarbeiter*—have substantially altered the ethnic mix in formerly unicultural cities of Western Europe. The restaurant shown here is in an Algerian neighborhood of Paris, France.

[1.] From Walter E. Eyl, "The New Americans," *Harper's Magazine* 129 (1914): 615. Copyright © 1914 Harper's Magazine Foundation, New York, NY.

PATTERNS OF DIVERSITY AND UNITY

setting a minority group off from a surrounding majority culture, consideration of ethnicity flows logically from the discussions of language and religion in Chapter 5.

Our examination of ethnic patterns will concentrate on North America, an area originally occupied by a multitude of territorially, culturally, and linguistically distinctive Native American people who were overwhelmed and displaced by immigrants—and their descendants—representing a wide spectrum of the Old World's ethnic groups. While North America lacks the homelands that gave territorial identity to immigrant ethnics in their countries of origin, it has provided a case study of how distinctive culture groups partition space and place their claims and imprints on it. It shows, as well, the durability of the idea of ethnic distinction even under conditions and national myths that emphasize intermixing and homogenization of population as the accepted norm. Examples drawn from other countries and environments will serve to highlight ways in which American-based generalizations may be applied more broadly or in which the North American experience reflects a larger world scene.

Ethnic Diversity and Separatism

Each year on a weekend in May, New York City has celebrated its cultural diversity and vitality by closing off to all but pedestrian traffic a 1-mile stretch of street to conduct the Ninth Avenue International Festival. Along the reserved route from 37th to 57th streets, a million or more New Yorkers have come together to sample the foods, view the crafts, and hear the music of the great number of the world's cultures represented among the citizens of the city. As a resident of the largest U.S. metropolis, each of the merchants and artists contributing one of the several hundred separate storefront, stall, or card-table displays of the festival became a member of the North American culture realm. Each has, however, preserved a distinctive small-group identity within that larger collective "realm" (Figure 6.2).

The threads of diversity exhibited in the festival are expressions of **ethnicity,** a term derived from the Greek word *ethnos,* meaning a "people" or "nation." Intuitively we recognize that the literal translation is incomplete. Ethnic groups are composed of individuals who share some prominent traits or characteristics, some evident physical or social identifications setting them apart both from the majority population and from other distinctive minorities among whom they may live.

No single trait denotes ethnicity. Group recognition may be based on language, religion, national origin, unique customs, or an ill-defined concept of "race" (see "The Matter of Race"). Whatever may establish the identity of a group, the common unifying bonds of ethnicity are a shared ancestry and cultural heritage, the retention of a set of distinctive traditions, and the maintenance of in-group interactions and relationships. The principal racial and ethnic groups of the United States are identified in Tables 6.1 and 6.2 and of Canada in Table 6.4.

FIGURE 6.2 The Ninth Avenue International Fair in New York City became one of the largest of its kind. Similar festivals celebrating America's ethnic diversity are found in cities and small towns across the country.

TABLE 6.1	Estimated U.S. Resident Population by Race and Hispanic Origin, 1995	
RACE	NUMBER (MILLIONS)	PERCENT OF U.S. POPULATION
Total by Race		
White	218.3	82.9
Black	33.1	12.6
Asian and Pacific Islander	9.8	3.7
American Indian, Eskimo, and Aleut	2.2	0.8
Resident Population	**263.4**	**100.0**
Hispanic Origin[a]	26.8	10.2

Note: Race as reported "reflects self-identification [and] does not denote . . . biological stock."

[a]Persons of Hispanic origin may be of any race.

Source: U.S. Bureau of the Census.

Ethnocentrism is the term describing a tendency to evaluate other cultures against the standards of one's own. It implies the feeling that one's own ethnic group is superior. Ethnocentrism can divide multiethnic societies by establishing rivalries and provoking social and spatial discord and isolation. It can, as well, be a sustaining and identifying emotion, giving familiar values and support to the individual in the face of the complexities of life. The ethnic group uman populations may be differentiated from one another on any number of bases: gender, nationality, stage of economic development, and so on. One common form of differentiation is based on recognizable inherent physical characteristics, or *race*.

A **race** is usually understood to be a population subset whose members have in common some hereditary biological characteristics that set them apart physically from other human groups. The spread of human beings over the earth and their occupation of different environments were accompanied by the development of physical variations in skin pigmentation, hair texture, facial characteristics, blood composition, and other traits largely related to soft tissue. Some subtle skeletal differences among peoples also exist. Such differences have formed the basis for the segregation, by some anthropologists, of humanity into different racial groups. Caucasoid, Negroid, Mongoloid, Amerindian, Australoid and other races have been recognized in a process of classification invention, modification, and refinement that began at least two centuries ago. Racial differentiation as commonly understood is old and can reasonably be dated at least to the Paleolithic (100,000 to about 11,000 years ago) spread and isolation of population groups.

Although racial classifications vary by author, most are based on recognized geographical variations of populations. Thus, Mongoloids are associated with northern and eastern Asia; Australoids are the aboriginal people of Australasia; Amerindians developed in the Americas, and so on. If all of humankind belongs to a single species that can freely interbreed and produce fertile offspring, how did this areal differentiation by race occur? Why is it that despite millennia of mixing and migration, people with distinct combinations of physical traits appear to be clustered in particular areas of the world?

Two causative forces appear to be most important. First, through evolutionary **natural selection** or **adaptation,** characteristics are transmitted that enable people to adapt to particular environment conditions, such as climate. Studies have suggested some plausible relationship between, for example, solar radiation and skin color, and between temperature and body size. In its carrier state, sickle-cell anemia, afflicting mainly people of African descent, protects against malaria. The second force, **genetic drift,** refers to a heritable trait (such as flatness of face) that appears by chance in one group and becomes accentuated through inbreeding. If two populations are too separated spatially for much interaction to occur (*isolation*), a trait may develop in one but not in the other. Unlike natural selection, genetic drift differentiates populations in nonadaptive ways.

Natural selection and genetic drift promote racial differentiation. Countering them is **gene flow** via interbreeding (also called *admixture*), which acts to homogenize neighboring populations. Genetically, it has been observed, there is no such thing as a "pure" race since people breed freely outside their local group. Opportunities for interbreeding, always part of the spread and intermingling of human populations, have accelerated with the growing mobility and migrations of people in the past few centuries. While we may have an urge to group humans "racially," we cannot use biology to justify it and anthropologists have largely abandoned the idea of race as a scientific concept.

Nor does race have meaningful application to any human characteristics that are culturally acquired. That is, race is *not* equivalent to ethnicity or nationality and has no bearing on differences in religion or language. There is no "Irish" or "Hispanic" race, for example. Such groupings are based on culture, not genes. Culture summarizes the way of life of a group of people, and members of the group may adopt it irrespective of their individual genetic heritage, or race.

maintains familiar cultural institutions and shares traditional food and music. More often than not, it provides the friends, spouses, business opportunities, and political identification of ethnic group members.

Territorial isolation is a strong and sustaining trait of ethnic separatism and assists individual groups to retain their identification. In Europe, Asia, and Africa, ethnicity and territorial identity are inseparable. Ethnic minorities are first and foremost associated with *homelands*. This is true of the Welsh, Bretons, and Basques of Western Europe; the Slovenes, Croatians, or Bosnians of Eastern Europe; the non-Slavic "nationalities" of Russia, and the immense number of ethnic communities of South and Southeast Asia. These minorities have specific spatial identity even though they may not have political independence.

Where ethnic groups are intermixed and territorial boundaries imprecise—former Yugoslavia is an example—or where a single state contains disparate, rival populations—the case of many African and Asian countries—conflict between groups can be serious if peaceful relations or central governmental control break down. "Ethnic cleansing," a polite term with grisly implications, has become a past or present justification and objective for civil conflict in parts of the former Soviet Union and Eastern Europe and in several African and Southeast Asian countries. Its outcome is not only an alteration of the ethnic composition of states, but of the ethnic

TABLE 6.2	Leading Ethnic Affiliations Claimed by U.S. Census Respondents, 1990	
ANCESTRY	NUMBER (000)	PERCENTAGE OF TOTAL POPULATION
German	57,947	23.3
Irish	38,736	15.6
English	32,682	13.1
African American	23,777	9.6
Italian	14,665	5.9
Mexican	11,589	4.7
French	10,321	4.1
Polish	9,366	3.8
American Indian	8,708	3.5

Note: More than 12 million persons listed "American" for ancestry. The tabulation is based on self-identification of respondents, not on objective criteria. Many persons reported their ancestry in two or three ethnic groups and were tabulated by the Census Bureau under each claimed ancestry.

Source: U.S. Bureau of the Census.

encouragement of minority linguistic rights, and other evidences of group self-awareness and promotion. In some multiethnic societies, second- and third-generation descendants of immigrants, now seeking "roots" and identity, embrace the ethnicity that their forebears sought to deny.

Immigration Streams

The ethnic diversity found on the North American scene today is the product of continuous flows of immigrants—some 60 million of them by the mid-1990s—representing, at different periods, movements to this continent of members of nearly all of the cultures and races of the world (Figure 6.3). For the United States, that movement took the form of three distinct immigrant waves, all of which, of course, followed much earlier Amerindian arrivals.

The first wave, lasting from pioneer settlement to about 1870, was made up of two different groups. One comprised white arrivals from western and northern Europe, with Britain and Germany best represented. Together with the Scots and Scotch-Irish, they established a majority society controlled by Protestant Anglo-Saxons and allied groups. The Europeans dominated numerically the second group of first-wave immigrants, blacks brought involuntarily to the New World, who made up nearly 20% of U.S. population in 1790. The mass immigration that occurred beginning after the middle of the 19th century began to reduce both the northwest European dominance of American society and the percentage of blacks within the growing total population.

mix in, usually, adjacent countries to which displaced populations have fled as refugees.

Identifiable homelands do not exist within the North American cultural mix. However, the "Chinatowns" and "Little Italys" as created enclaves within North American cities have provided both the spatial refuge and the support systems essential to new immigrants in an alien culture realm. Asian and West Indian immigrants in London and other English cities and foreign *guest workers*—originally migrant and temporary laborers, usually male—that reside in Continental European communities assume similar spatial separation. While serving a support function, this segregation is as much the consequence of the housing market and of public and private restriction as it is simply of self-selection. In Southeast Asia, Chinese communities remain aloof from the majority culture not as a transitional phase to incorporation with it but as a permanent chosen isolation.

By retaining what is familiar of the old in a new land, ethnic enclaves have reduced cultural shock and have paved the way for the gradual process of adaptation that prepares both individuals and groups to operate effectively in the new, larger **host society.** The traditional ideal of the United States "melting pot," in which ethnic identity and division would be lost and full amalgamation of all minorities into a blended, composite majority culture would occur, was the expectation voiced in the chapter-opening quotation. For many even long-resident ethnic groups, however, that ideal has not become a reality.

Recent decades have seen a resurgence of cultural pluralism and an increasing demand for ethnic autonomy not only in North America but also in multiethnic societies around the world (see "Nations of Immigrants"). At least, recognition is sought for ethnicity as a justifiable basis for special treatment in the allocation of political power, the structure of the educational system, the toleration or

FIGURE 6.3 Although it was not opened until 1892, Ellis Island—the country's first federal immigration facility—quickly became the symbol of all the migrant streams to the United States. By the time it was closed in late 1954, it had processed 17 million immigrants. Today their descendants number over 100 million Americans. A major renovation project was launched in 1984 to restore Ellis Island as a national monument.

FOR YOUR CONSIDERATION

NATIONS OF IMMIGRANTS

Americans, steeped in the country's "melting pot" myth and heritage, are inclined to forget that many other countries are also "nations of immigrants" and that their numbers are dramatically increasing. In the United States, Canada, Australia, and New Zealand, early European colonists and, later, immigrants from other continents overwhelmed indigenous populations. In each, immigration has continued, contributing not only to national ethnic mixes but maintaining or enlarging the proportion of the population that is foreign born. In Australia, as one example, that proportion now equals 21%.

In Latin America, foreign population domination of native peoples was and is less complete and uniform than in Anglo America. While in nearly all South and Central American states, European and other nonnative ethnic groups dominate the social and economic hierarchy, in many they constitute only a minority of the total population. In Paraguay, for example, the vast majority of inhabitants are native Paraguayans who pride themselves on their Native American descent, and Amerindians comprise nearly half the population of Peru, Bolivia, and Ecuador. But European ethnics make up over 90% of the population of Argentina, Uruguay, Costa Rica, and southern Chile, and about 50% of the inhabitants of Brazil.

The original homelands of those immigrant groups are themselves increasingly becoming multiethnic, and several European countries are now home to as many or more of the foreign-born proportionately than is the United States. Over 8% of Britain's population and 11% of France's are of foreign birth, compared with America's 8.7%. Many came as immigrants and refugees fleeing unrest or poverty in post-communist Eastern Europe. Many are "guest workers" and their families that were earlier recruited in Turkey and North Africa; or they are immigrants from former colonial or overseas territories in Asia, Africa, and the Caribbean. More than 6% of Germany's inhabitants come from outside the European Union, as do over 3% of Holland's and Belgium's.

The trend of ethnic mixing is certain to continue and accelerate. Cross-border movements of migrants and refugees in Africa, Asia, the Americas, as well as in Europe, are continuing common occurrences of the later 20th century, reflecting growing incidences of ethnic strife, civil wars, famines, and economic hardships. But of even greater long-term influence are the growing disparities in population numbers and economic wealth between the older developed states and the developing world. The population of the world's poorer countries is growing twice as fast as Europe's of the late 19th century, when that continent fed the massive immigration streams across the Atlantic. The rich world, whose population is projected to stabilize well below 2 billion, will increasingly be a magnet for those from poorer countries where numbers will rise from some 4 billion to more than 7 billion by A.D. 2025 and to perhaps 10 billion in a half-century. The economic and population pressures building in the developing world insure greater international and intercontinental migration and a rapid expansion in the numbers of "nations of immigrants."

Many of those developed host countries are beginning to resist that flow. Although the Universal Declaration of Human Rights declares individuals are to be free to move within or to leave their own countries, no right of admittance to any other country is conceded. Political asylum is often—but not necessarily—granted; refugees or migrants seeking economic opportunity or fleeing civil strife or starvation have no claims for acceptance. Increasingly, they are being turned away. The Interior Minister of France advocates "zero immigration"; Germany's government closed its doors in 1993 by increasing border controls and changing its constitutional right to asylum; Britain in 1994 tightened immigration rules even for foreign students and casual workers. And all European Union countries except Ireland have measures for turning back refugees who come via another EU country. In 1995, the EU's members materially narrowed the definition of who may qualify for asylum.

Nor is Europe alone. Hong Kong ejects Vietnamese refugees; Zaire orders Rwandans to return to their own country; India tries to stem the influx of Bangladeshis; the United States rejects "economic refugees" from Haiti. Algerians are increasingly resented in France as their numbers and cultural presence increase. Turks feel the enmity of a small but violent group of Germans, and East Indians and Africans find growing resistance among the Dutch. In many countries, policies of exclusion or restriction appear motivated by unacceptable influxes of specific racial, ethnic, or national groups.

Questions:

1. *Do you think all people everywhere should have a universal right of admittance to a country of choice equivalent to their declared right to depart their homelands? Why or why not?*

2. *Do you think it appropriate that destination states make a distinction between political and economic refugees? Why or why not?*

3. *Do you think it legitimate for countries to establish immigration quotas based on national origin, or to classify certain potential immigrants as unacceptable or undesirable on the grounds that their national, racial, or religious origins are incompatible with the culture of the prospective host country? Why or why not?*

That second immigrant wave, from 1870 to 1921, was heavily weighted in favor of eastern and southern Europeans, who comprised more than 50% of new arrivals by the end of the century. The second period ended with congressional adoption of a quota system regulating both the numbers of individuals who would be accepted and the countries from which they could come. That system, plus a world depression and World War II (1939–1945), greatly slowed immigration until a third-wave migration was launched during the 1960s. At that time the old national quota system of immigrant regulation was replaced by one more liberal in its admission of Latin Americans. Along with more recent Asian arrivals, they became the largest segment of new arrivals. The changing source areas of the newcomers are traced in Table 6.3 and Figure 6.4.

Canada experienced three quite different immigration streams. Until 1760, most settlers came from France. After that date, the pattern abruptly altered as a flood of United Kingdom (English, Irish, and Scottish) immigrants arrived. Many came by way of the United States, fleeing, as Loyalists, to Canada during and after the American Revolutionary War. Others came directly from overseas. Another pronounced shift in arrival pattern occurred during the 20th century as the bulk of new immigrants began originating in Continental Europe and, more recently, in other continents. By 1991, one-sixth of all Canadians had been born outside of the country; the national ethnic mix at that date is reported in Table 6.4.

The United States' cultural diversity has increased as its immigration source regions have changed from the traditional European areas to Latin America and Asia. The dominant European ethnic groups had completed their major periods of arrival in the United States by the 1920s, and immigration essentially halted until after World War II. Except for a spurt of legal and illegal immigration from Eastern Europe and Russia after 1990, the modest postwar revival of inflow from Europe went largely unnoticed as the new entrants affiliated with already assimilated groups of the same cultural background.

More recent expanded immigration from new source regions has increased the number of visible and vocal ethnic communities and the regions of the country housing significant minority populations. Simultaneously, the proportion of foreign-born residents has increased in the U.S. population mix. In 1920, at the end of the period of the most active European immigration, more than 13% of the American population had been born in another country. That percentage declined each decade until a low of 4.7% foreign born was reported in 1970. So great was the inflow of aliens beginning in the 1970s, however, that by the mid-1990s some

TABLE 6.3	Immigrants to the United States: Major Flows by Origin	
ETHNIC GROUPS	TIME PERIOD	NUMBERS IN MILLIONS (APPROXIMATE)
Blacks	1650s–1800	1
Irish	1840s and 1850s	1.75
Germans	1840s–1880s	4
Scandinavians	1870s–1900s	1.5
Poles	1880s–1920s	1.25
East European Jews	1880s–1920s	2.5
Austro-Hungarians	1880s–1920s	4
Italians	1880s–1920s	4.75
Mexicans	1950s–1990s	4.5
Cubans	1960s–1980s	1
Asians	1960s–1990s	5

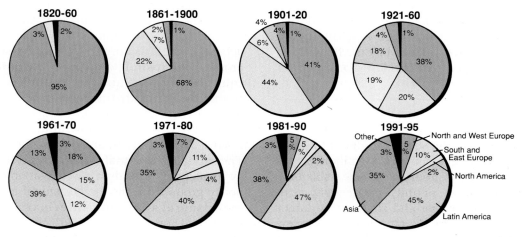

FIGURE 6.4   **Legal immigrants admitted to the United States by region of origin, 1820–1995.** The diagrams clearly reflect the dramatic change in geographic origins of immigrants. After 1965, immigration restrictions based on national origin were shifted to priorities based on family reunification and needed skills and professions. Those priorities underwent Congressional reconsideration in 1995 and 1996. What is not shown is the dramatic increase in the numbers of legal and illegal entrants to the United States in the 1980s and early 1990s, years that witnessed the highest legal and illegal immigrant and refugee numbers in the nation's history.

TABLE 6.4	Canadian Population by Selected Ethnic Origins, 1991	

	TOTAL	
ETHNIC GROUP	(000)	PERCENT (OF TOTAL POP.)
Single Origin[a]	**21,183.9**	**78.5**
French	6,146.6	22.8
English	3,958.4	14.7
Scottish	893.1	3.3
Irish	725.7	2.7
Other British[a]	2,018.0	7.5
German	911.6	3.4
Canadian	765.1	2.8
Italian	750.1	2.8
Chinese	586.6	2.2
Native Peoples	470.6	1.7
Ukrainian	406.6	1.5
Dutch (Netherlands)	358.2	1.3
East Indians, n.i.e.[b]	324.8	1.2
Polish	272.8	1.0
Multiple Origins[c]	**5,810.1**	**21.5**
Total Population	**26,994.0**	**100.0**

[a]Includes "British only" multiple origins.

[b]n.i.e. = not included elsewhere

[c]Mostly British and French, British and other, French and other, or British, French and other; excludes British only.

Source: Statistics Canada, *Ethnic Origin.* Ottawa: Industry, Science and Technology Canada, 1993.

8.5% of the population, or nearly 23 million people, had been born abroad, and over 30% of total population growth of the country between 1980 and 1995 was accounted for by legal and illegal immigration. As had been the case during the 19th century, growing influxes from new immigrant source regions prompted movements to halt the flow and to preserve the ethnic status quo (see "Backlash," p. 88).

Acculturation and Assimilation

In the United States, at least, the sheer volume of multiple immigration streams makes the concept of "minority" suspect when no single "majority" group exists (see Table 6.2). American society is a composite of unity and diversity, with immigrants both being shaped by and shaping the larger community they joined. The traditional "melting pot" view of ethnic integration has been more formally called **amalgamation theory,** which rejects the idea of immigrant conformity to a dominating Anglo-culture norm and views American society as the merger into a composite mainstream of the many traits of all ethnic groups entering it.

Nonetheless, as we shall see, all immigrant groups after the first found a controlling culture in place, with accustomed patterns of behavior and response and a dominating language of the workplace and government. The customs and practices familiar and expected among those already in place had to be learned by newcomers if they were to be accepted. The process of **acculturation** is that of the adoption by the immigrants of the values, attitudes, ways of behavior, and speech of the receiving society. In the process, the ethnic group loses its separate cultural identity as it accepts over time the culture of the larger host community.

Acculturation is a slow process for many immigrant individuals and groups, and the parent tongue may of choice or necessity be retained as an ethnically identifying feature even after fashions of dress, food, and customary behavior have been substantially altered in the new environment. In 1990, some 14% of U.S. census respondents reported speaking a language other than English in the home; for more than half of them, that language was Spanish. In the light of recent immigration trends, we can assume that the number of people speaking a foreign language at home is increasing. The retention of the native tongue is encouraged rather than hindered by American civil rights regulations that give to new immigrants the right to bilingual education and (in some cases) special assistance in voting in their own language (see "An Official U.S. Language?", p. 152).

The language barrier that has made it difficult for foreign-born groups, past and present, to gain quick entrance to the labor force has encouraged their high rate of initiation of or entry into small businesses. The consequence has been a continuing stimulus to the American economy and, through the creation of family-held neighborhood enterprises, the maintenance of the ethnic character of immigrant communities (Figure 6.5). The result has also been the gradual integration of the new arrivals into the economic and cultural mainstream of American society.

When that integration is complete, **assimilation** has occurred. Full assimilation may be seen as a two-part process. **Behavioral** (or **cultural**) **assimilation** is the rough equivalent of acculturation; it implies integration into a common cultural life through shared experience, language, intermarriage, and sense of history. **Structural assimilation** refers to the fusion of immigrant ethnics with the groups, social systems, and occupations of the host society. The extent of structural assimilation is frequently measured by the degree of residential segregation that sets off the minority group from the larger general community. Employment segregation and intermarriage rates are also indicative. For most of the "old" (pre-1921 European) immigrants and their descendants, both forms of assimilation are complete. For most of the "new" (post-1960s) immigrants, acculturation is proceeding or has already occurred, but for many of them and for racial minorities as well, structural assimilation has been elusive.

FUNCTIONAL VARIATION BY ETHNIC AREAS

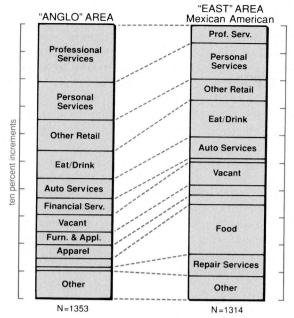

FIGURE 6.5 Variations in business establishments in Anglo and Mexican American neighborhoods of Los Angeles in the late 1970s. Although the total populations of the two areas were comparable, the Mexican American community had over three times more food stores because of the dominance of corner grocery stores over supermarkets. Bakeries (*tortillerías*) were a frequent expression of ethnic dietary habits. Neighborhood businesses conducted in Spanish and related to the needs of the community were the rule. Anglo neighborhoods, because of greater affluence, had greater numbers of professional services (doctors, lawyers) available.

Assimilation does not necessarily mean that ethnic consciousness is diminished or awareness of racial and cultural differences is reduced or lost. *Competition theory,* in fact, suggests that as ethnic minorities begin to achieve success and enter into mainstream social and economic life, awareness of ethnic differences may be heightened. Frequently, ethnic identity may be most clearly experienced and expressed by those who can most successfully assimilate but who choose to promote group awareness and ethnic mobilization movements. That promotion, the theory holds, is a reflection of pressures of American urban life and the realities of increased competition. Those pressures transform formerly isolated groups into recognized, self-assertive ethnic minorities pursuing goals and interests dependent on their position within the larger society.

While in the United States it is usually assumed that acculturation and assimilation are self-evidently advantageous, Canada established multiculturalism in the 1970s as the national policy designed to reduce tensions between ethnic and language groups and to recognize that each thriving culture is an important part of the country's priceless personal resources. Since 1988, multiculturalism has been formalized by act of the Canadian parliament and supervised by a separate government ministry. An example of its practical application can be seen in the way Toronto, Canada's largest and the world's most multicultural city, routinely sends out property tax notices in six languages—English, French, Chinese, Italian, Greek, and Portuguese. Nevertheless, Canada—which takes in more immigrants per capita than any other industrialized country—began in 1995 to reduce the number of newcomers it was prepared to admit.

Both Canada and the United States seek to incorporate their varied immigrant minorities into composite national societies. In other countries quite different attitudes and circumstances may prevail when indigenous—not immigrant—minorities feel their cultures and territories threatened. The Sinhalese comprise 75% of Sri Lanka's population, but the minority Tamils have waged years of guerilla warfare to defend what they see as majority threats to their culture, rights, and property. In India, Kashmiri nationalists fight to separate their largely Muslim valley from the Hindu majority society. And in many multiethnic African countries, single party governments seek to impose a sense of national unity on populations whose primary and nearly unshakable loyalties are rooted in their tribes and not the state that is composed of many tribes. Across the world, conflicts between ethnic groups within states have proliferated in recent years. Armenia, Azerbaijan, Burma, Burundi, Ethiopia, Iraq, Russia, Rwanda, and the former Yugoslavia are others in a long list of countries where ethnic tensions have erupted into civil conflict.

Basques and Catalans of Spain and Corsicans, Bretons, and Normans of France have only recently seen their respective central governments relax strict prohibitions on teaching or using the languages that identified those ethnic groups. On the other hand, in Bulgaria, ethnic Turks who unofficially comprise 10% of the total population officially ceased to exist in 1984, when the government obliged Turkish speakers and Muslims to replace their Turkish and Islamic names with Bulgarian and Christian ones. The government also banned their language and strictly limited practice of their religion. The intent was to impose an assimilation not sought by the minority.

Elsewhere, ethnic minorities—including immigrant minorities—have grown into majority groups, posing the question of who will assimilate whom. Ethnic Fijians sought to resolve that issue by staging a coup to retain political power when the majority immigrant ethnic Indians came to power by election in 1987. As these and innumerable other examples from all continents demonstrate, Anglo American experiences and expectations have limited application to other societies differently constituted and motivated.

Areal Expressions of Ethnicity

Throughout much of the world, the close association of territoriality and ethnicity is well recognized, accepted, and often politically disruptive. Indigenous ethnic groups have developed over time in specific locations and, through ties of kinship, language, culture, religion, and shared history, have established themselves in their own and others' eyes as distinctive peoples with defined homeland areas. The boundaries of most countries of the world encompass a number of racial or ethnic minorities, whose demands for special territorial recognition have increased rather than diminished with advances in economic development, education, and self-awareness (Figure 6.6).

The dissolution of the Soviet Union in 1991, for example, not only set free the 14 ethnically based union republics that formerly had been dominated by Russia and Russians, but also opened the way for many smaller ethnic groups to seek recognition and greater local control from the majority populations, including Russians, within whose territory their homelands lay. In Asia, the Indian subcontinent was subdivided to create separate countries with primarily religious-territorial affiliations, and the country of India itself has adjusted the boundaries of its constituent states to accommodate linguistic-ethnic realities. Other continents and countries show a similar acceptance of the importance of ethnic territoriality in their administrative structure. In some cases, as in the dismemberment of the Austro-Hungarian Empire after World War I, the recognition of ethnically defined homelands was the basis of new country formations (see "The Rising Tide of Nationalism").

With the exceptions of some—largely Canadian—Native American tribes and of French Canadians, there is not the coincidence in Anglo America between territorial claim and ethnic-racial distinctiveness so characteristic elsewhere in the world (Figure 6.7). The general absence of such claims is the result of the immigrant nature of American society. Even the Native American "homeland" reservations in the United States are dispersed, noncontiguous, and in large part artificial impositions. The spatial pattern of ethnicity that has developed is therefore more intricate and shifting than in many other pluralistic societies. It is not based on absolute ethnic dominance but on interplay between a majority culture and, usually, several competing minority groups. It shows the enduring consequences of early settlement and the changing structure of a fluid, responsive, freely mobile North American society.

Charter Cultures

Although, with the Canadian French and Native American exceptions noted, no single ethnic minority homeland area exists in present-day North America, a number of separate social and ethnic groups are of sufficient size and regional concentration to have put their impress on particular areas. Part of that imprint results from what the geographer Wilbur

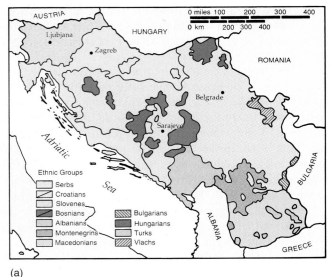

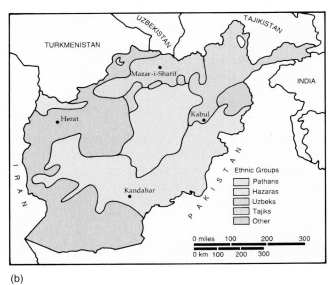

(a)   (b)

FIGURE 6.6 (a) **Ethnicity in former Yugoslavia.** Yugoslavia was formed after World War I (1914–1918) from a patchwork of Balkan states and territories, including the former kingdoms of Serbia and Montenegro, Bosnia-Herzegovina, Croatia-Slavonia, and Dalmatia. The authoritarian central government created in 1945 began to disintegrate in 1991 as non-Serb minorities voted for regional independence. In response, Serb guerillas backed by the Serb-dominated Yugoslav military engaged in a policy of territorial seizure and "ethnic cleansing" to secure areas claimed as traditional Serb "homelands." Religious differences between Eastern Orthodox, Roman Catholic, and Muslim adherents compound the conflicts rooted in nationality. (b) **Afghanistan** houses Pathan, Tajik, Uzbek, and Hazara ethnic groups speaking Pashto, Dari Persian, Uzbek, and several minor languages, and split between majority Sunni and minority Shia Muslim believers. Following Soviet military withdrawal in 1989, conflict between various Afghan groups hindered establishment of a unified state and government.

he 1990s are witness to spreading ethnic self-assertion and demands for national independence and cultural purification of homeland territories. To some, these demands and the conflicts they frequently engender are the expected consequences of the decline of strong central governments and imperial controls. It has happened before. The collapse of the Roman and the Holy Roman Empire was followed by the emergence of the nation-states of medieval and Renaissance Europe. The fall of Germany and the Austro-Hungarian Empire after World War I saw the creation of new ethnically based countries in Eastern Europe. The brief decline of post-czarist Russia permitted freedom for Finland, and for 20 years for Estonia, Latvia, and

Lithuania. The disintegration of British, French, and Dutch colonial control after World War II resulted in new state formation in Africa, South and East Asia, and Oceania.

Few empires have collapsed as rapidly and completely as did that of the Soviet Union and its Eastern European satellites in the late 1980s and early 1990s. In the subsequent loss of strong central authority, the ethnic nationalisms that communist governments had for so long tried to suppress asserted themselves in independence movements. At one scale, the Commonwealth of Independent States and the republics of Estonia, Latvia, Lithuania, and Georgia emerged from the former Soviet Union. At a lesser territorial scale, ethnic animosities and assertions led to bloodshed in the Caucasian republics of the former

USSR, in former Yugoslavia (Figure 6.6a), in Moldova, and elsewhere, while Czechs and Slovaks agreed to peacefully go their separate ways at the start of 1993.

Democracies, too, at least before legal protections for minorities are firmly in place, risk disintegration or division along ethnic, tribal, or religious lines. African states with their multiple ethnic loyalties (Figure 12.5) have frequently used those divisions to justify restricting political freedoms and continuing one-party rule. However, past and present ethnically-inspired civil wars and regional revolts in Somalia, Ethiopia, Nigeria, Uganda, Liberia, Angola, Rwanda, Burundi, and elsewhere show the fragility of the political structure on that continent.

FIGURE 6.7   Although all of North America was once theirs alone, Native Americans have become now part of a larger cultural mix. In the United States, their areas of domination have been reduced to reservations found largely in the western half of the country and to the ethnic provinces shown on Figure 6.11. These are often areas to which Amerindian groups were relocated, not necessarily the territories occupied by their ancestors at the time of European colonization.

Amerindians were never a single ethnic or cultural group and cannot be compared to a European national immigrant group in homogeneity. Arriving over many thousands of years, from many different origin points, with different languages, racial characteristics, customs, and skills, they are in no way comparable to a culturally uniform Irish or Slovak ethnic group arriving during the 19th century or Salvadorans or Koreans during the 20th. Unlike most other minorities in the American amalgam, Amerindians have generally rejected the goal of full and complete assimilation into the national mainstream culture.

Zelinsky termed the "doctrine of **first effective settlement.**" That principle holds that

> Whenever an empty territory undergoes settlement, or an earlier population is dislodged by invaders, the specific characteristics of the first group able to effect a viable, self-perpetuating society are of crucial significance for the later social and cultural geography of the area, no matter how tiny the initial band of settlers may have been.[2]

On the North American stage, the English and their affiliates, although few in number, were the first effective entrants in the eastern United States and shared with the French that role in eastern Canada. Although the French were ousted from parts of Seaboard Canada, they retained their cultural and territorial dominance in Quebec Province, where today their political power and ethnocentricity foster among some the determination to achieve separate nationhood. In the United States, British immigrants (English, Welsh, Scottish, and Scotch-Irish) constituted the main portion of the new settlers in eastern Colonial America and retained their significance in the immigrant stream until after 1870.

The English, particularly, became the **charter group,** the dominant first arrivals establishing the cultural norms and standards against which other immigrant groups were measured. It is understandable, then, in the light of Zelinsky's "doctrine," that: English became the national language; English common law became the foundation of the American legal system; British philosophers influenced the considerations and debates leading to the American Constitution; English place-names predominate in much of the country; and the influence of English literature and music remains strong. By their early arrival and initial dominance, the British established the majority culture of the Anglo American realm; their enduring ethnic impact is felt even today.

Somewhat comparable to the British domination in the East is the Hispanic influence in the Southwest. Mexican and Spanish explorers established settlements in New Mexico a generation before the Pilgrims arrived at Plymouth Rock. Spanish-speaking El Paso and Santa Fe were prospering before Jamestown, Virginia was founded in 1607. Although subsequently incorporated into an expanding "Anglo"-controlled cultural realm and dominated by it, the early established Hispanic culture, reinforced by continuing immigration, has proved enduringly effective. From Texas to California, Spanish-derived social, economic, legal, and cultural institutions and traditions remain an integral part of contemporary life—from language, art, folklore, and names on the land through Spanish water law to land ownership patterns reflecting Spanish tenure systems.

Ethnic Clusters

Because the British already occupied much of the agricultural land of the East, other, later immigrant streams from Europe were forced to "leapfrog" those areas and seek settlement opportunities in still available productive lands of the interior and western United States and Canada. The Scandinavians of the North Central states, the Germans in the Appalachian uplands, the upper Middle West, and Texas, various Slavic groups farther west on the Plains, and Italians and Armenians in California are examples of later arrivals occupying, ethnically influencing, and becoming identified with different sections of the United States even as they remained part of a larger cultural realm dominated by British roots. Such areas of ethnic concentration are known as **ethnic islands,** the dispersed and rural counterparts of urban ethnic neighborhoods (Figure 6.8).

Characterized usually by a strong sense of community, ethnic islands frequently placed their distinctive imprint on the rural landscape by retaining home country barn and house styles and farmstead layouts, while their inhabitants may have retained their own language, manner of dress, and customs. With the passing of the generations, rural ethnic identity has tended to diminish, and 20th-century adaptations and dispersions have occurred. When long-enduring through spatial isolation or group determination, ethnic islands have tended to be considered landscape expressions of folk culture rather than purely ethnic culture; we shall return to them in that context in Chapter 7.

Similar concentrations of immigrant arrivals are found in Canada. Descendants of French and British immigrants dominate its ethnic structure, both occupying primary areas too large to be considered ethnic islands. British origins are most common in all the provinces except Quebec, where 75% of the population is of French descent and over 80% of French Canadians make their home. French descendants are the second-largest ethnic group in Atlantic Canada and Ontario but fall to fifth or sixth position among minorities in the western provinces. Chinese have concentrated in British Columbia, Italians in Ontario and Quebec, and Ukrainians are the third-largest minority in the Prairie Provinces. The ethnic diversity of the central portion of Canada is suggested by Figure 6.9.

European immigrants arriving by the middle of the 19th century frequently took up tracts of rural land as groups rather than as individuals, assuring the creation of at least small ethnic islands. German and Ukrainian Mennonites in Manitoba and Saskatchewan, for example, Doukhobors in Saskatchewan, Mennonites in Alberta, Hutterites in South Dakota, Manitoba, Saskatchewan, and Alberta, the Pennsylvania Dutch (whose name is a corruption of *Deutsch,* or "German," their true nationality), Frisians in Illinois, and other ethnic groups settled as collectives. They sometimes acted on the advice and the land descriptions reported by advance agents sent out by the group. In most cases, sizable extents of rural territory received the imprint of a group of immigrants acting in concert.

---

2. *The Cultural Geography of the United States.* Rev. ed. (Englewood Cliffs, NJ: Prentice-Hall, 1992), p. 13.

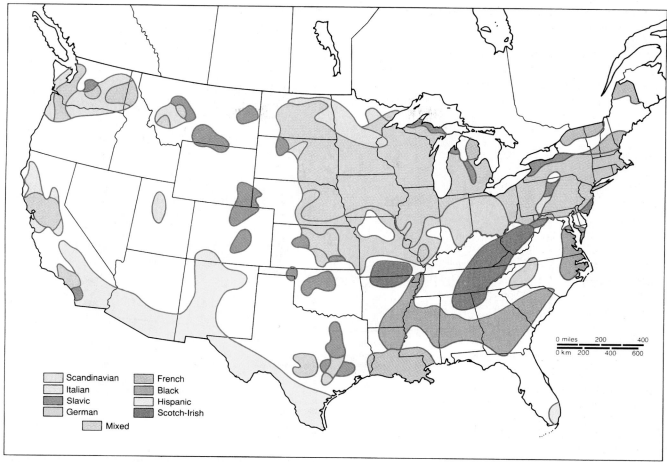

FIGURE 6.8   Ethnic islands in the United States.

Such **cluster migration** was not unique to foreign colonies. In a similar fashion, a culturally distinctive American group, the Latter-day Saints (Mormons), placed their enduring mark as the first and dominant settlers on a large portion of the West, focusing on Utah and adjacent districts (Figure 6.10). In general, however, later in the century and in the less arable sections of the western United States, the disappearance of land available for homesteading and the changing nature of immigrant flows reduced the incidence of cluster settlement. Impoverished individuals rather than financially solid communities sought American refuge and found it in urban locations and employment.

While cluster migration created some ethnic concentrations of Anglo America, others evolved from the cumulative effect of **chain migration**—the assemblage in one area of the relatives, friends, or unconnected compatriots of the first arrivals, attracted both by favorable reports and by familiar presences in specific locales of the New World (see also p. 87). Although such chain migration might not affect sizable districts, it could and did place a distinctive imprint on restricted rural ethnic islands and, particularly, urban areas. "Chinatown," "Little Sicily," and other urban enclaves, the concentration of Arab Americans in Dearborn, Michigan, and the Italian and Armenian farm communities of Cal-

ifornia's Central Valley, are examples of chain migrations and congregate settlement.

Black Dispersions

Some entire regions of North America—vastly larger than the distinctive ethnic islands—have become associated with larger ethnic or racial aggregations numbering in the thousands or millions. Such **ethnic provinces** include French Canadians in Quebec, African Americans in the United States Southeast, Native Americans in Oklahoma, the Southwest, the Northern Plains and Prairie Provinces, and Hispanics in the southern border states of the United States West (Figure 6.11). The identification of distinctive communities with extensive regional units persists, even though ethnicity and race have not been fully reliable bases for regionalization in North America. Cultural, ethnic, and racial mixing has been too complete to permit American counterparts of Old World ethnic homelands to develop, even in the instance of the now-inappropriate association of African Americans with southern states.

African Americans, involuntary immigrants to the continent, were nearly exclusively confined to rural areas of the South and Southeast prior to the Civil War (Figure 6.12). Even after emancipation, most remained on the land in the

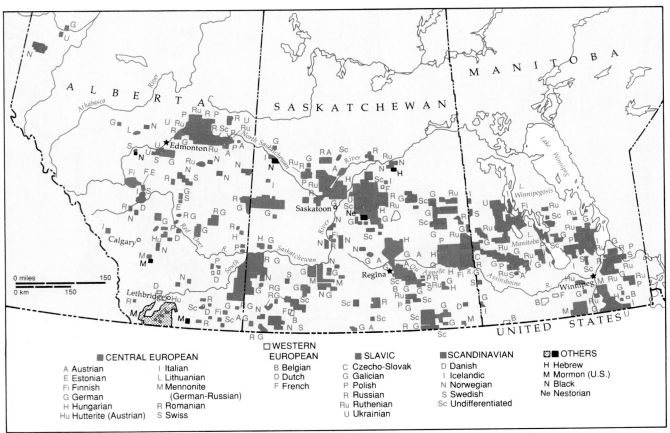

FIGURE 6.9 **Ethnic diversity in the Prairie Provinces of Canada.** In 1991, 69% of all Canadians claimed some French or English ancestry. For the Prairie Provinces with their much greater ethnic mixture, only 15% declared any English or French descent. Immigrants comprise a larger share of Canadian population than they do of the U.S. population. Early in the century most newcomers located in rural western Canada and by 1921 about half the population of the Prairie Provinces was foreign born. Later immigrants concentrated in the major metropolitan centers. Today, nearly 40% of Toronto's population is foreign born and 30% of Vancouver's. In the period 1981–1991, 48% of Canada's immigrants were from Asia and only 25% from Europe, the traditionally dominant source region.

Source: D.G.G. Kerr, *A Historical Atlas of Canada,* 2d ed., Thomas Nelson & Sons Ltd., 1966.

FIGURE 6.10 **The Mormon culture region** as defined by D. W. Meinig. To express the observed spatial gradations in Mormon cultural dominance and to approximate its sequential spread, Professor Meinig defined the Salt Lake City *core* region of Mormon culture as "a centralized zone of concentration . . . and homogeneity." The broader concept of *domain* identifies "areas in which the . . . culture is dominant" but less intensive than in the core. The *sphere* of any culture, Meinig suggests, is the zone of outer influence, where only parts of the culture are represented or where the culture's adherents are a minority of the total population.

PATTERNS OF DIVERSITY AND UNITY

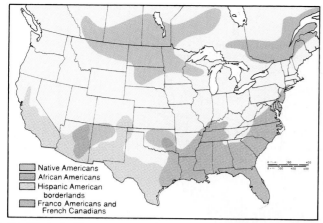

FIGURE 6.11 **Four North American ethnic groups and their provinces.** Note how this generalized map differs from the more detailed picture of ethnic distributions shown in Figure 6.8.

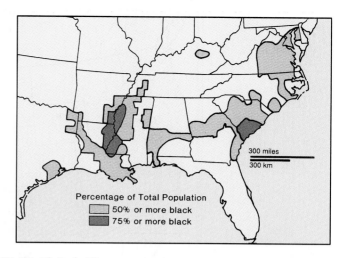

FIGURE 6.12 **African American concentrations, 1850.**

South. During the present century, however, established patterns of southern rural residence and farm employment have undergone profound changes, although southern regionalization of blacks is still evident (Figure 6.13). The decline of subsistence farming and sharecropping, the mechanization of southern agriculture, the demand for factory labor in northern cities starting with World War I (1914–1918), and the general urbanization of the American economy all affected traditional patterns of black residence and livelihood. The growing African American population (nearly 13% of all Americans in 1995) has become more urbanized than the general population; 84% were residents of metropolitan areas in 1990, compared to 77% for all Americans combined. Although recent national economic trends, including industrial growth in the Sunbelt, have encouraged a reverse migration, almost half of African Americans in 1995 resided outside the South (Figure 6.13).

African Americans, like Asian Americans and Hispanics, have had thrust on them an assumed common ethnicity that does not, in fact, exist. Because of prominent physical or linguistic characteristics, quite dissimilar ethnic groups have been categorized by the white, English-speaking majority in ways totally at odds with the realities of their separate national origins or cultural inheritances. Although the U.S. Census Bureau makes some attempt to subdivide Asian ethnic groups—Chinese, Filipino, and Korean, for example—these are distinctions not necessarily recognized by members of the white majority. But even the Census Bureau, in its summary statistics, has treated "Black" and "Hispanic Origin" as catchall classifications that suggest ethnic uniformities where none necessarily exist.

In the case of African Americans, such clustering is of decreasing relevance. Their spatial mobility was encouraged by the industrial urban labor requirements first apparent during World War I and continuing through the Vietnam era of the 1960s. Government intervention, mandating and promot-

ing racial equality, further deracialized the economic sector. As a result, the African American community has become subdivided along socioeconomic rather than primarily regional lines. No common native culture united the slaves brought to America; few of their transported traits or traditions could endure the generations of servitude. By long residence and separate experiences, African Americans have become as differentiated as comparably placed ethnics of any other heritage.

Hispanic Concentrations

Similarly, the members of the multiracial, multinational, and multicultural composite population crudely lumped by the Census Bureau into the single category of "Hispanic Origin" are not a homogeneous group either. Hispanic Americans represent as much diversity within the assumed uniform group as they do between that group and the rest of the population. They also constitute the most rapidly growing minority component of U.S. residents—increasing some 49% between 1985 and 1995. At present rates of growth, Hispanics of all national origins will surpass African Americans as the largest minority group early in the 21st century, as Table 6.5 indicates. Indeed, by 1990, Hispanics already outnumbered blacks in 4 of the country's 10 largest cities—Los Angeles, Houston, Phoenix, and San Antonio—and, by the middle of the decade, overtook African Americans in New York City, the biggest.

Mexican Americans account for over 60% of all Hispanic Americans (Table 6.6). They are overwhelmingly located in the five southwestern states that constitute the ethnic province called the Hispanic American borderland (Figure 6.11). Beginning in the 1940s, the Mexican populations in the United States became increasingly urbanized and dispersed, losing their earlier primary identification as agricultural *braceros* (seasonal laborers) and as residents of the rural areas of Texas, New Mexico, and Arizona. California

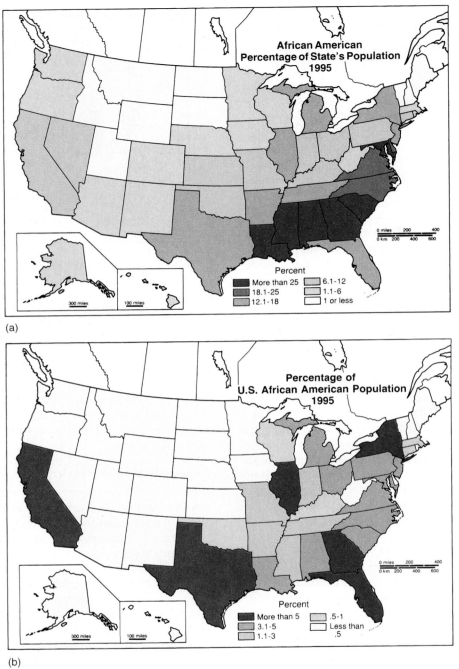

(a)

(b)

FIGURE 6.13   **Evidence of African American concentration** endures in the South, although African Americans, in response to employment opportunities in metropolitan areas of the North and West, are now more widely distributed than a century ago.

rapidly increased its Mexican American populations (Figure 6.14), as did the Midwest, particularly the chain of industrial cities from southeastern Wisconsin through metropolitan Chicago to Detroit. In the decade of the 1980s, the Mexican American population increased by nearly 55% and grew an additional 20% between 1990 and 1995, primarily the result of continuing immigration.

Mexican Americans, representing a distinctive set of cultural characteristics, have been dispersing widely across the United States, though increases in the Midwestern states

(nearly 50% between 1980 and 1995) have been particularly noticeable. In similar fashion, immigrants from equally distinctive South, Central, and Caribbean America countries have been spreading out from their respective initial geographic concentrations. Puerto Ricans, already citizens, first localized in New York City, now the largest Puerto Rican city anywhere in numerical terms. Since 1940, however, when 88% of mainland Puerto Ricans were New Yorkers, there has been an outward dispersal primarily to other major metropolitan areas of the northeastern part of the

TABLE 6.5 Projected U.S. Population Mix: 2000, 2025, and 2050

POPULATION GROUP	PERCENT OF TOTAL		
	2000	2025	2050
Non-Hispanic White	71.6	62.0	52.5
Hispanic	11.3	16.8	22.5
Black	12.8	14.2	15.7
Asian/Pacific Islander	4.4	7.5	10.3
Native American	0.8	1.0	1.1

Source: U.S. Bureau of the Census, based on middle series projections. Totals do not round to 100%.

TABLE 6.6 Estimated Composition of U.S. Hispanic Population, Mid-1990s

HISPANIC SUBGROUP	NUMBER (MILLIONS)	PERCENT
Mexican	17.2	64.3
Puerto Rican	2.8	10.6
Cuban	1.3	4.7
Central and South American	3.6	13.4
Other Hispanic origin[a]	1.9	7.0
Total Hispanic Origin	**26.8**	**100.0**

[a]"Other Hispanics" includes those with origins in Spain or who identify themselves as "Hispanic," "Latino," "Spanish American," etc.

Source: Based on Bureau of Census estimates in *Current Population Reports,* Series P-20.

FIGURE 6.14   Street mural in a Los Angeles *barrio*. Over 40% of Los Angeles' population in 1995 was Hispanic and overwhelmingly Mexican American. Their impact on the urban landscape—in choice of house colors, advertising signs, street vendors, and colorful wall paintings—is distinctive and pervasive.

country. The old industrial cities of New Jersey (Jersey City, Newark, Paterson, Passaic, and Hoboken); Bridgeport and Stamford, Connecticut; the Massachusetts cities of Lowell, Lawrence, and Brockton; and Chicago and other central cities and industrial satellites of the Midwest have received the outflow. By the mid-1990s, New York City retained only about one-third of the mainland Puerto Ricans.

Miami and Dade County, Florida, play the same magnet role for Cubans as New York City earlier did for Puerto Ricans. The first large scale movement of Cuban refugees from the Castro revolution occurred between 1959 and 1962. There followed a mixed period lasting until 1980 when emigration was alternately permitted and prohibited by the Cuban government. Suddenly and unexpectedly, in April 1980, a torrent of Cuban migration was released through the small port of Mariel. Although their flow was stopped after only five months, some 125,000 *Marielitos* fled from Cuba to the United States.

Early in the period of post-1959 Cuban influx, the federal government attempted a resettlement program to scatter the new arrivals around the United States. Some remnants of that program are still to be found in concentrations of Cubans in New York City, northern New Jersey, Chicago, and Los Angeles. The majority of early and late arrivals from Cuba, however, have settled in the Miami area and south Florida, home to over half of Cuban Americans.

Immigrants from the Dominican Republic, many of them undocumented and difficult to trace, appear to be concentrating in the New York City area. Within that same city, Central and South Americans have congregated in the borough of Queens, with the South American contingent, particularly Colombians, settling in the Jackson Heights section. Central American Hispanics—estimated in the mid-1990s to number between 1.5 and 2.5 million legal and illegal migrants—tend to cluster in certain sections of the country. Los Angeles is estimated to hold some 40% of the total. Other areas of concentration include San Francisco, New York City, and Washington, D.C.

Each concentration differs in its country of origin. Most Nicaraguans are found in the Miami area, most Hondurans in New Orleans. As noted, migrants from the Dominican Republic seek refuge in New York City; Salvadoran and Guatemalan migrants have dispersed themselves more widely. New arrivals tend to follow the paths of earlier countrymen. Chain migration and the security and support of an ethnically distinctive halfway community are as important for recent immigrants as for their predecessors of earlier times and different cultures. As the residential concentrations of these different Central American subgroups suggest, Hispanics as a whole are more urbanized than are non-Hispanic populations of the United States; in the mid-1990s, over 90% of Hispanic households were in urban areas, compared to less than 75% for non-Hispanic households.

Asian Contrasts

With their numbers more than doubling, Asians were the country's fastest-growing ethnic component between 1981 and 1990, continuing a pattern of rapid increase (141%) evident during the 1970s. By 1994, Asian Americans totalled nearly 7.5 million (see also Table 6.7), about 2.9% of the entire U.S. population. In 1980 they accounted for just 1.5% of the total. Their rapid growth has resulted from two different causes. First were changes in immigration law enacted in 1965 that abolished the older national origins system and favored family reunification as an admission criterion. Educated Asians, taking advantage of professional preference categories in the immigration laws to move to the United States (or remain here on adjusted student visas), could become citizens after five years and send for immediate family and other relatives without restriction. They in turn, after five years, could bring in other relatives. Chain migration was an important agency. Second, the flood of Southeast Asian refugees admitted during 1975–1980 under the Refugee Resettlement Program after the Vietnam War swelled the Asian numbers in the United States by over 400,000, with 2.4 million more Asian immigrants admitted between 1980 and 1990. By the early 1990s, Asians made up about 20% of the yearly immigrant flow to America.

Asia is a vast continent; successive periods of immigration have seen arrivals from many different parts of it, representing totally different ethnic groups and cultures. The major Asian American populations are detailed in Table 6.7, but even these groups are not homogeneous and cannot suggest the great diversity of ethnic groups—Burmese,

TABLE 6.7	U.S. Asian Population by Ethnicity, 1990	
ETHNICITY	NUMBER (000)	PERCENT OF ASIAN-AMERICAN TOTAL
Chinese	1643.6	22.6
Filipino	1403.6	19.3
Japanese	850.9	11.7
Asian Indian	814.5	11.2
Korean	800.0	11.0
Vietnamese	610.9	8.4
Laotian	149.0	2.0
Cambodian	147.4	2.0
Thai	91.0	1.3
Hmong	90.0	1.2
Pakistani	81.0	1.1
Other	590.7	8.1
Total	**7272.6**	**100.0**

Source: U.S. Bureau of the Census.

Cambodian, Hmong, Mien, Indonesians of great variety, and many more—who have joined the American realm. Although settled in all sections of the country and, like Hispanic Americans, differently localized by ethnic group, Asian Americans as a whole are relatively concentrated in residence—far more so than the rest of the population.

In 1994 59% of them resided in the West (and almost 40% in California alone), where only 21% of all Americans lived; 34% of the whole population lived in the South, but only 14% of Asian Americans were found there. Japanese and Filipinos are particularly concentrated in the western states, where more than half of the Chinese Americans also live. Only some 17% of all Asian Americans lived in the Northeast, but about one-third of the country's Asian Indians were localized there. The distribution of Koreans is most similar to that of the total American population. The Vietnamese, as a result of a refugee dispersal program, were initially more widely distributed than other major Asian American communities. Eventually, however, most Indochinese drifted to the milder climates of the West Coast; by 1990 about 40% were in California, concentrated particularly in the central valley south of San Francisco, although the largest Vietnamese community outside of Vietnam is found in Orange County, south of Los Angeles. In whatever part of the country they settled, Asian Americans (and Pacific Islanders) were drawn to metropolitan areas, where 95% of them lived in 1994—more than half in suburban areas.

French Uniformity

The stamp of the French charter group on the ethnic province of French Canada is overwhelming. Quebec Province—with ethnic extensions into New Brunswick and northernmost Maine—is the only extensive region of North America (except northern Canadian Native American homelands) where regional delimitation on purely ethnic lines is possible or appropriate. In language, religion, legal principals, system of land tenure, the arts, cuisine, philosophies of life, and landscapes of rural and urban occupance, Quebec stands apart from the rest of Canada (Figure 6.15). Its distinctiveness and self-assertion have won it special consideration and treatment within the political structure of the country.

Although the *Canadiens* of Quebec were the charter group of eastern Canada and for some 200 years the controlling population, they numbered only some 65,000 when the Treaty of Paris ended the North American wars between the British and the French in 1763. That treaty, however, gave them control over three primary aspects of their culture and lives: language, religion, and land tenure. From these, they created their own distinctive and enduring ethnic province of some 1.5 million square kilometers (600,000 sq. mi.) and 7.3 million people, 85% of whom have French as their native tongue (see Figure 5.16) and adhere to the Roman Catholic faith. Quebec City is the cultural heart of French Canada, though the bilingual Montreal metropolitan area with a population of over 3 million is the largest center of Quebec Province. The sense of cultural identity prevalent throughout French Canada imparted a sense of nationalism not similarly expressed in other ethnic provinces of North America. Laws and guarantees recognizing and strengthening the position of French language and culture within the province assure the preservation of this distinctive North American cultural region, even if the movement for full political separation from the rest of Canada is not successful.

(a)　　　　　　　　　　　　　　　　　　　　(b)

FIGURE 6.15 (*a*) The hotel Château Frontenac stands high above the lower older portion of Quebec City, where many streets show the architecture of French cities of the 18th century carried over to the urban heart of modern French Canada. (*b*) Rural Richelieu Valley in the Eastern Townships of Quebec Province.

Urban Ethnic Diversity and Segregation

"Little Havanas" and "Little Koreas" have joined the "Chinatowns," "Little Italys," and "Germantowns" of earlier eras as part of the American urban scene. The traditional practice of selective concentration of ethnics in their own frequently well-defined subcommunities is evidence of a much more inclusive, sharply defined social geography of urban America, in which ethnic neighborhoods have been a pronounced, enduring feature.

Protestant Anglo Americans created from colonial times the dominating host culture—the charter group—of urban North America. To that culture the mass migrations of the 19th and early 20th centuries brought individuals and groups representative of different religious and ethnic backgrounds, including Irish Catholics, eastern European Jews, and members of every nationality, ethnic stock, and distinctive culture of central, eastern, and southern Europe. To them were added, both simultaneously and subsequently, newcomers from Asia and Latin America and such urbanizing rural Americans as Appalachian whites and Southern blacks.

Each newcomer element sought both accommodation within the urban matrix established by the charter group and acceptable relationships with other in-migrant ethnic groups. That accommodation has characteristically been achieved by the establishment of the ethnic community or neighborhood—an area within the city where a particular culture group aggregates, which it dominates, and which

may serve as the core area from which diffusion or absorption into the host society can occur. The rapidly urbanizing, industrializing society of 19th-century America became a mosaic of such ethnic enclaves. Their maintenance as distinctive social and spatial entities depended on the degree to which the assimilation of their population occurred. Figure 6.16 shows the more recent ethnic concentrations that developed by the late 20th century in one major American city. The increasing subdivision of the immigrant stream and the consequent reduction in the size of identified enclaves make comparable maps of older U.S. cities such as New York and Chicago nearly unintelligibly complex.

Immigrant neighborhoods are a measure of the **social distance** that separates the minority from the charter group. The greater the perceived differences between the two groups, the greater the social distance and the less likely is the charter group to easily accept or assimilate the newcomer. Consequently, the ethnic community will endure longer as a place both of immigrant refuge and of enforced segregation.

Segregation is a shorthand expression for the extent to which members of an ethnic group are not uniformly distributed in relation to the rest of the population. A commonly employed measure quantifying the degree to which a distinctive group is segregated is the *index of residential dissimilarity*. It indicates the percentage difference between the distribution of two component groups of a population, with a theoretical range of values from 0 (no segregation) to 100 (complete segregation). Table 6.8 summarizes the differing degree of segregation faced by three major minority groups

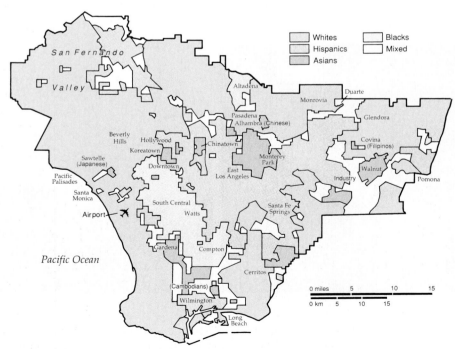

FIGURE 6.16 **Ethnic patterns in Los Angeles, 1990** are greatly generalized on this map, which conceals much of the complex intermingling of different ethnic groups in several sections of the city.

TABLE 6.8 Metropolitan Areas Ranked by Overall Segregation Levels, 1990

METRO AREA[a]	1990 POPULATION (MILLIONS)	OVERALL SEGREGATION INDEX[b]	INDEX OF DISSIMILARITY		
			BLACK	HISPANIC	ASIAN
1. Detroit, MI	4.4	83	89	42	48
2. Cleveland, OH	1.8	82	86	57	42
3. St. Louis, MO-IL	2.4	76	80	29	44
Chicago, IL	6.1	76	87	65	47
Newark, NJ	1.8	76	84	67	35
6. Philadelphia, PA-NJ	4.9	75	81	65	47
7. New York, NY	8.5	73	83	68	52
8. Baltimore, MD	2.4	71	75	35	42
9. Atlanta, GA	2.8	67	71	39	45
10. Boston, MA	2.9	62	72	59	46
Los Angeles-Long Beach, CA	8.9	62	74	63	48
12. Tampa-St. Petersburg-Clearwater, FL	2.1	61	74	47	39
13. Houston, TX	3.3	60	71	53	50
Nassau-Suffolk, NY	2.6	60	80	50	37
Dallas, TX	2.6	60	68	54	47
16. Washington, D.C.-MD-VA	3.9	59	67	43	35
17. Miami-Hialeah, FL	1.9	58	72	52	31
18. San Francisco, CA	1.6	54	66	51	51
19. Oakland, CA	2.1	51	66	48	34
Denver, CO	1.6	51	66	48	34
21. San Diego, CA	2.5	50	61	48	50
Phoenix, AZ	2.1	50	54	51	33

[a]Primary metropolitan statistical areas (PMSAs).

[b]The overall segregation index is a weighted average of the Index of Dissimilarity of the three minority groups.

Source: Data from U.S. Bureau of the Census.

in 22 large U.S. metropolitan centers. Evidence from cities throughout the world makes clear that most ethnic minorities tend to be sharply segregated from the charter group and that segregation on racial or ethnic lines is usually greater than would be anticipated from the socioeconomic levels of the groups involved.

Each world region and each country, of course, has its own patterns of national and urban immigration and immigrant residential patterns. Even when those population movements involve distinctive and contrasting ethnic groups, American models of spatial differentiation may not be applicable. Foreign migrants to West European cities, for example, frequently do not have the same expectations of permanent residence and eventual amalgamation into the host society as their American counterparts. Many came under labor contracts with no initial legal assurance of permanent residence. Although many now have been joined by their families, they often find citizenship difficult to acquire; in Germany, even German-born children of "guest workers" are considered aliens. Their residential choices are consequently influenced by difficulties or disinterest in integration or amalgamation, a high degree of migrant self-identity, restriction to housing units or districts specially provided for them, and the locational pull of chain migration. Culture and religion are important in that regard, as even small ethnically homogeneous groups, confined perhaps to part of a city block or to a single apartment building, help maintain the life-style and support systems of home territories.

The Islamic populations from North Africa and Turkey tend to be more tightly grouped and defensive against the surrounding majority culture of Western European cities than do African or South and East European Christian migrants. France, with some 5 million Muslim residents, most of them from North Africa, has tended to create bleak, distant, outer city ghettoes in which Arab legal and illegal immigrants remain largely isolated from mainstream French life.

Rapid urbanization in multiethnic India has resulted in cities of extreme social and cultural contrasts. Increasingly, Indian cities feature defined residential colonies segregated by village and caste origins of the immigrants. Chain migration has eased the influx of newcomers to specific new and old city areas; language, custom, religion, and tradition keep them confined. International and domestic migration within ethnically diverse Africa has had a similar residential outcome. In the Ivory Coast, for example, the rural-to-urban population shift has created city neighborhoods defined on tribal and village lines. In all continental and national urban contexts, the degree of immigrant segregation is at least in part conditioned by the degree of social distance felt between the newcomer population and the other immigrant and host societies among whom residential space is sought.

Constraints on assimilation and the extent of discrimination and segregation are greater for some minorities than for others. In general, the rate of assimilation of an ethnic minority by the host culture depends on two sets of controls: external, including attitudes toward the minority held by the charter group and other competing ethnic groups, and internal controls of group cohesiveness and defensiveness.

External Controls

When the majority culture or rival minorities perceive an ethnic group as threatening, the group tends to be spatially isolated by external "blocking" tactics designed to confine the rejected minority and to resist its "invasion" of already occupied urban neighborhoods. The more tightly knit the threatened group, the more adamant and overt are its resistance tactics. When confrontation measures (including, perhaps, threats and vandalism) fail, the invasion of charter-group territory by the rejected minority proceeds until a critical percentage of newcomer housing occupancy is reached. That level, the **tipping point,** may precipitate a rapid exodus by the former majority population. Invasion, followed by succession, then results in a new spatial pattern of ethnic dominance according to models of urban social geography developed for American cities and examined in Chapter 11, models less applicable to the European scene.

Racial or ethnic discrimination in urban areas generally expresses itself in the relegation of the most recent, most alien, most despised minority to the poorest available housing. That confinement has historically been abetted by the concentration of the newest, least assimilated ethnic minorities at the low end of the occupational structure. Distasteful, menial, low-paying service and factory employment unattractive to the charter group is available to those new arrivals even when other occupational avenues may be closed. The dockworkers, street cleaners, slaughterhouse employees, and sweatshop garment workers of earlier America had and have their counterparts in other regions. In England, successive waves of West Indians and Commonwealth Asians took the posts of low-pay hotel and restaurant service workers, transit workers, refuse collectors, manual laborers, and the like; Turks in West German cities and North Africans in France play similar low-status employment roles.

In the United States there has been a spatial association between the location of such employment opportunities—the inner city central business district (CBD) and its margins—and the location of the oldest, most dilapidated, and least desirable housing. Proximity to job opportunity and the availability of cheap housing near the CBD, therefore, combined to concentrate the United States immigrant slum near the heart of the 19th-century central city. In the second half of the 20th century, the suburbanization of jobs, the rising skill levels required in the automated offices of the CBD, and the effective isolation of inner city residents by the absence of public transportation or their inability to pay for private transport have maintained the association of the least competitive minorities and the least desirable housing area. But now, those locations lack the promise of entry-level jobs formerly close at hand.

That American spatial association does not necessarily extend to other cultures and urban environments. In Latin American cities, newest arrivals at the bottom of the economic and employment ladder are most apt to find housing in squatter or slum areas on the outskirts of the urban unit (Figure 11.40); prestigious housing claims room near the city center. European cities, too, have retained a larger proportion of upper-income groups at the urban center than have their American counterparts, with a corresponding impact on the distribution of lower-status, lower-income housing (Figure 11.36). In French urban agglomerations, at least, the outer fringes frequently have a higher percentage of foreigners than the city itself.

Internal Controls

Although part of the American pattern of urban residential segregation may be explained by the external controls of host-culture resistance and discrimination, the clustering of specific groups into discrete, ethnically homogeneous neighborhoods is best understood as the result of internal controls of group defensiveness and conservatism. The self-elected segregation of ethnic groups can be seen to serve four principal functions—defense, support, preservation, and "attack."

First, it provides *defense,* reducing individual immigrant isolation and exposure by physical association within a limited area. The walled and gated Jewish quarters of medieval European cities have their present-day counterparts in the clearly marked and defined "turfs" of street-gang members and the understood exclusive domains of the "black community," "Chinatown," and other ethnic or racial neighborhoods. In British cities, it has been observed that West Indians and Asians fill identical slots in the British economy and reside in the same sorts of areas, but they tend to avoid living in the *same* areas. West Indians avoid Asians; Sikhs isolate themselves from Muslims; Bengalis avoid Punjabis. In London, patterns of residential isolation even extend to West Indians of separate island homelands (see "The Caribbean Map in London").

Their own defined ethnic territory provides members of the group with security from the hostility of antagonistic social groups, a factor also underlying the white flight to "garrison" suburbs. That outsiders view at least some closely defined ethnic communities as homogeneous, impenetrable, and hostile is suggested by Figure 6.17, a "safety map" of Manhattan published in the newspaper *l'Aurore* for the guidance of French tourists.

Second, the ethnic neighborhood provides *support* for its residents in a variety of ways. The area serves as a halfway station between the home country and the alien society, to which admittance will eventually be sought. It acts as a place of initiation and indoctrination, providing supportive lay and religious ethnic institutions, familiar businesses, job opportunities where language barriers are minimal, and friendship and kinship ties to ease the transition to a new society.

Although the movement [to England] from the West Indies has been treated as if it were homogeneous, the island identity, particularly among those from the small islands, has remained strong. . . . [I]t is very evident to anyone working in the field that the process of chain migration produced a clustering of particular island or even village groups in their British destinations. . . .

The island identities have manifested themselves on the map of London. The island groups can still be picked out in the clusters of settlements in different parts of the city. There is an archipelago of Windward and Leeward islanders north of the Thames; Dominicans and St. Lucians have their core areas in Paddington and Notting Hill; Grenadians are found in the west in Hammersmith and Ealing; Montserratians are concentrated around Stoke Newington, Hackney and Finsbury Park; Antiguans spill over to the east in Hackney, Waltham Forest and Newham; south of the river is Jamaica.

That is not to say that Jamaicans are found only south of the river or that the only West Indians in Paddington are from St Lucia. The mixture is much greater than that. The populations overlap and interdigitate: there are no sharp edges. . . . [Nevertheless, north of the river] there is a west-east change with clusters of Grenadians in the west giving way to St Lucians and Dominicans in the inner west, through to Vincentians and Montserratians in the inner north and east and thence to Antiguans in the east.

Source: Ceri Peach, "The Force of West Indian Island Identity in Britain," in *Geography & Ethnic Pluralism*, ed. Colin Clarke, David Ley, and Ceri Peach (London: George Allen & Unwin, 1984).

Third, the ethnic neighborhood may provide a *preservation function,* reflecting the ethnic group's positive intent to preserve and promote such essential elements of its cultural heritage as language and religion. The preservation function represents a disinclination to be totally absorbed into the charter society and a desire to maintain those customs and associations seen to be essential to the conservation of the group. For example, Jewish dietary laws are more easily observed by, or exposure to potential marriage partners within the faith is more certain in, close-knit communities than when individuals are scattered.

Finally, ethnic spatial concentration can serve what has been termed the *attack function,* a peaceful and legitimate search for, particularly, political representation by a concentration of electoral power. Voter registration drives among African and Hispanic Americans represent concerted efforts to achieve the promotion of group interests at all governmental levels.

Shifting Ethnic Concentrations

Ethnic communities once established are not necessarily, or even usually, permanent. With recent diversified immigration, older homogeneous ethnic neighborhoods have become highly subdivided and polyethnic. In Los Angeles, for

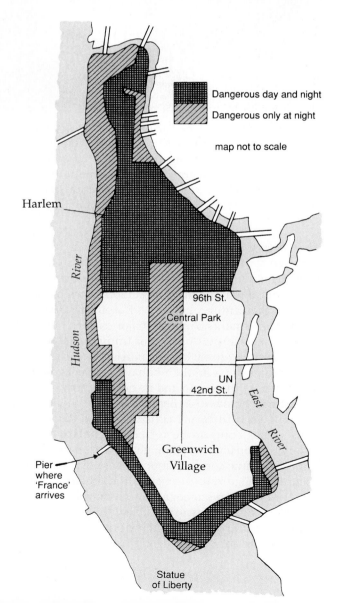

FIGURE 6.17 **A "safety map" of Manhattan.**
According to the editors of the French newspaper *l'Aurore,* any place north of 96th Street in Manhattan is best avoided both by day and by night. The perceived "danger area" includes all of central and east Harlem.

199

example, the great wave of immigrants from Mexico, Central America, and Asia has begun to push African Americans out of Watts and other well-established black communities, converting them from racially exclusive to multicultural areas. In New York, the Borough of Queens, once the stronghold of European ethnics, has now become home to more than 110 different, mainly non-European nationalities. In Woodside in Queens, Latin Americans and Koreans are prominent among the many replacements of the formerly dominant German and Irish groups. Elsewhere within the city, West Indians now dominate the old Jewish neighborhoods of Flatbush; Poles and Dominicans and other Central Americans have succeeded Germans and Jews in Washington Heights. Manhattan's Chinatown expands into old Little Italy, and a new Little Italy emerges in Bensonhurst.

Further, the new ethnic neighborhoods are intermixed in a way that enclaves of the turn of the century never were. The restaurants, bakeries, groceries, specialty shops, their customers and owners from a score of different countries and even different continents are now found within a two- or three-block radius. In the Kenmore Avenue area of East Los Angeles, for example, a half-square-mile (1.3 km²) area of former Anglo neighborhood now houses over 9000 people representing Hispanics and Asians of widely varied origin along with Pacific Islanders, Amerindians, African Americans, and a scattering of native-born whites. Students in the neighborhood school come from 43 countries and speak 23 languages, a localized ethnic intermixture unknown in the communities of single ethnicity so characteristic of earlier stages of immigration to the United States (see "Colonies of Immigrants").

Even when an ethnic community rejects or is denied assimilation into the larger society, it may both relocate and retain its coherence. "Satellite Chinatowns" are examples of migration from city centers outward to the suburbs or to outer boroughs—in Los Angeles, 7 miles east of the city to Monterey Park; in San Francisco, from the downtown area along Grant Avenue to the Richmond district 3 miles away. In New York City the satellite move was from the still-growing Canal Street area in lower Manhattan to Flushing, about 15 miles away (Figure 6.18), and to Elmhurst which, with immigrants from 114 different countries, is the city's most ethnically diverse neighborhood. Other growing, older ethnic communities—needing more space and containing newly affluent and successful members able to compete for better housing elsewhere—have followed a similar pattern of subdivision and relocation. For some ethnics, assimilation in job and society does not reduce the need for community identity.

Typologies and Spatial Results

When both the charter group and the ethnic group perceive the social distance separating them to be small, the isolation caused by external discriminatory and internal cohesiveness controls is temporary, and developed ethnic residential clusters quickly give way to full assimilation. While they endure, the clusters may be termed **colonies,** serving essentially as points of entry for members of the particular ethnic group.

FIGURE 6.18   The Flushing, Queens, area of New York City contains one of the newly developing "satellite Chinatowns." Like those in other cities, it reflects both the pressures exerted by a growing Chinese community upon their older urban enclaves and the suburbanization of an affluent younger generation that still seeks community coherence.

They persist only to the extent that new arrivals perpetuate the need for them. In American cities, many European ethnic colonies began to lose their vitality and purpose with the reduction of European immigration flows after the 1920s. Early in the century, however, European colonies were dynamic components of every major eastern and midwestern city, as the excerpt "Colonies of Immigrants" describes.

When an ethnic cluster persists because its occupants choose to preserve it, their behavior reflects the internal cohesiveness of the group and its desire to maintain an enduring **ethnic enclave** or neighborhood. When the cluster is perpetuated by external constraints and discriminatory actions, it has come to be termed a **ghetto.** In reality, the colony, the enclave, and the ghetto are spatially similar outcomes of ethnic concentrations whose origins are difficult to document. Figure 6.19 suggests the possible spatial expressions of these three recognized ethnic-cluster models.

Both discrimination and voluntarism determine the changing pattern of ethnic clustering within metropolitan areas. Where forced segregation limits residential choices,

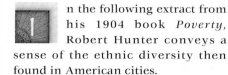

I n the following extract from his 1904 book *Poverty*, Robert Hunter conveys a sense of the ethnic diversity then found in American cities.

[In American cities] great colonies, foreign in language, customs, habits, and institutions, are separated from each other and from the distinctly American groups on national or racial lines. By crossing the Bowery one leaves behind him the great Jewish colony made up of Russians, Poles, and Roumanians and passes into Italy; to the northeast lies a little Germany; to the southwest a colony of Syrians; to the west lies an Irish community, a settlement of negroes, a remnant of the old native American stock; to the south lie a Chinese and a Greek colony. On Manhattan alone, either on the extreme west side or the extreme east side, there are other colonies of the Irish, the Jews, and the Italians, and, in addition, there is a large colony of Bohemians. In Chicago there are the same foreign poor. To my own knowledge there are four Italian colonies, two Polish,

a Bohemian, an Irish, a Jewish, a German, a negro, a Chinese, a Greek, a Scandinavian, and other colonies. So it is also in Boston and many other cities. In New York alone there are more persons of German descent than persons of native descent, and the German element is larger than in any city of Germany except Berlin. There are nearly twice as many Irish as in Dublin, about as many Jews as in Warsaw, and more Italians than in Naples or Venice. . . .

To live in one of these foreign communities is actually to live on foreign soil. The thoughts, feelings, and traditions which belong to the mental life of the colony are often entirely alien to an American. The newspapers, the literature, the ideals, the passions, the things which agitate the community are unknown to us except in fragments. . . .

While there is a great movement of population from all parts of the old world to all parts of the new, the migration to the United States is the largest and the most conspicuous. Literally speaking, millions of foreigners have established colonies in the very hearts of our urban and

industrial communities. . . . In recent years the flow of immigrants to the cities, where they are not needed, instead of to those parts of the country where they are needed, has been steadily increasing. Sixty-nine percent of the present immigration avows itself as determined to settle either in the great cities or in certain communities of the four great industrial states, Massachusetts, New York, Pennsylvania, and Illinois. According to their own statements, nearly 60 percent of the Russian and Polish Jews intend to settle in the largest cities. As a matter of fact, those who actually do settle in cities are even more numerous than this percentage indicates. As the class of immigrants, drawn from eastern and southern Europe, Russia, and Asia, come in increasing numbers to the United States, the tendency to settle in cities likewise increases.

Source: Robert Hunter, *Poverty* (New York: Macmillan, 1904).

---

ethnic or racial minorities may be confined to the older, low-cost housing areas, typically close to the city center. Growing ethnic groups that maintain voluntary spatial association frequently expand the area of their dominance by growth outward from the core of the city in a radial pattern. That process has long been recognized in Chicago (Figure 6.20) and has, in that and other cities, typically been extended beyond the central city boundaries into at least the inner fringe of the suburbs.

African Americans have, traditionally, found strong resistance to their territorial expansion from the Anglo charter group, though white-black urban relations and patterns of black ghetto formation and expansion have differed in different sections of the country. A revealing typology of African American ghettos is outlined in Figure 6.21. In the South, the white majority, with total control of the housing market, was able to assign residential space to blacks in accordance with white, not black, self-interest. In the *early southern* ghetto of such pre-Civil War cities as Charleston

and New Orleans, African Americans were assigned small dwellings in alleys and back streets within and bounding the white communities where they worked as (slave) house and garden servants. The *classic southern* ghetto for newly free blacks was composed of specially built, low-quality housing on undesirable land—swampy, perhaps, or near industry or railroads—and was sufficiently far from better-quality white housing to maintain full spatial and social segregation.

In the North, on the other hand, African Americans were open competitors with other claimants for space in a generalized housing market. The *early northern* ghetto represented a "toehold" location in high-density, aged, substandard housing on the margin of the central business district. The *classic northern* ghetto is a more recent expansion of that initial enclave to surround the CBD and to penetrate, through invasion and succession, contiguous zones as far as the numbers and the rent-paying ability of the growing African American community will carry. Finally, in new western and southwestern cities not tightly hemmed in by

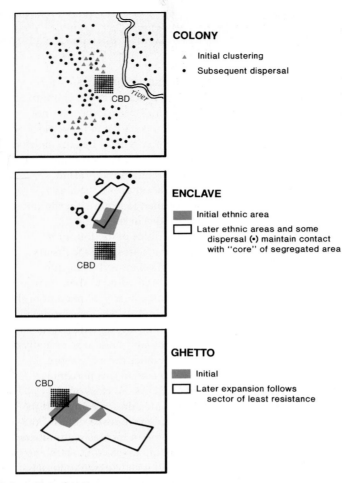

FIGURE 6.19   Types of ethnic areas.

COLONY
▲ Initial clustering
● Subsequent dispersal

ENCLAVE
▮ Initial ethnic area
▯ Later ethnic areas and some dispersal (•) maintain contact with "core" of segregated area

GHETTO
▮ Initial
▯ Later expansion follows sector of least resistance

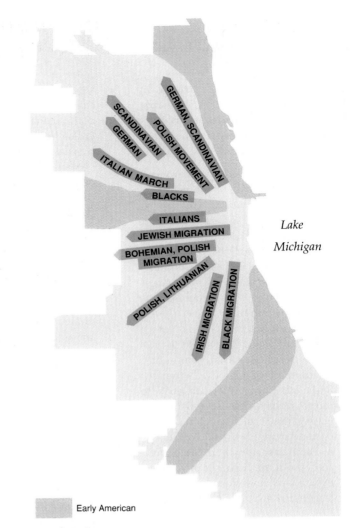

Early American

FIGURE 6.20   **The outward expansion of racial and nationality groups in Chicago.** "Often," Samuel Kincheloe observed in the 1930s, "[minority] groups first settle in a deteriorated area of a city somewhere near its center, then push outward along the main streets." More recently, many—particularly young, innovative, and entrepreneurial—immigrants have avoided traditional first locations in central cities and from their arrival have settled in metropolitan area suburbs and outlying cities where economic opportunity and quality of life is perceived as superior to conditions in the primary inner city.

resistant ethnic neighborhoods or ethnic suburbs, the black ghetto may display a linear expansion from the CBD to the suburban fringe.

Native Born Dispersals

The high degree of areal concentration of recent immigrant groups within the United States initiated a selective native born, particularly white, retreat, not only fleeing the cities for the suburbs but leaving entire metropolitan areas and states. California, with nearly one-quarter of its population foreign born in the mid-1990s, saw a departure of one native born white or black resident for nearly each foreign born arrival. Individual urban areas echoed California's state experience. The New York, Chicago, Los Angeles, Houston, and Boston metropolitan areas—5 of the top 11 immigrant destinations—lost 9 native residents for every 10 immigrant arrivals. For whites, top destinations were to cities and states away from coastal and southern border immigrant entry points, from San Francisco to Houston in the West, from Boston to Washington plus Miami in the East, and the Chicago district in the interior. African Americans, too, are leaving most of the high-immigration metropolitan areas with Atlanta, Georgia the preferred destination. A visible spatial consequence, then, of recent patterns of U.S. immigration and settlement is a de-

cline of the older ideal and reality of immigrant assimilation and of racial and cultural urban mixtures for one of increasing wholesale segregation and isolation by metropolitan areas and segments of the country.

Cultural Transfer

Immigrant groups arrive at their destinations with already existing sets of production techniques and skills. They bring established ideas of "appropriate" dress, foods, and building styles, and they have religious practices, marriage customs,

PATTERNS OF DIVERSITY AND UNITY

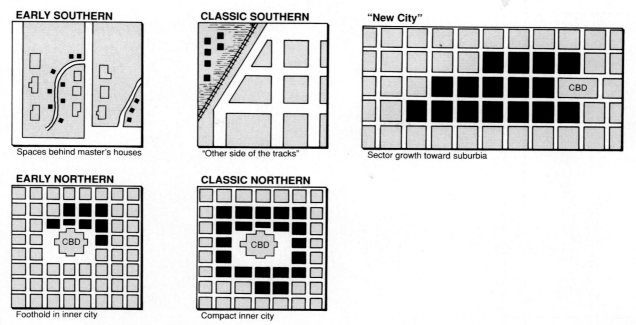

FIGURE 6.21   A typology of black ghettos in the United States.

and other cultural expressions in place and ingrained. That is, immigrants carry to their new homes a full complement of artifacts, sociofacts, and mentifacts. They may modify, abandon, or even pass these on to the host culture, depending on a number of interacting influences: (1) the background of the arriving group; (2) its social distance from the charter group; (3) the disparity between new home and origin-area environmental conditions; (4) the importance given by the migrants to the economic, political, or religious motivations that caused them to relocate; and (5) the kinds of encountered constraints that force personal, social, or technical adjustments on the new arrivals.

Immigrant groups rarely transferred intact all of their culture traits to North America. Invariably there have been modifications as a result of the necessary adjustment to new circumstances or physical conditions. In general, if a transplanted cultural element was usable in the new locale, it was retained. Simple inertia suggested there was little reason to abandon the familiar and comfortable when no advantage accrued. If a trait or a cultural complex was essential to group identity and purpose—the religious convictions of the rural Amish, for example, or of urban Hasidic Jews—its retention was certain. But ill-suited habits or techniques would be abandoned if superior American practices were encountered, and totally inappropriate practices would be dropped. German settlers in Texas, for example, found that the vine and the familiar midlatitude fruits did not thrive there. Old-country agricultural traditions were, they discovered, not fully transferable and had to be altered.

Finally, even apparently essential cultural elements may be modified in the face of unalterable opposition from the majority population. Although American in origin, the Latter-day Saints (Mormons) were viewed as outsiders whose practice of polygamy was alien and repugnant. To secure political and social acceptance, church members abandoned that facet of their religious belief. More recently, the some 30,000 Hmong and Mien tribespeople who settled in the Fresno, California, area after fleeing Vietnam, Thailand, and Laos found that their traditional practices of medicinal use of opium, of "capturing" young brides, and of ritual slaughtering of animals brought them into conflict with American law and customs and with the more Americanized members of their own culture group.

Every relocated ethnic group is subject to forces of attraction and rejection. The former tend toward assimilation into the host society; the latter, innate to the group, encourage retention of its self-identity. Acculturation tends to be responsive to economic advantage and to be accelerated if the immigrant group is in many basic traits similar to the host society, if it is relatively well educated, relatively wealthy, and if it finds political or social advantages in being "Americanized."

Rejection factors internal to the group that aid in the retention of cultural identification include the element of isolation. The immigrant group may seek physical separation in remote areas, or raise barriers of a social nature to assure its insulation from corrupting influences. Social isolation can be effective even in congested urban environments if it is buttressed by distinctive costume, beliefs, or practices (Figure 6.22). Group segregation may even result in the retention of customs, clothing, or dialects discarded in the original home area.

Rejection factors may also involve **culture rebound,** a belated adoption of group consciousness and reestablishment of identifying traits. These may reflect an attempt to reassert old values and to achieve at least a modicum of social separation. The wearing of dashikis, the adoption of "Afro" hairstyles, or the celebration of Kwanzaa by American blacks

FIGURE 6.22   Ultra-orthodox Hasidim, segregating themselves by dress and custom, seek social isolation and shun corrupting outside influences even in the midst of the congestion of New York City and the excitement of the New York Marathon.

seeking identification with African roots are examples of culture rebound. Ethnic identity is fostered by the nuclear family and ties of kinship, particularly when reinforced by residential proximity. It is preserved by such group activities as distinctive feasts or celebrations, by marriage customs, and by ethnically identified clubs, such as the Turnverein societies of German communities or the Sokol movement of athletic and cultural centers among the Czechs.

The Ethnic Landscape

Landscape evidence of ethnicity may be as subtle as the greater number and size of barns in the German-settled areas of the Ozarks or the designs of churches or the names of villages. The evidence may be as striking as the buggies of the Amish communities, the massive Dutch (really, German-origin) barns of southeastern Pennsylvania (Figure 6.23), or the adobe houses of Mexican American settlements in the Southwest. The ethnic landscape, however defined, may be a relic, reflecting old ways no longer pursued. It may contain evidence of artifacts or designs imported, found useful, and retained. In some instances, the physical or customary trappings of ethnicity may remain unique to one or a very few communities. In others, the diffusion of ideas or techniques may have spread introductions to areas beyond their initial impact. The landscapes and landscape evidences explored by cultural geographers are many and complex. The following paragraphs seek merely to suggest the variety of topics pursued in tracing the landscape impacts evident from the cultural diversity of Anglo America.

FIGURE 6.23   The Pennsylvania Dutch barn, with its origins in southern Germany, has two levels. Livestock occupy the ground level; on the upper level, reached by a gentle ramp, are the threshing floor, haylofts, and grain and equipment storage. A distinctive projecting forebay provides shelter for ground-level stock doors and unmistakably identifies the Pennsylvania Dutch barn. The style, particularly in its primitive log form, was exported from its eastern origins, underwent modification, and became a basic form in the Upland (i.e., off the Coastal Plain) South, Ohio, Indiana, Illinois, and Missouri. An example of a distinctive ethnic imprint on the landscape, the Pennsylvania Dutch barn also became an example of cultural transfer from an immigrant group to the charter group.

Land Survey

The charter group of any area had the option of designing a system for claiming and allotting land appropriate to its needs and traditions. For the most part, the English established land-division policies in the Atlantic Seaboard colonies. In New England, basic land grants were for "towns," relatively compact blocks ideally 6 miles (9.7 km) square. The established central village, with its meeting house and its commons area, was surrounded by larger fields subdivided into strips for allocation among the community members (Figure 6.24). The result was a distinctive pattern of nucleated villages and fragmented farms.

From Pennsylvania southward, the original royal land grants were made to "proprietors," who in turn sold or allotted holdings to settlers. In the southern colonies, the occupants claimed land in amounts approved by the authorities but unspecified in location. The land evaluated as best was claimed first, poor land was passed over, and parcel boundaries were irregular and unsystematic. The *metes-and-bounds* system of property description of the region, based largely on landform or water features or such temporary landscape elements as prominent trees, unusual rocks, or cairns, led to boundary uncertainty and dispute (Figure 6.25). It also resulted in "topographic" road patterns, such as those found in Pennsylvania and other eastern states, where routes are often controlled by the contours of the land rather than the regularity of a geometric survey.

When independence was achieved, the federal government decided that the public domain should be systematically surveyed and subdivided before being opened for settlement. The resulting township and range *rectangular survey* system, adopted in the Land Ordinance of 1785, established survey lines oriented in the cardinal directions and divided the land into townships 6 miles (9.7 km) square, which were further subdivided into sections 1 mile (1.6 km) on each side (Figure 6.25). The resultant rectilinear system of land subdivision and ownership was extended to all parts of the United States ever included within the public domain, creating the basic checkerboard pattern of minor civil divisions, the regular pattern of section-line and quarter-line country roads, the block patterns of fields and farms, and the gridiron street systems of American towns and cities.

Elsewhere in North America, the French and the Spanish constituted charter groups and established their own traditions of land description and allotment. The French impress has been particularly enduring. The *long-lot* system was introduced into the St. Lawrence Valley and followed French settlers wherever they established colonies in the New World: the Mississippi Valley, Detroit, Louisiana, and elsewhere. The long lot was a surveyed elongated holding typically about 10 times longer than wide stretching far back from a narrow river frontage (Figure 6.26). The back of the lot was indicated by a roadway roughly parallel to the line of the river, marking the front of a second series (or *range*) of

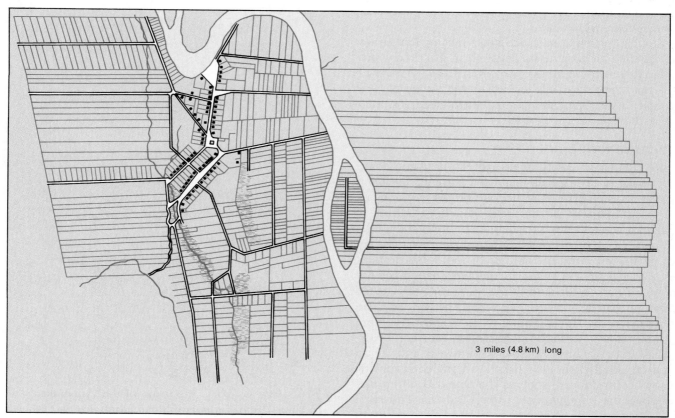

3 miles (4.8 km) long

FIGURE 6.24   **Wethersfield, Connecticut: 1640–1641.** The home lot and field patterns of 17th-century Wethersfield were typical of villages of rural New England.

FIGURE 6.25 **A contrast in survey systems.** The original metes-and-bounds property survey of a portion of the Virginia Military District of western Ohio is here contrasted with the regularity of surveyor's townships, made up of 36 numbered sections, each one mile (1.6 km) on a side.

long lots. The system had the advantage of providing each settler with a fair access to fertile land along the floodplain, lower-quality river terrace land, and remote poorer-quality back areas on the valley slopes serving as woodlots. Dwellings were built at the front of the holding, in a loose settlement alignment called a *côte,* where access was easy and the neighbors were close.

Although English Canada adopted a rectangular survey system, the long lot became the legal norm in French Quebec, where it controls land survey even in areas where river access is not significant. In the Rio Grande Valley of New Mexico and Texas, Spanish colonists introduced a similar long-lot system.

Settlement Patterns

The United States rural settlement pattern has been dominated by isolated farmsteads dispersed through the open countryside. It is an arrangement conditioned by the block pattern of land survey, by the homesteading tradition of "proving up" claims through residence on them, and by the regular pattern of rural roads. Other survey systems, of course, permitted different culturally rooted settlement choices. The French and Hispanic long lots encouraged the alignment of closely spaced, but separated, farmsteads along river or road frontage (Figure 6.27). The New England village reflected the transplanting of an English tradition. Agricultural villages were found as well in Mormon settlement areas, in the Spanish American Southwest, and as part of the cultural landscapes established by early communistic or religious communities, such as the Oneida Community of New York; the Rappites's Harmony, Indiana; Fountaingrove, California; and other, mostly short-lived "utopias" of the 19th and early 20th centuries.

To encourage the settlement of the prairies, the Mennonites were granted lands in Manitoba not as individuals but as communities. Their established agricultural villages

FIGURE 6.26 **A portion of the Vincennes, Indiana–Illinois, topographic quadrangle** (1944) showing evidence of original French long-lot survey. Note the importance of the Wabash River in both long-lot and Vincennes street-system orientations. This U.S. Geological Survey map was originally published at the fractional scale of 1:62,500.

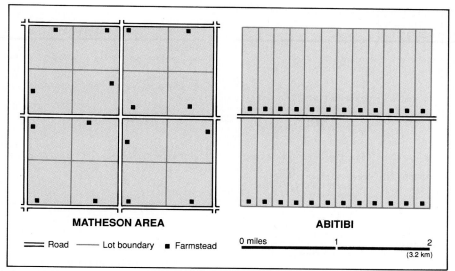

FIGURE 6.27 **Land survey in Canada.** Adjacent areas of Canada demonstrate the effects of different survey systems and cultural heritages on rural settlement patterns. The regular plots of Ontario in English Canada (left map) display the isolated farmsteads characteristic of much of rural Anglo America. The long-lot survey of Quebec in French Canada (right map) shows the lot-front alignments of rural dwellings.

with surrounding communal fields (Figure 6.28) recreated in North America the landscape of their European homelands. (Ethnically German, some Mennonites had colonized in Russia and Ukraine before relocating in North America.)

Ethnic Regionalism

Other world regions display even more pronounced contrasts in the built landscape, reflecting the more entrenched homeland pattern of long-established ethnic regionalism. In areas of intricate mixtures of peoples—eastern and southeastern Europe, for example—different house types, farmstead layouts, even the use of color can distinguish for the knowledgeable observer the ethnicity of the local population. The one-story "smoking-room" house of the northern Slavs with its covered entrance hall and stables all under one roof marks their areas of settlement even south of the Danube River. Blue-painted one-story, straw-roofed houses mark Croatian settlements. In the Danube Basin, areas of Slovene settlement are marked by the Pannonian house of wood and straw-mud. In Spain, the courtyard farmstead marks areas of Moorish influence.

It is impossible to delineate ethnic regions of the United States that correspond to the distinctive landscapes created by sharply contrasting cultural groups in Europe or other world areas. The reason lies in the mobility of Americans, the degree of acculturation and assimilation of immigrants and their offspring, and the significance of other than ethnic considerations in shaping the activities, the associations, and the material possessions of participants in an urbanized, mass communication society. What can be attempted is the delimitation of areas in which particular immigrant-group influences have played a recognizable or determinant role in shaping tangible landscapes and intangible regional "character."

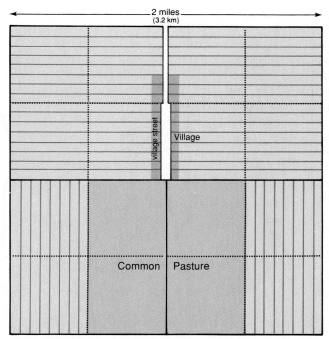

FIGURE 6.28 **A transplanted ethnic landscape.** The German-speaking Mennonites settled in Manitoba in the 1870s and recreated the agricultural village of their European homeland. Individual farmers were granted strip holdings in the separate fields to be farmed in common with the other villagers. The farmsteads themselves, with elongated rear lots, were aligned along both sides of a single village street in an Old World pattern.

REGION	APPROXIMATE DATES OF SETTLEMENT AND FORMATION	MAJOR SOURCES OF CULTURE (listed in order of importance)
NEW ENGLAND		
1a. Nuclear New England	1620–1750	England
1b. Northern New England	1750–1830	Nuclear New England, England
THE MIDLAND		
2a. Pennsylvania Region	1682–1850	England and Wales, Rhineland, Ulster, 19th-Century Europe
2b. New York Region or New England Extended	1624–1830	Great Britain, New England, 19th-Century Europe, Netherlands
THE SOUTH		
3a. Early British Colonial South	1607–1750	England, Africa, British West Indies
3b. Lowland or Deep South	1700–1850	Great Britain, Africa, Midland, Early British Colonial South, aborigines
3b-1. French Louisiana	1700–1760	France, Deep South, Africa, French West Indies
3c. Upland South	1700–1850	Midland, Lowland South, Great Britain
3c-1. The Bluegrass	1770–1800	Upland South, Lowland South
3c-2. The Ozarks	1820–1860	Upland South, Lowland South, Lower Middle West
THE MIDDLE WEST		
4a. Upper Middle West	1800–1880	New England Extended, New England, 19th-Century Europe, British Canada
4b. Lower Middle West	1790–1870	Midland, Upland South, New England Extended, 19th-Century Europe
4c. Cutover Area	1850–1900	Upper Middle West, 19th-Century Europe

REGION	APPROXIMATE DATES OF SETTLEMENT AND FORMATION	MAJOR SOURCES OF CULTURE (listed in order of importance)
THE WEST		
5a. Upper Rio Grande Valley	1590–	Mexico, Anglo America, aborigines
5b. Willamette Valley	1830–1900	Northeast U.S.
5c. Mormon Region	1847–1890	Northeast U.S., 19th-Century Europe
5d. Central California	(1775–1848) 1840–	(Mexico) Eastern U.S., 19th Century Europe, Mexico, East Asia
5e. Colorado Piedmont	1860–	Eastern U.S., Mexico
5f. Southern California	(1760–1848) 1880–	(Mexico) Eastern U.S., 19th and 20th-Century Europe, Mormon Region, Mexico, East Asia
5g. Puget Sound	1870–	Eastern U.S., 19th and 20th-Century Europe, East Asia
5h. Inland Empire	1880–	Eastern U.S., 19th and 20th-Century Europe
5i. Central Arizona	1900–	Eastern U.S., Southern California, Mexico
REGIONS OF UNCERTAIN STATUS OR AFFILIATION		
A. Texas	(1690–1836) 1821–	(Mexico) Lowland South, Upland South, Mexico, 19th-Century Central Europe
B. Peninsular Florida	1880–	Northeast U.S., the South, 20th-Century Europe, Antilles
C. Oklahoma	1890–	Upland South, Lowland South, aborigines, Middle West

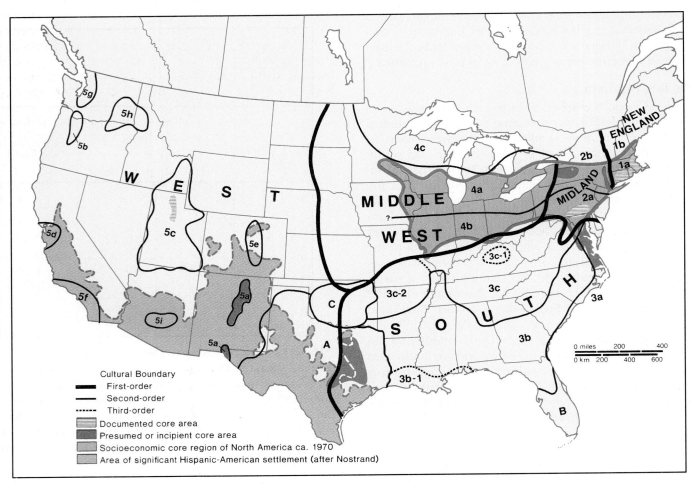

FIGURE 6.29   **Culture areas of the United States** based on multiple lines of evidence.

From Wilbur Zelinsky, *The Cultural Geography of the United States,* Rev. ed., 1992, pp. 118–119. Redrawn by permission of Prentice-Hall, Inc., Englewood Cliffs, NJ.

The "melting pot" producing a uniform cultural amalgam, we have seen, has been more American myth than reality. Therefore, there has occurred an inevitable, persistent disparity between the landscapes created by diverse immigrant groups and the national uniformity implicit either in the doctrine of first effective settlement or the concept of amalgamation. That disparity was summarized by Wilbur Zelinsky, as shown in Figure 6.29. The cultural areas are European in origin and can be seen as the expansionary product of three principal colonial culture hearths of the Atlantic Seaboard: the *New England,* the *South,* and the *Midland.* As the figure indicates, the "Middle West" is the product of the union of all three colonial regions. The popularly conceived American "West" probably exists not as a separate unit but as a set of subregions containing cross sections of national population with cultural mixing, but as yet with no achieved cultural uniformity.

Summary

Ethnic diversity is a reality in most countries of the world and is increasing in many of them. Immigration, refugee streams, guest workers, and job seekers all contribute to the mixing of peoples and cultures in an area. The mixing is not complete, however. Ethnicity—affiliation in a group sharing common identifying cultural traits—is fostered by territorial separation or isolation. In much of the world that separation identifies home territories within which the ethnic group is dominant and with which it is identified. In societies of immigrants—Anglo America, for example—such homelands are replaced by ethnic colonies, enclaves, or ghettos of self-selected or imposed separation from the larger host society. Cluster migration helped establish such colonies in rural America; chain migration encouraged their development in cities.

The 19th- and early 20th-century American central city displayed pronounced areal segregation as immigrant groups established and clung to protective ethnic neighborhoods while they gradually adjusted to the host culture. A continual population restructuring of urban areas occurred as older groups underwent acculturation, amalgamation, or assimilation, and new groups entered the urban social mix. The durability of ethnic neighborhoods has depended, among other considerations, on the degree of social distance separating the minority group from the host culture and on the significance the immigrant group places on long-term maintenance of their own cultural identity. That is, ethnic communities have been the product of both external and internal forces.

In other world regions, similar spatial separation of immigrant groups by racial, cultural, national, tribal, or village origin within the alien city is common. In Europe, because of the uncertain legal and employment status of many foreign populations and the restricted urban housing market they enter, ethnic enclaves have taken a different form, extent, and level of segregation than has been the case in North America.

Ethnicity is one of the threads of diversity in the spatial cultural fabric. Throughout the world, ethnic groups have imprinted their presence on the landscapes in which they have developed or to which they have transported their culture. In land division, house and farm building style, settlement patterns, and religious structures, the beliefs and practices of distinctive groups are reflected in the cultural landscape. Ethnicity is not, of course, the sole thread in the regional tapestry of societies. Folk culture joins ethnicity as a force creating distinctions between peoples and imparting special character to area. Countering those culturally based sources of separation is the behavioral unification and reduction of territorial distinctiveness that results from the leveling impact of popular culture. It is to these two additional strands in the cultural fabric—folk and popular culture—that we turn our attention in the following chapter.

KEY WORDS

acculturation 184
adaptation 180
amalgamation theory 184
assimilation 184
behavioral (cultural) assimilation 184
chain migration 189
charter group 188
cluster migration 189
colony 200
culture rebound 203

ethnic enclave 200
ethnic geography 178
ethnic group 178
ethnic island 188
ethnic province 189
ethnicity 179
ethnocentrism 179
first effective settlement 188
gene flow 180

genetic drift 180
ghetto 200
host society 181
natural selection 180
race 180
segregation 196
social distance 196
structural assimilation 184
tipping point 198

FOR REVIEW

1. How does *ethnocentrism* contribute to preservation of group identity? In what ways might an ethnic group sustain and support new immigrants?

2. How are the concepts of *ethnicity, race,* and *culture* related?

3. What have been some of the principal time patterns of immigration flows into the United States? Into Canada? How are those patterns important to an understanding of present-day social conflicts in either or both countries?

4. How may *segregation* be measured? Does ethnic segregation exist in the cities of world areas outside of North America? If so, does it take different form than in American cities?

5. What forces external to ethnic groups help to create and perpetuate immigrant neighborhoods? What functions beneficial to immigrant groups do ethnic communities provide?

6. What kinds of land survey were important in the allocation of property in the North American culture realm? With which *charter groups* were the different survey systems associated? How did survey systems affect settlement patterns?

SELECTED REFERENCES

Agócs, Carol. "Ethnic Groups in the Ecology of North American Cities." *Canadian Ethnic Studies/Études ethniques du Canada* 11, no. 2 (1979):1–13. Calgary, Alberta: Canadian Ethnic Studies Association, 1979.

Aiken, Charles S. "A New Type of Black Ghetto in the Plantation South." *Annals of the Association of American Geographers* 80 (1990):223–246.

Allen, James P., and Eugene Turner. "Spatial Patterns of Immigrant Assimilation." *Professional Geographer* 48, no. 2 (1996):140–155.

Allen, James Paul, and Eugene James Turner. *We the People: An Atlas of America's Ethnic Diversity.* New York: Macmillan, 1988.

Anderson, Kay J. "The Idea of Chinatown: The Power of Place and Institutional Practice in the Making of a Racial Category." *Annals of the Association of American Geographers* 77, no. 4 (1987):580–595.

Asante, Molefi K., and Mark T. Mattson. *Historical and Cultural Atlas of African Americans.* New York: Macmillan, 1991.

Bach, Robert L., et al. *Changing Relations: Newcomers and Established Residents in U.S. Communities.* New York: Ford Foundation, 1993.

Bean, Frank. D., and Marta Tienda. *The Hispanic Population of the United States.* New York: Russell Sage Foundation, 1990.

Bell-Fialkoff, Andrew. "A Brief History of Ethnic Cleansing." *Foreign Affairs* 72, no. 3 (Summer 1993):110–121.

Boal, F. W. "Ethnic Residential Segregation." In *Social Areas in Cities,* vol. 1, edited by D. Herbert and R. Johnston, pp. 41–79. New York: John Wiley & Sons, 1976.

Brass, Paul R. *Ethnicity and Nationalism: Theory and Comparison.* Newbury Park, CA: Sage, 1991.

Carlson, Alvar W. *The Spanish-American Homeland.* Baltimore, MD: Johns Hopkins University Press, 1990.

Cavalli-Sforza, L. Luca, Paolo Menozzi, and Alberto Piazza. *The History and Geography of Human Genes.* Princeton, NJ: Princeton University Press, 1994.

Clarke, Colin, David Ley, and Ceri Peach, eds. *Geography and Ethnic Pluralism.* London: George Allen & Unwin, 1984.

Conzen, Michael P. "Ethnicity on the Land." In *The Making of the American Landscape,* edited by Michael P. Conzen, pp. 221–248. Boston: Unwin Hyman, 1990.

Dawson, Carl A. *Group Settlement: Ethnic Communities in Western Canada.* Toronto: Macmillan Company of Canada, 1936.

Driedger, Leo, ed. *The Canadian Ethnic Mosaic: A Quest for Identity.* Vol. 6, Canadian Ethnic Studies Association series. Toronto: McClelland and Stewart, 1978.

Edmonston, Barry, and Jeffrey S. Passel, eds. *Immigration and Ethnicity: The Integration of America's Newest Arrivals.* Washington, D.C.: The Urban Institute Press, 1994.

"Ethnicity and Geography." *Geo Journal* 30, no. 3 (July 1993). Special issue.

Fellows, Donald Keith. *A Mosaic of America's Ethnic Minorities.* New York: John Wiley & Sons, 1972.

Fernández-Armesto, Felipe, ed. *The Times Guide to the Peoples of Europe.* Boulder, CO: Westview Press, 1995.

Fix, Michael, and Jeffrey S. Passel. *Immigration and Immigrants: Setting the Record Straight.* Washington, D.C.: The Urban Institute, 1994.

Fuchs, Lawrence H. *The American Kaleidoscope.* Hanover, NH: University Press of New England, 1990.

Gastil, Raymond D. *Cultural Regions of the United States.* Seattle: University of Washington Press, 1975.

"Geography and Ethnic Groups in Western Canada." *Canadian Ethnic Studies/Études ethniques du Canada* 9, no. 2 (1977). Special issue.

Glebe, Günther, and John O'Loughlin, eds. "Foreign Minorities in Continental European Cities." *Erdkundliches Wissen* 84 (1987). Stuttgart: Franz Steiner Verlag.

Godfrey, Brian J. *Neighborhoods in Transition: The Making of San Francisco's Ethnic and Nonconformist Communities.* Vol. 27, *University of California Publications in Geography.* Berkeley: University of California Press, 1988.

Halli, Shiva S., Frank Trovato, and Leo Driedger, eds. *Ethnic Demography: Canadian Immigrant, Racial and Cultural Variations.* Ottawa: Carleton University Press, 1990.

Harris, Chauncy. "New European Countries and Their Minorities." *Geographic Review* 83, no. 3 (1993):301–320.

Harris, Cole. "French Landscapes in North America." In *The Making of the American Landscape,* edited by Michael P. Conzen, pp. 63–79. Boston: Unwin Hyman, 1990.

Harvard Encyclopedia of American Ethnic Groups. Cambridge, MA: Harvard University Press, 1980.

Heberer, Thomas. *China and Its National Minorities.* Armonk, NY and London, England: M. E. Sharpe, 1989.

Higham, John. "Multiculturalism and Universalism: A History and Critique." *American Quarterly* 45, no. 2 (1993):195–219.

Horak, Stephan M. *Eastern European National Minorities, 1919–1980: A Handbook.* Littleton, CO: Libraries Unlimited, 1985.

Hornbeck, David. "Spanish Legacy in the Borderlands." In *The Making of the American Landscape,* edited by Michael P. Conzen, pp. 51–62. Boston: Unwin Hyman, 1990.

Jasso, Guillermina, and Mark R. Rosenzweig. *The New Chosen People: Immigrants in the United States.* For the National Committee for Research on the 1980 Census. New York: Russell Sage Foundation, 1990.

Jiobu, Robert M. *Ethnicity and Assimilation.* Albany: State University of New York Press, 1988.

Kaplan, David H. "Two Nations in Search of a State: Canada's Ambivalent Spatial Identities." *Annals of the Association of American Geographers* 84, no. 4 (1994):585–606.

Katz, Yossi, and John C. Lehr. "Jewish and Mormon Agricultural Settlement in Western Canada: A Comparative Analysis." *The Canadian Geographer/Le Géographe Canadien* 35, no. 2 (1991):128–142.

Lai, David C. *Chinatowns: Towns within Cities in Canada.* Vancouver: University of British Columbia Press, 1988.

Lee, Trevor R. *Race and Residence: The Concentration and Dispersal of Immigrants in London.* Oxford: Clarendon Press, 1977.

Lieberson, Stanley, and Mary C. Waters. *From Many Strands: Ethnic and Racial Groups in Contemporary America.* Census Monograph Series. New York: Russell Sage Foundation, 1988.

MacDonald, John S., and Leatrice D. MacDonald. "Chain Migration, Ethnic Neighborhood Formation and Social Networks." *Millbank Memorial Fund Quarterly* 42, no. 1 (January 1964):82–91.

Martin, Philip, and Elizabeth Midgley. "Immigration to the United States: Journey to an Uncertain Destination." *Population Bulletin* 48, no. 2. Washington, D.C.: Population Reference Bureau, 1994.

Meinig, Donald W. *Atlantic America, 1492–1800.* Vol. 1 of *The Shaping of America: A Geographical Perspective on 500 Years of History.* New Haven, CT: Yale University Press, 1986.

Meinig, Donald W. *Continental America, 1800–1867.* Vol. 2 of *The Shaping of America.* New Haven, CT: Yale University Press, 1993.

Murphy, Alexander B. "Territorial Policies in Multiethnic States." *Geographical Review* 79 (1989):410–421.

Noble, Allen G., ed. *To Build in a New Land: Ethnic Landscapes in North America.* Baltimore, MD: Johns Hopkins University Press, 1992.

Nostrand, Richard L. *The Hispano Homeland.* Norman: University of Oklahoma Press, 1992.

O'Hare, William P. "America's Minorities: The Demographics of Diversity." *Population Bulletin* 47, no. 4.

Washington, D.C.: Population Reference Bureau, 1992.

O'Hare, William P., and Judy C. Felt. "Asian Americans: America's Fastest Growing Minority Group." *Population Trends and Public Policy,* no. 19. Washington, D.C.: Population Reference Bureau, 1991.

O'Hare, William P., Kelvin M. Pollard, Taynia L. Mann, and Mary M. Kent. "African Americans in the 1990s." *Population Bulletin* 46, no. 1. Washington, D.C.: Population Reference Bureau, 1991.

Peach, Ceri, Vaughn Robinson, and Susan Smith, eds. *Ethnic Segregation in Cities.* London: Croom Helm, 1981.

Price, Edward T. *Dividing the Land: Early American Beginnings of Our Private Property Mosaic.* Geography Research Paper 238. Chicago: University of Chicago Press, 1995.

Raitz, Karl B. "Themes in the Cultural Geography of European Ethnic Groups in the United States." *Geographical Review* 69 (1979):79–94.

Roseman, Curtis C., Gunther Thieme, and Hans Dieter Laux, eds. *Ethnicity: Geographic Perspectives on Ethnic Change in Modern Cities.* Lanham, MD: Rowman & Littlefield, 1995.

Ross, Thomas E., and Tyrel G. Moore, eds. *A Cultural Geography of North American Indians.* Boulder, CO: Westview Press, 1987.

Shumway, J. Matthew, and Richard H. Jackson. "Native American Population Patterns." *Geographical Review* 85, no. 2 (1995): 185–201.

Sowell, Thomas. *Ethnic America: A History.* New York: Basic Books, 1981.

Winsberg, Morton D. "Ethnic Segregation and Concentration in Chicago Suburbs." *Urban Geography* 7, no. 2

FOLK AND POPULAR CULTURE:

DIVERSITY AND UNIFORMITY

FOLK CULTURAL DIVERSITY
AND REGIONALISM   215

North American Hearths   216
Folk Building Traditions   218
The Northern Hearths   220
   The Lower St. Lawrence Valley   220
   Southern New England   222
   The Hudson Valley   223
The Middle Atlantic Hearths   224
   The Delaware Valley   224
   Chesapeake Bay   224
The Southern Hearths   225
   The Southern Tidewater   225
   The Mississippi Delta   225
Interior and Western Hearths   226
Architectural Diffusions   226
Folk Fencing in North America   227
Nonmaterial Folk Culture   228
Folk Food and Drink Preferences   229
   Folk and Customary Foods   229
   Drink   231
Folk Music   232
Folk Medicines and Cures   234
The Oral Folk Tradition   235
**Folk Cultural Regions of Eastern United
   States   235**
**The Passing of Folk Cultural
   Regionalism   237**

PATTERNS OF POPULAR
CULTURE   238

National Uniformities   239
The Shopping Mall   240
Outside the Mall   242
Diffusion Tracks   243
Regional Emphasis   244
Vernacular Regions   247

SUMMARY   248
KEY WORDS   249
FOR REVIEW   249
SELECTED REFERENCES   249

*A commercial strip in Holbrook, Arizona,
forcefully advertises elements of American
popular culture.*

In rural and frontier America before 1850 the games people played were local, largely unorganized individual and team contests. Running, wrestling, weight lifting, shooting, or—if the Native American influence had been strong—shinny (field hockey), kickball, or lacrosse. In the growing cities, rowing, boxing, cricket, fencing, and the like involved the athletically inclined, sometimes as members of sporting clubs and sponsored teams. Everywhere, horse racing was an avid interest. In the countryside, sports and games relieved the monotony and isolation of life and provided an excuse, after the contests, for meeting friends, feasting, and dancing. Purely local in participation, games reflected the ethnic heritage of the local community—the games of the homeland—as well as the influence of the American experience. In the towns, they provided the outdoor recreation and exercise otherwise denied to shop-bound clerks and artisans. Without easy transportation, contests at a distance were difficult and rare; without easy communication, sports results were of local interest only.

The railroad and the telegraph changed all that. Teams could travel to more distant points, and scores could be immediately known to supporters at home and rivals in other cities. Baseball clubs were organized during the 1850s throughout the East and the Middle West. The establishment of the National Association of Base Ball Players in 1857 followed shortly after the railroad reached Chicago; even before the Civil War, New York teams were competing throughout that state. After the war, the expanding rail network turned baseball into a national craze. The National League was organized in 1876; Chicago, Boston, New York, Washington, Kansas City, Detroit, St. Louis, and Philadelphia all had professional teams by the 1880s, and innumerable local leagues were formed. Horse racing, prizefighting, amateur and professional cycling races, and intercollegiate sports—football, baseball, rowing, and track and field contests—pitted contestants and drew crowds over long distances. Sports and games had been altered from small-group participations to national events. They were no longer purely local, traditional, informal expressions of community culture; rather, organized sport had emerged as a unifying, standardized expression of national popular culture.

The kaleidoscope of culture presents an endlessly changing design, different for every society, world region, and national unit, and different over time. Ever present in each of its varied patterns, however, are two repeated fragments of diversity and one spreading color of uniformity. One distinctive element of diversity in many societies derives from *folk* culture—the material and nonmaterial aspects of daily life preserved by smaller groups partially or totally isolated from the mainstream currents of the larger society around them. A second source of diversity in composite societies, as we saw in Chapter 6, is surely and clearly provided by *ethnic* groups, each with its distinctive characterizing heritage and traditions and each contributing to the national cultural mix. Finally, given time, easy communication, and common interests, *popular* culture may provide a unifying and liberating coloration to the kaleidoscopic mix, reducing differences between formerly distinctive groups though perhaps not totally eradicating them. These three elements—folk, ethnic, and popular—of the cultural mosaic are intertwined. We will trace their connections particularly in the North American context, where diversified immigration provided the ethnic mix, frontier and rural isolation encouraged folk differentiation, and modern technology produced the leveling of popular culture. Along the way, we will see evidences of their separate influences in other societies and other culture realms.

FIGURE 7.1   Spectator sports emerged as a major element in American popular culture following the Civil War. The Cincinnati Red Stockings of 1869, shown in this photograph, were the first openly professional baseball team; the National League was established in 1876. Mark Twain, an early fan, wrote: "Baseball is the very symbol, the outward and visible expression of the drive and push and struggle of the raging, tearing, booming nineteenth century." Organized football was introduced as a college sport—also in 1869—when Rutgers played Princeton in the first intercollegiate game.

FOLK CULTURAL DIVERSITY AND REGIONALISM

Folk connotes traditional and nonfaddish, the characteristic or product of a homogeneous, cohesive, largely self-sufficient group that is essentially isolated from or resistant to outside influences, even of a larger society surrounding it. **Folk culture,** therefore, may be defined as the collective heritage of institutions, customs, skills, dress, and way of life of a small, stable, closely knit, usually rural community. Tradition controls folk culture, and resistance to change is strong. The homemade and handmade dominate in tools, food, music, story, and ritual. Buildings are erected without architect or blueprint, but with plan and purpose clearly in mind and by a design common to the local society using locally available building materials. When, as in North America, folk culture may represent a modification of imported ideas and techniques, local materials often substitute for a less-available original substance even as the design concepts are left unchanged.

Folk life is a cultural whole composed of both tangible and intangible elements. **Material culture** is made up of physical, visible things: everything from musical instruments to furniture, tools, and buildings. Collectively, material culture comprises the **built environment,** the landscape created by humans. At a different scale it also constitutes the contents of household and workshop. **Nonmaterial culture,** in contrast, is the intangible part, the mentifacts and sociofacts expressed in oral tradition, folk song and folk story, and customary behavior. Ways of speech, patterns of worship, outlooks and philosophies are parts of the nonmaterial component passed to following generations by teachings and examples.

Within Anglo America, true folk societies no longer exist; the universalizing impacts of industrialization, urbanization, and mass communication have been too pervasive for their full retention. Generations of intermixing of cultures, of mobility of peoples, and of leveling public education have altered the meaning of *folk* from the identification of a group to the recognition of a style, an article, or an individual preference in design and production. The Old Order Amish, with their rejection of electricity, the internal combustion engine, and other "worldly" accoutrements in favor of buggy, hand tools, and traditional dress are one of the least altered—and few—folk societies of the United States (Figure 7.2).

Canada, on the other hand, with as rich a mixture of cultural origins as the United States, has kept to a much later date clearly recognizable ethnically unique folk and decorative art traditions. One observer has noted that nearly all of the national folk art traditions of Europe can be found in one form or another well preserved and practiced somewhere in Canada. From the earliest arts and crafts of New France to the domestic art forms and folk artifacts of the Scandinavians, Germans, Ukrainians, and others who settled in western Canada in the late 19th and early 20th centuries, folk and ethnic are intertwined through transference of traditions from homelands and their adaptation to the Canadian context.

Folk culture today is more likely to be expressed by individuals than by coherent, isolated groups. The collector of folk songs, the artist employing traditional materials and styles, the artisan producing in wood and metal products

(a)

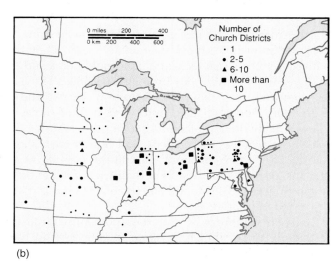

(b)

FIGURE 7.2   (*a*) Motivated by religious conviction that the "good life" must be reduced to its simplest forms, Amish communities shun all modern luxuries of the majority secular society around them. Children use horse and buggy, not school bus or automobile, on their daily trip to this rural school in east central Illinois. (*b*) **Distribution of Old Order Amish communities** in the United States.

identified with particular groups or regions, the quilter working in modern fabrics the designs of earlier generations all are perpetuating folk culture: material culture if it involves "things"; nonmaterial if the preserved tradition relates to song, story, recipe, or belief. In this respect, each of us bears the evidence of folk life. Each of us uses proverbs traditional to our family or culture; each is familiar with and can repeat childhood nursery rhymes and fables. We rap wood for luck and likely know how to make a willow whistle, how to plant a garden by phases of the moon, and what is the "right" way to prepare a favorite holiday dish.

When many persons share at least some of the same folk **customs**—repeated, characteristic acts, behavioral patterns, artistic traditions, and conventions regulating social life—and when those customs and artifacts are distinctively identified with any area long inhabited by a particular group, a *folk culture region* may be recognized. As with landscape evidence of ethnicity, folk culture in its material and nonmaterial elements may be seen to vary over time and space and to have hearth regions of origin and paths of diffusion.

Indeed, in many respects, ethnic geography and folk geography are extensions of each other and are logically intertwined. The variously named "Swiss" or "Mennonite" or "Dutch" barn introduced into Pennsylvania by German immigrants has been cited as physical evidence of ethnicity; in some of its many modifications and migrations, it may also be seen as a folk culture artifact of Appalachia. The folk songs of, say, western Virginia can be examined either as nonmaterial folk expressions of the Upland South or as evidence of the ethnic heritage derived from rural English forebears. In the New World, the debt of folk culture to ethnic origins is clear and persuasive. With the passage of time, of course, the dominance of origins recedes and new cultural patterns and roots emerge.

North American Hearths

North America is an amalgam of peoples who came as ethnics and stayed as Americans or Canadians. They brought with them more than tools and household items and articles of dress. Importantly, they brought clear ideas of what tools they needed, how they should fashion their clothes, cook their food, find a spouse, and worship their deity. They knew already the familiar songs to be sung and stories to be told, how a house should look and how a barn should be raised. They came, in short, with all the mentifacts and sociofacts to shape the artifacts of their way of life in their new home (Figure 7.3). (Mentifacts, sociofacts, and artifacts are discussed in Chapter 2.)

Their trappings of material and nonmaterial culture frequently underwent immediate modification in the New World. Climates and soils were often different from their homelands; new animal and vegetable foodstuffs were found for their larders. Building materials, labor skills, and items of manufacture available at their origins were different or lacking at their destinations. What the newcomers brought in

FIGURE 7.3 Reconstructed Plimoth Plantation. The first settlers in the New World carried with them fully developed cultural identities. Even their earliest settlements reflected established ideas of house and village form. Later they were to create a variety of distinctive cultural landscapes reminiscent of their homeland areas, though modified by American environmental conditions and material resources.

tools and ideas they began to modify as they adapted and adjusted to different American materials, terrains, and potentials. The settlers still retained the essence and the spirit of the old but made it simultaneously new and American.

The first colonists, their descendants, and still later arrivals created not one but many cultural landscapes of America, defined by the structures they built, the settlements they created, and the regionally varied articles they made or customs they followed. The natural landscape of America became settled, and superimposed on the natural landscape as modified by its Amerindian occupants, were the regions of cultural traits and characteristics of the European immigrants (see "Vanished American Roots"). In their later movements and those of their neighbors and offspring, they left a trail of landscape evidence from first settlement to the distant interior locations where they touched and intermingled.

The early arrivers established footholds along the East Coast. Their settlement areas became cultural hearths, nodes of introduction into the New World—through *relocation diffusion*—of concepts and artifacts brought from the Old. Locales of innovation in a new land rather than areas of new invention, they were—exactly as their ancient counterparts discussed in Chapter 2—source regions from which relocation and *expansion diffusion* carried their cultural identities deeper into the continent (Figure 7.4). Later arrivals, as we have seen in Chapter 6, not only added their own evidence of passage to the landscape but often set up independent secondary hearths in advance of or outside of the main paths of diffusion.

Each of the North American hearths had its own mix of peoples and, therefore, its own landscape distinctiveness. French settlement in the lower St. Lawrence Valley

merica, like every other world region, had its own primitive, naïve and indigenous original architecture. But this was the architecture of Indians—the bark houses of the Penobscots, the long houses of the Iroquois, the tipis of the Crows, the mounds of the Mandans, the pueblos of the Zuñi, the hogans of the Navajos, the [plank] dwellings of Puget Sound.

Some of these were even elegant, many contained seeds of promise; but we swept them all aside. Indian words and Indian foods passed into the American culture but nothing important from the Indian architecture, save a belated effort to imitate the form but not the function of the pueblos. (The so-called "Spanish" architecture of the Hispanic borderlands and northern Mexico, however—adobe walled with small windows and flat roofs supported by wooden beams—was of Amerindian, not European, origin.)

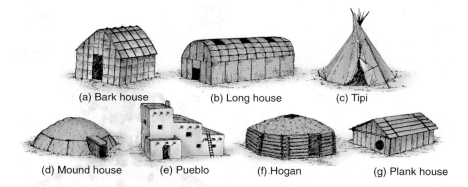

(a) Bark house   (b) Long house   (c) Tipi

(d) Mound house   (e) Pueblo   (f) Hogan   (g) Plank house

Source: From John Burchard and Albert Bush-Brown, *The Architecture of America: A Social and Cultural History*, (Boston: Little, Brown & Company, 1961), p. 57. © 1961, The American Institute of Architects.

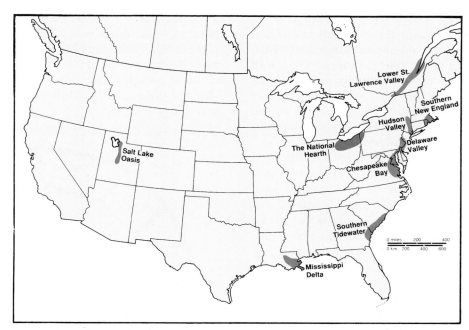

FIGURE 7.4   **Early North American culture hearths.** The interior "national hearth," suggested by Richard Pillsbury, represents a zone of coalescence in the eastern Midwest, from which composite housing ideas dispersed farther into the interior.

recreated there the long lots and rural house types of northwestern France. Upper Canada was English and Scottish with strong infusions of New England folk housing carried by Loyalists leaving that area during the Revolutionary War. Southern New England bore the imprint of settlers from rural southern England, while the Hudson Valley hearth showed the impress of Dutch, Flemish, English, German, and French Huguenot settlers.

In the Middle Atlantic area, the Delaware River hearth was created by a complex of English, Scotch-Irish, Swedish, and German influences. The Delaware Valley below Philadelphia also received the eastern Finns, or Karelians, who introduced, according to one viewpoint, the distinctive "backwoods" life-styles, self-sufficient economies, and log-building techniques and house designs of their forested homeland. It was their pioneering "midland" culture that was the catalyst for the rapid advance of the frontier and successful settlement of much of the interior of the continent and, later, of the Pacific Northwest.

Coastal Chesapeake Bay held English settlers, though Germans and Scotch-Irish were added elements away from the major rivers. The large landholdings of the area dispersed settlement and prevented a tightly or clearly defined culture hearth from developing, although distinctive house types that later diffused outward did emerge there. The Southern Tidewater hearth was dominantly English modified by West Indian, Huguenot, and African influences. The French again were part of the Delta hearth, along with Spanish and Haitian elements.

Later in time and deeper in the continental interior, the Salt Lake hearth marks the penetration of the distant West by the Mormons, considered an ethnic group by virtue of their self-identity through religious distinctiveness. Spanish American borderlands, the Upper Midwest Scandinavian colonies, English Canada, and the ethnic clusters of the Prairie Provinces could logically be added to the North American map of distinctive immigrant culture hearths.

The ethnic hearths gradually lost their identification with immigrant groups and became source regions of American architecture and implements, ornaments and toys, cookery and music. The evidence of the homeland was there, but the products became purely indigenous. In the isolated, largely rural American hearth regions, the ethnic culture imported from the Old World was partially transmuted into the folk culture of the New.

Folk Building Traditions

People everywhere house themselves and, if necessary, provide protection for their domesticated animals. Throughout the world, native rural societies established types of housing, means of construction, and use of materials appropriate to their economic and family needs, the materials and technologies available to them, and the environmental conditions they encountered. Because all these preconditions are spatially variable, rural housing and settlement patterns are comparably varied, a diversity increasingly lost as standardization of materials (corrugated metal, poured concrete, cinder block, and the like) and of design replace the local materials and styles developed through millennia by isolated folk societies.

The world is not yet, of course, totally homogenized. The family compound of the Bambara of Mali (Figure 7.5) is obviously and significantly different from the farmstead of a North American rural family. The Mongol or Turkic *yurt*, a movable low-rounded shelter of felt, skin, short poles, and rope, is a housing solution adapted to the needs and materials of nomadic herdsmen of the Asian grasslands (Figure 7.6*a*). A much different solution with different materials is reached by the Masai, a similar nomadic herding society but of the grasslands of eastern Africa. Their temporary home was traditionally the *manyatta*—an immovable, low-rounded hut made of poles, mud, and cow dung—which was abandoned as soon as local grazing and water supplies were consumed (Figure 7.6*b*). As the structures in Figure 7.7 can only slightly suggest, folk housing solutions in design and materials provide a worldwide mosaic of nearly infinite diversity and ingenuity.

Within the North American realm, although architectural diversity does not reach global proportions, the variety of ethnic and regional origins of immigrant streams and the differences in encountered environmental conditions assured architectural contrasts among the several settlement hearths of the New World. The landscapes of structures and settlements creating those contrasts speak to us of their creators' origins, travels, adaptations to new locales, and importations and retentions of the habits and customs of other places. One of the joys of travel in a world region as internally diverse as that of North America is to observe the variations in its cultural landscape, to listen to the many voices that tell of its creation through houses, barns, farmsteads, and village designs.

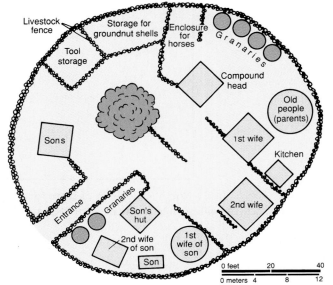

FIGURE 7.5　The extended family compound of the Bambara of Mali.

(a)

(b)

FIGURE 7.6   (*a*) A Uygur *yurt* in Xinjiang Province, China; (*b*) the Masai *manyatta*.

(a)

(b)

(c)

(d)

(e)

FIGURE 7.7   The common characteristics of preindustrial folk housing are an essential uniformity of design within a culture group and region, a lack of differentiation of interior space, a close adaptation to the conditions of the natural environment, and frequently ingenious use of available materials and response to the dictates of climate or terrain. (*a*) Stone house of Nepal; (*b*) Icelandic sod farm house; (*c*) reed dwelling of the Uros people on Lake Titicaca, Peru; (*d*) a Dogon village in Mali, West Africa; (*e*) traditional housing on Nias Island, off the west coast of Sumatera, Indonesia.

(*a*) and (*b*) Courtesy of Colin E. Thorn.

The folk cultural heritage is now passing; old farm structures are replaced or collapse with disuse as farming systems change. Old houses are removed, remodeled, or abandoned, and the modern, the popular, or the faddish everywhere replaces the evidences of first occupants. A close-knit community may preserve the past by resisting the present, but except where the efforts of preservationists have been successful in retaining and refurbishing one or a few structures or where outdoor museums and recreations have been developed, the landscapes—the voices—of the past are gradually lost. Many of those fading voices first took on their North American accents in the culture hearths suggested in Figure 7.4. They are still best heard in the house types associated with them.

The Northern Hearths

Vernacular house styles—those built in traditional form but without formal plans or drawings—were part of the material culture of early colonists that met new conditions in America. In the Northeast, colder, snowier winters posed different environmental challenges than did the milder, frequently wetter climates of northwestern Europe, and American stone and timber were more accessible and suitable construction materials than the clay and thatch common in the homeland. Yet the new circumstances at first affected not at all, or only slightly, the traditional housing forms (see "Log Cabin Myths and Facts").

The Lower St. Lawrence Valley

The St. Lawrence Valley (Figure 7.4) remains as one of the few areas with structural reminders of a French occupation that spread widely but impermanently over eastern North America (Figure 7.8). There, in French Canada, beginning in the middle of the 17th century, three major house types were introduced. All were styles still found in western France today.

In the lower valley below Quebec City, *Norman cottages* appear as near-exact replicas of houses of the Normandy region of northern France, with immense hipped

LOG CABIN MYTHS AND FACTS

First settlers to New England and Virginia brought with them familiarity with timber framing, wattle-and-daub infilling, and thatch roofing. They did not know of and did not construct the log cabins that are now commonly associated with pioneer settlement throughout the Eastern Seaboard. Log buildings were familiar, however, to the Swedes, Germans, and most particularly the eastern Finns, who introduced them into the Delaware Valley area. In Pennsylvania and much of the rest of North America, log construction—employing various building traditions and techniques—marked an initial settlement period. Log housing was not glorified by those who built and occupied it, however. As soon as affluence permitted, the log cabin was replaced (or concealed behind a new facade) by housing of greater prestige or social acceptability. Harold R. Shurtleff explains how the log cabin assumed a bigger role in American folklore than it had in the hearts and minds of its builders.

[T]o deny that log cabins or log dwelling houses existed in the early English settlements, or to maintain the fact that framed houses were built by the English without passing through a log cabin stage, is to take issue with an American belief that is both deep-seated and tenacious.

The reasons for this emotional basis for the Log Cabin Myth are not far to seek. In the nineteenth century Americans began to marvel at their own progress, and to make a virtue of their early struggles with the wilderness. The log cabin as a symbol of democracy was dramatized in two famous presidential campaigns, those of 1840 and 1860. In literature the popular "Log-Cabin to White House" series firmly fixed the log cabin as the proper scenario for the birth of a great American; as early as 1840 Daniel Webster was apologizing for not having been born in one, and as late as 1935, we are told, a "considerable legend" had already grown up around the "log-cabin origins" of Roy Harris, the Oklahoma composer. Thus, the log cabin came to be identified with "Old Hickory," "Tippecanoe," and Abraham Lincoln, with democracy and the frontier spirit, and with the common man and his dream of the good life, and those persons, types, and forces of

which Americans are justly proud. The log cabin, along with the Indian, the long rifle, and the hunting shirt is associated with one of the greatest of all conquests, the winning of the West. It gives us that sense of the dramatic which we seek in our history. . . . [W]e need not be surprised that careless historians projected it back into the earliest colonial settlements, or that many Americans today feel a sense of outrage when told that neither Captain John Smith [of Virginia colony] nor Governor Bradford [of Massachusetts Bay] nor any of the founding fathers dwelt in a log cabin, or ever saw one.

Reprinted by permission of the publisher from *The Log Cabin Myth: A Study of the Early Dwellings of the English Colonists in North America* by Harold R. Shurtleff, Cambridge, Mass.: Harvard University Press, Copyright © 1939 by the President and Fellows of Harvard College .

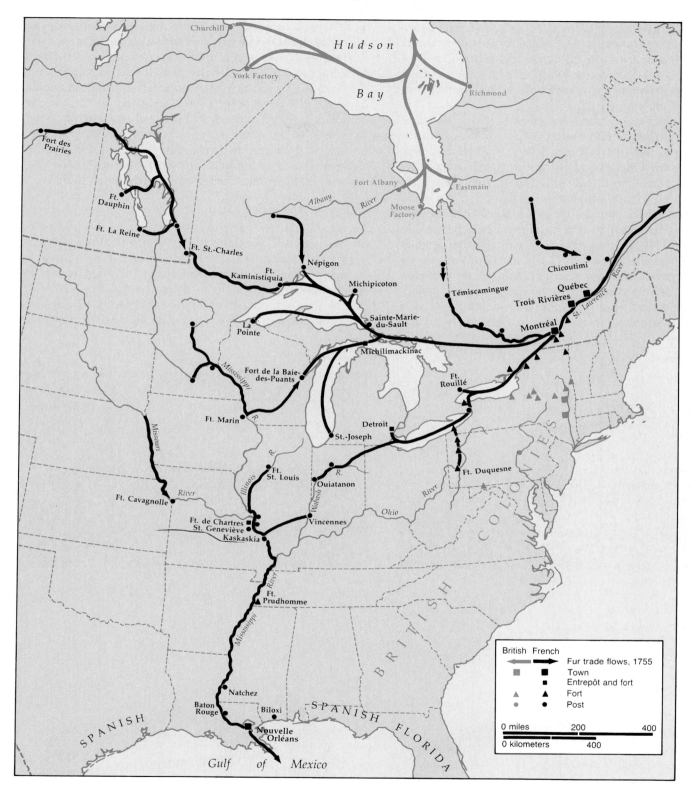

FIGURE 7.8 **The "arc of French settlement" about 1750.** The French were interested in the fur trade, not in the conversion of the wild landscape to one of farming and settlement. They needed the original forested environment, peopled not by settlers but by the Native American suppliers of the furs they sought. Except for the Lower St. Lawrence and parts of Atlantic Canada, most French influence was confined to their few larger towns, such as New Orleans and Detroit. French rural settlers were few; their impact on the landscape diminished rapidly away from towns and was more reflective of local than of French influences.

Sources: Based on Cole Harris, "French Landscapes in North America," in *The Making of the American Landscape*, ed. Michael P. Conzen (Boston: Unwin Hyman, 1990), Fig. 4.1, p. 66; and R. Cole Harris, *Historical Atlas of Canada*, vol. 1, *From the Beginning to 1800* (Toronto: University of Toronto Press, 1987), Plate 40.

roofs steeply pitched to wide or upturned (bell-cast) eaves (Figure 7.9*a*). In France, the bell-cast eaves threw water from the roof away from the clay base and earthen walls of the house. In the St. Lawrence Valley, the building material was fieldstone embedded in mortar, but inertia and custom preserved the traditional design.

The *Quebec cottage* was more widely distributed and more varied in construction materials than the Norman cottage. It featured two unequal rooms, a steeply pitched (but gabled) roof with wide, overhanging eaves and, frequently, an elevated front porch or galley. External walls were built of mortared and whitewashed stone rubble or, often, were framed and sheathed with sawn weatherboard (Figure 7.9*b*). Later versions usually had two chimneys, near but inside the gable ends. The *Montreal house*—so named because of its concentration in the Upper St. Lawrence Lowland—was a larger stone structure more characteristic of the crowded city than of the open countryside. It has distinctive heavy stone gables containing one or more chimney flues carried above the roof line as a protection against fire (Figure 7.9*c*).

As well as house styles, the French brought the characteristic *Quebec long barn,* stretching 50 or more feet wide with several bays and multiple barn functions efficiently contained within a single structure. It was an attractive design for keeping the farmer indoors in bitterly cold Canadian winters, though weather protection was not the primary purpose of the French original (Figure 7.9*d*). While the St. Lawrence Valley house types were found in other areas of French settlements in North America—Louisiana, the St. Genevieve area of Missouri, northern Maine (Figure 7.8)— the long barn was not carried outside of French Canada.

Southern New England

The rural southern English colonists who settled in New England carried memories of the heavily framed houses of their home countries: sturdy posts and stout horizontal beams held together by simple joinery and sided by overlapping clapboards. The series of New England vernacular houses that emerged in the new settlements all displayed that construction and were further distinguished by steep

(a)

(b)

(c)

(d)

FIGURE 7.9   Buildings of the Lower St. Lawrence hearth region. (*a*) The Norman cottage; (*b*) the Quebec cottage; (*c*) the Montreal house; (*d*) the Quebec long barn.

(*a*), (*b*), and (*c*) Courtesy of John A. Jakle. (*d*) Allen G. Noble, *Wood, Brick, and Stone*, vol. 2 (Amherst: University of Massachusetts Press, 1984), p. 18. Reprinted by permission.

roofs and massive central chimneys. Brick and stone buildings were rare in New England. Clay and lime for their construction were not easily available, and houses built of those materials had not been part of the home district culture of the settlers.

Among the primary house types evolved in the New England hearth were: (1) the *garrison house,* a two-story house with central chimney separating two rooms of roughly equal size on each floor. Its characteristic second floor overhang was a relict of urban house design in medieval Europe (Figure 7.10*a*); (2) the *saltbox house,* showing that same floor plan enlarged through a shed or lean-to addition giving extra rooms on the first floor to the rear and therefore having an asymmetrical gable roof (Figure 7.10*b*); and (3) the *New England large house,* a still larger structure of up to 10 rooms with lobby entrance, central chimney, and a symmetrical gable roof. Later, the central-chimney design gave way completely to the *Georgian* style with paired chimneys that reinforced the sense of balance (Figure 7.10*c*).

The New England hearth also created the *gable-front* house and its modification, the *upright-and-wing* or *lazy-T* house (Figure 7.10*d*). Versions of the upright-and-wing—undergoing modifications as they migrated—became landscape staples in both rural and urban areas from western New York into the Middle West. Among the rural outbuildings throughout the southern part of New England, the small rectangular English barn organized around its central threshing floor was the rule.

The Hudson Valley

An area settled by a complex mixture of Dutch, French, Flemish, English, and German settlers, the Hudson Valley showed a comparable mixture of common house forms. Little evidence of the once-dominant Dutch influence now remains. Dutch houses were usually of stone or brick, often one-and-a-half story, one-room-deep elongated structures, frequently with the gable end toward the front. Dutch barns, roughly square in plan with steep-pitched roof, horizontal

(a)

(b)

(c)

(d)

FIGURE 7.10   New England house types. (*a*) The garrison house; (*b*) the saltbox house; (*c*) the Georgian-style variant of the New England large house; (*d*) an upright-and-wing house, the wing representing a one-story extension of the basic gable-front house plan.

(*b*) and (*d*) Courtesy of John A. Jakle.

clapboard siding, and multiple entrances in the gable ends, were found throughout the area of Dutch settlement.

The Middle Atlantic Hearths

The Middle Atlantic hearths were also ethnically diverse and the sites of vernacular architecture more influential on North American housing styles than any other early settlement areas. The log cabin, later carried into Appalachia and the trans-Appalachian interior, evolved there. There, too, was introduced what would later be called the *I house*—a two-story structure one room deep with two rooms on each floor—that became prominent in the Upper South and the Lower Middle West in the 19th century.

The Delaware Valley

Dutch and Swedish settlers were less successful in colonizing the Delaware valley hearth area than were the English Quakers and Germans who arrived in the late 17th and early 18th centuries. The latter were joined by Finns, Welsh, and Scotch-Irish, each of whom contributed to the diversity of stone, brick, frame, and log housing of the district. Urban Quakers, arriving with the memory of the Great London Fire of 1666 still fresh in mind, built in red brick small versions of the Georgian-style houses then becoming fashionable in England. Germans, Scandinavians, and particularly, eastern Finns introduced the first New World log houses in the 17th century in Delaware and New Jersey. It was they, not the English colonists, who gave America that frontier symbol.

The Delaware Valley hearth (sometimes called the Pennsylvania hearth) is particularly noted for two vernacular house designs. The *four-over-four house*—so called in reference to its basic two-story floor plan with four rooms up and four down—was an amalgam of Georgian and Germanic house design wedded to a smaller Quaker plan (Figure 7.11*a*). The classic *I house* almost always was a "two-over-two" arrangement (7.11*b*).

A famous and widespread contribution of the Delaware Valley hearth to American architecture was not a house style but a barn—or rather a series of related designs of the German bank barn. Unlike the earlier English and Dutch barns that were essentially crop oriented, the bank barn combined animal shelter with the grain storage and threshing functions. The variously named German, Pennsylvania, Dutch, or Schweizer (Swiss) barn—in its several versions—was carried from its Pennsylvania origins to the continental interior and from the southern Appalachians northward to Ontario (Figure 6.23). Perhaps no other hearth region had as widespread an influence on American vernacular architecture as did the Pennsylvania hearth. Migrants from there carried their material culture southwestward along the Great Valley of Virginia, as well as due west into the Ohio Valley.

Chesapeake Bay

The area of dominantly English and Scotch-Irish settlement around Chesapeake Bay was rural and nearly devoid of large cities. Its settlers initially introduced wood-framed houses, though brick construction became increasingly common. Both building types featured raised foundations, outside end chimneys, and one-deep floor plans. Kitchens were often detached, and by the 18th century adaptation to the more southerly temperature conditions was reflected in added front porches and front-to-rear ventilation passages. Popular throughout the Middle Atlantic hearth regions, the classic I house was also part of the vernacular architecture of the Chesapeake Bay hearth (Figure 7.11*b*); it was early carried

(a)

(b)

FIGURE 7.11   House types of the Middle Atlantic hearths. (*a*) Four-over-four house; (*b*) the traditional or classic I house, with its two rooms on each floor separated by central hallways, had a varying number of façade openings and, usually, end chimneys located in the standard gable roof, but all symmetrically organized. This brick version, characteristic of the Upper South, has a detached summer kitchen.

(*a*) Courtesy of John A. Jakle.

into the Upper South and, after the 1850s, into the interior. Sometimes of brick but overwhelmingly of frame construction, its builders and building materials were brought by the new railroads to Indiana, Illinois, and Iowa (the *I*'s after which the house was named).

The Southern Hearths

Both climate and a new ethnic cultural mix altered the form of vernacular housing in the southern hearths along the Atlantic Coast and in the Gulf and Delta areas. Although local responses to these influences varied, the overall result was housing in a different style for different needs in the South than in the North.

The Southern Tidewater

Along the southeastern Atlantic coastal region of South Carolina and Georgia, English and Huguenot settlers faced problems of heat, humidity, and flooding not encountered farther to the north. The malaria, mosquitos, and extreme heat plaguing their inland plantations during the summer caused the wealthy to prefer hot-season residence in coastal cities such as Charleston, where sea breezes provided relief. The result was the characteristic *Charleston single house,* a name related to its single row of three or four rooms ranged from front to back and lined on the outside of each floor by a long veranda along one side of the structure (Figure 7.12). Set with its narrow end facing the street, the house was often raised on stilts above marshy land and to prevent flooding from hurricanes. The *Huguenot-plan house* introduced by French settlers was a square, hipped-roof design, usually two-story with a double file of rooms. Mostly brick in its later versions, the Huguenot-plan house was diffused throughout the southeast from its Tidewater origins.

The Mississippi Delta

The French, dominant in the Lower St. Lawrence Valley far to the north, established their second North American culture hearth in New Orleans and along the lower Mississippi during the 18th century (Figure 7.8). There, French influences from Nova Scotia and the French Caribbean islands—Haiti, specifically—were mixed with Spanish and African cultural contributions. Again, heat and humidity were environmental problems requiring distinctive housing solutions. The *grenier house* emerged as the standard design for rural Louisiana. Usually of frame construction with cypress siding, the structures were raised on posts or pillars several feet off the ground for cooling and protection against floodwaters, ground rot, and termites.

The *shotgun house* is a simple, inexpensive, and efficient house style identified with the Delta area but owing its origin to Africa by way of Port-au-Prince, Haiti, and introduced into America by free Haitian blacks who settled in the Delta before the middle of the 19th century. The shotgun house is easily recognized in both urban and rural settings by its narrow gable front, its considerable length of three or four rooms, and its front-to-back alignment of all room door openings (Figure 7.13). Quickly and cheaply made of sawed lumber, they found favor far beyond the delta area as affordable urban and rural housing.

FIGURE 7.12   The Charleston single house.

(a)

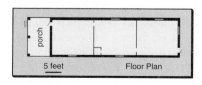

(b)

FIGURE 7.13   (*a*) Shotgun cottages in Claiborne County, Mississippi; (*b*) one variant of a shotgun cottage floor plan.

(*a*) Courtesy of John A. Jakle.

Interior and Western Hearths

Other immigrant groups, some from the eastern states, others from abroad—and all encountering still different environmental circumstances and building material sources—made their impress on local areas of the interior and North American West. Settlers of many different origins on the Great Plains initially built sod dugouts or rammed earth houses in the absence of native timber stands. Later, after the middle of the century, "balloon frame" construction—utilizing newly available cheap wire nails and light lumber milled to standard dimensions—became the norm in the interior where heavy timbers for traditional post and beam construction were not available. The strong, low-cost housing the new techniques and materials made possible owed less to the architectural traditions of eastern America than it did to the simplicity and proportional dimensions imposed by the standardized materials. Midwest vernacular house types developed—including the one-story gabled rectangle, double-wing, and two-story foursquare farmhouses, quickly constructed by local carpenters or the farmers themselves.

The thick-walled *Spanish adobe house,* long and single-storied with a flat or low-pitched earth-covered roof entered Anglo America through the Hispanic borderlands (Figure 6.11) but in most of its features owed more to indigenous Pueblo Indian design than to Spanish origins. In the Far West, Hispanic and Russian influences were locally felt, although housing concepts imported from the humid East predominated. In the Utah area, Mormon immigrants established the *central-hall house,*—related to both the I house and the four-over-four house—as the dominant house type.

A variety of ethnic and architectural influences met and intermingled in the Pacific Northwest. French Canadians produced a closely knit ethnic settlement on the Willamette River at French Prairie (between Salem and Portland, Oregon). Chinese came to the coal mines of Vancouver Island in the 1860s; later, thousands were employed in the construction of the Northern Pacific Railroad. By the 1870s an architecturally distinctive Chinatown was centered around the foot of Yesler Way and Occidental Avenue in Seattle, and similar enclaves were established in Tacoma, Portland, and other urban centers. But most immigrants to the British Columbia–Washington–Oregon regions were of North American not foreign birth, and the vast majority on the United States side came from midwestern roots, representing a further westward migration of populations whose forebears (or who themselves) were part of the Middle Atlantic culture hearths. Some—the earliest—carried to the Oregon and Washington forested regions the "midland" American backwoods pioneer culture and log-cabin tradition first encountered in the Delaware Valley hearth; others brought the variety of housing styles already well represented in the continental interior.

Architectural Diffusions

These vernacular architectural origins and movements were summarized by the cultural geographer Fred Kniffen, who thought that house types of the eastern United States and ultimately of much of Anglo America could be traced to three source regions on the Atlantic Coast, each feeding a separate diffusion stream: New England, Middle Atlantic, and Southern Coastal (Figure 7.14). *New England,* he argued, gave rise to a series of evolving house types based on a simple English original, variants of which spread westward with the settlers across New York, Ohio, Indiana, and Illinois and into Wisconsin and Iowa.

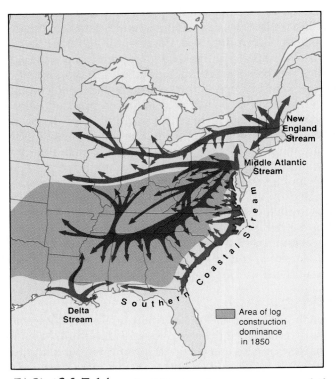

FIGURE 7.14   **Architectural source areas and the diffusion of building methods** from the Atlantic Seaboard hearths. The map emphasizes log and frame construction as of 1850. The variation in the width of stream paths suggests the strength of the influence of the various hearths on vernacular housing away from the coast. The Southern Coastal Stream was limited in its influence to the coastal plain. The Delaware Valley hearth not only exerted a strong influence on the Upland South but also became—along with other Middle Atlantic hearths—the dominant vernacular housing influence in the lower Middle West and the continental interior. By 1850 and farther to the west, new expansion cores were emerging around Salt Lake City, in coastal California, and in the Willamette Valley area of Oregon—all bearing the imprint of housing designs that first emerged in eastern hearths.

The *Middle Atlantic* source region had the most widespread folk housing influence of the three Atlantic Coast hearths. Its principal contributions were the English *I house* and the Finnish-German log building. Its major diffusion directions were southward along the Appalachian Uplands, with offshoots in all directions, and westward across Pennsylvania. Multiple paths of movement from this hearth converged in the Ohio Valley Midwest, creating an interior "national hearth" of several intermingled streams (Figure 7.4), and from there spread north, south, and west. In this respect, the narrow Middle Atlantic region played for vernacular architecture the same role its Midland dialect did in shaping the linguistic geography of the United States, as discussed on page 147.

The earliest diffusion from the Middle Atlantic hearth was the backwoods frontier culture that carried rough log carpentry to all parts of the forested East and, eventually, westward to the northern Rockies and the Pacific Northwest. The identifying features of that building tradition were the dogtrot and saddlebag house plans and double-crib barn designs. The basic unit of both house and barn was a rectangular "pen" ("crib" if for a barn) of four log walls that characteristically stood in tandem with an added second room that joined the first at the chimney end of the house. The resultant two-room central chimney design was called a *saddlebag house.* Another even more common expansion of the single-pen cabin was the *dogtrot* (Figure 7.15), a simple roofing-over of an open area left separating the two pens facing gable toward gable.

Although rough hewn log cabins and the better-built log houses that more permanent settlers constructed were soon replaced as the margin of denser settlement forced the frontier farther inland, both dogtrot and saddlebag houses and double-crib barns retained their favor in parts of the South. They were carried during the 19th century across the intervening grasslands to the wooded areas of the mountains and the Pacific Coast. The first log buildings of settlements and farmsteads of the Oregon territory, for example, were indistinguishable from their eastern predecessors of the preceding century.

The third source area, in the Lower Chesapeake, spread its remarkably uniform influence southward as the *Southern Coastal Stream,* diffusing its impact inland along numerous paths into the Upland South (Figure 7.14). In that area of complex population movements and topographically induced isolations, source area architectural styles were transformed into truly indigenous local folk housing forms. By 1850, diffusions from the eastern architectural hearths had produced a clearly defined folk housing geography in the eastern half of the United States and subsequently, by relocation and expansion diffusion, had influenced vernacular housing throughout Anglo America. The French and Caribbean influences of the Delta Stream, in contrast, were much more restricted and localized.

Folk Fencing in North America

Fencing, a nearly essential adjunct of agricultural land use, has been used as an indicator of the folk cultural traditions of farm populations, as a guide to settlement periods and stages, and as evidence of the resources and environmental conditions the settlers found. The stone fence, for example, was an obvious response to the need to clear glacial fieldstone before cultivation, and over 250,000 miles of stone fences were in existence in the 1870s in New York and New England. Elsewhere, angular or flat stones in sedimentary rock areas—in southern Ohio, Indiana, or parts of Kentucky, for example—made fences easier to build and maintain than did the rounded glacial boulders of New England.

The heavily forested eastern hearth regions provided an abundance of timber and poles for a variety of wooden fences, many based on European models. The "buck" fence, identical to some French folk fences, was reproduced in North America from French Canada southward into the Southern Appalachians (Figure 7.16a). The wattle fence of interlaced poles and branches (Figure 7.16b) was common in medieval Europe, known and briefly used by early settlers of Massachusetts and Virginia, but not found elsewhere in North America.

(a)

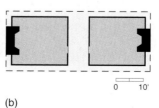

(b)

FIGURE 7.15   The "dogtrot" house.

FIGURE 7.16 Folk fencing of the eastern United States. (*a*) A buck fence; (*b*) a wattle or woven fence; (*c*) the angled-rail, snake, or worm fence; (*d*) a post-and-rail fence.

The angled-rail, "snake," or "worm" fence was a dominant American fence form for much of the 19th century until increasing labor costs and wood scarcity made it uneconomical. Its earlier attraction was its ease of construction—it required no post holes—and its use of abundant farm-produced wood; it was widely found in the South and in the eastern portion of the Middle West (Figure 7.16c). Indeed, wherever the backwoods pioneers temporarily settled, the zigzag log fence enclosed their forest clearings. The design was carried into the Pacific Northwest from Oregon to British Columbia, to be replaced only as new generations of farmers appeared and farm woodlots were reduced.

The post-and-rail fence, a form that consumed less land and fewer rails than did the angled fence, was particularly popular in southern New England and the Delaware Valley areas (Figure 7.16d). After the establishment of an American steel industry during the last half of the 19th century—and in the grasslands of the Great Plains—wire fenc-

ing, barbed wire in particular, became the commonly encountered form of stock enclosure or crop protection. Briefly, however, both sod fences and hedge fences (the Osage orange in particular) were popular from the forest margin westward to the mountains.

Nonmaterial Folk Culture

Houses burn, succumb to rot, are remodeled beyond recognition, or are physically replaced. Fences, barns, and outbuildings are similarly transitory features of the landscape, lost or replaced by other structures in other materials for other purposes as farms mechanize, consolidate, no longer rear livestock, are abandoned, or are subdivided for urban expansion. The folk housing and farm buildings that seem so solid a part of the built environment are, in reality, but temporary features of it.

Impermanent, too, for the most part are the tools and products of the folk craft worker. Some items of daily life and decoration may be preserved in museums or as household heirlooms; others may be exchanged among collectors of antiques. But inevitably, material folk culture is lost as the artifacts of even isolated groups increasingly are replaced by products of modern manufacture and standardized design. In many ways more permanent records of our folk heritages and differentials are to be found in the intangibles of our lives, in the nonmaterial folk culture that all of us possess and few recognize.

Ways of life change and the purposes of old tools are forgotten, but favorite foods and familiar songs endure. Nonmaterial characteristics may more indelibly mark origins and flows of cultures and peoples than physical trappings outmoded, replaced, or left behind. One important aspect of folk geography is the attention it pays to the spatial association of culture and environment. Folk societies, because of their subsistence, self-reliant economies and limited technologies, are deemed particularly responsive to physical environmental circumstances (see "Subsistence Household Economies"). Thus, foodstuffs, herbs, and medicinal plants naturally available or able to be grown locally—as well as shelter—have been especially subject to folk geographic study. Less immediately connected to the environment, but important indicators of the backgrounds and memories of a social group, are the stories, fables, and music traditional to it and transmitted within it.

Folk Food and Drink Preferences

Folk and Customary Foods

Cuisine, meaning the selection of foods and the style of cookery, is one of the most evident and enduring of the elements distinguishing cultural groups. Ethnic foods are the mainstay and the attraction of the innumerable fairs and "fests" held throughout the United States and Canada to celebrate the traditions of locally important groups. In the case of ethnic foods, of course, what is celebrated is the retention in a new environment of the food preferences, diets, and recipes that had their origin in a distant homeland. Folk food habits, on the other hand, are products of local circumstances; the dietary inputs are the natural foods derived from hunting, gathering, and fishing or the cultivated foods and domestic animals suited to the environmental conditions locally encountered.

The distinction between folk and ethnic is no clearer in foods than it is in other aspects of regional culture. Three observations may be made on this point. First, most societies have until recent times been intimately and largely concerned with food production on an individual and family basis. The close ties of people to environment—*folk* ties—are therefore particularly evident in food gathering and growing (Figure 7.17).

Second, most areas of the world have been occupied by a complex mix of peoples migrating in search of food and carrying food habits and preferences with them in their migrations. In the Americas, Australia, New Zealand, and a few

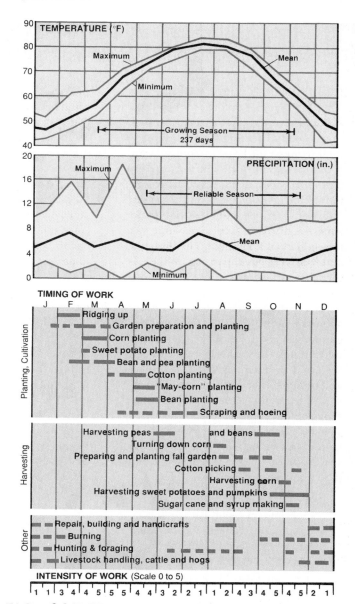

FIGURE 7.17 **The traditional "annual round" of folk culture farming** in the Upland South area of eastern Louisiana. The system and sequence of farming activities have varied little since the area was first settled around 1800. Frost danger dates and the phases of the moon are important in determining exact planting times. The corn, peas, and sweet potatoes assure the Upland farmer subsistence for family and animals. "The prudent folk farmer provides for subsistence first; then he turns to money crops"—in this case, cotton.

other regions of recent colonization and diversified settlement, we are aware of these differing *ethnic* origins and the recipes and customs they imply. In other world regions, ethnic and cultural intermixture is less immediately apparent. In Korea, for example, what outsiders see as a distinctive ethnic cookery best known, perhaps, for *kimch'i*—brined, pickled, and spiced vegetables in endless combinations and uniquely Korean—also incorporates Japanese and Chinese foodstuffs and dishes.

Whatever may be folk societies' regional differences based on the varying environments they occupy or the differing cultures they express, all have in common an economy of self-sufficiency based on family or small group cooperative effort. In the hearth regions and along the diffusion paths of settlement in Anglo America, the basic subsistence unit was the individual household. The husband and wife were equal partners in the enterprise, producing their own food, clothing, housing, furniture, and such necessary household goods as candles and soap. Beverly Sanders describes the gender division of labor in colonial households throughout much of the eastern hearth regions and the complex and arduous tasks assigned to women, who of necessity were masters of a wide range of folk crafts, artifacts, and skills. The essentials of women's responsibilities did not change in later years in the settlement of the United States or Canadian prairies or of the Northwest.

> By and large the man was responsible for building the house and furniture, clearing the land and planting crops, [and] slaughtering the larger animals. The woman was responsible for feeding and clothing all household members, manufacturing household necessities, housecleaning, nursing and child care. . . .
>
> Feeding a family involved far more than just cooking. The first care . . . was tending the fire. Throughout the year, the woman had to produce most of the food as well as cook it. She generally planted and tended a kitchen garden in which grew vegetables that could be stored in cold cellars for the winter, and others that could be dried. Fruits such as apples and berries were dried or preserved. The homemaker also cared for the barnyard animals. In order to have a chicken in the kettle for dinner, [she] had to slaughter, pluck and clean the fowl the same day. When cows and pigs were slaughtered she had the gigantic task of salting the beef to preserve it, and smoking the pig meat into ham and bacon. . . . Homemakers pickled a wide variety of foods. . . .
>
> Like food, clothing had to be made "from scratch." Fur and leather were popular materials for clothing [on the frontier] because they didn't need to be woven into cloth. Making linen cloth from the flax plant was a painstaking process that could take as long as sixteen months—from planting flax to spinning and bleaching thread. In wool making, the fleece from the sheep was cleaned, oiled and then combed to draw out the fibers to be spun into thread. Women wove the linen and woolen threads into cloth on a hand loom. . . . Clothing took a long time to make because it was generally worked on in odd hours that women could spare from more pressing chores. . . .
>
> [C]andle making had to be done during the busy autumn season before the long dark winter set in. Most were made from tallow, a rendered animal fat which was melted with boiling water in a large heavy kettle. Rows of candle wicks . . . were dipped into the melted tallow, cooled, then dipped again and again. . . . Since candles were always scarce, they were stored away very carefully, and used very sparingly.
>
> The most unpleasant chores of all were the cleaning of houses, clothing and people. Water was scarce and had to be carried into the house from a nearby stream. The cleaning agent—a soft soap—was manufactured by a tedious process that involved the combination of animal grease and lye, a caustic substance derived from ashes. . . . The busy homemaker could not possibly do laundry and housecleaning every day, but rather set aside special days for it once a month, or even once in three months. . . .
>
> Here is one day's work in the year 1775, set down in the diary of . . . a Connecticut girl:
>
> Fix'd gown for Prude,—Mend Mother's Riding-hood,—Spun short thread,—Fix'd two gowns for Welsh's girls,—Carded tow,—Spun linen,—Worked on Cheesebasket,—Hatchle'd flax with Hannah, we did 51 lbs. apiece,—Pleated and ironed,—Read a Sermon of Dodridge's,—Spooled a piece,—Milked the cows,—Spun linen, did 50 knots,—Made a Broom of Guinea wheat straw,—Spun thread to whiten,—Set a Red dye,—Had two Scholars from Mrs. Taylor's,—I carded two pounds of whole wool and felt Nationaly,—Spun harness twine,—Scoured the pewter.

Source: Beverly Sanders, *Women in the Colonial Era and the Early American Republic 1607–1820* (Newton, MA: WEEA/Education Development Center, 1979) pp. 18–21.

Third, food habits are not just matters of sustenance but are intimately connected with the totality of *culture* or *custom.* People eat what is available and also what is, to them, edible. Sheep's brains and eyeballs, boiled insects, animal blood, and pig intestines, which are delicacies in some cultures, may be abominations to others unfamiliar with the culture that offers them as special treats to guests. (For a special case of folk food habit, see "A Taste for Dirt.") Further, in most societies food and eating are considered a social, not just a personal, experience. Among Slavic peoples, to offer a guest bread and salt is a mark of esteem and welcome, and the bountiful and specially prepared meal as the mark of hospitality is common in nearly all cultures.

Hundreds of millions of people throughout the world eat dirt, usually fine clays, in a custom—called *geophagy*—so widespread it is usually considered to be within the range of normal human behavior. The practice is particularly common in sub-Saharan Africa, where hundreds of farmer and herder cultures consume dirt and, in some cases, sand. Africans brought as slaves to the United States carried the habit with them, and it is now prevalent among their descendants in the American South. It is also found widely in Asia, the Middle East, and parts of Latin America.

Wherever the custom is practiced, it is most common among pregnant women, though it may be more usual than reported among males as well. Some data indicate that from 30% to 50% of expectant mothers in large areas of Africa and among rural blacks in sections of the American South eat clay, as do hundreds of millions of women elsewhere in the world. Since dozens of animal species also consume clay, it is usually assumed that geophagy can supply minerals otherwise deficient in diets or can counteract nausea or diarrhea. (One of the most popular and widely available commercial remedies for diarrhea is based upon the clay *kaolin*). Heavy, chronic clay consumption can also cause serious ailments, including intestinal blockages, anemia, growth retardation, and zinc deficiency among some practitioners of the habit, however. As a folk food, clay may be specially selected for flavor (a sour taste is preferred). It is often mixed with bread dough or with vinegar and salt and baked, cooked, or smoked like bacon. It may also be used as a condiment or neutralizer. Nearly all varieties of wild potatoes growing in the Andes Mountains of South America (where the potato is native) contain toxic chemicals, as do some of the species cultivated and regularly eaten by the Indian populations there. To counteract intestinal distress caused by consuming the tubers, Indians either leach out the chemicals or, commonly, eat the potatoes with a dip made of clay and a mustardlike herb. That practice may have made it possible to domesticate this important food crop. Amerindians of the southwestern United States similarly use clay as a condiment with toxic wild tubers and acorns.

Like many other folk customs, geophagy is identified with specific groups rather than universally practiced. Like others, it seems to persist despite changes in the earlier dietary circumstances that may originally have inspired it and despite (in the United States) growing social pressure condemning the habit. Southern relatives may send favored varieties of clay to women who have moved to northern cities. Others, yielding to refined sensibilities, may substitute Argo starch, which has similar properties, for the clay consumption habits of their culture group.

The interconnections between the folk, the ethnic, and the customary in food habits and preferences are evident in the North American scene of mixed settlement and environmental diversity. Of course, the animals and plants nurtured, the basic recipes followed and flavorings added, and the specialized festive dishes of American folk groups have ethnic origins. Many originated abroad and were carried to and preserved in remote New World areas. Many were derived from the larder of the Amerindians and often varyingly used in different regional contexts. Turkey, squash, pumpkin, and cranberries were among them, as was the corn (maize) that appeared with time as southern grits, southwestern tortillas, and everywhere south of Pennsylvania the American replacement for wheat in the making of bread. Such classic American dishes as Brunswick stew, the clambake, smoked salmon, cornflakes, and beef jerky were originally Indian fare. Gradually, the environmental influences, isolation, and time spans implicit in the concept of folk culture created culinary distinctions among populations recognized as American rather than ethnic immigrants.

Shelves of cookbooks mark the general recognition of folk cuisines of the United States. Broad categories of New England, Creole, Southern, Chesapeake, Southwestern, and other regional cookery may be further refined into cookbooks containing Boston, Pennsylvania Dutch, Charleston, New Orleans, Tidewater, and other more localized recipes. Specific American dishes that have achieved fame and wide acceptance developed locally in response to food availability. New England seafood chowders and baked beans; southern pone, johnnycake, hush puppies, and other corn-(maize-) based dishes; the wild rice of the Great Lakes states; Louisiana crayfish (crawfish); southern gumbo; and salmon and shellfish dishes of the Pacific Coast are but a few of many examples of folk foods and recipes originally and still characteristic of specific cultural areas but subsequently made part of national food experience. Others, once locally known, effectively disappear as the culture or foodstuff source is lost. The "fern pie" of Oregon's frontier past and "pigeon pie" made with the now-extinct passenger pigeon are among many examples.

Drink

In the United States, drink also represents an amalgam between ethnic imports and folk responses and emphases. A colonial taste for rum was based on West Indian and Tidewater sugarcane and molasses. European rootstock was introduced, with mixed results, to develop vineyards in most seaboard settlements; the native scuppernong grape was tried for wine making in the South. Peach, cherry, apple, and other fruit brandies were distilled for home consumption. Whiskey was a barley-based import accompanying the Scots and the Scotch-Irish to America, particularly to the Appalachians. In the New World the grain base became native corn (maize), and whiskey making became a deeply rooted folk custom integral to the subsistence economy.

Whiskey also had cash economy significance. Small farmers of isolated areas far from markets converted part of their corn and rye crops into whiskey to produce a concentrated and valuable commodity conveniently transportable by horseback over bad roads. Such farmers viewed a federal excise tax imposed in 1791 on the production of distilled spirits as an intolerable burden not shared by those who could sell their grain directly. The tax led, first, to a short-lived tax revolt, the Whiskey Rebellion of 1794, in western Pennsylvania and, subsequently, to a tradition of moonshining—producing untaxed liquor in unlicensed stills. Figure 7.18 suggests the close association between its isolated Appalachian upland environment and illicit whiskey production in east Tennessee in the 1950s.

Folk Music

North American folk music began as transplants of familiar Old World songs carried by settlers to the New World. Each group of immigrants established an outpost of a European musical community, making the American folk song, in the words of Alan Lomax, "a museum of musical antiques from many lands." But the imported songs became Americanized, hybridization between musical traditions occurred, and American experience added its own songs of frontier life, of farming, courting, and laboring (see "The American Empire of Song"). Eventually, distinctive American styles of folk music and recognizable folk song cultural regions developed (Figure 7.19).

The *Northern* song area—including the Maritime Provinces of Canada, New England, and the Middle Atlantic states—in general featured unaccompanied solo singing in clear, hard tones. Its ballads were close to English originals, and the British connection was continuously renewed by new immigrants, including Scots and Irish. The traditional ballads and current popular songs brought by British immi-

grants provided the largest part of the Anglo-Canadian folk song heritage. On both sides of the border, the fiddle was featured at dances, and in the States, fife-and-drum bands became common in the early years of the Republic.

The *Southern Backwoods and Appalachian* song area, extending westward to east Texas, involved unaccompanied, high-pitched, and nasal solo singing. The music, based on English tradition and modified by Appalachian "hardscrabble" life, developed in isolation in upland and lowland settlement areas. Marked by moral and emotional conflict with an undercurrent of haunting melancholy, the backwoods style emerged in the modern period as the roots of the distinctive and popular genre of "country" music.

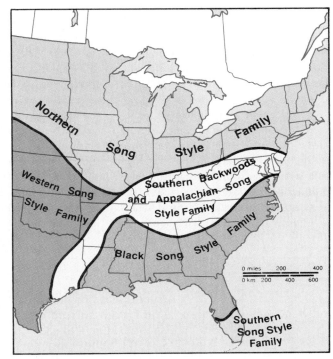

FIGURE 7.19   **Folk song regions of eastern United States.** Alan Lomax has indirectly outlined folk culture regions of the eastern United States by defining areas associated with different folk song traditions.

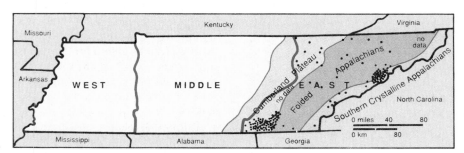

FIGURE 7.18   In the mid-1950s, official estimates put weekly moonshine production at 24,000 gallons in mountainous eastern Tennessee, at 6000 gallons in partially hilly middle Tennessee, and at 2000 gallons in flat western Tennessee. The map shows the approximate number of stills seized each month at that time in east Tennessee. Each dot indicates one still.

he map sings. The chanteys surge along the rocky Atlantic seaboard, across the Great Lakes and round the moon-curve of the Gulf of Mexico. The paddling songs of the French-Canadians ring out along the Saint Lawrence and west past the Rockies. Beside them, from Newfoundland, Nova Scotia, and New England, the ballads, straight and tall as spruce, march towards the West.

Inland from the Sea Islands, slave melodies sweep across the whole South from the Carolinas to Texas. And out on the shadows of the Smoky and Blue Ridge mountains the old ballads, lonesome love songs, and hoedowns echo through the upland South into the hills of Arkansas and Oklahoma. There in the Ozarks the Northern and Southern song families swap tunes and make a marriage.

The Texas cowboys roll the little doughies [*sic*] north to Montana, singing Northern ballads with a Southern accent. New roads and steel rails lace the Southern backwoods to the growl and thunder of Negro chants of labour—the axe songs, the hammer songs, and the railroad songs. These blend with the lonesome hollers of levee-camp mule-skinners to create the blues, and the blues, America's *cante hondo,* uncoils its subtle, sensual melancholy in the ear of all the states, then all the world.

The blues roll down the Mississippi to New Orleans, where the Creoles mix the musical gumbo of jazz—once a dirty word, but now a symbol of musical freedom for the West. The Creoles add Spanish pepper and French sauce and blue notes to the rowdy tantara of their reconstruction-happy brass bands, stir up the hot music of New Orleans and warm the weary heart of humanity. . . . These are the broad outlines of America's folk-song map.

The northern and southern traditions abutted in a transition zone along the Ohio Valley but blended together across the Mississippi to create the *Western* song area. There, factual narrative songs reflected the experiences of cowboy, riverman, sodbuster, and gold seeker. Natural beauty, personal valor, and feminine purity were recurring themes. Many songs appeared as reworked lumberjack ballads of the North or other modifications from the song traditions of the eastern United States.

Imported songs are more prominent among the traditional folk tunes of Canada than they are in the United States; only about one-quarter of Canadian traditional songs were composed in the New World. Most native Canadian songs—like their U.S. counterparts—reflected the daily lives of ordinary folk. In Newfoundland and along the Atlantic Coast, those lives were bound up with the sea, and songs of Canadian origin dealt with fishing, sealing, and whaling. Particularly in Ontario, it was the lumber camps that inspired and spread folk music. Anglo Canadian songs show a strong Irish character in pattern and tune and traditionally were sung solo and unaccompanied.

The *black* folk song tradition, growing out of racial and economic oppression, reflects a union of Anglo American folk song, English country dancing, and West African musical patterns. The African American folk song of the rural South or the northern ghetto was basically choral and instrumental in character; hands and feet were used to establish rhythm. A strong beat, a leader-chorus style, and deep-pitched mellow voices were characteristic.

Lomax dealt with and mapped only English-language folk song styles. To round out the North American scene, mention must also be made of French Canadian river and fur trader songs of the Northeast and the strong Mexican American musical tradition still vital and spreading in the Southwest.

Different folk music traditions have metamorphosed and spread in the 20th century as distinctive styles of popular music. Jazz emerged in New Orleans in the later 19th century as a union of minstrel show ragtime and the blues, a type of southern black music based on work songs and spirituals. Urban blues—performed with a harsh vocal delivery accompanied by electric guitars, harmonicas, and piano—was a Chicago creation, brought there largely by artists from Mississippi. Country music spread from its southern white ancestral areas with the development of the radio and the phonograph in the 20th century. It became commercialized, electrified, and amplified but remained at core modified folk music (Figure 7.20). Bluegrass style, a high-pitched derivative of Scottish bagpipe sound and church congregation singing tradition, is performed unamplified, true to its folk origins. Bluegrass identification with commercial singing groups bearing identities derived from place names emphasizes the ties of the people, the performers, and the land in the folk tradition.

As these examples of musical style and tradition show, the ethnic merges into the folk, and the folk blends into the popular—in music and in many other elements of culture. On the other hand, Anglo American religious folk songs

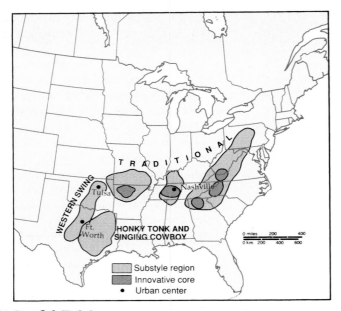

FIGURE 7.20 **Country music refuge areas.**
Traditional "old-timey" country music, little changed from that of the 18th and 19th centuries, was preserved into the 20th in five pockets of the Upland South, according to George Carney, before it turned modern and popular after World War II.

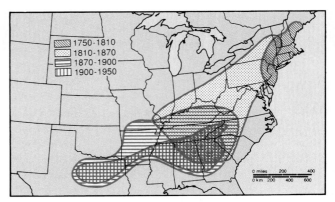

FIGURE 7.21 **The southward shift of white spirituals.** The southward shift and territorial contraction of the white spiritual folk song tradition in America is clearly shown on this map.

have become less popular and more spatially confined in an era of popular culture. The white spirituals, diffusing from their 18th-century New England hearth, covered much of the eastern United States during the 19th century, before contracting—far from their original core region—into the Lowland South during the 20th century (Figure 7.21).

The making of musical instruments is a recurring part of material folk culture traditions. For example, the zither was brought to the United States from northern and central Europe, but as the Pennsylvania Germans carried it southward into the southern Appalachians it became the American-made three- or four-stringed strummed or plucked dulcimer. The banjo has clear African origins, but by the end of the 19th century it had become a characteristically American folk instrument, versions of which—five-stringed and fretless—were homemade throughout the Southern Uplands. The fiddle was the preeminent Canadian folk instrument and—along with the bagpipe in Scottish communities—was the most common accompaniment for dancing. Both instruments were frequently homemade.

Folk Medicines and Cures

All folk societies—isolated and close to nature—have developed elaborate diversities of medicines, cures, and folk health wisdom based on the plants, barks, leaves, roots, and fruits of their areas of settlement and familiarity. Indeed, botanicals are a fundamental part of modern medicine, most of them initially employed by folk societies—quinine from the bark of the South American cinchona tree, for example, or digitalis, a heart stimulant derived from the dried leaf of the common foxglove.

In North America, folk medicine derived from the common wisdom of both the Old and the New World. The settlers assigned medicinal values to many garden herbs and spices they brought from Europe and planted everywhere in the eastern hearths. Basil, widely used in soups, stews, and salads, also was considered effective heart medicine and a cure for melancholy; thyme tea eased sorrow. Parsley was thought to be generally healthful, and fennel seeds, leaves, and roots properly prepared were deemed appropriate treatment for obesity. Sage was a specific for colds, balm was made into a tea for breaking fevers, marjoram was a cure-all for coughs, bronchitis, dropsy, and yellow jaundice. Lemon balm and rosemary were thought to prevent baldness, and boiled chervil roots, eaten cold, were healthful for the aged.

Native Americans provided Europeans with information and example of the curative values of a whole new set of plants and practices. Sassafras was a cure-all widely known in all the colonies—good as a purgative, as an ointment for bruises, as a "blood purifier," and as a means of curing fevers. Bearberry, a variety of cranberry, was an astringent and diuretic. Boneset (*Eupatoria*) was an emetic and purgative also used to cure intermittent fevers, arthritis, rheumatism, and gout. Goldenrod was a specific for fevers, pain in the chest, boils, and colds. American hemp was thought beneficial in dropsy, rheumatism, asthma, and as a diuretic. The list runs to the hundreds of medicinal plants from all sections of the country, cures (and practices such as sweat baths and cauterization) that were widely adopted by European newcomers, made part of their folk medicine and, in the case of some 200 different plants, incorporated into modern drug compendia.

Folkloric magic and symbolism were (and are) also important. Diseases of the head are best cured by tops of plants, while roots are specifics for leg problems. Brain fever should be treated by nut meats that resemble the brain. Scarlet fever should respond to wrapping patients in scarlet blankets and doctoring them with red medicine; yellow plants are good for jaundice. Wormroot, the Indians taught, is good for worms, and the red juice in bloodroot prevents bleeding.

Folk medicines, cures, and health wisdom in the United States have been best developed and preserved in the Upland South and Southern Appalachia, along the Texas-Mexican boundary in the Hispanic borderlands, and in the rural West among both white and Indian populations. But primitive peoples everywhere have their known cures and their folk wisdoms in matters medicinal, and all of us in our everyday references may unknowingly include reminders of that knowledge: "The hair of the dog that bit you" was not originally a recommendation for treating a hangover but an accepted remedy for curing the bite of a mad dog.

The Oral Folk Tradition

Folklore is the oral tradition of a group. It refers to ways of talking and interacting and includes proverbs, prayers, common expressions, and particularly, superstitions, beliefs, narrative tales, and legends. It puts into words the basic shared values of a group and informally expresses its ideals and codes of conduct. Folklore serves, as well, to preserve old customs and tales that are the identity of the folk group. The Brothers Grimm recorded German fairy tales early in the 19th century to trace the old mythologies and beliefs of the German people, not for the entertainment of the world's children.

Immigrant groups settling in the Americas brought with them different well-developed folklore traditions, each distinctive not only to the ethnic group itself but even to the part of the home country from which it came. In the New World, the established folklores of home areas became intermixed. The countries of North and South America contain many coexisting and interacting folklore traditions brought by early European colonizers, by transported African slaves, and by later diversified immigrant groups from both Europe and Asia.

The imported folk traditions serve to identify the separate groups in pluralistic societies. In some instances, the retention of folk identity and belief is long term because particular groups—Pennsylvania Dutch, Old Order Amish, and the Hasidim of Brooklyn, for example—isolate themselves from mainstream American culture. Other groups—in Appalachia, the Missouri Ozarks, and the Louisiana bayous—may retain or develop distinctive folklore traditions because isolation was thrust on them by remoteness or terrain.

Where immigrant groups intermixed, however, as in most New World countries, *syncretism*—the merging or fusion of different traditions—is characteristic. Old World beliefs, particularly in magic, begin to recede and are lost to later generations. Proverbs begin to be shared, common short jokes replace long folk tales as both entertainment and devices of instruction or ridicule of deviant behavior, and literacy reduces dependence on the reports and repetitions of knowledgeable elders. **Folkways**—the learned behavior shared by a society that prescribes accepted and common modes of conduct—become those of the country as a whole as acculturation and popularization dictate the ways of life of all.

With the passage of time, too, a new folklore of legend, myth, and hero develops. In the United States, Washington and the cherry tree, Patrick Henry's plea for liberty, the exploits of Jim Bowie or Davy Crockett, the song of John Henry the steel-driving man, or tales of Paul Bunyan become the common property and heritage of all Americans—a new national folklore that transcends regional boundaries or immigrant origins.

Folk Cultural Regions of Eastern United States

A small set of hearths or source regions of folk culture origin and dispersal have been recognized for the eastern United States. They are indicated in Figure 7.22. The similarity of the hearth locations and diffusion routes to the pattern of ethnically based architectural regions and flows shown in Figure 7.14 is unmistakable and a reminder that in the American context, "folk" and "ethnic" are intertwined and interchangeable when traced back to first settlement. Frontier settlers carrying to new, interior locations the artifacts and traditions of those hearth areas created a small set of indistinctly bounded eastern folk cultural regions (Figure 7.23). Although they have become blurred as folk traditions have died, their earlier contributions to American folk diversity remain clear.

From the small *Mid-Atlantic* region, folk cultural items and influences were dispersed into the North, the Upland South, and the Midwest. Southeastern Pennsylvania and the Delaware Valley formed its core and the Pennsylvania Dutch determined much of the Mid-Atlantic region's character. The eastern Finns added their log-building techniques and subsistence life-styles. Furniture styles, log-building techniques, decorative arts, house and barn types, and distinctive "sweet" cookery were among the purely European imports converted in the Mid-Atlantic hearth to American folk expressions.

The folk culture of the *Lowland South,* by contrast, derived from English originals and African admixtures. French influences in the Louisiana coastal extension and some down slope migrations from the highland areas add to the amalgam. Dogtrot and I houses became common; English cuisine was adapted to include black-eyed peas, turnip greens, sweet potatoes, small-bird pies, and syrups from sugarcane and sorghum. African origins influenced the widespread use of the banjo in music.

The *Upland South* showed a mixture of influences carried up from the Tidewater and brought south from the Mid-Atlantic folk region along the Appalachian highlands by settlers of German and Scotch-Irish stock. The sheltered isolation of the Upland South and its Ozark outlier encouraged the retention of traditional folk culture long after it had been lost in more accessible and exposed locations. Log houses and farm structures, rail fences, traditional art and music,

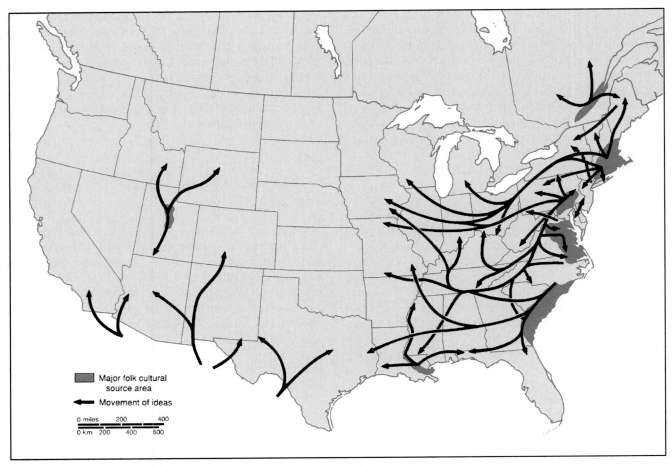

FIGURE 7.22   American folk culture hearths and diffusions.

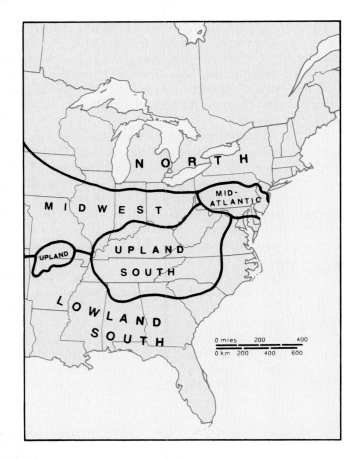

FIGURE 7.23   Material folk culture regions of the eastern United States.

and home-crafted quilts and furniture make the Upland South region a prime repository of folk artifacts and customs in the United States.

The *North*—dominated by New England, but including New York State, English Canada, Michigan, and Wisconsin—showed a folk culture of decidedly English origin. The salt-box house and Boston baked beans in pots of redware and stoneware are among characteristic elements. The New England–British domination is locally modified by French Canadian and central European influences.

The *Midwest*—a conglomerate of inputs from the Upland South, from the North, and particularly, from the Mid-Atlantic region—is the least distinctive, most intermixed and Americanized of the cultural regions. Everywhere the interior contains evidences, both rural and urban, of artifacts carried by migrants from the eastern hearths and by newly-arriving European immigrants. Folk geography in the Midwest is more the occasional discovery of architectural relics more or less pure in form, though frequently dilapidated, or the recognition of such unusual cultural pockets as those of the Amish, than it is a systematic survey of a defined cultural region.

The Passing of Folk Cultural Regionalism

By the early 20th century, the impacts of immigrant beginnings, settlement diffusions, and ethnic modifications had made themselves felt in a pattern of regionally differentiated rural cultural landscapes. The cities of the eastern and midwestern parts of the country were socially a world apart from the farms. Brash and booming with the economic success of rampant industrialization, the cities were in constant flux. Building and rebuilding, adding and absorbing immigrants and rural in-migrants, increasingly interconnected by passenger and freight railroad and by the national economic unification important since the 1870s, they were far removed in culture, outlook, and way of life from the agricultural areas in which they were physically but not emotionally located.

It was in the countryside that the most pronounced effects of regional cultural differentiation were to be discerned. Although the flow of young people to the city, responding to the push of farm mechanization and the pull of urban jobs and excitement, was altering traditional social orders and rhythms, the automobile, electrical appliances, and the lively mass medium of radio had not as yet obscured the distinction between urban and rural. The family farm, kinship and community ties, the traditions, ways of life, and artifacts of small-town and rural residence still existed as regionally varied composites. But those ways and artifacts, and the folk cultural regions they defined, were all being eroded and erased with the passage of time and the modernization of all segments of North American life and culture.

Regional character is a transient thing. New peoples, new economic challenges, and new technologies serve as catalysts of rapid change. By World War I and the Roaring Twenties, the automobile, the radio, motion pictures, and a national press began to homogenize America. The slowing of the immigrant stream and second-generation absorption of the common national culture served to blur and obliterate some of the most regionally distinctive cultural identifications. Mechanization, mass production, and mass distribution through mail order and market town diminished self-sufficiency and household crafts. Popular culture began to replace traditional culture in everyday life throughout the United States and Canada.

PATTERNS OF POPULAR CULTURE

In 1728, Mary Stith of Virginia wrote to a friend, then in England, "When you come to London pray favour me in your choice of a suit . . . suitably dressed with . . . whatever the fashion requires." In the 1750s, George Washington wrote to his British agent, Thomas Knox, to request "two pair of Work'd Ruffles . . . ; if work'd Ruffles shou'd be out of fashion send such as are not . . . ," noting "whatever Goods you may send me . . . you will let them be fashionable." In the 1760s, he asked another agent, Charles Lawrence, to "send me a Suit of handsome Cloth Cloaths. I have no doubts but you will choose a fashionable coloured Cloth as well as a good one and make it in the best taste. . . ." The American gentry might be distant and isolated, but they did not wish to be unstylish. The leading American women's magazine of the middle 19th century was *Godey's Lady's Book,* featuring hand-colored pictures of the latest foreign and American fashions in clothing and articles about household furnishings in the newest styles. Its contents influenced ladies of fashion in cities and towns throughout the settled United States. The Montgomery Ward and Sears, Roebuck catalogs appearing in the late 19th century served the same purpose for more ordinary goods, garments, and classes of customers.

Awareness of style and desire to copy the clothing, the manners, the new dances and entertainments, as they developed in the "fashion capitals" to which men and women looked for leadership, are nothing new to the 20th century. Indeed, the concept of style has been ascribed to the economic transformations in western Europe beginning in the 11th century that opened up the continent to long-distance travel and commerce, and introduced, through new production techniques, a wider variety of cloth and clothing possibilities than formerly known. The example in dress and manners of the rich and noble in leading capital cities was soon brought back by merchants and travelers to even the smallest provincial towns. Popular culture, based on fashions, standards, or fads developed in centers of influence and prestige, became a new and important reality over wide areas and across social strata.

By general understanding, popular culture stands in opposition to folk or ethnic culture. The latter two suggest individuality, small group distinctiveness, and above all, tradition. **Popular culture,** in contrast, implies the general mass of people, primarily but not exclusively urban based, constantly adopting, conforming to, and quickly abandoning ever-changing common modes of behavior and fads of material and nonmaterial culture. Popular culture presumably substitutes for and replaces folk and ethnic differences.

From another point of view, the distinctions between the three classes of culture are not that clear and precise. Popular culture has been defined as "our way of life"—how we act (and why), what we eat and wear, how we amuse ourselves, what we believe, whom we admire. Such a definition is appropriate as well for members of recognizable folk and ethnic groups. The distinction, if one is to be made, must be based on the universality of the "way of life" described. Ethnic culture is preserved as behavioral norms—along with material and nonmaterial components—that set a recognizable national, social, or religious minority group apart from a majority culture; their way of life is not accepted by the mass society among which they live. Folk culture, too, affects small groups; it is individually and community oriented, self-sufficient, reinforcing, and only slowly altered from within. Isolation or tradition keeps it separate and distinctive.

Popular culture then becomes the way of life of the mass of the population, reducing though perhaps not eliminating regional folk and ethnic differences. In so doing, it becomes both a leveling and a liberating force. It serves to obliterate those locally distinctive life-styles and material and nonmaterial cultures that develop when groups remain isolated and ethnocentric. Uniformity is substituted for differentiation, and group identity is eroded. At the same time, however, the individual is liberated through exposure to a much broader range of available opportunities—in clothing, foods, tools, recreations, and life-styles—than ever were available in a cultural environment controlled by the restrictive and limited choices imposed by custom and isolation. Although broad areal uniformity may displace localisms, it is a cultural uniformity vastly richer in content and possibilities than any it replaces.

That uniformity is frequently, though not exclusively, associated with national populations: the American or Canadian way of life distinguished from the English, the Japanese, or others. Even these distinctions are eroding as popular culture in many aspects of music, movies, sports (soccer, for example), and the like becomes internationalized (Figure 7.24). Popular culture becomes dominant with the wide dissemination of common influences and with the mixing of cultures that force both ethnic and folk communities to become aware of and part of a larger homogeneous society.

Initially, the printing press was the unifying agent. Later, industrialization, urbanization, television and national advertising, increased leisure time, and decreased self-sufficiency became the devices that in all advanced societies erode traditional differentiations and standardize behavior

FIGURE 7.24   Soccer has become the world's most popular sport, with a television audience approaching 2 billion worldwide for the quadrennial World Cup soccer finals. The game here is being played in Madrid, Spain.

among the general population and within the great number of subcultures (such as that of college students) that have emerged. The result is a material and nonmaterial cultural mix that is not necessarily better or worse than the folk and ethnic cultures lost. It is, however, certainly and obviously different from the traits and distinctions of the past.

National Uniformities

Landscapes of popular culture tend to acquire uniformity through the installation of standardized facilities. National motel chains announced by identical signs, advertised by repetitious billboards, and featuring uniform facilities and services may comfort travelers with the familiar but also deny them the interest of regional contrast. Fast-food restaurants—franchised, standardized, and merchandized as identical—carry single logos, building designs, and menus across cultural boundaries and national borders (Figure 7.25). They provide the assurance of the known and the tolerable but insulate the palate from the regionally distinctive. Even food outlets identified with ethnics have lost their cultural char-

FIGURE 7.25   Western fast-food chains, classics of standardized popular culture, have gone international—and bilingual—as this restaurant row in Shenyang, China reveals.

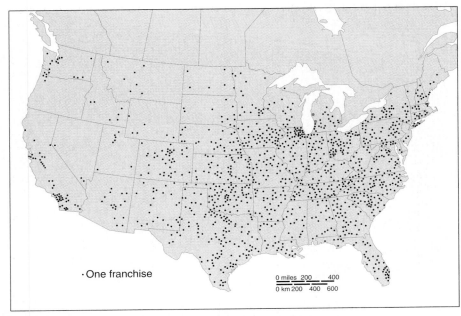

· One franchise

0 miles 200   400
0 km 200 400 600

FIGURE 7.26   The locations of pizza parlors of a single national chain.

acter. The pizza has become American, not Italian (Figure 7.26), just as the franchised Mexican American taco and burrito have escaped their regional and ethnic confines and been carried nationwide. Chain gas stations, discount stores, and other enterprises carry on the theme of familiarity of outlet and standardization of product and service wherever one resides or journeys.

Many of these elements of popular culture are oriented toward the automobile, the ubiquitous means of local and interregional travel (Figure 7.27). Advertisements' distinctiveness of design assures instant recognition, and their clustering along highways and main streets guarantees that whatever the incidence of regional character still remaining, the public face of town and highway is everywhere the same (Figure 7.28).

The Shopping Mall

That sameness of popular culture has been carried indoors into the design, merchants, and merchandize of the shopping mall. Major regional malls have been created in every part of North America that boasts a metropolitan population large enough to satisfy their carefully calculated purchasing-power requirements. Local and neighborhood malls extend the concept to smaller residential entities. With their mammoth parking lots and easy access from expressways or highways, America's 38,000 large and small malls are part of

the automobile culture that helped create them after World War II. Increasingly, however, they stand in standardized separation from the world of movement and of regional contrast. Enclosed, temperature controlled, without windows or other acknowledgment of a world outside, they cater to a full range of homogenized shopping and consuming wants with a repetitive assemblage of brand name products available in a uniform collection of national chain outlets.

Some assume monumental size, approximating the retail space contained in the central business districts of older medium-sized and large cities (Figure 7.29). For example, the West Edmonton Mall in Edmonton, Alberta, was at its completion in 1986 the world's largest shopping mall; it contains 836 stores, 110 restaurants, 20 movie theaters, a 360-room hotel, plus such other recreational features as roller coasters, carousels and other rides, a miniature golf course, a 600-foot water slide, and a hockey rink. A slightly smaller U.S. counterpart opened in Bloomington, Minnesota in 1992. More recently, expansion of established malls has outpaced development of new ones and by the end of 1995 both Woodfield Mall near Chicago and the King of Prussia mall near Philadelphia claimed the "world's largest" title after their renovation and enlargement. Malls are, it has been suggested, an idealized, Disneyland version of the American myth of small-town sanitized intimacy, itself a product of popular culture.

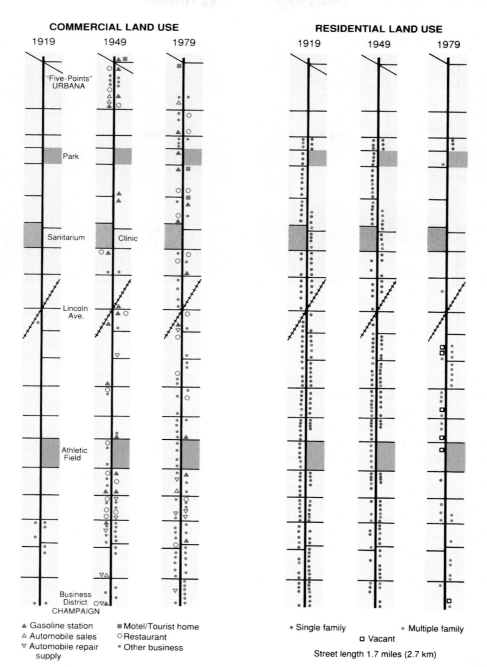

COMMERCIAL LAND USE

1919   1949   1979

"Five-Points" URBANA

Park

Sanitarium   Clinic

Lincoln Ave.

Athletic Field

Business District CHAMPAIGN

▲ Gasoline station   ■ Motel/Tourist home
△ Automobile sales   ○ Restaurant
▽ Automobile repair   • Other business
   supply

RESIDENTIAL LAND USE

1919   1949   1979

• Single family   • Multiple family
          □ Vacant
Street length 1.7 miles (2.7 km)

FIGURE 7.27   **A street transformation.** A residential street becomes a commercial strip in Champaign–Urbana, Illinois. After 60 years of automobile traffic on this main arterial street, residential land use has been replaced almost entirely by commercial uses, all depending on drive-in customer access or catering to automotive needs themselves. The major change in land use came after 1949.

Source: John A. Jakle and Richard L. Mattson, "The Evolution of a Commercial Strip," *Journal of Cultural Geography* 1 (Spring/Summer 1981): 14, 20. Redrawn by permission.

FIGURE 7.28   For some, the advertisements for commercialized popular culture constitute visual blight.

FIGURE 7.29   Massive, enclosed, and buffered from its surroundings, the modern metropolitan shopping mall is an external and internal built environment that summarizes the contrasts between popular culture standardization and folk and ethnic cultural individuality. This mall is in the center city area of Philadelphia, Pa.

The ubiquity of malls and the uniformity of their goods are clearly reflected in items of clothing. Fashion replaces personal preference, social position, occupation, or tradition as the arbiter of type or design of clothing. Whatever may be dictated nationally—miniskirt, leisure suit, designer jeans, or other fad—is instantly available locally, hurried to market by well-organized chains responding to well-orchestrated customer demand. A few national or international fashion centers dictate what shall be worn; a few designer names dominate the popularly acceptable range of choices. Since popular culture is, above all, commercialized culture, a market success by one producer is instantly copied by others. Thus, even the great number of individual shops within the mall is only an assurance of variations on the same limited range of clothing (or other) themes, not necessarily of diversity of choice. Yet, of course, the very wealth of variations and separate items permits an individuality of choice and selection of image not possible within constrained and controlled folk or ethnic groups.

Even culture in the sense of the arts is standardized within the malls. Chain bookstores offer identical bestsellers and paperbacks; multiscreen cinemas provide viewing choice only among the currently popular films; gift shops have nationally identical selections of figurines and pressed glass; and art stores stock similar lines of prints, photographs, and posters. It has been noted that Americans, at least, spend more of their time within malls than anywhere else except home and work. It is not unlikely that a standardized popular culture is, at least in part, traceable to the homogenized shopping mall.

Outside the Mall

Nonmaterial tastes and recreations are, in popular culture, subject to the same widespread uniformities as are the goods available within repetitive shopping complexes. Country music, we saw, was culturally associated with the Upland South. It has long since lost that regional exclusivity, and Nashville has become a product, not a place. By the late 1970s (Figure 7.30), no American with access to radio was denied exposure to electric guitar and melancholy lyric. Fad motion pictures are simultaneously released throughout the country; the same children's toys and adults' games are everywhere instantly available to satisfy the generated wants.

Wilbur Zelinsky reported on the speed of diffusion of a manufactured desire:

> In August, 1958, I drove from Santa Monica, California, to Detroit at an average rate of about 400 miles (650 km) per day; and display windows in almost every drugstore and variety store along the way were being hastily stocked with hula hoops just off the delivery trucks from Southern California. A national television program the week before had roused instant cravings. It was an eerie sensation, surfing along a pseudo-innovation wave.[1]

[1] *Cultural Geography of the United States* (Englewood Cliffs, NJ: Prentice-Hall, 1973), p. 80, fn. 18; rev ed. 1992.

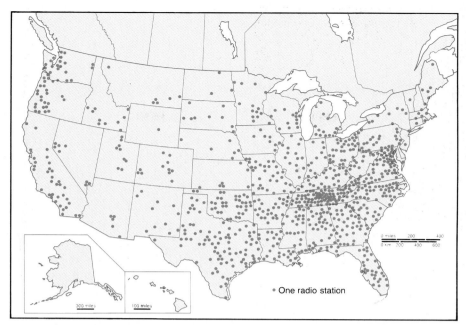

FIGURE 7.30   **Country music radio stations.** Although still most heavily concentrated in the Upland South, radio stations playing only country music had become a national commonplace by the late 1970s.

Diffusion Tracks

Popular culture is marked by the nearly simultaneous adoption over wide areas of an artifact or a nonmaterial element. Knowledge of an innovation is widely and quickly available; television and the national press inform without distance constraints. Mass manufacturing and imitative production place desired items, as Zelinsky discovered, in every store in a remarkably short time. For fads particularly, the tracing of diffusion tracks is difficult and probably meaningless. Recognizable culture hearths and migration paths are not clearly defined by the myriad introductions into the ever-changing popular culture pool. It is not particularly revealing to know that the origin of the Frisbee is apocryphally traced to the pie tins of the old Frisbie Baking Co. of Bridgeport, Connecticut, manufactured in plastic and carried as a game toy by college students throughout the United States, or that the Rubik's Cube puzzle was an invention of a Hungarian architect. The one has nothing to do with a New England culture hearth nor the other with East European ethnic influences.

Some more lasting popular changes have been recorded and do provide useful insight into the nature of diffusion and the sequence of acceptance and adoption of new cultural elements. The New Orleans origin of jazz, its upriver movement, and the gradual acceptance by white sophisticates of a new black musical form trace for us the origin, the diffusion path, and the adoption sequence of a major introduction. Cricket as a popular sport followed the spread of empire as British influences were implanted across the world. The names settlers and town founders gave to their communities provide another expression of popular culture and its diffusion (Figure 5.17). Professor Zelinsky has investigated the origin and spread of classical town names in the United States, documenting on the map America's 19th-century attraction to the Greco-Roman world. Neoclassical public architecture, Latin state mottoes, Latin and Greek personal names, and classical town nomenclature were all part of that Classical Revival. Figure 7.31 summarizes the patterns of innovation and dispersal that he discovered.

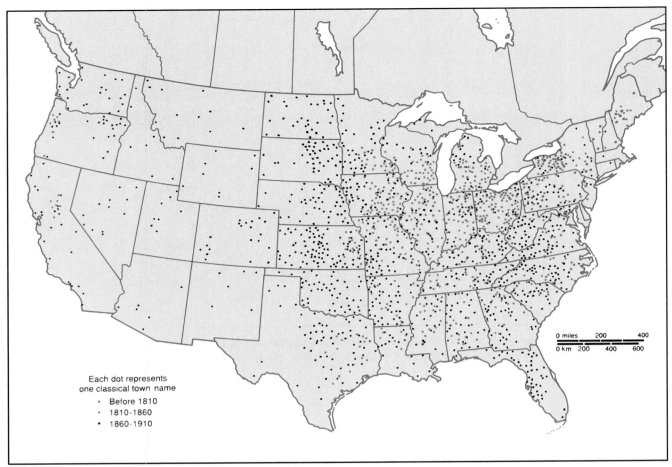

FIGURE 7.31 **Classical town names.** A permanent reminder of popular culture: the diffusion of classical town names in the United States to 1910.

Regional Emphasis

The uneven distribution of classical place-names suggests that not all expressions of popular culture are spatially uniform. Areal variations do exist in the extent to which particular elements in the general cultural pool are adopted. These variations impart an aspect of regional differentiation of interest to geographers.

Spatial patterns in sports, for example, reveal that the games played, the migration paths of their fans and players, and the landscape evidence of organized sports constitute regional variables, part of the areal diversity of North American—and world—life. Figure 7.32a, for example, shows that television interest in professional baseball is not universal despite the sport's reputation as "the national pastime." Studies and maps of many encountered regional differences in food and drink preferences, leisure activities, and personal and political tastes—a sampling is presented in Figure 7.32—are suggestive of the growing interest in how people behave and respond, not as echoes of the distant past but as participants in a vibrant and changing contemporary world that still retains evidence of regional contrast along with the commonalities of popular culture.

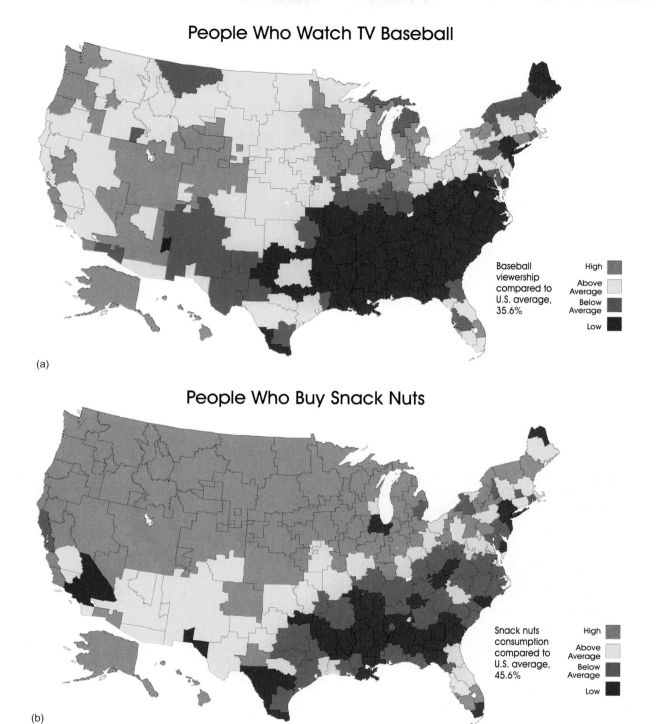

People Who Watch TV Baseball

Baseball viewership compared to U.S. average, 35.6%

High
Above Average
Below Average
Low

(a)

People Who Buy Snack Nuts

Snack nuts consumption compared to U.S. average, 45.6%

High
Above Average
Below Average
Low

(b)

FIGURE 7.32 **Regional variations in expressions of popular culture.** (*a*) Part of the regional variation in television viewing of baseball reflects the game's lack of appeal in the African American community and, therefore, its low viewership in the Southeast and in metropolitan centers where, additionally, attendance at games is an alternative to watching TV. (*b*) The sharp regional contrasts in snack nut consumption has been attributed to the presumed greater incidence of cocktail parties in the North and West and the higher incidence of religious conservatives (not usual cocktail party hosts or guests) in the Southeast. A map of Americans who habitually listen to religious radio broadcasts is essentially the reverse of this nut map. (*c*) Members of fraternal orders tend to concentrate in the rural west, where the clubs provide a social opportunity for rural or small town residents, and in retirement communities, for the younger generation seems less inclined to "join the lodge." (*d*) Even bad habits regionalize. The country's cigarette belt includes notably many of the rural areas where tobacco is grown.

From Michael J. Weiss, *Latitudes and Attitudes: An Atlas of American Tastes, Trends, Politics, and Passions.* Boston: Little, Brown and Company, 1994. Used by permission of the author.

Members of Fraternal Orders

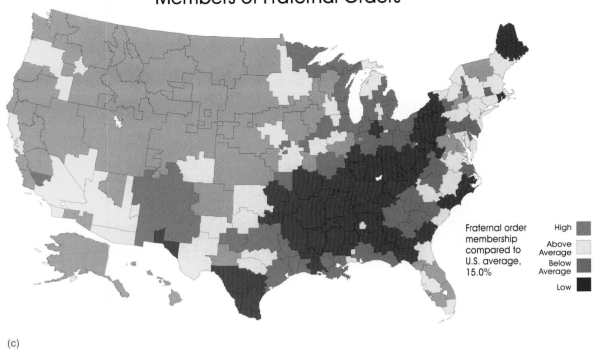

Fraternal order membership compared to U.S. average, 15.0%

High
Above Average
Below Average
Low

(c)

People Who Smoke Cigarettes

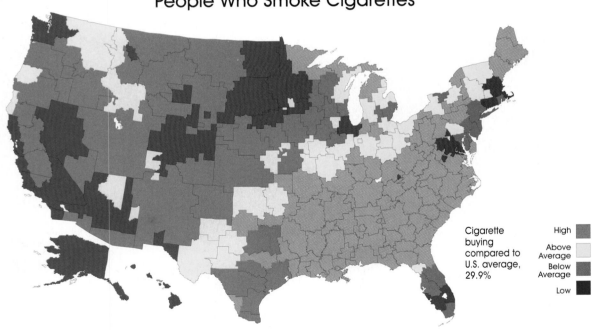

Cigarette buying compared to U.S. average, 29.9%

High
Above Average
Below Average
Low

(d)

FIGURE 7.32   *(continued)*

Vernacular Regions

Ordinary people have a clear view of space. They are aware of variations from place to place in the mix of phenomena, both physical and cultural. They use and recognize as meaningful such common regional names as Corn Belt, Sunbelt, and "the Coast." More important, people individually and collectively agree on where they live. They occupy regions that have reality in their minds and that are reflected in regional journals, in regional museums, and in regionally based names employed in businesses, by sports teams, or in advertising slogans.

These are **vernacular** or **popular regions;** they have reality as part of folk or popular culture rather than as political impositions or scholarly constructs. Geographers are increasingly recognizing that vernacular regions are significant concepts affecting the way people view space, assign their loyalties, and interpret their world. One geographer has drawn the boundaries of the large popular regions of North America on the basis of place names and locational identities found in the white pages of central-city telephone directories (Figure 7.33). The 14 large but subnational vernacular regions recognized accord reasonably well with cultural regions defined by more rigorous methods. However, particularly in the West, that accordance is not clearly demonstrated by comparison of the vernacular regions with Figure 6.29. Another, more subjective cultural regionalization of the United States is offered in Figure 7.34. The generalized "consensus" or vernacular regions suggested are based on an understood "sense of place" derived from current population and landscape characteristics as well as on historical differences that impart distinctive regional behaviors and attitudes.

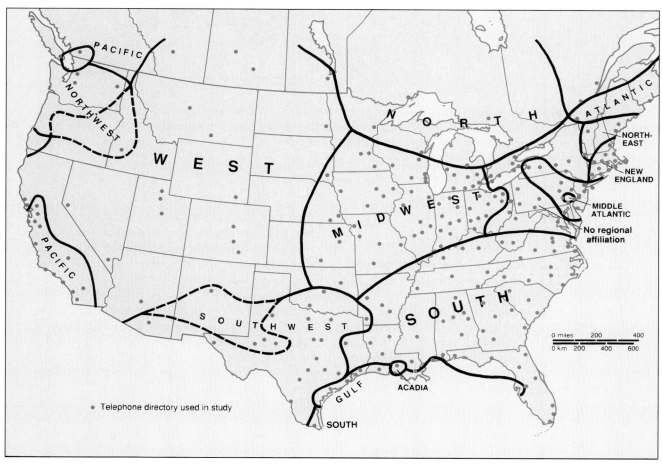

FIGURE 7.33   **Vernacular regions of North America** as determined by names of enterprises listed in central city telephone directories. Regions are those in which a given term or a cluster of closely related terms (e.g., Southern, Southland, Dixie) outnumber all other regional or locational references.

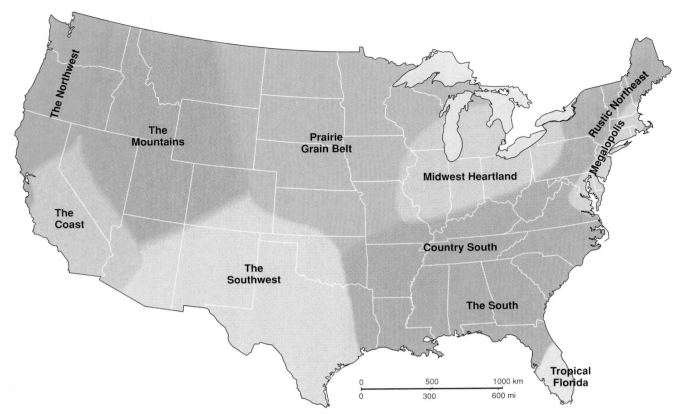

FIGURE 7.34   **Generalized U.S. culture regions.** "In spite of strong tendencies toward cultural homogenization and place obliteration, . . . regional identities persist," in the view of geographer Larry Ford, who suggests the 11 culture regions shown. Whatever the reasons for that persistence, "the different [culture] regions of the United States continue to have their own personalities and senses of place."

Summary

In the population mix that is the Anglo American, particularly United States, society, we may recognize two culture-based sources of separation and one of unification. Ethnic culture and folk culture tend to create distinctions between peoples and to impart a special character to the areas in which their influences are dominant. Popular culture implies behavioral unification and the reduction of territorial distinctiveness.

Early arriving ethnic groups were soon Americanized, and their imported cultures were converted from the distinctly ethnic traits of foreigners to the folk cultures of the New World. The foothold settlements of first colonists became separate culture hearths in which imported architectural styles, food preferences, music, and other elements of material and nonmaterial culture were mixed, modified, abandoned, or disseminated along clearly traceable diffusion paths into the continental interior. Ethnic culture was transmuted to folk culture when nurtured in isolated areas and made part of traditional America by long retention and by

modification to accommodate local circumstances. Distinctive and bearing the stamp of restricted sections of the nation, those folk cultures contributed both to eastern regional diversity and to the diffusion streams affecting midwestern and western cultural amalgams.

The territorial and social diversities implied by the concepts of *ethnic* and *folk* are modified by the general unifying forces of *popular* culture. Fads, foods, music, dress, toys, games, and other introduced tastes tend to be adopted within a larger society, irrespective of the ethnic or folk distinctions of its parts. Sport interests and rivalries, as we saw at the opening of this chapter, become regional and national—and, increasingly, international—surmounting older limitations of distance. The more modernized and urbanized a country, the more it is uniformly subjected to the mass media and to common entertainment sources, and the more will popular culture subdue the remnant social distinctions still imparted by folk and ethnic customs. At the same time, the greater will be the choices made available to individuals newly freed from the limiting constraints of folk and ethnic traditions.

The threads of diversity traced in Chapter 6 and in this chapter are those of the traits and characteristics of small groups as revealed by behavior and artifact. The reference has been, for the most part, to a single cultural realm and particularly to a single country, the United States, within that realm. The aim has been to impart a clearer understanding of the role of cultural differentiation and unification in the human geography of a region best known to most readers. With different emphases of topic, we could, of course, present similar discussions of cultural mosaics for all other culture realms and sizable countries of the world.

If we were to do so, one recurring condition of material and nonmaterial cultural differentiation would become evident. Much of human activity, including tools made and used, structures built, migrations undertaken, and social controls adopted, is related to economic life. Culture is conditioned by the necessities of production of food and material objects and, increasingly, of their exchange over space and between groups. Many of the threads in the fabric of cultural diversity—and, as well, many of its patterns of uniformity—are those woven by the traditions and technologies of livelihood. We must therefore next turn our attention to a consideration of the varied world of work and to the regional patterns of production and exchange revealed by that encompassing branch of human geography called *economic geography*.

KEY WORDS

built environment   215
custom   216
folk culture   215
folklore   235

folkways   235
material culture   215
nonmaterial culture   215
popular culture   238

popular region   247
vernacular house   220
vernacular region   247

FOR REVIEW

1. What contrasts can you draw between *folk culture* and *popular culture*? What different sorts of material and nonmaterial elements identify them?

2. How many of the early settlement cultural hearths of North America can you name? Did early immigrants create uniform *built environments* within them? If not, why not?

3. When and under what circumstances did popular culture begin to erode the folk and ethnic cultural differences between Americans? Thinking only of your own life and habits, what traces of folk culture do you carry? To what degree does popular culture affect your decisions on dress? On reading material? On recreation?

4. How are we able to recognize hearths and trace diffusions of folk cultural elements? Do items of popular culture have hearths and diffusions paths that are equally traceable? Why or why not?

5. What kinds of connections can you discern between the nature of the physical environment and the characteristics of different *vernacular house* styles in North America? In other parts of the world?

6. If, as some have observed, there is a close relationship between the natural environment and the artifacts of folk culture, is there likely to be a similar causal connection between the environment and expressions of popular culture? Why or why not?

SELECTED REFERENCES

Bale, John. *Landscapes of Modern Sport.* New York/Leicester, England: Leicester University Press, 1994.

Bale, John. *Sports Geography.* New York: E. & F. N. Spon, 1989.

Barer-Stein, Thelma. *You Eat What You Are: A Study of Ethnic Food Traditions.* Toronto: McClelland and Stewart, 1979.

Carney, George O., ed. *Fast Food, Stock Cars, and Rock-N-Roll: Space and Place in American Pop Culture.* Lanham, MD: Rowman & Littlefield, 1995.

Carney, George O., ed. *The Sounds of People and Places: Readings in the Geography of American Folk and Popular Music.* 3d ed. Lanham, MD: Rowman & Littlefield, 1994.

Coe, Sophie D. *America's First Cuisines.* Austin: University of Texas Press, 1994.

Conzen, Michael P., ed. *The Making of the American Landscape.* Boston: Unwin Hyman, 1990.

Dorson, Richard M., ed. *Folklore and Folklife: An Introduction.* Chicago: University of Chicago Press, 1972.

Ennals, Peter M. "Nineteenth-Century Barns in Southern Ontario." *The Canadian Geographer/Le Géographe Canadien* 16 (1972):256–270.

Ensminger, Robert F. *The Pennsylvania Barn.* Baltimore, MD: Johns Hopkins University Press, 1992.

Fowke, Edith. *Canadian Folklore.* Toronto: Oxford University Press, 1988.

Francaviglia, Richard V. *The Mormon Landscape.* New York: AMS Press, Inc., 1978.

Glassie, Henry. "The Appalachian Log Cabin." *Mountain Life & Work* 39 (1963):5–14.

Glassie, Henry. "Old Barns of Appalachia." *Mountain Life & Work* 41, no. 2 (1965):21–30.

Glassie, Henry. *Pattern in the Material Folk Culture of the Eastern United States.* Philadelphia: University of Pennsylvania Press, 1968.

Glassie, Henry. *Folk Housing in Middle Virginia*. Knoxville: University of Tennessee Press, 1975.

Gordon, Jean, and Jan McArthur. "Popular Culture, Magazines and American Domestic Interiors, 1898–1940." *Journal of Popular Culture* 22, no. 4 (1989):35–60.

Goss, John. "The 'Magic of the Mall': An Analysis of Form, Function, and Meaning in the Contemporary Retail Built Environment." *Annals of the Association of American Geographers* 83, no. l (1993):18–47.

Hart, John Fraser. *The Look of the Land*. Englewood Cliffs, NJ: Prentice-Hall, 1975.

Hart, John Fraser, and Eugene Cotton Mather. "The American Fence." *Landscape* 5, no. 3 (1957):4–9.

Howe, Barbara J., Dolores A. Fleming, Emory L. Kemp, and Ruth Ann Overbeck. *Houses and Homes: Exploring their History*. Nashville, TN: American Association for State and Local History, 1987.

Jackson, Edgar L., and Denis B. Johnson, eds. "The West Edmonton Mall and Mega-Malls." Feature Issue of *The Canadian Geographer/Le Géographe Canadien* 35, no. 3 (1991).

Jackson, John B. *Discovering the Vernacular Landscape*. New Haven, CT: Yale University Press, 1984.

Jakle, John A., Robert W. Bastian, and Douglas K. Meyer. *Common Houses in America's Small Towns: The Atlantic Seaboard to the Mississippi Valley*. Athens: University of Georgia Press, 1989.

Johnson, Paul. *The Birth of the Modern: World Society 1815–1830*. New York: HarperCollins, 1991.

Jordan, Terry. "Perceptual Regions in Texas." *Geographical Review* 68 (1978):293–307.

Jordon, Terry G., and Matti Kaups. "Folk Architecture in Cultural and Ecological Context." *Geographical Review* 77 (1987):52–75.

Jordan, Terry G., and Matti Kaups. *The American Backwoods Frontier*. Baltimore and London: Johns Hopkins University Press, 1989.

Kimber, Clarissa T. "Plants in the Folk Medicine of the Texas-Mexico Borderlands." *Proceedings of the Association of American Geographers* 5 (1973):130–133.

Kniffen, Fred B. "American Cultural Geography and Folklife." In *American Folklife*, edited by Don Yoder, pp. 51–70. Austin: University of Texas Press, 1976.

Kniffen, Fred B. "Folk Housing: Key to Diffusion." *Annals of the Association of American Geographers* 55 (1965):549–577.

Kniffen, Fred B., and Henry Glassie. "Building in Wood in the Eastern United States: A Time-Place Perspective." *Geographical Review* 56 (1966):40–66.

Kraybill, Donald B. *The Riddle of Amish Culture*. Baltimore: Johns Hopkins University Press, 1989.

Lewis, Pierce F. "Common Houses, Cultural Spoor." *Landscape* 19, no. 2 (January 1975):1–22.

Lomax, Alan. *The Folk Songs of North America in the English Language*. Garden City, NY: Doubleday, 1960.

Luedtke, Luther S., ed. *Making America: The Society & Culture of the United States*. Chapel Hill: University of North Carolina Press, 1992.

Mather, Eugene Cotton, and John Fraser Hart. "Fences and Farms." *Geographical Review* 44 (1954):201–223.

Meinig, Donald W. "The Mormon Culture Region: Strategies and Patterns in the Geography of the American West, 1847–1964." *Annals of the Association of American Geographers* 55 (1965):191–220.

Meinig, Donald W. *The Shaping of America: A Geographical Perspective on 500 years of History*. Vol. 1: *Atlantic America, 1492–1800;* Vol 2: *Continental America, 1800–1867*. New Haven, CT: Yale University Press, 1986 and 1993.

Miller, E. Joan Wilson. "The Ozark Culture Region as Revealed by Traditional Materials." *Annals of the Association of American Geographers* 58 (1968):51–77.

Mitchell, Robert D., ed. *Appalachian Frontiers Settlement, Society, and Development in the Preindustrial Era*. Lexington: University Press of Kentucky, 1991.

Morgan, John. *The Log House in East Tennessee*. Knoxville: University of Tennessee Press, 1990.

Noble, Allen G. *Wood, Brick, and Stone: The North American Settlement Landscape*. Vol. 1: *Houses;* Vol. 2: *Barns and Farm Structures*. Amherst: University of Massachusetts Press, 1984.

Noble, Allen G., and Richard K. Cleek. *The Old Barn Book*. New Brunswick, NJ: Rutgers University Press, 1995.

Noble, Allen G., and Gayle A. Seymour. "Distribution of Barn Types in Northeastern United States." *Geographical Review* 72 (1982):155–170.

Oliver, Paul. *Dwellings: The House across the World*. Austin: University of Texas Press, 1987.

Paredes, Américo. *Folklore and Culture on the Texas-Mexican Border*. Austin: University of Texas Press, 1995.

Peterson, Fred W. *Homes in the Heartland: Balloon Frame Farmhouses of the Upper Midwest, 1850–1920*. Lawrence: University Press of Kansas, 1992.

Price, Edward T. *Dividing the Land: Early American Beginnings of Our Private Property Mosaic*. Chicago: University of Chicago Press, 1995.

Price, Edward T. "Root Digging in the Appalachians: The Geography of Botanical Drugs." *Geographical Review* 50 (1960):1–20.

Purvis, Thomas L. "The Pennsylvania Dutch and the German-American Diaspora in 1790." *Journal of Cultural Geography* 6, no. 2 (1986):81–99.

Rapaport, Amos. *House Form and Culture*. Englewood Cliffs, NJ: Prentice-Hall, 1969.

Roark, Michael, ed. *French and Germans in the Mississippi Valley: Landscape and Cultural Traditions*. Cape Girardeau: Southeast Missouri State University, 1988.

Rooney, John F., Jr., and Richard Pillsbury. *Atlas of American Sport*. New York: Macmillan, 1992.

Rooney, John F., and Richard Pillsbury. "Sports Regions." *American Demographics* 14 (November 1993):30–39.

Rooney, John F., Jr., Wilbur Zelinsky, and Dean R. Louder, eds. *This Remarkable Continent: An Atlas of United States and Canadian Society and Cultures*. College

Station: Texas A&M University Press, 1982.

Rowe, W. John. "Old-World Legacies in America." *Folk Life: Journal of the Society for Folk Life Studies* 6 (1968):68–82.

Schlereth, Thomas J. *Victorian America: Transformations in Everyday Life, 1876–1915.* New York: HarperCollins, 1991.

Upton, Dell. *America's Architectural Roots: Ethnic Groups that Built America.* National Trust for Historic Preservation, *Building Watchers Series.* Washington, D.C.: Preservation Press, 1986.

Upton, Dell, and John Michael Vlach, eds. *Common Places: Readings in American Vernacular Architecture.* Athens: University of Georgia Press, 1986.

Vermeer, Donald E., and Dennis A. Frate. "Geophagy in a Mississippi County." *Annals of the Association of American Geographers* 65 (1975):414–424.

Vlach, John Michael. "The Shotgun House: An African Architectural Legacy." Parts 1, 2. *Pioneer America* 8 (January, July 1976):47–56, 57–70.

Voeks, Robert. "African Medicine and Magic in the Americas." *Geographical Review* 83, no. 1 (1993):66–78.

Vogel, Virgil J. *American Indian Medicine.* Norman: University of Oklahoma Press, 1970.

Waterman, Thomas T. *The Dwellings of Colonial America.* Chapel Hill: University of North Carolina Press, 1950.

Weatherford, Jack. *Indian Givers: How the Indians of the Americas Transformed the World.* New York: Ballantine Books, 1990.

Weiss, Michael J. *Latitudes and Attitudes: An Atlas of American Tastes, Trends, Politics, and Passions.* Boston: Little, Brown and Company, 1994.

Welsch, Roger L. "Sod Construction on the Plains." *Pioneer America* 1, no. 2 (July 1969):13–17.

Wilson, Eugene M. "The Single Pen Log House in the South." *Pioneer America* 2 (1970):21–28.

Wood, Joseph S. " 'Build, Therefore, Your Own World': The New England Village as Settlement Ideal." *Annals of the Association of American Geographers* 81, no. 1 (March 1991):32–50.

Yoder, Don, ed. *American Folklife.* Austin: University of Texas Press, 1976.

Zelinsky, Wilbur. *The Cultural Geography of the United States.* Rev. ed. Englewood Cliffs, NJ: Prentice-Hall, 1992.

Zelinsky, Wilbur. "North America's Vernacular Regions." *Annals of the Association of American Geographers* 70 (1980):1–16.

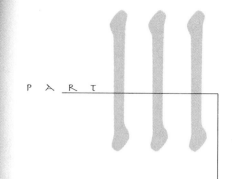

DYNAMIC PATTERNS OF THE SPACE ECONOMY

*A container ship at dock in Rotterdam harbor,
The Netherlands.*

The preceding chapters of Part II focused on prominent elements of unity and diversity of distinctive societies and culture realms of the world. Their theme stressed tradition and conservatism. The patterns of language, religion, ethnicity, and folk beliefs and customs that were recognized represent long-established and faithfully transmitted expressions of cultural identity that endure even in the face of profound changes affecting group life and activity. In the following chapters of Part III of our study of human geography, the theme switches from conservative cultural retentions to dynamic economic innovations. Change, as we have seen, is the recurring theme of human societies, and in few other regards is change so pervasive and eagerly sought as it is in the economic orientations and activities of countries and societies throughout the modern world.

Since many—though by no means all—of the material and nonmaterial expressions of cultural differentiation are rooted in the necessities of subsistence and livelihood, basic changes in spatial economic patterns also affect culture groups' established noneconomic sociofacts and mentifacts. Traditional preindustrial societies developed tools and other artifacts, evolved sequences of behavior, and created institutions and practices that were related to their continuing need for finding or producing food and essential materials. That need remains, but the culturally distinctive solutions of traditional societies are being steadily replaced by the shared technologies of modern economies.

Food and raw material production still dominates some economies and areas, but increasingly the world's people are engaging in activities—labeled secondary and tertiary—that involve the processing and exchange of produced primary materials and the provision of personal, business, and professional services to an increasingly interdependent world economy. Simultaneously, economically advanced societies are becoming "postindustrial" while those less advanced seek the prosperity and benefits that are promised by "development." Cultural convergence through shared technologies and intertwined economies has served to reduce the distinguishing contrasts that formerly were preserved in economic isolation. Increasingly, economic development of peoples in all parts of the world has imposed new pressures on the environment to accommodate new patterns of production and exploitation.

Our concern in the next three chapters will be with the dynamic changes in economic patterns and orientations of regions and societies that have emerged with the increasing development and integration of the world's space economy. These patterns of livelihood, production, and exchange augment and complement the understandings of regional cultural differentiation we have already developed. They add an awareness of the economic unity, diversity, and change so prominent in modern society and so essential to our fuller appreciation of the spatial mosaic of culture.

LIVELIHOOD AND ECONOMY:

PRIMARY ACTIVITIES

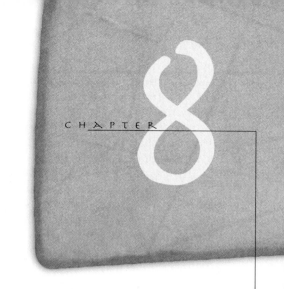

The Classification of Economic Activity and Economies 256
Categories of Activity 257
Types of Economic Systems 258
Primary Activities: Agriculture 260
Subsistence Agriculture 261
  Extensive Subsistence Agriculture 261
  Intensive Subsistence Systems 264
  Costs of Territorial Extension 266
  The Green Revolution 266
Commercial Agriculture 267
  Production Controls 268
  A Model of Agricultural Location 270
  Intensive Commercial Agriculture 271
  Extensive Commercial Agriculture 272
  Special Crops 275
  Agriculture in Planned Economies 276
Primary Activities: Resource Exploitation 278
Resource Terminology 278
Fishing 279
Forestry 282
Mining and Quarrying 283
  Metallic Minerals 284
  Nonmetallic Minerals 286
  Mineral Fuels 287
Trade in Primary Products 289
  SUMMARY 290
  KEY WORDS 291
  FOR REVIEW 291
  SELECTED REFERENCES 292

Processing the catch at Godthåb, Greenland.

The crop bloomed luxuriantly that summer of 1846. The disaster of the preceding year seemed over, and the potato, the sole sustenance of some 8 million Irish peasants, would again yield in the bounty needed. Yet within a week, wrote Father Mathew, "I beheld one wide waste of putrefying vegetation. The wretched people were seated on the fences of their decaying gardens . . . bewailing bitterly the destruction that had left them foodless." Colonel Gore found that "every field was black," and an estate steward noted that "the fields . . . look as if fire has passed over them." The potato was irretrievably gone for a second year; famine and pestilence were inevitable.

Within 5 years, the settlement geography of the most densely populated country in Europe was forever altered. The United States received a million immigrants, who provided the cheap labor needed for the canals, railroads, and mines that it was creating in its rush to economic development. New patterns of commodity flows were initiated as American maize for the first time found an Anglo-Irish market—as part of Poor Relief—and then entered a wider European market that had also suffered general crop failure in that bitter year. Within days, a microscopic organism, the cause of the potato blight, had altered the economic and human geography of two continents.

Although the Irish famine of the 1840s was a spatially localized tragedy, it dramatically demonstrated how widespread and intricate are the interrelations between widely separated peoples and areas of the earth. It made vividly clear how fundamental are human activity patterns that are rooted in economy and subsistence. These are the patterns that, within the broader context of human geography, economic geography isolates for special study.

Simply stated, **economic geography** is the study of how people earn their living, how livelihood systems vary by area, and how economic activities are spatially interrelated and linked. It applies geography's general concern with the study of spatial variation to the special circumstances of the production, exchange, and consumption of goods and services. In reality, of course, we cannot really comprehend the totality of the economic pursuits of nearly 6 billion human beings. We cannot examine the infinite variety of productive and service activities found everywhere on the earth's surface; nor can we trace all their innumerable interrelationships, linkages, and flows. Even if that level of understanding were possible, it would be valid for only a fleeting instant of time, for economic activities are constantly undergoing change.

Economic geographers seek consistencies. They attempt to develop generalizations that will aid in the comprehension of the maze of economic variations characterizing human existence. From their studies emerges a deeper awareness of the dynamic, interlocking diversity of human enterprise and of the impact of economic activity on all other facets of human life and culture. From them, too, comes appreciation of the increasing interdependence of differing national and regional economic systems. The potato blight, although it struck only one small island, ultimately affected the economies of continents. In like fashion, the depletion of America's natural resources and the "deindustrialization" of its economy are altering the relative wealth of countries, flows of international trade, domestic employment and income patterns, and more (Figure 8.l).

The Classification of Economic Activity and Economies

The search for understanding livelihood patterns is made more difficult by the complex environmental and cultural realities controlling the economic activities of humans. Many production patterns are rooted in the spatially variable circumstances of the *physical environment*. The staple crops of the humid tropics, for example, are not part of the agricultural systems of the midlatitudes; livestock types that thrive in American feedlots or on western ranges are not adapted to the Arctic tundra or to the margins of the Saharan

FIGURE 8.1   These Japanese cars unloading at Seattle are part of a continuing flow of imported goods capturing a share of the domestic market traditionally held by American manufacturers. Established patterns of production and exchange are constantly subject to change in a world of increasing economic and cultural interdependence and of changing relative competitive strengths.

desert. The unequal distribution of useful mineral deposits gives some regions and countries economic prospects and employment opportunities that are denied to others. Forestry and fishing depend on still other natural resources unequal in occurrence, type, and value.

Within the bounds of the environmentally possible, *cultural considerations* may condition economic or production decisions. For example, culturally based food preferences rather than environmental limitations may dictate the choice of crops or livestock. Maize is a preferred grain in Africa and the Americas, wheat in North America, Australia, Argentina, southern Europe and Ukraine, and rice in much of Asia. As we saw in Figure 5.18, pigs are not produced in Muslim areas.

Level of *technological development* of a culture will affect its recognition of resources or its ability to exploit them. **Technology** refers to the totality of tools and methods available to and used by a culture group in producing items essential to its subsistence and comfort. Preindustrial societies have no knowledge of or need for the iron ore or coking coal underlying their hunting, gathering, or gardening grounds. *Political decisions* may encourage or discourage—through subsidies, protective tariffs, or production restrictions—patterns of economic activity. And, ultimately, production is controlled by *economic factors* of demand, whether that demand is expressed through a free market mechanism, government instruction, or the consumption requirements of a single family producing for its own needs.

Categories of Activity

Regionally varying environmental, cultural, technological, political, and market conditions add spatial details to more generalized ways of classifying the world's productive work. One approach to that categorization is to view economic activity as ranged along a continuum of both increasing complexity of product or service and increasing distance from the natural environment. Seen from that perspective, a small number of distinctive stages of production and service activities may be distinguished (see Figure 8.2).

Primary activities are those that harvest or extract something from the earth. They are at the beginning of the production cycle, where humans are in closest contact with the resources and potentialities of the environment. Such activities involve basic foodstuff and raw material production. Hunting and gathering, grazing, agriculture, fishing, forestry, and mining and quarrying are examples. **Secondary activities** are those that add value to materials by changing their form or combining them into more useful—therefore more valuable—commodities. That provision of *form utility* may range from simple handicraft production of pottery or woodenware to the delicate assembly of electronic goods or space vehicles (Figure 8.3). Copper smelting, steelmaking, metalworking, automobile production, textile and chemical industries—indeed, the full array of *manufacturing and processing industries*—are included in this phase of the production process. Also included are the production of *energy* (the "power company") and the *construction* industry.

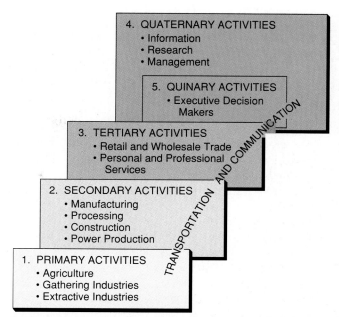

FIGURE 8.2 **The categories of economic activity.** The main sectors of the economy do not stand alone. They are connected and integrated by transportation and communication services and facilities not assigned to any single sector but common to all.

Tertiary activities consist of those business and labor specializations that provide *services* to the primary and secondary sectors, to the general community, and to the individual. These include financial, business, professional, clerical, and personal services. They constitute the vital link between producer and consumer, for tertiary occupations importantly include the wholesale and retail *trade* activities necessary in highly interdependent societies. Tertiary activities also provide essential information to manufacturers: the knowledge of market demand without which economically justifiable production decisions are impossible.

In economically advanced societies many individuals and some entire organizations are engaged in the processing and dissemination of information and in the administration and control of their own or other enterprises. The term **quaternary** is applied to this fourth class of economic activities, which is composed entirely of services rendered by "white collar" professionals working in education, government, management, information processing, and research. Sometimes, a subdivision of these management functions—**quinary activities**—is distinguished to recognize high-level decision-making roles in all types of large organizations, public and private. Transportation and communication services and facilities cut across the general categories of economic activity, unite them, and make possible the spatial interactions that all human enterprise requires (discussed in Chapter 3).

The term *industry*—in addition to its common meaning as a branch of manufacturing activity—is frequently employed as a substitute identical in meaning to *activity* as a designation of these categories of economic enterprise. That

FIGURE 8.3   These logs entering a lumber mill are products of *primary production*. Processing them into boards, plywood, or prefabricated houses is a *secondary activity* that increases their value by altering their form.

is, we can speak of the steel, automobile, or textile "industry" with all the impressions of factories, mills, raw materials, and products that each type of enterprise implies. But with equal logic we can refer in a more generalized way to the "entertainment" or the "travel" industries or, in the present context, to "primary," "secondary," and "tertiary" industries.

These categories of production and service activities or industries help us to see an underlying structure to the nearly infinite variety of things people do to earn a living and to sustain themselves. But by themselves they tell us little about the organization of the larger economy of which the individual worker or establishment is a part. For that broader organizational understanding we look to *systems* rather than *components* of economies.

Types of Economic Systems

Broadly speaking, national economies of, particularly, the latter half of the 20th century fall into one of three major types of systems: *subsistence, commercial,* or *planned.* None of these economic systems is "pure"; that is, none exists in isolation in an increasingly interdependent world. Each, however, displays certain underlying characteristics based on its distinctive forms of resource management and economic control.

In a **subsistence economy,** goods and services are created for the use of the producers and their kinship groups. Therefore, there is little exchange of goods and only limited

need for markets. In the **commercial economies** that have become dominant in nearly all parts of the world, producers or their agents freely market their goods and services, the laws of supply and demand determine price and quantity, and market competition is the primary force shaping production decisions and distributions. In the extreme form of **planned economies,** associated with the communist-controlled societies that have now collapsed in nearly every country where they were formerly created or imposed, producers or their agents dispose of goods and services through government agencies that controlled both supply and price. The quantities produced and the locational patterns of production were rigidly programmed by central planning departments without benefit of the cost or demand information a free market economy regularly supplies.

Even though rigidly planned economies no longer exist in their classical form—modified or dismantled now in favor of free market structures or only partially retained in a lesser degree of economic control associated with governmental supervision or ownership of selected sectors of increasingly market-oriented economies—their landscape evidence lives on. The physical structures, patterns of production, and imposed regional interdependencies they created remain to influence the economic decisions of successor societies.

In actuality, few people are members of only one of these systems, although one may be dominant. A farmer in India may produce rice and vegetables privately for the family's consumption but also save some of the produce to sell. In addition, members of the family may market cloth or other handicrafts they make. With the money derived from those sales, the Indian peasant is able to buy, among other things, clothes for the family, tools, and fuel. Thus, that Indian farmer is a member of at least two systems: subsistence and commercial.

In the United States, government controls on the production of various types of goods and services (such as growing wheat or tobacco, producing alcohol, constructing and operating nuclear power plants, and engaging in licensed personal and professional services) mean that the country does not have a purely commercial economy. To a limited extent, its citizens participate in a controlled and planned as well as in a free market environment. Many African, Asian, and Latin American market economies have been decisively shaped by government policies that encourage or demand production of export commodities rather than domestic foodstuffs, or promote through import restrictions the development of domestic industries not readily supported by the national market alone. Example after example would show that there are very few people in the world who are members of only one type of economic system.

Nonetheless, in a given country, one of the three economic systems tends to dominate, and it has in the past been relatively easy subjectively to classify countries by that dominance even while recognizing that some elements of the other two systems might exist within the controlling scheme. However, the one geographic certainty is that spatial patterns—including those of economic activities and systems—will change. For example, the commercial economies of Western European countries, some with sizable infusions of planned economy controls, are affected by new, supranational direction and both increased free market competition and centralized regulation under the single market of the European Union. Many of the countries of Latin America, Africa, Asia, and the Middle East that traditionally were dominated by subsistence economies are now adopting advanced technologies and simultaneously becoming both more commercial and more planned.

No matter what economic system may locally prevail, in all systems transportation is a key variable. No advanced economy can flourish without a well-connected transport network. All subsistence societies—or subsistence areas of developing countries—are characterized by their isolation from regional and world routeways (Figure 8.4). That isolation restricts their progression to more advanced forms of economic structure.

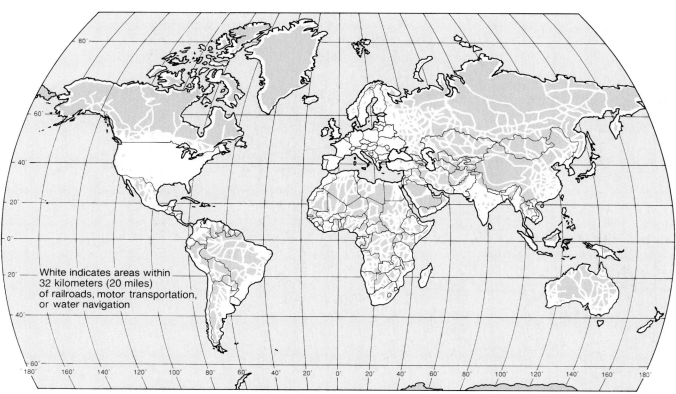

White indicates areas within 32 kilometers (20 miles) of railroads, motor transportation, or water navigation

FIGURE 8.4   **Patterns of access and isolation.** Accessibility is a key measure of economic development and of the degree to which a world region can participate in interconnected market activities. Isolated areas of countries with advanced economies suffer a price disadvantage because of high transportation costs. Lack of accessibility in subsistence economic areas slows their modernization and hinders their participation in the world market.

Although the former sharp contrasts in economic organization are becoming blurred and national economic orientations are changing, the evident contrasts between subsistence, planned, and commercial systems have differently affected national patterns of livelihood, production, and economic decision making. Indeed, both approaches to economic classification—by types of activities and by organization of economies—help us to visualize and understand world economic geographic patterns. In the remainder of this chapter we will center our attention on the primary industries. In Chapter 9 we will consider secondary through quinary activity patterns.

Primary Activities: Agriculture

Before there was farming, *hunting* and *gathering* were the universal forms of primary production. These preagricultural pursuits are now practiced by at most a few thousands of persons worldwide, primarily in isolated and remote pockets within the low latitudes and among the sparse populations of very high latitudes. The interior of New Guinea, rugged areas of interior Southeast Asia, diminishing segments of the Amazon rain forest, a few districts of tropical Africa and northern Australia, and parts of the Arctic regions still contain such preagricultural people.

Their numbers are few and declining, and wherever they are brought into contact with more advanced cultures, their way of life is eroded or lost.

Agriculture, defined as the growing of crops and the tending of livestock whether for the subsistence of the producers or for sale or exchange, has replaced hunting and gathering as economically the most significant of the primary activities. It is spatially the most widespread, found in all world regions where environmental circumstances permit (Figure 8.5). Crop farming alone covers some 15 million square kilometers (5.8 million sq. mi.) worldwide, about 10% of the earth's total land area. In many developing economies, at least three-fourths of the labor force is directly involved in farming and herding. In some, such as Nepal in Asia and Rwanda and Niger in Africa, the figure is more than 90%. In highly developed commercial economies, on the other hand, agriculture involves only a small fraction of the labor force: less than 10% in most of Western Europe, 5% in Canada, and less than 3% in the United States (for the world pattern of the agricultural labor force, see Figure 10.11). Indeed, a declining number or proportion of farm workers, along with farm consolidation and increasing output, are typical in all present-day highly developed commercial agricultural systems. On the other hand, agriculture remains a major component in the economies of many of the world's developing countries, producing for domestic

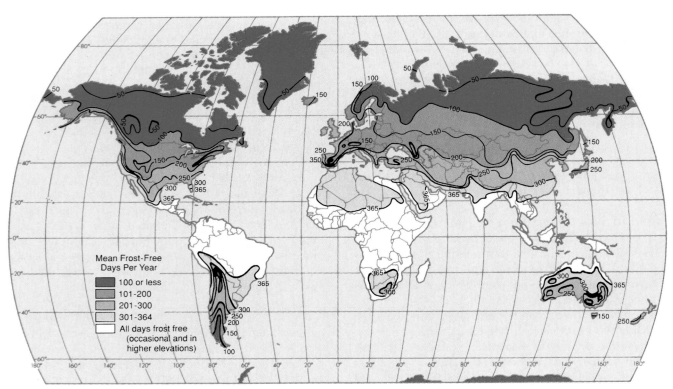

FIGURE 8.5 **Average length of growing season.** The number of frost-free days is an important environmental control on agriculture, as is the availability of precipitation sufficient in amount and reliability for crop production. Since agriculture is not usually practicable with less than a 90-day growing season, large parts of Russia and Canada have only limited cropping potential. Except where irrigation water is available, arid regions are similarly outside of the margins of regular crop production.

Courtesy Wayne M. Wendland.

markets and providing a major source of national income through exports (Figure 8.6).

It has been customary to classify agricultural societies on the twin bases of the importance of off-farm sales and the level of mechanization and technological advancement. *Subsistence, traditional* (or *intermediate*), and *advanced* (or *modern*) are usual terms employed to recognize both aspects. These are not mutually exclusive but rather are recognized stages along a continuum of farm economy variants. At one end lies production solely for family sustenance, using primitive tools and native plants. At the other is the specialized, highly capitalized, near-industrialized agriculture for off-farm delivery that marks advanced economies. Between these extremes is the middle ground of traditional agriculture, where farm production is in part destined for home consumption and in part oriented toward off-farm sale either locally or in national and international markets. We can most clearly see the variety of agricultural activities and the diversity of controls on their spatial patterns by examining the "subsistence" and "advanced" ends of the agricultural continuum.

Subsistence Agriculture

By definition, a *subsistence* economic system involves nearly total self-sufficiency on the part of its members. Production for exchange is minimal, and each family or close-knit social group relies on itself for its food and other most essential requirements. Farming for the immediate needs of the family is, even today, the predominant occupation of humankind. In most of Africa, south and east Asia, and much of Latin America, the majority of people are primarily concerned with feeding themselves from their own land and livestock.

Two chief types of subsistence agriculture may be recognized: *extensive* and *intensive*. Although each type has several variants, the essential contrast between them is realizable yield per unit of area used and, therefore, population-supporting potential. **Extensive subsistence agriculture** involves large areas of land and minimal labor input per hectare. Both product per land unit and population densities are low. **Intensive subsistence agriculture** involves the cultivation of small landholdings through the expenditure of great amounts of labor per acre. Yields per unit area and population densities are both high (Figure 8.7).

Extensive Subsistence Agriculture

Of the several types of *extensive subsistence* agriculture—varying one from another in their intensities of land use—two are of particular interest.

Nomadic herding, the wandering but controlled movement of livestock solely dependent on natural forage, is the most extensive type of land use system (Figure 8.7). That is, it requires the greatest amount of land area per per-

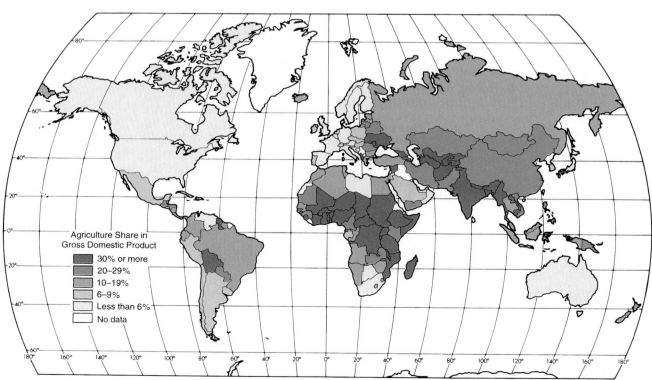

FIGURE 8.6 **Share of agriculture in gross domestic product.** Agriculture contributes 30% or more of gross domestic product (the total output of goods and services produced by an economy) of at least 50 countries worldwide. Most of them have developing economies, and collectively those 50 states—comprising some 31% of world population—average less than US $400 in per capita national income.

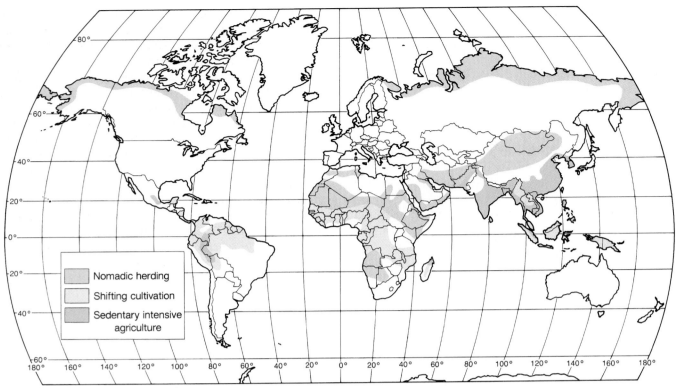

FIGURE 8.7 **Subsistence agricultural areas of the world.** Nomadic herding, supporting relatively few people, was the age-old way of life in large parts of the dry and cold world. Shifting or swidden agriculture maintains soil fertility by tested native practices in tropical wet and wet-and-dry climates. Large parts of Asia support millions of people engaged in sedentary intensive cultivation, with rice and wheat the chief crops.

son sustained. Over large portions of the Asian semidesert and desert areas, in certain highland zones, and on the fringes of and within the Sahara, a relatively small number of people graze animals for consumption by the herder group, not for market sale. Sheep, goats, and camels are most common, while cattle, horses, and yaks are locally important. The reindeer of Lapland were formerly part of the same system.

Whatever the animals involved, their common characteristics are hardiness, mobility, and an ability to subsist on sparse forage. The animals provide a variety of products: milk, cheese, and meat for food; hair, wool, and skins for clothing; skins for shelter; and excrement for fuel. For the herder, they represent primary subsistence. Nomadic movement is tied to sparse and seasonal rainfall or to cold temperature regimes and to the areally varying appearance and exhaustion of forage. Extended stays in a given location are neither desirable nor possible.

As a type of economic system, nomadic herding is declining. Many economic, social, and cultural changes are causing nomadic groups to alter their way of life or to disappear entirely. On the Arctic fringe of Russia, herders under communism were made members of state or collective herding enterprises. In northern Scandinavia, Lapps (Saami) are engaged in commercial more than in subsistence livestock farming. In the Sahel region of Africa on the margins

of the Sahara, oases formerly controlled by nomads have been taken over by farmers, and the great droughts of recent decades have forever altered the formerly nomadic way of life of thousands.

A much differently based and distributed form of extensive subsistence agriculture is found in all of the warm, moist, low-latitude areas of the world. There, many people engage in a kind of nomadic farming. Through clearing and use, the soils of those areas lose many of their nutrients (as soil chemicals are dissolved and removed by surface and groundwater or nutrients are removed from the land in the vegetables picked and eaten), and farmers cultivating them need to move on after harvesting several crops. In a sense, they rotate fields rather than crops to maintain productivity. This type of **shifting cultivation** has a number of names, the most common of which are *swidden* (an English localism for "burned clearing") and *slash-and-burn*.

Characteristically, the farmers hack down the natural vegetation, burn the cuttings, and then plant such crops as maize (corn), millet (a cereal grain), rice, manioc or cassava, yams, and sugarcane (Figure 8.8). Increasingly included in many of the crop combinations are such high-value, labor-intensive commercial crops as coffee, which provide the cash income that is evidence of the growing integration of all peoples into exchange economies. Initial yields—the first and second crops—may be very high, but they quickly be-

DYNAMIC PATTERNS OF THE SPACE ECONOMY

FIGURE 8.8 An African swidden plot burning. Any stumps or trees left in the clearing will remain after the burn.

come lower with each successive planting on the same plot. As that occurs, cropping ceases, native vegetation is allowed to reclaim the clearing, and gardening shifts to another newly prepared site. The first clearing will ideally not be used again for crops until, after many years, natural fallowing replenishes its fertility (see "Swidden Agriculture").

Nearly 5% of the world's people are still predominantly engaged in tropical shifting cultivation on more than one-fifth of the world's land area (Figure 8.7). Since the essential characteristic of the system is the intermittent cultivation of the land, each family requires a total occupance area equivalent to the garden plot in current use plus all land left fallow for regeneration. Population densities are traditionally low, for much land is needed to support few people. Here as elsewhere, however, population density must be considered a relative term. In actuality, although crude (arithmetic) density is low, people per unit area of *cultivated* land may be high.

SWIDDEN AGRICULTURE

The following account describes shifting cultivation among the Hanunóo people of the Philippines. Nearly identical procedures are followed in all swidden farming regions.

When a garden site of about one-half hectare (a little over one acre) has been selected, the swidden farmer begins to remove unwanted vegetation. The first phase of this process consists of slashing and cutting the undergrowth and smaller trees with bush knives. The principal aim is to cover the entire site with highly inflammable dead vegetation so that the later stage of burning will be most effective. Because of the threat of soil erosion the ground must not be exposed directly to the elements at any time during the cutting stage. During the first months of the agricultural year, activities connected with cutting take priority over all others. It is estimated that the time required ranges from 25 to 100 hours for the average-sized swidden plot.

Once most of the undergrowth has been slashed, chopped to hasten drying, and spread to protect the

soil and assure an even burn, the larger trees must be felled or killed by girdling (cutting a complete ring of bark) so that unwanted shade will be removed. The successful felling of a real forest giant is a dangerous activity and requires great skill. Felling in second growth is usually less dangerous and less arduous. Some trees are merely trimmed but not killed or cut, both to reduce the amount of labor and to leave trees to reseed the swidden during the subsequent fallow period.

The crucial and most important single event in the agricultural cycle is swidden burning. The main firing of a swidden is the culmination of many weeks of preparation in spreading and leveling chopped vegetation, preparing firebreaks to prevent flames escaping into the jungle, and allowing time for the drying process. An ideal burn rapidly consumes every bit of litter; in no more than an hour or an hour and a half, only smouldering remains are left.

Swidden farmers note the following as the benefits of a good burn: (1) removal of unwanted vegetation, resulting in a cleared swidden; (2) extermination of many animal and

some weed pests; (3) preparation of the soil for dibble (any small hand tool or stick to make a hole) planting by making it softer and more friable; (4) provision of an evenly distributed cover of wood ashes, good for young crop plants and protective of newly planted grain seed. Within the first year of the swidden cycle, an average of between 40 and 50 different types of crop plants have been planted and harvested.

The most critical feature of swidden agriculture is the maintenance of soil fertility and structure. The solution is to pursue a system of rotation of 1 to 3 years in crop and 10 to 20 in woody or bush fallow regeneration. When population pressures mandate a reduction in the length of fallow period, productivity of the region tends to drop as soil fertility is lowered, marginal land is utilized, and environmental degradation occurs. The balance is delicate.

Source: Based on Harold C. Conklin, *Hanunóo Agriculture,* FAO Forestry Development Paper No. 12.

Shifting cultivation is one of the oldest and most widely spread agricultural systems of the world. It is found on the islands of Kalimantan (Borneo), New Guinea, and Sumatera (Sumatra) in Indonesia. It is now retained, however, only in small parts of the uplands of South Asia in Vietnam, Thailand, Myanmar, and the Philippines. Nearly the whole of Central and West Africa away from the coasts, Brazil's Amazon basin, and large portions of Central America are all known for this type of extensive subsistence agriculture.

It may be argued that shifting cultivation is a highly efficient cultural adaptation where land is abundant in relation to population and levels of technology and capital availability are low. As those conditions change, the system becomes less viable. The basic change, as noted in Chapter 4, is that land is no longer abundant in relation to population in many of the less developed wet, tropical countries. Their growing populations have cleared and settled the forestlands formerly only intermittently used in swidden cultivation. The **Boserup thesis,** proposed by the economist Ester Boserup (1910–), is based on the observation that population increases necessitate increased inputs of labor and technology to compensate for reductions in the natural yields of swidden farming. It holds that population growth independently forces an increased use of technology in farming and—in a reversal of the Mathusian idea (page 125) that the supply of essential foodstuffs is basically fixed or only slowly expandable—requires a conversion from extensive to intensive subsistence agriculture.

Intensive Subsistence Systems

More than one-half of the people of the world are engaged in intensive subsistence agriculture, which predominates in areas shown in Figure 8.7. As a descriptive term, *intensive subsistence* is no longer fully applicable to a changing way of life and economy in which the distinction between subsistence and commercial is decreasingly valid. While families may still be fed primarily with the produce of their individual plots, the exchange of farm commodities within the system is considerable. Production of foodstuffs for sale in rapidly growing urban markets is increasingly vital for the rural economies of "subsistence farming" areas and for the sustenance of the growing proportion of national and regional populations no longer themselves engaged in farming. Nevertheless, hundreds of millions of Indians, Chinese, Pakistanis, Bangladeshis, and Indonesians plus further millions in other Asian, African, and Latin American countries remain small-plot, mainly subsistence producers of rice, wheat, maize, millet, or pulses (peas, beans, and other legumes). Most live in monsoon Asia, and we will devote our attention to that area.

Intensive subsistence farmers are concentrated in such major river valleys and deltas as the Ganges and the Chang Jiang (Yangtze) and in smaller valleys close to coasts—level areas with fertile alluvial soils. These warm, moist districts are well suited to the production of rice, a crop that under ideal conditions can provide large amounts of food per unit of land. Rice also requires a great deal of time and attention, for planting rice shoots by hand in standing fresh water is a tedious art (Figure 8.9). In the cooler and drier portions of

FIGURE 8.9 Transplanting rice seedlings requires arduous hand labor by all members of the family. The newly flooded diked fields, previously plowed and fertilized, will have their water level maintained until the grain is ripe. This photograph was taken in India. The scene is repeated wherever subsistence wet-rice agriculture is practiced.

Asia, wheat is grown intensively, along with millet and, less commonly, upland rice.

Rice is known to have been cultivated in parts of China and India for more than 7000 years. Today, wet, or lowland, rice is the mainstay of subsistence agriculture and diets of populations from Sri Lanka and India to Taiwan, Japan, and Korea. It is grown on over 80% of the planted area in Bangladesh, Thailand, and Malaysia and on over 50% in 6 other Asian countries. Almost exclusively used as a human food, rice provides 25% to 80% of the calories in the daily diet of over 2.8 billion Asians, or half the world's population. Its successful cultivation depends on the controlled management of water, relatively easy in humid tropical river valleys with heavy, impermeable, water-retaining soils though more difficult in upland and seasonally dry districts. Throughout Asia the necessary water management systems have left their distinctive marks on the landscape. Permanently diked fields to contain and control water, levees against unwanted water, and reservoirs, canals, and drainage channels to control its availability and flow are common sights. Terraces to extend level land to valley slopes are occasionally encountered as well (see Figure 4.23).

Intensive subsistence farming is characterized by large inputs of labor per unit of land, by small plots, by the intensive use of fertilizers, mostly animal manure, and by the promise of high yields in good years (see "The Economy of a Chinese Village"). For food security and dietary custom, some other products are also grown. Vegetables and some

THE ECONOMY OF A CHINESE VILLAGE

The village of Nanching is in subtropical southern China on the Zhu River delta near Guangzhou (Canton). Its pre-communist subsistence agricultural system was described by a field investigator, whose account is here condensed. The system is found in its essentials in other rice-oriented societies.

In this double-crop region, rice was planted in March and August and harvested in late June or July and again in November. March to November was the major farming season. Early in March the earth was turned with an iron-tipped wooden plow pulled by a water buffalo. The very poor who could not afford a buffalo used a large iron-tipped wooden hoe for the same purpose.

The plowed soil was raked smooth, fertilizer was applied, and water was let into the field, which was then ready for the transplanting of rice seedlings. Seedlings were raised in a seedbed, a tiny patch fenced off on the side or corner of the field. Beginning from the middle of March, the transplanting of seedlings took place. The whole family was on the scene. Each took the seedlings by the bunch, ten to fifteen plants, and pushed them into the soft inundated soil. For the first thirty or forty days the emerald green crop demanded little attention except keeping the water at a proper level. But after this period came the first weeding; the second weeding followed a month later. This was done by hand, and everyone old enough for such work participated. With the second weeding went the job of adding fertilizer. The grain was now allowed to stand to "draw starch" to fill the hull of the kernels. When the kernels had "drawn enough starch," water was let out of the field, and both the soil and the stalks were allowed to dry under the hot sun.

Then came the harvest, when all the rice plants were cut off a few inches above the ground with a sickle. Threshing was done on a threshing board. Then the grain and the stalks and leaves were taken home with a carrying pole on the peasant's shoulder. The plant was used as fuel at home.

As soon as the exhausting harvest work was done, no time could be lost before starting the chores of plowing, fertilizing, pumping water into the fields, and transplanting seedlings for the second crop. The slack season of the rice crop was taken up by chores required for the vegetables which demanded continuous attention, since every peasant family devoted a part of the farm to vegetable gardening. In the hot and damp period of late spring and summer, eggplant and several varieties of squash and beans were grown. The green-leafed vegetables thrived in the cooler and drier period of fall, winter, and early spring. Leeks grew the year round.

When one crop of vegetables was harvested, the soil was turned and the clods broken up by a digging hoe and leveled with an iron rake. Fertilizer was applied, and seeds or seedlings of a new crop were planted. Hand weeding was a constant job; watering with the long-handled wooden dipper had to be done an average of three times a day, and in the very hot season when evaporation was rapid, as frequently as six times a day. The soil had to be cultivated with the hoe frequently as the heavy tropical rains packed the earth continuously. Instead of the two applications of fertilizer common with the rice crop, fertilizing was much more frequent for vegetables. Besides the heavy fertilizing of the soil at the beginning of a crop, usually with city garbage, additional fertilizer, usually diluted urine or a mixture of diluted urine and excreta, was given every ten days or so to most vegetables.

Source: Adapted from C. K. Yang, *A Chinese Village in Early Communist Transition* (Cambridge, MA: Massachusetts Institute of Technology, 1959).

livestock are part of the agricultural system, and fish may be reared in rice paddies and ponds. Cattle are a source of labor and of food. Food animals include swine, ducks, and chickens, but since Muslims eat no pork, hogs are absent in their areas of settlement. Hindus generally eat little meat, mainly goat and lamb but not pork or beef. The large number of cattle in India are vital for labor, as a source of milk and cheese, and as producers of fertilizer and fuel.

Costs of Territorial Extension

Improved health care in this century has lowered infant and crude death rates and accelerated population growth rates in countries of intensive subsistence agriculture. The rising population, of course, puts increasing pressure on the land and, following the Boserup thesis, the response has been to increase further the intensity of agricultural production. Lands formerly considered unsuitable for farming by reason of low fertility, inadequate moisture, difficulty of clearing and preparation, isolation from settlement areas, and other factors have been brought into cultivation.

To till those additional lands, a price must be paid. Any economic activity incurs an additional (called *marginal*) cost in labor, capital, or other unit of expenditure to bring into existence an added unit of production. When the value of the added (marginal) production at least equals the added cost, the effort may be undertaken. In past periods of lower population pressure, there was no incentive to extend cultivation to less productive or more expensive unneeded lands. Now circumstances are different. In many intensive subsistence agricultural economies, however, possibilities for land conversion to agriculture are limited. More than 60% of the population of the developing world lives in countries in which some three-quarters of possible arable land is already under cultivation and where undeveloped cultivable land has low potential for settlement and use.

When population pressures dictate land conversion, serious environmental deterioration may result. Clearing of wet tropical forests in the Philippines and Indonesia has converted dense woodland to barren desolation within a very few years as soil erosion and nutrient loss have followed forest destruction. In Southeast Asia, some 10 million hectares (25 million acres) of former forestland are now wasteland, covered by useless sawgrasses that supply neither forage, food, nor fuel.

The Green Revolution

Increased productivity of existing cropland rather than expansion of cultivated area has accounted for most of the growth of agricultural production over the past few decades. **Green Revolution** is the shorthand reference to a complex of seed and management improvements adapted to the needs of intensive agriculture that have brought larger harvests from a given area of farmland. Between 1965 and 1995, world cereal production rose more than 90%; over three-quarters of that increase was due to increases in yields rather than expansions in cropland. For Asia as a whole, cereal yields grew by nearly one-third between 1980 and 1992 and increased by nearly 25% in South America. These yield increases and the improved food supplies they represent have been particularly important in densely populated, subsistence farming areas heavily dependent on rice and wheat cultivation (Figure 8.10). Indeed, the proportion of malnourished fell, the Food and Agriculture Organization (FAO) tells us, from 36% to 20% of the population of developing countries between 1965 and 1995.

Genetic improvements in rice and wheat have formed the basis of the Green Revolution. Dwarfed varieties have been developed that respond dramatically to heavy applications of fertilizer, that resist plant diseases, and that can tolerate much shorter growing seasons than traditional native

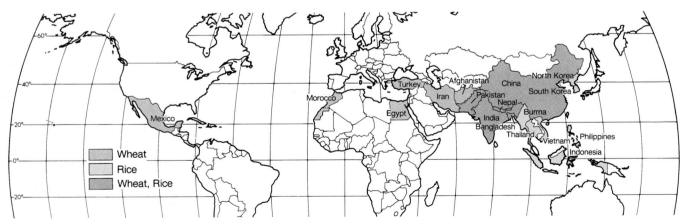

FIGURE 8.10   Chief beneficiaries of the Green Revolution. In the 11 countries that were early adopters of new rice varieties and cropping technologies, average yields increased by 52% between 1965 and 1983. In the rest of the world, they actually dropped by 4% during the same period. Wheat yields increased 66% in the 9 reporting countries (excluding Mexico); in the rest of the world they grew only 29%. By the early 1990s in the developing countries as a group, new high-yielding crop varieties were being used on 52% of the farmland planted in wheat, 54% of land planted in rice, and 51% of land planted in maize.

varieties. Adopting the new varieties and applying the irrigation, mechanization, fertilization, and pesticide practices they require have created a new "high-input, high-yield" agriculture. Most poor farmers on marginal and rain-fed (nonirrigated) lands, however, have not benefited from the new plant varieties requiring irrigation and high-chemical inputs.

Expanded food production made possible through the Green Revolution has helped alleviate some of the shortages and famines predicted for intensive subsistence agricultural regions since the early 1960s (Figure 8.11). But a price has been paid. Traditional and subsistence agriculture is being displaced. With it is lost the food security that distinctive locally adapted native crop varieties (*land races*) provided and

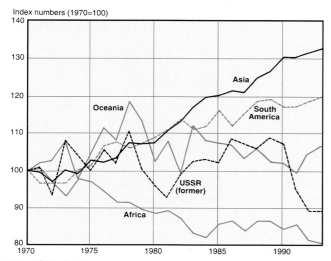

FIGURE 8.11 **Index of per capita food production by region, 1970–1993.** The average annual increase in world food production has declined over the past decades, dropping from 3% anually during the 1960's to 2.4% in the 1970s, and to 2.2% in the 1980s. Total food—particularly grain—production actually showed absolute declines during some years of the 1990s. As a result, the earlier upward trend in annual per capita food availability appears to have leveled off since 1985 as stagnant or declining agricultural output supplies an increasing total population.

From 1984 to the mid-1990s, world grain land output grew only 1% per year—below the pace of population growth. Earlier dramatic yield increases were largely due to the effective interactions of increasing fertilizer use, expanding irrigation, and the introduction of grain varieties responsive to heavy fertilizer applications. Up to 1984, each additional ton of fertilizer boosted world grain output 9 tons. Since 1984, fertilizer efficiency and use have dropped sharply as the limits of plant response were reached for each of the major cereals—wheat, rice, and corn.

Data from Food and Agriculture Organization, World Resources Institute, and U.S. Department of Agriculture.

the nutritional diversity and balance that multiple-crop, intensive gardening assured. Subsistence farming, wherever practiced, was oriented toward risk minimization. Many differentially hardy varieties of a single crop guaranteed some yield whatever adverse weather, disease, or pest problems might occur.

Commercial agriculture, however, aims at profit maximization, not minimal food security. Poor farmers unable to afford the capital investment the Green Revolution demands have been displaced by a commercial monoculture, one often oriented toward specialty and industrial crops designed for export rather than to food production for a domestic market. Traditional rural society has been disrupted, and landless peasants have been added to the urbanizing populations of affected countries. To the extent that land races are lost to monoculture, varietal distinction in food crops is reduced. "Seed banks" rather than native cultivation are increasingly needed to preserve genetic diversity for future plant breeding and as insurance against catastrophic pest or disease susceptibility of inbred varieties (Figure 8.12).

The presumed benefits of the Green Revolution are not available to all subsistence agricultural areas or advantageous to everyone engaged in farming (see "Women and the Green Revolution"). Africa is a case in point (Figure 8.11). Green Revolution crop improvements have concentrated on wheat, rice, and maize. Of these, only maize is important in Africa, where principal food crops include millet, sorghum, cassava, manioc, yams, cowpeas, and peanuts. Although new varieties of maize resistant to the drought and acidic soils common in Africa were announced in the middle 1990s, both belated research efforts directed to African crops and the great range of growing conditions on the continent suggest that the dramatic regionwide increases in food production experienced with rice in Southeast Asia will be delayed or perhaps never experienced in the African context.

Even in those world regions favorable for Green Revolution introductions, its advent has not always improved diets or reduced dependency on imported basic foodstuffs. Often, the displacement of native agriculture involves a net loss of domestic food availability. In many instances, through governmental directive, foreign ownership or management, or domestic market realities, the new commercial agriculture is oriented towards food and industrial crops for the export market or towards specialty crop and livestock production for the expanding urban market rather than food production for the rural population.

Commercial Agriculture

Few people or areas still retain the isolation and selfcontainment characteristic of pure subsistence economies. Nearly all have been touched by a modern world of trade and exchange and have adjusted their traditional economies in response. Modifications of subsistence agricultural systems have inevitably made them more complex by imparting to them at least some of the diversity and linkages of activity that mark the advanced economic systems of the more developed world. Farmers in those systems produce not for

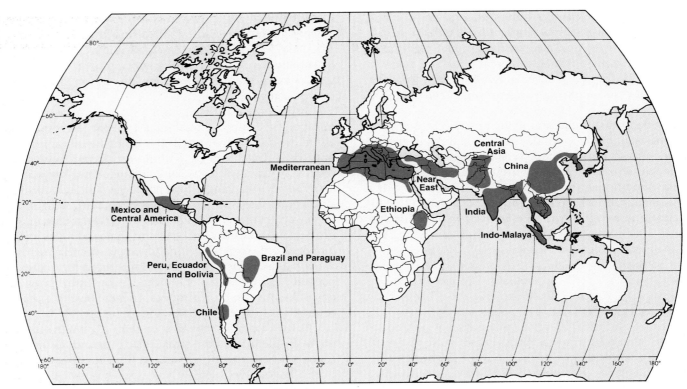

FIGURE 8.12   Areas with high current genetic diversity of crop varieties. Loss of crop varieties characterizes the commercial agriculture of much of the developed world. In place of the many thousands of species and subspecies (varieties) of food plants grown since the development of agriculture 15,000 or more years ago, fewer than 100 species now provide most of the world's food supply. Most of the diversity loss has occurred in the last century. In the United States, for example, 96% of commercial vegetable varieties listed by the Department of Agriculture in 1903 are now extinct. Crop breeders, however, require genetic diversity to develop new varieties that are resistant to evolving plant pest and disease perils. That need necessitates the protection of plant stocks and environments in those temperate and subtropical zones where food plants were first domesticated and are home to the wild relatives of our current food crops.

their own subsistence but primarily for a market off the farm itself. They are part of integrated exchange economies in which agriculture is but one element in a complex structure that includes employment in mining, manufacturing, processing, and the service activities of the tertiary and quaternary sectors. In those economies, agricultural patterns presumably mark production responses to market demand expressed through price, and are related to the consumption requirements of the larger society rather than to the immediate needs of farmers themselves.

Production Controls

Agriculture within modern, developed economies is characterized by *specialization*—by enterprise (farm), by area, and even by country; by *off-farm sale* rather than subsistence production; and by *interdependence* of producers and buyers linked through markets. Farmers in a free market economy supposedly produce those crops that their estimates of market price and production cost indicate will yield the greatest return. Theoretically, farm products in short supply will command an increased market price.

That, in turn, should induce increased production to meet the demand with a consequent reduction of market price to a level of equilibrium with production costs. In some developing countries, that equation between production costs and market price is broken and the farm economy distorted when government policy requires uneconomically low food prices for urban workers.

Where free market conditions prevail, however, the crop or the mix of crops and livestock that individual commercial farmers produce is a result of an appraisal of profit possibilities. Farmers must assess and predict prices, evaluate the physical nature of farmland, and factor in the possible weather conditions. The costs of production (fuel, fertilizer, capital equipment, labor) must be reckoned. A number of unpredictable conditions may thwart farmers' aspirations for profit. Among them are the uncertainties of growing season conditions that follow the original planting decision, the total volume of output that will be achieved (and therefore the unit cost of production), and the supply and price situation that will exist months or years in the future, when crops are ready for market.

omen farmers grow at least half of the world's food and up to 80% in some African countries. They are responsible for an even larger share of food consumed by their own families: 80% in sub-Saharan Africa and 60% in Asia. Further, women comprise between one-third and one-half of all agricultural laborers in developing countries. Despite their fundamental role, however, women do not share equally with men in the rewards from agriculture, nor are they always beneficiaries of presumed improvements in agricultural technologies and practices.

As a rule, women farmers work longer hours and have lower incomes than do male farmers. This is not because they are less educated or competent. Rather, it is due to restricting cultural and economic factors. First, most women farmers are involved in subsistence farming and food production for the local market that yields little cash return. Second, they have less access than men to credit at bank or government-subsidized rates that would make it possible for them to acquire the Green Revolution technology, such as hybrid seeds and fertilizers. Third, in some cultures women cannot own land and so are excluded from agricultural improvement programs and projects aimed at landowners. For example, many African agricultural development programs are based on the conversion of communal land, to which women have access, to private holdings, from which they are excluded.

At the same time, the Green Revolution and its greater commercialization of crops has generally required an increase in labor per hectare, particularly in tasks typically reserved for women, such as weeding, harvesting, and postharvest work. If women are provided no relief from their other daily tasks, the Green Revolution for them may be more burden than blessing. But when mechanization is added to the new farming system, women tend to be losers. Frequently, such predominantly female tasks as harvesting or dehusking and polishing of grain—all traditionally done by hand—are given over to machinery, displacing rather than employing women. Even the application of chemical fertilizers (a man's task) instead of cow dung (women's work) has reduced the female role in agricultural development programs.

If women are to benefit from the Green Revolution, new cultural norms will be required that permit them land-owning and other legal rights now denied, access to credit at favorable rates, and government assistance programs purged of traditional pro-male biases.

Beginning in the 1950s in the United States, specialist farmers and corporate purchasers developed strategies for minimizing those uncertainties. Processors sought uniformity of product quality and timing of delivery. Vegetable canners—of tomatoes, sweet corn, and the like—required volume delivery of raw products of uniform size, color, and ingredient content on dates that accorded with cannery and labor schedules. And farmers wanted the support of a guaranteed market at an assured price to minimize the uncertainties of their specialization and stabilize the return on their investment.

The solution was contractual arrangements or vertical integrations uniting contracted farmer with purchaser-processor. Broiler chickens of specified age and weight, cattle fed to an exact weight and finish, wheat with a minimum protein content, popping corn with prescribed characteristics, potatoes of the kind and quality demanded by particular fast-food chains, and similar product specification became part of production contracts between farmer and buyer-processor. In the United States, the percentage of total farm output produced under contractual arrangements or by vertical integration (where production, processing, and sales were all coordinated within one firm) rose from 19% in 1960 to well over one-third by the 1990s.

Supply, demand, and the market price mechanism are the presumed controls on agricultural production in commercial economies. In actuality, they are joined by a number of nonmarket governmental influences that may be as decisive as market forces in shaping farmers' options and spatial production patterns. If there is a glut of wheat on the market, for example, the price per ton will come down and the area sown should diminish. It will also diminish regardless of supply if governments, responding to economic or political considerations, impose acreage controls.

Distortions of market control may also be introduced to favor certain crops or commodities through subsidies, price supports, market protections, and the like. The political power of farmers in the European Union (EU), for example, secured for them generous product subsidies and for the EU immense unsold stores of butter, wine, and grains until 1992, when reforms began to reduce the unsold stockpiles even while increasing total farm spending. In Japan, the home market for rice is largely protected and reserved for Japanese rice farmers even though their production efficiencies are low and their selling price is high by world market standards. In the United States, programs of farm price supports, acreage controls, financial assistance, and other governmental involvements in agriculture are of long-standing

FIGURE 8.13 Open storage of 1 million bushels of Iowa corn. In the world of commercial agriculture, supply and demand are not always in balance. Both the bounty of nature in favorable crop years and the intervention of governmental programs that distort production decisions can create surpluses for which no market is readily available.

and of equally distorting effect (Figure 8.13). The result is international tension as market competition builds to dispose of unwanted farm surpluses.

A Model of Agricultural Location

Early in the 19th century, before such governmental influences were the norm, Johann Heinrich von Thünen (1783–1850) observed that lands of apparently identical physical properties were utilized for different agricultural purposes. Around each major urban market center, he noted, there developed a set of concentric land use rings of different farm products (Figure 8.14). The ring closest to the market specialized in perishable commodities that were both expensive to ship and in high demand. The high prices they could command in the urban market made their production an appropriate use of high-valued land near the city. Surrounding rings of farmlands farther away from the city were used for less perishable commodities with lower transport costs, reduced demand, and lower market prices. General farming and grain farming replaced the market gardening of the inner ring. At the outer margins of profitable agriculture, farthest from the single central market, livestock grazing and similar extensive land uses were found.

To explain why this should be so, von Thünen constructed a formal spatial model, perhaps the first developed to analyze human activity patterns. He deduced that the uses to which parcels were put was a function of the differ-ing "rent" values placed on seemingly identical lands. Those differences, he claimed, reflected the cost of overcoming the distance separating a given farm from a central market town ("A portion of each crop is eaten by the wheels," he observed). The greater the distance, the higher was the operating cost to the farmer, since transport charges had to be added to other expenses. When a commodity's production costs plus its transport costs just equaled its value at the market, a farmer was at the economic margin of its cultivation. A simple exchange relationship ensued: the greater the transportation costs, the lower the rent that could be paid for land if the crop produced was to remain competitive in the market.

Since in the simplest form of the model, transport costs are the only variable, the relationship between land rent and distance from market can be easily calculated by reference to each competing crop's *transport gradient*. Perishable commodities such as fruits and vegetables would encounter high transport rates per unit of distance; other items such as grain would have lower rates. Land rent for any farm commodity decreases with increasing distance from the central market, and the rate of decline is determined by the transport gradient for that commodity. Crops that have both the highest market price and the highest transport costs will be grown nearest to the market. Less perishable crops with lower production and transport costs will be grown at greater distances away (Figure 8.15). Since in this model

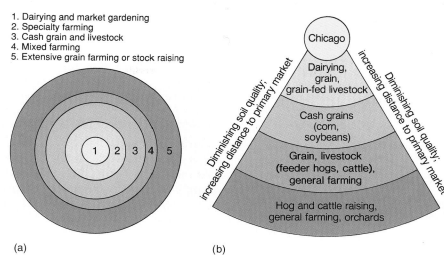

1. Dairying and market gardening
2. Specialty farming
3. Cash grain and livestock
4. Mixed farming
5. Extensive grain farming or stock raising

(a)

Chicago

Dairying, grain, grain-fed livestock

Cash grains (corn, soybeans)

Grain, livestock (feeder hogs, cattle), general farming

Hog and cattle raising, general farming, orchards

Diminishing soil quality; increasing distance to primary market

Diminishing soil quality; increasing distance to primary market

(b)

FIGURE 8.14   (a) **von Thünen's model.** Recognizing that as distance from the market increases, the value of land decreases, von Thünen developed a descriptive model of intensity of land use that holds up reasonably well in practice. The most intensively produced crops are found on land close to the market; the less intensively produced commodities are located at more distant points. The numbered zones of the diagram represent modern equivalents of the theoretical land use sequence von Thünen suggested over 150 years ago. As the metropolitan area at the center increases in size, the agricultural speciality areas are displaced outward, but the relative position of each is retained. Compare this diagram with Figure 8.18. (b) **A schematic view of the von Thünen zones** in the sector south of Chicago. There, farmland quality decreases southward as the boundary of recent glaciation is passed and hill lands are encountered in southern Illinois. On the margins of the city near the market, dairying competes for space with livestock feeding and suburbanization. Southward into flat, fertile central Illinois, cash grains dominate. In southern Illinois, livestock rearing and fattening, general farming, and some orchard crops are the rule.

transport costs are uniform in all directions away from the center, a concentric zonal pattern of land use called the **von Thünen rings** results.

The von Thünen model may be modified by introducing ideas of differential transport costs (Figure 8.16), variations in topography or soil fertility, or changes in commodity demand and market price. With or without such modifications, von Thünen's analysis helps explain the changing crop patterns and farm sizes evident on the landscape at increasing distance from major cities, particularly in regions dominantly agricultural in economy. Farmland close to markets takes on high value, is used *intensively* for high-value crops, and is subdivided into relatively small units. Land far from markets is used *extensively* and in larger units.

In dominantly industrial and post-industrial economies, it has been suggested, the basic forces determining agricultural land use near cities are those associated with urban expansion itself, and von Thünen regularities are less certain. Rather, irregularities and uncertainties of peripheral city growth, the encroachment on agricultural land by expansion from two or more cities, and the withholding of land from farming in anticipation of subdivision may locally reverse the von Thünen intensity rings. Where those urbanizing forces dominate, the agricultural pattern often may be one of increasing—rather than decreasing—intensity with distance from the city.

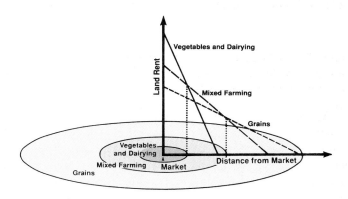

FIGURE 8.15   **Transport gradients and agricultural zones.**

Intensive Commercial Agriculture

Farmers who apply large amounts of capital (for machinery and fertilizers, for example) and/or labor per unit of land engage in **intensive commercial agriculture.** The crops that justify such costly inputs are characterized by high yields and high market value per unit of land. They include fruits, vegetables, and dairy products, all of which are highly perishable. Near most medium-sized and large cities, dairy farms and **truck farms** (horticultural or "market garden" farms) produce a wide range of vegetables and fruits. Since the produce is perishable, transport costs increase because

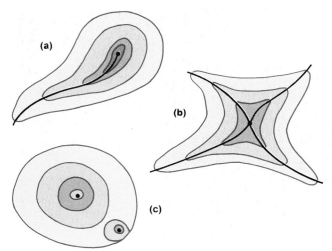

FIGURE 8.16 **Ring modifications.** Modifications of controlling conditions will alter the details but not change the underlying pattern of the *von Thünen rings*. For example, a change in demand and therefore market price of a commodity would merely expand its ring of production. An increase in transport costs would contract the production area, while reductions in freight rates would extend it. (*a*) If transport costs are reduced in one direction, the circularity—but not the sequence—of the rings will be affected. (*b*) If several roads are constructed or improved, land use sequences assume a star-shaped or digitate outline. (*c*) The addition of a smaller outlying market results in the emergence of a set of von Thünen rings subordinate to it.

of the required special handling, such as use of refrigerated trucks and custom packaging. This is another reason for locations close to market. Note the distribution of truck and fruit farming in Figure 8.17.

Livestock-grain farming involves the growing of grain to be fed on the producing farm to livestock, which constitute the farm's cash product. In Western Europe, three-fourths of cropland is devoted to production for animal consumption; in Denmark, 90% of all grains are fed to livestock for conversion not only into meat but also into butter, cheese, and milk. Although livestock-grain farmers work their land intensively, the value of their product per unit of land is usually less than that of the truck farm. Consequently, in North America at least, livestock-grain farms are farther from the main markets than are horticultural and dairy farms.

Normally the profits for marketing livestock (chiefly hogs and beef cattle in the United States) are greater per pound than those for selling corn or other feed, such as alfalfa and clover. As a result, farmers convert their corn into meat on the farm by feeding it to the livestock, efficiently avoiding the cost of buying grain. They may also convert farm grain at local feed mills to the more balanced feed modern livestock rearing requires. Where land is too expensive to be used to grow feed, especially near cities, feed must be shipped to the farm. The grain-livestock belts of the world are close to the great coastal and industrial zone markets. The "corn belt" of the United States and the livestock region of Western Europe are two examples.

Extensive Commercial Agriculture

Farther from the market, on less expensive land, there is less need to use the land intensively. Cheaper land gives rise to larger farm units. **Extensive commercial agriculture** is typified by large wheat farms and livestock ranching.

There are, of course, limits to the land use explanations attributable to von Thünen's model. While it is evident from Figure 8.18 that farmland values decline westward with increasing distance from the northeastern market of the United States, they show no corresponding increase with increasing proximity to the massive West Coast market region until the agricultural specialty areas of the coastal states themselves are reached. The western states are characterized by extensive agriculture, but as a consequence of environmental, not distance, considerations. Climatic conditions obviously affect the productivity and the potential agricultural use of an area, as do associated soils regions and topography. In Anglo America, of course, increasing distance westward from eastern markets is by chance associated with increasing aridity and the beginning of mountainous terrain. In general, rough terrain and subhumid climates rather than simple distance from market underlie the widespread occurrence of extensive agriculture.

Large-scale wheat farming requires sizable capital inputs for planting and harvesting machinery, but the inputs per unit of land are low; wheat farms are very large. Nearly half the farms in Saskatchewan, for example, are more than 400 hectares (1000 acres). The average farm in Kansas is over 400 hectares, and in North Dakota more than 525 (1300 acres). In North America, the spring wheat (planted in spring, harvested in autumn) region includes the Dakotas, eastern Montana, and the southern parts of the Prairie Provinces of Canada. The winter wheat (planted in fall, harvested in midsummer) belt focuses on Kansas and includes adjacent sections of neighboring states (Figure 8.19). Argentina is the only South American country to have comparable large-scale wheat farming. In the Eastern Hemisphere, the system is fully developed only east of the Volga River in northern Kazakhstan and the southern part of Western Siberia, and in southeastern and western Australia. Because wheat is an important crop in many agricultural systems—today, wheat ranks first in total production among all the world's grains and accounts for more than 20% of the total calories consumed by humans collectively—large-scale wheat farms face competition from commercial and subsistence producers throughout the world (Figure 8.20).

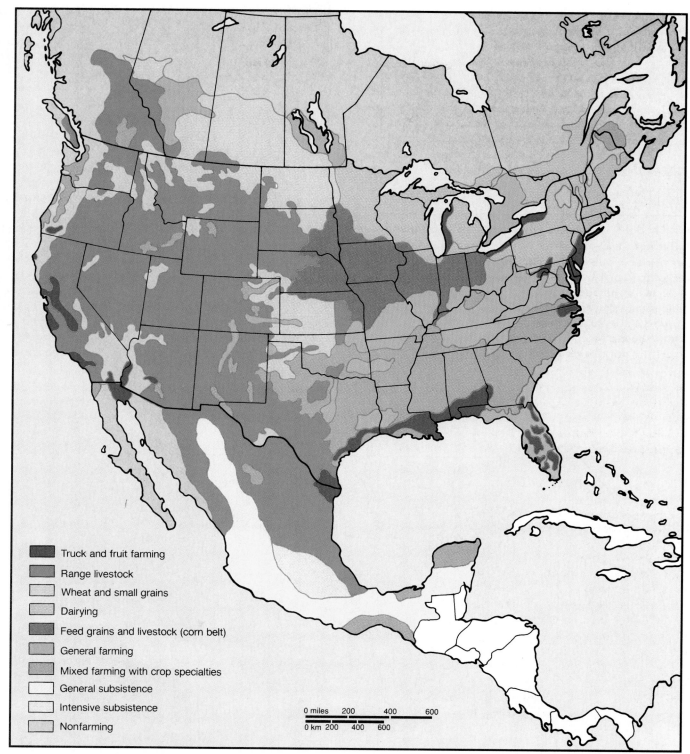

Legend

- Truck and fruit farming
- Range livestock
- Wheat and small grains
- Dairying
- Feed grains and livestock (corn belt)
- General farming
- Mixed farming with crop specialties
- General subsistence
- Intensive subsistence
- Nonfarming

0 miles | 200 | 400 | 600

0 km 200 | 400 | 600

FIGURE 8.17   Generalized agricultural regions of North America.

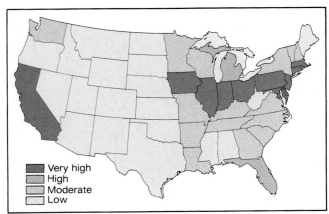

FIGURE 8.18   **Relative value per acre of farmland and buildings.** In a generalized way, per acre valuations support von Thünen's model. The major metropolitan markets of the Northeast, the Midwest, and California are in part reflected by high rural property valuations, and fruit and vegetable production along the Gulf Coast increases land values there. National and international markets for agricultural goods, soil productivity, climate, and terrain characteristics are also reflected in the map patterns.

FIGURE 8.19   Contract harvesters follow the ripening wheat northward through the plains of the United States and Canada.

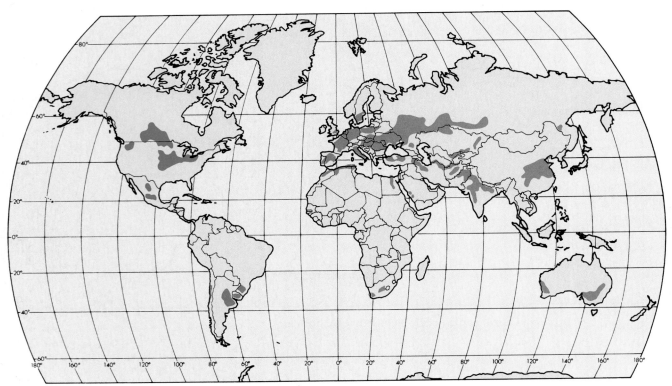

FIGURE 8.20   **Principal wheat-growing areas.** Only part of the world's wheat production comes from large-scale farming enterprises. In western and southern Europe, eastern and southern Asia, and North Africa, wheat growing is part of general or intensive subsistence farming. Recently, developing country successes with the Green Revolution and subsidized surpluses of the grain in Europe have altered traditional patterns of production and world trade in wheat.

DYNAMIC PATTERNS OF THE SPACE ECONOMY

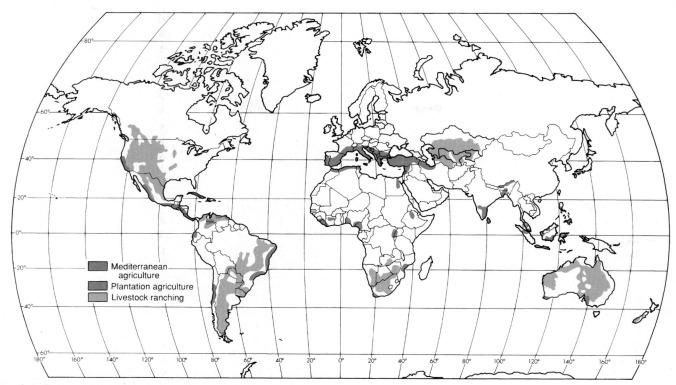

FIGURE 8.21 **Livestock ranching and special crop agriculture.** Livestock ranching is primarily a midlatitude enterprise catering to the urban markets of industrialized countries. Mediterranean and plantation agriculture are similarly oriented to the markets provided by advanced economies of Western Europe and North America. Areas of Mediterranean agriculture—all of roughly comparable climatic conditions—specialize in similar commodities, such as grapes, oranges, olives, peaches, and vegetables. The specialized crops of plantation agriculture are influenced by both physical geographic conditions and present or, particularly, former colonial control of the area.

Livestock ranching differs significantly from livestock-grain farming and, by its commercial orientation and distribution, from the nomadism it superficially resembles. A product of the 19th-century growth of urban markets for beef and wool in Western Europe and the northeastern United States, ranching has been primarily confined to areas of European settlement. It is found in the western United States and adjacent sections of Mexico and Canada (Figure 8.17); the grasslands of Argentina, Brazil, Uruguay, and Venezuela; the interior of Australia; the uplands of South Island, New Zealand; and the Karoo and adjacent areas of South Africa (Figure 8.21). All except New Zealand and the humid pampas of South America have semiarid climates. All, even the most remote from markets, were a product of improvements in transportation by land and sea, refrigeration of carriers, and of meat-canning technology.

In all of the ranching regions, livestock range (and the area exclusively in ranching) has been reduced as crop farming has encroached on their more humid margins, as pasture improvement has replaced less nutritious native grasses, and as grain fattening has supplemented traditional grazing. Recently, the midlatitude demand for beef has been blamed for expanded cattle ranching and extensive destruction of tropical rain forests in Central America and the Amazon basin.

In areas of livestock ranching, young cattle or sheep are allowed to graze over thousands of acres. In the United States, when the cattle have gained enough weight so that weight loss in shipping will not be a problem, they are sent to livestock-grain farms or to feedlots near slaughterhouses for accelerated fattening. Since ranching can be an economic activity only where alternative land uses are nonexistent and land quality is low, ranching regions of the world characteristically have low population densities, low capitalizations per land unit, and relatively low labor requirements.

Special Crops

Proximity to the market does not guarantee the intensive production of high-value crops should terrain or climatic circumstances hinder it. Nor does great distance from the market inevitably determine that extensive farming on low-priced land will be the sole agricultural option. Special circumstances, most often climatic, make some places far from markets intensively developed agricultural areas. Two special cases are agriculture in Mediterranean climates and in plantation areas (Figure 8.21).

Most of the arable land in the Mediterranean basin itself is planted to grains, and much of the agricultural area is used for grazing. *Mediterranean agriculture* as a specialized farming economy, however, is known for grapes, olives, oranges, figs, vegetables, and similar commodities. These crops need warm temperatures all year round and a great deal of sunshine in the summer. The Mediterranean agricultural lands indicated in Figure 8.21 are among the most productive in the world. Farmers can regulate their output in sunny areas such as these because storms and other inclement weather problems are infrequent. Also, the precipitation regime of Mediterranean climate areas—winter rain and summer drought—lends itself to the controlled use of water. Of course, much capital must be spent for the irrigation systems. This is another reason for the intensive use of the land for high-value crops that are, for the most part, destined for export to industrialized countries or areas outside the Mediterranean climatic zone and even, in the case of Southern Hemisphere locations, to markets north of the equator.

Climate is also considered the vital element in the production of what are commonly, but imprecisely, known as *plantation crops*. The implication of **plantation** is the introduction of a foreign element—investment, management, and marketing—into an indigenous culture and economy, often employing an introduced alien labor force. The plantation itself is an estate whose resident workers produce one or two specialized crops. Those crops, although native to the tropics, were frequently foreign to the areas of plantation establishment: African coffee and Asian sugar in the Western Hemisphere and American cacao, tobacco, and rubber in Southeast Asia and Africa are examples (Figure 8.22). Entrepreneurs in Western countries such as England, France, the Netherlands, and the United States became interested in the tropics partly because they afforded them the opportunity to satisfy a demand in temperate lands for agricultural commodities not producible in the market areas. Custom and convenience usually retain the term "plantation" even where native producers of local crops dominate, as they do in cola nut production in Guinea, spice growing in India or Sri Lanka, or sisal production in the Yucatán.

The major plantation crops and the areas where they are produced include tea (India and Sri Lanka), jute (India and Bangladesh), rubber (Malaysia and Indonesia); cacao (Ghana and Nigeria), cane sugar (Cuba and the Caribbean area, Brazil, Mexico, India, and the Philippines), coffee (Brazil and Colombia), and bananas (Central America). As Figure 8.21 suggests, for ease of access to shipping, most plantation crops are cultivated along or near coasts since production for export rather than for local consumption is the rule.

Agriculture in Planned Economies

As their name implies, planned economies have a degree of centrally directed control of resources and of key sectors of the economy that permits the pursuit of governmentally determined objectives. When that control is extended to the agricultural sector—as it was during particularly the latter part of the 20th century in communist-controlled Soviet Union, Eastern Europe, mainland China, and elsewhere—state and collective farms and agricultural communes replace private farms or subsistence gardens, crop

FIGURE 8.22 A Malaysian rubber plantation worker collects latex in a small cup attached to the tree and cuts a new tap just below the previous one. The scene typifies classical plantation agriculture in general. The plantation was established by foreign capital (English) to produce a nonnative (American) commercial crop for a distant, midlatitude market using nonnative (Chinese) labor supervised by foreign (English) managers. Present-day ownership, management, and labor may have changed, but the nature and market orientation of the enterprise remain.

production is divorced from market control or family need, and prices are established by plan rather than by demand or production cost.

Such extremes of rural control have in recent years been relaxed or abandoned in the formerly strictly planned economies. Wherever past centralized control of agriculture was imposed and long endured, however, traditional rural landscapes were altered, the organization of rural society was disrupted. The programs set in motion by Stalin and his successors in the former Soviet Union, for example, fundamentally restructured the geography of agriculture of that country. Together, **collective farms** ("voluntary"—actually, compulsory—producers' cooperatives whose unpaid members lost their own land and joined brigades of other workers assigned specific tasks during the crop year) and **state farms** (government enterprises operated by paid employees of the state) transformed the Soviet countryside from millions of small peasant holdings to a consolidated pattern of fewer than 50,000 centrally controlled operating units.

Only on the small private plots allowed to collective farm families was private farm enterprise permitted within the USSR. The result was that those carefully tended personal plots, together amounting to less than 5% of the country's farmland, yielded more than 25% of the value of its gross agricultural output and produced some 60% of the potatoes, 50% of the fruit, 35% of the eggs and vegetables, and 30% of the meat and milk of the former USSR at the time of its collapse. To compensate for declining per capita food and feed grain production under state and collective farm operations, the Soviet government launched the Virgin and Idle Lands program in 1954, extending farming into marginal semiarid grasslands of the east and expanding total cultivated land in the former USSR by 30% (Figure 8.23).

Conversion to private agriculture was undertaken quickly in Russia following the dissolution of the USSR in late 1991. By July of 1992, 120,000 newly created family farms represented the first phase of privatization of the 26,000 gigantic state and collective farms of the Soviet period. The process was facilitated by a 1993 decrees granting to former collective farmers entitlement certificates usable in bidding singly or in association with others for farmland, equipment, and livestock assets. And in March, 1996, President Yeltsin issued a decree permitting farmers the right to buy, sell, rent, or lease farm land for the first time since 1917. The same edict granted outright ownership of millions of small garden plots to the city dwellers who worked them.

A similar progression from private and peasant agriculture, through collectivization, and back to what is virtually a private farming system has taken place in the planned economy of the People's Republic of China. After its assumption of power in 1949, the Communist regime redistributed all farmlands to some 350 million peasants in inefficiently small (0.2 hectare, or 0.5 acre) subsistence holdings that were totally inadequate for the growing food needs of the country. By the end of 1957, some 90% of peasant households had been organized into about 700,000 communes, a number further reduced in the 1970s to 50,000 communes averaging some 13,000 members. Production goals and directives issued by local officials enforced central governmental agricultural plans.

After the death of Chairman Mao in 1976 what became effectively a private farming system was reintroduced when 180 million new farms were allocated for unrestricted use to

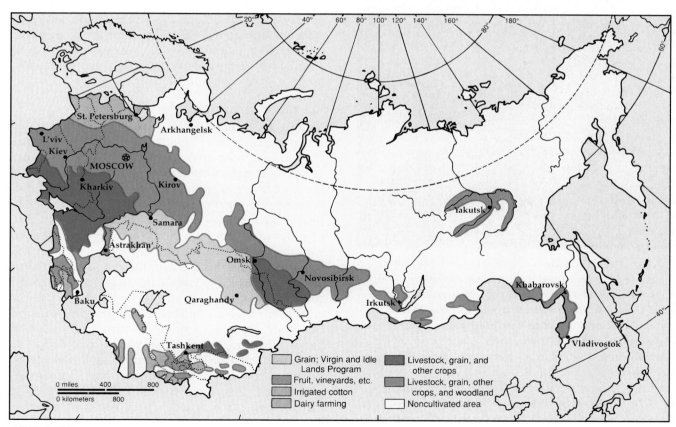

FIGURE 8.23 **The Virgin and Idle Lands** program extended grain production, primarily spring wheat, eastward onto marginal land. Wheat constituted nearly 90% of total Soviet food-grain production and 50% of all grains grown at the time of the state's collapse. Sown land totalled some 10% of the USSR, most of it in a "fertile triangle" wedged between the frigid northern and dry southern limits of farming. The eastward expansion released older western grain areas for vegetables, dairy products, and livestock production. Even before the country's dissolution, sown area was being reduced in the Virgin Lands and some segments—particularly in Kazakhstan—were being returned to grazing. (Note that the map indicates current, rather than Soviet-era, place names).

peasant families under rent-free leases. Most staple crops are still sold under enforced contracts at fixed prices to government purchasers, but increasingly vegetables and meat are sold on the free market (Figure 8.24), and a slow shift from grain production to vegetables and industrial crops is occurring. Total agricultural output increased by 50% between 1980 and 1990 and even allowing for population growth, per capita gains were impressive—up by about one-third. Disturbingly, China—with 20% of the world's population but only 7% of the world's arable land—is losing farmland rapidly to industry and urban development, and to environmental deterioration. Total farmland declined by 20% between the late 1950s and mid-1990s, raising again the prospect of shortages of domestically produced food.

Primary Activities: Resource Exploitation

In addition to agriculture, primary economic activities include fishing, forestry, and the mining and quarrying of minerals. These industries involve the direct exploitation of natural resources that are unequally available in the environment and differentially evaluated by different societies. Their development, therefore, depends on the occurrence of perceived resources, the technology to exploit their natural availability, and the cultural awareness of their value.

Fishing and forestry are **gathering industries** based on harvesting the natural bounty of renewable resources that are in serious danger of depletion through overexploitation. Livelihoods based on both of these resources are areally widespread and both involve subsistence and market-oriented components. Mining and quarrying are **extractive industries,** removing nonrenewable metallic and nonmetallic minerals, including the mineral fuels, from the earth's crust. They are the initial raw material phase of modern industrial economies.

Resource Terminology

Resources or **natural resources** are the naturally occurring materials that a human population, at any given state of economic development and technological awareness, perceives to be necessary and useful to its economic and material well-being. Their occurrence and distribution in the environment are the result of physical processes over which people have little or no direct control. The fact that things exist, however, does not mean that they are resources. To be considered such, a given substance must be *understood* to be a resource—and this is a cultural, not purely a physical, circumstance. Native Americans may have viewed the resource base of Pennsylvania, West Virginia, or Kentucky as composed of forests for shelter and fuel and as the habitat of the game animals (another resource) on which they depended for food. European settlers viewed the forests as the unwanted covering of the resource that *they* perceived to be of value: soil for agriculture. Still later, industrialists appraised the underlying coal deposits, ignored or unrecognized as a resource by earlier occupants, as the item of value for exploitation (Figure 8.25)

Resources may be classified as *renewable* or *nonrenewable.* **Renewable resources** are materials that can be consumed and then replenished relatively quickly by natural or by human-assisted processes. Food crops are renewable resources, for example, as are forests, grasslands, animals and fish, and other living things. Even renewable resources can be exhausted if exploited to extinction or destruction.

FIGURE 8.24 Independent street merchants, shop owners, and peddlers in modern China are members of both a planned and market system. In early 1995 the country's more than 15 million registered private businesses far exceeded the total number of private enterprises operating in 1949 when the Communists took power. Since government price controls on most food items were removed in May, 1985, free markets have multiplied. Increasingly manufacturing, too, is being freed of central government control. In 1978, state-owned firms accounted for 78% of China's industrial output; by 1995, they produced less than half, and by the year 2000, by Chinese government plan, no more than 25% of industrial production will be state controlled. Now, foreign investment is encouraged and capitalism with all its risks and rewards is replacing the security and distortions of communism in the economic sphere. The photo shows a portion of the produce market in Wuxi, Jiangsu Province.

FIGURE 8.25 The original hardwood forest covering these West Virginia hills was removed by settlers who saw greater resource value in the underlying soils. The soils, in their turn, were stripped away for access to the still more valuable coal deposits below. Resources are as a culture perceives them, though their exploitation may consume them and destroy the potential of an area for alternate uses.

Soils can be totally eroded; an animal species may be completely eliminated. The **maximum sustainable yield** of a resource is the maximum volume or rate of use that will not impair its ability to be renewed or to maintain the same future productivity. For fishing and forestry, for example, that level is marked by a catch or harvest equal to the net growth of the replacement stock. If that maximum exploitation level is exceeded, the renewable resource becomes a nonrenewable one—an outcome increasingly likely in the case of Atlantic cod and some other food fish species. **Nonrenewable resources** exist in finite amounts and either are not replaced by natural processes—at least not within any time frame of interest to the exploiting society—or are replaced at a rate slower than the rate of use.

Both types of resources are exploited by the nonagricultural primary industries. Fish as a food resource and forests as a source for building materials, cellulose, and fuel are heavily exploited renewable resources. Mining and quarrying extract from nature the nonrenewable minerals essential to industrialized economies.

Fishing

Fish provide more than 6% of the total daily protein intake of the developing world's population and over 7% of total protein supply worldwide. Reliance on fish is particularly great in developing countries of eastern and southeastern Asia (50% or more of animal protein supply), Africa (15% to 20%), and

parts of Latin America. Fish are also very important in the diets of some advanced states with well-developed fishing industries—Russia, Norway, Iceland, and Japan, for example.

While about two-thirds of the world annual fish catch is consumed by humans, up to one-third is processed into fish meal to be fed to livestock or used as fertilizer. Those two quite different markets have increased both the demand for and annual harvest of fish. Between 1950 and 1970, the total commercial fisheries catch rose steadily at an annual rate of about 6%. An abrupt decline in harvest was experienced in 1972, largely because of the sudden collapse of the Peruvian anchovy catch, which was then by far the largest single segment of the fishery industry. Between 1972 and 1982, slow annual increases of between 1% and 2% were recorded to a steady annual total of about 80 million tons. During the remainder of the 1980s, total catches again increased rapidly to reach nearly 100 million tons annually, but beginning in 1990 for the first time in well over a decade, the total global tonnage of fish caught declined—a warning of overexploitation and resource depletion.

Only about 10% to 12% of the annual fish supply comes from inland waters—lakes, rivers, and farm ponds. The other 88% to 90% of the harvest comes from the world's oceans—from marine fisheries. And most (99%) of that catch is made in coastal wetlands, estuaries, and the relatively shallow coastal waters above the *continental shelf*—the gently sloping extension of submerged land bordering most coastlines and reaching seaward for varying distances up to 150 kilometers (about 100 miles) or more where, at about the 100-fathom (600-foot or nearly 200-meter) line, an abrupt slope to much deeper water occurs (Figure 8.26). Near shore, shallow embayments and marshes provide spawning grounds, and river waters supply nutrients to an environment highly productive of fish. Offshore, ocean currents and upwelling water move great amounts of nutritive materials from the ocean floor through the sunlit surface waters, nourishing *plankton*—minute plant and animal life forming the base of the marine food chain. Increasingly, these are, as well, areas seriously affected by pollution from runoff and ocean dumping, an environmental assault so devastating in some areas that fish and shellfish stocks have been destroyed with little hope of revival.

The remaining 1% of maritime fish catch comes from the open seas that make up more than 90% of the world's oceans. Fishing in these comparatively barren waters is an expensive form of maritime hunting and gathering. An accepted equation in distant water fishing is that about one ton of diesel oil is burned for every ton of fish caught. In fact, all commercial marine fishing is costly. The Food and Agriculture Organization (FAO) reports that governments subsidize fishers with over $50 billion annually of low-cost loans and direct grants, in effect encouraging uneconomic over-exploitation of a decreasing resource.

Commercial fishing for market is largely a northern waters activity. Common and familiar food species—herring, cod, mackerel, haddock, flounder, pollock—are denizens of the northern seas, where warm and cold currents join and mix and where fish congregate or "school" on the broad continental shelves and *banks*—extensive elevated portions of the shelf where environmental conditions are most favorable for fish production. Two of the most heavily fished regions are the Northeast Atlantic, with a (early 1990s) catch of about 10 million tons per year, and the Northwest Pacific, where over 20 million tons per year are taken.

Tropical fish species tend not to school and, because of their high oil content and unfamiliarity, to be less acceptable in the commercial market. They are, however, of great importance for local consumption. Traditional or "artisan" fishermen, nearly all working in inshore waters within sight of land, are estimated to number between 8 and 10 million worldwide, harvesting some 24 million metric tons of fish and shellfish a year—a catch usually not included in world fishery totals. Since each coastal fisherman provides employment for two or three onshore workers, more than 25 million persons are involved in small-scale fisheries.

The rapid increase in world fish catch between 1950 and 1970 led to inflated projections of the eventual total annual catch and to the feeling that the resources of the oceans were inexhaustible. Quite the opposite has proved to be true. Both overfishing and pollution of coastal waters have seriously endangered the supply of traditional and desired food species. The collapse of the Peruvian anchovy industry in the early 1970s was the result of massive overfishing, though ecological change played a role. Pilchard stocks off South Africa and Namibia fell dramatically in 1974 from fishing pressure. Along the North American Atlantic Coast, the weakfish catch fell 85% between 1980 and 1994, the summer

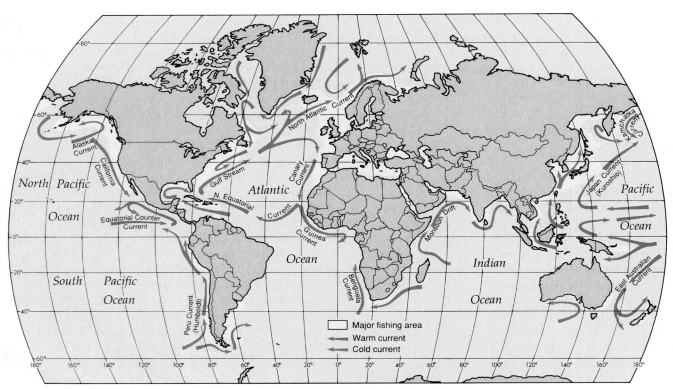

FIGURE 8.26   The major commercial marine fisheries of the world.

flounder take dropped 75% between 1989 and 1995, oysters are largely gone from Chesapeake Bay, and grouper and red snapper were mostly memories in the Gulf of Mexico. In 1993, Canada shut down its cod industry to allow stocks to recover, and U.S. authorities reported that 67 species were overfished and 61 were being harvested to capacity. Worldwide, all 17 of the principal marine fisheries have either reached or exceeded their natural limits and nine are in serious decline.

Overfishing is partly the result of the accepted view that the world's oceans are common property, a resource open to anyone's use with no one responsible for its maintenance, protection, or improvement. The result of this "open seas" principle is but one expression of the so-called **tragedy of the commons**[1]—the economic reality that when a resource is available to all, each user, in the absence of collective controls, thinks he or she is best served by exploiting the resource to the maximum even though this means its eventual depletion.

Increasingly since 1976, coastal states have been claiming a 200-nautical mile (370-km) exclusive economic zone (EEZ) within which they can regulate or prohibit foreign fishing fleets. Since most commercially attractive fish live in coastal waters, these claims, part of the United Nations Convention on the Law of the Sea treaty reviewed in Chapter 12 (pp. 438–439), brought many fisheries under control of the nearest country. In theory, the developed countries should

have benefited the most, for the bulk of distant water fishing is off their coasts and they—the United States and Canada, particularly—gained most in expanded control of fishery resources. Nevertheless, by the mid-1990s, overfishing in developed-country waters was worse than ever as governments failed to act on scientific management recommendations and as domestic fleets expanded to replace banned or restricted foreign fishing in territorial waters.

In 1995, more than 100 countries adopted a treaty—to become legally binding when ratified by 30 nations—to regulate fishing on the open oceans outside of territorial waters. Applying to such species as cod, pollock, and tuna, that is, to migratory and high seas species that together account for 20% of ocean fish stocks, the treaty requires fishermen to report the size of their catches to regional organizations that would set quotas and subject vessels to boarding to check for violations. These and other fishing control measures, if enforced and enforceable, at least hold out the hope of future sustainability of important food fish stocks.

If fully exploited, unconventional maritime food sources may return to the seas their earlier reputation as a near-inexhaustible supplier of protein. Calculations suggest that a sustained yield of 100 million tons per year of squid is reasonable and that tens of millions of tons of *krill*—tiny, shrimplike crustaceans enormously plentiful in Antarctic waters—could be harvested annually. More feasible is the steady expansion of harvesting of fish raised in farm ponds (*aquaculture*) or by fenced confinement in coastal lagoons (*mariculture*). Fish farming in ponds, canals, and rice paddies has been common in Asia for millennia (Figure 8.27);

---

[1] The *commons* refers to undivided land available for the use of everyone; usually, it meant the open land of a village that all used as pasture. The *Boston Common* originally had this meaning.

FIGURE 8.27   Harvesting fish at an aquaculture farm in Thailand.

catfish and crayfish farms are increasingly common in the southeastern United States. Maricultural production of shellfish is being practiced in France, Japan, and the United States. Together, aquaculture and mariculture produce about 15% of the total world fishery harvest, are growing at about 10% a year, and produce 90% of all commercially sold oysters, almost half of the tilapia, a third of all salmon, and more than 25% of all shrimps and prawns.

Forestry

After the retreat of continental glaciers some 11,000 years ago and before the rise of agriculture, the world's forests and woodlands probably covered some 45% of the earth's land area exclusive of Antarctica. They were a sheltered and productive environment for earlier societies that subsisted on gathered fruits, nuts, berries, leaves, roots, and fibers collected from trees and woody plants. Few such cultures remain, though the gathering of forest products is still an important supplemental activity, particularly among subsistence agricultural societies.

Even after millennia of land clearance for agriculture and, more recently, commercial lumbering, cattle ranching, and fuelwood gathering, forests still cover roughly 30% of the world's land area. As an industrial raw material source, however, forests are more restricted in area. Although forests of some type reach discontinuously from the equator northward to beyond the Arctic Circle and southward to the tips of the southern continents, *commercial forests* are restricted to two very large global belts. One, nearly continuous, is found in upper-middle latitudes of the Northern Hemisphere; the second is located in the equatorial zones of South and Central America, Central Africa, and Southeast Asia. (Figure 8.28). These forest belts differ in the types of trees they contain and in the type of market or use they serve.

The northern coniferous, or softwood, forest is the largest and most continuous stand, extending around the globe from Scandinavia across Siberia to North America, then eastward to the Atlantic and southward along the Pacific Coast. The pine, spruce, fir, and other conifers are used for construction lumber and to produce pulp for paper, rayon, and other cellulose products. On the south side of the northern midlatitude forest region are the deciduous hardwoods: oak, hickory, maple, birch, and the like. These and the trees of the mixed forest lying between the hardwood and softwood belts have been greatly reduced in areal extent by centuries of agricultural and urban settlement and development. In both Europe and North America, however, although they—like northern softwoods—have lately been seriously threatened by acid rain and atmospheric pollution, their area has been held constant through conservation, protection, and reforestation. They still are commercially important for hardwood applications: furniture, veneers, railroad ties, and the like. The tropical lowland hardwood forests are exploited primarily for fuelwood and charcoal, although an increasing

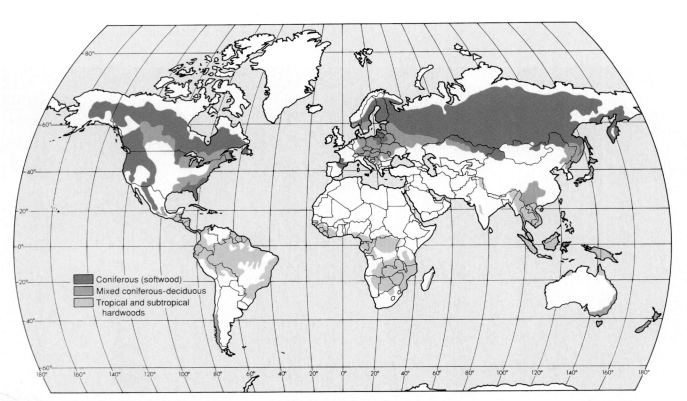

FIGURE 8.28 **Major commercial forest regions.** Much of the original forest, particularly in midlatitude regions, has been cut over. Many treed landscapes that remain do not contain commercial timber stands. Significant portions of the northern forest are not readily accessible and at current prices cannot be considered commercial. Deforestation of tropical hardwood stands involves more clearing for agriculture and firewood than for roundwood production.

DYNAMIC PATTERNS OF THE SPACE ECONOMY

quantity of special quality woods are cut for export as lumber. In fact, developing—particularly tropical—countries account for 90% of the world's hardwood log exports (Figure 8.29); some two-thirds of these in the early 1990s came from Malaysia alone, with the Malaysian state of Sarawak (on the island of Borneo and about the size of Mississippi) the source of one-half of the world's hardwood logs.

These contrasting uses document *roundwood* (log) production as a primary economic activity. About half of the world's annual logging harvest is for industrial consumption, almost all of it the output of industrialized countries from the middle-latitude forest belt. Half of all production of industrial wood is from the United States, Canada, and Russia. Chiefly because of their distance from major industrial wood markets, the developing countries as a group accounted for less than 25% of industrial wood production in the mid-1990s. The logic of von Thünen's analysis of transportation costs and market accessibility helps explain the pattern.

The other half of roundwood production is for fuelwood and charcoal; 85% of world fuelwood production comes from the forests of Africa, Asia, Oceania, and Latin America. Since the populations of developing countries are heavily dependent on fuelwood and charcoal (see "The Energy Crisis in LDCs," Chapter 10), their growing numbers have resulted in serious depletion of tropical forest stands. Indeed, about 60% (some 1.5 billion people) of those who depend on fuelwood as their principal energy source are cutting wood at a rate well above the maximum sustainable yield. In tropical areas as a whole, deforestation rates exceed reforestation by 10 to 15 times. Since the mid-1970s, tropical forests and woodlands have been converted to agricultural lands at a rate of 10 to 12 million hectares (25 to 30 million acres) annually. Additional millions of hectares, particularly in South and Central America, have been cleared for pasture for beef cattle destined primarily for the North American market.

These uses and conversions have serious implications not only ecologically but also economically. Forest removal without replenishment for whatever reason converts the renewable resource of a gathering industry into a destructively exploited nonrenewable one. Regional economies, patterns of international trade, and prospects of industrial development are all adversely affected. Some world and regional ecological consequences of deforestation are discussed in Chapter 13.

Mining and Quarrying

Societies at all stages of economic development can and do engage in agriculture, fishing, and forestry. The extractive industries—mining and drilling for nonrenewable mineral wealth—emerged only when cultural advancement and economic necessity made possible a broader understanding of the earth's resources. Now those industries provide the raw material and energy base for the way of life experienced by people in the advanced economies and are the basis for a major part of the international trade connecting the developed and developing countries of the world.

FIGURE 8.29   Teak logs for export stacked near Mandalay, Myanmar.

The extractive industries depend on the exploitation of minerals unevenly distributed in amounts and concentrations determined by past geologic events, not by contemporary market demand. In physically workable and economically usable deposits, minerals constitute only a tiny fraction of the earth's crust—far less than 1%. That industrialization has proceeded so rapidly and so cheaply is the direct result of an earlier ready availability of rich and accessible deposits of the requisite materials. Economies grew fat by skimming the cream. It has been suggested that should some catastrophe occur to return human cultural levels to a preagricultural state, it would be extremely unlikely that humankind ever again could move along the road of industrialization with the resources left at its disposal.

Our successes in exploiting mineral resources have been achieved not only at the expense of depleting usable world reserves but also at increasing monetary costs as the high-grade deposits are removed (Figure 8.30). Costs increase as more advanced energy-consuming technologies must be applied to extract the desired materials from ever greater depths in the earth's crust or from new deposits of smaller mineral content. That observation states a physical and economic reality relevant particularly to the exploitation of both the *metallic minerals* and the *mineral fuels*. It is less applicable to the third main category of extractive industry, the *nonmetallic minerals*.

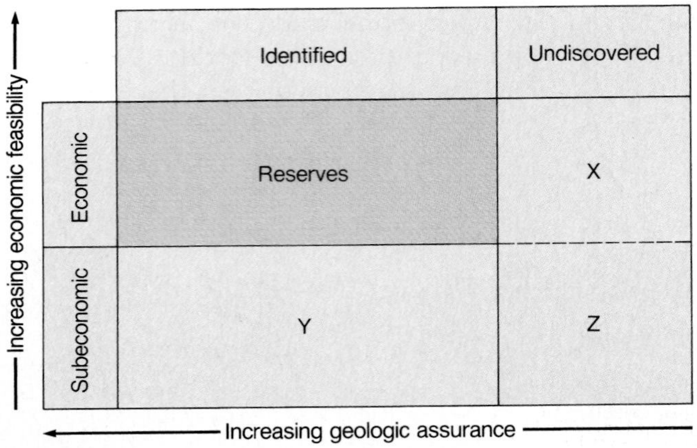

Metallic Minerals

Because usable mineral deposits are the result of geologic accident, it follows that the larger the country, the more probable it is that such accidents will have occurred within the national territory. And in fact, Russia, Canada, China, the United States, Brazil, and Australia possess abundant and diverse mineral resources. It is also true, however, that many smaller developing countries are major sources of one or more critical raw materials and become, therefore, important participants in the growing international trade in minerals.

The production of most metallic minerals, such as copper, lead, and iron ore, is affected by a balance of three forces: the quantity available, the richness of the ore, and the distance to markets. A fourth factor, land acquisition and royalty costs, may equal or exceed other considerations in mine development decisions (see "Public Land, Private Profit"). Even if these conditions are favorable, mines may not be developed or even remain operating if supplies from competing sources are more cheaply available in the market. In the 1980s, more than 25 million tons of iron ore-producing capacity was permanently shut down in the United States and Canada. Similar declines occurred in North American copper, nickel, zinc, lead, and molybdenum mining as market prices fell below domestic production costs. Of course, increases in mineral prices may be reflected in opening or reopening mines that, at lower returns, were deemed unprofitable. However, the developed industrial countries of market economies, whatever their former or even present mineral endowment, find themselves at a competitive disadvantage against developing country producers with lower-cost labor and state-owned mines with abundant, rich reserves.

When the ore is rich in metallic content, it is profitable to ship it directly to the market for refining. But, of course, the highest-grade ores tend to be mined first. Consequently, the demand for low-grade ores has been increasing in recent years as richer deposits have been depleted. Low-grade ores are often upgraded by various types of separation treatments at the mine site to avoid the cost of transporting waste materials not wanted at the market. Concentration of copper is nearly always mine oriented (Figure 8.31); refining takes place near areas of consumption. The large amount of waste in copper (98% to 99% or more of the ore) and in most other industrially significant ores should not be considered the mark of an unattractive deposit. Indeed, the opposite may be true. Because of the cost of extraction or the smallness of the reserves, many higher-content ores are left unexploited in favor of the utilization of large deposits of even very low-grade ore. The attraction of the latter is a size of reserve sufficient to justify the long-term commitment of development capital and, simultaneously, to assure a long-term source of supply.

FIGURE 8.30   **The variable definition of reserves.** Assume the large rectangle includes the total world stock of a particular resource. Some deposits of that resource have been discovered and are shown in the left column as "identified." Deposits not yet known are "undiscovered" reserves. Deposits that are economically recoverable with current technology are at the top of the diagram. Those below, labeled "subeconomic" reserves, are not attractive for any of several reasons—mineral content, accessibility, cost of extraction, and so on. Only the pink area can be properly referred to as **usable reserves.** These are deposits that have been identified and can be recovered at current prices and with current technology. *X* denotes reserves that would be attractive economically but are not yet discovered. Identified but not economically attractive reserves are labeled *Y. Z* represents undiscovered deposits that would not now be attractive even if they were known.

FOR YOUR CONSIDERATION

PUBLIC LAND, PRIVATE PROFIT

When U.S. President Ulysses S. Grant signed the Mining Act of 1872, the presidential and congressional goal was to encourage Western settlement and development by allowing any "hard-rock" miners (including prospectors for silver, gold, copper, and other metals) to mine federally owned land without royalty payment. It further permitted mining companies to gain clear title to publicly owned land and all subsurface minerals for no more than $12 a hectare ($5 an acre). Under those liberal provisions, mining firms have bought 1.3 million hectares (3.2 million acres) of federal land since 1872 and each year remove some $1.2 billion worth of minerals from government property. In contrast to the royalty-free extraction privileges granted to metal miners, oil, gas, and coal companies pay royalties of as much as 12.5% of their gross revenues for exploiting federal lands.

Whatever the merits of the 1872 law in encouraging economic development of lands otherwise unattractive to homesteaders, modern-day mining companies throughout the Western states have secured enormous actual and potential profits from the law's generous provisions. In Montana, a company claim to 810 hectares (2000 acres) of land would cost it less than $10,000 for an estimated $4 billion worth of platinum and palladium; in California, a gold-mining company in 1994 sought title to 93 hectares (230 acres) of federal land containing a potential of $320 million of gold for less than $1200. Foreign as well as domestic firms may be beneficiaries of the 1872 law. In 1994, a South African firm arranged to buy 411 hectares (1016 acres) of

Nevada land with a prospective $1.1 billion in gold from the government for $5100. A Canadian firm in 1994 received title to 800 hectares (nearly 2000 acres) near Elko, Nevada, that cover a likely $10 billion worth of gold—a transfer that Interior Secretary Bruce Babbitt dubbed "the biggest gold heist since the days of Butch Cassidy." And in 1995, Mr. Babbitt conveyed about $1 billion worth of travertine (a mineral used in whitening paper) under 45 hectares (110 acres) of Idaho to a Danish-owned company for $275.

The "gold heist" characterization summarized a growing administration and congressional feeling that what was good in 1872 and today for metal mining companies was not necessarily beneficial to the American public that owns the land. In part, that feeling results from the fact that mining companies commit environmental sins that require public funding to repair or public tolerance to accept. The mining firms may destroy whole mountains to gain access to low-grade ores and leave toxic mine tailings, surface water contamination, and open-pit scarring of the landscape as they move on or disappear. Projected public costs of cleaning up 56 of the most damaged abandoned mining sites are estimated at $32 billion.

A congressional proposal introduced in 1993 would require mining companies to pay royalties of 8% on gross revenues for all hard-rock ores extracted and prohibit them from outright purchase of federal land. The royalty provision alone would have yielded nearly $100 million annually at 1994 levels of company income. Mining firms claim that imposition of royalties might well destroy America's mining industry. They stress both the high levels of investment they must make to extract and process

frequently low-grade ores and the large number of high-wage jobs they provide as their sufficient contribution to the nation. The Canadian company involved in the Elko site, for example, reports that since it acquired the claims in 1987 from their previous owner, it has expended over $1 billion, and in addition has made donations for town sewer lines and schools and created 1700 jobs. The American Mining Congress estimates the proposed 8% royalty charge would cost 47,000 jobs out of 140,000, and even the U.S. Bureau of Mines assumes a loss of 1100 jobs.

Questions:

1. *Do you believe the 1872 Mining Law should be repealed or amended? If not, what are your reasons for arguing for retention? If so, would you advocate the imposition of royalties on mining company revenues? At what levels, if any, should royalties be assessed? Should hard-rock and energy companies be treated equally for access to public land resources? Why or why not?*

2. *Would you propose to prohibit outright land sales to mining companies? If not, should sales prices be determined by surface value of the land or by the estimated (but unrealized) value of mineral deposits it contains?*

3. *Do you think that cleanup and other charges now born by the public are acceptable in view of the capital investments and job creation of hard-rock companies? Do you accept the industry's claim that imposition of royalties would destroy American metal mining? Why or why not?*

FIGURE 8.31 Copper ore concentrating and smelting facilities at the Phelps-Dodge mine in Morenci, Arizona. Concentrating mills crush the ore, separating copper-bearing material from the rocky mass containing it. The great volume of waste material removed assures that most concentrating operations are found near the ore bodies. Smelters separate concentrated copper from other, unwanted minerals such as oxygen and sulfur. Because smelting is also a "weight-reducing" activity, it is frequently—though not invariably—located close to the mine as well.

At one time, high-grade magnetite iron ore was mined and shipped from the Mesabi area of Minnesota. Those deposits are now exhausted. Yet immense amounts of capital have been invested in the mining and processing into high-grade iron ore pellets of the virtually unlimited supplies of low-grade iron-bearing rock (taconite) still remaining. Such investments do not assure the profitable exploitation of the resource. The metals market is highly volatile. Rapidly and widely fluctuating prices can quickly change profitable mining and refining ventures to losing undertakings. Marginal gold and silver deposits are opened or closed in reaction to trends in precious metals prices. Taconite *beneficiation* (waste material removal) in the Lake Superior region has virtually ceased in response to the decline of the U.S. steel industry. In market economies, cost and market controls dominate economic decisions. In planned economies, cost may be a less important consideration than other concerns such as goals of national development and resources independence.

Nonmetallic Minerals

From the standpoint of volume and weight of material removed, the extraction of nonmetallic earth materials is the most important branch of the extractive industries. The minerals mined are usually classified by their end use. Of widest distribution, greatest use, and least long-distance movement are those used for *construction*: sand and gravel, building stone, and the gypsum and limestone that are the ingredients of cement. Transportation costs play a great role in determining where low-value minerals will be mined. Minerals such as gravel, limestone for cement, and aggregate are found in such abundance that they have value only when they are near the site where they are to be used. For example, gravel for road building has value if it is at or near the road-building project, not otherwise. Transporting gravel hundreds of miles is an unprofitable activity (Figure 8.32).

FIGURE 8.32 The Vancouver, British Columbia, municipal gravel quarry and storage yard. Proximity to market gives utility to low-value minerals unable to bear high transportation charges.

The mined *fertilizer* minerals include potash and phosphate, which do move in international trade because of their unequal distribution and market value. *Precious* and *semiprecious* stones are also important in the trade of some countries, including South Africa and Sri Lanka.

Mineral Fuels

The advanced economies have reached that status through their control and use of energy. By the application of energy, the conversion of materials into commodities and the performance of services far beyond the capabilities of any single individual are made possible. Energy consumption goes hand in hand with industrial production and with increases in per capita income (Figure 8.33). Further, the application of energy can overcome deficiencies in the material world that humans exploit. High-quality iron ore may be depleted, but by massive applications of energy, the iron contained in rocks of very low iron content, such as taconite, can be extracted and concentrated for industrial uses.

Because of the association of energy and economic development, a basic disparity between societies is made clear. Countries that can afford high levels of energy consumption through production or purchase continue to expand their economies and to increase their levels of living. Those without access to energy or those unable to afford it see the gap between their economic prospects and those of the developed states growing ever greater.

Except for the brief and localized importance of waterpower at the outset of the Industrial Revolution, modern economic advancement has been heavily dependent on the *mineral fuels:* coal, petroleum, and natural gas. Also known as *fossil fuels,* these nonrenewable energy sources represent the capture of the sun's energy by plants and animals in earlier geologic time and its storage in the form of hydrocarbon compounds in sedimentary rocks within the earth's crust.

Coal was the earliest in importance and is still the most plentiful of the mineral fuels. As the first of the major industrial energy sources, coal deposits—as we shall see in Chapter 9—were formerly very important in attracting manufacturing and urbanization in industrializing countries. Although coal is a nonrenewable resource, world supplies are so great—on the order of 10,000 billion (10^{13}) tons—that its resource life expectancy is measured in centuries, not in the tens of years usually cited for oil and natural gas. Worldwide, the most extensive deposits are concentrated in the industrialized middle latitudes of the Northern Hemisphere (Table 8.1). Two countries, the United States and China, accounted in roughly equal shares for over 40% of total world coal output in the early 1990s; Russia and Germany each produced only 8%.

Coal is not a resource of constant quality, varying in *rank* (a measure—from lignite to anthracite—of increasing carbon content and fuel quality) and *grade* (a measure of its waste material content, particularly ash and sulfur). The value of a coal deposit depends on these measures and on its accessibility, which is a function of the thickness, depth, and continuity of the coal seam. Much coal can be mined relatively cheaply by open-pit (surface) techniques, in which huge shovels strip off surface material and remove the exposed coal (see Figure 13.21). Much coal, however, is available only by expensive and more dangerous shaft mining, as in Appalachia and most of Europe.

Petroleum, first extracted commercially in the 1860s in both the United States and Azerbaijan, became a major power source and a primary component of the extractive industries only early in this century. The rapidity of its adoption as both a favored energy resource and a raw material important in a number of industries from plastics to fertilizers, along with the limited size and the speed of depletion of known and probable reserves, suggests that petroleum cannot long retain its present position of importance in the energy budget of countries. Although no one has more than a

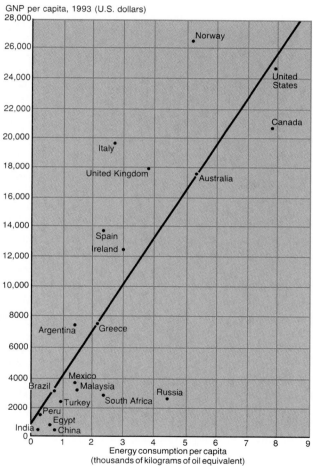

FIGURE 8.33 **Energy and GNP.** Energy consumption rises with increasing gross national product. Because the internal-combustion engine accounts for a large share of national energy consumption, this graph is a statement both of economic development and of the role of mass transportation, automotive efficiency, and mechanization of agriculture and manufacturing in different national economies.

TABLE 8.1   Petroleum, Natural Gas, and Coal Reserves, January 1, 1995

	SHARE OF TOTAL PETROLEUM (%)	SHARE OF TOTAL NATURAL GAS (%)	SHARE OF TOTAL COAL (%)
Anglo America	3.7	4.9	23.9
Western Europe	1.6	3.8	9.1
Former Soviet Union	*5.6*	*39.7*	*23.1*
Of which: Russian Fed.	4.9	34.1	
Others	0.7	5.5	
Other Eastern Europe	0.3	0.5	7.1
Latin America	12.5	5.2	1.0
Africa	6.2	6.8	5.9
Middle East[a]	65.4	32.0	—
Australia/New Zealand	0.2	0.5	8.7
Japan	—	—	0.1
China	2.4	1.2	11.0
Other Asia	1.8	5.4	10.1
Total World	**100.0**	**100.0**	**100**
Of which OPEC[b]	76.3	40.9	NA

[a]Middle East includes Arabian Peninsula, Iran, Iraq, Israel, Jordan, Lebanon, Syria.

[b]OPEC: Organization of Petroleum Exporting Countries. Member nations are, by world region:
Latin America: Venezuela
Middle East: Iran, Iraq, Kuwait, Qatar, Saudi Arabia, United Arab Emirates (Abu Dhabi, Dubai, and Sharjah)
North Africa: Algeria, Libya
West Africa: Gabon, Nigeria
Southeast Asia: Indonesia
Source: British Petroleum (BP), *BP Statistical Review of World Energy 1995.*

vague notion of how much oil (or natural gas) remains in the world or how long it will last, a U.S. Geological Survey estimate suggests that 1996 levels of production could be maintained for about 75 years, though even a modest 3% annual increase in consumption would exhaust reserves in only about 30 years. On a world basis, petroleum accounted for 47% of commercial energy in 1973, but had dropped to 40% by the mid-1990s as a reflection of its increasing cost and of conservation measures to offset those increases.

Petroleum is among the most unevenly distributed of the major resources. Eighty percent of proved reserves are concentrated in just 8 countries and 90% in 12; Iran and the Arab states of the Middle East alone control two-thirds of the world total (Table 8.1). The distribution of petroleum supplies differs markedly from that of the coal deposits on which the urban-industrial markets developed, but the substitution of petroleum for coal did little to alter earlier patterns of manufacturing and population concentration. Because oil is easier and cheaper to transport than coal, it was moved in enormous volumes to the existing centers of consumption via intricate and extensive national and international systems of transportation, a textbook example of spatial interaction, complementarity, and transferability (see Chapter 3).

The dependence of the United States and many other advanced industrial economies (those of Europe and Japan, for example) on imported oil gave the oil exporting states tremendous power, as reflected in the soaring price of petroleum in the 1970s. The oil "shocks" of 1973–1974 and 1979–1980 resulted from the supply and selling price control exerted by the Organization of Petroleum Exporting Countries (OPEC). Their expressions were worldwide recessions, large net trade deficits for some importers, and a reorientation of international monetary wealth. Oil price declines in the mid-1980s had the opposite effect, stimulating economic activity and increasing world consumption of the cheaper fuel. International tensions and conflict, as the Iraqi invasion of Kuwait in 1990 made clear, can again quickly alter established patterns of supply and abruptly increase world oil prices.

Natural gas has been called the nearly perfect energy resource. It is a highly efficient, versatile fuel that requires little processing and is environmentally benign. Geologists estimate that world recoverable gas reserves are sufficient to last to near the middle of the next century at 1995 levels of consumption. *Ultimately recoverable reserves,* those that may be found and recovered at very much higher prices, might last another 200 years.

As we saw for coal and petroleum, reserves of natural gas are very unevenly distributed (Table 8.1). In the case of gas, however, inequalities of supply are not so readily accommodated by massive international movements. Like oil, natural gas flows easily and cheaply by pipeline, but unlike petroleum it does not move freely in international trade by sea. Transoceanic shipment involves costly equipment for liquefaction and for special vessels to contain the liquid under appropriate temperature conditions. Where the fuel can be moved, even internationally, by pipeline, its consumption has increased dramatically. For the world as a whole, gas consumption rose almost 60% between 1974 and 1994, to nearly 25% of global energy consumption.

Trade in Primary Products

International trade expanded by more than 6% a year between 1950 and 1996, a rate over 50% faster than growth in total gross world product. Primary commodities—agricultural goods, minerals, and fuels—make up nearly one-third of the total dollar value of that international trade. The world distribution of supply and demand for those items in general results in an understandable pattern of commodity flow: from raw material producers located within less developed countries to processors, manufacturers, and consumers of the more developed ones (Figure 8.34). The reverse flow carries manufactured goods processed in the industrialized states back to the developing countries, a flow that accounted for 25% of total industrial country exports in 1995. The trade benefits the developed states by providing access to a continuing supply of industrial raw materials and foodstuffs not available domestically. It provides less developed countries with capital to invest in their own development or to expend on the importation of manufactured goods, food supplies, or commodities—such as petroleum—they do not themselves produce. The terms of this exchange have, however, been criticized as unequal and potentially damaging to commodity exporting countries.

Many developing countries rely greatly on the export of primary commodities—for example, on plantation agriculture crops such as coffee, cocoa, rubber, or sugar, or on unprocessed ores and metals, such as bauxite and copper. Developing countries send about two-thirds of both their total agricultural and industrial raw material exports to the industrial countries. Some 90% of Zambia's exports in the late 1980s were copper, and 90% of those of Mauritius were sugar; 60% of Jamaica's exports were either bauxite or alumina. Many developing states have tried to break this degree of dependency and, since 1950, have emphasized the expansion of their industrial capabilities and export of manufactured goods, but with mixed and incomplete results. In Latin America, primary commodities often constitute more than two-thirds of country exports, and in about half of the African states they account for 90% or more.

FIGURE 8.34   Sugar being loaded for export at the port of Cebu in the Philippines. Much of the developing world depends on exports of mineral and agricultural products to the developed economies for the major portion of its income. Fluctuations in market demand and price of some of those commodities can have serious and unexpected consequences.

LIVELIHOOD AND ECONOMY: PRIMARY ACTIVITIES

That dependency has left those countries exposed and weakened. Because commodity prices are volatile, rising sharply in periods of product shortage or international economic growth and, likely, falling abruptly with supply glut or international recession, commodity exporting countries risk disruptive fluctuations in levels of income. This, in turn, can create serious difficulties in economic planning and debt repayment. Commodity prices fell steeply in the decade of the 1980s, and between 1980 and 1995, average commodity prices dropped by more than half in real terms, representing an annual loss to developing countries of $100 billion in the early and mid-1990s. That long-term decline in real prices was the result of growth in demand lower than expansion of production capacity, the shifting of developed economies to activities that use fewer raw materials, and the development through technology of cheaper replacements for some raw materials—synthetic fibers for cotton and jute, synthetic for natural rubber, glass fibers for copper wire. Shorter-term fluctuations due to speculation, temporary glut, and recession are superimposed on those long-term declines.

While prices paid for commodities tend to be low, prices charged for the manufactured goods offered in exchange by the developed countries tend to be high. To capture processing and manufacturing profits for themselves, some developing states have placed restrictions on the export of unprocessed commodities. Malaysia, the Philippines, and Cameroon, for example, have limited the export of logs in favor of increased domestic processing of sawlogs and exports of lumber; in 1985 Indonesia introduced a total ban on unprocessed log exports. Some developing countries have also encouraged domestic manufacturing to reduce imports and to diversify their exports. Frequently, however, such exports meet with tariffs and quotas protecting the home markets of the industrialized states and with agricultural subsidies and price supports. As a result, the disparities in the economic roles and prospects of the developed and less developed countries (the "North-South" split reviewed later in Chapter 10) are continued in the established pattern of trade in primary commodities.

Over the longer term, it has been argued, depletion of their natural capital through export of nonrenewable or destructively exploited resources endangers the future financial well-being of countries dependent wholly or largely on those natural resources for jobs and national income. Even the intensification of that exploitation to compensate for uneconomically low prices cannot guarantee maintenance of their current income levels. Many developing regions heavily dependent on commodities have seen their share of global trade fall materially between 1970 and the mid-1990s: sub-Saharan Africa from 3.8% to 1%, Latin America from 5.6% to 3.3%, and the least developed countries from 0.8% to 0.4%.

Those relative declines are understandable in the light of greatly expanding international trade in manufactured goods from China, Korea, Mexico, and other rapidly industrializing states and from the expansion of trade in both manufactured goods and primary products between the industrialized countries themselves within newly established regional free-trade zones. For example, the developed countries acquire some three-quarters by value of their agricultural imports and 70% of their industrial raw materials from one another. The progressive elimination of tariff barriers within the European Union and the North American Free Trade Agreement—and under the provisions of the World Trade Organization—promises further expansion of the share of world trade carried on between the advanced countries.

In reaction to these felt inequities in world trade between the developed core and developing periphery countries (see The Core-Periphery Argument, p. 336), a demand for a new economic world order resulted in 1964 in the establishment of the United Nations Conference on Trade and Development, whose central constituency is the "Group of 77," now expanded to some 130 developing states demanding an increase in the prices and values of their exports, a system of import preferences for their manufactured goods, and a restructuring of international cooperation to stress trade promotion and recognition of the special needs of poor countries.

Summary

How people earn their living and how the diversified resources of the earth are employed by different peoples and cultures are of fundamental concern in human geography. The economic activities that support us and our society are constant preoccupations that color our perception of the world and its opportunities. At the same time, the totality of our culture—technology, religion, customary behavior—and the circumstances of our natural environment influence the economic choices we discern and the livelihood decisions we make.

In seeking spatial and activity regularities in the nearly infinite diversity of human economic activity, it is useful to generalize about systems of economic organization and control and about classes of productive effort and labor specialization. We can observe for example that, broadly speaking, there are three types of economic systems: subsistence, commercial, and planned. The first is concerned with production for the immediate consumption of individual producers and family members. In the second, economic decisions ideally respond to impersonal market forces and reasoned assessments of monetary gain. In the third, at least some nonmonetary social rather than personal goals influence production decisions. The three system forms are not mutually exclusive; all societies contain some intermixture of features of at least two of the three pure types, and some economies have elements of all three. Recognition of each type's respective features and controls, however, helps us to understand the forces shaping economic decisions and patterns in different cultural and regional settings.

Our search for regularities is furthered by a classification of economic activities according to the stages of production and the degree of specialization they represent. We can, for example, decide all productive activity is arranged along a continuum of increasing technology, labor specialization, value of product, or sophistication of service. With that assumption, we can divide our continuum into primary activities (food and raw material production), secondary production (processing and manufacturing), tertiary activities (distribution and general professional and personal service), and the quaternary activities (administrative, informational, and technical specializations) that mark highly advanced societies of either planned or commercial systems.

Agriculture, the most extensively practiced of the primary industries, is part of the spatial economy of both subsistence and advanced societies. In the first instance—whether it takes the form of extensive or intensive, shifting or sedentary production—it is responsive to the immediate consumption needs of the producer group and reflective of the environmental conditions under which it is practiced. Agriculture in advanced economies involves the application of capital and technology to the productive enterprises; as one sector of an integrated economy, it is responsive to consumption requirements expressed through free or controlled markets. Its spatial expression reflects assessments of profitability and the dictates of social and economic planning.

Agriculture, fishing, forestry, and the extractive (mining) industries are closely tied to the uneven distribution of earth resources. Their spatial patterns reflect those resource potentials, but they are influenced as well by the integration of all societies and economies through the medium of international trade and mutual dependence. The flows of primary products and of manufactured goods suggest the hierarchy of production, marketing, and service activities, which will be the subject of Chapter 9.

KEY WORDS

agriculture 260
Boserup thesis 264
collective farm 276
commercial economy 258
economic geography 256
extensive commercial agriculture 272
extensive subsistence agriculture 261
extractive industry 278
gathering industry 278
Green Revolution 266
intensive commercial agriculture 271

intensive subsistence agriculture 261
maximum sustainable yield 279
natural resource 278
nomadic herding 261
nonrenewable resource 279
planned economy 258
plantation 276
primary activity 257
quaternary activity 257
quinary activity 257
renewable resource 278

secondary activity 257
shifting cultivation 262
state farm 276
subsistence economy 258
technology 257
tertiary activity 257
tragedy of the commons 281
truck farm 271
usable reserves 284
von Thünen rings 271

FOR REVIEW

1. What are the distinguishing characteristics of the economic systems labeled *subsistence, commercial,* and *planned?* Are they mutually exclusive, or can they coexist within a single political unit?

2. What are the ecological consequences of the different forms of *extensive subsistence* land use? In what world regions are such systems found? What, in your opinion, are the prospects for these land uses and for the way of life they embody?

3. How is *intensive subsistence* agriculture distinguished from *extensive subsistence* agriculture? Why, in your opinion, have such

different land use forms developed in separate areas of the warm, moist tropics?

4. Briefly summarize the assumptions and dictates of von Thünen's agricultural model. How might the land use patterns predicted by the model be altered by an increase in the market price of a single crop? A decrease in the transportation costs of one crop but not of all crops?

5. What is the basic distinction between a *renewable* and a *nonrenewable* resource? Under what circumstances might the distinction between the two be blurred or obliterated?

6. What economic and ecological problems can you cite that do or might affect the viability and productivity of the *gathering industries* of forestry and fishing? What is meant by *the tragedy of the commons?* How is that concept related to the problems you discerned?

7. Why have the mineral fuels been so important in economic development? What are the mineral fuels and what are the prospects for their continued availability? What economic and social consequences might you anticipate if the price of mineral fuels should double? If it should be cut in half?

SELECTED REFERENCES

Andreae, Bernd. *Farming, Development and Space: A World Agricultural Geography.* New York: Walter de Gruyter, 1981.

Berry, Brian J. L., Edgar C. Conkling, and D. Michael Ray. *The Global Economy: Resource Use, Locational Choice, and International Trade.* Englewood Cliffs, NJ: Prentice-Hall, 1993.

Boserup, Ester. *The Conditions of Agricultural Change: The Economics of Agrarian Change under Population Pressure.* London, England: Allyn & Unwin, 1965.

Boserup, Ester. *Population and Technological Change: A Study of Long Term Trends.* Chicago: University of Chicago Press, 1981.

Bowler, Ian R. *Agriculture under the Common Agricultural Policy: A Geography.* Manchester, England: Manchester University Press, 1985.

Bowler, Ian R. *The Geography of Agriculture in Developed Market Economies.* New York: John Wiley & Sons, 1993.

Chang, Claudia, and Harold A. Kostner. *Pastoralists at the Periphery: Herders in a Capitalist World.* Tucson: University of Arizona Press, 1994.

Chapman, J. D. *Geography and Energy: Commercial Energy Systems and National Policies.* Burnt Mill, Essex, England, and New York: Longman Scientific and John Wiley & Sons, 1989.

Courtenay, Percy P. *Plantation Agriculture.* 2d ed. London: Bell and Hyman, 1980.

Crosson, Pierre R., and Norman J. Rosenberg. "Strategies for Agriculture." *Scientific American* 261, no. 3 (1989):128–35. Special issue, *Managing Planet Earth.*

Dixon, Chris. *Rural Development in the Third World.* London and New York: Routledge, 1990.

"Energy for Planet Earth." *Scientific American* 263 (September 1990). Special energy issue.

Feeny, David, Firket Berkes, Bonnie J. McCay, and James M. Acheson. "The Tragedy of the Commons: Twenty-two Years Later." *Human Ecology* 18 (1990):1–19.

Freeman, Michael. *Atlas of the World Economy.* New York: Simon & Schuster, 1991.

French, Hilary F. *Costly Tradeoffs: Reconciling Trade and the Environment.* Worldwatch Paper 113. Washington, D.C.: Worldwatch Institute, 1993.

Galaty, John G., and Douglas L. Johnson, eds. *The World of Pastoralism: Herding Systems in Comparative Perspective.* New York: Guilford Press, 1990.

Graham, Edgar, and Ingrid Floering, eds. *The Modern Plantations in the Third World.* New York: St. Martin's Press, 1984.

Grigg, David. *An Introduction to Agricultural Geography.* 2nd ed. New York: Routledge, 1995.

Hamilton, Ian. *Resources and Industry.* New York: Oxford University Press, 1992. The Illustrated Encyclopedia of World Geography.

Hardin, Garrett. "The Tragedy of the Commons." *Science* 162 (1968):1243–1248.

Harris, David R. "The Ecology of Swidden Agriculture in the Upper Orinoco Rain Forest, Venezuela." *Geographical Review* 61 (1971):475–495.

Hart, John Fraser. *The Land that Feeds Us.* New York: W. W. Norton, 1991.

Hartshorn, Truman A., and John W. Alexander. *Economic Geography.* 3d ed. Englewood Cliffs, NJ: Prentice-Hall, 1988.

Hartwick, John M., and Nancy D. Lewiler. *The Economics of Natural Resource Use.* New York: Harper & Row, 1986.

Johnson, Hildegard B. "A Note on Thünen's Circles." *Annals of the Association of American Geographers* 52 (1962):213–220.

Kane, Hal. "Growing Fish in Fields." *WorldWatch* 6, no. 5 (Sept.–Oct. 1993):20–27.

Krugman, Paul. *Geography and Trade.* Cambridge, MA: MIT Press, 1991.

Lele, Uma, and Steven W. Stone. *Population Pressure, the Environment, and Agricultural Intensification.* MADIA Discussion Paper 4. Washington, D.C.: The World Bank, 1989.

Millar, James R. *The Soviet Economic Experiment.* Urbana: University of Illinois Press, 1990.

Mitchell, Bruce. *Geography and Resource Analysis.* 2d ed. New York: John Wiley & Sons, 1989.

Peters, William J., and Leon F. Neuenschwander. *Slash and Burn: Farming in the Third World Forest.* Moscow: University of Idaho Press, 1988.

Postel, Sandra, and Lori Heise. *Reforesting the Earth.* Worldwatch Paper 83. Washington, D.C.: Worldwatch Institute, 1988.

Rees, Judith. *Natural Resources: Allocation, Economics and Policy.* 2d ed. New York: Routledge, 1990.

Sinclair, Robert. "Von Thünen and Urban Sprawl." *Annals of the Association of American Geographers* 57, no. 1 (1967):72–87.

Soussan, John. *Primary Resources and Energy in the Third World.* London and New York: Routledge, 1988.

Symons, Leslie. *Agricultural Geography.* 2d rev. ed. Boulder, CO: Westview Press, 1979.

Tarrant, John, ed. *Farming and Food.* The Illustrated Encyclopedia of World Geography. New York: Oxford University Press, 1991.

Turner, B. L. II, and Stephen B. Brush, eds. *Comparative Farming Systems.* New York: Guilford Press, 1987.

Wädekin, Karl-Eugen, ed. *Communist Agriculture: Farming in the Far East and Cuba.* New York: Routledge, 1990.

Weber, Peter. *Abandoned Seas: Reversing the Decline of the Oceans.* Worldwatch Paper 116. Washington, D.C.: Worldwatch Institute, 1993.

Weber, Peter. *Net Loss: Fish, Jobs, and the Marine Environment.* Worldwatch Paper 120. Washington, D.C.: Worldwatch Institute, 1994.

Wheeler, James O., and Peter Muller. *Economic Geography.* 3d ed. New York: John Wiley & Sons, 1997.

Wolf, Edward C. *Beyond the Green Revolution: New Approaches for Third World Agriculture.* Worldwatch Paper 73. Washington, D.C.: Worldwatch Institute, 1986.

World Resources . . . A Report by the World Resources Institute in collaboration with the United Nations Environment Programme and the United Nations Development Program. New York: Oxford University Press, annual or biennial beginning 1986.

Young, John E. *Mining the Earth.* Worldwatch Paper 109. Washington, D.C.: Worldwatch Institute, 1992.

LIVELIHOOD AND ECONOMY:

FROM BLUE COLLAR TO GOLD COLLAR

Components of the Space Economy   294
Concepts and Controls   295
Secondary Activities: Manufacturing   296
Locational Decisions in
    Manufacturing   296
  Principles of Location   297
  Raw Materials   297
  Power Supply   298
  Labor   298
  Market   299
  Transportation   299
Transportation and Location   302
Industrial Location Theories   304
  Least-Cost Theory   304
  Locational Interdependence Theory   305
  Profit-Maximization Approaches   306
Other Locational Considerations and
    Controls   307
  Agglomeration Economies   307
  Comparative Advantage   307
  Transnational Corporations   309
  Imposed Considerations   310
Industrial Location in Planned
    Economies   310
**Major Manufacturing Regions of the
    World   310**
Eastern Anglo America   312
  *Other Anglo American
      Concentrations   314*
Western and Central Europe   315
Eastern Europe   316
Eastern Asia   318
  Japan   318
  China   319
  The "Dragons"   321
High-Tech Patterns   323
Tertiary and Beyond   325

*Working leather in a Wanxian, China,
factory, part of the country's expanding
industrial base.*

SUMMARY   327
KEY WORDS   327
FOR REVIEW   328
SELECTED REFERENCES   328

Route 837 connects the four USX (United States Steel) plants stretched out along the Monongahela ("Mon") River south of Pittsburgh. Once, in the late 1960s, 50,000 workers labored in those mills, and Route 837 was choked with the traffic of their cars and of steel haulers' trucks. By 1979, fires were going out in the furnaces of the aging mills as steel imports from Asia and Europe flowed unchecked into domestic markets long controlled by American producers. By the mid-1980s, with employment in the steel plants of the Mon Valley well below 5000, the highway was only lightly traveled and only occasionally did anyone turn at the traffic lights into the closed and deserted mills.

At the same time, traffic was building along many highways in the northeastern part of the country. Four-lane Route 1 was clogged with traffic along the 42 kilometers (26 miles) of the "Princeton Corridor" in central New Jersey as that stretch of road in the 1980s had more office space, research laboratories, hotels, conference centers, and residential subdivisions planned and under construction than anywhere else between Washington, D.C. and Boston. Further to the south, around Washington itself, traffic grew heavy along the Capital Beltway in Virginia where vast office building complexes, defense-related industries, and commercial centers were converting rural land to urban uses. And east of New York City, traffic jams were monumental around Stamford, Connecticut in Fairfield County, as it became a leading corporate headquarters town with 150,000 daily in-commuters.

By the 1990s, traffic in Fairfield County had thinned as corporate takeovers, leveraged buyouts, and "downsizing" reorganizations reduced the number and size of companies and their need for both employees and office space. Vacancies exceeded 25% among the office buildings and research parks so enthusiastically built during the 1970s and 1980s, and vacant "corporate campuses" lined stretches of formerly clogged highways. But simultaneously, traffic was building elsewhere in the country as about a million Americans during the late 1980s and early 1990s gained technology-related jobs in a series of widely-spaced emerging "high-tech" hot spots clustered around such industries as computers, lasers, software, medical devices, and biotechnology.

These contrasting and fluctuating patterns of traffic flow symbolize the ever-changing nature and structure of the Anglo American space economy. The smokestack industries of the 19th and early 20th centuries have declined, replaced by research park industries, shopping centers, and office building complexes that in their turn experience variable prosperity and adversity. The continent's economic landscape and employment structure are inconstant at best (Figure 9.1). And North America is not alone. Change is the ever-present condition of contemporary economies, whether of the already industrialized, advanced countries or of those newly developing in an integrated world marketplace. Resources are exploited and exhausted; markets grow and decline; patterns of economic advantage, of labor skills, of industrial investment and productive capacity undergo alteration as countries and regions differentially develop, prosper, or experience reversals and decline. Such changes have profound impact on the spatial structure and processes of economic activity.

Components of the Space Economy

All human activity has spatial expression. In the economic sphere we recognize regions of industrial concentration, areas of employment and functional specialization, and specific factory sites and store locations. As geographers, we assume an underlying logic to those spatial economic patterns and seek, through observation and theory, an understanding and explanation of them. In a very preliminary fashion, that understanding has begun through classification of economic activity into *primary, secondary, tertiary,* and *quaternary* industries. (Remember, the term *industry* may be used in the narrow sense of type of manufacturing activity or enterprise as well as in the broader meaning of category of economic orientation.)

Primary industries, you will recall from Chapter 8, are tied to the natural resources they gather or exploit. Location is therefore predetermined by the distribution of minerals, fuels, forests, fisheries, or natural conditions affecting agriculture and herding. The later (beyond primary) stages of economic activity, however, are increasingly divorced from the conditions of the physical environment. In them, processing, distribution, communication, and management permit enterprise location in response to cultural and economic rather than physical influences. They are movable, rather than spatially tied activities. The locational decisions made and the economic patternings that result differ with the type or level of economic activity in question. Secondary industries involved in material processing and goods production have different spatial constraints than do the retailing activities of tertiary industry or the research parks or office complexes of quaternary activities. At every industrial or activity level, however, it is assumed that a recurring set of economic controls may be identified.

FIGURE 9.1   This idled Pennsylvania steel mill typifies the structural changes occurring in "postindustrial America"—and in other advanced economies where comparable dislocations and changes are taking place. The heavy industry of the secondary activity sector is frequently unable to compete in unregulated markets with lower-cost producers from developing countries or with those receiving production and export subsidies from their governments. Replacement employment must increasingly be found in the service industries of the tertiary and quaternary sectors.

Concepts and Controls

The controls that are assumed to exist are rooted in observations about human spatial behavior in general and economic behavior in particular. We have already explored some of those assumptions in earlier discussions. We noted, for example, that the intensity of spatial interaction decreases with increasing separation of places—distance decay, we called it. We observed the importance of complementarity and transferability in the assessment of resource value and trade potential. Von Thünen's model of agricultural land use, you will recall, was rooted in conjectures about transportation cost and land value relationships.

Such simplifying assumptions help us to understand a presumed common set of controls and motivations guiding human economic behavior. We assume, for example, that people are *economically rational;* that is, given the information at their disposal, they make locational, production, or purchasing decisions in light of a perception of what is most cost-effective and advantageous. From the standpoint of producers or sellers of goods or services, it is assumed each is intent on *maximizing profit.* To reach that objective, each may consider a host of production and marketing costs and political, competitive, and other limiting factors. But the ul-

timate goal of profit seeking remains clear. Finally, we assume that in commercial economies the best measure of the correctness of economic decisions is afforded by the *market mechanism.*

At root, that market control mechanism is measured by *price*—the price of land (rent), of labor (wages), of a college course (tuition), or of goods at the store. In turn, price is seen as a function of *supply* and *demand.* In large, complex economies where there are many producers, sellers, and buyers and many alternative products competing in the market place, price is the neutral measure of comparative value and profitability. The theoretical relationship between supply, demand, and price is simple. If demand for a good or service exceeds its available supply, scarcity will drive up the price it can command in the marketplace. That increased price will enhance the profitability of the sale which will encourage existing producers to increase output or induce new producers or sellers to enter the market (Figure 9.2a). That is, *the higher the price of a good, the more of it will be offered in the market.*

When the price is very high, however, relatively few people are inclined to buy. To dispose of their increased output, old and new producers of the commodity are forced to reduce prices to enlarge the market by making the good

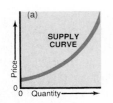
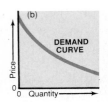
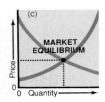

FIGURE 9.2 **Supply, demand, and market equilibrium.** (*a*) The *supply curve* tells us that as the price of a good increases, more of that good will be made available for sale. Countering any tendency for prices to rise to infinity is the market reality that the higher the price, the smaller the demand as potential customers find other purchases or products more cost-effective. (*b*) The *demand curve* shows how the market will expand as prices are lowered and goods are made more affordable and attractive to more customers. (*c*) *Market equilibrium* is marked by the point of intersection of the supply and demand curves and determines the price of goods, the total demand, and the quantity bought and sold.

affordable to a larger number of potential customers. That is, *at lower prices, more of a good will be purchased* (Figure 9.2*b*). If the price falls too low, production or sale becomes unprofitable and inefficient suppliers are forced out of business, reducing supply. **Market equilibrium** is marked by the price at which supply equals demand, satisfying the needs of consumers and the profit motivation of suppliers (Figure 9.2*c*).

These and other modifying concepts and controls of the economist treat supply, demand, and price as if all production, buying, and selling occurred at a single point. But as geographers, we know that human activities have specific locational settings and that neither people, nor resources, nor opportunities are uniformly distributed over the earth. We appreciate that the place or places of production may differ from the locations of demand. We understand that there are spatial relations and interactions based on supply, demand, and equilibrium price. We realize there is a *geography* of supply, a *geography* of demand, and a *geography* of cost.

Secondary Activities: Manufacturing

If we assume free markets, rational producers, and informed consumers, then locational production and marketing decisions should be based on careful consideration of spatially differing costs and opportunities. In the case of primary industries, those tied to the environment, points or areas of possible production are naturally fixed. The only decision is whether or not to exploit known resources. In the instance of secondary and higher levels of economic activity, however, the locational decision is more complex. It involves the weighing of the locational "pulls" of a number of cost considerations and profit prospects.

On the *demand* side, the distribution of populations and of purchasing power defines general areas of marketing opportunities. The regional location of tertiary—sales and service—activities may be nearly as fixed as are primary industries, though specific site decisions are more complex. On the *supply* side, decision making for manufacturers involves a more intricate set of equations. Manufacturers must consider costs of raw materials, distance from them and from markets, wages of labor, outlays for fuel, capital availability and rates, and a host of other inputs to the production and distribution process. It is assumed that the nature and the spatial variability of those myriad costs are known and that rational location decisions leading to profit maximization are based on that knowledge. For market economies, both observation and theory tend to support that assumption.

Locational Decisions in Manufacturing

Secondary activities involve transforming raw materials into usable products, giving them *form utility.* Dominant among them is manufacturing in all of its aspects, from pouring iron and steel to stamping out plastic toys, assembling computer components, or sewing dresses. In every case the common characteristics are the application of power and specialized labor to the production of standardized commodities in factory settings: in short, the characteristics of industrialization.

Manufacturing poses a different locational problem than does the gathering of primary commodities. It involves the assembly and the processing of inputs and the distribution of the output to other points and therefore presents the question of where the processing should take place. It is a question that has two spatial levels. One is regional and addresses the comparative attractions for different types of industry of different sections of the country or even of different countries at the international scale. The other is more localized and specific to an individual enterprise. It asks why a particular industrialist elects to locate production in a selected locale on a specific site. That is, we can ask at one level why northeastern United States–southeastern Canada exerted an earlier pull on industry in general and, at the other, why specific sites along the Monongahela Valley to the south of Pittsburgh were chosen by U.S. Steel Corporation for its mills.

In framing responses, one needs to consider a wide range of industrial pulls and attractions and the modifying influence of a number of physical, political, economic, and cultural constraints. Some of them have importance at both levels of questioning; others provide more limited locational insights. None, however, stands alone. The locational factors recognized are complexly interrelated, change over time in their relative significance, and differ between industries and regions. But all of them are tied to *principles of location* that are assumed to operate under all economic systems, though to be determinant, perhaps, only in free market, or commercial, economies.

Principles of Location

The principles or "ground rules" of location are simply stated.

1. Certain of the input costs of manufacturing are **spatially fixed costs,** that is, are relatively unaffected in their amount or relative importance no matter where the industry is located within a generalized regional or national setting. Wage rates set by national or areawide labor contracts, materials or components sold at a uniform delivered price without regard to distance from producer, and standardized rates charged for investment capital are examples of fixed costs that have no implication for comparative locational advantage.

2. Other of the input costs of manufacturing are **spatially variable costs;** that is, they show significant differences from place to place in both their amount and their relative contribution to the total cost of manufacturing (Figure 9.3). Substantial areal variation in wage rates, power costs, raw material delivered prices, and the like will influence locational choices.

3. The ultimate aim of the economic activity is *profit maximization.* In an economic environment of full and perfect competition, the profit objective is most likely to be achieved if the manufacturing enterprise is situated at the *least total cost* location. Under conditions of imperfect competition, considerations of sales and market may be more important than production costs in fixing "best" locations.

4. Since among the totality of production costs some inputs are approximately the same irrespective of location, fixed costs are not of major importance in determining optimum, or least-cost, locations. Rather, the industrialist bases the locational search on the minimization of variable costs. The locational determinant is apt to be the cost that is both an important component of total costs and shows the greatest spatial variation.

5. Transportation charges—the costs of accumulating inputs and of distributing products—are highly variable costs. As such, they (rather than the commodity transported) may become the locational determinant, imparting an unmistakable *orientation*—a term describing locational tendencies—to the plant siting decision.

6. Individual establishments rarely stand alone; they are part of integrated manufacturing sequences and environments in which *interdependence* increases as the complexity of industrial processes increases. The economies of structural and spatial interdependence may be decisive locational determinants for some industries. Interdependence may affect locational decisions based on *vertical integration* within a single firm of all stages of manufacturing from raw material processing through semifinished fabricating to final product assembly. For example, an integrated steel company might control ore and coking coal supplies and at one location operate coke ovens, blast furnaces, steel furnaces, and rolling mills and produce structural steel products, steel sheets, and finished metal goods. In other instances, *linkages* between firms may localize manufacturing in areas of industrial agglomeration where common resources—such as skilled labor—or multiple suppliers of product inputs—such as automobile component manufacturers—are found.

These principles are generalized statements about locational tendencies of industries. Their relative weight, of course, varies among industries and firms. Their significance also varies depending on the extent to which purely economic considerations—as opposed, say, to political or environmental constraints—dictate locational decisions.

Raw Materials

All manufactured goods have their origins in the processing of raw materials, but only a few industries at the early stages of the production cycle use raw materials directly from farms or mines. Most manufacturing is based on the further processing and shaping of materials already treated in some fashion by an earlier stage of manufacturing located elsewhere. In general, the more advanced the industrial economy of a nation, the smaller is the role played by truly *raw* materials in its economic structure.

For those industries in which unprocessed commodities are a primary input, however, the source and characteristics of the raw materials upon which they are based are

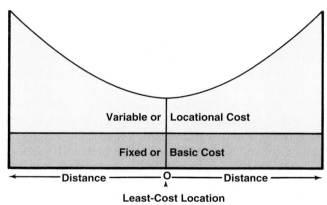

FIGURE 9.3 **The spatial implications of fixed and variable costs.** *Spatially fixed* (or *basic*) costs represent the minimum price that must be paid at any location for the necessary inputs of production of a given item. Here, for simplicity, a single raw material is assumed and priced at its cheapest source. *Spatially variable* (*locational*) costs are the additional costs incurred at alternate locations in overcoming distance, attracting labor, purchasing the plant site, and so forth. In the example, only the transportation cost of the single material away from its cheapest (source) location is diagrammed to determine *O,* the optimal or least-cost location.

important indeed. The quality, amount, or ease of mining or gathering of a resource may be a locational determinant if cost of raw material is the major variable and multiple sources of the primary material are available. Raw materials may attract the industries that process them when they are bulky, undergo great weight loss in the processing, or are highly perishable. Copper smelting and iron ore beneficiation are examples of weight- (impurity-) reducing industries localized by their ore supplies (see pp. 284–286). Pulp, paper, and sawmills are, logically, found in areas within or accessible to timber. Fruit and vegetable canning in California, midwestern meat packing, and Florida orange juice concentration and freezing are different but comparable examples of raw **material orientation.** The reason is simple; it is cheaper and easier to transport to market a refined or stabilized product than one filled with waste material or subject to spoilage and loss.

Multiple raw materials might dictate an intermediate plant location. Least cost may be determined not by a single raw material input but by the spatially differing costs of accumulating several inputs. Steel mills at Gary, Indiana, or Cleveland, Ohio, for example, were not based on local raw material sources but on the minimization of the total cost of collecting at a point the necessary ore, coking coal, and fluxing material inputs for the production process (Figure 9.4). Steel mills along the U.S. east coast—at Sparrows Point, Maryland, or the Fairless Works near Philadelphia—were localized where imported ores were unloaded from ocean carriers, avoiding expensive transshipment costs. In this latter avoidance, both the Great Lakes and the coastal locations are similar.

Power Supply

For some industries, power supplies that are immobile or of low transferability may serve to attract the activities dependent on them. Such was the case early in the Industrial Revolution when water power sites localized textile mills and fuel (initially charcoal, later coking coal) drew the iron and steel industry. Metallurgical industries became concentrated in such coal-rich regions as the Midlands of England, the Ruhr district of Germany, and the Donets Basin of Ukraine.

Massive charges of electricity are required to extract aluminum from its processed raw material, *alumina* (aluminum oxide). Electrical power accounts for between 30% and 40% of the cost of producing the aluminum and is the major variable cost influencing plant location in the industry. The Kitimat plant on the west coast of Canada or the Bratsk plant near Lake Baikal in eastern Siberia are examples of industry placed far from raw material sources or market but close to vast supplies of cheap power—in these instances, hydroelectricity.

Labor

Labor also is a spatial variable affecting location decisions and industrial development. Three different considerations—price, skill, and amount—of labor may be determinant singly or in combination. For some activities, a cheap labor supply is a necessity (see "Wage Rates and the Cloth

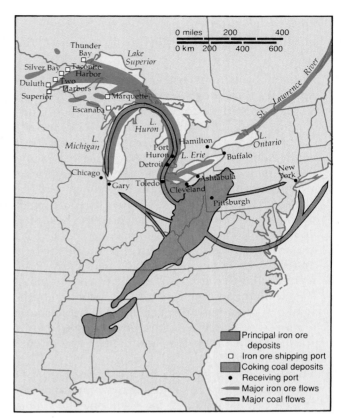

FIGURE 9.4   **Material flows in the steel industry.** When an industrial process requires the combination of several heavy or bulky ingredients, an intermediate point of assembly of materials is often a least-cost location. Earlier in this century, the iron and steel industry of eastern United States showed this kind of localization—not at the source of any single input but where coking coal, iron ore, and limestone could be brought together at the lowest price.

Trades"). For others, labor skills may constitute the locational attraction and regional advantage. Machine tools in Sweden, precision instruments in Switzerland, optical and electronic goods in Japan are examples of industries that have created and depend on localized labor skills. In an increasingly high-tech world of automation, electronics, and industrial robots, labor skills—even at high unit costs—are more in demand than an unskilled, uneducated workforce.

In some world areas, of course, labor of any skill level may be poorly distributed to satisfy the developmental objectives of government planners or private entrepreneurs. In the former Soviet Union, for example, long-standing economic plans called for the fuller exploitation of the vast resources of sparsely populated Siberia, an area generally unattractive to a labor force more attuned to the milder climates and greater amenities of the settled European portion of the country. At the same time, labor surpluses were growing in Soviet Central Asia, where resources were few and rates of natural population increase were high, but whose Muslim populations resisted resettlement outside of their homeland areas (Figure 9.5).

DYNAMIC PATTERNS OF THE SPACE ECONOMY

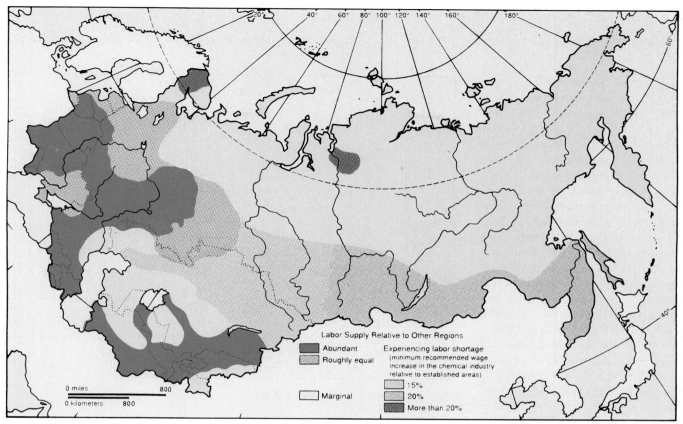

FIGURE 9.5 **Labor surplus and shortage in the former Soviet Union, mid-1960s.** Because labor was in short supply outside of the densely settled European part of the country, development programs for Siberia and the northern territories encountered greatly increased costs to induce workers to relocate to new industrial areas. The price of any commodity in short supply at isolated locations tends to increase, raising total variable costs of manufacture at those points.

Market

Goods are produced to supply a market demand. Therefore, the size, nature, and distribution of markets may be as important in industrial location decisions as are raw material, energy, labor, or other inputs. Market pull, like raw material attraction, is at root an expression of the cost of commodity movement. When the transportation charges for sending finished goods to market are a relatively high proportion of the total value of the good (or can be significantly reduced by proximity to market), then the attraction of location near to the consumer is obvious and **market orientation** results.

The consumer may be either another firm or the general public. When a factory is but one stage in a larger manufacturing process—firms making wheels, tires, windshields, bumpers, and the like in the assembly of automobiles, for example—location near the next stage of production is an obvious advantage. The advantage is increased if that final stage of production is also near the ultimate consumer market. To continue our example, automobile assembly plants have been scattered throughout the North American realm in response to the existence of large regional markets and the cost of distribution of the finished automobile. This market orientation is further reflected by the location in North America of auto manufacturing or assembly plants of Asian

and European motor vehicle companies, although both foreign and domestic firms again appear to be reconcentrating the industry in the east central part of the United States.

People themselves, of course, are the ultimate consumers. Large urban concentrations represent markets, and major cities have always attracted producers of goods consumed by city dwellers. Admittedly, it is impossible to distinguish clearly between urbanites as market and urbanites as labor force. In either case, many manufacturing activities are drawn to major metropolitan centers. Certain producers are, in fact, inseparable from the immediate markets they serve and are so widely distributed that they are known as **ubiquitous industries.** Newspaper publishing, bakeries, and dairies, all of which produce a highly perishable commodity designed for immediate consumption, are examples.

Transportation

Transportation has been so much the unifying thread of all of these references to "factors" of industrial location that it is difficult to isolate its separate role. In fact, some of the earlier observations about manufacturing plant orientations can be restated in purely transportation cost terms. For example, copper smelting or iron ore beneficiation—described earlier as examples of raw material orientation—may also be seen as

I n the free market world, few industries have been as spatially responsive to labor costs as have textiles and garment making. While a great deal of labor is necessary to turn natural or artificial fibers into a finished product, it need not be skilled labor. In the United States, for example, the cotton and woolen cloth industry established in New England during the 1820s and 1830s drew extensively on a labor pool made up largely of underemployed daughters of the many families working small farms of the area. Later, immigrants provided the surplus unskilled labor supply in the cities and towns of the area. With time and further industrialization, wage rates began to increase in New England to levels unacceptable to the highly competitive textile industry. When (among other reasons) it became clear that a surplus of cheap labor was available in the Piedmont district of the Southeast, the industry quickly moved in that direction. Today, the United States textile industry that still remains in the face of foreign competition is concentrated in that region.

Much of the recent competition comes from *newly industrializing countries* (NICs) of Asia where the textile industry is seen as a near-ideal employer of an abundant labor force. Among them earlier were the major suppliers of the American market during the 1970s and 1980s: Taiwan, South Korea, and Hong Kong (which counted as a NIC industrially, though not politically). As industrialization grew and wage rates increased in these producing areas, however, their relative labor advantage was eroded. The

TEXTILE MILL PRODUCTS EMPLOYEES, 1992

Figures in thousands of workers

textile industry began to shift to still lower cost producers, including China, Bangladesh, Mexico, and Thailand. The trends of the textile industry confirm the observation that in commercial economies "best location" is only a transient advantage of specific sites, regions, or countries.

The point is emphasized in the experience of the apparel industry, which converts finished textiles into clothing. Like textile manufacturing, the apparel industry finds its most profitable production locations in areas of cheap labor. Repetitious, limited-skill, assembly-line operations are necessary for volume production of clothing for a mass market that is highly price competitive; labor costs are the chief locational determinant. Even the lowest-wage areas of the United States have difficulty competing

in the manufacture of standardized women's and children's clothing. Wage rates in the early 1990s for apparel production workers in the 20 major exporters of garments to the United States ranged from a low of 2% (Bangladesh) to a high of 25% (Singapore) of the level of their American counterparts. Those 20 low-wage countries accounted for nearly 90% of imported apparel, which, in turn, captured 60% of the U.S. domestic apparel market. That percentage began to rise in the later 1990s as requirements of the World Trade Organization reduced American import restrictions and quotas.

Data from *County Business Patterns.*

industries engaged in *weight reduction* designed to minimize transportation costs by removal of waste material prior to shipment. Some market orientation is of the opposite nature, reflecting *weight-gaining* production. Soft drink bottlers, for example, add large amounts of water to small amounts of concentrated syrup to produce a bulky product of relatively low value. All transport costs are reduced if only the concentrate is shipped to local bottlers, who add the water that is everywhere available and distribute only to local dealers. The frequency of this practice suggests the inclusion of soft drink bottlers among the ubiquitous industries.

No matter the specific characterization of attraction, modern industry is intimately and inseparably tied to transportation systems. The Industrial Revolution is usefully seen as initially and simultaneously a transportation revolution as successive improvements in the technology of movement of peoples and commodities enlarged the effective areas of spatial interaction and made integrated economic development and areal specialization possible. All advanced economies are well served by a diversity of transport media (see Figure 8.4); without them, all that is possible is local subsistence activity. All major industrial agglomerations are simultaneously important nodes of different transportation media, each with its own characteristic advantages and limitations.

Water transportation is the cheapest means of long-distance freight movement (Figure 9.6). Little motive power is required, right-of-way costs are low or absent, and operating costs per unit of freight are low when high-capacity vessels are used. Inland waterway improvement and canal construction marked the first phase of the Industrial Revolution in Europe and was the first stage of modern transport development in the United States. Because the ton-mile costs of water movement remain so relatively low, river ports and seaports have locational attractiveness for industry unmatched by alternative centers not served by water carriers. Although the disadvantages of water carriage of freight are serious, where water routes are in place, as in northwestern Europe or the Great Lakes–Mississippi systems of the United States, they are vital elements in regional industrial economies.

Railroads efficiently move large volumes of freight over long distances at low fuel and labor costs (Figure 9.7). They are, however, inflexible in route, slow to respond to

FIGURE 9.7 Increasingly, environmental protection requirements call for use of higher-grade coals—those of low content of the particulate matter that causes visible air pollution and lung damage and of the sulfur that is a major source of atmospheric sulfur dioxide and acid rain. In the United States, such coals are found mainly in the western states, far from the eastern consuming regions. The cost of long-distance transportation is reduced when the long-haul efficiencies of railroads are most economically exploited. *Unit trains* carrying only coal engage in a continuous shuttle movement between western strip mines and eastern utility companies.

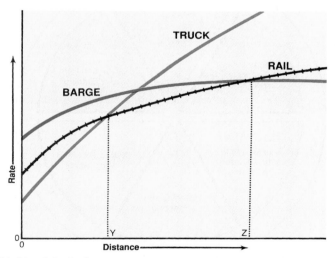

FIGURE 9.6 **The pattern of carrier efficiency.** Different transport media have cost advantages over differing distances. The usual generalization is that when all three media are available for a given shipment, trucks are most efficient and economical over short hauls of up to about 500 kilometers (about 300 miles), railroads have the cost advantage over intermediate hauls of 500 to 3200 kilometers (about 300 to 2000 miles), and water (barge) movement over longer distances (and, often, over shorter distance where speed of delivery of nonperishable commodities is not a consideration). The differing cost curves represent the differing amounts of fixed or variable costs incurred by each transport medium, as further illustrated in Figure 9.9.

changing industrial locational patterns, and expensive to construct and maintain. They require high volumes of traffic to be cost-effective. When for any reason traffic declines below minimum revenue levels, rail service may be uneconomic and the lines abandoned—a response of American railroads since the 1930s (Table 9.1).

High-volume, high-speed *motor trucks* operating on modern roadway and expressway systems have altered the competitive picture to favor highways over railways in many intercity movements in modern economies. Road systems provide great flexibility of service and are more quickly responsive than railroads to new traffic demands and changing origin and destination points. Intervening opportunities are more easily created and regional integration more cheaply achieved by highway than by railroad (or waterway systems). Disadvantages of highway transport include high maintenance costs of vehicles (and roads) and low efficiency in the long-distance, high-volume movement of bulky commodities.

Increasingly in the United States and elsewhere, greater transport cost efficiencies are achieved by combining short-haul motor carriage with longer-haul rail or ship movement of the same freight containers. Hauling a truck trailer on a railroad flatcar ("piggybacking") or on ship deck serves to minimize total freight rates and transport times by utilizing the most efficient carrier at different trip stages to move goods kept within a pre-packed container.

Pipelines provide efficient, speedy, and dependable transportation specifically suited to the movement of a variety of liquids and gases. They serve to localize along their routes the industries—particularly fertilizer and petrochemical plants—that use the transported commodity as raw material. In contrast, *air transport* has little locational significance for most industries despite its growing impor-

tance in long-distance passenger and high-value package freight movement. It contributes, of course, to the range of transport alternatives available to large population centers in industrially advanced nations and may increase the attractiveness of airport sites for high-tech and other industries shipping or receiving high-value, low-bulk commodities. Further, air transport may serve as the only effective connection with a larger national economy in the development of outposts of mining or manufacturing—as, for example, in Arctic regions or in interior Siberia. It is not, however, an effective competitor in the usual patterns of freight flow (see "A Comparison of Transport Media").

Transportation and Location

Figure 9.8 indicates the general pattern of industrial orientation related to variable transportation costs. In their turn, those costs are more than a simple function of the distance that goods are carried. Rather, they represent the application of differing **freight rates,** charges made for loading, transporting, and unloading of goods. Freight rates are said to *discriminate* between commodities on the basis of their assumed ability to bear transport costs in relation to their value. In general, manufactured goods have higher value,

TABLE 9.1	Total Length of Railway Operated in the United States	
	LENGTH (000)	
YEAR	KILOMETERS	MILES
1890	269	167
1900	310	193
1910	388	241
1920	418	260
1930	418	260
1940	377	234
1950	360	224
1960	351	218
1970	332	206
1980	288	179
1990	232	144
1995	203	126

Sources: *Statistical Abstract of the United States* and Association of American Railroads.

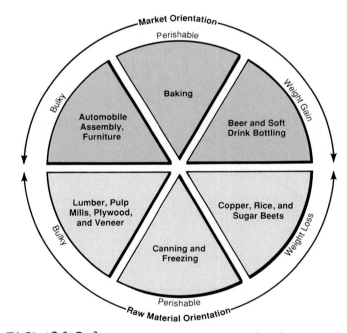

FIGURE 9.8 **Spatial orientation tendencies.** *Raw material orientation* is presumed to exist when there are limited alternative material sources, when the material is perishable, or when—in its natural state—it contains a large proportion of impurities or nonmarketable components. *Market orientation* represents the least-cost solution when manufacturing uses commonly available materials that add weight to the finished product, when the manufacturing process produces a commodity much bulkier or more expensive to ship than its separate components, or when the perishable nature of the product demands processing at individual market points.

A COMPARISON OF TRANSPORT MEDIA

MODE	USES	ADVANTAGES	DISADVANTAGES
Railroad	Intercity medium- to long-haul bulk and general cargo transport	Fast, reliable service on separate rights-of-way; essentially nonpolluting; energy efficient; adapted to steady flow of single commodities between two points; routes and modes provide intervening development opportunities	High construction and operating costs; inflexibility of routes; underutilized lines cause economic drain
Highway carrier	Local and intercity movement of general cargo and merchandise; pickup and delivery services; feeder to other carriers	Highly flexible in routes, origins, and destinations; individualized service; maximum accessibility; unlimited intervening opportunity; high speed and low terminal costs	Low energy efficiency; contributes to air pollution; adds congestion to public roads; high maintenance costs; inefficient for large volume freight
Inland waterway	Low-speed haulage of bulk, nonperishable commodities	High energy efficiency; low per mile costs; large cargo capacity	High terminal costs; low route flexibility; not suited for short haul; possible delays from ice or low water levels
Pipeline	Continuous flows of liquids, gases, or suspended solids where volumes are high and continuity is required	Fast, efficient, dependable; low per mile costs over long distances; maximum safety	Highly inflexible in route and cargo type; high development costs
Airways	Medium- and long-haul of high-value, low-bulk cargo where delivery speed is important	High speed and efficiency; adapted to goods that are perishable, packaged, of a size and quantity unsuited to other modes; high route flexibility; access to areas otherwise inaccessible	Very expensive, high mileage costs; some weather-related unreliability; inconvenient terminal locations; no intervening opportunities between airports

greater fragility, require more special handling, and can bear higher freight charges than can unprocessed bulk commodities. The higher transport costs for finished goods are therefore seen as a major reason for increasing the market orientation of industry in advanced economies with high-value manufacturing.

In addition to these forms of rate discrimination, each shipment of whatever nature must bear a share of both the *fixed costs* and the *variable costs* incurred by the transportation agency. Fixed costs of transportation—sometimes called **terminal costs**—are the overhead costs of the carrier, a share of which must be borne by every shipment and cannot easily be allocated among shipments. Variable costs of transportation—sometimes called **line-haul** or *over-the-road* **costs**—vary with the individual shipments and can be allocated to each according to equipment used, distance traveled, and expenses incurred. Total transport costs represent a combination of fixed and variable charges and are curvilinear rather than linear functions of distance. That is, carrier costs have a tendency to decline as the length of haul increases because scale economies in long-haul movement permit the averaging of fixed costs over a greater number of miles. The result is the *tapering principle* diagrammed in Figure 9.9.

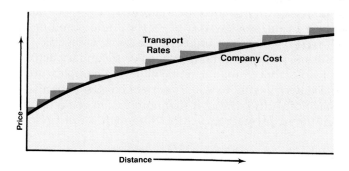

FIGURE 9.9   **The tapering principle.** The actual costs of transport, including terminal charges and line costs, increase at a decreasing rate as fixed costs are spread over longer hauls. The "tapering" of company cost is differently expressed among media because their mixes of fixed and variable costs are different, as Figure 9.6 diagrams. Note that actual rates charged move in stepwise increments to match the general pattern and level of company costs.

One consequence of the necessary assignment of fixed costs to *every* shipment regardless of distance moved is that factory locations intermediate between sources of materials and final markets are less attractive than location at either end of a single long haul. That is, two short hauls cost more than a single continuous haul over the same distance (Figure 9.10).

Two exceptions to this locational generalization are of practical interest. **Break-of-bulk points** are sites where goods have to be transferred or transshipped from one carrier to another—at ports, for example, where barge or ocean vessel must be unloaded and cargo reloaded to railcar or truck, or between railroad and truck line. When such transfer occurs, an additional fixed or terminal cost is levied against the shipment, perhaps significantly increasing its total transport costs (piggyback transfers reduce, but do not eliminate, those handling charges). There is a tendency for manufacturing to concentrate at such points to avoid the additional charges. As a traffic-generating inducement, **in-transit privilege** may be granted to a manufacturer by a transportation agency through the quotation of a special single rate from material source to market for a movement that may be interrupted for processing or manufacturing *en route*. Such a special rate obviously removes the cost disadvantage of two short hauls, and by equalizing shipping costs between locations tends to reduce the otherwise dominant attractions of either material or market locations.

Industrial Location Theories

In practice, enterprise locational decisions are based not on the impact of a single selected industrial factor but on the interplay and balance of a number of considerations. Implicit in our review has been the understanding that each type or branch of industry has its own specific set of significant plant siting conditions. For secondary activities as a whole, therefore, a truly bewildering complex of locational determinants exists. Theorists have set themselves the task of sorting through that complex in the attempt to define its underlying structure. Although a full review of

all of their contributions is beyond our scope and interest, it is useful to survey briefly the three fundamental approaches to the problem of plant location that they have proposed—*least-cost theory, locational interdependence theory,* and *profit-maximization approaches*—and the different conclusions they reach.

Least-Cost Theory

The classical model of industrial location theory, the **least-cost theory,** is based on the work of Alfred Weber (1868–1958) and sometimes called **Weberian analysis.** It explains the optimum location of a manufacturing establishment in terms of minimization of three basic expenses: relative transport costs, labor costs, and agglomeration costs. **Agglomeration** refers to the clustering of productive activities and people for mutual advantage. Such clustering can produce "agglomeration economies" through shared facilities and services. Diseconomies such as higher rents or wage levels resulting from competition for these resources may also occur.

Weber concluded that transport costs are the major consideration determining location. That is, the optimum location will be found where the costs of transporting raw materials to the factory and finished goods to the market are at their lowest. He noted, however, if variations in labor or agglomeration costs are sufficiently great, a location determined solely on the basis of transportation costs may not in fact be the optimum one.

Weber made five controlling assumptions: (1) An area is completely uniform physically, politically, culturally, and technologically. This is known as the **uniform** or **isotropic plain** assumption. (2) Manufacturing involves a single product to be shipped to a single market whose location is known. (3) Inputs involve raw materials from more than one known source location. (4) Labor is infinitely available but immobile in location. (5) Transportation routes are not fixed but connect origin and destination by the shortest path; and transport costs directly reflect the weight of items shipped and the distance they are moved.

Given these assumptions, Weber derived the least transport cost location by means of the *locational triangle* (Figure 9.11). It diagrams the cost consequences of fixed locations of materials and market and of movement in any direction of a given weight of commodity at a uniform cost per unit of distance. In Figure 9.11a, S_1 and S_2 are the two material sources for a product consumed at M. The problem is to locate the *optimum point of production* where the total ton-distance involved in assembling materials and distributing the product is at a minimum. Each corner of the triangle exerts its pull; each has a defined cost of production should it be chosen as the plant site. If we assume that the material weights are cut in half during manufacturing (so that the finished product weighs the same as each of the original raw materials), then location at either S_1 or S_2 on the diagram would involve a $3 shipping charge from the other raw material source plus $3 to move the product, for a total delivered cost at market of $6. If the market were selected as the plant site, two raw material shipments—again totalling $6—would be involved.

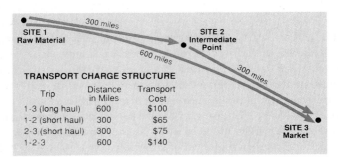

TRANSPORT CHARGE STRUCTURE

Trip	Distance in Miles	Transport Cost
1-3 (long haul)	600	$100
1-2 (short haul)	300	$65
2-3 (short haul)	300	$75
1-2-3	600	$140

FIGURE 9.10   **The short-haul penalty. Plant locations** intermediate between material and market are generally avoided because of the realities of transportation pricing that are shown here. Two short hauls simply cost more than a single long haul because two sets of fixed costs must be assigned to the interrupted movement.

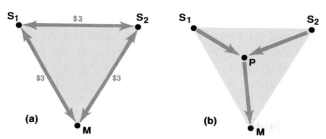

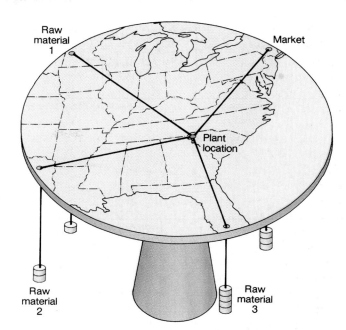

FIGURE 9.11 **Weber's locational triangle** with differing assumptions. (*a*) With one market, two raw material sources, and a finished product reflecting a 50% material weight loss, production could appropriately be located at S_1, S_2, or M since each length of haul is the same. In (*b*) the optimum production point, P, is seen to lie within the triangle, where total transport costs would be less than at corner locations. The exact location of P would depend on the weight-loss characteristics of the two material inputs if only transport charges were involved. P would, of course, be pulled toward the material whose weight is most reduced.

Weberian analysis, however, aims at the least transport cost location, which most likely will be an intermediate point somewhere within the locational triangle. Its exact position will depend on distances, the respective weights of the raw material inputs, and the final weight of the finished product, and may be either material or market oriented (Figure 9.11*b*). Material orientation reflects a sizable weight loss during the production process; market orientation indicates a weight gain. The optimum placement of P can be found by different analytical means, but the easiest to visualize is by way of a mechanical model of weights and strings (Figure 9.12).

Weber assumed that transport costs are uniform by distance and weight in any direction but labor costs are spatially variable because of differences in wage rates and efficiency of workforces. A location of high transportation costs (because of weight or distance considerations) might nonetheless be industrially attractive because of a cheap (or highly efficient) labor supply. Weber treated this circumstance as a "distortion" of a purely transport-based locational pattern and concluded that optimum location for a given firm would be at the point with the lowest combined transport and labor costs. If, as he observed, the long-term trend in transportation costs is downward, labor locations will be increasingly attractive for all industries.

A final distorting factor recognized by Weber is the tendency of industry to agglomerate to achieve economies of association. These can be calculated in specific cost terms and used to offset added transport costs for firms that otherwise might seek separated locations. Examples of such agglomeration economies include savings from shared business or financial services, benefits from a greater division of labor, shared public services, and the like.

FIGURE 9.12 **Plane table solution to a plant location problem.** This mechanical model, suggested by Alfred Weber, uses weights to demonstrate the least transport cost point where there are several sources of raw materials. When a weight is allowed to represent the "pull" of raw material and market locations, an equilibrium point is found on the plane table. That point is the location at which all forces balance each other and represents the least-cost plant location.

Locational Interdependence Theory

When the locational decision of one firm is influenced by locations chosen by its competitors, a condition of **locational interdependence** exists. It influences the manner in which competitive firms with identical cost structures arrange themselves in space to assure themselves a measure of *spatial monopoly* in their combined market. In locational interdependence theory, the concern is with *variable revenue analysis* rather than, as in the Weber model, with variable costs.

The simplest case concerns the locational decisions of two firms in competition with each other to supply identical goods to customers evenly spaced along a linear market. The usual example cited is of two ice cream vendors, each selling the same brand at the same price along a stretch of beach having a uniform distribution of people. All will purchase the same amount of ice cream (that is, demand is *inelastic*—is not sensitive to a change in the price) and will patronize the seller nearer to them. Figure 9.13 suggests that the two sellers would eventually cluster at the midpoint of the linear market (the beach) so that each vendor could supply customers at the extremities of the market without yielding locational advantage to the single competitor.

This is a spatial solution that maximizes return but does not minimize costs. The lowest total cost location for each of the two vendors would be at the midpoint of his or

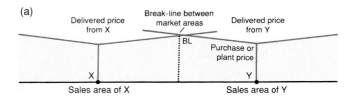

(a)

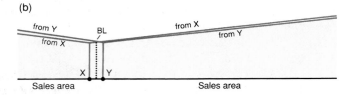

(b)

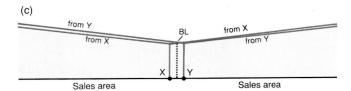

(c)

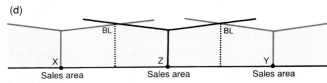

(d)

FIGURE 9.13   Competitive locations in a linear
market (Hotelling model). The initial *socially optimal*
locations (*a*) that minimize total distribution costs will be
vacated in the search for market advantage (*b*), eventually
resulting in *competitive equilibrium* at the center of the
market (*c*). Spatial dispersion will again occur if two or more
competitors either encounter elasticity of demand or
subdivide the market by agreement (*d*).

her half of the beach, as shown at the top of Figure 9.13,
where the total effort expended by customers walking to the
ice cream stands (or cost by sellers delivering the product) is
least. To maximize market share, however, one seller might
decide to relocate immediately next to the competitor (Figure 9.13*b*), dominating now three-fourths of the entire beach
market. The logical retaliation would be for the second vendor to jump back over the first to recapture market share.
Ultimately, side-by-side location at the center line of the
beach is inevitable and a stable placement is achieved since
neither seller can gain any further advantage from moving.
But now the customers collectively have to walk farther to
satisfy their ice-cream hunger than they did initially; that is,
total acquisition cost or delivered price (ice-cream purchase
plus effort expended) has increased.

The economist Harold Hotelling (1895–1973), who is
usually associated with the locational interdependence approach, expanded the conclusion about clustered ice cream
sellers to a more generalized statement explaining industrial
concentration by multiple producers under conditions of

identical production costs and inelastic market demand.
However, if the market becomes sensitive to price, sales to
more distant customers will be discouraged and producers
seeking to maximize sales will again separate rather than
aggregate. The conclusion then is that price sensitivity (elasticity of demand) will encourage industrial dispersion.

Profit-Maximization Approaches

Dissatisfaction with the simplicities and rigidities of the
least-cost and the locational interdependence explanations
has led many locational theorists to adopt the view expressed by the economist August Lösch (1906–1945) that
"the correct location [of a firm] lies where the net profit is
greatest." Since net profit represents the difference between
sales income and production costs, the entrepreneur's obligation is to find the production location where this difference
is the greatest. It is, however, extremely difficult to pinpoint
a single "best" location. For example, the **substitution principle** recognizes that in many industrial processes it is possible to replace a declining amount of one input—labor, for
example—with an increase in another, such as capital for
automated equipment, or to increase transportation costs
while simultaneously reducing land rent. With substitution,
a number of different points may be "optimal" locations.

Further, a manufacturer may take advantage of the
fact that both revenues and processing costs vary spatially.
Naturally, *profit maximization* will occur only at the single
point where the excess of total revenue is greatest, but a
whole series of points exists where total revenue just equals
total cost of producing a given output. These points, connected, mark the **spatial margin of profitability** and define the area within which profitable operation is possible
(Figure 9.14). The shape and extent of the area will reflect

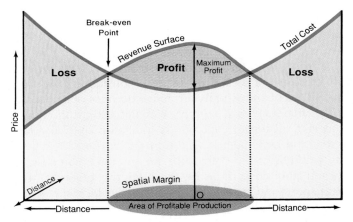

FIGURE 9.14   The spatial margin of profitability. In
the diagram, *O* is the single optimal profit-maximizing
location, but location anywhere within the area defined by
the intersects of the total cost and total revenue surfaces will
permit profitable operation. Some industries will have wide
margins; others will be more spatially constricted. Skilled
entrepreneurs may be able to expand the margins farther
than less able industrialists. Importantly, a *satisficing* location
may be selected by reasonable estimate even in the absence of
the totality of information required for an *optimal* decision.

the *cost surface* and *revenue surface* unique to each firm. The concept of the spatial margin permits less than optimal decisions to be introduced into locational theory, which otherwise concerns itself only with a single profit-maximizing possibility. Location anywhere within the margin assures some profit and tolerates both imperfect knowledge and personal (rather than economic) considerations. Such less-than-optimal, but still-acceptable, locations are considered **satisficing locations.**

For some firms, spatial margins may be very broad because transport costs are a negligible factor in production and marketing. Such firms are said to be **footloose**—that is, neither resource nor market oriented. For example, both the raw materials and the finished product in the manufacture of computers are so valuable, light, and compact that transportation costs have little bearing on where production takes place.

Other Locational Considerations and Controls

The behavior of individual firms seeking specific production sites under competitive commercial conditions forms the basis of most industrial location theory. But that theory does not fully explain world or regional patterns of industrial localization or specialization. Moreover, it does not account for locational behavior that is uncontrolled by objective "factors" or that is directed by noncapitalistic planning goals.

Agglomeration Economies

The cumulative and reinforcing attractions of industrial concentration and urban growth are recognized locational factors, but ones not easily quantified. Both cost-minimizing and profit-maximizing theories, as we have seen, make provision for *agglomeration,* the spatial concentration of people and activities for mutual benefit. That is, both recognize that areal grouping of industrial activities may produce benefits for individual firms that they could not experience in isolation. Those benefits—**agglomeration economies** or **external economies**—accrue in the form of savings from shared transport facilities, social services, public utilities, communication facilities, and the like. Collectively, these and other installations and services needed to facilitate industrial and other forms of economic development are called **infrastructure.**

Areal concentration may also create pools of skilled and ordinary labor, of capital, ancillary business services, and, of course, a market built of other industries and urban populations. New firms, particularly, may find significant advantages in locating near other firms engaged in the same activity, for labor specializations and support services specific to that activity are already in place. Some may find profit in being near other firms with which they are linked either as customers or suppliers.

A concentration of capital, labor, management skills, customer base, and all that is implied by the term *infrastructure* will tend to attract still more industries from other locations to the agglomeration. In Weber's terms, that is, economies of association distort or alter locational decisions that otherwise would be based solely on transportation and labor costs, and once in existence agglomerations will tend

to grow (Figure 9.15). Through a **multiplier effect,** each new firm added to the agglomeration will lead to the further development of infrastructure and linkages. As we shall see in Chapter 11, the "multiplier effect" also implies total (urban) population growth and thus the expansion of the labor pool and the localized market that are part of agglomeration economies.

Agglomeration—concentration—of like industries in small areas dates from the early industrial age and continues with many of the newest industries. Familiar examples include the town of Dalton, Georgia in or near which are found all but one of the top 20 U.S. carpet makers, and Akron, Ohio which, before 1930, held almost the entire 100 or so tire manufacturers of the country. Silicon Valley dating from the 1960s and other more recent high-tech specialized concentrations simply continue the tradition.

Admittedly, agglomeration can yield disadvantages as well as benefits. Overconcentration can result in diseconomies of congestion, high land values, pollution, increased governmental regulation, and the like. When the costs of aggregation exceed the benefits, a firm will actually profit by relocating to a more isolated position, a process called **deglomeration.** It is a process expressed in the suburbanization of industry within metropolitan areas or the relocation of firms to nonmetropolitan locations.

Comparative Advantage

The principle of **comparative advantage** tells us that areas tend to specialize in the production of those items for which they have the greatest relative advantage over other areas or for which they have the least relative disadvantage, as long as free trade exists. The principle, basic to the understanding of regional specializations, applies as long as areas have different relative advantages for two or more goods. Assume that two countries both have a need for and are domestically able to produce two commodities. Further assume that there is no transport cost consideration. No matter what its cost of production of either commodity, Country A will choose to specialize in only one of them if by that specialization and through exchange with Country B for the other, Country A stands to gain more than it loses. The key to comparative advantage is the utilization of resources in such a fashion as to gain, by specialization, a volume of production and a selling price that permit exchange for a needed commodity at a cost level that is below that of the domestic production of both.

At first glance, the concept of comparative advantage may at times seem to defy logic. For example, Japan may be able to produce airplanes and home appliances more cheaply than the United States, thereby giving it an apparent advantage in both goods. But it benefits both countries if they specialize in the good in which they have a comparative advantage. In this instance, Japan's manufacturing cost structure makes it more profitable for Japan to specialize in the volume production of appliances and to buy airplanes from the United States, where large civilian and military markets encourage aircraft manufacturing specialization and efficiency.

FIGURE 9.15   On a small scale, the planned industrial park furnishes its tenants external agglomeration economies similar to those offered by large urban concentrations to industry in general. An industrial park provides a subdivided tract of land developed according to a comprehensive plan for the use of (frequently) otherwise unconnected firms. Since the park developers, whether private companies or public agencies, supply the basic infrastructure of streets, water, sewage, power, transport facilities, and perhaps private police and fire protection, park tenants are spared the additional cost of providing these services themselves. In some instances, factory buildings are available for rent, still further reducing firm capital outlays. Counterparts of industrial parks for manufacturers are the office parks, research parks, science parks, and the like for "high-tech" firms and for enterprises in tertiary and quaternary services.

When other countries' comparative advantages reflect lower labor, land, raw material, and capital costs, manufacturing activities may voluntarily relocate from higher-cost market locations to lower-cost foreign production sites. Such voluntary **outsourcing**—producing parts or products abroad for domestic sale—by American manufacturers has employment and areal economic consequences no different from those resulting from successful competition by foreign companies or from industrial locational decisions favoring one section of the country over others.

A North American case in point is found along the northern border of Mexico. In the 1960s Mexico enacted legislation permitting foreign (specifically, American) companies to establish "sister" plants, called *maquiladoras,* within 20 kilometers (12 miles) of the U.S. border for the duty-free assembly of products destined for re-export. By the mid-1990s,

more than 2000 such assembly and manufacturing plants had been established to produce a diversity of goods including electronic products, textiles, furniture, leather goods, toys, and automotive parts. The plants generated direct and indirect employment for over a half-million Mexican workers (Figure 9.16). The North American Free Trade Agreement (NAFTA) creating a single Canadian–United States–Mexican production and marketing community turns "outsourcing" in the North American context from a search abroad for low-cost production sites to a review of best locations within a broadened unified economic environment. The United States also benefits from outsourcing by other countries. Japanese and European companies have established automobile and other manufacturing plants to take advantage of lower American production and labor costs, with at least part of the product re-exported to other markets.

FIGURE 9.16   American manufacturers, seeking lower labor costs, began in the 1960s to establish component manufacturing and assembly operations along the international border in Mexico. United States laws allowed finished or semifinished products to be brought into the country duty-free. In some cases, as here at a Hoover plant in Mexico City, factories farther from the border were more traditional manufacturers, though the product was still primarily destined for export. *Outsourcing* has moved a larger proportion of American electronics, small appliance, toy, and garment industries to offshore subsidiaries or contractors in Asia and Latin America.

Transnational Corporations

Outsourcing is but one small expression of the growing international structure of modern manufacturing and service enterprises. Business and industry are increasingly stateless and economies borderless as giant **transnational corporations (TNCs)**—private firms that have established branch operations in nations foreign to their headquarters country—become ever-more important in the world space economy. By the mid-1990s there were more than 37,000 transnational (or multinational) companies controlling some 210,000 foreign affiliates. They varied greatly in size and power with the top 100 multinationals (excluding those in finance and banking) accounting for some $3.5 trillion in global assets and for about half of all assets held by transnationals outside of their home countries.

TNCs are increasingly international in origin. In 1970, of the some 7000 multinational companies then identified by the United Nations, over half were from only two countries: the United States and Britain. By the mid-1990s, of the world's 100 largest TNCs—all based in 15 developed countries—more than half were in 10 European countries, a third in Anglo America, 16 in Japan, and one each in Australia and New Zealand. Those same leading 100 multinationals are reckoned to control some 16% of the world's productive assets, with the top 300 together controlling about one-quarter.

Most transnational corporations operate in only a few industries: computers, electronics, petroleum and mining, motor vehicles, chemicals, and pharmaceuticals. Their worldwide impact is broader than those company specializations suggest. Some dominate, for example, the market-ing and distribution of basic commodities; a few TNCs account for 85% or more of world trade in wheat, maize, coffee, cotton, iron ore, and timber. As a group, TNCs directly employ some 75 million persons at home and abroad, or about 10% of worldwide nonagricultural paid employment. But because of their outsourced purchases of raw materials, parts and components, and services, the total number of worldwide jobs associated with TNCs in the mid-1990s reached 150 million or more.

Some 60% of TNC employees work with the parent firm in the home country, however, and employees working for the companies' foreign affiliates make up just over 1% of the world's workforce. Even that foreign impact is limited to a relatively few developing countries and regions. Majority inflows of foreign direct investment (FDI) are concentrated in 10 to 15 countries, mainly in South, Southeast and East Asia (China is the largest developing-country recipient) and in Latin America and the Caribbean. The least-developed countries as a group—including nearly all African states—have received little FDI. Overall, however, the United States is not only the largest source of foreign direct investment but is its largest recipient as well.

Because they are international in operation with multiple markets, plants, and raw material sources, the TNCs are active and effective practitioners of the principle of comparative advantage. TNCs produce in that country or region where costs of materials, labor, or other production inputs are minimized, while maintaining operational control and declaring taxes in localities where the economic climate is most favorable. Indeed, one-third of all trade consists of intrafirm transactions. From a locational perspective, TNCs have internationalized the plant-siting decision process and carried it further than single-country firms by multiplying the number of locationally separated operations that must be economically assessed. Increasingly, service activities as well as manufacturing companies are international in scope, frequently under the control of "transnational integral conglomerates" that span a large spectrum of both service and industrial sectors.

Imposed Considerations

Locational theories dictate that in a pure, competitive economy, the costs of material, transportation, labor, and plant should be dominant in locational decisions. Obviously, neither in the United States nor in any other market economy do the idealized conditions exist. Other constraints—some representing cost considerations, others political or social impositions—also affect, perhaps decisively, the locational decision process. Land use and zoning controls, environmental quality standards, governmental area-development inducements, local tax-abatement provisions or developmental bond authorizations, noneconomic pressures on quasi-governmental corporations, and other considerations constitute attractions or repulsions for industry outside of the context and consideration of pure theory (see "Contests and Bribery"). If these noneconomic forces become compelling, the assumptions of the commercial economy classification no longer apply, and locational controls reminiscent of those imposed by centrally planned economies become determining.

Industrial Location in Planned Economies

The theoretical controls on plant location decisions that apply in commercial economies were not, by definition, determinant in the centrally planned Marxist economies of Eastern Europe and the former Soviet Union. In those economies, plant locational decisions were made by government agencies rather than by individual firms. Bureaucratic rather than company decision making did not mean that location assessments based on factor cost were ignored. It did mean that central planners were more concerned with other than purely economic considerations in the creation of new industrial plants and concentrations. Since such major capital investments are relatively permanent additions to the landscape, the results of the planners' often noneconomic political or philosophical decisions are fixed and remain to influence industrial regionalism and competitive efficiencies into the post-communist present and future.

Important in the former Soviet Union, for example, was a controlling policy of the *rationalization of industry* through full development of the resources of the country wherever they might be found and without regard to the cost or competitiveness of such development. Rationaliza-

tion reflected a Soviet application of the Marxist-Leninist call for *industrial diversification* and *regional self-sufficiency.* Those developmental goals required each section of the country to contain a variety of industrial types (and, if possible, a local agricultural base) to assure its independent operation even if its connections to other sections were to be severed.

The **territorial production complex** was the planning mechanism created to achieve such economic development. As an areally based organizational form, its responsibility was to develop necessary regional infrastructure, to facilitate the specialization of individual enterprises, and to promote overall regional economic growth and integration. National determination to achieve economic self-sufficiency dictated a conscious rejection of the logic of comparative advantage and required domestic production of goods more cheaply available abroad.

Inevitably, although the factors of industrial production are identical in capitalist and noncapitalist economies, the philosophies and patterns of industrial location and areal development will differ between them. In commercial economies, the locational focus is on the individual firm and its particular cost-minimization/profit-maximization goals. In noncapitalist planned economies, the objective may be overall regional development and economic balance that require inefficiently high-cost/low-return enterprise locations.

Major Manufacturing Regions of the World

Whether locational decisions are made by private entrepreneurs or central planner—and on whatever considerations those decisions are based—the results over many years have produced a distinctive world pattern of manufacturing. It shows a striking prominence of a relatively small number of major industrial concentrations localized within relatively few of the world's countries (Figure 9.17). These are not all countries of the "developed world," as a comparison with Figure 10.3 will indicate. Mexico, Brazil, China, and other countries of the "developing world" have created industrial regions of international significance, and the contribution to world manufacturing activity of the smaller newly industrializing countries (NICs) has been growing significantly.

Within the global industrial pattern outlined on Figure 9.17 are four commonly recognized major manufacturing regions: *Eastern Anglo America, Western and Central Europe, Eastern Europe,* and *Eastern Asia.* These most prominent manufacturing districts will receive our attention here. We should remember, however, that some of the secondary centers also shown within and outside of that globe-girdling industrial belt are beginning to assume the status of major concentrations in their own right.

FOR YOUR CONSIDERATION

CONTESTS AND BRIBERY

In 1985 it cost Kentucky over $140 million in incentives—some $47,000 a job—to induce Toyota to locate an automobile assembly plant in Georgetown, Kentucky. That was cheap. By 1993 Alabama spent $200,000 per job to lure Mercedes-Benz to that state and Kentucky bid $350,000 per job in tax credits to bring a Canadian steel mill there. The spirited auction for jobs is not confined to manufacturing. A University of Minnesota economist calculates that his state is to spend $500,000 for each of the 1500 or more permanent jobs to be created by Northwest Airlines at two new maintenance facilities. For some, the bidding between states and locales to attract new employers and employment gets too fierce. Kentucky withdrew from competition for a United Airlines maintenance facility, letting Indianapolis have it when Indiana's offered package exceeded $300 million.

Inducements to lure companies are not just in cash and loans—though both figure in some offers. For manufacturers, incentives may include workforce training, property tax abatement, subsidized costs of land and building or their outright gifts, below-market financing of bonds, and the like. Similar offers are regularly made by states, counties, and cities to wholesalers, retailers, major office-worker and other service activity employers. The objective, of course, is not just to

secure the new jobs represented by the attracted firm but to benefit from the general economic stimulus and employment growth that those jobs—and their companies—generate. Auto parts manufacturers are presumably attracted to new assembly plant locations; cities grow and service industries of all kinds—doctors, department stores, restaurants, food stores—prosper from the investments made to attract new basic employment.

Not everyone is convinced that those investments are wise, however. A poll of Minnesotans showed a majority opposed the generous offer made by the state to Northwest Airlines. In the late 1980s, the governor of Indiana, a candidate for Kentucky's governorship, and the mayor of Flat Rock, Michigan were all defeated by challengers who charged that too much had been spent in luring the Suburu-Isuzu, Toyota, and Mazda plants, respectively. Established businesses resent what often seems neglect of their interests in favor of spending their tax money on favors to newcomers. The Council for Urban Economic Development, surveying the escalating bidding wars, has actively lobbied against incentives, and many academic observers note that industrial attraction amounts to a zero-sum game: unless the attracted newcomer is a foreign firm, whatever one state achieves in attracting an expanding U.S. company comes at the expense of another state.

Some doubt that inducements matter much anyway. Although, sensibly,

companies seeking new locations will shop around and solicit the lowest-cost, best deal possible, their site choices are apt to be determined by more realistic business considerations: access to labor, suppliers, and markets; transportation and utility costs; weather; the nature of the workforce; and overall costs of living. Only when two or more similarly attractive locations have essentially equal cost structures might such special inducements as tax reductions or abatements be determining in a locational decision.

Questions:

1. *As citizen and taxpayer, do you think it is appropriate to spend public money to attract new employment to your state or community?*

2. *If not, why not? If yes, what kinds of inducements and what total amount offered per job seem appropriate to you? What reasons support your opinion?*

3. *If you believe that "best locations" for the economy as a whole are those determined by pure location theory, what arguments would you propose to discourage locales and states from making financial offers designed to circumvent decisions clearly justified on abstract theoretical grounds?*

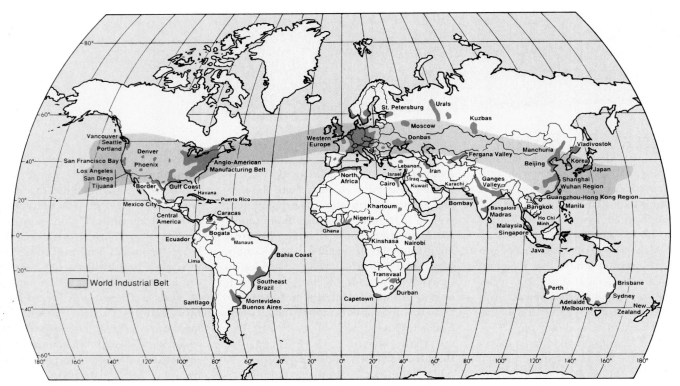

FIGURE 9.17 **World industrial regions.** Industrial districts are not as continuous or "solid" as the map suggests. Manufacturing is a relatively minor user of land even in areas of its greatest concentration. There is a loose spatial association of major industrial districts in an "industrial belt" extending from Western Europe eastward to the Ural Mountains and, through outliers in Siberia, to the Far East. The belt picks up again on the west coast of North America, though its major Anglo American concentration lies east of the Mississippi River. More than 75% of the volume and 80% of the value of manufacturing production of the world is found within this global industrial belt.

Eastern Anglo America

The importance of manufacturing in Anglo America, both as an employer of labor and as a contributor to the national income of Canada and the United States has been steadily declining. In 1960, the 25% of the labor force engaged in manufacturing generated nearly 30% of the region's wealth. By the mid-1990s, manufacturing employment had dropped to near 15% of a much larger labor force, and manufacturing contributed only about a fifth of the gross domestic product of the Anglo American realm. Nevertheless, the importance of the region as a major force in world industrial production is unquestioned.

Manufacturing is found particularly in the urbanized sections of North America, but is not uniformly distributed. Its primary concentration is in the northeastern part of the United States and adjacent sections of southeastern Canada, the *Anglo American Manufacturing Belt.* That belt extends from the St. Lawrence Valley on the north (though excluding northern New England) to the Ohio Valley, and from the Atlantic Coast westward to just beyond the Mississippi River (Figure 9.18). Covering less than 5% of the land area of Anglo America, the manufacturing belt contains the majority of the urban population of the two countries, their densest and best-developed transportation network, the largest number of their manufacturing establishments, and the preponderance of heavy industry. It is, as well, part of

the continent's agricultural heartland. These are all items of interrelated influence on the past history and present structure of industry within the belt.

Anglo American manufacturing began early in the 19th century in southern New England, where waterpowered textile mills, iron plants, and other small-scale industries began to free Canada and the new United States from total dependence on European—particularly English—sources. Although lacking the raw materials that later formed the industrial base of the continental interior, the eastern portion of the manufacturing belt contained early population centers, a growing canal and railroad network, a steady influx of immigrant skilled and unskilled labor, and concentrations of investment capital. Although the early manufacturing advantages of the Northeast were soon lost as settlement advanced across the Appalachians into the rich continental interior, the U.S. eastern seaboard remains an important producer of consumer goods, light industrial, and high-technology products on the basis of its market and developed labor skills. Important individual concentrations of both are found in *Megalopolis,*[1] a 1000-kilometer- (600-mile-) long city system stretching from southern Maine to

---

[1] A *megalopolis* or *conurbation* is an extended urbanized area formed by the gradual merger of several individual cities.

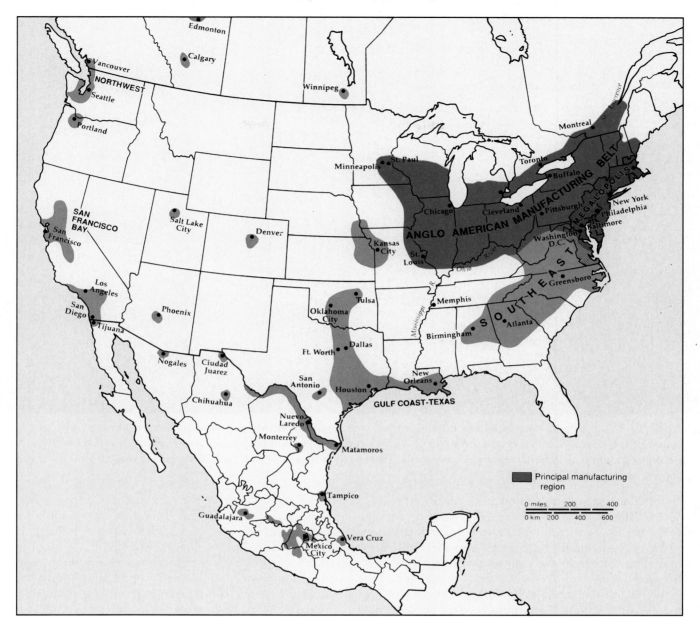

FIGURE 9.18   **North American manufacturing districts.** Although the preponderance of North American industry is still concentrated in Anglo America, Mexican manufacturing activity is rapidly growing and diversifying—for both expanding domestic and export markets. While Mexico City alone yields nearly half of the country's manufacturing output volume, industrial plants are also localized in the Central Plateau area and along the northern border with the United States, where most *maquiladoras* have been established.

Norfolk, Virginia—one of the longest, largest, most populous of the world's great metropolitan chains. As a major consumer concentration, it has attracted a tremendous array of market-oriented industries and thousands of individual industrial plants served by the largest and most varied labor force in the country.

Within Megalopolis, areal concentrations and specializations exist. New York City, for example, has printing, publishing, metal fabrication, electrical goods, the apparel industry, and food processing—and increasingly specializes in financial and administrative "industries" of the tertiary and quaternary sectors. Both Philadelphia and

Baltimore—on the southern margin of the manufacturing belt—have excellent port facilities and good rail connections to the industrial-agricultural interior. Imported iron ore and petroleum provide material inputs for steel plants and petrochemical works that show by their tidewater locations a raw material orientation at break-bulk points.

The heart of the Anglo American manufacturing belt developed across the Appalachians in the interior of the continent in the valleys of the Ohio River and its tributaries and along the shores of the Great Lakes. The rivers and the Great Lakes provided the early "highways" of the interior (Figure 9.19), supplemented by canals built throughout the

FIGURE 9.19   A barge "tow" passing St. Louis on the Mississippi River. About 15% of the total ton-miles of freight movement in the United States is by inland water carriers. Crude and refined petroleum accounts for three-fifths of the tonnage. Farm products, chemicals (including fertilizers), and nonmetallic minerals (sand, rock, and gravel) make up much of the rest.

eastern Middle West of the United States during the 1830s and 1840s. They were followed after the 1850s by the railroads that tied together the agricultural and industrial raw materials, the growing urban centers, and the multiplying manufacturing plants of the interior with both the established eastern and the developing western reaches of the continent. The raw material endowment of the region was impressive: anthracite and bituminous coking and thermal coals, iron ore, petroleum, copper, lead and other nonferrous metals, timber resources, and agricultural land of richness and extent unknown elsewhere in the world.

Changing circumstances have altered the earlier industrial strength and production mix of the interior portion manufacturing belt. Parts of it—the USX plants of the Mon Valley will serve as example—have been dubbed the "Rust Belt" to signify deterioration and abandonment of plants formerly dominating the metals industries but now outmoded and obsolete, unable to compete even in their home market with more efficient, cheaper, and more technologically advanced foreign producers or with smaller, market-oriented domestic mills. Raw material depletion, energy cost increases, water and air pollution control costs and restrictions, and direct and indirect labor costs that are high by the standards of competing countries have served to alter the industrial mix and patterns of success of the past.

Some of the same problems of change and competition have afflicted the Canadian portion of the Anglo American manufacturing belt. Canadian industry is highly localized. About one-half of the country's manufacturing labor force is concentrated in southern Ontario, every bit the equivalent in industrial development and mix of its United States counterparts in upstate New York and nearby Pennsylvania, Ohio, and eastern Michigan. Toronto forms the hub, but the industrial belt extends westward to Windsor, across from Detroit. Another third of Canadian manufacturing employment is found in Quebec, with Montreal as the obvious core but with important energy-intensive industries—particularly aluminum plants and paper mills—found along the St. Lawrence River and elsewhere in the province.

Other Anglo American Concentrations

For much of the 19th century and as recently as the late 1960s, the manufacturing belt just described contained from one-half to two-thirds of Anglo American industry. By the 1990s, however, its share had dropped to near 40%. Not only was the position of manufacturing declining in the Anglo American economy, but what remained was continuing a pattern of relocation reflecting national population shifts and changing material and product orientations.

Figure 9.18 suggests the location of some of the larger of these outlying industrial zones. In the *Southeast,* textiles (see "Wage Rates and the Cloth Trades," page 300), tobacco, food-processing, wood products, furniture, and a Birmingham-based iron and steel industry became important users of local resources. Atlanta has emerged as the diversified industrial-commercial regional capital, but all of the rapidly growing cities of the region are beneficiaries of the region's climate, low energy costs, and available, productive labor force. In the *Gulf Coast–Texas district* (actually extending northward into Oklahoma) petroleum and natural gas provide wealth, energy, and raw materials for a vast petrochemical industry; sulfur and salt support other branches of chemical production. The explosive growth of large metropolitan complexes has attracted a full array of market-oriented firms. Farther west, *Denver* and *Salt Lake City* have become major, though isolated industrial centers with important "high-tech" orientations, while on the West Coast, three distinctive industrial subregions have emerged to continental prominence. In the *Northwest,* from Vancouver to Portland, orientation to both a regional and a broader Asian–Pacific market is of greater significance than are the primary domestic markets of Canada and the United States, both more than 3000 kilometers (1800 miles) away. Seattle's aircraft industry has world significance, of course, and the booming software industry of the Northwest is, by the high value and small volume of its product, largely unaffected by transport costs to its world markets. The *San Francisco Bay district* is home to Silicon Valley and the electronics/computer/high-tech manufacturing that name implies. Food specializations (wine, for example) for a national market have their counterpart farther south in the *Los Angeles–San Diego corridor,* where fruits and vegetables are grown and packed. More important, however, is diversified, particularly consumer-goods, production for the rapidly growing California and western market.

Western and Central Europe

The Industrial Revolution that began in England in the 1730s and spread to the continent during the 19th century established Western and Central Europe as a premier manufacturing region and the source area for the diffusion of industrialization across the globe. By 1900 Europe accounted for 90% of the world's industrial output though, of course, its relative position has since eroded, particularly after World War II. Although industry is part of the economic structure of every section and every metropolitan complex of Europe, the majority of manufacturing output is concentrated in a set of distinctive districts stretching from the Midlands of England in the west to the Ural Mountains in the east (Figure 9.20). Within that broad band, a reasonable division may be made between the industrial concentrations of Western and Central Europe eastward through Germany, and an eastern component made up of Eastern European countries including European Russia.

The textile industry of England was the start of the Industrial Revolution and of the areal concentrations and specialization that accompanied its spread. Waterpowered mechanical spinning and weaving in Lancashire, Yorkshire, and the English Midlands established the model, but it was steam power, not waterpower, that provided the impetus for the industrialization of that country and of Europe as a whole. Consequently, coal fields, not rivers, were the sites of the new manufacturing districts in the English Midlands, Lancashire, Yorkshire, and the Scottish Lowlands. Although it was remote from coal deposits or other natural resources, London became the largest single manufacturing center of the United Kingdom. Already sizeable at the time of the Industrial Revolution, its consumers and labor force were potent magnets for new industry.

Technologies developed in Britain spread to the continent. The coal fields distributed in a band across northern France, Belgium, central Germany, the northern Czech Republic, southern Poland, and eastward to southern Ukraine, as well as iron ore deposits, localize the metallurgical industries to the present day. Other pronounced industrial concentrations focus on the major metropolitan districts and capital cities of the countries of Europe. In all districts, product specialization has been the tradition and the basis for regional exchange.

The largest and most important single industrial area of Europe today extends from the Sambre–Meuse area of the French–Belgium border to the Ruhr district of western Germany. Its core is the Ruhr, a compact, highly urbanized industrial concentration of more than 10 million inhabitants in over 50 major cities. Iron and steel, textiles, automobiles, chemicals, and all the metal-forming and metal-using industries of modern economies are found here in the now-declining hub of Germany's industrial structure (Figure 9.21).

In France, heavy industry located near the iron ore of Nancy and the coal of Lille, which also specialized in textile production. Like London, Paris lacks raw materials, but as an early center of population and commerce, with easy access to the sea and to the domestic market, it became and remains the major manufacturing center of France. Its population (including suburbs) of some 9 million makes it the largest city in mainland Western Europe, and its full range of consumer goods, of transport, electrical, and engineering equipment, and of such specialty items of perfumes, toiletries, and high-fashion garments reflects its market pull and labor skills.

Farther east, the Saxony district began to industrialize as early as the 1600s, in part benefiting from labor skills brought by immigrant artisans from France and Holland. Those skills have been preserved in a district noted for the quality of its manufactured goods, including porcelain in the Dresden area, textiles at Plauen and Chemnitz, chemicals at Halle, printing and publishing in Leipzig, and, in various locales, precision machinery and optical goods.

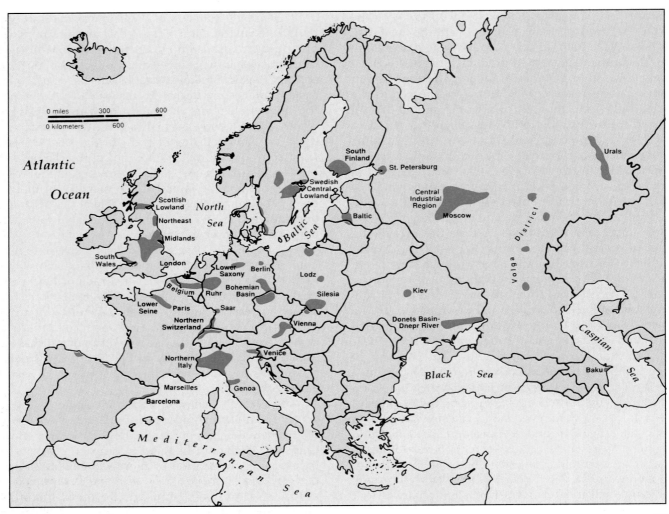

FIGURE 9.20   The industrial regions of Europe.

Western Europe is experiencing a *deindustrialization* accompanied by massive layoffs of workers in coal mining because of declining demand and in iron mining because of ore depletion. Iron and steel, textiles, and shipbuilding—the core industries of the Industrial Revolution—have been particularly hard hit among the secondary industries. Western European crude steel production reached its peak in 1974 and has declined steadily since then, buffeted by high wages, antiquated plants, and changing market demand. Tens of thousands of unemployed miners and factory workers and hundreds of idled plants in metals, textiles, and other mainstay industries signal a restructuring of the Western European economy.

Eastern Europe

Between the end of World War II and 1990, Eastern European industrial concentrations, such as that of Silesia in Poland and the Czech portion of the Bohemian Basin (Figure 9.20), were largely cut off from their earlier ties with the larger European market and economy. They were controlled by centralized industrial planning and tied to purely domestic concerns and to the regional economic plans imposed by the Soviet Union.

Czech industry, like that of former East German Saxony, was important in those plans for the diversity and quality of its output. In addition, it shares the emphasis on heavy industry—iron and steel, transportation equipment, armaments, chemicals, and the like—that characterizes the manufacturing pattern of Poland, Hungary, Bulgaria, Romania, and former Yugoslavia. Collectively, the earlier centrally planned industrial economies of Eastern Europe entered their post-Marxist period with a generally poorly conceived, technologically antiquated, uneconomic industrial structure that, in its creation and operation, not only was unresponsive to market realities but also wreaked immeasurable damage on the natural environment (see "Ideology, Industrialization, and Environmental Disaster").

Farther east, in Russia and Ukraine, two distinctly different industrial orientations predominate, both dating from Czarist times and strengthened under Soviet-era planning. One emphasis is on light industrial, market-oriented production primarily focused on Russia's Central Industrial

FIGURE 9.21   The scenic Rhine River serves as a main artery of industrial Western Europe, flowing past Europe's premier industrial complex, the Ruhr district. For western Germany, the Rhine is the convenient connection to the North Sea and the Atlantic through the port of Rotterdam in the Netherlands. Thanks to its massive volume of river and ocean traffic, Rotterdam is the leading port of Europe and the world's largest port in tonnage handled.

Region of Greater Moscow and surrounding areas (Figure 9.22). With no natural resources except poor quality brown coal, the district has been supported by major metropolitan markets, superior transportation systems, centrality within the European portion of the country, and a readily available labor force. St. Petersburg, a stand-alone industrial district of the northwest, has been noted for labor skills since its founder, Peter the Great, early in the 18th century brought Western European artisans, engineers, and craftsmen to build the city and to create there a modern industrial base. Its industries still reflect those labor skills.

The other orientation is heavy industrial. Its Czarist beginnings were localized in the southern Ukrainian Donets Basin–Dnepr River district where coking coal, iron ore, fluxing materials, and iron alloys are found near at hand. A modern iron and steel industry was begun there, largely with foreign capital, during the last third of the 19th century. Nearly Ruhr-like in its intensity of development and urbanization, the Donets Basin and adjacent areas remained the sole source of metallurgical industry throughout late Czarist times. Only the Stalinist Five-Year plans, with their emphasis on creation of multiple sources of supply of essential industrial goods, gave the district rivals elsewhere in the Soviet Union.

Prior to the Revolution of 1917, 90% of Russian industry was found west of the Volga River. The pattern of new industrial districts shown in Figure 9.22 represents the Stalinist (and later) determination to develop fully all the resources of the country, to create new industrial bases at resource locations, and to strengthen the national economy through construction of multiple districts of diversified industry. The industrialization of Russia's Volga, Urals, Kuznetsk Basin, Baikal, and Far East regions, and the industrial complexes of the Caucasus, Kazakhstan, and Central Asia resulted from those Soviet programs first launched in 1928. By 1991 and the collapse of the Soviet Union, these planned manufacturing centers and territorial production complexes together yielded 35–40% of national industrial output.

Since the collapse of communism, there has been a significant structural change in Eastern European industries. An obvious shift has occurred from Soviet dominance and mandates to a more market-oriented, nationally independent manufacturing structure. Eastern European and Russian industries have been either partly or fully privatized, often with investments from Western European or North American firms. Many, without the governmental market and financial support that formerly sustained them, have been idled or closed.

arxist theory maintained that under socialism there can be no environmental problems since, where there is no profit motive, humans and nature inherently are in harmony. That comforting philosophy did little to reduce the evident and growing environmental degradation that unrestricted and reckless industrial development brought to the Soviet Union and Eastern Europe under communism. Uncontrolled emissions from smelters, refineries, steel furnaces and coke ovens, chemical plants, and cities themselves have imposed enormous damages on the forests, rivers, air, and soil of the region and on the health and life expectancy of its populations.

A Russian ecologist reports that industrial pollution made one-sixth of the territory of the former Soviet Union environmentally hazardous, two-thirds of its almost 150 million population is exposed to pollution between 5 and 10 times normal, and that 50 million people live in cities where air pollution is more than 10 times greater than maximum safe levels. Within Russia, nearly 100,000 barrels of oil—roughly 10% of total output—are spilled each day, permanently destroying the contaminated ground. The Baltic Sea is dying, a quarter of its bottom effectively a marine desert devoid of life. Sediments of St. Petersburg harbor contain 1000 times the normal levels of lead and cadmium.

Poland has identified 27 ecologically endangered areas. Five of these, containing 35% of the nation's population, have been described as "ecological disasters." In them, the incidence of cancer is one-quarter to one-third higher than the national average, respiratory diseases are 50% higher, and life expectancy averages at least 2 years less than in the rest of the country. In Poland as a whole, air, water, and soil pollution are severe to the point that the health of at least one-third of the population is at serious risk. Essentially all of its river water is unfit for human consumption, and 50% is so toxic it is unfit even for industrial use. A quarter of the country's soil is probably too contaminated for safe farming, and the lead and cadmium content of Upper Silesian soil is so high that the government contemplated banning vegetable farming in response to the great increase there in the number of children with mental impairments. Dumping of untreated industrial and urban waste has so polluted the Vistula River that citizens are advised not to give babies tap water, even after boiling it. Nearly 450 cities and 3600 industrial plants are totally without facilities to treat wastewater.

Poland, which has more detailed and restrictive regulations for environmental protection than any of the other Eastern European countries, is simply the worst of a series of bad situations. In former East Germany, air pollution from power plant emissions has effectively destroyed the forests around Halle and Leipzig, where more than half of the country's power stations were concentrated. Life expectancy is reported to be considerably lower there than elsewhere in Germany. Hungary produces some 5 million tons of hazardous waste each year and until recently was importing for paid disposal thousands of additional tons from Austria, Switzerland, and West Germany—all without adequate disposal facilities. Former Czechoslovakia's communist rulers forbade emigration from heavily industrialized northern Bohemia, but offered citizens higher wages—a form of "hazardous duty" pay—to compensate them for the health dangers of remaining in areas of extreme pollution.

In their drive to establish strong national economies and to match the level of industrial development of Western Europe, the centrally planned economies of Eastern Europe ignored the environmental consequences of their programs. They—and areas far beyond their borders affected by airborne pollutants—are now suffering from their philosophy and decisions. Ideological assumptions cannot alter industrial realities.

Eastern Asia

The Eastern Asian sphere is rapidly becoming the most productive of the world's industrial districts. Japan has emerged as the overall second-ranked manufacturing nation. China—building on a rich resource base, massive labor force, and nearly insatiable market demand—is industrializing rapidly and ranks among the top 10 producers of a number of major industrial commodities. Hong Kong, South Korea, and Taiwan are three of the "four dragons," newly industrializing Asian economies (the fourth is Singapore in Southeast Asia) that have become major presences in markets around the world.

Japan

Japanese industry was rebuilt from near total destruction during World War II to second rank in the world—and first in some areas of electronics and other high-tech production. That recovery was accomplished largely without a domestic raw material base and primarily with the export market in mind. Dependence on imports of materials and exports of product has encouraged a coastal location for most factories. The industrial core of modern Japan is the heavily urbanized belt from Tokyo to northern Kyushu (Figure 9.23). In turn, this zone has two major and two secondary subregions.

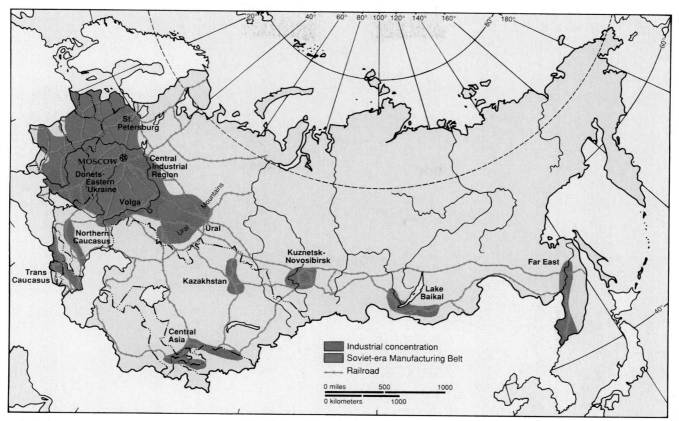

FIGURE 9.22 **Industrial regions under central planning in the former Soviet Union.** The Volga, the Central Industrial, and the St. Petersburg (Leningrad) concentrations within the former Soviet manufacturing belt were dependent on transportation, labor, and market pulls. All the other planned industrial regions had a strong orientation to materials and were developed despite their distance from the population centers and markets of the west.

The Tokyo megalopolis is the manufacturing heart of the country as well as its principal population concentration. In addition to Tokyo itself (the capital and largest city of Japan), the subarea contains Yokohama (the principal port), Kawasaki, Chiba, and a number of lesser centers. Manufacturing activities of all types are localized here, where some one-fifth of the nation's population produces between one-fourth and one-third of its industrial output. Iron and steel plants, petroleum refining and petrochemicals, shipbuilding, automobiles, motorcycles, and more are part of the vast industrial complex, and all are based on imported raw materials. The Kobe-Osaka district, including the ancient capital of Kyoto, focuses on the Inland Sea, intensively utilized as a transport connection between the cities of the industrial core. This second-ranked industrial subregion, temporarily severely damaged in an earthquake in 1995, is responsible for about one-fifth of total Japanese manufactures. Shipbuilding, iron and steel, textiles, oil refining and petrochemicals, machine tools, and all the other types of production suggested by the descriptive term "diversified industry" are found in the district.

The two subordinate subregions of the Japanese industrialized belt are the Nagoya district and fourth-ranked Kitakyushu (Figure 9.23). Nagoya, with less than 20% of national production, also can be described as "diversified," with its traditional emphasis on textiles more recently being augmented by heavy industry and automobile assembly. Kitakyushu, the southernmost industrial center, is one of the few places in Japan where industry is based on local raw materials—here, coal and iron ore. Their presence encouraged the early development of heavy industry, though increasingly manufacturing is dependent on imported materials. The slowest-growing of the industrial subregions, Kitakyushu's proximity to mainland China suggests a brighter future as trade relations between the two countries continue to expand.

China

When the communists assumed control of China's still war-damaged economy in 1949, that country was essentially unindustrialized. Most manufacturing was small-scale production geared to local subsistence needs. Those larger textile and iron and steel plants that did exist were coastal in

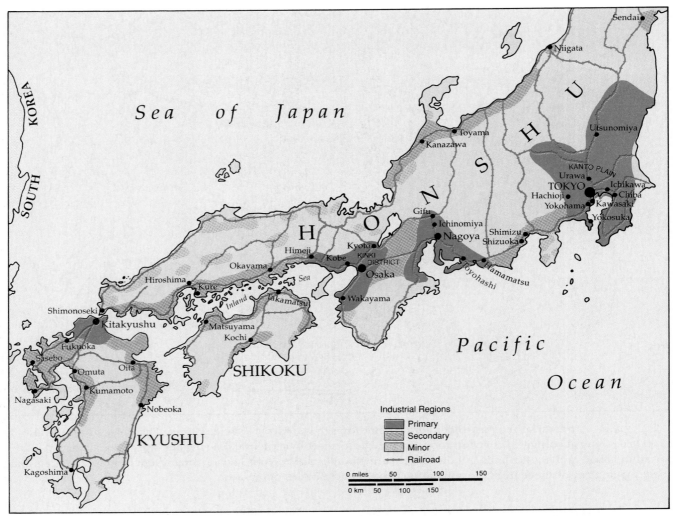

FIGURE 9.23   **The industrial regions of Japan** are primarily coastal and dependent on imported raw materials and access to the world's markets.

From Richard H. Jackson and Lloyd E. Hudman, *World Regional Geography,* 2d ed. Copyright © 1986 John Wiley & Sons, Inc., New York. NY. Reprinted by permission of John Wiley & Sons, Inc.

location, built or owned by foreigners (including the Japanese who had long occupied the northeast of the country) and oriented toward exports to the owners' home markets. A massive industrialization program initiated by the new regime—with some assistance up to the mid-1960s from the Soviet Union—greatly increased the volume, diversity, and dispersion of manufacturing in China.

Until 1976 under Mao-Zedong, domestic needs rather than foreign markets were the principal concern of an industrial development totally controlled by the state and the communist party. After Mao's death, the decision was made in 1978 that economic growth had to take precedence over rigid communist orthodoxy. Manufacturing activities were freed from absolute state control, factory managers were authorized to sign contracts with suppliers, most goods could be sold to any able buyer, and workers could be hired and fired according to factory needs. Industrial output grew

rapidly with most dramatic gains coming not from state enterprises but from quickly multiplying rural collectives (see "China's Separate Path").

Unlike Japan, China possesses a relatively rich and diversified domestic raw material base of ores and fuels. In coal, China ranks third in the world; petroleum and natural gas have been the object of intensive and successful exploration. Iron ore is found in several locations, and a wide array of iron alloys and nonferrous metals is also known and exploited. The pattern of resource distribution in part accounts for the spatial pattern of industry, though coastal locations, urban agglomerations, and market orientations are equally important (Figure 9.24). Overall, the distributional pattern is one of discontinuous industrial regions extending from Harbin in the Northeast to Guangzhou (Canton) on the south coast and, since the early 1990s, to Hainan Island in the South China Sea.

DYNAMIC PATTERNS OF THE SPACE ECONOMY

n 1978, two years after Mao's death, China's leaders redirected the country's economy away from earlier-held Stalinist principles of central planning, state ownership, and import substitution and toward a market economy in food produced on what became basically family farms. The subsequent enrichment of the peasantry and countryside generated the surplus of rural savings needed to finance the industrialization of the country, which found its most dramatic expression in competitive rural factories. In 1978, just prior to the reforms, state-owned firms accounted for 78% of China's industrial production. By 1995, state-owned industry produced just over 40%, and government plans were for that share to drop to 25% by 2000. Thanks to its new economic policies, China's real gross national product grew by an average of 9.5% a year between 1980 and 1995—

some 6.5 percentage points faster than U.S. growth. China is the world's tenth-largest economy by traditional exchange rate measures and probably the world's second- or third-largest economy with more than 6% of worldwide output of goods and services (behind the United States and either just behind or just ahead of Japan) based on comparisons of purchasing power.

The engine of that growth and success was the development of industries, mainly in the countryside, that are not owned by the central government but are nonprivate "collectives." Technically known as "township and village enterprises" these rural manufacturing enterprises are controlled by units of local government. Management is answerable to local officials and to private householders who have started or invested in the enterprise. These rural firms have remade both the Chinese industrial economy and the economic structure of the countryside.

In 1978 there were 1.5 million nonstate industrial firms in rural areas employing 28 million people. By 1995 there were over 20 million rural industrial enterprises with more than 100 million employees. And by the mid-1990s, rural factories were responsible for more than 40% of China's industrial employment, over 25% of industrial output, and some 25% of national exports. At the same time, rural China has been restructured. At the start of the reforms, farming accounted for 70% of rural output and industry for only 20%; more recently, industry and farming each accounted for about 45%. If the rate of national economic growth, spurred by China's permissive industrial policy, continues at the rate it has shown since 1978, it will be the world's biggest economy by 2010—a vastly different prospect from that of Russia despite their common ideological roots.

The Northeast (called Dongbei by the Chinese and formerly known as Manchuria) became a core region of Chinese industry, accounting for some 13% by value of China's factory output and 18% of its heavy industry in the early 1990s. Similar to the Ruhr of Germany and the Donets Basin of Ukraine in its raw material orientation, industrial mix, and urbanization, Dongbei exploits the iron ore, coal, timber, and petroleum of the region. With older, state-owned plants dominant and largely untouched by the economic restructuring of the 1980s, the Northeast—first developed by the Japanese prior to World War II—now suffers from slow growth and rising unemployment. It is increasingly eclipsed in industrial importance by the dynamic southern coastal provinces of China.

A second major industrial district—and first in total value of production, with over one-third of China's output—extends along the coast from Qingdao (Tsingtao) in the north to Shanghai on the south. Referred to as the East, this heavily populated coastal district includes China's biggest industrial city, Shanghai—with textile, metal, chemical, and a vast array of light manufacturing plants—and has access to the interior via the country's most important river, the Chang Jiang (Yangtze). Shanghai itself and the larger Chang Jiang delta together account for nearly one-third of all China's output, the result of industrial growth rates in the

first half of the 1990s a third higher than in China as a whole. Upstream on the Chang Jiang is the Chang district from Wuhan (iron and steel and heavy industry) westward to Chongqing (Chunking).

Between the East and the Northeast districts lies the North China subregion, centering on the national capital, Beijing, and including the port city of Tianjin (Tientsin). A major coal-producing district, the region has iron and steel mills at several different locations, as well as textiles, food processing, transportation equipment, and consumer goods. Altogether, some 20% of China's industrial output comes from this areally limited district. The fourth-largest industrial production region, the Central-South, is focused on Guangzhou (Canton) and its province, Guangdong, where consumer goods industrial output has soared since 1980 in a thriving, market-driven manufacturing economy that is becoming a "fifth dragon" competitor in exports of light industrial goods.

The "Dragons"

Four smaller Asian economies—Hong Kong, Taiwan, South Korea, and Singapore—have become major manufacturing and trading forces in the world market. Maturing beyond their earlier designation as NICs (newly industrializing countries), all four have now outgrown their "developing

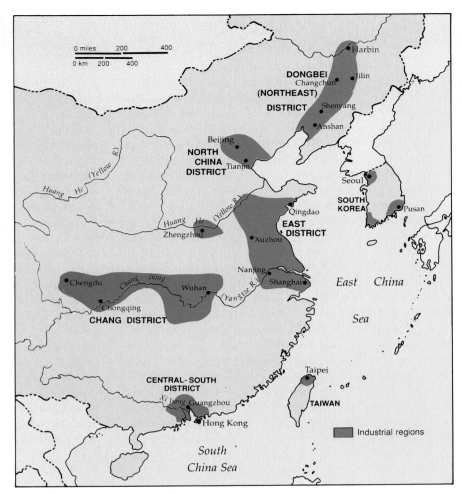

FIGURE 9.24   **Industrialized China and the "dragons".**

country" status and effectively have become advanced industrialized economies. Their rise to prominence has been rapid, and their share of market in those branches of industry in which they have chosen to specialize has increased dramatically. Although the specifics of their industrial successes have differed, in each case an educated, trainable labor force, economic and social systems encouraging industrial enterprise, and national programs directed at capital accumulation, industrial development, and export orientation fueled the programs. Rising production and labor costs in the four dragons have caused some foreign-owned factories to relocate to a newer set of rapidly expanding Southeast Asian economies: Thailand, Malaysia, and Indonesia, as well as to mainland China.

Hong Kong, with some 6 million population, lies just off-shore from Guangzhou (Figure 9.24). Its industrial production—textiles, plastics, electrical goods, small appliances, and electronics—is oriented to export. Presumably, the significant addition to the total value of manufacture of the East Asian district made by Hong Kong, a British crown colony since 1841, will continue after it is returned to Chinese sovereignty in 1997. Taiwan, an island some 200 kilometers (125 miles) off the southeast coast of China is, like Hong

Kong, crowded and without a significant resource base (except for small coal deposits around Taipei at the north end of the island and hydroelectric potential along its mountainous spine). Also largely oriented toward the Western market and imported raw materials, Taiwan has become a major producer of textiles, of electrical and electronic goods, plastics, toys, small appliances, and the like (Figure 9.25) and has developed domestic iron and steel, aluminum, and chemical industries.

South Korea was kept from the communist orbit after World War II and the Korean conflict and sustained with massive American aid. North Korea kept possession of the bulk of the coal and iron ore, the majority of other minerals, and most of the hydroelectric potential of the divided country as well as the only developed heavy industrial district around the northern capital of Pyongyang. South Korea initially was largely agricultural and impoverished, but since the mid-1950s experienced rapid growth in all branches of industry. By the early 1990s it had developed the world's seventeenth-largest economy and became the twelfth-largest trading nation. It possesses the world's largest steel plant, builds automobiles and military aircraft, has major shipyards and ship repair facilities, rivals and strongly

FIGURE 9.25 Industrialization in Taiwan began in the 1950s with low-skill textiles, plastic toys, simple appliances, and housewares production for export. In the 1960s, television, bicycles, refrigerators, radios, electrical goods, and the like represented more advanced manufacturing processes and products. In the 1970s, under governmental planning, factories for intermediate goods and producers goods—petrochemicals, machine tools, heavy machinery, and the like—were developed to support an expanding industrial base. The 1980s saw the rise of science-based high-technology industries fully competitive in the world market. For the 1990s, further telecommunication, consumer electronic, aerospace, and pharmaceutical industry expansions are emphasized.

competes with Japan in the production of consumer electronic and electrical goods, and in general shows a range and volume of industrial production impressive for any nation and astounding for one of South Korea's size and population.

Singapore, in southeastern Asia at the southern tip of the Malay Peninsula, is the smallest—and richest—of the "dragons." With fewer than 3 million population on only 600 square kilometers (240 sq. mi.), this island state has prospered since its independence from Malaysia in 1965 by enticing foreign investors with its well-trained, highly disciplined, and low-cost labor force. Now specializing in high-tech manufacturing, electronic technology, and financial and research services, Singapore also serves as a major transshipment port of Southeast Asia.

Although the "dragons" have received most recognition for their outstanding successes, other Asian manufacturing concentrations are also emerging as important participants in the world's industrial economy. India benefits from expanding industrial bases centered in metropolitan Karachi, Bombay, Delhi, Calcutta, and elsewhere, each with its own developing specializations. Thailand, Malaysia, and the Philippines are emerging as both independent and "outsourcing" manufacturing economies duplicating in some product lines the earlier successes and specializations of the "dragons" themselves.

High-Tech Patterns

Major industrial districts of the world developed over time as entrepreneurs and planners established traditional secondary industries according to the pulls and orientations predicted by classical location theories. The Midlands of England, the Ruhr of Germany, and the Donets Basin of Ukraine are unmistakably raw-material oriented; the market and labor force attractions of a Shanghai, London, or Paris are clear-cut; and the importance of transportation is evident in the coastal locations of Japanese manufacturing. Those theories are less applicable in explaining the location of the latest generation of manufacturing activities: the high technology—or *high-tech*—processing and production that is increasingly part of the advanced economies. For these firms, new and different patterns of locational orientation and advantage have emerged based on other than the traditional regional and site attractions.

High technology is more a concept than a definition. It probably is best understood as the application of intensive research and development efforts to the creation and manufacture of products of an advanced scientific and engineering character. Professional—"white collar"—workers make up a large share of the total workforce. They include research scientists, engineers, and skilled technicians. When these high-skill specialists are added to administrative, supervisory, marketing, and other professional staffs they may greatly outnumber actual production workers in a firm's employment structure. Although only a few types of industrial activity are generally reckoned as exclusively high tech—electronics, computers, software, biotechnology, and the like—advanced technology is increasingly a part of the structure of all forms of industry. Robotics on the assembly line, computer-aided design and manufacturing, electronic controls of smelting and refining processes, and the constant development of new products of the chemical and pharmaceutical industries are cases in point.

The impact of high-tech industries on patterns of economic geography is expressed in at least three different ways. First, high-tech activities are becoming major factors in employment growth in the advanced economies. In the United States, for example, between 1972 and 1995, the high-tech industries added some 2 million new jobs to the secondary sector of the economy, helping to replace thousands of other workers who lost jobs to outsourcing, foreign competition, changing markets, and deindustrialization. England, Germany, Japan, and other advanced countries—though not yet those of Eastern Europe—have had similar employment shifts.

Second, high-tech industries have tended to become regionally concentrated in their countries of development and within those regions they frequently form self-sustaining, highly specialized agglomerations. California, for example, has a share of U.S. high-tech employment far in excess of its share of American population. Along with California, the Pacific Northwest (including British Columbia), New England, New Jersey, Texas, and Delaware all have proportions of their workers in high-tech industries above the national average. And within these and other states or regions of high-tech concentration, specific locales have achieved prominence: "Silicon Valley" of Santa Clara County near San Francisco, the "Silicon Forest" near Seattle, North Carolina's Research Triangle, Utah's "Software Valley," Route 128 around Boston, Ottawa, Canada's "Silicon Valley North," or the Canadian Technology Triangle west of Toronto are familiar Anglo American examples. Within such concentrations, specialization is often the rule: medical technologies in Minneapolis and Philadelphia, biotechnology around San Antonio, computers and semiconductors in eastern Virginia and at Austin, Texas, biotechnology and telecommunications in New Jersey's Princeton Corridor. Elsewhere, Scotland's Silicon Glen or England's Sunrise Strip are other examples of industrial landscapes characterized by low, modern, dispersed office-plant-laboratory buildings rather than by massive factories, mills, or assembly structures, freight facilities, and storage areas. Not all areas that thrive on high-tech growth, however, necessarily retain their strength; the same competitive forces that weakened traditional industry in established economies can damage or destroy high-tech specializations and concentrations (Figure 9.26).

FIGURE 9.26   The Boott cotton mills at Lowell, Massachusetts, in 1852. Lowell was America's first industrial city, built in the 1820s at a water power site on the Merrimack River as a direct copy of British cotton-mill cities. The eventual decline of the textile industry left Lowell industrially destitute, with an unemployment rate of 12.5% in 1975. By the late 1980s it had transformed itself into a center of modern enterprise: 24% of its nearly-full employment was in high-technology industry, compared to 10% for Massachusetts as a whole. At least part of that industry was housed in the city's older vacated textile mills, showing high tech is not the exclusive property of the Sunbelt or of research parks in rural settings. In May 1991, Lowell's unemployment rate again hit 12.5%. Its high-tech industry had been dominated by a single large employer and a single product, the mini-computer. When both lost market shares, Lowell's high-tech boom faded.

The new distributional patterns of high-tech industries suggest they respond to different localizing forces than those controlling older generation industries. At least five locational tendencies have been recognized: (1) proximity to major universities or research facilities and to a large pool of scientific and technical labor skills; (2) avoidance of areas with strong labor unionization where contract rigidities might slow process innovation and workforce flexibility; (3) locally available venture capital and entrepreneurial daring; (4) location in regions and major metropolitan areas with favorable "quality of life" reputations—climate, scenery, recreation, good universities, and an employment base sufficiently large to supply needed workers and provide job opportunities for professionally trained spouses; (5) availability of first-quality communication and transportation facilities to unite separated stages of research, development, and manufacturing and to connect the firm with suppliers, markets, finances, and the government agencies so important in supporting research.

Agglomerating forces are also important. The formation of new firms is frequent and rapid in industries where discoveries are constant and innovation is continuous. Since many are "spin-off" firms founded by employees leaving established local companies, areas of existing high-tech concentration tend to spawn new entrants and to provide necessary labor skills. Agglomeration, therefore, is both a product and a cause of spatial associations.

Not all phases of high-tech production must be concentrated, however. The spatial attractions affecting the professional, scientific, and knowledge-intensive aspects of high tech have little meaning for many of the component manufacturing and assembly operations, which may be highly automated or require little in the way of labor skills. These tasks, in our earlier locational terminology, are "footloose"; they require highly mobile capital and technology investments but may be adequately or advantageously performed by young women in low-wage areas at home or—more likely—in countries such as Taiwan, Hong Kong, Malaysia, or Mexico. Through manufacturing *transfers of technology* and *outsourcing*, therefore, high-tech activities are spread to newly industrializing countries—from the center to the periphery, in the developmental terms we will explore in Chapter 10. This areal transfer and dispersion represents the third impact of high-tech activities on world economic geographic patterns.

Tertiary and Beyond

Primary activities, you will recall, gather, extract, or grow things. Secondary industries, we have seen in this chapter, give *form utility* to the products of primary industry through manufacturing and processing efforts. **Tertiary activities** consist of those business and labor specializations that pro-vide support to the primary and secondary sectors, to the general community, and to the individual. They involve services, not the production of tangible commodities.

True, some services are concerned with the wholesaling or retailing of goods, providing what economists call *place utility* to items produced elsewhere. They fulfill the exchange function of advanced economies and provide the market exchanges necessary in highly interdependent societies. In commercial economies, tertiary activities also provide vitally needed information about market demand, without which economically justifiable production decisions are impossible. But most tertiary activities are concerned with personal and business services performed in shops and offices that, typically, cluster in cities large and small. The spatial patterns of the tertiary sector are identical to the spatial distribution of *effective demand*—that is, wants made meaningful through purchasing power. We shall look at those patterns as part of our examination of the characteristics of cities that function as "service centers," and as part of the land use patterning of all cities, in Chapter 11.

Tertiary activities represent a mark of contrast between advanced and subsistence societies, and the greater their proliferation, the greater the interdependence of the society of which they are a part. Their expansion has been great in both the commercial and the formerly planned economies. The decisive element is the development level of the society, not the form of economic administration. Within the United States, 80% of nonfarm employment in the mid-1990s (and 70% of its gross domestic product) was accounted for by "services"; manufacturing provided about 16% of employment (Table 9.2) and only some 20% of GDP.

TABLE 9.2 U.S. Employment Patterns, 1965–1995[1]	PERCENT OF NONFARM JOBS 1965	1995	PERCENT INCREASE IN JOBS 1965–1995
In Services			
Miscellaneous services[2]	14.9	28.1	+259
Retail trade	15.5	17.9	+121
State and local government	12.7	14.1	+113
Finance, insurance	5.0	6.0	+129
Wholesale trade	5.4	5.4	+90
Transport and utilities	6.6	5.3	+53
Federal government	3.9	2.4	+18
Total	**64.0**	**79.2**	**+136**
In Goods Production			
Manufacturing	29.8	15.9	+2
Construction	5.2	4.4	+63
Mining	1.0	0.5	−8
Total	**36.0**	**20.8**	**+11**
Nonfarm Jobs (millions)	60.8	116.2	+91

[1]Payroll employees only; self-employed not included.

[2]Includes education, health, food and lodgings, etc.

Source: Bureau of Labor Statistics, *Employment and Earnings*.

In 1965, services were far less dominant, and "goods production" occupied more than 35% of the employed labor force. Nearly 25 million new jobs were created in the United States between 1980 and 1995, all of them, after discounting for job losses in other employment sectors, in services. Comparable changes are found in other countries. By the 1990s between 60% and 80% of jobs in such commercial economies as Japan, Canada, Australia, and all major Western European countries were in the service sector; Russia and Eastern Europe averaged 40–50% in services.

The **quaternary** sector may realistically be seen as an advanced form of service, or tertiary, activity involving specialized knowledge, technical skills, communication ability, or administrative competence. These are the activities carried on in office buildings, elementary and university classrooms, hospitals and doctors' offices, theaters, television stations, and the like. In advanced economies many individuals and groups are engaged in business and institutional services and management, advertising, professional services and the like for hire or for specific enterprises. In fact, over half of all workers in rich economies are employed in the "knowledge sector" alone—in the production, storage, retrieval, or distribution of knowledge.

Quaternary-sector jobs are not spatially tied to resources, affected by the environment, or localized by market. Information, administration, and the "knowledge" activities in their broadest sense are dependent on communication. Improvements in the technology of communication have freed them from their former concentrations in larger central business districts and in regional and national economic and political capitals, though they may remain close to those centers of power and population (Figure 9.27). Among the knowledge industries least tied locally or nationally is that of computer software generation. Skilled programmers in India and Eastern Europe, for example, are taking an increasing share of the world software generation, reaping the advantage given by wage and salary rates far below those of their Anglo American, Japanese, or European counterparts.

And, finally, there are the **quinary** activities, the "gold collar" professions of the chapter title, another separately recognized subdivision of the tertiary sector representing the special and highly paid skills of top business executives, government officials, research scientists, financial and legal consultants, and the like. These people find their place of business in major metropolitan centers, in and near major

FIGURE 9.27   "Office parks" such as this complex at Tysons Corner, Virginia, outside of Washington, D.C., are increasingly familiar concentrations of quaternary workers in the outlying zones of major metropolitan centers. In the middle 1990s more than 80,000 office workers were employed in this "suburban downtown."

DYNAMIC PATTERNS OF THE SPACE ECONOMY

universities and research parks, at first-rank medical centers, and in cabinet and department-level offices of political capitals. Within their cities of concentration they may be highly localized by prestigious street addresses (Park Avenue, Wall Street) or post offices (Princeton, New Jersey), or by notable "signature" office buildings (Transamerica Building, Seagram Building). Their importance in the structure of advanced economies far outweighs their numbers.

The list of tertiary, quaternary, and quinary employment is long. Its diversity and familiarity remind us of the complexity of modern life and of how far removed we are from the subsistence economies. As societies advance economically, the share of employment and national income generated by the primary, secondary, tertiary, and quaternary sectors continually changes; the spatial patterns of human activity reflect those changes. The shift is steadily away from production and processing, and toward the trade, personal, and professional services of the tertiary sector and the information and control activities of the quaternary and quinary. The transition is recognized by the now-familiar term *postindustrial*.

Summary

The spatial patterns of the world's manufacturing regions represent the landscape evidence of industrial location theories. Those theories are based on assumed regularities of human economic behavior that is responsive to profit and price motivations and on simplifying assumptions about fixed and variable costs of manufacturing and distribution. In commercial economies, market mechanisms and market prices guide investment and production decisions.

Industrial cost components considered theoretically important are raw materials, power, labor, market accessibility, and transportation. Weberian analysis argues that least-cost locations are optimal and are strongly or exclusively influenced by transportation charges. Locational interdependence theory suggests that firms situate themselves to assure a degree of market monopoly in response to the location of competitors. Profit maximization concepts accept the possibility of multiple satisficing locations within a spatial margin of profitability. Agglomeration economies and the multiplier effect may make attractive locations not otherwise predicted for individual firms, while comparative advantage may dictate production, if not location, decisions of entrepreneurs.

Major industrial districts of Eastern Anglo America, Western and Central Europe, Eastern Europe, and Eastern Asia are part of a world-girdling "industrial belt" in which the vast majority of global secondary industrial activity occurs. The most advanced countries within that belt, however, are undergoing deindustrialization as newly industrializing countries with more favorable cost structures compete for markets. In the advanced economies, tertiary, quaternary, and quinary activities become more important as secondary-sector employment and share of gross national product declines. The new high-tech and postindustrial spatial patterns are not necessarily identical to those developed in response to theoretical and practical determinants of manufacturing success.

The nearly empty highway of the Mon Valley and the crowded expressways of high-tech and office park corridors are symbols of those changes in North America. As economic activity becomes less concerned with raw materials and freight rates, it becomes freer of the locational constraints of an older industrial society. Increasingly it is skills, knowledge, communication, and population concentrations that attract and hold the newer economic sectors in the most advanced economies. At the same time, much of the less developed world is striving for the transfer of manufacturing technology from developed economies and for the industrial growth that are seen as the path to their future prosperity. Those aspirations for economic development and the contrasts they imply in the technological subsystems of the countries of the world are topics of concern in Chapter 10.

KEY WORDS

agglomeration 304
agglomeration (external) economies 307
break-of-bulk point 304
comparative advantage 307
deglomeration 307
fixed cost 297
footloose firm 307
freight rates 302
infrastructure 307
in-transit privilege 304
least-cost theory 304
line-haul costs 303

locational interdependence 305
market equilibrium 296
market orientation 299
material orientation 298
multiplier effect 307
outsourcing 308
quaternary activities 326
quinary activities 326
satisficing location 307
secondary activities 296
spatial margin of profitability 306
spatially fixed costs 297

spatially variable costs 297
substitution principle 306
terminal costs 303
territorial production complex 310
tertiary activities 325
transnational (multinational) corporation (TNC) 309
ubiquitous industry 299
uniform (isotropic) plain 304
variable cost 297
Weberian analysis 304

FOR REVIEW

1. What are the six *principles of location* outlined in this chapter? Briefly explain each and note its contribution to an entrepreneur's spatial search.

2. What is the difference between *fixed* and *variable* costs? Which of the two is of interest in the plant locational decision? What kinds of variable costs are generally reckoned as most important in locational theory?

3. What role do prices play in the allocation of resources in commercial economies? Are prices a factor in resource allocation in planned economies? What differences in locational patterns of industry are implicit in the different treatment of costs in the two economies?

4. *Raw materials, power, labor, market,* and *transportation* are "factors of location" usually considered important in industrial placement decisions. Summarize the role of each, and cite examples of where each could be decisive in a firm's location.

5. What were Weber's controlling assumptions in his theory of plant location? What "distortions" did he recognize that might alter the locational decision?

6. With respect to plant siting, in what ways do the concepts and conclusions of *locational interdependence theory* differ from those of *least-cost theory*?

7. What is the *spatial margin of profitability?* What is its significance in plant location practice?

8. How have the concepts or practices of *comparative advantage* and *outsourcing* affected the industrial structure of advanced and developing countries?

9. In what ways are the locational constraints for *high-tech* industries significantly different from those of more basic secondary activities?

10. As high-tech industries and *quaternary* and *quinary* employment become more important in the economic structure of advanced nations, what consequences for economic geographic patterns do you anticipate? Explain.

SELECTED REFERENCES

Barnet, Richard J., and John Cavanagh. *Global Dreams: Imperial Corporations and the New World Order.* New York: Simon & Schuster, 1994.

Berry, Brian J. L., Edgar C. Conkling, and D. Michael Ray. *The Global Economy: Resource Use, Locational Choice, and International Trade.* Englewood Cliffs, NJ: Prentice Hall, 1993.

Boycko, Maxim, Andrei Shleifer, and Robert Vishny. *Privatising Russia.* Washington, D.C.: Brookings Institution, 1994.

Breheny, Michael J., and Ronald McQuaid, eds. *The Development of High Technology Industries: An International Survey.* London: Croom Helm, 1987.

Bressand, Albert, and Kalypso Nicolaïdis, eds. *Strategic Trends in Services: An Inquiry into the Global Service Economy.* New York: Harper and Row, 1989.

Carter, F. W., and David Turnock. *Environmental Problems in Eastern Europe.* New York: Routledge, 1993.

Chapman, Keith, and David Walker. *Industrial Location.* 2d ed. Oxford, England: Basil Blackwell, 1991.

Chavance, Bernard. *The Transformation of Communist Systems: Economic Reform Since the 1950s.* Charles Hauss, trans. Boulder, CO: Westview Press, 1994.

Chinese Academy of Sciences. Institute of Geography, et al. *The National Economic Atlas of China.* New York: Oxford University Press, 1994.

Clark, David. *Post-Industrial America: A Geographical Perspective.* New York and London: Methuen, 1985.

Corbridge, Stuart. *World Economy.* The Illustrated Encyclopedia of World Geography. New York: Oxford University Press, 1993.

Daniels, P. W. *The Global Economy in Transition.* White Plains, NY: Longman, 1996.

Daniels, P. W. *Service Industries in the World Economy.* Series: Institute of British Geographers Studies in Geography. Cambridge, MA: Blackwell Publishers, 1993.

Dicken, Peter. *Global Shift: The Internationalization of Economic Activity.* 2d ed. New York: Guilford Press, 1992.

Dicken, Peter, and Peter E. Lloyd. *Location in Space: Theoretical Perspectives in Economic Geography.* 3d ed. New York: Harper & Row, 1990.

Ettlinger, Nancy. "The Roots of Competitive Advantage in California and Japan." *Annals of the Association of American Geographers* 81, no. 3 (1991):391–407.

Feshbach, Murray, and Alfred Friendly, Jr. *Ecocide in the U.S.S.R.* New York: Basic Books, 1992.

Freeman, Michael. *Atlas of the World Economy.* New York: Simon & Schuster, 1991.

Gottmann, Jean. *Megalopolis: The Urbanized Northeastern Seaboard of the United States.* New York: Twentieth Century Fund, 1961.

Greenhut, Melvin L. *Plant Location in Theory and in Practice.* Chapel Hill: University of North Carolina Press, 1956. Reprint. Westport, CT: Greenwood Press, 1982.

Hall, Peter, and Ann Markusen, eds. *Silicon Landscapes.* Boston: Allen & Unwin, 1985.

Hamilton, Ian, ed. *Resources and Industry.* The Illustrated Encyclopedia of World Geography. New York: Oxford University Press, 1992.

Harrington, James W., Jr. "Producer Services Research in U.S. Regional Studies." *Professional Geographer* 47, no. 1 (1995):87–96.

Hartshorn, Truman A., and John W. Alexander. *Economic Geography.* 3d ed. Englewood Cliffs, NJ: Prentice-Hall, 1988.

Henderson, Jeffrey. *The Globalization of High Technology Production.* New York: Routledge, 1991.

Hepworth, Mark E. *Geography of the Information Economy.* New York: Guilford Press, 1990.

Hoover, Edgar M. *The Location of Economic Activity.* New York: McGraw-Hill, 1948.

Knox, Paul L., and John A. Agnew. *The Geography of the World Economy.* 2nd ed. London: Edward Arnold, 1994.

Krugman, Paul. "Technology's Revenge." *The Wilson Quarterly* 18, no. 4 (Autumn 1994):56–64.

Malecki, Edward J. "Industrial Location and Corporate Organization in High Technology Industries." *Economic Geography* 61, no. 4 (1985):345–369.

Malecki, Edward J. "The Geography of High Technology." *Focus* 35, no. 4 (1985):2–9.

Markusen, Ann, Peter Hall, and Amy Glasmeier. *High Tech America.* Boston: Allen & Unwin, 1986.

Marshall, J.N. *Services and Space: Aspects of Urban and Regional Development.* White Plains, NY: Longman, 1995.

Martin, Ron, and Bob Rowthorn, eds. *The Geography of Deindustrialization.* London: Macmillan, 1986.

Reich, Robert B. "Who is Us?" *Harvard Business Review* 68, no. 1 (1990):53–64.

South, Robert B. "Transnational 'Maquiladora' Location." *Annals of the Association of American Geographers* 80, no. 4 (1990):549–570.

United Nations Conference on Trade and Development (UNCTAD). *Transnational Corporations, Employment and the Workplace.* World Investment Report 1994. New York and Geneva: United Nations, 1994.

Vogel, Ezra F. *The Four Little Dragons: The Spread of Industrialization in East Asia.* Cambridge, MA: Harvard University Press, 1991.

Watts, H. D. *Industrial Geography.* New York: Longman Scientific & Technical/John Wiley & Sons, 1987.

Webber, Michael J. *Industrial Location.* Scientific Geography Series, vol. 3. Newbury Park, CA: Sage, 1984.

Weber, Alfred. *Theory of the Location of Industries.* Translated by Carl J. Friedrich. Chicago: University of Chicago Press, 1929. Reissue. New York: Russell & Russell, 1971.

Wheeler, James O., and Peter O. Muller. *Economic Geography.* 3d ed. New York: John Wiley & Sons, 1997.

PATTERNS OF DEVELOPMENT AND CHANGE

Development as a Cultural Variable   333

Dividing the Continuum: Definitions of Development   333

Explanations of Underdevelopment   335

The Core-Periphery Argument   336

Economic Measures of Development   336

The Diffusion of Technology   338

The Complex of Development   340

Gross National Product and PPP Per Capita   340

Energy Consumption Per Capita   342

Percentage of the Workforce Engaged in Agriculture   344

Landlessness   344

Poverty, Calories, and Nutrition   348

Composite Assessment of Economic Development   349

A Model for Economic Development   350

Noneconomic Measures of Development   352

Education   352

Public Services   354

Health   354

Aggregate Measures of Development and Well-Being   358

The Role of Women   360

SUMMARY   366

KEY WORDS   366

FOR REVIEW   366

SELECTED REFERENCES   367

In developing economies, the traditional—in dress and transportation—mixes freely with the modern. Pujili, Ecuador.

The Hindu funeral pyres burned day and night; Muslims were buried five and more together in common graves. Countless dead cattle, buffalo, and dogs were hastily gathered and dumped in pits. In a sense, on that unseasonably cold December night in central India, all had died for economic development. Some 40% of the Indian population exists in poverty. Eager to attract modern industry to its less developed states, to create additional industrial and urban employment, and to produce domestically the chemicals essential to its drive for agricultural self-sufficiency, the Indian government in 1969 granted Union Carbide Corporation a license to manufacture pesticides at a new plant built on vacant land on the outskirts of Bhopal. A principal ingredient was deadly methyl isocyanate gas, the silent killer that escaped from its storage tank that winter night of 1984 after a sudden and unexplained build-up of its temperature and pressure.

To assure the plant's success, Union Carbide had been exempted from many local taxes, and land, water, and power costs were heavily subsidized. To yield maximum benefit to the local economy and maximum transfer of technology and skills, 50% ownership in the enterprise was retained for Indian investors along with total local control of construction and operation of the plant. The 1000 jobs were considered so important by the state and local governments that despite six accidents and one death in the years before the night of disaster, reports critical of plant safety and operation were shelved and ignored. A local official who had called for the removal of the factory to a more isolated area was himself removed from office.

By the time of the fatal accident, Bhopal had grown from 300,000 to over 900,000 people. More than 130,000 residents lived in the slums and shantytowns they built for themselves just across the street from a factory they thought produced "plant medicine" to keep crops healthy; they were the principal victims. Before the week was over, almost 3000 people had died. Another 300,000 had been affected by exposure to the deadly poison, and perhaps 150,000 of those suffer long-term permanent disabilities—blindness, sterility, kidney and liver infections, and brain damage.

FIGURE 10.1   Burning the dead at Bhopal. At the time of the tragedy, India was more prepared than many developing countries to accept the transfer of advanced technology. In 1984 it ranked among the top 15 countries in manufacturing output and supplied most basic domestic needs from its own industry. India still sought modern plants and processes and, particularly, industry supporting agricultural improvement and expansion.

Development as a Cultural Variable

Whatever its immediate cause of equipment failure or operator error, the tragedy of Bhopal is witness to the lure of economic development so eagerly sought that safety and caution are sacrificed to achieve it. That lure is nearly irresistible for those countries and regions that look to industrialization and urban employment as their deliverance from traditional economies no longer able to support their growing populations or to satisfy their hopes for an improved quality of life.

Any view of the contemporary world quickly shows great—almost unbelievable—contrasts from place to place in levels of economic development and people's material well-being. Variations in these are indicative of the tools, energy sources, and other *artifacts* (p. 51) differing societies employ in production and the kinds of economic activities in which they engage, and underlie the social organizations and behavior patterns they have developed. A look around tells us that these interrelated economic and social structures are not shared by all societies; they vary between cultures and countries. The plaintive comment that "poor people have poor ways" or the ready distinction that we make between the "Gold Coast" and the "slum" indicate that different groups have differential access to the wealth, tools, and resources of the global and national societies of which they are a part.

At an international scale, we distinguish between "advanced" or "rich" nations, such as Canada or Switzerland, and "less developed" or "poor" countries, like Bangladesh or Burkina Faso, though neither class of states may wish those adjectives applied to its circumstances. Hunter-gatherers of southwest Africa or Papua New Guinea, shifting gardeners of Amazonia, or subsistence farmers of southeastern Asia may be largely untouched by the modernization, industrialization, or urbanization of society commonplace elsewhere.

Development differentials exist within countries, too. The poverty of drought- and hunger-plagued northeastern Brazil stands in sharp contrast to the prosperous, industrialized modernity of São Paulo state or city (Figure 10.2), while in the United States, farmers of the hillsides of Appalachia live in a different economic and cultural reality than do midwestern cash grain farmers.

Dividing the Continuum: Definitions of Development

Countries display different levels of development. **Development** in that comparative sense means simply the extent to which the resources of an area or country have been brought into full productive use. It may also carry in common usage the implications of economic growth, modernization, and improvement in levels of material production and consumption. For some, it may also suggest changes in traditional social, cultural, and political structures to resemble more nearly those displayed in countries and economies deemed "advanced." Many of the attributes of development under an economic definition can be quantified by reference to statistics of national production, per capita income, energy consumption, nutritional levels, labor force characteristics, and the like. Taken together, such variables might calibrate a scale of achievement against which the level of development of a single country may be compared.

Such a scale would reveal that countries lie along a continuum from the least advanced in technology, industrialization, or urbanization to the most developed in those and similar characteristics. Geographers (and others) attempt to classify and group countries along the continuum in ways that are conceptually revealing and spatially informative. The extremes are easy; the middle ground is less clear-cut, and the terminology referring to it is mixed.

(a)

(b)

FIGURE 10.2   The modern high-rise office and apartment buildings of prosperous São Paulo (*a*), a city which generates over one-third of Brazil's national income, stand a world apart from the poverty and peasant housing of northeastern Brazil (*b*). The evidences and benefits of "development" are not equally shared by all segments of any country or society.

In the broadest view, "developed" countries stand in easy contrast to the "underdeveloped," "less developed," or "developing" world. (*Developing* was the term introduced by President Harry S. Truman in 1949 as a replacement for *backward,* the unsatisfactory and unflattering reference then in use.) **Underdevelopment** from a strictly economic point of view suggests the possibility or desirability of applying additional capital, labor, or technology to the resource base of an area to permit the present population to improve its material well-being or to allow populations to increase without a deterioration in their quality of life.

The catch-all category of *underdeveloped,* however, does not tell us in which countries such efforts at improvement have occurred or been effective. With time, therefore, more refined subdivisions of development have been introduced, including such indistinctly relative terms as *moderately, less,* or *least developed* countries.[1] Since development is commonly understood to imply industrialization and to be reflected in improvements in national and personal income, the additional terms *newly industrializing countries* (NICs) (which we encountered in Chapter 9) and *middle income countries* have been employed.

In a corruption of its original meaning, the term **Third World** is often applied to the developing countries as a group, though when first used that designation was a purely political reference to nations not formally aligned with a "First World" of industrialized free market (capitalist) nations or a "Second World" of centrally controlled (communist bloc) economies. Although the fundamental political changes in the former communist bloc has made Third World meaningless in its earlier sense, the term is still retained and useful as a composite designation for developing countries that have not yet achieved the income levels or qualities of life of the advanced industrial economies.

In 1980 the contrasting terms *North* and *South* were introduced (by the Independent Commission on International Development Issues, commonly called the "Brandt Report")[2] as a broad and not wholly accurate generalization to emphasize the distinctions between the rich, advanced, developed countries of the Northern Hemisphere (to which Southern Hemisphere Australia and New Zealand are added)—the *North*—and, roughly, all the rest of the world—the *South* (Figure 10.3). This

[1]In 1971 the General Assembly of the UN listed 24 least developed countries identified by per capita gross domestic product, share of manufacturing in GDP, and literacy. By 1981, their ranks were increased to 31, to 41 in 1989, and to 45 by the mid-1990s.

[2]*North-South: A Programme for Survival.* The Commission was established in 1977 at the suggestion of the chairman of World Bank. Under its charge, "global issues arising from economic and social disparities of the world community" were to be studied and "ways of promoting adequate solutions to the problems involved in development" were to be proposed. The former Soviet Union was at that time included within the North, and its successor states retain that association.

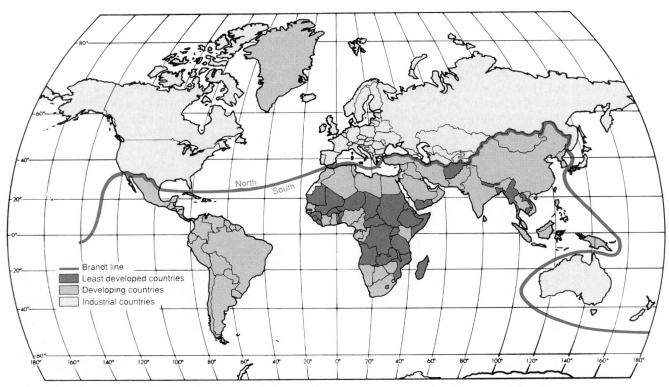

FIGURE 10.3 **Comparative development levels.** The "North–South" line of the 1980 *Brandt Report* suggested a simplified world contrast of development and underdevelopment based largely on degree of industrialization and per capita wealth. More recently, the United Nations General Assembly recognized 45 "least developed countries." That recognition reflects low ratings in three indicators: gross domestic product, share of manufacturing in the GDP, and literacy rate. The "industrial countries" are those identified in 1995 as most developed by the United Nations Development Program.

split agreed with the United Nations classification that placed all of Europe and North America, plus Australia, Japan, New Zealand, and the former USSR in a *more developed country* category, with all other states classed as *less developed countries* (LDCs).

The variety of terms devised—not all of them accurately descriptive or acceptable to those countries designated—represent honest efforts to categorize countries whose developmental circumstances are defined by a variety of economic and social measures along a continuum of specific or composite characteristics. In the remainder of this chapter, broad developmental contrasts between countries or regions will conform to the "North–South" and the UN "more developed–less developed" categorizations. Our primary attention in maps and text, however, will be given to the developing countries of the "South."

The terminology of development is usually applied to country units, but it is equally meaningful at the regional and local levels within them, for few countries are uniformly highly developed or totally undeveloped. Many developing countries contain pockets—frequently the major urban centers—of productivity, wealth, and modernity not shared by the rest of the state. For example, Mexico is a leading NIC, but more than 50% of its industrial workers and over 60% of value of manufacturing are located in metropolitan Mexico City. Many other parts of the country and, particularly, its Indian population, remain untouched by the development concentrated in the capital city. Even within the most advanced societies some areas and populations remain outside the mainstream of progress and prosperity enjoyed by the majority.

Explanations of Underdevelopment

It is one thing to devise categories of relative development and to assign countries to them; it is quite another to see in those categories an explanation of their spatial pattern. Why are different countries arranged as they are along the continuum of advancement? What conditions underlie their relative degrees of development? Are those conditions common to all countries at the same level of technology? And do those conditions have spatial expression and spatial explanation?

The Brandt report hints at one frequent but simplistic spatial explanation: Development is a characteristic of the rich "North"—the midlatitudes, more precisely; poverty and underdevelopment are tropical conditions. Proponents of the latitudinal explanation support their conviction not only by reference to such topical maps as Figures 10.3, 10.7, or 10.10, but by noting as well that similar differences in development and wealth exist within individual countries. Brazilians of the southeastern temperate highlands, for example, have average incomes several times higher than their compatriots of tropical Amazonia. Annual average incomes of Mexicans of the temperate north far exceed those of southern Yucatán. Australians of the tropical north are poorer than Australians of the temperate south. Unfortunately for the search for easy explanation, many of the poorer nations

of the "South" lie partially or wholly within the midlatitudes or at temperate elevations—Afghanistan, North Korea, and Mongolia are examples—while equatorial Singapore and Malaysia prosper.

Other generalizations are similarly inconclusive: (1) Resource poverty is cited as a limit to developmental possibilities. Although some developing countries are deficient in raw materials, others are major world suppliers of both industrial minerals and agricultural goods—bauxite, cacao, and coffee, for example. Admittedly, a Third World complaint is that their materials are underpriced in the developed world markets to which they flow, but that is a matter of marketing and economics, not resources. Further, economists have long held that reliance on natural resource wealth and exports by less developed countries undermines their prospects for growth by interfering with their development of industry and export-oriented manufacturing. (2) Overpopulation and overcrowding are frequently noted as common denominators of national underdevelopment, but Hong Kong prospers with 5600 per square kilometer (15,000 per sq. mi.) while impoverished Mali is empty with 8 per square kilometer (20 per sq. mi.) (Figure 10.4). (3) Former colonial status is often blamed for present underdevelopment, which may be a surprise to the ex-colonies of Australia, New Zealand, Canada, Singapore, or the United States—and to Ethiopia, which never was colonized but is a case study in underdevelopment. There appears to be no

FIGURE 10.4 Land-locked and subject to severe droughts, Mali is one of the poorest of the "least developed" countries. Low densities of population are not necessarily related to prosperity, or high densities to poverty. Mali has 8 people per square kilometer (20 per sq. mi.); Japan has nearly 332 per square kilometer (860 per sq. mi.). These Dogon women crossing a parched millet field near Sanga are on their way to get water—a time- and energy-consuming daily task.

single, simple explanation of Third World status, just as there is no single measure of underdevelopment that accounts for every Third World case.

The Core-Periphery Argument

Core-periphery models are based on the observation that within many spatial systems sharp territorial contrasts exist in wealth, economic advancement, and growth—in "development"—between economic heartlands and outlying subordinate zones. Wealthy urban cores and depressed rural peripheries, or prospering "high-tech" concentrations and declining "rust belts," are contrasts found in many developed countries. On the international scene, core-periphery contrasts are discerned between, particularly, Western Europe, Japan, and the United States as prosperous cores and the Third World as underdeveloped periphery. At all spatial scales, the models assume that at least partially and temporarily the growth and prosperity of core regions is at the expense of exploited peripheral zones.

That conclusion is drawn from the observation that linkages and interactions exist between the contrasting parts of the system. As one variant of the model suggests, if for any reason (perhaps a new industrial process or product) one section of a country experiences accelerated economic development, that section by its expanding prosperity becomes increasingly attractive for investors and other entrepreneurs. Assuming national investment capital is limited, growth in the developing core must come at the expense of the peripheries of the country. A process of **circular and cumulative causation** has been set in motion that continues to polarize development and leads to a permanent division between prosperous (and dominating) cores and depressed (and exploited) peripheral districts that are milked of surplus labor, raw materials, and profits. In different Marxist and non-Marxist forms, this version of core-periphery theory sees the developing world as effectively held captive by the leading industrial nations. It is drained of wealth and deprived of growth by remaining largely a food and raw material exporter and an importer of manufactured commodities—and frequently suffering price discrimination in both their sales and purchases. A condition of *neocolonialism* is said to exist in which economic and even political control is exercised by developed states over the economies and societies of legally independent countries of the underdeveloped world.

A more hopeful variant of the model observes that regional income inequalities exist within all countries, but that they tend to be greater in less developed countries than in the developed ones. That is, within market economies income disparities tend to be reduced as developmental levels increase. In Brazil, for example, the poorest fifth of the population have just 2% of all income, the richest fifth have 68%, and only 10% of the population controls 51% of all income. But in Canada, the poorest fifth have 6% of all income while the richest fifth have only 40%. Eventually, convergence will occur as **trickle-down effects** or *spread effects* work to diffuse benefits outward from the center in the

form of higher prices paid for needed materials or through the dispersion of technology to branch plants or contract suppliers in lower-cost regions of production. On the international scale, such spread effects will reduce the dominance of formerly exploitative cores and equalize incomes between world regions. Penetration of European and American markets by Asian-produced goods ranging from cheap textiles to expensive automobiles and high-technology electronics are cited in support of this model variant.

In this view, core-periphery contrasts are but a stage in a four-stage sequence of the space-economy. Those stages are (1) a preindustrial society with localized, self-sufficient economies, (2) the core-periphery stage, (3) dispersion of economic activity and the passing of control of portions of the economy into parts of the periphery, and (4) creation of spatial integration in which the spatially separate and fully developed components of the economy relate in an interdependent fashion. Whatever the descriptive value of these stages for individual countries may be, their applicability to the world space economy appears demonstrated by the growing productivity, wealth, and share of world trade attributable to developing world economies as a group.

Core-periphery models stress economic relationships and spatial patterns of control over production and trade. Indeed, the usual measures and comparisons of development are stated in economic terms. As we shall see later in this chapter, noneconomic measures may also be employed, though usually not without reference to their relationships to national or per capita income or to other measures of wealth and productivity. We shall also see that composite measures of developmental level are perhaps more useful and meaningful than those restricted to single factors or solely to matters of either economy or social welfare.

Economic Measures of Development

The developing countries as a group have made significant progress along the continuum of economic development. Between 1965 and the mid-1990s, their economies collectively grew at an average annual rate of over 5.3% compared to slightly less than 3.5% per year for the industrial states. As a result of those growth differentials and of overall changes in the composition of their gross domestic products, the less developed states are in a decisively different relative position at the end of the 20th century than they were at its start. In 1913, on the eve of World War I, the 20 or so countries now known as the rich industrial economies produced almost 80% of world manufacturing. In 1950, the United States alone accounted for around half of world output, about the share produced by all the developed economies together in the mid-1990s.

Particularly after midcentury, the spread effects of technology transfer, industrialization, and expanding world trade substantially reduced—though have not yet eliminated—the core-periphery contrasts in productivity and structure of gross domestic product that formerly seemed insurmountably great. Significantly, manufactured goods in the mid-1990s accounted for about 60% of all exports of developing countries as a group, up from only 5% in 1955, and their share of world exports of manufactures jumped from 5% in 1970 to nearly 25% in 1995. Their growing importance in manufacturing exports clearly marks the restructuring of the economies of many developing states away from subsistence agriculture and primary commodity production.

In 1965, 30% of the developing countries' combined income came from agriculture and another 30% from industry; by the 1990s, agriculture's share had dropped to about 17% while industry grew to account for nearly 40% of their collective national earnings. Not all of the employment shifts and structural changes within developing countries, however, are accounted for by official statistics (Figure 10.5).

The world and regional impacts of these shifts in global economic balance are obscured by traditional market exchange rate estimates of the relative size of national economies. Those estimates measure gross national product or per capita share of gross domestic product in U.S. dollar equivalents, making no assessment of relative price levels in different countries or of the value of non-traded goods and services. Seeking a more realistic measure of national economies, the International Monetary Fund and the World Bank now use **purchasing power parity (PPP),** which takes account of what money actually buys in each country. When the new PPP measure was introduced in 1993, it gave a clearer picture of the world economy and radically changed traditional assessments of it. Overnight the relative importance of the Third World doubled. Using purchasing power parity, Asia's share of world output jumped from 7%

FIGURE 10.5   "Informal sector" initiative in Ecuador. Between 1965 and 1995, the percentage of the labor force in agriculture dropped precipitously in all countries of Latin America. That decline was not matched by a proportional increase in employment in manufacturing and other industries. In Ecuador, employment in agriculture fell from 55% to 32% of the total between 1965 and 1995, but the share of workers in industry remained constant at less than 20%. However, many of the former rural workers found urban jobs in the "informal" sector. They became errand runners, street vendors, odd-job handymen, open-air dispensers of such personal services as barbering, shoe shining, clothes mending, and the like, as well as workers in small-scale construction and repair shops. The informal sector accounts for 30% of all jobs in Latin America—and 60% of those in Africa. In Peru, the informal sector occupies 48% of the total labor force and creates 38% of the nation's gross domestic product. If the informal economy did not exist in Bolivia, the country's unemployment rate of 7% would increase to 35%. Unmeasured informal sector contributions correct and improve official assessments of gross domestic product and national prosperity.

to 17%, and the revised weight for all developing states vaulted from 18% to 34%. Add in Eastern Europe and the former Soviet Union and the total for the less-developed world rises to 46%. That is, the rich industrial economies in the mid-1990s accounted for just 54% of total global output using PPPs, a marked come-down from their assumed 73% contribution under the old exchange rate system. If present trends hold, the World Bank forecasts, industrial economies will account for less than half of world output by the end of the 1990s, and by 2020 the current "rich world's" share of global output could shrink to less than two-fifths.

Impressive as the shifts in global economic balance between the industrial and developing countries may be, they do little to reduce the contrasts that remain between the richest of the North and the poorest of the South. While as a group the developing countries—134 of them as usually defined—are catching up to the developed world in total productivity, a good part of the aggregate gain is lost in per capita terms (see "Poverty and Development"). With the South's population increasing at about a 2% per annum rate (slightly more than 2% without China), growing national prosperity has to be shared among an increasing number of claimants. In the early 1990s, the South had to divide its recalculated one-third share of *gross global product* (the total value of goods and services produced by the world economy) among more than three-fourths of world population. And the very rich, in contrast, continue to get richer. Countries with the wealthiest 20% of world population increased their share of gross global product from 70% in 1965 to 85% in the early 1990s while countries with the poorest 20% of world population experienced a decline from 2.3% to 1.4%.

Further, as core-periphery theory suggests, the industrial economies still account for three-quarters of world exports and dominate the international financial markets. And the South's economies are far more (though decreasingly) oriented toward raw material production than are those of the developed world. For example, in 1965, over 80% of the exports from developing countries—but less than one-third of those from industrial market countries—were minerals and agricultural products. By the 1990s, the disparity had materially lessened; minerals and agricultural goods represented only 40% by value of the developing countries'[3] exports and for 20% of those from industrial market economies.

The Diffusion of Technology

Composite figures mask the disparities that exist within the ranks of developing countries. The world's 45 "least developed" states in 1992 produced less than 1% of global wealth, measured at market exchange rates. In contrast, the small, rapidly industrializing "four dragons"—Hong Kong, Singapore, South Korea, and Taiwan—alone contributed over 3% to gross world product. Obviously, there are differences within the developing world in the successful application of technology to the creation of wealth.

[3]Excluding high-income petroleum exporting countries.

Technology refers to the totality of tools and methods available to and used by a culture group in producing items essential to its subsistence and comfort. We saw in Chapter 2 how in antiquity there emerged *culture hearths*—centers of technological innovation, of new ideas and techniques that diffused or were carried out from the core region. Innovation is rarely a single event; as cultures advance, needs multiply and different solutions develop to meet expanding requirements. The ancient hearths (Figure 2.16; Table 2.1) were locales of such multiple invention and innovation. Their modern counterparts are the highly urbanized, industrialized advanced nations whose creativity is recorded by patent registrations and product and process introductions. The changing rate of innovation over time is suggested by Figure 2.21.

In all periods there has existed between hearths and outlying regions a **technology gap,** a contrast in the range and productivity of artifacts introduced at the core and those known or employed at the periphery. That gap has widened at an accelerating rate as technology has moved farther away from the shared knowledge of earlier periods. During the Industrial Revolution, the technological distance between cottage hand looms of 18th-century English villagers and the power looms of their neighboring factories was one of only moderate degree (Figure 10.6). Far greater is the gap

FIGURE 10.6 Early in the Industrial Revolution, new techniques that diffused most readily from the English hearth were those close to handicraft production processes. In some industries, the important innovation was the adoption of power and volume production, not radically new machines or products. For textiles and similar light industries, capital requirements were low and workers required little training in new skills. The picture shows carding, drawing, and spinning machinery built by memory in the United States in 1790 by Samuel Slater, an Englishman who introduced the new technology despite British prohibitions on exports of drawings or models of it.

A ccording to the World Bank and the United Nations Human Development Programme (UNDP), almost one-third of the total population of developing countries—some 1.3 billion people—experience "absolute poverty." They exist on an annual income (1995) of less than $440 per year in purchasing power parity, a figure below which, it is usually reckoned, people are unable to buy adequate food, shelter, and other necessities. Although the dollar definition of poverty is applied as if it were a worldwide constant, in reality poverty is comprised of two separate elements that are regional variables. One of these is the reasonably objective observation that you are impoverished if you can't afford a minimum standard of nutrition. The other element is more subjective and equates poverty with inability to buy basic goods that other citizens of your country regard as necessities.

Thanks to its own forecasts of continuing significant economic growth in developing countries, the World Bank predicts their one-third population in poverty in the early 1990s will fall to only 18% by 2000, a drop of over 300 million people. That expected improvement would con-

tinue progress made in many developing countries since the 1960s. Indonesia, for example, reduced its incidence of absolute poverty from nearly 60% to less than 25% between 1965 and 1992, and China saw average life expectancy (a presumed measure of poverty conditions) rise from 52 to 70 years between 1960 and 1995. The Human Development Programme is less optimistic. It calculates that poor people in developing countries will increase by 100 million by the turn of the century and still account for some 26% of their population.

Both the Bank and the UNDP recognize Africa as a continuing problem region. Because of its rapid population growth, stagnation or decline in per capita food production, weakness in infrastructure and facilities systems, periodic drought, and devastating civil wars, sub-Saharan Africa is projected to have 360 million people or 40% of its population in poverty in 2010, an increase of 180 million over 1985. The Bank anticipates that while Asia's share of the world's poor should decline to 53% by the end of the century (down from 72% in 1985), Africa's will likely double, from 16% to 32%. The more pessimistic Human Development Programme anticipates that 40% of the world's poor will reside in Africa by 2000.

Whatever the value of economic indicators of poverty, social indicators often present a different and more favorable picture. People in most African, Asian, and Latin American countries are living longer under better and improving conditions. In Africa, infant mortality declined from 1980 to the mid-1990s, life expectancy increased in 33 out of 42 countries, illiteracy rates have declined, and access to safe water has improved. In Latin America, too, infant deaths decreased during the 1980s, life expectancy increased or at least stayed constant, vaccination rates increased and there was at least no increase in child malnutrition despite population growth. Worldwide, the UNDP observes, 70% of people lived in "abysmal" conditions as recently as 1960, but less than a third did in 1995.

The key to improving both the economic and social lot of the "poorest of the poor," the World Bank and United Nations argue, is to target public spending on their special needs of education and health care and to pursue patterns of investment and economic growth that can productively employ the underutilized and growing labor force so abundant in the least developed countries.

---

between the range of traditional crafts known throughout the world and the modern technologies of the most advanced societies. It is much more difficult now for a less developed society to advance to the "state of the art" by its own efforts than it was for British colonies or the rest of Europe to recreate the textile or iron-making industries first developed in England.

The persistence and expansion of the technology gap suggest that the idea of **cultural convergence**—the increasing similarity in technologies and ways of life among societies at the same levels of development—does not as well unite the most and the least advanced economies. In the modern world, as we saw in Chapter 2 (p. 49), there is a widespread sharing of technologies, organizational forms, and developed cultural traits. But not all countries are at the same developmental state. Not all are equally able to draw

on advanced technology to create the same products with identical efficiency and quality, although all peoples are increasingly aware of the existence of those products and the benefits of their use.

The technology gap matters. At any given level of technology, the resources of an area will have a limited population supporting capacity. As population growth approaches or exceeds those limits, as it has in many less developed areas of the globe, poverty, famine, and political and social upheaval can result. Understandably, all countries aspire to expand their resource base, increase its support levels through application of improved technologies, or enter more fully into an income-producing exchange relationship with other world regions through economic development. Their objective is a **technology transfer,** placing in their own territory and under their own control the productive plants and processes marking the more advanced countries. The chemical plant of Bhopal was one item in a technology transfer sought by the state of Madhya Pradesh and the government of India, one step in the process of moving the region and country further along the continuum from less developed to more developed status.

The Complex of Development

Technology transfer is only one aspect of economic development. The process as a whole intricately affects all facets of social and economic life. The terms *level of living* and *standard of living* bring to mind some of the ways in which economic advancement implies both technological and societal change, including amount of personal income, levels of education, food consumption, life expectancy, and the availability of health care. The complexity of the occupational structure, the degree of specialization in jobs, the ways in which natural resources are used, and the level of industrialization are also measures of development and of the innovation or adoption of technology within a society.

The generalized summary table "Relative Characteristics of Development" outlines some of the many implications and attributes of development. It also makes clear why no single measure is sufficient to assess the comparative stage of economic development or level of living of a society. We might, for example, simplistically assume that national contrasts in average per capita income would serve to measure the level of living in all of its aspects; but personal income figures are particularly hard to compare across national borders. An income of (U.S.) $50,000 in Sweden is taxed at a much higher rate than a similar income in the United States. But social welfare programs, higher education, and medicine receive greater central governmental funding in Sweden; the American family must set aside a larger portion of its income for such services.

Further, identical incomes will be spent on different amounts and types of goods and services in different countries. Americans, it is generally agreed, spend a smaller proportion of their personal income on food than do the residents of most European states or Japan; those living in northern climates must buy fuel and heavy clothing not necessary in tropical household budgets; and price levels may vary widely in different economies for similar essential goods. Of course, national average personal income figures do not indicate how earnings are distributed among the citizenry. In some countries the wealthiest 5% of the population control over 50% of the income, whereas in others revenues are more uniformly distributed.

To broaden the limited view afforded by per capita income figures, therefore, a variety of more specific and descriptive measures has been employed to suggest national levels of development. Each such measure can present only part of a total picture of developmental status. Taken together, however, the comparative criteria tend to show a high, but not perfect, correlation that collectively supports the accepted North–South global split. The primarily economic measures discussed here are among those commonly accepted as most revealing of the relative progress of countries of the "South" along the scale of development. They are: (1) gross national product and purchasing power parity (PPP) per capita, (2) per capita energy consumption, (3) percent of the workforce engaged in agriculture, and (4) calorie intake per capita.

Gross National Product and PPP Per Capita

Gross national product (GNP) is a commonly available statistic that reports the total market value of goods and services[4] produced within an economy within a given time period, usually a year. Expressed in per capita terms (see Appendix B), GNP is the most frequently used indicator of a country's economic performance (Figure 10.7). Like any other single index of development, gross national product tells only part of a complex story. Indeed, its concept, and that of the related gross domestic product, is under increasing attack for its assumed distortions of reality. One group, including environmentalists, argues that the GNP overstates the wealth of a society by ignoring the cost of ecological damage and the drain modern economies place on natural resources. An opposing group holds that GNP understates the strength of economic growth by overlooking much of the quality and productivity improvements brought by technology (safer automobiles, faster, more powerful computers, etc.).

Of course, gross national product per capita is not a personal income figure, but simply a calculated assignment of each individual's share of a national total. Change in total population or in total national product will alter the average per capita figure but need have no impact on the personal finances of any individual citizen. As expected, the countries with the highest GNP per capita are those in northwestern Europe, where the Industrial Revolution began, and in the midlatitude colonial areas—North America, Australia, and New Zealand—to which the new technologies were first transplanted. In the middle position are found many of the countries of Latin America and of southern and eastern Europe. Large sections of Africa and Asia, in contrast, are at the low end of average income figures.

Per capita GNP is not a totally realistic summary of developmental status. Indeed, the pattern shown on Figure 10.7 distorts the more inclusive picture of underdevelopment summarized on Figure 10.3 by overemphasizing the purely monetary circumstances of countries. Since the market value of goods may experience rapid short-term

---

[4]Adjusted by deducting income earned by foreign interests and adding income accruing to residents from foreign investments or remittances. Without these adjustments the statistic is called **gross domestic product,** itself subject to different adjustments.

RELATIVE CHARACTERISTICS OF DEVELOPMENT

Less Developed

1. Per capita incomes are low, and capital is scarce.
2. Wealth is unevenly distributed within individual countries (e.g., in Colombia 2.6% of population owns 40% of the national wealth, and in Gabon 1% owns 56% of total wealth).
3. Primary industries (farming, forestry, quarrying, mining, fishing) dominate national economies.
4. High proportion (over 50%) of population engaged in agriculture.
5. Farming is mostly at the subsistence level and is characterized by inefficient methods and underemployment. Farm holdings are small, mechanization is limited, and crop yields are low.
6. Populations are dominantly rural, though impoverished urban numbers are growing.
7. Birth and death rates are high, and life expectancy is low. There tends to be a high proportion of children. Rates of natural increase are high.
8. Inadequate or unbalanced diets resulting from a relatively low consumption of protein; hunger and malnutrition are common.
9. Infectious, respiratory, and parasitic diseases are common; medical services are poor.
10. Overcrowding, poor housing, few public services, and bad sanitation yield poor social conditions.
11. Poor educational facilities and high levels of illiteracy hinder scientific and technological advancement. (In sub-Saharan Africa, nearly 50% of population is illiterate.)
12. Women may be held in inferior position in society.

Developed

1. Per capita incomes are high, and capital is readily available.
2. Wealth within individual countries is comparatively evenly distributed (e.g., in Canada, 10% of the population owns 24% of national wealth).
3. Manufacturing and service industries dominate national economies.
4. Very small proportion (under 10%) of population is engaged in agriculture.
5. Farming is mostly commercial, efficient, and highly mechanized. Farm holdings are generally large, and crop yields are high.
6. Populations are predominantly urban, with over 70% living in towns and cities.
7. Birth and death rates are low, and life expectancy is high. There is often a high proportion of people over 60 years of age. Rates of natural increase are low.
8. Generally adequate supplies of food and balanced diets; overeating is sometimes a problem.
9. There is a low incidence of disease, and good medical services are available.
10. Social conditions are generally good, with adequate housing space and a high level of public health facilities and sanitation.
11. Highly developed educational facilities and low levels of illiteracy are the norm. Technical proficiency is advanced.
12. Women are increasingly treated on equal terms with men.

Adapted with permission from Charles Whynne-Hammond, *Elements of Human Geography*, 2d ed. (London: Unwin Hyman Limited, 1985).

---

fluctuations, a country's GNP may quickly change and the relative national standings shown on Figure 10.7 may be both misleading and temporary.

Finally, we have seen, the GNP does not accurately represent the economic circumstances of countries with dominantly subsistence economies, for example, many of the nations of Asia and Africa with low income figures. Gross national product stated in U.S. dollar terms does not assess reliably the money value of the nontraded goods and services that subsistence farmers provide for themselves and their communities. That is, the GNP systematically understates the real value of developing world output, a problem partly resolved, you will recall, by calculating what are sometimes called "real per capita gross domestic products," but more usually summarized as *purchasing power parities* (Figure 10.8). That statistic, international agencies now agree, presents a more realistic comparison of developing country conditions and economies relative to those of the industrialized world.

Rapid industrialization and successful development of home and foreign markets have dramatically raised the productivity and income of such newly industrializing countries

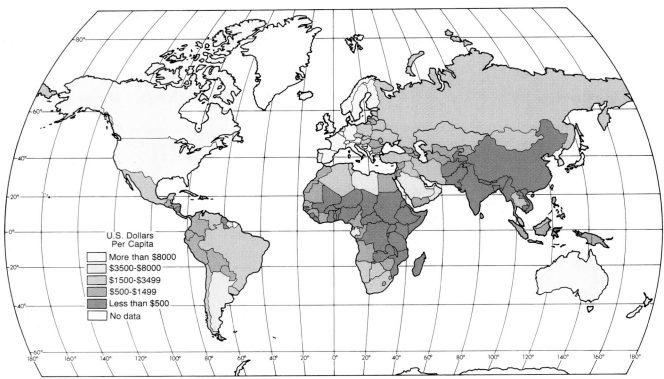

FIGURE 10.7   **Gross national product per capita.** GNP per capita is a frequently employed summary of degree of economic advancement, though high incomes in sparsely populated, oil-rich countries may not have the same meaning in developmental terms as do comparable per capita values in industrially advanced states. The map implies an unrealistic precision. For many states, when uncertain GNP is divided by unreliable population totals, the resulting GNP per capita is at best a rough approximation that varies between reporting agencies. A comparison of this map and Figure 10.11 presents an interesting study in regional contrasts.

as Mexico and the East Asian "four dragons." A similar path of industrialization and market penetration earlier raised Japan from postwar poverty to its current state of prosperity. Elsewhere, the industrial development and the commercial agriculture programs of many countries are rapidly increasing their gross national products in monetary terms and raising their status among nations according to this single index of technological development. National averages, of course, even if valid, may at a different scale be misleading. For large diversified countries, particularly, they tend to conceal regional variation (Figure 10.9).

Energy Consumption Per Capita

Per capita energy consumption is a common measure of technological advancement of nations because it loosely correlates with per capita income, degree of industrialization, and use of advanced technology (Figure 8.33). In fact, the industrialized countries use about 10 times more energy on a per capita basis than developing economies do. The consumption rather than the production of energy is the concern. Many of the highly developed countries consume large amounts of energy but produce relatively little. Japan, for

example, must import from abroad the energy supplies its domestic resource base lacks. In contrast, many less developed countries have very high per capita or total energy production figures but primarily export the resource (petroleum). Libya, Nigeria, and Brunei are cases in point. The data presented in Figure 10.10 refer to commercial forms of inanimate energy (petroleum, coal, lignite, natural gas, hydropower, nuclear energy, etc.) converted into oil equivalents. Not included, and thus distorting the world picture, are animate energy inputs (human and animal labor) and the firewood, dung, peat, and other domestic fuels used by subsistence populations.

The advanced countries developed their economic strength through the use of cheap energy and its application to industrial processes. But energy is cheap only if immense capital investment is made to produce it at a low cost per unit. The less advanced nations, unable to make those necessary investments or lacking domestic energy resources, use expensive animate energy or such decreasingly available fuels as firewood (see "The Energy Crisis in LDCs"), and they must forgo energy-intensive industrial development. Anything that increases the cost of energy

DYNAMIC PATTERNS OF THE SPACE ECONOMY

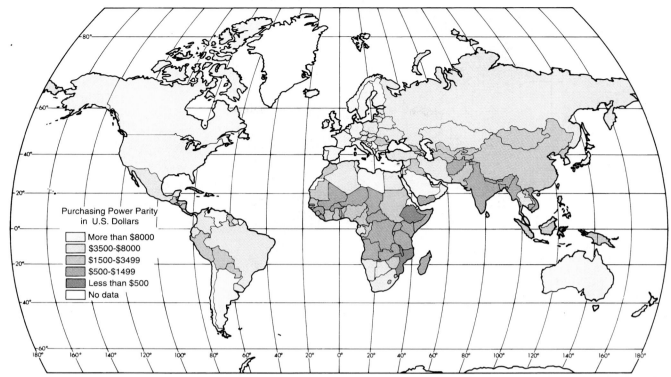

FIGURE 10.8 **Purchasing power parity (PPP).** When local currency gross domestic product is converted into purchasing power parities, there is a twofold revision of the usual view of world economic status. The first result is a sharp increase in developing countries' share of total world output. By varying calculations, China now falls somewhere between the world's second and ninth largest economy, and India, Brazil, and Mexico all emerge as bigger than Canada. Second, the abject poverty suggested by per capita gross national or gross domestic product is seen to be much reduced in many developing countries. India, for example, shows a 1992 gross domestic product per capita at market exchange rates of $310; in purchasing power parity, the figure rises to over $1200, and Pakistan's people jump from $420 to nearly $3000. Compare this map with Figure 10.7 to see how PPP changes our impressions of some countries' economic status.

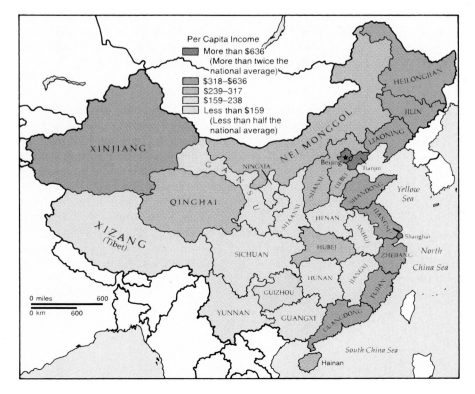

FIGURE 10.9 **Average per capita income in China, 1992.** The striking regional variation shown on the map reminds us that generalizations at the national level may be misstatements at the local scale. The map conversion of yuan to dollar amounts is made at China's officially managed exchange rate of 5.46 yuan to the dollar in 1992. In that year, per capita share of national income was 1736 yuan, or $318—far below the national purchasing power parity average of more than $3000.

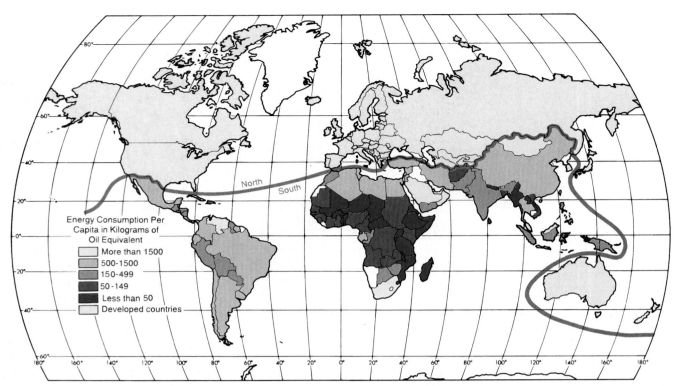

FIGURE 10.10   The South: per capita annual consumption of commercial energy. Large volume use of inanimate energy is usually—but not invariably—an indicator of industrialization and mechanization of agriculture. Saudi Arabia and the United Arab Emirates, for example, have high consumption but relatively low indices of manufacturing or farm machinery use. All countries of the North have per capita commercial energy consumption of more than 1500 kilograms of oil equivalent. Some, like Canada, approach or exceed 10,000.

further removes it from easy acquisition by less developed countries. The "oil shocks" of the 1970s and 1980s and the consequent increase in the price of all purchased energy supplies served to widen further the gulf between the technological subsystems of the rich and the poor countries of the world.

Percentage of the Workforce Engaged in Agriculture

A high percentage of employment in agriculture (Figure 10.11) is almost invariably associated with low per capita gross national product and low energy consumption, that is, with underdevelopment (Table 10.1). Economic development always means a range of occupational choices far greater than those available in a subsistence agricultural society. Mechanization of agriculture increases the productivity of a decreasing farm labor force; surplus rural workers are made available for urban industrial and service

employment, and if jobs are found, national and personal prosperity increases. When a labor force is primarily engaged in agriculture, on the other hand, subsistence farming, low capital accumulation, and limited national economic development are usually indicated.

Landlessness

Third World economies devoid of adequate urban industrial or service employment opportunities can no longer accommodate population growth by bringing new agricultural land into cultivation. In the most densely settled portions of the developing world, rural population expansion increasingly means that new entrants to the labor force are denied access to land either through ownership or tenancy. The problem is most acute in southern Asia, particularly on the Indian subcontinent, where the landless rural population is estimated to number some 250 million—nearly as large as the total population of the United States. Additional millions he poor man's energy crisis" is a phrase increasingly applicable to the rising demand for and the decreasing supply of wood for fuel in the developing countries. It is a different kind of crisis from that faced by industrialized countries encountering rising prices and diminishing supplies of petroleum and natural gas. The crisis of the less developed societies involves cooking food and keeping warm, not running machines, cooling theaters, or burning lights.

The United Nations Food and Agriculture Organization (FAO) estimates that wood accounts for at least 60% of the fuel used in the developing countries and exceeds 90% in the poorest countries such as Ethiopia and Nepal. The agency reports that wood accounts for nearly two-thirds of all energy consumed in Africa (excluding Egypt and South Africa), more than 40% in the Far East (excluding China), 20% in Latin America, and 14% in the Near East. Increasing demand and declining supplies are having serious human and natural consequences. More than 100 million people consume amounts of energy—mainly fuelwood—"below minimum requirements" for cooking, heating, and other domestic purposes. Another 1.3 billion people meet their needs only by serious depletion of the wood reserves upon which they totally depend. Some two-thirds of those people live in Asia. The most serious shortages and depletions are in the drier areas of Africa (more than 50 million Africans face acute fuelwood shortages), in the mountainous districts of Asia—the Himalayas are particularly affected—and in the Andean uplands of Latin America. As a result of shortages and deforestations in such widely scattered areas as Nepal and Haiti, families have been forced to change their diets to primary dependence on less nutritious foods that need no cooking. Reports of whole villages reduced to only one cooked meal a day are common. With the average villager requiring a ton of wood per year, an increasing proportion of labor must be expended to secure even minimal supplies of fuel, to the detriment of food- or income-producing activities. In parts of Tanzania in East Africa, because of time involved in travelling to and from forest lands and gathering the wood itself, between 250 and 300 workdays are needed to fill the yearly firewood needs of a single household. The figure is 230 person-days in the highlands of Nepal. Growing populations assure that the problem of fuel shortages will continue to plague developing countries even though recently introduced improved stoves and greater availability of oil and natural gas have begun to lower per capita fuelwood use in many regions.

The obvious environmental consequences of the increasing demand for fuelwood involve total deforestation and the uprooting of shrubs and grasses over wide areas. Further soil erosion and desertification are inevitable in lands already poor and overpopulated. Worldwide, over-exploitation of fuelwood sources accounts for 7% of all seriously degraded soils, with Africa the most seriously affected. A common response to the fuel wood crisis is the substitution of animal dung for the unavailable wood. The result of that is a loss of manure for soil enrichment. An estimated 400 million tons of potential fertilizer are burned each year in Africa and Asia, inevitably lowering the productivity of already marginal lands.

Populations Projected to Experience Fuelwood Deficiencies in A.D. 2000 (millions of persons)		
	ACUTE SCARCITY OR DEFICIT	
REGION	TOTAL POPULATION	RURAL POPULATION
Africa	535	464
Near East and North Africa	268	158
Asia and Pacific	1671	1434
Latin America	512	342
Total	**2986**	**2398**

Source: FAO, *Fuelwood Supplies in Developing Countries*, Rome, 1983.

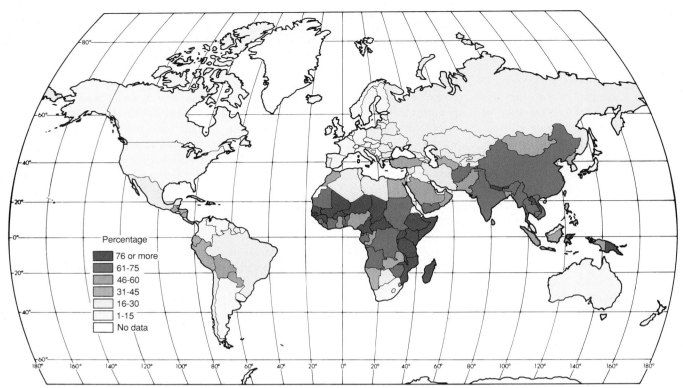

FIGURE 10.11   **Percentage of labor force engaged in agriculture.** For the world as a whole, agricultural workers make up slightly more than half of the total labor force. Highly developed economies usually have relatively low proportions of their labor forces in the agricultural sector. Most countries of the "North" have 15% or less of their labor force in farming, but some less industrialized Eastern European and former Soviet Central Asian states greatly exceed that percentage level. The contrast between advanced and underdeveloped countries in the agricultural labor force measure is diminishing. Rapid Third World population growth has resulted in increased rural landlessness and poverty from which escape is sought by migration to cities. The resulting reduction in the agricultural labor force percentage is an expression of relocation of poverty and unemployment, not of economic advancement.

TABLE 10.1   Economic Indicators and Agriculture's Share of Labor

COUNTRY GROUP	PER CAPITA GNP[A]	PER CAPITA ENERGY CONSUMPTION[B]	PERCENT OF LABOR FORCE IN AGRICULTURE
Least Developed Countries	213	48	74
All Developing Countries	982	527	58
Industrial Countries	16,065	4834	10

[A]U.S. dollars, 1992.

[B]Kilograms of oil equivalent, 1992; commercial energy only.

Source: United Nations Development Program, *Human Development Report 1995* (New York: Oxford University Press, 1995).

have access to parcels too small to adequately feed the average household. A landless agricultural labor force is also of increasing concern in Africa and Latin America (Figure 10.12).

Landlessness is in part a function of an imbalance between the size of the agricultural labor force and the arable land resource. It is also frequently a reflection of concentration of ownership by a few and consequent landlessness for many. Restricted ownership of large tracts of rural land

appears to affect not just the economic fortunes of the agricultural labor force itself but also to depress national economic growth through inefficient utilization of a valuable but limited resource. Large estates are often farmed carelessly, are devoted to production of crops for export with little benefit for low-paid farm workers, or even left idle. In some societies, governments concerned about undue concentration of ownership have imposed restrictions on total farm size—though not always effectively.

FIGURE 10.12   Throughout much of the developing world, growing numbers and proportions of rural populations are either landless agricultural laborers with at best tiny garden plots to provide basic food needs or independent holders of parcels inadequate in size or quality to provide food security for the family. In either case, size of land holding and poverty of farmer restrict the operator to rudimentary agricultural implements and practices. The photo shows hoe cultivation of a garden plot in Bali.

In Latin America, where farms are often huge and most peasants landless, land reform—that is, redistribution of arable land to farm workers—has had limited effect. The Mexican revolution early in the 20th century resulted in the redistribution of nearly half the country's agricultural land over the succeeding 60 years, but the rural discord in Chiapas in the mid-1990s reflects the persistence there of underutilized large estates and peasant landlessness. The Bolivian revolution of 1952 was followed by a redivision of 83% of the land. Some 40% of Peru's farming area was redistributed by the government during the 1970s. In other Latin American countries, however, land reform movements have been unattempted or less successful. In Guatemala, for example, 85% of rural households are landless or nearly so, and the top 1% of landowners control 34% of arable land. In Brazil, the top 2% of landowners possess 60% of arable land, 30% of farms are smaller than 1 hectare (2.5 acres) and together occupy just 1% of all farmland, and 70% of rural households are landless or so nearly so they lack enough land to support themselves. Programs of governmental expropriation of land have been delayed by innumerable lawsuits and by armed guards hired to protect from "squatter" occupation private lands slated for redistribution.

In India, where two-thirds of rural families either have no land at all or own less than 2 hectares (5 acres), a government regulation limits ownership of "good" land to 7 hectares (18 acres). That limitation has been effectively circumvented by owners distributing title to the excess land to their relatives. Population growth has reduced the amount of land available to the average farmer on the Indonesian island of Java to only 0.3 hectares (three-quarters of an acre), and the central government reports that over half of Java's farmers now work plots too small to support them.

The rural landless are the most disadvantaged segment of the poorest countries of the least developed regions of the world. Invariably, they have far higher levels of malnutrition and incidence of disease and lower life expectancies than other segments of their societies. In Bangladesh, for example, the rural landless consume only some 80% of the daily caloric intake of their landholding neighbors. To survive, many there and in other countries where landlessness is a growing rural problem leave the agricultural labor force and migrate to urban areas, swelling the number of shantytown residents but not necessarily improving their fortunes.

Poverty, Calories, and Nutrition

Poverty is the most apparent common characteristic of countries, regions, communities, or households afflicted by malnourishment. Availability of urban employment or rural access to arable land is far more important in determining national levels of undernourishment than is a country's aggregate per capita food production. During the Bangladesh famine of 1974, for example, total food availability per capita was at a long-term peak; starvation, according to World Bank reports, was the result of declines in real wages and employment in the rural sector and short-term speculative increases in the price of rice.

Nourishment levels, therefore, are as truly an indicator of economic development of a country as are any of the dollar-indexed measures of production and income or summary statements about the structure of national employment. Indeed, no other economic measure of national prosperity or development level can be as meaningful as the availability of food supplies sufficient in caloric content to meet individual daily energy requirements and so balanced as to satisfy normal nutritional needs. Food, as the essential universal consumption necessity and the objective of the majority of human productive activity, is the ultimate indicator of economic well-being.

Calorie requirements to maintain moderate activity vary according to a person's type of occupation, age, sex, and size, and to climate conditions. The Food and Agriculture Organization (FAO) of the UN specifies 2360 calories is the minimum necessary daily consumption level, but that figure has doubtful universal applicability. By way of a benchmark, per capita daily calorie availability in the United States is nearly 3700. Despite the limitations of the FAO standards, Figure 10.13 uses them to report calorie intake as a percentage of the minimum daily requirements.

Like other national indicators, caloric intake figures must be viewed with suspicion; the dietary levels reported by some states may more reflect self-serving estimates or fervent hopes than actual food availability. Even if accurate, of course, they report national averages, which may seriously obscure the food deprivation of large segments of a population. But even the data reported on Figure 10.13 show one-third of the world's population, exclusively in the less

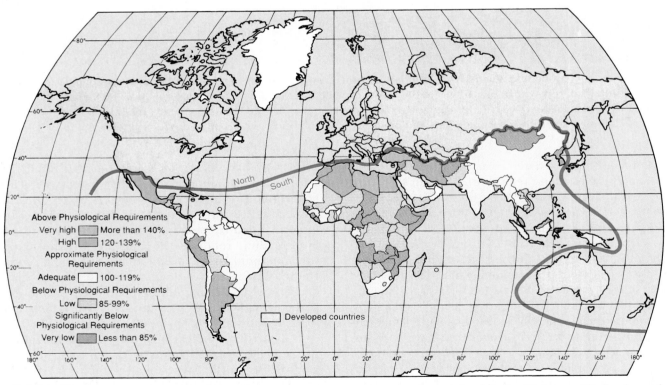

FIGURE 10.13 **The South: Percentage of required dietary energy supply received daily.** If the world's food supply were evenly divided, all would have an adequate diet; each person's share would be between 2600 and 2700 calories. Even Third World populations *as a group* would be adequately fed with between 2400 and 2500 calories each. In reality, roughly 780 million people in poor countries—20% of their population—do not get enough to eat. Yet progress in feeding the world's people has been made. In 1970, more than one of every three people living in poor countries—almost 950 million—was undernourished. Only in Africa has the hunger problem remained largely the same, a product of the continent's continuing poverty and a drop in food production by 20% between 1970 and 1992. In contrast to the regional variation shown on the map of the South, all countries of the North have average daily per capita caloric intake above 120% of physiological requirements.

DYNAMIC PATTERNS OF THE SPACE ECONOMY

FIGURE 10.14   The occasional and uncertain supplies of food dispensed by foreign aid programs and private charities are not sufficient to assure health, vigor, or normal development to these children in a Sudanese refugee camp.

developed countries, to be inadequately supplied with food energy (Figure 10.14). Areal or household incidences of hunger or malnutrition that exist in the more developed and affluent economies are masked within high national averages.

Low caloric intake is usually coupled with lack of dietary balance, reflecting an inadequate supply of the range and amounts of carbohydrates, proteins, fats, vitamins, and minerals needed for optimum physical and mental development and maintenance of health. The World Health Organization estimates that nearly 2 billion people worldwide suffer from some form of micronutrient malnutrition that leads to high infant and child mortality, impaired physical and mental development, and weakened immune responses. As Figure 10.13 indicates, dietary insufficiencies—with inevitable adverse consequences for life expectancy, physical vigor, and intellectual acuity—are most likely to be encountered in those developing countries that have large proportions of their populations in the young age groups (Figure 4.10). African states have been particularly hard hit by famine and malnutrition (Figure 10.15) as a result of recurring droughts, environmental degradation, and armed conflicts that disrupt production and distribution of food.

Composite Assessment of Economic Development

Although single-factor evaluations of technological development tend to identify the same set of countries as "less developed," the correspondence is not exact. For each measure selected for comparison, each country finds itself in the company of a slightly different set of peers. As a consequence, no one individual measure of technological

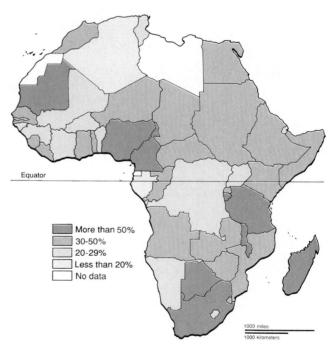

FIGURE 10.15   **Percentage of children under 5 years malnourished or with stunted growth, 1984–92.** The consequences of malnutrition are many and include premature births, low birth weights, abnormally low weight-for-height and weight-for-age ratios, mental retardation, and anemia. Here, the pattern of stunted growth resulting from malnutrition traces regional poverty, recurring drought and crop failure, and the changing pattern of war and civil unrest.

development, wealth, or economic well-being fully reflects the diversity of characteristics of individual countries, though revealing summary indexes have been prepared. Using data from the 1950s, Brian Berry compressed through factor analysis, 43 different, dominantly economic measurements of development for 95 separate countries into a single index of technological status.

More recent similar attempts at country ranking on an economic development scale show the earlier situation has changed very little with the passage of time. Some shifts have occurred, of course. Thanks to oil wealth, some petroleum exporting countries like Libya have moved out of the ranks of the "least developed." India placed relatively well in the 1950 rankings, but nearly 50 years later its low GNP per capita put it among the poorer countries of the world. Such relatively modest shifts emphasize rather than contradict the conclusion that improvements in a country's relative technological position and national wealth are difficult to achieve.

A Model for Economic Development

The realization that economic development is not automatic and inevitable has been a discouraging reversal of an earlier commonly held belief: that there was an inevitable process of development that all countries could reasonably expect to experience and that progress toward development would be marked by recognizable stages of achievement.

A widely cited model for economic advancement was proposed in the late 1950s by W. W. Rostow (1916–). Generalizing on the "sweep of modern history," Rostow theorized that all developing economies may pass through five successive stages of growth and advancement. *Traditional societies* of subsistence agriculture, low technology levels, and poorly developed commercial economies can have only

FOR YOUR CONSIDERATION

DOES FOREIGN AID HELP?

Since the 1970s, the industrial countries have annually spent about one-third of one percent of their gross domestic product on aid to developing countries. In addition, large sums have flowed from "North" to "South" (Figure 10.3) in the form of direct loans from individual countries and such international institutions as the World Bank, the International Monetary Fund, and regional development banks. Poor countries owed nearly $2 trillion in development-related debts to outside lenders in 1995.

The official goal of foreign aid is, usually, to help the poor and to develop the infrastructure essential to encourage economic and social development. In reality, much aid seems driven by the political interests of donor countries rather than by the developmental needs of the recipients. Whatever the motive, the results have been less substantial than the amounts donated or loaned.

True, aid proponents point to many past successes. In *food production,* advances in maize, wheat, and rice farming spurred the Green Revolution, greatly increasing food self-sufficiency in many countries, though often to the detriment of smaller, subsistence farmers. The *physical infrastructure* of various recipient states has been improved by new roads, power stations, irrigation and hydroelectric dams, sewage and water supply systems, and the like. Importantly, *health benefits* flowing from aid contributions to developing countries are measured by an increase since 1960 in life expectancy from 46 to 63 years and by the reduction by two-thirds in the number of children who die before their fifth birthday. The eradication of smallpox, provision and promotion of oral rehydration for diarrheal disease, widening distribution of standard immunizations, and provision of vitamin supplements are among the positive foreign aid achievements.

Despite these achievements, many analysts question the effectiveness of foreign aid. The argument that aid is needed to provide investment capital is countered by the observations that even the poorest countries have rich elites who save and invest little in their home countries, and that many of the major recipients of aid also enjoy large inflows of private capital. Further, analysis of aid flows to nearly 100 countries since the 1970s reveals that in almost all cases aid is spent entirely on consumption of goods and services—for the most part by governments and the already well-to-do elites—with rarely a big increase in investment. Even countries that receive aid equal to 15% of their GDP have no greater improvement in basic measures of human development or economic growth than countries receiving no aid.

low productivity per capita. The *preconditions for takeoff* are established when those societies, led by an enterprising elite, begin to organize as political rather than kinship units and to invest in transportation systems and other productive and supportive infrastructure.

The *takeoff* to sustained growth is the critical developmental stage, lasting perhaps 20 to 30 years, during which rates of investment increase, new industries are established, resources are exploited, and growth becomes the expected norm. The *drive to maturity* sees the application of modern technology to all phases of economic activity; diversification carries the economy beyond the industrial emphases first triggering growth, and the economy becomes increasingly self-sufficient. Finally, when consumer goods and services begin to rival heavy industry as leading economic sectors and most of the population has consumption levels far above basic needs, the economy has completed its transition to the *age of mass consumption*. More recently—and referring to most advanced economies (and discussed in Chapter 9)—a sixth stage, the *postindustrial,* has been recognized. Services replace industry as the principal sector of the economy, professional and technical skills assume preeminence in the labor force, and information replaces energy as the key productive resource.

Rostow's expectations of an inevitable progression of development proved illusory. Many LDCs remain locked in one of the first two stages of his model, unable to achieve the takeoff to self-sustained growth despite importation of technology and of foreign aid investment funds from the more developed world (see "Does Foreign Aid Help?"). Indeed, it has become apparent to many observers that despite the best efforts of the world community, the development gap between the most and the least advanced countries widens rather than narrows over time. A case in

---

Some contend that foreign aid is self-defeating; that the increases in population brought about by greater food production and better health care nullify any gain in modernization.

Increasingly, aid recipients are also debtor countries, saddled with repayment obligations that overwhelm their national budgets and prevent expenditures from domestic funds on health care, education, infrastructure development, and the like. For sub-Saharan Africa, debt is now higher than the region's entire output of goods and services. Debtor countries, further, are increasingly resentful of the tendency of international lending agencies and individual donors to make new or continued support contingent on changes in recipient states' economic and political policies. For them, aid and loans have proved more detrimental than advantageous as the burden of economic reform programs falls heavily on the poorest of their populations.

The foreign aid of the United States has for some years averaged no more than 1% of the federal budget, yet still amounts to billions of dollars—$437 billion between 1946 and 1995. Much of that money goes to a relatively few countries with which the U.S. has special relationships; Egypt and Israel, for example, together received 40% of the total in 1996. On a worldwide scale, critics contend, little of the aid from the rich "North" has been invested in places that need it most. In the early 1990s, while 10 countries accounted for 66% of the world's poorest people, they received only 32% of all development assistance. India alone, with 27% of the "absolute poor," got only 5% of the aid. Those who support continuation of U.S. foreign aid levels note that it benefits rather than weakens the national economy. Almost 75% of foreign assistance flows back in the form of tied purchases of American services and agricultural and manufactured goods.

Questions:

1. *Do you feel that the amount the U.S. spends on foreign aid is too much, too little, or about right? If too much, do you advocate cutting foreign aid? If too little, would you support an increase in the federal budget aid allocation? What are your reasons for your opinions?*

2. *Do you believe that U.S. foreign aid should be closely monitored to assure that assistance benefits the poor and the social and developmental programs that promise most effective improvement in their circumstances of life—even if such donor control is resented or rejected by recipient countries? Why or why not?*

3. *One widely-held opinion is that money now spent on direct and indirect foreign aid more properly should be spent on domestic programs dealing with poverty, unemployment, homelessness, inner-city decay, inequality, and the like. An equally strongly-held contrary view is that foreign aid should take priority, for it is needed to address world and regional problems of overpopulation, hunger, disease, destruction of the environment, and civil and ethnic strife those conditions foster. Assuming you had to choose one of the two polar positions, which view would you support, and why?*

point is sub-Saharan Africa; in the 1980s, per capita income declined by almost 2% a year, leaving all but a tiny elite significantly poorer at the end of the decade. Over the same period, income per head in the industrial market economies grew at a 2.5% annual rate, a growth differential that continued into the 1990s. The 1960s, 1970s, and 1980s were all proclaimed by United Nations resolutions as "Development Decades." They proved instead to be decades of dashed hopes—at least by economic measures—for many of the world's least developed states and for those who believed in definable and achievable "stages of development."

Other development theories and models try to address these realities. The concept of the "Big Push" concludes that underdeveloped economies can break out of their poverty trap by coordinated investment in both basic—but high wage—industries and infrastructure, creating simultaneously an expanding consumer base and steadily falling costs and rising volumes of production. These in turn encourage creation of backward- and forward-linked industries, further cost reductions, faster growth, and perhaps the industrial specializations that foster agglomeration economies and trade expansion.

Another viewpoint holds that national growth rate differentials are rooted in differing investments in "human capital," an ill-defined composite of skills, habits, schooling, and knowledge that—more importantly than labor force numbers or capital availability—contributes to successful economic development and sustained growth. A corollary concept concludes that for least-developed or newly industrializing countries, incentives encouraging foreign direct investment are the most important policy. When imported ideas and technology that help create "human capital" labor and intellectual skills are combined with domestic industrial control, encouragement of education, and local research and development, there will certainly follow industrial specializations, massive exports, and rising levels of living—as presumably they did for Taiwan, Singapore, and the other "dragons."

Obviously, not all less-developed countries have been able to follow that same path to success. Indeed, those countries where the poorest 20% of the world's people live were, in the early 1990s, 60 times worse off than those where the richest fifth live, and the gap between the two groups had doubled since the early 1960s. *Dependency theory* holds that these differentials are not accidental but the logical result of the ability and necessity of developed countries and power elites to exploit and subjugate other populations and regions to secure for themselves a continual source of new capital. Development aid where proffered, the theory holds, involves a forced economic dependency on donor countries and economies that continues an imposed cycle in which, in a sense, selective industrialization leads not to independent growth but to further dependent underdevelopment.

Balancing these polar extremes, we have seen, is the emerging world reality of accelerating economic growth for the developing countries as a group. Their present status as collective generators of nearly one-half of world output and

30% of world trade, holding over 45% of foreign-exchange reserves clearly suggests that, development theories aside, the best stimulus for economic growth has been the widespread relaxation of restrictive economic and political controls on all economies and on international trade flows in the past generation. Transnational corporations, technology transfer, pro-development national policies, trade restriction relaxations, and selective foreign aid and lending have all played a part. But the major impetus to the transition to Rostow's *takeoff* to sustained growth appears to be near worldwide conversion from controlled to free market economies.

Noneconomic Measures of Development

Development is measured by more than economic standards, though income and national wealth strongly affect the degree to which societies can invest in education, sanitation, health services, and other components of individual and group well-being. Indeed, the relationship between economic and social measures of development is direct and proportional. The higher the per capita gross national product is, for example, the higher the national ranking tends to be in such matters as access to safe drinking water, prevalence of sanitary waste treatment, availability of physicians and hospital beds, and educational and literacy levels. Conversely, the relationship between social–economic and demographic variables is usually inverse. Higher educational or income levels, for example, are usually associated with lower infant mortality rates, birth and death rates, rates of natural increase, and the like. However it is measured, the gap between the most and least developed countries in noneconomic characteristics is at least as great as it is in their economic–technological circumstances. As Table 10.2 shows, although the South as a whole has made progress in reducing its disadvantages in some human well-being measures, in others the gap between rich and poor is widening and, by all measures, disparities still remain after the three UN "development decades."

Education

A literate, educated labor force is essential for the effective transfer of advanced technology from the developed to developing countries. Yet in the poorest societies two-thirds or more of adults are illiterate; for the richest, the figure is 1% or less (Figure 10.16). The problem in part stems from a national poverty that denies funds sufficient for teachers, school buildings, books, and other necessities of the educational program. In part it reflects the lack of a trained pool of teachers and the inability to expand their number rapidly enough to keep up with the ever-increasing size of school-age populations. For the same number of potential pupils, the richest countries may have 20 to 25 times as many teachers as do the poorest countries. In Denmark in the mid-1990s

TABLE 10.2 North-South Disparity in Human Development, 1960–1992

	NORTH 1960	1992	SOUTH 1960	1992	ABSOLUTE DISPARITY 1960	1992
Narrowing disparity in human survival						
Life expectancy (years)	69.0	74.5	46.2	62.8	22.8	11.7
Adult literacy (%)	95	97	46	68	49	29
Nutrition (daily calorie supply as % of requirement)	124	133	90	112	34	21
Infant mortality (per 1000 live births)	37	12	149	70	112	58
Child mortality (per 1000 live births)	46	15	233	101	187	86
Access to safe water (% of population)	100	100	40	69	60	31
Widening disparity in human progress						
Mean years of schooling	9.1	10.0	3.5	3.9	5.6	6.1
Tertiary education enrollment ratio (%)[a]	18	37	3	8	15	29
Scientists and technicians (per 1000 people)[a]	51	85	6	9	45	76
Expenditure on research and development (U.S.$ billions)[a]	196	434	13	18	183	416
Telephones (per 1000 people)	130	479	9	31	121	448
Radios (per 1000 people)	449	1130	32	180	417	950

[a]1990

Source: United Nations Development Programme (UNDP), *Human Development Report 1992, 1994,* and *1995* (New York: Oxford University Press).

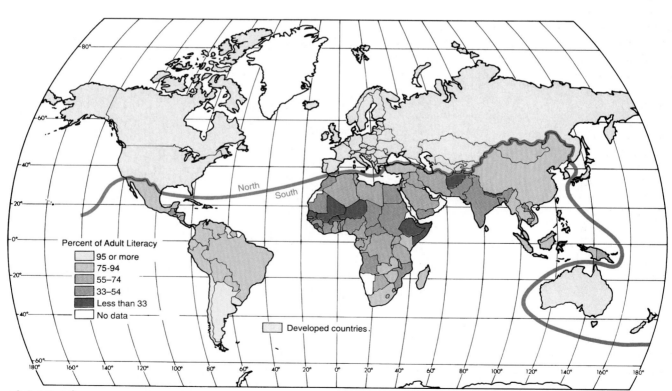

FIGURE 10.16 **The South: Adult literacy rate,** as a percentage of the adult population (over 15 years of age) able to read and write short, simple statements relating to their everyday life. With almost no exceptions, adult literacy was 95% or more in countries of the North.

there was 1 teacher for every 12 children of school age; in Burkina Faso the ratio was 1 to more than 270. Both wealth and commitment appear important in the student-teacher ratios, as Figure 10.17 makes clear. Oil-rich Qatar had 11 students per teacher; in similarly rich Saudi Arabia the figure was nearly 30. Israel had more teachers per 1000 students than did wealthier Switzerland or the United States.

Public Services

Development implies more than industrial expansion or agricultural improvement. The quality of public services and the creation of facilities to assure the health of the labor force are equally significant evidences of national advancement. Safe drinking water and the sanitary disposal of human waste are particularly important in maintaining human health (Figure 4.18). As Table 10.2 notes, disparities in access to safe water and sanitation are being steadily reduced between developed and developing countries. Nevertheless, their accepted presence in the North and general absence in, particularly, rural areas and urban slums in the less-developed world present a profound contrast between the two realms. Less than half of the rural populations of the predominantly rural least developed states have access to water safe to drink.

Within the expanding cities of the developing countries nearly a quarter-billion people live in shantytowns and slums devoid of adequate water supply or sanitary disposal facilities (Figure 10.18). Worldwide, 1.3 billion people in the developing countries do not have a dependable sanitary supply of water (Figure 10.19), more than 2 billion lack simple sanitary facilities essential to health, and water-related diseases kill approximately 10 million people every year. Yet, some progress has been made; during the 1980s more than 1 billion people worldwide were added to the ranks of those with access to potable water.

Health

Access to medical facilities and personnel is another spatial variable with profound implications for the health and well-being of populations. Within the less-developed world, as Figure 10.20 suggests, vast numbers of people are effectively denied services of physicians. There are simply too few trained health professionals to serve the needs of expanding populations. Those few who are in practice tend to congregate in urban areas, particularly in the capital cities. Rural clinics are few in number and the distance to them so great that many rural populations are effectively denied medical treatment of even the most rudimentary nature.

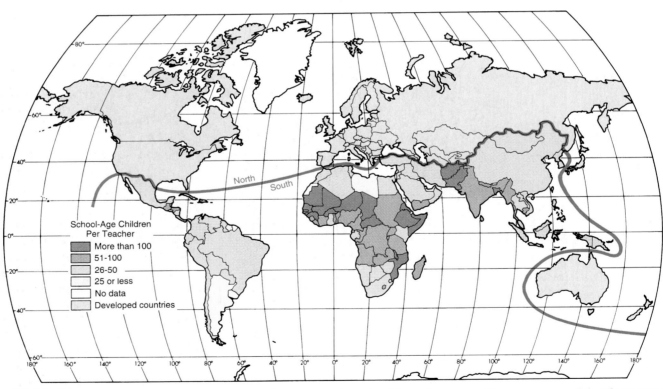

FIGURE 10.17 **The South: School-age population per teacher.** In this, as in many other measures of development and well-being, Africa makes the poorest showing. In more than 30 African nations in the early 1990s, more than half the children were not enrolled in school; in 8 of them, 3 out of 4 children were not in school. Between 1975 and 1990, however, the number of Third World teachers increased by nearly 45% and the teacher–pupil ratio improved greatly. With 2 or 3 Eastern European exceptions, all countries of the North had 25 or fewer school-age children per teacher.

FIGURE 10.18   Because they have no access to safe drinking water or sanitary waste disposal, impoverished populations of a developing country's unserved rural districts and urban slums—like this one in Bombay, India—are subject to water-borne and sanitation-related diseases: 900 million annual cases of diarrhea including 2 million childhood deaths, 900 million cases of roundworm, 200 million of schistosomiasis, and additional millions of other similarly related infections and deaths.

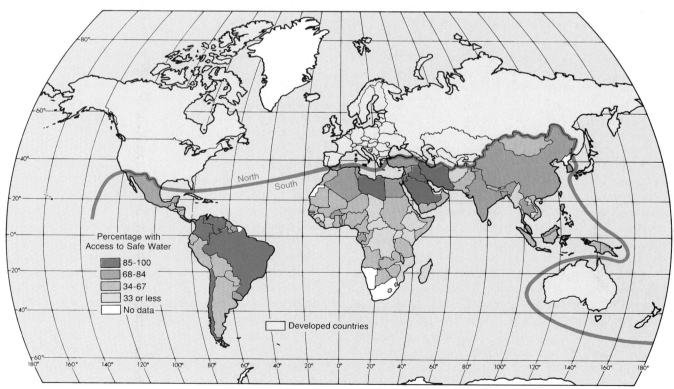

FIGURE 10.19   **Percentage of population with access to safe drinking water.** Between 1975 and 1995, access to safe water increased by more than two-thirds. The growing urban populations of the world benefited most; by the mid-1990s more than 80% of urbanites in the developing countries had access to safe water.

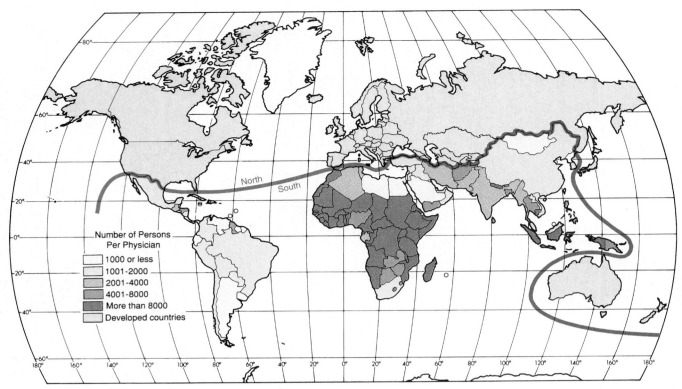

FIGURE 10.20   **Population per physician in developing countries.** In the industrial countries, on average, one physician serves 390 people. The corresponding figure for the developing world is nearly 6700. In Kenya it is about 71,000 people per physician and for all of sub-Saharan Africa, the ratio is 36,000 to 1. When the ratio rises above 4000 to 1, whole populations are denied any access to advanced medical attention.

Increasingly, the contrasts in conditions of health and disease between advanced and developing countries have become matters of international concern and attention. We saw in Chapter 4 how important for developing states' population growth is the transfer of advanced technologies of medicine and public health: insecticides, antibiotics, and immunization, for example. Together, these and other transfers have helped raise life expectancy in developing countries from 40 years in 1950 to 64 years in the mid-1990s. Most recently—and an important contributor to that longevity rise—childhood diseases and deaths in developing countries have come under coordinated attack by the World Health Organization under the Task Force for Child Survival program (Figure 10.21). Gains have been impressive. If the 1960 worldwide infant mortality rate had remained in 1990, 8.5 million more children would have died than in fact did. Yet stark contrasts between most developed and least developed societies remain. Based on the mortality levels for children under five in industrialized countries in 1990 (300,000), the United Nations estimated that 95% of the approximately 14.5 million infant and child deaths in developing countries in that year were preventable.

Taken at their extremes, advanced and developing countries occupy two distinct worlds of disease and health. One is affluent; its death rates are low, and the chief killers of its mature populations are cancers, heart attacks, and strokes. The other world is impoverished, often crowded, and prone to disease. The deadly dangers of its youthful populations are infectious, respiratory, and parasitic diseases made more serious by malnutrition.

In the 1960s and 1970s, developing countries with their own and international resources sought to improve health conditions with drugs, pesticides, and centralized hospitals that served mainly their urban populations. Clean water, sanitation, and rural health programs were coupled with family planning efforts to introduce improved living conditions. For the poorest, most explosively growing nations those approaches were unsuccessful. Their expanding, susceptible populations were making demands on health services greater than the financial resources of those nations, or the international community, could support. In 1978, the World Health Organization endorsed preventive, rather than curative, health care as a more attainable goal and adopted "health for all by the year 2000" as its official target. It was to be reached through primary health care: low technologies aimed at disease prevention in poorer nations.

The general determinants of health are well known: enough purchasing power to secure the food, housing, and medical care essential to it; a healthful physical environment that is both sanitary and free from infectious disease; and a particularly female educational level sufficient to comprehend the essentials of nutrition and hygiene. Family planning, health, and infrastructure and economic developmental programs have begun to increase the numbers in the developing world that now have access to at least rudimentary health services (Figure 10.22).

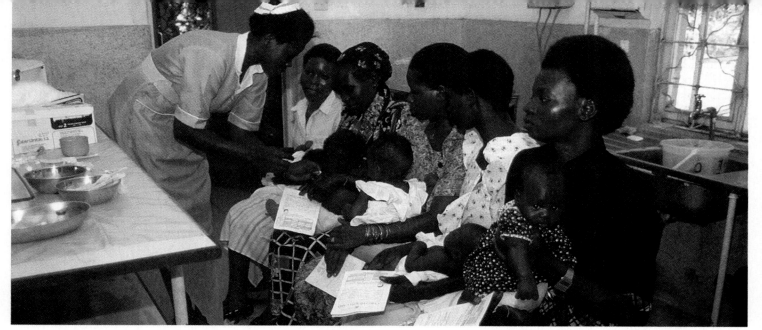

FIGURE 10.21   The World Health Organization (WHO) is the agency of the United Nations that helps bring modern preventive health care, safe water, and sanitation to the less developed world. WHO workers help to fight certain diseases, advise on nutrition and living conditions, and aid developing countries in strengthening their health services. When the organization launched its Expanded Programme on Immunization in 1974, only 5% of the world's children were immunized against measles, diphtheria, polio, tetanus, whooping cough, and tuberculosis, diseases claiming 5 million young lives annually. By 1990, immunization of the children of the developing world reached above 75%. The UN Children's Fund reported in 1995 that more than 90% of the developing world's children lived in countries making significant progress toward reducing malnutrition and preventing diseases. Pictured is preventive health care in a Kampala, Uganda, clinic.

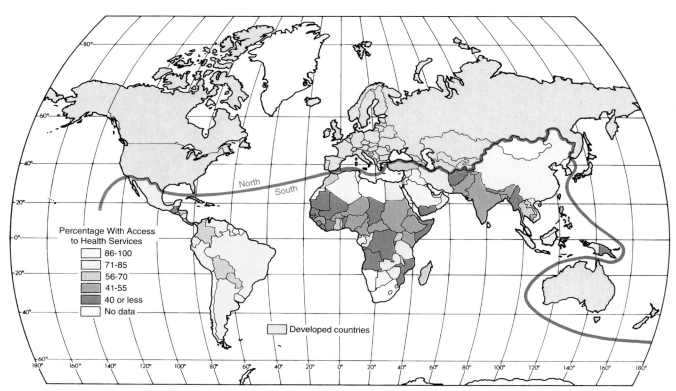

FIGURE 10.22   **The South: Access to health services.** The map reports the percentage of each country's population that is within one hour's reach of local health services on foot or by local means of transport. Although many, particularly African, countries are still poorly served by health personnel and facilities, two-thirds of the population of the developing countries now have such access.

Unfortunately, resurgence of old diseases and emergence of new ones may disrupt or reverse the hoped-for transition to better health in many world areas. Almost 10% of world population now suffer from one or more tropical diseases, many of which—malaria, affecting 200 to 300 million people annually, is an example—were formerly thought to be eradicable but now are spreading in drug-resistant form. Third World civil unrest and wars disrupt medical treatment and disease-control programs, while the high and rising costs of modern medications place unbearable burdens on strained budgets of developing states.

Those costs increasingly must include health care for the rapidly growing number of elderly in developing countries and for those exposed to the health risks that come with economic development and industrialization: higher consumption of alcohol, tobacco, and fatty foods, pollution, motor vehicle accidents, and the like. The World Health Organization is concerned that health services in poor developing countries may be overwhelmed by the twin burdens of poverty-related illness and health problems of industrialization and urbanization; heart disease and cancer now claim as many developing world as industrial world lives.

Poorer countries are also hardest hit by the spread of AIDS (acquired immune deficiency syndrome). In 1985, about half of the immunodeficiency virus infections known to cause AIDS were in the economically advanced countries, most in the United States. By 1990, two-thirds of those infections were in less-developed states. By 2000, the UN Global Program on AIDS predicts, 90% of a worldwide estimated 30–40 million adult and 10 million child cases of HIV infection will be found in the developing world. The population and economic consequences of AIDS, as an extreme example of new and spreading health problems, are immense. Beginning in 1990 as a direct consequence of AIDS, childhood mortality stopped declining and in some countries began to increase. Further, AIDS as a disease of young and middle-aged adults including business and government workers and members of social, economic, and political elites, poses the threat of economic and political destabilization in some developing states where those leadership groups are already small numerically and proportionally. Africa has been particularly hard hit, but AIDS, increasingly associated with heterosexual transmission, is spreading rapidly in Asia and Latin America as well.

Aggregate Measures of Development and Well-Being

As we have seen, no single measure adequately summarizes the different facets of national development or gives a definitive comparison of countries on the continuum of development. Composite measures to achieve that summary aim can, of course, be devised from the growing body of comparative statistics regularly published by United Nations agencies, the World Bank, and other sources. Many of those—Figure 10.3 is an example—have been criticized for being based too strongly on economic and infrastructural indicators: gross national product, per capita income, sectoral structure of national economies, import and export data, miles of railroad or paved highways, and the like.

Development, it is maintained, is more than the purely economic and physical, and personal development may have little or nothing to do with objective statistical measures. The achievement of development must also be seen in terms of individual and collective well-being: a safe environment, freedom from want, opportunity for personal growth and enrichment, and access to goods and services beyond the absolute minimum to sustain life (see "Measuring Happiness"). Health, safety, educational and cultural development, security in old age, political freedom, and similar noneconomic criteria are among the evidences of comparative developmental level that are sought in composite statistics. Also sought is a summary statistic of development that is value free; that is, the input data should not measure development by expenditure patterns or performance standards that are ethnocentric or colored by political agendas. The values of one culture—for example, in housing space per person, in educational levels achieved, or in distribution of national income—are not necessarily universally applicable or acceptable, and a true comparative statistic should not imply that they are.

Seeking a value-free measure of the extent to which minimum human needs are being satisfied among the world's countries, the Overseas Development Council devised a Physical Quality of Life Index (PQLI). Three indicators—infant mortality, life expectancy, and literacy—are each scored 0–100, with 0 an explicitly "worst" performance. A national achievement level is calculated by averaging the three indicators. The PQLI is but one of many attempts to recognize that national development and human welfare are complex achievements not measurable by a single indicator. Each approach has attempted to integrate into a composite index a larger or smaller number of national variables detailing physical, economic, political, and social conditions specific to country units. On the basis of the national rankings they derived, each has explicitly or implicitly ranked the countries of the world on a continuum from least to most developed.

One such ranking gaining increasing recognition is employed by the United Nations Development Programme. Its "human development index" (HDI) combines purchasing power (not just dollar amount of per capita GNP), life expectancy, and literacy (Figure 10.23). The HDI reflects the Programme's conviction that the important human aspirations are leading a long and healthy life, receiving adequate education, and having access to assets and income sufficient for a decent quality of life. The arbitrary weighting of the three input variables—longevity (measured by life

In an article in *The Times* (London) of 26 May 1975, "Introducing the Hedonometer, a New Way of Assessing National Performance *or* Why We Should Measure Happiness Instead of Income," Geraldine Norman compares England and Botswana under six headings.

Three years ago I spent my honeymoon in the eastern highlands of Rhodesia [now Zimbabwe] trying to construct a hedonometer, a means of measuring happiness per head of the population. I did not have a thermometer type of thing in mind: it was to be a statistical structure, on the lines of Keynesian national accounting, that would end up by measuring gross national happiness instead of gross national product. The unit of measurement would be psychological satisfaction rather than money. I envisaged my hedonometer as a tool for political policy making of such power that boring chat about economic growth would be ousted, forgotten and interred.

The motivation for this eccentric undertaking was a growing conviction that the accretion of wealth and/or the expansion of income, whether at national or individual level, was not necessarily a recipe for happiness. Indeed, I suspected that in some cases greater wealth reduced the likelihood of happiness—that in certain circumstances there could be a negative correlation between happiness and money. . . .

From my psychology book . . . I learnt that the two primary needs of a human being are security and achievement, achievement being the positive satisfaction of individual and species drives. Conning [the] book with attention—and using a bit of imagination—I arrived at the six principal factors which contribute to a happy life, the basis of my hedonometer. The list is as follows (the first two factors provide security and the next four require satisfaction for an adequate level of achievement):

1. *Understanding of your environment and how to control it.*

2. *Social support from family and friends.*

3. *Species drive satisfaction (sex and parental drives).*

4. *Satisfaction of drives contributing to physical well-being (hunger, sleep, etc.).*

5. *Satisfaction of aesthetic and sensory drives.*

6. *Satisfaction of the exploratory drive (creativity, discovery, etc.).*

You might like to modify the table by changing the relative importance of different factors, the scores, the countries, even the factors themselves. On the purely subjective judgement of Geraldine Norman, Botswana is a "happier" place than England. The measurement of happiness is indeed difficult and very subjective. The exercise is worthwhile, however, because it shows how the conventional measures of development such as energy consumption and GNP per inhabitant are really very subjective too.

© Times Newspapers Limited, 1975.

| | IMPORTANCE | ENGLAND | | BOTSWANA | |
		SATISFACTION (%)	PRODUCT (SCORE)	SATISFACTION (%)	PRODUCT (SCORE)
Understanding	15	50	750	70	1050
Social support	20	40	800	80	1600
Species satisfaction	10	70	700	70	700
Physical well-being	35	92	3220	72	2520
Aesthetic	5	40	200	60	300
Exploratory	15	30	450	60	900
Total	**100**		**6120**		**7070**

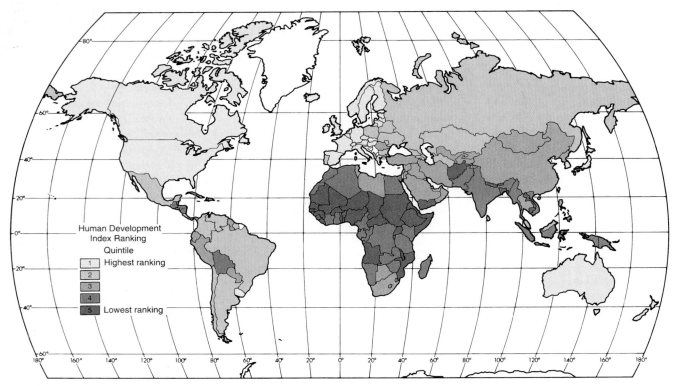

FIGURE 10.23 **Country rankings according to the Human Development Index** of the United Nations Development Programme. Since the index is intended to measure the absence of deprivation, it discounts incomes above PPP$5120, the global average real GDP per capita (1994), and therefore is uninformative in comparing the levels of development of the richest countries. The four measures that are used by the UNDP—life expectancy, adult literacy, mean years of schooling, and income—are highly correlated with one another. For that reason, it has been noted, the rankings derived by the HDI differ only slightly from income rankings adjusted for purchasing power parity. Fifth quintile countries, at the bottom of the Human Development Index, closely match the "least developed" countries recognized by the UN and shown on Figure 10.3.

Legend: Human Development Index Ranking Quintile — 1 Highest ranking, 2, 3, 4, 5 Lowest ranking

expectancy at birth), knowledge (indicated by weighted measures of adult literacy and mean years of schooling), and income (based on a poverty-adjusted statistic of gross domestic product per capita)—makes the derived national rankings subjective rather than fully objective. The HDI, like all attempts at measuring developmental levels of countries and categorizing their variations in qualities of life and human welfare, is a recognition both of the complexity of the economic and social structures involved and of the need to focus developmental efforts.

The Role of Women

Many of the common measures of development and change within and between countries take no account of the sex and age structures of the societies examined. Gross national product per capita, literacy rates, percentage of labor force in agriculture, and the like are statistics that treat all members (or all adult members) of the society uniformly. Yet among the most prominent strands in the fabric of culture are the social structures (*sociofacts*) and relationships that establish distinctions between males and females in the duties assigned and the rewards afforded to each.

Because gender relationships and role assignments vary among societies, the status of women is a cultural spatial variable. Because so much of that variation is related to the way economic roles and production and reward assignments are allocated by sex, we might well assume a close tie between the status of women in different societies and their level and type of economic development. Further, it would be logical to believe that advancement in the technological sense would be reflected in an enhancement of the status and rewards of both men and women in developing countries. Should that prove true, it would logically follow that contrasts between the developed and developing world in gender relationships and role assignments would steadily diminish.

The pattern that we actually observe is not quite that simple or straightforward, for gender relationships and role assignments are only partially under the control of the technological subsystem. **Gender** in the cultural sense refers to socially created—not biologically based—distinctions between femininity and masculinity. Therefore, religion and custom play their own important roles. Further, it appears that at least in the earlier phases of technological change and development, women generally lose rather than gain in status and rewards. Only recently and only in the most developed countries have gender-related contrasts been reduced within and between societies.

Hunting and gathering cultures observed a general egalitarianism; each sex had a respected, productive role in the kinship group (Figure 2.12). Gender is more involved and changeable in agricultural societies (see "Women and the Green Revolution," page 269). The Agricultural Revolution—a major change in the technological subsystem—altered the earlier structure of gender-related responsibilities. In the hoe agriculture found in much of sub-Saharan Africa and in South and Southeast Asia, women became responsible for most of the actual field work, while still retaining their traditional duties in child rearing, food preparation, and the like.

Plow agriculture, on the other hand, tended to subordinate the role of women and diminish their level of equality. Women may have hoed, but men plowed, and female participation in farm work was drastically reduced. This is the case today in Latin America and, increasingly, in sub-Saharan Africa where women are often more visibly productive in the market than in the field (Figure 10.24). As women's agricultural productive role declined, they were afforded less domestic authority, less control over their own lives, and few if any property rights independent of male family members.

Western industrial—"developed"—society emerged directly from the agricultural tradition of the subordinate female who was not considered an important element in the economically active population, no matter how arduous or essential the domestic tasks assigned and who was not afforded full access to education or similar amenities of an advancing society. European colonial powers introduced that attitude along with economic development into Third World cultures. Only within the later 20th century, and then largely in the more developed countries, has that subordinate role pattern changed.

The rate and extent of women's participation in the labor force has expanded everywhere in recent years. Between 1970 and 1990, both the percentage of the total labor force who are women and the percentage of women who

FIGURE 10.24   Women dominate the once-a-week *periodic* markets in nearly all developing countries. Here they sell produce from their gardens or the family farm and often offer processed goods for sale (to which their labor has added value)—oil pressed from seeds or, in Niger, for example, from peanuts grown on their own fields; cooked, dried, or preserved foods; simple pottery and baskets; or decorated gourds. In this photo, women are selling vegetables in Freetown, Sierra Leone. More than half the economically active women in sub-Saharan Africa and southern Asia and about one-third in northern Africa and the rest of Asia are self-employed, working primarily in the informal sector. In the developed world, only about 14% of active women are self-employed.

are economically active[5] increased in nearly every world region—developed and developing (Figure 10.25). The effects of the worldwide economic restructuring during the 1980s and early 1990s varied by region in developing countries. In general, women bore the brunt of coping with inflation-stabilization programs that increased living costs by removing food and other subsidies; many who had not previously participated in the formal economy sought to become economically active (see "Empowering Women Financially").

Considering all work—paid and unpaid economic activity and unpaid housework—women spend more hours per day working than do men in all developed and developing regions except Anglo America and Australia. Everywhere women are paid less than men for comparable employment, but in most world regions the percentage of economically active women holding wage or salaried posi-

tions is about equal to the rate for men. Exceptions are Latin America, where a higher proportion of active women than men are wage earners and Africa, where wage-earning opportunities for women are few; in several African states less than 10% of economically active women are wage earners.

Despite these and similar widely-applicable generalizations, the present world pattern of gender-related institutional and economic role assignments is varied. It is influenced by a country's level of economic development, by the persistence of the religious and customary restrictions its culture imposes on women, and by the specific nature of its economic—particularly agricultural—base. The first control is reflected in contrasts between the developed and developing world; the second and third are evidenced in variations within the developing world itself.

The differential impact of these and other conditions is evident in Figures 10.26, 10.27, and 10.28. The patterns show a distinct gender-specific regionalization among the countries of the Third World. Among the Arab or Arab-influenced Muslim areas of western Asia and North Africa, the recorded proportion of the female population that is economically active is low. Religious tradition restricts women's acceptance in economic activities outside of the home, a tradition that results in probable underreporting of female

[5]The International Labor Office defines "economically active" work as that "producing significant amounts of 'economic' (that is, marketable) goods, or of visible income." Included in the "economically active population" are all employed and unemployed persons seeking employment and all wage earners, unpaid family workers, and members of producers' cooperatives.

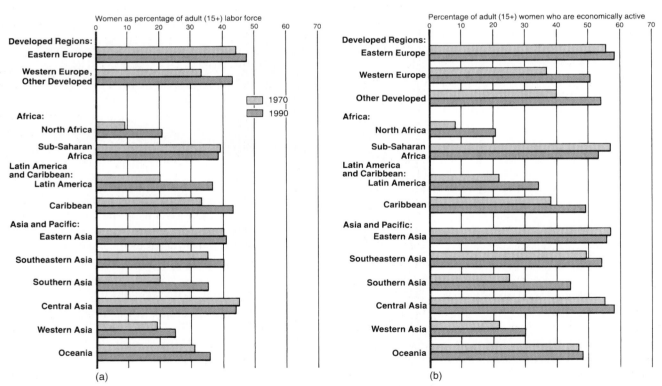

FIGURE 10.25 (a) **Women's share of the labor force** increased in almost all world regions between 1970 and 1990. Worldwide in 1992, women were recorded at 37% of the total labor force. (b) **Women's economic activity rates** showed a similar pattern of increase in most of the developing and developed world. More than half of the world's female labor force lived in Asia and the Pacific area in 1995, and although the regional share of economically active women varies widely, it is estimated that women will make up half the labor force in most countries and regions shortly after 2000.

The Fourth World Conference on Women held in Beijing during September, 1995, called on all governments to formulate strategies, programs, and laws designed to assure women their full human rights to equality and development. The Conference's final declaration detailed recommended policies in the areas of sexuality and child-bearing, violence against women, discrimination against girls, female inheritance rights, and family protection. Its particular emphasis, however, focused on efforts to "insure women's equal access to economic resources including land, credit, . . . and markets as a means to further advancement and empowerment of women and girls."

Two-thirds of the total amount of work women do is unpaid, but that unpaid work amounts to an $11 trillion addition to the total world economy. The Beijing Conference declaration was a recognition that women's economic contribution would be even greater—and of more social and personal benefit—were governments to grant them equal opportunity through financial support to engage as owners in small-scale manufacturing, trade, or service enterprises. In fact, both the model and proof of success in granting women access to credit were already in place.

In 1976 a Bangladeshi economist, Muhammad Yunus, wandered into a poor village and got an idea that has captured international interest and changed accepted beliefs and practices of banking in developing countries. The concept behind the Grameen Bank he established is simple: if individual borrowers are given access to credit they will be able to identify and engage in viable income-producing activities such as pottery-making, weaving, sewing, buying and marketing simple consumer goods, or providing transportation and other basic services. Declaring that "Access to credit should be a human right," Mr. Yunus was a pioneer in extending "micro-credit" for "micro-enterprises" with women emerging as the primary borrowers and beneficiaries of Grameen Bank's practice of lending money without collateral and at low rates of interest. To be eligible for the average loan of about U.S.$100, women without assets must join or form a "cell" of five women, of whom only two can borrow at first though all five are responsible for repayment. When the first two begin to repay, two more can borrow, and so on. As a condition of the loan, clients must also agree to increase their savings, observe sound nutritional practices, and educate their children.

By 1995, the bank had made over 2 million loans in 35,000 villages in Bangladesh. More than 93% of the borrowers are women and repayment rates reach 97%. The average household income of Grameen Bank members has risen to about 59% higher than that of nonmembers in the same villages, with the landless benefiting most and marginal landowner families following closely. Because of enterprise incomes resulting from the lending program, there has been a sharp reduction in the number of Grameen Bank members living below the poverty line—to 20% compared to nearly 60% for nonmembers. There has also been a marked shift from low-status agricultural labor to self-employment in simple manufacturing and trading.

The Grameen concept has spread from its Bangladesh origins to elsewhere in Asia and to Latin America and Africa. By 1995, some 10 million customers of micro-credit institutions and small credit cooperatives were operating worldwide, but these represent only 2% of the estimated 500 million women worldwide who have virtually no access to credit—or to the economic, social, educational, and nutritional benefits that come from its availability. It is that globally enormous number of women now effectively denied credit equality that the resolutions of the Fourth World Conference on Women seek to benefit.

employment by the countries involved. The same cultural limitations do not apply under the different rural economic conditions of Muslims in southern and southeastern Asia, where labor force participation by women in Indonesia and Bangladesh, for example, is much higher than it is among the western Muslims.

In Latin America, women have been overcoming cultural restrictions on their employment outside the home and their active economic participation has been increasing. That participation is occurring almost entirely outside of the agricultural realm, where the high degree of farm labor tenancy as well as custom limits the role of females. Sub-Saharan Africa, highly diverse culturally and economically, in general is highly dependent on female farm labor and market income. The historical role of strongly independent, property-owning females formerly encountered under traditional agricultural and village systems, however, has increasingly been replaced by subordination of women with modernization of agricultural techniques and introduction of formal, male-dominated financial and administrative farm sector institutions.

For the developing world in general, a series of indicators has been combined by the International Fund for Agricultural Development to establish a "women's status index" and ranking (Figure 10.28); it clearly displays regional differentials in the position of women in different cultures and world regions. A related "gender empowerment measure" devised by the United Nations Development Programme emphasizes female participation in national economic, political, and professional affairs (Figure 10.29).

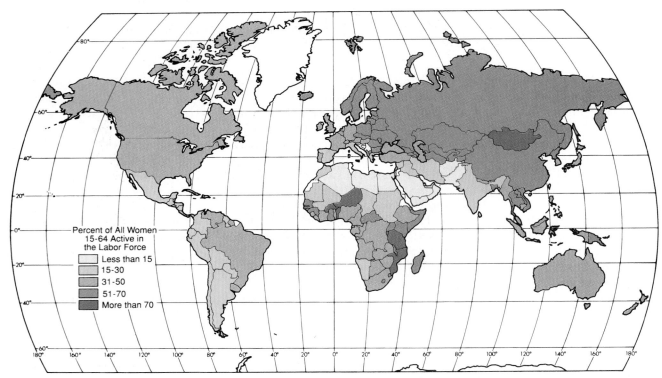

FIGURE 10.26   **Economically active women, 1994.** Since female participation in the labor force is reported by individual countries with differing definitions of "economically active," international comparisons may be misleading. The International Labor Office definition is given as a footnote on page 362.

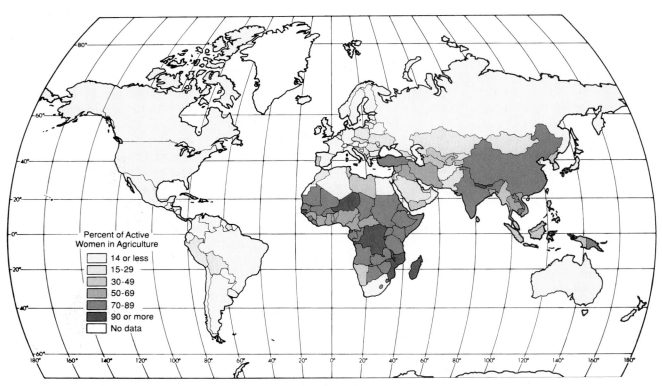

FIGURE 10.27   **Percentage of economically active women engaged in agriculture, 1994.** The role of women in agriculture is difficult to document and is generally poorly estimated or ignored in many parts of the world. Nevertheless, some studies indicate that women have become increasingly important in food production in developing regions thanks to men's increased migration to cities and towns. A high proportion of women in agriculture work without wages on their own or their families' farms—about 40% in all developing regions except Latin America.

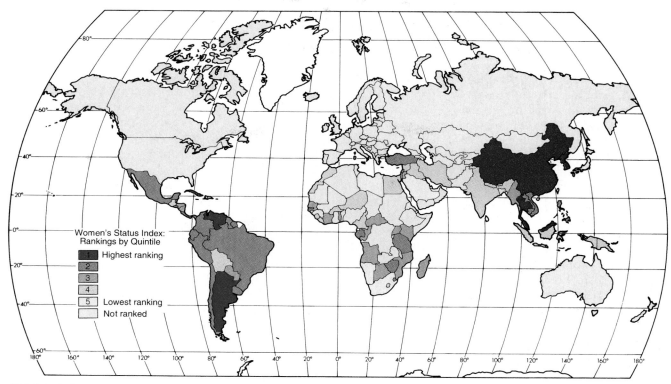

FIGURE 10.28   **The women's status index** is a summary statistic that attempts to measure quantitatively the relative position of women in different countries and cultural settings. Calculated by the International Fund for Agricultural Development for 114 countries, the index is derived from inputs that include: maternal mortality rate, percentage of women using contraceptives, female adult literacy rate, gross primary and secondary school female enrollment, female/male wage ratio in agriculture or nonagriculture employment, and female labor force participation rate. Among the developing regions, women's status is generally lowest in Africa and South Asia and highest in Latin America.

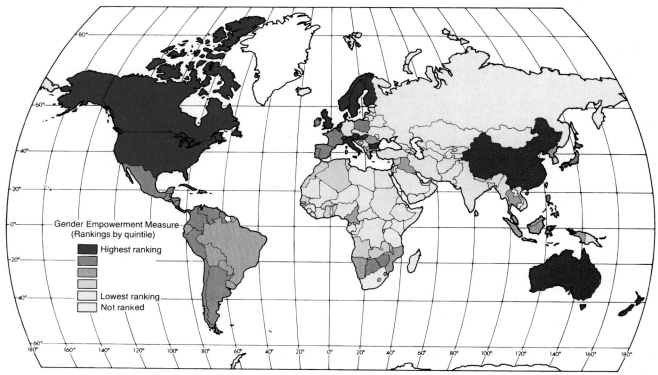

FIGURE 10.29   **The gender empowerment measure (GEM)** summarizes women's access to political and economic power based on three variables: female share of parliamentary seats; share of professional, technical, administrative, and managerial jobs; and earning power, determined by access to jobs and wages. The GEM rankings show that gender equality in political, economic, and professional activities is not necessarily related to level of national wealth or development. Some developing countries according to this measure—China, for example—outperform industrialized France and Spain. Only 116 countries are ranked; in most, women are in a distinct minority in the exercise of economic power and decision making on the site.

Summary

Development as a concept and process implies change and improvement. It suggests the fuller and more productive use of the resources of an area through the application of advanced levels of technology. The result is presumed to be improved conditions of life and well-being for constant or growing populations and, for the society undergoing development, a fuller integration into—and more equal share of—the world space economy.

Development in that light can be seen as a cultural variable with a distinctive spatial patterning. No two countries have exactly the same position on the continuum of development in all of its many different possible economic and noneconomic measures. For this reason, precise classification of countries by developmental level is impossible and a variety of general descriptive terms has been introduced, including: developed, developing, underdeveloped, least (or less) developed, Third World, and the like. Whatever the terms, the overall world pattern of development is clear: The advanced and relatively wealthy countries of the economic core are those of Europe, North America, Japan, Australia, and New Zealand. The rest of the world is considered to be "developing" on the economic periphery, where individual countries are progressing at different rates and with different degrees of success.

A variety of comparative economic and noneconomic data is available to help identify the relative position of individual countries. *Gross national product* and *purchasing power parity per capita* document the basic core–periphery pattern while making clear the diversity among the developing countries in the monetary success of their economies. *Per capita consumption of commercial energy* reveals the immense size of the technology gap between most and least developed states, for energy use may be loosely equated with modern industrial plant and transportation facilities. A high percentage of a country's *workforce in agriculture* is associated with less developed subsistence economies with low labor productivity and low levels of national wealth. The price of underdevelopment—and of the relative poverty it implies—is malnutrition. Although the correlation is not exact, countries registering *average caloric intake* below daily requirements are also countries registering poorly on all purely economic measures of development.

Earlier hopes that underdevelopment was simply the common starting point in a series of expected and inevitable stages of advancement have been dashed. Many countries appear unable to accumulate the capital, develop the skills, or achieve the technology transfer necessary to carry them along the path to fuller economic development and prosperity. Without that development, countries score poorly on noneconomic measures such as literacy, safe water, and conditions of health. With it, they can—as the experience of newly industrializing countries demonstrates—experience growing cultural and technological convergence with the most advanced states. That convergence, in fact, is increasing and the share of the *gross world product* attributable to what is still called the "developing" world continues to grow and amounted to over 45% in the mid-1990s.

Development implies pervasive changes in the organizational and institutional structuring of peoples and space. Urbanization of populations and employment has invariably accompanied economic development, as has a more complete and rigorous political organization of space. We turn our attention in the following chapters to these two important expressions of human geographic variation, beginning first with an examination of city systems and of the spatial variations observable in the structure of urban units.

KEY WORDS

circular and cumulative causation   336
core-periphery model   336
cultural convergence   339
development   333
gender   361

gross domestic product   340
gross national product (GNP)   340
purchasing power parity (PPP)   337
spread effect   336
technology   338

technology gap   338
technology transfer   339
Third World   334
trickle-down effect   336
underdevelopment   334

FOR REVIEW

1. How does the *core–periphery* model help us understand observed contrasts between developed and developing countries? In what way is *circular and cumulative causation* linked either to the perpetuation or the reduction of those contrasts? How does the concept of *trickle-down effects* or *spread effects* explain the equalization of development and incomes on a regional or international scale?

2. What are some of the reasons that have been given to explain why some countries are *developed* and others are *underdeveloped*?

3. What different ways and measures do we have to indicate degrees of development of particular countries or regions? Do you think these measures can be used to place countries or regions into uniform *stages of development?*

4. Why should any country or society concern itself with *technology transfer* or with the *technology gap?* What do these concepts have to do with either development or societal well-being?

5. What kinds of material and nonmaterial economic and noneconomic contrasts can you cite that differentiate more-developed from less-developed societies?

6. Assume you are requested to devise a composite index of national development and well-being. What *kinds* of characteristics would you like to include in your composite?

Why? What specific *measures* of those characteristics would you like to cite?

7. Why is energy *consumption* per capita considered a reliable measure of level of national economic development? If a country has a large per capita *production* of energy, can we assume that it also has a high level of development? Why or why not?

8. Have both males and females shared equally in the benefits of economic development in its early stages? What are the principal contrasts in the status of women between the developed and developing worlds? What regional contrasts within the developing world are evident in the economic roles assigned to women?

SELECTED REFERENCES

Agnew, John A. "Bringing Culture Back In: Overcoming the Economic-Cultural Split in Development Studies." *Journal of Geography* 86, no. 6 (1987):276–281.

Andrews, Alice C. "The Status of Women in the Third World." In *The Third World: States of Mind and Being,* edited by Jim Norwine and Alfonso Gonzalez, pp. 125–137. Winchester, MA: Unwin Hyman, 1988.

Berry, Brian J. L. "An Inductive Approach to the Regionalization of Economic Development." In *Essays on Geography and Economic Development,* edited by Norton Ginsburg, pp. 78–107. Chicago: University of Chicago, Department of Geography, *Research Paper No. 62.* 1960.

Boserup, Ester. *Woman's Role in Economic Development.* London: Allen & Unwin, 1970.

Brydon, Lynne, and Sylvia Chant. *Women in the Third World: Gender Issues in Rural and Urban Areas.* New Brunswick, NJ: Rutgers University Press, 1989.

Butz, David, Steven Lonergan, and Barry Smit. "Why International Development Neglects Indigenous Social Reality." *Canadian Journal of Development Studies* 12, no. 1 (1991):143–157.

Chandra, Rajesh. *Industrialization and Development in the Third World.* Introductions to Development series. London, England: Routledge, 1992.

Charlton, Sue Ellen M. *Women in Third World Development.* Boulder, CO: Westview Press, 1984.

Cole, John P. *Development and Underdevelopment: A Profile of the Third World.* London and New York: Methuen, 1987.

Crow, Ben, and Alan Thomas. *Third World Atlas.* The Open University Press. Philadelphia: Milton Keynes, 1985.

Dickenson, John, ed. *Geography of the Third World.* New York: Routledge, 1996.

Dixon, Chris J. *Rural Development in the Third World.* London and New York: Routledge, 1990.

Fellmann, Jerome D. "Spatial Patterns of Disease and Health: One World or Two?" In *The Third World: States of Mind and Being,* edited by Jim Norwine and Alfonso Gonzalez, pp. 112–124. Boston: Unwin Hyman, 1988.

Gilbert, Alan, and Joseph Gugler. *Cities, Poverty and Development: Urbanization in the Third World.* New York: Oxford University Press, 1992.

Hanson, Susan, and Geraldine Pratt. *Gender, Work and Space.* New York: Routledge, 1995.

Independent Commission on International Development Issues. *North–South: A Programme for Survival.* Cambridge, MA: MIT Press, 1980.

International Bank for Reconstruction and Development/The World Bank. *World Development Report.* New York: Oxford University Press, Annual.

Jacobson, Jodi L. *Gender Bias: Roadblock to Sustainable Development.* Worldwatch Paper 110. Washington, D.C.: Worldwatch Institute, 1992.

Joekes, Susan P. *Women in the World Economy.* New York: Oxford University Press, 1987.

Kelley, Allen C. "The Human Development Index: 'Handle with Care.' " *Population and Development Review* 17, no. 2 (1991):315–324.

Knox, Paul L., and John A. Agnew. *The Geography of the World Economy.* 2d ed. London: Edward Arnold, 1994.

Kurian, George T. *Atlas of the Third World.* 2d. ed. New York: Facts on File, 1992.

Kurian, George T. *Encyclopedia of the Third World.* 4th ed. New York: Facts on File, 1992.

Lenssen, Nicholas. *Empowering Development: The New Energy Equation.* Worldwatch Paper 111. Washington, D.C.: Worldwatch Institute, 1992.

Momsen, Janet H. *Women and Development in the Third World.* New York: Routledge, 1991.

Momsen, Janet H., and Vivian Kinnaird. *Different Places, Different Voices: Gender and Development in Africa, Asia and Latin America.* New York: Routledge, 1993.

Nuss, Shirley, in collaboration with Ettore Denti and David Viry. *Women in the World of Work: Statistical Analysis and Projections to the Year 2000.* Geneva, Switzerland: International Labor Office, 1989.

Pacione, Michael, ed. *The Geography of the Third World.* London and New York: Routledge, 1988.

Phillips, David R. *Health and Health Care in the Third World.* London: Longman, 1990.

Phillips, David R., and Yola Verhasselt, eds. *Health and Development.* New York: Routledge, 1994.

Rostow, Walter W. *The Stages of Economic Growth.* London: Cambridge University Press, 1960, 1971.

Simpson, Edward S. *The Developing World: An Introduction.* 2d. ed. Harlow, England and New York: Longman/John Wiley & Sons, 1994.

Sivard, Ruth Leger. *Women . . . A World Survey.* 2d ed. Washington, D.C.: World Priorities, 1995.

Tata, Robert J., and Ronald R. Schultz. "World Variation in Human Welfare: A New Index of Development Status." *Annals of the Association of American Geographers* 78, no. 4 (1988):580–593.

Thomas, Alan, et al. *Third World Atlas.* 2nd ed. Bristol, PA.: Taylor and Francis, 1994

UNICEF. *The State of the World's Children.* New York: United Nations, Annual.

United Nations. *Women in a Changing Global Economy: 1994 World Survey on the Role of Women in Development.* New York: United Nations, 1995.

United Nations. *The World's Women 1970–1990: Trends and Statistics.* Social Statistics and Indicators, Series K, no. 8. New York: United Nations, 1991.

United Nations. *The World's Women 1995: Trends and Statistics.* Social Statistics and Indicators, Series K, no. 12. New York: United Nations, 1995.

United Nations Development Programme. *Human Development Report.* New York: Oxford University Press, Annual.

Unwin, Tim, ed. *Atlas of World Development.* New York: John Wiley & Sons, Inc., 1995.

World Bank. *World Development Report.* New York: Oxford University Press. Annual.

World Development 17, no. 7 (July 1989). Special issue: *Beyond Survival: Expanding Income-Earning Opportunities for Women in Developing Countries.*

LANDSCAPES OF FUNCTIONAL ORGANIZATION

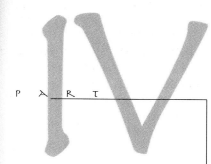

PART IV

The skyline of Seattle, Washington.

The more advanced a region's space economy, the more highly developed and integrated are its organizational controls. Subsistence economies of hunting, gathering, and shifting agriculture were locally based, self-sufficient, small-group ways of life. As the preceding chapters make clear, they have nearly everywhere been replaced by more advanced and spatially integrated economies based on secondary, tertiary, and "postindustrial" activities. These newer forms of economic orientation require more concentrated and structured systems of production and a more formal organization of society and territory than any previously experienced. They have inevitably given rise to distinctive urban and political landscapes.

Urbanization has always accompanied economic advancement. Manufacturing and trade imply concentrations of workers, managers, merchants, and supporting populations and institutions. They require a functional organization and control of space far more pervasive and extensive than any guiding the subsistence economies that went before. Chapter 11, the first of the two chapters of this section of our study of human geography, looks at the systems of cities, which contain an increasing proportion of the population of all culture realms and in which are concentrated a growing share of the world's productive activities.

Cities, we shall see, are functional entities producing and exchanging goods, performing services, and administering the space economy for the larger society of which they are the operational focus. The functions they house and the kind of economy that has shaped them help determine the size and spatial patterns of the urban systems that have developed in different parts of the world. Within those systems, each city is a separate landscape entity, distinct from surrounding nonurban areas. Internally, each displays a complex of land use arrangements and social geographies, in part unique to it but in part, as well, influenced by the cultural, economic, and ideological setting that it reflects. Both city systems and internal city structures are fundamental features of spatial organization and of cultural differentiation.

Advancement in cultural and economic development beyond the local and the self-sufficient also implies hierarchies of formal territorial control and administration. Structured political landscapes have been created as the accompaniment of the economic development and urbanization of societies and regions. In Chapter 12, the second of the chapters of this section, we examine the variety of forms and levels—from local to international—of the political control of space as another key element in the contemporary human geographic mosaic.

IV

URBAN SYSTEMS AND URBAN STRUCTURES

The Urbanizing Century 373
Merging Metropolises 373
Settlement Roots 377
The Nature of Cities 379
Some Definitions 380
The Location of Urban Settlements 380
The Functions of Cities 381
The Economic Base 381
Base Ratios 382
Systems of Urban Settlements 383
The Urban Hierarchy 383
Rank-Size and Primacy 384
Urban Influence Zones 385
Central Places 385
Inside the City 388
The Competitive Bidding for Land 388
Land Values and Population Density 390
Models of Urban Land Use Structure 392
Social Areas of Cities 393
Social Status 393
Family Status 394
Ethnicity 394
Institutional Controls 396
Suburbanization in the United States 396
Central City Change 398
World Urban Diversity 400
The Anglo American City 400
The West European City 403
The East European City 404
Cities in the Developing World 406
The Asian City and African City 408
The Latin American City 410
SUMMARY 411
KEY WORDS 412
FOR REVIEW 412
SELECTED REFERENCES 412

*Downtown Auckland, New Zealand,
at the waterfront.*

In the 1930s Mexico City was described as perhaps the handsomest city in North America and the most exotic capital city of the hemisphere, essentially unchanged over the years and timeless in its atmosphere. It was praised as beautifully laid out, with wide streets and avenues, still the "city of palaces" that Baron von Humboldt called it in the 19th century. The 70-meter-wide (200-ft.) Paseo de la Reforma, often noted as "one of the most beautiful avenues in the world," was shaded by a double row of trees and lined with luxurious residences.

By the 1950s, with a population of over 2 million and an area of 52 square kilometers (20 sq. mi.), Mexico City had changed. The old, rich families who formerly resided along the Paseo de la Reforma had fled from the noise and crowding. Their "palaces" were being replaced by tall blocks of apartments and hotels. Industry was expanding and multiplying, tens of thousands of peasants were flocking in from the countryside every year. By the mid-1990s, with a population above 20 million and its area at over 1350 square kilometers (522 sq. mi.), metropolitan Mexico City was adding over a half-million immigrants each year as well as growing prodigiously by its own 3% natural increase.

The toll exacted by that growth is heavy. Each year the city pours more than 5 million tons of pollutants into its air. Some 80% comes from unburned gas leaked from the residents' stoves and heaters and from the exhausts of their estimated 4 million motor vehicles; the rest is produced by nearly 35,000 industrial plants. More than 5 million people citywide have no access to tap water; in many squatter neighborhoods less than half do. Some 4 million residents have no access to the sewage system. About one-third of all families—and they average five people—live in but a single room, and that room generally is in a hovel in one of the largest slums in the world.

The changes in Mexico City since the 1930s have been profound (Figure 11.1). Already one of the world's most populous metropolitan areas, Greater Mexico City is expected to swell further to 25 million or more by the year 2000. And Mexico City is only a worst case scenario of an urban explosion that sees an increasing proportion of the world's population housed within a growing number of immense cities.

FIGURE 11.1   Surrounded by mountains, Mexico City endures frequent atmospheric inversions—most commonly on winter mornings—when cold air is trapped beneath a layer of warm air. The pollutants surging into the air each day are therefore unable to rise and drift away from the city. The result is suggested in this early morning, late November photo—frequent deadly smog as visibility drops to less than 500 meters and citizens are afflicted with respiratory problems and eye irritation.

The Urbanizing Century

Figure 11.2 gives evidence that this has been the century of cities. Some 300 metropolitan areas had a population in excess of 1 million people in 1996; at the beginning of the century there were only 13. At least 19 metropolises (Beijing, Bombay, Buenos Aires, Cairo, Calcutta, Delhi, Jakarta, Los Angeles, Manila, Mexico City, Moscow, New York, Osaka–Kobe, Rio de Janeiro, São Paulo, Seoul, Shanghai, Tehran, and Tokyo) had populations of over 10 million people (Figure 11.3). In 1900, none was of that size. Of course, as we saw in Chapter 4, it follows that since the world's population has greatly increased, so too would the urban component increase. But the fact remains that urbanization and metropolitanization have increased more rapidly than the growth of total population. The amount of urban growth differs from continent to continent and from country to country (Figure 11.4), but nearly all countries have two things in common: the proportion of their people living in cities is rising, and the cities themselves are large and growing.

Table 11.1 shows world urban population by region. Note that the most industrialized parts of the world, North America, Europe, and East Asia (including Japan, Taiwan, South Korea, and Hong Kong) are the most urbanized—that is, have the highest percentages of their populations living in cities—while Africa and most of Asia have the lowest proportions of urban population (Figure 4.26). What is evident is that the industrialization process has also been one of urbanization. As the world, especially the developing world, continues to industrialize, we can expect further large increases of urban population. With urban growth at 3.8% a year, the World Bank projects that by 2020, 3.6 billion people will inhabit urban areas while about 3 billion will remain in rural districts. It is interesting to note in Table 11.1 that even though China, Southeast Asia (Vietnam, Indonesia, etc.), and South Asia (India, Pakistan, and Bangladesh) have relatively low proportions of people in cities, the absolute number of people in urban areas is extraordinarily high. Given the huge populations in Asia, and the relatively heavy emphasis on agriculture (excluding Japan and Korea), it sometimes escapes us that many very large cities exist throughout parts of the world where most people are still subsistence farmers.

Merging Metropolises

When separate major metropolitan complexes expand along the superior transportation facilities connecting them, they may eventually meet, bind together at their outer margins, and create the extensive metropolitan regions or **conurbations** suggested on Figure 11.3. Where this increasingly common pattern has emerged, the urban landscape can no longer be described in simple terms. No longer is there a single city with a single downtown area set off by open countryside from any other urban unit in its vicinity. Rather, we must now recognize extensive regions of continuous urbanization made up of multiple centers that have come together at their edges.

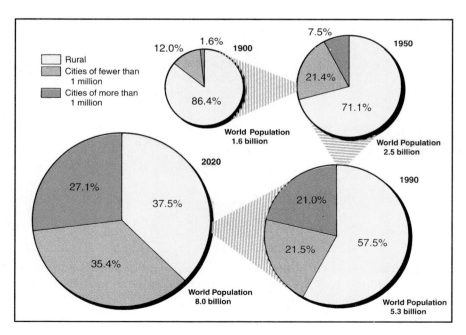

FIGURE 11.2   Trends of world urbanization.

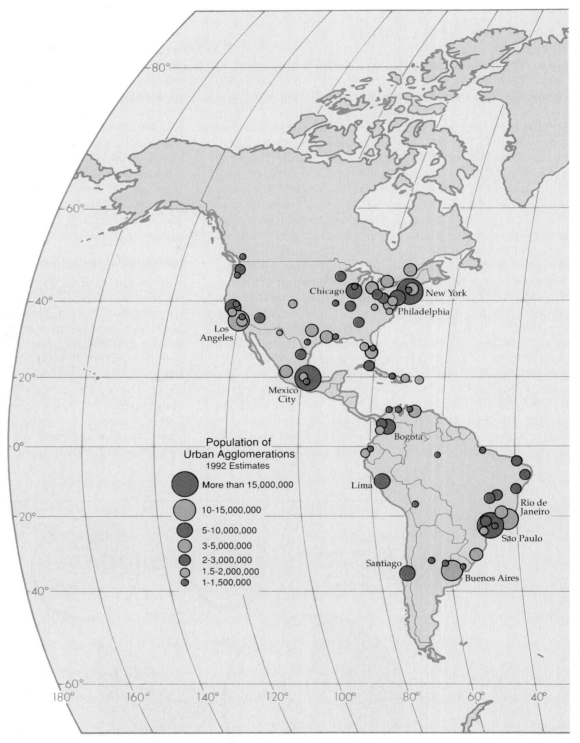

FIGURE 11.3 **World metropolitan areas of 1 million or more.** Massive urbanized districts are no longer characteristic only of the industrialized, developed nations. They are now found on every continent, in all latitudes, as part of most economies and societies. Not all cities in congested areas are shown.

Population of
Urban Agglomerations
1992 Estimates

More than 15,000,000

10-15,000,000

5-10,000,000

3-5,000,000

2-3,000,000

1.5-2,000,000

1-1,500,000

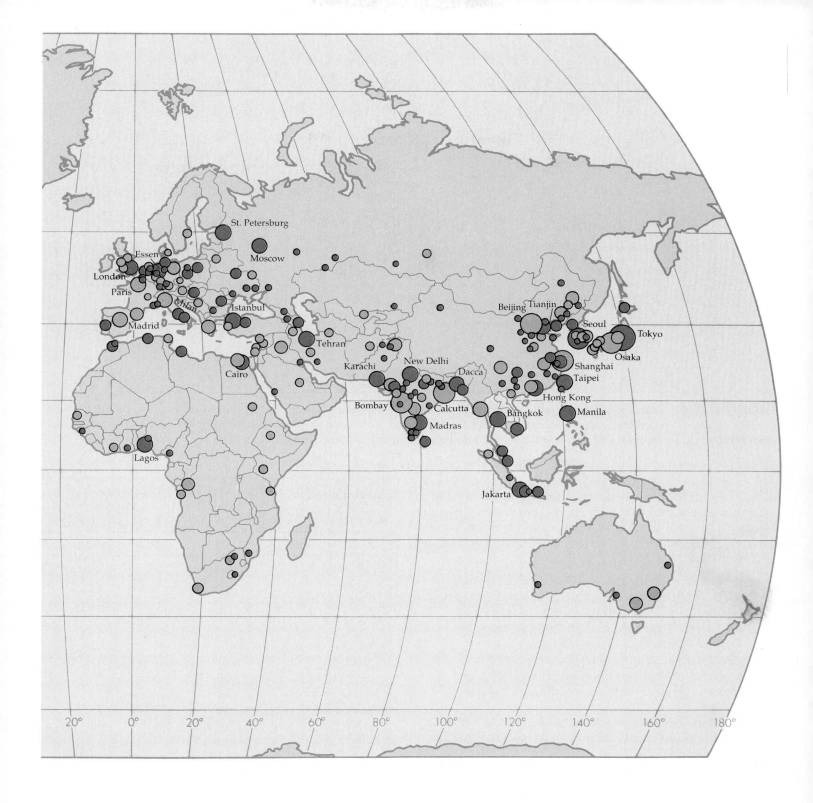

St. Petersburg
Essen
London
Paris
Milan
Madrid
Istanbul
Tehran
Cairo
Moscow
Karachi
New Delhi
Dacca
Bombay
Calcutta
Bangkok
Madras
Lagos
Jakarta
Beijing
Tianjin
Seoul
Tokyo
Osaka
Shanghai
Taipei
Hong Kong
Manila

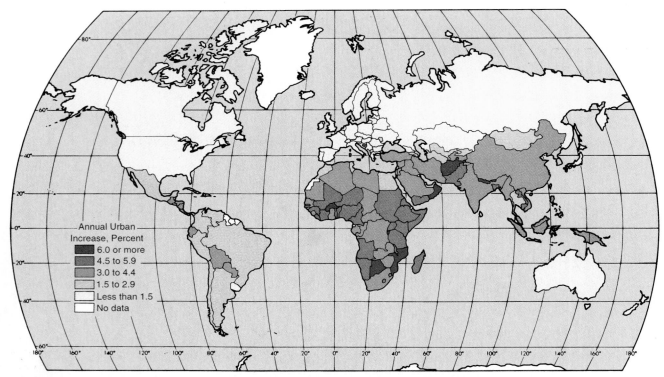

FIGURE 11.4   Annual urban population growth rates, 1995–2000. In general, developing countries show the highest percent increases in their urban populations, and the already highly urbanized and industrialized countries have the lowest—less than 1% per annum in most of Europe. UN data are based on recent years' trends projected to 2000.

Megalopolis, already encountered in Chapter 9 (page 312), is the major conurbation of North America, a nearly continuous urban string that stretches from north of Boston (southern Maine) to south of Washington, D.C. (southern Virginia). Other North American present or emerging conurbations include

- the southern Great Lakes region stretching from north of Milwaukee through Chicago and eastward to Detroit, Cleveland, and Pittsburgh;
- the Coastal California zone of San Francisco–Los Angeles–San Diego–Tijuana, Mexico;
- the Canadian "core region" conurbation from Montreal to Windsor, opposite Detroit, Michigan, where it connects with the southern Great Lakes region;
- Vancouver–Willamette strip ("Cascadia") in the West, and the Gulf Coast and the Coastal Florida zones in the Southeast (Figure 11.5).

Outside North America, examples of conurbations are numerous and growing, still primarily in the most industrialized European and East Asian (Japanese) districts, but forming as well in the other major world urban regions. Prominent Eurasian megalopolises include

- the north of England, including Liverpool, Manchester, Leeds, Sheffield, and the several dozen industrial towns in between;
- the London region with its many cities and suburbs;

TABLE 11.1	Estimated Urban Share of Total Population, 1950 and 1990, with Projections to 2000		
REGION	1950	1990	2000
North America	64%	74%	78%
Europe	56	75	79
Russia	45	74	79
East Asia (except China)	43	73	79
China	12	23	50
Southeast Asia	—	27	38
South Asia	15	26	39
Latin America	41	69	77
Africa	15	31	45
Oceania	61	70	74
World	29	47	55

Sources: Lester R. Brown and Jodi L. Jacobson, *The Future of Urbanization.* Worldwatch Paper 77 (Washington, D.C.: Worldwatch Institute, 1987), p. 8; Population Reference Bureau; and other estimates.

- the Ruhr of Germany, with a dozen large connected cities such as Essen and Düsseldorf;
- the Tokyo–Yokohama–Kawasaki region of Japan.

Were it not for the mountains between Tokyo and Nagoya, and between Nagoya and Osaka–Kobe–Kyoto, there is no doubt that these huge metropolises would by now be one

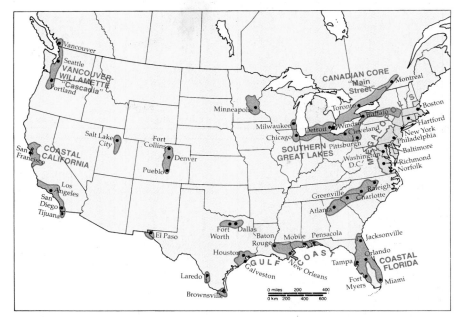

FIGURE 11.5 **Megalopolis and developing North American conurbations.** The northeastern U.S. Boston-to-Norfolk urban corridor comprises the original and largest *Megalopolis* and contains the economic, political, and administrative core of the United States. A Canadian counterpart core region—dubbed *Main Street* by the geographer Maurice Yeates—connects with other U.S. conurbations through Buffalo, New York, and Detroit, Michigan. For some of their extent, conurbations fulfill their classic definition of continuous built-up urban areas. In other portions, they are more statistical than landscape entities, marked by counties that qualify as "urban" or "metropolitan" even though land uses may appear dominantly rural.

Settlement Roots

The major cities of today had humbler origins, their roots lying in the clustered dwellings which everywhere have been the rule of human settlement. People are gregarious and cooperative. Even Stone Age hunters and gatherers lived and worked in groups, not as single individuals or isolated families. Primitive cultures are communal for protection, cooperative effort, sharing of tasks by age and sex, and for more subtle psychological and social reasons. Communal dwelling became the near-universal rule with the advent of sedentary agriculture wherever it developed, and the village became the norm of human society.

In most of the world still, most rural people live in nucleated settlements, that is, in villages or hamlets, rather than in dispersed dwellings or isolated farmsteads. Only in North America, parts of northern and western Europe, and in Australia and New Zealand do rural folk tend to live apart, with houses and farm buildings located on land that is individually worked. In those regions, farmsteads tend to be spatially separate one from another, and the farm village is a much less common settlement form. Communal settlements were not, of course, unknown in North America.

giant megalopolitan area. Large metropolises are being created in developing countries as well, as we shall review later in this chapter.

Mormon Utah, Mennonite Manitoba, and other districts of cluster migration (see p. 189) were frequently village-centered, as were such cooperative and utopian communities as Oneida, New York; Amana, Iowa; New Harmony, Indiana; the various Shaker settlements; and others of the 19th century. Elsewhere in the world, villages and hamlets were the settlement norm, though with size and form that varied by region and culture. Intensity of agricultural land use, density of population, complexity and specialization of life and livelihood, and addition of functions other than the purely residential affected the size, distribution, external form, and internal structure of settlements (Figures 11.6 and 11.7).

Rural settlements in developing countries are often considered as expressions of subsistence economic systems in which farming and fishing cultures produce no more than their individual families can consume. That clearly is not always the case. Even in the poorest farm settlements of India or Bangladesh, for example, there is a good deal of trading, buying, and selling of farm goods and family crafts for other needed commodities, and at least some village land is used for other than residential purposes (Figure 11.8). The farm or fishing settlement itself, however, may be nearly self-contained, with little commercial exchange with neighboring villages or between villages and distant cities.

When trade does develop between two or more rural settlements, they begin to take on new physical characteristics as their inhabitants engage in additional types of occupations. The villages lose the purely social and residential

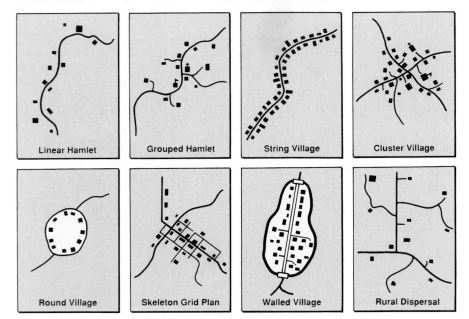

Linear Hamlet Grouped Hamlet String Village Cluster Village

Round Village Skeleton Grid Plan Walled Village Rural Dispersal

FIGURE 11.6   **Basic settlement forms.** The smallest organized rural clusters of houses and nonresidential structures are commonly called *hamlets,* and may contain only 10–15 buildings. *Villages* are larger agglomerations, though not as sizeable or functionally complex as urban *towns.* The distinction between village and town is usually a statistical definition that varies by country.

Redrawn from *Introducing Cultural Geography,* 2d ed., by Joseph E. Spencer and William L. Thomas. Copyright © 1978 John Wiley & Sons, Inc. Used by permission of John Wiley & Sons, Inc.

(a)

(b)

(c)

FIGURE 11.7   Rural settlements in largely subsistence economies vary from the rather small populations characteristic of compact African villages, such as the Zulu village, or kraal, in South Africa shown in (*a*), to more dispersed and populous settlements, such as the Nepalese high pasture summer village of Konar seen in (*b*), to the very large, densely populated Indian rural communities like that seen in (*c*). (*b*) Courtesy of Colin Thorn.

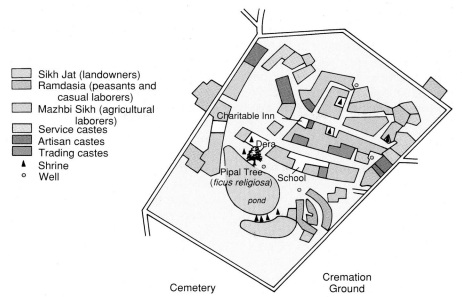

Sikh Jat (landowners)
Ramdasia (peasants and casual laborers)
Mazhbi Sikh (agricultural laborers)
Service castes
Artisan castes
Trading castes
▲ **Shrine**
○ **Well**

Charitable Inn

Dera

Pipal Tree
(*ficus religiosa*)

School

pond

Cemetery

Cremation
Ground

FIGURE 11.8   A village in the Punjab region, India. In the 1960s, Kunran village had some 1000 inhabitants of several different occupational castes. Most numerous were the Sikh Jat (landowners: 76 households), Ramdasia (peasants and casual laborers: 27 households), and Mazhbi Sikh (agricultural laborers: 12 households). Other castes (and occupations) included Tarkhan (carpenter), Bazigar (acrobat), Jhiwar (water carrier), Sunar (goldsmith), Nai (barber), and Bania (shopkeeper). The trades, crafts, and services they (and others) pursued created a more complex land use pattern than is implied by the generalized village forms depicted on Figure 11.6.

Redrawn with permission from Jan O. M. Broek and John M. Webb, *A Geography of Mankind,* copyright © 1968 McGraw-Hill, Inc.

character of subsistence agricultural settlements and assume urban features. There is a tendency for the houses to cluster along the main road or roads, creating a linear, cross, or starlike pattern. No longer are the settlements nearly completely self-contained; they become part of a system of communities. The beginnings of urbanization are seen in the types of buildings that are erected and in the heightened importance of the main streets and of the roads leading to other settlements. The location of villages relative to one another becomes significant as the once self-sufficient rural settlements become towns and cities engaged in urban activities and interchange.

The Nature of Cities

Cities are among the oldest marks of civilization. Dating from 4000 to 6000 years or more ago, they originated in—or diffused from—the culture hearths that first developed sedentary agriculture (Table 2.1, page 48). They are as well among the newest experiences of a growing share of the world's population, as Table 11.1 suggests. Whether ancient or modern, all cities show recurring themes and regularities appropriate to their time and place of existence.

First, all of them perform functions—have an economic base—generating the income necessary to support themselves and their contained population. Second, none exists in a vacuum; each is part of a larger society and economy with which it has essential reciprocal connections. That

is, each is a unit in a system of cities and a focus for a surrounding nonurban area. Third, each urban unit has a more or less orderly internal arrangement of land uses, social groups, and economic functions. These arrangements may be partially planned and controlled and partially determined by individual decisions and market forces. Finally, all cities, large or small, ancient or modern, have experienced problems of land use, social conflict, and environmental concern. Yet cities, though flawed, remain the capstone of our cultures, the organizing focuses of modern societies and economies, the magnet of people everywhere.

Whatever their size, age, or location, urban settlements exist for the efficient performance of functions required by the society that creates them. They reflect the saving of time, energy, and money that the agglomeration of people and activities implies. The more accessible the producer to the consumer, the worker to the work place, the citizen to the town hall, the worshiper to the church, or the lawyer or doctor to the client, the more efficient is the performance of their separate activities, and the more effective is the integration of urban functions.

Urban areas may provide all or some of the following types of functions: retailing, wholesaling, manufacturing, professional and personal services, entertainment, business and political administration, military defense, educational and religious functions, and transportation and communication services. Because all urban functions and people cannot be located at a single point, cities themselves must take up space, and land uses and populations must have room within them. Because interconnection is essential, the nature of the transportation system will have an enormous bearing on the total number of services that can be performed and the efficiency with which they can be carried out. The totality of people and functions of a city constitutes a distinctive cultural landscape whose similarities and differences from place to place are the subjects for urban geographic analysis.

Some Definitions

Urban units are not of a single type, structure, or size. What they have in common is that they are nucleated, nonagricultural settlements. At one end of the size scale, urban areas are hamlets or small towns with at most a single short main street of shops; at the opposite end, they are complex multifunctional metropolitan areas or supercities (Figure 11.9). The word *urban* is often used to describe such places as a town, city, suburb, and metropolitan area, but it is a general term, not used to specify a particular type or size of settlement. Although the terms designating the different types of urban settlement, such as *city*, are employed in common speech, not everyone uses them in the same way. What is recognized as a city by a resident of rural Vermont or West Virginia might not at all be afforded that name and status by an inhabitant of California or New Jersey. It is necessary in this chapter to agree on the meanings of terms commonly employed but varyingly interpreted.

The words **city** and **town** denote nucleated settlements, multifunctional in character, including an established central business district and both residential and nonresidential land uses. Towns have smaller size and less functional complexity than cities, but still have a nuclear business concentration. **Suburb** implies a subsidiary area, a functionally specialized segment of a larger urban complex. It may be dominantly or exclusively residential, industrial, or commercial, but by the specialization of its land uses and functions, a suburb is not self-sufficient. It is part of—and correlated with—an urbanized area outside its boundaries. Suburbs can, however, be independent political entities. For large cities having many suburbs, it is common to call that part of the urban area contained within the official boundaries of the main city around which the suburbs have been built the **central city.**

Some or all of these urban types may be associated into larger landscape units. The **urbanized area** refers to a continuously built-up landscape defined by building and population densities with no reference to political boundaries. It may be viewed as the *physical city* and may contain a central city and many contiguous cities, towns, suburbs, and other urban tracts. A **metropolitan area,** on the other hand, refers to a large-scale *functional* entity, perhaps containing several urbanized areas, discontinuously built-up but nonetheless operating as an integrated economic whole. Figure 11.10 shows these areas in a hypothetical American county.

The Location of Urban Settlements

Urban centers are functionally connected to other cities and to rural areas. In fact, the reason for the existence of an urban unit is not only to provide services for itself, but for others outside of it. The urban center is a consumer of food, a processor of materials, and an accumulator and dispenser of goods and services. But it must depend on outside areas for its essential supplies and as a market for its products and activities.

In order to adequately perform the tasks that support it and to add new functions as demanded by the larger economy, the city must be efficiently located. That efficiency may be marked by centrality to the area served. It may derive from the physical characteristics of its site. Or placement may be related to the resources, productive regions, and transportation network of the country, so that the effective performance of a wide array of activities is possible.

(a)

(b)

FIGURE 11.9　The differences in size, density, and land use complexity between New York City and a small U.S. town are immediately apparent. Clearly, one is a city, one is a town, but both are *urban*.

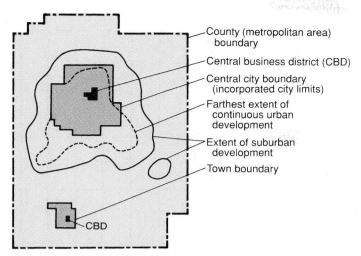

FIGURE 11.10   **A hypothetical spatial arrangement of urban units within a metropolitan area.** Sometimes official limits of the central city are very extensive and contain areas commonly considered suburban or even rural. Older eastern U.S. cities more often have restricted limits and contain only part of the high-density land uses associated with them.

In discussing urban settlement location, geographers usually mention the significance of site and situation, concepts already introduced in Chapter 1 (see p. 10 and Figures 1.6 and 1.7). You will recall that *site* refers to the exact terrain features associated with the city, as well as—less usefully—to its absolute (globe grid) location. Classifications of cities according to site characteristics have been proposed, recognizing special placement circumstances: *break-of-bulk* locations, for example, such as river crossing points where cargos and people must interrupt a journey; *head-of-navigation* or *bay head* locations where the limits of water transportation are reached; or *railhead* locations where the railroad ended. In Europe, security and defense—island locations or elevations—were considerations in earlier settlement locations and figure in site classifications. Waterpower sites of earlier stages and coalfield sites of later phases of the Industrial Revolution were noted in Chapters 8 and 9 and represent a union of environmental and cultural-economic considerations.

If site suggests absolute location, *situation* indicates relative location that places a settlement in relation to the physical and cultural characteristics of surrounding areas. Very often it is important to know what kinds of possibilities and activities exist in the area near a settlement, such as the distribution of raw materials, market areas, agricultural regions, mountains, and oceans. Although in many ways more important than site in understanding the functions and growth potentials of cities, situation is more nearly unique to each settlement and does not lend itself to easy generalization.

The site or situation that originally gave rise to an urban unit may not remain the essential ingredient for its growth and development for very long. Agglomerations originally successful for whatever reason may by their success attract people and activities totally unrelated to the initial localizing forces (Figure 11.11). By a form of "circular and cumulative causation" (see p. 336), a successful urban unit may acquire new populations and functions attracted by the already existing markets, labor force, and urban facilities.

The Functions of Cities

The key concept is *function*—what cities actually do within the larger society and economy that established them. No city stands alone. Each is linked to other towns and cities in an interconnected city system; each provides services and products for its surrounding tributary region—its *hinterland* or trade area. Those linkages reflect complementarity and the processes of spatial interaction that we explored in Chapter 3; they are rooted in the different functions performed by different units within the urban system. However, not all of the activities carried on within a city are intended to connect that city with the outside world. Some are necessary simply to support the city itself. Together, these two levels of activity make up the **economic base** of an urban settlement.

The Economic Base
Part of the employed population of an urban unit is engaged either in the production of goods or the performance of services for areas and people outside the city itself. They are workers engaged in "export" activities, whose efforts result in money flowing into the community. Collectively, they constitute the **basic sector** of the city's total economic structure. Other workers support themselves by producing goods or services for residents of the urban unit itself. Their efforts, necessary to the well-being and the successful operation of the settlement, do not generate new money for it but comprise a **service** or **nonbasic sector** of its economy. These people are responsible for the internal functioning of the urban unit. They are crucial to the continued operation

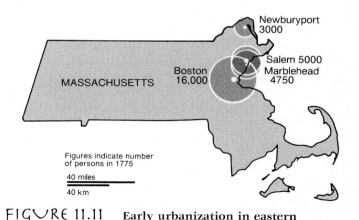

FIGURE 11.11   **Early urbanization in eastern Massachusetts.** Maritime activities, situational advantages, port characteristics, and diversity of functions helped localize individual settlements and led to the early rise of urban agglomerations in eastern Massachusetts. Their development and success encouraged continued urbanization despite changing economic conditions.

of its stores, professional offices, city government, local transit, and school systems.

The total economic structure of an urban area equals the sum of its basic and nonbasic activities. In actuality, it is the rare urbanite who can be classified as belonging entirely to one sector or another. Some part of the work of most people involves financial interaction with residents of other areas. Doctors, for example, may have mainly local patients and thus are members of the nonbasic sector, but the moment they provide a service to someone from outside the community, they bring new money into the city and become part of the basic sector.

Variations in basic employment structure among urban units characterize the specific functional role played by individual cities. Most centers perform many export functions, and the larger the urban unit, the more multifunctional it becomes. Nonetheless, even in cities with a diversified economic base, one or a very small number of export activities tends to dominate the structure of the community and to identify its operational purpose within a system of cities.

Such functional specialization permits the classification of cities into categories: manufacturing, retailing, wholesaling, transportation, government, and so on. Such specialization may also evoke images when the city is named: Detroit, Michigan, or Tokyo, Japan, as manufacturing centers; Tulsa, Oklahoma, for oil production; Nice, France, as a resort; Ottawa, Canada, in government; and so on. Certain large regional, national, or world capitals—as befits major multifunctional concentrations—call up a whole series of mental associations, such as New York with banking, the stock exchange, entertainment, the fashion industry, port activities, and others.

Base Ratios

Assuming it were possible to divide with complete accuracy the employed population of a city into totally separate basic and service (nonbasic) components, a ratio between the two employment groups could be established. With exception for some high-income communities, this *basic/nonbasic ratio* is roughly similar for urban units of similar size irrespective of their functional specializations. Further, as a city increases in size, the number of nonbasic personnel grows faster than the number of new basic workers. Thus, in centers with a population of 1 million, the ratio is about two nonbasic workers for every basic worker. The addition of ten new basic employees implies the expansion of the labor force by 30 (10 basic, 20 nonbasic) and an increase in total population equal to the added workers plus their dependents. A **multiplier effect** thus exists, associated with economic growth. The term implies the addition of nonbasic workers and dependents to a city's total employment and population as a supplement to new basic employment. The size of the multiplier effect is determined by the community's basic/nonbasic ratio (Figure 11.12).

The changing numerical relationships shown in Figure 11.12 are understandable when we consider how settlements add functions and grow in population. A new industry selling services to other communities requires new workers who thus increase the basic workforce. These new employees in turn demand certain goods and services, such as clothing, food, and medical assistance, which are provided locally. Those who perform such services must themselves have services available to them. For example, a grocery clerk must also buy groceries. The more nonbasic workers a city has, the more nonbasic workers are needed to support them, and the application of the multiplier effect becomes obvious.

We have also seen that the growth of urban centers may be self-generating—"circular and cumulative" in a way related not to the development of basic industry but to the attraction of what would be classified as *service* activity. Banking and legal services, a sizeable market, a diversified labor force, extensive public services, and the like may generate additions to the labor force not basic by definition.

In much the same way as settlements grow in size and complexity, so do they decline. When the demand for the goods and services of an urban unit falls, obviously there is a need for fewer workers, and both the basic and the services components of a settlement system are affected. There is, however, a resistance to decline that impedes the process and delays its impact. That is, cities can grow rapidly as migrants respond quickly to the need for more workers, but under conditions of decline those that have developed roots in the community are hesitant to leave or may be financially unable to move to another locale. Figure 11.13 shows that in recent years urban areas in the South and West of the United States have been growing, while decline is evident in the Northeast and the North Central regions.

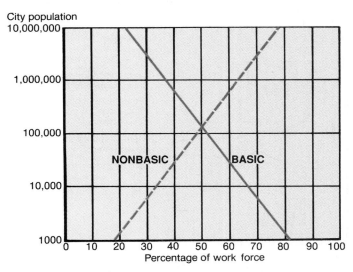

City population

Percentage of work force

FIGURE 11.12 **A generalized representation of the proportion of the work force engaged in basic and nonbasic activities by city size.** As settlements become larger, a greater proportion of the work force is employed in nonbasic activities. Larger centers are therefore more self-contained.

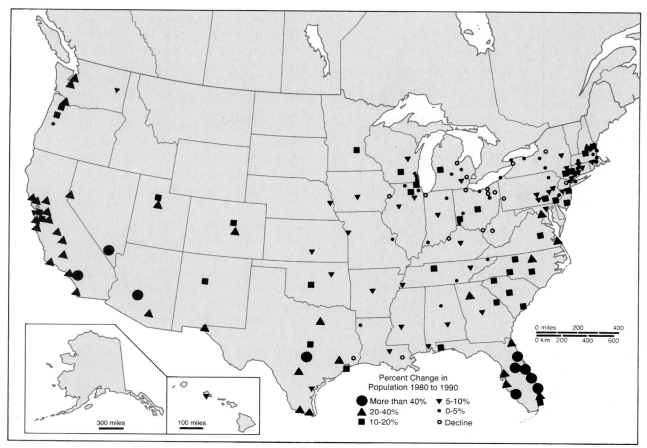

FIGURE 11.13 The pattern of metropolitan growth and decline in the United States, 1980–1990.

Systems of Urban Settlements

The functional structure of a settlement affects its current size and growth prospects. At the same time, its functions are a reflection of that community's location and its relationships with other urban units in the larger city system of which all are a part. A simple but revealing threefold functional classification of urban settlements recognizes them as either transportation centers, special-function cities, or central places. Each class has its own characteristic spatial arrangement; together, the three classes help explain the distributional pattern and the size and functional hierarchies of the entire city system.

The spatial pattern of *transportation centers* is that of alignment—along seacoasts, major and minor rivers, canals, or railways. Routes of communication form the orienting axes along which cities developed and on which at least their initial functional success depended (Figure 11.14). *Special-function cities* are those engaged in mining, manufacturing, or other activities the localization of which is related to raw material occurrence, agglomeration economies, or the circular and cumulative attractions of constantly growing market and labor concentrations. Special-function cities show a pattern of urban clustering—as the mining and manufacturing cities of the Ruhr district, the Midlands of Eng-

land, or the Donets Basin, for example. More familiarly, they appear in the form of the multifunctional metropolitan concentrations recognized by the Metropolitan Statistical Areas of the United States, the Census Metropolitan Areas of Canada, or in such massive urbanized complexes as metropolitan Tokyo, Moscow, Paris, London, Buenos Aires, and others worldwide.

A common property of all settlements is centrality, no matter what their recognized functional specializations. Every urban unit provides goods and services for a surrounding area tributary to it. For many, including mining or major manufacturing centers, service to tributary areas is only a very minor part of their economic base. Some settlements, however, have that rural service and trade function as their dominant role, and these make up the third simplified category of cities: *central places.*

The Urban Hierarchy

Perhaps the most effective way to recognize how systems of cities are organized is to consider the **urban hierarchy,** a ranking of cities based on their size and functional complexity. One can measure the numbers and kinds of functions each city or metropolitan area performs. The hierarchy is then like a pyramid; a few large and complex cities are at the top and many smaller, simpler ones are at the bottom. There

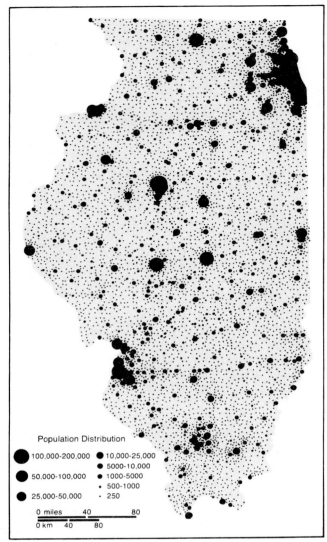

FIGURE 11.14 **Urban alignments in Illinois.**
Railroads preceded settlement in much of the North American continental interior, and urban centers were developed—frequently by the railroad companies themselves—as collecting and distributing points expected to grow as the farm populations increased. Located at constant 8- to 10-kilometer (5- to 6-mile) intervals in Illinois, the rail towns were the focal points of an expanding commercial agriculture. The linearity of the town pattern in 1940, at the peak of railroad influence, unmistakably marks the rail routes. Also evident are such special-function clusterings as the Chicago and St. Louis metropolitan districts and the mining towns of Southern Illinois.

Population Distribution

● 100,000–200,000	● 10,000–25,000
● 50,000–100,000	• 5000–10,000
	• 1000–5000
● 25,000–50,000	· 500–1000
	· 250

0 miles 40 80
0 km 40 80

are always more smaller cities than larger ones. One can envisage, for example, a six-level hierarchy where the complexity of urban centers increases as one rises in the pyramid.

When a spatial dimension is added to the hierarchy as in Figure 11.15, it becomes clear that a spatial system of metropolitan centers, large cities, small cities, and towns exists. Goods, services, communications, and people flow up and down the hierarchy. The few high-level metropolitan areas provide specialized functions for large regions while the smaller cities serve smaller districts. Note that the separate centers interact with the area around them, but since cities of the same level provide roughly the same services, those of the same size tend not to serve each other unless they provide some very specialized activity, such as housing a political capital of a region or a major university. Thus, the settlements of a given level in the hierarchy are not independent but interrelated with communities of other levels in that hierarchy. Together, all centers at all levels in the hierarchy constitute an urban system.

Rank-Size and Primacy

The observation that there are many more small than large cities within an urban system ("the larger the fewer") is a statement about hierarchy. For many large countries of great regional diversity and, usually but not always, advanced economy, the city size hierarchy is summarized by the **rank-size rule.** It tells us that the nth largest city of a national system of cities will be $1/n$ the size of the largest city. That is, the second largest settlement will be 1/2 the size of the largest, the 10th biggest will be 1/10 the size of the first-ranked city.

The rank-size ordering may describe the urban-size patterning in countries where urban history is long and urbanizing forces are many and widely distributed. Although no national city system exactly meets the requirements of the rank-size rule, that of the United States closely approximates it. It is less applicable to countries where the urban size hierarchy has been distorted through concentration of functions in a single, paramount center.

In some countries the urban system is dominated by a **primate city,** one that is far more than twice the size of the second-ranked city. In fact, there may be no obvious "second city" at all, for a characteristic of a primate city hierarchy is one very large city, few or no intermediate-sized cities, and many subordinate smaller settlements. For example, Seoul contains over one-quarter of the total population and 35% of the urban population of South Korea, and Luanda has nearly two-thirds of Angola's urban folk. The capital cities of many developing countries display that kind of overwhelming primacy. In part, their primate city pattern is a heritage of their colonial past, when economic development, colonial administration, and transportation and trade activities were concentrated at a single point (Figure 11.16). In other instances—Egypt (Cairo) or Mexico (Mexico City), for example—development and population growth have tended to concentrate disproportionately in a capital city whose very size attracts further development and growth. Many European countries—Austria, the United Kingdom, and France are familiar examples—also show a primate structure, often ascribed to the former concentration of economic and political power around the royal court in a capital city that was, perhaps, also the administrative and trade center of a larger colonial empire.

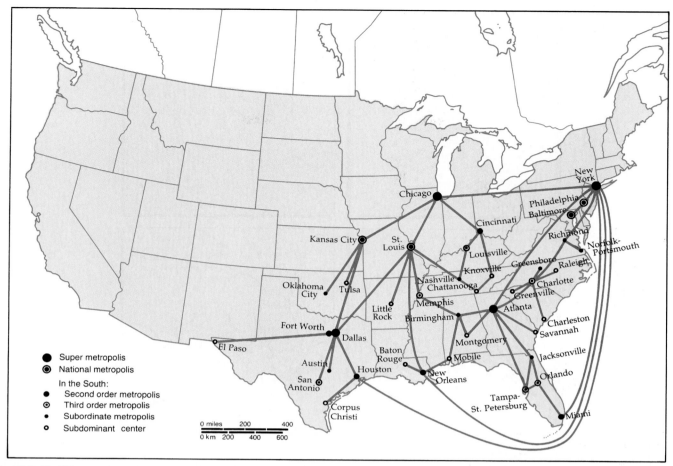

FIGURE 11.15   **Hierarchical relationships among southern U.S. cities.**

Urban Influence Zones

Whatever its position in its particular urban hierarchy, every urban settlement exerts an influence on its immediately surrounding area. A small city may influence a local region of some 65 square kilometers (25 sq. mi.) if, for example, its newspaper is delivered to that district. Beyond that area, another city may be the dominant influence. **Urban influence zones** are the areas outside of a city that are still affected by it. As the distance away from a community increases, its influence on the surrounding countryside decreases (recall the idea of distance decay discussed in Chapter 3). The sphere of influence of an urban unit is usually proportional to its size.

A large city located at a distance away from the small city may influence that and other small cities through its banking services, its TV stations, and its large shopping malls. Consequently, influence zones are very much like the market areas of central place theory. There is an overlapping hierarchical arrangement, and the influence of the largest cities is felt over the widest areas (Figure 11.15).

Intricate relationships and hierarchies are common. Consider Grand Forks, North Dakota, which for local market purposes dominates the rural area immediately surrounding it. However, Grand Forks is influenced by political decisions made in the state capital, Bismark. For a variety of cultural, commercial, and banking activities, Grand Forks is influenced by Minneapolis. As a center of wheat production, Grand Forks and Minneapolis are subordinate to the grain market in Chicago. Of course, the pervasive agricultural and other political controls exerted from Washington, D.C., on Grand Forks, Minneapolis, and Chicago indicate how large and complex are urban zones of influence.

Central Places

An effective way to appreciate the meaning of influence zones and to grasp how cities and towns are interrelated is to consider urban settlements as central places. A **central place** is an urban focal point for the distribution of economic goods and services to surrounding nonurban populations. It is at the same time an essential link in a system of interdependent urban settlements. Central places show size and spacing regularities not seen where special function or transportation cities predominate. That is, instead of showing patterns of clustering or alignment, central places display a regularity of distribution, with towns of about the same size and performing about the same number and kind of functions located about the same distance from each other.

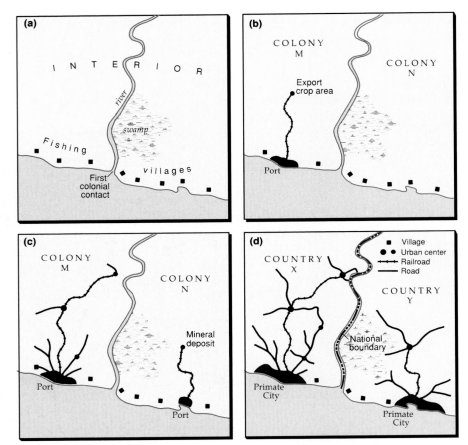

FIGURE 11.16 **Primate city evolution.** At first colonial contact (*a*), settlements are coastal and unconnected with each other. Joining a newly productive hinterland by European-built railroad to a new colonial port (*b*) begins to create a pattern of core–periphery relations and to focus European administration, trade, and settlement at the port. Mineral discoveries and another rail line in a neighboring colony across the river (*c*) mark the beginnings of a new set of core–periphery relationships and of a new multifunctional colonial capital nearby but unconnected by land with its neighbor. With the passage of time and further transport and economic development, two newly-independent nations (*d*) display *primate city* structures in which further economic and population growth flows to the single dominating centers of countries lacking balanced regional transport networks, resource development, and urban structures. Both populations and new functions continue to seek locations in the primate city where their prospects for success are greatest.

In 1933, the German geographer **Walter Christaller** (1893–1969) attempted to explain those observed regularities of size, location, and interdependence of settlements. He recognized that his **central place theory** could best be visualized in rather idealized, simplified circumstances. Christaller assumed that the following propositions were true.

1. Towns that provide the surrounding countryside with such fundamental goods as groceries and clothing would develop on a uniform plain with no topographic barriers, channelization of traffic, or variations in farm productivity.
2. The farm population would be dispersed in an even pattern across that plain.
3. The characteristics of the people would be uniform; that is, they would possess similar tastes, demands, and incomes.

4. Each kind of product or service available to the dispersed population would have its own *threshold*, or minimum number of consumers needed to support its supply. Because such goods as sports cars or fur coats are either expensive or not in great demand, they would have a high threshold, while fewer customers within smaller tributary areas would be needed to support a small grocery store.
5. Consumers would purchase goods and services from the nearest opportunity (store or supplier).

When all of Christaller's assumptions are considered simultaneously, they yield the following results.

1. Since each customer patronizes the nearest center offering the needed goods, the agricultural plain is automatically divided into noncompeting market areas—*complementary regions*—where each individual town (and its merchants) has a sales monopoly.

LANDSCAPES OF FUNCTIONAL ORGANIZATION

2. Those market areas will take the form of a series of hexagons that cover the entire plain. Since the hypothetical plain must be completely subdivided, no area can be unserved and none can have equal service from two competing centers. That means that complementary regions cannot be circular (Figure 11.17). Rather, they take the form of hexagons, the most compact geometric form into which the entire hypothetical surface can be subdivided, leaving no unserved hinterland and no areas unassigned to a closest central place (Figure 11.18).

3. There will be a central place at the center of each of the hexagonal market areas.

4. The largest central places (with the largest market areas) will supply all the goods and services the consumers in that area demand and can afford.

5. The size of the market area of a central place will be proportional to the number of goods and services offered from that place.

6. Contained within or at the edge of the largest market areas are central places serving a smaller population and offering fewer goods and services. As Figure 11.18 indicates, the central place pattern shows a "nesting" of complementary regions in which part or all of multiple lower-order service areas are contained within the market area of a higher-order center.

Christaller reached two important conclusions. First, the system of central places is interdependent. If one town were eliminated, the entire system would have to readjust in its spatial pattern, its offered goods, or both, in order to provide consumers with the needed variety and availability of central place items. The equilibrium of the system of central places must be maintained or reestablished when disturbed. That stability is reflected in the regularity of the central place size hierarchy. Where central places dominate,

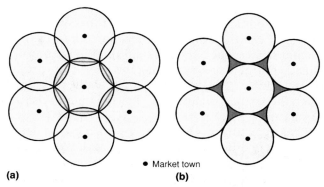

• Market town

(a)   **(b)**

FIGURE 11.17   **The derivation of complementary regions.** (*a*) If the hypothetical region were totally covered by circular complementary regions, areas of overlap would occur. Since Christaller's assumption was that people will only shop at the nearest center, areas of overlap must be divided so that those on each side of the boundary are directed to their nearest service point. (*b*) Circular areas too small to cover the region completely result in impermissible unserved populations.

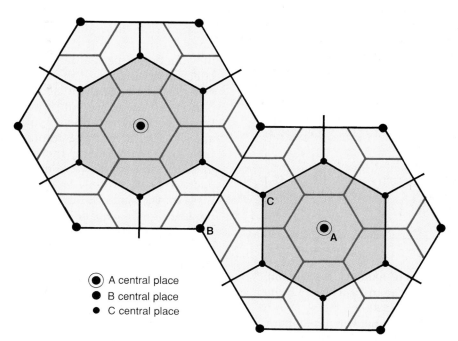

⊙ A central place
● B central place
• C central place

FIGURE 11.18   **Complementary regions and the pattern of central places.** The two *A* central places are the largest on this diagram of one of Christaller's models. The *B* central places offer fewer goods and services for sale and serve only the areas of the intermediate-sized hexagons. The many *C* central places, which are considerably smaller and more closely spaced, serve still smaller market areas. The goods offered in the *C* places are also offered in the *B* and *A* places, but the latter offer considerably more and more specialized goods. Notice that places of the same size are equally spaced.

the pattern is one of a relatively small number of city size classes and distinct size differences separating the classes.

Second, towns at the same size (functional level) in the central place system will be evenly spaced, and larger towns (higher-order places) will be farther apart than smaller ones. This means that there will be many more small than large settlements. In Figure 11.18 the ratio of the number of small towns to towns of the next larger size is 3 to 1. The distinct, steplike series of towns in size classes differentiated by both size and function is called a *hierarchy of central places*. The towns containing many goods and services become regional retailing centers, and the small central places serve just the people immediately in their vicinity. The higher the threshold of a desired product, the farther, on average, the consumer must travel to purchase it.

These conclusions have been shown to be generally valid in widely differing areas of the world. When varying incomes, cultures, landscapes, and transportation systems are taken into account, the results, though altered, hold up rather well. They are particularly applicable to agricultural areas, especially with regard to the size and spacing of cities and towns, as Figure 11.19 suggests. One has to stretch things a bit to see the model operating in highly industrialized areas where cities are more than just retailing centers. However, if we combine a Christaller-type approach with the ideas that help us understand the cluster patterns of special-function cities and the alignments of transportation-based cities, we have a fairly good understanding of the distribution of the majority of cities and towns.

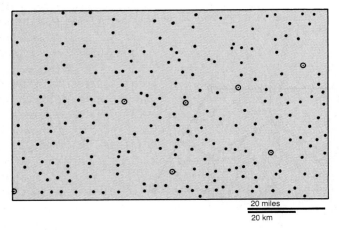

FIGURE 11.19   **The pattern of hamlets, towns, and cities in a portion of Indiana.** The map displays the former urban distribution in an area 132 by 82 kilometers (32 by 51 mi.) just north of Indianapolis. Cities that contained more than 10,000 people are circled. Notice that the pattern was remarkably even and included a number of linear arrangements corresponding to highways and railroads.

Inside the City

The structure, patterns, and spatial interactions of systems of cities make up only half of the story of urban settlements. The other half involves the distinctive cultural landscapes that are the cities themselves. An understanding of the nature of cities is incomplete without a knowledge of their internal characteristics. So far we have explored the location, the size, and the growth and decline tendencies of cities. Now we look into the city itself in order to better understand how its land uses are arranged, how social areas are formed, and how institutional controls such as zoning regulations affect its development. We will begin on familiar ground and focus our discussion primarily on United States cities. Later in this chapter we will review urban land use patterns and social geographies in different world settings.

It is a common observation that recurring patterns of land use arrangements and population densities exist within urban areas. There is a certain sameness to the ways cities are internally organized, especially within one particular culture sphere like Latin America or Western Europe. Older central cities of eastern North America also display land use and social area regularities. The major variables responsible for shaping those North American regularities were: differential accessibility, the transportation technologies available during the periods of urban growth, the operations of a free market in land, and the collective consequences of individual residential, commercial, and industrial locational decisions.

The Competitive Bidding for Land

For its effective operation, the city requires close spatial association of its functions and people. As long as those functions were few and the population small, pedestrian movement and pack-animal haulage were sufficient for the effective integration of the urban community. With the advent of large-scale manufacturing and the accelerated urbanization of the economy during the 19th century, however, functions and populations—and therefore city areas—grew beyond the interaction capabilities of pedestrian movement alone. Increasingly efficient and costly mass transit systems were installed. Even with their introduction, however, only land within walking distance of the mass transit routes or terminals could successfully be incorporated into the expanding urban structure.

Usable—because accessible—land, therefore, was a scarce commodity, and by its scarcity it assumed high market value and demanded intensive, high-density utilization. Because of its limited supply of usable land, the industrial city of the mass transit era (the late 19th and early 20th centuries) was compact, was characterized by high residential and structural densities (Figure 11.20), and showed a sharp break on its margins between urban and nonurban uses. The older central cities of, particularly, the northeastern United States and southeastern Canada were of that vintage and pattern.

FIGURE 11.20 Duplexes, apartment buildings, and row houses like these in the Crown Heights district of Brooklyn were characteristic 19th-century residential responses to the price and scarcity of developable urban land. Where detached single-family dwellings were built, they were usually placed on far smaller lots than became the rule during the middle 20th century.

Within the mass transit city, parcels of land were allocated among alternate potential users on the basis of the relative ability of those users to outbid their competitors for a chosen site. There was, in gross generalization, a continuous open auction in land in which users would locate, relocate, or be displaced in accordance with "rent-paying ability." The attractiveness of a parcel, and therefore the price that it could command, was a function of its accessibility. Ideally, the most desirable and efficient location for all the functions and the people of a city would be at the single point at which the maximum possible interchange could be achieved. Such total coalescence of activity is obviously impossible.

Because users must therefore arrange themselves spatially, the attractiveness of a parcel is rated by its relative accessibility to all other land uses of the city. Store owners wish to locate where they can easily be reached by potential customers; factories need a convenient assembling of their workers and materials; residents desire easy connection with jobs, stores, and schools. Within the older central city, the radiating mass transit lines established the elements of the urban land use structure by freezing in the landscape a clear-cut pattern of differential accessibility. The convergence of that system on the city core gave that location the highest accessibility, the highest desirability, and hence, the highest land values of the entire built-up area. Similarly, transit junction points were accessible to larger segments of the city than locations along single traffic routes; the latter were more desirable than parcels lying between the radiating lines (Figure 11.21).

Society deems certain functions desirable without regard to their economic competitiveness. Schools, parks, and public buildings are granted space without being participants in the auction for land. Other uses, through the process of that auction, are assigned spaces by market forces. The merchants with the widest variety and highest order of goods and the largest threshold requirements bid most for and occupy parcels within the **central business district (CBD),** which became localized at the convergence of mass transit lines. The successful bidders for slightly less accessible CBD parcels were the developers of tall office buildings of major cities, the principal hotels, and similar land uses.

Comparable, but lower-order, commercial aggregations developed at the outlying intersections—transfer points—of the mass transit system. With time a distinctive retailing hierarchy emerged within the urban settlement, an intracity central place pattern based on the purchasing power thresholds and complementary regions of city populations them-

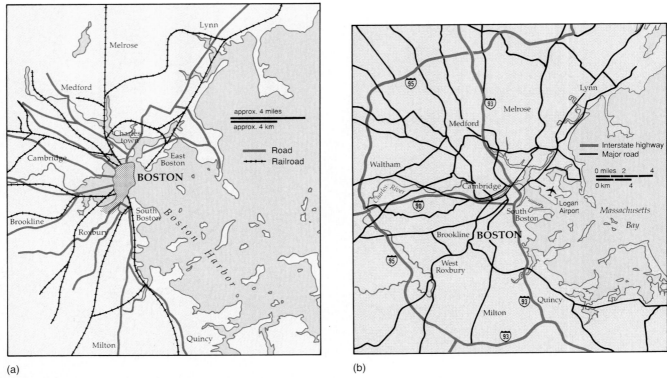

(a)   (b)

FIGURE 11.21   Major access lines in Boston in 1872 and 1994. (*a*) The convergence of mass transit lines in the 19th century gave to the central city and its downtown core a centrality reduced or lost with (*b*) the freeway pattern and motor vehicle dominance in 1994 Boston. See also Figure 11.34.

selves. Industry took control of parcels adjacent to essential cargo routes: rail lines, waterfronts, rivers, or canals. Strings of stores, light industries, and high-density apartment structures could afford and benefit from location along high-volume transit routes. The least accessible locations within the city were left for the least competitive uses: low-density residences. A diagrammatic summary of this repetitive allocation of space among competitors for urban sites in American mass transit cities is shown in Figure 11.22. Compare it to the generalized land use map of Calgary, Alberta, shown in Figure 11.27.

The land use regularities of the older, eastern mass transit central cities were not fully replicated in the 20th-century urban centers of western United States. Those newer cities are more influenced in their density and land use structures by the automobile than by mass transit systems. They spread more readily, evolved at lower densities, and therefore display less tightly structured and standardized land use patterns than their eastern predecessors.

Land Values and Population Density

Theoretically, the open land auction should yield two separate although interconnected distance decay patterns, one related to land values and the other to population density (as distance increases away from the CBD, population density decreases). If one views the land value surface of the older central city as a topographic map (Figure 11.23), with hills representing high

valuations and depressions showing low prices, a series of peaks, ridges, and valleys would reflect the differentials in accessibility marked by the pattern of mass transit lines, their intersections, and the unserved interstitial areas.

Dominating these local variations, however, is an overall decline of valuations with increasing distance away from the *peak land value intersection,* the most accessible (by mass transit) and costly location of the central business district. As would be expected in a distance decay pattern, the drop in valuation is precipitous within a short linear distance from that point, and then the valuation declines at a lesser rate to the margins of the built-up area.

With one important variation, the population density pattern of the central city shows a comparable distance decay arrangement, as suggested by Figure 11.24. The exception is the tendency to form a hollow *at the center,* the CBD, which represents the inability of all but the most costly apartment houses to compete for space against alternative users desiring these supremely accessible parcels. Yet accessibility is attractive to a number of residential users and brings its penalty in high land prices. The result is the high-density residential occupancy of parcels *near the center* of the city—by those who are too poor to afford a long-distance journey to work; who are consigned by their poverty to overcrowding in obsolescent slum tenements near the heart of the inner city; or who are self-selected occupants of luxury apartments whose high rents are made necessary by the price of land. Other urbanites, if

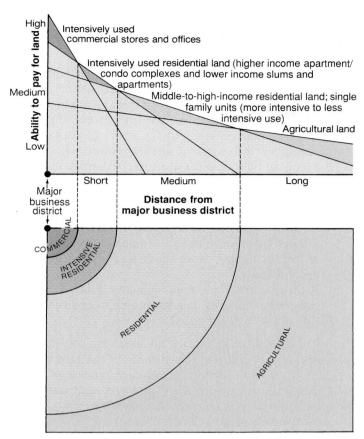

FIGURE 11.22   Generalized urban land use pattern. The model depicts the location of various land uses in an idealized city where the highest bidder gets the most accessible land.

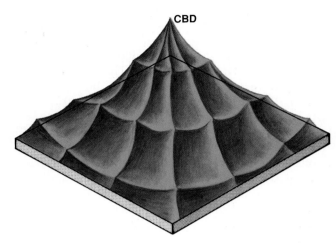

FIGURE 11.23   Generalized pattern of land values. The "topography" represented on this diagram shows the major land-value peak of the CBD. The ridges radiating from that point mark mass transit lines and major business thoroughfares. Regularly occurring minor peaks indicate commercial agglomerations at intersections of mass transit lines or main traffic routes, which are points of accessibility superior to those of the interstitial troughs.

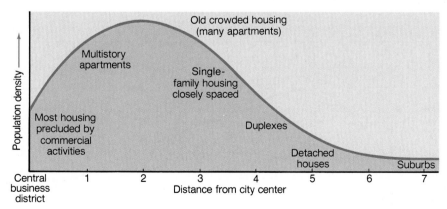

FIGURE 11.24   A summary population density curve. As distance from the area of multistory apartment buildings increases, the population density declines.

financially able, may opt to trade off higher commuting costs for lower-priced land and may reside on larger parcels away from high-accessibility, high-congestion locations. Residential density declines with increasing distance from the city center as this option is exercised.

As a city grows in population, the peak densities no longer increase, and the pattern of population distribution becomes more uniform. Secondary centers begin to compete with the CBD for customers and industry, and the residential areas become less associated with the city center and more dependent on high-speed transportation arteries. Peak densities in the inner city decline, and peripheral areas increase in population concentration. These generalizations are clearly documented in the series of density gradients drawn for Cleveland, Ohio, for the late industrial to postindustrial period (Figure 11.25).

Models of Urban Land Use Structure

Generalized models of urban growth and land use patterns were proposed during the 1920s and 1930s describing the results of these controls on the observed structure of the central city. Their starting point is the distinctive central business district found in every older central city. The core of this area displays intensive land development: tall buildings, many stores and offices, and crowded streets. Framing the core is a fringe area of wholesaling activities, transportation terminals, warehouses, new-car dealers, furniture stores, and even light industries. Just beyond the central business district frame is the beginning of residential land uses.

The land use models shown in Figure 11.26 differ in their explanation of patterns outside the CBD. The **concentric zone model** (Figure 11.26a), developed to explain the sociological patterning of American cities in the 1920s, sees the urban community as a set of nested rings. It recognizes four concentric circles of mostly residential diversity at increasing distance in all directions from the wholesaling, warehousing, and light industry border of the high-density CBD core:

* A zone in transition marked by the deterioration of old residential structures abandoned, as the city expanded, by the former wealthier occupants and now containing high-density, low-income slums, rooming houses, and perhaps ethnic ghettos.
* A zone of "independent working people's homes" occupied by industrial workers, perhaps second-generation Americans able to afford modest but older homes on small lots.
* A zone of better residences, single-family homes, or high-rent apartments occupied by those wealthy enough to exercise choice in housing location and to afford the longer, more costly journey to CBD employment.
* A commuters' zone of low-density, isolated residential suburbs, just beginning to emerge when this model was proposed.

The model is dynamic; it imagines the continuous expansion of inner zones at the expense of the next outer developed circles and suggests a ceaseless process of *invasion* and *succession* that yields a restructured land use pattern and population segregation by income level.

The **sector model** (Figure 11.26b) also concerns itself with patterns of housing and wealth, but it arrives at the conclusion that high-rent residential areas are dominant in city expansion and grow outward from the center of the city along major arterials. New housing for the wealthy, the model concludes, is added in an outward extension of existing high-rent axes as the city grows. Middle-income housing sectors lie adjacent to the high-rent areas, and low-income residents occupy the remaining sectors of growth. There tends to be a *filtering-down* process as older areas are aban-

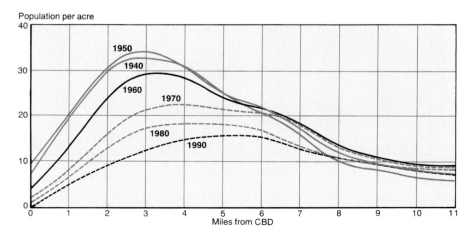

FIGURE 11.25   **Population density gradients for Cleveland, 1940–1990.** The progressive depopulation of the central core and flattening of the density gradient to the city margin is clearly seen as Cleveland passed from mass transit to automobile domination.

Source: Redrawn from "Population Density Gradient Changes of a Postindustrial City—Cleveland Ohio (1960-1990)" by Anupa Mukhopadhyay and Ashok K. Dutt. *GeoJournal* 34 (1994), Figure 2, p. 517.

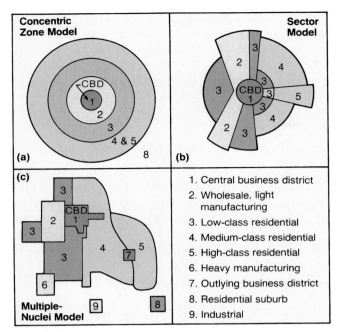

1. Central business district
2. Wholesale, light manufacturing
3. Low-class residential
4. Medium-class residential
5. High-class residential
6. Heavy manufacturing
7. Outlying business district
8. Residential suburb
9. Industrial

FIGURE 11.26   **Three classic models of the internal structure of cities.**

doned by the outward movement of their original inhabitants, with the lowest-income populations (closest to the center of the city and farthest from the current location of the wealthy) becoming the dubious beneficiaries of the least desirable vacated areas. The accordance of the sector model with the actual pattern that developed in Calgary, Canada, is suggested in Figure 11.27.

The concentric circle and sector models assume urban growth and development outward from a single central core, the site of original urban settlement that later developed into the central business district. These "single-node" models are countered by a **multiple-nuclei model** (Figure 11.26c), which maintains that large cities develop by peripheral spread from several nodes of growth, not just one. Individual nodes of special function—commercial, industrial, port, residential—are originally developed in response to the benefits accruing from the spatial association of like activities. Peripheral expansion of the separate nuclei eventually leads to coalescence and the meeting of incompatible land uses along the lines of juncture. The urban land use pattern, therefore, is not regularly structured from a single center in a sequence of circles or a series of sectors but based on separately expanding clusters of contrasting activities.

Social Areas of Cities

Although too simplistic to be fully satisfactory, these classical models of American city structure receive some confirmation from modern interpretations of social segregation within urban areas. The larger and more economically and socially complex cities are, the stronger is the tendency for

their residents to segregate themselves into groups based on *social status, family status,* and *ethnicity.* In a large metropolitan region with its diversified population, this territorial behavior may be a defense against the unknown or the unwanted, a desire to be among similar kinds of people, a response to income constraints, or a result of social and institutional barriers.

Most people feel more secure when they are near those with whom they can easily identify. In traditional societies, these groups are the families and tribes. In modern society, people group according to income or occupation (social status), stages in the life cycle (family status), and language or race (ethnic characteristics). Many of these groupings are fostered by the size and the value of the available housing. Land developers, especially in cities, produce homes of similar quality in specific areas. Of course, as time elapses, there is a change in the condition and quality of that housing, and new groups may replace previous tenants. In any case, neighborhoods of similar social characteristics evolve.

Social Status

The social status of an individual or a family is determined by income, education, occupation, and home value, though it may be measured differently in different cultures. In the United States, high income, a college education, a professional or managerial position, and high home value constitute high status. High home value can mean an expensive rental apartment as well as a large house with extensive grounds.

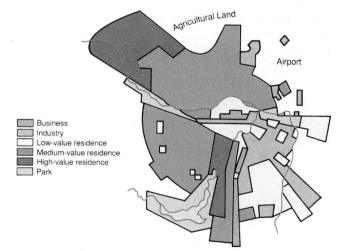

FIGURE 11.27   **The land use pattern in and around Calgary, Alberta, in 1981.** The circular arrangement of uses suggested by the concentric zone theory (Figure 11.26a) might result if a city developed on a flat surface. In reality, hills, rivers, railroads, and highways affect land uses in uneven ways. Physical and cultural barriers and the evolution of cities over time tend to result in a sectoral pattern of similar land uses. Calgary's central business district is the focus for many of the sectors.

A good housing indicator of social status is persons per room. A low number of persons per room tends to indicate high status. Low status characterizes people with low-income jobs living in low-value housing. There are many levels of status, and people tend to filter out into neighborhoods where most of the heads of households are of similar rank.

Social-status patterning agrees with the sector model, and in most cities, people of similar social status are grouped in sectors whose points are in the innermost urban residential areas (Figure 11.28). The pattern in Chicago is illustrated in Figure 11.29. If the number of people within a given social group increases, they tend to move away from the central city along an arterial connecting them with the old neighborhood. Major transport routes leading to the city center are the usual migration routes out from the center.

Family Status

As the distance from the city center increases, the average age of the head of the household declines, or the size of the family increases, or both. Within a particular sector—say, that of high status—older people whose children do not live with them or young professionals without families tend to live close to the city center; both covet the accessibility to the cultural and business life of the city. Young families seeking space for child rearing may locate farther out, at or beyond the central city margin. However, where inner-city life is unpleasant, there is a tendency for older people to migrate to the suburbs or to retirement communities.

Within lower-status sectors, the same pattern tends to emerge. Transients and single people are housed in the inner city, and families, if they find it possible or desirable, live farther from the center. The arrangement that emerges is a concentric circle patterning according to family status, as Figure 11.28 suggests. In general, inner-city areas house older people and outer-city areas house younger populations.

Ethnicity

For some groups, ethnicity is a more important residential location determinant than is social or family status. Areas of homogeneous ethnic identification appear in the social geography of cities as separate clusters or nuclei, reminiscent of the multiple-nuclei concept of urban structure (see Figure 11.28). For some ethnic groups, cultural segregation is both sought and vigorously defended, even in the face of pressures for neighborhood change exerted by potential competitors for housing space, as we saw in Chapter 6. The durability of "Little Italys" and "Chinatowns" and of Polish, Greek, Armenian, and other ethnic neighborhoods in many American cities is evidence of the persistence of self-maintained segregation (see "The Los Angeles Puzzle").

Certain ethnic or racial groups, especially African Americans, have had segregation in nuclear communities forced on them. Every city in the United States has one or more black areas which in many respects may be considered cities within a city with their own self-contained social geographies of social status, income, and housing quality. Figure 6.16 (page 196) illustrates the concentration of blacks, Hispanics, and other ethnic groups in Los Angeles, while Table 6.8 (page 197) indicates the degree of segregation experienced by African Americans, Hispanics, and, Asians in 22 United States metropolitan areas.

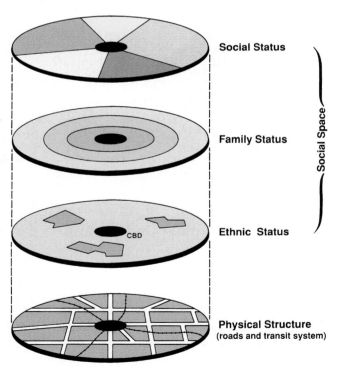

FIGURE 11.28   The social geography of American and Canadian cities.

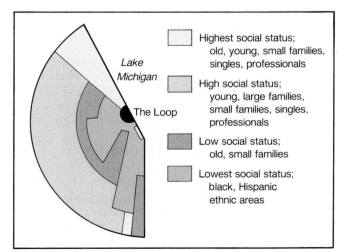

FIGURE 11.29   A diagrammatic representation of the major social areas of the Chicago region. The central business district of Chicago is known as the "Loop."

D ifferent ethnic and racial groups fit together in a large American metropolis much as separate pieces make up a giant jigsaw puzzle. Unlike an ordinary puzzle, however, the urban ethnic pattern is never complete or constant. Pieces change shape and move, and more pieces may have to be squeezed within expanding borders of the puzzle, as the Los Angeles experience demonstrates.

The population of the Los Angeles metropolitan area topped 15 million by the mid-1990s, with continuing growth projected to the end of the decade. With that expansion have come major shifts in the ethnic and racial structure of the region—in the size and shape of the puzzle pieces and the locations where they fit. Economic restructuring and job loss in the region—and the negative impacts of the Los Angeles riot (1992), devastating fires (1993), and the severe Northridge earthquake (1994)—led to an outmigration of some Angelenos, primarily of whites and blacks, during the 1980s and 1990s. At the same time, immigrants from other countries streamed into California and metropolitan Los Angeles. In 1970, the Los Angeles basin was dominated by white Protes-

tant migrants from the Midwest. Within 25 years, whites had decreased from 77% to less than 40% of the total, and blacks had dropped from 18% to less than 11%.

Hispanics represent the largest influx of immigrants; Mexicans alone grew from fewer than 350,000 in Los Angeles County in 1960 to over 2.5 million by the mid-1990s. Together with Central American immigrants, particularly from El Salvador, they swelled the Hispanic component of county population to over 40%. Asians also arrived in large numbers during the 1980s and 1990s, coming chiefly from the Philippines, Vietnam, Korea, China (Hong Kong), and Japan. Collectively, Asians accounted for at least 11% of Los Angeles County population in the mid-1990s, up from just 5.8% in 1980.

By 1995, one of every four people in Los Angeles County was foreign-born. Like migrants before them, these new arrivals tended to cluster in separate ethnic communities. South Central Los Angeles, once predominantly black, became almost half Hispanic and is projected to be largely so by 2000. Many Vietnamese live or own businesses in the Westminster area (known as "Little Saigon"). Asians, especially Chinese, are now the largest group in both Alhambra and Monterey Park, communities that

had negligible Asian populations only 20 years earlier.

These and other newcomers in part displaced whites and blacks and in part merely replaced them as they left the region. White outmigration—some of it following relocating jobs, some fleeing the troubles and congestion of a city growing faster than its service sector could handle—was primarily to other western states, to both small towns and such growing metropolitan areas as Seattle, Portland, Las Vegas, Salt Lake City, Phoenix, and Tucson. Between 1985 and 1990, 7% of Los Angeles County African Americans over the age of 5 moved out, a relocation that continued into the mid-1990s, carrying Angeleno blacks not only to outlying areas of metropolitan Los Angeles but the other states as well, particularly to the South. Generally, they leapfrogged the Los Angeles suburban areas favored by relocating whites and headed eastward toward Riverside and San Bernardino counties or northward to Ventura County. The metropolitan Los Angeles jigsaw puzzle continues to reshape and re-form as new pieces are added and old ones shrink or are lost or relocated.

Table 11.2 demonstrates the extent of isolation facing African Americans in 1990 in the ten largest United States metropolitan areas and documents that the barriers to movement outside the areas assigned to segregated minorities have always been high. It also suggests that black segregation is a spatial variable within the country. Chicago, St. Louis, Detroit, and Philadelphia have more than half of their black residents living in segregated neighborhoods, and Detroit, Cleveland, Buffalo, Cincinnati, and New York actually had greater black segregation in 1990 than in 1980. On the other hand, southern and western metropolitan areas are much less segregated than those of the Northeast and Midwest. San Diego is fully integrated, while segregation of blacks into predominantly black districts in Los Angeles declined from 20% in 1980 to 7% in 1990, one result of the influx into their communities of Hispanic and Asian immigrants (see "The Los Angeles Puzzle").

TABLE 11.2	Black Segregation[a] in Large U.S. Metropolitan Central Cities, 1990	
CITY	PERCENT IN ISOLATION 1990	CHANGE SINCE 1980
Chicago	71	–9.1
Detroit	61	+4.0
Philadelphia	53	+0.1
Atlanta	43	–6.1
Washington, D.C.	37	–9.3
New York	31	+3.0
Houston	30	–19.5
Dallas	29	–21.6
Boston	19	–5.6
Los Angeles	7	–12.6

[a]Percent of African Americans living in "block groups" (spatial units containing 300–400 people) that are at least 90% black.

Source: Knight-Ridder newspapers and The Economist.

Of the three social geographic patterns depicted in Figure 11.28, family status has undergone the most widespread change in recent years. Today, the suburbs house large numbers of singles and childless couples, as well as two-parent families, and areas near the central business district have become popular for young professionals. Much of this is a result of changes in family structure and the advent, during the 1970s and 1980s, of large numbers of new jobs for professionals in the suburbs and central business districts, but not in between. With more women in the workforce than ever before, and as a result of multiple-earner families, residential site selection has become a more complex undertaking.

Institutional Controls

Within this century, and particularly since World War II, institutional controls have strongly influenced the land use arrangements and growth patterns of most United States cities. Indeed, the governments—local and national—of most urbanized societies have instituted a myriad of laws to control all aspects of urban life with particular emphasis on the ways in which individual property and city areas can be developed and used. In the United States, emphasis has been on land use planning, subdivision control and zoning ordinances, and building, health, and safety codes. All have been designed to assure a legally acceptable manner and pattern of urban development, and all are based on broad applications of the police powers of municipalities to assure public health, safety, and well-being even when private property rights are infringed.

These nonmarket controls on land use are designed to minimize incompatibilities (residences adjacent to heavy industry, for example), provide for the creation in appropriate locations of public uses (the transportation system, waste disposal facilities, government buildings, parks), and private uses (colleges, shopping centers, housing) needed for and conducive to a balanced, orderly community. In theory, such careful planning should prevent the emergence of slums, so often the result of undesirable adjacent uses, and should stabilize neighborhoods by reducing market-induced pressures for land use change.

Zoning ordinances and land use planning have sometimes been criticized as being unduly restrictive and unresponsive to changing land use needs and patterns of economic development. Zoning and subdivision control regulations that specify acre or larger residential building lots and large house-floor areas have been particularly criticized. They are charged with being devices to exclude from upper-income areas lower-income populations or those who would choose to build or occupy other forms of residences: apartments, special housing for the aged, and so forth. Bitter court battles have been waged, with mixed results, over "exclusionary" zoning practices that in the view of some serve to separate rather than to unify the total urban structure and to maintain or increase diseconomies of land use development.

All institutional controls, of course, whatever their origin or objective, interfere with the open auction in urban land which initially gave rise to the city structure we have been reviewing. Also interfering with that auction and the market allocation of urban land it implies are such nongovernmental actions as those of real estate agents who "steer" people of certain racial and ethnic groups into neighborhoods that the agent thinks are appropriate.

Suburbanization in the United States

The 20 years before World War II (1939–1945) saw the creation of a technological, physical, and institutional structure that resulted after that war in a sudden and massive alteration of past urban forms. The improvement of the automobile increased its reliability and range, freeing its owner from dependence on fixed-route public transit for travel to home, work, or shopping. The new movement flexibility opened up vast new acreages of cheap rural land for urban development. The acceptance of a maximum 40-hour work week guaranteed millions of Americans the time for a commuting journey not possible when workdays of 10 or more hours were common.

Finally, to stimulate the economy by the ripple effect associated with expanding home construction, the Federal Housing Administration was established as part of the New Deal programs under President Franklin D. Roosevelt. It guaranteed creditors the security of their mortgage loans, thus reducing down-payment requirements and lengthening mortgage repayment periods, and made owned rather than rented housing possible for working-class Americans. In addition, veterans of World War II were granted generous terms on new residences.

Demand for housing, pent up by years of economic depression and wartime restrictions, was loosed in a flood after 1945 and a massive suburbanization of people and urban functions altered the existing pattern of urban America. Between 1950 and 1970, the two most prominent patterns of population growth were the metropolitanization of people and, within metropolitan areas, their suburbanization. During the 1960s the interstate highway system was substantially completed and major metropolitan expressways put in place, allowing sites 30 to 45 or more kilometers (20 to 30 or more miles) from workplaces to be within acceptable commuting distance from home. The major metropolitan areas rapidly expanded in area and population. Growth patterns for the Chicago area, reflecting those developments, are shown in Figure 11.30. The high energy prices of the 1970s slowed the rush to the suburbs, but in the next decade suburbanization again proceeded apace, although the tendency was as much for "filling in" as it was for continued sprawl.

Residential land uses led the rush to the suburbs. Individually uniform, spatially discontinuous housing developments beyond the boundaries of most older central cities were the rule initially. The new design was an unfocused sprawl because it was not tied to mass transit lines and the channelized pattern of nodes and links they imposed. Further, it represented a massive relocation of purchasing power to which retail merchants were quick to respond. The

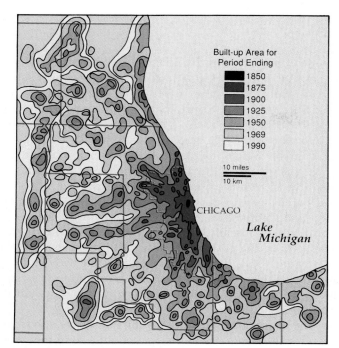

FIGURE 11.30 **A history of urban sprawl.** In Chicago, as in most larger and older U.S. cities, the slow peripheral expansion recorded during the late 19th and early 20th centuries suddenly accelerated as the automobile suburbs began developing after 1945.

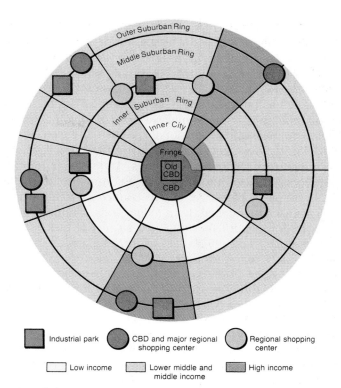

FIGURE 11.31 **A diagram of the U.S. metropolitan area.** Note that aspects of the concentric zone, sector, and multiple-nuclei patterns are evident and carried out into the suburban fringe. The "major regional shopping centers" of this earlier, mid-1970s model are increasingly the cores of newly developing "outer cities."

planned major regional shopping center became the suburban counterpart to higher-order central places and the central city's major outlying commercial districts. Smaller shopping plazas and a multiplying number of the strip shopping centers that had initially preceded the larger malls gradually completed the retailing hierarchy.

Faced with a newly suburbanized labor force, industry followed the outward move, drawn as well by the economies derived from modern single-story plants with plenty of parking space for employees, and the new freedom from railroad access made possible by the motor truck and the expanding highway system (Figure 9.15). Service industries were also attracted by suburbanizing purchasing power and labor force, and along with the new shopping malls, office building complexes began to be developed; like the malls these localized at freeway intersections and along freeway frontage roads and major connecting highways.

In time, in the United States, new metropolitan land use and functional patterns emerged that could no longer be satisfactorily explained by the classic ring, sector, or multiple-nuclei models. Yet traces of the older generation concepts seemingly remained applicable. Multiple nuclei of specialized land uses appeared, expanded, and coalesced. Sectors of high-income residential use continued their outward extension beyond the central city limits, usurping the most scenic and most desirable suburban areas and segregating them by price and zoning restrictions. As shown in Figure 11.31, middle-, lower-middle-, and lower-income

groups found their own income-segregated portions of the fringe. Ethnic minorities were frequently relegated to the inner city and to some older industrial suburbs.

By the 1990s, a new urban America had emerged on the perimeters of the major metropolitan areas. With increasing sprawl and the rising costs implicit in the ever-greater spatial separation of the functional segments of the fringe, peripheral expansion slowed, the supply of developable land was reduced (with corresponding increases in its price), and the intensity of land utilization grew. The suburbs, no longer dependent on the central city, were reborn as vast, collectively self-sufficient outer cities, marked by landscapes of skyscraper office parks, massive retailing complexes, established industrial parks, and a proliferation of apartment and condominium districts (see "The Self-Sufficient Suburbs"). The new suburbia became more focused than formerly as its employment and service nodes began to rival older central business districts in size and complexity, though not necessarily in convenience of access.

Collectively, the new centers surpassed the central cities as generators of employment and income. Individually, each of the major suburban centers established its own particular role in the metropolitan economy, cooperatively sharing with both the old central business district and other new suburban downtowns the performance of the myriad tertiary and quaternary services that mark the postindustrial metropolis. During the 1980s, more office space was created in the suburbs than in the central cities of America. Tysons Corner, Virginia, for example, became the ninth largest central business district in the United States (Figure 9.27). Regional and national headquarters of leading corporations, banking, professional services of all kinds, major hotel complexes and recreational centers—all formerly considered immovable keystones of central business districts—became parts of the new outer cities. And these outer cities themselves filled in and made more continuous the urban landscape of all North American conurbations. Journalist Joel Garreau has dubbed them "edge cities," defined as having 5 million square feet (465,000 sq. m) of office space, 500,000 square feet (46,500 sq. m) of retail space in malls, and more jobs than residents.

Those edge cities, the landscape realities of the postindustrial service and information economy, now exist in all regions of urbanized North America. The South Coast Metro Center in Orange County, California, the City Post Oak-Galleria center on Houston's west side, King of Prussia and the Route 202 corridor northwest of Philadelphia, the Meadowlands, New Jersey west of New York City, and Schaumburg, Illinois in the western Chicago suburbs, are but a very few examples of the new urban forms. The metropolis has become polynucleated and urban regions are increasingly "galactic"; that is, galaxies of economic activity nodes organized primarily around the freeway systems (Figure 11.32). Commuting across the galaxy is far more common than journeys-to-work between suburbs and central cities.

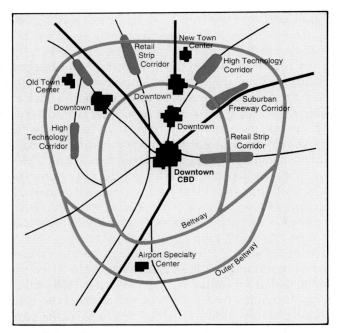

FIGURE 11.32 **The galactic city's multiple downtowns and special function nodes and corridors are linked by the metropolitan expressway systems in this conceptualization proposed by Truman Hartshorn and Peter Muller.**

Central City Change

The economic base and the financial stability of the central city have been grievously damaged by the process of suburbanization and the creation of new outer cities. In earlier periods of growth, as new settlement areas developed beyond the political margins of the city, annexation absorbed the new growth within the corporate boundaries of the expanding older city. The additional tax base and employment centers became part of the municipal whole. But in states that recognized the right of separate incorporation for the new growth areas—particularly in the eastern part of the United States—the ability of the city to continue to expand was restricted. Where possible, suburbanites opted for a separation from the central city and for aloofness from the costs, the deterioration, and the adversities associated with it. Their homes, jobs, shopping, schools, and recreation all existed outside the confines of the city from which they had divorced themselves.

The redistribution of population caused by suburbanization resulted not only in the spatial but also in the political segregation of social groups of the metropolitan area. The upwardly mobile resident of the city—younger, whiter, wealthier, and better educated—took advantage of the automobile and the freeway to leave the central city. The poorer, older, least-advantaged urbanites were left behind. The central cities and the suburbs became increasingly differentiated. Large areas within the cities now contain only the poor and minority groups, including women (see "Women in the City"), a population little able to pay the rising costs of the social services that their numbers, neighborhoods, and condition require.

The services needed to support the poor include welfare payments, social workers, extra police and fire protection, health delivery systems, and subsidized housing. Central cities, by themselves, are unable to raise the taxes needed to support such an array and intensity of social services since they have lost the tax bases represented by suburbanized commerce, industry, and upper-income residential uses. Lost, too, are the job opportunities that were formerly a part of the central city structure. Increasingly, the poor and minorities are trapped in a central city without the possibility of nearby employment and are isolated by distance, immobility, and unawareness from the few remaining low-skill jobs, which are now largely in the suburbs.

About two-thirds of the 200 largest metropolitan areas show this pattern of American urban separatism in which most poor blacks and Hispanics are confined within the inner cities surrounded by predominantly white suburbs. Many African Americans, however, also joined the exodus from central cities and helped reduce, rather than increase, metropolitan segregation. As early as the 1970s, for example, the Central Harlem and Bedford-Stuyvesant black communities of New York City lost a third of their populations; parts of the South Bronx lost two-thirds. Similar outmigrations are continuing in other metropolitan areas.

The suburbanization of the American population and of the commerce and industry dependent on its purchasing power and labor has led to more than the simple physical separation of the suburbanite from the central city. It has created a metropolitan area, many of whose inhabitants have no connection with the core city, feel no ties to it, and find satisfaction of all their needs within the peripheral zone.

A 1978 *New York Times* "suburban poll" revealed a surprising lack of interest in New York City on the part of those usually assumed to be intimately involved in the economic, cultural, and social life of the "functional city," the metropolitan area dominated by New York. The poll discovered that in 80% of suburban households, the principal wage earner did not work in New York City. The concept of the commuter zone obviously no longer has validity if *commuting* implies, as it formerly did, a daily journey to work in the central city.

Just as employment ties have been broken, now that the majority of suburbanites work in or near their outlying areas of residence, the cultural and service ties that were traditionally thought to bind the metropolitan areas into a single unit dominated by the core city have also been severed. The *Times* survey found that one-half of the suburbanites polled made fewer than five nonbusiness visits to New York City each year; one-quarter said that they never went there and 39% said that events in the city had "hardly any impact" on their daily lives. A second *Times* poll of late 1991 found even less concern with central city matters: 51% of suburbanites disclaimed any impact on their lives from New York affairs. In part that was apparently related to the fact that 59% of the 1991 poll respondents in the 14-county surrounding area had never lived in New York City proper, and thus were not tied to it by familiarity or nostalgia.

Even the presumed concentration in the city of high-order goods and services—those with the largest service areas—did not constitute an attraction for most suburbanites. More than three-quarters of those surveyed in 1991 said they would not need to journey to New York City to see doctors, lawyers, or accountants; more than two-thirds rarely or never shopped in the city; and more than 40% said that they could satisfy their concert- and play-going close to home. Even needs at the upper reaches of the central place hierarchy were satisfied within the fringe.

The suburbs, as the *Times* surveys documented, have outgrown their former role as bedroom communities and have emerged as a chain of independent, multinucleated urban complexes. Together, they are largely self-sufficient and divorced from the central city, and have little feeling of subordination to or dependence on that city. As the urban scholar Brian Berry has so aptly put it, we are creating an "urban civilization without cities."

Miami's traditional black neighborhoods have lost between a quarter and one-half of their residents; Chicago's black population fell by 113,000 during the 1980s, Atlanta lost 125,000, and Washington, D.C. saw the departure of 225,000 through the early 1990s. During the 1980s alone, the black suburban population of the 39 largest metropolitan areas increased by 38%. Other upwardly mobile minorities joined the movement; the suburban Hispanic population increased by 70% in the 1980s and that of Asians by 126%. White suburbanites increased by only 9% in the same decade.

Abandonment of the central city by people and functions has nearly destroyed the traditional active, open auction of urban land which formerly led to the replacement of obsolescent uses and inefficient structures in a continuing process of urban modernization. In the vacuum left by the departure of private investors, the federal government, particularly after the landmark Housing Act of 1949, initiated urban renewal programs with or without provisions for a partnership with private housing and redevelopment investment. Under a wide array of programs, slum areas were cleared; public housing was built (Figure 11.33); cultural complexes and industrial parks were created; and city centers have been reconstructed.

With the continuing erosion of the urban economic base and the disadvantageous restructuring of the central city population base, the hard-fought governmental battle to maintain or revive the central city is frequently judged to be a losing one. Public assistance programs—themselves undergoing massive alterations and reductions in the 1990s—have not reduced the central city burden of thousands of homeless people (see "The Homeless"), nor have central city economies, with their high land and housing values, limited unskilled job opportunities, and inadequate resources for social services offered them prospects for change. At the start of the 20th century, the burgeoning cities of the United States were dynamic source areas for the economic growth and growing prosperity of the nation. At the start of the 21st century, the central city stands weakened by changing technologies, mobilities, and social tensions, and by seemingly unmanageable economic reverses.

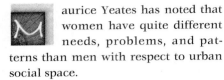

Maurice Yeates has noted that women have quite different needs, problems, and patterns than men with respect to urban social space.

In the first place, women are more numerous in large central cities than are men. Washington, D.C. probably is the most female-dominant (numerically) of any city in North America, with a "sex ratio" of eighty-seven (or 115 females for every 100 males). In Minneapolis it is eighty-four. The preponderance of women in central cities is related to an above-average number of household units headed by women, and to the larger numbers of women among the elderly.

A second characteristic is that women, along with their children, constitute the bulk of the poor. This feminization of poverty among all races is a consequence of the low wage rates, part-time work, and lack of security of employment in many "women's jobs." Central cities, with their low-cost but often low-quality rental housing units, house the vast majority of poor women.

A third spatial characteristic of women in urban areas is that they have shorter journeys to work and rely more heavily upon public transportation than do men, a reflection of the lower incomes received by women, the differences in location of "female jobs," and the concentration of women in the central cities. Women on the whole simply cannot afford to spend as much on travel costs as men and make greater use of public transportation, which in the United States is usually inferior and often dangerous. The concentration of employment of women in clerical, sales, service jobs, and nursing also influences travel distances because these "women's jobs" are spread around the metropolitan area more than "men's jobs," which tend to be concentrated. It might well be argued that the more widespread location of "women's jobs" helps maintain the relative inaccessibility of many higher-paid "men's jobs" to a large number of women.

Given the allocation of roles, the resulting inequities, and the persistence of these inequities, there are spatial issues that impinge directly upon women. One is that many women find that their spatial range of employment opportunities is limited as a result of the inadequate availability of child-care facilities within urban areas. A second spatial issue relates to the structure of North American metropolitan areas and to the design of housing in general. North American cities are the outcome of male-dominant traits. Suburbs, in particular, reflect a male-paid work and female-home/children ethos. The suburban structure mitigates against women by confining them to a place and role in which there are very few meaningful choices. It has been argued that suburban women really desire a greater level of accessibility to a variety of conveniences and services, more efficient housing units, and a range of public and private transportation that will assure higher levels of mobility. These requirements imply higher-density urban areas.

World Urban Diversity

The city, Figure 11.3 reminds us, is a global phenomenon. It is also a regional and cultural variable. The descriptions and models that we have used to study the functions, land use arrangements, suburbanization trends, and other aspects of the United States city would not in all—or even many—instances help us understand the structures and patterns of cities in other parts of the world. Those cities have been created under different historical, cultural, and technological circumstances. They have developed different functional and structural patterns, some so radically different from our United States model that we would find them unfamiliar and uncharted landscapes indeed. The city is universal; its characteristics are cultural and regional.

The Anglo American City

Even within the seemingly homogeneous Anglo American culture realm the city shows subtle but significant differences—not only between older eastern and newer western U.S. cities, but between cities of Canada and those of the United States. Although the urban expression is similar in the two countries, it is not identical. The Canadian city, for example, is more compact than its U.S. counterpart of equal population size, with a higher density of buildings and people and a lesser degree of suburbanization of populations and functions (Figure 11.34).

Space-saving multiple-family housing units are more the rule in Canada, so a similar population size is housed on a smaller land area with much higher densities, on average, within the central area of cities. The Canadian city is better

FIGURE 11.33   Many elaborate—and massive—public housing projects have been failures. Chicago's Robert Taylor Homes, shown here—with 4400 apartments in 28 16-story buildings, the largest public housing unit in the world—has been partly abandoned, a victim of soaring vandalism and crime rates. The growing awareness that public high-rise buildings intended to revive the central city do not meet the housing and social needs of their inhabitants led to the razing of thousands of the more than 1.3 million public housing units in cities around the country during the 1990s, many to be replaced by low-rise apartment or mix-use developments. In 1995, the federal Housing Secretary proposed to replace public housing with a rent subsidy program and to demolish projects that could not command market-based rents.

FIGURE 11.34   The central and outlying business districts of Toronto, easily visible in this photo, are still rooted firmly by mass transit convergence and mass transit usage. On a per capita basis, Canadian urbanites are two and a half times more dependent on public transportation than are American city dwellers. That reliance gives form, structure, and coherence to the Canadian central city, qualities now irretrievably lost in the sprawled and fragmented U.S. metropolis.

THE HOMELESS

In the 1980s and 1990s, the number of homeless people in the United States rose dramatically: to anywhere between 600,000 and 3 million in 1995 according to various "official" counts. Their existence and persistence raise a multitude of questions—with the answers yet to be agreed upon by public officials and private Americans. Who are the homeless, and why do their numbers increase? Who should be responsible for coping with the problems they present? Are there ways to eliminate homelessness?

Some people believe the homeless are primarily the impoverished victims of a rich and uncaring society. They view them as ordinary people, but ones who have had a bad break and been forced from their homes by job loss, divorce, domestic violence, or incapacitating illness. They point to the increasing numbers of families, women, and children among the homeless, less visible than the "loners" (primarily men) because they tend to live in cars, emergency shelters, or doubled-up in substandard buildings. Advocates of the homeless argue that government policies of the 1980s and 1990s that led to a dire shortage of affordable housing are partly to blame. Federal outlays for building low-income and subsidized housing were more than $30 billion in 1980 but dropped to $7.5 billion a decade later. Simultaneously, local governments pursued policies of destruction of low-income housing, especially single-room-occupancy hotels and encouraged **gentrification** (private, middle-and upper-income group residential renovation of deteriorated, often historic, portions of the inner city). In addition, federal regulations and reduced state funding for mental hospitals cast institutionalized patients onto the streets to join people displaced by gentrification, job loss, or rising rents.

A contrary view is presented by those who see the homeless chiefly as people responsible for their own plight, not unlike the skid row denizens of former years. In the words of one commentator, the homeless are "deranged, pathological predators who spoil neighborhoods, terrorize passersby, and threaten the commonweal." They point to studies showing that nationally between 66% and 85% of all homeless suffer from alcoholism, drug abuse, or mental illness, and argue that people are responsible for the alcohol and drugs they ingest; they are not helpless victims of disease.

Communities have tried a number of strategies to cope with their homeless populations. Some set up temporary shelters, especially in winter; some subsidize permanent housing and/or group homes. They encourage private, nonprofit groups to establish soup kitchens and food banks. Others attempt to drive the homeless out of town or at least to parts of town where they will be less visible. They forbid loitering in city parks or on beaches after midnight, install sleep-proof seats on park benches and bus stations, and outlaw aggressive panhandling.

Still other observers believe that homelessness is more than simply a lack of shelter, that it is a matter of a mostly disturbed population with severe problems that requires help getting off the streets and into treatment. What the homeless need, they say, is a "continuum of care"—an entire range of services that includes education; treatment for drug and alcohol abuse and mental illness; and job training.

Questions:

1. *What is the nature of the homeless problem in the community where you live or with which you are most familiar?*

2. *Where should responsibility for the homeless lie: at the federal, state, or local governmental level? Is it best left to private groups such as churches and charities? Or is it ultimately best recognized as a personal matter to be handled by homeless individuals themselves? What reasons form or support your response?*

3. *Some people argue that giving money, food, or housing but no therapy to street people makes one an "enabler" or accomplice of addicts. Do you agree? Why or why not?*

A homeless man finds shelter on a bench near the White House in Washington, D.C.

served by and more dependent on mass transportation than is the U.S. city. Since Canadian metropolitan areas have only one-quarter the number of miles of expressway lanes per capita as U.S. metropolises—and at least as much resistance to constructing more—suburbanization of peoples and functions is less extensive north of the border than south.

In social as well as physical structure, Canadian–United States contrasts are apparent. While cities in both countries are ethnically diverse—Canadian communities, in fact, have the higher proportion of foreign born—U.S. central cities exhibit far greater internal distinctions in race, income, and social status and more pronounced contrasts between central city and suburban residents. That is, there has been much less "flight to the suburbs" by middle-income Canadians. As a result, the Canadian city shows greater social stability, higher per capita average income, more retention of shopping facilities, and more employment opportunities and urban amenities than its U.S. central city counterpart. In particular, it does not have the rivalry from well-defined competitive "edge cities" of suburbia that so spread and fragment United States metropolitan complexes.

The West European City

If such significant urban differences are found even within the tightly knit Anglo American region, we can only expect still greater divergences from the U.S. model at greater linear and cultural distance and in countries with long urban traditions and mature cities of their own. The political history of France, for example, has given to Paris an overwhelmingly primate position in its system of cities. Political, economic, and colonial history has done the same for London in the United Kingdom. On the other hand, Germany and Italy came late to nationhood and no overwhelmingly dominant cities developed in their systems.

Nonetheless, a generally common heritage of medieval origins, Renaissance restructurings, and industrial period extensions has given to the cities of Western Europe features distinctly different from those of cities in other regions founded and settled by European immigrants. Despite wartime destructions and postwar redevelopments, many still bear the impress of past occupants and technologies, even back to Roman times in some cases. An irregular system of narrow streets may be retained from the random street pattern developed in medieval times of pedestrian and pack-animal movement. Main streets radiating from the city center and cut by circumferential "ring roads" tell us the location of primary roads leading into town through the gates in city walls now gone and replaced by circular boulevards. Broad thoroughfares, public parks, and plazas mark Renaissance ideals of city beautification and the esthetic need felt for processional avenues and promenades.

Although each is unique historically and culturally, West European cities as a group share certain common features that set them off from the United States model, though they are less far removed from the Canadian norm. Cities of Western Europe have, for example, a much more compact form and occupy less total area than American cities of comparable population; most of their residents are apartment dwellers. Residential streets of the older sections tend to be narrow, and front, side, or rear yards or gardens are rare.

European cities were developed for pedestrians and still retain the compactness appropriate to walking distances. The sprawl of American peripheral or suburban zones is generally absent. At the same time, compactness and high density do not mean skyscraper skylines. Much of urban Europe predates the steel-frame building and the elevator. City skylines tend to be low, three to five stories in height, sometimes (as in central Paris) held down by building ordinance (Figure 11.35), or by prohibitions on private structures exceeding the height of a major public building, often the central cathedral.

Compactness, high densities, and apartment dwelling encouraged the development and continued importance of public transportation, including well-developed subway systems. The private automobile has become much more common of late, though most central city areas have not yet been significantly restructured with wider streets and parking facilities to accommodate it. The automobile is not the universal need in Europe that it has become in American cities. Home and work are generally more closely spaced in Europe—often within walking or bicycling distance—while most sections of towns have first-floor retail and business establishments (below upper-story apartments) bringing both places of employment and retail shops within convenient distance of residences.

A very generalized model of the social geography of the West European city has been proposed (Figure 11.36). Its exact counterpart can be found nowhere, but many of its general features are part of the spatial social structure of most major European cities. In the historic core, now increasingly gentrified, residential units for the middle class, the self-employed, and the older generation of skilled artisans share limited space with preserved historic buildings, monuments, and tourist attractions.

The old city fortifications may mark the boundary between the core and the surrounding transitional zone of substandard housing, 19th-century industry, and recent immigrants. The waterfront has similar older industry; newer plants are found on the periphery. Public housing and some immigrant concentrations may be near that newer industry, while other urban socioeconomic groups aggregate themselves in distinctive social areas within the body of the city.

The European city does not always feature the ethnic neighborhoods of United States cities although some, like London, do (see The Caribbean Map in London, p. 199), particularly for immigrants of non-European origin. Nor is it characterized by inner-city deterioration and out-migration. Its core areas tend to be stable in population and to attract rather than repel the successful middle class and the upwardly mobile, conditions far different from comparable sections of older American central cities.

FIGURE 11.35   Even in their central areas, many European cities show a low profile, like that of Paris seen here from the Eiffel Tower. Although taller buildings—20, 30, even 50 or more stories in height—have become more common in major cities since World War II, they are not the universal mark of central business districts that they have become in the United States, nor the generally welcomed symbols of city progress and pride.

The East European City

Cities of Eastern Europe, including Russia and the former European republics of the Soviet Union, make up a separate urban class—the East European city. It is an urban form that shares many of the traditions and practices of West European cities, but it differs from them in the centrally administered planning principles that were in the communist period designed to shape and control both new and older settlements. For reasons both ideological and practical, the particular concerns were, first, limitation on size of cities to avoid supercity growth and metropolitan sprawl; second, assurance of an internal structure of neighborhood equality and self-sufficiency; and third, strict land use segregation. The planned East European city fully achieved none of these objectives, but by attempting them it has emerged as a distinctive urban form.

In general structural terms, the city is compact, with relatively high building and population densities reflecting the nearly universal apartment dwelling, and with a sharp break between urban and rural land uses on its margins. Like the older generation West European city, the East European city depends nearly exclusively on public transportation.

During the communist period, it differed from its Western counterpart in its purely governmental rather than market control of land use and functional patterns. That control dictated that the central area of cities should be reserved for public use (and called the Central Cultural District), not occupied by retail establishments or office buildings on the Western, capitalist model. A large central square ringed by administrative and cultural buildings was the preferred pattern. Nearby, space was provided for a large recreational and commemorative park. Neither a central business district nor major outlying business districts were required or provided, for residential areas were expected to be largely self-contained in the provision of at least low-order goods and services, minimizing the need for a journey to centralized shopping locations.

Residential areas are made up of *microdistricts,* assemblages of uniform apartment blocks housing perhaps 10,000 to 15,000 persons, surrounded by broad boulevards, and containing centrally sited nursery and grade schools, grocery and department stores, theaters, clinics, and similar neighborhood necessities and amenities (Figure 11.37a). Plans called for effective separation of residential quarters from industrial districts by landscaped buffer zones, but in practice many microdistricts were built by factories for their own workers and were located immediately adjacent to the workplace. Since microdistricts were most easily and rapidly constructed on open land at the margins of expanding cities, high residential densities have been carried to the outskirts of town (Figure 11.37b). The distance decay curve of declining population densities outlined on Figure 11.24 does not apply to the East European city of communist origin.

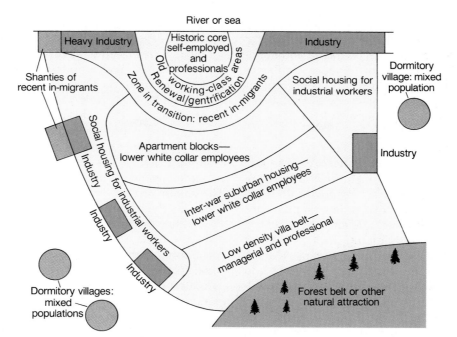

FIGURE 11.36 **A diagrammatic representation of the West European city.**

Paul White, *The West European City: A Social Geography.* (Essex, England: Longman Group UK Limited, 1984). Redrawn by permission.

(a)

(b)

FIGURE 11.37 (*a*) This scene from Bucharest, Romania, clearly shows important recurring characteristics of the socialist city design: mass transit service to boulevard-bordered "superblocks" of self-contained apartment house microdistricts that contain their own shopping, schools, and other facilities. (*b*) High-density apartment houses bordered by wheat fields mark the urban margin of Poprad, Slovakia; the Tatra Mountains are in the background.

These characteristic patterns will change in the decades to come as market principles of land allocation are adopted. Now that private interests can own land and buildings, the urban areas may take on forms more similar to those of the West European city. Currently, a prominent trend is to construct more spacious privately owned apartments and single-family houses for the newly rich.

Cities in the Developing World

Still farther removed from the United States urban model are the cities of Africa, Asia, and Latin America. Industrialization has come to them only recently or not at all, modern technologies in transportation and public facilities are barely known or sparsely available, and the structures of cities and the cultures of their inhabitants are far different from the urban world familiar to North Americans. The developing world is vast in extent and diverse in physical and social content; generalizations about it or its urban landscapes lack certainty and universality. Islamic cities of North Africa, for example, are entities sharply distinct from the sub-Saharan African, the Southeast Asian, or the Latin American city.

Yet, by observation and consensus, some common features of developing-world cities are recognizable. All, for example, have endured massive in-migrations from rural areas, and most have had even faster rates of natural increase than of immigration. As a result, most are ringed by vast squatter settlements high in density and low in public facilities and services (see "The Informal Housing Problem"). All, apparently, have populations greater than their formal functions and employment bases can support. In all, large numbers support themselves in the "informal" sector—as snack-food vendors, peddlers of cigarettes or trinkets, street-side barbers or tailors, errand runners or package carriers, and the like outside the usual forms of wage labor (Figure 10.5).

But the extent of acceptable generalization is limited, for the backgrounds, developmental histories, and current economies and administrations of developing-world cities vary so greatly. Some are still preindustrial, with only a modest central commercial core or central bazaar; they lack industrial districts, public transportation, or any meaningful degree of land use separation. Some are the product of Western colonialism, established as ports or outposts of administration and exploitation, built by Europeans on the Western

THE INFORMAL HOUSING PROBLEM

B etween one-third and two-thirds of the population of most developing-world cities is crowded into shantytowns and squatter settlements built by the inhabitants, often in defiance of officialdom. These unofficial communities usually have little or no access to publicly provided services such as water supply, sewerage and drainage, paved roads, and garbage removal. In such megacities as Rio de Janeiro, São Paulo, Mexico City, Bangkok, Madras, Cairo, or Lagos, millions find refuge in the shacks and slums of the "informal housing sector." Crumbling tenements house additional tens of thousands, many of whom are eventually forced into shantytowns by the conversion of tenements into commercial property or high-income apartments.

No more than 20% of the new housing in Third World cities is produced by the formal housing sector; the rest develops informally, ignoring building codes, zoning restrictions, property rights, and infrastructure standards. As the graph indicates, informal settlements house varying percentages of these populations, but for low-income developing countries as a whole during the 1980s and early 1990s, only one formal housing unit was added for every nine new households, and between 70% and 90% of all new households found shelter in shanties or slums. Peripheral squatter settlements, though densely built, may provide adequate household space and even water, sewers, and defined traffic lanes through the efforts of the residents. More usually, however, overcrowding transforms these settlements into vast zones of disease and squalor subject to constant danger from landslides, fire, and flooding.

Source: Graph data from *Human Development Report 1990*, Oxford University Press, New York, NY, and other sources.

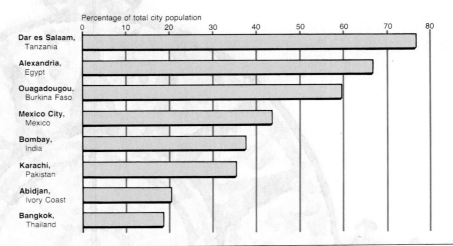

LANDSCAPES OF FUNCTIONAL ORGANIZATION

FIGURE 11.38   The Grand Bazaar of Istanbul, Turkey, with its miles of crowded streets, was built in the mid-17th century and now houses more than 3000 shops. It is a vibrant reminder that a successful, thriving commercial economy need not be housed in Western-style business districts.

model, though increasingly engulfed by later, indigenous urban forms. In some, Western-style skyscraper central areas and commercial cores have been newly constructed; in others, commerce is conducted in different forums and formats (Figure 11.38).

Wherever the automobile or modern transport systems are an integral part of the growth of developing-world cities, the metropolis begins to take on Western characteristics. On the other hand, in places like Bombay (India), Lagos (Nigeria), Jakarta (Indonesia), Kinshasa (Zaire), and Cairo (Egypt), where the public transport system is limited, the result has been overcrowded cities centered on a single major business district in the old tradition. In such societies, the impact of urbanization and the responses to it differ from the patterns and problems observable in the cities of the United States.

The developing countries, emerging from formerly dominant subsistence economies, have experienced disproportionate population concentrations, particularly in their national and regional capitals. Lacking or relatively undeveloped is the substructure of maturing, functionally complex smaller and medium-sized centers characteristic of more advanced and diversified economies. The primate city dominates their urban systems (Figure 11.16). More than a quarter of all Nicaraguans live in Managua, and Libreville contains nearly one-third of the populace of Gabon. Vast numbers of surplus, low-income rural populations have been attracted to these developed seats of wealth and political centrality in the hope of finding a job.

Although attention may be lavished on creating urban cores on the skyscraper model of Western cities (Figure 11.39), most of the new urban multitudes have little choice but to pack themselves into squatter shanty communities on the fringes of the city, isolated from the sanitary facilities, the public utilities, and the job opportunities that are found only at the center. In the sprawling slum district of Nairobi, Kenya, called Mathare Valley some 250,000 people are squeezed into 15 square kilometers (6 sq. mi.) and are

FIGURE 11.39 **Downtown Nairobi, Kenya, is a busy, modern, urban core complete with high-rise commercial buildings.**

increasing by 10,000 inhabitants per year. Such impoverished squatter districts exist around most major cities in Africa, Asia, and Latin America (Figure 11.40), creating an *inverse concentric zone* pattern where the elite and upper class reside in central areas and social status declines with increasing distance from the center. Proposed models of developing-world urban structures demonstrate the limits of these generalizations. The same models (and others) help define some of the regional and cultural contrasts that distinguish those cities (Figure 11.41).

The Asian City and African City

Many large cities of Asia and Africa were founded and developed by European colonialists. For example, the British built Calcutta and Bombay in India and Nairobi and Harare (formerly Salisbury) in Africa, the French developed Ho Chi

FIGURE 11.40 Millions of people of the developing world live in shantytown settlements on the fringes of large cities, without benefit of running water, electricity, sewage systems, or other public services. The hillside slum pictured here is one of the many *favelas* that are home for nearly half of Rio de Janeiro's more than 11 million residents.

(a) SOUTHEAST ASIAN CITY

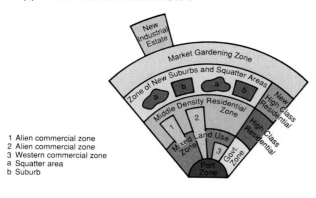

1 Alien commercial zone
2 Alien commercial zone
3 Western commercial zone
a Squatter area
b Suburb

(b) COLONIAL-BASED SOUTH ASIAN CITY

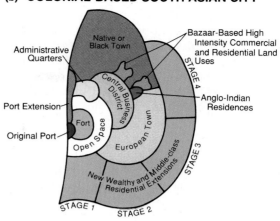

(c) BAZAAR-BASED (Traditional) SOUTH ASIAN CITY

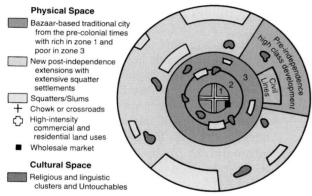

Physical Space

Bazaar-based traditional city from the pre-colonial times with rich in zone 1 and poor in zone 3

New post-independence extensions with extensive squatter settlements

Squatters/Slums

+ Chowk or crossroads

High-intensity commercial and residential land uses

■ Wholesale market

Cultural Space

Religious and linguistic clusters and Untouchables

(d) LATIN AMERICAN CITY

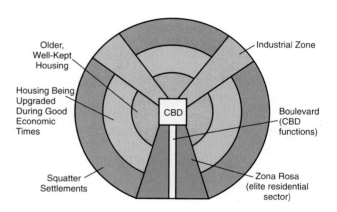

FIGURE 11.41   **Developing world urban models.**

Minh City (Saigon) in Vietnam and Dakar in Senegal. The Dutch had as their main outpost Jakarta in Indonesia, and many colonial countries established Shanghai. These and many other cities in Asia and Africa have certain important similarities derived in part from their colonial heritage and the imprint of alien cultures which they still bear.

The large *Southeast Asian* city is shown in Figure 11.41*a* as a composite. The port and its associated areas were colonial creations, retained and strengthened in independence. Around them are found a Western-style central business district with European shops, hotels, and restaurants; one or more "alien commercial zones" where merchants of the Chinese and, perhaps, Indian communities have established themselves; and the more widespread zone of mixed residential, light industrial, and indigenous commercial uses. Central slums and peripheral squatter settlements house up to two-thirds of the total city population. Market gardening and recent industrial development mark the outer metropolitan limits.

The *South Asian* city appears in two forms. Figure 11.41*b* summarizes the internal structure of the colonial-based city, making clear the spatial separation of local and European residential areas, the mixed-race enclave between

them, and the 20th-century new growth areas housing the wealthier local elites. Figure 11.41*c* depicts the traditional bazaar city, its city center focused on a crossroads around which are found the houses of the wealthier residents. Merchants live above or behind their shops, and the entire city center is characterized by mixed residential, commercial, and manufacturing land uses. Beyond the inner core is, first, an upper-income residential area shared (but not in the same structures) with poorer servants. Still farther out are the slums and squatter communities, generally sharply segregated according to ethnic, religious, caste, or native village of their inhabitants.

Asia's past and projected urban growth is explosive. From 1960 to 1990, some 45% of the continent's total population growth came within its urban areas. The United Nations estimates that essentially all of Asia's net population increase between 1990 and 2020 will be in cities, raising Asia's urban population from 850 million to 2.25 billion. That annual average growth of 47 million new city dwellers will certainly exaggerate the already considerable problems of environmental degradation posed by urban growth unsupported by adequate infrastructure development in water, sewer, and other facilities.

Most Asian governments, recognizing the problems of substandard housing, inadequate public services, and environmental deterioration their dominantly primate city population concentrations create, have adopted policies encouraging the establishment of intermediate-sized cities to disperse urbanization and its developmental benefits more widely across their territories. China has achieved more success in this regard than have, for example, India or Pakistan.

The *African city* is less easily generalized. Sub-Saharan Africa, with less than one-third of its people living in cities, is the least urbanized segment of the developing world. It has, however, the fastest urban growth rates. No more than half of their growth reflects the natural increase of populations already in the cities, and future African urban expansion will largely come from rural to urban migration and the incorporation of villages into spreading metropolitan complexes.

As they did in Asia, European colonialists created new centers of administration and exploitation. Many were designed with spread-out, tree-lined European residential districts separated by open land from the barracks built for African laborers. Disregarding local climate, building materials, and wisdom, British colonists imposed English building codes more concerned with snow-load than tropical heat. Since independence, these former colonial outposts have grown apace, with the largest cities expanding at rates upwards of 10% per year in some countries. That explosive growth reflects the centralization of government and the concentration of wealth and power in single cities that the small urban elites view as symbols of their countries' economic growth and modernity.

Many, like Lagos, Nigeria, present a confused landscape of teeming, dirt-street shanty developments, unserved by running water or sewerage lines surrounding a modern urban core of high-rise buildings, paved streets and expressways, and modern facilities, and the older, lower-building commercial, governmental, and residential district near the harbor. In contrast, others like Abidjan in the Ivory Coast are clean, well-designed, and orderly cities nearly Western in appearance.

In all African cities, however, spatial contrasts in social geography are great and in most sub-Saharan cities socioeconomic divisions are coupled with a partition of, particularly, squatter slum areas into ethnically-based subdivisions. Former greenbelts have been densely filled with cardboard and sheet metal shacks of the poor who are still denied access to the spacious suburbs of the well-to-do and influential. The richest 10% of Nairobi's population, for example, occupy two-thirds of the city's residential land.

The Latin American City

"City life" is the cultural norm in Latin America. The vast majority of the residents of Mexico, Venezuela, Brazil, Argentina, Chile, and other countries live in cities, and very often in the primate city. The urbanization process is rapidly making Latin cities among the largest in the world. Analysts predict that by the year 2010, six of the largest 28 cities will be in Latin America, and Rio de Janeiro and São Paulo, Brazil, will have merged into a continuous megalopolis 350 miles long with almost 40 million inhabitants.

The limited wealth of Latin cities confines most commercial activity to the central business district (CBD) (Figure 11.41d). The entire transportation system focuses on the downtown, where the vast majority of jobs are found. The city centers are lively and modern with many tall office buildings, clubs, restaurants, and stores of every variety. Condominium apartments house the well-to-do who prefer living in the center because of its convenience to workplaces, theaters, museums, friends, specialty shops, and restaurants (Figure 11.42). Thousands of commuters pour into the CBD each day, some coming from the outer edge of the city (perhaps an hour or two commuting time) where the poorest people live.

Two features figure prominently in the Latin American urban land use model suggested in Figure 11.41d. One is the *spine,* which is a continuation of the features of the CBD outward along the main wide boulevard. Here one finds the upper-middle-class housing stock, which is again apartments and town houses. The second is the concentric rings around the center housing ever poorer people as distance increases from the center. This social patterning is just the opposite of many United States cities. The slums (*barrios, favelas*) are on the outskirts of the city. In rapidly growing centers like Mexico City, the barrios are found in the farthest concentric ring, which is several miles wide.

Once Latin residents establish themselves in the city, they tend to remain at their original site, and as income permits they improve their homes. When times are good, there is a great deal of house repair and upgrading activity. Those in the city for the longest time are generally the most prosperous. As a result, the quality of housing continually improves inward toward the city center. The homes closest to the center are substantial and need little upgrading, but even farther out where slums were once in evidence, one now finds modest houses with new additions being built.

Each of the idealized land use models in Figure 11.41 presents a variant of the developing world's collective urban dilemma: an urban structure not fully capable of housing the peoples so rapidly thrust upon it. The great increases in city populations exceed urban support capabilities and unemployment rates are nearly everywhere disastrously high. There is little chance to reduce them as additional millions continue to swell cities already overwhelmed by poverty. The problems, cultures, environments, and economies of developing-world cities are tragically unique to them. The urban models which give us understanding of United States cities are of little assistance or guidance in such vastly different culture realms.

FIGURE 11.42   **Buildings along the Paseo de la Reforma in Mexico City.** Part of the central business district, this area contains apartment houses, theaters and nightclubs, and commercial high rises.

Summary

The city is the essential focus of every society advanced beyond the subsistence level. Although cities are among the oldest marks of civilization, only in this century have they become the home of the majority of the people in the industrialized countries and both the commercial crossroads and place of refuge for uncounted millions in the developing world. At the global scale, four major world urban regions have emerged: Western Europe, South Asia, East Asia, and North America.

All cities growing beyond their village origins take on functions uniting them to the countryside and to a larger system of cities. As they grow, they become functionally complex. Their economic base, composed of both *basic* and *service* activities, may become diverse. Basic activities represent the functions performed for the larger economy and urban system, while service (nonbasic) activities satisfy the needs of the urban residents themselves. Functional classifications distinguish the economic roles of urban centers, while simple description of them as transportation and special-function cities or as central places helps define and explain their functional and size hierarchies and the spatial patterns they display within a system of cities.

As Anglo American urban centers expanded in population size and diversity, they developed more or less structured land use and social patterns based on market allocations of urban space, channelization of traffic, and largely voluntary socioeconomic aggregation. The observed regularity of land use arrangements has been summarized for U.S. cities by the concentric circle, sector, and multiple-nuclei models. Social area counterparts of land use specializations were based on social status, family status, and ethnicity. Since 1945, these older models of land uses and social areas have been modified by the suburbanization of people and functions that has led to the creation of new and complex outer cities and to the deterioration of the older central city itself.

Urbanization is a global phenomenon, and the North American models of city systems, land use, and social area patterns are not necessarily or usually applicable to other cultural contexts. In Europe, stringent land use regulations have brought about a compact urban form ringed by greenbelts. The East European urban areas still show a pattern of density and land use reflecting recent communist principles of city structure. Models descriptive of developing-world cities do little to convey the fact that those settlements are currently growing faster than it is possible to provide employment, housing, safe water, sanitation, and other minimally essential services and facilities.

KEY WORDS

basic sector 381
central business district (CBD) 389
central city 380
central place 385
central place theory 386
Christaller, Walter 386
city 380
concentric zone model 392

conurbation 373
economic base 381
gentrification 402
metropolitan area 380
multiple-nuclei model 393
multiplier effect 382
nonbasic (service) sector 381
primate city 384

rank-size rule 384
sector model 392
service (nonbasic) sector 381
suburb 380
town 380
urban hierarchy 383
urban influence zone 385
urbanized area 380

FOR REVIEW

1. Consider the city or town in which you live, attend school, or with which you are most familiar. In a brief paragraph, discuss that community's *site* and *situation*. Point out the connection, if any, between its site and situation and the basic functions that it earlier or now performs.

2. Describe the *multiplier effect* as it relates to the population growth of urban units.

3. What area does a *central place* serve, and what kinds of functions does it perform? If an urban system were composed solely of central places, what summary statements could you make about the spatial distribution and the urban size hierarchy of that system?

4. Is there a hierarchy of retailing activities in the community with which you are most familiar? Of

how many and of what kinds of levels is that hierarchy composed? What localizing forces affect the distributional pattern of retailing within that community?

5. Briefly describe the urban land use patterns predicted by the *concentric circle,* the *sector,* and the *multiple-nuclei* models of urban development. Which one, if any, best corresponds to the growth and land use pattern of the community most familiar to you? How well does Figure 11.31 or 11.32 depict the land use patterns in the metropolitan area with which you are most familiar?

6. In what ways do *social status, family status,* and *ethnicity* affect the residential choices of households? What expected distributional patterns of urban social areas are associated with each? Does the

social geography of your community conform to the predicted pattern?

7. How has suburbanization damaged the economic base and the financial stability of the United States central city?

8. In what ways does the Canadian city differ from the pattern of its U.S. counterpart?

9. What are *primate cities*? Why are primate cities so prevalent in the developing world? How are some governments attempting to reduce their relative importance in their national systems of cities?

10. What are the significant differences in the generalized pattern of land uses of North American, West European, East European, Asian, and African cities?

SELECTED REFERENCES

Borchert, John R. "America's Changing Metropolitan Regions." *Annals of the Association of American Geographers* 62 (1972):352–373.

Bourne, Larry S., and David F. Ley, eds. *The Changing Social Geography of Canadian Cities.* Canadian Association of Geographers Series in Canadian Geography. Montreal: McGill-Queen's University Press, 1993.

Bourne, Larry S., Robert Sinclair, and K. Dziewnski, eds. *Urbanization and Settlement Systems: International Perspectives.* New York: Oxford University Press, 1984.

Brunn, Stanley D., and Jack F. Williams. *Cities of the World: World Regional Urban Development.* 2d ed. New York: Harper & Row, 1993.

Bunting, Trudi, and Pierre Filion, eds. *Canadian Cities in Transition.* Toronto: Oxford University Press, 1991.

Burgess, Ernest W. "The Growth of the City." In *The City,* edited by Robert E. Park, Ernest W. Burgess, and Roderick D. McKenzie, pp. 47–62. Chicago: University of Chicago Press, 1925.

Burtenshaw, D., M. Bateman, and G. J. Ashworth. *The European City: A Western Perspective.* New York: John Wiley & Sons, 1991.

Carter, Harold. *The Study of Urban Geography.* 4th ed. London: Arnold, 1995

Christaller, Walter. *Central Places in Southern Germany.* (Translated by C. W. Baskin.) Englewood Cliffs, NJ: Prentice-Hall, 1966.

Christian, Charles M., and Robert A. Harper, eds. *Modern Metropolitan Systems.* Columbus, OH: Charles E. Merrill, 1982.

Costa, Frank J., Ashok K. Dutt, Lawrence J. C. Ma, and Allen G. Noble, eds. *Urbanization in Asia: Spatial Dimensions and Policy Issues.* Honolulu: University of Hawaii Press, 1989.

Davies, Wayne K. D., and David T. Herbert. *Communities within Cities: An Urban Social Geography.* London: Bellhaven Press, 1993.

Dogan, Mattei, and John D. Kasarda, eds. *The Metropolis Era.* Vol. 1, *A World of Giant Cities;* Vol. 2, *Mega-Cities.* Newbury Park, CA: Sage Publications, 1988.

Drakakis-Smith, David. *The Third World City.* London and New York: Methuen, 1987.

Drakakis-Smith, David, ed. *Economic Growth and Urbanization in Developing Areas.* London and New York: Routledge, 1990.

Dutt, Ashok K., et al., eds. *The Asian City: Processes of Development, Characteristics and Planning.* Dordrecht/Boston/London: Kluwer Academic Publishers, 1994.

Erickson, Rodney A., and Marylynn Gentry. "Suburban Nucleations." *Geographical Review* 75 (1985):19–31.

Ewing, Gordon O. "The Bases of Differences between American and Canadian Cities." *The Canadian Geographer/Le Géographie Canadien* 36, no. 3 (1992):266–279.

Farley, Reynolds, and William H. Frey. "Changes in the Segregation of Whites from Blacks during the 1980s: Small Steps Toward a More Integrated Society." *American Sociological Review* 59 (1994):23–45.

Ford, Larry R. *Cities and Buildings: Skyscrapers, Skid Rows, and Suburbs.* Baltimore: Johns Hopkins University Press, 1994.

Garreau, Joel. *Edge City: Life on the New Frontier.* New York: Doubleday & Co., 1991.

Getis, Arthur, and Judith Getis. "Christaller's Central Place Theory." *Journal of Geography* 65 (1966):220–226.

Gilbert, Alan, and Josef Gugler. *Cities, Poverty and Development: Urbanization in the Third World.* 2d rev. ed. New York: Oxford University Press, 1992.

Ginsburg, Norton, et al., eds. *The Extended Metropolis: Settlement Transition in Asia.* Honolulu: University of Hawaii Press, 1991.

Goldberg, Michael A., and John Mercer. *The Myth of the North American City.* Vancouver: University of British Columbia Press, 1986.

Griffin, Ernst, and Larry Ford. "A Model of Latin American City Structure." *Geographical Review* 70 (1980):397–422.

Harris, Chauncy D., and Edward L. Ullman. "The Nature of Cities." *Annals of the American Academy of Political and Social Science* 242 (1945):7–17.

Hartshorn, Truman. *Interpreting the City.* 3d ed. New York: John Wiley & Sons, 1997.

Herbert, David T., and Colin J. Thomas. *Cities in Space: City as Place.* Lanham, MD: Barnes & Noble, 1990.

Hornby, William F., and Melvyn Jones. *An Introduction to Settlement Geography.* New York: Cambridge University Press, 1991.

Hoyt, Homer. *The Structure and Growth of Residential Neighborhoods in American Cities.* Washington, D.C.: Government Printing Office, 1939.

Jefferson, Mark. "The Law of the Primate City." *Geographical Review* 29 (1939):226–232.

Karan, P. P., and W. A. Bladen. "Arabic Cities." *Focus* 33, no. 3 (1983).

Kariel, Herbert G., and S. L. Walling. "A Nodal Structure for a Set of Canadian Cities Using Graph Theory and Newspaper Datelines." *Canadian Geographer* 21 (1977):148–173.

King, Leslie J. *Central Place Theory.* Newbury Park, CA: Sage Publications, 1984.

Knox, Paul L. *Urban Social Geography: An Introduction.* 3d ed. White Plains, NY: Longman 1995.

Knox, Paul L. *Urbanization: An Introduction to Urban Geography.* Englewood Cliffs, NJ: Prentice-Hall, 1994.

Kosambi, Meera, and John E. Brush. "Three Colonial Port Cities in India." *Geographical Review* 78, no. 1 (1988):32–47.

Lowder, Stella. *The Geography of Third World Cities.* Totowa, NJ: Barnes & Noble, 1986.

McGee, T. G. *The Southeast Asian City.* New York: Praeger, 1967.

Medvedkov, Olga. *Soviet Urbanization.* London and New York: Routledge, 1990.

Muller, Peter O. *Contemporary Suburban America.* Englewood Cliffs, NJ: Prentice-Hall, 1981.

Pannell, Clifton. "China's Urban Transition." *Journal of Geography* 94, no. 3 (1995):394–403.

Preston, Richard E. "The Structure of Central Place Systems." *Economic Geography* 47 (1971):136–155.

Rose, Harold. *The Black Ghetto: A Spatial Behavioral Perspective.* New York: McGraw-Hill, 1971.

Roseman, Curtis C., Gunther Thieme, and Hans Dieter Laux, eds. *EthniCity: Geographic Perspectives on Ethnic Change in Modern Cities.* Lanham, MD: Rowman & Littlefield, 1995.

Short, John R., ed. *Human Settlement.* The Illustrated Encyclopedia of World Geography. New York: Oxford University Press, 1992.

Simon, David. *Cities, Capital, and Development: African Cities in the World Economy.* New York: John Wiley & Sons, 1992.

Smith, Neil, and Peter Williams, eds. *Gentrification of the City.* Winchester, MA: Allen & Unwin, 1986.

Stelter, Gilbert, and Alan F. J. Artibise, eds. *Power and Place: Canadian Urban Development in the North American Context.* Vancouver: University of British Columbia Press, 1986.

Stimpson, Catharine R., Elsa Dixler, Martha J. Nelson, and Kathryn B. Yatrakis. *Women and the American City.* Chicago: University of Chicago Press, 1981.

White, Paul. *The West European City: A Social Geography.* London and New York: Longman, 1984.

Wood, Joseph S. "Suburbanization of Center City." *Geographical Review* 78, no. 3 (1988):325–329.

Yeates, Maurice. *The North American City.* 4th ed. New York: Harper & Row, 1990.

THE POLITICAL ORDERING OF SPACE

CHAPTER 12

National Political Systems 417

States, Nations, and Nation-States 417

The Evolution of the Modern State 419

Geographic Characteristics of States 419

   Size 420

   Shape 420

   Location 424

   Cores and Capitals 425

Boundaries: The Limits of the State 425

   Classification of Boundaries 426

   Boundary Disputes 428

State Cohesiveness 429

   Nationalism 429

   Unifying Institutions 430

   Organization and Administration 431

   Transportation and
      Communication 431

Nationalism and Centrifugal Forces 433

The Projection of Power 434

   Geopolitical Assessments 435

International Political Systems 436

The United Nations and Its Agencies 437

   Maritime Boundaries 438

   An International Law of the Sea 438

Regional Alliances 439

   Economic Alliances 440

   Military and Political Alliances 443

**Local and Regional Political
Organization 443**

The Geography of Representation: The
Districting Problem 444

The Fragmentation of Political
Power 445

   Unified Government 449

   Predevelopment Annexation 450

   SUMMARY 450

   KEY WORDS 451

   FOR REVIEW 451

   SELECTED REFERENCES 452

A view of Parliament, London, England.

They met together in the cabin of the little ship on the day of the landfall. The journey from England had been long and stormy. Provisions ran out, a man had died, a boy had been born. Although they were grateful to have been delivered to the calm waters off Cape Cod that November day of 1620, their gathering in the cramped cabin was not to offer prayers of thanksgiving but to create a political structure to govern the settlement they were now to establish (they had originally been bound for Virginia). The Mayflower Compact was an agreement among themselves to "covenant and combine our selves togeather into a civill Body Politick . . . to enacte, constitute, and frame such just and equall Lawes, Ordinances, Acts, Constitutions, and Offices . . . convenient for ye Generall good of ye Colonie. . . ." They elected one of their company governor, and only after those political acts did they launch a boat and put a party ashore.

The land they were to colonize had for more than 100 years been claimed by the England they had left. The New World voyage of John Cabot in 1497 had invested their sovereign with title to all of the land of North America and a recognized legal right to govern his subjects dwelling there. That right was delegated by royal patent to colonizers and their sponsors, conferring upon them title to a defined tract and the right to govern it. Although the Mayflower settlers were originally without a charter or patent, they recognized themselves as part of an established political system. They chose their governor and his executive department annually by vote of the General Court, a legislature composed of all freemen of the settlement.

As the population grew, new towns were established too distant for their voters to attend the General Court. By 1636 the larger towns were sending representatives to cooperate with the executive branch in making laws. Each town became a legal entity, with election of local officials and enactment of local ordinances the prime purpose of the town meetings that are still common in New England today.

The Mayflower Compact, signed by 41 freemen as their initial act in a New World, was the first step in a continuing journey of political development for the settlement and for the larger territory of which it became a part. From company patent to crown colony to rebellious commonwealth under the Continental Congress to state in a new nation, Massachusetts (and Plimoth Plantation) were part of a continuing process of the political organization of space.

FIGURE 12.1   Signing the Mayflower Compact. This voluntary agreement of self-government provided for a form of popular rule and was the first written constitution in North America.

That process is as old as human history. From clans to kingdoms, human groups, have laid claim to territory and have organized themselves and administered their affairs within it. Indeed, the political organizations of society are as fundamental an expression of culture and cultural differences as are forms of economy or religious beliefs. Geographers are interested in that structuring because it is both an expression of the human organization of space and is closely related to other spatial evidences of culture, such as religion, language, and ethnicity.

Political geography is the study of the organization and distribution of political phenomena, including their impact on other spatial components of society and culture. Nationality is a basic element in cultural variation among people, and political geography traditionally has had a primary interest in country units, or *states* (Figure 12.2). Of central concern have been spatial patterns that reflect the exercise of central governmental control, such as questions of boundary delimitation and effect. Increasingly, however, attention has shifted both upward and downward on the political scale. On the world scene, international alliances, regional compacts, and producer cartels—some requiring the surrender of at least a portion of national sovereignty—have increased in prominence since World War II, representing new forms of spatial interaction. At the local level, voting patterns, constituency boundaries and districting rules, and political fragmentation have directed public attention to the significance of area in the domestic political process.

In this chapter we consider some of the characteristics of political entities, examine the problems involved in defining jurisdictions, seek the elements that lend cohesion to a political entity, explore the implications of partial surrender of sovereignty, and consider the significance of the fragmentation of political power. We begin with states (countries) and end with local political systems.

FIGURE 12.2   These flags, symbols of separate member states, grace the front of the United Nations building in New York City. Although central to political geographic interest, states are only one level of the political organization of space.

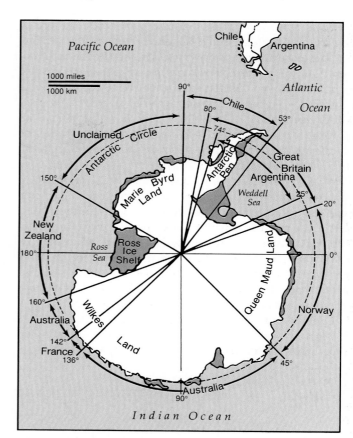

FIGURE 12.3   **Territorial claims in Antarctica.** Although seven countries claim sovereignty over portions of Antarctica, and three of the claims overlap, the continent has no permanent inhabitants or established local government.

Emphasis here on political entities should not make us lose sight of the reality that states are rooted in the operations of the economy and society they represent, that social and economic disputes are as significant as border confrontations, and that in some regards transnational corporations and other nongovernmental agencies may exert more influence in international affairs than do the separate states in which they are housed or operate. Nor should we forget that, increasingly, world and local conflicts are rooted in clashes of civilizations and cultures and not just in interstate rivalries. Some of those expanded political considerations are alluded to in the discussions that follow; others were developed more fully in Chapter 10.

National Political Systems

One of the most significant elements in cultural geography is the nearly complete division of the earth's land surface into separate national units, as shown on the Countries of the World map inside the book's cover. Even Antarctica is subject to the rival territorial claims of seven countries, although these claims have not been pressed because of the Antarctic Treaty of 1961 (Figure 12.3). A second element is that this division into country units is relatively recent. Although countries and empires have existed since the days of early Egypt and Mesopotamia, only in the last century has the world been almost completely divided into independent governing entities. Now people everywhere accept the idea of the state and its claim to sovereignty within its borders as normal.

States, Nations, and Nation-States

Before we begin our consideration of political systems, we need to clarify some terminology. Geographers use the words *state* and *nation* somewhat differently than the way they are used in everyday speech; sometimes confusion arises because each word has more than one meaning. A state can be defined as either (1) any of the political units forming a federal government (e.g., one of the United States) or as (2) a recognized independent political entity holding sovereignty over a territory (e.g., the United States). In this latter sense, *state* is synonymous with *country* or *nation*. That is, a nation can also be defined as (1) an independent political unit holding sovereignty over a territory (e.g., a member of the United Nations). But it can also be used to describe (2) a community of people with a common ancestry, culture, and territory (e.g., the Kurdish nation). The second definition is *not* synonymous with state or country.

To avoid confusion, we shall define a **state** on the international level as an independent political unit occupying a defined, permanently populated territory and having full sovereign control over its internal and foreign affairs. We will use *country* as a synonym for the territorial and political concept of "state." Not all recognized territorial entities are states. Antarctica, for example, has neither established government nor permanent population, and it is, therefore, not a state. Nor are *colonies* or *protectorates* recognized as states. Although they have defined extent, permanent inhabitants, and some degree of separate governmental structure, they lack full control over all of their internal and external affairs. More importantly, they lack recognition as states by the international community, a decisive consideration in the proper use of the term "state."

We use nation in its second sense, as a reference to people, not to political structure. A **nation** is a group of people with a common culture occupying a particular territory, bound together by a strong sense of unity arising from shared beliefs and customs. Language and religion may be unifying elements, but even more important are an emotional conviction of cultural distinctiveness and a sense of ethnocentrism. The Cree nation exists because of its cultural uniqueness, not by virtue of territorial sovereignty.

The composite term **nation-state** properly refers to a state whose territorial extent coincides with that occupied by a distinct nation or people or, at least, whose population shares a general sense of cohesion and adherence to a set of common values (Figure 12.4). That is, a nation-state is an entity whose members feel a natural connection with each other by virtue of sharing language, religion, or some other cultural characteristic strong enough both to bind them together and to give them a sense of distinction from all others outside the community. Although all countries strive for consensus values and loyalty to the state, few can claim to be ethnic nation-states. Iceland, Denmark, and Poland are often cited as acceptable European examples. Japan is an Asian illustration, Eritrea an African one.

A *binational* or *multinational state* is one that contains more than one nation. Often, no single ethnic group dominates the population. In the constitutional structure of the former Soviet Union before 1988, one division of the legislative branch of the government was termed the Soviet of Nationalities. It was composed of representatives from civil divisions of the Soviet Union populated by groups of officially recognized "nations": Ukrainians, Kazakhs, Tatars, Estonians, and others. In this instance, the concept of nationality was territorially less than the extent of the state.

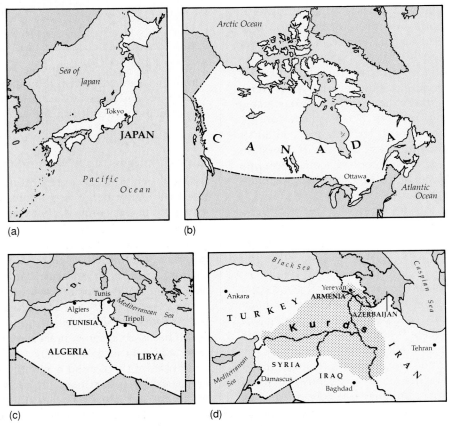

FIGURE 12.4   **Types of relationships between "states" and "nations."** (*a*) **A nation-state.** Japan is an example of a state occupied by a distinct nation, or people. (*b*) **A multinational state.** Canada contains three distinct nations (native Canadians and those of British or French origin) and has two official languages, English and French. (*c*) **A part-nation state.** The Arab nation extends across and dominates many states in northern Africa and the Middle East. (*d*) **A stateless nation.** An ancient group with a distinctive language and culture, the Kurds are concentrated in Turkey, Iran, and Iraq. Smaller numbers live in Syria, Armenia, and Azerbaijan.

LANDSCAPES OF FUNCTIONAL ORGANIZATIONS

Alternatively, a single nation may be dispersed across and be predominant in two or more states. This is the case with the *part-nation state*. Here, a people's sense of nationality exceeds the areal limits of a single country. An example is the Arab nation, which dominates 17 states.

Finally, there is the special case of the *stateless nation*, a nation without a country. The Kurds, for example, are a nation of some 20 million people divided among six states and dominant in none (Figure 12.4d). Kurdish nationalism has survived over the centuries, and many Kurds nurture a vision of an independent Kurdistan. Other stateless nations are Macedonians, Basques, and Palestinians. The Palestine Liberation Organization (PLO) took over administrative control of the Gaza Strip and Jericho from Israel in 1994 and of additional towns and districts within the West Bank region in 1995 and 1996, steps that Palestinians expect to lead to independent statehood.

The Evolution of the Modern State

Whether we think in terms of nation or state, the concept and practice of political organization of space and people arose independently in many parts of the world. Certainly, one of the distinguishing characteristics of very early culture hearths—including those shown on Figure 2.16—was the political organization of their peoples and areas. The larger and more complex the economic structures they developed, the more sophisticated became their mechanisms of political control and territorial administration.

Our Western orientations and biases may incline us to trace ideas of spatial political organization through their Near Eastern, Mediterranean, and Western European expressions. Mesopotamian and classical Greek city states, the Roman Empire, and European colonizing kingdoms and warring principalities were, however, neither unique nor particularly unusual. Southern, southeastern and eastern Asia had their counterparts, as did sub-Saharan Africa and the Western Hemisphere. It is true that Western European models and colonization strongly influenced the forms and structures of modern states in both hemispheres, but the cultural roots of statehood run deeper and reach further back in many parts of the world than European example alone suggests.

The now universal idea of the modern state was developed by European political philosophers in the 18th century. Their views advanced the concept that people owe allegiance to a state and the people it represents rather than to its leader, such as a king or feudal lord. The new concept coincided in France with the French Revolution and spread over Western Europe, to England, Spain, and Germany.

Many states are the result of European expansion during the 17th, 18th, and 19th centuries, when much of Africa, Asia, and the Americas was divided into colonies. Usually these colonial claims were given fixed and described boundaries where none had earlier been formally defined. Of course, precolonial indigenous populations had relatively fixed home areas of control within which there was recognized dominance and border defense and from which there were, perhaps, raids of plunder or conquest of neighboring "foreign" territories. Beyond tribal territories, great empires arose, again with recognized outer limits of influence or control: Mogul and Chinese; Benin and Zulu; Incan and Aztec. Upon them where they still existed, and upon the less formally organized spatial patterns of effective tribal control, European colonizers imposed their arbitrary new administrative divisions of the land. In fact, tribes that had little in common were often joined in the same colony (Figure 12.5). The new divisions, therefore, were not usually based on meaningful cultural or physical lines. Instead, the boundaries simply represented the limits of the colonizing empire's power.

As these former colonies have gained political independence, they have retained the idea of the state. They have generally accepted—in the case of Africa, by a conscious decision to avoid precolonial territorial or ethnic claims that could lead to war—the borders established by their former European rulers (Figure 12.6). The problem that many of the new countries face is "nation building"—developing feelings of loyalty to the state among their arbitrarily associated citizens. Zaire, the former Belgian Congo, contains some 270 frequently antagonistic ethnic groups. Only if past tribal animosities can be converted into an overriding spirit of national cohesion will countries like Zaire truly be nation-states.

The idea of separate statehood grew slowly at first and, more recently, has accelerated rapidly. At the time of the Declaration of Independence of the United States in 1776, there were only some 35 empires, kingdoms, and countries in the entire world. By the start of World War II at the end of the 1930s, their number had only doubled to about 70. Following that war, the end of the colonial era brought a rapid increase in the number of sovereign states. From the former British Empire and Commonwealth, there have come the independent countries of India, Pakistan, Bangladesh, Malaysia, and Singapore in Asia, and Ghana, Nigeria, Kenya, Uganda, Tanzania, Malawi, Botswana, Zimbabwe, and Zambia in Africa. Even this extensive list is not complete. A similar process has occurred in most of the former overseas possessions of the Netherlands, Spain, Portugal, and France. By 1990, independent states totalled nearly 200 and their number increased again following—among other political geographic developments—the disintegration of the former USSR and Yugoslavia during the early 1990s (Figure 12.7).

Geographic Characteristics of States

Every state has certain geographic characteristics by which it can be described and that set it apart from all other states. A look at the world political map inside the cover of this book confirms that every state is unique. The size, shape, and location of any one state combine to distinguish it from all others. These characteristics are of more than academic interest, because they also affect the power and stability of states.

FIGURE 12.5   **The discrepancies between tribal and national boundaries in Africa.** Tribal boundaries were ignored by European colonial powers. The result has been significant ethnic diversity in nearly all African countries.

Size

The area that a state occupies may be large, as is true of China, or small, as is Liechtenstein. The world's largest country, Russia, occupies over 17 million square kilometers (6.5 million sq. mi.), some 11% of the earth's land surface—nearly as large as the whole continent of South America and more than 1 million times as large as Nauru, one of the *ministates* or *microstates* found in all parts of the world (see "The Ministates").

An easy assumption would be that the larger a state's area, the greater is the chance that it will include the ores, energy supplies, and fertile soils from which it can benefit. In general, that assumption is valid, but much depends on accidents of location. Mineral resources are unevenly distributed, and size alone does not guarantee their presence within a state. Australia, Canada, and Russia, though large in territory, have relatively small areas capable of supporting productive agriculture. Great size, in fact, may be a disad-

vantage. A very large country may have vast areas that are remote, sparsely populated, and hard to integrate into the mainstream of economy and society. Small states are more apt than large ones to have a culturally homogeneous population. They find it easier to develop transportation and communication systems to link the sections of the country, and, of course, they have shorter boundaries to defend against invasion. Size alone, then, is not critical in determining a country's stability and strength, but it is a contributing factor.

Shape

Like size, a country's shape can affect its well-being as a state by fostering or hindering effective organization. Assuming no major topographical barriers, the most efficient form would be a circle with the capital located in the center. In such a country, all places could be reached from the center in a minimal amount of time and with the least expenditure for roads, railway lines, and so on. It would also have

LANDSCAPES OF FUNCTIONAL ORGANIZATIONS

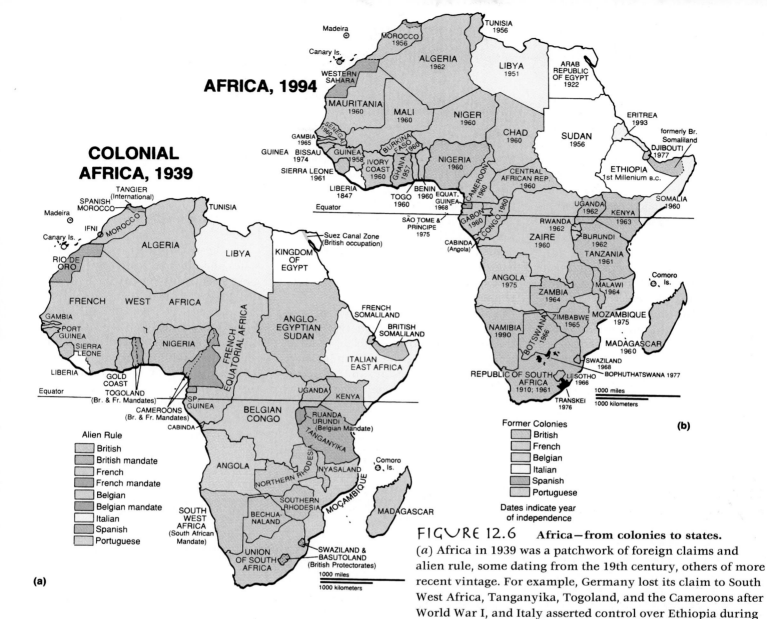

COLONIAL AFRICA, 1939

AFRICA, 1994

Madeira ⊖

Canary Is. ⊘

TANGIER (International)

SPANISH MOROCCO

IFNI ⊘ MOROCCO

RIO DE ORO

ALGERIA

TUNISIA

LIBYA

KINGDOM OF EGYPT

Suez Canal Zone (British occupation)

FRENCH WEST AFRICA

GAMBIA

PORT. GUINEA

SIERRA LEONE

LIBERIA

GOLD COAST

TOGOLAND (Br. & Fr. Mandates)

CAMEROONS (Br. & Fr. Mandates)

CABINDA

NIGERIA

SP. GUINEA

ANGOLA

FRENCH EQUATORIAL AFRICA

ANGLO-EGYPTIAN SUDAN

FRENCH SOMALILAND

BRITISH SOMALILAND

ITALIAN EAST AFRICA

UGANDA

KENYA

BELGIAN CONGO

RUANDA URUNDI (Belgian Mandate)

TANGANYIKA

NORTHERN RHODESIA

NYASALAND

Comoro Is. ⊘

SOUTHERN RHODESIA

MOÇAMBIQUE

MADAGASCAR

SOUTH WEST AFRICA (South African Mandate)

BECHUANA-LAND

UNION OF SOUTH AFRICA

SWAZILAND & BASUTOLAND (British Protectorates)

Equator

1000 miles

1000 kilometers

Alien Rule

- British
- British mandate
- French
- French mandate
- Belgian
- Belgian mandate
- Italian
- Spanish
- Portuguese

(a)

Madeira ⊘

Canary Is. ⊘

WESTERN SAHARA

MOROCCO 1956

ALGERIA 1962

TUNISIA 1956

LIBYA 1951

ARAB REPUBLIC OF EGYPT 1922

MAURITANIA 1960

MALI 1960

NIGER 1960

CHAD 1960

SUDAN 1956

ERITREA 1993

formerly Br. Somaliland

DJIBOUTI 1977

ETHIOPIA 1st Millenium B.C.

GAMBIA 1965

SENEGAL 1960

GUINEA BISSAU 1974

GUINEA 1958

SIERRA LEONE 1961

LIBERIA 1847

BURKINA FASO 1960

IVORY COAST 1960

GHANA 1957

TOGO 1960

BENIN 1960

EQUAT. GUINEA 1968

NIGERIA 1960

CAMEROON 1960

CENTRAL AFRICAN REP. 1960

SÃO TOMÉ & PRÍNCIPE 1975

GABON 1960

CONGO 1960

CABINDA (Angola)

SOMALIA 1960

UGANDA 1962

KENYA 1963

RWANDA 1962

BURUNDI 1962

ZAIRE 1960

TANZANIA 1961

ANGOLA 1975

ZAMBIA 1964

MALAWI 1964

Comoro Is. ⊘

MOZAMBIQUE 1975

NAMIBIA 1990

ZIMBABWE 1965

BOTSWANA 1966

MADAGASCAR 1960

SWAZILAND 1968

BOPHUTHATSWANA 1977

REPUBLIC OF SOUTH AFRICA 1910; 1961

LESOTHO 1966

TRANSKEI 1976

Equator

1000 miles

1000 kilometers

(b)

Former Colonies

- British
- French
- Belgian
- Italian
- Spanish
- Portuguese

Dates indicate year of independence

FIGURE 12.6 **Africa—from colonies to states.**
(*a*) Africa in 1939 was a patchwork of foreign claims and alien rule, some dating from the 19th century, others of more recent vintage. For example, Germany lost its claim to South West Africa, Tanganyika, Togoland, and the Cameroons after World War I, and Italy asserted control over Ethiopia during the 1930s. (*b*) Africa in the 1990s is a mosaic of separate states. Their dates of independence are indicated on the map. French West Africa and French Equatorial Africa have been extensively subdivided, and Ethiopia and Somaliland emerged from Italian control. Most of the current countries retain the boundaries of their former colonial existence.

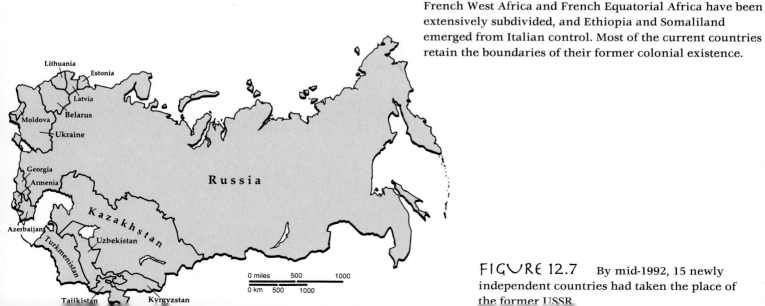

Lithuania

Estonia

Latvia

Belarus

Moldova

Ukraine

Georgia

Armenia

Russia

Kazakhstan

Azerbaijan

Uzbekistan

Turkmenistan

Tajikistan

Kyrgyzstan

0 miles 500 1000

0 km 500 1000

FIGURE 12.7 By mid-1992, 15 newly independent countries had taken the place of the former USSR.

otally or partially autonomous political units that are small in area and population pose some intriguing questions. Should size be a criterion for statehood? What is the potential of ministates to cause friction among the major powers? Under what conditions are they entitled to representation in international assemblies like the United Nations?

Almost half the world's independent countries contain fewer than 5 million people. Of these, 45 have under 1 million, the population size adopted by the United Nations as the upper limit defining "small states," though not too small to be members of that organization. Nauru has about 10,000 inhabitants on its 21 square kilometers (8.2 sq. mi.). Other areally small states like Singapore (580 sq. km; 224 sq. mi.) have populations (3 million) well above the UN criterion. Many are island territories located in the West Indies and the Pacific Ocean (such as Grenada and Tonga Islands), but Europe (Vatican City and Andorra), Asia (Bahrain), and Africa (Djibouti and Equatorial Guinea) have their share.

Many ministates are vestiges of colonial systems that no longer exist. Some of the small countries of West Africa and on the Arabian peninsula fall into this category. Others, such as Mauritius, served primarily as refueling stops on transoceanic shipping lanes. However, some occupy strategic locations (such as Bahrain, Malta, and Singapore), and others contain valuable minerals (Kuwait, Nauru, and Trinidad). The possibility of claiming 370-kilometer-wide (200-nautical-mile) zones of adjacent seas

(see "Specks and Spoils," p. 440) adds to the attraction of yet others.

Their strategic or economic value can expose small islands and territories to unwanted attention from larger neighbors. The 1982 war between Britain and Argentina over the Falkland Islands (claimed as the Islas Malvinas by Argentina) and the Iraqi invasion of Kuwait in 1990 demonstrate the ability of such areas to bring major powers into conflict and to receive world attention that is out of proportion to their size and population.

The proliferation of tiny countries raises the question of their representation and their voting weight in international assemblies. Should there be a minimum size necessary for participation in such bodies? Should countries receive a vote proportional to their population? Within the United Nations, the Small Island Developing States

(SIDS) recently have emerged as a significant power bloc, controlling more than one-fifth of UN General Assembly votes. Since forming themselves into the Alliance of Small Island States (AOSIS) in November 1990, they have proved to have unexpected clout and played a key role in placing New Zealand on the Security Council in 1993.

The influence of the United States and other major powers in the United Nations has already been eroded by the small states. Although the United States pays 25% of the UN budget and has about one and one-half times the population of all the small countries combined, its vote can be balanced by that of any of them. The fact that as many as 50 additional territories may gain independence in the next few years underscores the international interest in them.

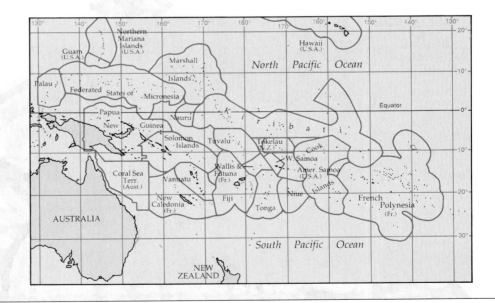

the shortest possible borders to defend. Uruguay, Zimbabwe, and Poland have roughly circular shapes, forming a **compact state** (Figure 12.8).

Prorupt states are nearly compact but possess one or sometimes two narrow extensions of territory. Proruption may simply reflect peninsular elongations of land area, as in the case of Myanmar and Thailand. In other instances, the extensions have an economic or strategic significance, recording a past history of international negotiation to secure access to resources or water routes or to establish a buffer zone between states that would otherwise adjoin. The proruptions of Afghanistan, Zaire, and Namibia fall into this category. The Caprivi Strip of Namibia, for example, which extends eastward from the main part of the country, was designed by the Germans to give what was then their colony of Southwest Africa access to the Zambezi River. Whatever their origin, proruptions tend to isolate a portion of a state.

The least efficient shape administratively is represented by countries like Norway, Vietnam, or Chile, which are long and narrow. In such **elongated states,** the parts of the country far from the capital are likely to be isolated because great expenditures are required to link them to the core. These countries are also likely to encompass more diversity of climate, resources, and peoples than compact states, perhaps to the detriment of national cohesion or, perhaps, to the promotion of economic strength.

A fourth class of **fragmented states** includes countries composed entirely of islands (e.g., the Philippines and Indonesia), countries that are partly on islands and partly on the mainland (Italy and Malaysia), and those that are chiefly on the mainland but whose territory is separated by another state (The United States). Pakistan was a fragmented country until 1971, when the eastern part—1600 kilometers (1000 mi.) distant—broke away from the west and declared itself the independent state of Bangladesh. Fragmentation and isolation can weaken centralized control of state territory and increase the regionalism that may lead to separatist movements. That was the case with Bangladesh; it also is a problem in the Philippines and Indonesia, the latter made up of over 13,000 islands stretched out along a 5100 kilometer (3200 mi.) arc.

A special case of fragmentation occurs when a territorial outlier of one state is located within another. Before German unification, West Berlin was an outlier of West

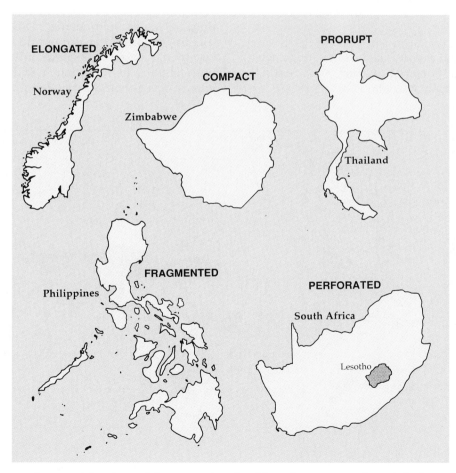

FIGURE 12.8 **Shapes of states.** The sizes of the countries should not be compared. Each is drawn on a different scale.

Germany within the eastern German Democratic Republic. Europe has many such **exclaves,** outlying bits of one country inside another country. Kleinwalsertal, for example, is a patch of Austria accessible only from Germany. Baarle-Hertog is a fragment of Belgium inside Holland; Campione d' Italia is an Italian outlier in Switzerland and Büsingen is a German one; and Llivia is a totally Spanish (Catalan) town of 930 residents 3 miles inside France. Exclaves are not limited to Europe, of course. African examples include Cabinda, an exclave of Angola, and Mililla and Ceuta, two Spanish exclaves in Morocco.

The counterpart of an exclave, an **enclave,** helps to define the fifth class of country shapes, the **perforated state.** A perforated state completely surrounds a territory that it does not rule as, for example, the Republic of South Africa surrounds Lesotho. The enclave, the surrounded territory, may be independent or may be part of another country. Two of Europe's smallest independent states, San Marino and Vatican City, are enclaves that perforate Italy. As an *exclave* of former West Germany, West Berlin perforated the national territory of former East Germany and was an *enclave* in it. The stability of the perforated state can be weakened if the enclave is occupied by people whose value systems differ from those of the surrounding country.

Location

The significance of size and shape as factors in national well-being can be modified by a state's location, both absolute and relative. Although both Canada and Russia are extremely large, their *absolute* location in upper middle latitudes reduces their size advantages when agricultural potential is considered. To take another example, Iceland has a reasonably compact shape, but its location in the North Atlantic Ocean, just south of the Arctic Circle, means that most of the country is barren, with settlement confined to the rim of the island.

A state's *relative* location, its position compared to that of other countries, is as important as its absolute location. *Landlocked* states, those lacking ocean frontage and surrounded by other states, are at a commercial and strategic disadvantage. They lack easy access to both maritime (sea-borne) trade and the resources found in coast waters and submerged lands. Bolivia gained 480 kilometers (300 mi.) of sea frontier along with its independence in 1825, but lost its ocean frontage by conquest to Chile in 1879. Its annual Day of the Sea ceremony reminds Bolivians of their loss and of continuing diplomatic efforts to secure an alternate outlet. The number of landlocked states—about 40—increased greatly with the dissolution of the Soviet Union and the creation of new, smaller nation-states out of such former multinational countries as Yugoslavia and Czechoslovakia (Figure 12.9).

In a few instances, a favorable relative location constitutes the primary resource of a state. Singapore, a state of only 580 square kilometers (224 sq. mi.) and 3 million population, is located at a crossroads of world shipping and commerce. Based on its port and commercial activities and buttressed by its more recent industrial development, Singapore has become a notable Southeast Asian economic

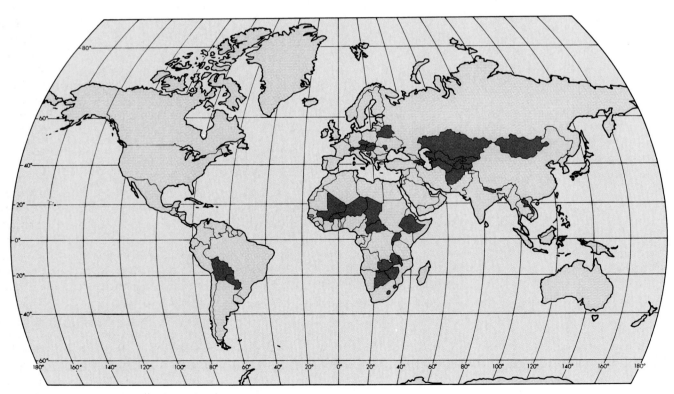

FIGURE 12.9 **Landlocked states, 1995.**

LANDSCAPES OF FUNCTIONAL ORGANIZATIONS

success. In general, history has shown that countries benefit from a location on major trade routes, not only from the economic advantages such a location carries, but also because they are exposed to the diffusion of new ideas and technologies.

Cores and Capitals

Many states have come to assume their present shape, and thus the location they occupy, as a result of growth over centuries. They grew outward from a central region, gradually expanding into surrounding territory. The original nucleus, or **core area,** of a state usually contains its most developed economic base, densest population and largest cities, the best developed transportation systems, and—at least formerly if no longer—the resources which sustained it. All of these elements become less intense away from the national core. Transportation networks thin, urbanization ratios and city sizes decline, and economic development is less intensive. The outlying resource base may be rich, but generally is of more recent exploitation with product and benefit tending to flow to the established heartlands. The developed cores of states, then, can be contrasted to their subordinate peripheries just as we saw the core-periphery idea applicable in an international developmental context in Chapter 10.

Easily recognized and unmistakably dominant national cores include the Paris Basin of France, London and southeastern England, Moscow and the major cities of European Russia, northeastern United States and southeastern Canada, and the Buenos Aires megalopolis in Argentina. Not all countries have such clearly defined cores—Chad, or Mongolia, or Saudi Arabia, for example—and some may have two or more rival core areas. Ecuador, Nigeria, Zaire, and Vietnam are examples of multicore states.

The capital city of a state is usually within its core region and frequently is the very focus of it, dominant not only because it is the seat of central authority but because of the concentration of population and economic functions as well. That is, in many countries the capital city is also the largest or *primate* city, dominating the structure of the entire country. Paris in France, London in the United Kingdom, and Mexico City are examples of that kind of political, cultural, and economic primacy (see p. 384 and Figure 11.16).

This association of capital with core is common in what have been called the *unitary states,* countries with highly centralized governments, relatively few internal cultural contrasts, a strong sense of national identity, and borders that are clearly cultural as well as political boundaries. Most European cores and capitals are of this type. It is also found in many newly independent countries whose former colonial occupiers established a primary center of exploitation and administration and developed a functioning core in a region that lacked an urban structure or organized government. With independence, the new states retained the established infrastructure, added new functions to the capital and, through lavish expenditures on governmental, public, and commercial buildings, sought to create prestigious symbols of nationhood.

In *federal states,* associations of more or less equal provinces or states with strong regional governmental responsibilities, the national capital city may have been newly created or selected to serve as the administrative center. Although part of a generalized core region of the country, the designated capital was not its largest city and acquired few of the additional functions to make it so. Ottawa, Canada; Washington, D.C.; and Canberra, Australia, are examples (Figure 12.10).

All other things being equal, a capital located in the center of the country provides equal access to the government, facilitates communication to and from the political hub, and enables the government to exert its authority easily. Many capital cities, such as Washington, D.C., were centrally located when they were designated as seats of government but lost their centrality as the state expanded.

Some capital cities have been relocated outside of peripheral national core regions, at least in part to achieve the presumed advantages of centrality. Two examples of such relocation are from Karachi inland to Islamabad in Pakistan and from Istanbul to Ankara, in the center of Turkey's territory. A particular type of relocated capital is the *forward-thrust capital* city, one that has been deliberately sited in a state's interior to signal the government's awareness of regions away from a peripheral core and its interest in encouraging more uniform development. In the late 1950s, Brazil relocated its capital from Rio de Janeiro to the new city of Brasilia to demonstrate its intent to develop the vast interior of the country. The West African country, Nigeria, has been building the new capital of Abuja near its geographic center since the late 1970s, with relocation there of government offices and foreign embassies in the early 1990s. The British colonial government relocated Canada's capital six times between 1841 to 1865, in part seeking centrality to the mid-19th-century population pattern and in part seeking a location that bridged that colony's cultural divide (Figure 12.11).

Boundaries: The Limits of the State

We noted earlier that no portion of the earth's land surface is outside the claimed control of a national unit, that even uninhabited Antarctica has had territorial claims imposed upon it (Figure 12.3). Each of the world's states is separated from its neighbors by *international boundaries,* or lines that establish the limit of each state's jurisdiction and authority. Boundaries indicate where the sovereignty of one state ends and that of another begins.

Within its own bounded territory, a state administers laws, collects taxes, provides for defense, and performs other such governmental functions. Thus, the location of the boundary determines the kind of money people in a given area use, the legal code to which they are subject, the army they may be called upon to join, and the language

FIGURE 12.10   Canberra, the planned capital of Australia, was deliberately sited away from the country's largest cities, Sydney and Melbourne. Planned capitals are often architectural showcases, providing a focus for national pride.

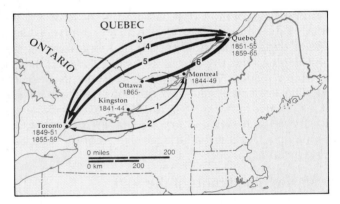

FIGURE 12.11   **Canada's migratory capital.** Kingston was chosen as the first capital of the united Province of Canada in preference to either Quebec, capital of Lower Canada, or Toronto, that of Upper Canada. In 1844, governmental functions were relocated to Montreal where they remained until 1849, after which they shifted back and forth—as the map indicates—between Toronto and Quebec. An 1865 session of the provincial legislature was held in Ottawa, the city that became the capital of the Confederation of Canada in 1867.

Redrawn with permission from David B. Knight, *A Capital for Canada* (Chicago: University of Chicago, Department of Geography, Research Paper No. 182, 1977), Figure 1, p. vii.

and perhaps the religion children are taught in school. These examples suggest how boundaries serve as powerful reinforcers of cultural variation over the earth's surface.

Territorial claims of sovereignty, it should be noted, are three-dimensional. International boundaries mark not only the outer limits of a state's claim to land (or water) surface, but are also projected downward to the center of the earth in accordance with international consensus allocating rights to subsurface resources. States also project their sovereignty upward, but with less certainty because of a lack of agreement on the upper limits of territorial airspace. Properly viewed, then, an international boundary is a line without breadth; it is a vertical interface between adjacent state sovereignties.

Before boundaries were delimited, nations or empires were likely to be separated by *frontier zones*, ill-defined and fluctuating areas marking the effective end of a state's authority. Such zones were often uninhabited or only sparsely populated and were liable to change with shifting settlement patterns. Many present-day international boundaries lie in former frontier zones, and in that sense the boundary line has replaced the broader frontier as a marker of a state's authority.

Classification of Boundaries

Geographers have traditionally distinguished between "natural" and "geometric" boundaries. **Natural** (or *physical*) **boundaries** are those based on recognizable physiographic features, such as mountains, rivers, and lakes. Although they might seem to be attractive as borders because they actually exist in the landscape and are visible dividing elements, many natural boundaries have proved to be unsatisfactory. That is, they do not effectively separate states.

Many international boundaries lie along mountain ranges, for example in the Alps, Himalayas, and Andes, but while some have proved to be stable, others have not. Mountains are rarely total barriers to interaction. Although they do not invite movement, they are crossed by passes, roads, and tunnels. High pastures may be used for seasonal grazing, and the mountain region may be the source of water for irrigation or hydroelectric power. Nor is the definition of a boundary along a mountain range a simple matter. Should it follow the crests of the mountains or the *water divide* (the line dividing two drainage areas)? The two are not always the same. Border disputes between China and India are in part the result of the failure of mountain crests and headwaters of major streams to coincide (Figure 12.12).

Rivers can be even less satisfactory as boundaries. In contrast to mountains, rivers foster interaction. River valleys are likely to be agriculturally or industrially productive, and to be densely populated. For example, for hundreds of miles the Rhine River serves as an international boundary in Western Europe. It is also a primary traffic route lined by chemical plants, factories, blast furnaces, and power stations, and dotted by the castles and cathedrals that make it one of Europe's major tourist attractions (Figure 9.21). It is more a common intensively used resource than a barrier in the lives of the nations it borders. Further, rivers tend to change their path, requiring redefinition of the boundaries they mark. They also invite dispute over whether the boundary should be along one bank or the other, along the main navigation channel, or along the middle of the stream.

The alternative to natural boundaries are **geometric** (or *artificial*) **boundaries.** Frequently delimited as segments of parallels of latitude or meridians of longitude, they are found chiefly in Africa, Asia, and the Americas. The western portion of the United States–Canada border, which follows the 49th parallel, is an example of a geometric boundary (Figure 12.13). Many such were established when the areas in question were colonies, the land was only sparsely settled, and detailed geographic knowledge of the frontier region was lacking.

Boundaries can also be classified according to whether they were laid out before or after the principal features of the cultural landscape were developed. An **antecedent boundary** is one drawn across an area before it is well populated, that is, before most of the cultural landscape features were put in place. To continue our earlier example, the western portion of the United States–Canada boundary is such an antecedent line, established by a treaty between the United States and Great Britain in 1846.

Boundaries drawn after the development of the cultural landscape are termed **subsequent.** One type of subsequent boundary is **consequent** (also called *ethnographic*), a

FIGURE 12.12   Several international borders run through the jumble of the Himalayas. The mountain boundary between India and China has long been in dispute.

FIGURE 12.13   The international Peace Arch at Blaine, Washington. Its position is determined by the globe grid rather than by topography or drainage systems. *Geometric boundaries* like that between most of the United States and Canada are unrelated to landscape features.

border drawn to accommodate existing religious, linguistic, ethnic, or economic differences between countries. An example is the boundary drawn between Northern Ireland and Eire (Ireland). Subsequent **superimposed boundaries** may also be forced on existing cultural landscapes, a country, or a people by a conquering or colonizing power that is unconcerned about preexisting cultural patterns. The colonial powers in 19th-century Africa superimposed boundaries upon established African cultures without regard to the tradition, language, religion, or tribal affiliation of those whom they divided (Figure 12.5).

When Great Britain prepared to leave the Indian subcontinent after World War II, it was decided that two independent states would be established in the region: India and Pakistan. The boundary between the two countries, defined in the partition settlement of 1947, was thus both a *subsequent* and a *superimposed* line. As millions of Hindus migrated from the northwestern portion of the subcontinent to seek homes in India, millions of Muslims left what would become India for Pakistan. In a sense, they were attempting to insure that the boundary would be *consequent,* that is, that it would coincide with a division based on religion.

If a former boundary line that no longer functions as such is still marked by some landscape features or differences on the two sides, it is termed a **relict boundary** (Figure 12.14). The abandoned castles dotting the former frontier zone between Wales and England are examples of a relict boundary. They are also evidence of the disputes that sometimes attend the process of boundary making.

Boundary Disputes

Boundaries create many possibilities and provocations for conflict. Since World War II, almost half of the world's sovereign states have been involved in border disputes with neighboring countries. Just like householders, states are far more likely to have disputes with their neighbors than with more distant parties. It follows that the more neighbors a state has, the greater the likelihood of conflict. Although the causes of boundary disputes and open conflict are many and varied, they can reasonably be placed into four categories.

1. **Positional disputes** occur when states disagree about the interpretation of documents that define a boundary and/or the way the boundary was delimited. Such disputes typically arise when the boundary is antecedent, preceding effective human settlement in the border region. Once the area becomes populated and gains value, the exact location of the boundary becomes important.

   The boundary between Argentina and Chile, originally defined during Spanish colonial rule, was to follow the highest peaks of the southern Andes and the watershed divides between east- and west-flowing rivers. Because the terrain had not been adequately explored, it was not apparent that the two do not always coincide. In some places, the water divide is many miles east of the highest peaks, leaving a long, narrow area of several hundred square miles in dispute (Figure 12.15). During the late 1970s, Argentina and Chile nearly went to war over the disputed territory, whose significance had been increased by the discovery of oil and natural gas deposits.

2. **Territorial disputes** over the ownership of a region often, though not always, arise when a boundary that has been superimposed on the landscape divides an

FIGURE 12.14   Like Hadrian's Wall in the north of England or the Great Wall of China, the Berlin Wall was a demarcated boundary. Unlike them, it cut across a large city and disrupted established cultural patterns. The Berlin Wall, therefore, was a *subsequent superimposed* boundary. The dismantling of the wall in 1990 marked the reunification of Germany; any of it that remains standing as a historic monument is a *relict* boundary.

FIGURE 12.15 **Areas of international dispute in Latin America.** Among the countries disputing the precise location of their boundaries are Argentina and Chile, Peru and Ecuador, Venezuela and Guyana, and Honduras and El Salvador. Early in 1995 the controversy between Peru and Ecuador erupted into a local border war, as it has done periodically since 1942, when the Protocol of Rio de Janeiro awarded the disputed land to Peru.

ethnically homogeneous population. Each of the two states then has some justification for claiming the territory inhabited by the ethnic group in question. We noted previously that a single nation may be dispersed across several states (Figure 12.4*d*). Conflicts can arise if the people of one state want to annex a territory whose population is ethnically related to that of the state but now subject to a foreign government. This type of expansionism is called **irredentism.** In the 1930s, Hitler used the existence of German minorities in Czechoslovakia and Poland to justify German invasion and occupation. More recently, Somalia has had many border clashes with Ethiopia over the rights of Somalis living in that country.

3. Closely related to territorial conflicts are **resource disputes.** Neighboring states are likely to covet the resources—whether they be valuable mineral deposits, fertile farmland, or rich fishing grounds—lying in border areas and to disagree over their use. In recent years, the United States has been involved in disputes with both its immediate neighbors: with Mexico over the shared resources of the Colorado River and Gulf of Mexico and with Canada over the Georges Bank fishing grounds in the Atlantic Ocean.

One of the causes of the 1990–91 war in the Persian Gulf was the huge oil reservoir known as the Rumaila field, lying mainly under Iraq with a small extension into Kuwait. Because the two countries were unable to agree on percentages of ownership of the rich reserve, or a formula for sharing production costs and revenues, Kuwait pumped oil from Rumaila without any international agreement. Iraq helped justify its invasion of Kuwait by contending that the latter had been stealing Iraqi oil in what amounted to economic warfare.

4. **Functional disputes** arise when neighboring states disagree over policies to be applied along a boundary. Such policies may concern immigration, the movement of traditionally nomadic groups, customs regulations, or land use. U.S. relations with Mexico, for example, have been affected by the increasing number of illegal aliens entering the United States from Mexico (Figure 12.16). In Central America, relations between Honduras and El Salvador, two countries that have long disputed their common boundary, worsened in the late 1970s, when Honduras expelled Salvadoran farmers who had illegally occupied available agricultural land in western Honduras.

State Cohesiveness

At any moment in time, a state is characterized by forces that promote unity and national stability and by others that disrupt them. Political geographers refer to the former as **centripetal forces.** These are factors that bind together the people of a state, that enable it to function and give it strength. **Centrifugal forces,** on the other hand, destabilize and weaken a state. If centrifugal forces are stronger than those promoting unity, the very existence of the state will be threatened. In the sections that follow we examine four centripetal (uniting) forces: nationalism, unifying institutions, effective organization and administration of government, and systems of transportation and communication.

Nationalism

One of the most powerful of the centripetal forces is **nationalism,** an identification with the state and the acceptance of national goals. Nationalism is based on the concept of allegiance to a single country and the ideals and the way of life it represents; it is an emotion that provides a sense of identity and loyalty and of collective distinction from all other peoples and lands.

States purposely try to instill feelings of allegiance in their citizens, for such feelings give the political system strength. People who have such allegiance are likely to accept common rules of action and behavior and to participate in the decision-making process establishing those rules. In light of the divisive forces present in most societies, not everyone, of course, will feel the same degree of commit-

(a)

(b)

FIGURE 12.16 (a) To stem the flow of undocumented migrants entering California from Baja California, the United States, in 1993, constructed a fence 3 meters (10 ft) high along the border. (b) Protesters on the Mexican side of the border expressed their anger over the construction.

ment or loyalty. The important consideration is that the majority of a state's population accepts its ideologies, adheres to its laws, and participates in its effective operation. For many countries, such acceptance and adherence has come only recently and partially; in some, it is frail and endangered.

We noted earlier that true nation-states are rare; in only a few countries do the territory occupied by the people of a particular nation and the territorial limits of the state coincide. In a multicultural society, nationalism helps integrate different groups into a unified population. This kind of consensus nationalism has emerged in countries such as the United States and Canada, where different culture groups, few or none with defined North American homelands, have joined together to create political entities commanding the loyalties of all their citizens.

National anthems and other patriotic songs; flags, national sports teams, and officially designated or easily identified flowers and animals; and rituals and holidays are all developed by states to promote nationalism and attract allegiance (Figure 12.17). By ensuring that all citizens, no matter how diverse the population may be, will have at least these symbols in common, they impart a sense of belonging to a political entity called, for example, Japan or Canada. In some countries, certain documents, such as the Magna Charta in England or the Declaration of Independence in the United

States, serve the same purpose. Royalty may fill the need: in Sweden, Japan, and Great Britain, the monarchy functions as the symbolic focus of allegiance. Such symbols are significant, for symbols and beliefs are major components of the ideological subsystem (p. 51) of every culture.

Unifying Institutions

Institutions as well as symbols help to develop the sense of commitment and cohesiveness essential to the state. Schools, particularly elementary schools, are among the most important of these. Children learn the history of their own country and relatively little about other countries. Schools are expected to instill the society's goals, values, and traditions, to teach the common language that conveys them, and to guide youngsters to identify with their country.

Other institutions that advance nationalism are the armed forces and, sometimes, a state church. The armed forces are of necessity taught to identify with the state. They see themselves as protecting the state's welfare from what are perceived to be its enemies. In some countries, the religion of the majority of the people may be designated a state church. In such cases the church sometimes becomes a force for cohesion, helping to unify the population. This is true of the Roman Catholic church in the Republic of Ireland, Islam in Pakistan, and Judaism in Israel. In countries like these,

FIGURE 12.17   The ritual of the pledge of allegiance is just one way in which schools in the United States seek to instill a sense of national identity in students.

the religion and the church are so identified with the state that belief in one is transferred to allegiance to the other.

The schools, the armed forces, and the church are just three of the institutions that teach people what it is like to be members of a state. As institutions, they operate primarily on the level of the sociological subsystem of culture, helping to structure the outlooks and behaviors of the society. But by themselves, they are not enough to give cohesion, and thus strength, to a state.

Organization and Administration

A further bonding force is public confidence in the effective organization of the state. Can it provide security from external aggression and internal conflict? Are its resources distributed and allocated in such a way as to be perceived to promote the economic welfare of all its citizens? Are all citizens afforded equal opportunity to participate in governmental affairs (see "Legislative Women")? Do institutions that encourage consultation and the peaceful settlement of disputes exist? How firmly established are the rule of law and the power of the courts? Is the system of decision making responsive to the people's needs (Figure 12.18)?

The answers to such questions, and the relative importance of the answers, will vary from country to country, but they and similar ones are implicit in the expectation that the state will, in the words of the Constitution of the United States, "establish justice, insure domestic tranquility, provide for the common defence, [and] promote the general welfare. . . ." If those expectations are not fulfilled, the loyalties promoted by national symbols and unifying institutions may be weakened or lost.

FIGURE 12.18   The Supreme Court of Canada building, Ottawa. Continuity, impartiality, and efficiency are attributes of government important in securing public confidence and loyalty.

Transportation and Communication

A state's transportation network fosters political integration by promoting interaction between areas and by joining them economically and socially. The role of a transportation network in uniting a country has been recognized since ancient times. The saying that all roads lead to Rome had its origin in the impressive system of roads omen, a majority of the world's population, in general get a raw deal in the allocation of such resources as primary and higher education, employment opportunities and income, and health care. That their lot is improving is encouraging. In every developing country women have been closing the gender gap in literacy, school enrollment, and acceptance in the job market—facts that may in time close the status gap.

But in the political arena—where power ultimately lies—women's share of influence is increasing slowly, if at all. In 1995, only nine countries out of a world total of some 200 had women as heads of government—presidents or prime ministers. Nor did they fare much better as members of parliaments. Women in early 1996 held more than 20% of national legislative seats in only thirteen countries. Eight of them were European democracies—five of them Nordic (Sweden was the most feminist, with 41% female members) plus Germany, Luxembourg, and Netherlands. South Africa, Seychelles, Mozambique, and nondemocractic China and North Korea completed the roster. Earlier in the decade ten members of the "communist bloc" of Eastern Europe and the Soviet Union were included in the 1990 group of 16 countries with 20% or more female members of legislative bodies. It would appear that one way to have women in parliament was not to have free and open elections, though five Arab states with no elections at all also had no women in their parliaments.

Certainly, most Western democracies' legislatures are vastly unbalanced in favor of men. For the European Union as a whole, women in 1994 accounted for 17% of legislature members, but for only 5% of France's National Assembly, 9% of Britain's House of Commons, 15% of the lower house of the Spanish Parliament, and 8% of Italy's Chamber of Deputies. Women had but 2% of the seats in Japan's Diet and only 11% of the U.S. House of Representatives (7% of the Senate). In many instances, however, even those paltry proportions represented an improvement over the situation 4 to 5 years earlier when, for example, Britain's House of Commons had only 6.3% women and the American Congress only 5.3%.

Women's legislative opportunities did not improve after the democratic revolutions in the former Soviet Union and other communist countries. About one-third of the parliamentary seats in the Soviet Union were held by women; that had fallen to about 15% in 1991. In Albania, women's representation dropped from 29% to 3% after the 1991 elections, and in Hungary the number of women in parliament dropped from 21% under communism to 7%.

Poor as their success in elections may be, women fare even worse in appointive posts of importance. Worldwide, they held less than 7% of all national ministerial and departmental head positions, and only 5.6% of economic ministries in 1994. Even in the United Nations, despite a pledge to fill 25% of executive jobs with women by 1995, only 15% were held by them.

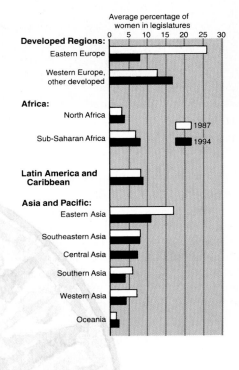

Source: Graph redrawn from United Nations, *The World's Women*, 1995.

that linked Rome to the rest of its empire. Centuries later, a similar network was built in France, linking Paris to the various departments of the country. Often the capital city is better connected to other cities than the outlying cities are to one another. In France, for example, it can take less time to travel from one city to another by way of Paris than by direct route.

Roads and railroads have played a historically significant role in promoting political integration. In the United States and Canada, they not only opened up new areas for settlement but increased interaction between rural and urban districts. Because transportation systems play a major role in a state's economic development, it follows that the more economically advanced a country is, the more extensive its transport network is likely to be (Figure 8.4). At the same time, the higher the level of development, the more resources there are to be invested in building transport routes. The two reinforce one another.

Transportation and communication, while encouraged within a state, are frequently curtailed or at least controlled between them as a conscious device for promoting state cohesion through limitation on external spatial interaction (Figure 12.19). The mechanisms of control include restrictions on trade through tariffs or embargoes, legal barriers to immigration and emigration, and limitations on travel through passports and visa requirements.

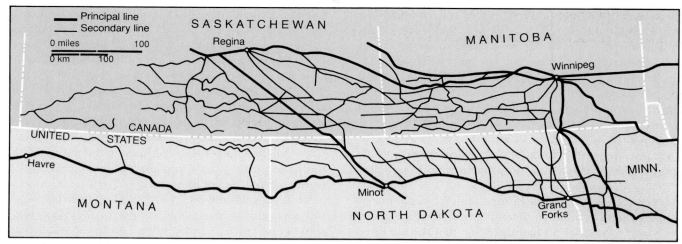

FIGURE 12.19   Canadian–U.S. railroad discontinuity. Canada and the United States developed independent railway systems connecting their respective prairie regions with their separate national cores. Despite extensive rail construction during the 19th and early 20th centuries, the pattern that emerged even before recent track abandonment was one of discontinuity at the border. Note how the political boundary restricted the ease of spatial interaction between adjacent territories. Many branch lines approached the border, but only eight crossed it. In fact, for over 480 kilometers (300 miles), no railway bridged the boundary line. The international border—and the cultural separation it represents—inhibits other expected degrees of interaction. Telephone calls between Canadian and U.S. cities, for example, are far less frequent than would be expected if distance alone were the controlling factor.

Nationalism and Centrifugal Forces

State cohesion is not easily achieved or, once gained, invariably retained. Destabilizing *centrifugal forces* are ever-present, sowing internal discord and challenges to the state's authority.

We said previously that nationalism is one of the most powerful of the centripetal forces. Paradoxically, it is also a potent disruptive centrifugal force. The idea of the nation-state is that states are formed around and coincide with nations. It is a small step from that to the notion that every nation has the right to its own state or territory. Any country that contains one or more important national minorities is susceptible to nationalist challenges from within its borders *if* the minority group has an explicit territorial identification.

A dissident minority that has total or partial secession from the state as its primary goal is said to be guided by *separation* or **autonomous nationalism.** In recent years, such nationalism has created currents of unrest within many countries, even long-established ones. In Western Europe, for example, five countries (the United Kingdom, France, Belgium, Italy, and Spain) house separatist political movements whose members reject the existing sovereign state and who claim to be the core of a separate national entity (Figure 12.20). Their basic demand is for regional autonomy, usually in the form of self-government or "home rule" rather than complete independence. Both the Welsh and the Scottish nationalists would like independence for their regions and commonwealth status within the United Kingdom, for example.

FIGURE 12.20   Regions in Western Europe demanding autonomy. Each was once an independent entity, incorporated within a larger state. Despite long-standing efforts to assimilate them, each of these historic nations contains a political movement that has recently sought or is currently seeking a degree of separatism that recognizes its individual identity.

Separatist movements affect many states outside of Western Europe and indeed are more characteristic of developing countries, especially those formed since the end of World War II and containing disparate groups more motivated by enmity than affinity. The Basques of Spain and the Bretons of France have their counterparts in the Palestinians in Israel, the Sikhs in India, the Moros in the Philippines, the Tamils in Sri Lanka, and many others. Separatist movements have attracted the attention of political geographers because they are expressions of **regionalism,** minority group self-awareness and identification with a region rather than with the state.

The countries of Eastern Europe and the republics of the former Soviet Union have recently seen an explosion of regionally-rooted nationalist feelings. Now that the forces of ethnicity, religion, language, and culture are no longer suppressed by communism, ancient rivalries are more evident than at any time since World War II. The end of the Cold War aroused hopes of decades of peace. Instead, the collapse of communism and the demise of the USSR have spawned dozens of smaller wars. Numerous ethnic groups large and small are asserting their identities and what they perceive to be their right to *self-determination,* the freedom to control their own political status.

The national independence claimed in the early 1990s by the 15 former Soviet constituent republics did not assure the satisfaction of all separatist movements within them. Many of the new individual countries are themselves subject to strong destabilizing forces that threaten their territorial integrity and survival. The Russian Federation itself, the largest and most powerful remnant of the former USSR, contains 21 ethnically and culturally varied republics and a number of other nationality regions, many of which are rich in natural resources, have non-Russian majorities, and seek greater autonomy within the federation. Some, indeed, want total independence. One, the predominantly Muslim Caucasian republic of Chechnya, in 1994 claimed the right of self-determination and attempted to secede from the federation, provoking a bloody civil war. Under similar separatist pressures, Yugoslavia shattered into five pieces in 1991–1992 (see "The Disintegration of Yugoslavia"); more peacefully, Czechs and Slovaks agreed to split former Czechoslovakia into two ethnically-based states in 1993.

Recently, several European governments have moved peacefully in the direction of regional recognition and **devolution**—the allowance by a central government of a degree of political autonomy to recognized political subunits. In France, 22 regional governments were established in 1986; Spain has a program of devolution for its 17 "autonomous communities," a program that Portugal is beginning to emulate. Italy, Germany, and the Nordic countries have, or are developing, similar recognitions of regional communities with granted powers of local administration and relaxation of central controls.

The two preconditions common to all regional autonomist movements are *territory* and *nationality.* First, the group must be concentrated in a core region that it claims as a national homeland. It seeks to regain control of land and power that it believes were unjustly taken from it. Second, certain cultural characteristics must provide a basis for the group's perception of separateness and cultural unity. These might be language, religion, or distinctive group customs and institutions which promote feelings of group identity at the same time that they foster exclusivity. Normally, these cultural differences have persisted over several generations and have survived despite strong pressures toward assimilation.

Other characteristics common to many separatist movements are a *peripheral location* and *social and economic inequality.* Troubled regions tend to be peripheral, often isolated in rural pockets, and their location away from the seat of central government engenders feelings of alienation and exclusion. They perhaps sense what has been called the *law of peripheral neglect,* which observes that the concern of the capital for its controlled political space decreases with increasing distance from it. Second, the dominant culture group is often seen as an exploiting class that has suppressed the local language, controlled access to the civil service, and taken more than its share of wealth and power. Poorer regions complain that they have lower incomes and greater unemployment than prevail in the remainder of the state, and that "outsiders" control key resources and industry. Separatists in relatively rich regions believe that they could exploit their resources for themselves and do better economically without the constraints imposed by the central state.

The Projection of Power

Territorial and political influence or control by a state need not necessarily halt at its recognized land borders. Throughout history states have projected power beyond their home territories where such power could credibly be applied or asserted. Imperial powers such as Rome, Tsarist Russia, and China extended control outward over adjacent peoples and territories through conquest or *suzerainty*—control over vassal states. The former Soviet Union, for example, not only conquered and incorporated such adjacent states as Estonia, Latvia, and Lithuania but also, claiming to be first among equals, asserted the right to intervene militarily to preserve communist regimes wherever they appeared threatened.

Colonial empires such as those of England, France, Spain, and Portugal exerted home state control over noncontiguous territories and frequently retain influence even after their formal colonial dominion has been lost. The Commonwealth (originally, the British Commonwealth of Nations), for example, is a free association of some 50 countries that recognize the British sovereign as head of the Commonwealth and retain use of the English language and legal system. The French Community comprises autonomous states formerly part of the French colonial empire that opted to remain affiliated with the Community, that generally retain the French language and legal system, have various contractual cooperative arrangements with the former ruling state, and have in the instance of African members occasionally called on France to intervene militarily to protect established regimes.

The history of Yugoslavia in this century demonstrates how difficult it is for a state to be stable, how easy it can be for centrifugal forces to tear it apart. "I was born in one Yugoslavia, grew up in another, and now I'm a citizen of a third, and it is the smallest of the three," a woman complained as she watched the ceremony proclaiming a new Yugoslav state in 1992.

The first Yugoslavia was a kingdom created in 1918 when Serbia was joined by Croatia and Slovenia, both previously part of the Austro-Hungarian Empire. A combination of distinct groups, the new country was far from homogeneous. Slovenes and Croatians were primarily Roman Catholic and wrote in the Roman alphabet. Serbs, previously part of the Ottoman Empire, practiced the Eastern Orthodox religion and wrote in Cyrillic. Muslims were the largest ethnic group in Bosnia-Herzegovina.

The second Yugoslavia began life in 1946 as a centrally controlled communist state. It was a federation of six republics, but an uneasy federation. The two largest republics, Serbia and Croatia, had been on opposing sides during World War II. Indeed, thousands of Serbs had died in concentration camps run by the Nazi puppet government in Croatia.

In large part, this Yugoslavia was held together by the leadership of Josip Broz Tito, who had led the partisan army opposing the Nazis. He played down ethnic rivalries, brought a measure of economic prosperity to the country, and kept open ties to the West.

The federation began unraveling after Tito's death in 1980 and the decline of communism. As Yugoslavia's new political leaders appealed to nationalist feelings, ethnic, religious, and cultural differences came to the fore. Fearing domination by the Serbs (the largest ethnic group, with 36% of the population), four of the six republics seceded from the federation in 1991.

In its third incarnation, Yugoslavia consists only of Serbia and Montenegro. It has less than half the area and half the population of its predecessor.

Geopolitical Assessments

Geopolitics is a branch of political geography that considers the strategic value of land and sea area in the context of national economic and military power and ambitions. In that light, geopolitical concerns and territorial assessments have always influenced the policies of governments. "Manifest Destiny" rationalized the westward territorial spread of the United States; the Monroe Doctrine declared the Western Hemisphere off-limits to further European colonization; creation of a "Greater East Asia Co-Prosperity Sphere" justified Japan's Asian and Pacific aggression before and during World War II.

Modern geopolitics was rooted in the early 20th-century concern of an eminent English geographer, Halford Mackinder (1861–1947), with the world balance of power at a time of British expansion and overseas empire. He drew attention to the strategic advantages of land over sea power and developed what came to be known as the **heartland theory.** The greatest land power, he argued, would be sited in Eurasia, the "World-Island" containing the world's largest landmass in both area and population. Its interior or heartland, he warned, would provide a base for world conquest, and Eastern Europe was the core of that heartland (Figure 12.21). Mackinder warned, "Who rules East Europe commands the Heartland, who rules the Heartland commands the World-Island, who rules the World-Island commands the World."

Even earlier, Alfred Mahan (1840–1914) recognized the core position of Russia in the Asian landmass and anticipated conflict between Russian land power and British sea power, though Mahan argued that control of the world's sea lanes to protect commerce and isolate an adversary was the key to national strength. Near the end of the Second World War, Nicholas Spykman (1893–1943) also agreed that Eurasia was the likely base for potential world domination, but argued that the coastal fringes of the landmass, not its heartland, were the key (Figure 12.21). The continental margins, Spykman reasoned, contained dense populations, abundant resources, and had controlling access both to the seas and to the continental interior. His **rimland theory,** published in 1944, stated "Who controls the Rimland rules Eurasia, who rules Eurasia controls the destinies of the world" and concluded that it was in the interest of both the United States and the USSR to assure that the historical political fragmentation of the rimland be maintained.

By the end of World War II, the Heartland was equated in American eyes with the USSR. To prevent Soviet domination of the World-Island, U.S. foreign policy during the Cold War was based on the notion of containment, or confining the USSR within its borders by means of a string of regional alliances in the Rimland: The North Atlantic Treaty Organization (NATO) in Western Europe, the Central Treaty Organization (CENTO) in West Asia, and the Southeast Asia Treaty Organization (SEATO). Military intervention was deemed necessary where communist expansion, whether Soviet or Chinese, was a threat—in Berlin, the Middle East, and Korea, for example.

A simple spatial model, the **domino theory,** was used as an adjunct to the policy of containment. According to this analogy, adjacent countries are lined up like dominoes; if one topples, the rest will fall. In the early 1960s, the domino theory was invoked to explain and justify U.S. intervention in Vietnam, and in the 1980s the theory was applied to involvement in Central America.

These (and other) models aimed at realistic assessments of national power and foreign policy stand in contrast to "organic state theory" based on the 19th-century idea of German geographer Friedrich Ratzel (1844–1904) that the state was an organism conforming to natural laws and forced to grow and expand into new territories (*Lebensraum*) in order to secure the resources needed for survival. Without that growth, the state would wither and die. These ideas, later expanded in the 1920s by the German Karl Haushofer (1869–1946) as *Geopolitik,* were used by the Nazi party as the presumed intellectual basis for wartime Germany's theories of race superiority and need for territorial conquest. Repudiated by events and Germany's defeat, *Geopolitik* for many years gave bad odor to any study of geopolitics, which only recently has again become a serious subfield of political geography.

In a rapidly changing world, many analysts believe the older geopolitical concepts and ideas of geostrategy no longer apply. A number of developments have rendered them obsolete: the dissolution of the USSR and the presumed end of the Cold War; the proliferation of nuclear technology; the declining influence of the United States; and the rise of Japan, China, and Western Europe to world power status. Geopolitical reality is now seen less in terms of military advantage and confrontation—the East–West rivalry of the Cold War era—and more as a reflection of two other forms of competition.

One is economic rivalry within the developed world and between economic core countries and emerging peripheral states—the North–South split introduced in Chapter 10 and expressed in the development of international blocs aligned by economic interests. The other is competition rooted in more fundamental and perhaps enduring conflicts between different "civilizations." It has been suggested that the world will increasingly be shaped by the interactions and conflicts among 7 or 8 major civilizations: Western, Confucian, Japanese, Islamic, Hindu, Slavic, Latin American, and possibly African. The differences between such civilizations, it is thought, are basic and antagonistic, rooted in enduring differences of history, language, culture, tradition, and religion. These differences are less easily resolved than purely political and economic ones and underlie such recent clashes as Indian rivalries between Hindus and Muslims, those of Sri Lanka between Tamils and Buddhists, conflicts in former Yugoslavia and between Armenians and Azeris in the Caucasus, and between and within other states and areas where "civilizations" come in contact and competition.

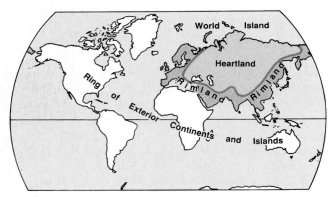

FIGURE 12.21   **Geopolitical viewpoints.** Both Mackinder and Spykman believed that Eurasia possessed strategic advantages, but they disagreed on whether its heartland or rimland provided the most likely base for world domination. Mahan recognized sea power as the key to national strength, advocating American occupation of the Hawaiian Islands, control of the Caribbean, and construction of an interocean canal through Central America.

International Political Systems

As changing geopolitical theories and outlooks suggest, in many ways individual countries are now weaker than ever before. Many are economically frail, others are politically unstable, and some are both. Strategically, no country is safe from military attack, for technology now enables us to shoot weapons halfway around the world. Some people believe that no national security is possible in the atomic age.

LANDSCAPES OF FUNCTIONAL ORGANIZATIONS

The recognition that a country cannot by itself guarantee either its prosperity or its own security has led to increased cooperation among states. In a sense, these cooperative ventures are replacing the empires of yesterday. They are proliferating quickly, and they involve countries everywhere.

The United Nations and Its Agencies

The United Nations (UN) is the only organization that tries to be universal, and even it is not all-inclusive. The UN is the most ambitious attempt ever undertaken to bring together the world's nations in international assembly and to promote world peace. Stronger and more representative than its predecessor, the League of Nations, it provides a forum where countries may discuss international problems and regional concerns and a mechanism, admittedly weak but still significant, for forestalling disputes or, when necessary, for ending wars (Figure 12.22). The United Nations also sponsors 40 programs and agencies aimed at fostering international cooperation with respect to specific goals. Among these are the World Health Organization (WHO), the Food and Agriculture Organization (FAO), and the United Nations Educational, Scientific, and Cultural Organization

(UNESCO). Many other UN agencies and much of the UN budget are committed to assisting member states with matters of economic growth and development.

Member states have not surrendered sovereignty to the UN, and the world body is legally and effectively unable to make or enforce a world law. Nor is there a world police force. Although there is recognized international law adjudicated by the International Court of Justice, rulings by this body are sought only by countries agreeing beforehand to abide by its arbitration. The United Nations has no authority over the military forces of individual countries.

A pronounced change both in the relatively passive role of the United Nations and in traditional ideas of international relations has begun to emerge, however. Long-established rules of total national sovereignty which allowed governments to act internally as they saw fit, free of outside interference, are fading as the United Nations increasingly applies a concept of "interventionism." The Persian Gulf War of 1991 was UN authorized under the old rules prohibiting one state (Iraq) from violating the sovereignty of another (Kuwait) by attacking it. After the war, the new interventionism sanctioned UN operations within Iraq against the Iraqi government's will to protect Kurds within the country.

FIGURE 12.22   United Nations peacekeeping forces on duty in Bosnia-Herzegovina. Under the auspices of the UN, soldiers from many different countries staff peacekeeping forces and military observer groups in many world regions in an effort to halt or mitigate conflicts. Demand for peacekeeping and observer operations is indicated by recent deployment of UN forces in Cambodia, Cyprus, Lebanon, Israel, Syria, Iran, Iraq, India, Pakistan, Mozambique, Angola, Somalia, Western Sahara, and Namibia, among others.

Later, the UN intervened with troops and relief agencies in Somalia, Bosnia, and elsewhere, invoking an "international jurisdiction over inalienable human rights" that prevails without regard to state frontiers or sovereignty considerations.

Whatever the long-term prospects for interventionism replacing absolute sovereignty, for the short-term the United Nations remains the only institution where the vast majority of the world's countries can collectively discuss matters of international political and economic concerns and attempt peacefully to resolve their differences. It has been particularly influential in formulating a law of the sea.

Maritime Boundaries

Boundaries define political jurisdictions and areas of resource control. But claims of national authority are not restricted to land areas alone. Water covers about two-thirds of the earth's surface, and increasingly countries have been projecting their sovereignty seaward to claim adjacent maritime areas and resources. A basic question involves the right of states to control water and the resources that it contains. The inland waters of a country, such as rivers and lakes, have traditionally been considered within the sovereignty of that country. Oceans, however, are not within any country's borders. Are they, then, to be open to all states to use, or may a single country claim sovereignty and limit access and use by other states?

For most of human history, the oceans remained effectively outside individual national control or international jurisdiction. The seas were a common highway for those daring enough to venture on them, an inexhaustible larder for fishermen, and a vast refuse pit for the muck of civilization. By the end of the 19th century, however, most coastal countries claimed sovereignty over a continuous belt 3 or 4 nautical miles wide (a *nautical mile*, or *nm*, equals 1.15 statute miles, or 1.85 km). At the time, the 3-mile limit represented the farthest range of artillery and thus the effective limit of control by the coastal state. Though recognizing the rights of others to innocent passage, such sovereignty permitted the enforcement of quarantine and customs regulations, allowed national protection of coastal fisheries, and made claims of neutrality effective during other people's wars. The primary concern was with security and unrestricted commerce. No separately codified laws of the sea existed, however, and none seemed to be needed until after World War I.

A League of Nations Conference for the Codification of International Law, convened in 1930, inconclusively discussed maritime legal matters and served to identify areas of concern that were to become increasingly pressing after World War II. Important among these was an emerging shift from interest in commerce and national security to a preoccupation with the resources of the seas, an interest fanned by the *Truman Proclamation* of 1945. Motivated by a desire to exploit offshore oil deposits, the federal government under this doctrine laid claim to all resources on the continental shelf contiguous to its coasts. Other states, many claiming even broader areas of control, hurried to annex their own adjacent marine resources. Within a few years, a quarter of the earth's surface was appropriated by individual coastal countries.

Unrestricted extensions of jurisdiction and disputes over conflicting claims to maritime space and resources led to a series of United Nations conferences on the Law of the Sea. Meeting over a period of years, delegates from over 150 countries attempted to achieve consensus on a treaty that would establish an internationally agreed-upon "convention dealing with all matters relating to the Law of the Sea." The meetings culminated in a draft treaty in 1982, the **United Nations Convention on the Law of the Sea.**

An International Law of the Sea

The convention delimits territorial boundaries and rights by defining four zones of diminishing control (Figure 12.23):

* A *territorial sea* of up to 12 nm (19 km) in breadth over which coastal states have sovereignty, including exclusive fishing rights. Vessels of all types normally have the right of innocent passage through the territorial sea, though under certain circumstances noncommercial (primarily military and research) vessels can be challenged.

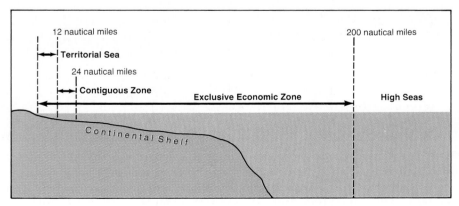

FIGURE 12.23   **Territorial claims permitted by the 1982 United Nations Convention on the Law of the Sea (UNCLOS).**

- A *contiguous zone* to 24 nm (38 km). Although a coastal state does not have complete sovereignty in this zone, it can enforce its customs, immigration, and sanitation laws and has the right of hot pursuit out of its territorial waters.
- An **exclusive economic zone (EEZ)** of up to 200 nm (370 km) (Figure 12.24) in which the state has recognized rights to explore, exploit, conserve, and manage the natural resources, both living and nonliving, of the seabed and waters. Countries have exclusive rights to the resources lying within the continental shelf when this extends farther, up to 350 nm (560 km), beyond their coasts. The traditional freedoms of the high seas are to be maintained in this zone.
- The *high seas* beyond the EEZ. Outside any national jurisdiction, they are open to all states, whether coastal or landlocked. Mineral resources in the international deep seabed area beyond national jurisdiction are declared the common heritage of humankind, to be managed for the benefit of all the peoples of the earth.

By the end of the 1980s, most coastal countries, including the United States, had used the UNCLOS provisions to proclaim and reciprocally recognize jurisdiction over 12-nm territorial seas and 200-nm economic zones. Despite reservations held by the United States and a few other industrial countries about the deep seabed mining provisions, the convention received the necessary ratification by 60 states and became international law in November, 1994.

Regional Alliances

Countries have shown themselves to be willing to relinquish some of their independence to participate in smaller multinational systems. These groupings may be economic, military, or political, and many have been formed since 1945. Cooperation in the economic sphere seems to come more easily to states than does political or military cooperation.

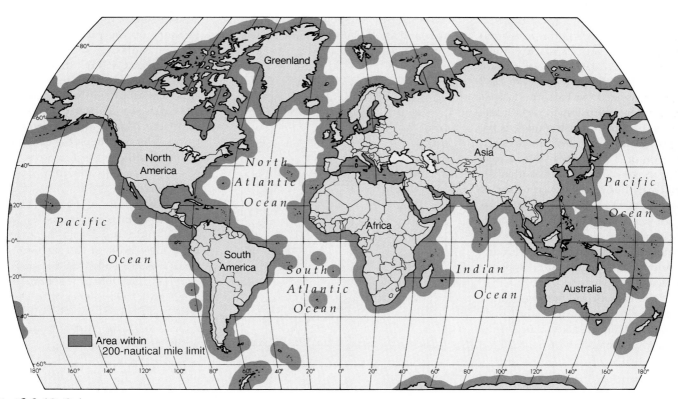

FIGURE 12.24   **The 200-nautical mile exclusive economic zone (EEZ) claims of coastal states.** The provisions of the Law of the Sea Convention have in effect changed the maritime map of the world. Three important consequences flow from the 200-nm EEZ concept: (1) islands have gained a new significance (see "Specks and Spoils"), (2) countries have a host of new neighbors, and (3) the EEZ lines result in overlapping claims. EEZ lines are drawn around a country's possessions as well as around the country itself. Every island, no matter how small, has its own 200-nm EEZ. This means that while the United States shares continental borders only with Canada and Mexico, it has maritime boundaries with countries in Asia, South America, and Europe. All told, the United States may have to negotiate some 30 maritime boundaries, which is likely to take decades. Other countries, particularly those with many possessions, will have to undertake similar lengthy negotiations.

he Convention on the Law of the Sea gives to owners of islands claims over immense areas of the surrounding sea and, of course, to the fisheries and mineral resources in and under them. Tiny specks of land formerly too insignificant in size or distant in location to arouse the emotions of any nation now are avidly sought and fervently claimed. Remote Rockall, a British islet far west of Scotland, was used by Britain in 1976 to justify extending its fishing rights claim farther into the North Atlantic than otherwise was possible. Argentina nearly went to war with Chile in 1978 over three islands at the tip of South America at the Atlantic end of the Beagle Channel. Chile had lodged its claim of ownership hoping to gain access to known South Atlantic fish resources and hoped-for petroleum deposits. In 1982 Argentina seized the Falkland Islands from Britain, ostensibly to reclaim the Malvinas (their Spanish name) as national territory, but with an underlying economic motive as well. British forces retook the islands and subsequently used sovereignty over them to claim a sea area three times as large as Britain. Japan has encased a disappearing islet in concrete to maintain territorial claims endangered through erosion of the speck of land supporting them.

The Paracel and Spratly Islands, straddling trade routes in the South China Sea, have attracted more attention and claimants than most island groups, thanks to presumed large reserves of oil and gas in their vicinities. The Japanese seized the Paracels from China during World War II and at its end surrendered them to Nationalist Chinese forces that soon retreated to Taiwan. South Vietnam took them over until 1974, when they were forcibly ejected by the mainland Chinese. In 1979, a united Vietnam reasserted its claims, basing them on 17th- and 18th-century maps. China countered with reference to 3rd-century explorations by its geographers and maintained its control.

The location of the Paracels to the north, near China, in the South China Sea places them in a different and less difficult status than that of the Spratlys, whose nearest neighbors are the Philippines and Malaysia. Mere dots in the sea,

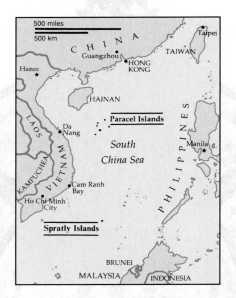

the largest of the Spratlys is about 100 acres—no more than one-eighth the size of New York's Central Park. But under the Convention on the Law of the Sea, possession of the island group would confer rights to the resources (oil, it is hoped) found beneath about 400,000 square kilometers (150,000 sq. mi.) of sea. That lure has made rivals of six governments and posed the possibility of conflict. Until early in 1988, Vietnam, the Philippines, Malaysia, Taiwan, and tiny Brunei had all maintained in peaceful coexistence garrisons on separate islets in the Spratly group. Then China landed troops on islands near the Vietnamese holdings, sank two Vietnamese naval ships, and accused Vietnam of seizing "Chinese" territory on the pretext of searching for their missing sailors. Although China agreed in 1992 that ownership disputes in the Spratlys should be resolved without violence it also, in 1993, passed a law repeating its claims to all the islands and its determination to defend them. In early 1995, China occupied "Mischief Reef," close to—and already claimed by—the Philippines.

Assertions of past discovery, previous or present occupation, proximity, and simple wishful thinking have all served as the basis for the proliferating claims to seas and seabeds. The world's oceans, once open and freely accessible, are increasingly being closed by the lure of specks of land and the spoils of wealth they command.

Economic Alliances

The World Trade Organization, which came into existence at the start of 1995, is charged with enforcing the global trade accord that grew out of years of international negotiations under the terms of the General Agreement on Tariffs and Trade (GATT). The basic principle behind the WTO is that the 100-plus member countries should work to cut tariffs, dismantle nontariff barriers to trade, liberalize trade in services, and treat all other countries uniformly in matters of trade; any preference granted to one should be available to all. Increasingly, however, regional rather than global trade agreements are being struck and free trade areas (FTAs) are proliferating. Such regional alliances, it is held, make world trade less free by scrapping tariffs on trade among member states but retaining them separately or as a group on exchanges with nonmembers.

Among the most powerful and far-reaching of the economic alliances are those that have evolved in Europe, particularly the European Union and its several forerunners. Shortly after the end of World War II, the Benelux countries (Belgium, the Netherlands, and Luxembourg) formed an economic union to create a common set of tariffs and to eliminate import licenses and quotas. Formed at about the same time were the Organization for European Cooperation (1948), which coordinated the distribution and use of Marshall Plan funds, and the European Coal and Steel Community (1952), which integrated the development of that industry in the member countries. A few years later, in 1957, the *European Economic Community* (EEC) or *Common Market,* was created, composed at first of only six states: France, Italy, West Germany, and the Benelux countries.

To counteract these Inner Six, as they were called, other countries in 1960 formed the European Free Trade Association (EFTA). Known as the Outer Seven, they were the United Kingdom, Norway, Denmark, Sweden, Switzerland, Austria, and Portugal (Figure 12.25). Between 1973 and 1986, three members (the United Kingdom, Denmark, and Portugal) left EFTA for membership in the Common Market and were replaced by Iceland and Finland. Other Common Market additions were Greece in 1981, and Spain and Portugal in 1986. After 23 years of associate status, Turkey ap-

plied for full membership in 1987, but will not achieve it for some years. Austria, Finland, and Sweden became members in 1995. Negotiations for the admittance of 10 Eastern European states are to begin by the end of 1997.

Over the years, members of the **European Union (EU),** as the organization embracing the Common Market is now called, have taken many steps to integrate their economies and coordinate their policies in such areas as transportation, agriculture, and fisheries. A Council of Ministers, a Commission, a European Parliament, and a Court of Justice give the European Union supranational institutions with effective ability to make and enforce laws. By January 1, 1993, the EU had abolished most remnant barriers to free trade and the free movement of capital and people, creating a single European market (Figure 12.26), with 7 members abolishing all border controls and passport restrictions between themselves in 1995. Plans call for monetary integration and a single European currency for at least some countries by 1999.

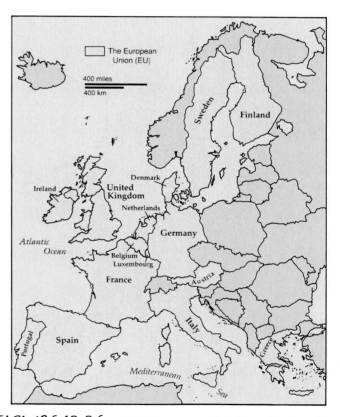

FIGURE 12.26   **The European Union** on January 1, 1995, expanded from 12 to 15 members as Austria, Finland, and Sweden joined the organization. The EU now spreads from the Mediterranean to the Arctic. In addition, some 70 states in Africa, the Caribbean, and the Pacific have been affiliated with the EU by the Lomé Convention, which provides for developmental aid (amounting to $39 billion since 1975) and favored trade access to EU markets. In late 1995, the EU decided to terminate those affiliation benefits in 2000.

FIGURE 12.25   **The original "Inner Six" and "Outer Seven" of Europe.**

We have traced this European development process to illustrate the fluid process by which regional alliances are made. Countries come together in an association, some drop out, and others join. New treaties are made, and new coalitions emerge. It seems safe to predict that although the alliances themselves will change, the idea of economic associations has been permanently added to that of political and military leagues, which are as old as nation-states themselves.

Three further points about economic unions are worth noting. The first, which also applies to military and political alliances, is that the formation of a coalition in one area often stimulates the creation of another alliance by countries left out of the first. Thus, the union of the Inner Six gave rise to the treaty among the Outer Seven. Similarly, a counterpart of the Common Market was the Council of Mutual Economic Assistance (CMEA), also known as Comecon, which linked the former communist countries of Eastern Europe and the USSR through trade agreements.

Second, the new economic unions tend to be composed of contiguous states (Figure 12.27). This was not the case with the recently dissolved empires, which included far-flung territories. Contiguity facilitates the movement of people and goods. Communication and transportation are simpler and more effective among adjoining countries than among those far removed from one another.

Finally, it does not seem to matter whether countries are alike or distinctly different in their economies, as far as joining economic unions is concerned. There are examples of both. If the countries are dissimilar, they may complement each other. This was one basis for the European Common Market. Dairy products and furniture from Denmark are sold in France, freeing that country to specialize in the production of machinery and clothing—although the EU is faced by expensive gluts of agricultural goods produced in more than one country. On the other hand, countries that produce the same raw materials hope that by joining together in an economic alliance, they might be able to enhance their control of markets and prices for their products. The Organization of Petroleum Exporting Countries (OPEC), discussed in Chapter 8, is a case in point. Other attempts to form commodity cartels and price agreements between producing and consuming nations are represented by the International Tin Agreement, the International Coffee Agreement, and others.

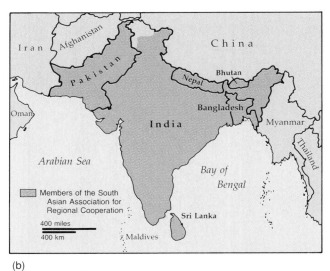

(a) (b)

FIGURE 12.27 (*a*) **The North American Free Trade Agreement (NAFTA)** is intended to unite Canada, the United States, and Mexico in a regional free trade zone. Under the terms of the treaty, tariffs on all agricultural products and thousands of other goods are to be eliminated by the end of 1999. In addition, all three countries are to ease restrictions on the movement of business executives and professionals. If fully implemented, the treaty will create one of the world's richest and largest trading blocs. (*b*) **Members of the South Asian Association for Regional Cooperation.** Formed in December 1985 to promote cooperation in such areas as agriculture and rural development, transportation, and telecommunications, the Association is composed of seven neighboring states that contain about one-fifth of the world's population. Many other regional economic associations have been formed or proposed, including: the Arab Maghreb Union (of North African states); the Asean Free Trade Area (Southeast Asia); the Southern Cone Common Market (Mercosur) and the Andean Group (both in South America); the Caribbean Group and Common Market; and the Southern African Development Community.

Military and Political Alliances

Countries form alliances for other than economic reasons. Strategic, political, and cultural considerations may also foster cooperation. *Military alliances* are based on the principle that in unity there is strength. Such pacts usually provide for mutual assistance in the case of aggression. Once again, action breeds reaction when such an association is created. The formation of the North Atlantic Treaty Organization (NATO), a defensive alliance of many European countries and the United States, was countered by the establishment of the Warsaw Treaty Organization, which joined the USSR and its satellite countries of Eastern Europe. Both pacts allowed the member states to base armed forces in one another's territories, a relinquishment of a certain degree of sovereignty unique to this century.

Military alliances depend on the perceived common interests and political goodwill of the countries involved. As political realities change, so do the strategic alliances. NATO was created to defend Western Europe and North America against the Soviet military threat. When the dissolution of the USSR and the Warsaw Pact removed that threat, the purpose of the NATO alliance became less clear and, during the 1990s, its relationships with Eastern European states and Russia were under review and change as most of those countries sought ways to foster cooperation with NATO.

All international alliances recognize communities of interest. In economic and military associations, common objectives are clearly seen and described, and joint actions are agreed on with respect to the achievement of those objectives. More generalized common concerns or appeals to historical interest may be the basis for primarily *political alliances*. Such associations tend to be rather loose, not requiring their members to yield much power to the union. Examples are the Commonwealth of Nations (formerly the British Commonwealth), composed of many former British colonies and dominions, and the Organization of American States, both of which offer economic as well as political benefits.

There are many examples of abortive political unions that have foundered precisely because the individual countries could not agree on questions of policy and were unwilling to subordinate individual interests to make the union succeed. The United Arab Republic, the Central African Federation, the Federation of Malaysia and Singapore, and the Federation of the West Indies fall within this category.

Although many such political associations have failed, observers of the world scene speculate about the possibility that "superstates" will emerge from one or more of the economic or political alliances that now exist. Will a "United States of Europe," for example, under a single government be the logical outcome of the successes of the EU? No one knows, but as long as the individual state·is regarded as the highest form of political and social organization (as it is now) and as the body in which sovereignty rests, such total unification is unlikely.

Local and Regional Political Organization

The most profound contrasts in cultures tend to occur between, rather than within, states, one reason political geographers traditionally have been primarily interested in country units. The emphasis on the state, however, should not obscure the fact that for most of us it is at that local level that we find our most intimate and immediate contact with government and its influence on the administration of our affairs. In the United States, for example, an individual is subject to the decisions and regulations made by the school board, the municipality, the county, the state, and, perhaps, a host of special-purpose districts—all in addition to the laws and regulations issued by the federal government and its agencies. Among other things, local political entities determine where children go to school, the minimum size lot on which a person can build a house, and where one may legally park a car. Adjacent states of the United States may be characterized by sharply differing personal and business tax rates; differing controls on the sale of firearms, alcohol, and tobacco; variant administrative systems for public services; and different levels of expenditures for them (Figure 12.28).

All of these governmental entities are *spatial systems*. Because they operate within defined geographic areas and because they make behavior-governing decisions, they are topics of interests to political geographers. In the concluding sections of this chapter we examine two aspects of political organization at the local and regional level. Our emphasis will be on the United States and Canadian scene simply because their local political geography is familiar to most of

FIGURE 12.28   The Four Corners Monument, marking the meeting of Utah, Colorado, Arizona, and New Mexico. Jurisdictional boundaries within countries may be precisely located but are usually not highly visible in the landscape. At the same time, those boundaries may be very significant in citizens' personal affairs and in the conduct of economic activities.

us. We should remember, however, North American structures of municipal governments, minor civil divisions, and special-purpose districts have counterparts in other regions of the world (Figure 12.29).

The Geography of Representation: The Districting Problem

There are more than 85,000 local governmental units in the United States. Slightly more than half of these are municipalities, townships, and counties. The remainder are school districts, water-control districts, airport authorities, sanitary districts, and other special-purpose bodies. Around each of these districts, boundaries have been drawn. Although the number of districts does not change greatly from year to year, many boundary lines are redrawn in any single year.

FIGURE 12.29 The Rathaus—city hall—of Munich, Germany. Before the rise of strong central governments, citizens of wealth and power in medieval and renaissance Europe focused their loyalties upon their home cities and created within them municipal buildings and institutions that would reflect their pride and substance. The city hall was frequently the grandest public building of the community, prominently located in the center of town.

For example, the ruling of the U.S. Supreme Court in 1954 in *Brown v. Board of Education of Topeka, Kansas,* that the doctrine of "separate but equal" school systems was unconstitutional, led to the redrawing of thousands of attendance boundaries of school districts. Likewise, the court's "one person, one vote" ruling in *Baker v. Carr* (1962) signified the end of overrepresentation of sparsely populated rural districts in state legislatures and led to the frequent adjustment of electoral districts within states and cities to attain roughly equal numbers of voters. Such *redistricting* or *reapportionment* is made necessary by shifts in population, as areas gain or lose people.

The analysis of how boundaries are drawn around voting districts is one aspect of **electoral geography,** which also addresses the spatial patterns yielded by election results and their relationship to the socioeconomic characteristics of voters. In a democracy, it might be assumed that election districts should contain roughly equal numbers of voters, that electoral districts should be reasonably compact, and that the proportion of elected representatives should correspond to the share of votes cast for a given political party. Problems arise because the way in which the boundary lines are drawn can maximize, minimize, or effectively nullify the power of a group of people.

Gerrymandering is the practice of drawing the boundaries of voting districts so as to unfairly favor one political party over another, to fragment voting blocs, or to achieve other nondemocratic objectives (Figure 12.30). A number of strategies have been employed over the years for that purpose. *Stacked* gerrymandering involves drawing circuitous boundaries to enclose pockets of strength or weakness of the group in power; it is what we usually think of as gerrymandering. The *excess vote* technique concentrates the votes of the opposition in a few districts, which they can win easily, but leaves them few potential seats elsewhere. Conversely, the *wasted vote* strategy dilutes the opposition's strength by dividing its votes among a number of districts.

Assume that X and O represent two groups with an equal number of voters but different policy preferences. Although there are equal numbers of Xs and Os, the way electoral districts are drawn affects voting results. In Figure 12.31*a*, the Xs are concentrated in one district and will probably elect only one representative of four. The power of the Xs is maximized in Figure 12.31*b*, where they may control three of the four districts. The voters are evenly divided in Figure 12.31*c*, where the Xs have the opportunity to elect two of the four representatives. Finally, Figure 12.31*d* shows how both political parties might agree to delimit the electoral districts to provide "safe seats" for incumbents.

Figure 12.31 depicts a hypothetical district, compact in shape with an even population distribution and only two groups competing for representation. In actuality, voting districts are often oddly shaped because of such factors as the city limits, current population distribution, and transportation routes—as well as past gerrymandering. Further, in any large area many groups vie for power. Each electoral inter-

THE GERRY-MANDER. (Boston, 1811.)

FIGURE 12.30 **The original gerrymander.** The term *gerrymander* originated in 1812 from the shape of an electoral district formed in Massachusetts while Elbridge Gerry was governor. When an artist added certain animal features, the district resembled a salamander and quickly came to be called a gerrymander.

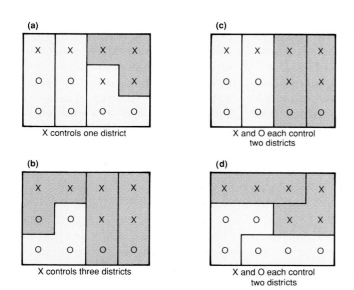

FIGURE 12.31 **Alternative districting strategies.** *X*s and *O*s might represent Republicans and Democrats, Liberals and Conservatives, urban and rural voters, blacks and whites, or any other distinctive groups.

est group promotes its version of fairness in the way boundaries are delimited. Minority interests seek representation in proportion to their numbers, so that they will be able to elect representatives who are concerned about and responsive to their needs (see "Voting Rights and Race").

Of course, gerrymandering is not always and automatically successful. First, a districting arrangement that appears to be unfair may be appealed to the courts. Further, voters are not unthinking party loyalists; key issues may cut across party lines, scandal may erode, or personal charm increase, votes unexpectedly; and the amount of candidate financing or number of campaign workers may determine election outcome if compelling issues are absent.

The Fragmentation of Political Power

Boundary drawing at any electoral level is never easy, particularly when political groups want to maximize their representation and minimize that of opposition groups. Furthermore, the boundaries that we may want for one set of districts may *not* be those that we want for another. For example, sewage districts must take natural drainage features into account, whereas police districts may be based on

FOR YOUR CONSIDERATION

VOTING RIGHTS AND RACE

The irregularly shaped Congressional voting districts shown here represent a deliberate attempt to balance voting rights and race. They have been called extreme examples of racial gerrymandering, however, and at least in part ruled unconstitutional by the Supreme Court.

All of the districts shown contain a majority of black voters. They were created by state legislatures after the 1990 census to make minority representation in Congress more closely resemble minority presence in the state's total population. Specifically, they were intended to comply with the federal Voting Rights Act's charge to remedy past discrimination against black voters by increasing their elected representation.

In North Carolina, for example, although 24% of the population of the state is black, past districting had divided black voters among a number of districts, with the result that blacks had not elected a single Congressional representative in the 20th century. In 1991, the Justice Department ordered North Carolina to redistrict so that at least two districts would contain black majorities. Because of the way the black population is distributed, the only way to form black-majority districts was to string together cities, towns, and rural areas. The two newly created districts had slim (53%) black majorities.

The redistricting in North Carolina and other states had immediate effects. Black membership in the House of Representatives increased from 26 in 1990 to 39 in 1992; blacks constituted nearly 9% of the House as against 12% of African Americans in the total population. Within a year, those electoral gains were threatened as lawsuits challenging the redistricting were filed in a number of states. The chief contention of the plaintiffs was that the irregular shapes of the districts were a product of racial gerrymandering and amounted to reverse discrimination against whites.

In June 1993, a sharply-divided Supreme Court ruled in *Shaw v. Reno* that North Carolina's 12th Congressional District may violate the constitutional rights of white voters and ordered a district court to review the case. The 5–4 ruling gave evidence that the country had not yet reached agreement on how to comply with the Voting Rights Act. It raised a central question: should a state maximize the rights of racial minorities or not take racial status into consideration? A divided Court provided answers in 1995 and 1996 rulings that rejected Congressional redistricting maps for Georgia, Texas, and North Carolina on the grounds that "race cannot be the predominant factor" in drawing election district boundaries, no matter the laudable objectives of the Voting Rights Act of 1965.

One way to eliminate gerrymandering and its distortion of voter representation is through a modified at-large voting system called *preference* or *cumulative voting*. Under this system, voters elect several candidates in a larger district rather than just one in a traditional district. North Carolina, for example, might contain three Congressional districts instead of its current 12, with the divisions along county lines. The districts would be assigned a number of representatives proportional to their population. If one district had four representatives, voters would have four votes to assign however they liked. They could cast all four for one candidate or spread them among two, three, or four candidates. by concentrating their votes, minority groups could increase the chances that their candidates would be elected. Preference voting is common in Europe and on corporate boards in the United States. Although it is used in a number of American communities, no state employs the system.

the distribution of the population or the number of miles of street to be patrolled, and school attendance zones must consider the numbers of school-aged children and the capacities of individual schools.

As these examples suggest, the United States is subdivided into great numbers of political administrative units whose areas of control are spatially limited. The 50 states are partitioned into more than 3000 counties ("parishes" in Louisiana), most of which are further subdivided into townships, each with a still lower level of governing power. This political fragmentation is further increased by the existence of nearly innumerable special-purpose districts whose boundaries rarely coincide with the standard major and minor civil divisions of the country or even with each other (Figure 12.32). Each district represents a form of political al-

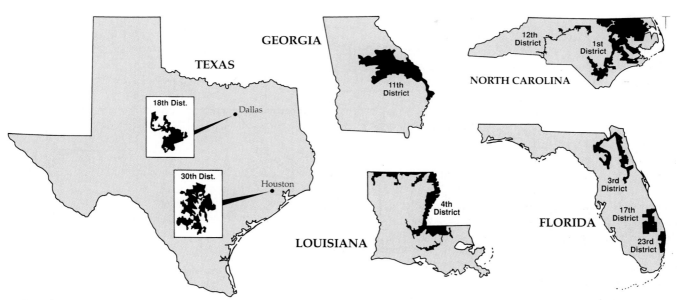

Questions:

1. Do you believe that race should be a consideration in the electoral process? Why or why not? If so, do you believe that voting districts should be drawn to increase the likelihood that representatives of racial or ethnic minorities will win elections?

2. With which of the following arguments in Shaw v. Reno do you agree? Why? ". . . Racial gerrymandering, even for remedial purposes, may balkanize us into competing racial factions; it threatens to carry us further from the goal of a political system in which race no longer matters." (Justice Sandra Day O'Connor) ". . . Legislators will have to take race into account in order to avoid dilution of minority voting strength." (Justice David Souter)

3. One of the candidates in North Carolina's 12th Congressional District said, "I love the district because I can drive down I-85 with both car doors open and hit every person in the district." Given a good transportation and communication network, how important is it that voting Districts be compact?

4. Blacks apparently face difficult obstacles in being elected in districts that do not have a black majority, as witness their numerical underrepresentation in most legislative bodies. But critics of "racial gerrymandering" contend that blacks have been and can continue to be elected in white-majority districts and that white politicians can and do adequately represent the needs of all, including black, voters in their districts. Do you agree? Why or why not?

location of territory to achieve a specific aim of local need or legislative intent (see "Too Many Governments").

Canada, a federation of 10 provinces and two territories,[1] has a similar pattern of political subdivision. Each of the provinces contains minor civil divisions—municipalities—under provincial control, and all (cities, towns, villages and rural municipalities) are governed by elected councils. Ontario and Quebec also have counties that group smaller

[1]The two territories—the Yukon and the Northwest Territories—will be joined before the turn of the century by a third, Nunavut (meaning "Our Land" in the Inuktitut language). Nunavut will be carved from the eastern portion of present Northwest Territories, dividing the predominantly Inuit (Eskimo) population of the eastern and central Arctic from the primarily Indian and nonnative peoples of the west.

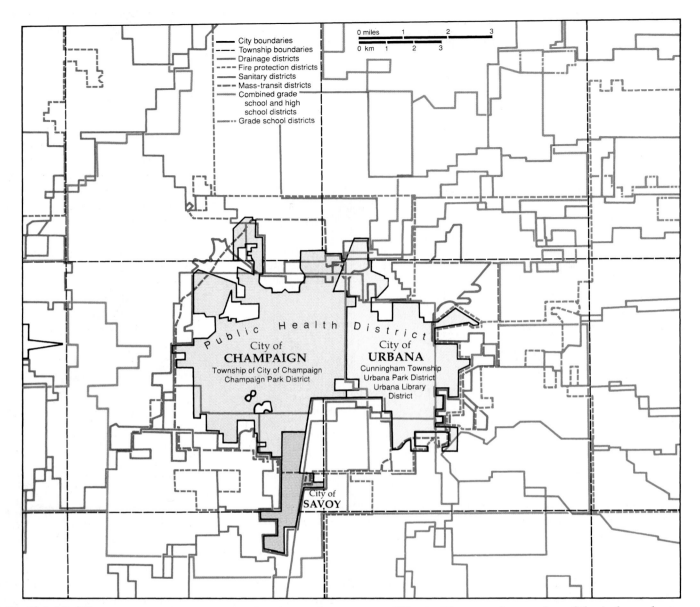

FIGURE 12.32 **Political fragmentation in Champaign County, Illinois.** The map shows a few of the independent administrative agencies with separate jurisdictions, responsibilities, and taxing powers in a portion of a single Illinois county. Among the other such agencies forming the fragmented political landscape are Champaign County itself, a forest preserve district, a public health district, a mental health district, the county housing authority, and a community college district.

municipal units for certain purposes. In general, municipalities are responsible for police and fire protection, local jails, roads and hospitals, water supply and sanitation, and schools, duties which are discharged either by elected agencies or appointed commissions.

Most North Americans live in large and small cities. In the United States these, too, are subdivided, not only into wards or precincts for voting purposes but also into special districts for such functions as fire and police protection, water and electricity supply, education, recreation, and sanitation. These districts almost never coincide with one another, and the larger the urban area, the greater the proliferation of small, special-purpose governing and taxing units. Although no Canadian community has quite the multiplication of governmental entities as, for example, Chicago, Illinois, with well over 1000 special- and general-purpose governments, major Canadian cities may find themselves with complex and growing systems of similar nature. Metropolitan Toronto, for example, has more than 100 identified authorities that can be classified as "local governments."

If you are a property owner in Wheeling Township in the city of Arlington Heights in Cook County, Illinois, here's who divvies up your taxes: the city, the county, the township, an elementary school district, a high school district, a junior college district, a fire protection district, a park district, a sanitary district, a forest preserve district, a library district, a tuberculosis sanitarium district, and a mosquito abatement district.

Lest you attribute this to population density or the Byzantine ways of Cook County politics, it's not that much different elsewhere in Illinois—home to more governmental units than any other state in the United States. According to late-1980s figures from the U.S. Bureau of the Census, there were 6626 local government units in Illinois. Second-place Pennsylvania had 4956 governments—1670 fewer than Illinois—and the average for all states was 1663.

Along with its 102 counties, Illinois has nearly 1300 municipalities, more than 1400 townships, and over 1000 school districts; but the biggest factor in the governmental unit total are single-function special districts. These were up from 2600 in 1982 to nearly 2800 in 1985, with no end to their increase in sight. Special districts range from Chicago's Metropolitan Sanitary District to the Caseyville Township Street Lighting District. Most of these governments have property-taxing power. Some also impose sales or utility taxes.

This proliferation is in part a historical by-product of good intentions. The framers of the state's 1870 constitution, wanting to prevent overtaxation, limited the borrowing and taxing power of local governments to 5% of the assessed value of properties in their jurisdictions. When this limit was reached and the need for government services continued to grow with population, voters and officials circumvented the constitutional proscription by creating new taxing bodies—special districts. Illinois' special districts grew because they could get around municipality debt limitations and because they could be fitted to service users without regard to city or county boundaries.

Critics say all these governments result in duplication of effort, inefficiencies, higher costs, and higher taxes. Supporters of special districts, townships, and small school districts argue that such units fulfill the ideal of a government close and responsive to its constituents.

Adapted with permission from J. M. Winski and J. S. Hill, "Illinois: A Case of Too Much Government," *Illinois Business,* Winter 1985, pp. 8–12. Copyright 1985 by Crain Communications Inc.

The existence of such a great number of districts in metropolitan areas may cause inefficiency in public services and hinder the orderly use of space. *Zoning ordinances,* for example, controlling the uses to which land may be put, are determined by each municipality. Unfortunately, in large urban areas, the efforts of one community may be hindered by the practices of neighboring communities. Thus land zoned for an industrial park or shopping mall in one city may abut land zoned for single-family residences in an adjoining municipality. Each community pursues its own interests, which may not coincide with those of its neighbors or the larger region.

Inefficiency and duplication of effort characterize not just zoning but many of the services provided by local governments. The efforts of one community to avert air and water pollution may be, and often are, counteracted by the rules and practices of other towns in the region, although state and national environmental protection standards are now reducing such potential conflicts. Social as well as physical problems spread beyond city boundaries. Thus, nearby suburban communities are affected when a central city lacks the resources to maintain high-quality schools or to attack social ills. The provision of health care facilities, electricity and water, transportation, and recreational space affects the whole region and, many professionals think, should be under the control of a single unified metropolitan government.

The growth in the number and size of metropolitan areas has increased awareness of the problems of their administrative fragmentation. In response, new approaches to the integration of those areas have been proposed and adopted. The aims of all plans of metropolitan government are to create or preserve coherence in the management of areawide concerns and to assure that both the problems and the benefits of growth are shared without regard to their jurisdictional locations. Two approaches—*unified government* and *predevelopment annexation*—have been followed to secure the efficient administration of extensive urbanized areas.

Unified Government

The modern concept of metropolitan government was developed early in the 20th century in the United States as a means of coping with urban growth. The applied North American model of **unified government**—sometimes called *Unigov* or *Metro*—is found, however, in the Province of Ontario, Canada, and, particularly, in metropolitan Toronto. The provincial government undertook the reorganization of Ontario's 900-plus cities, towns, and villages into some 30 two-tiered systems of metropolitan government. The upper tier provided broad-scale direction and fiscal control, the lower tier preserved some measure of local autonomy.

The Metropolitan Government of Toronto, established in 1954, was the prototype. The province federated the city of Toronto and its suburbs as a metropolitan corporation and assigned it responsibility for public transportation, water and sewerage, police protection, regional parks, and centralized land use planning. To preserve a sense of identity and to free Metro government from concern with problems best handled locally, the area municipalities retained their separate names and continued to perform such tasks as maintaining local roads and parks, providing fire protection, and collecting garbage. Metropolitan-wide school boards, independent of both the metropolitan corporation and area municipalities, are responsible for the administration and financing of the public schools. Metro Toronto served as a model for other Unigov introductions in Canada. The Montreal, Calgary, and Vancouver regions (among others) have Metro governments, though not all are structured identically to that of Toronto.

Unigov has won many adherents and some successes in the United States as well, where a variety of approaches to region-wide administration and planning have been tried. Nashville–Davidson County, Tennessee, and Indianapolis–Marion County, Indiana, are among the areas where city-county consolidation has occurred. A different system operates in Metropolitan Dade County, Florida, which includes Miami and 26 other municipalities. There, local governments have retained some powers (such as police and fire services), but others (like land use planning and tax collection) have been transferred to the county. Other Metro government operations are found in Jacksonville, Florida; Portland, Oregon; Seattle, Washington, and elsewhere.

Yet another approach to regionalism is represented by the Metropolitan Council of the Twin Cities area of Minneapolis/St. Paul. Here, Minnesota's two largest cities, some 130 smaller municipalities, seven counties, and great numbers of special-purpose agencies were partially subordinated to a metropolitan council responsible for activities that demand centralized, areawide administration (Figure 12.33). These include sewage, water supply, airport location, highway routes, and the preservation of open space. Local communities kept their own forms of government and the control of fire and police services, schools, street maintenance, and other local functions.

Predevelopment Annexation

The preservation of the tax base and the retention of expansion room for the central city are the driving forces behind the **predevelopment annexations** permitted under the laws of some states, particularly in the West. Cities such as Oklahoma City (650 square miles; 1680 km²) and Houston (510 square miles; 1320 km²) have taken advantage of such permissive regulation to assure that they will not be constricted by a ring of incorporated suburbs that would siphon off growth, population, jobs, and income generated by the

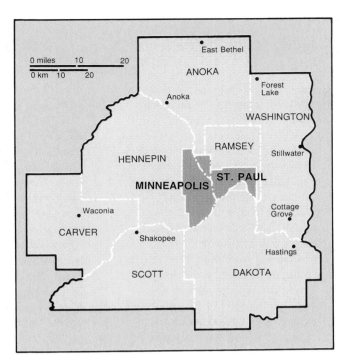

FIGURE 12.33   The Metropolitan Council of the Twin Cities Area, created in 1967, is responsible for the orderly development of a seven-county area that contains over 300 local units of government, including Minneapolis and St. Paul. The council coordinates such services as sewers and solid-waste disposal and the development of highways and parks. It reviews all land use plans of individual governments and can delay their implementation for 60 days while it attempts to coordinate them with regional goals.

presence of the central city itself. However, because all incorporated communities of a specific minimum size possess such annexation rights over contiguous unincorporated areas, rival communities may initiate unseemly "land grabs" to the detriment of both undeveloped rural areas and the rational control of logically single metropolitan areas.

Both Unigov and predevelopment annexation have proved beneficial to the well-being and stability of major cities. A recent study indicates that in politically integrated metro areas, areawide poverty, dependency, and crime rates are below those experienced in cities without metropolitan government, and that those able to annex a large inventory of undeveloped land—"elastic cities"—have been able to retain much of their suburban growth and white, middle-class tax base with less consequent racial and economic segregation.

Summary

The sovereign state is the dominant entity in the political subdivision of the world. It constitutes an expression of cultural separation and identity as pervasive as that inherent in language, religion, or ethnicity. A product of 18th-century political philosophy, the idea of the state was diffused globally by colonizing European powers. In most instances, the colonial boundaries they established have been retained as their international boundaries by newly independent countries.

The greatly varying physical characteristics of states contribute to national strength and stability. Size, shape, and relative location influence countries' economies and international roles, while national cores and capitals are the heartlands of states. Boundaries, the legal definition of a state's size and shape, determine the limits of its sovereignty. They may or may not reflect preexisting cultural landscapes and in any given case may or may not prove to be viable. Whatever their nature, boundaries are at the root of many international disputes. Maritime boundary claims, particularly as reflected in the UN Convention on the Law of the Sea, add a new dimension to traditional claims of territorial sovereignty.

State cohesiveness is promoted by a number of centripetal forces. Among these are national symbols, a variety of institutions, and confidence in the aims, organization, and administration of government. Also helping to foster political and economic integration are transportation and communication connections. Destabilizing centrifugal forces, particularly ethnically based separatist movements, threaten the cohesion and stability of many states.

Although the state remains central to the partitioning of the world, a broadening array of political entities affects people individually and collectively. Recent decades have seen a significant increase in the number and variety of global and regional alliances to which states have surrendered some sovereign powers. At the other end of the spectrum, expanding Anglo American urban areas and governmental responsibilities raise questions of fairness in districting procedures and of effectiveness when political power is fragmented. Metropolitan government and predevelopment annexation are two approaches to region-wide administration and planning.

KEY WORDS

antecedent boundary   427
autonomous nationalism   433
centrifugal force   429
centripetal force   429
compact state   423
consequent (ethnographic)
  boundary   427
core area   425
devolution   434
domino theory   436
electoral geography   444
elongated state   423
enclave   424
European Union (EU)   441
exclave   424

exclusive economic zone (EEZ)   439
fragmented state   423
functional dispute   429
geometric (artificial) boundary   427
geopolitics   435
gerrymandering   444
heartland theory   435
irredentism   429
nation   418
nationalism   429
nation-state   418
natural (physical) boundary   426
perforated state   424
political geography   416

positional dispute   428
predevelopment annexation   450
prorupt state   423
regionalism   434
relict boundary   428
resource dispute   429
rimland theory   436
state   417
subsequent boundary   427
superimposed boundary   427
territorial dispute   428
unified government   449
United Nations Convention on the Law
  of the Sea   438

FOR REVIEW

1. What are the differences between a *state*, a *nation*, and a *nation-state*? Why is a colony not a state? How can one account for the rapid increase in the number of states since World War II?

2. What attributes differentiate states from one another? How do a country's size and shape affect its power and stability? Can a piece of land be both an *enclave* and an *exclave*?

3. How may boundaries be classified? How do they create opportunities for conflict? Describe and give examples of three types of border disputes.

4. How does the *United Nations Convention on the Law of the Sea* define zones of diminishing national control? What are the consequences of the concept of the 200-nm *exclusive economic zone?*

5. Distinguish between *centripetal* and *centrifugal* political forces. What are some of the ways national cohesion and identity are achieved?

6. What characteristics are common to all or most regional autonomist movements? Where are some of these movements active? Why do they tend to be on the periphery rather than at the national core?

7. What types of international organizations and alliances can you name? What were the purposes of their establishment? What generalizations can you make regarding economic alliances?

8. How did Mackinder and Spykman differ in their assessments of Eurasia as a likely base for world conquest? What post-1945 developments suggest that there may be no enduring correlation between location and national power?

9. Why does it matter how boundaries are drawn around electoral districts? Theoretically, is it always possible to delimit boundaries "fairly"? Support your answer.

10. What reasons can you suggest for the great political fragmentation of the United States? What problems stem from such fragmentation? Describe two approaches to insuring the more efficient administration of large urban areas.

SELECTED REFERENCES

Agnew, John, and Stuart Corbridge. *Mastering Space: Hegemony, Territory and International Political Economy.* New York: Routledge, 1996.

Archer, J. Clark, and Fred M. Shelley. *American Electoral Mosaics.* Washington, D.C.: Association of American Geographers, 1986.

Blouet, Brian W. "The Political Geography of Europe: 1900-2000 A.D." *Journal of Geography* 95, no. 1 (1996):5-14.

Boyd, Andrew. *An Atlas of World Affairs.* 9th ed. New York: Routledge, 1992.

Christopher, A. J. "Continuity and Change of African Capitals." *Geographical Review* 75 (1985):44–57.

Cohen, Saul B. "Global Geopolitical Change in the Post-Cold War Era." *Annals of the Association of American Geographers* 81, no. 4 (1991):551–580.

Cohen, Saul B. "The World Geopolitical System in Retrospect and Prospect." *Journal of Geography* 89, no. 1 (1990):2–12.

Cole, John, and Francis Cole. *The Geography of the European Community.* New York: Routledge, 1993.

Dawson, Andrew H. *A Geography of European Integration.* New York: John Wiley & Sons, 1993.

Demko, George J., and William B. Wood, eds. *Reordering the World: Geopolitical Perspectives on the Twenty-First Century.* Boulder, CO: Westview Press, 1994.

Gibb, Richard, and Wieslaw Michalak, eds. *Continental Trading Blocs: The Growth of Regionalism in the World Economy.* New York: John Wiley & Sons, 1994.

Glassner, Martin I. *Neptune's Domain: A Political Geography of the Sea.* Winchester, MA: Unwin Hyman, 1990.

Glassner, Martin I. *Political Geography.* 2d ed. New York: John Wiley & Sons, 1996.

Goertz, Gary, and Paul Diehl. *Territorial Changes and International Conflict.* New York: Routledge, 1992.

Grofman, Bernard. *Political Gerrymandering and the Courts.* New York: Agathon, 1990.

Hartshorne, Richard. "The Functional Approach in Political Geography." *Annals of the Association of American Geographers* 40 (1950):95–130.

Hooson, David, ed. *Geography and National Identity.* Oxford, England: Blackwell Publishers, 1994.

Huntington, Samuel P. "The Clash of Civilizations?" *Foreign Affairs* 72, no. 3 (Summer 1993):22–49.

Johnston, Douglas M., and Phillip M. Saunders, eds. *Ocean Boundary Making: Regional Issues and Developments.* London and New York: Croom Helm, 1988.

Johnston, Ronald J., David B. Knight, and E. Kofman, eds. *Nationalism, Self-Determination and Political Geography.* London and New York: Croom Helm, 1988.

Johnston, Ronald J., Fred M. Shelley, and Peter J. Taylor, eds. *Developments in Electoral Geography.* New York: Routledge, 1990.

Kaiser, Robert J. *The Geography of Nationalism in Russia and the USSR.* Princeton, NJ: Princeton University Press, 1994.

Knight, David B. "Identity and Territory: Geographical Perspectives on Nationalism and Regionalism." *Annals of the Association of American Geographers* 72 (1982):514–531.

The Law of the Sea. New York: United Nations, 1983.

Mackinder, Halford J. *Democratic Ideals and Reality.* London: Constable, 1919.

Mackinder, Halford J. "The Geographical Pivot of History." *Geographical Journal* 23 (1904):421–437.

Mackinder, Halford J. "The Round World and the Winning of the Peace." *Foreign Affairs* 21 (July 1943):595–605.

Mellor, Roy E. H. *Nation, State, and Territory: A Political Geography.* New York: Routledge, 1989.

Morrill, Richard. "Gerrymandering." *Focus* 41, no. 3 (Fall 1991):23–27.

Morrill, Richard. *Political Redistricting and Geographic Theory.* Washington, D.C.: The Association of American Geographers, 1981.

Murphy, Alexander B. "Historical Justification for Territorial Claims." *Annals of the Association of American Geographers* 80, no. 4 (1990):531–548.

O'Loughlin, John, ed. *Dictionary of Geopolitics.* Westport, CT: Greenwood Publishing Group, 1994.

O'Loughlin, John. "The Identification and Evaluation of Racial Gerrymandering." *Annals of the Association of American Geographers* 72 (1982):165–184.

"The Political Geography of the Post Cold War World." *The Professional Geographer* 44, no. 1 (February 1992):1–29.

Prescott, J. R. V. *The Maritime Political Boundaries of the World.* London: Methuen, 1986.

Prescott, J. R. V. *Political Frontiers and Boundaries.* New York: HarperCollins Academic, 1990.

Renner, Michael. *Critical Juncture: The Future of Peacekeeping.* Worldwatch Paper 114. Washington, D.C.: Worldwatch Institute, 1993.

"The Rise of Europe's Little Nations." *The Wilson Quarterly* 18, no. 1 (Winter 1994):50–81.

Rumley, Dennis, and Julian V. Minghi, eds. *The Geography of Border Landscapes.* New York: Routledge, 1991.

Sanger, Clyde. *Ordering the Oceans: The Making of the Law of the Sea.* Toronto: University of Toronto Press, 1987.

Scholfield, Clive H., ed. *Global Boundaries.* World Boundaries Series. Vol. 1. London: Routledge, 1994.

Shelley, Fred M., J. Clark Archer, Fiona M. Davidson, and Stanley D. Brunn. *Political Geography of the United States.* New York: Guilford Publications, 1996.

Short, John R. *An Introduction to Political Geography.* 2d ed. New York: Routledge, 1993.

Smith, Anthony D. *The Ethnic Origins of Nations.* Oxford, England: Basil Blackwell, 1986.

Spykman, Nicholas J. *The Geography of the Peace.* New York: Harcourt Brace, 1944.

Taylor, Peter J. *Political Geography: World Economy, Nation-State and Locality.* 3d ed. New York: John Wiley & Sons, 1993.

Taylor, Peter J., ed. *Political Geography of the Twentieth Century: A Global Analysis.* New York: Bellhaven Press, 1993.

Taylor, Peter J., ed. *World Government.* Rev. ed. The Illustrated Encyclopedia of World Geography. New York: Oxford University Press, 1995.

Van der Wüsten, Herman, and John V. O'Loughlin. *A Political Geography of International Relations.* New York: Guilford, 1991.

HUMAN ACTIONS AND ENVIRONMENTAL IMPACTS

A portion of the Itaipu Dam across the Paraná River on the Brazil/Paraguay border.

he final chapter of our study of human geography brings to the fore the recurring theme of all geographic study and the unifying thread running through each of the preceding chapters: human activities and physical environments in interaction. In those chapters we have come to understand how over the past several thousand years people in their increasing numbers and growing technological skills have placed their mark on the natural landscape, altering it to conform to their needs. In some instances, such as that of modern cities, the human imprint may be so complete that the original landscape of nature has been totally wiped away and replaced by a created cultural environment. People, we now understand, are the dominant agents in the continuing drama of human–environmental interaction. Ecological alteration, damage, or destruction may be the unplanned and unwanted consequences of the power they possess.

We need that understanding, for increasingly evident environmental deterioration has become an ever-present and growing concern of people and governments throughout the world. Ecological damage or change is no longer occasional and localized; it has now become permanent and generalized. Climatic modification, air and water pollution, soil erosion, natural vegetation destruction, and loss of productive lands to advancing deserts are just part of the testimony of destructive cultural pressures that has aroused widespread public and private discussion. Increasingly, the inseparable interplay of the cultural and physical environments—seen in the imprint of humans on the endowment of nature—is apparent and accepted.

For convenience and focus, geographers may arbitrarily separate the physical and human systems that together comprise the reality of the earth's surface we occupy. We have made such a separation in our study of human geography, for our primary concern has been with the processes and patterns of human spatial organization. In addition to exploring the structure and logic of social spatial systems, that focus has also prepared us to evaluate the relationship of those systems to the physical environment humans occupy and alter. With the insights we have gained we can now bring a more informed voice to discussion of the interaction of human cause and environmental consequence. Further background for that discussion is offered in our concluding chapter, "Human Impacts on Natural Systems." Its subject matter bridges our temporarily convenient subdivision of the discipline and brings back into focus the inseparable unity of human and physical geography.

HUMAN IMPACTS ON NATURAL SYSTEMS:

GEOGRAPHIC OUTLOOKS ON GLOBAL CONCERNS

Physical Environments and Cultural Impacts   456

Climates, Biomes, and Change   457

Global Warming   460

Acid Rain   464

The Trouble with Ozone   465

Land Use and Land Cover   467

Tropical Deforestation   468

Desertification   470

Soil Erosion   472

Water Supply and Water Quality   475

Patterns of Availability   476

Water Use and Abuse   476

Garbage Heaps and Toxic Wastes   478

Solid Wastes and Rubbish   480

  Landfill Disposal   481

  Incineration   481

  Ocean Dumping   483

Toxic Wastes   483

  Radioactive Wastes   483

Exporting Waste   484

Prospects and Perspectives   486

  SUMMARY   487

  KEY WORDS   487

  FOR REVIEW   487

  SELECTED REFERENCES   488

Human abuse of wetlands in New York state.

When the daily tides come in, a surge of water high as a person's head moves up the rivers and creeks of the world's largest delta, formed where the Ganges and Brahmaputra rivers meet the Bay of Bengal in the South Asian country of Bangladesh. Within that Wisconsin-sized country that is one-fifth water, millions of people live on thousands of alluvial islands known as "chars." These form from the silt of the rivers and are washed away by their currents and by the force of cyclones that roar upstream from the bay during the annual cyclone period. As the chars are swept away so, too, are thousands and tens of thousands of their land-hungry occupants who fiercely battled each other with knives and clubs to claim and cultivate them.

Late in April of 1991, an atmospheric low-pressure area moved across the Malay Peninsula of Southeast Asia and gained strength in the Bay of Bengal, generating winds of nearly 240 kilometers (150 miles) per hour. As it moved northward the storm sucked up and drew along with it a wall of water 6 meters (20 feet) high. At 1:00 A.M. on April 30, with a full moon and highest tides, the cyclone and its battering ram of water slammed across the chars and the deltaic mainland. When it had passed, some of the richest rice fields in Asia were gray with the salt that ruined them, islands totally covered with paddies were left as giant sand dunes, others—densely populated—simply disappeared beneath the swirling waters. An estimated 200,000 lives were lost to the storm and to subsequent starvation, disease, and exposure.

Each year lesser variants of the tragedy are repeated; each year survivors return to rebuild their lives on old land or new, still left after the storms or created as the floods ease and some of the annual 2.5 billion tons of river-borne silt is deposited to form new chars. Deforestation in the Himalayan headwaters of the rivers increases erosion there and swells the volume of silt flowing into Bangladesh. Dams on the Ganges River in India alter normal flow patterns, releasing more water during floods and increasing silt deposits during seasonal droughts. And, always, population growth adds to the number of desperate people seeking homes and fields on lands more safely left as the realm of river and sea.

Physical Environments and Cultural Impacts

The people of the chars live with an immediate environmental contact that is not known to most of us in the highly developed, highly urbanized countries of the world. In fact, much of the content of the preceding chapters has detailed ways that humans isolate themselves from the physical environment and how they superimpose cultural landscapes on it to accommodate the growing needs of their growing numbers.

Many cultural landscape changes are minor in themselves. The forest clearing for swidden agriculture or the terracing of hillsides for subsistence farming are modest alterations of nature. Plowing and farming the prairies, harnessing major river systems by dams and reservoirs, building cities and their connecting highways, or opening vast open-pit mines (Figure 13.1) are much more substantial modifications. In some cases the new landscapes are apparently completely divorced from the natural ones which preceded them—as in enclosed, air-conditioned shopping malls and office towers. The original minor modifications have cumulatively become totally new cultural creations.

But suppression of the physical landscape does not mean eradication of human–environmental interactions. They continue, though in altered form, as humans increasingly become the active and dominant agents of environmental change. More often than not, the changes we have set in motion create unplanned cultural landscapes and unwanted environmental conditions. We have altered our climates, polluted our air and water and soil, destroyed natural vegetation and land contours while stripping ores and fuels from the earth. At the same time, we have found it increasingly difficult and costly to provide with food and resources our growing populations. Such adverse consequences of human impact on the environment are fundamental elements in our human geographic study. They are the unforeseen creations of the landscapes of culture we have been examining and analyzing.

Environment is an overworked word that means the totality of things that in any way affect an organism. Humans exist within a natural environment—the sum of the physical world—that they have modified by their individual and collective actions. Those actions include clearing forests, plowing grasslands, building dams, and constructing cities. On the natural environment, then, we have erected our cultural environment, modifying, altering, or destroying the conditions of nature that existed before human impact was expressed.

Even in the absence of humans, those conditions were marked by constant alteration and adjustment that nonetheless preserved intact the **biosphere** (or **ecosphere**), the thin

FIGURE 13.1 The Bingham Canyon open-pit copper mine in Utah is one of the largest man-made holes on earth. It measures over 450 meters (1500 feet) deep and involves operations covering more than 4000 hectares (10,000 acres). Giant machinery and intensive application of capital and energy make possible such monumental reshapings of contours and landscapes.

film of air, water, and earth within which we live. This biosphere is composed of three interrelated parts: (1) the *atmosphere*, a light blanket of air enveloping the earth, with more than half of its mass within 6.5 kilometers (4 miles) of the surface and 98% within 26 km (16 mi.); (2) the *hydrosphere*, the surface and subsurface waters in oceans, rivers, lakes, glaciers, and groundwater; and (3) the *lithosphere*, the upper reaches of the earth's crust containing the soils that support plant life, the minerals that plants and animals require for life, and the fossil fuels and ores that humans exploit. The biosphere is an intricately interlocked system, containing all that is needed for life, all that is available for life to use, and, presumably, all that ever will be available. The ingredients of the thin ecosphere must be and are constantly recycled and renewed in nature: plants purify the air; the air helps to purify the water; plants and animals use the water and the minerals, which are returned to the system for reuse. Anything that upsets the interplay of the ecosphere or diminishes its ability to recycle itself or to sustain life endangers all organisms within it, including humans.

Climates, Biomes, and Change

The structure of the ecosphere is not eternal and unchanging. On the contrary, alteration is the constant rule of the physical environment and would be so even in the absence of humans and their distorting impacts. Climatic change, year-to-year variations in weather patterns, fires, windstorms, floods, diseases, or the unexplained rise and fall of predator and prey populations all call for new environmental configurations and forever prevent the establishment of a single, constant "balance of nature." Remember that we began to track cultural geographic patterns from the end of the last continental glaciation, some 11,000 years ago. Our starting point, then, was a time of environmental change when humans were too few in number and primitive in technology to have had any impact on the larger structure of the biosphere. Their numbers increased and their technologies became vastly more sophisticated and intrusive with the passage of time, but for nearly all of the period of cultural development to modern times human impact on the world environment was absorbed and accommodated by it with no more than local distress. The rhythm and the regularity of larger global systems proceeded largely unaffected by people.

Over the millennia since the last glaciation—with a few periods of unusual warming or cooling as the exceptions—a relatively stable pattern of climatic regions emerged, a global system of environmental conditions within which human cultures developed and differentiated. That pattern reflected enduring physical controls and balances: the tilt of the earth's axis; the earth's rotation and its movement about the sun; its receipt of energy from the sun and the seasonal variations in energy effectiveness in the Northern and Southern Hemispheres; the reradiation of some of that received energy back through the atmosphere in the form of heat; and in finer detail the pattern of land and water distribution and of ocean and atmospheric currents (Figure 13.2).

In combination these and other controls determine global patterns of temperature and precipitation, the basic variables in world climatic systems. The continual warmth of the tropical (equatorial) regions is replaced by the seasonal temperature variations of the midlatitudes, where land and water contrasts also affect the temperatures recorded even at the same latitude. Summers become cooler and shorter farther towards the poles until, finally, permanent ice cap conditions prevail. Precipitation patterns are more complexly determined than are those of temperature but are important constituents of regional environmental variation.

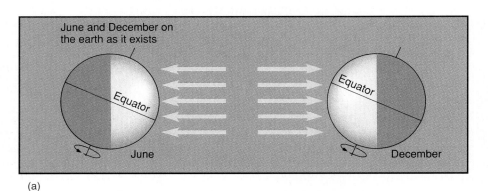
(a)

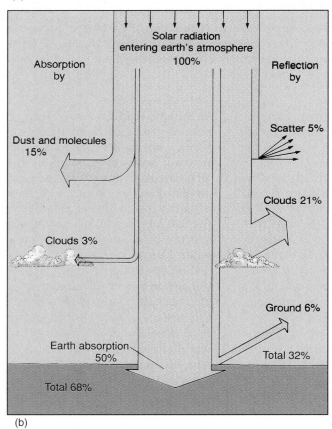
(b)

FIGURE 13.2   **Incoming solar energy** is indicated by the yellow arrows in (*a*). Because of the tilt of the earth's axis, the most intense of the sun's rays are received north of the equator in June and south of the equator in December. The tilt plus the earth's daily rotation on its axis also means that every point in the Northern (or Southern) Hemisphere summer has more hours of daylight than of darkness each day. The more direct rays received over longer daylight periods assure seasonal differences in hemispheric heating and cooling. (*b*) Consider the incoming solar radiation as 100%. The portion that is absorbed into the earth (50%) is eventually released to the atmosphere and then reradiated into space. Notice that the outgoing radiation is equal to 100%, showing that there is an energy balance on the earth.

The pattern of global climates that these physical controls established (Figure 13.3) was, at the same time, a pattern of biomes. **Biomes** are major communities of plants and animals occupying extensive areas of the earth's surface in response to climatic conditions. We know them by such descriptive names as *desert, grassland* or *steppe* or as the *tropical rain forest* and *northern coniferous forest* (see Chapter 8). Biomes, in turn, contain smaller, more specialized **ecosystems:** self-contained, self-regulating, and interacting communities adapted to local combinations of climate, topography, soil, and drainage conditions.

Ecosystems were the first to feel the destructive hand of humans and the cultural landscapes they made. We saw in Chapter 2 the results of human abuse of the local environment in the Chaco Canyon and Easter Island deforestations. Forest removal, overgrazing, and ill-considered agriculture turned lush hillsides of the Mediterranean Basin into sterile and impoverished landscapes by the end of the Roman Empire. Other similar local and even regional alterations of natural environmental conditions occurred and increased as humans multiplied and exerted growing pressure on the resources and food potentials of the areas they occupied.

At a global scale, however, human impact was minimal. Long-term and short-term deviations from average conditions were induced by natural, not cultural, conditions (Figure 13.4; see also "Our Inconstant Climates"). But slowly, unnoticed at first, human activity began to have a global impact, carrying the consequences of cultural abuse of the biosphere far beyond the local scene. The atmosphere, the one part of the biosphere that all the world shares, began to react measurably during the last half of the 20th century to damage that humans had done to it since the beginning of the Industrial Revolution in the 18th century. If those reactions prove permanent and cumulative, then established patterns of climates and the biomes based on them are destined to be altered in fundamental ways.

At first it appeared the danger was from over-cooling, an onset of a new glacial stage. The cause is implicit in Figure 13.2b. Part of incoming solar energy is intercepted by clouds and by solid and liquid particles—*aerosols*—and reradiated back to space. An increase in reflectors decreases energy receipts at the earth's surface, and a cooling effect, the **icebox effect,** is inevitable. Aerosols are naturally injected into the atmosphere from such sources as dust storms, forest fires, or volcanos. Indeed, increases in volcanic eruptions are thought by some not only to be triggering events for years-long cooling cycles but possibly even for ice age development itself. The famous "year without a summer," 1816, when snow fell in June in New England and frost occurred in July, was probably the climatic reflection of the 1815 eruption of the Indonesian volcano, Tambora. That

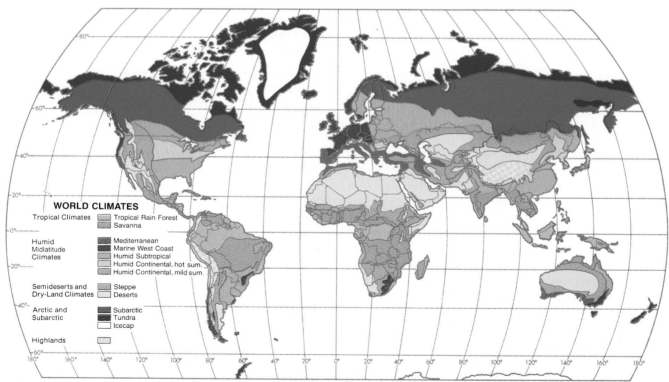

FIGURE 13.3   **Climates of the world.** Complex interrelationships of latitude, land and water contrasts, ocean currents, topography, and wind circulation, make the global pattern of climates more intricate than this generalized map reveals.

n 1125 William of Malmesbury favorably compared the number and productivity of the vineyards of England with those of France; England has almost no vineyards today. In the 10th century, the Vikings established successful colonies in Greenland; by 1250, that island was practically cut off by extensive drift ice, and by the early 15th century its colonies were forgotten and dead. The "little climatic optimum," which lasted from A.D. 800 to 1200, was marked by the warmest climate that had occurred in the Northern Hemisphere for several thousand years. Glaciers retreated and agricultural settlement spread throughout Europe. Those permissive conditions were not to last, however. Change and fluctuation in environmental conditions are the rules of nature.

In recent years archaeologists and historians have found evidence that ancient seats of power—such as Sumeria in the Middle East, Mycenae in southern Greece, and Mali in Africa—may have fallen not to bar-barians but to unfavorable alterations in the climates under which they came to power. Climatic change certainly altered the established structure of European society when, between 1550 and 1850, a "little ice age" descended on the Northern Hemisphere. Arctic ice expanded, glaciers advanced, Alpine passes were closed to traffic, and crop failures were common. Systems of agriculture, patterns of trade, designs of buildings, styles of clothing, and rhythms of life responded to climatic conditions vastly less favorable than those of the preceding centuries.

A new pronounced warming trend began about 1890 and lasted to the early 1940s. During that period, the margin of agriculture was extended northward, the pattern of commercial fishing shifted poleward, and the reliability of crop yields increased. But by the 1950s, natural conditions again seemed poised to change. From the late 1940s to the 1970s, the mean temperature of the globe declined. The growing season in England became two weeks shorter; disastrous droughts occurred in Africa and Asia; and unexpected freezes altered crop patterns in Latin America.

This time, humans were aware that changes in the great natural systems were partly traceable to things that they themselves were doing. The problem was, they were doing so many things, with such contrary consequences, that the combined and cumulative impact was unclear. One scenario predicted the planet would slowly cool over the next few centuries and enter a new ice age, helped along that path by the large amount of soot and dust in the atmosphere traceable to human activity that prevents incoming solar energy from reaching and warming the earth. A quite different scenario foretold a planet warming dangerously as different human stresses on the atmosphere overcame a natural cycle of cooling. Instead of nature's refrigerator, a man-made sauna may be the more likely prospect. A third conclusion maintains that fundamental climatic changes result from natural conditions essentially unaffected by human activities.

explosion ejected an estimated 200 million tons of gaseous aerosols—water vapor, sulfur dioxide, hydrogen chloride, and others—and upward of 50 cubic kilometers (30 cubic miles) of dust and ash into the atmosphere. The reflective cooling effect lasted for years. (A similar, but less extreme, Northern Hemisphere summer temperature drop in the early 1990s was attributed to the eruption of Mount Pinatubo in the Philippines in 1991).

Aerosols in solid and gaseous form are products of human activities as well. Ever-increasing amounts of them are ejected from the smoke stacks of factories, power plants, and city buildings and from the tail pipes of vehicles and exhaust plumes of jet aircraft. The global cooling that became noticeable by the late 1940s seemed to presage a new ice age, partly the product of natural conditions but hastened and deepened by human pressures upon the atmosphere.

The fears those pressures generated began to be replaced, in the 1980s, by a three-part package of different concerns: (1) a global warming caused by the "greenhouse" effect; (2) acid rain; and (3) ozone depletion. These, too, are presumed threats ascribed to human introduction into the atmosphere of kinds and amounts of materials that natural systems apparently cannot handle or recycle. Some lines of evidence and projections based on them indicate that these changing conditions may well alter the composition of the atmosphere and the pattern of climates established as the expected norm over the past few decades. Other scientifically plausible evidence, however, suggests that concerns and reactions based on the fear of human-induced global warming, acid precipitation, and ozone destruction are exaggerated and in large measure unwarranted.

Global Warming

To those who fear its reality, the evidence of global atmospheric warming seems compelling and modern civilization's role in its occurrence appears easily traced. Humankind's massive assault on the atmosphere, it is observed, began with the Industrial Revolution. First coal and then increasing amounts of petroleum and natural gas have been burned to power industry, heat and cool cities, and drive vehicles.

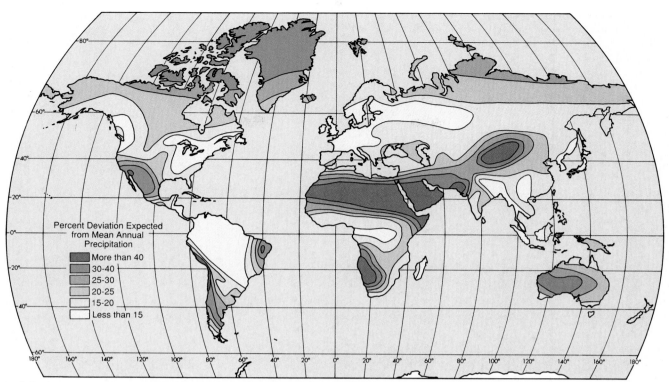

FIGURE 13.4   **The pattern of precipitation variability.** Note that regions of low total precipitation tend to have high variability. In general, the lower the amount of long-term annual precipitation, the lower is the probability that the "average" will be recorded in any single year. Short-run variability and long-term progressive change in climatic conditions are the rule of nature and occur independent of any human influence.

Their burning has turned fuels into carbon dioxide and water vapor. At the same time, the world's forest lands—most recently its tropical rain forests—have been destroyed wholesale by logging and to clear land for agriculture. With more carbon dioxide in the atmosphere and fewer trees to capture the carbon and produce oxygen, carbon dioxide levels have risen steadily. They now total 150% of their levels at the start of the Industrial Revolution, with some 280 billion tons of carbon having been added to the atmosphere. Carbon dioxide concentrations in the atmosphere increased by 25% between 1958 and 1988 alone.

That extra carbon dioxide makes the atmosphere just a bit less transparent to the long-wave heat energy radiated back into space from the earth. Along with three other partially man-made gases (methane, nitrous oxides, and chlorofluorocarbons), the carbon dioxide traps the heat before it can escape. That so-called **greenhouse effect** is far less benign and nurturing than the name implies (Figure 13.5). Slowly but inexorably the retained heat raises the average temperature of the earth; slowly but unavoidably, if the process continues, new patterns of climates and biomes must result.

During the first century of the Industrial Revolution, from 1780 to 1880, mean global temperature rose 0.3 degree Celsius (0.5 degree Fahrenheit). In the next hundred years—even allowing for the slight cooling in the 30 years after 1945—average temperatures increased about 0.6°C (a bit over 1°F). They rose another half degree Celsius in the last half of the 1980s alone. Apparently the rate of heating was increasing. The ten warmest years between 1880 and 1995 all occurred in the final 13 years of that period, with 1995 global temperature averaging nearly 60°F. Because of the time lag in developing the greenhouse effect, temperatures would continue to rise even if carbon dioxide amounts were stabilized at today's levels. If temperatures rise by 1.1°C to 3.9°C (2–7°F) over the next century as some analysts consider probable, the effects on world climates could be profound. But the outcome is not clearly foreseeable; climate prediction is not an exact science.

The role of humans in global warming has been disputed. Skeptics note that nearly half the observed atmospheric warming occurred before 1940 even though almost all the increased production of carbon dioxide and other greenhouse gases came after that date. Doubters further

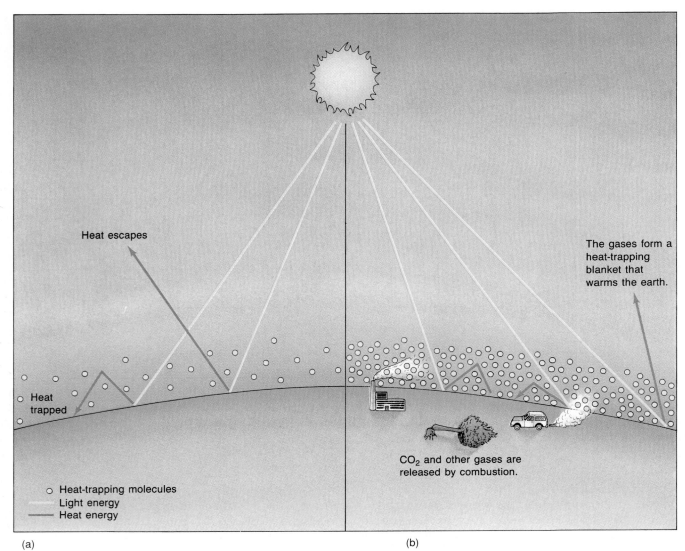

FIGURE 13.5   Creating the greenhouse effect. When there is a low level of carbon dioxide (CO_2) in the air, as in (*a*), incoming solar radiation strikes the earth's surface, heating it up, and the earth radiates the energy back into space as heat. The "greenhouse" effect, depicted in (*b*), is the result of the billions of tons of CO_2 that the burning of fossil fuels has added to the atmosphere. The carbon dioxide molecules intercept some of the reradiated energy, deflecting it groundward and preventing it from escaping from the atmosphere.

note that every millennium since the end of the last Ice Age has had one or two centuries in which temperatures have risen by at least as much as they have in the last century. It is reasonable, they claim, to assume that recent atmospheric temperature increases are part of a natural warming cycle and have nothing to do with carbon dioxide. That skepticism was apparently countered by an Intergovernmental Panel on Climate Change report in 1995 concluding that the warming of the last century, and especially of the last few years, "is unlikely to be entirely due to natural causes, and . . . a pattern of climatic response to human activities is identifiable in the climatic record." The panel, a United Nations group of 2500 scientists from around the world, advises governments negotiating reductions in greenhouse gases.

Whatever the attributable causes of global heating, climatologists agree on certain of its general consequences should it continue. Increases in sea temperatures would cause ocean waters to expand slightly and the polar ice caps to melt at least a bit. Inevitably, sea levels would rise, perhaps 0.5 to 3 meters (1.5 to 10 feet) within a hundred years. Even a conservative 1-meter (3-foot) rise would be enough to cover the Maldives and other low lying island countries. The homes of between 50 and 100 million people would be inundated, a fifth of Egypt's arable land in the Nile Delta would be flooded, and the impact on the people of the Bangladesh chars would be catastrophic.

Other water problems would result from changes in precipitation patterns. Shifts in weather conditions might well increase the aridity of some of the world's already dry

HUMAN ACTIONS AND ENVIRONMENTAL IMPACTS

areas, such as Africa's Sahel, and increase rainfall in some already wet areas, such as the British Isles. Almost certainly, much of the continental interiors of middle latitudes would receive less precipitation than they do now and suffer at least periodic drought if not absolute aridity. Precipitation might decline by as much as 40% in the U.S. corn and wheat belts, drastically reducing agricultural productivity, bringing to near ruin the rural economy, and altering world patterns of food supply and trade (Figure 13.6). That same 40% reduction of rainfall would translate into significantly reduced flows of such western rivers as the Colorado, cutting back the water supply of major southwestern cities and irrigated farming districts.

Climate change may also be expressed as short-term extremes of weather. Temperature and precipitation records from 1980 through 1995 show the incidence of extreme one-day precipitation, overall precipitation, above normal temperatures, and drought have risen in many parts of the United States. Those increases in weather extremes—the eastern states' blizzards of 1995 are recent examples—are directly attributable, scientists conclude, to the increase in greenhouse gases.

On the global and long-term scales, of course, some areas would benefit from general temperature rises. Parts of Russia, Scandinavia, and Canada would get longer growing seasons. In North America, crop patterns would shift northward, making the northern Great Lakes states and Canada the favored agricultural heartland climatically, though without the soil base supporting the present patterns and volumes of production. Global warming would tend to reduce latitudinal differences in temperature; higher latitudes would become relatively more heated than equatorial regions.

These are generally (but not completely) agreed upon scenarios of change, but local details are highly uncertain. Temperature differences are the engine driving the global circulation of winds and ocean currents and help create conditions inducing or inhibiting winter and summer precipitation and daily weather conditions. Exactly how those vital climatic details would express themselves locally and regionally is uncertain. The only realistic certainty is that the patterns of climates and biomes developed since the last glaciation and shown on Figure 13.3 would be drastically altered.

Global warming and climatic change would impact most severely, of course, on developing countries highly dependent on natural, unmanaged environments for their economic support. Agriculture, hunting and gathering, forestry, and coastal fishing have that dependency, but even in those economic sectors the impact of greenhouse warming is not certain. Studies suggest that warming would reduce yields in many crops, but also that the associated fertilization effect of higher carbon dioxide content would probably offset the negative impact of warming, at least for the next century. But certainly, small and poor countries with great dependence on agriculture are potentially most at risk from projected climatic changes. The lower-latitude states would be most vulnerable as increased heat and higher evaporation rates would greatly stress wheat, maize, rice, and soybean crops. Most economic activities in industrialized countries do not have a close dependency on natural ecosystems. The consensus is that the impacts of climate change on diversified developed countries are likely to be small, at least over the next half-century.

Nevertheless, on the world scene, any significant continuing deviation from the present norm would at the very least disrupt existing patterns of economy, productivity, and population-supporting potential. At the worst, severe and pervasive changes could result in a total restructuring of the landscapes of culture and the balances of human–environmental relationships presently established. Nothing, from population distributions to the relative strength of countries, would ever be quite the same again.

Such grim predictions were addressed at the Earth Summit held in Rio de Janeiro in June 1992. The Framework Convention on Climate Change signed then and subsequently ratified by more than 120 nations calls on industrialized countries to try to cap emissions of greenhouse gases at 1990 levels by the year 2000 as a necessary first step to prevent disruption of world agriculture and natural ecosystems. Small island countries, fearing their possible obliteration with rising seas, have proposed an addition to the treaty that would require industrialized states to reduce emissions to 20% below 1990 levels by 2005. The European Union and the United States have largely based their plans for compliance on hoped-for improved energy efficiencies. China and some other developing countries, not yet bound by any precise targets or timetables, strongly reject being subject to treaty provisions that would limit their economic growth prospects by limiting industrialization and the rapid expansion of fossil fuel use such growth implies.

FIGURE 13.6 Many climatologists noted that the parched cornfields in the U.S. Midwest during the summer of 1988 were a sample of what could be expected on a recurring basis if a worst-case scenario of global warming were to be realized. In actuality, the 1988 drought was a natural climatic fluctuation—much like the abundant rain and floods of 1993—but an event whose probability of recurrence is increased by the long-term accumulation of greenhouse gases.

A cautionary note is needed. A scenario of general global warming through a human-induced greenhouse effect may be countered by an equally plausible outline of the ecological and cultural consequences of a replenished Northern Hemisphere glacial cover. The onset of a new ice age is predicted on solid climatic reasoning that greenhouse-induced temperature increases would likely warm upper latitudes sufficiently to permit heavy snowfall to commence in regions—like northern Greenland—where it is now so cold that snow rarely falls. That increase in upper-latitude precipitation would yield a dramatic accumulation of polar ice and its subsequent expansion as continental glaciers to the point that their own frigid mass would nullify the moderate warming that triggered their growth. Recent evidence, it is claimed, indicates that glacial regions did, in fact, grow slightly warmer before the onset of the last glacial period, just as the greenhouse effect is warming them now.

Should that sequence of climatic changes occur rather than the one predicted under the usual global warming hypothesis, an equally profound, but quite different, set of human consequences would ensue—one still triggered by the greenhouse effect, but with a new ice age outcome.

Acid Rain

The acid rain that is the second of the recent trio of environmental concerns is in part traceable to actions taken in previous decades to alleviate a widespread source of atmospheric pollution dangerous to public health and damaging to public and private property. Smoke and soot poured into the skies from the chimneys of power plants, mills, and factories in industrial areas of all countries were increasingly blamed for high incidences of respiratory disease, lowered life expectancies, and vast damage to property. Urban smoke abatement and clean air programs usually incorporated prohibitions against the discharge of atmospheric pollutants damaging to areas near the discharge point. The response was to raise chimneys to such a height that smoke, soot, and gases were carried far from their origin points by higher elevation winds (Figure 13.7).

But when power plants, smelters, and factories were fitted with tall smokestacks to free local areas from pollution, the sulfur dioxide and nitrogen oxides in the smoke instead of being deposited locally were pumped high into the atmosphere. There they mixed with water and other chemicals and turned into sulfuric and nitric acid that was carried to distant areas. They were joined in their impact by other sources of acid gases. Motor vehicles are particularly prolific producers of nitrogen oxides in their exhausts, and volcanos can add immense amounts of acidic gases, as the Tambora eruption demonstrated.

When acids from all sources are washed out of the air by rain, snow, or fog the result is **acid rain,** though *acid precipitation* is a more precise designation. Acidity levels are described by the *pH factor,* the measure of acidity/alkalinity on a scale of 0 to 14. The average pH of normal rainfall is 5.6, slightly acidic, but acid rainfalls with a pH of

FIGURE 13.7   Before concern with acid rain became widespread, the U.S. Clean Air Act of 1970 set standards for ground-level air quality that could be met most easily by building smokestacks high enough to discharge pollutants into the upper atmosphere. Stacks 300 meters (1000 feet) and higher are now a common sight at utility plants and factories, far exceeding the earlier norm of 60–90 meters (200–300 feet). What helped cleanse one area of pollution greatly increased damage elsewhere. The farther and higher the noxious emissions go, the longer they have to combine with other atmospheric components and moisture to form acids. Thus, the taller stacks have directly aggravated the acid rain problem. Recognizing this, the Environmental Protection Agency in 1985 issued rules discouraging the use of tall smokestacks to disperse emissions. The Clean Air Act Amendments of 1990 required that sulfur dioxide and nitrogen oxide emissions from smokestacks be cut in half.

2.4—approximately the acidity of vinegar and lemon juice—have been recorded. Primarily occurring in developed nations, acid rain has become a serious problem in many parts of Europe, North America, and Japan. It expresses itself in several forms, though the most visible are its corrosive effects on marble and limestone sculptures and buildings and on metals such as iron and bronze (Figure 13.8) and in the destruction of forests. Trees at higher elevations are particularly susceptible, with widespread forest loss clearly apparent on the hillsides and mountain tops of New England, Scandinavia, and Germany, where acid rain had apparently degraded much of that country's famous forests by the early 1990s.

Damage to lakes, fish, and soils is less immediately evident, but more widespread and equally serious (Figure 13.9). Acid rain has been linked to the disappearance of fish in thousands of streams and lakes in New England, Canada, and Scandinavia, and to a decline in fish populations else-where. It leaches toxic constituents such as aluminum salts from the soil and kills soil microorganisms that break down organic matter and recycle nutrients through the ecosystem.

Acid deposition can damage and decrease yields of many food crops and increase the content of poisonous heavy metals in drinking water supplies. The culprit acids are borne in the atmosphere and so may wreak their damage far from the power plants or cities (or volcanos) that put them in the air. In North America, midwestern coal-burning power stations and industries are blamed for acid rain contamination in New England. They, along with other United States industries, power plants, and automobiles, are credited with the widespread acid rain damage in Canada (including some 2000 lakes totally dead to fish life and another 150,000 in danger). Canada itself has major urban and industrial pollution sources contributing to its acid rain incidence.

The Trouble with Ozone

The forest damage usually blamed exclusively on acid rain has, on closer investigation, proved to be at least partially the product of ozone poisoning. **Ozone** is a molecule consisting of three oxygen atoms rather than the two of normal oxygen. Sunlight produces it from standard oxygen, and a continuous but thin layer of ozone accumulates at upper levels in the atmosphere. There it blocks the cancer-causing ultraviolet (UV) light that damages DNA, the molecule of heredity and cell control. That upper atmospheric shield now appears in danger of destruction by chemicals released into the air by humans (see "Depleting the Ozone Layer").

FIGURE 13.8   The destructive effect of acid rain is evident on this limestone statuary at the cathedral in Reims, France.

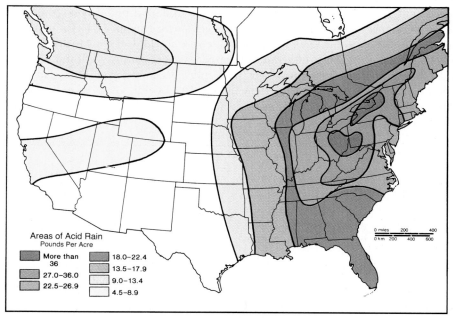

Areas of Acid Rain
Pounds Per Acre

More than 36	18.0–22.4
27.0–36.0	13.5–17.9
22.5–26.9	9.0–13.4
	4.5–8.9

FIGURE 13.9   **Where acid rain falls.** In general, the areas that receive the most acid rain in the eastern United States and Canada are those that are least able to tolerate it. Their surface waters tend to be acidic rather than alkaline and are unable to neutralize the acids deposited by rain or snow. Ironically, the highly industrialized Ohio Valley and southern Great Lakes districts have high natural resistance to soil and water acidification.

In the summer of 1986, scientists for the first time verified that a "hole" had formed in the ozone layer over Antarctica, a discovery that received immediate worldwide attention. In fact, the ozone was not entirely absent, but it had been reduced from earlier recorded levels by some 40%. As a result, Antarctic life—particularly the microscopic ocean plants (phytoplankton) at the base of the food chain—that had lived more or less in ultraviolet (UV) darkness was suddenly getting a trillionfold (1 followed by 12 zeros) increase above the natural rate of UV receipt.

The ozone hole typically occurs over Antarctica during late August through early October and breaks up in mid-November. From 1987 when the ozone loss was 60% to 1993 when it was effectively 100%, the hole has become larger, lasted longer, and spread farther outward each year toward South America and Australia. The NASA satellite images show the progression of ozone depletion during 1992, a year in which the hole covered 4.5 million square kilometers (1.7 million sq. mi.). (Blues and purples mark the areas of greatest ozone loss; missing data are indicated by black areas.)

Ozone depletion is an increasing and spreading atmospheric problem; ozone levels in August, 1995, for example, were 10% lower than the previous year, marking a new record low, and the "hole" covered 9.9 million square kilometers (3.86 million sq. mi.), an area about the size of Europe. Worldwide, the ozone layer decreased by 30% to 35% between 1957 and 1995. Most scientists now attribute the continuing decline to pollution from chlorofluorocarbons (CFCs), used as coolants, cleansing agents, and propellants for aerosols, and also used in insulating foams. In a chain reaction of oxygen destruction, each of the chlorine atoms released can over time destroy upwards of 10,000 ozone molecules.

Why should the hole in the ozone layer have appeared first so prominently over Antarctica? In most parts of the world, horizontal winds tend to keep chemicals in the air well mixed. But circulation patterns are such that the freezing whirlpool of air over the south polar continent in winter is not penetrated by air currents from the warmer earth regions. In the absence of sunlight and atmospheric mixing, the CFCs work to destroy the ozone. During summer, sunlight works to replenish it. The important unanswered question is whether that replenishment can continue indefinitely. A similar ozone hole about the size of Greenland opens in the Arctic, too, and the ozone shield over the midlatitudes dropped significantly from 1978 to 1992 (with only a slight thickening during the winter of 1993–1994), so perhaps the answer is no.

The depletion of the ozone layer is expected to have a number of adverse consequences. Among other things, increased exposure to UV radiation increases the incidence of skin cancer and, by suppressing bodily defense mechanisms, increases vulnerability to a variety of infectious diseases. Many crop plants are sensitive to UV radiation, and the very existence of the microscopic plankton at the base of the marine food chain is threatened by it. Some climatologists warn that the CFC accumulation and ozone depletion in the upper atmosphere may both cool that layer and contribute to the greenhouse warming closer to the earth's surface.

Some scientists dispute both the existence and the cause of ozone layer depletion. One report forcefully concludes that "there is no observed change in global ozone concentrations that is outside the bounds of natural variability" and another claims "there is no observational evidence that man-made chemicals like CFCs are dangerously thinning the ozone layer . . ." Nevertheless, production and use of CFCs is being phased out under the Montreal Protocol, a 1987 international agreement made effective in 1992, that requires production of CFCs be ended in developed countries at the end of 1995 and to cease in developing states by 2010.

At lower levels, however, the problem is accumulation, not depletion, of ozone. Relatively harmless to humans, ozone is damaging to plants. Exposed to too much of it, their growth may be stunted, their yields reduced (by as much as 30% for wheat), or they may even die. That, apparently, is an important contributor to forest damage and destruction commonly attributed to acid rain. In the lower atmosphere, ozone is produced in *photochemical smogs* by sunlight and pollution, with the main pollutant being motor vehicle exhaust fumes (Figure 13.10). Their nitrogen oxides and hydrocarbons are particularly good at converting oxygen to ozone. The increasing use of automobiles in Europe, not acid rain, has done the damage to that continent's forests, a fact that explains the rise of forest destruction during the same years that sulfur dioxide emissions from power plants were being significantly reduced.

There is an element of presumed irreversibility in both the greenhouse effect and ozone depletion. Once the processes creating them are launched, they tend to become cumulative and continuous. Even if carbon dioxide levels stayed as they are now, temperatures would continue to climb. Even if all CFCs were immediately banned and no more were released into the atmosphere, it would take more than a century to replenish the ozone already lost. Since population growth, industrial development, and chemical pollution will continue—though perhaps under tighter control—assaults upon the atmosphere will also continue rather than cease. The same disquieting irreversibility seems to

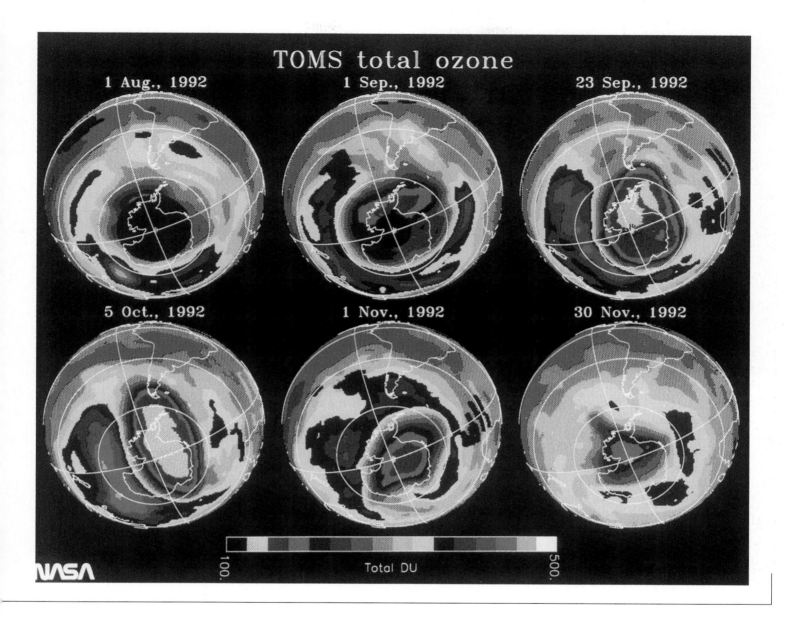

TOMS total ozone

1 Aug., 1992   1 Sep., 1992   23 Sep., 1992

5 Oct., 1992   1 Nov., 1992   30 Nov., 1992

100.   Total DU   500.

NASA

characterize three other processes of environmental degradation: *tropical deforestation; desertification* of cropland, grazing areas, and deforested lands; and air, land, and water *pollution.* Each stands alone as an identified problem of global concern, and each is a component part of cumulative human pressures upon the biosphere greater than its recuperative powers can handle.

Land Use and Land Cover

Human-induced alterations in land use and vegetative cover affect the radiation balance of the earth and, therefore, contribute to climatic change. Since the beginning of the 19th

century, vast portions of the earth's surface have been modified, whole ecosystems destroyed, and global biomes altered or eliminated. North American and European native forests have largely vanished, the grasslands of interior United States, Canada, and Ukraine have been converted into farmland. Marshes and wetlands have been drained, dams built, and major water impoundments created. Steppe lands have become deserts; deserts have blossomed under irrigation.

At least locally, every such change alters surface reflectivity for solar radiation, land and air temperature conditions, and water balances. In turn, these changes in surface conditions affect the climates of both the local area and of areas downwind. On a global basis their cumulative impact

(a)

(b)

FIGURE 13.10   (*a*) Photochemical smog in sunny California during the late 1970s. When air remains stagnant over Los Angeles, it can accumulate increasing amounts of automobile and industrial exhausts, reducing afternoon sunlight to a dull haze and sharply lifting ozone levels. Such occurrences are increasingly rare in Los Angeles—where peak levels of ozone have dropped to a quarter of their 1955 levels—and in other major cities with past serious smog and ozone dangers. From 1982 to 1992 overall U.S. smog occurrence dropped by 8%; carbon monoxide pollution fell 30%; and airborne sulfur dioxide declined by 20%. Mandates of the Clean Air Act of 1990 and, particularly, newer model cars assure continued improvements in metropolitan air quality. (*b*) The Germans call it *Waldsterben*—forest death—a term now used more widely to summarize the destruction of trees by a combination of ozone and acidity in clouds, rain, snow, and dust. It first strikes at higher elevations where natural stresses are greatest and acidic clouds most prevalent, but it slowing moves down slope until entire forests are gone. Here at Mount Mitchell in North Carolina, *Waldsterben* is thought to result from pollution traveling eastward from the Ohio and Tennessee valleys. Forests all along the Eastern Seaboard northward into Canada display evidence of similar pollution-related damage.

is less clear, but certain generalizations are agreed upon. The generation of methane gas, an important contributor to the greenhouse effect, is almost certainly reduced by drainage of swamps, but it is also greatly increased as a by-product of expanding paddy rice production and of growing herds of cattle on pastureland. Heavy applications of nitrogen fertilizers are thought to be important in increasing the nitrous oxide content of the atmosphere. When they enter streams and lakes through farm runoff, the fertilizers encourage the algal growth that alters water surface reflectivity and evaporation rates.

But unquestionably the most important of the land surface changes has been that of clearing of forests and plowing of grasslands. Both effect drastic environmental changes that alter temperature conditions and water balances and release—through vegetative decomposition—large quantities of carbon dioxide and other gases to the atmosphere. The destruction of both biomes represents, as well, the loss of major "sinks" that extract carbon dioxide from the atmosphere and hold it in plant tissue.

Tropical Deforestation

Forests, we saw in Chapter 8, still cover some 30% of the earth's land surface (Figure 8.28), though the forest biomes have suffered mightily as human pressures upon them have increased. Forest clearing accompanied the development of agriculture and spread of people throughout Europe, Central Asia, the Middle East, and India. European colonization had much the same impact upon the temperate forests of eastern North America and Australasia. In most midlatitude developed countries, although original forest cover is largely gone, replanting and reversion of cropland to timber has tended to replenish woodlands at about their rate of cutting.

Now it is the tropical rain forest—also known as the tropical moist forest—biome that is feeling the pressure of growing population numbers, the need for more agricultural land, expanded demand for fuel and commercial wood, and a midlatitude market for beef that can be satisfied profitably by replacing tropical forest with cleared grazing land. These disappearing forests extend across parts of Asia, Africa, and Latin America, and are the world's most diverse and least understood biome. About 45% of their original expanse has already been cleared or degraded. Africa has lost more than half of its original rain forest; nearly half of Asia's is gone; 70% of the moist forests of Central America and some 40% of those of South America have disappeared. Every year at least an additional 200,000 square kilometers (77,000 sq. mi.)—about the size of Nebraska or South Carolina—are lost. Tropical forest removal raises three principal global concerns and a host of local ones.

First, on a worldwide basis, all forests play a major role in maintaining the oxygen and carbon balance of the earth. This is particularly true of tropical forests because of their total area and volume. Humans and their industries consume oxygen; vegetation replenishes it through photosynthesis and the release of oxygen back into the atmosphere as a by-product. At the same time, plants extract the carbon from atmospheric carbon dioxide, acting as natural retaining sponges for the gas so important in the greenhouse effect. Each year, each hectare (2.47 acres) of Amazon rain forest absorbs a ton of carbon dioxide. When the tropical rain forest is cleared, not only is its role as a carbon "sink" lost but the act of destruction itself through decomposition or burning releases as carbon dioxide the vast quantities of carbon the forest had stored.

A second global concern is also climate related. Forest destruction changes surface and air temperatures, moisture content, and reflectivity. Conversion of forest to grassland, for example, increases surface temperature, raises air temperatures above the treeless ground, and therefore increases the water-holding capacity of the warmer air. As winds move the hotter, drier air, it tends to exert a drying effect on adjacent forest and agricultural lands. Trees and crops outside the denuded area experience heat and aridity stresses not normal to their geographical locations. It is calculated that cutting the forests of South America on a wide scale should raise regional temperatures from 3°C to 5°C (5.5–9°F), which in turn would extend the dry season and greatly disrupt not only regional but global climates.

In some ways, the most serious long-term global consequence of the eradication of tropical rain forests will be the loss of a major part of the biological diversity of the planet. Of the estimated 5–10 million plant and animals species believed to exist on earth, a minimum of 40% to 50% are native to the tropical rain forest biome. Many of the plants have become important world staple food crops: rice, millet, cassava, yam, taro, banana, pineapple, and sugarcane to name but a very few well-known ones. Unknown additional potential food species remain as yet unexploited. Reports from Indonesia suggest that in that country's forests

alone, some 4000 plant species have proved useful to native peoples as foodstuffs of one sort or another, though less than one-tenth have come into wide use. The rain forests are, in addition, the world's main storehouse of drug-yielding plants and insects, including thousands with proven or prospective anticancer properties and many widely used as sources of alkaloids, steroids, anesthetics, and other medicinal agents. The loss of the zoological and botanical storehouse that the rain forests represent would deprive humans of untold potential benefits that might never be realized.

On a more local basis, tropical forests play for their inhabitants and neighbors the same role taken by forests everywhere. They protect watersheds and regulate water flow. After forest cutting, unregulated flow accentuates the problems of high and low water variations, increases the severity of valley flooding, and makes more serious and prolonged the impact of low water flow on irrigation agriculture, navigation, and urban and rural water supply. Accelerated **soil erosion**—the process of removal of soil particles from the ecosystem, usually by wind or running water—quickly removes the always thin, infertile tropical forest soils from deforested areas. Lands cleared for agriculture almost immediately become unsuitable for that use partially because of soil loss (Figure 13.11). The surface

FIGURE 13.11   Wholesale destruction of the tropical rain forest guarantees environmental degradation so severe that the forest can never naturally regenerate itself. Exposed soils quickly deteriorate in structure and fertility and are easily eroded, as this growing gully in Amazonia clearly shows.

material removed is transported and deposited downstream, changing valley contours, extending the area subject to flooding, and filling irrigation and drainage channels. Or it may be deposited in the reservoirs behind the increasing number of major dams on rivers within the tropical rain forests or rising there (see "Dam Trouble in the Tropics").

Desertification

The tropical rain forests can succumb to deliberate massive human assaults and be irretrievably lost. With much less effort, and with no intent to destroy or alter the environment, humans are assumed to be similarly affecting the arid and semiarid regions of the world. The process is called **desertification,** the spread of desertlike landscapes into arid and semiarid environments. While the Earth Summit of 1992 defined desertification broadly as "land degradation in arid, semiarid and dry subhumid areas, resulting from climatic variations and human activities," the process is usually charged to increasing human pressures exerted through overgrazing, deforestation for fuel wood, clearing of original vegetation for cultivation, and burning, and implies a continuum of ecological alteration from slight to extreme (Figure 13.12).

Whatever its degree of development, when the process results from human rather than climatic causes, it begins in the same fashion: the disruption or removal of the native cover of grasses and shrubs through farming or overgrazing (Figure 13.13). If the disruption is severe enough, the original vegetation cannot reestablish itself and the exposed soil is made susceptible to erosion during the brief, heavy rains that dominate precipitation patterns in semiarid regions. Water runs off the land surface instead of seeping in, carrying soil particles with it and leaving behind an *erosion pavement.* When the water is lost through surface flow rather than seepage downward, the water table is lowered. Eventually, even deep-rooted bushes are unable to reach groundwater, and all natural vegetation is lost. The process is accentuated when too many grazing animals pack the earth down with their hooves, blocking the passage of air and water through the soil. When both plant cover and soil moisture are lost, desertification has occurred.

It happens with increasing frequency in many areas of the earth as pressures on the land continue. Worldwide, desertification affects about 900 million people in over 100 countries and impacts about 1.2 billion hectares—about the size of China and India combined. Africa is most at risk; the United Nations has estimated that 40% of that continent's nondesert land is in danger of human-induced desertification. But nearly a third of Asia's lands and a fifth of Latin America's are similarly endangered. In countries where desertification is particularly extensive and severe (Algeria,

DAM TROUBLE IN THE TROPICS

The great tropical river systems have a sizable percentage of the world's undeveloped power potential. The lure of that power and its promise for economic development and national modernization have proved nearly irresistible. But the tropical rain forests have been a particularly difficult environment for dam builders. The dams (and their reservoirs) often carry a heavy ecological price, and the clearing and development of the areas they are meant to serve often assure the destruction of the dam projects themselves.

The creation of Brokopondo in Suriname in 1964 marked the first large reservoir in a rain forest locale. Without being cleared of their potentially valuable timber, 1480 square kilometers (570 sq. mi.) of dense tropical forest disappeared underwater. As the trees decomposed, producing hydrogen sulfide, an intolerable stench polluted the atmosphere for scores of miles downwind. For more than two years, employees at the dam wore gas masks at work. Decomposition of vegetation produced acids that corroded the dam's cooling system, leading to costly continuing repairs and upkeep.

Water hyacinth spreads rapidly in tropical impoundments, its growth hastened by the rich nutrients released by tree decomposition. Within a year of the reservoir's completion, a 130-square-kilometer (50-sq.-mi.) blanket of the weed was afloat on Lake Brokopondo, and after another year almost half the reservoir was covered. Another 440 square kilometers (170 sq. mi.) were claimed by a floating fern, *Ceratopteris*. Identical problems plague most rain forest hydropower projects.

The expense, the disruption of the lives of valley residents whose homes are to be flooded, and the environmental damage of dam projects in the rain forest all may be in vain. Deforestation of river banks and clearing of vegetation for permanent agriculture usually results in accelerated erosion, rapid sedimentation of reservoirs, and drastic reduction of electrical generating capacity. The Ambuklao Reservoir in the Philippines, built with an expected payback period of 60 years, now appears certain to silt up in half that time. The Anchicaya Reservoir in Colombia lost 25% of its storage capacity only two years after it was completed and was almost totally filled with silt within 10 years. The Peligre Dam in Haiti was completed in 1956 with a life expectancy of at least 50 years; siltation reduced its usefulness by some 15 years. El Cajon Dam in Honduras, Arenal in Costa Rica, Chixoy in Guatemala and many others—all built to last decades or even centuries—have, because of premature siltation, failed to repay their costs or fulfill their promise. The price of deforestation in wet tropics is high indeed.

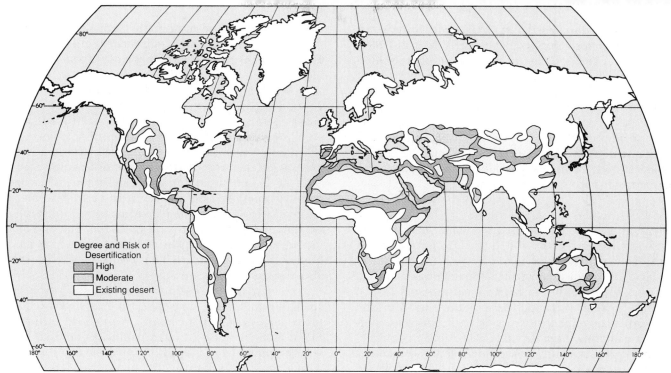

FIGURE 13.12   **Desertification** is usually understood to imply the steady advance of the margins of the world's deserts into their bordering drylands, converting through human mistreatment formerly productive or usable pastures and croplands into barren and sterile landscapes. Satellite measurements, however, are forcing a reassessment of what is really happening to arid and semiarid drylands along the perimeter of the Sahara and other major world deserts. Imagery from 1980 through 1990 indicates that the Sahel drylands region on the southern border of the Sahara, for example, did not move steadily south as usually assumed. Rather, the vegetation line fluctuated back and forth in response to variable rainfall patterns, with year to year shifts ranging between 30 and 150 miles. Since Africa's drylands climate has shifted back and forth between periods of extended drought and higher rainfall for at least 10,000 years, many scientists now believe climate variation keeps the drylands in a continual state of disequilibrium. That, rather than human abuse of the land, is thought to be the major influence on dryland ecology and the shifting margins of deserts. Because of different criteria, areas shown as "desert" here are not identical to desert regions of Figure 13.3. See also Figure 13.15.

FIGURE 13.13   The margin of the desert. Intensive grazing pressure destroys vegetation, compacts soil, and leads to soil degradation and desertification, as this desert-margin view from Burkina Faso suggests.

Ethiopia, Iraq, Jordan, Lebanon, Mali, and Niger) per capita food production declined by nearly half between 1950 and the mid-1990s. The resulting threat of starvation spurs populations of the affected areas to increase their farming and livestock pressures on the denuded land, further contributing to their desertification. It has been suggested that Mali may be the first country in the world rendered uninhabitable by environmental destruction. Many of its some 9 million (1995) inhabitants begin their day by shoveling their doorways clear of the night's accumulation of sand (Figure 13.14).

Soil Erosion

Desertification is but one expression of land deterioration leading to accelerated soil erosion, a worldwide problem of biosphere deterioration. Over much of the earth's surface, the thin layer of topsoil upon which life depends is only a few inches deep, usually less than 30 centimeters (1 ft.). Below it, the lithosphere is as lifeless as the surface of the moon. A **soil** is a complex mixture of rock particles, inorganic mineral matter, organic material, living organisms, air, and water. Under natural conditions, soil is constantly being formed by the physical and chemical decomposition of rock material and by the decay of organic matter. It is simultaneously being eroded, for soil erosion is as natural a process as soil formation and occurs even when land is to-

tally covered by forests or grass. Under most natural conditions, however, the rate of soil formation equals or exceeds the rate of soil erosion, so that soil depth and fertility tend to increase with time.

When land is cleared and planted to crops or when the vegetative cover is broken by overgrazing, deforestation, or other disturbances, the process of erosion inevitably accelerates. When its rate exceeds that of soil formation, the life-sustaining veneer of topsoil becomes thinner and eventually disappears, leaving behind only sterile subsoil or barren rock. At that point the renewable soil resource has been converted through human impact into a nonrenewable and dissipated asset. Carried to the extreme of bare rock hillsides or wind-denuded plains, erosion spells the total end of agricultural use of the land. Throughout history, such extreme human-induced destruction has occurred and been observed with dismay.

Any massive destruction of the soil resource could spell the end of the civilization it had supported. For the most part, however, farmers—even those in difficult climatic and topographic circumstances—devised ingenious ways to preserve and even improve the soil resource upon which their lives and livelihoods depended. Particularly when farming was carried on outside of fertile, level valley lands, farmers' practices were routinely based on some combination of crop rotation, fallowing, and terracing.

FIGURE 13.14   Windblown dust is engulfing the scrub forest in this drought-stricken area of Mali, near Timbuktu. The district is part of the Sahel region of Africa where desertification has been accelerated by both climate and human pressures on the land. From the late 1930s to 1990, some 650,000 square kilometers (250,000 sq. mi.) were added to the southern Sahara. It has expanded on its northern and eastern margins as well. On an annual basis, marginal fluctuation rather than steady expansion is the rule and some scientists prefer to speak of an "ebb and flow" of the Sahara margins and of land degradation rather than of permanent conversion to true desert.

Rotation involves the planting of two or more crops simultaneously or successively on the same area to preserve fertility or to provide a plant cover to protect the soil. **Fallowing** leaves a field idle (uncropped) for one or more years to achieve one of two outcomes. In semiarid areas the purpose is to accumulate soil moisture from one year to apply to the next year's crop; in tropical wet regions, as we saw in Chapter 8, the purpose is to renew soil fertility of the swidden plot. **Terracing** (Figure 4.23) replaces steep slopes with a series of narrow layered, level fields providing crop land where little or none existed previously. In addition, because water moving rapidly down slope has great erosive power, breaking the speed of flow by terracing reduces the amount of soil lost. Field trials in Nigeria indicate that cultivation on a 1% slope (a drop of one foot in elevation over 100 feet of horizontal distance) results in soil loss at or below the rate of soil formation; farming there on a 15% slope would totally strip a field of its soil cover in only 10 years (see "Maintaining Soil Productivity").

Farming skills have not declined in recent years. Rather, pressures on farmlands have increased with population growth. Farming has been forced higher up on steeper slopes, more forest land has been converted to cultivation, grazing and crops have been pushed farther and more intensively into semiarid areas, and existing fields have had to be worked more intensively and less carefully. Many traditional agricultural systems and areas that were ecologically stable and secure as recently as 1950, when world population stood at 2.5 billion, are disintegrating under the pressures of nearly 6 billion.

The evidence of that deterioration is found in all parts of the world (Figure 13.15) and expresses itself in two ways: through decreasing yields of cultivated fields themselves and in increased stream sediment loads and downstream deposition of silt. In Guatemala, for example, some 40% of the productive capacity of the land has been lost through erosion, and several areas of the country have been abandoned because agriculture has become economically impracticable; the figure is 50% in El Salvador. In Turkey, a reported 75% of the land is affected and 54% is severely or very severely eroded. Haiti has no high-value soil left at all. A full one-quarter of India's total land area has been significantly eroded: some 13 million hectares (32 million acres) by wind and nearly 74 million hectares (183 million acres) by water. Between 1960 and the mid-1990s, China lost about 15% of its total arable land to erosion, desertification, or conversion to nonagricultural use; 700,000 hectares (1.7 million acres) of cultivated land were taken by construction during 1994 alone. Its Huang River is the most sediment-laden of any stream on earth; in its middle course it is about 50% silt by

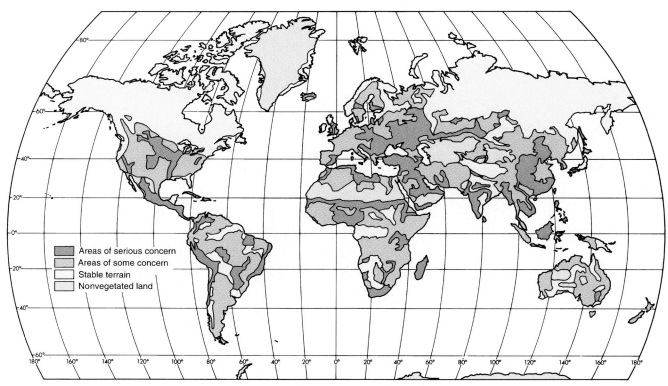

FIGURE 13.15 **The world pattern of soil degradation concern.** Between 1945 and 1995, nearly 2 billion hectares (almost 5 billion acres) of the world's 8.7 billion hectares (21.5 billion acres) of cropland, pastures, and forests used in agriculture—an area as large as Russia and India combined—have been degraded. Globally, about 18% of forest area, 21% of pastures, and 37% of cropland have undergone moderate to severe degradation. Water erosion accounted for 56% of that recorded deterioration, wind erosion for 28%, chemical deterioration (salinization and nutrient loss) for 12%, and physical degradation (e.g., compaction and waterlogging) for 4%.

n much of the world, increasing population numbers are largely responsible for accelerated soil erosion. In the United States in the 1970s and 1980s, economic conditions contributed to a rate of soil erosion equal to that registered during the Dust Bowl era of the 1930s. Of the roughly 167 million hectares (413 million acres) of land intensively cropped in the United States, over one-third are losing topsoil faster than it can be replaced naturally. In parts of Illinois and Iowa, where the topsoil was once a foot deep, less than half of it remains.

Federal tax laws and the high farmland values of the 1970s encouraged farmers to plow virgin grasslands and to tear down windbreaks to increase their cultivable land and yields. The secretary of agriculture exhorted farmers to plant all of their land "from fencerow to fencerow," to produce more grain for export. Land was converted from cattle grazing to corn and soybean production as livestock prices declined. When prices of both land and farm products declined in the 1980s, farmers felt impelled to produce as much as possible in order to meet their debts and make any profit at all. To maintain or increase productivity, many neglected conservation practices, plowing under marginal lands and suspending proven systems of fallowing and crop rotation.

Conservation techniques were not forgotten, of course. They were both practiced by many and persistently advocated by farm organizations and soil conservation groups. Techniques to reduce erosion by holding soil in place in North America are similar to those known and practiced elsewhere in the world. They include contour plowing, terracing, strip cropping and crop rotation, erecting windbreaks and constructing water diversion channels, and practicing no-till or minimum tillage farming (allowing crop residue such as cut corn stalks to remain on the soil surface when crops are planted instead of turning them under by plowing).

Since the mid-1980s, federal farm programs have attempted to reverse some of the damage resulting from past economic pressures and farming practices. One objective has been to retire for conservation purposes some 18.6 million hectares (46 million acres) of crop lands that were eroding faster than three times the natural rate of soil formation. Only by reducing the economic pressures that lead to abuse of farmlands and by continuing to practice known soil conservation techniques can the country maintain the long-term productivity of soil, the resource base upon which all depend.

Map source: USDA Soil Conservation Service.

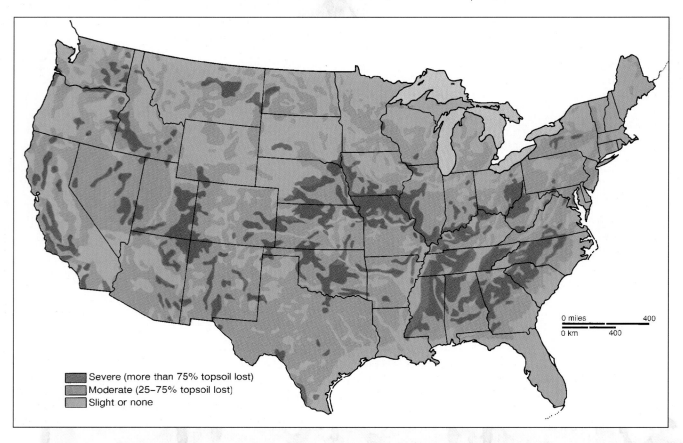

Severe (more than 75% topsoil lost)
Moderate (25–75% topsoil lost)
Slight or none

0 miles   400
0 km   400

weight, just under the point of liquid mud. Worldwide, an estimated 6 to 7 million hectares (15–17 million acres) of existing arable land are lost to erosion each year.

Experiments in the United States, Mexico, Nigeria, and elsewhere document the steep decline in yields as topsoil is progressively removed. United States corn and wheat production on test plots decreased on average by 6% for each inch (2.5 cm) of eroded topsoil. In Mexico, productivity of land deprived of 18 centimeters (7 in.) of topsoil dropped from 3.8 to 0.6 tons of corn per hectare (1.5–0.25 tons per acre) farmed. Significant declines can also occur as fertility or soil quality is reduced through excessive farming pressures even if soil is not physically lost from the surface.

Off-farm erosion evidence is provided by siltation loads carried by streams and rivers and by the downstream deposition that results. In the United States, about 3 billion tons of sediment are washed into waterways each year; off-site damage in the form of reduced reservoir capacity, fish kills, dredging costs, and the like, is estimated at over $6 billion annually. The world's rivers deliver about 24 billion tons of sediment to the oceans each year, while additional billions of tons settle along stream valleys or are deposited in reservoirs (see "Dam Trouble in the Tropics").

Agricultural soil depletion through erosion—and through salt accumulation and desertification—has been called "the quiet crisis." It continues inexorably and unfolds gradually, without the abrupt attention attracted by an earthquake or volcanic explosion. It frequently is accelerated by practices that give a temporary increase in crop yields, suggesting—erroneously—that improvement rather than degradation in productivity is occurring. Few governments have responded meaningfully to the loss of national wealth and food security that soil erosion threatens. In many cases, land degradation has proceeded so far that reclamation is no longer economically possible even if the need is appreciated.

Unfortunately, silent or not, erosion is a crisis of growing importance and immediacy, not just in the countries of its occurrence but—because of international markets and relief programs—throughout the world. A Worldwatch Institute report of the mid-1980s projected a 19% decline in cropland per person between that time and the end of the century. But, ominously, it also projected—at then current rates of soil loss and population growth—a 32% reduction in topsoil per person by the year 2000. The two rates of decline have profound significance for food production trends and for economic and political stability in the world.

Water Supply and Water Quality

Solar energy and water are the indispensable ingredients of life on earth. The supply of both is essentially constant and beyond the scope of humans to increase or alter although, as we saw with aerosols and atmospheric gases, humans can affect the quality and utility of an otherwise fixed resource. Any threat of reduction in availability or lessening of quality

of a material so basic to our very lives as water is certain to arouse strong emotions and deep concerns. In many parts of the world and for many competitors for limited freshwater supplies, those emotions and concerns are already real.

The problem is not with the global amount of water, but with its distribution, its availability, and its quality. The total amount of water on the earth is enormous, though only a small part of the *hydrosphere* (see p. 457) is suitable or available for use by humans, plants, or animals (Figure 13.16). And the total amount remains constant; water is a renewable resource. The **hydrologic cycle** assures that water, no matter how often used or how much abused, will return over and over to the earth for further exploitation (Figure 13.17). Enough rain and snow fall on the continents each year to cover the earth's total land area with 83 centimeters (33 in.) of water. It is usually reckoned that the volume of freshwater annually renewed by the hydrologic cycle could meet the needs of a world population 5 to 10 times its present size.

Yet in many parts of the world water supplies are inadequate and dwindling. Insufficient water for irrigation periodically endangers crops and threatens famine; permanent streams have become intermittent in flow; fresh and saltwater lakes are shrinking; and from throughout the world come reports of rapidly falling water tables and wells that have gone dry. Reduced availability and reliability of supply are echoed in a reduced quality of the world's freshwater inventory. Increased silt loads of streams, pollution of surface and groundwater supplies, and lakes acidified and biologically dead or prematurely filled by siltation and algal growth are evidences of adverse human impact upon an indispensable component of the biosphere.

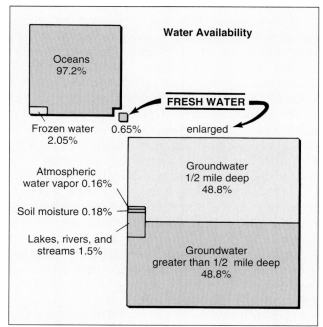

FIGURE 13.16 Less than 1% of the world's water supply is available for human use in freshwater lakes and rivers and from wells. An additional 2% is effectively locked in glaciers and polar ice caps.

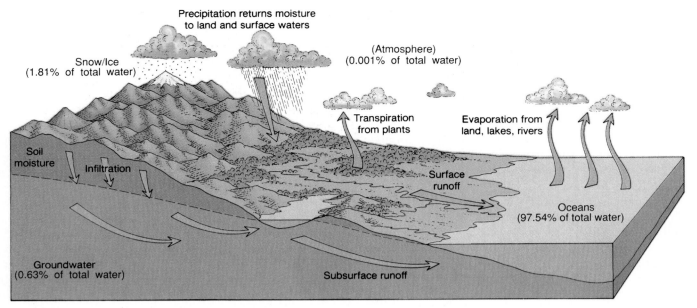

FIGURE 13.17 **The hydrologic cycle.** Water may change form and composition, but under natural environmental circumstances it is marvelously purified in the recycling process and is again made available with appropriate properties and purity to the ecosystems of the earth. The sun provides energy for the evaporation of fresh and ocean water. The water is held as vapor until the air becomes supersaturated. Atmospheric moisture is returned to the earth's surface as solid or liquid precipitation to complete the cycle. Precipitation is not uniformly distributed and moisture is not necessarily returned to areas in the same quantity as it has evaporated from them. The continents receive more water than they lose; the excess returns to the seas as surface water or groundwater. A global water balance, however, is always maintained.

Patterns of Availability

Observations about global supplies and renewal cycles of freshwater ignore the ever-present geographic reality: things are not uniformly distributed over the surface of the earth. There is no necessary relationship between the earth's pattern of freshwater availability and the distribution of consuming populations and activities. Three different world maps help us to understand why. The first, Figure 13.18, shows the spatially variable world pattern of precipitation. The second, Figure 13.4, reminds us that, as a rule, the lower the average amount of precipitation received in an area, the greater is the variability of precipitation from year to year. The recurring droughts and famines of the Sahel region of Africa are witness to the deadly impact of those expected fluctuations in areas of already low rainfall. Finally, Figure 13.19 takes account of the relationship between precipitation receipts and losses through *evapotranspiration,* the return of water from the land to the atmosphere through evaporation from soil and plants and by transpiration through plant leaves. These losses are higher in the tropics than in middle and upper latitudes, where lower rainfall amounts under cooler conditions may be more effective and useful than higher amounts received closer to the equator.

The distribution and vegetative sufficiency of precipitation are givens and, except for human impact upon climatic conditions, are largely independent of cultural influences. Regional water sufficiency, however, is also a function of the size of the population using the resource, its pattern of water use, and the amount of deterioration in quantity and quality the water supply experiences in the process of its use and return to the system. These are circumstances under human, not natural, control.

Water Use and Abuse

For the world as a whole, irrigated agriculture accounts for nearly three-quarters (73%) of freshwater use; in the poorest countries, the proportion is 90%. Industry uses about one-fifth (21%), and domestic and recreation needs account for the remainder. World figures conceal considerable regional variation. Irrigation agriculture produces about one-third of the world's harvest from about 17% of its cropland (Figure 13.20). Unfortunately, in many instances the crops that are produced are worth less than the water itself; the difference is made up in the huge subsidies that governments everywhere offer to irrigation farming. In areas and economies as different as California's Napa Valley or Egypt's Nile Valley, farmers rarely pay over a fifth of the operating costs of public irrigation projects or any of their capital costs. Unfortunately as well, much of the water used for agriculture is lost to the regional supply through evaporation and transpiration; often less than half of the water withdrawn for irrigation is returned to streams or **aquifers** (porous,

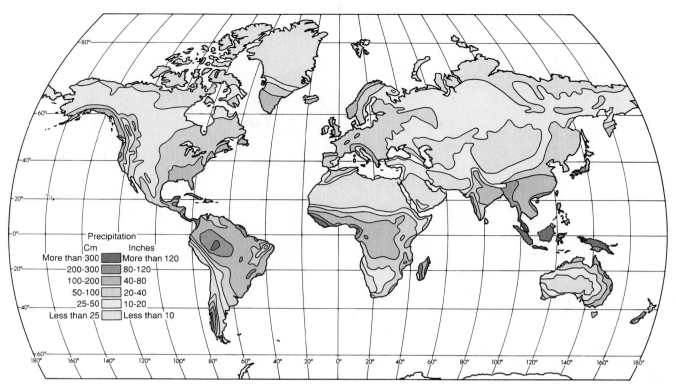

FIGURE 13.18   **Mean annual precipitation.** Regional contrasts of precipitation receipts clearly demonstrate that natural phenomena are unequally distributed over the surface of the earth. High and very high rainfall amounts are recorded in equatorial and tropical areas of Central and South America, Africa, and South and Southeast Asia. Productive agricultural regions of North America and Europe have lower moisture receipts. The world's desert regions—in North Africa, Inner Asia, the southwestern United States, and interior Australia—are clearly marked by low precipitation totals. But not all areas of low moisture receipt are arid, as Figure 13.19 makes clear.

water-bearing layers of sand, gravel, and rock) for further use. Much of that returned water, moreover, is heavily charged with salts removed from irrigated soils, making it unfit for reuse.

On the other hand, most of the water used for manufacturing processes and power production is returned to streams, lakes, or aquifers, but often in a state of pollution that renders it unsuitable for alternate and subsequent uses. Industrial water use rises dramatically with economic development, and in the developing countries growing industrial demands compete directly with increasing requirements for irrigation and urban water supply.

Although municipal wastewater treatment is increasing in the most developed countries, domestic and municipal sewage in the developing world is often discharged totally untreated, contaminating surface water supplies, endangering drinking water sources, and destroying aquatic life. Fully 70% of total surface waters in India are polluted, in large part because only about 200 of its more than 3000 sizable urban centers have full or partial sewage treatment. Of Taiwan's 20 million people, only 600,000 are served by sewers. Hong Kong each day pours 1 million tons of un-

treated sewage and industrial waste into the sea. Mainland China's rivers also suffer from increasing pollution loads. More than 80% of major rivers are polluted to some degree, over 20% to such an extent that their waters cannot be used for irrigation. Four-fifths of China's urban surface water is contaminated, only six of the country's 27 largest cities have drinking water within the state standards, and the water to be impounded by the massive Three Gorges Dam project, it is predicted, will be seriously contaminated by untreated raw sewerage from the dozens of cities along the new reservoir. In Malaysia, more than 40 major rivers are so polluted that they are nearly devoid of fish and aquatic mammals. And even in developed countries of formerly communist Eastern Europe and Russia, sewage and, particularly, industrial waste seriously pollute much of the surface water supply (see "Ideology, Industrialization, and Environmental Disaster" in Chapter 9, p. 318).

When humans introduce wastes into the biosphere in kinds and amounts that the biosphere cannot neutralize or recycle, the result is **environmental pollution.** In the case of water, pollution exists when water composition has been so modified by the presence of one or more substances that

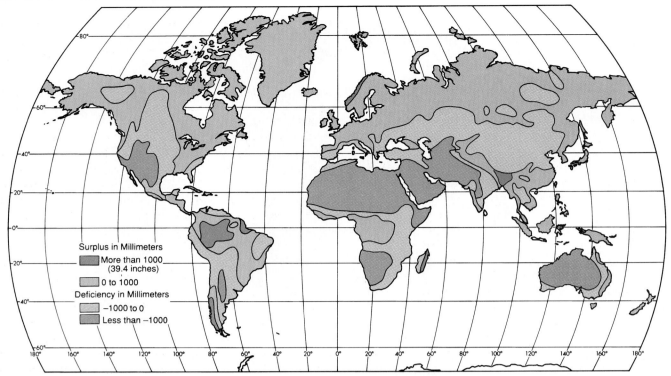

Surplus in Millimeters

Surplus in Millimeters
■ More than 1000 (39.4 inches)
■ 0 to 1000
Deficiency in Millimeters
■ −1000 to 0
■ Less than −1000

FIGURE 13.19 **World water supplies.** The pattern of surplus and deficit is seen in relation to the demands of the vegetation cover. Water is in surplus when precipitation is sufficient to satisfy or exceed the demands of the vegetation cover. When precipitation is lower than this potential demand, a water deficit occurs. By this measure, most of Africa (except the tropical rain forest areas of West Africa), much of the Middle East, the southwestern United States, and almost all of Australia are areas of extreme moisture deficit.

A comparison of this map with Figure 13.4 helps demonstrate the **limiting factor principle,** which notes that the single factor that is most deficient in an ecosystem is the one that determines what kind of plant and animal associations will exist there. Moisture surplus or deficit is the limiting factor that dictates whether desert, grassland, or forest will develop under natural, undisturbed conditions.

FIGURE 13.20 Irrigation in the Lake Argyle project of Western Australia. Since 1950, growing world food needs have extended irrigation to between 5 and 6 million additional hectares (12 to 15 million acres) annually. Usually, much more water is transported and applied to fields than crops actually require, using unnecessary amounts of a scarce resource. "Drip irrigation," a process of delivering water directly to plant roots through small perforated tubes laid across the field, reduces water consumption and salinization and, therefore, the economic and environmental costs of irrigation farming.

either it cannot be used for a specific purpose or it is less suitable for that use than it was in its natural state. In both developed and developing countries, human pressures upon freshwater supplies are now serious and pervasive concerns. If current trends of use and water abuse continue, freshwater will certainly—and soon—become a limiting factor for economic activity, food production, and maintenance of health in many parts of the world (see "A World of Water Woes"). Although a few governments have begun to face the water problem—one every bit as serious potentially or actually as atmospheric pollution, soil erosion, deforestation, and desertification—much remains to be done.

Garbage Heaps and Toxic Wastes

Humans have always managed to leave their mark on the landscapes they occupy. The search for minerals, for example, has altered whole landscapes, beginning with the pockmarks and pits marking Neolithic diggings into chalk cliffs to obtain flints or early Bronze Age excavations for tin and culminating with modern open-pit and strip-mining operations that tear minerals from the earth and create massive new landforms of depressions and rubble (Figures 13.1 and

Water covers almost three-quarters of the surface of the globe, yet "scarcity" is the word increasingly used to describe water-related concerns in both the developed and developing world. Globally, freshwater is abundant. Each year, an average of over 7000 cubic meters (some 250,000 cubic feet) per person enters rivers and underground reserves. But rainfall does not always occur when or where it is needed. Already, 80 countries with 40% of the world's population have water shortages that threaten to cripple agriculture and industry; 22 of them have renewable water resources of less than 1000 cubic meters (35,000 cubic feet)—a level generally understood to mean that water scarcity is a severe constraint on the economy and public health. Another 18 countries have less than 2000 cubic meters per capita on average, a dangerously low figure in years of rainfall shortage. Most of the water-short countries are in the Middle East, North Africa, and sub-Saharan Africa, the regions where populations (and consumption demands) are growing fastest.

In several major crop-producing regions, water use exceeds sustainable levels, threatening future food supplies. America's largest underground water reserve, stretching from west Texas northward into South Dakota, is drying up, partially depleted by more than 150,000 wells pumping water for irrigation, city supply, and industry. In some areas, the wells no longer yield enough to permit irrigation and farmed land is decreasing; in others, water levels have fallen so far that it is uneconomical to pump it to the surface for any use. In many agricultural districts of northern China, west and south India, and Mexico water scarcity limits agriculture even though national supplies are adequate. In Uzbekistan and adjacent sections of Central Asia and Kazakhstan, virtually the entire flow of the area's two primary rivers—the Amu Darya and the Syr Darya—is totally used for often wasteful irrigation, with none left to maintain the Aral Sea or supply growing urban populations. In Poland, the draining of bogs that formerly stored rainfall, combined with unimaginable pollution of streams and groundwater, has created a water shortage as great as that of any Middle Eastern desert country. And salinity now seriously affects productivity—or prohibits farming completely—on nearly 10% of the world's irrigated lands.

Water scarcity is often a region-wide concern. More than 200 river systems draining over half the earth's land surface, are shared by two or more countries. Egypt draws on the Nile for 86% of its domestic consumption, but virtually all of that water originates in eight upstream countries. Turkey, Iraq, and Syria have frequently been in dispute over the management of the Tigris and Euphrates rivers, and the downstream states fear the effect on them of Turkish impoundments and diversions. Mexico is angered at American depletion of the Colorado before it reaches the international border.

Many coastal communities face saltwater intrusions into their drinking water supplies as they draw down their underlying freshwater aquifers, while both coastal and inland cities dependent on groundwater may be seriously depleting their underground supplies. In China 50 cities face acute water shortages as groundwater levels drop 1 to 2 meters (3–6 ft.) each year. In Mexico City, groundwater is pumped at rates 40% faster than natural recharge, and millions of citizens of major cities throughout the world have had their water rationed as underground and surface supplies are used beyond recharge or storage capacity.

13.21). Ancient irrigation systems still visible on the landscape document both the engineering skills and the environmental alterations of early hydraulic civilizations in the Near East, North Africa, and elsewhere. The raised fields built by the Mayas of Yucatán are still traceable 1000 years after they were abandoned, and aerial photography reveals the sites of villages and patterns of fields of medieval England.

Among the most enduring of landscape evidences of human occupance, however, are not the holes deliberately dug or the structures built but the garbage produced and discarded by all societies everywhere. Prehistoric dwelling sites are located and analyzed by their *middens,* the refuse piles containing the kitchen wastes, broken tools, and other debris of human settlement. We have learned much about Roman and medieval European urban life and life-styles by examination of the refuse mounds that grew as man-made hills in their vicinities. In the Near East, whole cities gradually rose on the mounds of debris accumulating under them (Figure 13.22).

Modern cultures differ from their predecessors by the volume and character of their wastes, not by their habits of discard. The greater the society's population and material wealth, the greater the amount and variety of its garbage. Developed countries of the late 20th century are increasingly discovering that their material wealth and technological advancements are submerging them in a volume and variety of wastes—solid and liquid, harmless and toxic—that threaten both their environments and their established ways of life. The United States may serve as an example of situations all too common worldwide.

FIGURE 13.21   About 400 square kilometers (some 150 sq. mi.) of land surface in the United States are lost each year to the strip-mining of coal and other minerals; far more is chewed up worldwide. On flat or rolling terrain, strip-mining leaves a landscape of parallel ridges and trenches, the result of stripping away the unwanted surface material. That material— *overburden*—taken from one trench to reach the underlying mineral, is placed in an adjacent one, leaving the wavelike terrain shown here. Besides altering the topography, strip-mining interrupts surface and subsurface drainage patterns, destroys vegetation, and places sterile and frequently highly acidic subsoil and rock on top of the new ground surface. Current law not always successfully requires stripped areas to be returned to their original contours.

FIGURE 13.22   Tell Hesi, northeast of Gaza, Israel. Here and elsewhere in the Middle East, the debris of millennia of human settlement gradually raised the level of the land surface, producing *tells,* or occupation mounds. The city literally was constantly rebuilt at higher elevations on the accumulation of refuse of earlier occupants. In some cases, these striking landforms may rise hundreds of feet above the surrounding plains.

Solid Wastes and Rubbish

North Americans produce rubbish and garbage at a rate of 200 million tons per year, or about 1.6 kilograms (3.5 pounds) per person per day. As populations grow, incomes rise, and consumption patterns change, the volume of disposable materials continues to expand. Relatively little residue is created in subsistence societies that move food from garden to table, and wastes from table to farm animals or compost heaps. The problem comes with urban folk who purchase packaged foods, favor plastic wrappings and containers for every commodity, and seek (and can afford) an ever-broadening array of manufactured goods, both consumer durables such as refrigerators and automobiles and many designed for single use and quick disposal.

The wastes that communities must somehow dispose of include newspapers and beer cans, toothpaste tubes and old television sets, broken stoves and rusted cars. Such ordinary household and municipal trash does not meet the usual designation of *hazardous waste:* discarded material that may pose a substantial threat to human health or the environment when improperly stored or disposed of. Much of it, however, does have a component of danger to health or to the environment. Paints and paint removers, used motor oils, pesticides and herbicides, bleaches, many kinds of plastics, and the like pose problems significantly different from apple cores and waste paper.

Landfill Disposal

The supply of open land and a free-enterprise system of waste collection and disposal led most American communities to opt for dumping urban refuse in landfills. In earlier periods, most of these were simply open dumps on the land, a menace to public health and an esthetic blot on the landscape. Beginning in the 1960s, more stringent federal controls began to require waste disposal in what was considered a more environmentally sound manner: the *sanitary landfill.* This involves depositing refuse in a natural depression or excavated trench, compacting it, and then covering it each day with soil to seal it (Figure 13.23). Open dumping was outlawed in 1976.

Some 75% of the country's municipal waste is disposed of by landfill (1995), but the available, affordable, or permitted sites are rapidly disappearing. Some two-thirds of all landfills in operation in the late 1970s were filled and closed by 1990, and more than half the cities on the East Coast were without any local landfill sites in the mid-1990s. Remaining dumps are filling rapidly. New York City places most of the 24,000 tons of waste it produces each day into the world's largest dump, Fresh Kills on Staten Island, which on completion is slated to tower 135 feet above the torch on the Statue of Liberty. Generating 140,000 cubic meters (5 million cubic feet) of methane gas annually and already illegally exuding contaminated water, Fresh Kills symbolizes the rising tide of refuse engulfing cities, endangering the environment, and forcing ever more expensive and exotic disposal solutions (see "Odyssey of the *Mobro*").

Incineration

For cities and regions awash in solid waste, alternatives to local landfill are few, expensive, and strongly resisted. One possibility is incineration, a waste-to-energy option of burning refuse to produce steam or electricity that usually also involves sorting, recapturing, and recycling useful rubbish components, such as paper, glass, metals, and the like. Incinerators also produce air pollution, including highly toxic dioxin, so control equipment is required. Acid gases and heavy metals are also released by waste burning. The gases add to atmospheric pollution and acid rain, although "scrubbers" and fabric filters on modern incinerators reduce emissions to very low levels while the metals contribute to the toxicity of the ash that is the inevitable product of incineration and that requires landfill disposal.

The likelihood of pollution from one or many incinerator by-products has sparked strong protest to their construction in the United States, though they are more accepted abroad. A Supreme Court ruling of 1994 that incinerator ash was not exempt from the nation's hazardous waste law recognized the potential danger and mandated more expensive ash disposal procedures. Nonetheless, the 125 waste-to-energy incinerators operating in the United States in 1995 continued to burn about one-fifth of the country's municipal garbage (Figure 13.24). The seriousness of

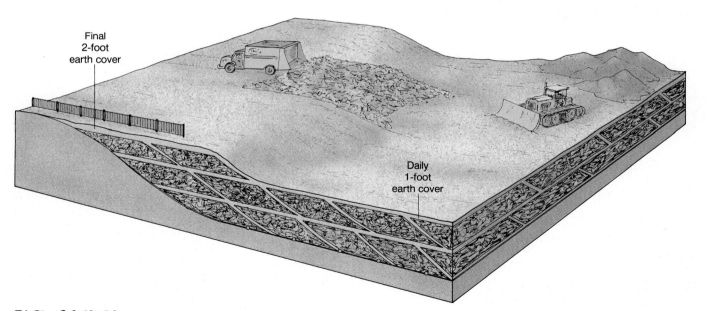

FIGURE 13.23   **A sanitary landfill.** Each day's deposit of refuse is compacted and isolated in a separate cell by a covering layer of soil or clay. The base of the landfill should be of impermeable clay sufficiently thick to prevent liquid *leachate* (chemically contaminated drainage from the landfill) from entering the ground water. Plastic sheets and leachate collector pipes, pits, and treatment systems, and methane monitoring sites are also features required under Environmental Protection Agency regulations of 1993. Even such precautions are probably no sure guarantee that leakage and water and soil contamination will not occur.

n March 22, 1987, the 70-meter (230-foot) barge *Mobro* was loaded with 3186 tons of baled garbage that had been turned away for lack of room from the landfill in the Long Island, New York, town of Islip. That was the beginning of a 5-month saga that captured headlines, aroused resentment, triggered court actions, and inspired humorists around the world. The 9500-kilometer (6000-mile), $1 million journey of the barge, pulled by the tugboat *Break of Dawn,* began with a purpose and a point in mind: it was to be moved to a garbage-to-methane gas operation in North Carolina to prove it was cheaper to move garbage by water than overland and that the methane gas to be recovered from it would make the shipment economically sound.

But the barge was turned away from North Carolina for lack of permits, and its fruitless journey in search of a destination began. It was rejected angrily by Alabama, Mississippi, Louisiana, Texas, and Florida. Seeking a better reception abroad, it called at—and was repulsed by—Mexico, Belize, and the Bahamas. Each rejection compounded incorrect public and private fears that the cargo was toxic and that previous refusals had been based upon the noxious and dangerous nature of the load. Finally after two months, tug and barge returned the garbage to New York. After court challenges and another three months' delay, permission was granted for incineration in Brooklyn. The ashes were then trucked off for burial at the Islip landfill where the saga of the *Mobro* began.

FIGURE 13.24   This waste-to-energy incinerator at Peekskill, New York, is one of the new generation of municipal plants expected to convert over one-quarter of the country's municipal waste to energy by A.D. 2000. A recent Supreme Court ruling that the ash they produce had to be tested for hazardous toxicity and appropriately disposed in protected landfills will raise the operating costs of present incinerators and alter the economic assessments of new construction.

HUMAN ACTIONS AND ENVIRONMENTAL IMPACTS

the dioxin and toxic ash problem, however, has aroused concern everywhere. Some European countries called at least temporary halts to incinerator construction while their safety was reconsidered, and increasingly landfills are refusing to take their residue.

Ocean Dumping

For coastal communities around the world the ocean has long been the preferred sink for not only municipal garbage, but for (frequently untreated) sewage, industrial waste, and all the detritus of an advanced urban society. The practice has been so common and long-standing, that by the 1980s the oceans were added to the list of great environmental concerns of the age. While the carcinogenic effect of ozone reduction had to be assumed from scientific report, the evidence of serious ocean pollution was increasingly apparent to even the most casual observer.

Along the Atlantic coast of North America from Massachusetts to Chesapeake Bay, reports of dead dolphins, raw sewage, tar balls, used syringes, vials of contaminated blood and hospital waste, diapers, plastic products in unimagined amounts and varieties, and other foul refuse kept swimmers from the beach, closed coastal shellfisheries, and elicited health warnings against wading or even breathing salt spray (Figure 13.25). The Gulf of Mexico coast is also tainted and polluted by accumulations of urban garbage, litter from ships and offshore oil rigs, and the toxic effluent of petrochemical plants. Long stretches of Pacific shoreline are in similar condition.

Elsewhere, the Adriatic, Aegean, Baltic, and Irish seas and the Sea of Japan—indeed, all the world's coastal waters—are no better. Environmental surveys of the shores of the Mediterranean Sea show serious damage and pollution. Around Italy, the Mediterranean waters are cloudy with raw sewage and industrial waste and some of the world's most beautiful beaches are fouled by garbage. The Bay of Guanabara, the grand entryway to Rio de Janeiro, Brazil, has graphically been called a cesspool.

An international treaty to regulate ocean dumping of hazardous trash was drafted in 1972 and another, the Ocean Dumping Ban to control marine disposal of wastes, was negotiated in 1988, but their effectiveness has yet to be demonstrated. In light of the length of the world's coastline, the number of countries sharing it, and the great growth of urban populations in the vicinity of the sea, serious doubt has been raised whether any international agreement can be fully effective or enforced. Many portents—from beach litter to massive fin- and shellfish kills—suggest that the oceans' troubled waters have reached the limit of the abuse they can absorb.

Whether the solution to solid waste disposal be sought by land, by fire, or by sea, humanity's rising tide of refuse threatens to overwhelm the environments that must deal with it. The problem is present, growing, and increasingly costly to manage. Solutions are still to be found, a constant reminder for the future of the threatening impact of the environments of culture upon those of nature.

FIGURE 13.25 Warning signs and beaches littered with sewage, garbage, and medical debris are among the increasingly common and distressing evidences of ocean dumping of wastes.

Toxic Wastes

The problems of municipal and household solid-waste management are daunting; those of treatment and disposal of hazardous and toxic wastes seem overwhelming. The definitions of the terms are imprecise, and *hazardous* and *toxic* are frequently used interchangeably, as we shall do here. More strictly defined, **toxic waste** is a relatively limited concept, referring to materials that can cause death or serious injury to humans or animals. **Hazardous waste** is a broader term referring to all wastes, including toxic ones, that pose an immediate or long-term human health risk or that endanger the environment (see definition on p. 480).

Such wastes contaminate the environment in different ways and by different routes. Because most hazardous debris is disposed of by dumping or burial on land, groundwater is most at risk of contamination. In all, some 2% of North America's groundwater supply could have hazardous waste contamination. No comparable world figures exist, but in all industrial countries at least some drinking water contamination from highly toxic solvents, hydrocarbons, pesticides, trace metals, and polychlorinated biphenyls (PCBs) has been detected. Toxic waste impoundments are also a source of air pollutants through the evaporation of volatile organic compounds. Finally, careless or deliberate distribution of toxic materials outside of confinement areas can cause unexpected, but deadly, hazards. Although methods of disposal other than containment techniques have been developed—including incineration, infrared heating, and bacterial decomposition—none is fully satisfactory and none is as yet in wide use.

Radioactive Wastes

Every organization that either uses or produces radioactive materials generates at least *low-level waste*. Nuclear power plants produce about half the total low-level waste in the form of used resins, filter sludges, lubricating oils, and detergent wastes. Industries that manufacture radio-pharmaceuticals, smoke alarms, and other consumer goods produce such wastes in the form of machinery parts, plastics, and organic solvents. Research establishments, universities, and hospitals are also producers of radioactive waste materials.

High-level waste is nuclear debris with a relatively dangerous level of radioactivity. It consists primarily of spent power reactor fuel assemblies and such "military waste" as the by-product of nuclear weapons manufacture. The volume of civilian waste alone is great. Each year the approximately 110 nuclear power stations in the United States produce about 1500 tons of spent fuel, most of it very highly radioactive; by 1995 roughly 30,000 tons of it had already accumulated.

No satisfactory method of radioactive waste disposal has yet been devised. Although sealing liquids with a radioactive life measured in the thousands of years within steel drums expected to last no more than 40 years seems an unlikely solution to the disposal problem, it is one that has been widely practiced. Often the drums are dumped at sea in the expectation that the depth of their resting place and the dilution of seawater will render their contents, when leaked, relatively innocuous. Nearly 50,000 drums of radioactive waste were dumped from 1946 to 1970 into the Pacific Ocean some 30 miles west of San Francisco; by 1990, many were known to have corroded and burst from water pressure, leaking plutonium and cesium. Land storage in specially protected tanks (Figure 13.26) and stabilizing ra-

dioactive waste through filtering, evaporation, and sealing of the residual sludge by mixing it with cement to form storable concrete blocks or melding it into logs of glass are other solutions (see "Yucca Mountain").

A much less constructive response, according to increasing complaints, has been the export of radioactive materials—in common with other hazardous wastes—to willing or unwitting recipient countries with less restrictive or costly controls and its illegal and unrecorded dumping at sea—now banned by the legally binding London Convention of 1993.

Exporting Waste

Regulations, community resistance, and steeply rising costs of disposal of hazardous wastes in the developed countries encouraged producers of those unwanted commodities to seek alternate areas for their disposition. Transboundary shipments of dangerous wastes became an increasingly attractive option for producers. In total, such cross-border movement amounted to tens of thousands of shipments annually by the early 1990s, with destinations including debt-ridden Eastern European countries and impoverished developing ones outside of Europe that were willing to trade a hole in the ground for hard currency. It was a trade, however, that increasingly aroused the ire and resistance of destination countries and, ultimately, elicited international agreements among both generating and receiving countries to cease the practice.

FIGURE 13.26 Storage tanks under construction in Hanford, Washington. Built to contain high-level radioactive waste, the tanks are shown before they were encased in concrete and buried underground. By the early 1990s, 66 of the 177 underground tanks were already known to be leaking.

The storage problem grows in size and complexity. Under current (1993) law, the federal government is to take possession of all spent fuel in 1998 and have a permanent storage site ready by 2010, but the proposed repository under Nevada's Yucca Mountain has been blocked by both technical difficulties and fierce political opposition. In the absence of an effective national program of radioactive waste storage, a 1995 decision by a federal Court of Appeals has, without public hearings or environmental studies of any kind, made more than 70 communities near nuclear generating plants the long-term repositories for spent nuclear fuel by permitting utilities to store radioactive wastes indefinitely at their nuclear power plants.

HUMAN ACTIONS AND ENVIRONMENTAL IMPACTS

For Your Consideration

YUCCA MOUNTAIN

If the U.S. government has its way, a long, low ridge in the basin-and-range region of Nevada will become America's first permanent repository for the deadly radioactive waste that nuclear power plants generate. If the opponents of the project have their way, however, Yucca Mountain will become a symbol of society's inability to solve a basic problem posed by nuclear power production: where to dispose of the used fuel. At present, no permanent disposal site for radioactive waste exists anywhere in the world.

In 1982, Congress ordered the Department of Energy (DOE) to construct a permanent repository by 1998 for the spent fuel of civilian nuclear power plants, as well as vast quantities of waste from the production of nuclear weapons. Yucca Mountain in southern

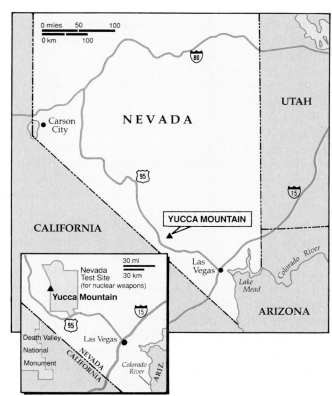

Nevada was selected in 1987 as the site for this high-level waste facility, which is intended to safely store wastes for 10,000 years, until radioactive decay has rendered them less hazardous than they are today. Most of the waste would be in the form of radioactive fuel pellets sealed in metal rods; these would be encased in extremely strong glass and placed in steel canisters entombed in chambers 300 meters (1000 ft.) below the Nevada desert. The steel containers would corrode in one or two centuries, after which the volcanic rock of the mountain would be responsible for containing radioactivity.

Plans now call for opening the repository in 2010, but many doubt that the Yucca Mountain facility will ever be completed and licensed. Three lines of concern have emerged. First, the storage area is vulnerable to both volcanic and earthquake activity, which could cause groundwater to well up suddenly and flood the repository. Yucca Mountain itself was formed from volcanic eruptions that occurred about 12 to 15 million years ago; some geologists are concerned that a new volcano could erupt within the mountain. Seven small cinder cones in the immediate area have erupted in recent times, the latest just 10,000 years ago. In addition, a number of seismic faults lie close to Yucca Mountain. One, the Ghost Dance Fault, runs right through the depository site. The epicenter of the 1992 earthquake at Little Skull Mountain was only 19 kilometers (12 mi.) from the proposed dump site.

Second, rainwater percolating down through the mountain could dissolve the waste itself, and the resulting toxic brew could seep down into the water table.

Finally, the Yucca Mountain site lies between the Nevada Test Site, which the DOE used as a nuclear bomb testing range, and the Nellis Air Force Base Bombing and Gunnery Range. Questions have been raised about the wisdom of locating a waste repository just a few kilometers from areas subject to underground explosions or aerial bombardment.

Questions:

1. *What are the advantages and disadvantages of permitting nuclear plants to operate when no system for disposing of their hazardous wastes exists?*

2. *Considering the uncertainties that would attend the irreversible underground entombment of high-level waste, do you think the government should instead pursue above-ground storage in a form that would allow for the continuous monitoring and retrieval of the wastes? Why or why not?*

3. *Plutonium, a spent fuel component, remains dangerously radioactive for 240,000 years. In your opinion, should such a material be stored in a repository intended to safely hold wastes for only 10,000 years? Do you think it realistic in any event to attach assurances of stability to any natural or human-designed containment facility over a period of tens of thousands of years? Why or why not?*

The Organization of African Unity in 1988 adopted a resolution condemning the dumping of all foreign wastes on that continent. More broadly and under the sponsorship of the United Nations, 117 countries in March of 1989 adopted a treaty—the Basel Convention on the Control of Transboundary Movements of Hazardous Wastes and Their Disposal—aimed at regulating the international trade in wastes. That regulation was to be achieved by requiring exporters to obtain consent from receiving countries before shipping waste and by requiring both exporter and importer countries to insure that the waste would be disposed of in an environmentally sound manner.

A still more restrictive convention was reached in March, 1994 when—with the United States dissenting—most Western industrialized countries agreed to ban the export of all poisonous or hazardous industrial wastes and residues to the developing world, the countries of Eastern Europe, and the former Soviet Union. United States' objections concerned the assumed prohibition on export of such materials as scrap metals for recycling within consenting receiving countries. Acknowledging those objections, the March, 1994, agreement was designed to take effect in two stages. The first was immediately effective and banned the 24 Western industrialized countries belonging to the Organization for Economic Cooperation and Development (except the United States) from sending hazardous waste for disposal in any nonmember country. The second stage, making it illegal to export wastes for "recycling and recovery"—believed to amount to about 90% of all such waste movements—was scheduled to become effective after December 31, 1997 following the September, 1995 treaty approval by members of the Basel Convention.

Prospects and Perspectives

Not surprisingly, the realities of the human impacts upon the environment that we have looked at in this chapter bring us directly back to ideas first presented in Chapter 2, at the start of our examination of the meaning of culture and the development of human geographic patterns on the surface of the earth. We noted there and see more clearly now that humans, in their increasing numbers and technical sophistication, have been able since the end of the last glaciation to alter for their own needs the physical landscapes they occupy. Humans, it is often observed, are the ecological dominant in the human–environmental equation that is the continuing focus of geographic inquiry.

That dominance has reflected itself in the increasing divergence of human societies as they increasingly separated themselves from common hunting-gathering origins, altering the environment they occupied as they each created their own cultural solutions to common concerns of sustenance and growth. Separate systems of exploitation of the environment were developed in and diffused from distinctive culture hearths. They were modified by the ever-expanding numbers of people occupying earth areas of differing carrying capacities and available resources. Gradually developing patterns of spatial interaction and exchange did not halt the creation of areally distinctive subsystems of culture or assure common methods of utilization of unequally distributed earth resources or environments. Sharp contrasts in levels of economic development and well-being emerged and persisted even as cultural convergence through shared technology began increasingly to unite societies throughout the world.

Each culture separately placed its imprint on the environment it occupied. In many cases—Chaco Canyon and Easter Island were our earlier examples—that imprint was ultimately destructive of the resources and environments upon which the cultures developed and depended. For human society collectively or single cultures separately, environmental damage or destruction is the unplanned consequence of the ecological dominance of humans. Our perpetual dilemma lies in the reality that what we need and want in support and supply from the environments we occupy generally exceeds in form and degree what they are able to yield in an unaltered state. To satisfy their felt needs, humans have learned to manipulate their environment. The greater those needs and the larger the populations with both needs and technical skills to satisfy them, the greater is the manipulation of the natural landscape. For as long as humans have occupied the earth the implicit but seldom addressed question has been not should we exploit and alter the environment, but how can we extract our requirements from the natural endowment without dissipating and destroying the basis of our support.

This final chapter detailing a few of the damaging pressures placed upon the environment by today's economies and cultures is not meant as a litany of despair. Rather it is a reminder of the potentially destructive ecological dominance of humans. Against the background of our now fuller understanding of human geographic patterns and interactions, this chapter is also meant to remind us yet again of the often repeated truism that everything is connected to everything else; we can never do just *one* thing. The ecological crises defined in this chapter and the human geographic patterns of interaction, contrast, and—occasionally—conflict observed in the preceding chapters show clearly and repeatedly how close and complex are the connections within the cultural world, and how intimately our created environment is joined to the physical landscape we all share.

There is growing awareness of those connections, of the adverse human impacts upon the natural world, and of the unity of all cultural and physical landscapes. Climatic change, air and water pollution, soil loss and desertification, refuse contamination, and a host of other environmental consequences and problems of intensifying human use of the earth are all matters of contemporary public debate and consideration. Awareness and concern of individuals are increasingly reflected by policies of environmental protection introduced by governments and supported or enforced by international conferences, compacts, and treaties. Acceptance of the interconnectedness and indivisibility of cultural and natural environments—the human creation and the physical endowment—is now more the rule than the exception.

Our understanding of those relationships is advanced by what we have learned of the human side of the human–environmental structure. We have seen that the seemingly infinitely complex diversity of human societies, economies, and interrelations is in fact logical, explicable, and far from random or arbitrary. We now have developed both a mental map of the cultural patterns and content of areas and an appreciation of the dynamics of their creation and operation. We must have that human geographic background—that sense of spatial interaction and unity of cultural, economic, and political patterns—to understand fully the relationship between our cultural world and the physical environment on which it ultimately depends. Only with that degree of human geographic awareness can we individually participate in an informed way in preserving and improving the increasingly difficult and delicate balance between the endowment of nature and our landscapes of culture.

activities, from the simplest forms of agriculture to modern industry, have an impact upon the biosphere. Cumulatively, in both developed and developing countries, that impact is now evident in the form of serious and threatening environmental deterioration. The atmosphere unites us all, and its global problems of greenhouse heating, ozone depletion, and particulate pollution endanger us all. Desertification, soil erosion, and tropical deforestation may appear to be local or regional problems, but they have worldwide implications of both environmental degradation and reduced population-supporting capacity. Freshwater supplies are deteriorating in quality and decreasing in sufficiency through contamination and competition. Finally, the inevitable end product of human use of the earth—the garbage and hazardous wastes of civilization—are beginning to overwhelm both sites and technologies of disposal.

We do not end our study of human geography on a note of despondency, however. We end with the conviction that the fuller knowledge we now have of the spatial patterns and structures of human cultural, economic, and political activities will aid in our understanding of the myriad ways in which human societies are bound to the physical landscapes they occupy—and which they have so substantially modified.

Summary

Cultural landscapes may buffer but cannot isolate societies from the physical environments they occupy. All human

KEY WORDS

acid rain   464
aquifer   476
biome   459
biosphere (ecosphere)   456
desertification   470
ecosystem   459
environment   456

environmental pollution   477
fallowing   473
greenhouse effect   461
hazardous waste   483
hydrologic cycle   475
icebox effect   459
limiting factor principle   478

ozone   465
rotation   473
soil   472
soil erosion   469
terracing   473
toxic waste   483

FOR REVIEW

1. What does the term *environment* mean? What is the distinction between the natural and the cultural environments? Can both be part of the physical environment we occupy?

2. What is the *biosphere* or *ecosphere?* What are its parts? How is the concept of *biome* related to that of the ecosphere?

3. Were there any evidences of human impact upon the natural environment prior to the Industrial Revolution? If so, can you provide examples? If not, can you explain why not?

4. Do we have any evidence of physical environmental change that

we cannot attribute to human action? Can we be certain that environmental change we observe today is attributable to human action? How?

5. What lines of reasoning and evidence suggest that human activity is altering global climates? What kind of alteration has occurred or is expected to occur? What do the terms *greenhouse* and *icebox effect* have to do with possible climatic futures?

6. What is *desertification?* What types of areas are particularly susceptible to desertification? What kinds of land uses are associated with it? How easily can its effects be overcome or reversed?

7. What agricultural techniques have been traditionally employed to reduce or halt soil erosion? Since these are known techniques that have been practiced throughout the world, why is there a current problem of soil erosion anywhere?

8. What effects has the increasing use of fossil fuels over the past 200 years had on the environment? What is *acid rain*, and where is it a problem? What factors affect the type and degree of air pollution found at a place? What is the relationship of *ozone* to *photochemical smog?*

9. Describe the chief sources of water pollution of which you are aware. How has the supply of freshwater

been affected by pollution and human use? When water is used, is it forever lost to the environment? If so, where does it go? If not, why should there be water shortages now in regions of formerly ample supply?

10. What methods do communities use to dispose of solid waste? Can *hazardous wastes* be treated in the same fashion? Since disposition of waste is a technical problem, why should there be any concern with waste disposal in modern advanced economies?

11. Suggest ways in which your study of human geography has increased your understanding of the relationship between the environments of culture and those of nature.

SELECTED REFERENCES

Abrahamson, Dean E., ed. *The Challenge of Global Warming.* Covelo, CA: Island Press, 1989.

Abramowitz, Janet N. *Imperiled Waters, Impoverished Future: The Decline of Freshwater Ecosystems.* Worldwatch Paper 128. Washington D.C.: Worldwatch Institute, 1996.

Bailey, Robert G. *Ecosystem Geography.* New York/Berlin: Springer Verlag, 1995.

Bell, Melinda. "Is Our Climate Unstable?" *Earth* 3, no. 1 (January 1994):24–31.

Broecker, Wallace S. "Global Warming on Trial." *Natural History* (April 1992):6–14.

Brown, Lester R., et al. *State of the World.* Washington, D.C.: Worldwatch Institute. Annual.

Brown, Lester R., and Edward C. Wolf. *Soil Erosion: Quiet Crisis in the World Economy.* Worldwatch Paper 60. Washington, D.C.: Worldwatch Institute, 1984.

Canada. Environment Canada. *The State of Canada's Environments.* Ottawa: Canada Communication Group–Publishing, 1992.

Carter, F. W., and David Turnock, eds. *Environmental Problems in Eastern Europe.* New York: Routledge, Chapman & Hall, 1993.

Cunningham, William P., and Barbara W. Saigo. *Environmental Science: A Global Concern.* 4th ed. Dubuque, IA: Wm. C. Brown, 1997.

Cutter, Susan, Hilary L. Renwick, and William H. Renwick. *Exploitation, Conservation, Preservation: A Geographical Perspective on Natural Resource Use.* 2d ed. New York: John Wiley & Sons, 1991.

"Desertification after the UNCED, Rio 1992." *GeoJournal* 31, no. 1 (September 1993). Special issue.

Dregne, Harold E. *Desertification of Arid Lands.* New York: Harwood Academic Publishers, 1983.

Durning, Alan T. *Saving the Forests: What Will It Take?* Worldwatch Paper 117. Washington, D.C.: Worldwatch Institute, 1993.

Durning, Alan T., and Holly B. Brough. *Taking Stock: Animal Farming and the Environment.* Worldwatch Paper 103. Washington, D.C.: Worldwatch Institute, 1991.

Elsom, Derek. *Atmospheric Pollution: A Global Problem.* 2d ed. Cambridge, MA: Blackwell, 1992.

Enger, Eldon D., and Bradley F. Smith. *Environmental Science: A Study of Interrelationships.* 5th ed. Dubuque, IA: Wm. C. Brown, 1995.

Falkenmark, Malin, and Carl Widstrand. "Population and Water Resources: A Delicate Balance." *Population Bulletin* 47, no. 1. Washington, D.C.: Population Reference Bureau, 1992.

Feshbach, Murray, and Alfred Friendly, Jr. *Ecocide in the USSR.* New York: Basic Books, 1992.

Flavin, Christopher. *Slowing Global Warming.* Worldwatch Paper 91. Washington, D.C.: Worldwatch Institute, 1989.

French, Hilary F. *Clearing the Air: A Global Agenda.* Worldwatch Paper 94. Washington, D.C.: Worldwatch Institute, 1990.

Getis, Judith. *You CAN Make a Difference: Help Protect the Earth.* Dubuque, IA: Wm. C. Brown, 1991.

Goldsmith, Edward, Peter Bunyard, Nicholas Hildyard, and Patrick McCully. *Imperiled Planet: Restoring Our Endangered Ecosystems.* Cambridge, MA: MIT Press, 1991.

Goudie, Andrew. *The Human Impact on the Natural Environment.* 4th ed. Cambridge, MA: Blackwell, 1993.

Goudie, Andrew, and Heather Viles. *The Earth Transformed: An Introduction to the Human Impact on the Environment.* Cambridge, MA: Blackwell, 1997.

Grainger, Alan. *Desertification: How People Make Deserts, How People Can Stop, and Why They Don't.* London: Earthscan/International Institute for Environment and Development, 1982.

Grove, Noel. "Air: An Atmosphere of Uncertainty." *National Geographic Magazine.* (April 1987):502–536.

Harrison, Paul. *The Third Revolution: Environment, Population, and a Sustainable World.* New York: St. Martin's Press, 1992.

Hulme, Mick, and Mick Kelly. "Desertification and Climate Change." *Environment* 35, no. 6 (July/August 1993):4–11, 39–45.

Jacobsen, Judith E., and John Firor, eds. *Human Impact on the Environment: Ancient Roots, Current Challenges.* Boulder, CO: Westview Press, 1992.

Jacobson, Jodi L. "Holding Back the Sea." *The Futurist.* (September/October 1990):20–27.

Kemp, David D. *Global Environmental Issues: A Climatological Approach.* 2d ed. New York: Routledge, 1995.

Lean, Geoffrey, and Don Hinrichsen, eds. *Atlas of the Environment.* World Wide Fund for Nature. Oxford, England: Helicon, 1992.

Lenssen, Nicholas. *Nuclear Waste: The Problem That Won't Go Away.* Worldwatch Paper 106. Washington, D.C.: Worldwatch Institute, 1991.

Longman, K. A., and J. Jeník. *Tropical Forest and Its Environment.* 2d ed. New York: Longman Scientific & Technical/John Wiley & Sons, 1987.

Mannion, A. M. *Global Environmental Change: A Natural and Cultural Environmental History.* New York: John Wiley & Sons, 1991.

Mason, Robert J., and Mark T. Mattson. *Atlas of U.S. Environmental Issues.* New York: Macmillan, 1991.

National Academy of Sciences. *One Earth, One Future: Our Changing Global Environment.* Washington, D.C.: National Academy Press, 1990.

Neal, Homer, and J. R. Schubel. *Solid Waste Management and the Environment.* Englewood Cliffs, NJ: Prentice-Hall, 1987.

Park, Chris C. *Tropical Rainforests.* London and New York: Routledge, 1992.

Postel, Sandra. *Air Pollution, Acid Rain, and the Future of Forests.* Worldwatch Paper 58. Washington, D.C.: Worldwatch Institute, 1984.

Postel, Sandra. *Last Oasis: Facing Water Scarcity.* New York: W. W. Norton, 1992.

Pryde, Phillip R., ed. *Environmental Resources and Constraints in the Former Soviet Republics.* Boulder, CO: Westview Press, 1995.

Pye, Veronica I., Ruth Patrick, and John Quarles. *Groundwater Contamination in the United States.* Philadelphia: University of Pennsylvania Press, 1983.

Roberts, Neil. *The Changing Global Environments.* Cambridge, MA: Blackwell, 1994.

Ryan, John C. *Life Support: Conserving Biological Diversity.* Worldwatch Paper 108. Washington, D.C.: Worldwatch Institute, 1992.

Scientific American 261, no. 3 (September 1989). Special issue: *Managing Planet Earth.*

Shukla, J., C. Nobre, and P. Sellers. "Amazon Deforestation and Climate Change." *Science* (March 16, 1990):1322–1325.

Simmons, I. G. *Changing the Face of the Earth: Culture, Environment, History.* 2nd ed. Cambridge, MA: Blackwell, 1997.

Simmons, I. G. *Earth, Air and Water: Resources and Environment in the Late 20th Century.* New York: Edward Arnold, 1991.

Thomas, David S. G., and Nicholas J. Middleton. *Desertification: Exploding the Myth.* New York: John Wiley & Sons, 1994.

Thomas, David S. G., and Nicholas J. Middleton. *World Atlas of Desertification.* United Nations Environmental Programme. London: Edward Arnold, 1992.

Thomas, William, ed. *Man's Role in Changing the Face of the Earth.* Chicago: University of Chicago Press, 1956.

Turner, B. L., II, et al. *The Earth as Transformed by Human Action: Global and Regional Changes in the Biosphere over the Past 300 Years.* Cambridge, England: Cambridge University Press, 1990.

Vogel, S. "Has Global Warming Begun?" *Earth* 4, no. 7 (December 1995):24–34.

"Water: The Power, Promise, and Turmoil of North America's Fresh Water." Special edition of *National Geographic* 184, no. 5A (November 1993).

Weber, Peter. *Abandoned Seas: Reversing the Decline of the Oceans.* Worldwatch Paper 116. Washington, D.C.: Worldwatch Institute, 1993.

White, R. M. "The Great Climate Debate." *Scientific American* 263 (1990):36–43.

Whyte, Ian D. *Climatic Change and Human Society.* New York: John Wiley and Sons, 1996.

Wilbanks, Thomas J. " 'Sustainable Development' in Geographic Perspective." *Annals of the Association of American Geographers* 84, no. 4 (1994):541–556.

Williams, Michael, ed. *Planet Management.* New York: Oxford University Press, 1993. The Illustrated Encyclopedia of World Geography.

World Bank. *Monitoring Environmental Progress: A Report on Work in Progress.* Washington, D.C.: The World Bank, 1995.

World Resources Institute/International Institute for Environment and Development. *World Resources.* Annual or biennial. New York: Oxford University Press.

Wyman, Richard L. *Global Climate Change and Life on Earth.* New York: Routledge, Chapman & Hall, 1991.

Young, John E. *Discarding the Throwaway Society.* Worldwatch Paper 101. Washington, D.C.: Worldwatch Institute, 1991.

Young, John E. *Mining the Earth.* Worldwatch Paper 109. Washington, D.C.: Worldwatch Institute, 1992.

Appendix A
Map Projections

 map projection is simply a system for displaying the curved surface of the earth on a flat sheet of paper. The definition is easy; the process is more difficult. No matter how one tries to "flatten" the earth, it can never be done in such a fashion as to show all earth details in their correct relative sizes, shapes, distances, or directions. Something is always wrong, and the cartographer's—the mapmaker's—task is to select and preserve those earth relationships important for the purpose at hand and to minimize or accept those distortions that are inevitable but unimportant.

Round Globe to Flat Map

The best way to model the earth's surface accurately, of course, would be to show it on a globe. But globes are not as convenient to use as flat maps and do not allow one to see the entire surface of the earth all at once. Nor can they show very much of the detailed content of areas. Even a very large globe of, say, 3 feet (nearly 1 meter) in diameter, compresses the physical or cultural information of some 130,000 square kilometers (about 50,000 sq. mi.) of earth surface into a space 2.5 centimeters (1 in.) on a side.

Geographers make two different demands on the maps they use to represent reality. One requirement is to show at one glance generalized relationships and spatial content of the entire world; the many world maps used in this and other geography textbooks and in atlases have that purpose. The other need is to show the detailed content of only portions of the earth's surface—cities, regions, countries, hemispheres—without reference to areas outside the zone of interest. Although the needs and problems of both kinds of maps differ, each starts with the same requirement: to transform a curved surface into a flat one.

If we look at the globe directly, only the front—the side facing us—is visible; the back is hidden (Figure A.1). To make a world map, we must decide on a way to flatten the

FIGURE A.1   An orthographic projection gives us a visually realistic view of the globe; its distortion towards the edges suggests the normal perspective appearance of a sphere viewed from a distance. Only a single hemisphere—one half of the globe—can be seen at a time, and only the central portion of that hemisphere avoids serious distortion of shape.

globe's curved surface on the hemisphere we can see. Then we have to cut the globe map down the middle of its hidden hemisphere and place the two back quarters on their respective sides of the already visible front half. In simple terms, we have to "peel" the map from the globe and flatten it in the same way we might try to peel an orange and flatten the skin. Inevitably, the peeling and flattening process will produce a resulting map that either shows tears or breaks in the surface (Figure A.2a) or is subject to uneven stretching or shrinking to make it lie flat (Figure A.2b).

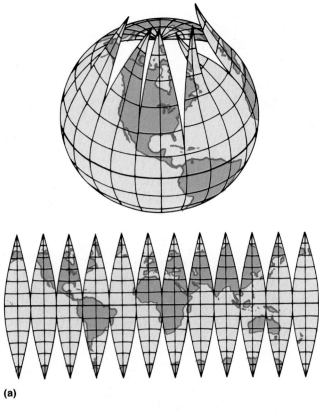

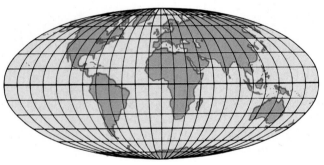

(a)

(b)

FIGURE A.2 (*a*) A careful "peeling" of the map from the globe yields a set of tapered "gores" which, although individually not showing much stretching or shrinking, do not collectively result in a very useful or understandable world map. (*b*) It is usually considered desirable to avoid or reduce the number of interruptions by depicting the entire global surface as a single flat circular, oval, or rectangular shape. That continuity of area, however, can be achieved only at the cost of considerable alteration of true shapes, distances, directions, or areas. Although the homolographic (Mollweide) projection shows areas correctly, it distorts shapes.

Projections—Geometrical and Mathematical

Of course, mapmakers do not physically engage in cutting, peeling, flattening, or stretching operations. Their task, rather, is to construct or *project* on a flat surface the network of parallels and meridians (the **graticule**) of the globe grid (see page 20). The idea of projections is perhaps easiest visualized by thinking of a transparent globe with an imagined light source located inside. Lines of latitude and longitude (or of coastlines or any other features) drawn on that globe will cast shadows on any nearby surface. A tracing of that shadow globe grid would represent a geometrical map projection.

In **geometrical** (or **perspective**) **projections,** the graticule is in theory visually transferred from the globe to a geometrical figure, such as a plane, cylinder, or cone, which in turn can be cut and then spread out flat (or *developed*) without any stretching or tearing. The surfaces of cylinders, cones, and planes are said to be **developable surfaces**—cylinders and cones can be cut and laid flat without distortion and planes are flat at the outset (Figure A.3). In actuality, geometrical projections are constructed not by tracing shadows but by the application of geometry and the use of lines, circles, arcs, and angles drawn on paper.

The location of the theoretical light source in relation to the globe surface can cause significant variation in the projection of the graticule on the developable geometric surface. An **orthographic** projection results from placement of the light source at infinity. A **gnomonic** projection is produced when the light source is at the center of the earth. When the light is placed at the *antipode*—the point exactly opposite the point of tangency (point of contact between globe and map)—a **stereographic** projection is produced (Figure A.4).

Although a few useful and common projections are based on these simple geometric means of production, most map designs can only be derived mathematically from tables of angles and dimensions separately developed for specific projections. The objective and need for **mathematical projections** is to preserve and emphasize specific earth relationships that cannot be recorded by the perspective globe and shadow approach. The graticule of each mathematical projection is orderly and "accurate" in the sense of displaying the correct locations of lines of latitude and longitude. Each projection scheme, however, presents a different arrangement of the globe grid to minimize or eliminate some of the distortions inherent in projecting from a curved to a flat surface. Every projection represents a compromise or deviation from reality to achieve a selected purpose, but in the process of adjustment or compromise each inevitably contains specific, accepted distortions.

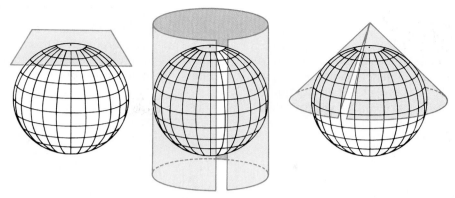

FIGURE A.3   The theory of *geometrical projections*. The three common geometric forms used in projections are the plane, the cylinder, and the cone.

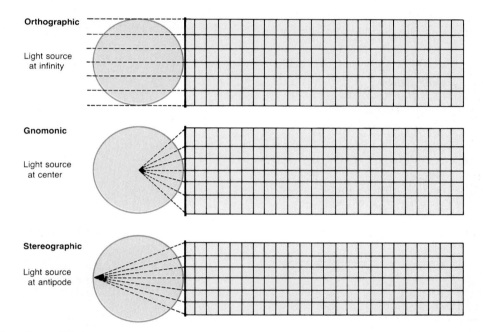

FIGURE A.4   The effect of light source location on planar surface projections. Note the variations in spacing of lines of latitude that occur when the light source is moved.

Globe Properties and Map Distortions

The true properties of the global grid are detailed on pages 20–21. Not all of those grid realities can ever be preserved in any single projection; projections invariably distort some or all of them. The result is that all flat maps, whether geometrically or mathematically derived, also distort in different ways and to different degrees some or all of the four main properties of actual earth surface relationships: area, shape, distance, and direction.

Area

Cartographers use **equal-area** or **equivalent** projections when it is important for the map to show the *areas* of regions in correct or constant proportion to earth reality—as it

is when the map is intended to show the actual areal extent of a phenomenon on the earth's surface. If we wish to compare the amount of land in agriculture in two different parts of the world, for example, it would be very misleading visually to use a map that represented the same amount of surface area at two different scales.[1] To retain the needed size comparability, our chosen projection must assure that a unit area drawn anywhere on it will always represent the same

[1]**Scale** is the relationship between the size of a feature or length of a line on the map and that same feature or line on the earth's surface. It may be indicated on a map as a ratio—for example, 1:1,000,000—that tells us the relationship between a unit of measure on the map and that same unit on the earth's surface. In our example, 1 centimeter of map distance equals 1 million centimeters (or 10 kilometers) of actual earth distance. See Figure 1.20.

number of square kilometers (or similar units) on the earth's surface. To achieve *equivalence,* any scale change that the projection imposes in one direction must be offset by compensating changes in the opposite direction. As a result, the shape of the portrayed area is inevitably distorted. A square on the earth, for example, may become a rectangle on the map, but that rectangle has the correct area (Figure A.5). *A map that shows correct areal relationships always distorts the shapes of regions,* as Figure A.6*a* demonstrates.

Shape

Although no projection can reproduce correct shapes for large areas, some do accurately portray the shapes of small areas. These true-shape projections are called **conformal,** and the importance of *conformality* is that regions and features "look right" and have the correct directional relationships. They achieve these properties for small areas by assuring that lines of latitude and longitude cross each other

at right angles and that the scale is the same in all directions at any given location. Both these conditions exist on the globe but can be retained for only relatively small areas on maps. Because that is so, the shapes of large regions—continents, for example—are always different from their true

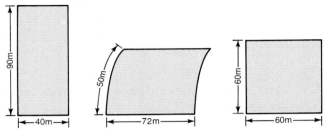

FIGURE A.5   These three figures are all equal in area despite their different dimensions and shapes.

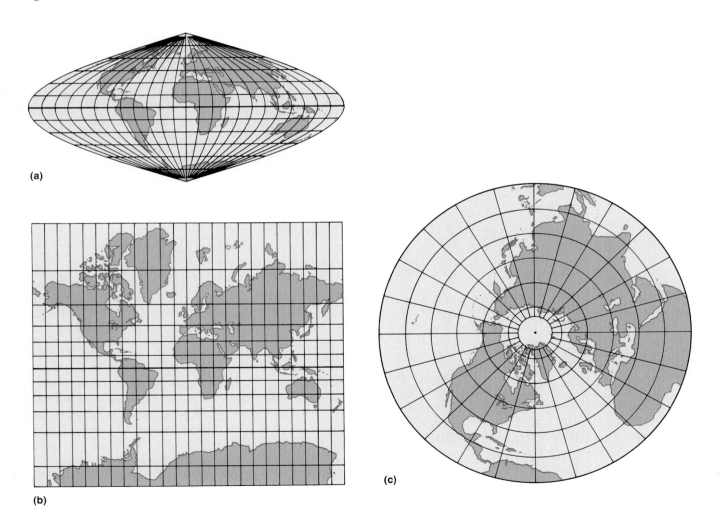

(a)

(b)

(c)

FIGURE A.6   Sample projections demonstrating specific map properties. (*a*) The equal-area sinusoidal projection retains everywhere the property of *equivalence.* (*b*) The mathematically-derived Mercator projection is *conformal,* displaying true shapes of individual features but greatly exaggerating sizes and distorting shapes away from the equator. (*c*) A portion of an azimuthal *equidistant* projection, polar case. Distances from the center (North Pole) to any other point are true; extension of the grid to the Southern Hemisphere would show the South Pole infinitely stretched to form the circumference of the map.

earth shapes even on conformal maps. Except for maps for very small areas, *a map cannot be both equivalent and conformal;* these two properties are mutually exclusive, as Figure A.6*b* suggests.

Distance

Distance relationships are nearly always distorted on a map, but some projections do maintain true distances in one direction or along certain selected lines. True distance relationships simply mean that the length of a straight line between two points on the map correctly represents the *great circle* distance between those points on the earth. (An arc of a great circle is the shortest distance between two points on the earth's curved surface; the equator is a great circle and all meridians of longitude are half great circles.) Projections with this property can be designed, but even on such **equidistant** maps true distance in all directions is shown only from one or two central points. Distances between all other locations are incorrect and, quite likely, greatly distorted as Figure A.6*c* clearly shows.

Direction

As is true of distances, directions between all points on a map cannot be shown without distortion. On **azimuthal** projections, however, true directions are shown from one central point to all other points. (An *azimuth* is the angle formed at the beginning point of a straight line, in relation to a meridian.) The azimuthal property of a projection is not exclusive but may be combined with equivalency, conformality, and equal distance. The azimuthal equal-distance ("equidistant") map shown as Figure A.6*c* is, as well, a true-direction map from the same North Pole origin. Another more specialized example is the gnomonic projection, displayed as Figure A.7.

Classes of Projections

Although there are many hundreds of different projections, the great majority of them can be grouped into four primary classes or families based on their origin. Each family has its own distinctive outline, set of similar properties, and pattern of distortions. Three of them are easily seen as derived from the geometric or perspective projection of the globe grid onto the developable surfaces of cylinders, cones, and planes. The fourth class is mathematically derived; its members have a variety of attributes but share a general oval design (Figure A.8).

Cylindrical Projections

Cylindrical projections are developed geometrically or mathematically from a cylinder wrapped around the globe. Usually, the cylinder is tangent at the equator, which thus becomes the **standard line**—that is, transferred from the globe without distortion. The result is a globe grid network with meridians and parallels intersecting at right angles. There is no scale distortion along the standard line of tan-

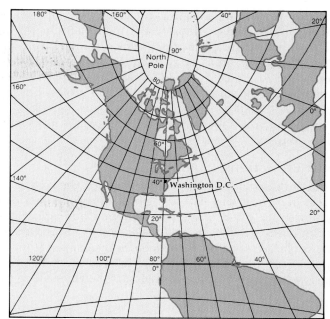

FIGURE A.7   A gnomonic projection centered on Washington, D.C. In this geometrical projection the light source is at the center of the globe (see Figure A.4) and the capital city marks the "standard point" where the projection plane is in contact with the globe. The rapid outward increase in graticule spacing makes it a projection impractical for more than a portion of a hemisphere. A unique property of the gnomonic projection is that it is the only projection on which all great circles appear as straight lines.

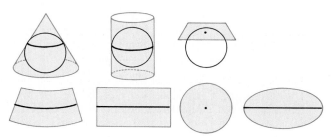

FIGURE A.8   Shape consistencies within families of projections. When the surface of cone, cylinder, or plane is made *tangent*—that is, comes into contact with the globe—at either a point or along a circle and then "developed," a characteristic family outline results. The tangent lines and point are indicated. A fourth common shape, the oval, may reflect a design in which the long dimension is a great circle comparable to the tangent line of the cylinder.

gency, but distortion increases with increasing distance away from it. The result is a rectangular world map with acceptable low-latitude representation, but with enormous areal exaggeration toward the poles.

The mathematically derived Mercator projection invented in 1569 is a special familiar but commonly misused cylindrical projection (Figure A.6*b*). Its sole original purpose was to serve as a navigational chart of the world with the special advantage of showing true compass headings, or *rhumb lines,* as straight lines on the map. Its frequent use in wall or book maps gives grossly exaggerated impressions of the size of land areas away from the tropics. Equal-area alternatives to the conformal Mercator map are available, and a number of "compromise" cylindrical projections that are neither equal area nor conformal (for example, the Miller projection, Figure A.9*a*) are frequently used bases for world maps.

Conic Projections

Of the three developable geometric surfaces, the cone is the closest in form to one-half of a globe. **Conic projections,** therefore, are often employed to depict hemispheric or smaller parts of the earth. In the *simple conic* projection the cone is placed tangent to the globe along a single standard parallel, with the apex of the cone located above the pole. The cone can also be made to intersect the globe along two or more lines, with a *polyconic* projection resulting; the increased number of standard lines reduces the distortion which otherwise increases away from the standard parallel. The projection of the grid on the cone yields evenly spaced straight-line meridians radiating from the pole and parallels that are arcs of circles. Although conic projections can be adjusted to minimize distortions and become either equivalent or conformal, by their nature they can never show the whole globe. In fact, they are most useful for and generally restricted to maps of midlatitude regions of greater east-west than north-south extent. The Albers equal-area projection often used for United States maps is a familiar example (Figure A.9*b*).

Planar (Azimuthal) Projections

Planar (or **azimuthal**) **projections** are constructed by placing a plane tangent to the globe at a single point. Although the plane may touch the globe anywhere the cartographer

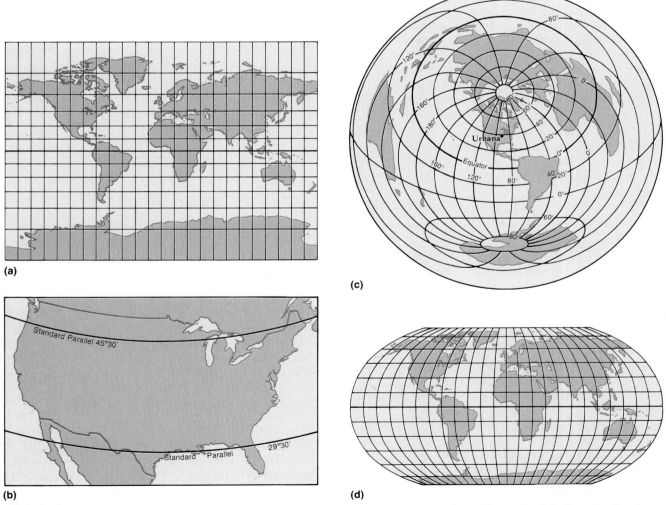

FIGURE A.9 Some sample members of the principal projection families. (*a*) The Miller cylindrical projection is mathematically derived. (*b*) The Albers equal-area conic projection, used for many official United States maps, has two standard parallels: 29 1/2° and 45 1/2° (*c*) A planar or azimuthal equidistant projection centered on Urbana, Illinois. (*d*) The Robinson projection of the oval family; neither conformal or equivalent, it was designed as a visually satisfactory world map.

wishes, the polar case with the plane centered on either the North or the South Pole is easiest to visualize (Figure A.6c). This equidistant projection is useful because it can be centered anywhere, facilitating the correct measurement of distances from that point to all others. When the plane is tangent at places other than the poles, the meridians and the parallels become curiously curved (Figure A.9c).

Planar maps are commonly used in atlases because they are particularly well suited for showing the arrangement of polar landmasses. Depending on the particular projection used, true shape, equal area, or some compromise between them can be depicted. The special quality of the planar gnomonic projection has already been shown in Figure A.7.

Oval or Elliptical Projections

Oval or elliptical projections have been mathematically developed usually as compromise projections designed to display the entire world in a fashion that is visually acceptable and suggestive of the curvature of the globe. In most, the equator and a central meridian (usually the prime meridian) are the standard lines. They cross in the middle of the map which thus becomes the point of no distortion. Parallels are, as a rule, parallel straight lines; meridians, except for the standard meridian, are shown as curved lines. In some instances the oval projection is a modification of one of different original shape. The world maps in this text, for example, are an oval adjustment of the circular (but not azimuthal) Van der Grinten projection (Figure A.10a), a compromise projection that achieves acceptable degrees of equivalence and conformality in lower and middle latitudes but becomes increasingly and unacceptably distorted in polar regions.

Other Projections and Manipulations

Projections can be developed mathematically to show the world or a portion of it in any shape that is desired: ovals are most common, but hearts, trapezoids, stars, and other—sometimes bizarre—forms have been devised for special purposes. One often-seen projection is the equal-area Goode's homolosine, an "interrupted" projection that is actually a product of fitting together the least distorted portions of two different projections and centering the split map along multiple standard meridians to minimize distortion of either (as desired) land or ocean surfaces (Figure A.10b).

The homolosine map clearly shows how projections may be manipulated or adjusted to achieve desired objectives. Since most projections are based on a mathematically consistent rendering of the actual globe grid, possibilities for such manipulation are nearly unlimited. Map properties to be retained, size and shape of areas to be displayed, and overall map design to be achieved may influence the cartographer's choices in reproducing the globe grid on the flat map.

Special effects and properties may also be achieved geometrically by adjusting the aspect of the projection.

Aspect simply means the positional relationship between the globe and the developable surface on which it is visually projected. Although the fundamental distortion pattern of any given projection system onto any of the developable surfaces will remain constant, shifting of the point or line of tangency will materially alter the appearance of the graticule and of the geographical features shown on the map.

Although an infinite number of aspects are possible for any of the geometric projections, three classes of aspects are most common. Named according to the relation of the axis of the globe to the cylinder, plane, or oval projection surface, the three classes are usually called *equatorial, polar,* and *oblique.* In the equatorial, the axis of the globe parallels the orientation of the plane, cylinder, or cone; a parallel, usually the central equator, is the line of tangency. In the polar aspect, the axis of the globe is perpendicular to the orientation of the developable surface. In the oblique aspect, the axis of the globe makes an oblique angle with the orientation of the developable surface and a complex arrangement of the graticule results.

A Cautionary Reminder

Mapmakers must be conscious of the properties of the projections they use, selecting the one that best suits their purposes. It is not ever possible to transform the globe into a flat map without distortion. But cartographers have devised hundreds of possible mathematical and geometrical projections in various modifications and aspects to display to their best advantage the variety of earth features and relationships they wish to emphasize. Some projections are highly specialized and properly restricted to a single limited purpose; others achieve a more general acceptability and utility.

If the map shows only a small area, the choice of a projection is not critical—virtually any can be used. The choice becomes more important when the area to be shown extends over a considerable longitude and latitude; then the selection of a projection clearly depends on the purpose of the map. As we have seen, Mercator or gnomonic projections are useful for navigation. If numerical data are being mapped, the relative sizes of the areas involved should be correct and equivalence is the sought-after map property. Conformality and equal distance may be required in other instances.

While selection of an appropriate projection is the task of the cartographer, understanding the consequences of that selection and recognizing and allowing for the distortions inevitable in all flat maps are the responsibility of the map reader. When skillfully designed maps are read by knowledgeable users, clear and accurate conveyance of spatial information and earth relationships is made convenient and natural.

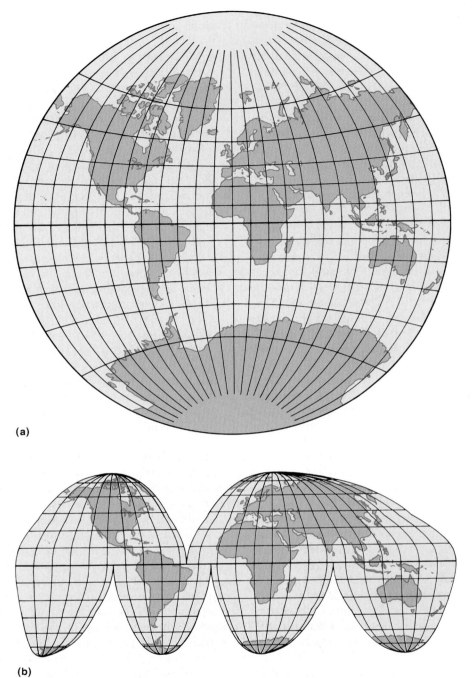

FIGURE A.10 (*a*) The full Van der Grinten projection; (*b*) Goode's interrupted homolosine grafts an upper latitude homolographic (Mollweide) onto a sinusoidal projection.

SELECTED REFERENCES

American Cartographic Association, Committee on Map Projections. *Choosing a World Map: Attributes, Distortions, Classes, Aspects.* Special Publication No. 2. Falls Church, VA: American Congress on Surveying and Mapping, 1988.

American Cartographic Association, Committee on Map Projections. *Matching the Map Projection to the Need.* Special Publication No. 3. Bethesda, MD: American Congress on Surveying and Mapping, 1991.

American Cartographic Association, Committee on Map Projections. *Which Map is Best? Projections for World Maps.* Special Publication No. 1. Falls Church, VA: American Congress on Surveying and Mapping, 1986.

Campbell, John. *Introductory Cartography.* 2d ed. Dubuque, IA: Wm. C. Brown, 1991.

Campbell, John. *Map Use and Analysis.* 2d ed. Dubuque, IA: Wm. C. Brown, 1991.

Deetz, Charles H., and Oscar S. Adams. *Elements of Map Projection.* United States Department of Commerce, Special Publication No. 68. Washington, D.C.: USGPO, 1945.

Snyder, John P. *Flattening the Earth: Two Thousand Years of Map Projections.* Chicago, IL: University of Chicago Press, 1993.

Snyder, John P. *Map Projections—A Working Manual.* U.S. Geological Survey Professional Paper 1395. Washington, D.C.: Department of the Interior, 1987.

Steers, J. A. *An Introduction to the Study of Map Projections.* London: University of London Press, 1962.

APPENDIX B
1996 WORLD POPULATION DATA

	Population Mid-1996 (millions)	Births per 1,000	Deaths per 1,000	Natural Increase (annual, %)	"Doubling Time" in Years at Current Rate	Projected Population (millions) 2010	Projected Population (millions) 2025	Infant Mortality Rate[a]	Total Fertility Rate[b]	Percent Age <15	Percent Age 65+	Life Expectancy at Birth (years) Total	Male	Female	Percent Urban	Adult Literacy Rate (%)	% with Access to Safe Water	Per Capita GNP 1994 (US $)
World	5,771	24	9	1.5	46	6,974	8,193	62	3.0	32	6	66	64	68	43	—	—	$4,740
More Developed	1,171	12	10	0.1	501	1,231	1,268	9	1.6	20	14	74	70	78	75	—	—	18,130
Less Developed	4,600	27	9	1.9	37	5,743	6,925	68	3.4	35	5	64	62	65	35	68	69	1,090
Less Developed (Excluding China)	3,383	31	10	2.2	32	4,356	5,433	73	4.0	38	4	61	60	63	38	—	—	1,320
Africa	732	41	13	2.8	25	1,039	1,462	91	5.7	44	3	55	53	56	31	—	—	660
Sub-Saharan Africa	597	44	14	2.9	24	867	1,248	96	6.1	46	3	52	51	54	27	54	43	550
Northern Africa	164	32	8	2.4	29	215	272	64	4.3	40	4	64	62	65	45	—	—	1,100
Algeria	29.0	30	6	2.4	29	38.0	47.2	55	4.3	40	4	67	67	68	50	57	78	1,690
Egypt	63.7	30	7	2.2	31	80.7	97.6	62	3.6	40	4	64	62	65	44	49	90	710
Libya	5.4	45	8	3.7	19	8.9	14.4	63	6.4	45	3	64	62	66	85	72	97	—
Morocco	27.6	29	6	2.2	31	34.2	40.7	57	4.0	38	5	68	66	70	47	41	61	1,150
Sudan	28.9	42	12	3.0	23	41.5	58.4	80	6.1	43	3	54	53	55	27	43	48	—
Tunisia	9.2	23	6	1.7	41	11.3	13.4	43	3.4	37	5	68	67	69	60	63	68	1,800
Western Sahara	0.2	47	19	2.8	25	0.3	0.4	152	7.0	—	—	46	45	47	—	—	—	—
Western Africa	204	45	14	3.1	23	310	463	92	6.1	46	3	53	52	54	24	—	—	330
Benin	5.6	49	18	3.1	22	8.3	12.3	86	7.1	47	3	48	46	49	36	33	50	370
Burkina Faso	10.6	47	19	2.8	24	14.5	20.9	94	6.9	48	3	45	44	46	15	17	56	300
Cape Verde	0.4	27	8	1.9	36	0.6	0.7	65	4.1	45	6	65	64	66	44	66	74	910
Côte d'Ivoire	14.7	50	15	3.5	20	22.1	33.4	88	5.7	47	2	51	50	52	46	37	83	510
Gambia	1.2	48	21	2.7	26	1.6	2.1	90	5.9	45	2	50	48	52	26	36	77	360
Ghana	18.0	42	12	3.0	23	26.6	38.0	66	5.5	45	3	56	54	58	36	61	56	430
Guinea	7.4	44	20	2.4	29	9.5	13.1	139	5.9	44	3	44	42	46	29	33	33	510
Guinea-Bissau	1.1	43	21	2.1	32	1.5	2.0	140	5.8	43	3	44	42	45	22	52	25	240
Liberia	2.1	44	12	3.1	22	4.5	6.8	113	6.4	44	3	58	55	60	44	35	54	—
Mali	9.7	52	20	3.1	22	15.0	23.7	106	7.3	48	3	46	44	48	26	27	49	250
Mauritania	2.3	39	14	2.5	28	3.3	4.4	101	5.0	45	4	52	50	53	39	36	66	480

	Population Mid-1996 (millions)	Births per 1,000	Deaths per 1,000	Natural Increase (annual, %)	"Doubling Time" in Years at Current Rate	Projected Population (millions)		Infant Mortality Rate[a]	Total Fertility Rate[b]	Percent Age		Life Expectancy at Birth (years)			Percent Urban	Adult Literacy Rate (%)	% with Access to Safe Water	Per Capita GNP 1994 (US $)
						2010	2025			< 15	65 +	Total	Male	Female				
Niger	9.5	53	19	3.4	21	14.8	22.4	123	7.4	49	3	47	45	48	15	12	59	230
Nigeria	103.9	43	12	3.1	22	162.0	246.0	87	6.0	45	3	56	55	58	16	53	46	280
Senegal	8.5	43	16	2.7	26	12.2	16.9	68	6.0	45	3	49	48	50	43	31	55	610
Sierra Leone	4.6	46	19	2.7	26	6.4	8.7	143	6.2	44	3	46	44	47	35	29	42	150
Togo	4.6	47	11	3.6	19	7.4	11.7	89	6.9	49	2	57	55	59	30	48	71	320
Eastern Africa	**227**	**45**	**15**	**2.9**	**24**	**322**	**456**	**106**	**6.3**	**47**	**3**	**50**	**48**	**51**	**21**	**—**	**—**	**210**
Burundi	5.9	46	16	3.0	23	8.6	12.2	102	6.6	46	4	50	48	52	6	33	37	150
Comoros	0.6	47	11	3.6	20	0.9	1.4	80	6.8	48	3	58	56	60	29	56	—	510
Djibouti	0.6	38	16	2.2	32	0.8	1.1	115	5.8	41	2	48	47	50	77	43	43	780
Eritrea	3.6	43	15	2.8	25	5.2	7.0	105	6.1	44	3	50	49	52	17	—	—	—
Ethiopia	57.2	46	16	3.1	23	90.0	129.7	120	6.8	49	3	50	48	52	15	33	18	130
Kenya	28.2	40	13	2.7	25	38.0	49.1	62	5.4	48	3	51	49	52	27	75	28	260
Madagascar	15.2	44	12	3.2	22	23.3	34.4	93	6.1	46	3	57	55	58	26	81	30	230
Malawi	9.5	50	20	3.0	23	12.7	18.5	134	6.7	48	3	46	45	46	17	54	53	140
Mauritius	1.1	20	7	1.3	54	1.3	1.5	18.1	2.4	29	6	69	65	73	44	81	100	3,180
Mozambique	16.5	45	19	2.7	26	24.7	35.1	148	6.5	46	2	46	45	48	33	37	24	80
Reunion	0.7	21	6	1.6	44	0.8	0.9	8	2.3	31	6	73	69	77	73	—	—	—
Rwanda	6.9	44	17	2.7	25	9.2	13.7	110	6.2	48	3	47	46	49	5	57	64	210
Seychelles	0.1	23	8	1.5	46	0.1	0.1	12.9	2.7	31	7	70	68	73	50	—	—	6,210
Somalia	9.5	50	19	3.2	22	14.5	21.3	122	7.0	48	3	47	45	49	24	27	56	—
Tanzania	29.1	43	14	3.0	23	38.7	56.3	92	6.3	47	3	49	47	50	21	64	52	90
Uganda	22.0	52	19	3.3	21	26.7	37.4	115	7.3	47	3	45	44	46	11	59	21	200
Zambia	9.2	45	15	3.0	23	12.6	18.5	107	6.5	47	3	49	48	50	42	75	59	350
Zimbabwe	11.5	35	9	2.5	28	14.1	17.3	53	4.4	45	3	62	61	62	31	83	36	490
Middle Africa	**86**	**46**	**16**	**2.9**	**24**	**126**	**189**	**106**	**6.3**	**46**	**3**	**49**	**47**	**51**	**33**	**—**	**—**	**—**
Angola	11.5	47	20	2.7	26	17.7	26.6	137	6.5	45	3	46	44	48	32	43	50	—
Cameroon	13.6	41	12	2.9	24	20.2	29.2	65	5.9	44	4	56	55	58	41	60	34	680
Central African Republic	3.3	42	17	2.5	28	3.9	5.2	97	5.1	43	3	49	47	52	39	54	12	370
Chad	6.5	44	18	2.6	27	9.3	12.9	122	5.9	41	3	48	46	49	22	45	—	190
Congo	2.5	40	17	2.3	31	3.2	4.2	109	5.2	44	3	46	44	48	58	71	20	610
Equatorial Guinea	0.4	41	15	2.6	27	0.6	0.9	103	5.3	43	4	52	50	54	37	75	—	430
Gabon	1.2	29	14	1.5	47	1.4	1.8	95	5.0	34	5	55	52	58	73	59	72	3,550
Sao Tome and Principe	0.1	35	9	2.6	26	0.2	0.2	50.8	4.5	47	4	63	62	65	46	—	—	250
Zaire	46.5	48	16	3.2	22	69.1	107.6	108	6.6	48	3	48	46	50	29	74	34	—
Southern Africa	**51**	**32**	**8**	**2.4**	**29**	**66**	**82**	**49**	**4.3**	**38**	**4**	**65**	**62**	**67**	**53**	**—**	**—**	**2,840**
Botswana	1.5	38	11	2.7	26	2.2	3.0	41	5.0	43	5	66	64	71	46	67	56	2,800
Lesotho	2.1	38	12	2.6	27	2.9	3.8	79	5.2	41	5	55	54	57	16	69	46	700
Namibia	1.6	37	11	2.7	26	2.2	3.0	57	5.4	42	5	59	58	60	32	40	52	2,030
South Africa	44.5	31	8	2.3	30	57.5	70.1	46	4.1	37	5	66	63	68	57	81	—	3,010
Swaziland	1.0	43	11	3.2	22	1.6	2.5	93	6.1	46	2	56	52	61	30	74	30	1,160
North America	**295**	**15**	**9**	**0.6**	**114**	**331**	**372**	**7**	**2.0**	**22**	**13**	**76**	**73**	**79**	**75**	**+**	**+**	**25,220**
Canada	30.0	13	7	0.6	116	33.6	36.6	6.2	1.6	21	12	78	74	81	77	+	+	19,570
United States	265.2	15	9	0.6	114	297.7	335.1	7.5	2.0	22	13	76	72	79	75	+	+	25,860

	Population Mid-1996 (millions)	Births per 1,000	Deaths per 1,000	Natural Increase (annual, %)	"Doubling Time" in Years at Current Rate	Projected Population (millions) 2010	Projected Population (millions) 2025	Infant Mortality Rate[a]	Total Fertility Rate[b]	Percent Age <15	Percent Age 65+	Life Expectancy Total	Life Expectancy Male	Life Expectancy Female	Percent Urban	Adult Literacy Rate (%)	% with Access to Safe Water	Per Capita GNP 1994 (US $)
Latin America and the Caribbean	**486**	**26**	**7**	**1.9**	**36**	**584**	**678**	**43**	**3.1**	**35**	**5**	**69**	**66**	**72**	**71**	**86**	**80**	**3,290**
Central America	**127**	**28**	**5**	**2.3**	**30**	**162**	**197**	**37**	**3.4**	**37**	**4**	**71**	**68**	**74**	**65**	**—**	**—**	**3,310**
Belize	0.2	38	5	3.3	21	0.3	0.4	34	4.5	44	4	72	70	74	48	96	73	2,550
Costa Rica	3.6	26	4	2.2	31	4.6	5.5	13.0	3.1	34	5	76	74	79	44	94	94	2,380
El Salvador	5.9	32	6	2.6	27	7.4	9.2	41	3.8	40	4	68	65	70	45	70	43	1,480
Guatemala	9.9	36	7	2.9	24	13.4	17.0	51	5.1	45	3	65	62	67	39	54	61	1,190
Honduras	5.6	34	6	2.8	25	7.6	9.7	50	5.2	45	3	68	66	71	47	71	70	580
Mexico	94.8	27	5	2.2	32	119.0	142.1	34	3.1	36	4	73	70	76	71	89	78	4,010
Nicaragua	4.6	33	6	2.7	26	6.7	9.1	49	4.6	44	3	65	62	68	63	65	53	330
Panama	2.7	22	4	1.8	39	3.2	3.8	18	3.0	33	5	73	71	75	55	90	83	2,670
Caribbean	**36**	**23**	**8**	**1.5**	**45**	**41**	**47**	**42**	**2.8**	**31**	**7**	**69**	**67**	**72**	**60**	**—**	**—**	**—**
Antigua and Barbuda	0.1	18	6	1.2	58	0.1	0.1	18	1.7	25	6	73	71	75	31	96	100	6,970
Bahamas	0.3	18	5	1.3	52	0.3	0.4	23.8	1.9	29	5	72	68	75	84	98	100	11,790
Barbados	0.3	14	9	0.5	133	0.3	0.3	9.1	1.6	24	12	76	73	78	38	97	100	6,530
Cuba	11.0	14	7	0.7	102	11.8	12.4	9.4	1.5	22	9	75	73	77	74	95	98	—
Dominica	0.1	20	7	1.3	55	0.1	0.1	18.4	2.1	32	10	78	74	80	61	97	96	2,830
Dominican Republic	8.1	29	6	2.3	31	9.9	11.7	52	3.3	37	4	68	66	71	61	81	67	1,320
Grenada	0.1	29	6	2.4	29	0.1	0.2	12	3.8	43	5	71	68	73	—	98	—	2,620
Guadeloupe	0.4	18	6	1.2	56	0.5	0.5	10.3	2.0	26	9	75	71	78	48	—	—	—
Haiti	7.3	35	12	2.3	30	8.8	11.2	74	4.8	40	4	57	55	58	32	43	41	220
Jamaica	2.6	24	5	1.8	38	2.9	3.3	24.0	3.0	34	7	74	71	76	53	84	100	1,420
Martinique	0.4	15	6	0.9	75	0.5	0.5	6	1.7	24	10	76	73	79	81	—	—	—
Netherlands Antilles	0.2	20	7	1.3	53	0.2	0.3	6.3	2.2	26	7	75	72	78	92	—	—	—
Puerto Rico	3.8	17	8	1.0	71	4.0	4.3	11.5	2.1	27	10	74	70	79	73	—	—	7,000[g]
St. Kitts-Nevis	0.04	22	9	1.3	54	0.1	0.1	24	2.4	32	9	69	66	71	42	99	100	4,760
Saint Lucia	0.1	26	6	2.0	35	0.2	0.2	23.0	3.1	37	7	72	69	75	48	93	—	3,450
St. Vincent and the Grenadines	0.1	25	7	1.8	38	0.1	0.2	17	3.1	37	6	73	71	74	25	98	89	2,120
Trinidad and Tobago	1.3	18	7	1.2	60	1.3	1.4	12.2	2.2	31	6	71	68	73	65	97	96	3,740
South America	**323**	**25**	**7**	**1.8**	**39**	**380**	**434**	**46**	**3.0**	**34**	**5**	**68**	**65**	**71**	**75**	**—**	**—**	**3,360**
Argentina	34.7	20	8	1.2	58	40.9	46.5	22.9	2.7	31	9	72	69	76	87	96	71	8,060
Bolivia	7.6	36	10	2.6	27	10.2	13.1	71	4.8	41	4	60	59	62	58	81	66	770
Brazil	160.5	25	8	1.7	41	181.9	202.3	58	2.8	34	4	66	64	69	76	82	87	3,370
Chile	14.5	21	6	1.6	45	16.5	18.1	13.1	2.5	30	7	72	69	76	85	95	86	3,560
Colombia	38.0	27	6	2.1	33	45.9	52.7	28	3.0	33	4	69	66	72	67	90	92	1,620
Ecuador	11.7	29	6	2.3	31	14.9	17.8	40	3.6	36	4	69	66	71	59	88	70	1,310
Guyana	0.7	25	7	1.8	39	0.8	0.8	48	2.6	38	4	65	62	68	33	98	—	530
Paraguay	5.0	34	6	2.8	25	7.0	9.4	38	4.5	42	4	69	66	71	50	91	34	1,570
Peru	24.0	29	7	2.1	33	29.4	33.9	60	3.5	36	4	66	64	68	70	87	58	1,890
Suriname	0.4	23	6	1.6	43	0.5	0.6	28	2.4	35	5	70	68	73	49	92	—	870
Uruguay	3.2	18	10	0.8	84	3.5	3.7	20.1	2.3	26	12	73	69	76	90	97	84	4,650
Venezuela	22.3	26	5	2.1	33	28.7	34.8	23.5	3.1	38	4	72	69	75	84	90	89	2,760

	Population Mid-1996 (millions)	Births per 1,000	Deaths per 1,000	Natural Increase (annual, %)	"Doubling Time" in Years at Current Rate	Projected Population (millions) 2010	Projected Population (millions) 2025	Infant Mortality Rate[a]	Total Fertility Rate[b]	Percent Age <15	Percent Age 65+	Life Expectancy Total	Life Expectancy Male	Life Expectancy Female	Percent Urban	Adult Literacy Rate (%)	% with Access to Safe Water	Per Capita GNP 1994 (US $)
Asia	**3,501**	**24**	**8**	**1.6**	**43**	**4,240**	**4,898**	**62**	**2.9**	**32**	**5**	**65**	**64**	**67**	**33**	**—**	**—**	**2,150**
Asia (Excl. China)	**2,283**	**28**	**9**	**1.9**	**37**	**2,853**	**3,406**	**68**	**3.5**	**35**	**5**	**63**	**62**	**64**	**35**	**—**	**—**	**3,110**
Western Asia	**176**	**32**	**7**	**2.4**	**29**	**243**	**328**	**48**	**4.4**	**39**	**4**	**67**	**65**	**69**	**63**	**—**	**—**	**3,840**
Armenia	3.8	14	7	0.7	98	3.8	4.1	15	1.7	31	7	71	68	74	69	+	—	670
Azerbaijan	7.6	21	7	1.4	50	9.0	10.3	25	2.2	33	5	71	66	75	53	+	100	500
Bahrain	0.6	29	3	2.6	27	0.8	0.9	19	3.7	32	2	73	71	76	88	84	100	7,500
Cyprus	0.7	16	8	0.9	81	0.9	1.0	9	2.2	25	11	77	75	79	53	—	100	10,380
Gaza	0.9	55	5	5.0	14	1.7	3.8	32	8.0	51	3	71	70	72	94	—	—	—
Georgia	5.4	11	9	0.2	330	5.7	6.0	18	1.3	24	10	73	69	76	55	+	—	580
Iraq	21.4	44	7	3.7	19	34.5	52.6	67	6.7	47	3	66	65	67	70	55	93	—
Israel	5.8	21	6	1.5	47	6.9	8.0	6.9	2.9	30	9	77	75	79	90	+	100	14,410
Jordan	4.2	32	6	2.6	27	6.1	8.3	34	4.6	42	3	68	66	70	78	84	99	1,390
Kuwait	1.8	26	2	2.3	30	2.9	3.4	12	3.6	29	1	75	73	77	96	77	100	19,040
Lebanon	3.8	25	5	2.0	34	5.0	6.1	28	2.9	33	7	75	73	78	86	91	98	—
Oman	2.3	53	4	4.9	14	3.6	5.5	24	6.9	36	3	71	70	72	12	35	64	5,200
Qatar	0.7	18	2	1.6	43	0.8	0.9	11	3.6	30	1	73	70	75	91	78	—	4,540
Saudi Arabia	19.4	36	4	3.2	22	31.1	50.3	24	5.5	43	2	70	69	72	79	61	95	7,240
Syria	15.6	44	6	3.7	19	23.3	31.7	44	6.9	49	4	66	65	67	51	68	79	—
Turkey	63.9	23	7	1.6	43	78.3	91.8	47	2.7	33	5	68	65	70	63	81	92	2,450
United Arab Emirates	1.9	23	4	1.9	36	2.5	3.0	23	4.1	32	15	72	70	74	82	78	100	21,420
West Bank	1.7	45	5	4.0	17	2.5	3.4	33	4.3	48	4	71	69	72	—	—	—	—
Yemen	14.7	53	21	3.2	22	23.7	36.6	83	7.7	52	3	52	51	53	23	41	—	280
South Central Asia	**1,385**	**30**	**10**	**2.1**	**34**	**1,752**	**2,105**	**80**	**3.8**	**37**	**4**	**59**	**59**	**60**	**27**	**—**	**—**	**340**
Afghanistan	21.5	50	22	2.8	24	34.0	45.3	163	6.9	41	3	43	43	44	18	29	21	—
Bangladesh	119.8	31	11	2.0	35	149.2	175.8	88	3.7	40	3	57	57	57	16	36	80	230
Bhutan	0.8	39	16	2.3	30	1.1	1.5	121	5.4	39	4	51	51	50	17	39	32	400
India	949.6	29	10	1.9	37	1,182.7	1,384.6	79	3.4	36	4	59	58	59	26	50	75	310
Iran	63.1	36	7	2.9	24	84.2	106.8	57	5.1	44	3	67	65	68	58	65	89	—
Kazakstan	16.5	18	9	0.9	81	18.4	20.5	27	2.3	31	6	69	64	73	56	+	—	1,110
Kyrgyzstan	4.6	25	8	1.6	43	5.6	7.0	29	3.1	38	5	68	64	72	35	+	—	610
Maldives	0.3	43	7	3.6	19	0.4	0.6	50	6.2	47	3	65	63	66	26	92	51	900
Nepal	23.2	39	12	2.6	26	32.4	43.5	98	5.2	42	3	55	56	53	10	26	36	200
Pakistan	133.5	39	10	2.9	24	176.4	232.9	91	5.6	41	3	61	61	61	28	36	56	440
Sri Lanka	18.4	20	5	1.5	47	21.2	23.2	18.4	2.3	35	4	73	70	75	22	89	60	640
Tajikistan	5.9	28	7	2.1	33	9.2	13.1	47	3.7	43	4	68	65	71	28	+	—	350
Turkmenistan	4.6	32	8	2.4	29	5.9	7.9	46	3.9	41	4	66	62	69	45	+	—	—
Uzbekistan	23.2	29	7	2.3	30	31.9	42.3	28	3.5	41	4	69	66	72	39	+	—	950
Southeast Asia	**496**	**27**	**8**	**1.9**	**37**	**614**	**727**	**52**	**3.3**	**36**	**4**	**64**	**62**	**66**	**30**	**—**	**—**	**1,240**
Brunei	0.3	27	3	2.4	29	0.4	0.4	7.4	3.1	35	3	74	73	76	67	86	95	14,240
Cambodia	10.9	45	16	2.9	24	15.7	22.8	111	5.8	46	3	49	48	51	13	38	36	—
Indonesia	201.4	24	8	1.6	43	240.6	276.5	66	2.9	35	4	63	61	65	31	83	42	880
Laos	5.0	43	15	2.9	24	7.2	9.8	102	6.1	45	3	52	50	53	19	54	29	320
Malaysia	20.6	28	5	2.4	29	27.5	34.5	11	3.3	36	4	72	70	75	51	82	79	3,520
Myanmar (Burma)	46.0	31	12	1.9	37	58.2	72.2	49	4.0	36	4	61	60	62	25	82	33	—
Philippines	72.0	30	9	2.1	33	93.9	113.5	34	4.1	38	4	65	63	66	49	94	81	960

	Population Mid-1996 (millions)	Births per 1,000	Deaths per 1,000	Natural Increase (annual, %)	"Doubling Time" in Years at Current Rate	Projected Population (millions) 2010	Projected Population (millions) 2025	Infant Mortality Rate[a]	Total Fertility Rate[b]	Percent Age <15	Percent Age 65+	Life Expectancy at Birth (years) Total	Male	Female	Percent Urban	Adult Literacy Rate (%)	% with Access to Safe Water	Per Capita GNP 1994 (US $)
Singapore	3.0	16	5	1.1	62	3.3	3.6	4.0	1.8	23	7	76	74	79	100	90	100	23,360
Thailand	60.7	20	6	1.4	48	68.5	75.1	35	2.2	30	4	70	68	72	19	94	72	2,210
Vietnam	76.6	30	7	2.3	30	99.0	118.8	42	3.7	40	5	65	63	67	19	92	50	190
East Asia	**1,443**	**16**	**7**	**1.0**	**70**	**1,630**	**1,739**	**40**	**1.8**	**26**	**7**	**71**	**69**	**73**	**36**	**—**	**—**	**3,940**
China	1,217.6	17	7	1.1	66	1,387.0	1,492.0	44	1.8	27	6	70	68	72	29	79	78	530
Hong Kong	6.4	12	5	0.7	99	7.4	8.1	5.0	1.2	19	9	78	75	81	—	91	100	21,650
Japan	125.8	10	7	0.2	315	130.4	125.8	4.2	1.5	16	15	80	77	83	78	+	+	34,630
Korea, North	23.9	24	6	1.9	38	28.5	32.1	28	2.4	29	4	70	67	73	61	95	—	—
Korea, South	45.3	15	6	0.9	75	49.7	50.8	11	1.7	23	6	72	68	76	74	97	93	8,220
Macao	0.4	15	3	1.2	58	0.5	0.6	6	1.6	24	7	69	67	71	97	—	—	—
Mongolia	2.3	22	8	1.4	51	3.0	3.6	61	3.8	40	4	64	62	65	55	81	66	340
Taiwan	21.4	15	5	1.0	70	24.0	25.5	5.1	1.8	24	7	74	72	78	75	—	—	—
Europe	**728**	**11**	**11**	**–0.1**	**—**	**745**	**743**	**11**	**1.5**	**19**	**14**	**73**	**68**	**77**	**74**	**—**	**—**	**12,310**
Northern Europe	**94**	**13**	**11**	**0.2**	**445**	**98**	**100**	**6**	**1.7**	**20**	**15**	**76**	**73**	**79**	**83**	**+**	**+**	**18,340**
Denmark	5.2	13	12	0.2	462	5.4	5.4	5.4	1.8	17	15	75	73	78	85	+	+	28,110
Estonia	1.5	9	15	–0.5	—	1.4	1.4	15	1.4	20	13	70	64	75	70	+	+	2,820
Finland	5.1	13	10	0.3	224	5.2	5.2	4.7	1.8	19	14	77	73	80	64	+	+	18,850
Iceland	0.3	17	7	1.0	68	0.3	0.3	3.4	2.1	25	11	79	77	81	91	+	+	24,590
Ireland	3.6	13	9	0.5	144	3.7	3.8	5.9	1.9	25	11	76	74	79	57	+	+	13,630
Latvia	2.5	9	16	–0.7	—	2.4	2.3	19	1.3	21	13	67	61	73	69	+	+	2,290
Lithuania	3.7	12	12	–0.1	—	3.8	3.9	14	1.5	22	12	69	63	75	68	+	+	1,350
Norway	4.4	14	10	0.4	182	4.7	5.0	5.2	1.9	19	16	78	75	81	73	+	+	26,480
Sweden	8.8	12	11	0.1	630	9.2	9.6	4.4	1.9	19	17	78	76	81	83	+	+	23,630
United Kingdom	58.8	13	11	0.2	385	61.1	62.5	6.2	1.7	19	16	77	74	79	90	+	+	18,410
Western Europe	**181**	**11**	**10**	**0.1**	**716**	**189**	**187**	**6**	**1.4**	**18**	**15**	**77**	**73**	**80**	**79**	**+**	**+**	**24,900**
Austria	8.1	11	10	0.1	866	8.2	8.2	5.5	1.4	18	15	77	73	80	65	+	+	24,950
Belgium	10.2	12	10	0.1	630	10.4	10.5	7.6	1.6	18	16	76	73	80	97	+	+	22,920
France	58.4	12	9	0.3	217	61.7	63.6	6.1	1.7	20	15	78	74	82	74	+	+	23,470
Germany	81.7	9	11	–0.1	—	83.4	79.3	5.5	1.3	16	15	76	72	79	85	+	+	25,580
Liechtenstein	0.03	12	7	0.5	139	0.03	0.03	5.6	1.3	19	10	72	68	75	—	+	+	—
Luxembourg	0.4	14	9	0.4	169	0.4	0.4	5.3	1.7	18	14	76	73	79	86	+	+	39,850
Netherlands	15.5	13	9	0.4	173	16.8	17.4	5.5	1.6	18	13	77	74	80	61	+	+	21,970
Switzerland	7.1	12	9	0.3	231	7.6	7.5	5.1	1.5	18	15	78	75	82	68	+	+	37,180
Eastern Europe	**309**	**10**	**14**	**–0.4**	**—**	**315**	**319**	**16**	**1.4**	**21**	**12**	**68**	**62**	**73**	**68**	**+**	**—**	**2,310**
Belarus	10.3	10	13	–0.3	—	10.8	11.2	13	1.4	22	12	69	64	74	69	+	—	2,160
Bulgaria	8.4	9	13	–0.4	—	8.1	7.9	15.5	1.4	19	15	71	68	75	68	94	—	1,160
Czech Republic	10.3	10	11	–0.1	—	10.4	10.6	7.9	1.4	19	13	73	70	77	75	+	—	3,210
Hungary	10.2	11	14	–0.3	—	9.9	9.3	11.5	1.6	18	14	70	65	74	64	+	—	3,840
Moldova	4.3	14	12	0.3	277	4.8	5.1	23	2.0	27	9	68	64	71	47	+	—	870
Poland	38.6	12	10	0.2	462	40.4	40.5	13.5	1.7	23	11	72	68	76	62	+	—	2,470
Romania	22.6	10	12	–0.2	—	22.2	21.2	23.9	1.3	21	12	70	66	73	55	+	—	1,230
Russia	147.7	9	15	–0.5	—	149.5	153.1	18	1.4	21	12	65	57	71	73	+	—	2,650
Slovakia	5.4	12	10	0.3	248	5.7	6.1	11.2	1.7	23	11	72	68	77	57	+	—	2,230
Ukraine	51.1	10	15	–0.5	—	53.0	54.0	14	1.5	20	14	68	63	73	68	+	—	1,570

	Population Mid-1996 (millions)	Births per 1,000	Deaths per 1,000	Natural Increase (annual, %)	"Doubling Time" in Years at Current Rate	Projected Population (millions) 2010	Projected Population (millions) 2025	Infant Mortality Rate[a]	Total Fertility Rate[b]	Percent Age <15	Percent Age 65+	Life Expectancy at Birth (years) Total	Male	Female	Percent Urban	Adult Literacy Rate (%)	% with Access to Safe Water	Per Capita GNP 1994 (US $)
Southern Europe	**143**	**10**	**9**	**0.1**	**652**	**144**	**137**	**11**	**1.3**	**17**	**14**	**76**	**73**	**79**	**75**	**—**	**—**	**14,180**
Albania	3.3	23	6	1.7	41	4.0	4.6	33.2	2.8	33	6	72	70	76	37	85	—	360
Bosnia-Herzegovina	3.6	13	7	0.6	122	3.9	3.9	—	—	23	7	72	70	75	—	—	—	—
Croatia	4.4	11	11	0.0	—	4.4	4.2	10.2	1.5	20	12	71	66	75	54	—	—	2,530
Greece	10.5	10	9	0.1	1,386	10.2	10.0	8.3	1.3	18	13	77	75	80	72	93	—	7,710
Italy	57.3	9	10	0.0	—	57.7	54.4	8.3	1.2	15	16	77	74	80	58	97	+	19,270
Macedonia	2.1	16	8	0.8	86	2.3	2.3	24.1	2.1	24	8	72	70	74	58	—	—	790
Malta	0.4	13	7	0.6	120	0.4	0.4	9.1	1.9	22	11	77	75	79	89	87	—	7,970
Portugal	9.9	11	10	0.1	866	10.2	10.0	7.9	1.4	18	14	75	71	78	48	85	—	9,370
San Marino	0.03	11	8	0.3	204	0.03	0.03	7.5	1.2	15	15	76	73	79	91	—	—	—
Slovenia	2.0	10	10	0.0	6,931	2.0	2.0	6.5	1.3	19	12	73	69	77	50	—	—	7,140
Spain	39.3	9	9	0.1	1,155	37.8	34.6	7.2	1.2	17	15	77	73	81	64	+	—	13,280
Yugoslavia[c]	10.2	13	10	0.3	224	10.6	10.6	18.6	1.9	22	11	72	69	74	57	93	—	—
Oceania	**29**	**19**	**7**	**1.1**	**60**	**34**	**39**	**24**	**2.5**	**26**	**10**	**73**	**71**	**76**	**70**	**—**	**—**	**13,770**
Australia	18.3	14	7	0.8	92	20.8	23.1	5.8	1.8	21	12	78	75	81	85	+	+	17,980
Federated States of Micronesia	0.1	38	8	3.0	23	0.1	0.2	52	5.6	43	3	64	62	66	26	—	—	1,890
Fiji	0.8	25	5	2.0	34	1.0	1.1	19	3.0	38	3	63	61	65	39	87	80	2,320
French Polynesia	0.2	26	5	2.1	34	0.3	0.4	13	3.1	36	3	70	68	72	57	—	71	—
Guam	0.2	30	4	2.6	27	0.2	0.2	9.7	3.5	30	4	74	72	76	38	—	94	—
Marshall Islands	0.1	26	4	2.2	31	0.1	0.2	63	5.9	51	3	62	60	63	65	—	91	1,680
New Caledonia	0.2	26	6	2.0	34	0.2	0.3	8	3.0	33	5	72	70	75	70	—	—	—
New Zealand	3.6	16	8	0.9	82	4.0	4.3	7.0	2.0	23	12	76	73	79	85	+	+	13,190
Palau	0.02	22	8	1.4	50	0.02	0.02	25	3.1	30	6	67	—	—	69	—	—	—
Papua-New Guinea	4.3	34	10	2.3	30	5.8	7.5	63	4.7	42	2	56	56	57	15	70	33	1,160
Solomon Islands	0.4	39	5	3.4	20	0.6	0.8	28	5.7	47	3	70	68	73	13	24	69	800
Vanuatu	0.2	38	9	2.9	24	0.2	0.3	45	5.3	44	4	63	—	—	18	65	70	1,150
Western Samoa	0.2	31	8	2.3	30	0.2	0.3	21	4.8	41	4	65	—	—	21	98	70	970

[a]Infant deaths per 1000 live births.

[b]Average number of children born to a woman in her lifetime at current birth rate.

[c]On April 27, 1992, Serbia and Montenegro formed a new state, the Federal Republic of Yugoslavia.

A dash (—) indicates data unavailable or inapplicable.

A plus sign (+) indicates that according to UNESCO, adult literacy is 95% or more. For countries of the industrialized "North," the "+" also implies essentially 100% access to safe water.

Urban population data are the percentage of the total population living in areas termed urban by that country.

Table modified from the *1996 World Population Data Sheet* of the Population Reference Bureau. Data for safe water supply are based on World Health Organization reports. Data on adult literacy are based on UNESCO sources.

APPENDIX C
NORTH AMERICAN REFERENCE MAP

GLOSSARY

Terms in italics identify related glossary items.

A

absolute direction
Direction with respect to cardinal east, west, north, and south reference points.

absolute distance
(*syn:* geodesic distance) The shortest-path separation between two places measured on a standard unit of length (miles or kilometers, usually); also called real distance.

absolute location
(*syn:* mathematical location) The exact position of an object or place stated in spatial coordinates of a grid system designed for locational purposes. In geography, the reference system is the *globe grid* of parallels of *latitude* north or south of the *equator* and of meridians of *longitude* east or west of a *prime meridian.* Absolute globe locations are cited in degrees, minutes, and (for greater precision) seconds of latitude and longitude north or south and east or west of the equatorial and prime meridian base lines.

absorbing barrier
A condition that blocks the *diffusion* of an *innovation* or prevents its adoption.

accessibility
The relative ease with which a destination may be reached from other locations; the relative opportunity for *spatial interaction.* May be measured in geometric, social, or economic terms.

acculturation
Cultural modification or change that results when one *culture* group or individual adopts traits of a dominant or *host society;* cultural development or change through "borrowing."

acid rain
Precipitation that is unusually acidic; created when oxides of sulfur and nitrogen change chemically as they dissolve in water vapor in the *atmosphere* and return to earth as acidic rain, snow, or fog.

activity space
The area within which people move freely on their rounds of regular activity.

adaptation
A presumed modification of heritable traits through response to environmental stimuli.

agglomeration
The spatial grouping of people or activities for mutual benefit; in *economic geography,* the concentration of productive enterprises for collective or cooperative use of *infrastructure* and sharing of labor resources and market access.

agglomeration economies
(*syn:* external economies) The savings to an individual enterprise derived from locational association with a cluster of other similar economic activities, such as other factories or retail stores.

agriculture
The science and practice of farming, including the cultivation of the soil and the rearing of livestock.

amalgamation theory
In *ethnic geography,* the concept that multiethnic societies become a merger of the *culture traits* of their member groups.

anecumene
See *nonecumene.*

animism
A belief that natural objects may be the abode of dead people, spirits, or gods who occasionally give the objects the appearance of life.

antecedent boundary
A *boundary* line established before the area in question is well populated.

antipode
The point on the earth's surface that is diametrically opposite the observer's location.

aquaculture
Production and harvesting of fish and shellfish in land-based ponds.

aquifer
A porous, water-bearing layer of rock, sand, or gravel below ground level.

arable land
Land that is or can be cultivated.

arithmetic density
See *crude density.*

artifacts
The material manifestations of *culture,* including tools, housing, systems of land use, clothing, and the like. Elements in the *technological subsystem* of culture.

artificial boundary
See *geometric boundary.*

aspect
In *map projections,* the positional relationship between the globe and the *developable surface* on which it is visually projected.

assimilation
A two-part *behavioral* and *structural* process by which a minority population reduces or loses completely its identifying cultural characteristics and blends into the *host society.*

atmosphere
The air or mixture of gases surrounding the earth.

autonomous nationalism
Movement by a dissident minority intent to achieve partial or total independence of territory it occupies from the *state* within which it lies.

awareness space
Locations or places about which an individual has knowledge even without visiting all of them; includes *activity space* and additional areas newly encountered or about which one acquires information.

azimuth
Direction of a line defined at its starting point by its angle in relation to a *meridian.*

azimuthal projection
See *planar projection*

basic sector
Those products or services of an *urban* economy that are exported outside the city itself, earning income for the community.

behavioral assimilation
(*syn:* cultural assimilation) The process of integration into a common cultural life through acquisition of the sentiments, attitudes, and experiences of other groups.

beneficiation
The enrichment of low-grade ores through concentration and other processes to reduce their waste content and increase their *transferability.*

bilingualism
Describing a society's use of two *official languages.*

biomass
The total dry weight of all living organisms within a unit area; plant and animal matter that can in any way be used as a source of energy.

biome
A major ecological community, including plants and animals, occupying an extensive earth area.

biosphere
(*syn:* ecosphere) The thin film of air, water, and earth within which we live, including the *atmosphere,* surrounding and subsurface waters, and the upper reaches of the earth's crust.

birth rate
The ratio of the number of live births during one year to the total population, usually at the midpoint of the same year, expressed as the number of births per year per 1000 population.

Boserup thesis
The view that population growth independently forces a conversion from extensive to intensive subsistence agriculture.

boundary
A line separating one political unit from another; see *international boundary.*

boundary dispute
See *functional dispute.*

Brandt Report
Entitled *North-South: A Program for Survival,* a report of the Independent Commission on International Development Issues, published 1980 and named for the commission chairman, Willy Brandt.

break-of-bulk point
A location where goods are transferred from one type of carrier to another (e.g., from barge to railroad).

Buddhism
A *universalizing religion,* primarily of eastern and central Asia, based on teachings of Siddhartha Gautama, the Buddha, that suffering is inherent in all life but can be relieved by mental and moral self-purification.

built environment
That part of the *physical landscape* that represents *material culture;* the buildings, roads, bridges, and similar structures large and small of the *cultural landscape.*

carrying capacity
The maximum population numbers that an area can support on a continuing basis without experiencing unacceptable deterioration; for humans, the numbers supportable by an area's known and used resources—usually agricultural ones.

cartogram
A map that has been simplified to present a single idea in a diagrammatic way; the base is not normally true to scale.

caste
One of the hereditary social classes in *Hinduism* that determine one's occupation and position in society.

central business district (CBD)
The nucleus or "downtown" of a city, where retail stores, offices, and cultural activities are concentrated, mass transit systems converge, and land values and building densities are high.

central city
That part of the *metropolitan area* contained within the boundaries of the main city around which suburbs have developed.

central place
An *urban* or other settlement node whose primary function is to provide goods and services to the consuming population of its *hinterland, complementary region,* or trade area.

central place theory
A deductive theory formulated by Walter *Christaller* (1893–1969) to explain the size and distribution of settlements through reference to competitive supply of goods and services to dispersed rural populations.

centrifugal force
1: In *urban geography,* economic and social forces pushing households and businesses outward from central and inner-city locations. **2:** In *political geography,* forces of disruption and dissolution threatening the unity of a *state.*

centripetal force
1: In *urban geography,* a force attracting establishments or activities to the city center. **2:** In *political geography,* forces tending to bind together the citizens of a *state.*

chain migration
The process by which *migration* movements from a common home area to a specific destination are sustained by links of friendship or kinship between first movers and later followers.

channelized migration
The tendency for *migration* to flow between areas that are socially and economically allied by past migration patterns, by economic and trade connections, or by some other affinity.

charter group
In plural societies, the early arriving ethnic group that created the *first effective settlement* and established the recognized cultural norms to which other, later groups are expected to conform.

chlorofluorocarbons (CFCs)
A family of synthetic chemicals that have significant commercial applications but whose emissions are contributing to the depletion of the *ozone* layer.

choropleth map
A *thematic map* presenting spatial data as average values per unit area.

Christaller
Walter Christaller (1893–1969), German geographer credited with developing *central place theory* (1933).

Christianity
A *monotheistic, universalizing religion* based on the teachings of Jesus Christ and of the Bible as sacred scripture.

circular and cumulative causation
A process through which tendencies for economic growth are self-reinforcing; an expression of the *multiplier effect,* it tends to favor major cities and *core* regions over less-advantaged *peripheral* regions.

city
A multifunctional nucleated settlement with a *central business district* and both residential and nonresidential land uses.

climate
A summary of weather conditions in a place or region over a period of time.

cluster migration
A pattern of movement and settlement resulting from the collective action of a distinctive social or *ethnic group.*

cognitive map
See *mental map.*

cohort
A population group unified by a specific common characteristic, such as age, and subsequently treated as a statistical unit during their lifetimes.

collective farm
In the former Soviet *planned economy,* the cooperative operation of an agricultural enterprise under state control of production and market, but without full status or support as a state enterprise.

colony
In *ethnic geography,* an urban ethnic area serving as point of entry and temporary *acculturation* zone for a specific immigrant group.

commercial economy
A system of production of goods and services for exchange in competitive markets where price and availability are determined by supply and demand forces.

commercial energy
Commercially traded fuels, such as coal, oil, or natural gas; excluding wood, vegetable or animal wastes, or other *biomass.*

compact state
A *state* whose territory is nearly circular.

comparative advantage
The principle that an area produces the items for which it has the greatest ratio of advantage or the least ratio of disadvantage in comparison to other areas, assuming free trade exists.

complementarity
The actual or potential relationship of two places or regions that each produce different goods or services for which the other has an effective demand, resulting in an exchange between the locales.

complementary region
The area served by a *central place*.

concentration
In *spatial distributions*, the clustering of a phenomenon around a central location.

concentric zone model
A model describing urban land uses as a series of circular belts or rings around a core *central business district*, each ring housing a distinct type of land use.

conformality
The map property of correct angles and shapes of small areas.

conformal projection
A *map projection* that retains correct shapes of small areas; lines of *latitude* and *longitude* cross at right angles and *scale* **(1)** is the same in all directions at any point on the map.

Confucianism
A Chinese *value system* and *ethnic religion* emphasizing ethics, social morality, tradition, and ancestor worship.

conic projection
A *map projection* employing a cone placed tangent or secant to the globe as the presumed *developable surface.*

connectivity
The directness of routes linking pairs of places; an indication of the degree of internal connection in a transport *network*. More generally, all of the tangible and intangible means of connection and communication between places.

consequent boundary
(*syn:* ethnographic boundary) A *boundary* line that coincides with some cultural divide, such as religion or language.

conservation
The wise use or preservation of natural resources so as to maintain supplies and qualities at levels sufficient to meet present and future needs.

contagious diffusion
A form of *expansion diffusion* that depends on direct contact. The process of dispersion is centrifugal, strongly influenced by distance, and dependent on interaction between actual and potential adopters of the *innovation.* Its name derives from the pattern of spread of contagious diseases.

continental shelf
A gently sloping seaward extension of the landmass found off the coasts of many continents; its outer margin is marked by a transition to the ocean depths at about 200 meters (660 feet).

conurbation
A continuous, extended *urban* area formed by the growing together of several formerly separate, expanding cities.

Convention on the Law of the Sea
See *United Nations Convention on the Law of the Sea.*

core area
1: In *economic geography,* a "core region," the national or world districts of concentrated economic power, wealth, innovation, and advanced technology. **2:** In *political geography,* the heartland or nucleus of a *state,* containing its most developed area, greatest wealth, densest populations, and clearest national identity.

core-periphery model
A model of the spatial structure of an economic system in which underdeveloped or declining peripheral areas are defined with respect to their dependence on a dominating developed *core region.*

core region
See *core area* **(1)**.

counter migration
(*syn:* return migration) The return of migrants to the regions from which they earlier emigrated.

country
See *state.*

creole
A *language* developed from a *pidgin* to become the native tongue of a society.

critical distance
The distance beyond which cost, effort, and/or means play a determining role in the willingness of people to travel.

crop rotation
The annual alteration of crops that make differential demands on or contributions to soil fertility.

crude birth rate (CBR)
See *birth rate.*

crude death rate (CDR)
See *death rate.*

crude density
(*syn:* arithmetic density) The number of people per unit area of land.

cultural assimilation
See *behavioral assimilation.*

cultural convergence
The tendency for *cultures* to become more alike as they increasingly share *technology* and organizational structures in a modern world united by improved transportation and communication.

cultural divergence
The likelihood or tendency for *cultures* to become increasingly dissimilar with the passage of time.

cultural ecology
The study of the interactions between societies and the natural *environments* they occupy.

cultural geography
A branch of *systematic geography* that focuses on culturally determined human activities, the impact of *material* and *nonmaterial* human *culture* on the environment, and the human organization of space.

cultural integration
The interconnectedness of all aspects of a *culture;* no part can be altered without creating an impact on other components of the culture.

cultural lag
The retention of established *culture traits* despite changing circumstances rendering them inappropriate.

cultural landscape
The *natural landscape* as modified by human activities and bearing the imprint of a *culture* group or society; the *built environment.*

culture
1: A society's collective beliefs, symbols, values, forms of behavior, and social organizations, together with its tools, structures, and artifacts created according to the group's conditions of life; transmitted as a heritage to succeeding generations and undergoing adoptions, modifications, and changes in the process. **2:** A collective term for a group displaying uniform cultural characteristics.

culture complex
A related set of *culture traits* descriptive of one aspect of a society's behavior or activity. Culture complexes may be as basic as those associated with food preparation, serving, and consumption or as involved as those associated with religious beliefs or business practices.

culture hearth
A nuclear area within which an advanced and distinctive set of *culture traits,* ideas, and *technologies* develops and from which there is *diffusion* of those characteristics and the *cultural landscape* features they imply.

culture realm
A collective of *culture regions* sharing related culture systems; a major world area having sufficient distinctiveness to be perceived as set apart from other realms in terms of cultural characteristics and complexes.

culture rebound
The readoption by later generations of *culture traits* and identities associated with immigrant forebears or ancestral homelands.

culture region
A *formal* or *functional region* within which common cultural characteristics prevail. It may be based on single *culture traits,* on *culture complexes,* or on political, social, or economic integration.

culture system
A generalization suggesting shared, identifying traits uniting two or more *culture complexes.*

culture trait
A single distinguishing feature of regular occurrence within a *culture,* such as the use of chopsticks or the observance of a particular caste system. A single element of learned behavior.

cumulative causation
See *circular and cumulative causation.*

custom
The body of traditional practices, usages, and conventions that regulate social life.

cylindrical projection
A *map projection* employing a cylinder wrapped around the globe as the presumed *developable surface.*

D

Daoism
See *Taoism.*

death rate
(*syn:* mortality rate) A mortality index usually calculated as the number of deaths per year per 1000 population.

deforestation
The clearing of land through total removal of forest cover.

deglomeration
The process of deconcentration; the location of industrial or other activities away from established *agglomerations* in response to growing costs of congestion, competition, and regulation.

deindustrialization
The cumulative and sustained decline in the contribution of manufacturing to a national economy.

demographic equation
A mathematical expression that summarizes the contribution of different demographic processes to the population change of a given area during a specified time period.

demographic momentum
(*syn:* population momentum) The tendency for population growth to continue despite stringent family planning programs because of a relatively high concentration of people in the childbearing years.

demographic transition
A model of the effect of economic development on population growth. A first stage involves stable numbers with both high *birth rates* and *death rates;* the second displays high birth rates, falling death rates, and population increases. Stage three shows reduction in population growth as birth rates decline to the level of death rates. The fourth and final stage again implies a population stable in size but with larger numbers than at the start of the transition process. An idealized summary of population history of industrializing Europe, its application to newly developing countries is questioned.

demography
The scientific study of population, with particular emphasis on quantitative aspects.

density
The quantity of anything (people, buildings, animals, traffic, etc.) per unit area.

dependency ratio
The number of dependents, old or young, that each 100 persons in the economically productive years must on average support.

desertification
Extension of desertlike landscapes as a result of overgrazing, destruction of the forests, or other human-induced changes, usually in semiarid regions.

developable surface
Projection surface (such as a plane, cone, or cylinder) that is or can be made flat without distortion.

development
The process of growth, expansion, or realization of potential; bringing regional resources into full productive use.

devolution
The transfer of certain powers from the *state* central government to separate political subdivisions within the state's territory.

dialect
A *language* variant marked by vocabulary, grammar, and pronunciation differences from other variants of the same common language. When those variations are spatial or regional, they are called *geographic dialects;* when they are indicative of socioeconomic or educational levels, they are called *social dialects.*

dialect geography
See *linguistic geography.*

dibble
Any small hand tool or stick to make a hole for planting.

diffusion
The spread or movement of a phenomenon over space or through time. The dispersion of a *culture trait* or characteristic or new ideas and practices from an origin area (e.g., *language,* plant *domestication,* new industrial *technology*). Recognized types include *relocation, expansion, contagious,* and *hierarchical* diffusion.

diffusion barrier
Any condition that hinders the flow of information, the movement of people, or the spread of an *innovation.*

direction bias
A statement of *movement bias* observing that among all possible directions of movement or flow, one or only a very few are favored and dominant.

dispersion
In *spatial distributions,* a statement of the amount of spread of a phenomenon over area or around a central location. Dispersion in this sense represents a continuum from clustered, concentrated, or agglomerated (at one end) to dispersed or scattered (at the other).

distance bias
A statement of *movement bias* observing that short journeys or interchanges are favored over more distant ones.

distance decay
The declining intensity of any activity, process, or function with increasing distance from its point of origin.

domestication
The successful transformation of plant or animal species from a wild state to a condition of dependency on human management, usually with distinct physical change from wild forebears.

domino theory
A *geopolitics* theory made part of American containment (of the former Soviet Union) policy beginning in the 1950s. The theory maintained that if a single country fell under Soviet influence or control, its neighbors would likely follow, creating a ripple effect like a line of toppling dominos.

doubling time
The time period required for any beginning total experiencing a compounding growth to double in size.

E

ecology
The scientific study of how living creatures affect each other and what determines their distribution and abundance.

economic base
The manufacturing and service activities performed by the *basic sector* of a city's labor force; functions of a city performed to satisfy demands external to the city itself and, in that performance, earning income to support the urban population.

economic geography
The branch of *systematic geography* concerned with how people support themselves, with the spatial patterns of production, distribution, and consumption of goods and services, and with the areal variation of economic activities over the surface of the earth.

ecosphere
See *biosphere.*

ecosystem
A population of organisms existing together in a small, relatively homogeneous area (pond, forest, small island), together with the energy, air, water, soil, and chemicals upon which it depends.

ecumene
That part of the earth's surface physically suitable for permanent human settlement; the permanently inhabited areas of the earth.

electoral geography
The study of the geographical elements of the organization and results of elections.

elongated state
A *state* whose territory is long and narrow.

enclave
A small bit of foreign territory lying within a *state* but not under its jurisdiction.

environment
Surroundings; the totality of things that in any way may affect an organism, including both physical and cultural conditions; a region characterized by a certain set of physical conditions.

environmental determinism
The view that the physical *environment,* particularly *climate,* controls human action, molds human behavior, and conditions cultural development.

environmental perception
The concept that people of different *cultures* will differently observe and interpret their *environment* and make different decisions about its nature, potentialities, and use.

environmental pollution
See *pollution.*

epidemiologic transition
The reduction of periodically high mortality rates from epidemic diseases as those diseases become essentially continual within a population that develops partial immunity to them.

equal-area (equivalent) projection
A *map projection* designed so that a unit area drawn anywhere on the map always represents the same area on the earth's surface.

equator
An imaginary east-west line that encircles the globe halfway between the North and South poles.

equidistant projection
A *map projection* showing true distances in all directions from one or two central points; all other distances are incorrect.

equivalence/equivalent projection
In *map projections,* the characteristic that a unit area drawn on the map always represents the same area on the earth's surface, regardless of where drawn. See also *equal-area projection.*

erosion
The wearing away and removal of rock and soil particles from exposed surfaces by agents such as moving water, wind, or ice.

ethnic enclave
A small area occupied by a distinctive minority *culture.*

ethnic geography
The study of spatial distributions and interactions of *ethnic groups* and of the cultural characteristics on which they are based.

ethnic group
People sharing a distinctive *culture,* frequently based on common national origin, *religion, language,* or *race.*

ethnic island
A small rural area settled by a single, distinctive *ethnic group* that placed its imprint on the landscape.

ethnicity
Ethnic quality; affiliation with a group whose racial, cultural, religious, or linguistic characteristics or national origins distinguish it from a larger population within which it is found.

ethnic province
A large territory, urban and rural, dominated by or closely associated with a single *ethnic group.*

ethnic religion
A *religion* identified with a particular *ethnic group* and largely exclusive to it. Such a religion does not seek converts.

ethnic separatism
Desired *regional autonomy* expressed by a culturally distinctive group within a larger, politically dominant *culture.*

ethnocentrism
Conviction of the evident superiority of one's own *ethnic group.*

ethnographic boundary
See *consequent boundary.*

European Union (EU)
An economic association established in 1957 by a number of Western European countries to promote free trade among members; often called the Common Market; expanded on January 1, 1995 to include 15 member states.

evapotranspiration
The return of water from the land to the *atmosphere* through evaporation from the soil surface and transpiration from plants.

exclave
A portion of a *state* that is separated from the main territory and surrounded by another country.

exclusive economic zone (EEZ)
As established in the *United Nations Convention on the Law of the Sea,* a zone of exploitation extending 200 nautical miles (370 km) seaward from a coastal state that has exclusive mineral and fishing rights over it.

expansion diffusion
The spread of ideas, behaviors, or articles through a culture area or from one *culture* to neighboring areas through contact and exchange of information; the dispersion leaves the phenomenon intact or intensified in its area of origin.

extensive agriculture
A crop or livestock system characterized by low inputs of labor per unit area of land. It may be part of either a *subsistence* or a *commercial* economy.

external economies
See *agglomeration economies.*

extractive industries
Primary activities involving the mining and quarrying of *nonrenewable* metallic and nonmetallic mineral resources.

F

fallowing
The practice of allowing plowed or cultivated land to remain (rest) uncropped or only partially cropped for one or more growing seasons.

federal state
A *state* with a two-tier system of government and a clear distinction between the powers vested in the central government and those residing in the governments of the component regional subdivisions.

fertility rate
The average number of live births per 1000 women of childbearing age.

filtering
In *urban geography,* a process whereby individuals of a lower-income group replace, in a portion of an urban area, residents who are of a higher-income group.

first effective settlement
The influence that the characteristics of an early dominant settlement group exert on the later *social* and *cultural geography* of an area.

fixed cost
An activity cost (as of investment in land, plant, and equipment) that must be met without regard to level of output; an input cost that is spatially constant.

fixed costs of transportation
See *terminal costs.*

folk culture
The body of institutions, customs, dress, *artifacts,* collective wisdoms, and traditions of a homogeneous, isolated, largely self-sufficient, and relatively static social group.

folklore
Oral traditions of a *folk culture,* including tales, fables, legends, customary observations, and moral teachings.

folkway
The learned manner of thinking and feeling and a prescribed mode of conduct common to a traditional social group.

footloose
A descriptive term applied to manufacturing activities for which the cost of transporting material or product is not important in determining location of production; an industry or firm showing neither *market* nor *material orientation.*

formal region
(*syn:* uniform region, homogeneous region, structural region) A *region* distinguished by a uniformity of one or more characteristics that can serve as the basis for areal generalization and of contrast with adjacent areas.

form utility
A value-increasing change in the form—and therefore in the "utility"—of a raw material or commodity.

forward-thrust capital
A capital city deliberately sited in a *state's* frontier zone.

fossil fuel
(*syn:* mineral fuel) Any of the fuels derived from decayed organic material converted by earth processes; especially, coal, petroleum, and natural gas, but also including tar sands and oil shales.

fragmented state
A *state* whose territory contains isolated parts, separated and discontinuous.

frame
In *urban geography,* that part of the *central business district* characterized by such low-intensity uses as warehouses, wholesaling, and automobile dealers.

freight rate
The charge levied by a transporter for the loading, moving, and unloading of goods; includes *line-haul costs* and *terminal costs.*

friction of distance
A measure of the retarding or restricting effect of distance on *spatial interaction.* Generally, the greater the distance, the greater the "friction" and the less the interaction or exchange, or the greater the cost of achieving the exchange.

frontier
That portion of a country adjacent to its boundaries and fronting another political unit.

frontier zone
A belt lying between two *states* or between settled and uninhabited or sparsely settled areas.

functional dispute
(*syn:* boundary dispute) In *political geography,* a disagreement between neighboring *states* over policies to be applied to their common border; often induced by differing customs regulations, movement of nomadic groups, or illegal immigration or emigration.

functional region
(*syn:* nodal region) A *region* differentiated by what occurs within it rather than by a homogeneity of physical or cultural phenomena; an earth area recognized as an operational unit based on defined organizational criteria. The concept of unity is based on interaction and interdependence between different points within the area.

G

gathering industries
Primary activities involving the *subsistence* or *commercial* harvesting of *renewable* natural resources of land or water. Primitive gathering involves local collection of food and other materials of nature, both plant and animal; commercial gathering usually implies forestry and fishing industries.

gender
In the cultural sense, a reference to socially created—not biologically based—distinctions between femininity and masculinity.

gene flow
The passage of genes characteristic of one breeding population into the gene pool of another by interbreeding.

genetic drift
A chance modification of gene composition occurring in an isolated population and preserved and accentuated through inbreeding.

gentrification
The movement into the inner portions of American cities of middle- and upper-income people who replace low-income populations, rehabilitate the structures they occupied, and change the social character of neighborhoods.

geodesic distance
See *absolute distance.*

geographic dialect
(*syn:* regional dialect) See *dialect.*

geometric boundary
(*syn:* artificial boundary) A boundary without obvious physical geographic basis; often a section of a *parallel of latitude* or a *meridian of longitude.*

geometrical projection
(*syn:* perspective projection; visual projection) The trace of the *graticule* shadow projected on a *developable surface* from a light source placed relative to a transparent globe.

geophagy
The practice of eating earthy substances, usually clays.

geopolitics
That branch of *political geography* treating national power, foreign policy, and international relations as influenced by geographic considerations of location, space, resources, and demography.

gerrymander
To redraw voting district boundaries in such a way as to give one political party maximum electoral advantage and to reduce that of another party, to fragment voting blocks, or to achieve other nondemocratic objectives.

ghetto
A forced or voluntarily segregated residential area housing a racial, ethnic, or religious minority.

globe grid
The set of imaginary lines of *latitude* and *longitude* that intersect at right angles to form a coordinate reference system for locating points on the surface of the earth.

gnomonic projection
A *geometrical projection* produced with the light source at the center of the earth.

GNP
See *gross national product.*

graphic scale
A graduate line included in a map legend by means of which distances on the map may be measured in terms of ground distances.

graticule
The network of meridians and parallels on the globe; the *globe grid.*

gravity model
A mathematical prediction of the interaction between two bodies (places) as a function of their size and of the distance separating them. Based on Newton's law, the model states that attraction (interaction) is proportional to the product of the masses (population sizes) of two bodies (places) and inversely proportional to the square of the distance between them.

great circle
Line formed by the intersection with the earth's surface of a plane passing through the center of the earth; an arc of a great circle is the shortest distance between two points on the earth's surface.

greenhouse effect
Heating of the earth's surface as shortwave solar energy passes through the *atmosphere,* which is transparent to it but opaque to reradiated long-wave terrestrial energy; also, increasing the opacity of the atmosphere through addition of increased amounts of carbon dioxide and other gases that trap heat.

Green Revolution
A term suggesting the great increases in food production, primarily in subtropical areas, accomplished through the introduction of very high-yielding grain crops, particularly wheat, maize, and rice.

grid system
See *globe grid.*

gross domestic product (GDP)
The total value of goods and services produced within the borders of a country during a specified time period, usually a calendar year.

gross national product (GNP)
The total value of goods and services (with some adjustments) including income received from abroad, produced by the residents of a country during a specified period (usually a year).

groundwater
Subsurface water that accumulates in the pores and cracks of rock and *soil.*

guest worker
A foreign worker, usually male and frequently under contract, who migrates to secure permanent work in a host country without intention to settle permanently in that country; particularly, workers from North Africa and countries of eastern, southern, and southeastern Europe employed in industrialized countries of Western Europe.

H

hazardous waste
Discarded solid, liquid, or gaseous material that poses a substantial threat to human health or to the *environment* when improperly disposed of or stored.

heartland theory
The belief of Halford Mackinder that the interior of Eurasia provided a likely base for world conquest.

hierarchical diffusion
A form of *diffusion* in which spread of an *innovation* can proceed either upward or downward through a hierarchy.

hierarchical migration
The tendency for individuals to move from small places to larger ones. See also *step migration*.

hierarchy of central places
The steplike series of *urban* units in classes differentiated by both size and function.

high-level waste
Nuclear waste with a relatively high level of radioactivity.

Hinduism
An ancient and now dominant *value system* and *religion* of India, closely identified with Indian *culture* but without central creed, single doctrine, or religious organization. Dharma (customary duty and divine law) and *caste* are uniting elements.

hinterland
The market area or region served by an *urban* center.

homeostatic plateau
(*syn:* carrying capacity) The application of the concept of homeostasis, or relatively stable state of equilibrium, to the balance between population numbers and areal resources; the equilibrium level of population that available resources can adequately support.

horticultural farming
See *truck farming*.

host society
The established and dominant society within which immigrant groups seek accommodation.

human geography
One of the two major divisions (the other is *physical geography*) of *systematic geography;* the spatial analysis of human populations, their *cultures,* their activities and behaviors, and their relationship with and impact on the physical landscapes they occupy.

hunter-gatherer/hunting-gathering
An economic and social system based primarily or exclusively on the hunting of wild animals and the gathering of food, fiber, and other materials from uncultivated plants.

hydrologic cycle
The natural system by which water is continuously circulated through the *biosphere* by evaporation, condensation, and *precipitation*.

hydrosphere
All water at or near the earth's surface that is not chemically bound in rocks, including the oceans, surface waters, *groundwater,* and water held in the *atmosphere*.

I

icebox effect
The tendency for certain kinds of air pollutants to lower temperatures on earth by reflecting incoming sunlight back into space and thus preventing it from reaching (and heating) the earth.

iconography
In *political geography,* a term denoting the study of symbols that unite a country.

ideological subsystem
The complex of ideas, beliefs, knowledge, and means of their communication that characterize a *culture*.

incinerator
A facility designed to burn waste.

independent invention
(*syn:* parallel invention) *Innovations* developed in two or more unconnected locations by individuals or groups acting independently. See also *multilinear evolution*.

Industrial Revolution
The term applied to the rapid economic and social changes in agriculture and manufacturing that followed the introduction of the factory system to the textile industry of England in the last quarter of the 18th century.

infant mortality rate
A refinement of the *death rate* to specify the ratio of deaths of infants age 1 year or less per 1000 live births.

infrastructure
The basic structure of services, installations, and facilities needed to support industrial, agricultural, and other economic development; included are transport and communications, along with water, power, and other public utilities.

innovation
Introduction of new ideas, practices, or objects; usually, an alteration of *custom* or *culture* that originates within the social group itself.

insolation
The solar radiation received at the earth's surface.

intensive agriculture
Any agricultural system involving the application of large amounts of capital and/or labor per unit of cultivated land; this may be part of either a *subsistence* or a *commercial economy*.

interaction model
See *gravity model*.

international boundary
The outer limit of a *state's* claim to land or water surface, projected downward to the center of the earth and, less certainly, upward to the height the state can effectively control.

International Date Line
By international agreement, the designated line where each new day begins, generally following the 180th *meridian*. The line compensates for accumulated 1-hour time changes for each 15 degrees of longitude by adding (from east to west) or subtracting (from west to east) 24 hours for travelers crossing the line.

interrupting barrier
A condition that delays the rate of *diffusion* of an *innovation* or that deflects its path.

intervening opportunity
The concept that closer opportunities will materially reduce the attractiveness of interaction with more distant—even slightly better—alternatives; a closer alternative source of supply between a demand point and the original source of supply.

in-transit privilege
The application of a single-haul *freight rate* from origin to destination even though the shipment is halted for processing en route, after which the journey is completed.

irredentism
The policy of a *state* wishing to incorporate within itself territory inhabited by people who have ethnic or linguistic links with the country but lies within a neighboring state.

Islam
A *monotheistic, universalizing* religion that includes belief in Allah as the sole deity and in Mohammed as his prophet completing the work of earlier prophets of *Judaism* and *Christianity*.

isochrone
A line connecting points equidistant in travel time from a common origin.

isogloss
A mapped boundary line marking the limits of a particular linguistic feature.

isoline
A map line connecting points of equal value.

isotropic plain
A hypothetical portion of the earth's surface assumed to be an unbounded, uniformly flat plain with uniform and unvarying distribution of population, purchasing power, transport costs, accessibility, and the like.

J

J-curve
A curve shaped like the letter **J**, depicting exponential or geometric growth (1, 2, 4, 8, 16 . . .).

Judaism
A *monotheistic, ethnic religion* first developed among the Hebrew people of the ancient Near East; its determining conditions include descent from Israel (Jacob), the Torah (law and scripture), and tradition.

K

krill
A form of marine *plankton* composed of crustaceans and larvae.

L

landlocked
Describing a *state* which lacks a sea coast.

land race
A genetically diverse, naturally adapted, native food plant.

language
The system of words, their pronunciation, and methods of combination used and mutually understood by a community of individuals.

language family
A group of *languages* thought to have descended from a single, common ancestral tongue.

latitude
Angular distance north or south of the *equator,* measured in degrees, minutes, and seconds. Grid lines marking latitudes are called *parallels.* The equator is 0°, the North Pole is 90° N, the South Pole is 90° S. Low latitudes are considered to fall within the tropics (23° 30′ N and 23° 30′ S); midlatitudes extend from the tropics to the Arctic and Antarctic circles (66° 30′ N and S); high latitudes occur from those circles to the North and South poles.

law of peripheral neglect
The observation that a government's awareness of or concern with regional problems decreases with the square of the distance of an outlying region from the capital city.

leachate
The contaminated liquid discharged from a *sanitary landfill* to either surface or subsurface land or water.

least-cost theory
(*syn:* Weberian analysis) The view that the optimum location of a manufacturing establishment is at the place where the costs of transport and labor and the advantages of *agglomeration* or *deglomeration* are most favorable.

limiting factor principle
The distribution of an organism or the structure of an *ecosystem* can be explained by the control exerted by the single factor (such as temperature, light, water) that is most deficient, that is, that falls below the levels required.

line-haul costs
(*syn:* over-the-road costs; variable costs of transportation) The costs involved in the actual physical movement of goods (or passengers); costs of haulage (including equipment and routeway costs), excluding *terminal costs.*

lingua franca
Any of various auxiliary *languages* used as common tongues among people of an area where several languages are spoken; literally, "Frankish language."

linguistic geography
(*syn:* dialect geography; dialectology) The study of local variations within a speech area by mapping word choices, pronunciations, or grammatical constructions.

link
A transportation or communication connection or route within a *network.*

lithosphere
The earth's solid crust.

locational interdependence
The circumstance under which the locational decision of a particular firm is influenced by the locations chosen by competitors.

locational triangle
A simple graphic model in *Weberian analysis* to illustrate the derivation of the least-transport-cost location of an industrial establishment.

longitude
Angular distance of a location in degrees, minutes, and seconds measured east or west of a designated *prime meridian* given the value of 0°. By general agreement, the *globe grid* prime meridian passes through the old observatory of Greenwich, England. Distances are measured from 0° to 180° both east and west, with 180° E and W being the same line. For much of its extent the 180° meridian also serves as the *International Date Line.* Because of the period of the earth's axial rotation, 15 degrees of longitude are equivalent to a difference of 1 hour in local time.

long lot
A farm or other property consisting of a long, narrow strip of land extending back from a river or road.

low-level waste
Nuclear waste with relatively moderate levels of radioactivity.

M

malnutrition
Food intake insufficient in quantity or deficient in quality to sustain life at optimal conditions of health.

Malthus
Thomas R. Malthus (1766–1843). English economist, demographer, and cleric who suggested that unless self-control, war, or natural disaster checks population, it will inevitably increase faster than will the food supplies needed to sustain it. This view is known as Malthusianism. See also *neo-Malthusianism.*

map projection
A systematic method of transferring the *globe grid* system from the earth's curved surface to the flat surface of a map. Projection automatically incurs error, but an attempt is usually made to preserve one or more (though never all) of the characteristics of the spherical surface: equal area, correct distance, true direction, proper shape.

map scale
See *scale.*

marginal cost
The additional cost of producing each successive unit of output.

mariculture
Production and harvesting of fish and shellfish in fenced confinement areas along coasts and in estuaries.

market equilibrium
The point of intersection of demand and supply curves of a given commodity; at equilibrium the market is cleared of the commodity.

market gardening
See *truck farming.*

market orientation
The tendency of an economic activity to locate close to its market; a reflection of large and variable distribution costs.

material culture
The tangible, physical items produced and used by members of a specific *culture* group and reflective of their traditions, life styles, and technologies.

material orientation
The tendency of an economic activity to locate near or at its source of raw material; this is experienced when material costs are highly variable spatially and/or represent a significant share of total costs.

mathematical location
See *absolute location.*

mathematical projection
The systematic rendering of the *globe grid* on a *developable surface* to achieve *graticule* characteristics not obtainable by visual means of *geometrical projection.*

maximum sustainable yield
The maximum rate at which a *renewable resource* can be exploited without impairing its ability to be renewed or replenished.

Mediterranean agriculture
An agricultural system based on the mild, moist winters, hot, sunny summers, and rough terrain of the Mediterranean basin. It involves cereals as winter crops, summer tree and vine crops (olives, figs, dates, citrus and other tree fruits, and grapes), and animals (sheep and goats).

megalopolis
1: A large, sprawled *urban* complex with contained open, nonurban land, created through the spread and joining of separate *metropolitan areas.* **2:** When capitalized, the name applied to the continuous functionally urban area of coastal northeastern United States from Maine to Virginia.

mental map
(*syn:* cognitive map) The maplike image of the world, country, region, city, or neighborhood a person carries in mind. The representation is therefore subjective; it includes knowledge of actual locations and spatial relationships and is colored by personal perceptions and preferences related to place.

mentifacts
The central, enduring elements of a *culture* expressing its values and beliefs, including *language, religion, folklore,* artistic traditions, and the like. Elements in the *ideological subsystem* of culture.

Mercator projection
A true *conformal cylindrical projection* first published in 1569, useful for navigation.

meridian
A north-south line of *longitude;* on the *globe grid,* all meridians are of equal length and converge at the poles.

Mesolithic
Middle Stone Age. The *culture* stage of the early postglacial period, during which earliest stages of *domestication* of animals and plants occurred, refined and specialized tools were developed, pottery was produced, and semipermanent settlements were established as climate change reduced the game-animal herds earlier followed for food.

metes-and-bounds survey
A system of property description using natural features (streams, rocks, trees, etc.) to trace and define the boundaries of individual parcels.

Metro
See *unified government.*

metropolitan area
In the United States, a large functionally integrated settlement area comprising one or more whole county units and usually containing several *urbanized areas;* discontinuously built up, it operates as a coherent economic whole.

microdistrict
The basic neighborhood planning unit characteristic of new urban residential construction in the planned East European city under communism.

microstate
(*syn:* ministate) An imprecise term for a *state* or territory small in both population and area. An informal definition accepted by the United Nations suggests a maximum of 1 million population combined with a territory of less than 700 km² (270 sq.mi.).

migration
The permanent (or relatively permanent) relocation of an individual or group to a new, usually distant, place of residence and employment.

migration field
The area from which a given city or place draws the majority of its in-migrants.

mineral
A natural inorganic substance that has a definite chemical composition and characteristic crystal structure, hardness, and density.

mineral fuel
See *fossil fuel.*

ministate
See *microstate.*

model
An idealized representation, abstraction, or simulation of reality. It is designed to simplify real-world complexity and eliminate extraneous phenomena in order to isolate for detailed study causal factors and interrelationships of *spatial systems.*

monoculture
Agricultural system dominated by a single crop.

monolingualism
A society's or country's use of only one *language* of communication for all purposes.

monotheism
The belief that there is but a single God.

mortality rate
See *death rate.*

movement bias
Any aggregate control on or regularity of movement of people, commodities, or communication. Included are *distance bias, direction bias,* and *network bias.*

multilinear evolution
A concept of independent but parallel cultural development advanced by the anthropologist Julian Steward (1902–1972) to explain cultural similarities between widely separated peoples existing in similar environments but who could not have benefited from shared experiences, borrowed ideas, or diffused technologies. See *independent invention.*

multilingualism
The common use of two or more *languages* in a society or country.

multinational corporation (MNC)
A large business organization operating in a number of different national economies; the term implies a more extensive form of *transnational corporation.*

multiple-nuclei model
The postulate that large cities develop by peripheral spread not from one *central business district* but from several nodes of growth, each of specialized use. The separately expanding use districts eventually coalesce at their margins.

multiplier effect
The direct, indirect, and induced consequences of change in an activity. **1:** In industrial *agglomerations,* the cumulative processes by which a given change (such as a new plant opening) sets in motion a sequence of further industrial employment and *infrastructure* growth. **2:** In *urban geography,* the expected addition of *nonbasic* workers and dependents to a city's total employment and population that accompanies new *basic* employment.

N

nation
A culturally distinctive group of people occupying a specific territory and bound together by a sense of unity arising from shared *ethnicity,* beliefs, and *customs.*

nationalism
A sense of unity binding the people of a *state* together; devotion to the interests of a particular country or *nation;* an identification with the state and an acceptance of national goals.

nation-state
A *state* whose territory is identical to that occupied by a particular *ethnic group* or *nation.*

natural boundary
(*syn:* physical boundary) A *boundary* line based on recognizable physiographic features, such as mountains or rivers.

natural hazard
A process or event in the physical environment that has consequences harmful to humans.

natural increase
The growth of a population through excess of births over deaths, excluding the effects of immigration or emigration.

natural landscape
The physical *environment* unaffected by human activities. The duration and near totality of human occupation of the earth's surface assure

that little or no "natural landscape" so defined remains intact. Opposed to *cultural landscape.*

natural resource
A physically occurring item that a population perceives to be necessary and useful to its maintenance and well-being.

natural selection
The process of survival and reproductive success of individuals or groups best adjusted to their environment, leading to the perpetuation of those genetic qualities most suited to that environment.

natural vegetation
The plant life that would exist in an area if humans did not interfere with its development.

neocolonialism
A disparaging reference to economic and political policies by which major developed countries are seen to retain or extend influence over the economies of less developed countries and peoples.

Neolithic
New Stone Age. The *culture* (succeeding that of the *Mesolithic*) of the middle postglacial period, during which polished stone tools were perfected, the economy was solely or largely based on cultivation of crops and *domestication* of animals, and the arts of spinning, weaving, smelting, and metal working were developed. More formalized societies and *culture complexes* emerged as cities developed and trade routes were established.

neo-Malthusianism
The advocacy of population control programs to preserve and improve general national prosperity and well-being.

net migration
The difference between in-migration and out-migration of an area.

network
The areal pattern of sets of places and the routes (*links*) connecting them along which movement can take place.

network bias
The view that the pattern of *links* in a *network* will affect the likelihood of flows between specific *nodes.*

nodal region
See *functional region.*

node
In *network* theory, an origin, destination, or intersection in a communication network.

nomadic herding
Migratory but controlled movement of livestock solely dependent on natural forage.

nonbasic sector
(*syn:* service sector) Those economic activities of an urban unit that supply the resident population with goods and services and that have no "export" implication.

nonecumene
(*syn:* anecumene) That portion of the earth's surface that is uninhabited or only temporarily or intermittently inhabited. See also *ecumene.*

nonmaterial culture
The oral traditions, songs, and stories of a *culture* group along with its beliefs and customary behaviors.

nonrenewable resource
A *natural resource* that is not replenished or replaced by natural processes or is used at a rate that exceeds its replacement rate.

North
The general term applied in the *Brandt Report* to the developed countries of the Northern Hemisphere plus Australia and New Zealand.

O

official language
A governmentally designated *language* of instruction, of government, of the courts, and other official public and private communication.

orthographic projection
A *geometrical projection* that results from placing the light source at infinity.

outsourcing
1: Producing abroad parts or products for domestic use or sale. **2:** Subcontracting production or services rather than performing those activities "in house."

overpopulation
A value judgement that the resources of an area are insufficient to sustain adequately its present population numbers.

over-the-road costs
See *line-haul costs.*

ozone
A gas molecule consisting of three atoms of oxygen (O_3) formed when diatomic oxygen (O_2) is exposed to *ultraviolet radiation.* In the upper *atmosphere* it forms a normally continuous, thin layer that blocks ultraviolet light; in the lower atmosphere it constitutes a damaging component of *photochemical smog.*

P

Paleolithic
Old Stone Age. An early stage of human *culture* largely coinciding with the *Pleistocene* glacial period. Characterized by *hunting-gathering* economies and the use of fire and simple stone tools, especially those made from flint.

parallel of latitude
An east-west line of *latitude* indicating distance north or south of the equator.

parallel invention
See *independent invention.*

pattern
The design or arrangement of phenomena in earth space.

peak value intersection
The most accessible and costly parcel of land in the *central business district* and, therefore, in the entire *urbanized area.*

perception
The acquisition of information about a place or thing through sensory means; the subjective organization and interpretation of acquired information in light of cultural attitudes and individual preferences or experiences. See *environmental perception.*

perceptual region
A *region* perceived to exist by its inhabitants or the general populace. Also known as a *vernacular region* or popular region, it has reality as an element of *popular culture* or *folk culture* represented in the *mental maps* of average people.

perforated state
A *state* whose territory is interrupted ("perforated") by a separate, independent state totally contained within its borders.

periodic market
A market operating at a particular location (village, city, neighborhood) on one or more fixed days per week or month.

periphery/peripheral
The outer regions or boundaries of an area. See also *core-periphery model.*

permeable barrier
An obstacle raised by a culture group or one culture group's reluctance to accept some, but not all, innovations diffused from a related but different *culture.* Acceptance or rejection may be conditioned by religious, political, ethnic, or similar considerations of suitability or compatibility.

personal communication field
An area defined by the distribution of an individual's short-range informal communications. The size and shape of the field are defined by work, recreation, school, and other regular contacts and are affected by age, sex, employment, and other personal characteristics.

personal space
An invisible, usually irregular area around a person into which he or she does not willingly admit others. The sense (and extent) of personal space is a situational and cultural variable.

perspective projection
See *geometrical projection.*

photochemical smog
A form of polluted air produced by the interaction of hydrocarbons and oxides of nitrogen in the presence of sunlight.

physical boundary
See *natural boundary.*

physical geography
One of two major divisions (the other is *human geography*) of *systematic geography;* the study of the structures, processes, distributions, and change through time of the natural phenomena of the earth's surface that are significant to human life.

physical landscape
The *natural landscape* plus visible elements of *material culture.*

physiological density
The number of persons per unit area of cultivable land.

pidgin
An auxiliary *language* derived, with reduced vocabulary and simplified structure, from other languages. Not a native tongue, it is used for limited communication between people with different languages.

place perception
See *perception.*

place utility
1: In human movement and *migration* studies, a measure of an individual's perceived satisfaction or approval of a place in its social, economic, or environmental attributes. **2:** In *economic geography,* the value imparted to goods or services by *tertiary* activities that provide things needed in specific markets.

planar projection
(*syn:* azimuthal projection) A *map projection* employing a plane as the presumed *developable surface.*

plankton
Microscopic freely floating plant and animal organisms of lakes and oceans.

planned economy
A system of production of goods and services, usually consumed or distributed by a governmental agency, in quantities, at prices, and in locations determined by a governmental program.

plantation
A large agricultural holding, frequently foreign owned, devoted to the production of a single export crop.

Pleistocene
The geological epoch dating from 2 million to 11 thousand years ago during which four stages of continental glaciation occurred.

political geography
A branch of *human geography* concerned with the spatial analysis of political phenomena.

pollution
The introduction into the biosphere of materials that because of their quantity, chemical nature, or temperature have a negative impact on the *ecosystem* or that cannot be readily disposed of by natural recycling processes.

polytheism
Belief in or worship of many gods.

popular culture
The constantly changing mix of material and nonmaterial elements available through mass production and the mass media to an urbanized, heterogeneous, nontraditional society.

popular region
See *vernacular region.*

population density
A measurement of the numbers of persons per unit area of land within predetermined limits, usually political or census boundaries. See also *physiological density.*

population geography
A division of *human geography* concerned with spatial variations in distribution, composition, growth, and movements of population and the relationship of those concerns with the geographic character of areas.

population momentum
See *demographic momentum.*

population projection
A statement of a population's future size, age, and sex composition based on the application of stated assumptions to current data.

population pyramid
A bar graph in pyramid form showing the age and sex composition of a population, usually a national one.

positional dispute
(*syn:* boundary dispute) In *political geography,* disagreement about the actual location of a *boundary.*

possibilism
The philosophical viewpoint that the physical *environment* offers human beings a set of opportunities from which (within limits) people may choose according to their cultural needs and technological awareness. The emphasis is on a freedom of choice and action not allowed under *environmental determinism.*

postindustrial
A stage of economic development in which service activities become relatively more important than goods production; professional and technical employment supersedes employment in agriculture and manufacturing; and level of living is defined by the quality of services and amenities rather than by the quantity of goods available.

potential model
A measurement of the total interaction opportunities available under *gravity model* assumptions to a center in a multicenter system.

precipitation
All moisture—solid and liquid—that falls to the earth's surface from the *atmosphere.*

predevelopment annexation
The inclusion within the *central city* of nonurban peripheral areas for the purpose of securing to the city itself the benefits of their eventual development.

primary activities
Those parts of the economy involved in making *natural resources* available for use or further processing; included are mining, *agriculture,* forestry, fishing and hunting, and grazing.

primate city
A country's leading city, disproportionately larger and functionally more complex than any other; a city dominating an urban hierarchy composed of a base of small towns and an absence of intermediate-sized cities.

prime meridian
An imaginary line passing through the Royal Observatory at Greenwich, England, serving by agreement as the 0° line of *longitude.*

private plot
In the planned economies under communism, a small garden plot allotted to collective farmers and urban workers.

projection
See *map projection.*

prorupt state
A *state* of basically *compact* form but with one or more narrow extensions of territory.

protolanguage
An assumed, reconstructed, or recorded ancestral *language.*

proved reserves
That portion of a *natural resource* that has been identified and can be extracted profitably with current technology.

psychological distance
The way an individual perceives distance.

pull factors
Characteristics of a locale that act as attractive forces, drawing migrants from other regions.

purchasing power parity (PPP)
A monetary measurement which takes account of what money actually buys in each country.

push factors
Unfavorable characteristics of a locale that contribute to the dissatisfaction of its residents and impel their emigration.

Q

quaternary activities
Those parts of the economy concerned with research, with the gathering and dissemination of information, and with administration—including administration of the other economic activity levels; often considered only as a specialized subdivision of *tertiary activities.*

quinary activities
A sometimes separately recognized subsection of *tertiary activity* management functions involving highest-level decision making in all types of large organizations. Also deemed the most advanced form of the *quaternary* subsector.

R

race
A subset of human population whose members share certain distinctive, inherited biological characteristics.

rank-size rule
An observed regularity in the city-size distribution of some countries. In a rank-size hierarchy, the population of any given town will be inversely proportional to its rank in the hierarchy; that is, the *n*th-ranked city will be 1/*n* the size of the largest city.

rate
The frequency of an event's occurrence during a specified time period.

rate of natural increase
Birth rate minus the *death rate,* suggesting the annual rate of population growth without considering *net migration.*

reapportionment
The process and outcome of a reallocation of electoral seats to defined territories, such as congressional seats to states of the United States.

recycling
The reuse of disposed materials after they have passed through some form of treatment (e.g., melting down glass bottles to produce new bottles).

redistricting
The drawing of new electoral district boundary lines in response to changing patterns of population or changing legal requirements.

region
Any earth area with distinctive and unifying physical or cultural characteristics that set it off and make it substantially different from surrounding areas. A region may be defined on the basis of its homogeneity or its functional integration as a single organizational unit. Regions and their boundaries are devices of areal generalization, intellectual concepts rather than visible landscape entities.

regional autonomy
A measure of self-governance afforded a subdivision of a *state.*

regional concept
The view that physical and cultural phenomena on the surface of the earth are rationally arranged by complex, diverse, but comprehensible interrelated spatial processes.

regional dialect
(*syn:* geographic dialect) See *dialect.*

regional geography
The study of geographic *regions;* the study of areal differentiation.

regionalism
In *political geography,* group—frequently ethnic group—identification with a particular region of a *state* rather than with the state as a whole.

relational direction
See *relative direction.*

relative direction
(*syn:* relational direction) A culturally based locational reference, as the Far West, the Old South, or the Middle East.

relative distance
A transformation of *absolute distance* into such relative measures as time or monetary costs. Such measures yield different explanations of human spatial behavior than do linear distances alone. Distances between places are constant by absolute terms, but relative distances may vary with improvements in transportation or communication technology or with different psychological perceptions of space.

relative location
The position of a place or activity in relation to other places or activities. Relative location implies spatial relationships and usually suggests the relative advantages or disadvantages of a location with respect to all competing locations.

relict boundary
A former *boundary* line that is still discernable and marked by some *cultural landscape* feature.

religion
A personal or institutionalized system of worship and of faith in the sacred and divine.

relocation diffusion
The transfer of ideas, behaviors, or articles from one place to another through the *migration* of those possessing the feature transported; also, spatial relocation in which a phenomenon leaves an area of origin as it is transported to a new location.

renewable resource
A *natural resource* that is potentially inexhaustible either because it is constantly (as solar radiation) or periodically (as *biomass*) replenished as long as its use does not exceed its *maximum sustainable yield*.

replacement level
The number of children per woman that will supply just enough births to replace parents and compensate for early deaths, with no allowance for *migration* effects; usually calculated at between 2.1 and 2.5 children.

representative fraction
The *scale* of a map expressed as a ratio of a unit of distance on the map to distance measured in the same unit on the ground, e.g., 1:250,000.

resource
See *natural resource*.

resource dispute
In *political geography,* disagreement over the control or use of shared resources, such as boundary rivers or jointly claimed fishing grounds.

return migration
See *counter migration*.

rhumb line
A directional line that crosses each successive *meridian* at a constant angle.

rimland theory
The belief of Nicholas Spykman that domination of the coastal fringes of Eurasia would provide a base for world conquest.

rotation
See *crop rotation*.

roundwood
Timber as it is harvested, before squaring, sawing, or pulping.

S

Sahel
The semiarid zone between the Sahara Desert and the grassland areas to the south in West Africa; a district of recurring drought, famine, and environmental degradation and *desertification*.

salinization
The process by which *soil* becomes saturated with salt, rendering the land unsuitable for *agriculture.* This occurs when land that has poor drainage is improperly irrigated.

sanitary landfill
Disposal of solid wastes by spreading them in layers covered with enough soil to control odors, rodents, and flies; sited to minimize water pollution from runoff and *leachate.*

satisficing location
A less than ideal best location, but one providing an acceptable level of utility or satisfaction.

scale
1: In cartography, the ratio between the size of area on a map and the actual size of that same area on the earth's surface. **2:** In more general terms, scale refers to the size of the area studied, from local to global.

S-curve
The horizontal bending, or leveling, of an exponential or *J-curve.*

secondary activities
Those parts of the economy involved in the processing of raw materials derived from *primary activities* and in altering or combining materials to produce commodities of enhanced utility and value; included are manufacturing, construction, and power generation.

sector model
A description of urban land uses as wedge-shaped sectors radiating outward from the *central business district* along transportation corridors. The radial access routes attract particular uses to certain sectors, with high-status residential uses occupying the most desirable wedges.

secularism
A rejection of or indifference to *religion* and religious practice.

segregation
A measure of the degree to which members of a minority group are not uniformly distributed among the total population.

separatism
See *ethnic separatism.*

service sector
See *nonbasic sector.*

shamanism
A form of *tribal religion* based on belief in a hidden world of gods, ancestral spirits, and demons responsive only to a shaman, or interceding priest.

shifting cultivation
(*syn:* slash-and-burn agriculture; swidden agriculture) Crop production on tropical forest clearings kept in cultivation until their quickly declining fertility is lost. Cleared plots are then abandoned and new sites are prepared.

Shinto
The *polytheistic, ethnic religion* of Japan that includes reverence of deities of natural forces and veneration of the emperor as descendent of the sun-goddess.

site
The *absolute location* of a place or activity described by local relief, landform, and other physical (or sometimes cultural) characteristics.

situation
The *relative location* of a place or activity in relation to the physical and cultural characteristics of the larger regional or *spatial system* of which it is a part. Situation implies spatial interconnection and interdependence.

slash-and-burn cultivation
See *shifting cultivation.*

social area
An area identified by homogeneity of the social indices (age group, socioeconomic status, *ethnicity*) of its population.

social dialect
See *dialect.*

social distance
A measure of the perceived degree of social separation between individuals, *ethnic groups,* neighborhoods, or other groupings; the voluntary or enforced *segregation* of two or more distinct social groups for most activities.

social geography
The branch of *cultural geography* that studies *social areas* and the social use of space, especially urban space; the study of the *spatial distribution* of social groups and of the processes underlying that distribution.

sociofacts
The institutions and links between individuals and groups that unite a *culture,* including family structure and political, educational, and religious institutions. Components of the *sociological subsystem* of culture.

sociological subsystem
The totality of expected and accepted patterns of interpersonal relations common to a *culture* or subculture.

soil
The complex mixture of loose material including minerals, organic and inorganic compounds, living organisms, air, and water found at the earth's surface and capable of supporting plant life.

soil erosion
See *erosion.*

solar energy
Radiation from the sun, which is transformed into heat primarily at the earth's surface and secondarily in the *atmosphere.*

South
The general term applied in the *Brandt Report* to the poor, developing countries of the world, generally (but not totally) located in the Southern Hemisphere.

space-time convergence
An expression of the extent to which improvements in transportation and communication have reduced distance barriers.

space-time prism
A diagram of the volume of space and the length of time within which our activities are confined by constraints of our bodily needs (eating, resting) and the means of mobility at our command.

spatial
Of or pertaining to space on the earth's surface. Often a synonym for *geographical* and used as

an adjective to describe specific geographic concepts or processes, as *spatial interaction* or *diffusion*.

spatial diffusion
See *diffusion*.

spatial distribution
The arrangement of things on the earth's surface; the descriptive elements of spatial distribution are *density, dispersion,* and *pattern*.

spatial interaction
The movement (e.g., of people, goods, information) between different places; an indication of interdependence between different geographic locations or areas.

spatial margin of profitability
The set of points delimiting the area within which a firm's profitable operation is possible.

spatial search
The process by which individuals evaluate the alternative locations to which they might move.

spatial system
The arrangement and integrated operation of phenomena produced by or responding to spatial processes on the earth's surface.

spatially fixed cost
An input cost in manufacturing that remains constant wherever production is located.

spatially variable cost
An input cost in manufacturing that changes significantly from place to place in its amount and its relative share of total costs.

speech community
A group of people having common characteristic patterns of vocabulary, word arrangement, and pronunciation.

spine
In *urban geography,* a continuation of the features of the *central business district* outward along the main wide boulevard characteristic of Latin American cities.

spread effect
(*syn:* trickle-down effect) The diffusion outward of the benefits of economic growth and prosperity from the power center or *core area* to poorer districts and people.

spring wheat
Wheat sown in spring for ripening during the summer or autumn.

standard language
A *language* substantially uniform with respect to spelling, grammar, pronunciation, and vocabulary and representing the approved community norm of the tongue.

standard line
Line of contact between a projection surface and the globe; transformed from the sphere to the plane surface without distortion.

state
(*syn:* country) An independent political unit occupying a defined, permanently populated territory and having full sovereign control over its internal and foreign affairs.

state farm
In the former Soviet Union (and other planned economies), a government agricultural enterprise operated with paid employees.

step (stepwise) migration
A *migration* in which an eventual long-distance relocation is undertaken in stages as, for example, from farm to village to small town to city. See also *hierarchical migration*.

stereographic projection
A *geometrical projection* that results from placing the light source at the *antipode*.

structural assimilation
The distribution of immigrant ethnics among the groups and social strata of a *host society,* but without their full *behavioral assimilation* into it.

subsequent boundary
A *boundary* line that is established after the area in question has been settled and that considers the cultural characteristics of the bounded area.

subsistence agriculture
Any of several farm economies in which most crops are grown for food nearly exclusively for local or family consumption.

subsistence economy
An economic system of relatively simple technology in which people produce most or all of the goods to satisfy their own and their family's needs; little or no exchange occurs outside of the immediate or extended family.

substitution principle
In industry, the tendency to substitute one factor of production for another in order to achieve optimum plant location.

suburb
A functionally specialized segment of a large *urban* complex located outside the boundaries of the *central city;* usually, a relatively homogeneous residential community, separately incorporated and administered.

superimposed boundary
A *boundary* line placed over and ignoring an existing cultural pattern.

sustained yield
The practice of balancing harvesting with growth of new stocks so as to avoid depletion of the *resource* and ensure a perpetual supply.

swidden agriculture
See *shifting cultivation*.

syncretism
The development of a new form of *culture trait* by the fusion of two or more distinct parental elements.

systematic geography
A division of geography that selects a particular aspect of the physical or cultural *environment* for detailed study of its areal differentiation and interrelationships. Branches of systematic geography are labeled according to the topic studied (e.g., recreational geography) or the related science with which the branch is associated (e.g., *economic geography*).

systems analysis
An approach to the study of large systems through (1) segregation of the entire system into its component parts, (2) investigation of the interactions between system elements, and (3) study of inputs, outputs, flows, interactions, and boundaries within the system.

T

Taoism
(*syn:* Daoism) A Chinese *value system* and *ethnic religion* emphasizing conformity to Tao (Way), the creative reality ordering the universe.

tapering principle
A *distance decay* observation of the diminution or tapering of costs of transportation with increasing distance from the point of origin of the shipment because of the averaging of *fixed costs* over a greater number of miles of travel.

technological subsystem
The complex of material objects together with the techniques of their use by means of which people carry out their productive activities.

technology
The integrated system of knowledge, skills, tools, and methods developed within or used by a *culture* to successfully carry out purposeful and productive tasks.

technology gap
The contrast between the *technology* available in developed *core regions* and that present in *peripheral areas* of *underdevelopment*.

technology transfer
The *diffusion* to or acquisition by one *culture* or *region* of the *technology* possessed by another, usually more developed, society.

terminal costs
(*syn:* fixed costs of transportation) The costs incurred, and charged, for loading and unloading freight at origin and destination points; costs charged each shipment for terminal facility use and unrelated to distance of movement or *line-haul costs*.

terracing
The practice of planting crops on steep slopes that have been converted into a series of horizontal steplike level plots (terraces).

territorial dispute
(*syn:* boundary dispute; functional dispute) In *political geography,* disagreement between *states* over the control of surface area.

territorial production complex
A design in former Soviet economic planning for large regional industrial, mining, and agricultural development leading to regional self-sufficiency, diversification, and the creation of specialized production for a larger national market.

territoriality
An individual or group attempt to identify and establish control over a clearly defined territory considered partially or wholly an exclusive domain; the behavior associated with the defense of the home territory.

tertiary activities
Those parts of the economy that fulfill the exchange function, that provide market availability of commodities, and that bring together consumers and providers of services; included are wholesale and retail trade, associated transportational and governmental services, and personal and professional services of all kinds.

thematic map
A map depicting a specific *spatial distribution* or statistical variation of abstract objects (e.g., unemployment) in space.

Third World
Originally (1950s), designating countries uncommitted to either the "First World" Western capitalist bloc or the Eastern "Second World" communist bloc; subsequently, a term applied to countries considered not yet fully developed or in a state of *underdevelopment* in economic and social terms.

threshold
In *economic geography* and *central place theory,* the minimum market needed to support the supply of a product or service.

tipping point
The degree of neighborhood racial or ethnic mixing that induces the former majority group to move out rapidly.

toponym
A place name.

toponymy
The place names of a region or, especially, the study of place names.

total fertility rate (TFR)
The average number of children that would be born to each woman if during her childbearing years she bore children at the current year's rate for women that age.

town
A nucleated settlement that contains a *central business district* but that is small and less functionally complex than a *city.*

toxic waste
Discarded chemical substances that can cause serious illness or death.

traditional religion
See *tribal religion.*

tragedy of the commons
The observation that in the absence of collective control over the use of a resource available to all, it is to the advantage of all users to maximize their separate shares even though their collective pressures may diminish total yield or destroy the resource altogether.

transferability
Acceptable costs of a spatial exchange; the cost of moving a commodity relative to the ability of the commodity to bear that cost.

transnational corporation (TNC)
A large business organization operating in at least two separate national economies; a form of *multinational corporation.*

tribal religion
(*syn:* traditional religion) An *ethnic religion* specific to a small, localized, preindustrial culture group.

trickle-down effect
See *spread effect.*

tropical rain forest
Tree cover composed of tall, high-crowned evergreen deciduous species, associated with the continuously wet tropical lowlands.

truck farming
(*syn:* horticultural farming; market gardening) The intensive production of fruits and vegetables for market rather than for processing or canning.

U

ubiquitous industry
A *market-oriented* industry whose establishments are distributed in direct proportion to the distribution of population.

ultraviolet (UV) radiation
Electromagnetic radiation from the sun with wavelengths shorter than the violet end of visible light and longer than X rays.

underdevelopment
A level of economic and social achievement below what could be reached—given the natural and human resources of an area—were necessary capital and technology available.

underpopulation
A value statement reflecting the view that an area has too few people in relation to its resources and population-supporting capacity.

unified government
(*syn:* Unigov; Metro) Any of several devices federating or consolidating governments within a *metropolitan* region.

uniform plain
See *isotropic plain.*

uniform region
See *formal region.*

Unigov
See *unified government.*

unitary state
A *state* in which the central government dictates the degree of local or *regional autonomy* and the nature of local governmental units; a country with few cultural conflicts and with a strong sense of national identity.

United Nations Convention on the Law of the Sea (UNCLOS)
A code of maritime law approved by the United Nations in 1982 that authorizes, among other provisions, territorial waters extending 12 nautical miles (22 km) from shore and 200-nautical-mile-wide (370-km-wide) *exclusive economic zones.*

universalizing religion
A *religion* that claims global truth and applicability and seeks the conversion of all humankind.

urban
Characteristic of, belonging to, or related to a city or town; the opposite of rural. An agglomerated settlement whose inhabitants are primarily engaged in nonagricultural occupations.

urban geography
The geographical study of cities; the branch of *human geography* concerned with the spatial aspects of (1) the locations, functional structures, size hierarchies, and intercity relationships of national or regional systems of cities, and (2) the *site,* evolution, *economic base,* internal land use, and social geographic patterns of individual cities.

urban hierarchy
A ranking of cities based on their size and functional complexity.

urban influence zone
An area outside of a *city* that is nevertheless affected by the city.

urbanization
Transformation of a population from rural to *urban* status; the process of city formation and expansion.

urbanized area
A continuously built up *urban* landscape defined by building and population densities with no reference to the political boundaries of the city; it may contain a *central city* and many contiguous towns, *suburbs,* and unincorporated areas.

usable reserves
Mineral deposits that have been identified and can be recovered at current prices and with current technology.

 V

value system
Mentifacts of the *ideological subsystem* of a *culture* summarizing its common beliefs, understandings, expectations, and controls.

variable cost
A cost of enterprise operation that varies either by output level or by location of the activity.

variable costs of transportation
See *line-haul costs.*

verbal scale
A statement of the relationship between units of measure on a map and distance on the ground, as "one inch represents one mile."

vernacular
1: The nonstandard indigenous *language* or *dialect* of a locality. **2:** Of or related to indigenous arts and architecture, such as a *vernacular house.* **3:** Of or related to the perceptions and understandings of the general population, such as a *vernacular region.*

vernacular house
An indigenous style of building constructed of native materials to traditional plan, without formal drawings.

vernacular region
A region perceived and defined by its inhabitants, usually with a popularly given or accepted nickname.

von Thünen model
Model developed by Johann H. von Thünen (1783–1850) to explain the forces that control the prices of agricultural commodities and how those variable prices affect patterns of agricultural land utilization.

von Thünen rings
The concentric zonal pattern of agricultural land use around a single market center proposed in the *von Thünen model*.

W

water table
The upper limit of the saturated zone and therefore of *groundwater*.

wattle and daub
A building technique featuring walls of interwoven twigs, branches, or poles (wattles) plastered (daubed) with clay and mud.

Weberian analysis
See *least-cost theory*.

winter wheat
Wheat sown in fall for ripening the following spring or summer.

Z

zero population growth (ZPG)
A term suggesting a population in equilibrium, fully stable in numbers with births (plus immigration) equaling deaths (plus emigration).

zoning
Designating by ordinance areas in a municipality for particular types of land use.

CREDITS

PHOTOS

Part Openers

1: © David Ryan/Uniphoto Picture Agency;
2: © John Lewis Stage/The Image Bank;
3: © DC Productions/The Image Bank;
4: © John Elk III; **5:** © Robert Fried/Stock, Boston

Chapter 1

Opener: © Uniphoto, Inc.; **1.1:** © Karl Weatherly/Corbis Media; **1.10:** © W. Frerck/Odyssey Productions/Chicago; **1.11:** NASA; **1.12:** USGS; **1.13:** From Chicago Area Transportation Study, Final Report 1959, Vol. 1, p. 44, Fig. 22. *Desire Lines of International Automobile Driver Trips.*

Chapter 2

Opener: © Wolfgang Kaehler; **2.1A:** © Ian Murphy/Tony Stone Images; **2.1B:** © Robert Eckert/EKM-Nepenthe; **2.2A:** © Walter Gans/The Image Works; **2.2B:** © Genzo Sugino/Tom Stack & Associates; **2.3:** © Kennan Ward/Corbis Media; **2.5:** © Paul Almasy/Corbis Media; **2.6:** © Aubrey Lang/Valan Photos; **2.7:** John Kreul; **p. 39:** © Don Johnston/Photo Nats, Inc.; **2.12:** © Aubrey Lang/Valan Photos; **2.15:** © Travel Ink/Abbie Enock/Corbis Media; **2.17:** Joyce Gregory Wyels; **2.18A:** © Dave G. Houser/Hillstrom Stock Photo, Inc.; **2.18B:** © R. Aguirre and G. Switkes/Amazonia Films; **2.19A:** © Cary Wolinsky/Stock, Boston; **2.19B:** © John Eastcott/The Image Works; **2.19C:** © Yigal Pardo/Hillstrom Stock Photo, Inc.; **2.19D:** © Paul Conklin/PhotoEdit; **2.20A:** © Mark Antman/The Image Works; **2.20B:** © W. Marc Bernsau/The Image Works; **2.20C:** © Owen Franken/Stock, Boston; **2.24A:** © Jeff Dunn/The Picture Cube; **2.24B:** © Philip M. Zito; **2.24C:** © Diane Bosley-Taylor; **2.24D,E,F:** © 1994 Margaret Berg/Picture Perfect-TM; **2.25:** © Geoffrey Hiller/Leo de Wys Inc.

Chapter 3

Opener: © Hans Wolf/The Image Bank; **3.1:** © Melinda Berge/Photographers Aspen, Inc.; **3.7A:** © Robert Frerck/Odyssey Productions/Chicago; **3.7B:** © Charles Gupton/Tony Stone Images; **3.22:** Bettmann Archive; **3.23:** © Alexander Sassaki/Gamma-Liaison; **3.28:** Bettmann Archive

Chapter 4

Opener: © Dagmar Fabricius/Stock, Boston; **4.2:** © Herb Snitzer/Stock, Boston; **p. 100:** © Owen Franken/Corbis Media; **4.11:** © Patrick Ward/Stock, Boston; **4.17:** Stock Montage, Inc.; **4.18:** © Steve McCutcheon/Visuals Unlimited; **4.23:** Bill Cardoni; **4.24:** © William E. Ferguson; **4.27:** United Nations Photo Library; **4.29:** © Carl Purcell/Words & Pictures; **4.30:** © Barry Wilson/Stock & Search

Chapter 5

Opener: © Sujoy Das/Stock, Boston; **5.1:** © Chuck Wyrostok/Appalight; **5.7:** © Mark Antman/The Image Works; **5.24:** © David A. Burney; **5.27B:** © David Brownell; **5.28:** © Topham/The Image Works; **5.30:** © Arvind Garg/Corbis Media; **5.31:** © Porterfield/Chickering/Photo Researchers, Inc.; **5.32:** © Fred Bruemmer/Valan Photos; **5.34:** © Wolfgang Kaehler; **5.35:** © Charlotte Kaehler

Chapter 6

Opener: © Robert Fried/Stock, Boston; **6.1:** © Philippe Gontier/The Image Works; **6.2:** © J. Messerschmidt/Bruce Coleman, Inc.; **6.3:** © Stacy Pick/Stock, Boston; **6.7:** © Chromosohm Media/The Image Works; **6.14:** © Joyce Gregory Wyels; **6.15A:** © Joseph Pearce/Valan Photos; **6.15B:** © Harold V. Green/Valan Photos; **6.18:** © Margot Granitsas/The Image Works; **6.22:** © Martha Cooper/Peter Arnold, Inc.; **6.23:** © Susan Reisenweaver

Chapter 7

Opener: © Michael Dwyer/Stock, Boston; **7.1:** Culver Pictures, Inc.; **7.2A:** © Jean Fellmann; **7.3:** Courtesy of Plimoth Plantation, Inc., Plymouth, MA, USA/Ted Curtain, Photographer; **7.6A:** © Ira Kirschenbaum/Stock, Boston; **7.6B:** © Pam E. Hickman/Valan Photos; **7.7A,B:** Courtesy of Professor Colin E. Thorn; **7.7C,E:** © Wolfgang Kaehler; **7.7D:** © Tony Stone Images, Inc.; **7.9A-C; 7.10B,D; 7.11A; 7.13A:** Courtesy of Professor John A. Jakle; **7.10A:** © Peter Menzel/Stock, Boston; **7.10C; 7.11B; 7.15A; 7.16A-C:** © Susan Reisenweaver; **7.12:** © Sharon Wildman; **7.16D:** © Jared Fellmann; **7.24:** © Larry Mangnio/The Image Works; **7.25:** Elizabeth J. Leppman; **7.28:** © Bob Coyle; **7.29:** © Joseph Nettis 1995/Stock, Boston

Chapter 8

Opener: © John Elk III; **8.1:** © John Maher/EKM-Nepenthe; **8.3:** © Mark E. Gibson; **8.8:** © Wolfgang Kaehler; **8.9:** © V. Crowl/Visuals Unlimited; **8.13:** © Bill Gillette/Stock, Boston; **8.19:** © Jim Pickerell/Stock, Boston; **8.22:** © Barry Wilson/Stock & Search; **8.24:** © Ric Ergenbright/Corbis Media; **8.25:** © David Muench/Corbis Media; **8.27:** © Cameramann International Ltd.; **8.29:** © Larry Tackett/Tom Stack & Associates; **8.31:** © Cameramann International, Ltd.; **8.32:** © Thomas Kitchin/Valan Photos; **8.34:** United Nations Photo Library

Chapter 9

Opener: © Wolfgang Kaehler; **9.1:** © Cary Wolinsky/Stock, Boston; **9.7:** © John Spagens Jr./Photo Researchers, Inc.; **9.15:** © Cameramann International, Ltd.; **9.16:** John Kreul; **9.19:** © Peter Pearson/Tony Stone Images; **9.21:** © Aubrey Diem/Valan Photos; **9.25:** Bert Schmid; **9.26:** Culver Pictures, Inc.; **9.27:** Courtesy of the Fairfax County Economic Development Authority

Chapter 10

Opener: © Wolfgang Kaehler;
10.1: © Dilip Mehta/Contact Press Images;
10.2A: © Cameramann International, Ltd.;
10.2B: © Jason Clay/Anthro Photo;
10.4: © Wolfgang Kaehler; **10.5:** © William E.
Ferguson; **10.6:** Bettmann Archive;
10.12: © Wendy Stone/Odyssey
Productions/Chicago; **10.14:** © D.
Willetts/Camera Pix Agency, Inc./Gamma-
Liaison; **10.18:** © Barry W. Barker;
10.21: © Wendy Stone/Odyssey
Productions/Chicago; **10.24:** © Topham/The
Image Works

Chapter 11

Opener: © Wolfgang Kaehler; **11.1:** © John
Kreul; **11.7A:** © William E. Ferguson;
11.7B: Courtesy of Professor Colin E. Thorn;
11.7C: © Wolfgang Kaehler; **11.9A:** © Carl
Purcell/Words & Pictures; **11.9B:** © Susan
Reisenweaver; **11.20:** © Robert Brenner/Photo
Edit; **11.33:** © Marc Pokempner/Tony Stone
Images; **11.34:** © Thomas Kitchin/Tom Stack &
Associates; **11.35:** © Chapman & Parry/The
Image Works; **11.37A:** © Aubrey Diem/Valan
Photos; **11.37B:** © Eastcott/Momatuik/The
Image Works; **p. 404:** Bettmann Archive;
11.38: © Dave G. Houser/Corbis Media;
11.39: AP/Wide World Photos; **11.40:** © Luiz
Claudio Marigo/Peter Arnold, Inc.; **11.42:**
© Byron Augustine/Tom Stack & Associates

Chapter 12

Opener: © Bernard Van Berg/The Image Bank;
12.1: Courtesy of the Pilgrim Society,
Plymouth, Massachusetts; **12.2:** © Chromosohm
Media/The Image Works; **12.10:** Australian
Information Service; **12.12:** © Fred Bavendam/
Peter Arnold, Inc.; **12.13:** © Jeannie R.
Kemp/Valan Photos; **12.14:** AP/Wide World
Photos; **12.16A,B:** © San Diego *Union Tribune*,
John Nelson; **12.17:** © Michael Siluk; **12.18:**
© Michael J. Johnson/Valan Photos;
12.22: United Nations Photo;
12.28: © Cameramann International, Ltd.;
12.29: © Keystone/The Image Works;
12.30: Bettmann Archive

Chapter 13

Opener: © Ted Russell/The Image Bank;
13.1: Courtesy Kennecott; **13.6:** © Rick
Maiman/Sygma; **13.7:** © Robert V. Eckert
Jr./EKM-Nepenthe; **13.8:** © William E.
Ferguson; **p. 467:** Goddard Space Flight
Center/NASA; **13.10A:** Exxon Corporation and
the American Petroleum Institute;
13.10B: © Susan Reisenweaver; **13.11:** © Martin
Wendler/Peter Arnold, Inc.; **13.13:** Jim
Whitmer; **13.14:** © Wolfgang Kaehler;
13.20: © Robert Frerck/Odyssey
Productions/Chicago; **13.21:** © Stephen Trimble;
13.22: © Lawrence E. Stager/Anthro-Photo;
13.24: © Mark Antman/The Image Works;
13.25: © Roger A. Clark/Photo Researchers,
Inc.; **13.26:** © Illustrator's Stock Photos

LINE ART

Chapter 1

Figure 1.8: Redrawn by permission from *The
Los Angeles Metropolitan Experience,* Howard J.
Nelson and William A. V. Clark, p. 49,
Association of American Geographers, 1976.
Figure 1.16: Sources: (a) John H. Garland, ed.,
The North American Midwest (New York: John
Wiley & Sons, Inc. 1955); (b) John R. Borchert
and Jane McGuigan, *Geography of the New World*
(Chicago; Rand McNally, 1961); and (c) Otis P.
Starkey and J. Lewis Robinson, *The Anglo-
American Realm* (New York; McGraw Hill,
1969). **Figure 1.19:** Redrawn by permission
from *Annals of the Association of American
Geographers,* John R. Borchert, vol. 62, p. 358,
Association of American Geographers, 1972.
Figure 1.23: William C. Adams, "As New
Hampshire Goes . . ." in *Media and Momentum:
The New Hampshire Primary and Nomination
Politics,* ed. Gary R. Orren and Nelson W.
Polsby (Chatham, NJ: Chatham House, 1987),
p. 43. Reprinted by permission. **Figures 1.26,
1.27:** Source: U.S. Geological Survey.
Figure 1.30: From Los Angeles Department of
City Planning, *The Visual Environment of Los
Angeles,* 1971. Reprinted by permission.

Chapter 2

Figure 2.14: Source: L. Luca Cavalli-Sforza,
Paolo Menozzi, and Alberto Piazza, *The History
and Geography of Human Genes.* Copyright © 1994
Princeton University Press, Princeton, NJ.
Figure 2.22: Redrawn by permission from
Spatial Diffusion, by Peter R. Gould, Resource
Paper No. 4, page 4, Association of American
Geographers, 1969. **Figure 2.23a:** Based on
Gerald F. Pyle and K. David Patterson, *Ecology of
Disease,* 2, no. 3, (1984): p. 179. **Figure 2.23b:**
Redrawn by permission from *Resource
Publications for College Geography, Spatial
Diffusion,* by Peter R. Gould, page 6, Association
of American Geographers, 1969. **Page 58:**
Source: Redrawn from data in Zvi Griliches,
"Hybrid Corn and the Economics of Innovation"
in *Science* 132(3422):277 (July 29, 1960), figure 3.

Chapter 3

Figure 3.2: Source: Data from BP International
Limited, *BP Statistical Review of World Energy
1995.* **Figure 3.4c:** Source: (c) Data from
Chicago Area Transportation Study, *A
Summary of Travel Characteristics, 1977.*
Figure 3.12: Robert A. Murdie, "Cultural
Differences in Consumer Travel," *Economic
Geography* 41, no. 3 (Worcester, Mass.: Clark
University, 1965). Redrawn by permission.
Page 75: Based on Risa Palm and Alan Pred, *A
Time-Geographic Perspective on Problems of
Inequality for Women,* Institute of Urban and
Regional Development, Working Paper no. 236,
University of California, Berkeley. **Figure 3.13:**
Source: *Metropolitan Toronto and Region
Transportation Study,* figure 42, The Queen's
Printer, Toronto, 1966. **Figure 3.14:** Frederick
P. Stutz, "Distance and Network Effects on

Urban Social Travel Fields," *Economic
Geography* 49, no. 2 (Worcester, Mass.: Clark
University, 1973), p. 139. Redrawn by
permission. **Figure 3.15:** Source: Data from
Historical Statistics of the United States, National
Association of Regulatory Utility
Commissioners, and AT&T. **Figure 3.18:** John
A. Jakle, Stanley Brunn and Curtis C. Roseman,
Human Spatial Behavior: A Social Geography,
p. 130, copyright 1976, 1985 by Waveland Press,
Inc., Prospect Heights, Illinois. Used by
permission of the author. **Figure 3.19:**
Courtesy of Hilary Hope Getis. **Figure 3.20:**
Herbert A. Whitney, "Preferred Locations in
North America: Canadians, Clues, and
Conjectures," *Journal of Geography* 83, no. 5
(Indiana, PA: National Council for Geographic
Education, 1984). Redrawn by permission.
Figure 3.21: Source: U.S. Environmental
Protection Agency, August 1987. **Figure 3.24:**
Map courtesy of Clyde Surveys Ltd., Berkshire,
England. **Figure 3.25a:** Source: Adrienne Kols
and Dana Lewison, *Migration, Population
Growth, and Development.* Population Reports,
Series M, No. 7 (Baltimore, MD.: Johns Hopkins
University, Population Information Program,
1983). **Figure 3.25b:** Source: Data from
Gunther Glebe and John O'Loughlin, eds.,
Foreign Minorities in Continental European Cities,
vol. 84, *Erdkundliches Wissen,* vol. 84
(Wiesbaden, Germany: Franz Steiner Verlag,
1987). **Figure 3.29a:** Redrawn by permission
from *Proceedings of the Association of American
Geographers,* C. C. Roseman, vol. 3, p. 142,
Association of American Geographers, 1971.
Figure 3.29b: Based on data from K. C.
Zachariah and Julien Conde, *Migration in West
Africa: Demographic Aspects,* copyright © 1981
by the International Bank for Reconstruction
and Development/The World Bank. **Figure
3.30:** Source: T. Hagerstand, *Innovation
Diffusion as a Spatial Process.* Copyright © 1967
The University of Chicago Press, Chicago, IL.
Figure 3.31: Source: U.S. Bureau of the Census,
Geographical Mobility: March 1990 to March 1991.
Current Population Reports P20-463.

Chapter 4

Figure 4.1a: Sources: (a) Estimates from
Population Reference Bureau and United
Nations Population Fund. **Figure 4.1b:**
(b) Based on United Nations, U.S. Bureau of the
Census, and Population Reference Bureau
projections. **Figure 4.3:** Source: Data from
Population Reference Bureau. **Figure 4.4:**
Sources: Projections based on Population
Reference Bureau, U.S. Bureau of the Census,
and United Nations figures. **Figures 4.5, 4.6:**
Source: Data from Population Reference
Bureau. **Figure 4.7:** Source: Data from U.S.
Bureau of the Census and Population
Reference Bureau. **Figure 4.8:** Sources: Data
from World Bank; the United Nations;
Population Reference Bureau; and Carl Haub,
"Population Change in the Former Soviet
Republics," *Population Bulletin* Vol. 49, No. 4,
December 1994. **Figure 4.9:** Source: Redrawn
from Lori S. Ashford, "New Perspectives on
Population: Lessons from Cairo," *Population

Bulletin Vol. 50, No. 1 (Washington, DC: Population Reference Bureau, Inc., March 1995, based on data from United Nations, *The Sex and Age Distribution of the World Populations: The 1992 Revisions,* 1993. **Figure 4.10:** Source: Data from Population Reference Bureau. **Figure 4.12:** Source: U.S. Bureau of the Census. **Figure 4.13:** Source: Data from Population Reference Bureau. **Figure 4.14:** Source: Population Reference Bureau, *1989 World Population Data Sheet.* **Figure 4.19:** Source: Revised and redrawn from Elaine M. Murphy, *World Population: Toward the Next Century,* rev. ed. (Washington, DC.: Population Reference Bureau, 1989), based on United Nations Population Division. **Figure 4.20:** Source: Shaded zones after Daniel Noin, *Geographie de la Population* (Paris: Masson, 1979), p. 85. **Figure 4.25:** World Bank, *Population Growth and Policies in Sub-Saharan Africa* (A World Bank Policy Study), 1986. Redrawn by permission. **Figure 4.26:** Source: Data from Population Reference Bureau.

Chapter 5

Figure 5.5: Data from various sources, including C. F. and F. M. Voegelin, *Map of North American Indian Languages* (Seattle: University of Washington Press, 1986). **Figure 5.10:** Adapted from Gordon R. Wood, *Vocabulary Change: A Study of Variation in Regional Words in Eight of the Southern States* (Carbondale: Southern Illinois University Press, 1971), Map 81, p. 357. Used by permission of the publisher. **Figure 5.11:** Redrawn from *A Word Geography of the Eastern United States,* by Hans Kurath, fig. 3. Copyright © by the University of Michigan, 1949. Used by permission. **Figure 5.12:** Sources: Raven I. McDavid, Jr., "The Dialects of American English" in W. Nelson Francis, *The Structure of American English,* pp. 580–581, (New York: The Ronald Press, 1958); "Regional Dialects in the United States," *Webster's New World Dictionary,* 2d College Edition, (New York: Simon and Schuster, 1980); and Gordon R. Wood, *Vocabulary Change,* (Carbondale: Southern Illinois University Press, 1971), Map 83, p. 358. **Figure 5.13:** Redrawn with permission from Alva L. Davis, *A Word Atlas of the Great Lakes States,* Ph.D. dissertation, University of Michigan, 1948. **Figure 5.14:** Source: Adapted from Bernd Heine, *Status and Use of African Lingua Francas* (Munich, Germany: Weltforum Verlag; and New York: Humanities Press, 1970). **Figure 5.16:** Source: Commissioner of Official Languages, Government of Canada. **Figure 5.17:** With kind permission of the American Name Society. **Figure 5.18:** Sources: J. F. Simoons, *Eat Not This Flesh* (Madison: University of Wisconsin Press, 1961); United Nations, Food and Agriculture Organization; and *Narodnoye Khozyaystvo SSR.* **Figure 5.25a:** Source: Based on "Christian Denominations in the Conterminous United States" in *Historical Atlas of the Religions of the World,* ed. Isma'il R. al-Faruqi and David E. Sopher (New York: Macmillan, 1974). **Figure 5.25b:** Source: Based on Statistics Canada, *Population: Religion* (Ottawa, 1984); and *The National Atlas of Canada.* **Figure 5.26a:** Redrawn

by permission from *Annals of the Association of American Geographers,* Wilbur Zelinsky, vol. 51, Association of American Geographers, 1961. **Figure 5.26b:** Ingolf Vogeler, University of Wisconsin-Eau Claire.

Chapter 6

Figure 6.4: Sources: Data from Leon F. Bouvier and Robert W. Gardner, "Immigration to the United States: The Unfinished Story," *Population Bulletin,* 41, no. 4 (Washington D.C.: Population Reference Bureau, 1986); and Immigration and Naturalization Service. **Figure 6.5:** Redrawn by permission from *Annals of the Association of American Geographers,* Keith D. Harries, vol. 61, p. 739, Association of American Geographers, 1971. **Figure 6.8:** Redrawn with permission from Russel Gerlach, *Settlement Patterns in Missouri* (Columbia: University of Missouri Press, 1986), p. 41. **Figure 6.10:** Redrawn by permission from *Annals of the Association of American Geographers,* D. W. Meinig, vol. 55, p. 214, Association of American Geographers, 1965. **Figure 6.13a,b:** Source: Data from U.S. Bureau of the Census. **Figure 6.16:** Source: Data from Eugene Turner and James P. Allen, "An Atlas of Population Patterns in Metropolitan Los Angeles and Orange Counties, 1990," *Occasional Publication* no. 8, Center for Geographical Studies, California State University, Northridge. **Figure 6.17:** Source: *The New York Times* as reproduced in Peter Jackson, *Ethnic Groups and Boundaries,* School of Geography, Oxford University, 1980. **Figures 6.19, 6.21:** David T. Herbert and Colin J. Thomas, *Urban Geography,* London: David Fulton Publishers, 1987. Redrawn by permission. **Figure 6.20:** Source: *The American City and its Church* by Samuel Kincheloe. Copyright 1938 by Friendship Press, New York. **Figure 6.24:** Source: Charles M. Andrews, "The River Towns of Connecticut" in *Johns Hopkins University Studies in Historical and Political Science,* 7th series, VII-VIII-IX (1899), opposite p. 5. **Figure 6.25:** Redrawn by permission from *Original Survey and Land Subdivision,* Monograph Series No. 4, Norman J. W. Thrower, p. 46, Association of American Geographers, 1966. **Figure 6.26:** Source: U.S. Geological Survey map. **Figure 6.27:** Redrawn by permission from *Annals of the Association of American Geographers,* George I. McDermott, vol. 51, p. 263, Association of American Geographers, 1961. **Figure 6.28:** Source: Redrawn from Carl A. Dawson, *Group Settlement: Ethnic Communities in Western Canada* Vol. 7, *Canadian Frontiers of Settlement* (Toronto: Macmillan Company of Canada, 1936), p. 111.

Chapter 7

Figure 7.2b: Redrawn by permission from *Annals of the Association of American Geographers,* William K. Crowley, vol. 68, p. 262, Association of American Geographers, 1978. **Figure 7.4:** Source: Based on Allen G. Noble, *Wood, Brick, and Stone,* vol. 1 (Amherst: University of Massachusetts Press, 1984); and

Annals of the Association of American Geographers, vol. 60, p. 446, Association of American Geographers, 1970. **Figure 7.5:** Redrawn with permission from Reuben K. Udo, *The Human Geography of Tropical Africa* (Ibadan: Heinemann Education Books (Nigeria) Ltd., 1982), p. 50. **Figure 7.8:** Source: Based on Cole Harris, "French Landscapes in North American," in *The Making of the American Landscape,* ed. Michael P. Conzen (Boston: Unwin Hyman, 1990), Fig. 4.1, p. 66; and R. Cole Harris, *Historical Atlas of Canada,* vol. 1, *From the Beginning to 1800* (Toronto: University of Toronto Press, 1987), Plate 40. **Figure 7.9d:** Reprinted from *Wood, Brick, and Stone: The North American Settlement Landscape,* volume 2, by Allen G. Noble. Drawing by M. Margaret Geib (Amherst: University of Massachusetts Press, 1984), copyright © 1984 by the University of Massachusetts Press. **Figure 7.14:** Sources: F. Kniffen, *Annals of the Association of American Geographers,* 55:560, 1965; Fred Kniffen and Henry Glassie, "Building in Wood in the Eastern United States" in *Geographical Review* 56:60, © 1966 The American Geographical Society; and Terry G. Jordan and Matti Kaups, *The American Backwooods Frontier,* pp. 8–9, © 1989 The Johns Hopkins University Press. **Figure 7.17:** Milton Newton, Jr., "The Annual Round in the Upland South: The Synchronization of Man and Nature Through Culture," *Pioneer America* 3, no. 2, (Akron, Ohio: Pioneer Society of America, 1971), p. 65. Redrawn by permission. **Figure 7.18:** Redrawn by permission from Loyal Durand, "Mountain Moonshining in East Tennessee," *Geographical Review* 46 (New York: American Geographical Society, 1956), p. 171. **Figure 7.19:** Redrawn "Map depicting folk song regions of the Eastern U.S." by Rafael Palacios, from *Folk Songs of North America* by Alan Lomax. Copyright © 1960 by Alan Lomax. Used by permission. **Figure 7.20:** Redrawn by permission from George O. Carney, "Country Music and the South," *Journal of Cultural Geography* 1 (Fall/Winter, 1980), p. 25. **Figure 7.21:** Reproduced by permission of the American Folklore Society from *Journal of American Folklore* 65:258, October–December 1952. Not for further reproduction. **Figure 7.22:** Source: Based on Henry Glassie, *Pattern in the Material Folk Culture of the Eastern United States,* pp. 37–38, copyright © 1968 by the Trustees of the University of Pennsylvania; and Michael P. Conzen, ed., *The Making of the American Landscape* (Winchester, MA.: Unwin Hyman, 1990), 373. **Figure 7.23:** Redrawn with permission from Henry Glassie, *Pattern in the Material Folk Culture of the Eastern United States,* p. 39, copyright © 1968 by the Trustees of the University of Pennsylvania. **Figure 7.26:** Source: Floyd M. Henderson and J. Russel, unpublished drawing. **Figure 7.27:** Redrawn with permission from John A. Jakle and Richard Mattson, "The Evolution of a Commercial Strip," *Journal of Cultural Geography* 1 (Spring/Summer 1981), pp. 14 and 20. **Figure 7.30:** Redrawn by permission from George O. Carney, "From

Down Home to Uptown," *Journal of Geography,* 76 (Indiana, Pa.: National Council for Geographic Education, 1977), p. 107.
Figure 7.31: Redrawn by permission from Wilbur Zelinsky, "Classical Town Names in the United States," *Geographical Review* 57 (New York: American Geographical Society, 1967).
Figure 7.33: Redrawn by permission from the *Annals of the Association of American Geographers,* W. Zelinsky, vol. 70, p. 14, Fig. 9, Association of American Geographers, 1980.
Figure 7.34: From Arthur Getis and Judith Getis, eds., *The United States and Canada: The Land, the People.* Copyright © 1995 Times Mirror Higher Education Group, Inc., Dubuque, Iowa. Reprinted by permission. All Rights Reserved.

Chapter 8

Figure 8.4: Sources: *Hammond Comparative World Atlas,* New Revised and Expanded Edition, Hammond Inc., Maplewood, NJ; *Goode's World Atlas,* 19th ed., Rand McNally & Company, Chicago, IL., 1995.
Figure 8.5: Courtesy Wayne M. Wendland.
Figure 8.6: Source: *The World Bank Atlas.*
Figure 8.10: Redrawn by permission from Robert E. Huke, "The Green Revolution," *Journal of Geography,* 84, no. 6 (Indiana, PA.: National Council for Geographic Education).
Figure 8.11: Source: Data from Food and Agriculture Organization, World Resources Institute, and U.S. Department of Agriculture.
Figure 8.12: Sources: J. G. Hawkes, *The Diversity of Crop Plants,* (Cambridge, MA: Harvard University Press, 1983); and Walter V. Reid and Kenton R. Miller, *Keeping Options Alive: The Scientific Basis for Conserving Biodiversity* (Washington, DC: World Resources Institute, 1989), fig. 5, p. 24. **Figure 8.14b:** Modified with permission from Bernd Anreae, *Farming Development and Space: A World Agricultural Geography,* trans. Howard F. Gregor (Berlin: Walter de Gruyter and Co., 1981). **Figure 8.17:** Sources: U.S. Bureau of Agricultural Economics; Agriculture Canada; and Secretaria de Agricultural y Recursos Hidraulicos, Mexico. **Figure 8.18:** Source: *Statistical Abstract of the United States.*
Figure 8.30: Source: U.S. Geological Survey.
Figure 8.33: Source: Data from World Bank.

Chapter 9

Figure 9.5: Redrawn from Leslie Dienes, *Locational Factors and Locational Developments in the Soviet Chemical Industry,* University of Chicago Research Dissertation no. 119, 1964, p. 116. Used by permission of the author.
Page 300: Source: Data from *County Business Patterns.*

Chapter 10

Figure 10.3: Sources: Data from World Bank and United Nations. **Figure 10.7:** Sources: Data from World Bank and Population Reference Bureau, Inc. **Figure 10.8:** Sources: Data from International Monetary Fund and World Bank. **Figure 10.9:** Source: Base data from *Statistical Yearbook of China, 1994.*

Figure 10.10: Sources: Data from United Nations and World Bank. **Figure 10.11:** Sources: Data from U.S. Department of Agriculture, *World Agriculture: Trends and Indicators;* the International Research Section, U.S. Bureau of the Census; and World Bank, *Social Indicators of Development.* **Figure 10.13:** Source: Data from *Human Development Report* and FAO. **Figure 10.15:** Sources: Data from World Health Organization; World Bank; and UNICEF. **Figures 10.16, 10.17:** Source: Data from UNESCO. **Figure 10.19:** Source: Data from United Nations. **Figure 10.20:** Source: Data from World Heath Organization.
Figure 10.22: Source: Data from UNICEF and International Fund for Agricultural Development. **Figure 10.23:** Source: Country rankings are made and reported by United Nations Development Programme in Table 1, "Human Development Index," in *Human Development Report 1995* (New York: Oxford University Press, 1995). **Figure 10.25:** Source: Redrawn from charts 5.4A and 5.4B of United Nations, *The World's Women 1995: Trends and Statistics.* Social Statistics and Indicators, Series K, No. 12. (New York: United Nations, 1995). **Figure 10.26:** Source: United Nations, *The World's Women 1995.* **Figure 10.27:** Sources: Data from United Nations, *The World's Women 1995,* and the International Labour Office. **Figure 10.28:** Source: Rankings from International Fund for Agricultural Development. **Figure 10.29b:** Source: United Nations Development Programme, *Human Development Report 1995,* pp. 84–85.

Chapter 11

Figure 11.2: Source: Estimates and projections from Population Reference Bureau and other sources. **Figure 11.3:** Data from Population Division, United Nations, and other sources. **Figure 11.4:** Source: Data from World Bank, *World Development Report 1992;* and United Nations. **Figure 11.13:** Source: Data from U.S. Bureau of the Census. **Figure 11.16:** Source: E. S. Simpson, *The Developing World: An Introduction.* (Harlow, Essex, England: Longman Group UK Limited, 1987).
Figure 11.18: Arthur Getis and Judith Getis, "Christaller's Central Place Theory," *Journal of Geography, 1966.* Used with permission of the National Council for Geographic Education.
Figure 11.23: Redrawn with permission from B. J. L. Berry, *Commercial Structure and Commercial Blight,* Research Paper 85, University of Chicago, 1963. **Figure 11.25:** Anupa Mukhopadhyay and Ashok K. Dutt, "Population Density Gradient Changes of a Postindustrial City—Cleveland, Ohio 1860–1990," *GeoJournal* 34:517, no. 4, 1994. Used by permission of Kluwer Academic Publishers and Ashok K. Dutt. **Figure 11.26:** Redrawn from "The Nature of Cities" by C. D. Harris and E. L. Ullmann in volume no. 242 of *The Annals of the American Academy of Political and Social Science.* Copyright © 1945 The American Academy of Political and Social

Science, Philadelphia, PA. Used by permission of the publisher and authors. **Figure 11.27:** Redrawn with permission from P. J. Smith, "Calgary: A Study in Urban Patterns," *Economic Geography* Vol. 38, No. 4, p. 32, © 1962 Clark University, Worcester, MA. **Figure 11.28:** Redrawn with permission from Robert A. Murdie, *Factorial Ecology of Metropolitan Toronto,* Research Paper 116, Department of Geography *Research Series,* University of Chicago, 1969. **Figure 11.30:** Redrawn with permission from B. J. L. Berry, *Chicago: Transformation of an Urban System,* (Cambridge, MA.: Ballinger, 1976), with additions from other sources. **Figure 11.31:** Figure 4.10 (Re-drawn) from *THE NORTH AMERICAN CITY,* 4th ed. by Maurice Yeates. Copyright © 1990 by Harper & Row, Publishers, Inc. Redrawn by permission of HarperCollins Publishers, Inc. **Figure 11.32:** Redrawn with permission from V. H. Winston & Son, Inc., "Suburban Downtowns and the Transformation of Atlanta's Business Landscape," *Urban Geography,* 10:382 (Silver Spring, MD.: V. H. Winston & Son, Inc., 1989). **Figure 11.41a:** T. G. McGee, *The Southeast Asian City* (New York: Praeger Publishers, 1967), p. 128. Redrawn by permission of Greenwood Publishing Group, Inc., Westport, CT. **Figure 11.41b,c:** Figures 9.7/9.9 Ashok K. Dutt—"Cities of South Asia," from *CITIES OF THE WORLD: WORLD REGIONAL DEVELOPMENT,* by Stanley D. Brun and Jack F. Williams. Copyright © 1993 by Harper & Row, Publishers, Inc. Redrawn by permission of HarperCollins Publishers, Inc. **Figure 11.41d:** Redrawn by permission from Ernst Griffin and Larry Ford, "A Model of Latin American City Structure," in *Geographical Review* 70 (1980), American Geographical Society.

Chapter 12

Figure 12.5: From *World Regional Geography: A Question of Place* by Paul Ward English, figure 5 on p. 248. Copyright 1977. Used by permission of the author.

Chapter 13

Figure 13.9: Source: Data from Canadian government. **Figure 13.12:** Sources: Based on H. E. Dregne, *Desertification of Arid Lands* (New York: Harwood Academic Publishers, 1983), Fig. 1.2; and *A World Map of Desertification,* UNESCO/FAO. **Figure 13.15:** Sources: *World Resources 1992–93;* and International Soil Reference and Information Center. **Figure 13.19:** Source: Malin Falkenmark, "Water and Mankind—A Complex System of Mutual Interaction," *Ambio* 6 (1977):5.

Appendixes

Figures A-2, A-8: Redrawn with permission from American Congress on Surveying and Mapping, *Choosing a World Map,* Special Publication No. 2 of the American Cartographic Association, Bethesda, MD. Copyright 1988 American Congress on Surveying and Mapping.

INDEX

Bold page numbers indicate figures, illustrations, and boxed material. Italicized page numbers indicate tables.

A

absolute direction, 10
absolute distance, 11
absolute location, 9
absorbing barrier, 57
accessibility, 14–15
acculturation, 60, **152,** 184
acculturation of languages, 141
acid rain, 464–65
acquired immune deficiency syndrome (AIDS)
  in developing countries, 358
  projected deaths from, 113
activity space, 71
  for family of five, diagram of, **71**
adaptation and racial differentiation, **180**
advanced countries
  agriculture in, characteristics of, 268
  AIDS in, 358
  birth and death rates after World War II, **114**
  birth rates in, 98–99, **114**
  defined, 334–35
  demographic transition model of population growth, 110–13
  energy consumption by, 287, 288, 342, 344, *346*
  foreign aid, effectiveness of, **349, 350–51**
  in models for economic advancement, 351–52
  North–South disparity in human development, *353*
  polarization between developing countries and, 113
  production of industrial wood from, 282, 283
  reduction of gender-related contrasts in, 361
  relative characteristics of development, *341*
  role of women in, 361–62

total global output, share of, 337–38
urbanization in, 373, **376**
advertising, popular culture and, 240, **242**
aerosols, role in icebox effect, 459, 460
Afghanistan, ethnic groups in, **186**
Africa. *See also individual countries*
  Arab nation as example of part-nation state, **418**
  Bantu advance, Khoisan retreat, **141**
  birth rates in, 98–99, **101**
  carrying capacity and potentials in sub-Saharan, 121
  children under 5 malnourished or with stunted growth, percentage of, **349**
  cities of, characteristics of, 408–9, 410
  colonial division and ramifications, 419, **421**
  from colonies to states, **421**
  Dinka chief on attempts at African unification, quote from, **134**
  early culture hearths, 47–49
  folk housing, 218, **219**
  forced migrations, 83, 85, 86
  fuelwood, effects of using, **345**
  Fulani movement paths, **83**
  geophagy in, **231**
  Green Revolution, effect of, 267
  infant mortality rates, 102–3
  "informal sector" of economy in, **337**
  languages spoken in, 137, **138–39, 141,** 142
  lingua francas of, **150**
  natural population increase that has permanently emigrated, percentage of, *116*
  nonnative ethnic groups in, response to, **182**
  official languages designated in, 149, **150**
  population
    growth of, **97**
    pyramid for Sub-Saharan, 104, **105**

poverty, data on persons living in, **339**
rural settlements, examples of, **378**
segregation in, 197
swidden plot burning, **263**
tribal and national boundaries, discrepancies between, **420**
urbanization in, 122
women as food producers in, **269**
African Americans
  abandonment of central city by, 398, 399
  black English vernacular, differentiation of, 148
  black segregation in large U.S. cities, *395*
  concentrations, 191, **192**
  culture rebound in, 203–4
  dispersion in U.S., 189, 191, **192**
  ethnic provinces of, 189, 191
  forced segregation of, in nuclear communities, 394, 395
  in Los Angeles, California, **395**
  in projected U.S. population, *193*
  representation created in North Carolina mandated for, **446–47**
  typology of African American ghettos, 201–2, **203**
Afro-Asiatic language family, 137, **138–39,** 141
age
  effect on activity space, 71
  in migration decisions, 89, 91
  of population and demand for services, 105, **107**
  world population and, 127
agglomerated phenomenon, 16
agglomeration
  economies, 304, 307, **308**
  high-tech industries and, 324–25
agriculture
  commercial. (*see* commercial agriculture)
  corn, diffusion patterns of hybrid, **58**
  cultural differences in farming practices, **34**

in culture hearths, 48
defined, 260
development, universality of early, 54–55
domestication of plants and animals, beginnings of, 44, **45, 46–47**
folk culture farming in Louisiana, "annual round" of, **229**
food production by region, **267**
freshwater use for irrigated, 476–77
gross domestic product, share of agriculture in, **261**
growing season, world map of, **260**
hunter-gatherers, conflict between agriculturalists and, 46
Mesolithic period, beginnings of, 44, **45,** 46
Neolithic innovations, 46–47
origins and diffusions, 44, **45,** **46–47**
population pressures to extend land for, 266
as primary economic activity, 257, 260–61
slash-and-burn, 262–64
soil erosion and, 472–73, **474,** 475
subsistence, 261–67. (*see* subsistence agriculture)
swidden, 262–64
swine production areas affected by religions, **157**
trade in primary products, 289–90
tropical deforestation for, results of, 469
value of farmland and buildings in U.S., 272, **274**
women engaged in, percentage of economically active, **364**
workforce engaged in, 344, 346–47
worldwide involvement in, 260–61
air transport, manufacturing decisions and, 302, **303**

Alliance of Small Island States (AOSIS), influence of, **422**

amalgamation theory, 184

Amerindians. *See* Native Americans

Amish
cultural landscape created by Amish farmers, **1**
Old Order Amish communities in U.S., distribution of, **215**
as remaining folk culture in U.S., 215
rural school in Illinois, picture of, **215**

Anasazi Indians (Arizona, New Mexico), ecological disaster created by, **39**

anecumene
characteristics of, 118
tundra vegetation and landscape, **120**

Anglo America
cities, characteristics of, 400, **401,** 403
colonial division and ramifications, 419
folk music in, 232–34
household as basic subsistence unit, **230**
reference map, **507**
space economy. (*see* space economy)
true folk societies no longer exist, 215

Anglo Americans
in Los Angeles, California, **395**
in projected U.S. population, *193*

animal domestication
beginnings, 44, **45,** 46
centers, **45**

animism, 157

Antarctica, territorial claims in, 417

antecedent boundary, defined, 427

aquaculture, 281–82

aquifers, 476–77

architecture
American indigenous, **217**
Buddhism and, 172, **173**
cathedrals in Christianity, importance of, **162**
ethnic regionalism in, 207
folk housing. (*see* folk housing)
French, in Quebec City, Canada, **195**
Hindu, 169–70
importance of Christian church in cultural landscape, **162,** 163, **166**
log cabin myths and facts, **220**
material culture, 215
Muslim, 168
nonmetallic minerals mined for construction industry, 286
Pennsylvania Dutch barn, example of, **204**
Shinto shrine at Honshu Island, Japan, **173**
shopping mall, 240, 241, **242**
Swedagon pagoda at Yangon, Myanmar, **173**

area
effect of scale on area and detail, 11–12
environmental limitations on use of, 37
in map projections, 493–94
space-time prism, 72, **73, 75**

arithmetic density, 15
of population, 119

Arizona
commercial strip advertising in Holbrook, as popular culture, **213**
copper ore facilities at Phelps-Dodge mine in Morenci, **286**
ecological disaster created by Anasazi Indians, **39**

armed forces, as unifying institutions, 430, 431

artifacts
as components of culture, 51, **52, 54**
technology gap of, 338–40

artificial boundaries, characteristics of, 427

Asia. *See also individual countries*
birth rates, 98–99, **101**
cities, characteristics of, 408–10
colonial division and ramifications, 419
conurbations, 376–77
early culture hearths, 47–49
East Asian ethnic religions, 172–73
fuelwood, effects of using, **345**
indigenous languages as divisive issue, 154
intermediate-sized cities, governmental program to establish, 410
Kurds as stateless nation, **418,** 419
languages spoken, 137, **138–39**
manufacturing regions of eastern, 318–23
Middle East. (*see* Middle East)
natural population increase that has permanently emigrated, *116*
Near East. (*see* Near East)
nonnative ethnic groups, response to, **182**
population
distribution, 117
growth of, **97**
urban areas, projected growth in, 409
South Asian Association for Regional Cooperation, **442**
textile industry in, **300**
urbanization, 122

Asian Americans
dispersion, 194–95
in Los Angeles, California, **395**
U.S. Asian population by ethnicity, *194*

Asian/Pacific Islanders, in projected U.S. population, *193*

aspiration level, in migration decisions, 87

assimilation
behavioral, 184
cultural, 184
structural, 184

atlal, **42**

atmosphere, 457
assault by humans on, 460, 461–62
ozone
hole in the ozone layer, **466–67**
problems with, 465–67

Australia
Canberra as planned capital of federal state, **426**
forced migration to, 83, 85
Lake Argyle irrigation project, **478**

Australian language family, 137, **138–39**

Austria
living conditions in Vienna in the 1870s, **111**
population pyramid for, **105**

Austro-Asiatic language family, 137, **138–39**

automobile, popular culture oriented toward, 240, **241,** 242

autonomous nationalism
as centrifugal force, 433
regions in Western Europe demanding autonomy, **433**

awareness space, 71

azimuthal projections, 495, 496–97

B

Babbitt, Bruce, **285**

Baker v. Carr (1962), 444

Bali, cultivation of a garden plot in, **347**

Bangladesh
chars as inhabited islands in, **456**
cycle of flood and resettlement, **456**
Grameen Bank, **363**
migration into, following 1970 cyclone, 80

barriers
diffusion, 57
to information, 78
to language spread, 142

barrios, 410

baseball
development in U.S., **214**
Japanese acculturation of, 60
regional variables in, 244, **245**

Basel Convention on the Control of Transboundary Movements of Hazardous Wastes and Their Disposal, 486

basic costs, 297

basic sector of city economy, 381

Basques, linguistic uniqueness of, 142

beer brewing by primitive cultures, 44

behavioral assimilation, 184

beneficiation, 286

Berry, Brian, 350

Bilingual Education Act of 1974, **152**

bilingualism, 149

binational state, 418

biome(s)
acid rain, 464–65
dam building in tropical moist forest, **470**
defined, 459
global heating, consequences of, 462–63

biosphere. *See also* environment
characteristics, 456–57
dumping of untreated sewage, impact of, 477
ozone
hole in the ozone layer, **466–67**
problems with, 465–67
soil erosion, 472–73, **474,** 475

birth rates, 98–99, **100, 101**

black Americans. *See* African Americans

Boserup, Ester, 264, 266

Boserup thesis, 264, 266

Bosnia-Herzegovina, UN peacekeeping forces in, **437**

Botswana, happiness in, **359**

boundaries
breaking point of cities trade area, computing, 68
as characteristics of regions, 17, **18**
classification of, 426–28
disputes over, 428–29, **430**
international, as three-dimensional, 426
as limits of states, 425, 426–29
and representation, 444–45, **446**
tribal and national boundaries in Africa, discrepancies between, **420**

Brazil
Earth Summit, attempts to reduce global warming at, 463
hillside locations occupied by Rio de Janeiro poor, **82, 408**
Itaipu Dam across the Paraná River, portion of, **453**
prosperity and poverty in, **333**

breaking point (BP) of cities trade area, computing, 68

break-of-bulk points, 304

Brown v. Board of Education of Topeka, Kansas (1954), 444

Buddhism, 170–72, **173**
innovation areas and diffusion routes of, **160**
Swedagon pagoda at Yangon, Myanmar, **173**
Tibetan lamas in exile at Sikkim monastery, **133**

built environment, 215

burin, **42**

Burkina Faso, desert margin view from, **471**

C

Cabot, John, 416
Cairo plan, 115
calendar, development of, 48
California
  cultural landscapes along California–Mexico border, contrasting, **13**
  Hispanic Americans celebrating heritage at Cinco de Mayo festival, **177**
  illegal immigrants, response to, **88**
  Los Angeles. (see Los Angeles, California)
  photochemical smog in, during late 1970s, **468**
caloric intake, as measure of economic development, 348–49
caloric intake, minumum daily, 348
Canada
  acid rainfall, location of, **465**
  agricultural regions of North America, generalized, **273**
  charter cultures, 188
  cities in, characteristics of, 400, **401,** 403
  culture hearths, 216, **217,** 218
  ethnic
    diversity in Prairie Provinces, 188, **190**
    islands, 188
    origin of population, *184*
    farmed fields of Canadian prairies, extensively, **34**
  folk
    music, 233
    traditions, 215
    forward-thrust capital city of, 425, **426**
  French Canada. (see French Canada)
  immigration streams, 183
  Indian and Inuit place names, return of, 155
  land use pattern in and around Calgary, Alberta, **393**
  language(s)
    bilingualism in, 149, 151
    Official Languages Act of 1969, 151
    preservation of native tongues, 151
  Main Street conurbation, **377**
  major conurbations in, 376, **377**
  manufacturing regions of, 312, **313,** 314
  Mennonite village as transplanted ethnic landscape in Manitoba, **207**
  Metropolitan Government of Toronto, establishment of, 450
  multiculturalism, 185
  as multinational state, **418**
  municipal gravel quarry and storage yard, Vancouver, **286**

nonecumene area of Northwest Territories, **120**
North American Free Trade Agreement, **442**
political fragmentation, 447–48
population distribution, 118
regional dialects, 146
religions, 163, **164**
residential preferences, **79**
rural settlement patterns, 206–7
ski development at Whistler Mountain, British Columbia, **3**
social geography of American and Canadian cities, **394**
Supreme Court of Canada building, as bonding force for state, **431**
survey system for, 206, **207**
Toronto
  as typical Canadian city, **401**
  unified government, 449–50
travel behaviors of midwestern Canadians, 74
U.S.–Canadian railroad discontinuity, map of, **433**
Windsor, Ontario sewage treatment plant, **112**
work and nonwork trips, frequency distribution of, **74**
capitals of states, characteristics of, 425, **426**
carbon dioxide
  in greenhouse effect, 461–62
  increase in atmospheric, 460, 461
Carey, Henry C., 68
carrying capacity, 43–44
  demographers projecting, **124**
  of land, 121
cartogram, 21, **22**
caste structure of Hindu society, 169
Caucasian language family, **138–39,** 142
cemeteries in Christian countries, land use for, 163
census
  problematic but improving worldwide data collection, 123–24
  taking in China, **123**
Central African Republic, world view after listening to VOA, **78**
central business district (CBD)
  in Calgary, Alberta, as point of focus, **393**
  importance of, in Latin American cities, 410
  land value in, 389, **391**
  Paseo de la Reforma in Mexico City, part of, **411**
  Tysons Corner, Virginia, as suburban, 398
central city
  Canadian city rooted in mass transit usage, **401**
  defined, 380
  effects of suburbanization on, 398, 399, **400**
centralized pattern of distribution, 16

central place theory, 386–88
centrifugal forces
  nationalism and, 433–34, **435**
  in state cohesiveness, 429
centripetal force, in state cohesiveness, 429
chain migration, 87, 189
  by ethnic minorities to urban areas, 197
change
  in attributes of place, 13–14
  as recurring theme in culture, 52, 54–57, **58**
channelized migration flows, 89, **90**
chars as inhabited islands in Bangladesh, **456**
charter cultures, 186, 188
charter group, 188
  invasion of, territory by minority, 197
Chesapeake Bay
  as cultural hearth, **217,** 218, 227
  folk housing, 224–25
Chicago, Illinois
  confirmation scene at Ukranian church, **131**
  government entities, multiplication of, 448
  racial and nationality groups, outward expansion of, **202**
  regions of interaction created during late 1950s, changing, **15**
  Robert Taylor Homes as example of public housing project, **401**
  situation of, **10**
  social areas of the Chicago region, **394**
  urban sprawl in, history of, **397**
  von Thünen zones in sector south of Chicago, schematic view of, **271**
children
  activity space, 71
  AIDS and childhood mortality in developing countries, 358
  critical distance, 73
  diseases of, under attack by WHO, 356, **357**
  infant mortality rates, 102–3
  malnourished or with stunted growth in Africa, **349**
  mental maps of neighborhood drawn by, **25**
  preparation of, for culture group membership, 53
Chile, infant mortality rate, **103**
China
  agriculture and planned economies, 276, 277–78
  birth rates, 99, **100, 101**
  census taking, **123**
  culture hearth emerging in, 47–49
  economy of village engaged in subsistence agriculture, **265**
  folk housing, **219**
  geography, ancient involvement in, 3
  Himalaya Mountains as natural boundary, **427**

ideographs among Chinese, common, 135
income, average per capita, 343
industrial regions, map of, **322**
industry in, 319–21
languages spoken, 137, **138–39**
pollution of freshwater, 477
population
  control program, **100**
  pyramid, 107
religion, 172–73
Spratly Islands, claimant to, **440**
street merchants in Wuxi, Jiangsu Province, independent, **278**
Tangshen area earthquake of 1976, response to, 80
Tibetan lamas in exile at Sikkim monastery, **133**
total fertility rate, 102
"township and village enterprises," **321**
Western fast-food chains in Shenyang, **239**
working leather in a Wanxian, China, factory, **293**
choropleth map, 21, **22**
Christaller, Walter, 386–88
Christianity, 160–61, **162,** 163, **164, 165, 166**
  Baptists and Lutherans in U.S., concentration of, **165**
  cathedrals, importance of, **162**
  church's position in cultural landscape, importance of, 163, **166**
  diffusion paths of, **160, 162**
  innovation areas and diffusion routes, **160**
  New England spired church, example of, **166**
  Notre Dame Cathedral in Paris, **162**
  regions and landscapes, 163, **164–66**
  religious affiliation in conterminous U.S., **164**
church, as unifying institution, 430, 431
cigarette smoking and popular culture, **245–46**
circular and cumulative causation in core-periphery model, 336
cities. *See also* urban areas; urbanization; world urban diversity
  accessibility as major factor in development, 388–90, **391**
  base ratios for, 382, **383**
  bazaar-based cities, **407,** 409
  central cities, defined, 380
  as central places, 383, 385, 386–88
  defined, 380
  economic base, 381–82
  functional classifications, 382, 383, **384**
  functions, 381–82, **383**
  galactic city, diagram of, **398**
  growth of, in past century, 373, 376–77
  homeless persons in U.S., **402**

inside the city, 388–96
internal structure of. (*see* urban land use)
land, competitive bidding for, 388–90, **391**
location, 380–81
nature of, 379–81
poor and minorities as being trapped in, 398, 399, **402**
rank-size rule, 384
self-sufficiency of persons living in suburbs from cities, 397, **399**
settlement roots, 377, **378,** 379
social areas, 393–96
social geography of American and Canadian, **394**
urban hierarchy, 383–85, **386**
women in, **400**
workforce engaged in basic and nonbasic activities, **382**
world urban diversity. (*see* world urban diversity)
civilization, components of, 47
Clean Air Act, **464, 468**
climate(s)
changes in, **460**
global heating, consequences of, 462–63
precipitation variability, patterns of, **461**
special crops and, 275–76
tropical deforestation and changes to, 469
world climates, map of, **459**
world climatic systems, recent patterns in, 457–60, **461**
clothing, Canadian travel patterns for purchase of, **74**
clustered phenomenon, 16
cluster migration, 189
coal
increased carbon dioxide in atmosphere from burning, 460, 461
Industrial Revolution use of, 37–38
mining of, 287
reserves, *288*
transportation of, for manufacturing, **301**
cohort measures in demography, 98
collective farms, 276–77
colonies, 200, **201, 202**
"colonies of immigrants," book excerpt by Robert Hunter, **201**
division of Africa, Asia, and Americas into, 419, **421**
as lacking characteristics of a state, 418
commercial agriculture, 267–68, 269–72, **273–74,** 275–78. *See also* agriculture
agricultural regions of North America, **273**
extensive, 272, **274,** 275
genetic diversity of crop varieties, world areas with high, **268**
intensive, 271–72, **273**

Mediterranean agriculture, 275–76
planned economies, modifications by, 276–78
plantation crops, 276
production controls, 268, 269, **270**
special crops, 275–76
von Thünen's model of agricultural location, 270–71, **272**
commercial economies, 258
commodities
primary, trade in, 289–90
spatial interaction and movement of, 64–65
volume of expected flow of a good, reduction of, **67**
Common Market, formation, 441
communication
effect of technology on spatial interaction, 73, 76
as factor in state cohesiveness, 431, 432
personal communication field, 76
space-cost convergence in telephone tolls, **76**
communism
agricultural control through planned economies, 276–78
Buddhist problems in communist countries, 172
economic planning and, 258
environmental damage by industry under, 316, **318**
ethnic groups seeking independence, 186
typical socialist city, characteristics of, 404, **405,** 406
compact state, defined, 423
comparative advantage in manufacturing location, principle of, 307–8, **309**
competition theory, ethnic differences and, 185
complementarity, 65
complementary regions
in central place theory, 386–87
derivation, **387**
and pattern of central places, **387**
concentration, as element of spatial distribution, 15–16
concentric zone model of urban land use, 392, **393**
Confucianism, 172
conic projections, 496
connectivity, 15, **19**
consequent boundary, defined, 427, 428
contact diffusion, Buddhism spread through, 171
contagious diffusion, 56
of Buddhism, 171
of Christianity, 160
of Hinduism, 168
continental shelf, 279–80
contour line, 23
contraception
Cairo plan and, 115
in developing countries, 113

population control program promotion in Bombay, India, **126**
conurbations
creation of larger U.S., after World War II, 396–98
defined, 373
location, **374–75,** 376–77
coordinate systems, use of, 9–10
copper mining, 284, **286**
core areas of states, 425
core-periphery model of development, 336
corn, diffusion patterns of hybrid, **58**
corporations
inducements by governments to lure companies, **311, 332,** 333
transnational corporations, locational perspective of, 309–10
Union Carbide tragedy at Bhopal (India), **332,** 333
cost(s)
as factor of distance, 67–68
space-cost convergence in telephone calls, **76**
in spatial interaction, 65–66, **67**
spatially
fixed costs, 297, 303–4
variable costs, 297, 303
tapering principle, **303**
transportation costs, in manufacturing, 302–4
counter migration, 89
country, defined, 417–18
country music
as popular culture, 242, **243**
refuge areas, **234**
creole languages, 149
critical distance, 72, **73**
critical isochrone, **73**
crude
birth rate, 98–99
death rate, 102, **103, 104**
density of population, 119
cuba, senior citizens exercising in Havana, **127**
cultural
assimilation, 184
attributes of place, 12–13
convergence, 49, 51, 339
divergence, 43
ecology, 36
integration, 52
lag, 54
modification and adoption, 60
transfer, 202–4
cultural landscape
attributes of, **1,** 12–13
process of change in a, **14**
culture
change in, 52, 54–57, **58**
components, 35–36, **37**
defined, 34
development as cultural variable, 333
and diffusion, 55–57, **58**
effect on economic activity, 257
environment
environments as controls, 37–38

human impacts, 38–40
interaction of people and, 36–40
female death rates and, 102, **104**
folk. (*see* folk culture)
hearth areas. (*see* culture hearths)
ideological subsystem of culture, 51, **54**
and innovation, 54–55
material, 215
modification and adoption of, 60
natural resources as viewed by, 278, **279**
nonmaterial, 215
physical environments and cultural impacts, 456–57
popular. (*see* popular culture)
realm, 36, **37**
region, 36
regions, contact between, 57, **59,** 60
and religion, 156, **157, 167**
roots, 40–41, **42,** 43
sociological subsystem, 51–52, **53, 54**
structure, 51–52, **53–54**
in study of human geography, 32
techological subsystem, 51, **52, 54**
culture complex, 36
culture hearths, 47–51
of colonial Atlantic Seaboard, 209
early culture hearths of the Old World and the Americas, **47**
North American, 216, **217,** 218
periods and developmental features of emerging, *48–49*
culture rebound, 203
culture traits, 35–36
cumulative voting, **446**
cuneiform, development of, 48
customs, folk, 216
cylindrical projections, 495–96

D

dam building in tropical rainforests, **470**
death rates, 102–4
European, 111, **112,** 113
technological lowering in developing countries, 113
deglomeration, 307
deindustrialization, 316
Delaware, folk housing in, 224
Delaware Valley (U.S.)
as culture hearth, **217,** 218
folk housing, 224
Delmarva Peninsula (U.S.), hierarchical arrangement of regions and, **18**
demographic equation, 113–14, 116
demographic momentum, 127
demographic transition model, 109–13, **114,** 115
polarization between developing and advanced countries, 113
stagnation of European population, **112**
Western experience, 110–13

demography
 carrying capacity of earth, projections for, **124**
 data collection, problems with, 123–24
 defined, 96
 population measures used in, 98
 population projections. (*see* population projections)
density, as element of spatial distribution, 15, **16**
dependency ratio, 105, **106**
dependency theory of economic development, 352
desertification, 470, **471,** 472
developable surfaces, 492
developed countries. *See* advanced countries
developing countries, 334
 adult literacy rate, **353**
 age and population, relationship of, 127
 AIDS in, 358
 birth rates, 98–99
 census data unreliable in, 123–24
 cities in, characteristics of, 406–10
 contraception and family planning, 113, **115**
 defined, 334–35
 depletion of natural capital in, danger of, 290
 dietary energy supply received daily in the South, **348**
 energy consumption by, 287, 342, 344, **345,** *346*
 foreign aid, effectiveness of, **349, 350–51**
 forest products, harvesting of, 283
 fuelwood, use of, **345**
 government control of primary commodity trading, 290
 Grameen Bank, value of, **363**
 Green Revolution in, 266–67, **269**
 hazardous waste transported to, 484, 486
 health services in the South, access to, **357**
 landlessness and, 344, 346–47
 migration in, **87**
 models for economic development, 350, 351, 352
 mortality rates in, 113
 newly industrializing countries, **300,** 310
 North–South disparity in human development, *353*
 periodic markets, domination of women in, **361**
 physician, population per, **356**
 polarization between advanced countries and, 113
 population
  control, attempts at, **100**
  "population explosion" after World War II, **114**
  projections for, 96, **97**
  school-age population per teacher, **354**
 poverty, persons living in, **339**
 prices and values of exports, demand for increase in, 290

purchasing power parity, 341–42, **343**
 relative characteristics of development, *341*
 role of women, 360–63, **364–65**
 sanitation or waste-disposal, lack of, 354, **355**
 technology
 technology gap and, 338–40
 technological advances and falling death rates, 113
 total global output, share of, 337–38
 unofficial housing in, problems with, **406,** 407, **408,** 410
 urbanization in, 122
 urban models of, **409**
 women, closing education and employment gap, **432**
development
 accessibility as key measure of economic, **259**
 birth rates and, 98–99
 "Brandt report" on contrasts in world, 334–35
 carrying capacity of land and, 121
 comparative levels of, world map of, **334**
 as cultural variable, 333
 death rates affected by level of, 102
 definitions of, 333–36
 economic measures of. (*see* economic measures of development)
 energy controlled and used for, 287–89
 evidences of, not equally shared, **333**
 hedonometer, attempt at measuring happiness, **359**
 human development index by UN Development Programme, 358, 360
 location decisions in manufacturing. (*see* locational decisions in manufacturing)
 models for economic development, 350, 351, 352
 noneconomic measures of. (*see* noneconomic measures of development)
 North–South disparity in human development, *353*
 Physical Quality of Life Index, 358
 population growth and, relationship between, 110–13
 poverty, persons living in, **339**
 relative characteristics, 340, *341*
 and well-being, aggregate measures of, 358, **359,** 360
 women in, role of, 360–63, **364–65**
devolution, defined, 434
dialects, 145, 146–47
 boundaries, **146**
 male and female language, **146**
 Old English dialect regions, **143**
Dictionary of Samuel Johnson, 143
diffusion
 architectural, 226–27
 barriers, 57

corn, diffusion patterns of hybrid, **58**
 culture and, 55–57, **58**
 folk culture, 235–36
 of languages, 141–42
 popular culture, 243
 religions
  Buddhism, 171, **172**
  Christianity, 160–61, **162,** 163
  Hinduism, 168
  Islam, 166, **167**
  Judaism, 159–60, **161**
  of world's major religions, **160**
 spatial, 15
 of technology, 338, 339–40
dioxin, 481, 483
direction
 bias, 69, 78
 in map projections, 495
 as spatial concept, 10–11
dirt, consumption of, **231**
discrimination in urban areas, racial or ethnic, 198
dispersed phenomenon, 16
dispersion, as element of spatial distribution, 15–16
distance
 as absorbing barrier, 57
 as barrier to information flow, 78
 and human interaction, 72–73, **74, 75**
 interpersonal exchanges, effect of distance on, **75**
 in map projections, 495
 psychological transformation of linear, 11
 social interaction as function of, **75**
 as spatial concept, 11
 von Thünen's model of agricultural location, 270–71, **272**
distance decay, 14, 57, 67–68
 in migration, 89
 shape of, **67**
doctrine of "first effective settlement" (Zelinsky), 188
domino theory, 436
dot map, 21, **22**
doubling time of population, 108–10
Douglas, William O., **152**
"Dragons," emerging manufacturing and trading force, 321–23
Dravidian language family, **138–39**
drink
 in Anglo-American folk culture, 231–32
 moonshine production in east Tennessee, **232**
drip irrigation, **478**

E

earth
 geography and study of, 2

population distribution, 116–18, **119**
earthquakes
 human perceptions of hazards accompanying, 80
 San Francisco earthquake and fire (1906), **81**
Earth Summit (1992)
 desertification defined, 470
 measures taken to reduce global heating, 463
East Asian ethnic religions, 172–73
Easter Island, impact of humans on environment, 40
economic activity
 accessibility as key measure of, **259**
 categories, 257–58
 classification, 256–60
 Japanese cars unloading at Seattle dock, **256**
 types of economic systems, 258–60
economic alliances of countries, 440–42
economic base of urban settlement, 381–82
economic control(s)
 planned economies, 276–78
 of primary commodity trading, 290
 production controls on agriculture, 268, 269, **270**
economic development. *See* development
economic geography, defined, 256
economic measures of development, 336–42, **343,** 344, **345,** 346–52
 agriculture, percentage of workforce engaged in, 344, 346–47
 complex of development, 340, *341*
 composite assessment of economic development, 349, 350, 351, 352
 energy consumption per capita, 342, 344, **345,** *346*
 global economic output, shift in, 336–38
 gross national product per capita, 340, 341–42
 models for economic development, 350, 351, 352
 poverty
  calories, and nutrition as, 348–49
  data on persons living in, **339**
 purchasing power parities, 341–42, **343**
 technology, diffusion of, 338–40
 total global output, measurement of, 337–38
ecosphere. *See* biosphere
ecosystem
 defined, 459
 limiting factor principle, **478**

Ecuador
"informal sector" initiative in, **337**
traditional and modern in Pujili street scene, mix of, **331**
ecumene, 118, **119**
edge cities, 398, 403
Edrisi, **5**
education
geography in public education programs, **6,** 8–9
as noneconomic measure of development, 352–54
standards for study of geography, **8**
Egypt
culture hearth emerging, 47–49
infant mortality rate, **103**
pyramids as independent inventions, 57
urbanization, 122
electoral geography, defined, 444
elliptical projections, 497
Ellis Island, importance of, **181**
elongated state, defined, 423
enclave
as description of states, 424
ethnic, 200, **202**
energy
consumption per capita as measure of development, 342, 344, **345,** *346*
fuelwood, use of, **345**
power supplies in manufacturing, 298
relationship with economic development, 287–89
England. *See also* Great Britain
as charter group in North America, 188
happiness in, **359**
Midlands industrial complex, 38
view of Parliament, London, **415**
English language
development, 142–43
eclectic vocabulary, 142–43, **144**
international English, **144**
Old English dialect regions, **143**
regional dialects, 146
environment
acid rain, effects of, 464–65
Bingham Canyon open-pit copper mine as example of reshaping landscapes, **457**
coals, use of higher-grade coals, **301**
defined, 456
desertification, 470, **471,** 472
effect on economic activity, 256–57
fuelwood, effects from use of, **345**
garbage. (*see* garbage)
global warming of the, 460, 461–64
human-environment relationship
abuse of wetlands in New York state, **455**
environments as controls, 37–38
human impacts, 12–13, 38–40
interaction of people and environment, 36

industrial damage to, by industries of Marxist countries, 316, **318**
as interrupting barrier, 57
limits on population growth by, 118
material culture, 215
modification of, 12–13
natural hazards, perceptions of, 79–82
perception of, 77–79
physical environments and cultural impacts, 456–57
population growth on the environment, effect of, 97
refugees, environmental, **87**
restructuring of environment during Neolithic period, 46
environmental determinism, loss of support for, 37
Environmental Protection Agency (EPA)
legislation on smokestack emissions, **464**
need for, 12
epidemiologic transition, 111, **112**
equal-area projection, 493–94
equivalent projections, 493–94
Eratosthenes, 2
ethnic cleansing, 180
ethnic clusters, 188–89, **190**
models, 200–202
ethnic culture, contrasted with folk and popular culture, 238–39
ethnic diversity
festival celebrating America's, **179**
and separatism, 179–81, **182**
of United States, 178
urban ethnic diversity. (*see* urban ethnic diversity)
ethnic enclave, 200, **202**
ethnic foods, 229–31
ethnic geography, 178
ethnic groups
acculturation and assimilation, 184–85
areal expressions of ethnicity, 186–96
attraction and rejection forces operating on, 203–4
concentrations, shifting, 199–200
defined, 132, 178
Ellis Island, importance of, **181**
ethnic affiliations
Canada, *184*
U.S., *181*
ethnic diversity and separatism, 179–81, **182**
"guest workers" effect on ethnic mix of unicultures, **178**
immigration streams, 181, 183–84
minorities, assertion of rights by, 185
"nations of immigrants," many countries as, **182**
race and classification of populations, **180**
suburbanization and, 397, 398, 399

urban ethnic diversity. (*see* urban ethnic diversity)
U.S. resident population by race and Hispanic origin, *179*
ethnic islands, 188, **189**
ethnicity, 178–79
areal expressions, 186–96
cities and, 394, 395–96
in former Yugoslavia, **186**
landscape evidence of, 204, 216
ethnic provinces, 189
ethnic regionalism, 207
ethnic religions, **131,** 157
East Asian, 172–73
ethnic separatism, 179–81, **182**
ethnic status, cities and, 394, 395–96
ethnocentrism, 179
ethnographic boundary, defined, 427
Europe. *See also individual countries*
acculturation, 60
agricultural development, 44, **45**
autonomy movement within, 434, **435**
Basques, linguistic uniqueness of, 142
birth rates, 98–99, **101**
conurbations, 376
demographic transition model applied to, 110–13
devolution movement, 434
early culture hearths, *47, 49*
Eastern European manufacturing regions, 316–17, **319**
economic alliances, 441–42
environmental damage by Marxist industry, 316, **318**
ethnic regionalism in the built landscape, 207
European Economic Community, formation of, 441
European Union, map of, **441**
forced migrations, 83, 85
"guest workers" effect on ethnic mix of unicultures, **178**
Ice Age environment, 40–41
indigenous languages, treatment of, 152–53
Inner Six and Outer Seven of, 441, 442
languages spoken, **138–39,** 141, 142
late Paleolithic environments, **41**
migrations in, 83, **84**
nonnative ethnic groups in, response to, **182**
population
distribution, 118
growth, **97**
natural population increase that has permanently emigrated, *116*
pyramid for Western, 104, **105**
stagnation of population levels, **112**
racial and ethnic discrimination in urban areas, 198
regions in Western Europe demanding autonomy, **433**

Rhine River flowing past Ruhr District, **317**
road conditions in Medieval, as barrier to spatial interaction, **66**
social geography of Western European city, model of, 403, **405**
tourism and migration places, favored, 79
typical Eastern European (socialist) city, characteristics of, 404, **405,** 406
Western and Central European manufacturing regions, 315–16, **318**
Western European city, characteristics of typical, 403, **404, 405**
European Union (EU)
economic activity and the, 259
government policies as market controls, 269
Euskara language, 142
evapotranspiration, 476
excess vote gerrymandering technique, 444
exclave, as description of states, 424
exclusive economic zone (EEZ)
development of, 439
world map delineating, **439**
expansion diffusion, 55, 56
of Christianity, 160
of East Coast (U.S.) settlers, 216, **217**
of Islam, 166, **167**
language spread by, 141
extensive
commercial agriculture, 272, **274,** 275
subsistence agriculture, 261–64
external economies, 307, **308**
extractive industries, resource exploitation by, 278

F

Faeroe Islands, regional dialects, 146–47
fallowing, as way to protect or enhance soil, 473
family planning
Cairo plan and, 115
in developing countries, 113
neo-Malthusianism and, 126
population control program in Bombay, India, **126**
family status, cities and, 394, 396
farming. *See* agriculture
fauna
destruction through human intervention, 39–40
domestication, beginnings of, 44, **45,** 46
favelas, 410
in Brazil, **408**
Federal Housing Administration (FHA), establishment of, 396

federal state(s), 425
  Canberra, Australia, as planned
    capital of, **426**
females. *See* women
fencing in North America, folk,
  227–28
fertility rates, 99, **100, 101,** 102
Finland, human advancement
  into, 41
fire as human tool, impact of, 38
fishing
  harvesting at aquaculture farm
    in Thailand, **281**
  major commercial marine
    fisheries of the world, map
    of, **280**
  as primary economic activity,
    257, 279–82
  resource exploitation through,
    278–79
fixed costs, 297, 303–4
flora
  destruction through human
    intervention, 39–40
  domestication, beginnings of,
    44, **45,** 46
folk culture
  "annual round" of folk culture
    farming in Louisiana, **229**
  contrasted with ethnic and
    popular culture, 238–39
  defined, 132, 214, 215
  household as basic subsistence
    unit, **230**
  "national hearth," **217**
  nonmaterial. (*see* nonmaterial
    folk culture)
  North American hearths, 216,
    217, 218
  Old Order Amish as, 215
  Plimoth Plantation,
    reconstructed, **216**
  present day expressions of,
    215–16
  regions, 216
    of eastern U.S., 235–36
    passing of folk cultural
      regionalism, 237
folk cures, 234–35
folk fencing in North America,
  227–28
folk housing, 218, **219,** 220
  American indigenous, **217**
  architectural
    diffusions, 226–27
    source areas and diffusion of
      building methods, **226**
  dogtrot house, 227
  extended family compound of
    Bambara of Mali, **218**
  house types
    Middle Atlantic, 224, **227**
    New England, 222–23
    preindustrial, **219**
    Southern, 225
    St. Lawrence region, 220, 222
  interior and Western hearths, 226
  log cabin myths and facts, **220**
  Masai manyatta, 218, **219**
  Middle Atlantic, 224–25, 227
  Northern hearths, 220, **221,**
    222–23
  Southern hearths, 225

Uygur yurt, **219**
folk life, 215
folklore traditions, 235
folk medicines, 234–35
folk music, 232–34
  "American Empire of Song," **232**
  folk song regions of eastern
    U.S., **232**
  refuge areas of country
    music, **234**
  white spirituals, southward shift
    of, **234**
folkways, 235
Food and Agriculture
  Organization (FAO)
  food shortage predictions, 121
  fuelwood, data on use of, **345**
  minimum daily caloric intake
    specified by, 348
  as part of UN effort, 437
food(s)
  dirt, consumption of, **231**
  ethnic, 229, 230–31
  folk and customary, 229, 230–31
  Native American contributions
    to folk, 231
  per capita food production by
    region, **267**
  pizza in popular culture, 240
  preferences, popular culture
    and, 244, **245**
  uniformity in, of popular
    culture, 239–40
footloose firms in profit-
  maximization approaches
  to industrial location, 307
forced migrations, 83
Ford, Larry, **248**
forestry
  major commercial forest regions
    of the world, 282
  as primary economic activity,
    257, **258,** 282–83
  resource exploitation through,
    278–79
formal region, 17–18
form utility, 257, **258**
forward-thrust capital city,
  425, **426**
fossil fuels, extraction of,
  287–89
Four Corners Monument, **443**
"four noble truths" in
  Buddhism, 170
fragmented states, defined,
  423–24
France
  acid rain damage to statuary at
    Reims, **465**
  as charter group in eastern
    Canada, 188
  "guest workers" effect on ethnic
    mix of unicultures, **178**
  infant mortality rate, **103**
  low profile of Paris as seen from
    Eiffel Tower, **404**
  Notre Dame Cathedral in
    Paris, **162**
  "safety map" of Manhattan for
    tourists, **199**
fraternal orders, popular
  culture and, **245–46**

freight rates, 302
French Canada
  cultural obstacles, 57
  French architecture in Quebec
    City, **195**
  French charter group, influence
    of, 195
  survey system for, 206, **207**
frictionless zone, **73**
friction of distance, 14, 67–68
  in migration decisions, 89
frontier zones, 426
fuels, extraction of, 287–89
fuelwood, world shortage of, **345**
functional boundary disputes,
  429, **430**
functional regions, 18, **19**

G

galactic city, diagram of, **398**
games, in American popular
  culture, **214**
garbage
  exportation, 484, 486
  hazardous waste. (*see* hazardous
    waste)
  incineration of solid waste, 481,
    482, 483
  landfill
    disposal in, 481, **482**
    sanitary landfill, use of, 481
    tells as ancient landfills, **480**
  Mobro, odyssey of the, **482**
  as most enduring evidence of
    human occupation, 479, **480**
  ocean dumping of wastes, 483
  solid wastes and rubbish, 480–81
  toxic wastes, disposal of,
    483–84, **485**
Garreau, Joel, 398
gathering industries, resource
  exploitation by, 278
gender
  defined, 361
  mortality and, preferences
    among societies, **106**
  women and development,
    360–63, **364–65**
gender empowerment measure
  (GEM), **365**
gene flow, **180**
General Agreement on Tariffs
  and Trade (GATT), 440
genetic classification of
  language, 136
genetic drift, **180**
"genre de vie," 32
gentrification, **402**
geographic dialects, 146–47
geography
  basic concepts
    direction, 10–11
    distance, 11
    location, 9–10
    physical and cultural
      attributes, 12–13
    place. (*see* place)
    regions, 16–18, **19**
    size and scale, 11–12
  career opportunities in, **6**

defined, 2
educational standards for, **8**
evolution of discipline, 2–3, **4, 5**
fundamental questions of, 2, 8, 9
in public education programs,
  6, 8–9
and space, 2, **3,** 8, 9
subdivisions, 3–4, **5**
value of, 2
Geography for Life, 8–9
geometrical projections, 492
geometric boundaries,
  characteristics of, 427
geophagy, **231**
geopolitics, defined, 435
Georgia, folk housing in, 225
Germanic languages, 136
Germany
  Berlin Wall as subsequent
    superimposed and relict
    boundary, **428**
  economic and social interaction
    on autobahn, **63**
  environmental damage by
    Marxist industry, **318**
  Rathaus of Munich as source of
    pride and substance, **444**
  regional boundaries in Aachen
    in 1649, **18**
  Ruhr industrial complex, 38
Gerry, Elbridge, 445
gerrymandering, techniques,
  444–45
ghettos, 200, **202**
  typology of African American,
    201–2, **203**
glaciers
  as agents of change, 13
  maximum extent of glaciation, **40**
global warming, 460, 461–64
globe
  grids, characteristics of, 20–21
  map projections and the, 491–95
  orthographic projection, **491**
  reality of relative location, **10**
gnomonic projection, 492, **495**
*Goals 2000: Educate America
  Act,* **6, 8**
government(s). *See also*
  international political
  systems; local and
  regional political
  organization; national
  political systems
  beginnings, 47
  employment patterns for,
    U.S., *325*
  government policies as market
    controls, 268, 269, **270**
  inducements by, to lure
    companies, **311, 332,** 333
  institutional controls on urban
    land use, 396
  proliferation of governmental
    units in Illinois, **449**
  public housing projects, 399, **401**
  unified, 449–50
  urban renewal programs, 399, **401**
Grameen Bank, value of, **363**
Grant, Ulysses S., signing Mining
  Act of 1872, **285**
graphic scale, **20**

graticule, 492
gravity model
    in migration decisions, 89
    of spatial interaction, 68, **69**
Great Britain. *See also individual countries*
    Caribbean Islanders, self-elected segregation in London, 198, **199**
    drawing subsequent and superimposed boundaries in Indian subcontinent, 428
    happiness in, **359**
    regional dialects, 146, 147
Greece, ancient contributions to geography, 2–3
greenhouse effect
    consequences of global heating, 462–63
    creation, 461–62
Greenland, processing the catch at Godthåb, **255**
Green Revolution in intensive subsistence agriculture, 266–67, **269**
grid pattern of distribution, 16
grid system for maps, 20–21
gross global product, 338
gross national product (GNP)
    and energy consumption, **287**
    per capita, measuring development with, 340, 341–42
    world map, **342, 343**
growth rates, European population, 110–13
guest workers, 181
    effect on ethnic mix of unicultures, **178**

H

hamlets, **388**
    basic settlement forms of, **378**
happiness, attempt at measuring, **359**
Harris, Roy, **220**
Hartshorn, Truman, **398**
Haun, Catherine, migrant from Iowa to California in 1849, 64
Haushofer, Karl, 436
Hayakawa, S.I., **153**
hazardous waste, 483–84
    Basel Convention on the Control of Transboundary Movements of Hazardous Wastes and Their Disposal, 486
    defined, 480
    exportation to developing countries, 484, 486
health as noneconomic measure of development, 354, 356, **357,** 358
heartland theory, 435, **436**
hedonometer, attempt at measuring happiness, **359**
hexagonal pattern of distribution, 16

hierarchical diffusion, 56
    of Christianity, 160–61
    language spread by, 142
hieroglyphics, development of, 48
high-level waste disposal, 484
high-tech industries, location of, 323–25
Himalaya Mountains, as natural boundaries, 427
Hinduism, 168–70
    innovation areas and diffusion routes, **160**
    pilgrims at dawn in Ganges River at Varanasi, **169**
    religion in the village of Nanpur, India, **171**
    temple complex at Khajraho in central India, **170**
Hispanic Americans
    businesses in Anglo and Mexican American neighborhoods, **185**
    celebrating heritage at Cinco de Mayo festival, **177**
    as charter group in Southwest, 188
    concentrations, 191–92, 194
    dispersion, 191–92, 193
    diversity within assumed uniform group, 191, *193*
    in Los Angeles, California, **395**
    population
        composition of Hispanic, *193*
        in projected U.S. population, *193*
    street mural in a barrio, **193**
    urban separatism and, 398–99
Hispanic origin, U.S. population by race and, *179*
homelands, 180
homeless persons in U.S., **402**
homeostatic plateau, 125
Hong Kong, as emerging manufacturing and trading force, 321, 322
host society, 181
Hotelling, Harold, 306
household as basic subsistence unit in Anglo America, **230**
housing, folk. *See* folk housing
Housing Act of 1949, 399
Hudson Valley (U.S.)
    as cultural hearth, **217,** 218
    folk housing, 223–24
human development, North–South disparity in, *353*
human-environment relationship. *See also* environment
    environments as controls, 37–38
    human abuse of wetlands in New York state, **455**
    human impacts, 12–14, 38–40, 460, 461
    interaction of people and environment, 36
human geography
    areas covered by, 4–5

basic observations underlying study of, 32
    career opportunities, **6**
    defined, 4
    subdivisions, 4, **5**
human spatial behavior. *See* spatial behavior
Hunter, Robert, **201**
hunter-gatherers
    agriculturalists and, conflict between, 46
    innovation and, **55**
    modern practitioners, 260
    Paleolithic, 40–41, **42,** 43
    women's contribution, 44
Huxley, Julian, 51
hydrologic cycle, 475, **476**
hydrosphere, 457

I

icebox effect, 459
Iceland, folk housing, **219**
identity and language, 152–54
ideological subsystem of culture, 51
Idrisi, **5**
Illinois
    Chicago. (*see* Chicago, Illinois)
    planar or azimuthal equidistant projection centered on Urbana, **496**
    political fragmentation in Champaign County, **448**
    population density, maps of, **12**
    proliferation of governmental units, **449**
    residential street transformation to commercial strip in Champaign, **241**
    urban alignment, **384**
    von Thünen zones in sector south of Chicago, **271**
immigration streams, 181, 183–84
imposed considerations in manufacturing locations, 310, **311**
incineration of solid waste, 481, **482,** 483
independent invention, 57
index of residential dissimilarity, 196, *197*
India
    Bhopal tragedy, **332,** 333
    birth rates, **101**
    chain migration, 89
    Great Britain drawing boundaries of Pakistan and, 428
    Himalaya Mountains as natural boundary, **427**
    Hindu pilgrims at dawn in Ganges River at Varanasi, **169**
    infant mortality rate, **103**
    landlessness in, 347
    languages spoken, **138–39,** 141–42

occupational castes in Kunran village, **379**
    population control program promotion in Bombay, **126**
    religion in village of Nanpur, **171**
    rush hour in Jaipur, **31**
    safe drinking water and waste disposal in, lack of, **355**
    segregation, 197
    subsistence agriculture in, **264**
Indiana, patterns of hamlets, towns, and cities in, **388**
Indo-European language cluster, 136, **137, 138–39**
    spread of, 141
Indonesia
    folk housing of Nias Island, **219**
    reluctant relocation from Jawa, 85
industrial countries, **334**
industrial location theories, 304–7
industrial parks, agglomeration economies in, **308**
Industrial Revolution
    development of new textile machinery, 338
    diffusion of subsystems, 56
    impact of, 52, **55**
    as a transportation revolution, 301
    use of natural resources, 37–38
industry. *See* manufacturing
Indus Valley (Pakistan)
    culture hearth emerging, 47–49
    environmental disaster (2000 BC), **50**
infant mortality rates, 102–3
"informal sector" of economy, **337**
information
    accumulation of, about spatial interactions, 73, 76–77
    flows, 76–77
    perception and, in spatial interaction, 77–82
infrastructure of industries, 307
innovation
    culture and, 54–55
    rate of, through human history, **55**
intensive
    commercial agriculture, 271–72, **273**
    subsistence agriculture, 261, 264–66
interaction potential in spatial interactions, 69
intercontinental movements, 83
interior culture hearths (U.S.), 226
International Conference on Population and Development, **115**
International Court of Justice, 437
International Fund for Agricultural Development, women's status index, **365**

International Monetary Fund
as distributor of foreign aid, **350–51**
purchasing power parity assessment model, 337–38
international political systems
economic alliances, 440–42
regional alliances, 439, 440–43
UN Convention on the Law of the Sea, 438–39, **440**
United Nations and its agencies, 437–38
interregional migrations, 83, **84**
interrupting barrier, 57
intervening opportunity, 66, **67**
interventionism by United Nations, 437–38
intracontinental migrations, 83, **84**
intransit privilege, 304
inverse concentric zone pattern of urban areas, 408
Iowa, open storage of corn, **270**
Iraq, resource dispute with Kuwait over Rumaila field, 429
Ireland, potato famine, 256
irrigation, majority of freshwater used for, 476–77
Islam, 166, **167,** 168
ancient contributions to geography, 3, **5**
expansion diffusion, 55
"five pillars," observance of, 166, **167**
hajj, worshippers gathered during, **167**
imprint of mosque on cultural landscape, 166, 168
innovation areas and diffusion routes, **160**
spread and extent of, **167**
Islands, Convention on the Law of the Sea and, **440**
isogloss, 146, **148**
isoline maps, 23, **25**
generalization of areal data, **25**
isotherm, 23
isotropic plain assumption, 304
Israel, Tell Hesi near Gaza as ancient landfill, **480**
Italy
infant mortality rate, **103**
regional dialects, 146

J

Japan
baseball, acculturation of, 60
birth rates, 99, **101**
commuter scene in Tokyo, **35**
cultural diffusion with America, 60
government policies as market controls, 269
industry in, 318–19, **320**
infant mortality rate, **103**
Japanese cars unloading at Seattle dock, **256**
languages spoken, **138–39**
nation-state, as example of, **418**
rice farmer of rural, **35**

Shinto shrine at Nikko Park, Honshu Island, **173**
social structure, **35**
Japanese-Korean language family, **138–39**
J-curve population growth, 108–9, **110**
Johnson, Samuel, 143
Judaism
dispersion, 159–60, **161**
innovation areas and diffusion routes, **160**
self-segregation of Hasidim, **204**

K

Kansas, newspaper coverage in 1970s, **77**
Kenya
fire, government program to limit use of, 38
Masai
cattle in culture of, **36**
culture complex of, 36
modern urban core of downtown Nairobi, **408**
population pyramid, 104, **105**
tropical savanna, view of, **38**
Khoisan language family, **138–39, 141**
Kincheloe, Samuel, **202**
Kniffen, Fred, 226
Kurds as stateless nation, **418,** 419
Kuwait, resource dispute with Iraq over Rumaila field, 429

L

labor
basic/nonbasic ratio in cities, 382
international labor migration flows, **84**
labor surplus and shortage in former Soviet Union, **299**
manufacturing decisions affected by, 298, **299, 300**
landfills. See garbage
landlessness in developing countries, 344, 346–47
landlocked states, 424
landscape
Bingham Canyon open-pit copper mine as example of reshaping landscapes, **457**
cultural landscape created by Amish farmers, **1**
desertification, 470, **471,** 472
ethnicity, evidence of, 204
garbage. (see garbage)
religion's imprint on, 156
rice cultivation, imprint of, 265
strip mining in U.S., results of, 457, **480**
land survey, 205–6
contrasting survey systems, **206**
Land Ordinance of 1785, 205

lot and field patterns of Wethersfield, Connecticut, **205**
rectangular system of, 9–10
land use
basic settlement forms, **378**
carrying capacity of land, 121
cemeteries in Christian countries, 163
desertification, 470, **471,** 472
ecumene, 118, **119**
physiological density of populations, 119–20
process of change in, **14**
residential street transformed to commercial strip, **241**
soil erosion, 472–73, **474,** 475
tropical deforestation, 468–70
urban. (see urban land use)
von Thünen's model of agricultural location, 270–71, **272**
language family, 135
language(s)
changes in, 142–43, 144
Chinese dialects, common ideographs among, **135**
classification, 135–36, **137**
creoles, 149
defined, 132, 135
dialects. (see dialects)
Dinka chief on attempts at African unification, quote from, **134**
English. (see English language)
genetic classification, 136
identity and, 152–54
languages spoken by more than 40 million people, 136
lingua franca, 149, **150**
as mentifact of culture, 134
official, 149, **150,** 151, **152**
pidgin, 149
political forces on, 144
sex differentiation in, **146**
spread of, 137, 141–42
standard, 144–45
territoriality and, 152–54
toponyms, 154–55
value of, 135
world
language families, **138–39**
pattern of, 136–37, **138–40,** 141–42
Latin America. See also individual countries
areas of international dispute, **429**
birth rates, **99, 101**
cities of, characteristics of, 410, **411**
early culture hearths, **47,** 49
human advancement into, **42**
"informal sector" of economy, **337**
landlessness, 347
migration of residents to U.S., 87, **88**
nonnative ethnic groups, **182**
personal space needed by residents, 70
population
growth, **97,** 410
natural population increase that has permanently emigrated, 116

racial and ethnic discrimination in urban areas, 198
latitude
absolute locations described by, 9
in globe grids, 20–21
Latter-day Saints (Mormons)
cluster migration, 189
Mormon culture region, **190**
law of peripheral neglect, 434
law of retail gravitation (Reilly), 68, **69**
law of universal gravitation (Newton), 68
leachate, **481**
least-cost theory of industrial location, 304–5
least developed countries, 334
Lebanon, religious regions of, **159**
less-developed countries. See developing countries
level of living, 340
life cycle stage, effect on activity space, 71
limiting factor principle, **478**
linear pattern of distribution, 16
line-haul costs, 303
lingua franca, 149, **150**
linguistic geography, 146
toponymy as aspect of, 154
Linton, Ralph, **59**
lithosphere, 457
livelihood. See economic activity
livestock
livestock-grain farming, 272, **273**
nomadic herding, 261–62
ranching, **273,** 275
local and regional political organization
the districting problem, 444–45, **446**
fragmentation of political power, 445, 446, 447–49
predevelopment annexation, 450
unified government, 449–50
location
agricultural model, 270–71, **272**
as characteristics of regions, 17
of cities, 380–81
manufacturing and. (see locational decisions in manufacturing)
as spatial concept, 9–10
of states, 424–25
locational costs, 297
locational decisions in manufacturing, 296–99, **300,** 301–2, **303**
agglomeration economies, 307, **308**
comparative advantage, principle of, 307–8, **309**
competitive locations in a linear market, **306**
high-tech industries, location of, 323–25
imposed considerations, 310, **311**
industrial location theories, 304–7
labor, 298, **299, 300**

long-haul efficiency of railroads, **301**
market, 299
material flows in the steel industry, **298**
planned economies, 310
power supply, 298
principles of location, 297
raw materials, 297–98
short-haul penalty, **304**
spatial
  margin of profitability, 306
  orientation tendencies, **302**
transnational corporations, 309–10
transportation, 299, 301–4
transport media, comparison of, **303**
wage rates and cloth trades, **300**
locational interdependence theory, 305–6
locational triangle, 304–5
Lomax, Alan, 232, 233
longitude
  absolute locations described by, 9
  in globe grids, 20–21
Los Angeles, California
  businesses in Anglo and Mexican American neighborhoods, **185**
  ethnic
    make-up, changing, **395**
    patterns in 1990, **196**
  lines of equal travel time, map of, **11**
  mental maps of, **26**
  street mural in a barrio, **193**
Lösch, August, 306
Louisiana, folk housing in, 225
low-level waste, disposal, 483–84

M

Mackinder, Halford, 435, **436**
Madagascar, environmental damage, 40
Mahan, Alfred, 435, **436**
maize, Green Revolution crop improvements of, 267
Malayo-Polynesian language family, **138–39, 141**
Malaysia, rubber farming in, **276**
males
  male and female language, **146**
  migrants, characteristics of, 89, 91
Mali
  Dogon dancers, **33**
  folk housing, **218**
  as one of least developed countries, **335**
  scrub forest in drought-stricken area near Timbuktu, **472**
malnutrition as measure of economic development, 348–49
Malthus, Thomas Robert, 125–26
manufacturing

agglomeration economies, 307, **308**
Bhopal, India, tragedy, **332,** 333
comparative advantage, principle of, 307–8, **309**
employment patterns, U.S., *325*
high-tech industries, location of, 323–25
idled Pennsylvania steel mill, **295**
inducements by governments to lure companies, **311, 332,** 333
locational decisions. (*see* locational decisions in manufacturing)
major manufacturing regions of the world. (*see* manufacturing regions of the world)
material flows in the steel industry, **298**
newly industrializing countries, **300,** 310
as secondary economic activity, 257, 296
suburbanization, 397
textile industry, **300**
transnational corporations, locational perspective of, 309–10
transportation, manufacturing decisions and, 299, 301–4
water use for, 477
working leather in a Wanxian, China factory, **293**
manufacturing regions of the world, 310
barge tow on Mississippi River passing St. Louis, **314**
eastern Anglo America, 312–14
Eastern Asia, 318–23
Eastern Europe, 316–17, **319**
European industrial regions, map of, **316**
industrial regions, world map of, **312**
other Anglo American concentrations, 314–15
Rhine River flowing past Ruhr district in Europe, **317**
Western and Central Europe, 315–16, **317**
Maoris (New Zealand), faunal destruction by, 39
Mao-Zedong
  agriculture under, 277
  industrial development under, 320
map projections, 491–98
maps
  data on maps, showing, 21, **22,** 23, **24**
  early development, 3, **4**
  globe grid, characteristics of, 20–21
  mental, 23, 25, **26**
  relative location and flat, **10**
  scale, 11–12, 19–20
  spatial system analysis with, 27
  symbols, **24**
  topographic. (*see* topographic maps)
  value of, 18–19
maquiladoras, establishment of, 308, **313**

mariculture, 281–82
maritime boundaries
  settling disputes over, 438–39, **440**
  UN Convention on the Law of the Sea, 438–39, **440**
market, industrial location decisions based on, 299
market equilibrium, relationship between supply, demand and, 296
market mechanism, 295
market orientation, 299, **302**
Maryland, folk housing in, 224
Masai (Kenya, Tanzania)
  cattle in culture of, **36**
  culture complex of, 36
Massachusetts
  Boott cotton mills at Lowell in 1852, **324**
  early urbanization in eastern, **381**
  fading of textile and high-tech industries in Lowell, **323**
  major access lines in Boston in 1872 and 1994, **390**
  Mayflower Compact as first political system in New World, **416**
  original gerrymander, **445**
  Plimoth Plantation, reconstructed, **216**
  scale on maps of Boston area, effects of, **20**
mass communication
  information flows and, 76–77
  Voice of America, world view after listening to, **78**
mass transit city, land use in, 388–90, **391**
material culture, 215
material orientation, 298, **302**
maternal mortality ratio, **104**
mathematical
  location, 9
  projections, 492
maximum sustainable yield, 279
Mayan pyramids as independent inventions, 57
Mayflower Compact as first political system in New World, **416**
media, mass, information flows and, 76–77
Mediterranean agriculture, 275–76
Mediterranean scratch plow, **46**
Megalopolis
  Main Street (Canadian/U.S.), **377**
  as major North American conurbation, 312–13, 376, **377**
Meiji, 173
men
  male and female language, **146**
  migrants, characteristics of, 89, 91
mental maps, 23, 25, **26**
  places having superior climates or landscapes, rating of, 79
  Voice of America, world view after listening to, **78**

mentifacts
  as components of culture, 51, **54**
  language and religion as, 134
Mercator projections, **494,** 495–96
meridians, in globe grids, 20–21
Mesolithic period
  domestication of plants and animals, 44, **45,** 46
  as transition period from food collection to production, 44–46
Mesopotamia, culture hearths emerging in, 47–49
metallic minerals, mining and quarrying of, 284, **285,** 286
metro government, 449–50
metropolitan areas
  administrative fragmentation, 448–49
  black segregation in large U.S., 394, 395
  defined, 380
  diagram of the U.S. metropolitan area, **397**
  galactic nature, 398
  history of urban sprawl in Chicago, 397
  Metropolitan Council of the Twin Cities as unified government, 450
  metropolitan growth and decline in U.S., patterns of, **383**
  predevelopment annexation, 450
  ranked by segregation levels, U.S., *197*
  spatial arrangement of urban units within, **381**
  suburbanization and, 396–98, **399**
  unified government, 449–50
  women in, **400**
Mexico
  air pollution in Mexico City, **372**
  cultural landscapes along California-Mexico border, contrasting, **13**
  effects of growth on Mexico City, 372
  Hoover Plant in Mexico City, **309**
  levels of development in, 335
  major conurbations, 376
  manufacturing regions, 313
  maquiladoras, establishment of, 308, **313**
  Mayan pyramids as independent inventions, 57
  migration of residents to U.S., 87, **88**
  North American Free Trade Agreement, **442**
  Paseo de la Reforma in Mexico City, part of central business district, **411**
  response to U.S. attempts to stop illegal aliens, 429, **430**
  urbanization at Teotihuacán, **50**
microdistricts in socialist land use, 404, **405**
middens, 479, **480**
Middle Atlantic culture hearths, 224–25, 227

Middle East. *See also individual countries*
  Arab nation as example of part-nation state, **418**
  Kurds as stateless nation, **418,** 419
  Palestinians as stateless nation, 419
  tells in, as ancient landfills, **480**
Middle Stone Age, transition from collecting food to producing, 44–46
Midwestern states (U.S.)
  bundled isoglosses in Midwest defining dialect regions, **148**
  center of U.S. population, westward moving, **84**
  channelized migration flows, **90**
  parched cornfields in, during summer of 1988, **463**
  population densities, map of, **12**
  as seen by different professional geographers, **17**
migration
  chain, 189
  cluster, 189
  controls, 85–91
  defined, 82–83
  in demographic equation, 114, 116
  Fulani (Africa) movement paths, **83**
  immigration impacts, 114, 116
  "laws of migration" by E.G. Ravenstein, 89
  natural population increase that has permanently emigrated, *116*
  patterns of, 83, **84**
  principal migrations of recent centuries, **116**
  push-pull factors, 86, **87**
  refugees, origin and destination countries, *86*
  relocation of population, 114, 116
  response to, **88**
  types of, 83, 85, 86
  undocumented migrants from Mexico, U.S. attempts to stop, 429, **430**
migration fields, 89
military alliances of countries, 443
Mining Act of 1872, **285**
mining and quarrying
  Bingham Canyon open-pit copper mine as example of reshaping landscapes, **457**
  employment patterns for, U.S., *325*
  metallic minerals, 284, **285,** 286
  mineral fuels, 287–89
  Mining Act of 1872, **285**
  municipal gravel quarry and storage yard, Vancouver, **286**
  nonmetallic minerals, 286–87
  as primary economic activity, 283–84
  reserves, variable definition of, **284**
  resource exploitation, 278–79
  royalties, controversy over, **285**
ministates, influence of, **422**

Minnesota, Metropolitan Council of the Twin Cities as unified government, 450
Mississippi Delta
  as cultural hearth, **217,** 218
  folk housing, 225
Missouri, barge tow on Mississippi River passing St. Louis, **314**
mobility, effect on activity space, 71
Mobro, odyssey of the, **482**
models, in spatial systems analysis, 27
monotheism, 157
Montreal Protocol, attempt to reduce CFCs, **466**
Mormons (Latter-day Saints)
  cluster migration, 189
  Mormon culture region, **190**
mortality rate, 102, **103, 104**
mosque, imprint of, on cultural landscape, 166, 168
motor trucks, manufacturing decisions and, 302, **303**
movement bias, 69
Muller, Peter, **398**
multilinear evolution, 49
multilingualism, 149
multinational state, 418
multiple-nuclei model of urban land use, 393
multiplier effect
  in agglomeration economies, 307
  in city growth, 382
music
  folk. (see folk music)
  popular culture and, 242, **243**
Muslim. *See* Islam
Myanmar (Burma)
  Swedagon pagoda at Yangon, **173**
  teak logs for export stacked near Mandalay, **283**

N

nation, defined, 418, 419
National Geography Standards 1994, **8**
nationalism
  and centrifugal forces, 433–34, **435**
  value of, 429, 430
national political systems. *See also* international political systems; local and regional political organization; states
  boundaries. (see boundaries)
  country, defined, 417–18
  evolution of the modern state, 419, **420, 421**
  geopolitical assessments, 435–36
  Mayflower Compact as first political system in New World, **416**
  nation, defined, 418, 419
  projection of power, 434–36
  state

cohesiveness, 429, 430–32, **433**
  defined, 417–18
national uniformities, 239–40, **241,** 242
nation-state, defined, 418
Native Americans
  contribution to folk foods, 231
  ecological disaster created by Anasazi Indians, **39**
  folk housing, **217**
  folk medicine, contribution to American, 234
  forced migrations of southeastern, **85**
  language families, 137, **138–39,** 140
  as part of larger cultural mix, 186, **187**
  in projected U.S. population, *193*
  use of fire, 38
natural boundaries, 426–27
natural gas
  extraction, 288–89
  Industrial Revolution use of, 37
  reserves, *288*
natural hazards
  perceptions of, 79–82
  responses to uncertainty of, *81*
natural landscape attributes, **1,** 12–13
natural resources
  defined, 278
  exploitation, 278–79
  maximum sustainable yield, 279
  nonrenewable resources, 279
  organization and administration of, as bonding force for state, 431
  renewable resources, 278
  reserves, variable definition of, **284**
  tragedy of the commons, 281
natural selection, and racial differentiation, **180**
Near East. *See also individual countries*
  agricultural development, 44, **45**
  early culture hearths, 47–49
  Neolithic period in, 46
neocolonialism, 336
Neolithic period
  agricultural development during, 46–47
  cultural hearths emerging during, 47, *48–49*
  restructuring of environment, 46
neo-Malthusianism, 126
Nepal
  folk housing, **219**
  high pasture summer village of Konar, picture of, **378**
Netherlands
  container ship at dock in Rotterdam harbor, **253**
  senior citizens, Dutch, **106**
network bias, 69–70
networks, 15
Nevada, Yucca Mountain repository for radioactive waste, **484, 485**
New Deal, establishment of Federal Housing

Administration, 396
New England, folk housing, 222–23, 226
New Jersey, folk housing, 224
newly industrializing countries (NICs), **300,** 310
New Mexico, ecological disaster created by Anasazi Indians, **39**
New Stone Age. *See* Neolithic period
Newton, Isaac, 68
New York
  Chinatowns in New York City, developing satellite, **200**
  cultural diversity, festival celebrating, 179
  cultural landscape of Long Island, changing, **14**
  Earth Day, crowd celebrating, **95**
  folk housing in Hudson Valley, 223–24
  housing in Crown Heights, Brooklyn, **389**
  human abuse of wetlands in, **455**
  Mobro, odyssey of the, **482**
  "safety map" of Manhattan for tourists, **199**
  self-segregation of Hasidim, **204**
  self-sufficiency of persons living in suburbs of New York City, **399**
  waste-to-energy incinerator at Peekskill, **482**
New Zealand
  downtown Aukland at the waterfront, **371**
  faunal destruction by Maoris, 39
Nicaragua, infant mortality rate, **103**
Niger-Congo language family, **138–39,** 141
nodal region, 18, **19**
nomadic herding, 261–62
nonbasic sector of city economy, 381
noneconomic measures of development
  education, 352–54
  health, 354, 356, **357,** 358
  literacy rate in the South, **353**
  North–South disparity in human development, *353*
  public services, *353,* 354, **355**
  safe drinking water and waste disposal in India, lack of, **355**
  school-age population per teacher in the South, **354**
nonecumene
  characteristics of, 118
  tundra vegetation and landscape, **120**
nonmaterial culture, 215
nonmaterial folk culture, 228–35
  drink, 231–32
  folk music. (see folk music)
  foods, folk and customary, 229, 230–31
  medicines and cures, 234–35

moonshine production in
east Tennessee
(mid-1950s), **232**
oral folk tradition, 235
nonmetallic minerals, mining
and quarrying, 286–87
nonrenewable resources, 279
Norman, Geraldine, **359**
North America. *See also
individual countries*
agricultural regions of, **273**
Anglo American cities,
characteristics of, 400,
401, 403
birth rates, 98–99, **101**
charter cultures, 186, 188
as cultural composite, 178
culture hearths, **47,** 49, 216,
217, 218
ethnic groups and their
provinces, **191**
French Canadians, cultural
obstacles of, 57
human advancement into, **42**
humans modifying
environment, impact of,
38, **39**
language
dialects in, 147–48
eastern U.S., dialect areas
of, 147
languages spoken in,
138–39, 140
Native American language
families, 137, **138–39, 140**
speech regions and dialect
diffusion, **148**
vernacular regions, **247**
major conurbations, 376, **377**
manufacturing regions, 312–14
Mayan pyramids as
independent
inventions, 57
Midwestern states, U.S. *See*
Midwestern states (U.S.)
migrations, 83
Native Americans as part of
larger cultural mix,
186, **187**
personal space needed by
residents, 70
political fragmentation, 445,
446, 447–49
population
distribution, 118
growth, **97**
reference map of, 507
rubbish and garbage, production
of, 480
rural settlement patterns, 206–7
space economy. (*see* space
economy)
wheat farming, large-scale, 272,
273, 274
North American Free Trade
Agreement (NAFTA), **442**
effect on outsourcing, 308
North Carolina
black majority Congressional
districts, **446–47**
forest death at Mount
Mitchell, **468**

O

occupations, development of
specialized, 47
ocean(s)
dumping of waste in, 483
settling boundary disputes
involving, 438–39, **440**
UN Convention on the Law of
the Sea, 438–39, **440**
off-farm sale in agriculture, 268
office parks, sample in Tysons
Corner, Virginia, **326**
official languages, 149, **150,**
151, **152**
oil. *See* petroleum
Old Stone Age
hunter-gatherers during, 40–41,
42, 43
tools, **42,** 43
opportunity, effect of, on
activity space, 71–72
oral folk tradition, 235
organic state theory, 436
Organization of Petroleum
Exporting Countries
(OPEC), 288
orthographic projection, **491,** 492
outsourcing of parts or
products, 308, **309**
oval projections, 497
overburden in strip
mining, **480**
overfishing, 280–81
Overland Trail, 64
overpopulation, 120–21
over-the-road costs, 303
ozone, problems with, 465–67

P

Pacific basin, settlement of, **42**
Pakistan
Great Britain drawing
boundaries of India
and, 428
Indus Valley
culture hearth emerging,
47–49
environmental disaster
(2000 BC), **50**
Paleo-Asiatic language family,
137, **138–39**
Paleolithic period
hunter-gatherers during, 40–41,
42, 43
tools, **42,** 43
Palestinians as stateless
nation, 419
Paracel Islands, claimants
to, **440**
parallel invention, 57
Paraguay, Itaipu Dam across
the Paraná River, **453**
pattern, as element of spatial
distribution, 16
peak value land
intersection, 390

Pennsylvania
cultural landscape created by
Amish farmers, **1**
folk housing in Pennsylvania
hearth, 224
idled steel mill, **295**
Pennsylvania Dutch barn,
55, 204
site of Philadelphia, 10
perception
in choice of migration
destination, 86, 87
information and, in spatial
interaction, 77–82
perceptual regions, 18
perforated state, defined,
423, 424
permeability of diffusion
barriers, 57
personal communication
field, 76
personal space, 70
perspective projections, 492
Peru, folk housing, **219**
petroleum
extraction, 287–88
Industrial Revolution use of, 37
interregional trade in, 1994, 65
reserves, *288*
trade, complementarity in, 65
Philippines
shifting agriculture among
Hanunóo people, **263**
sugar being loaded for export at
Cebu, **289**
terraced hillsides at Malegcong
on Luzon Island, **119**
photochemical smog, 466, **468**
physical attributes of place, 12–13
physical boundaries,
characteristics of, 426–27
physical geography, 4
Physical Quality of Life Index
(PQLI), 358
physicians per population in
developing countries, **356**
physiological density, 15
pidgin language, 149
Pillsbury, Richard, **217**
pipelines, manufacturing
decisions and, 302, **303**
pizza in popular culture, 240
place
basic characteristics, 9
direction, 10–11
distance, 11
interaction among places, 14–15
location, 9–10
physical and cultural attributes,
12–13
similarity defined by regions,
15–18
size and scale, 11–12
structured content, 15–16
place names
classical, in popular culture,
243, **244**
study of, 154–55
place perception, 77
place utility, 87, 325
planar projections, 496–97

plankton, 280
planned economies, 258, 310
planning, as institutional
control, 396
plantation crops, 276
plant domestication, 44, **45, 46**
centers of, **45**
Pleistocene overkill, 39
poisons, hunter-gatherers use
of, 44
Poland, environmental damage
by Marxist industry, **318**
political
alliances of countries, 443
power, fragmentation of, 445,
446, 447–49
political geography, 416, **417**
political systems, national. *See*
national political systems
politics
effect on economic activity, 257
local and regional political
organization. (*see* local and
regional political
organization)
pollution
incineration of solid waste,
481, **482,** 483
wastewater treatment, 477
Polynesians, faunal destruction
by, 39
polytheism, 157
poor countries. *See* developing
countries
popular culture, 132, 214
automobile as driving force, 240,
241, 242
baseball in, 244, **245**
classical town names, 243, **244**
commercial strip advertising in
Holbrook, Arizona,
as, **213**
contrasted with folk and ethnic
culture, 238–39
diffusion of, 243
national uniformities, 239–40,
241, 242
regional emphasis, 244, **245–46**
shopping mall, 240, 241, 242
soccer as world's most popular
sport, **239**
spectator sports in
American, **214**
popular regions, 247, **248**
population
age of, and demand for services,
105, **107**
aging, 127
arithmetic density, 119
birth rates, 98–99, **100, 101**
Boserup thesis, 264
carrying capacity, 43–44
center of U.S. population,
westward moving, **84**
controls, 125–26
data, 122–24
death rates, 102–4
demographic
equation, 113–14, 116
momentum, 127
transition model of growth,
109–13, **114,** 115
density. (*see* population density)

developing countries, effect of current growth rate on, 113
doubling times, 108–10
family planning
  Cairo plan and, 115
  effects on population growth, 113
fertility rates, 99, **100, 101,** 102
growth, 96–98
immigration impacts, 114, 116
"nations of immigrants," many countries as, **182**
natural increase in, 107, **109**
overpopulation, 120–21
projections. (*see* population projections)
pyramids, 104–7
race and classification of populations, **180**
relocation, degree of, 114, 116
shifting cultivation and, 264
structure, four patterns of, **105**
subsistence agriculture and pressures of rising, 266
suburbanization as cause of redistribution in U.S., 396–98, **399**
U.S. population center, westward shift of, **84**
world. (*see* world population)
zero population growth, **112**
population controls, 125–26
population density, 119–22
crude density of, 119
densities for selected countries, comparative, *120*
gradients for Cleveland, 1940-1990, *392*
land values and, 390, **391,** 392
map scale showing, **12**
overpopulation, 120–21
physiological density, 119–20
summary population density curve, urban, **391**
urbanization, 122
population geography, 96
population projections, 122–24
need for environmental component, **124**
positional boundary disputes, 428, **429**
possibilism, 37
postindustrial, 327
potential model of spatial interactions, 69
Poverty, **201**
poverty
as measure of economic development, 348–49
persons living in, data on, **339**
power, projection of, 434–36
precipitation
in hydrologic cycle, 475, **476**
mean annual, **477**
patterns of variability, **461**
variations, **461,** 476, **477, 478**
predevelopment annexation, 450
preference voting, **446**
price, relationship between supply, demand and, 295–96
primary commodities

sugar being loaded for export at Cebu, Philippines, **289**
trade in, 289–90
primary economic activities, 257, **258**
trade resulting from, 289–90
primate city
in developing countries, 407
in urban systems, 384, **386**
prime meridian, 20
Principles of Social Science, 68
printed materials, dissemination of, 77
production controls in commercial agriculture, 268, 269, **270**
profit-maximization approaches to industrial location, 306–7
projections, map, 19–20, 491–98
prorupt state, defined, 423
protectorates, 418
proto-Indo-European language cluster, 136, **137, 138–39**
spread of, 142
protolanguage, 135
Ptolemy (Claudius Ptolemaeus), world map by, **4**
public housing projects, 399, **401**
public services as noneconomic measure of development, *353,* 354, **355**
pull factors for migration, 86, **87**
purchasing power parity (PPP)
economic assessment model, 337–38
measuring development with, 341–42, **343**
world map of, **343**
push factors for migration, 86, **87**
pyramids as independent inventions, 57

Q

quarrying. *See* mining and quarrying
quaternary economic activities, 257, 326
office parks as, **326**
quinary economic activities, 257, 326–27

R

race
and classification of populations, **180**
forced segregation in nuclear communities based on, 394, 395
Los Angeles, changing racial make-up of, **395**
redistricting and, **446–47**
radioactive waste, disposal, 483–84, **485**
radon levels, U.S. areas with high, **80**

railroads
as factor in state cohesiveness, 432, **433**
manufacturing decisions and, 301–2, **303**
railway operated in U.S., total length of, *302*
unit trains, use of, **301**
rainforest
dam building, **470**
danger to, from deforestation, 469–70
ranching, livestock, **273,** 275
random pattern of distribution, 16
rank-size rule of city size hierarchy, 384
rate of natural increase of population, 107, **109**
rates, population measured by, 98
Ratzel, Friedrich, 436
Ravenstein, E.G., 89
raw materials
in manufacturing process, 297–98
orientation, 298, **302**
reapportionment, 444
recreation
popular culture and, **214,** 242, **243**
regional variables, 244, **245–46**
soccer, as world's most popular sport, **239**
rectilinear pattern of distribution, 16
redistricting, 444
regional concept, 17
regional dialects, 146–47
regional geography, 4
regionalism, as centrifugal force, 434
regions
agricultural regions of North America, **273**
characteristics, 17, **18**
commercial forest regions, 282
complementary regions in central place theory. (*see* complementary regions)
contact between, 57, **59,** 60
defined, 16–17
folk culture, 216
of eastern U.S., 235–36
passing of folk cultural regionalism, 237
international regional alliances, 439, 440–43
manufacturing regions of the world. (*see* manufacturing regions of the world)
place similarity and, 15–18
popular culture and, 247, **248**
regions in Western Europe demanding autonomy, **433**
types, 17–18, **19**
vernacular, 247
Reilly, William J., 68
relational direction, 10–11
relative
direction, 10–11
distance, 11
location, 9–10

relict boundary, 428
religion. *See also specific religions*
and birth rates, relationship of, 99
classification of, 156–57
and culture, 156, **157, 167**
defined, 156
development of formalized, 47
diffusion routes of major religions, **160**
Dinka chief on attempt to make one single people in Africa, quote from, **134**
East Asian ethnic religions, 172–73
innovation areas and diffusion routes of major religions, **160**
as mentifact of culture, 134
pattern, numbers, and flows, 158–59, **160, 161**
religious diversity in U.S., advertised evidence of, **134**
swine production areas affected by, **157**
world religions, 158–59, 160, 161, **162**
relocation diffusion, 55
of Christianity, 161
of East Coast (U.S.) settlers, 216
of Islam, 166
of Judaism, **161**
language spread by, 141
reluctant relocation, 85
renewable resources, 278
replacement level of populations, **112**
representative fraction, **20**
reserves, variable definition of, **284**
resource boundary disputes, 429
resources. *See* natural resources
return migration, 89
rice
Green Revolution and, 266–67
production of, by subsistence agriculture, 264–65
rich nations. *See* advanced countries
rimland theory, 436
roads, as factor in state cohesiveness, 432
"Roger's Book" (Roger II, Sicily), 3, **5**
Romance languages, 135, 136
Romania, Bucharest as typical socialist city, **405**
Rome, ancient contributions to geography, 3, **4**
Roosevelt, Franklin D., 396
Rostow, W.W., 350, 351, 352
rotation, as way to protect or enhance soil, 473, **474**
rural settlements
basic settlement forms, **378**
in developing countries, 377, **378,** 379
patterns of living, 377
in subsistence economies, **378**
Russia. *See also* Soviet Union
autonomy movement within, 434

birth rates, 98–99, **101**
conversion to private agriculture, 277
direction bias, 78
ethnic groups seeking independence, 186, **187**
human advancement into, 41
population pyramids for, 104, **105**
Rwanda, refugees fleeing 1994 civil war, **86**

S

Saharan language family, **138–39, 141**
Salt Lake area
  as cultural hearth, **217,** 218
  folk housing, 226
Sanders, Beverly, **230**
sanitary landfill, use of, 481
San people (South Africa), 43
satisficing industrial locations, 307
scale
  effect of scale on area and detail, **20**
  map, 19–20
  as spatial concept, 11–12
scattered phenomenon, 16
schools, as unifying institutions, 430, 431
S-curve population growth, 125
seas. *See* ocean(s)
secondary economic activities, 257, **258,** 296
sector model of urban land use, 392–93
secularism, 159
segregation
  in African cities, 410
  Caribbean Islanders, self-segregation in London, 198, **199**
  defined, 196
  external controls on, 198
  Hasidim, self-segregation of, **204**
  internal controls on, 198–99
  suburbanization and, 397, 398, 399
  U.S.
    metropolitan areas ranked by segregation levels, 197
    urban areas, 196, 197, 198
self-determination, 434
Senegal, international migration streams into, **90**
separation nationalism
  as centrifugal force, 433
  regions in Western Europe demanding autonomy, **433**
service sector of city economy, 381
sewage
  dumping of untreated, impact of, 477
  systems, growth in Europe and North America, 111, **112**
sex. *See also* gender
  male and female language, **146**
  in migration decisions, 89, 91

ratio of women to men in central cities, **400**
shamanism, 157
shape
  in map projections, 494–95
  of states as important factor, 420, 423–24
Shaw v. Reno (1993), **446**
shifting cultivation, 262–64
Shintoism, 173
shopping malls, 240, 241, 242
  suburban counterpart to higher-order central places, 397
short-haul penalty, **304**
Shurtleff, Harold R., **220**
Sierra Leone, women selling vegetables at Freetown periodic market, **361**
Singapore
  as emerging manufacturing and trading force, 321, 323
  latitude and longitude of, **9**
  zero population growth campaign, effects of, **96**
Sino-Tibetan language family, 137, **138–39**
site
  defined, 10
  in location of cities, 381
situation
  defined, 10, **11**
  in location of cities, 381
size
  as spatial concept, 11–12
  of states, 420, **422**
slash-and-burn agriculture, 262–64
Slater, Samuel, **338**
Slovakia, high density housing in Poprad, **405**
Small Island Developing States (SIDS), influence of, **422**
Smith, Mary, 238
snack nuts, **245**
soccer, as world's most popular sport, **239**
social
  interaction as function of distance, **75**
  status, cities and, 393–94
  structure in culture, 35
social areas of cities, 393–96
social dialects, 145
social distance, 196
social geography
  of North American cities, **394**
  Western European city, model of, 403, **405**
sociofacts, as components of culture, 51–52, **53, 54**
sociological subsystem of culture, 51–52, **53**
soil
  defined, 472
  degradation, world pattern of, **473**
soil erosion
  agriculture and, 472–73, **474,** 475
  from tropical deforestation, 469–70

in the United States, **474,** 475
solar energy
  in greenhouse effect, **462**
  intensity and absorbtion/reflection of incoming, **458**
solid wastes and rubbish, 480–81. *See also* garbage
South Africa
  "built environment" of Cape Town, **38**
  San people, culture of, 43
South America. *See also* individual countries
  destruction of rain forest causing environmental degradation in Amazonia, **469**
  early culture hearths, **47,** 49
  forced migrations, 83, 85
  human advancement into, **42**
  nonnative ethnic groups, **182**
  personal space needed by residents, 70
South Carolina, folk housing, 225
Southern cultural hearths, 225
Southern Tidewater area
  as cultural hearth, **217,** 218
  folk housing, 225
South Korea, as emerging manufacturing and trading force, 321, 322–23
Soviet Union. *See also* Russia
  agricultural control through planned economies, 276–77
  ethnic nationalism and break-up of, 186, **187**
  independent countries formed from former, map of, **421**
  industrial
    environmental damage by industry, 316, **318**
    location decisions under planned economies, 310
    regions under central planning, **319**
  labor surplus and shortage in former, **299**
  Virgin and Idle Lands program, 277
space
  geography and, 2, **3,** 8, 9
  personal, 70
  space-cost convergence in telephone calls, **76**
  space-time path for college student, **73**
space economy
  components, 294
  concepts and controls, 295–96
  effects of, **294, 295**
  supply, demand and market equilibrium, relationship between, 295–96
space-time prism, 72, **75**
Spain
  Basques, linguistic uniqueness of, 142
  crowded beach along Costa Blanca, **70**
spatial analysis, demographers' use of, 96
spatial behavior
  demanded personal space, 70

distance and, 72–73, **74, 75**
  individual activity space, 70–72
  social interaction as function of distance, **75**
  time and, 72, **75**
spatial diffusion, 15
spatial distribution, 15–16
spatial extent, as characteristics of regions, 17
spatial implications of fixed and variable costs, **297**
spatial interaction, 14–15
  bases for, 64–70
  conditions affecting, 65–66, **67**
  defined, 64
  information
    accumulation of, 73, 76–77
    flows, 76–77
    and perception, 77–82
  measuring, 66–70
  migration. (*see* migration)
  19th century migration in U.S., difficulties of, 64
  summarizing model, 65–66, **67**
spatially
  fixed costs, 297, 303–4
  variable costs, 297, 303
spatial margin of profitability, 306
spatial science, geography as, 2, 8, 9
spatial search behavior, 87
spatial systems
  analysis, 27
  government entities as, 443
special function cities, 383
specialization in commercial agriculture, 268
speech community, defined, 144
spine, in Latin American cities, 410
sports
  regional variables, 244, **245**
  soccer, as world's most popular sport, **239**
  spectator, in American popular culture, **214**
Spratly Islands, claimants to, **440**
spread effects in core-periphery model, 336
Spykman, Nicholas, 435–36
St. Lawrence Valley, lower (U.S.)
  arc of French settlement, **221**
  early North American culture hearth, 216, **217,** 218
  French influence in housing styles, 220, 222
stacked gerrymandering, 444
Stalin, Joseph, 276
standard language, 144–45
standard line in cylindrical projections, 495
standard of living, 340
starvation, 125
state farms, 276–77
states. *See also* national political systems
  boundaries. (*see* boundaries)

cohesiveness, 429, 430–32, **433**
  communication as cohesion factor, 431, 432
  cores and capitals, 425, **426**
  defined, 417–18
  economic alliances of, 440–42
  evolution of the modern state, 419, **420, 421**
  exclusive economic zone claims of coastal, **439**
  geographic characteristics, 419, 420, **422,** 423–25, **426**
  international regional alliances, 439, 440–43
  landlocked, 424
  location, 424–25
  maritime boundaries, settling disputes over, 438–39, **440**
  military alliances, 443
  ministates, influence, **422**
  nationalism
    and centrifugal forces, 433–34, **435**
  value of, 429, 430
  organization and administration as bonding force, 431, 432
  political alliances, 443
  projection of power, 434–36
  shape, as important factor, 420, 423–24
  size, 420, **422**
  states, nations and nation-states, 417–19
  transportation as cohesion factor, 431, 432, **433**
  unifying institutions, 430, 431
statistical map, defined, 21
step migration, 87
stereographic projection, 492, **493**
Steward, Julian, 49
Stone Age
  burial of hunter, **34**
  hunter-gatherers during, 40–41, **42,** 43
  Mesolithic period. (*see* Mesolithic period)
  Neolithic period. (*see* Neolithic period)
  Pleistocene overkill, 39
Strabo, 2
structural assimilation, 184
subsequent boundary, 427, **428**
subsistence agriculture
  areas of the world practicing, map of, **262**
  defined, 261
  extensive subsistence agriculture, 261–64
  intensive
    costs of territorial extension, 266
    Green Revolution in, 266–67, **269**
    subsistence agriculture, 261, 264–66
subsistence economies, 258
substitution principle in industrial processes, 306
suburbanization
  effects on central city, 398, 399, **400, 402**
  galactic city, diagram of, **398**
  self-sufficient suburbs, 397, **399**
  in U.S., 396–98, **399**

suburbs
  defined, 380
  mobility of wealthy suburbanites, 71
Sudan, food disbursement at refugee camp, **349**
Sudanic language family, **138–39, 141**
superimposed boundaries, **420,** 427–28
supply
  and demand in spatial interaction, 65–66, **67**
  relationship between price, demand and, 295–96
Suriname, creation of Brokopondo Dam, **470**
suzerainty, 434
Sweden
  human advancement into, 41
  migration, distance between old and new residences, *91*
  population pyramid, 104, **105**
swidden agriculture, 262–64
symbols
  promoting nationalism through, 430, **431**
  U.S. Geological Survey topographic map, **24**
syncretism, 57, **59**
  folklore and, 235
  religions, 172
syntax, changes in, 142
systematic geography, 4

T

Taiwan
  as emerging manufacturing and trading force, 321, 322, **323**
  industrialization, **323**
Tanzania
  Masai
    cattle in culture of, role of, **36**
    culture complex of, 36
    refugees fleeing 1994 Rwandan civil war, **86**
Taoism, 173
technology
  defined, 257, 338
  diffusion, 338, 339–40
  effect on economic activity, 257
  high-tech industries, location of, 323–25
  textile industry during Industrial Revolution, **338**
technology gap, 338–40
technology transfer, 339–40
technological subsystem of culture, 51, **52, 54**
tells in Middle East, as ancient landfills, **480**
Tennessee, moonshine production in eastern (mid-1950s), **232**
terminal costs, 303
terracing to minimize soil erosion, 473, **474**
territorial boundary disputes, 428–29

territoriality, 70
  and language, 152–54
territorial production complex in planned economies, 310
tertiary economic activities, 257, 325–26
Texas, petrochemical contamination near Texas City, **13**
Thailand, fish harvesting at aquaculture farm, **281**
thematic map, defined, 21
Third World. *See also* developing countries
  cities, characteristics of, 406–10
  unofficial housing in, problems with, **406,** 407, **408,** 410
  use of term, 334
Tibet, lamas in exile at Sikkim monastery, **133**
time
  distance measured by, 11
  as factor of distance, 67–68
  space-time path for college student, **73**
  spatial behavior restricted by, 72, **73, 75**
time-geography, 72
tipping point in urban environments, 198
Tito, Josip Broz, **435**
Tobler, W., **67**
tools
  early agricultural, 44, **46**
  Mediterranean scratch plow, **46**
  Neolithic, 46
  Paleolithic, **42,** 43
  in structure of culture, 51, **52**
topographic maps
  description of, 23
  French long-lot survey, topographic quadrangle showing, **206**
  Santa Barbara, California, portion of, **23**
  symbols, **24**
toponymy, 154–55
total fertility rate (TFR), 99, **101,** *102*
  in today's Europe, **112**
town names
  classical, in popular culture, 243, **244**
  study of, 154–55
towns
  city and, compared, 380
  defined, 380
  patterns of hamlets, towns, and cities in portion of Indiana, **388**
  village and, difference between, **378**
toxic waste, disposal, 483–84, **485**
trade
  factors in structure of, 64–65
  law of retail gravitation, 68, **69**
  in primary products, 289–90
traditional religions, 157
tragedy of the commons, 281
transferability, 65–66

transistor radio, as purveyor of information, 77
transitional birth rates, 99
transnational corporations (TNCs), locational perspective of, 309–10
transportation
  centers, cities classified as, 383, **384**
  employment patterns for, U.S., 325
  as factor in state cohesiveness, 431, 432, **433**
  manufacturing decisions and, 299, 301–4
  spatial orientation tendencies, **302**
  tapering principle, **303**
  traditional and modern in Ecuador street scene, **331**
  transport media, comparison of, **303**
trash. *See* garbage
tribal religions, 157
trickle-down effects in core-periphery model, 336
tropical rainforest
  dam building in, **470**
  deforestation, 468–70
tropical savanna, human impact on, 38
truck farms, 271–72, **273**
Truman, Harry S., 334
Turkey, thriving commerce of Grand Bazaar in Istanbul, **407**
Twain, Mark, **214**

U

ubiquitous industries, 299
Ullman, Edward, 65
underdevelopment
  defined, 334
  explanations of, 335–36
  world map of development and, **334**
underpopulation, 120
undeveloped countries. *See* developing countries
unified government, 449–50
uniform assumption, 304
uniform regions, 17–18
unifying institutions, 430, 431
unigov (government), 449–50
Union of Soviet Socialist Republics. *See* Soviet Union
unitary states, 425
United Nations. *See also individual agencies, conferences or programs*
  Conference on Trade and Development, 290
  Convention on the Law of the Sea, 438–39, **440**
  flags in front of UN building in New York City, **417**
  influence of ministates, **422**

International Conference on Population and Development, **115**
interventionism, 437–38
levels of development, classification of, 334, **335**
peacekeeping forces on duty in Bosnia-Herzegovina, **437**
reduction in greenhouse gases, advising governments on, 462
role in international community, 437–38
United Nations Development Programme (UNDP)
human development index, 358, 360
world poverty, measurement, **339**
United Nations Educational, Scientific, and Cultural Organization (UNESCO), 437
United States. *See also individual regions, states and cities*
acid rainfall, location, **465**
agricultural regions of North America, **273**
amalgamation theory, 184
assimilation of immigrants, **178**
average morning in life of "100% American," reflections on, **59**
Canadian-U.S. railroad discontinuity, map of, **433**
cartogram of news coverage of presidential nomination contest, **22**
center of population, westward changing, **84**
charter cultures, 188
Chinatowns in New York City, developing satellites, **200**
cities in, characteristics of, 400, **401,** 403
conurbations, 376, **377**
cross country movement as spatial interaction, 64
culture
areas, **208**
cultural diffusion with Japan, 60
hearths, 216, **217,** 218
regions, **248**
Delmarva Peninsula, nesting of regions and, **18**
direction bias, 78
Ellis Island, importance of, **181**
employment patterns, *325*
ethnic
affiliations claimed by census respondents, *181*
ethnicity in, 188
islands, 188, **189**
racial and ethnic discrimination in urban areas, 198
farmland and buildings, value of, 272, **274**
fire as tool, impact of, 38
folk music, 232–34
folk song regions of eastern U.S., **232**
foreign aid, effectiveness of, **350–51**
Four Corners Monument, **443**

government policies as market controls, 269, **270**
hierarchical relationships among southern cities, 385
high-tech industries, location, 324
homeless persons in, **402**
illegal immigrants, response to, **88**
immigration streams, 181, 183
incinerators, opposition to construction of, 481
infant mortality rate, **103**
interregional moves, reasons for, 91
landfill problems, 481, **482**
Land Ordinance of 1785, 205
language(s)
dialects, 147–48
eastern U.S., dialect areas of, 147
"English only" movement, **152–53**
linguistic diversity, **152**
speech regions and dialect diffusion, **148**
Main Street conurbation, **377**
manufacturing regions of, 312–14
metropolitan growth and decline, patterns of, **383**
Midwestern states. (*see* Midwestern states (U.S.))
migration decisions by citizens of, 91
mining controversy, **285**
multilingual education, **152**
nationalism, attempts to instill, **431**
Native Americans as part of larger cultural mix, 186, **187**
nonnative ethnic groups in, response to, **88, 182**
ocean dumping, results of, 483
origin of immigrants, 181, 183–84
political fragmentation, 445, 446, 447–49
population
density in, 119
distribution, 118
mix 1995–2050, *193*
projections, **107**
racial and ethnic discrimination in urban areas, 198
radon levels, areas with high, **80**
railway operated in U.S., total length of, *302*
religion
Baptists and Lutherans, concentration of, **165**
central position of church in cultural landscape, 163, **166**
diversity in, advertised evidence of, **134**
New England spired church, **166**
religions, 163, **164–67**
resident population by race and Hispanic origin, *179*
return migration in, 89
rural settlement patterns, 206
"safety map" of Manhattan for tourists, **199**

social geography of American and Canadian cities, **394**
soil erosion in, **474,** 475
St. Lawrence Valley. (*see* St. Lawrence Valley, lower)
strip mining in U.S., results of, **480**
tall smokestacks to meet ground-level air quality, **464**
textile industry, **300**
toponyms
Andover as town name, spreading of, **154**
Old World names in New World, 154–55
undocumented migrants from Mexico, efforts to halt, 429, **430**
unigov attempted, 450
urban influence zones, hierarchical structure, 385
universalizing religions, 157
Uralic-Altaic language family, **138–39,** 142
urban, defined, 380
urban areas. *See also* cities; urbanization
black English vernacular, differentiation of, 148
boundaries, **18**
breaking point of cities trade area, computing, 68
definitions concerning, 380
differences in size, density, and land use complexity, **380**
ethnic diversity. (*see* urban ethnic diversity)
functions supplied by, 379–80
galactic nature of, 398
homeless persons in U.S., **402**
increase in populations, 122
inverse concentric zone pattern, 408
metropolitan growth and decline in U.S., **383**
mobility of persons in inner-city slums, 71
national populations classified as urban, percentage of, **122**
native born dispersals, 202
patterns in, 16
population density curve, summary, **391**
racial and ethnic discrimination, 198
rank-size rule, 384
"safety map" of Manhattan for tourists, **199**
segregation, 196–98
spatial adjustment to natural hazards within, lack of, 82
suburbanization and effect on, 398, 399, **400, 402**
urban
alignment in Illinois, **384**
hierarchy, 383–85, **386**
influence zones, 385
urban sprawl in Chicago, history of, **397**
U.S. metropolitan area, diagram of, **397**
women in, **400**
world metropolitan areas of 1 million or more, map of, **374–75**

world urban diversity. (*see* world urban diversity)
urban ethnic diversity
Caribbean Islanders, self-elected segregation in London, 198, **199**
Chinatowns, developing satellites, **200**
"colonies of immigrants" in U.S. cities, **201**
ethnic
areas, types of, 200, **202**
cluster models, 200–202
enclaves in U.S., creation of, 196, *197*
groups in Los Angeles, distribution of, **196**
external controls on, 198
internal controls on, 198–99
metropolitan areas ranked by segregation levels, U.S., *197*
native born dispersals, 202
segregation. (*see* segregation)
urban influence zones, 385
urbanization. *See also* cities; urban areas
as characteristic of culture hearths, 47, 48, **50**
early, in eastern Massachusetts, **381**
increase in, 122, 373
trends of world, **373**
urban
population growth rates, 373, **376**
share of total population, *376*
world metropolitan areas of 1 million or more, map of, **374–75**
urbanized area. *See also* urban areas
defined, 380
urban land use
in Anglo American cities, 400, **401,** 403
Calgary, Alberta, land use pattern in and around, **393**
developing world
cities in, 406–10
urban models, **409**
following suburbanization, 398, 399, **401**
generalized land use pattern, **391**
housing in Crown Heights, Brooklyn, New York, **389**
inside the city, 388–96
institutional controls, 396
land values and population density, 390, **391,** 392
major access lines in Boston in 1872 and 1994, **390**
models of, and land use structure, 392–93
population density gradients for Cleveland, 1940–1990, **392**
in socialist countries, 404, **405,** 406
spine used in Latin American cities, 410
suburbanization and, 396–98
unofficial housing in developing countries, problems with, **406,** 407, **408**
in Western European cities, 403, **404, 405**

U.S. Geological Survey
    petroleum reserves estimate
        by, 288
    topographic maps, 23, **24**
usable reserves, **284**
Utah
    Bingham Canyon open-pit
        copper mine as example of
        reshaping landscapes, **457**
    folk housing, 226

V

value systems, 156
Van der Grinten projection,
    497, **498**
variable costs, 297, 303
vehicles of Buddhism, 171, **172**
verbal scale, **20**
vernacular, 145
    house, 220
    regions, 18, 247
vertical integration, 297
villages, basic settlement forms
    of, **378**
Virgin and Idle Lands program
    (Soviet Union), 277
Virginia
    office park in Tysons Corner,
        sample, **326**
    Tysons Corner, as suburban
        central business district, 398
Voice of America (VOA), world
    view after listening to, **78**
volcanos, distribution of
    aerosols by, 459–60
voluntary migration, 83, 85, **87**
von Thünen, Johann Heinrich
    model of agricultural location,
        270–71, **272**
    von Thünen's rings, 270–71, **272**
voting districts
    alternative districting
        strategies, **445**
    black majority Congressional
        districts in North Carolina,
        446–47
    gerrymandering, 444–45
Voting Rights Act, redistricting
    in North Carolina to
    comply with, **446–47**

W

Waldsterben, **468**
Washington
    Peace Arch at Blaine, as
        example of geometric
        boundary, **427**
    radioactive waste storage tanks
        in Hanford, **484**
    Seattle skyline, picture of, **369**

Washington, D.C., gnomonic
    projection centered
    on, **495**
Washington, George, 238
waste. *See* garbage
wasted vote strategy, 444
water
    agricultural use, 476–77
    availability, **475,** 476, **477, 479**
    hydrologic cycle, 475, **476**
    pollution, 477–78
    precipitation. (*see* precipitation)
    sanitary
        development of systems in
            Europe, 111, **112**
        importance in maintaining
            human health, *353,*
            354, **355**
        safe drinking water, map of
            population with, **355**
    scarcity of, worldwide, **479**
    use and abuse, 476–78, **479**
    wastewater treatment as source
        of pollution, 477
    world water supplies, map
        of, **478**
water divide, 427
water transportation, 301,
    303, 314
Weber, Alfred
    locational triangle, 305
    plane table solution to plant
        location problem, **305**
    Weberian analysis of industrial
        location, 304–5
Webster, Daniel, **220**
Western culture hearths
    (U.S.), 226
West Virgina, hardwood
    forests, **279**
wheat
    Green Revolution, 266–67
    growing areas of the world, map
        of, **274**
    large-scale wheat farming, 272,
        273, 274
White, Leslie, 51
William of Malmesbury, **460**
women
    agriculture, percentage of
        economically active,
        engaged in, **364**
    contributions to hunter-gatherer
        society, 44
    domestic duties of, in
        settlement of North
        America, **230**
    economically active women,
        percentage of, **364**
    Fourth World Conference on
        Women (Beijing), **363**
    gender empowerment
        measure, **365**
    Green Revolution and, **269**
    in Hindu society, **171**

labor force, women's share
    of, **362**
male and female language, **146**
migrants, motivation of, 89, 91
mortality
    due to cultural gender
        preferences, **106**
    female death rates, world,
        102, **104**
    maternal mortality
        ratio, **104**
in periodic marketplace of
    developing countries, **361**
in political system, slowly
    gaining influence, **432**
role of, in development, 360–63,
    364–65
space-time prism of, **75**
status index, **365**
urban areas, needs of women
    in, **400**
World Bank
    as distributor of foreign aid,
        350–51
    use of purchasing power parity
        assessment model, 337–38
    world poverty, measurement
        of, **339**
World Health Organization
    (WHO)
    health services in developing
        countries, providing,
        356, **357**
    micronutrient malnutrition,
        data on effects of, 349
    as part of UN effort, 437
World Hunger Project,
    calculation of
    maximum population
    for ecosystem, **124**
world population
    age and population, 127
    annual rate of natural
        increase, **109**
    Cairo plan for stabilizing, 115
    controls. (*see* population
        controls)
    data for 1996, 501–6
    death rates, improvement
        in, 102–4
    demographic momentum, 127
    density, **117**
    distribution, 116–18, **119**
    doubling time, decrease in, 108
    economic development and
        population growth, 98–99,
        110–13
    at end of Paleolithic period, 41
    "explosion" after World War
        II, **114**
    fifteen years of age, percentage
        of population under, **106**
    growth
        8000 BC to AD 2000, **110**
        yielded by 2 percent rate of
            increase, *108*
    historical growth and doubling
        times of, *108*

immigration impacts, 114, 116
international labor flows, **84**
J-curve growth of, 108–9, **110**
life expectancies, improvement
    in, 103–4
metropolitan areas of 1 million
    or more, map of, **374–75**
national populations classified
    as urban, percentage of, **122**
"nations of immigrants," many
    countries as, **182**
natural population increase
    that has permanently
    emigrated, *116*
Northern Hemisphere,
    population dominance of,
    117, **118**
projections. (*see* population
    projections)
prospects for, 126–27
race and classification of, **180**
recent, 96, **97**
regional contributions to, **101**
relocation, degree of, 114, 116
total fertility rates and, 99,
    101, 102
World Trade Organization,
    300, 440
world urban diversity, 400,
    401, 403–10, **411**
    Anglo American city, 400,
        401, 403
    developing world urban
        models, **409**
    Latin American city, 410, **411**
    Western European city, 403,
        404, 405
writing, development of, 48–49

Y

Yeates, Maurice, **377, 400**
Yugoslavia
    centrifugal forces operating
        on, **435**
    ethnicity in former, **186**
    UN peacekeeping forces on duty
        in Bosnia-Herzegovina, **437**
Yunus, Muhammad, **363**

Z

Zaire (Belgian Congo), ethnic
    groups in, 419
Zelinsky, Wilbur, 186, 188,
    242, 243
    culture areas of U.S., **208,** 209
zero population growth, in
    Europe, **112**
Zimbabwe, subsistence maize
    plot in, **34**
zoning, as institutional control
    on urban land use, 396